The Oxford Study Thesaurus

The Oxford Study Thesaurus

Compiled by

Alan Spooner

Oxford University Press

Oxford University Press, Walton Street, Oxford OX2 6DP

Oxford New York Toronto
Delhi Bombay Calcutta Madras Karachi
Petaling Jaya Singapore Hong Kong Tokyo
Nairobi Dar es Salaam Cape Town
Melbourne Auckland

and associated companies in
Berlin Ibadan

Oxford is a trade mark of Oxford University Press

First published 1991
Reprinted 1991, 1992
Paperback published 1992
Reprinted 1992, 1993

ISBN 0 19 910232 5 (Non-net hardback)
ISBN 0 19 910257 0 (Net hardback)
ISBN 0 19 910270 8 (Paperback)

A CIP catalogue record for this book
is available from the British Library

Typeset by Latimer Trend & Company Ltd, Plymouth
Printed in Great Britain
by HarperCollins Manufacturing, Glasgow

Preface

This thesaurus is designed to be sufficiently advanced in vocabulary and treatment to match the needs of older students in schools and colleges, while at the same time being friendly and easy to use. It is less daunting than some larger thesauruses, whose complex indexing and cross-referencing can be confusing, but more comprehensive than smaller synonym dictionaries. It will, I hope, make an ideal volume not only for school and college students, but also for adults who want a quick-reference thesaurus.

In selecting the vocabulary for this book, my principle has been to include all words *which we are likely to use in everyday writing*: at school, at college, at home, and at work. I have deliberately not included rare or archaic terms, which may delight students of language and quiz-game fanatics, but which would look eccentric in everyday English. Nor do I give the specialized jargon of academic subjects, trades, professions, and so on, except when the terms have passed into the general vocabulary and have become acceptable in ordinary situations. I have included a lot of words which are used informally; but, with a few exceptions, I have left out slang expressions, which are often ephemeral or specific to a restricted geographical area or social group. I have not included words which might give offence.

Although I want this to be an accessible book, I am aware that a thesaurus is a dangerous tool if used thoughtlessly. Ill-considered plundering of a thesaurus for synonyms can lead to pretentiousness, or to the writing of sheer nonsense. I hope that people who use this book may want to browse and ponder on the extraordinary diversity of English synonyms—and may become aware of how surprisingly seldom they are in fact interchangeable. I hope, too, that the occasional notes on word-building, etymology, and other linguistic matters may encourage a curiosity about how language works. I should be pleased if this thesaurus might help not only to extend the vocabularies of those who use it, but also to increase their awareness of the complexity and subtlety of our language, and to enhance their concern to use language *creatively*.

I want to record my sincere thanks to all who have helped in the preparation of the book: members of the Oxford University Press, especially Rob Scriven and Mary Worrall for their support and patience; Rosemary Burt for her invaluable help with the preparation of the manuscript; and Genevieve Hawkins for her sharp-eyed and constructive work on proofs.

Nottingham Polytechnic AJS
August 1990

Before you use this thesaurus . . .

What is a thesaurus for?

A thesaurus helps you find the words you need to make your language more effective in communicating what you want to say.

How does this thesaurus help?

This thesaurus works basically in four ways:

- It lists words with a similar meaning to the word you look up [synonyms], so that you can choose the best word for your purpose.
- It refers you to places where you can find words of opposite meanings [antonyms].
- It provides useful 'families' of words which are related in other ways: names of colours, medical terms, kinds of vehicle, and so on.
- It gives information to help you understand the meanings and uses of words.

A thesaurus does *not* give definitions. If you want a definition of a word, you need to look the word up in a dictionary.

How is this thesaurus arranged?

Headwords
The first word of each entry (the *headword*) is printed in **bold** type. Each headword is followed by a 'part-of-speech' label (noun, verb, etc.) to indicate its grammatical function. All the headwords are arranged in alphabetical order.

Notes
From time to time, we include notes about interesting facts or problems. If a note refers to a group of words, it is displayed between horizontal lines; if it refers to just one word, it appears in square brackets within the entry concerned.

Antonyms
If you want opposites, we give you a simple cross-reference so that you know where to find them.

Numbers
When a headword can be used in more than one sense, numbers identify the main meanings or uses of the word.

Illustrative examples
Phrases or sentences printed in *italics* illustrate how the headword can be used.

Sub-entries
When a headword is commonly part of a phrase, the phrase may appear in small bold type at the end of the main entry. This is a 'sub-entry'.

peculiarity noun *We all have our peculiarities.* abnormality, characteristic, eccentricity, foible, idiosyncrasy, mannerism, oddity, peculiar feature [SEE **peculiar**], quirk, singularity, speciality, trait, uniqueness.

pecuniary adjective SEE **financial**.

pedagogue noun SEE **teacher**.

A number of English words such as *pedal, pedestal, pedestrian* are related to Latin *pes, pedis=foot.*

---

pedal verb SEE **travel** verb.

pedantic adjective 1 *a pedantic use of long words.* academic, bookish, formal, humourless, learned, old-fashioned, pompous, scholarly, schoolmasterly, stilted.
OPPOSITES: SEE **informal**.
2 *pedantic observance of the rules.* inflexible, [*informal*] nit-picking, precise, strict, unimaginative.
OPPOSITES: SEE **flexible**.

peddle verb SEE **sell**.

pedestal noun SEE **base** noun.

pedestrian adjective 1 *a pedestrian precinct.* pedestrianized, traffic-free.
2 *a pedestrian performance.* SEE **ordinary**.

pedestrian noun foot-traveller, walker.

pedigree adjective *a pedigree animal.* pure-bred, thoroughbred.

pedigree noun *a dog's pedigree.* ancestry, descent, SEE **family**, family history, line.

pedlar noun *a pedlar of cheap goods.* [*old-fashioned*] chapman, door-to-door salesman, hawker, seller, street-trader, vendor.

peek noun, verb SEE **look** noun, verb.

peel noun *orange peel.* rind, skin.

peel verb *to peel an orange. to peel off a covering.* denude, pare, skin, strip.

peep noun, verb SEE **look** noun, verb.
peep of day SEE **dawn**.

peer verb SEE **look** verb.

peer, peeress nouns aristocrat, noble, nobleman, noblewoman, titled person.
OPPOSITE: commoner.

TITLES OF BRITISH PEERS: baron, baroness, duchess, duke, earl, lady, lord, marchioness, marquis or marquess, viscount, viscountess.

OTHER TITLES: SEE **title** noun.

Synonyms
Most entries include one or more lists of synonyms. But remember: one word seldom means *exactly* the same as another, so think carefully about the words you have to choose from. Which gives *most exactly* your meaning? Which is *most suitable* for your purpose? Do you want a friendly or informal word, or a more formal one? Do you want an obvious everyday word, or a surprising, unusual word? And so on.

Cross-references
If we don't have space for a full entry under a particular headword, or if there is useful additional information elsewhere in the thesaurus, we suggest that you refer to another entry. This is called *cross-referencing*.

Usage warnings
If you need to be careful about the use of a word (for example if it is normally *informal, uncomplimentary, old-fashioned*, etc.) we put a warning in *italics*.

Related words
In addition to synonyms and antonyms, this thesaurus often lists words which are related to the headword in other ways. To distinguish these lists from lists of synonyms, we display them between horizontal ruled lines.

A

aback adverb **taken aback** SEE **surprised**.

abandon verb 1 *to abandon ship*. desert, evacuate, forsake, leave, quit, vacate, withdraw from.
2 *to abandon a friend*. desert, drop, forsake, jilt, leave behind, leave in the lurch, maroon, renounce, repudiate, strand, wash your hands of.
3 *to abandon a plan*. cancel, [*slang*] chuck in, discard, discontinue, [*informal*] ditch, drop, finish, forgo, give up, postpone, scrap.
4 *to abandon a right*. cede, drop, forfeit, forgo, give up, relinquish, renounce, resign, surrender, waive, yield.

abase verb **to abase yourself** SEE **humiliate**.

abashed adjective SEE **ashamed**.

abate verb *The storm abated*. SEE **lessen**.

abattoir noun slaughterhouse.

abbey noun cathedral, SEE **church**, convent, friary, monastery, nunnery, priory.

abbreviate verb SEE **abridge**.

abdicate verb *to abdicate the throne*. SEE **resign**.

abdomen noun belly, [*slang*] guts, [*insulting*] paunch, [*insulting*] pot, stomach, [*informal*] tummy.
OTHER PARTS OF THE BODY: SEE **body**.

abduct verb SEE **kidnap**.

aberrant adjective SEE **abnormal**.

aberration noun SEE **abnormality**.

abet verb SEE **encourage**.

abettor noun SEE **accomplice**.

abeyance noun **in abeyance** SEE **suspended**.

abhor verb SEE **hate** verb.

abhorrent adjective *Torture is abhorrent to civilized people*. abominable, detestable, disgusting, distasteful, execrable, hateful, horrible, horrid, horrifying, loathsome, nauseating, obnoxious, odious, offensive, repellent, repugnant, repulsive, revolting.

abide verb 1 [*old-fashioned*] *Abide with me*. SEE **stay**.
2 *I can't abide cigarette smoke*. accept, bear, endure, put up with, stand, [*informal*] stomach, suffer, tolerate.
to abide by *Abide by the rules*. accept, act in accordance with, adhere to, carry out, conform to, follow, keep to, obey, observe, stand by, submit to.

abiding adjective SEE **permanent**.

ability noun 1 *The rich have the ability to buy what they want*. capability, capacity, chance, means, opportunity, potential, potentiality, power, resources, scope, way, wherewithal.
2 *She has the ability to be a good artist*. aptitude, bent, brains, calibre, capability, cleverness, competence, expertise, facility, faculty, flair, genius, gift, intelligence, knack, [*informal*] know-how, knowledge, power, proficiency, prowess, qualification, skill, strength, talent, training.

abject adjective SEE **miserable**.

ablaze adjective afire, aflame, alight, blazing, burning, fiery, flaming, incandescent, lit up, on fire, raging.

able adjective 1 *I'm able to stay*. allowed, at liberty (to), authorized, available, eligible, equipped, fit, free, permitted, prepared, ready, willing.
OPPOSITES: SEE **unable**.
2 *She's an able player*. accomplished, adept, capable, clever, competent, effective, efficient, experienced, expert, gifted, [*informal*] handy, intelligent, masterly, practised, proficient, qualified, skilful, skilled, strong, talented, trained.
OPPOSITES: SEE **incompetent**.

ablutions noun SEE **wash** noun.

abnegation noun SEE **denial**.

abnormal adjective *abnormal behaviour*. aberrant, anomalous, atypical, [*informal*] bent, bizarre, curious, deviant, eccentric, erratic, exceptional, extraordinary, freak, funny, heretical, irregular, [*informal*] kinky, odd, peculiar, perverse, perverted, queer, singular, strange, unaccountable, uncharacteristic, uncommon, unexpected, unnatural, unpredictable, unrepresentative, untypical, unusual, wayward, weird.
OPPOSITES: SEE **normal**.

abnormality noun aberration, anomaly, deformity, deviation, eccentricity, idiosyncrasy, irregularity, oddity, peculiarity, perversity, singularity, strangeness, waywardness.

aboard adverb **to go aboard** SEE **embark**.

abode noun SEE **home**.

abolish verb *to abolish a law*. abrogate, annul, cancel, destroy, do away with, eliminate, end, eradicate, finish, [*informal*] get rid of, invalidate, nullify, overturn, put an end to, quash, repeal, remove, rescind, revoke, suppress, terminate, withdraw.
OPPOSITES: SEE **create**.

abominable adjective *abominable tortures.* abhorrent, appalling, atrocious, awful, base, beastly, brutal, contemptible, cruel, despicable, detestable, disgusting, distasteful, dreadful, execrable, foul, hateful, heinous, horrible, horrid, horrifying, inhuman, loathsome, nasty, nauseating, obnoxious, odious, offensive, repellent, repugnant, repulsive, revolting, terrible, unpleasant, vile.
OPPOSITES: SEE **humane**.

abominate verb SEE **hate** verb.

aboriginal adjective *the aboriginal inhabitants of a country.* ancient, earliest, first, indigenous, native, original, primal, primeval.

abort verb **1** *The foetus aborted.* be born prematurely, die, miscarry.
2 *to abort take-off.* call off, end, halt, nullify, stop, terminate.

abortion noun **1** *Her pregnancy ended in an abortion.* miscarriage, premature birth, termination of pregnancy.
2 *The ogre was portrayed as an abortion.* SEE **monster**.

abortive adjective *an abortive attempt.* fruitless, futile, ineffective, ineffectual, pointless, stillborn, unavailing, unfruitful, unproductive, unsuccessful, useless, vain.
OPPOSITES: SEE **successful**.

abound verb SEE **plentiful (to be plentiful)**.

abounding adjective SEE **plentiful**.

about-turn noun *His sudden about-turn surprised me.* about-face, change of direction, reversal, U-turn, volte face.

abrade verb SEE **graze** verb.

abrasion noun SEE **graze** noun.

abrasive adjective *an abrasive manner.* biting, caustic, galling, grating, harsh, hurtful, irritating, rough, sharp, SEE **unkind**.
OPPOSITES: SEE **kind** adjective.

abrasive noun VARIOUS ABRASIVES: emery, glass paper, grinding compound, sandpaper, scouring powder.

abridge verb *The play was abridged for TV.* abbreviate, compress, condense, curtail, cut, digest, edit, precis, prune, reduce, shorten, summarize, truncate.
OPPOSITES: SEE **expand**.

abridged adjective *an abridged version.* condensed, cut, edited, [*informal*] potted, shortened.

abridgement noun *an abridgement of a book.* abbreviation, condensation, digest, precis, short version, summary, synopsis.

abroad adverb *to travel abroad.* overseas.

abrogate verb SEE **abolish**.

abrupt adjective **1** *an abrupt ending.* hasty, headlong, hurried, precipitate, quick, rapid, sudden, swift, unexpected, unforeseen, unpredicted.
2 *an abrupt drop.* precipitous, sharp, sheer, steep.
OPPOSITES: SEE **gradual**.
3 *an abrupt manner.* blunt, brusque, curt, discourteous, gruff, impolite, rude, unceremonious, uncivil, ungracious.
OPPOSITES: SEE **polite**.
4 *an abrupt way of talking.* brisk, broken, disconnected, jerky, snappy, terse.

abscess noun SEE **boil** noun.

abscond verb SEE **escape** verb.

absent adjective **1** *absent from work.* away, [*slang*] bunking off, missing, playing truant, [*informal*] skiving.
OPPOSITES: SEE **present** adjective.
2 *an absent expression.* absent-minded, abstracted, blank, day-dreaming, distracted, dreamy, far-away, inattentive, oblivious, preoccupied, unaware, unthinking, vacant, vague, woolgathering.
OPPOSITES: SEE **alert** adjective.

absenteeism noun SEE **truancy**.

absent-minded adjective careless, forgetful, heedless, impractical, inattentive, scatterbrained, thoughtless, unheeding, unthinking, vague.
OPPOSITES: SEE **alert** adjective.

absolute adjective **1** *absolute silence. absolute happiness. an absolute certainty.* categorical, certain, complete, conclusive, decided, definite, downright, entire, full, genuine, implicit (*implicit faith*), inalienable (*an inalienable right*), indubitable, infallible, [*informal*] out-and-out, perfect, positive, pure, sheer, stark (*stark reality*), supreme, sure, thorough, total, unadulterated, unalloyed, unambiguous, unconditional, unequivocal, unmitigated, unmixed, unqualified, unquestionable, unreserved, unrestricted, utter.
2 *an absolute ruler.* almighty, autocratic, despotic, dictatorial, omnipotent, sovereign, totalitarian, tyrannical, undemocratic, unrestricted.
3 *the absolute opposite.* [*informal*] dead, diametrical, exact, precise.

absolution noun SEE **forgiveness**.

absolve verb SEE **forgive**.

absorb verb **1** *Our bodies absorb nutrients from our food.* assimilate, consume, devour, digest, drink in, fill up with, hold, imbibe, incorporate, [*formal*] ingest,

receive, retain, soak up, suck up, take in, utilise.
OPPOSITES: SEE **emit**.
2 *Buffers absorb the shock of impact.* cushion, deaden, lessen, reduce, soften.
3 *The game totally absorbed us.* captivate, engage, engross, enthral, fascinate, interest, involve, occupy, preoccupy, rivet.

absorbed adjective *absorbed in a book.* engrossed, SEE **interested**, [*informal*] lost, occupied, preoccupied, rapt.
to be absorbed SEE **concentrate** verb.

absorbing adjective *an absorbing hobby.* SEE **interesting**.

absorbent adjective *Absorbent substances soak up liquids.* absorptive, permeable, pervious, porous, spongy.
OPPOSITES: SEE **impervious**.

abstain verb **to abstain from** *to abstain from alcohol.* avoid, cease, decline, deny yourself, desist from, eschew, forgo, give up, go without, refrain from, refuse, reject, renounce, resist, shun, stop.
OPPOSITES: SEE **indulge (indulge yourself)**.

abstemious adjective *an abstemious way of life.* ascetic, austere, frugal, moderate, restrained, self-denying, self-disciplined, sober, sparing, teetotal [= *abstaining from alcohol*], temperate.
OPPOSITES: SEE **self-indulgent**.

abstract adjective 1 *abstract ideas.* abstruse, academic, general, hypothetical, indefinite, intangible, intellectual, metaphysical, philosophical, theoretical, unpractical, unreal, unrealistic.
OPPOSITES: SEE **concrete**.
2 *abstract art.* non-pictorial, non-representational.
OPPOSITES: SEE **representational**.

abstract noun SEE **summary** noun.

abstract verb SEE **remove** verb.

abstruse adjective *abstruse ideas.* complex, cryptic, deep, devious, difficult, enigmatic, esoteric, hard, incomprehensible, mysterious, mystical, obscure, perplexing, problematical, profound, puzzling, recherché, recondite, unfathomable.
OPPOSITES: SEE **obvious**.

absurd adjective 1 *an absurd explanation.* anomalous, illogical, incongruous, irrational, SEE **mad**, meaningless, nonsensical, paradoxical, preposterous, senseless, silly, stupid, unreasonable, untenable.
OPPOSITES: SEE **sensible**.
2 *absurd antics.* amusing, comic, crazy, [*informal*] daft, farcical, foolish, funny, grotesque, humorous, laughable, ludicrous, ridiculous, zany.
OPPOSITES: SEE **serious**.

abundant adjective *an abundant supply of food. an abundant growth of weeds.* ample, bounteous, bountiful, copious, excessive, flourishing, full, generous, lavish, liberal, luxuriant, overflowing, plenteous, plentiful, prodigal, profuse, rampant, rank, rich, well-supplied.
OPPOSITES: SEE **scarce**.

abuse noun 1 *Politicians should beware of the abuse of power.* misuse.
2 *We deplore the physical abuse of any human being.* assault, cruel treatment, ill-treatment, maltreatment.
3 *They yelled abuse at us.* curses, insults, invective, obscenities, slander.

abuse verb 1 *to abuse a thing, a machine, or a person* [*physically*]. batter, damage, harm, hurt, ill-treat, injure, maltreat, manhandle, misuse, molest, spoil, treat roughly.
2 *to abuse a person* [*verbally*]. affront, be rude to, [*informal*] call someone names, castigate, criticize, curse, defame, denigrate, disparage, insult, inveigh against, libel, malign, revile, slander, [*informal*] slate, [*informal*] smear, sneer at, swear at, traduce, upbraid, vilify, vituperate, wrong.

abusive adjective *abusive language.* acrimonious, angry, censorious, contemptuous, critical, cruel, defamatory, denigrating, derisive, derogatory, disparaging, harsh, hurtful, impolite, insulting, libellous, obscene, offensive, opprobrious, pejorative, rude, scathing, scurrilous, slanderous, vituperative.
OPPOSITES: SEE **friendly**, **polite**.

abut verb SEE **border** verb.

abysmal adjective 1 *abysmal despair.* bottomless, boundless, complete, deep, extreme, immeasurable, incalculable, infinite, profound, unfathomable, vast.
2 [*informal*] *The film was so abysmal that I fell asleep.* appalling, awful, SEE **bad**, dreadful, terrible, worthless.

abyss noun *a bottomless abyss.* chasm, crater, fissure, gap, gulf, hole, opening, pit, rift, void.

academic adjective 1 *A university is an academic institution.* educational, pedagogical, scholastic.
2 *an academic student.* bookish, brainy, clever, erudite, highbrow, intelligent, learned, scholarly, studious, well-read.
OPPOSITES: SEE **stupid**.
3 *academic studies.* abstract, intellectual, pure (*pure science*), theoretical.
OPPOSITES: SEE **applied**.

4 *Ideas about time-travelling are purely academic.* conjectural, hypothetical, impractical, notional, speculative, unpractical.
OPPOSITES: SEE **practical.**

academic noun *The professor is a real academic.* [*informal*] egghead, highbrow, intellectual, scholar, thinker.

academy noun SEE **college.**

accede verb SEE **agree.**

accelerate verb **1** *The bus accelerated.* [*informal*] get a move on, go faster, hasten, pick up speed, quicken, speed up.
2 *The factory must accelerate production.* [*formal*] expedite, promote, spur on, step up, stimulate.

accent noun **1** *an Irish accent.* brogue, cadence, dialect, enunciation, inflection, intonation, pronunciation, sound, tone.
2 *Play the first note with a strong accent.* accentuation, beat, emphasis, force, pulse, rhythm, stress.

accept verb **1** *I accepted her gift.* acquire, get, [*informal*] jump at, receive, take, welcome.
2 *She accepts responsibility.* acknowledge, admit, assume, bear, suffer, undertake.
3 *He accepted my arguments.* abide by, accede to, acquiesce in, adopt, agree to, approve, believe in, be reconciled to, consent to, defer to, grant, recognize, resign yourself to, [*informal*] stomach, submit to, [*informal*] swallow, take in, tolerate, [*informal*] wear, yield to.
OPPOSITES: SEE **reject.**

acceptable adjective **1** *an acceptable gift.* agreeable, appreciated, gratifying, pleasant, pleasing, welcome, worthwhile.
2 *an acceptable standard of work.* adequate, admissible, appropriate, moderate, passable, satisfactory, suitable, tolerable, unexceptionable.
OPPOSITES: SEE **unacceptable.**

acceptance noun *I wrote a letter of acceptance when he offered me the job.* acquiescence, agreement, approval, consent, willingness.
OPPOSITES: SEE **refusal.**

accepted adjective *an accepted fact.* acknowledged, agreed, canonical, indisputable, recognized, standard, undeniable, undisputed, unquestioned.
OPPOSITES: SEE **controversial.**

access noun SEE **entrance** noun.

accessible adjective *Make sure the first aid box is accessible.* at hand, available, convenient, [*informal*] get-at-able, [*informal*] handy, reachable, within reach.
OPPOSITES: SEE **inaccessible.**

accessory noun **1** *accessories for an electric drill.* addition, appendage, attachment, extension, extra, fitting.
2 *an accessory to a crime.* SEE **accomplice.**

accident noun **1** *a tragic accident.* calamity, catastrophe, collision, [*usually joking*] contretemps, crash, derailment, disaster, misadventure, mischance, misfortune, mishap, [*informal*] pile-up, [*slang*] shunt, wreck.
2 *an unforeseen accident. It happened by accident.* chance, coincidence, contingency, fate, fluke, fortune, hazard, luck, [*informal*] pot luck, serendipity.

accidental adjective *an accidental mistake.* adventitious, arbitrary, casual, chance, coincidental, [*informal*] fluky, fortuitous, fortunate, haphazard, inadvertent, lucky, random, unconscious, unexpected, unforeseen, unfortunate, unintended, unintentional, unlooked for, unplanned, unpremeditated.
OPPOSITES: SEE **intentional.**

acclaim verb SEE **praise** verb.

acclimatize verb SEE **accustom.**

accolade noun SEE **praise** noun.

accommodate verb **1** *If you need anything, we'll try to accommodate you.* aid, assist, furnish, help, oblige, provide, serve, supply.
2 *The hostel can accommodate thirty guests.* billet, board, cater for, entertain, harbour, hold, house, lodge, provide for, [*informal*] put up, quarter, shelter, take in.
3 *We quickly accommodated ourselves to our new surroundings.* SEE **accustom.**

accommodating adjective SEE **helpful.**

accommodation noun *holiday accommodation. temporary accommodation.* board, housing, lodgings, pied-à-terre, shelter.

KINDS OF ACCOMMODATION: apartment, barracks, bed and breakfast, [*informal*] bedsit, bedsitter, billet, boarding house, [*informal*] digs, flat, guest house, hall of residence, SEE **home**, hostel, hotel, married quarters, motel, rooms, self-catering, timeshare, youth hostel.

---

accompany verb **1** *A friend accompanied me.* attend, chaperon, conduct, convoy, escort, follow, go with, guard, guide, look after, partner, [*informal*] tag along with, travel with, usher.

2 *A cough often accompanies a cold.* belong with, be present with, coexist with, coincide with, complement, occur with, supplement.

accompanying adjective associated, attendant, concomitant, connected, related.

accomplice noun *The thief had an accomplice.* abettor, accessory, associate, collaborator, confederate, conspirator, SEE **helper**, [*informal*] henchman, partner.

accomplish verb *We accomplished our task.* achieve, attain, bring off, carry out, complete, conclude, consummate, discharge, do successfully, effect, execute, finish, fulfil, perform, realize, succeed in.

accomplished adjective SEE **skilful**.

accomplishment noun SEE **skill**.

accord noun SEE **agreement**.

accord verb SEE **agree**, **award** verb.

accost verb SEE **waylay**.

account noun **1** *The waiter gave us our account.* bill, check, invoice, receipt, reckoning, [*informal*] score, statement, tally.
2 *Money is of little account compared with your health.* advantage, benefit, concern, consequence, consideration, importance, interest, merit, profit, significance, standing, use, value, worth.
3 *I wrote an account of my trip.* chronicle, commentary, description, diary, disquisition, explanation, history, log, memoir, narration, narrative, portrayal, record, report, story, tale, version, [*informal*] write-up.

account verb *Can you account for his odd behaviour?* clarify, elucidate, explain, give reasons for, justify, make excuses for, rationalize, vindicate.

accountable adjective SEE **responsible**.

accountancy noun book-keeping.

accoutrements noun SEE **equipment**.

accredited adjective SEE **official** adjective.

accretion noun SEE **growth**.

accrue verb SEE **accumulate**.

accumulate verb **1** *I accumulate a lot of rubbish.* agglomerate, aggregate, amass, assemble, bring together, collect, gather, heap up, hoard, mass, pile up, [*informal*] stash away, stockpile, store up.
OPPOSITES: SEE **disperse**.
2 *The interest on your savings will accumulate.* accrue, build up, grow, increase, multiply.
OPPOSITES: SEE **decrease** verb.

accumulation noun *an accumulation of odds and ends.* [*informal*] build-up, collection, conglomeration, heap, hoard, mass, pile, stock, store, supply.

accurate adjective **1** *an accurate description.* authentic, close, factual, faithful, faultless, reliable, right, sound, strict, true, truthful, veracious.
2 *accurate measurements.* careful, correct, exact, meticulous, minute, perfect, precise, scrupulous.
3 *accurate aim.* certain, [*informal*] spot-on, sure, unerring.
OPPOSITES: SEE **inaccurate**.

accursed adjective *an accursed place where witches dance.* bewitched, damned, diabolical, evil.
OPPOSITES: SEE **holy**.

accusation noun *She denied the accusation completely.* allegation, alleged offence, charge, complaint, indictment, summons.

accuse verb *to accuse someone of a crime.* blame, bring charges against, censure, charge, condemn, denounce, impeach, impugn, incriminate, indict, inform against, make allegations against, prosecute, summons, tax.
OPPOSITES: SEE **defend**.

accustomed adjective *We had our accustomed bedtime drink.* common, conventional, customary, established, expected, familiar, habitual, normal, ordinary, prevailing, regular, routine, set, traditional, usual, wonted.
to get accustomed *You'll soon get accustomed to new surroundings.* acclimatize, adapt, adjust, become conditioned, become hardened, become inured, become seasoned, become trained, familiarize yourself (with), get broken in, get used (to), orientate yourself.

ace noun *an ace at athletics.* SEE **expert** noun.

acerbity noun SEE **asperity**.

ache noun *Exercise made the ache worse.* anguish, discomfort, hurt, pang, SEE **pain** noun, smart, soreness, suffering, throbbing, twinge.

ache verb *The swollen ankle ached when I walked.* be painful, be sore, hurt, smart, sting, suffer, throb.

achieve verb **1** *to achieve an ambition.* accomplish, attain, bring off, carry out, complete, conclude, consummate, discharge, do successfully, effect, execute, finish, fulfil, manage, perform, succeed in.
2 *They achieved fame overnight.* acquire, earn, gain, get, obtain, procure, reach,

score (*They scored a great success*), strike, win.

achievement noun SEE **feat, success**.

aching adjective SEE **painful**.

acid adjective **1** *Lemons taste acid.* sharp, sour, stinging, tangy, tart, vinegary.
2 *She has an acid tongue.* SEE **sharp**.

acknowledge verb **1** *I acknowledge that you are right.* accede, accept, admit, affirm, agree, allow, concede, confess, confirm, declare, endorse, grant, own, profess, yield.
OPPOSITES: SEE **deny**.
2 *Please acknowledge my letter.* answer, notice, react to, reply to, respond to, return (*a signal or greeting*).
3 *He acknowledged me with a smile.* greet, hail, recognize, salute, [*informal*] say hullo to.

acknowledged adjective SEE **accepted**.

acme noun *the acme of perfection.* SEE **apex**, crown, height, highest point, maximum, peak, pinnacle, summit, top.

acolyte noun SEE **assistant**.

acoustic adjective *the acoustic properties of a room.* auditory.

acquaint verb **to acquaint with** *She acquainted us with her discovery.* advise of, announce, apprise of, brief about, disclose, divulge, enlighten about, inform of, make familiar with, notify, reveal, tell about.

acquaintance noun SEE **friend**.

acquiesce verb SEE **agree**.

acquiescent *adjective* SEE **submissive**.

acquire verb SEE **get**.

acquisition noun *a new acquisition for the library.* accession, addition, [*informal*] buy, gain, possession, prize, property, purchase.

acquisitive adjective SEE **greedy**.

acquit verb *The judge acquitted the prisoner.* absolve, clear, declare innocent, discharge, dismiss, [*formal*] exculpate, excuse, exonerate, free, [*informal*] let off, liberate, release, reprieve, set free, vindicate.
to acquit yourself *We acquitted ourselves well in the competition.* act, behave, conduct yourself, operate, perform, work.

acrid adjective *an acrid smell of burning.* bitter, caustic, harsh, pungent, sharp, unpleasant.

acrimonious adjective *acrimonious insults.* abusive, acerbic, angry, bad-tempered, biting, bitter, caustic, censorious, churlish, cutting, hostile, hot-tempered, ill-natured, ill-tempered, irascible, mordant, peevish, petulant, pungent, SEE **quarrelsome**, rancorous, sarcastic, sharp, spiteful, tart, testy, venomous, virulent, waspish.
OPPOSITES: SEE **peaceable**.

acrimony noun SEE **bitterness**.

acrobat noun contortionist, gymnast, tumbler.

act noun **1** *a brave act.* action, deed, effort, enterprise, exploit, feat, operation, proceeding, step, undertaking.
2 *an act of parliament.* bill [=*draft of an act before it is passed*], decree, edict, law, order, regulation, statute.
3 *an act in a concert.* item, performance, routine, sketch, turn.
to put on an act SEE **pretend**.

act verb **1** *He acted like a baby.* behave, conduct yourself, seem to be.
2 *The medicine didn't act.* function, have an effect, operate, serve, take effect, work.
3 *to act a role. to act in a play.* appear (as), assume the character of, characterize, enact, imitate, impersonate, mime, mimic, perform, personify, play, portray, pose as, represent, simulate.
4 *Stop acting!* SEE **pretend**.

acting adjective *acting captain.* deputy, interim, provisional, stand-by, stopgap, substitute, surrogate (*surrogate mother*), temporary, vice (*vice-captain*).

action noun **1** *a brave action. a prompt action.* act, deed, effort, endeavour, enterprise, exploit, feat, measure, performance, proceeding, process, step, undertaking, work.
2 *a holiday packed with action.* activity, drama, energy, excitement, exercise, exertion, liveliness, movement, vigour, vitality.
3 *the action of a play.* events, happenings, incidents, story.
4 *the action of a watch.* functioning, mechanism, operation, working, works.
5 *a military action.* SEE **battle** noun.

actionable adjective SEE **illegal**.

activate verb *to activate a fire-alarm. to activate someone's enthusiasm.* actuate, animate, arouse, energize, excite, fire, galvanize, [*informal*] get going, initiate, mobilize, motivate, prompt, rouse, set in motion, set off, start, stimulate, stir, trigger off.

active adjective **1** *an active person. an active scene.* agile, animated, bustling, busy, energetic, enterprising, enthusiastic, functioning, live, lively, militant, nimble, [*informal*] on the go, spirited, sprightly, vigorous, vital, vivacious.

2 *an active supporter.* assiduous, busy, committed, dedicated, devoted, diligent, employed, engaged, enthusiastic, hard-working, industrious, involved, occupied, sedulous, staunch, working, zealous.
OPPOSITES: SEE **inactive**.
3 *an active volcano.* erupting, smoking, smouldering.
OPPOSITE: extinct.

activist noun *a political activist.* militant.

activity noun **1** *The market-place was full of activity.* action, animation, bustle, commotion, excitement, hurly-burly, hustle, industry, life, liveliness, motion, movement, stir.
2 *spare-time activities.* hobby, interest, job, labour, occupation, pastime, project, pursuit, scheme, task, undertaking, venture, work.

actor, actress nouns artist, artiste, SEE **entertainer**, lead, leading lady, performer, player, star, supporting actor, trouper, walk-on part.
GROUP WORD: cast, company, troupe.

actual adjective *I saw the actual place where it happened.* authentic, bona fide, certain, confirmed, definite, existing, factual, genuine, indisputable, legitimate, real, realistic, tangible, true, truthful, unquestionable, verifiable.
OPPOSITES: SEE **imaginary**.

actuate verb SEE **activate**.

acumen noun SEE **intelligence**.

acute adjective **1** *an acute mind.* analytical, astute, canny, SEE **clever**, incisive, intelligent, keen, observant, penetrating, perceptive, perspicacious, quick, sharp, shrewd, [*informal*] smart, subtle.
OPPOSITES: SEE **dull, stupid**.
2 *acute pain.* exquisite, extreme, fierce, intense, keen, piercing, racking, severe, sharp, shooting, sudden, violent.
OPPOSITES: SEE **mild**.
3 *an acute problem.* compelling, crucial, decisive, immediate, important, overwhelming, pressing, serious, urgent, vital.
OPPOSITES: SEE **continual**.
4 *an acute illness.* critical, sudden.
OPPOSITES: SEE **chronic**.
5 *an acute angle.* pointed, sharp.
OPPOSITE: obtuse.

ad noun SEE **advertisement**.

adamant adjective SEE **determined**.

adapt verb **1** *to adapt yourself to new ways.* acclimatize, accommodate, accustom, adjust, attune, fit, habituate, harmonize, orientate, reconcile, suit, tailor, turn.
2 *to adapt something for a new purpose.* alter, amend, change, convert, metamorphose, modify, process, rearrange, rebuild, reconstruct, refashion, remake, remodel, reorganize, reshape, transform, vary.
3 *to adapt a play for TV.* SEE **edit**.

adaptable adjective **1** *an adaptable tool.* SEE **adjustable**.
2 *an adaptable person.* SEE **amenable**.

add verb *to add one thing to another.* annex, append, attach, combine, integrate, join, put together, [*informal*] tack on, unite.
OPPOSITES: SEE **deduct**.
to add to *Our shouts only added to the confusion.* amplify, augment, enlarge, increase, supplement.
to add up 1 *Add up the scores.* calculate, compute, count, do a sum, reckon up, [*informal*] tot up, work out.
2 [*informal*] *Her story doesn't add up.* be convincing, be reasonable, [*informal*] hold water, make sense, [*informal*] ring true.
to add up to *What does the cost add up to?* amount to, come to, make, total.

added adjective SEE **additional**.

addendum noun SEE **appendix**.

addict noun **1** alcoholic, [*slang*] dope-fiend, [*slang*] junkie, [*informal*] user.
2 *a snooker addict.* SEE **enthusiast**.

addiction noun alcoholism [= *addiction to alcohol*], compulsion, craving, dependence, fixation, habit, obsession.

addition noun accession (*to a library*), accessory, accretion, addendum (*to a document*), additive, adjunct, admixture, afterthought, amplification, annexe (*to a building*), appendage, appendix (*to a book*), appurtenance, attachment, continuation, development, enlargement, expansion, extension, extra, increase, increment (*to salary*), postscript (*to a letter*), supplement.

additional adjective *additional resources.* added, extra, further, increased, more, new, other, spare, supplementary.

addled adjective *addled eggs.* SEE **rotten**.

address noun **1** *the address on an envelope.* directions.
2 *The vicar delivered an address.* discourse, [*formal*] disquisition, harangue, [*now often joking*] homily, lecture, [*formal*] oration, sermon, speech, talk.

address verb *A stranger addressed me.* accost, apostrophize, approach, [*informal*] buttonhole, engage in conversation, greet, hail, salute, speak to, talk to.

to address yourself to *Address yourself to your work.* apply yourself to, attend to, concentrate on, devote yourself to, engage in, focus on, get involved in, settle down to, tackle, undertake.

adduce verb SEE **cite**.

adept adjective SEE **skilful**.

adequate adjective *an adequate standard of work.* acceptable, competent, fair, good enough, passable, presentable, respectable, satisfactory, sufficient, suitable, tolerable.
OPPOSITES: SEE **inadequate**.

adhere verb SEE **stick** verb.

adherent noun SEE **supporter**.

adhesive adjective SEE **sticky**.

adhesive noun SEE **glue** noun.

adieu SEE **goodbye**.

adipose adjective SEE **fat** adjective.

adjacent adjective SEE **adjoining**.

adjoin verb SEE **border** verb.

adjoining adjective *the garden adjoining ours.* abutting, adjacent to, alongside, beside, bordering, closest to, contiguous with, juxtaposed to, nearest, neighbouring, next to, touching.
OPPOSITES: SEE **distant**, **separate**.

adjourn verb *to adjourn a meeting.* break off, defer, discontinue, dissolve, interrupt, postpone, prorogue (*parliament*), put off, stop temporarily, suspend.

adjournment noun *an adjournment of a meeting.* break, delay, interruption, pause, postponement, prorogation, recess, stay, stoppage, suspension.

adjudicate verb SEE **judge** verb.

adjunct noun SEE **addition**.

adjure verb SEE **command** verb, **request** verb.

adjust verb **1** *I adjusted the TV picture.* alter, amend, arrange, balance, change, modify, position, put right, rectify, regulate, set, temper, tune, vary.
2 *I adjusted myself to my new work.* acclimatize, accommodate, accustom, adapt, convert, fit, habituate, harmonize, modify, reconcile, refashion, remake, remodel, reorganize, reshape, tailor.

adjustable adjective *an adjustable handle.* adaptable, alterable, changeable, flexible, modifiable, movable, variable.
OPPOSITES: SEE **fixed**.

ad-lib adjective *ad-lib remarks.* extempore, impromptu, improvised, impulsive, made-up, [*informal*] off the cuff, [*informal*] off the top of your head, spontaneous, unplanned, unprepared, unrehearsed.

ad-lib verb *I had to ad-lib when I lost my notes.* extemporize, improvise, make it up, [*informal*] play it by ear.

administer verb **1** *The Head administers the school.* administrate, command, conduct the affairs of, control, direct, govern, head, lead, look after, manage, organize, oversee, preside over, regulate, rule, run, superintend, supervise.
2 *A nurse administered my medicine.* apply, deal out, dispense, distribute, dole out, give, hand out, measure out, mete out, provide, supply.

administrate verb SEE **administer**.

administrator noun bureaucrat, civil servant, executive, SEE **manager**, organizer.

admirable adjective *She has many admirable qualities.* commendable, creditable, deserving, enjoyable, estimable, excellent, exemplary, fine, SEE **good**, honourable, laudable, likeable, lovable, marvellous, meritorious, pleasing, praiseworthy, valued, wonderful, worthy.
OPPOSITES: SEE **contemptible**.

admiration noun *Her skill won our admiration.* appreciation, approval, commendation, esteem, hero-worship, high regard, honour, praise, respect.
OPPOSITES: SEE **contempt**.

admire verb **1** *I admire her skill.* applaud, approve of, esteem, have a high opinion of, hero-worship, [*formal*] laud, look up to, marvel at, praise, respect, revere, think highly of, value, wonder at.
2 *We admired the view.* appreciate, be delighted by, enjoy, like, love.
OPPOSITES: SEE **despise**.

admirer noun SEE **fan** noun, **lover**.

admiring adjective *admiring glances.* appreciative, approving, complimentary, flattering, respectful.
OPPOSITES: SEE **contemptuous**.

admissible adjective SEE **permissible**.

admission noun **1** *Admission is by ticket.* access, admittance, entrance, entry.
2 *an admission of guilt.* acceptance, acknowledgement, affirmation, avowal, confession, declaration, profession, revelation.
OPPOSITES: SEE **denial**.

admit verb **1** *to admit someone to hospital.* accept, allow in, grant access, let in, provide a place (in), receive, take in.
OPPOSITES: SEE **exclude**.
2 *to admit your guilt.* accept, acknowledge, agree, allow, concede, confess,

declare, disclose, divulge, grant, own up, profess, recognize, reveal, say reluctantly.
OPPOSITES: SEE **deny**.

admixture noun addition, amalgamation, blend, combination, fusion, mingling.

admonish verb SEE **reprimand** verb.

admonition noun SEE **reprimand** noun.

ado noun SEE **commotion**.

adolescence noun boyhood, girlhood, growing up, puberty, [*informal*] your teens, youth.

adolescent adjective *adolescent behaviour*. [These words are often used by adults to suggest that they are superior to young people.] boyish, girlish, immature, juvenile, puerile, teenage, youthful.

adolescent noun boy, girl, [*formal*] juvenile, minor, [*informal*] teenager, youngster, youth.

adopt verb **1** *We adopted their suggestion.* accept, appropriate, approve, back, champion, choose, embrace, endorse, espouse, follow, [*informal*] go for, support, take up.
2 *We adopted a stray cat.* befriend, foster, patronize, stand by, take in, [*informal*] take under your wing.

adorable adjective SEE **lovable**.

adoration noun SEE **love** noun, **worship** noun.

adore verb **1** *She adores her grandad.* dote on, glorify, idolize, love, revere, venerate, worship.
2 [*informal*] *I adore toffee!* SEE **like** verb.
OPPOSITES: SEE **hate** verb.

adorn verb SEE **decorate**.

adornment noun SEE **decoration**.

adrift adjective **1** *adrift on the ocean.* afloat, anchorless, drifting, floating, rudderless.
2 *adrift in a strange city.* aimless, astray, directionless, lost, purposeless, rootless.

adroit adjective SEE **skilful**.

adulation noun SEE **flattery**.

adult adjective developed, full-size, fully grown, grown-up, marriageable, mature, of age.
OPPOSITES: SEE **immature**.

adulterate verb *He adulterated the expensive wine with a cheaper brand.* contaminate, corrupt, debase, defile, dilute, [*informal*] doctor, pollute, taint, thin, water down, weaken.

adultery noun extramarital relations, having an affair, infidelity, unfaithfulness.

advance noun *You can't stop the advance of science.* development, evolution, forward movement, growth, headway, progress.

advance verb **1** *As the army advanced, the enemy fled.* approach, bear down, come near, forge ahead, gain ground, go forward, make headway, make progress, [*informal*] make strides, move forward, press ahead, press on, proceed, progress, [*informal*] push on.
OPPOSITES: SEE **retreat** verb.
2 *Computer technology has advanced enormously.* develop, evolve, grow, improve, increase, prosper, thrive.
OPPOSITES: SEE **regress**.
3 *Passing your exams will advance your career.* accelerate, assist, benefit, boost, expedite, facilitate, further, help the progress of, promote.
OPPOSITES: SEE **hinder**.
4 *He advanced an interesting theory.* adduce, cite, furnish, give, present, propose, submit, suggest.
5 [*informal*] *She advanced me a couple of pounds.* lend, loan, offer, pay, proffer, provide, supply.

advanced adjective **1** *advanced technology.* latest, modern, sophisticated, ultra-modern, up-to-date.
OPPOSITES: SEE **obsolete**.
2 *advanced ideas.* avant-garde, contemporary, experimental, forward-looking, futuristic, imaginative, innovative, inventive, new, novel, original, pioneering, precocious, progressive, revolutionary, trend-setting, unconventional, unheard of, [*informal*] way-out.
OPPOSITES: SEE **old-fashioned**.
3 *advanced mathematics.* complex, complicated, difficult, hard, higher.
OPPOSITES: SEE **elementary**.
4 *advanced for her age.* grown-up, mature, sophisticated, well-developed.

advantage noun *We had the advantage of a following wind.* aid, asset, assistance, benefit, boon, convenience, favour, gain, help, profit, service, use, usefulness.
to take advantage of SEE **exploit** verb.

advantageous adjective SEE **helpful**.

advent noun SEE **arrival**.

adventitious adjective SEE **accidental**.

adventure noun **1** *a dangerous adventure.* enterprise, escapade, exploit, gamble, incident, occurrence, operation, risk, undertaking, venture.
2 *a sense of adventure.* danger, excitement, hazard.

adventurous adjective 1 *adventurous explorers.* bold, daring, enterprising, heroic, intrepid, valiant, venturesome.
2 *an adventurous life.* challenging, dangerous, eventful, exciting, perilous, risky.
OPPOSITES: SEE **unadventurous**.

adversary noun SEE **enemy**.

adverse adjective 1 *an adverse report.* antagonistic, attacking, censorious, critical, derogatory, disapproving, hostile, hurtful, inimical, negative, uncomplimentary, unfavourable, unfriendly, unkind, unsympathetic.
2 *adverse conditions, adverse effects.* contrary, deleterious, detrimental, disadvantageous, harmful, inappropriate, inauspicious, opposing, prejudicial, uncongenial, unfortunate, unpropitious.
OPPOSITES: SEE **favourable**.

adversity noun SEE **misfortune**.

advert noun SEE **advertisement**.

advertise verb announce, broadcast, display, flaunt, make known, market, merchandise, notify, [*informal*] plug, proclaim, promote, promulgate, publicize, [*informal*] push, show off, [*informal*] spotlight, tout.

advertisement noun [*informal*] ad, [*informal*] advert, announcement, bill, [*informal*] blurb, [*informal*] break [*on TV*], classified advertisement [*in newspaper*], commercial [*on TV*], display, hand-out, leaflet, notice, placard, [*informal*] plug, poster, promotion, publicity, [*old-fashioned or joking*] puff, sign, [*informal*] small ad.

advice noun *He gave me some advice.* admonition, caution, counsel, guidance, help, opinion, recommendation, suggestion, tip, warning.

advisable adjective *The doctor said a rest was advisable.* prudent, recommended, wise.
OPPOSITES: SEE **inadvisable**.

advise verb 1 *The doctor advised her to rest.* admonish, advocate, caution, counsel, encourage, [*formal*] enjoin, [*formal*] exhort, instruct, prescribe, recommend, suggest, urge, warn.
2 *They advised us that the plane would be delayed.* SEE **inform**.

adviser noun consultant, counsellor, mentor.

advocate noun 1 *an advocate of reform.* SEE **supporter**.
2 *an advocate in a lawcourt.* SEE **lawyer**.

advocate verb SEE **recommend**.

aegis noun SEE **sponsorship**.

aeon noun SEE **time** noun.

aerate verb SEE **ventilate**.

aerial adjective *an aerial railway.* elevated, overhead, raised.

aerodrome noun airfield, airport, airstrip, landing-strip.

aeronautics noun aviation, flying.

aeroplane noun SEE **aircraft**.

aesthete noun artistic person.

aesthetic adjective SEE **artistic**.

affable adjective SEE **friendly**.

affair noun 1 *business affairs.* activity, business, concern, interest, matter, operation, project, question, subject, topic, transaction, undertaking.
2 *The crash was a mysterious affair.* circumstance, episode, event, happening, incident, occasion, occurrence, thing.
3 *a passionate affair.* attachment, intrigue, involvement, liaison, love affair, relationship, romance.

affect verb [Don't confuse *affect* with *effect.*] 1 *Acid rain affects trees. The storm affected the train service.* act on, alter, attack, change, have an effect on, have an impact on, [*informal*] hit, impinge on, influence, modify, pertain to, relate to, transform.
2 *The bad news affected us.* agitate, concern, disturb, grieve, impress, move, perturb, stir, touch, trouble, upset.
3 *She affects a posh accent.* assume, feign, SEE **pretend**, [*informal*] put on.

affectation noun [Don't confuse *affectation* with *affection.*] *Her posh accent is pure affectation.* insincerity, mannerism, SEE **pretence**, pretension.

affected adjective 1 *an affected way of talking.* insincere, SEE **pretentious**, [*informal*] put on.
2 *We sent aid to the affected areas.* damaged, distressed, hurt, infected, injured, poisoned, stricken, troubled.

affection noun *We can show affection by hugs and kisses.* amity, attachment, devotion, feeling, fondness, friendliness, friendship, liking, love, partiality, regard, [*informal*] soft spot, tenderness, warmth.
OPPOSITES: SEE **hatred**.

affectionate adjective SEE **loving**.

affianced adjective SEE **engaged**.

affidavit noun SEE **testimony**.

affiliate verb *Our club is affiliated to a national organization.* ally, amalgamate, associate, band together, combine, connect, couple, federate, incorporate, join,

join forces, link up, merge, syndicate, unite.

ffinity noun 1 *She has a natural affinity with animals.* SEE **sympathy**.
2 *The film doesn't have much affinity with the book.* SEE **similarity**.

ffirm verb SEE **declare**.

ffirmation noun SEE **declaration**.

ffirmative adjective *an affirmative answer.* agreeing, assenting, concurring, confirming, consenting, positive, saying 'yes'.
OPPOSITES: SEE **negative**.

ffix verb SEE **fasten**.

fflict verb *He is afflicted by illness. A plague of locusts afflicted the land.* annoy, bedevil, beset, burden, cause suffering, distress, harass, harm, hurt, oppress, pain, pester, plague, rack, torment, torture, trouble, try, vex, worry, wound.

ffliction noun SEE **evil, illness, pain**.

ffluent adjective 1 *an affluent life-style.* comfortable, expensive, gracious, lavish, luxurious, opulent, pampered, self-indulgent, sumptuous.
2 *an affluent businessman.* flourishing, [*informal*] flush, [*slang*] loaded, moneyed, [*often joking*] plutocratic, prosperous, rich, wealthy, [*informal*] well-heeled, well-off, well-to-do.
OPPOSITES: SEE **poor**.

fford verb 1 *Can you afford the cost?* find enough, manage to give, spare, [*informal*] stand.
2 *Our plan affords a solution to the problem.* SEE **provide**.

float adjective aboard, adrift, at sea, floating, on board ship, under sail.

fraid adjective 1 *I was afraid of the danger.* aghast, agitated, alarmed, anxious, apprehensive, cowardly, cowed, daunted, diffident, faint-hearted, fearful, frightened, hesitant, horrified, intimidated, jittery, nervous, pusillanimous, reluctant, scared, terrified, timid, timorous, uneasy, unheroic, [*informal*] yellow.
OPPOSITES: SEE **brave, confident**.
2 [*informal*] *I'm afraid I may be late.* regretful, sorry, unhappy.
to be afraid dread, fear, quake, tremble, worry.

fterlife noun SEE **eternity**, heaven, hell, the hereafter, the next world.

ftermath noun SEE **consequence**.

fterthought noun addendum, addition, appendix, extra, postscript.

ge noun 1 *What is your age?* date of birth.
2 *Age is catching up on me.* decrepitude, dotage, old age, senility.
3 *the Victorian age.* days, epoch, era, generation, period, time.
4 [*informal*] *It's an age since we met.* aeon, lifetime, long time.

age verb 1 *He's aged since we last saw him.* decline, degenerate, look older.
2 *Wine needs to age.* develop, grow older, mature, mellow, ripen.

aged adjective SEE **old**.

Several English words, including *agenda* and *agent*, are related to Latin *agere = to do.*

---

agenda noun [In Latin, *agenda* is plural = *things to be done*, but in English it is often used as if it were singular.] list, plan, programme, schedule, timetable.

agent noun *He employs an agent to act on his behalf.* broker, delegate, emissary, executor, [*old-fashioned*] functionary, go-between, intermediary, mediator, middleman, negotiator, representative, trustee.

agglomerate verb SEE **collect**.

agglutinate verb SEE **stick** verb.

aggrandizement noun SEE **glorification**.

aggravate verb [See note above *grave* (*adj.*). Some people think that the informal use of *aggravate = annoy* is incorrect.]
1 *The medicine only aggravated the pain.* add to, augment, compound, exacerbate, exaggerate, heighten, increase, inflame, intensify, magnify, make more serious, make worse, worsen.
OPPOSITES: SEE **alleviate**.
2 [*informal*] *Their teasing aggravated us.* annoy, bother, exasperate, irk, irritate, [*informal*] needle, nettle, [*informal*] peeve, provoke, trouble, vex.

aggregate noun SEE **total** noun.

aggression noun SEE **attack** noun, **hostility**.

aggressive adjective *aggressive behaviour.* antagonistic, assertive, attacking, bellicose, belligerent, bullying, [*slang*] butch, contentious, destructive, hostile, jingoistic, [*slang*] macho, militant, offensive, provocative, pugnacious, pushful, [*informal*] pushy, quarrelsome, violent, warlike, zealous.
OPPOSITES: SEE **friendly**.

aggressor noun SEE **attacker**.

aggrieved adjective SEE **resentful**.

aghast adjective SEE **horrified**.

agile adjective acrobatic, active, adroit, deft, fleet, graceful, limber, lissom,

lithe, lively, mobile, nimble, quick-moving, sprightly, spray, supple, swift.
OPPOSITES: SEE **clumsy, slow** adjective.

agitate verb **1** *The wind agitated the surface of the water.* beat, churn, convulse, ferment, froth up, ruffle, shake, stimulate, stir, toss, work up.
2 *The storm agitated the animals.* alarm, arouse, confuse, disconcert, disturb, excite, fluster, incite, perturb, rouse, stir up, trouble, unsettle, upset, worry.
OPPOSITES: SEE **calm** verb.

agitated adjective anxious, confused, distraught, disturbed, edgy, excited, feverish, fidgety, flustered, nervous, restive, restless, ruffled, [*informal*] tossing and turning, unsettled, upset.
OPPOSITES: SEE **serene**.

agitator noun demagogue, revolutionary, troublemaker.

agnostic adjective SEE **uncertain**.

agnostic noun doubter, sceptic.
COMPARE: atheist, believer.

agog adjective SEE **eager**.

agonize verb *I agonized over the decision.* be in agony [SEE **agony**], SEE **hurt**, labour, struggle, suffer, worry, wrestle.

agonizing adjective SEE **painful**.

agony noun anguish, distress, pain, suffering, torment, torture.

agrarian adjective *an agrarian economy.* agricultural, rural.
OPPOSITES: SEE **industrial**.

agree verb **1** *I agree to pay my share. He agreed to my proposal.* accede (to), accept, acknowledge, acquiesce (in), admit, allow, assent (to), be willing, concede, consent (to), [*formal*] covenant, grant, make a contract, pledge yourself, promise, undertake.
2 *I'm glad that we agree. We both added the figures up, but our answers didn't agree.* accord, be unanimous, be united, coincide, concur, conform, correspond, fit, get on, harmonize, match, [*informal*] see eye to eye, suit (*each other*).
OPPOSITES: SEE **disagree**.
to agree on *We agreed on a price.* choose, decide, establish, fix, settle.
to agree with *I don't agree with capital punishment.* advocate, argue for, [*informal*] back, defend, support.

agreeable adjective SEE **pleasant**.

agreement noun **1** *There's a large measure of agreement between us.* accord, affinity, compatibility, compliance, concord, conformity, congruence, consensus, consent, consistency, correspondence, harmony, similarity, sympathy, unanimity, unity.
OPPOSITES: SEE **disagreement**.
2 *The two sides signed an agreement.* acceptance, alliance, armistice, arrangement, bargain, bond, compact, concordat, contract, convention, covenant, deal, [*French*] entente, pact, pledge, protocol, settlement, treaty, truce, understanding.

agricultural adjective *an agricultural community.* agrarian, [*poetic or joking*] bucolic, pastoral, rural.

agriculture noun [*formal*] agronomy, crofting, cultivation, farming, growing, husbandry, tilling.

aground adjective *The ship was aground.* beached, grounded, high-and-dry, marooned, stranded, stuck.

aid noun *Poorer countries need aid from richer ones.* advice, assistance, backing, benefit, collaboration, co-operation, contribution, donation, encouragement, guidance, help, loan, patronage, prop, relief, sponsorship, subsidy, succour, support.

aid verb *to aid the poor. to aid a partner.* abet, assist, back, benefit, collaborate with, co-operate with, contribute to, encourage, help, [*informal*] lend a hand to, promote, prop up, [*informal*] rally round, relieve, subsidize, [*formal*] succour, support, sustain.

aide noun SEE **assistant**.

ail verb, **ailing** adjective SEE **ill**.

ailment noun SEE **illness**.

aim noun *What's your aim in life?* ambition, aspiration, cause, design, desire, destination, direction, dream, end, goal, hope, intention, mark, object, objective, plan, purpose, target, wish.

aim verb **1** *to aim a missile at someone.* address, beam, direct, level, line up, point, send, sight, take aim, train, turn, zero in on.
2 *to aim to do something.* aspire, attempt, design, endeavour, essay, intend, mean, plan, propose, resolve, seek, strive, try, want, wish.

aimless adjective SEE **rambling, random**.

air noun **1** *the air above us.* airspace, atmosphere, ether, heavens, sky, [*poetic*] welkin.
2 *We went out to get some air.* breath of air, breeze, draught, oxygen, waft, wind, [*poetic*] zephyr.
3 *She has the air of one who gets her own way.* ambience, appearance, aspect, aura, bearing, character, demeanour,

effect, feeling, impression, look, manner, mien, mood, quality, style.

air verb **1** *to air a room. to air clothes.* aerate, dry off, freshen, ventilate.
2 *to air opinions.* SEE **express** verb.

aircraft noun aeroplane, [*old-fashioned*] flying-machine, plane.

KINDS OF AIRCRAFT: airliner, airship, balloon, biplane, bomber, delta wing, dirigible, fighter, flying boat, glider, gunship, hang-glider, helicopter, jet, jumbo jet, jump-jet, microlight, monoplane, seaplane, STOL (short take-off and landing), supersonic aircraft, turboprop, VTOL (vertical take-off and landing).

PARTS OF AIRCRAFT: aileron, cabin, cargo hold, cockpit, elevator, fin, flap, fuselage, jet engine, joy-stick, passenger cabin, propeller, rotor, rudder, tail, tailplane, undercarriage, wing.

---

airfield noun SEE **airport**.

air force noun SEE **armed services**.

airless adjective SEE **stuffy**.

airliner noun SEE **aircraft**.

airman noun aviator, flier, pilot.

airport noun aerodrome, airfield, air strip, heliport, landing-strip, runway.

airship noun SEE **aircraft**.

airy adjective **1** *an airy room.* blowy, breezy, draughty, fresh, open, spacious, ventilated.
OPPOSITES: SEE **stuffy**.
2 *an airy manner.* SEE **cheery**.

aisle noun corridor, gangway, passage, passageway.

akin adjective SEE **similar**.

alacrity noun SEE **eagerness, speed**.

alarm noun **1** *Did you hear the alarm?* alarm-clock, alert, bell, fire-alarm, gong, signal, siren, tocsin, warning.
2 *We were filled with alarm.* anxiety, apprehension, consternation, dismay, distress, fear, fright, nervousness, panic, terror, trepidation, uneasiness.

alarm verb *The noise alarmed us.* agitate, daunt, dismay, distress, disturb, frighten, panic, [*informal*] put the wind up, scare, shock, startle, surprise, terrify, unnerve, upset, worry.
OPPOSITES: SEE **reassure**.

albino adjective colourless, pale, white.

album noun SEE **book** noun, **record** noun.

alcohol noun [*slang*] bevvy, [*informal*] booze, SEE **drink** noun, hard stuff, intoxicant, liquor, spirits, wine.

alcoholic adjective *alcoholic drink.* brewed, distilled, fermented, [*informal*] hard, intoxicating, [*old-fashioned*] spirituous, [*informal*] strong.

alcoholic noun addict, dipsomaniac, SEE **drunkard**, hard drinker, inebriate, toper.
OPPOSITES: SEE **teetotaller**.

alcoholism noun SEE **addiction**.

alcove noun SEE **recess**.

ale noun beer.

alert adjective *Stay alert!* alive (to), attentive, awake, careful, circumspect, heedful, lively, observant, on the alert, on the lookout, [*informal*] on the qui vive, on your guard, perceptive, quick, ready, sharp-eyed, vigilant, wary, watchful, wide awake.
OPPOSITES: SEE **dull** adjective, **inattentive**.

alert noun SEE **alarm** noun.
on the alert SEE **alert** adjective.

alert verb *We alerted them to the danger.* caution, forewarn, give the alarm, inform, make aware, notify, signal, tip off, warn.

alfresco adjective open-air, outdoor.

Several English words, including *alias* and *alien*, are related to Latin *alius* = *other*.

---

alias noun SEE **pseudonym**.

alibi noun SEE **excuse** noun.

alien adjective **1** *alien beings.* exotic, extra-terrestrial, foreign, outlandish, remote, strange, unfamiliar.
2 *Their ways are quite alien to me.* SEE **uncongenial**.

alien noun SEE **foreigner**.

alienate verb SEE **antagonize**.

alight adjective ablaze, afire, aflame, bright, burning, fiery, ignited, illuminated, lit up, on fire, shining.

alight verb *to alight from a bus.* descend, disembark, dismount, get down, get off.
2 *The bird alighted on a branch.* come down, come to rest, land, perch, settle, touch down.

align verb **1** *I aligned the marker pegs.* arrange in line, line up, place in line, straighten up.
2 *He aligns himself with the socialists.* affiliate, agree, ally, associate, co-operate, join, side, sympathize.

alike adjective *These paintings are alike.* akin, analogous, close, cognate, comparable, corresponding, equivalent, identical, indistinguishable, like, parallel, related, resembling, similar, the same, twin, uniform.

alimony noun SEE **payment**.

alive adjective **1** *Are the goldfish still alive?* SEE **active**, animate, breathing, existing, extant, flourishing, in existence, live, living, [*old-fashioned*] quick, surviving.
OPPOSITES: SEE **dead**.
2 *She's alive to recent developments.* SEE **alert** adjective.
to be alive with *Our garden's alive with ants.* SEE **swarm** verb.

allay verb *to allay someone's fears.* alleviate, assuage, calm, check, compose, diminish, ease, lessen, lull, mitigate, moderate, mollify, pacify, quell, quench (*your thirst*), quiet, quieten, reduce, relieve, slake (*your thirst*), soften, soothe, subdue.
OPPOSITES: SEE **increase, stimulate**.

allegation noun *The allegations against him were never proved.* accusation, assertion, charge, claim, declaration, statement, testimony.

allege verb *She alleged that he was a thief.* adduce, affirm, assert, [*formal*] asseverate, attest, aver, avow, claim, contend, declare, [*formal*] depose, insist, maintain, make a charge, [*formal*] plead, state.

allegiance noun *allegiance to your king.* devotion, duty, faithfulness, [*old-fashioned*] fealty, fidelity, loyalty, obedience.

allergic adjective [*informal*] *I'm allergic to work.* antagonistic, antipathetic, averse, disinclined, hostile, incompatible (with), opposed.

alleviate verb *to alleviate suffering.* abate, allay, ameliorate, assuage, check, diminish, ease, lessen, lighten, make lighter, mitigate, moderate, pacify, palliate, quell, quench (*your thirst*), reduce, relieve, slake (*your thirst*), soften, soothe, subdue, temper.
OPPOSITES: SEE **aggravate**.

alley noun SEE **road**.

alliance noun *an alliance between two countries or parties.* affiliation, agreement, association, bloc, bond, cartel, coalition, combination, compact, concordat, confederation, connection, consortium, covenant, entente, federation, guild, league, marriage, pact, partnership, relationship, syndicate, treaty, understanding, union.

alligator noun crocodile.

allocation noun SEE **allowance**.

allocate verb SEE **allot**.

allot verb *We alloted fair shares to all.* allocate, allow, apportion, assign, award, deal out, [*informal*] dish out, [*informal*] dole out, dispense, distribute, divide out, give out, grant, mete out, ration, set aside, share out.

allotment noun SEE **garden**.

allow verb **1** *We don't allow smoking.* approve, authorize, bear, endure, enable, grant permission for, let, license, permit, [*informal*] put up with, sanction, [*informal*] stand, suffer, support, tolerate.
OPPOSITES: SEE **forbid**.
2 *The shop allowed £40 for our old gas fire.* allot, allocate, deduct, give, grant, provide, remit, set aside.
3 *I allow that he's right.* SEE **admit**.

allowance noun **1** *a daily allowance of food.* allocation, allotment, amount, measure, portion, quota, ration, share.
2 *I can just live on my allowance.* annuity, grant, SEE **payment**, pension, pocket money, subsistence.
3 *They offered us an allowance for our old cooker.* deduction, discount, rebate, reduction, remittance, subsidy.
to make allowances for SEE **tolerate**.

alloy noun *an alloy of two metals.* amalgam, blend, combination, composite, compound, fusion, mixture.
VARIOUS METAL ALLOYS: SEE **metal**.

all right [Although *alright* is common, *all right* is still the better spelling.] *Are you all right? The food's all right.* SEE **healthy, safe, satisfactory**.

all-round adjective SEE **general**.

allude verb **to allude to** *Please don't allude to her illness.* hint at, make an allusion to, mention, refer to, speak of, suggest, touch on.

allure verb *allured by a smell of cooking.* attract, beguile, bewitch, cajole, charm, coax, decoy, draw, entice, fascinate, inveigle, lead on, lure, magnetize, persuade, seduce, tempt.

alluring adjective SEE **attractive**.

allusion noun hint, mention, reference, suggestion.

ally noun abettor, accessory, accomplice, associate, collaborator, colleague, companion, confederate, friend, helper, helpmate, [*informal*] mate, partner.
OPPOSITES: SEE **enemy**.

ally verb *With which side do you ally yourself?* affiliate, amalgamate, associate, band together, collaborate, combine, confederate, co-operate, form an alliance (SEE **alliance**), fraternize, join, join forces, league, [*informal*] link up, marry, merge, side, [*informal*] team up, unite.

almanac noun annual, calendar, year-book.

almighty adjective **1** *Almighty God.* all-powerful, omnipotent, supreme.
2 [*informal*] *an almighty bang.* SEE **big**.

almost adverb about, all but, approximately, around, as good as, just about, nearly, not quite, practically, virtually.

alms noun *alms for the poor.* SEE **charity**.

alone adjective *She lives alone.* apart, desolate, forlorn, friendless, isolated, lonely, lonesome, on your own, separate, single, solitary, solo, unaccompanied.

aloof adjective *He's hard to know—he's so aloof.* cold, cool, dispassionate, distant, formal, frigid, haughty, inaccessible, indifferent, remote, reserved, reticent, self-contained, self-possessed, [*informal*] standoffish, supercilious, unapproachable, unconcerned, undemonstrative, unforthcoming, unfriendly, unresponsive, unsociable, unsympathetic.
OPPOSITES: SEE **approachable**.

aloud adverb *to read aloud.* audibly, clearly, distinctly, out loud.
OPPOSITE: silently.

alp noun SEE **mountain**.

alphabet noun [*informal*] ABC, characters, letters.

alpine adjective, noun SEE **mountainous**.

alright SEE **all right**.

also adverb additionally, besides, furthermore, in addition, moreover, [*joking*] to boot, too.

Several English words, including *alter, alteration, alternate,* and *alternative,* are related to Latin *alter = other*.

---

alter verb adapt, adjust, amend, become different, SEE **change** verb, convert, edit, emend, enlarge, make different, modify, reconstruct, reduce, reform, remake, remodel, reorganize, reshape, revise, transform, vary.

alteration noun adaptation, adjustment, amendment, SEE **change** noun, difference, modification, reorganization, transformation.

altercation noun SEE **quarrel** noun. [Don't confuse *altercation* with *alteration.*]

alternate verb *Two actors will alternate in the leading role.* act alternately, come alternately, follow each other, interchange, oscillate, replace each other, rotate, [*informal*] see-saw, substitute for each other, take turns.

alternative noun **1** *I had no alternative.* choice, option.
2 *There are alternatives to coal.* back-up, replacement, substitute.

Several English words, including *altimeter* and *altitude,* are related to Latin *altus = high.*

---

altitude noun elevation, height.

altogether adverb *I'm not altogether satisfied.* absolutely, completely, entirely, fully, perfectly, quite, thoroughly, totally, utterly, wholly.

altruistic adjective SEE **unselfish**.

always adverb consistently, constantly, continually, continuously, endlessly, eternally, everlastingly, evermore, forever, [*informal*] for ever and ever, invariably, perpetually, persistently, regularly, repeatedly, unceasingly, unfailingly, unremittingly.

amalgam noun SEE **alloy**.

amalgamate verb *Two teams amalgamated. We amalgamated two teams.* affiliate, ally, associate, band together, coalesce, combine, come together, confederate, form an alliance, fuse, integrate, join, join forces, league, [*informal*] link up, marry, merge, put together, synthesize, [*informal*] team up, unite.

amass verb SEE **accumulate**.

amateur adjective *an amateur player. an amateur worker.* inexperienced, unpaid, unqualified, untrained.
OPPOSITE: professional.

amateur noun *unpaid amateurs.* dabbler, dilettante, enthusiast, layman, non-professional.
OPPOSITE: professional.

amateurish adjective *amateurish work.* clumsy, crude, [*informal*] do-it-yourself, incompetent, inept, inexpert, [*informal*] rough-and-ready, second-rate, shoddy, unpolished, unprofessional, unskilful, unskilled, untrained.
OPPOSITES: SEE **skilled**.

amaze verb astonish, astound, bewilder, confound, confuse, daze, disconcert, dumbfound, [*informal*] flabbergast, perplex, [*informal*] rock, shock, stagger, startle, stun, stupefy, surprise.

amazed adjective astonished, astounded, confused, dazed, dumbfounded, [*informal*] flabbergasted, nonplussed, speechless, staggered, stumped, stunned, surprised, [*informal*] thunderstruck.

amazing adjective awe-inspiring, breathtaking, exceptional, extraordinary, [*informal*] fantastic, incredible, miraculous, notable, phenomenal, prodigious, remarkable, [*informal*] sensational, special, staggering, stunning, stupendous, unusual, [*informal*] wonderful.

ambassador noun attaché, chargé d'affaires, consul, diplomat, emissary, envoy, legate (*of the pope*), nuncio (*of the pope*), plenipotentiary, representative.

amber adjective SEE **yellow**.

ambience noun SEE **atmosphere**.

ambiguous adjective *an ambiguous message.* ambivalent, confusing, enigmatic, equivocal, indefinite, indeterminate, puzzling, uncertain, unclear, vague, woolly.
OPPOSITES: SEE **definite**.

ambition noun **1** *She's got the ambition to succeed.* drive, enterprise, enthusiasm, [*informal*] push, pushfulness, self-assertion, thrust, zeal.
2 *Her ambition is to run in the Olympics.* aim, aspiration, desire, dream, goal, hope, ideal, intention, object, objective, target, wish.

ambitious adjective **1** *You must be ambitious to succeed in business.* assertive, committed, eager, energetic, enterprising, enthusiastic, go-ahead, [*informal*] go-getting, hard-working, industrious, keen, [*informal*] pushy, zealous.
OPPOSITES: SEE **apathetic**.
2 *She has ambitious ideas.* [*informal*] big, far-reaching, grand, grandiose, large-scale, SEE **unrealistic**.
OPPOSITES: SEE **modest**.

ambivalent adjective *His ambivalent reply means I still don't know what he wants.* ambiguous, backhanded (*a backhanded compliment*), confusing, doubtful, equivocal, inconclusive, inconsistent, indefinite, self-contradictory, [*informal*] two-faced, uncertain, unclear, uncommitted, unresolved, unsettled.

amble verb SEE **walk** verb.

ambush noun *The patrol set up an ambush.* ambuscade, attack, snare, surprise attack, trap.

ambush verb *The patrol ambushed the outlaws.* attack, ensnare, entrap, intercept, pounce on, surprise, swoop on, trap, waylay.

ameliorate verb SEE **improve**.

amenable adjective *He was quite amenable to our suggestions.* accommodating, acquiescent, adaptable, agreeable, biddable, complaisant, compliant, co-operative, deferential, docile, open-minded, persuadable, responsive, submissive, tractable, willing.
OPPOSITES: SEE **obstinate**.

amend verb *I hope that naughty dog will soon amend its ways.* adapt, adjust, alter, change, correct, emend, improve, mend, modify, put right, rectify, reform, remedy, revise.

amends noun **to make amends** SEE **atone**.

amenity noun SEE **facility**.

amiable, amicable adjectives SEE **friendly**.

amiss adjective SEE **wrong** adjective.

amity noun SEE **friendship**.

ammunition noun buckshot, bullet, cartridge, grenade, missile, projectile, round, shell, shrapnel.

amnesia noun forgetfulness, loss of memory.

amnesty noun SEE **pardon** noun.

amok, amuck adverb **to run amok, amuck** SEE **rampage** verb.

amoral adjective *an amoral way of life.* lax, loose, unethical, unprincipled, without standards.
OPPOSITES: SEE **moral**.
[Compare *amoral* with *immoral*.]

amorous adjective *amorous advances.* affectionate, ardent, carnal, doting, enamoured, erotic, fond, impassioned, loving, lustful, passionate, [*slang*] randy, sexual, [*informal*] sexy.
OPPOSITES: SEE **frigid**.

amorphous adjective SEE **shapeless**.

amount noun *a cheque for the full amount.* aggregate, entirety, quantum, reckoning, sum, total, whole.
2 *a large amount of rubbish.* bulk, lot, mass, measure, SEE **quantity**, supply, volume.

amount verb **to amount to** *What does it all amount to?* add up to, aggregate, be equivalent to, come to, equal, make, mean, total.

ample adjective **1** *an ample supply of food.* abundant, big, bountiful, capacious, commodious, considerable, copious, extensive, generous, great, large, lavish, liberal, munificent, plentiful, profuse, roomy, spacious, substantial, voluminous.
OPPOSITES: SEE **inadequate**.

2 *No more, thanks—that's ample.* [*informal*] heaps, [*informal*] lots, [*informal*] masses, more than enough, [*informal*] oodles, [*informal*] piles, plenty, [*informal*] stacks, sufficient.
OPPOSITES: SEE **insufficient**.

amplify verb **1** *I amplified what I had written in my notes.* add to, augment, broaden, develop, dilate upon, elaborate, enlarge, expand, expatiate on, extend, fill out, lengthen, make fuller, make longer, supplement.
OPPOSITES: SEE **condense**.
2 *to amplify sound.* boost, heighten, increase, intensify, make louder, magnify, raise the volume.
OPPOSITES: SEE **decrease**.

amputate verb *to amputate a limb.* chop off, cut off, dock (*a dog's tail*), lop off (*a branch*), poll or pollard (*a tree*), remove, sever, truncate.

amuse verb **1** *A comedian tries to amuse people.* cheer up, delight, divert, enliven, entertain, gladden, make laugh, raise a smile, [*informal*] tickle.
2 *The crossword amused me for a while.* absorb, beguile, engross, interest, involve, occupy, please.
OPPOSITES: SEE **bore** verb.
to amuse yourself *How do you like to amuse yourself?* be entertained, disport yourself, pass the time.

amusement noun **1** *We tried not to show our amusement.* hilarity, laughter, merriment, mirth.
2 *What's your chief amusement?* delight, distraction, diversion, enjoyment, entertainment, fun, game, hobby, interest, joke, leisure activity, pastime, play, pleasure, recreation, sport.

amusing adjective diverting, enjoyable, entertaining, SEE **funny**, pleasing.

anaemic adjective bloodless, colourless, feeble, frail, pale, pallid, pasty, sallow, sickly, wan, weak.

anaesthetic noun analgesic, painkiller.
KINDS OF ANAESTHETIC: chloroform, ether, laughing-gas.

analogous adjective SEE **similar**.

analogy noun *To explain the circulation of the blood she used the analogy of a central heating system.* comparison, likeness, metaphor, parallel, resemblance, similarity, simile.

analyse verb *We analysed the results of our experiment.* break down, dissect, evaluate, examine, interpret, investigate, scrutinize, separate out, study.

analysis noun *What did your analysis of the figures show?* breakdown, enquiry, evaluation, examination, interpretation, investigation, [*informal*] postmortem, scrutiny, study, test.

analytical adjective *an analytical mind.* analytic, critical, [*informal*] in-depth (*an in-depth investigation*), inquiring, investigative, logical, methodical, penetrating, questioning, rational, searching, systematic.
OPPOSITES: SEE **superficial**.

anarchist noun [These synonyms apply when you use the word informally, not in its strict political sense.] rebel, revolutionary, terrorist.

Several English words, including *anarchy* and *monarchy*, are related to Greek *arkho = to rule.* Greek *anarkhia = leaderless, without a ruler; monarkhia = rule of one.*

---

anarchy noun *There would be anarchy if we had no police.* bedlam, chaos, confusion, disorder, disorganization, insurrection, lawlessness, misgovernment, misrule, mutiny, pandemonium, riot.

anatomy noun physiology.

ancestor noun antecedent, forebear, forefather, forerunner, precursor, predecessor, progenitor.
OPPOSITE: **descendant**.

ancestry noun *Their family is of German ancestry.* blood, derivation, descent, extraction, family, genealogy, heredity, line, lineage, origin, parentage, pedigree, roots, stock.

anchor verb **1** *to anchor a ship.* berth, make fast, moor, tie up.
2 *to anchor something firmly.* SEE **fix**.

anchorage noun *a safe anchorage for ships.* harbour, haven, marina, moorings, port, refuge, sanctuary, shelter.

ancient adjective **1** *ancient buildings.* aged, [*often joking*] antediluvian, antiquated, antique, archaic, fossilized, obsolete, old, old-fashioned, outmoded, out-of-date, passé, [*often joking*] superannuated, venerable.
2 *ancient times.* bygone, early, [*poetic*] immemorial (*time immemorial*), [*old-fashioned*] olden, past, prehistoric, primeval, primitive, primordial, remote, [*old-fashioned*] of yore.
OPPOSITES: SEE **modern**.

ancillary adjective SEE **auxiliary**.

android noun SEE **robot**.

anecdote noun SEE **story**.

angel noun **1** archangel, cherub, divine messenger, seraph.

2 [*joking*] *Be an angel and make a cup of tea.* SEE **good (good person)**.

angelic adjective 1 *an angelic expression. angelic music.* beatific, SEE **beautiful**, blessed, celestial, cherubic, divine, ethereal, heavenly, holy, seraphic, spiritual.
2 *angelic behaviour.* exemplary, SEE **good**, innocent, pious, pure, saintly, unworldly, virtuous.
OPPOSITES: SEE **devilish**.

anger noun *filled with anger.* angry feelings [SEE **angry**], annoyance, bitterness, [*old-fashioned*] choler, exasperation, fury, hostility, indignation, [*old-fashioned*] ire, irritability, outrage, passion, pique, rage, [*formal*] rancour, resentment, tantrum, temper, vexation, wrath.

anger verb *Don't anger the bull!* [*informal*] aggravate, SEE **annoy**, antagonize, [*slang*] bug, displease, enrage, exasperate, incense, incite, inflame, infuriate, irritate, madden, make angry [SEE **angry**], [*informal*] needle, provoke, [*informal*] rile, [*informal*] rub up the wrong way, vex.
OPPOSITES: SEE **pacify**.

angle noun 1 *an angle between two walls or lines.* bend, corner, crook, nook.
2 *The speaker took an interesting angle on the topic.* approach, outlook, perspective, point of view, position, slant, standpoint, viewpoint.

angle verb *Angle the light so that it shines on me.* bend, SEE **bevel**, slant, turn, twist.

angler noun fisherman.

angry adjective [*informal*] aerated, annoyed, apoplectic, bad-tempered, bitter, [*informal*] bristling, [*informal*] choked, [*old-fashioned*] choleric, SEE **cross** adjective, disgruntled, enraged, exasperated, fiery, fuming, furious, heated, hostile, [*informal*] hot under the collar, ill-tempered, incensed, indignant, infuriated, [*informal*] in high dudgeon, irascible, irate, livid, mad, [*informal*] miffed, outraged, [*informal*] peeved, piqued, provoked, [*informal*] put out, raging, [*informal*] ratty, raving, resentful, riled, seething, [*slang*] shirty, [*informal*] sore, vexed, [*informal*] ugly (*in an ugly mood*), wild, wrathful.
OPPOSITES: SEE **calm** adjective.
an angry person [*informal*] cross-patch, [*informal*] sourpuss, [*informal*] spitfire.
to be angry, to become angry [*informal*] be in a paddy, [*informal*] blow up, boil, bristle, flare up, [*informal*] fly off the handle, fulminate (= *talk angrily*), fume, [*informal*] get steamed up, lose your temper, rage, rant, rave, [*informal*] see red, seethe, snap, storm.
to make someone angry SEE **anger** verb.

anguish noun agony, anxiety, distress, grief, heartache, misery, pain, sorrow, suffering, torment, torture, tribulation, woe.

anguished adjective SEE **pain (in pain)**.

angular adjective *the angular shape of sharp rocks.* bent, crooked, indented, jagged, sharp-cornered, zigzag.

animal adjective *animal passions.* bestial, bodily, brutish, carnal, fleshly, inhuman, instinctive, physical, savage, sensual, wild.
OPPOSITES: SEE **spiritual**.

animal noun beast, being, brute, creature, [*formal, plural*] fauna, [*plural*] wildlife.
KINDS OF ANIMAL: amphibian, arachnid, biped, SEE **bird**, carnivore, SEE **fish**, herbivore, hibernating animal, SEE **insect**, invertebrate, mammal, marsupial, mollusc, monster, nocturnal animal, omnivore, pet, predator, quadruped, SEE **reptile**, rodent, scavenger, vertebrate.

SOME LIVING ANIMALS: aardvark, antelope, ape, armadillo, baboon, badger, bear, beaver, bison, buffalo, camel, caribou, cat, chamois, cheetah, chimpanzee, chinchilla, chipmunk, coypu, deer, dog, dolphin, donkey, dormouse, dromedary.
elephant, elk, ermine, ferret, fox, frog, gazelle, gerbil, gibbon, giraffe, gnu, goat, gorilla, grizzly bear, guinea-pig, hamster, hare, hedgehog, hippopotamus, horse, hyena, ibex, impala, jackal, jaguar, jerboa.
kangaroo, koala, lemming, lemur, leopard, lion, llama, lynx, marmoset, marmot, marten, mink, mongoose, monkey, moose, mouse, musquash, ocelot, octopus, opossum, orang-utan, otter, panda, panther, pig, platypus, polar bear, polecat, porcupine, porpoise.
rabbit, rat, reindeer, rhinoceros, roe, salamander, scorpion, seal, sea-lion, sheep, shrew, skunk, snake, spider, squirrel, stoat, tapir, tiger, toad, vole, wallaby, walrus, weasel, whale, wildebeest, wolf, wolverine, wombat, yak, zebra.

FEMALE ANIMALS: bitch (*dog, wolf*), cow (*cattle, elephant, whale, etc.*), doe (*deer, hare, rabbit*), ewe (*sheep*), filly (*horse*), hen (*bird*), hind (*deer*), nanny goat, lioness, mare (*horse*), sow (*pig*), tigress, vixen (*fox*).

MALE ANIMALS: billy goat, buck (*deer, hare, rabbit*), bull (*cattle, elephant, whale*), cob (*swan*), cock (*bird*), dog (*dog, fox, wolf*), drake (*duck*), gander (*goose*), hart (*deer*), ram (*sheep*), stag (*deer*), stallion (*horse*), steer (*cattle*), tom (*cat*).

YOUNG ANIMALS: calf (*cattle*), chick, colt (*male horse*), cub (*fox, lion, etc.*), cygnet (*swan*), duckling, fawn (*deer*), filly (*female horse*), fledgling (*bird*), foal (*horse*), fry (*fish*), gosling (*goose*), heifer (*cow*), kid (*goat*), kitten (*cat*), lamb (*sheep*), leveret (*hare*), piglet, pup (*dog, seal, etc.*), whelp (*dog*).

GROUPS OF ANIMALS: brood (*of chicks*), covey (*of partridges*), flock (*of birds, sheep*), gaggle (*of geese*), herd (*of cattle*), leap (*of leopards*), litter (*of puppies*), pack (*of wolves*), pride (*of lions*), school (*of porpoises*), shoal (*of fish*), swarm (*of bees*).

SOME EXTINCT ANIMALS: brontosaurus, dinosaur, dodo, mastodon, pterodactyl, pterosaur, quagga.

---

animate adjective *Animals are animate, stones are not.* alive, breathing, conscious, feeling, live, living, sentient.
OPPOSITE: **inanimate**.

animate verb *The captain tried to animate her weary team.* activate, arouse, brighten up, [*informal*] buck up, cheer up, encourage, energize, enliven, excite, exhilarate, fire, galvanize, incite, inspire, invigorate, kindle, liven up, make lively, move, [*informal*] pep up, [*informal*] perk up, quicken, rejuvenate, revitalize, revive, rouse, spark, spur, stimulate, stir, urge, vitalize.

animated adjective *animated chatter.* active, alive, bright, brisk, bubbling, busy, cheerful, eager, ebullient, energetic, enthusiastic, excited, exuberant, gay, impassioned, lively, passionate, quick, spirited, sprightly, vibrant, vigorous, vivacious, zestful.
OPPOSITE: **lethargic**.
an animated film cartoon.

animation noun *a scene of lively animation.* activity, briskness, eagerness, ebullience, energy, enthusiasm, excitement, exhilaration, gaiety, high spirits, life, liveliness, [*informal*] pep, sparkle, spirit, sprightliness, verve, vigour, vitality, vivacity, zest.
OPPOSITE: **lethargy**.

animosity noun *animosity between two fighters.* acerbity, acrimony, animus, antagonism, antipathy, asperity, aversion, bad blood, bitterness, dislike, enmity, grudge, hate, hatred, hostility, ill will, loathing, malevolence, malice, malignancy, malignity, odium, rancour, resentment, sarcasm, sharpness, sourness, spite, unfriendliness, venom, vindictiveness, virulence.
OPPOSITE: **friendliness**.

animus noun SEE **animosity**.

annals noun SEE **history**.

annex verb *to annex territory.* acquire, appropriate, conquer, occupy, purloin (*goods or property*), seize, take over, usurp (*someone's position or authority*).

annexe noun **1** *an annexe to a hotel.* attached building, extension, wing.
2 [*formal*] *an annexe to a document.* SEE **appendix**.

annihilate verb *Nuclear weapons could annihilate the world.* abolish, destroy, eliminate, eradicate, erase, exterminate, extinguish, [*formal*] extirpate, [*informal*] finish off, [*informal*] kill off, [*informal*] liquidate, [*formal*] nullify, obliterate, raze, slaughter, wipe out.

annihilation noun SEE **destruction**.

Several English words, including *anniversary, annual,* and *superannuation,* are related to Latin *annus*=*year.*

---

anniversary noun annual celebration.
SPECIAL ANNIVERSARIES: bicentenary, birthday, centenary, coming-of-age, jubilee, silver/golden/diamond/ruby wedding.

annotate verb *to annotate a document.* make notes on, write annotations in [SEE **annotation**].

annotation noun *I wrote annotations in the margin of the book.* comment, commentary, [*formal*] elucidation, explanation, footnote, gloss, interpretation, note.

announce verb **1** *The boss announced his decision.* advertise, broadcast, declare, disclose, divulge, intimate, notify, proclaim, promulgate, publish, report, reveal, state.
2 *The DJ announced the next record.* introduce, lead into, preface, present.

announcement noun advertisement, bulletin, [*official*] communiqué, declaration, [*formal*] intimation, notification, [*official*] proclamation, [*formal*] promulgation, publication, report, revelation, statement.

announcer noun broadcaster, commentator, compère, [*poetic*] harbinger, herald, messenger, newscaster, newsreader, reporter, town crier.

annoy verb [*informal*] aggravate, SEE **anger** verb, antagonize, [*informal*] badger, be an annoyance to, bother, [*slang*] bug, chagrin, displease, exasperate, [*informal*] get on your nerves, grate, harass, harry, irk, irritate, jar, madden, make cross, molest, [*informal*] needle, [*informal*] nettle, offend, [*joking*] peeve, pester, pique, [*informal*] plague, provoke, rankle, [*informal*] rile, [*informal*] rub up the wrong way, ruffle, tease, trouble, try (*He tries me sorely*), upset, vex, worry.
OPPOSITE: **please.**

annoyance noun **1** *Her annoyance was obvious.* SEE **anger** noun, chagrin, crossness, displeasure, exasperation, irritation, pique, vexation.
2 *Is the dog an annoyance to you?* [*informal*] aggravation, harassment, irritant, offence, provocation, worry.

annoyed adjective SEE **angry**, chagrined, cross, displeased, exasperated, [*informal*] huffy, irritated, jaundiced, [*informal*] mad, [*informal*] miffed, [*informal*] needled, [*informal*] nettled, offended, [*informal*] peeved, piqued, [*informal*] riled, [*informal*] shirty, [*informal*] sore, upset, vexed.
OPPOSITES: SEE **pleased.**
to be annoyed [*informal*] go off in a huff, take offence, [*informal*] take umbrage.

annoying adjective [*informal*] aggravating, displeasing, exasperating, galling, grating, irksome, irritating, jarring, maddening, offensive, provocative, provoking, tiresome, troublesome, trying, upsetting, vexatious, vexing, worrying.

annual adjective *an annual event.* yearly.

annuity noun SEE **income.**

annul verb SEE **abolish.**

anoint verb **1** *to anoint a king.* bless, consecrate, dedicate, hallow, sanctify.
2 *to anoint a wound with ointment.* embrocate, grease, lubricate, oil, rub, smear.

anomalous adjective, **anomaly** noun SEE **abnormal, abnormality.**

anonymous adjective **1** *an anonymous poet.* incognito, nameless, unacknowledged, unidentified, unknown, unnamed, unspecified, unsung.
2 *an anonymous letter.* unattributed, unsigned.
3 *an anonymous style.* characterless, impersonal, nondescript, unremarkable.

anorak noun SEE **coat** noun.

answer noun **1** *an answer to a question.* acknowledgement, [*informal*] comeback, reaction, rejoinder, reply, response, retort, [*joking*] riposte.
2 *an answer to a problem.* explanation, outcome, solution.
3 *an answer to a charge or accusation.* countercharge, defence, plea, rebuttal, refutation, vindication.

answer verb **1** *I answered her question.* acknowledge, give an answer to, react to, reply to, respond to.
2 *"I'm quite well," I answered.* rejoin, reply, respond, retort, return.
3 *The dictionary answered our problem.* explain, resolve, solve.
4 *How did she answer the accusation?* refute.
5 *Will £10 answer your immediate need?* correspond to, echo, fit, match up to, meet, satisfy, serve, suffice, suit.
to answer back SEE **argue.**

answerable adjective SEE **responsible.**

antagonism noun SEE **animosity.**

antagonist noun SEE **opponent.**

antagonistic adjective SEE **hostile.**

antagonize verb *Don't antagonize the neighbours by making a noise.* alienate, anger, annoy, embitter, estrange, irritate, make an enemy of, offend, provoke, upset.
OPPOSITE: **please.**

Many English words have the prefix *ante-*. This is related to Latin *ante = before.* So *antecedent = going before; antediluvian = before the Flood.*
Don't confuse the prefix *ante-* with the quite different prefix *anti-*.

---

antecedent noun SEE **ancestor.**

antedate verb *The pottery we found antedates the fragments in the museum.* be older than, come before, go before, precede, predate.

antediluvian adjective SEE **antiquated.**

ante-room noun SEE **lobby.**

anthem noun canticle, chant, chorale, hymn, introit, paean, psalm.

anthology noun *an anthology of poems.* collection, compendium, compilation, digest, miscellany, selection, treasury.

anticipate verb **1** *I anticipated his blow and fended it off.* forestall, pre-empt.
2 [*informal*] *I anticipate that the result will be a draw.* expect, forecast, foresee, foretell, hope, predict. [Many people think this is an incorrect use of *anticipate.*]

Many English words, including *anticlimax, antidote, antiperspirant*, etc., have the prefix *anti-*. This is related to Greek *anti-=against*.
Don't confuse the prefix *anti-* with the quite different prefix *ante-*.

anticlimax noun *It was an anticlimax when they abandoned the game.* bathos, [*informal*] come-down, [*informal*] damp squib, disappointment, [*informal*] let-down.

antics noun *The children laughed at the clown's antics.* buffoonery, capers, clowning, escapades, foolery, fooling, [*informal*] larking about, pranks, [*informal*] skylarking, tomfoolery, tricks.

anticyclone noun area of high pressure, high.

antidote noun antitoxin, corrective, countermeasure, cure, neutralizing agent, remedy.

antipathy noun SEE **animosity, distaste**.

antiperspirant noun deodorant.

antiquarian noun antiquary, antiques expert, collector, dealer.

antiquated adjective *antiquated ideas. an antiquated machine.* aged, anachronistic, ancient, antediluvian, antique, archaic, dated, obsolete, SEE **old**, old-fashioned, out-dated, outmoded, out-of-date, passé, [*informal*] past it, [*informal*] prehistoric, [*informal*] primeval, primitive, quaint, [*joking*] superannuated, unfashionable.
OPPOSITES: SEE **new**.

antique adjective *antique furniture.* ancient, antiquarian, SEE **antiquated**, historic, old-fashioned, traditional, veteran (*cars*), vintage (*cars*).

antique noun bygone, curio, curiosity.

antiquity noun SEE **past** noun.

antirrhinum noun [*informal*] snapdragon.

anti-Semitic adjective SEE **racist**.

antiseptic adjective **1** *an antiseptic dressing.* aseptic, clean, disinfected, germ-free, hygienic, medicated, sanitized, sterile, sterilized, unpolluted.
2 *antiseptic ointment.* disinfectant, germicidal, sterilizing.

antisocial adjective *antisocial behaviour. antisocial hooligans.* alienated, anarchic, disagreeable, disorderly, disruptive, misanthropic, nasty, obnoxious, offensive, rebellious, rude, troublesome, uncooperative, undisciplined, unfriendly, unruly, unsociable.
OPPOSITES: SEE **friendly, sociable**.

antithesis noun SEE **opposite** noun.

antithetical adjective SEE **opposite** adjective.

antitoxin noun SEE **antidote**.

antler noun *a deer's antlers.* horn.

antonym noun opposite.

anxiety noun **1** *anxiety about the future.* apprehension, concern, disquiet, distress, doubt, dread, fear, foreboding, fretfulness, misgiving, nervousness, qualm, scruple, strain, stress, tension, uncertainty, unease, worry.
OPPOSITES: SEE **calmness**.
2 *anxiety to do your best.* desire, eagerness, enthusiasm, impatience, keenness, willingness.

anxious **1** *anxious about the future.* afraid, agitated, alarmed, apprehensive, concerned, distressed, disturbed, edgy, fearful, [*informal*] fraught, fretful, [*informal*] jittery, nervous, [*informal*] nervy, overwrought, perturbed, solicitous, tense, troubled, uneasy, upset, worried.
OPPOSITES: SEE **calm** adjective, **carefree**.
2 *anxious to do your best.* avid, careful, desirous, [*informal*] dying, eager, impatient, intent, [*informal*] itching, keen, willing, yearning.
to be anxious SEE **worry** verb.

apart adverb asunder, separately.
to keep apart, to take apart SEE **separate** verb.

apartheid noun SEE **racism**.

apartment noun flat.

apathetic adjective *You won't succeed if you are apathetic.* cool, dispassionate, emotionless, impassive, inactive, indifferent, lethargic, listless, passive, phlegmatic, sluggish, tepid, torpid, unambitious, uncommitted, unconcerned, unenthusiastic, unfeeling, uninterested, uninvolved, unmotivated.
OPPOSITES: SEE **enthusiastic**.

apathy noun coolness, inactivity, indifference, lassitude, lethargy, listlessness, passivity, torpor.
OPPOSITES: SEE **enthusiasm**.

ape noun SEE **monkey**.

ape verb SEE **imitate**.

aperient noun enema, laxative, purgative.

aperture noun SEE **opening** noun.

apex noun **1** *the apex of a pyramid or mountain.* crest, crown, head, peak, pinnacle, point, summit, tip, top, vertex.
OPPOSITES: SEE **bottom** noun.
2 *the apex of her career.* acme, apogee, climax, consummation, crowning moment, culmination, height, zenith.
OPPOSITES: SEE **nadir**.

aphorism noun SEE **saying**.

aphrodisiac adjective *an aphrodisiac potion.* arousing, erotic, [*informal*] sexy, stimulating.

apiary noun beehive, hive.

aplomb noun SEE **confidence**.

apocalyptic adjective SEE **prophetic**, ruinous.

apocryphal adjective SEE **fictitious**.

apogee noun SEE **apex**.

apologetic adjective *He was apologetic about his mistake.* contrite, penitent, regretful, remorseful, repentant, rueful, sorry.
OPPOSITES: SEE **unrepentant**.

apologize verb *He apologized for being rude.* be penitent, express regret, make an apology, repent, say sorry.

apology noun *He made an apology for his rudeness.* acknowledgement, confession, defence, excuse, explanation, justification, plea.

apophthegm noun SEE **saying**.

apoplectic adjective SEE **angry**.

apostate noun SEE **deserter**.

apostle noun crusader, evangelist, messenger, missionary, preacher, propagandist, proselytizer, teacher.
the Apostles Christ's disciples, Christ's followers.

apostrophize verb SEE **address** verb.

apothecary noun SEE **chemist**.

appal verb *Their injuries appalled us.* alarm, disgust, dismay, distress, frighten, harrow, horrify, nauseate, outrage, revolt, shock, sicken, terrify, unnerve.

appalling adjective **1** *appalling injuries. appalling behaviour.* alarming, atrocious, disgusting, distressing, dreadful, frightening, frightful, gruesome, harrowing, horrendous, horrible, horrific, horrifying, nauseating, outrageous, revolting, shocking, sickening, terrifying, unnerving.
2 [*informal*] *an appalling piece of work.* SEE **bad**.

apparatus noun appliance, contraption, device, equipment, gadget, [*informal*] gear, instrument, machine, machinery, mechanism, [*informal*] set-up, system, [*informal*] tackle, tool.

apparel noun SEE **clothes**.

apparent adjective *There was no apparent reason for the crash.* blatant, clear, conspicuous, detectable, discernible, evident, manifest, noticeable, observable, obvious, ostensible, overt, patent, perceptible, recognizable, self-explanatory, unconcealed, visible.
OPPOSITES: SEE **concealed**.

apparition noun chimera, ghost, hallucination, illusion, manifestation, phantasm, phantom, presence, shade, spectre, spirit, [*informal*] spook, vision, wraith.

appeal noun **1** *an appeal for help.* call, cry, entreaty, petition, request, supplication.
2 *She had a great appeal for the audience.* allure, attractiveness, charisma, charm, [*informal*] pull, seductiveness.

appeal verb *to appeal for aid.* ask earnestly, beg, beseech, call, canvass, cry out, entreat, implore, invoke, petition, plead, pray, request, solicit, supplicate.
to appeal to *His good looks don't appeal to me.* SEE **attract**.

appealing adjective SEE **attractive**.

appear verb **1** *Our visitors appeared. A light appeared upstairs. Snowdrops appear in the spring.* arise, arrive, attend, begin, be seen, [*informal*] bob up, come, come into view, [*informal*] crop up, enter, develop, emerge, [*informal*] heave into sight, loom, materialize, occur, show, [*informal*] show up, spring up, surface, turn up.
2 *I once appeared in a play.* feature, figure, SEE **perform**.
3 *My magazine appears on Saturdays.* be published, come out.
4 *It appears that he was asleep.* look, seem, transpire, turn out.

appearance noun **1** *His early appearance surprised us.* SEE **arrival**.
2 *He has the appearance of one who's had no sleep.* aspect, exterior, impression, likeness, SEE **look** noun, semblance.

appease verb *They offered a sacrifice to appease the gods.* assuage, calm, conciliate, humour, mollify, pacify, placate, propitiate, quiet, reconcile, satisfy, soothe, [*informal*] sweeten, tranquillize, win over.
OPPOSITES: SEE **anger** verb.

appellation noun SEE **name** noun.

append verb SEE **attach**.

appendage noun SEE **addition**.

appendix noun *an appendix to a book.* addendum, addition, annexe, codicil (*to a will*), epilogue, postscript, rider, supplement.

appertaining adjective SEE **relevant**.

appetizing adjective *appetizing food.* delicious, [*informal*] mouthwatering, tasty, tempting.
WORDS TO DESCRIBE HOW THINGS TASTE: SEE **taste** verb.

appetite noun *an appetite for food. an appetite for adventure.* craving, demand, desire, eagerness, greed, hankering, hunger, keenness, longing, lust, passion, predilection, relish, [*informal*] stomach, taste, thirst, urge, willingness, wish, yearning, [*informal*] yen, zeal, zest.

applaud verb *to applaud a performance.* acclaim, approve, [*informal*] bring the house down, cheer, clap, commend, compliment, congratulate, eulogize, extol, give an ovation, [*formal*] laud, praise, salute.
OPPOSITES: SEE **criticize**.

applause noun approval, clapping, ovation, plaudits, SEE **praise** noun.

apple noun [*old-fashioned*] pippin.
KINDS OF APPLE: cooker, crab, eater, eating apple.
OTHER FRUITS: SEE **fruit**.

appliance noun SEE **apparatus**.

DOMESTIC APPLIANCES: carpet-sweeper, cooker, dish-washer, freezer, fridge, microwave, vacuum cleaner, washing machine.

---

applicable adjective SEE **appropriate** adjective.

applicant noun *an applicant for a job.* aspirant, candidate, competitor, entrant, interviewee, participant, postulant [=*applicant to join a religious order*].

applied adjective *applied science.* practical, utilitarian.
OPPOSITE: **pure**.

apply verb **1** *Apply ointment to the wound.* administer, bring into contact, lay on, put on, spread.
2 *The rules apply to everyone.* appertain, be relevant, pertain, refer, relate.
3 *Apply your skill.* bring into use, employ, exercise, implement, practise, use, utilize, wield.
to apply for *I applied for a refund.* ask formally for, [*informal*] put in for, request, solicit, sue for.
to apply yourself SEE **concentrate**.

appoint verb **1** *to appoint a time for a meeting.* arrange, decide on, determine, fix, ordain, settle.
2 *Who did they appoint to do the job?* choose, co-opt, delegate, depute, designate, detail, elect, make an appointment, name, nominate, [*informal*] plump for, select, settle on, vote for.

appointment noun **1** *an appointment with the dentist.* arrangement, assignation, consultation, date, engagement, fixture, interview, meeting, rendezvous, session, [*old-fashioned*] tryst.
2 *the appointment of a new member of staff.* choice, choosing, commissioning, election, naming, nomination, selection.
3 *Did you apply for the appointment?* job, office, place, position, post, situation.

apportion verb SEE **allot**.

apposite adjective SEE **relevant**.

appraise verb SEE **assess**.

appreciable adjective SEE **considerable**.

appreciate verb **1** *I appreciate what she did for me.* admire, approve of, be grateful for, be sensitive to, cherish, enjoy, esteem, like, prize, regard highly, respect, sympathize with, treasure, value, welcome.
OPPOSITES: SEE **despise**.
2 *I appreciate that you can't afford much.* acknowledge, apprehend, comprehend, know, realize, recognize, see, understand.
OPPOSITES: SEE **disregard**.
3 *The value of property may appreciate.* build up, escalate, gain, go up, grow, improve, increase, inflate, mount, rise, soar, strengthen.
OPPOSITES: SEE **depreciate**.

appreciative adjective SEE **admiring, grateful**.

apprehend verb SEE **arrest, understand**.

apprehension noun SEE **fear** noun, **understanding**.

apprehensive adjective SEE **anxious**.

apprentice noun beginner, learner, novice, probationer, pupil, starter, [*joking*] tiro, trainee.

apprise verb SEE **inform**.

approach noun **1** *Footsteps signalled their approach.* advance, advent, arrival, coming, nearing.
OPPOSITES: SEE **retreat** noun.
2 *The easiest approach is from the west.* access, doorway, entrance, entry, passage, road, way in.
3 *She has a positive approach to her work.* attitude, course, manner, means, method, mode, procedure, style, system, technique, way.
4 *I made an informal approach to the bank manager.* appeal, application, invitation, offer, overture, proposal, proposition.

approach verb **1** *The lion approached its prey.* advance on, bear down on, catch up with, come near, draw near, gain on, move towards, near.
2 *We approached the job cheerfully.* SEE **begin, undertake**.

3 *I approached the bank manager for a loan.* SEE **contact** verb.

approaching adjective *approaching traffic.* advancing, looming, nearing, oncoming.

approachable adjective *an approachable person.* accessible, affable, agreeable, congenial, cordial, friendly, informal, kind, [*informal*] matey, open, sociable, sympathetic, [*informal*] unstuffy, welcoming, well-disposed.
OPPOSITES: SEE **aloof, formal.**

approbation noun SEE **approval.**

appropriate adjective *appropriate clothes. an appropriate moment to ask a question.* applicable, apposite, [*joking*] apropos, apt, becoming, befitting, correct, deserved, due, felicitous, fit, fitting, germane, happy, just, [*old-fashioned*] meet, opportune, pertinent, proper, relevant, right, seasonable, seemly, suitable, tactful, tasteful, timely, well-judged, well-suited, well-timed.
OPPOSITES: SEE **inappropriate.**

appropriate verb *to appropriate someone else's property.* commandeer, confiscate, gain control of, [*informal*] hijack, requisition, seize, steal, take, take over, usurp.

approval noun **1** *We cheered to show our approval.* acclaim, acclamation, admiration, applause, appreciation, approbation, commendation, esteem, favour, liking, plaudits, praise, regard, respect, support.
OPPOSITES: SEE **disapproval.**
2 *The committee gave its approval to our plan.* acceptance, acquiescence, agreement, assent, authorization, [*informal*] blessing, confirmation, consent, endorsement, [*informal*] go-ahead, [*informal*] green light, licence, mandate, [*informal*] OK, permission, ratification, sanction, seal (*of approval*), stamp (*of approval*), support, [*informal*] thumbs up, validation.
OPPOSITES: SEE **refusal, veto.**

approve verb *The boss approved my request for leave.* accede to, accept, agree to, allow, assent to, authorize, [*informal*] back, [*informal*] bless, confirm, consent to, countenance, endorse, give in to, pass, permit, ratify, [*informal*] rubber-stamp, sanction, sign, subscribe to, support, tolerate, uphold, validate.
OPPOSITES: SEE **refuse** verb, **veto.**
to approve of *She approves of what I did.* acclaim, admire, applaud, appreciate, commend, esteem, favour, like, love, praise, respect, value, welcome.
OPPOSITES: SEE **condemn.**

approximate adjective *an approximate calculation.* close, estimated, inexact, near, rough.
OPPOSITES: SEE **exact** adjective.

approximate verb **to approximate to** *Does the price approximate to what you expected?* approach, be close to, be similar to, border on, come near to, equal roughly, look like, resemble.

approximately adverb about, round, circa (*born circa 1750*), close to, just about, loosely, more or less, nearly, [*informal*] nigh on, [*informal*] or thereabouts, [*informal*] pushing, roughly, round about.

appurtenance noun SEE **addition.**

apropos adjective SEE **appropriate** adjective.

apt adjective **1** *an apt remark.* SEE **appropriate** adjective.
2 *apt to fall asleep.* SEE **likely.**
3 *an apt pupil.* SEE **clever.**

aptitude noun SEE **ability.**

Several English words, including *aquarium, aquatic, aqueduct,* and *sub-aqua,* are related to Latin *aqua* = *water.*

---

aquamarine adjective SEE **blue** adjective.

aquaplane verb SEE **skid.**

aquarium noun fish-tank.

aquatic adjective *aquatic sports.* water.

aqueduct noun SEE **bridge** noun.

aqueous adjective SEE **watery.**

aquiline adjective *an aquiline nose.* hooked.

arabesque noun SEE **decoration.**

arable adjective *arable land.* cultivated.
OPPOSITE: **pasture.**

arachnid noun ARACHNIDS INCLUDE: mite, scorpion, spider.

arbiter noun SEE **judge** noun.

arbitrary adjective **1** *an arbitrary decision.* capricious, casual, chance, fanciful, illogical, indiscriminate, irrational, random, subjective, unplanned, unpredictable, unreasonable, whimsical, wilful.
OPPOSITES: SEE **methodical, rational.**
2 *an arbitrary show of force.* absolute, autocratic, despotic, dictatorial, high-handed, imperious, summary, tyrannical, tyrannous.

arbitrate verb *to arbitrate in a dispute.* adjudicate, decide the outcome, intercede, judge, make peace, mediate, negotiate, pass judgement, referee, settle, umpire.

arbitration noun *The arbitration of an independent judge settled the dispute.* adjudication, decision, [*informal*] good offices, intercession, judgement, mediation, negotiation, settlement.

arbitrator noun adjudicator, arbiter, go-between, intermediary, judge, mediator, middleman, negotiator, ombudsman, peacemaker, referee, [*informal*] trouble-shooter, umpire.

arboreal adjective SEE **silvan**.

arboretum noun SEE **park** noun.

arbour noun SEE **garden**.

arc noun SEE **curve** noun.

arcane adjective SEE **secret** adjective.

arch noun arc, archway, bridge, SEE **curve** noun, vault.

arch verb *The cat arched its back.* arc, bend, bow, curve.

archaic adjective SEE **old-fashioned**.

archbishop noun SEE **clergyman**.

archetypal adjective SEE **original** adjective.

archetype noun classic, example, ideal, model, original, paradigm, pattern, precursor, prototype, standard.

architect noun designer.

archives noun *Historians searched the archives for information.* annals, chronicles, documents, history, libraries, memorials, museums, papers, records, registers.

archivist noun curator, historian, researcher.

archway noun SEE **arch** noun.

arctic adjective *arctic weather.* SEE **cold** adjective.

ardent adjective *ardent kisses.* SEE **fervent**.

arduous adjective *arduous work.* backbreaking, daunting, demanding, difficult, exhausting, fatiguing, formidable, gruelling, hard, harsh, heavy, herculean, [*informal*] killing, laborious, onerous, punishing, rigorous, severe, strenuous, taxing, tough, uphill, wearisome.
OPPOSITES: SEE **easy**.

area noun **1** *an area of land or water.* breadth, expanse, extent, patch, sector, sheet, space, stretch, surface, tract, width.
2 *an urban area.* district, environment, environs, locality, neighbourhood, part, precinct, province, region, sector, terrain, territory, vicinity, zone.
3 *an area of study.* field, sphere, subject.

arena noun *a sports arena.* amphitheatre, field, ground, park, pitch, playing area, ring, rink, stadium.

arguable adjective SEE **debatable**.

argue verb **1** *Whenever I make a suggestion you argue!* [*informal*] bandy words, bicker, demur, differ, disagree, dispute, dissent, expostulate, fall out, feud, fight, have an argument [SEE **argument**], object, protest, quarrel, remonstrate, squabble, take exception, wrangle.
OPPOSITES: SEE **agree**.
2 *He argued over the price.* bargain, haggle.
3 *The lawyer argued that the accused was innocent.* assert, claim, contend, demonstrate, maintain, prove, reason, show, suggest.
to argue about *We argue about politics.* debate, deliberate, discuss.

argument noun **1** *a violent argument.* altercation, clash, controversy, difference, disagreement, dispute, expostulation, feud, fight, quarrel, remonstration, row, [*informal*] set-to, squabble, wrangle.
2 *a civilized argument.* consultation, debate, defence, deliberation, [*formal*] dialectic, discussion, exposition, polemic, reasoning.
3 *Did you follow the argument of the lecture?* abstract, case, contention, gist, hypothesis, idea, line of reasoning, outline, plot, summary, synopsis, theme, thesis, view.

argumentative adjective SEE **quarrelsome**.

arid adjective **1** *arid desert.* barren, desert, dry, fruitless, infertile, lifeless, parched, sterile, torrid, unproductive, waste, waterless.
OPPOSITES: SEE **fruitful**.
2 *an arid subject.* boring, dreary, dull, pointless, tedious, uninspired, uninteresting, vapid.
OPPOSITES: SEE **interesting**.

arise verb *Perhaps the matter won't arise.* SEE **appear**, come up, crop up.
2 *We arose at dawn.* SEE **rise** verb.

aristocrat noun grandee, lady, lord, noble, nobleman, noblewoman, patrician, titled person [SEE **peer, peeress** nouns].

aristocratic adjective *an old aristocratic family.* [*informal*] blue-blooded, courtly, élite, gentle, highborn, lordly, noble, patrician, princely, royal, thoroughbred, titled, upperclass.

arithmetic noun SEE **mathematics**.

arm noun appendage, bough, branch, extension, limb, offshoot, projection.

arm verb *We armed ourselves with sticks.* equip, fortify, furnish, provide, supply.

armada noun *an armada of ships.* convoy, fleet, flotilla, navy, squadron, task-force.

Armageddon noun SEE **battle** noun.

armaments noun WEAPONS: SEE **weapons.**

armchair noun SEE **seat** noun.

armed services

VARIOUS GROUPS OF FIGHTING MEN: air force, army, battalion, brigade, cavalry, cohort, company, corps, garrison, fleet, foreign legion, infantry, legion, militia, navy, patrol, platoon, rearguard, regiment, reinforcements, squad, squadron, task-force, vanguard.

SERVICEMEN & WOMEN INCLUDE: aircraftman, aircraftwoman, cavalryman, commando, infantryman, marine, mercenary, paratrooper, recruit, sailor, soldier, [*plural*] troops.

SEE ALSO **fighter, officer, rank** noun.

---

armistice noun *An armistice ended the fighting.* agreement, cease-fire, entente, league, moratorium, pact, peace, suspension of hostilities, treaty, truce, understanding.

armour noun *a knight's armour.* chain-mail, mail, protection.
PARTS OF MEDIEVAL ARMOUR: breastplate, gauntlet, greave, habergeon, helmet, visor.

armoury noun *an armoury of weapons.* ammunition-dump, arsenal, depot, magazine, ordnance depot, stockpile.

army noun SEE **armed services.**
RANKS IN THE ARMY: SEE **rank** noun.

aroma noun bouquet, fragrance, odour, perfume, scent, smell, whiff.

arouse verb *The controversial plan aroused strong feelings.* SEE **cause** verb, kindle, quicken, provoke, spark off, stimulate, stir up, [*informal*] whip up.
OPPOSITES: SEE **allay.**

arrange verb **1** *to arrange flowers. to arrange information.* adjust, align, array, categorize, classify, collate, display, dispose, distribute, grade, group, lay out, line up, marshal, order, organize, [*informal*] pigeon-hole, position, put in order, put out, range, rank, set out, sift, sort, sort out, space out, systematize, tabulate, tidy up.
2 *to arrange an outing.* contrive, coordinate, devise, fix, manage, organize, plan, prepare, see to, settle, set up.
3 *to arrange music.* adapt, harmonize, orchestrate, score, set.

arrangement noun **1** *the arrangement of the furniture in a room. the arrangement of words on a page.* adjustment, alignment, SEE **array** noun, design, display, disposition, distribution, grouping, layout, marshalling, organization, planning, setting out, spacing, tabulation.
2 *a business arrangement.* agreement, bargain, compact, contract, deal, pact, scheme, settlement, terms, understanding.
3 *a musical arrangement.* adaptation, harmonization, orchestration, setting, version.

arrant adjective *arrant nonsense.* SEE **complete** adjective.

array noun *a gleaming array of vintage cars.* arrangement, assemblage, SEE **collection**, demonstration, display, exhibition, formation, [*informal*] line-up, muster, panoply, parade, presentation, show, spectacle.

array verb **1** *His trophies were arrayed on the mantelpiece.* SEE **arrange.**
2 *We were arrayed in our best clothes.* adorn, apparel, attire, clothe, deck, decorate, dress, equip, fit out, garb, rig out, robe, wrap.

arrears noun backlog, overdue payment.

arrest verb **1** *A landslide arrested our progress.* bar, block, check, delay, end, halt, hinder, impede, inhibit, interrupt, obstruct, prevent, retard, slow, stem, stop.
2 *The police arrested the suspect.* apprehend, [*informal*] book, capture, catch, [*informal*] collar, detain, [*informal*] have up (*They had me up for speeding*), hold, [*informal*] nab, [*informal*] nick, [*informal*] pinch, restrain, [*informal*] run in, seize, take into custody, take prisoner.

arrival noun **1** *A crowd awaited the star's arrival.* advent, appearance, approach, coming, entrance, homecoming, landing, return, touchdown.
2 *Have you met the new arrivals yet?* caller, newcomer, visitor.

arrive verb **1** *When is she due to arrive?* appear, come, disembark, drive up, enter, get in, land, [*informal*] roll in, [*informal*] roll up, show up, touch down, turn up.
2 [*informal*] *Now he's got a posh car, he thinks he's arrived.* get to the top, make good, [*informal*] make it, succeed.
to arrive at *We arrived at the terminus.* attain, come to, get to, [*informal*] make, reach.

arrogant adjective *an arrogant manner.* boastful, bumptious, cavalier, [*informal*] cocky, conceited, condescending, disdainful, haughty, [*informal*] high and mighty, high-handed, imperious, insolent, lordly, overbearing, pompous, presumptuous, proud, scornful, self-important, snobbish, [*informal*] stuck-up, supercilious, superior, vain.
OPPOSITES: SEE **modest**.

arsenal noun SEE **armoury**.

arson noun fire-raising, incendiarism.

arsonist noun fire-raiser, incendiary, pyromaniac.

art noun **1** artistry, artwork, craft, craftsmanship, draughtsmanship.
a work of art artefact, objet d'art.

ARTS AND CRAFTS INCLUDE: architecture, batik, cameo, caricature, carpentry, cartoon, cloisonné, collage, commercial art, crochet, draughtsmanship, drawing, embroidery, enamelling, engraving, etching, fashion design, graphics, handicraft, illustration, jewellery, knitting, linocut, lithography, marquetry, metalwork, mobiles, modelling, monoprint, mosaic, needlework, origami, SEE **painting**, patchwork, photography, portraiture, pottery, printing, print, SEE **sculpture**, sewing, sketching, spinning, stencilling, stone carving, weaving, wicker-work, woodcut, woodwork.

ARTISTS AND CRAFTSMEN: SEE **artist**.

---

2 *There's an art in lighting a bonfire.* aptitude, cleverness, craft, dexterity, expertise, facility, knack, proficiency, skilfulness, skill, talent, technique, touch, trick.

artefact noun SEE **thing**.

artful adjective [*usually uncomplimentary*] *That was an artful trick!* astute, canny, clever, crafty, cunning, deceitful, designing, devious, [*informal*] fly, [*informal*] foxy, ingenious, knowing, scheming, shrewd, skilful, sly, smart, subtle, tricky, wily.
OPPOSITES: SEE **ingenuous**.

article 1 *Have you any unwanted articles for the jumble sale?* SEE **thing**.
2 *Did you read my article in the magazine?* SEE **writing**.

articulate adjective *an articulate speaker.* clear, coherent, comprehensible, distinct, eloquent, expressive, fluent, [*uncomplimentary*] glib, intelligible, lucid, understandable, vocal.
OPPOSITES: SEE **inarticulate**.

articulate verb SEE **speak**.

articulated adjective *an articulated lorry.* bending, flexible, hinged, jointed.

artificial adjective **1** *an artificial beard. an artificial cheeriness.* affected, assumed, bogus, contrived, counterfeit, factitious, fake, false, feigned, imitation, mock, [*informal*] phoney, [*informal*] put on, pretended, pseudo, sham, simulated, spurious, unreal.
OPPOSITES: SEE **genuine**.
2 *artificial fertilizers.* fabricated, made-up, man-made, manufactured, synthetic, unnatural.
OPPOSITES: SEE **natural**.

artillery noun SEE **gun**.

artist noun **1** craftsman, craftswoman, designer.

ARTISTS AND CRAFTSMEN INCLUDE: architect, blacksmith, caricaturist, carpenter, cartoonist, commercial artist, draughtsman, draughtswoman, engraver, goldsmith, graphic designer, illustrator, mason, miniaturist, old master, painter, photographer, portrait painter, potter, printer, sculptor, silversmith, smith, weaver.

ARTS AND CRAFTS: SEE **art**.

---

2 *a music-hall artist.* SEE **performer**.

artistic adjective *an artistic arrangement of flowers.* aesthetic, attractive, beautiful, creative, cultured, decorative, imaginative, ornamental, tasteful.
OPPOSITES: SEE **crude, ugly**.

artless adjective SEE **simple**.

arty adjective SEE **pretentious**.

ascend verb **1** *to ascend a hill.* climb, come up, go up, mount, move up, scale.
2 *The plane ascended.* defy gravity, fly up, levitate, lift off, rise, soar, take off.
3 *The road ascends to the church.* slope up.
OPPOSITES: SEE **descend**.

ascension noun SEE **ascent**.

ascent noun *a steep ascent.* ascension, climb, elevation, gradient, hill, incline, ramp, rise, slope.
OPPOSITES: SEE **descent**.

ascertain verb *We ascertained that our passports were in order.* confirm, determine, discover, establish, find out, identify, learn, make certain, make sure, settle, verify.

ascetic adjective *The hermit followed an ascetic life-style.* abstemious, austere, celibate, chaste, frugal, harsh, hermit-like, plain, puritanical, restrained, rigorous, self-controlled, self-denying,

self-disciplined, severe, spartan, strict, temperate.
OPPOSITES: SEE **self-indulgent**.

ascribe verb SEE **attribute**.

aseptic adjective SEE **antiseptic**.

asexual adjective *asexual reproduction.* sexless.

ash noun *ash from a fire.* burnt remains, cinders, clinker, embers.

ashamed adjective **1** *ashamed of doing wrong.* apologetic, blushing, chagrined, chastened, conscience-stricken, contrite, discomfited, distressed, guilty, humbled, humiliated, mortified, penitent, red-faced, remorseful, repentant, rueful, shamefaced, sorry, upset.
OPPOSITES: SEE **unrepentant**.
2 *too ashamed to take his clothes off.* abashed, bashful, demure, diffident, embarrassed, modest, prudish, self-conscious, sheepish, shy.
OPPOSITES: SEE **shameless**.

ashen adjective SEE **pale**.

asinine adjective SEE **stupid**.

ask verb **1** *to ask a question. to ask for help.* appeal, apply, badger, beg, beseech, [*formal*] catechize, crave, demand, enquire, entreat, implore, importune, inquire, interrogate, petition, plead, pose a question, pray, press, query, question, quiz, request, seek, solicit, sue, supplicate.
2 *to ask someone to a party.* [*old-fashioned*] bid, invite, [*formal*] request the pleasure of the company of.
to ask for *He asked for trouble!* attract, cause, court, encourage, generate, incite, provoke, [*informal*] stir up, tempt.

askance adverb **to look askance** SEE **disapprove**.

askew adjective SEE **crooked**.

asleep adjective **1** *asleep in bed.* comatose, [*informal*] dead to the world, dormant, dozing, [*informal*] fast off, [*informal*] having a nap, hibernating, inactive, inattentive, napping, resting, sedated, sleeping, slumbering, snoozing, [*informal*] sound off, unconscious, under sedation.
OPPOSITES: SEE **awake**.
2 *My foot's asleep.* SEE **numb**.

aspect noun **1** *There's an aspect of this affair I don't understand.* angle, circumstance, detail, facet, feature, side, standpoint.
2 *The place had a peaceful aspect. He had a belligerent aspect.* air, appearance, attitude, bearing, countenance, demeanour, expression, face, look, manner, mien, visage.
3 *The house has a southern aspect.* direction, orientation, outlook, position, prospect, situation, view.

asperity noun *We were hurt by the asperity of his manner.* acerbity, acidity, acrimony, astringency, bitterness, churlishness, crossness, harshness, hostility, irascibility, irritability, peevishness, rancour, roughness, severity, sharpness, sourness, venom, virulence.
OPPOSITES: SEE **mildness**.

aspersions noun **to cast aspersions on** SEE **criticize**.

asphyxiate verb SEE **suffocate**.

aspirant noun SEE **applicant**.

aspirate verb SEE **pronounce**.

aspiration noun SEE **ambition**.

aspire verb **to aspire to** *He aspires to the top position in the business.* aim for, crave, desire, dream of, have ambitions to or for, hope for, long for, pursue, seek, set your sights on, strive after, want, wish for, yearn for.

aspiring adjective *an aspiring politician.* budding, [*informal*] hopeful, intending, potential, [*informal*] would-be.

assail verb *They assailed us with missiles.* assault, SEE **attack** verb, bombard, pelt, set on.

assassinate verb SEE **kill**.

assassination noun SEE **murder** noun.

assault noun, verb SEE **attack** noun, verb.

assay verb SEE **assess**, **test** verb.

assemble verb **1** *A crowd assembled.* accumulate, collect, come together, congregate, converge, crowd together, flock together, gather, group, herd, join up, meet, rally round, swarm, throng round.
2 *We assembled our luggage. The general assembled his troops.* amass, bring together, convene, gather, get together, marshal, mobilize, muster, pile up, rally, round up.
OPPOSITES: SEE **disperse**.
3 *These cars are assembled in Britain.* build, construct, erect, fabricate, fit together, make, manufacture, piece together, produce, put together.
OPPOSITES: SEE **dismantle**.

assembly noun **1** *a political assembly.* conclave, conference, congregation [=*assembly for worship*], congress, convention, convocation, council, gathering, SEE **meeting**, parliament, rally, synod [=*church assembly*].
2 *an assembly of people.* SEE **crowd** noun.

assent noun *We need the Head's assent before we do anything.* acceptance, accord, acquiescence, agreement, approbation, approval, compliance, consent, [*informal*] go-ahead, permission, sanction, willingness.
OPPOSITES: SEE **refusal**.

assent verb *He assented to our proposals.* accede, accept, acquiesce, agree, approve, be willing, comply, concede, concur, consent, express agreement, give assent, say 'yes', submit, yield.

assert verb *The accused asserted that he was innocent.* affirm, allege, argue, asseverate, attest, claim, contend, declare, emphasize, insist, maintain, proclaim, profess, protest, state, stress, swear, testify.
to assert yourself *Don't give in: assert yourself!* be assertive [SEE **assertive**], be resolute, insist, make demands, persist, stand firm, [*informal*] stick to your guns.

assertive adjective *His assertive personality dominated the meeting.* aggressive, assured, authoritative, bold, confident, decided, decisive, dogmatic, domineering, emphatic, firm, forceful, insistent, [*uncomplimentary*] opinionated, positive, [*uncomplimentary*] pushy, self-assured, strong, strong-willed, [*uncomplimentary*] stubborn, uncompromising.
OPPOSITES: SEE **submissive**.

assess verb *The garage assessed the damage to the car.* appraise, assay (*quality of metals*), calculate, compute, consider, determine, estimate, evaluate, fix, gauge, judge, price, reckon, review, [*informal*] size up, value, weigh up, work out.

asset noun **1 assets** capital, estate, funds, goods, holdings, means, money, possessions, property, resources, savings, securities, wealth, [*informal*] worldly goods.
2 *Good health is a great asset.* advantage, aid, blessing, benefit, boon, [*informal*] godsend, good, help, profit, support.

asseverate verb SEE **assert**.

assiduous adjective SEE **diligent**.

assign verb **1** *He assigned the most responsible jobs to experienced people.* allocate, allot, apportion, consign, dispense, distribute, give, hand over, share out.
2 *He assigned me to the sweeping up.* appoint, choose, consign, delegate, designate, nominate, put down, select, specify, stipulate.
3 *I assign my success to pure luck.* accredit, ascribe, attribute, credit.

assignation noun SEE **appointment**.

assignment noun *We were given a hard assignment.* duty, errand, job, mission, post, project, responsibility, task, work.

assimilate verb SEE **absorb**, **learn**.

assist verb *We'll do the job more quickly if you assist us.* abet, advance, aid, back, benefit, boost, collaborate, co-operate, facilitate, further, help, [*infomal*] lend a hand, [*informal*] rally round, reinforce, relieve, second, serve, succour, support, sustain.
OPPOSITES: SEE **hinder**.

assistance noun aid, backing, collaboration, co-operation, contribution, encouragement, help, patronage, sponsorship, subsidy, succour, support.
OPPOSITES: SEE **hindrance**.

assistant noun abettor, accessory, accomplice, acolyte, aide, ally, associate, auxiliary, backer, collaborator, colleague, companion, confederate, deputy, helper, helpmate, [*informal*] henchman, mainstay, [*uncomplimentary*] minion, partner, [*informal*] right-hand man or woman, second, second-in-command, stand-by, subordinate, supporter.

associate noun SEE **assistant**.

associate verb **1** *I hope you don't associate with that mob!* ally yourself, be friends, consort, fraternize, [*informal*] gang up, mix, side, socialize.
OPPOSITES: SEE **dissociate**.
2 *I don't associate sunbathing with the North Pole.* bracket together, connect, put together, relate, [*informal*] tie up.

association noun **1** *The association between us lasted many years.* SEE **friendship**, **relationship**.
2 *an association of youth clubs.* affiliation, alliance, amalgamation, body, brotherhood, cartel, clique, club, coalition, combination, company, confederation, consortium, co-operative, corporation, federation, fellowship, group, league, marriage, merger, organization, partnership, party, society, syndicate, trust, union.

assonance noun SEE **harmony**.

assorted adjective *assorted colours.* different, differing, [*old-fashioned*] divers, diverse, diversified, heterogeneous, manifold, miscellaneous, mixed, motley, multifarious, several, sundry, varied, various.

assortment noun *an assortment of sandwiches.* array, choice, collection, diversity, medley, mélange, miscellany, mixture, selection, variety.

assuage verb SEE **soothe**.

assume verb 1 *I assume you'd like some tea.* believe, deduce, expect, guess, [*informal*] have a hunch, have no doubt, imagine, infer, presume, presuppose, suppose, surmise, suspect, take for granted, think, understand.
2 *The new boss assumes his duties next week.* accept, embrace, take on, undertake.
3 *She assumed a disguise.* acquire, adopt, don, dress up in, feign, put on, wear.

assumed adjective *an assumed name.* SEE **false**.

assumption noun *My assumption is that we can average 40 miles an hour.* belief, conjecture, expectation, guess, hypothesis, premise or premiss, supposition, surmise, theory.

assurance noun SEE **promise** noun.

assure verb 1 *He assured me the work would be done by Friday.* SEE **promise** verb.
2 *He wanted to assure himself that all was well.* SEE **reassure**.

assured adjective *an assured manner.* SEE **confident**.

Several English words, including *asterisk, asteroid, astronaut, astronomy*, etc., are related to Greek *aster=star*.

---

asterisk noun star.

asteroid noun SEE **astronomy**.

astonish verb amaze, astound, baffle, bewilder, confound, daze, [*informal*] dazzle, dumbfound, electrify, flabbergast, leave speechless, nonplus, shock, stagger, startle, stun, stupefy, surprise, take aback, take by surprise, [*informal*] take your breath away, [*slang*] wow.

astound verb SEE **astonish**.

astray adverb *to go astray.* adrift, amiss, awry, lost, off course, [*informal*] off the rails, wide of the mark, wrong.

astringent adjective SEE **caustic**.

astrology noun [*informal*] your stars. [Don't confuse *astronomy* with *astrology*.]

astronaut noun cosmonaut, space-traveller.

astronautics noun space-travel.

astronomer noun star-gazer.

astronomy noun star-gazing.

SOME ASTRONOMICAL TERMS: asteroid, comet, constellation, cosmos, eclipse, galaxy, meteor, meteorite, moon, nebula, nova, planet, pulsar, quasar, satellite, shooting star, space, sun, supernova, universe, world.

---

astute adjective *an astute tactician. an astute move.* acute, adroit, artful, canny, clever, crafty, cunning, discerning, [*informal*] fly, [*informal*] foxy, ingenious, intelligent, knowing, observant, perceptive, perspicacious, sagacious, sharp, shrewd, sly, subtle, wily.
OPPOSITES: SEE **stupid**.

asunder adverb apart.

asylum noun 1 *The travellers sought asylum from the storm.* cover, haven, refuge, retreat, safety, sanctuary, shelter.
2 [*old-fashioned*] *a lunatic asylum.* These synonyms are used in insulting contexts: bedlam, institution, loony-bin, madhouse, mental home, nuthouse. Politer synonyms are: mental hospital, psychiatric unit.

asymmetrical adjective *asymmetrical shapes.* awry, crooked, distorted, irregular, lop-sided, unbalanced, uneven, [*informal*] wonky.
OPPOSITES: SEE **symmetrical**.

atheist noun heathen, pagan, unbeliever.
OPPOSITES: SEE **believer**.

athlete noun SEE **sportsperson**.

athletic adjective *an athletic person. athletic pursuits.* acrobatic, active, energetic, fit, in condition, muscular, powerful, robust, sinewy, [*informal*] sporty, [*informal*] strapping, strong, sturdy, vigorous, well-built, wiry.
OPPOSITES: SEE **feeble**.

athletics noun OTHER SPORTS: SEE **sport**.

VARIOUS ATHLETIC EVENTS: cross-country, decathlon, discus, field events, high jump, hurdles, javelin, long jump, marathon, pentathlon, pole-vault, relay race, running, shot, sprinting, triple jump.

---

atmosphere noun 1 *We still let harmful gases escape into the atmosphere.* aerospace, air, ether, heavens, ionosphere, sky, stratosphere, troposphere.
2 *There was a happy atmosphere at the party.* ambience, aura, character, climate, environment, feeling, mood, spirit, tone, undercurrent, [*informal*] vibes, vibrations.

atoll noun SEE **island**.

atom noun [*informal*] bit, crumb, grain, iota, jot, molecule, morsel, particle, scrap, speck, spot, trace.

atom bomb OTHER WEAPONS: SEE **weapon**.

atomize verb SEE **powder** verb.

atonal adjective *atonal music.* keyless, [*informal*] tuneless, twelve-tone.

atone verb **to atone for** be punished for, compensate for, do penance for, expiate, make amends for, make reparation for, make up for, pay for, pay the penalty for, pay the price for, recompense for, redeem yourself, redress (*to redress a wrong*).

atrocious adjective *an atrocious attack.* abominable, barbaric, bloodthirsty, brutal, brutish, callous, cruel, diabolical, evil, execrable, fiendish, grim, hateful, heartless, hideous, horrifying, inhuman, merciless, monstrous, outrageous, sadistic, savage, terrible, vicious, vile, villainous, wicked.

atrocity noun SEE **outrage**.

atrophy verb decay, decline, degenerate, deteriorate, diminish, dwindle, fade, lose weight, shrink, shrivel, waste away, wither.

attach verb **1** *to attach one thing to another.* add, affix, anchor, append, bind, combine, connect, couple, SEE **fasten**, fix, join, link, secure, stick, tie, unite, weld.
2 *to attach importance to something.* ascribe, assign, associate, attribute, impute, place, put, relate to.
OPPOSITES: SEE **detach**.

attaché noun SEE **ambassador**.

attached adjective *The twins are very attached to each other.* affectionate, close, dear, devoted, fond, friendly, loving, loyal, warm.

attack noun **1** *an attack against the enemy.* aggression, ambush, assault, [*legal*] battery, blitz, bombardment, broadside, cannonade, charge, counter-attack, foray, incursion, invasion, offensive, onslaught, raid, rush, sortie, strike.
2 *She was upset by his attack on her character.* abuse, censure, criticism, diatribe, impugnment, invective, outburst, tirade.
3 *a heart attack. an attack of coughing.* bout, convulsion, fit, outbreak, paroxysm, seizure, spasm, stroke, [*informal*] turn.

attack verb **1** *to attack an enemy.* ambush, assail, assault, [*informal*] beat up, [*informal*] blast, bombard, charge, counterattack, descend on, [*informal*] do over, fall on, fly at, invade, jump on, lash out at, [*informal*] lay into, mob, mug, [*informal*] pitch into, pounce on, raid, rush, set about, set on, storm, strike at, [*informal*] wade into.
2 *He attacked her reputation.* abuse, censure, criticize, denounce, impugn, inveigh against, libel, malign, round on, slander, snipe at, traduce, vilify.
OPPOSITES: SEE **defend**.
3 *We attacked the job enthusiastically.* SEE **begin**.

attacker noun aggressor, assailant, critic, detractor, enemy, SEE **fighter**, intruder, invader, mugger, opponent, persecutor, raider, slanderer.

attacking adjective SEE **aggressive**.

attain verb *to attain your objective.* accomplish, achieve, acquire, arrive at, complete, earn, fulfil, gain, get, grasp, [*informal*] make, obtain, [*informal*] pull (it) off, procure, reach, realize, secure, touch, win.

attainment noun SEE **achievement**.

attempt noun *You made a good attempt.* assault (*an assault on a mountain*), bid, endeavour, [*informal*] go (*Let me have a go*), start, try.

attempt verb *We attempted to beat the record.* aim, aspire, do your best, endeavour, essay, exert yourself, [*informal*] have a go, make an assault, make a bid, make an effort, put yourself out, seek, [*informal*] spare no effort, strive, [*informal*] sweat blood, tackle, try, undertake, venture.

attend verb **1** *Attend to what I say.* concentrate on, follow carefully, hear, heed, listen, mark, mind, note, notice, observe, pay attention, think about, watch.
2 *I attended an interview.* appear at, be present at, go to, present yourself at, visit.
3 *The bride was attended by two bridesmaids.* accompany, assist, chaperon, escort, follow, guard, usher, wait on.
to attend to *Nurses attended to the wounded.* care for, help, look after, make arrangements for, mind, minister to, nurse, see to, take care of, tend.

attendant noun SEE **servant**.

attention noun **1** *Give proper attention to your work.* alertness, awareness, care, concentration, concern, diligence, heed, notice, recognition, thought, vigilance.
2 *Thank you for your kind attention.* attentiveness, civility, consideration, courtesy, gallantry, good manners, kindness, politeness, regard, respect, thoughtfulness.

attentive adjective SEE **alert** adjective, **polite**.

attenuated adjective SEE **thin** adjective.

attest verb SEE **testify**.

attic noun garret, loft, roof-space.

attire noun accoutrements, apparel, array, clothes, clothing, costume, dress, finery, garb, garments, [*informal*] gear, [*old-fashioned*] habit, outfit, [*old-fashioned*] raiment, wear, weeds (*widow's weeds*).

attire verb **to attire yourself** SEE **dress** verb.

attitude noun **1** *a light-hearted attitude.* air, approach, bearing, behaviour, demeanour, disposition, frame of mind, manner, mien, mood, posture, stance.
2 *What's your attitude towards smoking?* belief, feeling, opinion, outlook, position, standpoint, thought, view.

attorney noun SEE **lawyer**.

attract verb *Baby animals attract crowds at the zoo. Magnets attract iron.* allure, appeal to, beguile, bewitch, bring in, captivate, charm, decoy, drag, draw, enchant, entice, fascinate, induce, interest, inveigle, lure, magnetize, pull, seduce, tempt, tug at.
OPPOSITES: SEE **repel**.

attractive adjective **1** *an attractive person. an attractive dress.* agreeable, alluring, adorable, appealing, artistic, beautiful, bewitching, [*informal*] bonny, captivating, [*informal*] catchy (*tune*), charming, [*informal*] cute, desirable, enchanting, endearing, engaging, enticing, fascinating, fetching, glamorous, good-looking, gorgeous, handsome, hypnotic, interesting, inviting, irresistible, lovable, lovely, magnetic, personable, pleasant, pleasing, [*usually negative*] prepossessing (*not very prepossessing*), pretty, quaint, seductive, stunning, [*informal*] taking, tempting, winsome.
OPPOSITES: SEE **repulsive**.
2 *an attractive salary.* enviable, sought after.

attribute verb *To what do you attribute your success?* accredit, ascribe, assign, blame, charge, credit, impute, put down, refer, trace back.

attrition noun chafing, erosion, fretting, friction, grinding down, rubbing, wearing away, wearing down.

atypical adjective SEE **abnormal**, uncharacteristic, unrepresentative.
OPPOSITES: SEE **typical**.

auburn adjective SEE **red**.

auction noun SEE **sale**.

auctioneer noun SEE **salesman**.

audacious adjective SEE **bold**.

audacity noun [Although *audacious* means *bold* or *brave, audacity* is more often used in the uncomplimentary sense of *insolence.*] **1** *We admired her audacity.* SEE **bravery**.
2 [*uncomplimentary*] *I was amazed that she had the audacity to ask for money.* [*informal*] cheek, effrontery, forwardness, impertinence, impudence, presumptuousness, rashness, [*informal*] sauce, temerity.

Several English words, including *audible, audience, audio, auditorium,* etc., are related to Latin *audire = to hear.*

---

audible adjective *an audible voice.* clear, detectable, distinct, high, loud, noisy, strong, recognizable.
OPPOSITES: SEE **inaudible**.

audience noun assembly, congregation, crowd, gathering, the house (*in a theatre*), listeners, meeting, onlookers, ratings [*= numbers in a TV audience*], spectators, [*informal*] turn-out, viewers.

audio equipment noun play-back equipment, sound-recording equipment.

AUDIO EQUIPMENT: amplifier, cassette recorder, earphones, gramophone, headphones, hi-fi, high-fidelity equipment, juke-box, loudspeaker, microphone, music-centre, personal stereo, pick-up, [*old-fashioned*] phonograph, radio, [*old-fashioned*] radiogram, recorder, record-player, stereo, stylus, tape-deck, tape-recorder, tuner, turntable, [*informal*] walkman.

---

audio-visual adjective **audio-visual equipment** teaching aids, study aids.

VARIOUS TEACHING AND STUDY AIDS: SEE **audio equipment**, epidiascope, film-projector, interactive video, language laboratory, microfiche-reader, microfilm-reader, overhead-projector, slide-projector, tape-slide equipment, television, VCR, video, video-disc equipment.

---

audit noun SEE **examine**.

audition noun, verb SEE **test** noun, verb.

auditorium noun assembly room, concert-hall, hall, theatre.

augment verb *to augment your resources.* add to, amplify, boost, eke out, enlarge,

expand, extend, fill out, grow, increase, intensify, magnify, make larger, multiply, raise, reinforce, strengthen, supplement, swell.
OPPOSITES: SEE **decrease** verb.

augur verb *The signs augur well for tomorrow's weather.* bode, forebode, foreshadow, forewarn, give an omen, herald, portend, predict, promise, prophesy, signal.

augury noun SEE **omen**.

august adjective SEE **majestic**.

au pair noun SEE **servant**.

aura noun SEE **atmosphere**.

au revoir SEE **goodbye**.

auspices plural noun SEE **omen**.
under the auspices of SEE **sponsorship**.

auspicious adjective *auspicious signs.* [*informal*] hopeful, positive, promising.
OPPOSITES: SEE **ominous**.

austere adjective **1** *an austere person.* cold, exacting, forbidding, formal, grave, hard, harsh, self-disciplined, serious, severe, stern, [*informal*] straight-laced, strict.
OPPOSITES: SEE **genial**.
2 *an austere life-style.* abstemious, ascetic, chaste, economical, frugal, hermit-like, parsimonious, puritanical, restrained, rigorous, self-denying, sober, spartan, thrifty, unpampered.
OPPOSITES: SEE **lavish**.
3 *an austere building.* modest, plain, simple, unadorned, unfussy.
OPPOSITES: SEE **elaborate**.

authentic adjective **1** *an authentic antique.* actual, bona fide, certain, genuine, legitimate, original, real, true, valid.
OPPOSITES: SEE **fake** adjective.
2 *an authentic account.* accurate, authoritative, dependable, factual, honest, reliable, truthful, veracious.
OPPOSITES: SEE **false**.

authenticate verb SEE **certify**.

author noun **1** *the author of a book, etc.* composer, creator, dramatist, novelist, playwright, poet, scriptwriter, SEE **writer**.
2 *the author of an idea.* architect, begetter, designer, father, founder, initiator, inventor, maker, mover, organizer, originator, parent, planner, prime mover, producer.

authoritarian adjective SEE **bossy**.

authoritative adjective SEE **definitive**.

authority noun **1** *I have the boss's authority to park here.* approval, authorization, consent, licence, mandate, permission, permit, sanction, warrant.
2 *If you're the boss, you can assert your authority.* charge, command, control, domination, force, influence, jurisdiction, might, power, prerogative, right, sovereignty, supremacy, sway, weight.
3 *He's an authority on steam trains.* [*informal*] boffin, connoisseur (of), expert, specialist.
the authorities administration, government, management, officialdom, [*informal*] the powers that be.

authorize verb *The director authorized the purchase of a computer.* accede to, agree to, allow, approve, [*informal*] back, commission, consent to, empower, endorse, entitle, legalize, license, mandate, [*informal*] OK, pass, permit, ratify, [*informal*] rubber-stamp, sanction, sign the order or warrant, validate.

autobiography noun memoirs, reminiscences.

autocrat noun SEE **ruler**.

autocratic adjective SEE **dictatorial**.

autograph noun **1** *He signed his autograph.* signature.
2 *The museum bought the autograph.* manuscript, original document.

automate verb computerize, program.

automated adjective *an automated production-line.* SEE **automatic**, computerized, electronic, programmable, programmed, robotic.
OPPOSITES: hand-operated, labour-intensive, manually controlled.

automatic adjective **1** *an automatic reaction.* habitual, impulsive, instinctive, involuntary, natural, reflex, spontaneous, unconscious, unintentional, unthinking.
2 *an automatic machine.* automated, computerized, mechanical, programmed, robotic, self-regulating, unmanned.
automatic machine SEE **robot**.

automaton noun SEE **robot**.

automobile noun SEE **car**.

autonomous adjective *an autonomous country.* free, independent, self-determining, self-governing, sovereign.
OPPOSITES: enslaved, owned.

autopsy noun post-mortem.

auxiliary adjective **1** *auxiliary engines.* additional, ancillary, assisting, [*informal*] back-up, emergency, extra, helping, reserve, secondary, spare, subsidiary, substitute, supplementary, supporting, supportive.

avail noun, verb SEE **help** noun, verb.

available adjective *available cash.* accessible, at hand, convenient, disposable,

free, handy, obtainable, procurable, ready, to hand, uncommitted, unengaged, unused, usable.
OPPOSITES: SEE **inaccessible**.

avant-garde adjective SEE **modern**.

avarice noun SEE **greed**.

avaricious adjective SEE **greedy, miserly**.

avenge verb *to avenge a wrong someone has done to you.* exact punishment for, [*informal*] get your own back for, repay, requite, take revenge for.

avenue noun SEE **road**.

average adjective [*informal*] *an average sort of day.* common, commonplace, everyday, indifferent, mediocre, medium, middling, moderate, normal, ordinary, passable, regular, [*informal*] run of the mill, [*informal*] so-so, typical, usual.
OPPOSITES: SEE **extraordinary**.

average noun *the mathematical average.* mean, mid-point.

average verb equalize, even out, normalize, standardize.

averse adjective SEE **hostile**.

aversion noun SEE **hostility**.

avert verb *to avert disaster. to avert a blow.* change the course of, deflect, draw off, fend off, parry, prevent, stave off, turn aside, turn away, ward off.

aviary noun bird-cage.

aviation noun aeronautics, flying.

aviator noun airman, pilot.

avid adjective SEE **eager, greedy**.

avoid verb *to avoid a blow. to avoid a subject. to avoid work.* abstain from, be absent from, [*informal*] beg the question, [*informal*] bypass, circumvent, dodge, [*informal*] duck, elude, escape, eschew, evade, fend off, find a way round, get out of the way of, [*informal*] get round, [*informal*] give a wide berth to, help (*I couldn't help hearing*), ignore, keep away from, keep clear of, refrain from, run away from, shirk, shun, sidestep, skirt round, [*informal*] skive [=*avoid work*], steer clear of.
OPPOSITES: SEE **seek**.

avow verb SEE **declare**.

await verb *I await your reply.* be ready for, expect, hope for, lie in wait for, look out for, wait for.

awake adjective *Are you awake?* alert, attentive, aware, conscious, lively, observant, on the lookout, open-eyed, ready, restless, sleepless, vigilant, wakeful, watchful, wide awake.
OPPOSITES: SEE **asleep**.

awaken verb *The alarm awakened us. The TV programme awakened my interest.* alert, animate, arouse, awake, call, excite, kindle, revive, rouse, stimulate, stir up, wake, waken.
OPPOSITES: SEE **calm** verb, **sedate** verb.

award noun VARIOUS AWARDS: badge, cap, cup, decoration, medal, prize, reward, scholarship, trophy.

award verb *They awarded him first prize.* accord, allot, assign, bestow, confer, endow, give, grant, hand over, present.

aware adjective **aware of** *Are you aware of the rules?* acquainted with, alive to, appreciative of, attentive to, cognisant of, conscious of, conversant with, familiar with, heedful of, informed about, knowledgeable about, mindful of, observant of, responsive to, sensible of, sensitive to, versed in.
OPPOSITES: SEE **ignorant, insensitive**.

awash adjective SEE **wet** adjective.

awe noun *We watched in awe as the volcano erupted.* admiration, amazement, apprehension, dread, fear, respect, reverence, terror, veneration, wonder.

awe-inspiring adjective *The erupting volcano was an awe-inspiring sight.* amazing, awesome, [*old-fashioned*] awful, breathtaking, dramatic, grand, imposing, impressive, magnificent, [*informal*] marvellous, overwhelming, solemn, [*informal*] stunning, stupendous, sublime, [*informal*] wonderful, [*poetic*] wondrous.
OPPOSITES: SEE **insignificant**.

awesome adjective SEE **awe-inspiring**.

awful adjective **1** [*old-fashioned*] *The erupting volcano was an awful sight.* SEE **awe-inspiring**.
2 *awful handwriting.* SEE **bad**.
3 *an awful crime.* SEE **hateful**.

awkward adjective **1** *an awkward thing to handle.* bulky, cumbersome, inconvenient, unmanageable, unwieldy.
OPPOSITES: SEE **convenient**.
2 *awkward with your hands.* blundering, bungling, clumsy, gauche, gawky, [*informal*] ham-fisted, inept, inexpert, maladroit, uncoordinated, ungainly, unskilful.
OPPOSITES: SEE **skilful**.
3 *an awkward problem.* annoying, difficult, perplexing, thorny, [*informal*] ticklish, troublesome, trying, vexatious, vexing.
OPPOSITES: SEE **straightforward**.
4 *an awkward silence.* embarrassing, uncomfortable, uneasy.
OPPOSITES: SEE **reassuring**.

5 *an awkward customer.* [*informal*] bloody-minded, disobliging, exasperating, obstinate, perverse, [*informal*] prickly, rude, stubborn, touchy, unco-operative.
OPPOSITES: SEE **co-operative.**
6 *an awkward pupil.* [*slang*] bolshie, defiant, disobedient, intractable, misbehaving, naughty, rebellious, refractory, undisciplined, unruly, wayward.
OPPOSITES: SEE **well-behaved.**

awning noun canopy, fly-sheet, screen, shade, shelter, tarpaulin.

awry adjective *His hat was awry.* askew, asymmetrical, crooked, not straight, off-centre, twisted, uneven, [*informal*] wonky.
OPPOSITES: SEE **straight.**

axe noun battleaxe, chopper, cleaver, hatchet, tomahawk.

axe verb *They axed our bus service. The firm axed 20 workers.* cancel, cut, discharge, discontinue, dismiss, eliminate, get rid of, [*informal*] give the chop to, make redundant, [*euphemistic*] rationalize, remove, sack, terminate, withdraw.

axiom noun SEE **saying.**

axis noun centre-line, pivot.

axle noun rod, shaft, spindle.

azure adjective SEE **blue** adjective.

B

babble verb SEE **talk** verb.

baboon noun SEE **monkey.**

baby noun babe, child, infant, papoose, toddler, [*uncomplimentary*] weakling.

babyish adjective [All these words are uncomplimentary. Compare *childlike.*] childish, immature, infantile, juvenile, puerile.
OPPOSITES: SEE **mature.**

bachelor SEE **unmarried.**

back adjective *the back legs of an animal.* dorsal (*dorsal fin*), end, hind, hinder, hindmost, last, rear, rearmost.
OPPOSITES: SEE **front** adjective.

back noun 1 *the back of a train.* end, rear, tail-end.
2 *the back of a ship.* stern.
3 *the back of an envelope.* reverse, verso.
4 *the back of an animal.* hindquarters, posterior, rear, tail.
OPPOSITES: SEE **front** noun.

back verb 1 *to back into a corner.* back away, back off, back-pedal, backtrack, [*informal*] beat a retreat, give way, go backwards, move back, recede, recoil, retire, retreat, reverse.
OPPOSITES: SEE **advance** verb.
2 *to back a plan.* SEE **support** verb.
3 *to back horses.* SEE **gamble** verb.
to back down SEE **retreat** verb.
to back out SEE **withdraw.**

backbiting noun SEE **slander** noun.

backbone noun spine, the vertebrae.

backbreaking adjective SEE **arduous.**

backchat noun SEE **rudeness.**

backer noun SEE **sponsor** noun.

backfire verb SEE **explode, rebound** verb.

background noun 1 *the background of a picture.* context, setting, surroundings.
OPPOSITES: SEE **foreground.**
2 *the background to the Second World War.* circumstances, context, history, [*informal*] lead-up.
3 *a family with a military background.* breeding, culture, education, experience, [*formal*] milieu, tradition, upbringing.

backhanded adjective SEE **ambivalent.**

backhander noun SEE **bribe** noun.

backing noun 1 *We had the backing of the Principal.* aid, assistance, encouragement, endorsement, help, loan, patronage, sponsorship, subsidy, support.
2 *a musical backing.* accompaniment, orchestration, scoring.

backlash noun SEE **reaction.**

backlog noun arrears.

back-pedal verb SEE **back** verb.

backside noun SEE **buttocks.**

backslider noun SEE **deserter.**

backtrack verb SEE **back** verb.

backward adjective 1 *a backward movement.* regressive, retrograde, retrogressive, reverse.
OPPOSITES: SEE **forward.**
2 *a backward pupil.* handicapped, immature, late-starting, retarded, slow, SEE **stupid**, subnormal, underdeveloped, undeveloped.
OPPOSITES: SEE **precocious.**
3 *Don't be backward—ask for his autograph.* afraid, bashful, coy, diffident, hesitant, inhibited, modest, reluctant, reserved, reticent, self-effacing, shy, timid, unforthcoming.
OPPOSITES: SEE **confident.**

bacon noun gammon, ham, rashers.

bacteria noun SEE **microorganism**.

bad adjective [We use the word *bad* to describe almost anything we don't like. There are, therefore, hundreds of possible synonyms, depending on the context in which the word is used. We give synonyms here for some main senses of the word, but you can look in other places for synonyms to suit particular contexts. For example, in the case of *bad handwriting*, you might find synonyms under *illegible*; in the case of *bad visibility*, under *foggy*; and so on.] **1** *a bad man. a bad deed.* abhorrent, base, beastly, blameworthy, corrupt, criminal, SEE **cruel**, dangerous, delinquent, deplorable, depraved, detestable, evil, guilty, immoral, infamous, malevolent, malicious, malignant, mean, mischievous, nasty, naughty, offensive, regrettable, reprehensible, rotten, shameful, sinful, unworthy, vicious, vile, villainous, wicked, wrong.
2 *a bad accident. a bad illness.* appalling, awful, calamitous, dire, disastrous, distressing, dreadful, frightful, ghastly, grave, hair-raising, hideous, horrible, painful, serious, severe, shocking, terrible, unfortunate, SEE **unpleasant**, violent.
3 *bad behaviour. a bad driver. bad work.* abominable, abysmal, appalling, awful, cheap, [*informal*] chronic, defective, deficient, diabolical, disgraceful, dreadful, egregious, execrable, faulty, feeble, [*informal*] grotty, hopeless, imperfect, inadequate, incompetent, incorrect, ineffective, inefficient, inferior, [*informal*] lousy, pitiful, poor, [*informal*] ropy, shoddy, [*informal*] sorry (*in a sorry state*), substandard, unsound, unsatisfactory, useless, weak, worthless.
4 *bad conditions.* adverse, deleterious, detrimental, discouraging, [*informal*] frightful, harmful, harsh, hostile, inappropriate, inauspicious, prejudicial, uncongenial, unfortunate, unhelpful, unpropitious.
5 *bad eggs. a bad smell.* decayed, decomposing, diseased, foul, loathsome, mildewed, mouldy, nauseating, noxious, objectionable, obnoxious, odious, offensive, polluted, putrid, rancid, repellent, repulsive, revolting, sickening, rotten, smelly, sour, spoiled, tainted, vile.
6 *Smoking is bad for you.* SEE **harmful**.
7 *I felt so bad I went to bed.* SEE **ill**.
8 *I feel bad about not phoning.* SEE **sorry**.

badge noun *an identifying badge.* chevron, crest, device, emblem, insignia, logo, mark, medal, rosette, sign, symbol, token.

badinage noun SEE **banter**.

bad-tempered adjective acrimonious, angry, cantankerous, churlish, crabbed, cross, [*informal*] crotchety, disgruntled, dyspeptic, gruff, grumbling, grumpy, hot-tempered, ill-humoured, ill-tempered, irascible, irritable, moody, morose, peevish, petulant, quarrelsome, querulous, rude, short-tempered, shrewish, snappy, [*informal*] stroppy, sulky, sullen, testy, truculent.
OPPOSITES: SEE **good-tempered**.

baffle verb **1** *The problem baffled us.* [*informal*] bamboozle, bemuse, bewilder, confound, confuse, defeat, [*informal*] floor, [*informal*] flummox, foil, frustrate, mystify, perplex, puzzle, [*informal*] stump, thwart.

baffling adjective *a baffling problem.* bewildering, confusing, extraordinary, frustrating, inexplicable, inscrutable, insoluble, mysterious, mystifying, perplexing, puzzling, unfathomable.
OPPOSITES: SEE **straightforward**.

bag noun basket, carrier, carrier-bag, case, SEE **container**, handbag, holdall, sack, satchel, shopping-bag, shoulder-bag.

bag verb [*informal*] *to bag a seat.* SEE **capture, reserve** verb.

bagatelle noun SEE **small (small thing)**.

baggage noun accoutrements (*of a soldier*), bags, belongings, cases, [*informal*] gear, [*joking*] impedimenta, luggage, paraphernalia, suitcases, trunks.

baggy adjective *baggy clothes.* SEE **loose**.

bailey noun SEE **castle**.

bailiff noun SEE **official** noun.

bairn noun SEE **child**.

bait noun allurement, attraction, bribe, carrot, decoy, enticement, inducement, lure, temptation.

bait verb **1** *to bait a trap* = *to put bait in a trap.*
2 *to bait an animal.* annoy, goad, hound, jeer at, [*informal*] needle, persecute, pester, provoke, tease, torment.

bake verb SEE **cook** verb.

balance noun **1** *weighed in the balance.* scales, weighing-machine.
2 *to lose your balance.* equilibrium, equipoise, poise, stability, steadiness.
3 *We want to get a balance of girls and boys.* correspondence, equality, equivalence, evenness, parity, symmetry.
4 *I spend half my wages and put the balance in the bank.* difference, remainder, residue, rest, surplus.

balance verb **1** *If I carry one bag in each hand, they balance each other.* counteract,

counterbalance, counterpoise, equalize, even up, level, make steady, match, neutralize, offset, parallel, stabilize, steady.
2 *He balanced ten baskets on his head.* keep, keep balanced, keep in equilibrium, poise, steady, support.

balanced adjective 1 *a balanced shape.* even, regular, symmetrical
2 *a balanced argument.* even-handed, fair, impartial.
3 *a balanced personality.* equable, sane, stable.
4 *a balanced diet.* all-round, well-planned.
OPPOSITES: SEE **unbalanced**.

bald adjective 1 *a bald man.* baldheaded, hairless, [*slang*] slaphead, thin on top.
2 *bald tyres.* bare, smooth.
3 *a bald statement.* direct, forthright, plain, simple, stark, straightforward, unadorned, uncompromising

balderdash noun SEE **nonsense**.

bale noun bunch, bundle, pack, package, truss.

bale verb **to bale out** *to bale out of an aircraft.* eject, escape, jump out, parachute down.

baleful adjective SEE **destructive**.

ball noun 1 drop, globe, globule, orb, shot, sphere, spheroid.
2 *Cinderella went to a ball.* dance, disco, party, social.

ballerina noun ballet-dancer, dancer.

ballet noun SEE **dance** noun.

balloon noun airship, dirigible, hot-air balloon.

balloon verb SEE **billow** verb.

ballot noun election, plebiscite, poll, referendum, vote.

ball-point noun SEE **pen** noun.

ballyhoo noun SEE **publicity**.

balmy adjective *a balmy evening.* gentle, mild, peaceful, pleasant, soft, soothing, summery.

bamboo noun cane.

bamboozle verb SEE **mystify**, **trick** verb.

ban noun *a ban on smoking.* embargo, moratorium, prohibition, veto.

ban verb *to ban smoking.* banish, bar, debar, disallow, exclude, forbid, [*formal*] interdict, make illegal, ostracize, outlaw, prevent, prohibit, proscribe, put a ban on [SEE **ban** noun], restrict, stop, suppress, veto.
OPPOSITES: SEE **permit** verb.

banal adjective *an exciting film spoiled by a banal ending.* boring, clichéd, cliché-ridden, commonplace, [*informal*] corny, dull, hackneyed, obvious, ordinary, over-used, pedestrian, platitudinous, predictable, stereotyped, trite, unimaginative, uninteresting, unoriginal, vapid.
OPPOSITES: SEE **interesting**.

band noun 1 *a band of colour.* belt, hoop, line, loop, ribbon, ring, strip, stripe, swathe.
2 *a band of devoted followers.* association, body, clique, club, company, crew, flock, gang, group, herd, horde, party, society, troop.
3 *a concert band.* ensemble, group, orchestra.
OTHER MUSICAL GROUPS: SEE **music**.

band verb SEE **group** verb.

bandage noun dressing, gauze, lint, plaster.

bandit noun brigand, buccaneer, desperado, footpad, gangster, gunman, highwayman, hijacker, marauder, outlaw, pirate, robber, thief.

bandwagon noun **to climb on a bandwagon** be fashionable, follow the trend.

bandy adjective bandy-legged, bowed, bow-legged.

bandy verb *Various ideas were bandied about.* exchange, interchange, pass, swap, throw, toss.
to bandy words SEE **argue**.

bane noun *the bane of my life.* SEE **misfortune**.

bang noun 1 *a bang on the head.* blow, [*informal*] box, bump, collision, cuff, hit, knock, punch, slam, smack, stroke, thump, [*slang*] wallop, whack.
2 *a loud bang.* blast, boom, clap, crash, explosion, pop, report, thud, thump.

bang verb VARIOUS SOUNDS: SEE **sound** noun.

banish verb *He was banished to an island.* deport, eject, evict, exile, expatriate, expel, outlaw, send away, ship away, transport.
2 *Would you want to banish bad news from the papers?* ban, bar, [*informal*] black, debar, eliminate, exclude, forbid, get rid of, make illegal, ostracize, oust, prohibit, proscribe, put an embargo on, remove, restrict, stop, suppress, veto.
OPPOSITES: SEE **reinstate**.

bank noun 1 *a grassy bank.* dike, earthwork, embankment, mound, rampart, ridge.
2 *a river bank.* brink, edge, margin, shore, side.
3 *a steep bank.* camber, [*formal*] declivity, gradient, incline, ramp, rise, slope, tilt.

4 *a bank of navigational instruments.* array, collection, display, file, group, line, rank, row, series.

bank verb 1 *The plane banked.* cant, heel, incline, lean, list, pitch, slant, slope, tilt, tip.
2 *I banked my wages.* deposit, keep in a bank, save.

banker noun bank manager, financier.

banknote noun SEE **money**.

bankrupt adjective 1 *a bankrupt business.* failed, [*slang*] gone bust, insolvent, ruined.
OPPOSITES: SEE **solvent**.
2 [*informal*] broke, destitute, [*formal*] impecunious, penniless, SEE **poor**, [*informal*] short, [*slang*] skint, [*informal*] spent-up, [*slang*] stony-broke.
OPPOSITES: SEE **wealthy**.

banner noun *banners fluttering in the wind.* colours, ensign, flag, pennant, pennon, standard, streamer.

banquet noun [*informal*] binge, [*slang*] blow-out, dinner, feast, SEE **meal**, [*formal*] repast, [*informal*] spread.

bantam noun SEE **chicken**.

bantamweight noun SEE **boxing**.

banter noun *good-humoured banter.* badinage, chaffing, joking, [*formal*] persiflage, pleasantry, raillery, repartee, ribbing, ridicule, teasing, word-play.

bar noun 1 *iron bars.* beam, girder, pole, rail, railing, rod, shaft, stake, stick, strut.
2 *a bar of chocolate, soap, etc.* block, cake, chunk, hunk, ingot, lump, nugget, piece, slab, wedge.
3 *a bar to invaders.* barricade, barrier, check, deterrent, hindrance, impediment, obstacle, obstruction.
4 *a bar for refreshments.* café, canteen, counter, inn, lounge (*coffee lounge*), pub, saloon, tavern.
the bar LEGAL TERMS: SEE **law**.

bar verb 1 *She was barred from the club.* ban, banish, debar, exclude, forbid to enter, keep out, ostracize, outlaw, prevent from entering, prohibit, proscribe.
2 *A fallen tree barred our way.* arrest, block, check, deter, halt, hinder, impede, obstruct, prevent, stop, thwart.

barbarian adjective SEE **uncivilized**.

barbarian noun [Compare *barbaric, barbarous. Barbarian* originally referred to any foreigner with different customs, etc. *Barbarian* and the synonyms given here are especially insulting when used to refer to foreigners.] heathen, hun, pagan, Philistine, savage, vandal.

barbaric adjective *a barbaric attack.* barbarous, brutal, SEE **cruel**, inhuman, primitive, savage, uncivilized, wild.
OPPOSITES: SEE **civilized, humane**.

barbarous SEE **barbaric**.

barbecue noun SEE **meal, party**.

barbecue verb SEE **cook** verb.

barber noun hairdresser.

barbican noun SEE **castle**.

bard noun SEE **poet**.

bare adjective 1 *bare legs. a bare patch.* bald, denuded, exposed, naked, nude, stark-naked, stripped, unclad, unclothed, uncovered, undressed.
2 *a bare landscape.* barren, bleak, desolate, featureless, open, treeless, unwooded, windswept.
3 *bare trees.* defoliated, leafless.
4 *a bare room.* austere, empty, plain, simple, unfurnished, vacant.
5 *a bare wall.* blank, clean, unadorned, undecorated, unmarked.
6 *the bare facts.* explicit, honest, literal, plain, straightforward, unconcealed, undisguised, unembellished.
7 *the bare necessities.* basic, essential, just adequate, just sufficient, minimum.

bare verb *to bare your private thoughts.* betray, communicate, disclose, expose, lay bare, make known, publish, reveal, show, uncover, unveil.

barefaced adjective SEE **shameless**.

bargain noun 1 *I made a bargain with the salesman.* agreement, arrangement, compact, contract, deal, negotiation, pact, pledge, promise, settlement, transaction, treaty, understanding.
2 *The coat I bought was a bargain.* discounted item, [*informal*] give-away, good buy, loss-leader, reduced item, [*informal*] snip, special offer.

bargain verb *to bargain about the price.* argue, barter, discuss (*terms*), do a deal, haggle, negotiate.
to bargain on *I didn't bargain on him bringing his family.* anticipate, be prepared for, contemplate, expect, foresee, imagine, plan for, reckon on.

barge noun VARIOUS SHIPS: SEE **vessel**.

bargee noun SEE **sailor**.

bark verb 1 *to bark your shin.* abrade, chafe, graze, rub, score, scrape, scratch.
2 *The dog barked fiercely.* growl, yap.

barley noun SEE **cereal**.

barmaid, barman nouns attendant, server, steward, stewardess, waiter, waitress.
OTHER PEOPLE WHO SERVE: SEE **servant**.

barmy adjective SEE **mad**.

barn noun SEE **farm** noun.

baron, baroness nouns ARISTOCRATIC TITLES: SEE **title** noun.
RELATED ADJECTIVE: baronial.

barrack verb SEE **jeer**.

barracks noun *military barracks.* accommodation, billet, camp, garrison, lodging, quarters.

barrage noun **1** *a barrage across a river.* barrier, dam, embankment, wall
2 *a barrage of artillery fire.* assault, attack, battery, bombardment, cannonade, fusillade, gunfire, onslaught, salvo, storm, volley.

barrel noun butt, cask, drum, hogshead, keg, tub, tun, water-butt.
OTHER CONTAINERS: SEE **container**.

barren adjective **1** *barren desert.* arid, bare, desert, desolate, dried-up, empty, infertile, lifeless, non-productive, treeless, useless, uncultivated, unproductive, untilled, waste.
2 *a barren tree.* fruitless, unfruitful.
3 *a barren woman.* childless, infertile, sterile, sterilized.
OPPOSITES: SEE **fertile**.

barricade noun *a barricade across a road.* barrier, blockade, bulwark, fence, obstacle, obstruction, palisade, stockade.

barrier noun **1** *a barrier to keep spectators off the track.* bar, barricade, fence, hurdle, obstacle, obstruction, railing, wall.
2 *a barrier across a river.* barrage, boom, dam.
3 *a barrier to progress.* check, drawback, handicap, hindrance, impediment, limitation, restriction, stumbling-block.

barrister noun SEE **lawyer**.

barrow noun cart, handcart, wheelbarrow.

barter verb bargain, deal, exchange, negotiate, swap, trade, traffic.

base adjective *a base crime.* contemptible, cowardly, depraved, despicable, detestable, dishonourable, evil, ignoble, immoral, low, mean, scandalous, selfish, shameful, sordid, vile, wicked.
OPPOSITES: SEE **sublime**.

base noun **1** *the base of a wall. a base on which to build.* basis, bed, bedrock, bottom, core, essentials, foot, footing, foundation, fundamentals, groundwork, pedestal, plinth, rest, stand, substructure, support.
2 *the base of an expedition.* camp, depot, headquarters, post, station.

base verb *The building was based on rock. The story was based on fact.* build, construct, establish, found, ground, locate, set up, station.

basement noun cellar, crypt, vault.

bash verb SEE **hit** verb.

bashful adjective *Don't be bashful—speak up for yourself.* abashed, backward, blushing, coy, demure, diffident, embarrassed, faint-hearted, inhibited, modest, nervous, reserved, reticent, retiring, self-conscious, self-effacing, sheepish, shy, timid, timorous, unforthcoming.
OPPOSITES: SEE **assertive**.

basic adjective *the basic facts. basic needs.* central, chief, crucial, elementary, essential, foremost, fundamental, important, intrinsic, key, main, necessary, primary, principal, radical, underlying, vital.
OPPOSITES: SEE **unimportant**.

basilica noun SEE **church**.

basin noun bowl, dish, sink, stoup.

basis noun *the basis on which something is built. the basis of a rumour.* base, core, footing, foundation, ground, premise, principle, starting-point, support.

bask verb *to bask in the sun. to bask in applause.* enjoy, expose yourself (to), feel pleasure, glory, lie, lounge, luxuriate, relax, sunbathe, wallow.

basket noun bag, hamper, pannier, punnet, shopping-basket, skip, trug.
OTHER CONTAINERS: SEE **container**.

bas-relief noun SEE **sculpture** noun.

bass adjective *a bass note.* bottom, low.
OTHER MUSICAL TERMS: SEE **music**.

bastard noun [Nowadays *bastard* is often used as an insult. The synonyms are politer words.] illegitimate child, [*old-fashioned*] love-child, natural child.

baste verb SEE **cook** verb.

bastion noun SEE **stronghold**.

bat noun *Hit the ball with the bat.* club, racket, racquet.

bat verb **1** *to bat a ball.* SEE **hit** verb.
2 *She didn't bat an eyelid.* SEE **flutter**.

batch noun *a batch of cakes.* SEE **group** noun.

bath noun **1** *a bath of water.* SEE **container**.
2 *to have a bath.* douche, jacuzzi, sauna, shower, [*informal*] soak, [*informal*] tub, wash.

bathe verb **1** *to bathe a wound.* clean, cleanse, immerse, moisten, rinse, soak, steep, swill, wash.
2 *to bathe in the sea.* go swimming, paddle, plunge, splash about, swim, [*informal*] take a dip.

bathing-costume noun [*informal*] bathers, bathing-suit, bikini, one-piece, swimming costume, swimsuit, trunks.

bathos noun anticlimax, [*informal*] come-down, disappointment, [*informal*] let-down.
OPPOSITES: SEE **climax**.

bathroom noun

BATHROOM FITTINGS: bath, bidet, extractor fan, jacuzzi, lavatory, medicine cabinet, mirror, shaver-point, shower, taps, tiles, toilet, towel-rail, ventilator, wash-basin.

OTHER THINGS YOU FIND IN A BATHROOM: bath-mat, bath salts, comb, SEE **cosmetics**, curlers, flannel, foam bath, hair-brush, hair-drier, loofah, nail-brush, nail-scissors, pumice-stone, razor, scales, shampoo, shaver, soap, sponge, toiletries, toilet-roll, toothbrush, towel, tweezers.

---

batman noun SEE **servant**.

baton noun *a policeman's baton*. cane, club, cudgel, rod, staff, stick, truncheon.

battalion noun SEE **armed services**.

batten verb SEE **fasten**.

batter verb *to batter on a door*. SEE **beat** verb, bludgeon, cudgel, keep hitting, pound.

battery noun **1** *a battery of guns*. artillery-unit, emplacement, SEE **group** noun.
2 *an electric battery*. accumulator, cell.
3 [*legal*] *assault and battery*. assault, attack, [*informal*] beating-up, blows, onslaught, thrashing, violence.

battle noun *Many died in the battle*. action, air-raid, Armageddon, attack, blitz, brush, campaign, clash, combat, conflict, confrontation, contest, crusade, [*informal*] dogfight (=*air battle*), dispute, encounter, engagement, fight, fray, hostilities, offensive, pitched battle, pre-emptive strike, [*informal*] punch-up, row, scrap, [*informal*] shoot-out, siege, skirmish, strife, struggle, war, warfare.

battle verb *They battled to control the fire*. SEE **fight** verb, **struggle** verb.

battlefield noun area of hostilities, arena, battleground, theatre of war.

battleship noun SHIPS: SEE **vessel**.

batty adjective SEE **mad**.

bauble noun SEE **ornament** noun.

baulk verb SEE **frustrate**, **refuse** verb.

bawdy adjective *a bawdy comedy*. **1** Synonyms not implying adverse criticism: broad, earthy, erotic, lusty, [*informal*] naughty, racy, [*informal*] raunchy, ribald, [*informal*] sexy, [*informal*] spicy.
2 Synonyms implying adverse criticism: [*informal*] blue, coarse, dirty, immoral, improper, indecent, indecorous, indelicate, lascivious, lecherous, lewd, licentious, obscene, pornographic, prurient, risqué, rude, salacious, smutty, suggestive, titillating, vulgar.
OPPOSITES: SEE **proper**.

bawl verb SEE **shout** verb.

bay noun **1** *a sandy bay*. bight, cove, creek, estuary, fjord, gulf, harbour, indentation, inlet, ria, sound.
2 *an unloading bay*. alcove, booth, compartment, niche, nook, opening, recess.

bazaar noun *a fund-raising bazaar*. auction, boot-sale, bring-and-buy, fair, fête, jumble sale, market, sale.

be verb **1** *To be, or not to be?* be alive, breathe, endure, exist, live.
2 *Will you be here long?* continue, dwell, inhabit, keep going, last, occupy a position, persist, remain, stay, survive.
3 *When will your next holiday be?* arise, befall, come about, happen, occur, take place.
4 *She wants to be a writer*. become, develop into.

beach noun *a sandy beach*. coast, coastline, foreshore, sand, sands, seashore, seaside, shore, [*poetic*] strand.

beacon noun bonfire, flare, lighthouse, signal.

bead noun **1** *pretty beads*. SEE **jewellery**.
2 *beads of sweat*. blob, drip, drop, droplet, globule, pearl.

beagling noun SEE **hunting**.

beak noun *a bird's beak*. bill, mandible.

beaker noun *a beaker of water*. cup, glass, goblet, jar, mug, tankard, tumbler, wine-glass.

beam noun **1** *a wooden beam*. bar, boom, girder, joist, plank, post, rafter, spar, stanchion, support, timber.
2 *a beam of light*. gleam, ray, shaft, stream.

beam verb **1** *to beam radio waves towards a satellite*. aim, broadcast, direct, emit, radiate, send out, shine, transmit.
2 *to beam happily*. grin, laugh, look radiant, radiate happiness, smile.
OPPOSITES: SEE **glower**.

bean noun legume, pulse.

KINDS OF BEAN: broad bean, butter-bean, French bean, haricot, kidney bean, runner bean, soya bean.

bear noun VARIOUS ANIMALS: SEE **animal** noun.

bear verb **1** *The rope won't bear my weight.* carry, hold, prop up, support, take.
2 *The gravestone bears an inscription.* display, exhibit, have, possess, show.
3 *They bore the coffin into the church.* bring, carry, convey, deliver, fetch, move, take, transfer, transport.
4 *I can't bear pain.* abide, accept, brook, cope with, endure, live with, permit, put up with, [*informal*] stand, [*informal*] stomach, suffer, sustain, tolerate, undergo.
5 *The bitch bore six puppies. The tree bore a lot of fruit.* breed, [*old-fashioned*] bring forth, develop, give birth to [SEE **birth**], produce, yield.
to bear down on *The runaway truck bore down on us.* SEE **approach** verb.
to bear out *The news bears out what I heard.* SEE **confirm**.
to bear witness SEE **testify**.

bearable adjective SEE **tolerable**.

bearing noun **1** *a military bearing.* air, appearance, behaviour, carriage, demeanour, deportment, look, manner, mien, poise, posture, presence, style.
2 *Your evidence has no bearing on the case.* connection, import, pertinence, reference, relationship, relevance, significance.
bearings *I lost my bearings in the fog.* aim, course, direction, line, location, orientation, path, position, road, sense of direction, tack, track, way, whereabouts.

beast noun *wild beasts.* SEE **animal** noun, brute, creature, monster.

beastly 1 *beastly cruelty.* SEE **brutal**.
2 [*informal*] *beastly weather.* SEE **nasty**.

beat noun **1** *music with a strong beat.* accent, pulse, rhythm, stress, throb.
2 *a policeman's beat.* course, itinerary, journey, path, rounds, route, way.

beat verb **1** *to beat with a stick.* batter, bludgeon, buffet, cane, clout, cudgel, flail, flog, hammer, SEE **hit** verb, knock about, lash, [*informal*] lay into, manhandle, pound, punch, scourge, strike, [*informal*] tan, thrash, thump, trounce, [*informal*] wallop, whack, whip.
2 *to beat eggs.* agitate, blend, froth up, knead, mix, pound, stir, whip, whisk.
3 *My heart beat faster.* flutter, palpitate, pound, pulsate, race, thump.
4 *Our opponents beat us.* best, conquer, crush, defeat, excel, get the better of, [*informal*] lick, master, outclass, outdistance, outdo, outpace, outrun, outwit, overcome, overpower, overthrow, overwhelm, rout, subdue, surpass, [*informal*] thrash, top, trounce, vanquish, win against, worst.
to beat about the bush SEE **prevaricate**.
to beat up SEE **attack** verb.

beatific adjective SEE **happy**.

beautiful adjective [*Beautiful* has many shades of meaning. The words given here are only a selection of the synonyms you could use.] *a beautiful bride. beautiful pictures. beautiful scenery.* admirable, aesthetic, alluring, appealing, artistic, attractive, bewitching, brilliant, captivating, charming, [*old-fashioned*] comely, dainty, delightful, elegant, exquisite, [*old-fashioned*] fair, fascinating, fetching, fine, good-looking, glamorous, glorious, gorgeous, graceful, handsome, imaginative, irresistible, lovely, magnificent, neat, picturesque, pleasing, pretty, quaint, radiant, ravishing, scenic, seductive, sensuous, spectacular, splendid, stunning, superb, tempting.
OPPOSITES: SEE **ugly**.

beautify verb *The church was beautified with flowers.* adorn, deck, decorate, embellish, make beautiful, ornament, prettify, [*uncomplimentary*] tart up.
OPPOSITES: SEE **disfigure**.

beauty noun *the beauty of the landscape.* allure, appeal, attractiveness, charm, elegance, fascination, glamour, glory, grace, handsomeness, loveliness, magnificence, prettiness, radiance, splendour.
OPPOSITES: SEE **ugliness**.

beaver verb **to beaver away** SEE **work** verb.

becalmed adjective *a becalmed ship.* helpless, idle, motionless, still, unmoving.
OPPOSITE: storm-tossed.

beck noun SEE **stream** noun.

beckon verb SEE **gesture** verb, **signal** verb.

become verb **1** *Little puppies become big dogs!* change into, develop into, grow into, turn into.
2 *That colour becomes you.* be appropriate to, be becoming to, befit, enhance, fit, flatter, harmonize with, set off, suit.

becoming adjective *a becoming dress.* appropriate, apt, attractive, befitting, charming, decent, decorous, fit, fitting, flattering, [*old-fashioned*] meet, pleasing, proper, seemly, suitable, tasteful.

bed noun **1** *a bed to sleep in.*

KINDS OF BED: air-bed, berth, bunk, cot, couch, couchette, cradle, crib, divan, four-poster, hammock, pallet, palliasse, truckle bed, water-bed.

PARTS OF A BED: bedpost, bedstead, headboard, mattress, springs.

THINGS YOU USE TO MAKE A BED: bed linen, bedspread, blanket, bolster, continental quilt, counterpane, coverlet, duvet, eiderdown, electric blanket, mattress, pillow, pillowcase, pillowslip, quilt, sheet, sleeping-bag.

---

2 *a bed of concrete.* base, foundation, groundwork, layer, substratum.
3 *a river bed.* bottom, channel, course, watercourse.
4 *a flower bed.* border, garden, patch, plot.

bedclothes noun bedding.
SEE PANEL ABOVE.

bedevil verb *His life was bedevilled with health problems.* SEE **afflict**.

bedlam noun SEE **asylum, uproar**.

bedraggled adjective *bedraggled from the rain.* dirty, dishevelled, messy, scruffy, sodden, soiled, stained, unkempt, untidy, wet.
OPPOSITES: SEE **spruce** adjective.

bedridden adjective SEE **ill**.

bedrock noun SEE **base** noun.

bedroom noun dormitory, sleeping quarters.
OTHER ROOMS: SEE **room**.

bedsit, bedsitter nouns SEE **accommodation**.

bee noun bumble-bee, drone, honey-bee, queen, worker.
a home for bees apiary, beehive, hive.
a bee in your bonnet SEE **obsession**.

beefy adjective SEE **muscular**.

beer noun ale, [*informal*] bitter, lager, [*informal*] mild, stout.
OTHER DRINKS: SEE **drink** noun.

beetling adjective *a beetling cliff.* jutting, overhanging, projecting, protruding.

befall verb [*old-fashioned*] *Who knows what may befall?* be the outcome, [*old-fashioned*] betide, chance, come about, [*informal*] crop up, eventuate, happen, occur, take place, [*informal*] transpire.

befitting adjective SEE **appropriate** adjective.

before adverb earlier, in advance, previously, sooner.

befriend verb SEE **friend (make friends with)**.

beg verb **1** *to beg for food.* ask for alms, [*informal*] cadge, scrounge, sponge.
2 *to beg for a favour.* ask, beseech, crave, entreat, implore, importune, petition, plead, pray, request, [*formal*] supplicate.
to beg the question SEE **avoid**.

beget verb *He begot three children. War begets misery.* breed, bring about, cause, create, engender, father, generate, give rise to, procreate, produce, propagate, result in, sire, spawn.

beggar noun destitute person, down-and-out, homeless person, mendicant, pauper, poor person, ragamuffin, tramp, vagrant.
RELEVANT ADJECTIVES: SEE **poor**.

beggarly adjective SEE **mean** adjective.

beggary noun SEE **poverty**.

begin verb **1** *to begin something new.* activate, attack, be first with, broach, commence, conceive, create, embark on, enter into, found, [*informal*] get cracking on, [*informal*] get something going, inaugurate, initiate, inspire, instigate, introduce, kindle, launch, launch into, lay the foundations of, move into, open up, originate, pioneer, precipitate, provoke, set in motion, set about, set up, [*informal*] spark off, start, take the initiative, take up, touch off, trigger off, undertake.
OPPOSITES: SEE **finish** verb.
2 *How did your new idea begin?* appear, arise, break out, come into existence, crop up, emerge, get going, happen, materialize, originate, spring up.
OPPOSITES: SEE **end** verb.

beginner noun **1** *Who was the beginner of it all?* creator, founder, initiator, inspiration, instigator, originator, pioneer.
2 *I'm only a beginner.* apprentice, fresher (*at university or college*), greenhorn, initiate, learner, novice, recruit, starter, tiro, trainee.

beginning noun **1** *the beginning of life. the beginning of a new career.* birth, commencement, conception, creation, dawn, embryo, emergence, establishment, foundation, genesis, germ, inauguration, inception, initiation, instigation, introduction, launch, onset, opening, origin, outset, point of departure, rise, source, start, starting-point, threshold.
2 *the beginning of a book.* preface, prelude, prologue.
OPPOSITES: SEE **end** noun.

begrudge verb *Don't begrudge his just reward.* be bitter about, covet, envy, grudge, mind, object to, resent.

beguile verb SEE **amuse, deceive**.

behave verb **1** *Try to behave well.* acquit yourself, act, conduct yourself, function, operate, perform, react, respond, run, work.
2 *I wish those kids would behave!* be good, be on best behaviour, be virtuous.

behaviour noun *Their behaviour was excellent.* actions, attitude, bearing, comportment, conduct, courtesy, dealings, demeanour, deportment, manners, performance, reaction, response, ways.

behead verb decapitate, guillotine.

behind noun SEE **buttocks**.

behold verb SEE **see**.

beige adjective SEE **brown** adjective.

being noun **1** *She loves him with all her being.* actuality, essence, existence, life, living, reality, solidity, soul, spirit, substance.
2 *a mortal being.* animal, creature, individual, person.

belated adjective *belated thanks.* behindhand, delayed, last-minute, late, overdue, posthumous, tardy, unpunctual.

belch verb **1** *Cucumber makes me belch.* break wind, [*informal*] burp, emit wind.
2 *The chimney belched smoke.* discharge, emit, erupt, fume, gush, send out, smoke, spew out, vomit.

beleaguer verb SEE **besiege**.

belfry noun SEE **tower** noun.

belief noun **1** *belief in Santa Claus.* certainty, confidence, credence, reliance, sureness, trust.
OPPOSITES: SEE **disbelief**, **scepticism**.
2 *religious belief.* assurance, attitude, conviction, creed, doctrine, dogma, ethos, faith, feeling, ideology, morality, notion, opinion, persuasion, principles, religion, standards, tenets, theories, views.

believe verb **1** *I believe all he says.* accept, be certain about, count on, credit, depend on, endorse, have faith in, reckon on, rely on, subscribe to, [*informal*] swallow, swear by, trust.
OPPOSITES: SEE **disbelieve**.
2 *I believe she cheated.* assume, consider, [*informal*] dare say, feel, gather, guess, imagine, judge, know, maintain, [*formal*] postulate, presume, speculate, suppose, take it for granted, think.

believer noun *a religious believer.* adherent, devotee, disciple, fanatic, follower, proselyte, supporter, upholder, zealot.
OPPOSITES: SEE **agnostic**, **atheist**.

belittle verb SEE **criticize**.

bell noun *Did you hear the bell?* alarm, carillon, chime, knell, peal, signal.
RELEVANT VERBS: chime, clang, clink, jangle, jingle, peal, ping, resonate, resound, reverberate, ring, sound the knell, strike, tinkle, toll.

bellicose adjective SEE **belligerent**.

belligerent adjective *a belligerent fighter.* aggressive, antagonistic, argumentative, bellicose, bullying, combative, contentious, defiant, fierce, hostile, martial, militant, militaristic, provocative, pugnacious, quarrelsome, unfriendly, violent, warlike, warmongering, warring.
OPPOSITES: SEE **peaceable**.

bellow verb SEE **shout**.

belly noun abdomen, [*slang*] guts, paunch, [*uncomplimentary*] pot, stomach, [*informal*] tummy.

belong verb **1** *This book belongs to me.* be owned by, go with, pertain to, relate to.
2 *I belong to the squash club.* be affiliated with, be a member of, be connected with, [*informal*] be in with.
3 *I don't feel I belong here.* be at home, feel welcome, have a place.

belongings noun [*old-fashioned*] chattels, effects, [*informal*] gear, goods, [*joking*] impedimenta, possessions, property, things.

beloved adjective SEE **loved**.

belt noun **1** *a belt round the waist.* cummerbund, girdle, girth (*on a horse*), sash, strap, waistband.
2 *a fan-belt.* band, circle, loop.
3 *a belt of woodland.* area, district, line, stretch, strip, swathe, tract, zone.
a seat-belt safety-harness, safety-belt.

belt verb **1** [*informal*] *to belt someone.* SEE **hit** verb.
2 [*informal*] *to belt along.* SEE **hurry** verb.

bemuse verb SEE **bewilder**.

ben noun SEE **mountain**.

bench noun **1** *a park bench.* form, pew, seat, settle.
2 *the magistrate's bench.* court, courtroom, judge, magistrate, tribunal.
3 *a carpenter's bench.* counter, table, work-bench, work-table.

bend noun *a bend in the road.* angle, arc, bow, corner, crank, crook, curvature, curve, loop, turn, twist, zigzag.

bend verb **1** *to bend wire.* arch, bow, buckle, coil, contort, curl, curve, distort, flex, fold, loop, mould, refract (*light rays*), shape, turn, twist, warp, wind.
2 *Wire bends.* be flexible, [*informal*] give, yield.
to bend down bow, crouch, duck, kneel, lean, stoop.

Several English words, including *benediction*, *benefactor*, *beneficial*, *benevolent*, etc., are related to Latin *bene = well*. Contrast words beginning *male-*, such as *malefactor*, *malevolent*, etc.

benediction noun blessing.

benefactor noun *An anonymous benefactor paid for my trip.* backer, [*uncomplimentary*] do-gooder, donor, [*informal*] fairy godmother, patron, philanthropist, promoter, sponsor, supporter, well-wisher.
OPPOSITES: malefactor, SEE **wrongdoer**.

beneficial adjective *beneficial to health.* advantageous, benign, constructive, favourable, good, healthy, helpful, improving, nourishing, nutritious, profitable, rewarding, salutary, useful, valuable, wholesome.
OPPOSITES: SEE **harmful**.

beneficiary noun *a beneficiary under a will.* heir, heiress, inheritor, legatee, recipient, successor (*to a title*).

benefit noun **1** *the benefits of living in the country.* advantage, asset, blessing, [*old-fashioned*] boon, convenience, gain, good thing, help, privilege, prize, profit, use.
OPPOSITES: SEE **handicap** noun.
2 *unemployment benefit.* allowance, assistance, [*informal*] dole, [*informal*] hand-out, grant, income support, payment, social security, welfare.

benefit verb *The money will benefit the poor.* advance, advantage, aid, assist, better, boost, do good to, enhance, further, help, improve, profit, promote, serve.
OPPOSITES: SEE **hinder**.

benevolence noun altruism, SEE **charity**, consideration, generosity, goodness, humanity, kindness, liberality, magnanimity, mercy, philanthropy, sympathy.

benevolent adjective *a benevolent sponsor.* altruistic, caring, charitable, considerate, friendly, generous, good, helpful, humane, humanitarian, SEE **kind** adjective, kindly, liberal, magnanimous, merciful, philanthropic, supportive, sympathetic, warm-hearted.
OPPOSITES: malevolent, SEE **malicious**.

benign adjective **1** *a benign smile.* SEE **kind** adjective.
2 *a benign influence.* SEE **beneficial**.
OPPOSITES: SEE **malignant**.

bent adjective **1** *bent wire. a bent back.* angled, arched, bowed, buckled, coiled, contorted, crooked, curved, distorted, folded, hunched, looped, twisted, warped.
OPPOSITES: SEE **straight**.
2 [*informal*] *a bent businessman.* corrupt, criminal, dishonest, immoral, untrustworthy, wicked.
OPPOSITES: SEE **honest**.

bent noun SEE **aptitude, bias** noun.

bequeath verb *She bequeathed her money to her grandchildren.* endow, hand down, leave, pass on, settle, will.

bequest noun *He received a bequest under his grandmother's will.* endowment, gift, inheritance, legacy, settlement.

bereave verb **to be bereaved** be orphaned, be widowed, lose a loved one.

bereavement noun *a bereavement in the family.* death, loss.

bereft adjective *bereft of reason.* deprived, destitute, devoid, lacking, robbed, wanting.

berry noun SEE **fruit**.

berserk adjective *The dog went berserk when a wasp stung him.* [*informal*] beside yourself, crazy, demented, deranged, frantic, frenetic, frenzied, furious, infuriated, insane, mad, maniacal, rabid, violent, wild.
OPPOSITES: SEE **composed**.
to go berserk lose control, rampage, rave, run amok, run riot, [*informal*] see red.

berth noun **1** *a sleeping-berth.* SEE **bed**, bunk, hammock.
2 *a berth for a ship.* anchorage, dock, harbour, haven, landing-stage, moorings, pier, port, quay, slipway, wharf.
to give a wide berth to SEE **avoid**.

berth verb *The ship berthed.* anchor, dock, drop anchor, land, moor, tie up.

beseech verb SEE **ask**.

beset verb SEE **surround**.

besiege verb **1** *The Greeks besieged Troy for 10 long years.* beleaguer, beset, blockade, cut off, encircle, encompass, isolate, surround.
2 *The superstar was besieged by reporters.* SEE **pester**.

besom noun SEE **broom**.

besotted adjective SEE **infatuated**.

best adjective *my best friend. best quality.* first-class, foremost, incomparable, leading, matchless, optimum, outstanding, pre-eminent, supreme, top, unequalled, unrivalled, unsurpassed.

bestial adjective *bestial cruelty.* animal, beast-like, beastly, brutal, brutish, inhuman, SEE **savage** adjective, subhuman.

bestow verb SEE **give**.

bet noun **1** *I had a bet that she would win* [*informal*] flutter, gamble, [*informal*] punt, speculation, wager.
2 *How much was the bet?* bid, stake.

bet verb *He bet everything he had. I bet occasionally.* bid, gamble, do the pools, enter a lottery, [*informal*] have a flutter, hazard, lay bets, [*informal*] punt, risk, speculate, stake, venture, wager.

bête noire noun SEE **hate** noun.

betide verb SEE **happen**.

betray verb **1** *to betray someone.* abandon, be a Judas to, be a traitor to, cheat, conspire against, deceive, desert, double-cross, [*informal*] grass on, inform on, jilt (*a lover*), let down, [*informal*] rat on, [*informal*] sell down the river, sell out, [*informal*] shop, [*informal*] tell tales about, [*informal*] turn Queen's evidence on.
2 *to betray a secret.* disclose, divulge, expose, give away, indicate, let out, let slip, manifest, reveal, show, tell.

betrothed adjective SEE **engaged**.

better adjective *Are you better after your flu?* back to normal, convalescent, cured, fitter, healed, healthier, improved, [*informal*] none the worse, [*informal*] on the mend, progressing, recovered, recovering, restored, well.
better half SEE **spouse**.

better verb SEE **improve, surpass**.

bevel verb *The carpenter bevelled the edges.* angle, cant, chamfer, give an angle to, give a diagonal or oblique or sloping edge to, mitre, slant.

beverage noun SEE **drink** noun.

bevy noun SEE **group** noun.

beware verb **to beware of** *Beware of the bull.* avoid, be alert to (SEE **alert**), be cautious about, guard against, heed, keep clear of, look out for, mind, shun, steer away from, take heed of, take precautions against, watch out for.

bewilder verb baffle, [*informal*] bamboozle, bemuse, confound, confuse, daze, disconcert, disorientate, distract, floor, [*informal*] flummox, mislead, muddle, mystify, perplex, puzzle, stump, stun.

bewitch verb SEE **charm** verb.

bewitching adjective SEE **attractive**.

bias noun **1** *She has a bias towards science.* aptitude, bent, inclination, leaning, liking, partiality, penchant, predilection, predisposition, preference, proclivity, proneness, propensity, tendency.
2 *The ref was guilty of bias.* bigotry, chauvinism, favouritism, imbalance, injustice, nepotism, one-sidedness, partiality, partisanship, prejudice, racism, sexism, unfairness.

bias verb SEE **influence** verb.

biased adjective *a biased decision. a biased referee.* bigoted, blinkered, chauvinistic, distorted, influenced, interested (*an interested party*), loaded, one-sided, partial, partisan, prejudiced, racist, sexist, slanted, tendentious, unfair, unjust, warped.
OPPOSITES: SEE **unbiased**.

bicker verb SEE **quarrel** verb.

Many English words which incorporate the idea *two* or *double*—including *bicycle, biennial, bifocal, bilingual,* etc.—use the Latin prefix *bi-* = *two.*

---

bicycle noun [*informal*] bike, cycle, penny-farthing, [*informal*] push-bike, racer, tandem, [*informal*] two-wheeler.

bid noun **1** *a bid at an auction.* offer, price, proposal, proposition, tender.
2 *a bid to beat a record.* attempt, [*informal*] crack, effort, endeavour, [*informal*] go, try, venture.

bid verb **1** *to bid at an auction.* make an offer, offer, proffer, propose, tender.
2 [*formal or old-fashioned*] *He bade them enter.* SEE **command** verb.

biddable adjective SEE **amenable**.

bidding noun SEE **command** noun.

bide verb SEE **wait** verb.

bier noun SEE **funeral**.

biff verb SEE **hit** verb.

bifocals noun SEE **glass (glasses)**.

big adjective **1** *a big amount. a big woman. a big box.* [*informal*] almighty, ample, bulky, burly, capacious, colossal, commodious, considerable, elephantine, enormous, extensive, SEE **fat** adjective, gargantuan, giant, gigantic, grand, great, heavy, hefty, high, huge, [*informal*] hulking, husky, immeasurable, immense, impressive, incalculable, infinite, [*informal*] jumbo, large, lofty, mammoth, massive, mighty, monstrous, monumental, mountainous, prodigious, roomy, sizeable, spacious, substantial, tall, titanic, towering, [*informal*] tremendous, vast, voluminous, weighty.

2 *a big decision. the big match.* grave, important, influential, leading, main, major, momentous, notable, powerful, prime, principal, prominent, serious, significant.
3 *a big noise.* SEE **loud**.

bight noun SEE **bay** noun.

bigot noun chauvinist, fanatic, prejudiced person [SEE **prejudiced**], racist, sexist, zealot.

bigoted adjective SEE **prejudiced**.

bigotry noun SEE **prejudice** noun.

bigwig noun SEE **celebrity**.

bike noun SEE **bicycle**.

bikini noun SEE **bathing-costume**.

bilge noun SEE **nonsense**.

bilingual adjective polyglot.

bilious adjective *He's feeling bilious.* SEE **ill**, liverish, nauseated, queasy, sick.

bilk verb SEE **cheat** verb.

bill noun 1 *a bill showing what you pay.* account, invoice, receipt, statement.
2 *a bill advertising a sale.* advertisement, broadsheet, bulletin, circular, handbill, handout, leaflet, notice, placard, poster, sheet.
3 *a Parliamentary bill.* draft law, proposed law. [*A bill* becomes an *Act* when passed.]
4 *a bird's bill.* beak, mandible.

billet noun SEE **lodgings**.

billhook noun scythe.

billow noun SEE **wave** noun.

billow verb *The sheets billowed on the washing-line.* balloon, belly, bulge, fill out, heave, puff out, rise, roll, surge, swell, undulate.

billy-goat noun SEE **goat**.

bin noun CONTAINERS: SEE **container**.

binary adjective SEE **two**.

bind verb 1 *to bind something with string.* attach, clamp, connect, SEE **fasten**, hitch, join, lash, link, rope, secure, strap, tie, truss.
2 *Loyalty to our leader bound us together.* combine, fuse, hold together, unify, unite, weld.
3 *The nurse bound the wound.* bandage, cover, dress, encase, swathe, wrap.
4 *I was bound by oath to tell the truth.* compel, constrain, force, necessitate, oblige, require.

binder noun *a binder for papers.* SEE **file** noun.

binding adjective *a binding agreement.* compulsory, contractual, formal, irrevocable, legally enforceable, mandatory, necessary, obligatory, permanent, required, [*informal*] signed and sealed, statutory, unalterable, unavoidable, unbreakable.
OPPOSITES: SEE **informal**.

binge noun SEE **celebration**.

binoculars noun SEE **optical (optical instruments)**.

Several English words, including *biography*, *biology*, and *biopsy*, are related to Greek *bios=life*.

---

biographer noun SEE **writer**.

biography noun autobiography, history, life, life-story, memoirs, recollections.
OTHER KINDS OF WRITING: SEE **writing**.

biology noun botany, life science, nature study, zoology.

bionic adjective SEE **robot**.

biopsy noun SEE **operation**.

bipartite adjective SEE **two**.

biped noun KINDS OF ANIMAL: SEE **animal**.

biplane noun OTHER AIRCRAFT: SEE **aircraft**.

birch verb SEE **whip** verb.

bird noun [*childish*] birdie, [*joking*] feathered friend, fowl.
female bird hen.
male bird cock, drake (*duck*), gander (*goose*).
young bird chick, cygnet (*swan*), duckling, fledgeling, gosling (*goose*), nestling.
a home for birds aviary, cage, nest, nesting-box.
the study of birds ornithology.

KINDS OF BIRD: gamebird, seabird, wader, waterfowl, wildfowl.

VARIOUS BIRDS: albatross, auk, bittern, blackbird, budgerigar, bullfinch, bunting, bustard, buzzard, canary, carrion crow, cassowary, chaffinch, chicken, chiff-chaff, chough, cockatoo, coot, cormorant, corncrake, crane, crow, cuckoo, curlew, dabchick, dipper, dove, duck, dunnock.
eagle, egret, emu, falcon, finch, flamingo, flycatcher, fulmar, goldcrest, goldfinch, goose, grebe, greenfinch, grouse, gull, hawk, hedge-sparrow, heron, hoopoe, hornbill, humming bird, ibis, jackdaw, jay, kestrel, kingfisher, kite, kiwi, kookaburra, lapwing, lark, linnet.

macaw, magpie, martin, mina bird, moorhen, nightingale, nightjar, nuthatch, oriole, osprey, ostrich, ousel, owl, parakeet, parrot, partridge, peacock, peewit, pelican, penguin, peregrine, petrel, pheasant, pigeon, pipit, plover, ptarmigan, puffin, quail, raven, redbreast, redstart, robin, rook.

sandpiper, seagull, shearwater, shelduck, shrike, skua, skylark, snipe, sparrow, sparrowhawk, spoonbill, starling, stonechat, stork, swallow, swan, swift, teal, tern, thrush, tit, toucan, turkey, turtle-dove, vulture, wagtail, warbler, waxwing, wheatear, woodcock, woodpecker, wren, yellowhammer

PARTS OF A BIRD: beak, bill, claw, crest, down, feathers, mandible, plumage, tail, talon, wing.

GROUPS OF BIRDS: brood (*of chicks*), covey (*of partridges*), flock, gaggle (*of geese*).

Biro noun SEE **pen** noun.

birth noun **1** *the birth of a baby.* breech birth, Caesarian, childbirth, confinement, delivery, labour, nativity (*of Christ*), [*formal*] parturition.
SEE ALSO **pregnant**.
MEDICAL SPECIALIST IN CHILDBIRTH: obstetrician.
2 *of noble birth.* ancestry, background, blood, breeding, derivation, descent, extraction, family, genealogy, line, lineage, parentage, pedigree, race, stock, strain.
3 *the birth of a new idea.* SEE **beginning**.
to give birth (to) bear, SEE **begin**, calve, farrow, foal.
RELATED ADJECTIVE: natal (*ante-natal, post-natal*).

birth-control noun SEE **contraception**.

birthday noun SEE **anniversary**.

birthmark noun SEE **blemish**.

biscuit noun [*American*] cookie, cracker, crispbread, digestive, ginger-nut, pretzel, rusk, shortbread, wafer.

bisect verb *The lines bisect each other.* cross, cut in half, divide, halve, intersect.

bisexual adjective [Compare *heterosexual* and *homosexual.*] hermaphrodite.

bishop noun SEE **clergyman**.
RELATED ADJECTIVE: episcopal.

bistro noun SEE **restaurant**.

bit noun **1** *a bit of chocolate. a bit of stone.* atom, block, chip, chunk, crumb, division, dollop, fraction, fragment, grain, helping, hunk, iota, lump, morsel, part, particle, piece, portion, scrap, section, segment, share, slab, slice, snippet, speck.
2 *Can you wait a bit?* instant, [*informal*] jiffy, minute, moment, second, [*informal*] tick, time, while.

bitch noun SEE **dog** noun.

bitchy adjective SEE **malicious**.

bite noun **1** *a nasty bite.* nip, pinch, sting, SEE **wound** noun.
2 *a bite to eat.* bit, morsel, mouthful, nibble, piece, snack, taste.

bite verb **1** champ, chew, crunch, cut into, gnaw, [*formal*] masticate, munch, nibble, nip, rend, snap, tear at, wound.
2 *An insect bit me.* pierce, sting.
3 *The worn thread of the screw wouldn't bite.* grip, hold.

biting adjective **1** *biting wind.* SEE **cold** adjective.
2 *a biting remark.* SEE **sharp**.

bitter adjective **1** *a bitter taste.* acid, acrid, harsh, sharp, sour, unpleasant.
OPPOSITES: SEE **mild**, **sweet** adjective.
2 *a bitter experience.* calamitous, dire, distasteful, distressing, galling, hateful, heartbreaking, painful, poignant, sorrowful, unhappy, unwelcome, upsetting.
OPPOSITES: SEE **pleasant**.
3 *bitter remarks.* acerbic, acrimonious, angry, cruel, cynical, embittered, envious, hostile, jaundiced, jealous, malicious, rancorous, resentful, savage, sharp, spiteful, stinging, vicious, violent, waspish.
OPPOSITES: SEE **kind** adjective.
4 *a bitter wind.* biting, SEE **cold** adjective, fierce, freezing, perishing, piercing, raw.
OPPOSITES: SEE **gentle**.

bitterness noun SEE **animosity**.

bitumen noun pitch, tar.

bivalve noun SEE **shellfish**.

bivouac noun SEE **camp** noun.

bizarre adjective SEE **odd**.

blab verb SEE **talk** verb.

black adjective **1** blackish, coal-black, SEE **dark**, dusky, ebony, funereal, gloomy, inky, jet, jet-black, moonless, murky, pitch-black, pitch-dark, raven, sable, sooty, starless, unlit.
2 *black with dirt.* SEE **dirty** adjective.

black verb **1** *I blacked my shoes.* blacken, polish.
2 *They blacked the imported goods.* ban, bar, blacklist, boycott, put an embargo on, refuse to handle.

blackball verb SEE **blacklist**.

black-beetle noun cockroach.

blackberry noun bramble.

blacken verb SEE **darken**.

blackfly noun aphid, aphis.

blackguard noun [*old-fashioned*] cad, rogue, SEE **scoundrel**, villain.

blackhead noun SEE **blemish**.

blackleg noun strike-breaker, traitor.

blacklist verb ban, bar, blackball, boycott, debar, disallow, exclude, ostracize, preclude, proscribe, repudiate, snub, veto.

blackmail noun extortion.

blacksmith noun farrier, smith.
VARIOUS CRAFTSMEN: SEE **artist**.

blade noun dagger, edge, knife, razor, scalpel, SEE **sword**, vane.

blame noun *I accepted the blame*. accountability, accusation, castigation, censure, charge, complaint, condemnation, criticism, culpability, fault, guilt, imputation, incrimination, liability, onus, [*informal*] rap, recrimination, reprimand, reproach, reproof, responsibility, [*informal*] stick, stricture.

blame verb *They blamed me for the accident*. accuse, admonish, censure, charge, chide, condemn, criticize, denounce, [*informal*] get at, hold responsible, incriminate, rebuke, reprehend, reprimand, reproach, reprove, round on, scold, tax, upbraid.
OPPOSITES: SEE **excuse** verb.

blameless adjective SEE **innocent**.

blanch verb become white, pale, whiten.
OPPOSITES: SEE **blush**.

bland adjective **1** *a bland flavour*. boring, flat, insipid, mild, nondescript, smooth, tasteless, unappetizing, uninteresting, watery, weak.
OPPOSITES: SEE **sharp, tasty**.
2 *a bland personality. bland remarks*. affable, amiable, banal, calm, characterless, dull, gentle, [*informal*] smooth, soft, soothing, suave, trite, unexciting, uninspiring, uninteresting, vapid, weak, [*informal*] wishy-washy.
OPPOSITES: SEE **interesting**.

blank adjective **1** *blank paper. blank tape*. clean, clear, empty, plain, spotless, unmarked, unused, void.
OPPOSITES: SEE **used**.
2 *a blank look*. apathetic, baffled, baffling, dead, [*informal*] deadpan, emotionless, expressionless, featureless, glazed, immobile, impassive, inane, inscrutable, lifeless, poker-faced, uncomprehending, unresponsive, vacant, vacuous.
OPPOSITES: SEE **responsive**.

blank noun **1** *My mind was a blank*. emptiness, nothingness, [*formal*] vacuity, vacuum, void.
2 *Fill in the blanks*. break, gap, space.
blank verse SEE **verse**.

blanket noun SEE **bed**.

blare verb VARIOUS SOUNDS: SEE **sound** noun.

blarney noun SEE **flattery**.

blasé adjective SEE **indifferent**.

blaspheme verb, **blasphemy** noun SEE **curse** noun, verb.

blasphemous adjective *blasphemous language*. godless, impious, irreligious, irreverent, profane, sacrilegious, ungodly, wicked.
OPPOSITES: SEE **reverent**.

blast noun **1** *a blast of air*. SEE **wind** noun.
2 *a bomb blast*. SEE **explosion**.

blast verb SEE **attack** verb, **destroy, explode**.
to blast off SEE **launch** verb.

blatant adjective *a blatant mistake. blatant rudeness*. apparent, bare-faced, bold, brazen, conspicuous, evident, flagrant, glaring, obtrusive, obvious, open, overt, shameless, stark, unconcealed, undisguised, unmistakable, visible.
OPPOSITES: SEE **concealed**.

blaze noun SEE **fire** noun.

blaze verb SEE **burn** verb.

blazer noun SEE **coat** noun.

bleach verb blanch, discolour, etiolate (*leaves of a plant*), fade, lighten, pale, peroxide (*hair*), whiten.

bleak adjective *a bleak hillside. a bleak outlook*. bare, barren, blasted, cheerless, SEE **cold** adjective, comfortless, depressing, desolate, dismal, dreary, exposed, grim, hopeless, joyless, uncomfortable, unpromising, windswept, wintry.
OPPOSITES: SEE **reassuring, warm** adjective.

bleary adjective *bleary eyes. bleary vision* blurred, [*informal*] blurry, cloudy, dim, filmy, fogged, foggy, fuzzy, hazy, indistinct, misty, murky, obscured, smeary, unclear, watery.
OPPOSITES: SEE **clear** adjective.

bleat verb VARIOUS SOUNDS: SEE **sound** noun.

bleed verb **1** *Liquid was bleeding out*. SEE **flow** verb.
2 *to bleed oil from the sump*. SEE **drain** verb.

bleep verb VARIOUS SOUNDS: SEE **sound** noun.

blemish noun **1** *a blemish in your work*. blot, defect, eyesore, fault, flaw, imperfection, mark, mess, smudge, speck, stain, ugliness.

2 *a blemish on the skin.* birthmark, blackhead, blister, blotch, callus, corn, deformity, disfigurement, freckle, mole, naevus, pimple, pustule, scar, spot, verruca, wart, whitlow, [*slang*] zit.

blench verb SEE **flinch**.

blend noun *a blend of various ingredients.* alloy (*of metals*), amalgam, amalgamation, combination, composite, compound, concoction, fusion, mélange, mix, mixture, synthesis, union.

blend verb 1 *to blend into a crowd.* amalgamate, coalesce, combine, fuse, harmonize, integrate, intermingle, intermix, merge, mingle, synthesize, unite.
2 *to blend ingredients for a cake.* beat, compound, mix, stir together, whip, whisk.

blender noun food processor, liquidizer, mixer.

bless verb 1 *to bless someone or something to make it holy.* anoint, consecrate, dedicate, grace, hallow, make sacred, ordain, sanctify.
OPPOSITES: SEE **condemn, desecrate**.
2 *to bless God's name.* exalt, extol, glorify, magnify, praise.
OPPOSITES: SEE **curse** verb.

blessed adjective 1 *God's blessed name.* adored, divine, hallowed, holy, revered, sacred, sanctified.
2 [*informal*] *a blessed relief.* SEE **happy**.

blessing 1 *The priest pronounced a blessing.* benediction, grace, prayer.
OPPOSITES: SEE **curse** noun.
2 *Our parents gave their blessing to our marriage.* approbation, approval, backing, [*formal*] concurrence, consent, leave, permission, sanction, support.
OPPOSITES: SEE **disapproval**.
3 *Central heating is a blessing in the winter.* advantage, asset, benefit, [*old-fashioned*] boon, comfort, convenience, godsend, help.
OPPOSITES: SEE **evil** noun.

blether verb SEE **talk** verb.

blight noun *blight in the potatoes. a blight on society.* affliction, ailment, [*old-fashioned*] bane, cancer, canker, curse, decay, disease, evil, illness, infestation, [*old-fashioned*] pestilence, plague, pollution, rot, scourge, sickness.

blight verb SEE **spoil**.

blighter noun SEE **scoundrel**.

blind adjective 1 WORDS TO DESCRIBE PEOPLE WITH IMPAIRED VISION: astigmatic, blinded, boss-eyed, colour-blind, cross-eyed, eyeless, long-sighted, myopic, near-sighted, short-sighted, sightless, suffering from cataract or glaucoma, unseeing, visually handicapped.
2 *blind devotion. blind to his faults.* blinkered, heedless, ignorant, inattentive, indifferent, insensible, insensitive, mindless, oblivious, prejudiced, unaware, unobservant.
OPPOSITES: SEE **aware**.

blind noun *Close the blind.* cover, curtain, screen, shade, shutters.

blind verb 1 *to blind someone with a bright light.* SEE **dazzle**.
2 [*informal*] *to blind someone with science.* SEE **deceive**.

blink verb *blinking lights.* flash, flicker, flutter, gleam, glimmer, twinkle, wink.

bliss noun *a life of bliss.* delight, ecstasy, euphoria, felicity, gladness, happiness, heaven, joy, paradise, pleasure, rapture.
OPPOSITES: SEE **misery**.

blissful adjective SEE **happy**.

blister noun SEE **spot** noun.

blistering adjective *a blistering attack.* SEE **savage** adjective.

blithe adjective SEE **happy**.

blitz noun SEE **attack** noun.

blizzard noun SEE **storm** noun.

bloated adjective *starving children with bloated stomachs.* dilated, distended, enlarged, inflated, swollen.

blob noun SEE **drop** noun.

bloc noun SEE **alliance**.

block noun 1 *a block of chocolate. a block of wood.* bar, brick, cake, chock, chunk, hunk, ingot, lump, mass, piece, slab.
2 *a mental block. a block in the system.* barrier, blockage, delay, hang-up, hindrance, impediment, jam, obstacle, obstruction, resistance, stoppage.

block verb 1 *The drain was blocked with leaves.* [*informal*] bung up, choke, clog, close, congest, constrict, dam, fill, jam, obstruct, plug, stop up.
2 *A parked car blocked our way.* bar, barricade, impede, obstruct.
3 *The boss blocked our plan.* deter, halt, hamper, hinder, hold back, prevent, prohibit, resist, [*informal*] scotch, [*informal*] stonewall, stop, thwart.

blockade noun SEE **siege**.

blockage noun *a blockage in a drain.* barrier, block, bottleneck, congestion, constriction, delay, hang-up, hindrance, impediment, jam, obstacle, obstruction, resistance, stoppage.

blockhead noun SEE **idiot**.

bloke noun SEE **man** noun.

blond, blonde adjective [This was originally a French word: *blond* is masculine, *blonde* is feminine.] *blond hair.* bleached, fair, flaxen, golden, light, platinum, silvery, yellow.

blood noun gore.

bloodcurdling adjective SEE **frightening.**

bloodshed noun *The battlefield was a scene of appalling bloodshed.* bloodletting, butchery, carnage, killing, massacre, murder, slaughter, slaying.

bloodthirsty adjective barbaric, brutal, SEE **cruel**, ferocious, fierce, inhuman, murderous, pitiless, ruthless, sadistic, savage, vicious, violent, warlike.

bloody adjective **1** *a bloody wound.* bleeding, blood-stained, raw.
2 *a bloody battle.* SEE **fierce**, gory, sanguinary.

bloom noun **1** *I cut my best blooms for the flower-show.* blossom, bud, flower.
2 *the bloom of youth.* beauty, blush, flush, glow, prime.

bloom verb *Most flowers bloom in summer.* be healthy, blossom, [*poetic*] blow, bud, burgeon, develop, flourish, flower, grow, open, prosper, sprout, thrive.
OPPOSITES: SEE **fade.**

blooming adjective SEE **healthy.**

blossom noun [*Blossom* often refers to a *mass of flowers* rather than a single flower.] *apple blossom.* blooms, buds, florets, flowers.

blossom verb SEE **bloom** verb.

blot noun **1** *a blot of ink.* blob, blotch, mark, smear, smudge, [*informal*] splodge, spot, stain.
2 *a blot on the landscape.* blemish, defect, eyesore, fault, flaw, ugliness.

blot verb *to blot a page.* bespatter, mar, mark, smudge, spoil, spot, stain.
to blot out *The fog blotted out the view.* cancel, conceal, cover, delete, eclipse, erase, expunge, hide, mask, obliterate, obscure, rub out, wipe out.
to blot your copybook SEE **misbehave.**

blotch noun SEE **mark** noun.

blotchy adjective *a blotchy skin.* blemished, marked, patchy, smudged, spotty, uneven.

blow noun **1** *a blow on the head.* bang, bash, [*informal*] belt, [*informal*] biff, box (*on the ears*), buffet, bump, clip, clout, clump, [*formal*] concussion, hit, jolt, knock, punch, rap, slap, [*informal*] slosh, smack, [*informal*] sock, stroke, swat, swipe, thump, wallop [*informal*] wap, welt, whack.
2 *The loss of her purse was a terrible blow.* affliction, [*informal*] bombshell, calamity, disappointment, disaster, misfortune, shock, surprise, upset.

blow verb *The heater blows out hot air.* blast, breathe, exhale, fan, puff, waft, whirl, whistle.
to blow up 1 *to blow up tyres.* dilate, expand, fill, inflate, pump up.
2 *to blow up a photo.* enlarge.
3 *to blow up a problem.* exaggerate, make worse, magnify, overstate.
3 *to blow up with explosive.* blast, bomb, burst, detonate, dynamite, erupt, explode, go off, set off, shatter.
4 [*informal*] *to blow up in a temper.* get angry [SEE **angry**], lose your temper, rage.

blow-out noun SEE **meal.**

blowy adjective SEE **windy.**

blowzy adjective SEE **untidy.**

bludgeon noun SEE **cudgel** noun.

bludgeon verb SEE **beat** verb.

blue adjective **1** SHADES OF BLUE: aquamarine, azure, cerulean, cobalt, indigo, navy, sapphire, sky-blue, turquoise, ultramarine.
OTHER COLOURS: SEE **colour** noun.
2 *a blue joke.* SEE **bawdy.**
3 [*informal*] *to feel blue.* SEE **sad.**

blue verb SEE **squander.**

bluebottle noun fly.

blueprint noun *a blueprint for a new invention.* basis, design, draft, model, outline, pattern, pilot, plan, project, proposal, prototype, scheme.

blues noun SEE **depression.**

bluff adjective *a bluff manner.* SEE **blunt** adjective.

bluff verb *He bluffed me.* SEE **deceive.**

blunder noun *I made a terrible blunder.* [*informal*] boob, [*informal*] botch, [*informal*] clanger, [*slang*] cock-up, error, fault, faux pas, gaffe, howler, indiscretion, miscalculation, misjudgement, mistake, slip, slip-up, [*formal*] solecism.

blunder verb *Someone has blundered!* be clumsy, [*informal*] botch (something) up, bumble, bungle, [*informal*] drop a clanger, err, [*informal*] foul (something) up, [*slang*] goof, go wrong, [*informal*] make a hash (of something), make a mistake, mess (something) up, miscalculate, misjudge, [*informal*] put your foot in it, slip up, stumble.

blunt adjective **1** *a blunt knife. a blunt instrument.* dull, rounded, thick, unpointed, unsharpened.
OPPOSITES: SEE **sharp.**

2 *a blunt remark. a blunt manner*. abrupt, bluff, brusque, candid, curt, direct, downright, forthright, frank, honest, insensitive, outspoken, plain-spoken, SEE **rude**, straightforward, tactless, unceremonious.
OPPOSITES: SEE **polite, tactful**.

blunt verb *to blunt your awareness. to blunt your hunger*. abate, allay, anaesthetize, dampen, deaden, desensitize, dull, lessen, numb, soften, take the edge off, weaken.
OPPOSITES: SEE **sharpen**.

blur verb 1 *The steamy windows blurred the view*. befog, blear, cloud, darken, dim, fog, mask, obscure, smear.
2 *The accident had blurred her memory*. confuse, muddle.

blurred adjective *a blurred memory. a blurred photo*. bleary, blurry, clouded, cloudy, confused, dim, faint, foggy, fuzzy, hazy, ill-defined, indefinite, indistinct, misty, nebulous, out of focus, smoky, unclear, unfocussed, vague.
OPPOSITES: SEE **clear** adjective.

blurt verb **to blurt out** be indiscreet, [*informal*] blab, burst out with, come out with, cry out, disclose, divulge, exclaim, [*informal*] give the game away, let out, let slip, reveal, [*informal*] spill the beans, tell.

blush verb colour, flush, glow, go red.
OPPOSITES: SEE **blanch**.

blushing adjective SEE **red**.

blustering adjective *I don't like his blustering manner*. angry, boasting, boisterous, bragging, bullying, crowing, defiant, domineering, hectoring, noisy, ranting, self-assertive, showing-off, storming, swaggering, threatening, vaunting, violent.
OPPOSITES: SEE **modest**.

blustery adjective gusty, squally, SEE **windy**.

board noun 1 *wooden boards*. blockboard, chipboard, clapboard, panel, plank, plywood, sheet, slab, slat, timber, weather board.
2 *the managing board*. committee, council, department, directorate, jury, panel.

board verb 1 *The fire victims were boarded in a hotel*. accommodate, billet, house, lodge, put up, quarter.
2 *We boarded the plane an hour before take-off*. catch, embark (on), enter, get on, go on board.

boarding-house noun SEE **accommodation**.

boarding-school noun SEE **school**.

boast verb [*slang*] be all mouth, [*informal*] blow your own trumpet, bluster, brag, crow, exaggerate, gloat, praise yourself, [*slang*] shoot a line, show off, [*informal*] sing your own praises, swagger, [*informal*] swank, talk big, vaunt.

boaster noun [*informal*] big-head, [*informal*] big-mouth, boastful person [SEE **boastful**], braggadocio, braggart, [*informal*] loudmouth, [*informal*] poser, show-off, swaggerer, swank.

boastful adjective [*informal*] big-headed, bragging, [*informal*] cocky, conceited, egotistical, proud, puffed up, swaggering, swanky, swollen-headed, vain, [*formal*] vainglorious.
OPPOSITES: SEE **modest**.

boat noun VARIOUS BOATS: SEE **vessel**.

boatman noun bargee, ferryman, gondolier, lighterman, oarsman, rower, SEE **sailor**, waterman, yachtsman.

bob verb *Something bobbed up and down in the water*. be agitated, bounce, dance, hop, jerk, jig about, jolt, jump, leap, move about, nod, oscillate, shake, toss about, twitch.
to bob up SEE **appear**.

bobbin noun cotton-reel, reel, spool.

bob-sleigh noun SEE **sledge**.

bode verb SEE **augur**.

bodily adjective *bodily contact*. SEE **physical**.

bodkin noun SEE **pin** noun.

body noun 1 *the human body*. anatomy, being, build, figure, form, frame, individual, physique, shape, substance.
2 *a blow to the body*. torso, trunk.
3 *a dead body*. cadaver, carcass, corpse, mortal remains, mummy, relics, remains, [*slang*] stiff.
4 *the governing body*. association, band, committee, company, corporation, SEE **group** noun, society.
5 *a large body of material*. accumulation, agglomeration, collection, corpus, mass.

PARTS OF THE HUMAN BODY: abdomen, Adam's apple, ankle, anus, aorta, arm, armpit, artery, backbone, bladder, bone, bowel, brain, breast, buttocks, calf, cartilage, cheek, chest, chin, clavicle, coccyx, cranium, duodenum, ear, eardrum, elbow, epiglottis, eye, fallopian tube, finger, foot, forehead.

genitals, gland, groin, gullet, gums, gut, hand, haunch, head, heart, heel, hip, instep, intestines, jaw, jugular, kidney, knee, kneecap, knuckle, larynx, leg, lip, liver, loins, lung, mastoid, midriff, mouth, muscle, navel, neck, nerves, nipple, nose.

oesophagus, ovary, pancreas, pelvis, pituitary, pore, prostate, rectum, rib, shin, shoulder, sinew, sinus, skeleton, skin, skull, spine, spleen, stomach, temple, tendon, testicle, thigh, thorax, throat, thyroid, tongue, tonsil, tooth, trachea, uterus, vein, vertebrae, waist, windpipe, womb, wrist.

SOME BODILY FLUIDS AND CHEMICALS: bile, blood, hormone, saliva.

---

bodyguard noun defender, guard, minder, protector.

boffin noun SEE **scientist**.

bog noun fen, marsh, marshland, mire, morass, mudflats, peat bog, quagmire, quicksands, salt-marsh, [*old-fashioned*] slough, swamp, wetlands.
to get bogged down be hindered, be slowed down, get into difficulties, get stuck, sink.

boggy adjective SEE **muddy**.

bogie noun SEE **wheel** noun.

bogus adjective SEE **counterfeit** adjective.

bogy noun SEE **spirit**.

Bohemian adjective [*Bohemian* can simply mean *from Bohemia*, but the word is often used to describe someone whose way of life is unconventional.] *Bohemian dress.* [*informal*] arty, [*old-fashioned*] beatnik, bizarre, eccentric, hippie, informal, non-conformist, off-beat, unconventional, unorthodox, [*informal*] way-out, weird.

boil noun *a boil on the skin.* abscess, blister, carbuncle, chilblain, eruption, gathering, gumboil, inflammation, pimple, pock, pustule, sore, spot, tumour, ulcer, [*slang*] zit.

boil verb **1** *I boiled the water. I boiled the potatoes.* bring to boiling point, SEE **cook** verb, heat, simmer, stew.
2 *Is the water boiling yet?* bubble, effervesce, foam, seethe, steam.
3 *to boil with anger.* SEE **angry (be angry)**.

boiler noun SEE **heater**.

boisterous adjective **1** *boisterous weather.* SEE **windy**.
2 *boisterous behaviour.* animated, cheerful, disorderly, exuberant, irrepressible, lively, loud, noisy, obstreperous, riotous, rollicking, rough, rowdy, tumultuous, unrestrained, unruly, uproarious, wild.
OPPOSITES: SEE **calm** adjective.

bold adjective **1** [*complimentary*] *a bold explorer.* adventurous, audacious, brave, confident, courageous, daring, dauntless, enterprising, fearless, forceful, gallant, heroic, intrepid, [*informal*] plucky, self-confident, valiant, valorous, venturesome.
OPPOSITES: SEE **cowardly, nervous**.
2 [*uncomplimentary*] *a bold request.* brash, brazen, cheeky, forward, fresh, impertinent, impudent, insolent, pert, presumptuous, rude, saucy, shameless, unashamed.
OPPOSITES: SEE **polite, reticent**.
3 *bold colours. bold writing.* big, bright, clear, conspicuous, eye-catching, large, obvious, prominent, pronounced, showy, striking, strong, vivid.
OPPOSITES: SEE **inconspicuous**.

boldness noun SEE **audacity, bravery**.

bole noun *the bole of a tree.* SEE **trunk**.

bollard noun SEE **post** noun.

boloney noun SEE **nonsense**.

Bolshie noun [Short for *Bolshevik*- =member of a Russian party in the early 20th century, in favour of an extreme form of socialism.] SEE **rebellious**.

bolster noun cushion, pillow.

bolster verb **support** verb.

bolt noun **1** *a bolt on a door.* bar, catch, fastening, latch, lock.
2 *nuts and bolts.* peg, pin, rivet, rod, screw.
bolt from the blue SEE **surprise** noun.

bolt verb **1** *Bolt the door.* bar, close, fasten, latch, lock, secure.
2 *The animals bolted.* abscond, dart away, dash away, escape, flee, fly, SEE **run**, rush off.
3 *Don't bolt your food.* devour, eat hastily, gobble, gulp, guzzle, stuff, wolf.

bolt-hole noun SEE **refuge**.

bomb noun OTHER WEAPONS: SEE **weapon**.

bomb verb SEE **bombard**.

bombard verb **1** *to bombard someone with missiles.* assail, assault, attack, beset, blast, blitz, bomb, fire at, pelt, pound, shell, shoot at, strafe.
2 *to bombard someone with questions.* badger, harass, importune, pester, plague.

bombardment noun *a bombardment of missiles.* attack, barrage, blast, blitz, broadside, burst, cannonade, discharge, fusillade, hail, salvo, volley.

bombastic adjective SEE **pompous**.

bomber noun OTHER AIRCRAFT: SEE **aircraft**.

bombshell noun SEE **surprise** noun.

bona fide SEE **genuine**.

bonanza noun SEE **prosperity**.

bon-bon noun SEE **sweet** noun.

bond noun 1 *The captive tried to undo his bonds*. chain, cord, fastening, fetters, handcuffs, manacles, rope, shackles.
2 *There's a bond between the twins*. affiliation, affinity, attachment, connection, link, relationship, tie, unity.
3 *His word is his bond*. agreement, compact, contract, covenant, guarantee, legal document, pledge, promise, word.

bond verb SEE **stick** verb.

bondage noun SEE **slavery**.

bone noun SEE **skeleton**.

bonehead noun SEE **idiot**.

bonfire noun SEE **fire** noun.

bonnet noun SEE **hat**.

bonny adjective SEE **attractive**.

bonus noun 1 *I got £25 as a Christmas bonus*. bounty, commission, dividend, gift, gratuity, payment, [*informal*] perk, reward, supplement, tip.
2 *an unexpected bonus*. addition, advantage, benefit, extra, [*informal*] plus.

bony adjective *a bony figure*. angular, emaciated, gangling, gawky, lanky, lean, scraggy, scrawny, skinny, thin, ungainly.
OPPOSITES: SEE **graceful, plump**.

boo verb SEE **jeer**.

booby noun SEE **idiot**.
booby trap SEE **trap** noun.

book noun SEE **booklet**, copy, edition, hardback, paperback, publication, [*old-fashioned*] tome, volume, work.

VARIOUS KINDS OF BOOK: album, annual, anthology, atlas, bestiary, [*old-fashioned*] chap-book, compendium, concordance, diary, dictionary, digest, directory, encyclopaedia, fiction, gazetteer, guidebook, handbook, hymnal, hymnbook, jotter, ledger, lexicon, SEE **magazine**, manual, manuscript, missal, non-fiction, notebook, omnibus, picture-book, prayer-book, primer, psalter, reading book, reference book, score (*musical score*), scrap-book, scroll, sketch-book, textbook, thesaurus, vade mecum.

PARTS OF A BOOK: appendix, bibliography, [*informal*] blurb, chapter, contents-page, cover, dust-jacket, epilogue, foreword, frontispiece, illustrations, index, introduction, plates, preface, prologue, text, title, title page.

VARIOUS KINDS OF WRITING: SEE **writing**.

---

book verb 1 *The policeman booked him for speeding*. SEE **arrest**, take your name, write down details.
2 *We booked tickets for the play*. buy, order, reserve.
3 *I've booked the disco for the party*. arrange, engage, organize, sign up.

bookcase noun bookshelves.

bookish adjective SEE **academic** adjective.

bookkeeping noun accountancy.

booklet noun brochure, leaflet, pamphlet, paperback.

bookmaker noun [*informal*] bookie, turf accountant.

boom noun 1 *the boom of big guns*. bang, blast, crash, explosion, reverberation, roar, SEE **sound** noun.
2 *a boom in trade*. bonanza, boost, expansion, growth, improvement, increase, SEE **prosperity**, spurt, upsurge, upturn.
OPPOSITES: SEE **slump** noun.
3 *a boom across a river*. SEE **barrier**.

boom verb 1 *The guns boomed*. VARIOUS SOUNDS: SEE **sound** noun.
2 *Business is booming*. SEE **prosper**.

boon noun SEE **benefit** noun.

boor noun SEE **lout**.

boorish adjective SEE **ill-mannered**.

boost noun SEE **impetus**.

boost verb *Advertising boosts sales*. advance, aid, assist, augment, bolster, build up, buoy up, encourage, enhance, enlarge, expand, foster, further, give an impetus to [SEE **impetus**], heighten, help, improve, increase, inspire, lift, promote, push up, raise, sustain.
OPPOSITES: SEE **depress, hinder**.

boot noun FOOTWEAR: SEE **shoe**.

booth noun *a telephone booth. a voting booth*. carrel, compartment, cubicle, hut, kiosk, stall, stand.

booty noun *The escaping thieves dropped their booty*. contraband, gains, haul, loot, pickings, pillage, plunder, spoils, [*informal*] swag, takings, trophies, winnings.

booze noun SEE **alcohol**.

booze verb SEE **drink** verb.

border noun 1 *the border of a tablecloth. the border of a lake*. brim, brink, edge, edging, frame, frieze, frill, fringe, hem, margin, perimeter, periphery, rim, surround, verge.
2 *You mustn't cross the border*. borderline, boundary, frontier, limit.
3 *a flower border*. bed.

border verb *Our garden borders the railway.* abut on, adjoin, be adjacent to, be alongside, join, share a border with, touch.

borderline noun SEE **boundary**.

bore verb **1** *to bore a hole.* burrow, drill, mine, penetrate, perforate, pierce, sink, tunnel.
OPPOSITES: SEE **fill**.
2 *to bore an audience.* alienate, [*informal*] leave people cold, tire, [*informal*] turn off, weary.
OPPOSITES: SEE **interest** verb.

boring adjective *a boring book. boring work.* arid, commonplace, dreary, dry, dull, flat, humdrum, long-winded, monotonous, repetitious, repetitive, stale, tedious, tiresome, trite, uneventful, unexciting, uninspiring, uninteresting, vapid, wearisome, wordy.
OPPOSITES: SEE **interesting**.

born adjective *a born comedian.* congenital, genuine, instinctive, natural, untaught.

borough noun SEE **town**.

borrow verb *to borrow a pen. to borrow someone's ideas.* adopt, appropriate, be lent, [*informal*] cadge, copy, crib, make use of, pirate, plagiarize, [*informal*] scrounge, take, use, usurp.
OPPOSITES: SEE **lend**.

bosh noun SEE **nonsense**.

bosom boun SEE **breast**.

boss noun SEE **chief** noun.

bossy adjective *We resented her bossy manner.* aggressive, assertive, authoritarian, autocratic, bullying, despotic, dictatorial, domineering, exacting, hectoring, high-handed, imperious, lordly, magisterial, masterful, SEE **officious**, oppressive, overbearing, peremptory, [*informal*] pushy, self-assertive, tyrannical.
OPPOSITES: SEE **servile**.

botch verb SEE **spoil**.

bother noun **1** *There was some bother in the youth club.* ado, difficulty, disorder, disturbance, fuss, [*informal*] hassle, problem, [*informal*] to-do, SEE **trouble** noun.
2 *Is the dog a bother to you?* annoyance, inconvenience, irritation, nuisance, pest, trouble, worry.

bother verb **1** *Do the wasps bother you?* annoy, concern, dismay, disturb, exasperate, harass, [*informal*] hassle, inconvenience, irk, irritate, molest, nag, pester, plague, trouble, upset, vex, worry.
2 *Don't bother to wash up.* be concerned, be worried, care, mind, take trouble.

bothersome adjective SEE **troublesome**.

bottle noun KINDS OF BOTTLE: carafe, carboy, decanter, flagon, flask, jar, jeroboam, magnum, phial, pitcher, vial, wine-bottle.
OTHER CONTAINERS: SEE **container**.

bottle verb **to bottle up** SEE **suppress**.

bottleneck noun SEE **blockage**.

bottom adjective **1** *the bottom rung of a ladder.* deepest, lowest.
2 *bottom marks.* least, minimum.
OPPOSITES: SEE **top** adjective.

bottom noun **1** *the bottom of a wall.* base, foot, foundation, pedestal, substructure, underside.
2 *the bottom of the sea.* bed, depths, floor, underneath.
3 *She was at the bottom of her fortunes.* lowest point, nadir.
4 *We tried to get to the bottom of his problem.* basis, essence, grounds, heart, origin, root, source.
5 *A wasp stung me on the bottom.* [*vulgar*] arse, backside, behind, [*informal*] bum, buttocks, [*formal or joking*] posterior, rear, rump, seat, [*informal*] sit-upon.

bottomless adjective SEE **deep**.

bough noun *a bough of a tree.* arm, branch, limb.

boulder noun *a beach strewn with boulders.* rock, stone.

boulevard noun SEE **road**.

bounce verb *The ball bounced up and down.* bob, bound, bump, jump, leap, move about, rebound, recoil, ricochet, spring.

bound adjective **1** *Our friends are bound to help.* certain, committed, compelled, destined, doomed, duty-bound, fated, forced, obliged, pledged, required, sure.
2 *His wrists were bound with rope.* connected, hitched together, joined, lashed together, linked, roped, strapped, tied, trussed up.
bound for *The rocket was bound for the moon.* aimed at, directed towards, going to, heading for, making for, off to, travelling towards.

bound verb *A dog bounded across the lawn.* bob, bounce, caper, frisk, gambol, hop, hurdle, jump, leap, pounce, skip, spring, vault.

boundary noun *The fence marks the boundary.* border, borderline, bounds, brink, circumference, confines, demarcation, edge, end, extremity, fringe, frontier, interface, limit, margin, perimeter, threshold, verge.

boundless adjective *boundless energy*. endless, everlasting, immeasurable, incalculable, inexhaustible, infinite, limitless, unbounded, unflagging, unlimited, untold, vast.

bounty noun *The rich are not always known for their bounty*. alms, altruism, benevolence, charity, generosity, giving, kindness, largesse, liberality, philanthropy, unselfishness.

bouquet noun **1** *a bouquet of flowers*. arrangement, bunch, buttonhole, corsage, garland, nosegay, posy, spray, wreath.
2 *the bouquet of wine*. SEE **smell** noun.

bourgeois adjective SEE **conventional**.

bourgeoisie noun middle class.
SOCIAL CLASS: SEE **class** noun.

bout noun **1** *a bout of coughing*. attack, fit, period, run, spell, stint, stretch, time, turn.
2 *a boxing bout*. battle, combat, competition, contest, encounter, engagement, fight, match, round, struggle.

boutique noun SEE **shop** noun.

bovine adjective cow-like, ox-like.

bow noun [Rhymes with *go*.] **1** *bows and arrows*. WEAPONS: SEE **weapon**.
2 *Tie it in a bow*. KNOTS: SEE **knot** noun.
3 [Rhymes with *cow*.] *the bow of a ship*. forward part, front.

bow verb **1** *to bow as a sign of respect*. bend, bob, curtsy, genuflect, incline, nod, stoop.
2 *to bow to someone's authority*. SEE **submit**.

bowdlerize verb SEE **censor**.

bowels nouns SEE **entrails**.

bower noun *a shady bower in the garden*. alcove, arbour, bay, gazebo, grotto, hideaway, pavilion, pergola, recess, retreat, sanctuary, shelter, summerhouse.

bowl noun *a bowl of soup*. basin, dish, tureen.

bowl verb *He bowled a faster ball*. fling, hurl, lob, pitch, throw, toss.

box noun carton, case, casket, chest, coffer, coffin, crate, pack, package, tea-chest, trunk.
OTHER CONTAINERS: SEE **container**.

boxer noun SEE **fighter**.

boxing noun [*informal*] fisticuffs.

VARIOUS BOXING WEIGHTS: bantamweight, cruiserweight, featherweight, flyweight, heavyweight, lightweight, middleweight, welterweight.

---

box-office noun booking-office, ticket-office.

boy noun [*uncomplimentary*] brat, [*informal*] kid, lad, schoolboy, son, [*joking*] stripling, [*uncomplimentary*] urchin, youngster, youth.

boycott noun *a boycott of imported goods*. ban, blacklist, embargo, prohibition.

boycott verb *to boycott a meeting. to boycott goods*. avoid, black, blackball, blacklist, exclude, [*informal*] give the cold-shoulder to, ignore, make unwelcome, ostracize, outlaw, prohibit, spurn, stay away from.

boyish adjective SEE **youthful**.

brace noun *a brace of partridge*. SEE **pair**.

bracelet noun wristlet.
OTHER JEWELLERY: SEE **jewellery**.

bracing adjective SEE **invigorating**.

bracken noun fern.

bracket noun *a bracket for a shelf*. SEE **support** noun.

brackish adjective SEE **salty**.

brag verb *I don't think you should brag about winning*. [*informal*] blow your own trumpet, boast, crow, gloat, show off, swank, talk big.

braggart noun SEE **boaster**.

braid noun lace, ribbon.

brain noun **1** PARTS OF THE BODY: SEE **body**.
2 *Use your brain!* brains, [*informal*] grey matter, intellect, intelligence, mind, [*informal*] nous, reason, sense, understanding, wisdom, wit.
RELATED ADJECTIVE: cerebral.

brain verb [*informal*] *to brain someone*. SEE **kill**.

brainwash verb *to brainwash political prisoners*. condition, indoctrinate, re-educate.

brainwave noun SEE **idea**.

brainy adjective SEE **clever**.

braise verb SEE **cook** verb.

bramble noun blackberry.

branch noun **1** *a branch of a tree*. arm, bough, limb, offshoot, prong.
2 *a branch of the armed services. a branch of a subject*. department, division, part, office, ramification, section, subdivision, wing.

branch verb *The road branches*. divide, fork.

to branch out *We branched out and opened another shop.* broaden out, develop, diversify, enlarge, expand, extend.

brand noun *a brand of margarine.* kind, label, line, make, sort, trademark, type, variety.

brand verb **1** *to brand cattle with a hot iron.* burn, identify, label, mark, scar, stamp.
2 *to brand someone as a trouble-maker.* censure, denounce, discredit, give (someone) the reputation of, stigmatize, vilify.

brandish verb SEE **wave** verb.

brash adjective SEE **bumptious, reckless.**

brass noun OTHER METALS: SEE **metal**.

BRASS INSTRUMENTS: bugle, cornet, euphonium, flugelhorn, horn, trombone, trumpet, tuba.

---

brasserie noun SEE **restaurant**.

brat noun SEE **child**.

bravado noun SEE **bravery**.

brave adjective *a brave act. a brave person.* adventurous, audacious, bold, chivalrous, cool, courageous, daring, dauntless, fearless, gallant, game, heroic, indomitable, intrepid, lion-hearted, [*uncomplimentary*] macho, [*sexist*] manly, noble, plucky, resolute, spirited, stalwart, stoical, tough, unafraid, uncomplaining, undaunted, unshrinking, valiant, valorous, venturesome.
OPPOSITES: SEE **cowardly**.

bravery noun *Everyone praised her bravery.* audacity, boldness, [*informal*] bottle, bravado [= *outward show of bravery*], courage, daring, determination, fearlessness, fortitude, gallantry, [*informal*] grit, [*informal*] guts, heroism, [*informal*] nerve, [*informal*] pluck, prowess, resolution, spirit, [*slang*] spunk, stoicism, valour.
OPPOSITES: SEE **cowardice**.

brawl noun *a brawl in the street.* affray, altercation, [*informal*] bust-up, clash, [*informal*] dust-up, SEE **fight** noun, fracas, fray, [*informal*] free-for-all, mêlée, [*informal*] punch-up, scrap, scuffle, [*informal*] set-to, tussle.

brawl verb SEE **fight** verb.

brawny adjective *a brawny wrestler.* SEE **muscular**.

brazen adjective *a brazen lie.* barefaced, blatant, cheeky, defiant, flagrant, impertinent, impudent, insolent, rude, shameless, unabashed, unashamed.
OPPOSITES: SEE **shamefaced**.

brazier noun SEE **fire** noun.

breach noun **1** *a breach of the rules.* breaking, contravention, failure, infringement, offence (against), transgression, violation.
2 *a breach between friends.* alienation, break, difference, disagreement, drifting apart, estrangement, quarrel, rift, [*formal*] schism (*in a church, etc.*), separation, split.
3 *a breach in a sea wall.* aperture, chasm, crack, fissure, gap, hole, opening, rent, rupture, space, split.

bread noun WAYS IN WHICH BREAD IS SOLD: brioche, cob, croissant, French bread, loaf, roll, stick of bread, toast.

break noun **1** *a break in a pipe.* breach, breakage, burst, chink, cleft, crack, crevice, cut, fissure, fracture, gap, gash, hole, leak, opening, rent, rift, rupture, slit, split, tear.
2 *a break in work.* [*informal*] breather, breathing-space, hiatus, interlude, intermission, interval, [*informal*] let-up, lull, pause, respite, rest, tea-break.
3 *a break in normal service.* disruption, halt, interruption, lapse, suspension.

break verb **1** *to break in half. to break into pieces.* breach, burst, [*informal*] bust, chip, crack, crumple, crush, damage, demolish, SEE **destroy**, fracture, fragment, knock down, ruin, shatter, shiver, smash, [*informal*] smash to smithereens, snap, splinter, split, squash, wreck.
2 *to break the law. to break a promise.* contravene, disobey, disregard, flout, go back on, infringe, transgress, violate.
3 *to break a record. to break the speed limit.* beat, better, do more than, exceed, excel, go beyond, outdo, outstrip, pass, surpass.
to break down SEE **analyse, demolish, fail.**
to break in SEE **interrupt, intrude.**
to break off SEE **finish** verb.
to break out SEE **begin, escape** verb.
to break up SEE **disintegrate, end** verb.

breakaway adjective SEE **rebel** adjective.

breakdown noun **1** *a mental breakdown. a mechanical breakdown.* collapse, disintegration, failure, fault (*a mechanical fault*), hitch, [*formal*] malfunction, stoppage.
2 *a breakdown of the figures.* analysis, classification, dissection, itemization.

breaker noun SEE **wave** noun.

break-in noun SEE **burglary**.

breakneck adjective *breakneck speed.* dangerous, SEE **fast** adjective, hasty, headlong, suicidal.

breakthrough noun *a scientific breakthrough.* advance, development, discovery, find, improvement, innovation, invention, leap forward, progress, revolution, success.

breakwater noun groyne, jetty, mole, pier, sea-defence.

breast noun bosom, bust, chest, front.

breath noun *a breath of wind.* breeze, pant, puff, sigh, waft, whiff, whisper.

breathe verb **1** *to breathe fresh air.* exhale, inhale, pant, puff, respire.
2 *Don't breathe a word of this!* hint, let out, SEE **speak**, whisper.

breathing-space noun SEE **break** noun.

breathless adjective *Running makes me breathless.* exhausted, gasping, out of breath, panting, puffing, tired out, wheezy.

breathtaking adjective SEE **amazing**.

breeches verb SEE **trousers**.

breed noun **1** *a breed of dog.* kind, pedigree, sort, species, strain, type, variety.
2 *a breed of people.* ancestry, clan, family, line, nation, progeny, race, stock.

breed verb **1** *Mice breed rapidly.* bear young ones, beget young ones, increase, multiply, procreate, produce young, propagate (*plants*), raise young ones, reproduce.
2 *Familiarity breeds contempt.* arouse, cause, create, cultivate, develop, engender, foster, generate, induce, nourish, nurture, occasion.

breeze noun SEE **wind** noun.

breezy adjective airy, draughty, fresh, SEE **windy**.

breviary noun missal, prayer-book.

brevity noun *Owing to the brevity of the speeches, we finished early.* briefness, compression, conciseness, curtness, economy, incisiveness, pithiness, shortness, succinctness, terseness.

brew noun [*often joking*] *What's that evil brew in the saucepan?* blend, compound, concoction, drink, hash, infusion, liquor, mixture, potion, preparation, punch, stew.

brew verb **1** *to brew beer. to brew tea.* ferment, infuse, make, steep, stew.
2 *They're brewing mischief.* concoct, contrive, [*informal*] cook up, develop, devise, foment, hatch, plan, plot, prepare, scheme, stir up.

bribable adjective SEE **corrupt** adjective.

bribe noun [*slang*] backhander, bribery, [*informal*] carrot, enticement, [*slang*] graft, gratuity, incentive, inducement, [*informal*] payola, protection money, [*informal*] sweetener, tip.

bribe verb *Don't try to bribe the vicar.* buy off, corrupt, entice, [*informal*] grease the palm of, influence, offer a bribe to [SEE **bribe** noun], pervert, reward, [*formal*] suborn, tempt, tip.

bric-à-brac noun antiques, baubles, curios, odds and ends, oddments, ornaments, trinkets.

brick noun *bricks used in building.* block, breeze-block, building block, flagstone, paving stone, set or sett, stone.

brickbat noun SEE **missile**.

bricklayer noun builder.

bridge noun *a bridge over a river.* arch, crossing, span, way over.

KINDS OF BRIDGE: aqueduct, Bailey bridge, causeway, drawbridge, flyover, footbridge, overpass, pontoon bridge, suspension bridge, swing bridge, subway, underpass, viaduct.

---

bridge verb *to bridge a gap.* connect, cross, fill, join, link, span, straddle, traverse, unite.

bridle verb SEE **restrain**.

brief adjective **1** *a brief visit. a brief journey.* cursory, fast, SEE **fleeting**, hasty, limited, little, momentary, passing, quick, sharp, short, short-lived, temporary, transient.
OPPOSITES: SEE **long** adjective.
2 *a brief summary of a story. a brief comment.* abbreviated, abridged, compact, compressed, concise, condensed, crisp, curt, curtailed, incisive, laconic, pithy, shortened, succinct, terse, thumbnail [*a thumbnail sketch*].
OPPOSITES: SEE **wordy**.

brief noun **1** *We were given the brief for our next job.* advice, briefing, data, description, directions, information, instructions, orders, outline, plan.
2 *a barrister's brief.* argument, case, defence, dossier, summary.

brief verb *The captain briefed her team before the match.* advise, direct, [*informal*] fill (someone) in, give (someone) the facts, guide, inform, instruct, prepare, [*informal*] put (someone) in the picture, prime.

briefs noun camiknickers, knickers, panties, pants, shorts, trunks, underpants.

brigade noun SEE **armed services**.

brigand noun bandit, buccaneer, desperado, footpad, gangster, highwayman, marauder, outlaw, pirate, robber, ruffian, thief.

bright adjective **1** *bright colours. a bright day.* blazing, brilliant, burnished, clear, dazzling, flashy, gaudy, glaring, gleaming, glistening, glittering, glowing, intense, light (*a light room*), luminous, lustrous, pellucid, radiant, resplendent, scintillating, shimmering, shining, shiny, showy, sparkling, sunny, twinkling, vivid.
OPPOSITES: SEE **dark, dull** adjective.
2 *a bright manner.* SEE **cheerful**.
3 *a bright idea.* SEE **clever**.

brighten verb **1** *Some fresh paint will brighten this place up.* cheer, enliven, gladden, illuminate, light up, perk up, revitalize, smarten up.
2 *The weather brightened.* become sunny, clear up, lighten.

brilliant adjective **1** *brilliant light.* blazing, bright, dazzling, glaring, gleaming, glittering, glorious, resplendent, scintillating, shining, showy, sparkling, splendid, vivid.
OPPOSITES: SEE **dull** adjective.
2 *a brilliant scientist.* SEE **clever**.
3 *a brilliant game.* SEE **excellent**.

brim noun *filled to the brim.* brink, circumference, edge, limit, lip, margin, perimeter, periphery, rim, top, verge.

brimming adjective SEE **full**.

brimstone noun sulphur.

briny adjective SEE **salt** adjective.

bring verb **1** *Did you bring the shopping home?* bear, carry, convey, deliver, fetch, take, transfer, transport.
2 *Bring your friends in.* accompany, conduct, escort, guide, lead, usher.
3 *Their performance brought great applause.* attract, cause, create, draw, earn, engender, generate, get, give rise to, induce, lead to, occasion, produce, prompt, provoke, result in.
to bring about *The head teacher brought about changes.* achieve, cause, create, effect, engineer, manage.
to bring in 1 *The charity appeal brought in many donations.* accrue, earn, gross, net, profit, realize, yield.
2 *The manufacturer is bringing in a new model.* initiate, introduce, make available, start.
to bring off *It was a difficult play to bring off.* accomplish, be successful in, do successfully, succeed in.
to bring on 1 *The warmth brings on the flowers.* accelerate, advance, encourage, speed up.
2 *Stress brings on his asthma.* aggravate, cause, give rise to, induce, lead to, occasion, precipitate, provoke.
to bring out 1 *We brought out a poetry magazine.* issue, print, produce, publish, release.
2 *Her description brings out the funny side.* accentuate, dwell on, emphasize, feature, foreground, highlight, make obvious, play up, point up, show clearly, spotlight, stress, underline.
to bring up 1 *Parents bring up children.* care for, educate, foster, look after, nurture, raise, rear, teach, train.
2 [*informal*] *Unfortunately, the baby brought up his dinner.* SEE **vomit**.

brink noun *the brink of the lake.* bank, border, boundary, brim, circumference, edge, fringe, limit, lip, margin, perimeter, periphery, rim, skirt, threshold, verge.

brisk adjective *brisk exercise. a brisk manner.* active, alert, animated, bright, businesslike, bustling, busy, crisp, decisive, energetic, fast, invigorating, keen, lively, nimble, quick, rapid, [*informal*] snappy, [*informal*] spanking (*at a spanking pace*), speedy, spirited, sprightly, spry, vigorous.
OPPOSITES: SEE **leisurely**.

bristle noun *bristles on a man's face. bristles in a brush.* hair, prickle, spine, stubble, whisker, wire.

bristle verb SEE **angry (to be angry)**.

bristling adjective **1** *bristling with problems.* SEE **plentiful**.
2 *bristling with indignation.* SEE **angry**.

bristly adjective SEE **hairy**.

brittle adjective *brittle bones. brittle toffee.* breakable, crackly, crisp, crumbling, delicate, easily broken, fragile, frail.
OPPOSITES: SEE **flexible, resilient**.

broach verb SEE **introduce**.

broad adjective **1** *a broad path. a broad expanse of countryside.* ample, capacious, expansive, extensive, great, large, open, roomy, spacious, sweeping, vast, wide.
OPPOSITES: SEE **narrow, small**.
2 *a broad outline of a story.* general, imprecise, indefinite, inexact, non-specific, undetailed, vague.
OPPOSITES: SEE **specific**.
3 *She had broad tastes in music.* all-embracing, catholic, comprehensive, eclectic, encyclopaedic, universal, wide-ranging.
OPPOSITES: SEE **narrow**.
4 *Her broad sense of humour made him blush.* bawdy, [*slang*] blue, coarse, earthy, improper, impure, indecent,

indelicate, racy, ribald, suggestive, vulgar.
OPPOSITES: SEE **narrow-minded**.

broadcast noun *a TV broadcast.* programme, relay, transmission.

broadcast verb **1** *They broadcast the concert on TV.* relay, send out, televise, transmit.
2 *I'll tell you a secret if you promise not to broadcast it.* advertise, announce, circulate, [*formal*] disseminate, make known, make public, proclaim, [*formal*] promulgate, publish, report, scatter about, spread.

broadcaster noun anchor-man, announcer, commentator, compère, disc jockey, DJ, SEE **entertainer**, linkman, newsreader, presenter.

broaden verb *to broaden your interests.* branch out (into something), build up, develop, diversify, enlarge, expand, extend, increase, open up, spread, widen.

broad-minded adjective *a broad-minded outlook.* all-embracing, balanced, broad, catholic, comprehensive, cosmopolitan, eclectic, enlightened, liberal, open-minded, permissive, tolerant, unbiased, unbigoted, unprejudiced, unshockable, wide-ranging.
OPPOSITES: SEE **narrow-minded**.

broadside noun SEE **attack** noun.

brochure noun *a travel brochure.* booklet, broadsheet, catalogue, circular, folder, handbill, leaflet, pamphlet, prospectus.

brogue noun **1** FOOTWEAR: SEE **shoe**.
2 *an Irish brogue.* SEE **accent**.

broil verb SEE **cook** verb.

broiler noun SEE **chicken**.

broke adjective SEE **poor**.

broken-hearted adjective SEE **heart-broken**.

broker noun SEE **agent**.

bronco noun SEE **horse**.

bronze adjective SEE **brown** adjective.

bronze noun OTHER METALS: SEE **metal**.

bronze verb SEE **brown** verb.

brooch noun badge, clasp, clip.

brood noun *a mother and her brood.* clutch (*of eggs*), children, issue, family, litter (*of pups*), offspring, progeny, young.

brood verb **1** *The hen was brooding her clutch of eggs.* hatch, incubate, sit on.
2 *Don't brood over past mistakes.* agonize, dwell (on), fret, meditate (on), mope, mull over, muse (on), ponder, reflect (on), sulk (about), think (about).

brook noun beck, burn, channel, [*poetic*] rill, rivulet, stream, watercourse.

brook verb SEE **tolerate**.

broom noun *Sweep the floor with a broom.* besom, brush.

broth noun clear soup, consommé, soup.

brother noun sibling.
FAMILY RELATIONSHIPS: SEE **family**.

brotherhood noun SEE **association**.

browbeat verb SEE **coerce**.

brown adjective SHADES OF BROWN: beige, bronze, buff, chestnut, chocolate, dun, fawn, khaki, ochre, russet, sepia, tan, tawny, terracotta, umber.

brown verb **1** *Brown the topping under the grill.* grill, toast.
2 *Do you brown quickly in the sun?* bronze, burn, colour, tan.

browned-off adjective SEE **depressed**.

browse verb **1** *The cattle browsed in the meadow.* crop grass, eat, feed, graze, pasture.
2 *I was browsing in a book.* dip in, flick through, leaf through, look through, peruse, read here and there, scan, skim, thumb through.

bruise noun black eye, bump, [*formal*] contusion, discoloration, [*informal*] shiner. SEE ALSO **wound** noun.

bruise verb blacken, crush, damage, discolour, injure, knock, mark, SEE **wound** verb.

brunette noun brown-haired woman, dark-haired woman.

brunt noun SEE **force** noun.

brush noun **1** *a brush to sweep with.* besom, broom.
2 *a brush with the police.* SEE **conflict** noun.

brush verb *Brush your hair.* comb, groom, tidy.
to brush up *to brush up your facts.* go over, improve, read up, refresh your memory of, relearn, revise, study, [*informal*] swot up.

brush-off noun SEE **snub** noun.

brusque adjective *a brusque reply.* SEE **curt**.

brutal adjective *a brutal murder.* atrocious, barbarous, beastly, bestial, bloodthirsty, bloody, brutish, callous, cold-blooded, cruel, dehumanized, ferocious, heartless, inhuman, inhumane, merciless, murderous, pitiless, remorseless, ruthless, sadistic, savage, uncivilized, unfeeling, vicious, violent, wild.
OPPOSITES: SEE **gentle**, **humane**.

brutalize verb *Long imprisonment brutalized the prisoners.* dehumanize, harden, inure, make brutal [SEE **brutal**].

brute adjective *brute force.* crude, physical, rough, unthinking.
OPPOSITES: SEE **sensitive**.

brute noun **1** SEE **animal** noun, beast, creature, dumb animal.
2 *The executioner was a cruel brute.* barbarian, bully, devil, lout, monster, SEE **ruffian**, sadist, savage, swine.

brutish adjective *We were horrified by their brutish behaviour.* animal, barbaric, barbarous, beastly, bestial, boorish, brutal, coarse, cold-blooded, crude, SEE **cruel**, [*informal*] gross, inhuman, insensitive, loutish, mindless, savage, senseless, stupid, subhuman, uncouth, unintelligent, unthinking.
OPPOSITES: SEE **humane**.

bubble noun ball, blister, hollow, [*formal*] vesicle.
bubbles *soap bubbles. bubbles in champagne.* effervescence, fizz, foam, froth, head, lather, suds.

bubble verb *The water bubbled.* boil, effervesce, fizz, fizzle, foam, froth, gurgle, seethe, sparkle.

bubbly adjective **1** *bubbly drinks.* carbonated, effervescent, fizzy, foaming, seething, sparkling.
OPPOSITE: flat.
2 [*informal*] *a bubbly personality.* SEE **lively**.

buccaneer noun adventurer, bandit, brigand, corsair, marauder, pirate, privateer, robber.

buck verb *The horse bucked.* bound, jerk, jump, leap, prance, spring, start, vault.
to buck up 1 [*informal*] *Buck up—we're late!* SEE **hurry**.
2 [*informal*] *After I lost the game, she tried to buck me up.* animate, cheer up, encourage, enliven, gladden, hearten, inspire, make cheerful, please, revitalize, revive.

bucket noun can, pail.

buckle noun *the buckle of a belt.* catch, clasp, clip, fastener, fastening, hasp.

buckle verb **1** *Buckle your safety belts.* clasp, clip, do up, fasten, hitch up, hook up, secure.
2 *The framework buckled under the weight.* bend, bulge, cave in, collapse, contort, crumple, curve, dent, distort, fold, twist, warp.

bucolic adjective SEE **rural**.

bud noun shoot, sprout.

bud verb *The trees are budding early this year.* begin to grow, burgeon, develop, shoot, sprout.

budding adjective *a budding actor.* aspiring, developing, embryonic, [*informal*] hopeful, incipient, inexperienced, intending, new, potential, promising, [*informal*] would-be, young.
OPPOSITES: SEE **established**.

buddy noun SEE **friend**.

budge verb **1** *The stubborn donkey wouldn't budge.* change position, give way, move, shift, stir, yield.
2 *We couldn't budge him.* alter, change, dislodge, influence, move, persuade, propel, push, remove, shift, sway.

budget noun *Don't spend more than your budget allows.* accounts, allocation of funds, allowance, estimate, financial planning, funds, means, resources.

budget verb *We've budgeted for a new carpet next year.* allocate money, allot resources, allow (for), estimate expenditure, plan your spending, provide (for), ration your spending.

buff adjective SEE **brown** adjective.

buff noun *a railway buff.* addict, admirer, connoisseur, devotee, enthusiast, expert, fan, fanatic, fancier, [*informal*] fiend, [*informal*] freak, [*informal*] nut, supporter.

buff verb *Buff up the paintwork with a soft cloth.* burnish, clean, polish, rub, shine, smooth.

buffer noun *buffers to soften the impact.* bulwark, bumper, cushion, fender, pad, safeguard, screen, shield, shock-absorber.

buffet noun **1** *We went to the buffet for a snack.* bar, café, cafeteria, counter, snack-bar.
2 *They prepared a buffet for the party.* SEE **meal**.

buffet verb SEE **hit** verb.

buffoon noun SEE **clown** noun.

bug noun **1** [*informal*] *Birds help to control bugs in the garden.* SEE **pest**.
2 [*informal*] *I had a bug which made me ill.* SEE **microorganism**.
3 *a bug in a computer program.* breakdown, defect, error, failing, fault, flaw, [*informal*] gremlin, imperfection, [*formal*] malfunction, mistake, [*informal*] snarl-up.

bug verb **1** *Spies had bugged the telephone.* intercept, interfere with, listen in to, tap.
2 [*slang*] *People who smoke in public bug me.* SEE **annoy**.

build verb **1** *to build a shed.* assemble, construct, erect, fabricate, form, [*informal*] knock together, make, put together, put up, raise, rear (*They reared a monument*), set up.
to build up 1 *He built up a large collection of records.* accumulate, amass, assemble, begin, bring together, collect, create, develop, enlarge, expand, raise.
2 *The excitement built up to a climax.* augment, escalate, grow, increase, intensify, rise, strengthen.

builder noun bricklayer, construction worker, labourer.
OTHER JOBS: SEE **job**.

building noun construction, edifice, erection, piece of architecture, [*informal*] pile, premises, structure.

VARIOUS BUILDINGS: arcade, art gallery, barn, barracks, basilica, boat-house, brewery, broiler-house, bungalow, cabin, castle, cathedral, chapel, château, SEE **church**, cinema, clinic, college, complex, cottage, crematorium, dovecote, factory, farmhouse, filling-station, flats, fort, fortress.

garage, gazebo, granary, grandstand, gymnasium, hall, hangar, hotel, SEE **house**, inn, library, lighthouse, mansion, mausoleum, mill, monastery, monument, mosque, museum, observatory, orphanage, outbuilding, outhouse.

pagoda, palace, pavilion, pier, pigsty, police station, post office, power-station, prison, pub, public house, restaurant, school, shed, SEE **shop**, silo, skyscraper, slaughterhouse, stable, storehouse, studio, summerhouse, synagogue, temple, theatre, tower, villa, warehouse, waterworks, windmill, woodshed.

ARCHITECTURAL FEATURES: arch, balcony, baluster, balustrade, banister, basement, battlement, bay window, belfry, boss, bow window, brickwork, buttress, capital, ceiling, cellar, chimney, cloister, colonnade, column, coping, corbel, cornice, corridor, courtyard, coving, crypt.

dome, dormer window, drawbridge, dungeon, eaves, finial, floor, foundation, foyer, gable, gallery, gateway, gutter, joist, keep, lobby, masonry, minaret, mullion.

parapet, pediment, pilaster, pillar, pinnacle, porch, portal, portcullis, quadrangle, rafter, rampart, roof, room, sill, spire, staircase, steeple, tower, tracery, turret, vault, veranda, wall, window, window-sill.

SOME BUILDING MATERIALS: asbestos, asphalt, brick, cement, concrete, fibreboard, fibreglass, glass, hardboard, metal, mortar, paint, perspex, plaster, plasterboard, plastic, plywood, polystyrene, polythene, putty, PVC, rubber, slate, stone, tar, tile, timber, vinyl, wood.

---

build-up noun SEE **increase** noun.

bulb noun corm, tuber.
SOME FLOWERS THAT GROW FROM BULBS: amaryllis, bluebell, crocus, daffodil, freesia, hyacinth, lily, snowdrop, tulip.
2 *an electric bulb.* lamp, light.

bulbous adjective *a bulbous shape.* bloated, bulging, convex, distended, ovoid, pear-shaped, potbellied, rotund, rounded, spherical, swollen, tuberous.
OPPOSITES: SEE **flat** adjective.

bulge noun *The bruise made a discoloured bulge under his skin.* bump, [*formal*] distension, hump, knob, lump, projection, [*formal*] protrusion, protuberance, rise, swelling.

bulge verb *The sails bulged in the wind.* belly, billow, dilate, distend, enlarge, expand, project, protrude, stick out, swell.

bulk noun **1** *The bulk of the aircraft amazed us.* amplitude, bigness, body, dimensions, extent, immensity, largeness, magnitude, mass, size, substance, volume, weight.
2 *We did the bulk of the work ourselves.* [*informal*] best part, greater part, majority, preponderance.

bulky adjective *a bulky parcel.* SEE **big**.

bulldoze verb **1** *to bulldoze a building.* SEE **demolish**.
2 [*informal*] *to bulldoze someone into doing something.* SEE **force** verb.

bullet noun SEE **missile**.

bulletin noun *a news bulletin.* announcement, communication, communiqué, dispatch, message, news-flash, notice, proclamation, report, statement.

bullfighter noun matador, toreador.

bullion noun *gold bullion.* bar, ingot, nugget, solid gold or silver, etc.

bull's-eye noun *Try to hit the bull's-eye.* bull, centre, middle, target.

bully noun SEE **ruffian**.

bully verb *to bully younger children.* bludgeon, browbeat, coerce, cow, domineer, frighten, hector, intimidate, oppress, persecute, [*informal*] push around, terrorize, threaten, torment, tyrannize.

bulwark noun earthwork, fortification, parapet, protection, rampart, wall.

bum noun SEE **buttocks**.

bumble verb SEE **blunder** verb.

bump noun 1 *a bump in the car*. bang, blow, collision, crash, hit, knock, smash, thud, thump.
2 *a bump on the head*. bulge, [*formal*] distension, hump, knob, lump, projection, [*formal*] protrusion, protuberance, rise, swelling.

bump verb 1 *He bumped us deliberately*. bang, collide with, crash into, jar, knock, ram, slam, smash into, strike, thump, wallop. SEE ALSO **hit** verb.
2 *We bumped up and down on the rough road*. bounce, jerk, jolt, shake.
to bump into SEE **meet**.
to bump off SEE **kill**.

bumper adjective SEE **plentiful**.

bumpkin noun SEE **peasant**.

bumptious adjective *I hated the bumptious way he acknowledged the applause*. arrogant, [*informal*] big-headed, boastful, brash, [*informal*] cocky, conceited, egotistic, forward, immodest, officious, overbearing, over-confident, pompous, presumptuous, pretentious, [*informal*] pushy, self-assertive, self-important, smug, [*informal*] stuck-up, [*informal*] snooty, swaggering, vain, vainglorious, vaunting.
OPPOSITES: SEE **modest**.

bumpy adjective 1 *a bumpy ride*. bouncy, jerky, jolting, rough.
2 *a bumpy surface*. irregular, knobbly, lumpy, uneven.

bunch noun 1 *a bunch of carrots. a bunch of keys*. batch, bundle, clump, cluster, collection, heap, lot, number, pack, quantity, set, sheaf, tuft.
2 *a bunch of flowers*. bouquet, posy, spray.
3 [*informal*] *a bunch of friends*. band, crew, crowd, flock, gang, gathering, group, mob, party, team, troop.

bunch verb *My friends bunched together in a corner*. assemble, cluster, collect, congregate, crowd, flock, gather, group, herd, huddle, mass, pack.
OPPOSITES: SEE **scatter**.

bundle noun *a bundle of papers*. bag, bale, bunch, carton, collection, pack, package, packet, parcel, sheaf, truss (*truss of hay*).

bundle verb 1 *to bundle things up together*. bale, bind, enclose, fasten, pack, roll, tie, truss, wrap.
2 *They bundled us into the back room*. dispose of, eject, move hurriedly or rudely, push away, put away, remove, send away, shove.

bung noun *the bung of a barrel*. cork, plug, stopper.

bung verb SEE **throw**.

bungalow noun SEE **house** noun.

bungle verb *If you bungle a job, you must do it again!* blunder, botch, [*slang*] cock up, [*informal*] foul up, fluff, [*informal*] make a hash of, [*informal*] make a mess of, [*informal*] mess up, mismanage, [*informal*] muff, ruin, spoil.

bunk noun 1 bed, berth.
2 [*slang*] *He talked bunk!* SEE **nonsense**.
to do a bunk SEE **escape** verb.

bunker noun *The soldiers sheltered in a bunker*. SEE **shelter** noun.

bunkum noun SEE **nonsense**.

buoy noun *A buoy marked the entrance to the anchorage*. beacon, float, marker, signal.

buoy verb **to buoy up** SEE **boost, lift** verb.

buoyant adjective 1 *A boat must be made of buoyant material*. floating, light.
2 *We were in a buoyant mood after winning our match*. SEE **cheerful**.

burble verb SEE **speak**.

burden noun 1 *a heavy burden*. cargo, encumbrance, load, weight.
2 *the burden of responsibility*. affliction, anxiety, care, duty, handicap, millstone, obligation, onus, problem, responsibility, sorrow, trial, trouble, worry.

burden verb *For years she was burdened by illness*. afflict, bother, encumber, hamper, handicap, load (with), [*informal*] lumber (with), oppress, overload (with), [*informal*] saddle (with), strain, tax, trouble, worry.

burdensome adjective *a burdensome task*. difficult, exacting, hard, heavy, irksome, onerous, taxing, tiring, troublesome, trying, wearisome, wearying, worrying.
OPPOSITES: SEE **easy**.

bureau 1 *a writing bureau*. desk.
2 *an information bureau*. agency, counter, department, office, service.

bureaucracy noun *They'd do things quicker if there was less bureaucracy!* administration, officialdom, paperwork, [*informal*] red tape, regulations.

bureaucrat noun SEE **administrator**.

burgeon verb SEE **grow**.

burgess noun SEE **citizen**.

burglar noun cat-burglar, housebreaker, intruder, robber, thief.

burglary noun break-in, forcible entry, house-breaking, larceny, pilfering, robbery, stealing, theft, thieving.

burgle verb *to burgle a house.* break in, pilfer, rob, steal from, thieve from.

burial noun *a burial service.* entombment, funeral, interment, obsequies.

burlesque noun *Our comic play was a burlesque of a Shakespearean tragedy.* caricature, imitation, mockery, parody, pastiche, satire, [*informal*] send-up, [*informal*] take-off, travesty.

burly adjective *a burly figure.* athletic, beefy, big, brawny, heavy, hefty, hulking, husky, muscular, powerful, stocky, stout, [*informal*] strapping, strong, sturdy, thickset, tough, well-built.
OPPOSITES: SEE **thin** adjective.

burn noun **1** *The victim's body was covered with burns.* blister, charring.
2 *a Scottish burn.* SEE **stream** noun.

burn verb **1** *The bonfire burned all day.* be alight, blaze, flame, flare, flash, flicker, glow, smoke, smoulder.
2 *The incinerator burns anything.* carbonize, consume, cremate, destroy by fire, ignite, incinerate, kindle, light, reduce to ashes, set fire to.
3 *The heat burnt his skin.* blister, brand, char, scald, scorch, sear, shrivel, singe, sting, toast.
OTHER RELATED WORDS: SEE **fire** noun, verb.

burning adjective **1** *a burning building.* ablaze, afire, alight, blazing, flaming, glowing, incandescent, lit up, on fire, raging, smouldering.
2 *a burning pain.* biting, blistering, boiling, fiery, hot, inflamed, scalding, scorching, searing, smarting, stinging.
3 *a burning substance* [=*a substance which burns you*]. acid, caustic, corrosive.
4 *a burning smell* [=*a smell of burning*]. acrid, pungent, reeking, scorching, smoky.
5 *a burning desire.* acute, ardent, consuming, eager, fervent, flaming, frenzied, heated, impassioned, intense, passionate, red-hot, vehement.
6 *a burning question.* crucial, important, pertinent, pressing, relevant, urgent, vital.

burning noun SEE **fire** noun.

burnish verb SEE **polish** verb.

burp verb SEE **belch**.

burrow noun *an animal's burrow.* (*a fox's or badger's*) earth, excavation, hole, retreat, (*a badger's*) set, shelter, tunnel, (*a rabbit's*) warren.

burrow verb *The rabbits burrowed under the fence.* delve, dig, excavate, mine, tunnel.

burst verb **1** *The door burst open. They burst open the door.* be forced open, break, crack, disintegrate, erupt, explode, force open, give way, open suddenly, part suddenly, puncture, rupture, shatter, split, tear.
2 *He burst into the room.* SEE **rush** verb.

bursting adjective **1** *The shopping bag was bursting with good things.* SEE **full**.
2 *She's bursting to help.* SEE **eager**.

bury verb *to bury something in the ground.* conceal, cover, embed, enclose, engulf, entomb, hide, immerse, implant, insert, inter, lay to rest, plant, put away, secrete, sink, submerge.

bus noun [*old-fashioned*] charabanc, coach, double-decker, minibus, [*old-fashioned*] omnibus.

bush noun SEE **shrub**.

bushy adjective *a bushy beard.* bristling, bristly, dense, fluffy, fuzzy, hairy, luxuriant, rough, shaggy, spreading, sticking out, tangled, thick, thick-growing, unruly, untidy.

business noun **1** *I have urgent business to see to.* affair, concern, duty, issue, matter, problem, question, responsibility, subject, task, topic.
2 *What sort of business do you want to go into?* calling, career, craft, employment, industry, job, line of work, occupation, profession, pursuit, trade, vocation, work.
3 *The new shop does a lot of business.* buying and selling, commerce, dealings, industry, marketing, merchandising, selling, trade, trading, transactions.
4 *He works for a sports equipment business.* company, concern, corporation, enterprise, establishment, firm, organization, [*informal*] outfit, practice, [*informal*] set-up, venture.

businesslike adjective efficient, hard-headed, methodical, orderly, practical, professional, prompt, systematic, well-organized.

businessman, businesswoman nouns dealer, entrepreneur, executive, financier, industrialist, magnate, manager, merchant, trader, tycoon.

busker noun SEE **entertainer**.

bust noun **1** *a bust of Napoleon.* SEE **statue**.
2 *a woman's bust.* SEE **breast**.

bust verb SEE **break** verb.

bustle noun *The airport lounge was full of bustle.* activity, agitation, commotion, excitement, flurry, fuss, haste, hurly-burly, hurry, hustle, movement, restlessness, scurry, stir, [*informal*] tearing about, [*informal*] to-do, [*informal*] toing and froing.

bustle verb *He bustled about the kitchen preparing dinner.* dart, dash, fuss, hasten, hurry, hustle, make haste, move busily, rush, scamper, scramble, scurry, scuttle, [*informal*] tear, whirl.

busy adjective **1** *busy in the garden. busy at work.* active, assiduous, bustling about, diligent, employed, energetic, engaged, engrossed, [*informal*] hard at it, industrious, involved, occupied, [*informal*] on the go, pottering, slaving, tireless, [*informal*] up to your eyes, working.
OPPOSITES: SEE **idle** adjective.
2 *It's busy in town on Saturdays.* bustling, frantic, full of people, hectic, lively.
OPPOSITES: SEE **quiet**.

busybody noun gossip, inquisitive person [SEE **inquisitive**], meddler, [*informal*] Nosy Parker, scandalmonger, snooper, spy.
to be a busybody SEE **interfere**.

butch adjective SEE **masculine**.

butler noun SEE **servant**.

butt noun **1** *a rifle butt.* haft, handle, shaft, stock.
2 *a water butt.* barrel, cask, water-butt.
OTHER CONTAINERS: SEE **container**.
3 *a cigar butt.* end, remains, remnant, stub.
4 *the butt of someone's ridicule.* mark, object, subject, target, victim.
butts rifle-range, shooting-gallery, shooting-range.

butt verb *It's not nice to be butted by a goat.* buffet, bump, jab, knock, poke, prod, punch, push, ram, shove, strike, thump.
SEE ALSO **hit** verb.
to butt in SEE **interrupt**.

butterfingers noun SEE **clumsy (clumsy person)**.

butterfly noun OTHER INSECTS: SEE **insect**.

buttocks noun [*impolite*] arse, backside, behind, bottom, [*sometimes impolite*] bum, haunches, hindquarters, [*joking*] posterior, rear, rump, seat.

button noun OTHER FASTENERS: SEE **fastener**.

button verb OTHER WAYS TO FASTEN THINGS: SEE **fasten**.

buttonhole verb SEE **waylay**.

buttress noun *a buttress supporting the church wall.* pier, prop, reinforcement, support.

buttress verb SEE **support** verb.

buxom adjective [Often used jokingly by men in sexist remarks about a woman's figure: *a buxom wench.*] ample, bosomy, full-figured, healthy-looking, plump, robust, rounded, voluptuous.
OPPOSITES: SEE **thin** adjective.

buy verb **1** *to buy a TV set.* acquire, gain, get, get on hire purchase, [*informal*] invest in, obtain, pay for, procure, purchase.
OPPOSITES: SEE **sell**.
2 *to buy someone's loyalty.* SEE **bribe** verb.

buyer noun customer, purchaser, shopper.
OPPOSITES: SEE **seller**.

buzz noun, verb VARIOUS SOUNDS: SEE **sound** noun.

bygone adjective SEE **past** adjective.

bygone noun SEE **antique** noun.

by-law noun SEE **regulation**.

bypass noun SEE **road**.

bypass verb *Her case was so urgent that they bypassed the usual admission procedure.* avoid, circumvent, dodge, evade, find a way round, get out of, go round, ignore, neglect, omit.

by-product noun *Becoming a baseball fan was a by-product of my research into sport on TV.* adjunct, complement, consequence, corollary, repercussion, result, side-effect.

by-road noun SEE **road**.

bystander noun *The police asked bystanders to describe the accident.* eyewitness, looker-on, observer, onlooker, passer-by, spectator, watcher, witness.

byway noun SEE **road**.

byword noun **1** *She was a byword for punctuality.* SEE **model** noun.
2 *"Punctuality"* was her byword. SEE **motto**.

C

cab noun SEE **taxi**.

cabal noun SEE **conspiracy, party**.

cabaret noun entertainment, floor-show, night-club, revue.
OTHER ENTERTAINMENTS: SEE **entertainment**.

cabbage noun greens.
OTHER VEGETABLES: SEE **vegetable**.

cabin noun **1** *a cabin in the hills.* chalet, hut, lodge, shack, shanty, shed, shelter.
2 *a cabin on a ship.* berth, compartment, deck-house, quarters.

cabinet noun *a china cabinet.* SEE **cupboard**.

cable noun **1** *an anchor cable.* chain, cord, hawser, line, mooring, rope.
2 *electric cable.* flex, lead, wire.
3 *They sent a message by cable.* message, telegram, wire.
cable railway cable-car.
cable television SEE **communication**.

cache noun *a cache of stores.* depot, dump, hiding-place, hoard, repository, reserve, stockpile, storehouse, supply.

cackle noun, verb VARIOUS SOUNDS: SEE **sound** noun.

cacophonous adjective *a cacophonous row.* SEE **discordant**, harsh, noisy, unmusical.
OPPOSITES: SEE **musical** adjective.

cacophony noun *a noisy cacophony.* atonality, caterwauling, din, discord, disharmony, dissonance, harshness, jangle, noise, racket, row, rumpus, tumult.
OPPOSITES: SEE **harmony**.

cad noun SEE **blackguard**.

cadaverous adjective SEE **gaunt**.

caddy noun *a tea caddy.* box, tin.

cadence noun *the cadences of the English language.* accent, beat, inflection, intonation, lilt, metre, pattern, rhythm, rise and fall, sound, stress, tune.

cadet noun *a cadet in the armed forces.* beginner, learner, recruit, trainee.

cadge verb *The cat from next door cadges for food.* ask, beg, scrounge, sponge.

cadre noun *a cadre of workers.* core, force, SEE **group** noun, nucleus, squad, staff, team.

Caesarian section noun SEE **birth**.

café noun bar, bistro, buffet, cafeteria, canteen, coffee bar, restaurant, snack-bar, take-away, tea-room.

cage noun *an animal's cage. a bird's cage.* aviary, coop, enclosure, hutch, pen, pound.

cagey adjective SEE **cautious**.

cagoule noun SEE **coat** noun.

cajole verb SEE **coax**.

cake noun **1** *cake for tea.* KINDS OF CAKE: bun, doughnut, éclair, flan, fruit cake, gateau, gingerbread, macaroon, Madeira, madeleine, meringue, muffin, sandwich, scone, shortbread, simnel cake, sponge, teacake.
2 *a cake of soap.* block, lump, mass, piece, slab.

cake verb **1** *Our shoes were caked with mud.* coat, clog, cover, encrust, make dirty, make muddy.
2 *Get the mud off before it cakes.* coagulate, congeal, dry, go solid, harden, solidify.

calamitous adjective *a calamitous mistake.* cataclysmic, catastrophic, deadly, devastating, dire, disastrous, dreadful, fatal, ghastly, ruinous, serious, terrible, tragic, unfortunate, unlucky, woeful.
OPPOSITES: SEE **fortunate**.

calamity noun *The fire was a terrible calamity.* accident, affliction, cataclysm, catastrophe, disaster, misadventure, mischance, misfortune, mishap, tragedy, tribulation.

calculate verb *to calculate figures.* add up, assess, compute, count, determine, do sums, enumerate, estimate, figure out, find out, gauge, judge, reckon, total, value, weigh, work out.

calculated adjective *a calculated insult.* SEE **deliberate**.

calculating adjective *a calculating expression.* SEE **crafty**.

calculus noun SEE **mathematics**.

calendar noun SEE **time** noun.

calf noun **1** *a new-born calf.* SEE **cattle**.
2 *My calves ache after running.* SEE **leg**.

calibre noun **1** *the calibre of a rifle.* bore, diameter, gauge, measure, size.
2 *They ought to win with players of such high calibre.* ability, capacity, character, distinction, excellence, genius, gifts, merit, proficiency, quality, skill, stature, talent, worth.

call noun **1** *a call for help.* cry, exclamation, scream, shout, yell.
2 *a bugle call.* signal, summons.
3 *Grandad made an unexpected call.* stay, stop, visit.
4 *There's no call for suntan oil in winter.* demand, need, occasion, request.

call verb **1** *He called in a loud voice.* clamour, cry out, exclaim, shout, yell.
2 *Grandad called on us.* drop in, visit.
3 *What did they call him?* baptize, christen, dub, name.
4 *What do you call your story?* entitle.
5 *On Saturdays mum calls me at nine.* arouse, awaken, get someone up, rouse, wake, waken.
6 *The boss called me to his office.* convene, gather, invite, order, summon.
7 *I tried to call, but the phone was dead.* contact, dial, phone, ring, telephone.
to call for 1 *This calls for a celebration!* demand, entail, necessitate, need, occasion, require.

2 *They don't deliver, so we must call for it.* collect, come for, fetch, pick up.
to call off *The weather was so bad we had to call the game off.* abandon, adjourn, cancel, discontinue, drop, end, halt, postpone.
to call someone names SEE **insult** verb.

calligraphy noun copperplate, handwriting, illumination, lettering, penmanship, script.

calling noun *your calling in life.* business, career, employment, job, line of work, occupation, profession, trade, vocation, work.

calliper noun *callipers on a lame leg.* irons, leg support, splint.

callous adjective *a callous murder.* cold, cold-blooded, SEE **cruel**, dispassionate, hard-bitten, [*informal*] hard-boiled, hard-hearted, heartless, inhuman, insensitive, merciless, pitiless, ruthless, [*informal*] thick-skinned, uncaring, unconcerned, unemotional, unfeeling, unsympathetic.
OPPOSITES: SEE **kind** adjective.

callow adjective [*often patronizing*] *a callow youth.* adolescent, [*informal*] born yesterday, [*informal*] green, immature, inexperienced, juvenile, naïve, unsophisticated, [*informal*] wet behind the ears, young.
OPPOSITES: SEE **experienced**.

callus noun SEE **blemish**.

calm adjective **1** *calm water. calm weather.* airless, even, flat, glassy, [*poetic*] halcyon (*halcyon days*), like a millpond, motionless, placid, quiet, slow-moving, smooth, still, unclouded, unruffled, unwrinkled, windless.
OPPOSITES: SEE **stormy**.
2 *a calm mood. a calm temperament.* collected, [*uncomplimentary*] complacent, composed, cool, dispassionate, equable, impassive, imperturbable, [*informal*] laid-back, level-headed, moderate, pacific, [*uncomplimentary*] passionless, patient, peaceful, quiet, relaxed, restful, restrained, sedate, self-possessed, sensible, serene, tranquil, unemotional, unexcitable, [*informal*] unflappable, unhurried, unperturbed, untroubled.
OPPOSITES: SEE **anxious, excitable**.

calm noun **1** *the calm after a storm.* calmness, flat sea, peace, quietness, stillness, tranquillity.
OPPOSITES: SEE **storm** noun.
2 *I admired his calm.* SEE **calmness**.

calm verb *to calm an angry person.* appease, compose, control, cool down, lull, mollify, pacify, placate, quieten, settle down, sober down, soothe, tranquillize.
OPPOSITES: SEE **upset** verb.

calmness noun *I was amazed by his calmness in the crisis.* [*uncomplimentary*] complacency, composure, equability, equanimity, imperturbability, level-headedness, peace of mind, sang-froid, self-possession, serenity, [*informal*] unflappability.
OPPOSITES: SEE **anxiety**.

calumny noun SEE **slander** noun.

calve verb SEE **birth (to give birth)**.

camaraderie noun SEE **friendship**.

camber noun SEE **slope** noun.

camel noun dromedary.

cameo noun SEE **picture** noun.

camera noun box-camera, ciné-camera, Polaroid camera, reflex camera, SLR [=*single lens reflex*], video camera.
PHOTOGRAPHIC EQUIPMENT: SEE **photography**.

camiknickers noun SEE **briefs**.

camouflage noun *They used branches of trees as camouflage.* blind, cloak, concealment, cover, disguise, front, guise, mask, protective colouring, screen, veil.

camouflage verb *We camouflaged our hide-out.* cloak, conceal, cover up, disguise, hide, mask, obscure, screen, veil.

camp adjective **1** *a camp tone of voice.* SEE **effeminate**.
2 *a camp performance.* SEE **exaggerated**.

camp noun **1** *a scout camp.* bivouac, camping-ground, camp-site, encampment.
2 *Which political camp do you belong to?* SEE **party**.

campaign noun *a military campaign. a campaign to save the whale.* action, battle, crusade, drive, fight, movement, offensive, operation, push, struggle, war.

campus noun *a college campus.* grounds, setting, site.

can noun *a can of lager.* canister, jar, tin.

can verb *to can fruit.* SEE **preserve** verb.

canal noun channel, waterway.

cancel verb **1** *to cancel a sporting fixture.* abandon, drop, give up, postpone, scrap, [*informal*] scrub.
2 *to cancel an instruction. to cancel a debt.* abolish, abort, [*formal*] abrogate (*a law*), annul, countermand, cross out, delete, eliminate, erase, expunge, invalidate, nullify, override, overrule, quash, repeal, repudiate, rescind, revoke, wipe out.
3 *to cancel a stamp.* frank.

to cancel out compensate for, counterbalance, make up for, neutralize, offset, outweigh, wipe out.

cancer noun canker (*of a plant or tree*), carcinoma, growth, malignancy, melanoma, tumour.
producing cancer adjective carcinogenic.

candelabra noun SEE **light** noun.

candid adjective *a candid opinion.* blunt, direct, fair, forthright, frank, honest, just, [*informal*] no-nonsense, open, outspoken, plain, sincere, straightforward, true, truthful, unbiased, undisguised, unflattering, unprejudiced.
OPPOSITES: SEE **devious, insincere**.

candidate noun *a candidate for a job or an examination.* applicant, aspirant, competitor, contender, contestant, entrant, [*informal*] possibility, pretender (*to the throne*), runner, [*old-fashioned*] suitor (*for a woman's hand in marriage*).

candle noun SEE **light** noun.

candour noun SEE **honesty**.

candy noun SEE **sweet** noun (**sweets**).

cane noun *a cane to support a tomato plant.* bamboo, rod, stick.
to give someone the cane=**cane** verb.

cane verb SEE **punish**.

canine adjective dog-like.

canine noun SEE **tooth**.

canister noun VARIOUS CONTAINERS: SEE **container**.

canker noun SEE **cancer**.

cannelloni noun SEE **pasta**.

cannon noun SEE **gun**.

cannon verb SEE **collide**.

cannonade noun SEE **attack** noun, **gunfire**.

canny adjective SEE **shrewd**.

canoe noun dug-out, kayak.
OTHER CRAFT: SEE **vessel**.

canoe verb SEE **travel** verb.

canon noun **1** *the canons of justice.* SEE **principle**.
2 *a canon of a cathedral.* SEE **clergyman**.

canonical adjective SEE **accepted**.

canopy noun *There was a waterproof canopy over the platform.* awning, cover, covering, shade, shelter, umbrella.

cant noun **1** *The cant of the floor made it hard to stand upright.* SEE **slope** noun.
2 *Don't believe the cant he talks.* SEE **hypocrisy**.
3 *thieves' cant.* SEE **jargon**.

cantaloup noun melon.

cantankerous adjective SEE **bad-tempered**.

cantata noun OTHER MUSIC FOR SINGING: SEE **song**.

canteen noun *We had a snack in the canteen.* bar, buffet, café, cafeteria, coffee-bar, restaurant, snack-bar.

canter verb SEE **run** verb.

canton noun SEE **country**.

canvass noun *a canvass of public opinion.* census, enquiry (into), examination, investigation, market research (into), opinion poll, poll, probe (into), scrutiny, survey.

canvass verb *to canvass for votes.* ask for, campaign (for), [*informal*] drum up, electioneer, seek, solicit.

canyon noun *a deep canyon.* defile, gorge, pass, ravine, valley.

cap noun **1** KINDS OF HAT: SEE **hat**.
2 *the cap off a ketchup bottle.* covering, lid, top.

cap verb SEE **cover** verb.

capable adjective *a capable mathematician.* able, accomplished, clever, competent, effective, efficient, experienced, expert, gifted, [*informal*] handy, intelligent, masterly, practised, proficient, qualified, skilful, skilled, talented, trained.
OPPOSITES: SEE **incompetent**.
capable of *She's capable of turning up without warning.* adept at, apt to, disposed to, equal to, liable to.
OPPOSITES: SEE **incapable**.

capacious adjective SEE **roomy**.

capacity noun **1** *the capacity of a container.* dimensions, magnitude, size, volume.
2 *your mental capacity. your physical capacity.* ability, capability, competence, SEE **intelligence**, power, skill, talent.
3 *In his capacity as captain he's got a right to tell us what to do.* appointment, function, job, office, position, post, role.

cape noun **1** *a waterproof cape.* cloak, coat, cope, mantle, robe, shawl, wrap.
2 *the Cape of Good Hope.* head, headland, peninsula, point, promontory.

caper verb *Lambs capered about the field.* bound, cavort, dance, frisk, frolic, gambol, hop, jig about, jump, leap, play, prance, romp, skip, spring.

capillary noun SEE **tube, vein**.

capital adjective **1** *the capital city.* chief, controlling, first, foremost, leading, main, pre-eminent, primary, principal.
2 [*old-fashioned*] *a capital idea.* SEE **excellent**.

3 *a capital offence.* punishable by death. **4** *capital letters.* big, block, initial, large, upper-case.

capital noun **1** *Paris is the capital of France.* chief city, centre of government. **2** *capital to start a new business.* assets, cash, finance, funds, investments, principal, money, property, [*slang*] the ready, resources, riches, savings, stock, wealth, [*informal*] the wherewithal.

capitalism noun OTHER POLITICAL TERMS: SEE **politics**.

capitalist noun SEE **rich (rich person)**.

capitalize verb SEE **profit** verb (**profit by**).

capitulate verb *They capitulated after a long fight.* be defeated, desist, fall, give in, submit, succumb, surrender, [*informal*] throw in the towel, yield.
OPPOSITES: SEE **persevere**.

capricious adjective *a capricious wind. a capricious personality.* changeable, erratic, fanciful, fickle, fitful, flighty, impulsive, inconstant, mercurial, moody, quirky, uncertain, unpredictable, unreliable, variable, wayward, whimsical.
OPPOSITES: SEE **predictable**, **steady** adjective.

capsize verb *The boat capsized.* flip over, invert, keel over, overturn, tip over, turn over, [*informal*] turn turtle, turn upside down.

capstan noun SEE **post** noun.

capsule noun **1** *The doctor gave her some capsules.* lozenge, medicine, pill, tablet. **2** *a space capsule.* WORDS TO DO WITH TRAVEL IN SPACE: SEE **space**.

captain noun **1** *the captain of a team.* boss, chief, head, leader.
2 *an army captain. a naval captain.* SEE **rank** noun.
3 *the captain of a ship. the captain of an aircraft.* commander, master, officer in charge, pilot, skipper.

caption noun *a caption to a picture.* description, explanation, heading, headline, [*formal*] superscription, title.

captious adjective SEE **critical**.

captivate verb **1** *The music captivated us. Her beauty captivated him.* attract, beguile, bewitch, charm, delight, enamour, enchant, enrapture, ensnare, enthral, entrance, fascinate, hypnotize, infatuate, mesmerize, seduce, [*informal*] steal your heart, [*informal*] turn your head.
OPPOSITES: SEE **repel**.

captivating adjective SEE **attractive**.

captive adjective *captive animals.* caged, captured, chained, confined, detained, enslaved, ensnared, fettered, gaoled, imprisoned, incarcerated, jailed, restricted, secure, taken prisoner.
OPPOSITES: SEE **free** adjective.

captive noun *captives in prison.* convict, detainee, hostage, internee, prisoner.

captivity noun *His enemies kept him in captivity.* bondage, confinement, custody, detention, duress (*under duress*), imprisonment, incarceration, internment [don't confuse with *interment*], SEE **prison**, protective custody, remand (*on remand*), restraint (*under restraint*), servitude, slavery.
OPPOSITES: SEE **freedom**.

capture verb **1** *to capture a criminal.* apprehend, arrest, [*informal*] bag, bind, catch, [*informal*] collar, corner, [*informal*] get, [*informal*] nab, overpower, secure, seize, take prisoner, SEE **trap** verb.
2 *to capture a castle.* SEE **conquer**.

car noun automobile, [*informal*] banger [=*old car*], [*joking*] bus, [*joking*] jalopy, motor, motor car, [*informal*] wheels.

KINDS OF CAR: convertible, coupé, Dormobile, estate, fastback, hatchback, jeep, Land Rover, limousine, Mini, patrol car, police car, saloon, shooting brake, sports car, tourer.

OTHER VEHICLES: SEE **vehicle**.

---

carafe noun SEE **bottle** noun.

caravan noun OTHER VEHICLES: SEE **vehicle**.

caravanning noun SEE **holiday**.

carbohydrate noun SEE **food**.

carbon noun CHEMICAL ELEMENTS: SEE **chemical**.
carbon copy SEE **duplicate** noun.

carboy noun SEE **bottle** noun.

carbuncle noun SEE **boil** noun.

carcass noun **1** *the carcass of an animal.* body, cadaver, corpse, meat, remains.
2 *the rusting carcass of an old car.* framework, hulk, remains, shell, skeleton, structure.

carcinoma noun SEE **cancer**.

card noun *a piece of card.* cardboard, SEE **paper**, pasteboard.

VARIOUS MESSAGE CARDS: birthday card, Christmas card, congratulations card, Easter card, get well card, greetings card, invitation, notelet, picture postcard, postcard, sympathy card, Valentine, visiting card.

---

cards *a game of cards.* playing-cards.
put your cards on the table SEE **honest** **(be honest).**

CARD-GAMES INCLUDE: bridge, canasta, cribbage, patience, poker, pontoon, rummy, snap, whist.

SUITS: clubs, diamonds, hearts, spades, trumps.

VALUES: ace, king, knave, jack, joker, numbers 2 to 10, queen.

---

cardboard noun card, pasteboard.

cardiac adjective SEE **heart**.

cardigan noun SEE **coat** noun.

cardinal objective **1** *a cardinal sin.* SEE **important**.
2 *cardinal red.* SEE **red**.
cardinal numbers whole numbers.

cardinal noun SEE **clergyman**.

care noun **1** *Drive with care.* attention. carefulness, caution, circumspection, concentration, concern, diligence, exactness, forethought, heed, interest, meticulousness, pains, prudence, solicitude, thoroughness, thought, vigilance, watchfulness.
OPPOSITES: SEE **carelessness**.
2 *He doesn't have a care in the world!* anxiety, burden, concern, difficulty, hardship, problem, responsibility, sorrow, stress, tribulation, trouble, vexation, woe, worry.
OPPOSITES: SEE **joy**.
3 *She left the baby in my care.* charge, control, custody, guardianship, keeping, management, protection, safekeeping, [*formal*] ward.

care verb *If you saw their suffering, you would care about them.* be troubled, bother, concern yourself, mind, worry.
to care for 1 *He cares for his dog.* attend to, cherish, guard, keep, [*informal*] keep an eye on, look after, mind, mother, nurse, protect, supervise, take care of, tend, watch over.
2 *Do you care for me?* SEE **love** verb.

careen verb SEE **tilt** verb.

career noun *a career in industry.* business, calling, employment, job, livelihood, occupation, profession, trade, vocation, work.
VARIOUS CAREERS: SEE **job**.

career verb *They careered along.* SEE **rush** verb.

carefree adjective **1** *a carefree attitude.* casual, cheerful, cheery, contented, debonair, easy, easy-going, happy, happy-go-lucky, [*informal*] laid-back, light-hearted, relaxed, unconcerned, unworried.
OPPOSITES: SEE **anxious, tense** adjective.
2 *a carefree holiday.* leisured, peaceful, quiet, relaxing, restful, trouble-free, untroubled.

careful adjective **1** *a careful worker. careful work.* accurate, conscientious, deliberate, diligent, exhaustive, fastidious, judicious, methodical, meticulous, neat, orderly, organized, painstaking, particular, precise, punctilious, responsible, rigorous, scrupulous, systematic, thorough.
OPPOSITES: SEE **careless, irresponsible**.
2 *Be careful not to upset anyone.* alert, attentive, cautious, chary, circumspect, heedful, mindful, observant, prudent, solicitous, thoughtful, vigilant, wary, watchful.
OPPOSITES: SEE **careless, thoughtless**.
to be careful be on your guard, look out, take care, watch out, [*informal*] watch your step.

careless adjective **1** *careless driving. careless talk.* absent-minded, heedless, ill-considered, imprudent, inattentive, incautious, inconsiderate, irresponsible, negligent, rash, reckless, thoughtless, uncaring, unguarded, unthinking, unwary.
OPPOSITES: SEE **attentive, careful**.
2 *careless work.* casual, confused, cursory, disorganized, hasty, imprecise, inaccurate, jumbled, messy, perfunctory, scatter-brained, shoddy, slapdash, slipshod, [*informal*] sloppy, slovenly, thoughtless, untidy.
OPPOSITES: SEE **accurate, careful**.

carelessness noun haste, inattention, irresponsibility, negligence, recklessness, [*informal*] sloppiness, slovenliness, thoughtlessness, untidiness.
OPPOSITES: SEE **care** noun.

caress noun *a loving caress.* cuddle, embrace, hug, kiss, pat, stroke, touch.

caress verb *to caress someone lovingly.* cuddle, embrace, fondle, hug, kiss, make love to, [*slang*] neck with, nuzzle, pat, pet, rub against, smooth, stroke, touch.

caretaker noun custodian, janitor, keeper, porter, superintendent, warden, watchman.

careworn adjective gaunt, grim, haggard, SEE **weary** adjective.

cargo noun *The cargo was transported in large containers.* consignment, freight, goods, [*formal*] lading (*bill of lading*), load, merchandise, payload, shipment.

caricature noun [Don't confuse with *character.*] *She drew a wickedly funny caricature of the teacher.* cartoon, parody, satire, [*informal*] send-up, [*informal*] take-off, travesty.

caricature verb *She caricatured his mannerisms.* burlesque, distort, exaggerate, imitate, lampoon, make fun of, mimic, mock, parody, ridicule, satirize, [*informal*] send up, take off.

carillon noun SEE **bell**.

caring adjective *a caring attitude.* SEE **concerned**.

caring noun SEE **concern** noun, kindness, nursing, solicitude.

carmine adjective SEE **red**.

Several English words, including *carnage, carnal,* and *carnivore*, are related to Latin *carnis=flesh.*

---

carnage noun *a scene of carnage.* bloodbath, bloodshed, butchery, havoc, holocaust, killing, massacre, pogrom, shambles, slaughter.

carnal adjective *carnal desires.* animal, bodily, erotic, fleshly, SEE **lustful**, natural, physical, sensual, sexual.

carnival noun *a bank-holiday carnival.* celebration, fair, festival, festivity, fête, fiesta, fun and games, gala, jamboree, merrymaking, pageant, parade, procession, revelry, show, spectacle.

carnivore noun KINDS OF ANIMAL: SEE **animal** noun.

carnivorous adjective flesh-eating, meat-eating.
COMPARE: herbivorous, omnivorous, vegetarian.

carol noun MUSIC FOR SINGING: SEE **song**.

carouse verb *They were carousing all night.* [*informal*] booze, celebrate, drink, [*formal*] imbibe, make merry, [*old-fashioned*] quaff, revel, [*old-fashioned*] wassail.

carp verb *to carp about small problems.* [*informal*] belly-ache, cavil, SEE **complain**, find fault, [*informal*] go on, grumble, object, quibble, [*informal*] split hairs.

carpenter noun joiner.

carpentry noun joinery, woodwork.

carpet noun SEE **floor (floor coverings)**.

carpet verb SEE **cover** verb.

carport noun garage.

carriage noun **1** OTHER VEHICLES: SEE **vehicle**.
2 *Military men have an upright carriage.* bearing, comportment, demeanour, gait, manner, mien, posture.

carriageway noun SEE **road**.

carrier noun **1** *a carrier of good news.* bearer, conveyor, courier, deliveryman or -woman, dispatch rider, errand-boy or -girl, messenger, postman, runner.
2 *the carrier of a disease.* contact, host, transmitter.

carrion noun SEE **flesh**.

carroty adjective SEE **red**.

carry verb **1** bring, fetch, haul, lift, [*informal*] lug, manhandle, move, remove, shoulder, take, transfer.
2 *Aircraft carry passengers and goods.* convey, ferry, ship, transport.
3 *Telegraph wires carry signals.* communicate, relay, transmit.
4 *The rear axle carries the greatest weight.* bear, hold up, support.
5 *Murder carries a heavy penalty.* demand, entail, involve, lead to, occasion, require, result in.
to carry on 1 *We carried on in spite of the rain.* continue, go on, keep on, last, persevere, persist, remain, stay, [*informal*] stick it out, survive.
2 *He carries on a small business.* administer, maintain, manage, run.
3 [*informal*] *Stop carrying on like that!* SEE **misbehave**.
to carry out *We carried out her orders.* accomplish, achieve, complete, do, enforce, execute, finish, perform.

cart noun barrow, dray, truck, wagon, wheelbarrow.

cartel noun SEE **group** noun.

carthorse noun SEE **horse**.

cartography noun map-drawing.

carton noun box, case, pack, package, packet.
OTHER CONTAINERS: SEE **container**.

cartoon noun **1** *a cartoon in the newspaper.* caricature, comic strip, drawing, SEE **picture** noun, sketch.
2 *a cartoon on TV.* animation, SEE **film** noun.

cartridge noun **1** *a cartridge of film. a cartridge of ink.* canister, capsule, case, cassette, cylinder, tube.
2 *a cartridge for a rifle.* magazine, round, shell.
OTHER CONTAINERS: SEE **container**.
cartridge paper SEE **paper** noun.

carve verb **1** *to carve meat.* SEE **cut** verb, slice.
2 *to carve a statue.* chisel, hew, [*informal*] sculpt.

carving noun SEE **sculpture** noun.

cascade noun cataract, torrent, waterfall.

case noun **1** *a packing case. a display-case.* box, cabinet, carton, casket, chest, crate, SEE **luggage**, pack, packaging, suitcase, trunk.
OTHER CONTAINERS: SEE **container**.
2 *an obvious case of favouritism.* example, illustration, instance, occurrence, specimen, state of affairs.
3 *Normally everyone has to help with the washing up, but in her case we made an exception.* circumstances, condition, context, plight, predicament, situation, state.
4 *The judge said he'd never known a case like this one.* argument, inquiry, investigation, law suit.

case verb SEE **enclose**.

casement noun SEE **window**.

cash noun bank notes, change, coins, currency, [*informal*] dough, funds, hard money, money, notes, [*informal*] the ready, [*informal*] the wherewithal.

cash verb **to cash in on** SEE **profit** verb.

cashier noun accountant, banker, check-out (person), clerk, [*formal*] teller, treasurer.

cashier verb *cashiered from the army.* SEE **dismiss**.

casing noun SEE **covering**.

cask noun *a cask of rum.* barrel, butt, hogshead, tub, tun, vat.

casket noun SEE **box**.

casserole noun SEE **dish**.

casserole verb SEE **cook** verb.

cassette noun SEE **recording**.

cast noun **1** *a plaster cast.* SEE **sculpture** noun.
2 *the cast of a play.* characters, company, dramatis personae, troupe.

cast verb **1** *to cast coins into a well.* bowl, chuck, drop, fling, hurl, impel, launch, lob, pelt, pitch, project, scatter, shy, sling, throw, toss.
2 *The sculptor cast his statue in bronze.* form, mould, SEE **sculpture** verb, shape.
to cast off 1 *to cast off clothes.* SEE **shed** verb.
2 *to cast off a ship.* SEE **untie**.

castaway noun ADJECTIVES WHICH DESCRIBE A CASTAWAY: abandoned, deserted, marooned, shipwrecked, stranded.

caste noun [Properly *caste* refers to the Hindu system of hereditary classes, but the word is often used more loosely.] class, degree, estate, grade, position, rank, station, status, stratum.

castigate verb censure, chasten, chastize, [*old-fashioned*] chide, SEE **criticize**, discipline, lash, punish, rebuke, reprimand, scold.

castigation noun SEE **censure** noun.

castle noun château, citadel, fort, fortress, palace, stronghold, tower.
RELATED ADJECTIVE = *like a castle*: castellated [*a castellated wall*].

PARTS OF A CASTLE: bailey, barbican, battlement, buttress, courtyard, donjon, drawbridge, dungeon, gate, keep, magazine, moat, motte, parapet, portcullis, rampart, tower, turret, wall.

---

castor noun *castors under an armchair.* runner, wheel.

castrate verb *Animals reared for meat are often castrated.* emasculate, geld, neuter, spay, sterilize, unsex.

casual adjective **1** *a casual meeting.* accidental, chance, fortuitous, incidental, random, unexpected, unforeseen, unintentional, unplanned, unpremeditated.
OPPOSITES: SEE **deliberate**.
2 *casual conversation. a casual attitude.* apathetic, blasé, careless, [*informal*] couldn't-care-less, easy-going, [*informal*] free-and-easy, lackadaisical, [*informal*] laid back, lax, negligent, nonchalant, offhand, relaxed, [*informal*] slap-happy, [*informal*] throwaway (*a throwaway remark*), unconcerned, unenthusiastic, unimportant, unprofessional.
OPPOSITES: SEE **committed**, **enthusiastic**.
3 *casual clothes.* informal.
OPPOSITE: formal.

casualty noun *It was a nasty accident, but there were few casualties.* dead person, death, fatality, injured person, injury, loss, victim, wounded person.

casuistry noun chicanery, equivocation, false reasoning [SEE **reasoning**], sophistry, speciousness.

cat noun kitten, [*informal*] moggy, [*informal*] pussy, tabby, tom, tomcat.
RELATED ADJECTIVES: [*informal*] catty [=*spiteful*], feline [=*characteristic of a cat*].
a cat's home cattery.

cataclysm noun SEE **catastrophe**.

catacombs noun crypt, sepulchre, tomb, underground passage, vault.

catafalque noun SEE **funeral**.

catalogue noun *a shopping catalogue. a library catalogue.* brochure, directory, index, inventory, list, record, register, roll, schedule, table.

catalogue verb *to catalogue a record collection.* classify, codify, file, index, list, make an inventory of, record, register, tabulate.

catapult verb SEE **hurl**.

cataract noun cascade, falls, rapids, torrent, waterfall.

catastrophe noun *The flood was a catastrophe for farmers.* blow, calamity, cataclysm, crushing blow, débâcle, devastation, disaster, fiasco, holocaust, mischance, misfortune, mishap, ruin, ruination, tragedy, upheaval.

catcall noun jeer.

catch noun **1** *an angler's catch.* bag, booty, haul, net, prey.
2 *The price is so low that there must be a catch.* difficulty, disadvantage, drawback, obstacle, problem, snag, trap, trick.
3 *a catch on a door.* bolt, clasp, clip, fastener, fastening, hasp, hook, latch, lock.
catch-22 SEE **dilemma**.

catch verb **1** *to catch a fish.* ensnare, entrap, hook, net, snare, trap.
2 *to catch a ball.* clutch, grab, grasp, grip, hang on to, hold, seize, snatch, take.
3 *to catch a thief.* apprehend, arrest, capture, [*informal*] cop, corner, detect, discover, expose, [*informal*] nab, [*informal*] nobble, stop, surprise, take by surprise, unmask.
4 *to catch a bus.* be in time for, get on.
5 *to catch an illness.* become infected by, contract, get.
to catch on 1 *Their latest record didn't catch on.* SEE **succeed**.
2 [*informal*] *Explain it again—I'm a bit slow to catch on.* SEE **understand**.
to catch up *If we run we'll catch them up.* come alongside, gain on, overtake.

catching adjective *a catching disease.* communicable, contagious, infectious, spreading, transmittable.
OPPOSITE: non-infectious.

catchment area noun SEE **locality**.

catch-phrase, catchword nouns SEE **slogan**.

catchy adjective *a catchy tune.* attractive, haunting, memorable, popular, singable, tuneful.

catechize verb SEE **question** verb.

categorical adjective *a categorical denial.* absolute, certain, complete, decided, definite, direct, downright, emphatic, explicit, forceful, [*informal*] out-and-out, positive, strong, total, unambiguous, unconditional, unequivocal, unmitigated, unqualified, unreserved, utter, vigorous.
OPPOSITES: SEE **tentative, uncertain**.

category noun class, classification, division, grade, group, heading, kind, order, rank, section, set, sort, type.

cater verb *We catered for twelve people at Christmas.* cook, make arrangements, provide, supply.

caterpillar noun grub, [*formal*] larva, maggot.

caterwaul verb SEE **cry** verb.

catgut noun SEE **cord**.

cathedral noun SEE **church**.

catholic adjective *catholic tastes in music.* all-embracing, broad, broad-minded, comprehensive, cosmopolitan, eclectic, general, liberal, universal, varied, wide, wide-ranging.

catnap noun, verb SEE **sleep** noun, verb.

cattle plural noun bulls, bullocks, calves, cows, heifers, livestock, oxen, steers.

catty adjective [*informal*] *catty remarks.* [*informal*] bitchy, ill-natured, malevolent, malicious, mean, nasty, rancorous, sly, spiteful, venomous, vicious.

caucus noun SEE **committee**.

cauldron noun pot, saucepan.

cause noun **1** *What was the cause of the trouble?* basis, beginning, genesis, grounds, motivation, motive, occasion, origin, reason, root, source, spring, stimulus.
2 *Who was the cause of it all?* agent, author, [*old-fashioned*] begetter, creator, initiator, inspiration, inventor, originator, producer.
3 *Do you know the cause of his absence?* explanation, excuse, pretext, reason.
4 *We were collecting for a good cause.* aim, belief, end, object, purpose, undertaking.

cause verb **1** *It'll cause trouble if we don't share things fairly.* arouse, begin, bring about, create, effect, effectuate, engender, foment, generate, give rise to, incite, kindle, lead to, occasion, precipitate, produce, provoke, result in, set off, trigger off, [*infomal*] whip up.
2 *His illness caused him to retire.* compel, force, induce, motivate.

causeway noun SEE **road**.

caustic adjective **1** *caustic substances.* acid, astringent, burning, corrosive.
2 *caustic criticism.* acidulous, biting, bitter, cutting, mordant, pungent, sarcastic, scathing, severe, sharp, stinging, virulent, waspish.

cauterize verb SEE **disinfect**.

caution noun **1** *Proceed with caution.* alertness, attentiveness, care, carefulness, circumspection, discretion, forethought, heed, heedfulness, prudence, vigilance, wariness, watchfulness.
2 *They let me off with a caution.* admonition, [*informal*] dressing-down, reprimand, [*informal*] talking-to, [*informal*] ticking-off, warning.

caution verb **1** *They cautioned us about the dangers of drugs.* advise, alert, counsel, forewarn, inform, [*informal*] tip off, warn.
2 *The police cautioned me.* admonish, censure, give a warning, reprehend, reprimand, [*informal*] tell off, [*informal*] tick off.

cautionary adjective *a cautionary story.* SEE **moral** adjective.

cautious adjective **1** *a cautious driver.* alert, attentive, careful, heedful, prudent, scrupulous, vigilant, watchful.
OPPOSITES: SEE **careless, reckless**.
2 *a cautious remark. a cautious attempt.* [*informal*] cagey, calculating, chary, circumspect, deliberate, discreet, gingerly (*a gingerly approach*), grudging, guarded, hesitant, judicious, non-committal, restrained, suspicious, tactful, tentative, unadventurous, wary, watchful.
OPPOSITES: SEE **forthright, impetuous**.

cavalcade noun march-past, parade, procession, spectacle, troop (*of horses*).

cavalry noun SEE **armed services**.

cave noun cavern, cavity, den, grotto, hole, pothole, underground chamber.
the study of caves speleology.

cave verb **to cave in 1** *The roof caved in.* SEE **collapse**.
2 [*informal*] *The opposition caved in.* SEE **surrender**.

caveat noun SEE **warning**.

caveman noun cave-dweller, troglodyte.

cavern noun SEE **cave** noun.

cavil verb SEE **carp**.

cavity noun cave, crater, dent, hole, hollow, pit.

cavort verb SEE **caper**.

cease verb *Cease work!* break off, call a halt to, conclude, cut off, desist (from), discontinue, end, finish, halt, [*informal*] kick (*to kick a habit*), [*informal*] knock off (*to knock off work*), [*informal*] lay off, [*informal*] pack in, refrain from, stop, terminate.
OPPOSITES: SEE **commence**.

cease-fire noun SEE **truce**.

ceaseless adjective *Their ceaseless noise annoyed the neighbours.* chronic, constant, continual, continuous, endless, everlasting, incessant, interminable, never-ending, non-stop, permanent, perpetual, persistent, relentless, unending, unremitting, untiring.
OPPOSITES: SEE **temporary**.

cede verb SEE **relinquish**.

ceilidh noun SEE **entertainment**.

celebrate verb **1** *Let's celebrate!* be happy, have a celebration [SEE **celebration**], let yourself go, [*informal*] live it up, make merry, rejoice, revel.
2 *to celebrate an anniversary.* commemorate, keep, observe, remember, solemnize.

celebrated adjective *a celebrated actor.* acclaimed, distinguished, eminent, exalted, famous, glorious, illustrious, legendary, notable, noted, [*uncomplimentary*] notorious, outstanding, popular, prominent, renowned, revered, well-known.

celebration noun KINDS OF CELEBRATION: anniversary, banquet, binge, birthday, carnival, commemoration, feast, festival, festivity, fête, gala, jamboree, [*joking*] jollification, jubilee, merry-making, orgy, party, [*informal*] rave-up, [*formal*] remembrance, reunion, [*informal*] shindig, wedding.

celebrity noun *a TV celebrity.* big name, [*informal*] bigwig, dignitary, famous person [SEE **famous**], idol, notability, personality, public figure, star, superstar, VIP, [*joking*] worthy.

celerity noun SEE **speed** noun.

celestial adjective **1** *celestial regions.* cosmic, galactic, interplanetary, interstellar, starry, stellar, universal.
2 *celestial music.* angelic, blissful, divine, ethereal, godlike, heavenly, seraphic, sublime, supernatural, transcendental, visionary.

celibate adjective *a celibate life.* chaste, continent, single, virgin, unmarried, unwedded.

celibacy noun *People in some religious orders take a vow of celibacy.* bachelorhood, chastity, spinsterhood, virginity.

cell noun **1** *a prison cell. a cell of a honeycomb.* cavity, compartment, cubicle, den, enclosure, living space, prison, room, space, unit.
2 *an electric cell.* battery.

cellar noun basement, crypt, vault, wine-cellar.

celluloid noun SEE **plastic** noun.

Celsius adjective centigrade.

cemetery noun burial-ground, churchyard, graveyard, [*formal*] necropolis [=*ancient cemetery*].
WORDS TO DO WITH FUNERALS: SEE **funeral**.

cenotaph noun SEE **monument**.

censor verb [Do not confuse with verb *censure*.] **1** [=*to remove certain parts only*] *They censored the violent film.* amend, bowdlerize, [*informal*] clean up, cut, edit, expurgate.
2 [=*to remove completely*] *They censored the violence.* ban, cut out, exclude, forbid, prohibit, remove.

censorious adjective SEE **disapproving**.

censure noun *He deserved the referee's censure for that foul.* accusation, admonition, blame, castigation, condemnation, criticism, denunciation, diatribe, disapproval, [*informal*] dressing-down, harangue, rebuke, reprimand, reproach, reprobation, reproof, [*informal*] slating, stricture, [*informal*] talking-to, [*informal*] telling-off, tirade, verbal attack, vituperation.

censure verb [Do not confuse with verb *censor*.] *The referee censured him.* admonish, berate, blame, [*informal*] carpet, castigate, caution, chide, condemn, criticize, denounce, lecture, rebuke, reproach, reprove, scold, take (someone) to task, [*slang*] tear (someone) off a strip, [*informal*] tell off, [*informal*] tick off, upbraid.

census noun *a traffic census.* count, survey, tally.

Several English words, including *bicentennial, centenary, centigrade, century,* etc., are related to Latin *centum* = *a hundred.*

---

centenary noun SEE **anniversary**.

centigrade adjective Celsius.

central adjective **1** *the central part of town.* focal, inner, innermost, interior, middle.
2 *the central facts.* chief, crucial, essential, focal, fundamental, important, key, main, major, overriding, pivotal, primary, principal, vital.
OPPOSITES: SEE **peripheral**.

centralize verb *The company built a new HQ to centralize their administration.* amalgamate, bring together, concentrate, rationalize, streamline, unify.
OPPOSITES: SEE **devolve, disperse**.

centre noun *the centre of a circle. the centre of town.* bull's-eye, core, focus, heart, hub, inside, interior, kernel, middle, mid-point, nucleus, pivot.
OPPOSITES: SEE **edge** noun, **outskirts**, **surface** noun.

centrifugal adjective *centrifugal force.* dispersing, diverging, moving outwards, spreading, scattering.
OPPOSITE: centripetal.

centripetal adjective converging.
OPPOSITE: centrifugal.

century noun SEE **time** noun.

ceramics noun SEE **pottery**.

cereal noun corn, grain.
CEREALS INCLUDE: barley, corn on the cob, maize, millet, oats, rice, rye, sweetcorn, wheat.

cerebral adjective [=*of the brain*] *cerebral activity.* SEE **intellectual**.

ceremonial adjective *a ceremonial occasion.* dignified, formal, [*in church*] liturgical, majestic, official, ritual, ritualistic, solemn, stately.
OPPOSITES: SEE **informal**.

ceremony noun **1** *a ceremony to mark an anniversary.* celebration, commemoration, [*informal*] do, event, formal occasion, function, occasion, parade, reception, rite, ritual, service [*church service*].
2 *a quiet wedding without a lot of ceremony.* ceremonial, decorum, etiquette, formality, grandeur, pageantry, pomp, pomp and circumstance, protocol, ritual, spectacle.

cerise adjective SEE **red**.

certain adjective **1** *I was certain I would win.* adamant, assured, confident, convinced, determined, firm, positive, resolved, satisfied, sure, undoubting, unshakable.
2 *a certain fact. certain proof.* absolute, authenticated, categorical, certified, clear, clear-cut, conclusive, convincing, definite, dependable, established, genuine, incontestable, incontrovertible, indubitable, infallible, irrefutable, known, official, plain, reliable, settled, sure, true, trustworthy, unarguable, undeniable, undisputed, undoubted, unmistakable, unquestionable, valid, verifiable.
3 *She faced certain disaster.* destined, fated, guaranteed, imminent, inescapable, inevitable, inexorable, predictable, unavoidable.
OPPOSITES: SEE **uncertain**.

4 *If the watch doesn't go, they are certain to refund your money.* bound, compelled, obliged, required, sure.
5 *Certain people are not telling the truth!* individual, particular, some, specific, unnamed.
for certain SEE **definitely.**
to be certain SEE **know.**
to make certain SEE **ensure.**

certainty noun **1** *I saw it happen, so I can speak with certainty.* assertiveness, assurance, authority, [*formal*] certitude, confidence, conviction, knowledge, positiveness, proof, sureness, truth, validity.
2 *It was a certainty that we'd quarrel sooner or later.* certain fact, [*informal*] foregone conclusion, foreseeable outcome, inevitability, necessity, [*informal*] sure thing.
OPPOSITES: SEE **impossibility.**

certificate noun *a certificate of airworthiness.* authorization, award, credentials, degree, diploma, document, guarantee, licence, pass, permit, qualification, warrant.

certify verb *The doctor certified that I was fit to go to work.* affirm, attest, authenticate, authorize, [*formal*] avow, confirm, declare, endorse, guarantee, notify, sign, testify, verify, vouch, witness.

cervical adjective of the neck.

cessation noun SEE **end** noun.

cesspit, cesspool nouns drainage, septic tank, sewer, soakaway.

chafe verb SEE **rub.**

chaff noun hay, husks, straw.

chaff verb SEE **tease.**

chagrin noun SEE **annoyance.**

chain noun **1** *iron chains.* bonds, coupling, fetters, handcuffs, irons, links, manacles, shackles.
2 *a chain of events. a human chain.* column, concatenation, cordon, line, progression, row, sequence, series, string, succession, train.

chain verb *The slaves were chained.* bind, [*old-fashioned*] clap in irons, SEE **fasten**, fetter, handcuff, link, manacle, shackle, tether, tie.

chainsaw noun SEE **saw.**

chair noun armchair, deck-chair, dining-chair, reclining-chair, rocking-chair, throne.
OTHER FURNITURE YOU SIT ON: SEE **seat** noun.

chairman noun *the chairman of a committee.* chair, chairperson, chairwoman, convener, director, organizer, president, speaker.

chalet noun SEE **house** noun.

chalice noun SEE **cup.**

challenge verb **1** *to challenge an intruder.* accost, confront, [*informal*] have a go at, take on, tax.
2 *to challenge someone to a duel.* dare, defy, [*old-fashioned*] demand satisfaction, provoke, summon.
3 *to challenge a decision.* argue against, dissent from, dispute, impugn, object to, oppose, protest against, query, question.

challenging adjective *a challenging task.* SEE **difficult**, inspiring, stimulating, testing, thought-provoking, worthwhile.
OPPOSITES: SEE **easy.**

chamber noun **1** *a council chamber.* SEE **room.**
2 *the chambers of the heart.* cavity, cell, compartment, space.

chambermaid noun SEE **servant.**

chamfer verb SEE **bevel.**

chamois noun **1** SEE **deer.**
2 [Pronounced *shammy,* = *chamois-leather*] cleaning cloth, leather, polishing cloth.

champ verb *to champ at the bit.* SEE **chew.**

champion adjective **1** *a champion athlete.* great, leading, record-breaking, supreme, top, unrivalled, victorious, winning, world-beating.
2 [*informal*] *I had a champion time.* SEE **good.**

champion noun **1** *The final game decides who is the champion.* conqueror, hero, medallist, prize-winner, record-breaker, superman, superwoman, title-holder, victor, winner.
2 *a great champion of civil rights.* backer, defender, guardian, patron, protector, supporter, upholder, vindicator.
3 [*old-fashioned*] *The lord sent his champion into the lists.* challenger, contender, contestant, fighter, knight, warrior.

champion verb SEE **support** verb.

championship noun *a snooker championship.* competition, contest, tournament.

chance adjective *a chance meeting.* accidental, [*formal*] adventitious, casual, coincidental, [*informal*] fluky, fortuitous, fortunate, haphazard, inadvertent, incidental, lucky, random, unexpected, unforeseen, unfortunate, unintentional, unlooked for, unplanned, unpremeditated.
OPPOSITES: SEE **intentional.**

chance noun **1** *It happened by chance.* accident, coincidence, destiny, fate,

fluke, fortune, gamble, hazard, luck, misfortune, serendipity.
2 *a chance of rain.* danger, liability, likelihood, possibility, probability, prospect, risk.
3 *Now it's your chance to try.* occasion, opportunity, time, turn.

chance verb **1** *I chanced to pass by.* SEE **happen.**
2 [*informal*] *Shall we chance it?* SEE **risk** verb.

chancy adjective *Gambling is a chancy way of making money.* dangerous, [*informal*] dicey, [*informal*] dodgy, hazardous, [*informal*] iffy, insecure, precarious, risky, speculative, ticklish, tricky, uncertain, unpredictable, unsafe.
OPPOSITES: SEE **predictable, safe.**

chandelier noun SEE **light** noun.

change noun **1** *a change in the weather. a change of policy. a change in the shape or appearance of something.* adaptation, adjustment, alteration, break, conversion, deterioration, development, difference, diversion, improvement, innovation, metamorphosis, modification, modulation, mutation, new look, rearrangement, refinement, reformation, reorganization, revolution, shift, substitution, swing, transfiguration, transformation, transition, translation, [*joking*] transmogrification, transmutation, transposition, [*informal*] turn-about, U-turn, variation, vicissitude, variety.
2 *Have you any change?* cash, coins, money, notes.

change verb **1** *to change your mind. to change your way of life. to change the shape or appearance of something.* acclimatize, accommodate, accustom, adapt, adjust, affect, alter, amend, convert, diversify, influence, modify, process, rearrange, reconstruct, refashion, reform, remodel, reorganize, reshape, restyle, tailor, transfigure, transform, translate, [*joking*] transmogrify, transmute, vary.
2 *to change clothes. to change places.* alternate, displace, exchange, replace, substitute, switch, swop, transpose.
3 *to change money.* barter, convert, trade in.
4 *Over a period, things do change.* alter, be transformed, [*informal*] chop and change, develop, fluctuate, metamorphose, move on, mutate, shift, vary.
to change into *Tadpoles change into frogs.* become, be changed into, turn into.
to change someone's mind SEE **convert.**
to change your mind be converted, reconsider, [*informal*] think better of it, [*informal*] think twice.

changeable adjective *changeable weather. changeable moods.* capricious, chequered (*a chequered career*), erratic, fickle, fitful, fluctuating, fluid, inconsistent, inconstant, irregular, mercurial, mutable, shifting, temperamental, uncertain, unpredictable, unreliable, unstable, unsteady, [*informal*] up and down, vacillating, variable, varying, volatile, wavering.
OPPOSITES: SEE **constant, steady** adjective.

channel noun **1** *a channel to take away water. a navigable channel.* canal, conduit, course, dike, ditch, duct, groove, gully, gutter, overflow, pipe, sound, strait, SEE **stream** noun, trough, watercourse, waterway.
2 *a channel of communication.* avenue, means, medium, path, route, way.
3 *a TV channel.* [*informal*] side (*Which side is the news on?*), station, waveband, wavelength.

channel verb *Channel your enquiries through reception.* convey, direct, guide, pass on, route, send, transmit.

chant verb SEE **sing.**

chaos noun anarchy, bedlam, confusion, disorder, disorganization, lawlessness, mayhem, muddle, pandemonium, shambles, tumult.
OPPOSITES: SEE **order** noun.

chaotic adjective **1** *My room's in a chaotic state.* confused, deranged, disordered, disorderly, disorganized, haphazard, [*informal*] haywire, [*informal*] higgledy-piggledy, jumbled, muddled, [*informal*] shambolic, [*informal*] topsy-turvy, untidy, [*informal*] upside-down.
OPPOSITES: SEE **neat, orderly.**
2 *During the famine, the country was in a chaotic state.* anarchic, lawless, rebellious, riotous, tumultuous, uncontrolled, ungovernable, unruly.
OPPOSITES: SEE **law-abiding, organized.**

chap noun SEE **man** noun.

chap verb SEE **sore (make sore).**

chapel noun SEE **church.**

chaperon noun escort.

chaperon verb SEE **escort** verb.

chaplain noun SEE **clergyman.**

chapman noun SEE **pedlar.**

chapter noun **1** *a chapter of a book.* act (*of a play*), canto (*of a poem*), division, episode, instalment, part, scene (*of a play*) section, subdivision.
2 *When you leave school you start a new chapter of your life.* SEE **part** noun.

char verb *The fire charred the woodwork* blacken, brown, burn, carbonize scorch, sear, singe.

charabanc noun SEE **bus**.

character noun **1** *This brand of tea has a character all of its own.* SEE **characteristic** noun, distinctiveness, flavour, idiosyncrasy, individuality, integrity, peculiarity, quality, stamp, taste, uniqueness.
2 *She has a forceful character.* attitude, constitution, disposition, individuality, make-up, manner, nature, personality, reputation, temper, temperament.
3 *She's a well-known character.* figure, human being, individual, person, personality, [*informal*] type.
4 *She made us laugh—she's such a character!* [*informal*] case, comedian, comic, eccentric, [*informal*] nut-case, oddity, [*uncomplimentary slang*] weirdo.
5 *a character in a play.* part, persona, portrayal, role.
6 *the characters of the alphabet.* cipher, figure, [*plural*] hieroglyphics (*Egyptian hieroglyphics*), ideogram, letter, mark, rune, sign, symbol, type.

characteristic adjective *I recognized his characteristic walk.* distinctive, distinguishing, essential, idiosyncratic, individual, particular, peculiar, recognizable, singular, special, specific, symptomatic, unique.

characteristic noun *He has some odd characteristics.* attribute, distinguishing feature, feature, hallmark, idiosyncrasy, peculiarity, symptom, trait.

characterize verb **1** *The play characterizes Richard III as a villain.* describe, delineate, depict, draw, portray, present.
2 *The cuckoo is characterized by its familiar call.* brand, differentiate, distinguish, identify, individualize, mark, recognize, typify.

charade noun *He wasn't really upset—his behaviour was just a charade.* acting, deceit, deception, fabrication, make-believe, masquerade, mockery, [*informal*] play-acting, pose, pretence, [*informal*] put-up job, sham.

charge noun **1** *an increase in charges.* cost, expenditure, expense, fare, fee, payment, postage, price, rate, terms, toll, value.
2 *They left the dog in my charge.* care, command, control, custody, keeping, protection, responsibility, safe-keeping, trust.
3 *a criminal charge.* accusation, allegation, imputation, indictment.
4 *Some of the horses fell in the charge.* assault, attack, incursion, invasion, offensive, onslaught, raid, rush, sortie, strike.

charge verb **1** *What do they charge for a coffee?* ask for, exact, levy, make you pay, require.
FOR VERBS WITH THE BUYER AS SUBJECT, SEE **pay** verb.
2 *They charged me with the duty of cleaning the hall.* burden, command, commit, empower, entrust, give, impose on.
3 *What crime did they charge him with?* accuse, blame, [*formal*] impeach, [*formal*] indict, prosecute, tax.
4 *The cavalry charged the enemy line.* assail, assault, attack, [*informal*] fall on, rush, set on, storm, [*informal*] wade into.

charger noun SEE **horse**.

chariot noun OTHER VEHICLES: SEE **vehicle**.

charisma noun SEE **charm** noun.

charitable adjective SEE **generous, kind**.

charity noun **1** *He helped us out of charity, not self-interest.* affection, altruism, benevolence, bounty, caring, compassion, consideration, generosity, goodness, helpfulness, humanity, kindness, love, mercy, philanthropy, sympathy, tender-heartedness, unselfishness, warm-heartedness.
OPPOSITES: SEE **selfishness**.
2 *The animals' hospital depends on our charity.* [*old-fashioned*] alms or alms-giving, bounty, donations, financial support, gifts, [*informal*] hand-outs, largesse, offerings, patronage, self-sacrifice.
3 *We collected for charity.* a good cause, the needy, the poor.

charlatan noun SEE **cheat** noun.

charm noun **1** *Everyone falls for his charm!* allure, appeal, attractiveness, charisma, fascination, hypnotic power, lovable nature, lure, magic, magnetism, power, pull, seductiveness, sex appeal.
2 *magic charms.* curse, enchantment, incantation, SEE **magic**, mumbo-jumbo, sorcery, spell, witchcraft, wizardry.
3 *a charm on a silver chain.* amulet, lucky charm, mascot, ornament, talisman, trinket.

charm verb *He charmed us with his singing.* allure, attract, beguile, bewitch, cajole, captivate, cast a spell on, decoy, delight, enchant, enrapture, entrance, fascinate, hold spellbound, intrigue, lure, mesmerize, please, seduce, soothe.

charming adjective *charming manners.* alluring, SEE **attractive**, disarming, endearing, lovable, seductive, winning, winsome.

chart noun **1** *a weather chart.* map, sketch-map.

2 *an information chart.* diagram, graph, plan, table.

charter noun SEE **document** noun.

charter verb *to charter an aircraft.* employ, engage, hire, lease, rent.

charwoman noun SEE **servant**.

chary adjective SEE **cautious**.

chase verb **1** *The dog chased a rabbit.* drive, follow, hound, hunt, pursue, track, trail.
2 [*informal*] *I chased round trying to finish my jobs.* SEE **hurry**.

chasm noun *a deep chasm.* abyss, canyon, cleft, crater, crevasse, drop, fissure, gap, gulf, hole, hollow, opening, pit, ravine, rift, split, void.

chaste adjective **1** *People in some religious orders remain chaste.* celibate, continent, [*formal*] immaculate, inexperienced, innocent, moral, pure, sinless, uncorrupted, undefiled, unmarried, virgin, virginal, virtuous.
OPPOSITES: SEE **immoral**.
2 *a chaste dress.* austere, becoming, decent, decorous, maidenly, modest, plain, restrained, simple, tasteful.
OPPOSITES: SEE **ornate, sexy, vulgar**.

chasten verb **1** *They chastened me for my slowness.* SEE **punish**.
2 *She was chastened by her failure to reach the finals.* SEE **humble** verb.

chastise verb SEE **punish**.

chastity noun *sexual chastity.* abstinence, celibacy, continence, innocence, maidenhood, purity, sinlessness, virginity, virtue.

chat noun, verb SEE **talk** noun, verb.

château noun SEE **castle**.

chattels noun SEE **possessions**.

chatter noun, verb SEE **talk** noun, verb.

chatterbox noun SEE **talkative (talkative person)**.

chatty adjective SEE **talkative**.

chauffeur noun driver.

chauvinism noun [*Chauvinism* means *exaggerated patriotism,* but is now also used to mean *sexism.*] SEE **patriotism**, sexism, SEE **prejudice** noun.

chauvinist, chauvinistic adjectives SEE **patriotic**, sexist, SEE **prejudiced**.

chauvinist noun SEE **prejudiced (prejudiced person)**.

cheap adjective **1** *a cheap buy. a cheap price.* bargain, budget, cut-price, [*informal*] dirt-cheap, discount, economical, economy, fair, inexpensive, [*informal*] knock-down, low-priced, reasonable, reduced, [*informal*] rock-bottom, sale, under-priced.
OPPOSITES: SEE **expensive**.
2 *cheap quality.* inferior, poor, second-rate, shoddy, tatty, tawdry, tinny, worthless.
OPPOSITES: SEE **superior**.
3 *cheap humour. cheap insults.* contemptible, crude, despicable, facile, glib, ill-bred, ill-mannered, mean, silly, tasteless, unworthy, vulgar.
OPPOSITES: SEE **worthy**.

cheapen verb *The actors' silly giggling cheapened the performance.* belittle, debase, degrade, demean, devalue, discredit, downgrade, lower the tone (of), popularize, prostitute, vulgarize.

cheat noun **1** *Don't trust him—he's a cheat.* charlatan, cheater, [*informal*] con-man, counterfeiter, crafty person, deceiver, double-crosser, extortioner, forger, fraud, hoaxer, impersonator, impostor, [*informal*] phoney, [*informal*] quack, racketeer, rogue, [*informal*] shark, swindler, trickster, [*informal*] twister.
2 *The whole thing was a cheat.* artifice, bluff, chicanery, [*informal*] con, confidence trick, deceit, deception, [*slang*] fiddle, fraud, hoax, imposture, lie, misrepresentation, pretence, [*informal*] put-up job, [*informal*] racket, [*informal*] rip-off, ruse, sham, swindle, [*informal*] swizz, treachery, trick.

cheat verb **1** *He cheated me by selling me an unroadworthy car.* bamboozle, beguile, bilk, [*informal*] con, deceive, defraud, [*slang*] diddle, [*informal*] do, double-cross, dupe, [*slang*] fiddle, [*informal*] fleece, fool, hoax, hoodwink, outwit, [*informal*] rip off, rob, [*informal*] short-change, swindle, take in, trick.
2 *to cheat in an examination.* copy, crib, plagiarize.

check adjective *a check pattern.* SEE **chequered**.

check noun **1** *We reached our destination without any check.* SEE **interruption**.
2 *I took the car to the garage for a check.* check-up, examination, [*informal*] going-over, inspection, investigation, [*informal*] once-over, scrutiny, test.
3 [*American*] *a check for 10 dollars.* SEE **cheque**.
to keep in check SEE **check** verb.

check verb **1** *to check someone's progress. to check a horse.* arrest, bar, block, bridle, control, curb, delay, foil, govern, halt, hamper, hinder, hold back, impede, inhibit, keep in check, obstruct, regulate, rein, repress, restrain, retard,

slow, slow down, stem (*to stem the tide*), stop, stunt (*to stunt growth*), thwart.
2 *We checked our answers. They checked the locks on the doors.* [*American*] check out, compare, cross-check, examine, inspect, investigate, monitor, research, scrutinize, test, verify.

check-up noun SEE **check** noun.

cheek noun [*informal*] *She's got a cheek!* arrogance, audacity, boldness, brazenness, effrontery, impertinence, impudence, insolence, [*informal*] lip, [*informal*] nerve, pertness, presumptuousness, rudeness, [*informal*] sauce, shamelessness, temerity.

cheeky adjective *a cheeky manner. a cheeky remark.* arrogant, audacious, bold, brazen, cool, discourteous, disrespectful, flippant, forward, impertinent, impolite, impudent, insolent, insulting, irreverent, mocking, pert, presumptuous, rude, [*informal*] saucy, shameless, [*informal*] tongue-in-cheek.
OPPOSITES: SEE **respectful**.

cheer noun **1** *Give the winners a hearty cheer!* acclamation, applause, cry of approval, encouragement, hurrah, ovation, shout of approval.
2 [*old-fashioned*] *Be of good cheer!* SEE **happiness**.

cheer verb **1** *We cheered the winners.* acclaim, applaud, clap, shout.
OPPOSITES: SEE **jeer**.
2 *The good news cheered us.* comfort, console, delight, divert, encourage, entertain, exhilarate, gladden, make cheerful, please, solace, uplift.
OPPOSITES: SEE **sadden**.
to cheer up *The weather cheered up. Cheer up—we're nearly home!* become more cheerful, brighten, [*informal*] buck up, make more cheerful, [*informal*] perk up, [*slang*] snap out of it, take heart.

cheerful adjective *a cheerful mood.* animated, bright, buoyant, cheery, [*informal*] chirpy, contented, convivial, delighted, elated, festive, gay, genial, glad, gleeful, good-humoured, SEE **happy**, hearty, jaunty, jocund, jolly, jovial, joyful, joyous, jubilant, laughing, light (*a light heart*), light-hearted, lively, merry, optimistic, [*informal*] perky, pleased, rapturous, sparkling, spirited, sprightly, sunny, warm-hearted.
OPPOSITES: SEE **sad**.

cheerfulness noun animation, brightness, cheeriness, elation, festivity, gaiety, good-humour, SEE **happiness**, jollity, laughter, merriment, optimism, sprightliness.
OPPOSITES: SEE **depression**.

cheerio interjection SEE **goodbye**.

cheerless adjective *a cheerless rainy day.* bleak, comfortless, dark, depressing, desolate, dingy, disconsolate, dismal, drab, dreary, dull, forbidding, forlorn, frowning, funereal, gloomy, grim, joyless, lack-lustre, melancholy, miserable, mournful, sad, sober, sombre, sullen, sunless, uncongenial, unhappy, uninviting, unpleasant, unpromising, woeful, wretched.
OPPOSITES: SEE **cheerful**.

cheery adjective *a cheery manner.* airy, blithe, carefree, SEE **cheerful**, good-humoured, pleasant.

chef noun cook.

chemical noun compound, element, substance.

SOME CHEMICALS: acid, alcohol, alkali, ammonia, arsenic, chlorine, fluoride, litmus.

CHEMICAL ELEMENTS AND THEIR SYMBOLS: actinium *Ac*, aluminium *Al*, americium *Am*, antimony *Sb*, argon *Ar*, arsenic *As*, astatine *At*, barium *Ba*, berkelium *Bk*, beryllium *Be*, bismuth *Bi*, boron *B*, bromine *Br*, cadmium *Cd*, caesium *Cs*, calcium *Ca*, californium *Cf*, carbon *C*, cerium *Ce*, chlorine *Cl*, chromium *Cr*, cobalt *Co*, copper *Cu*, curium *Cm*, dysprosium *Dy*, einsteinium *Es*, erbium *Er*, europium *Eu*.

fermium *Fm*, fluorine *F*, francium *Fr*, gadolinium *Gd*, gallium *Ga*, germanium *Ge*, gold *Au*, hafnium *Hf*, helium *He*, holmium *Ho*, hydrogen *H*, indium *In*, iodine *I*, iridium *Ir*, iron *Fe*, krypton *Kr*, lanthanum *La*, lawrencium *Lr*, lead *Pb*, lithium *Li*, lutetium *Lu*, magnesium *Mg*, manganese *Mn*, mendelevium *Md*, mercury *Hg*, molybdenum *Mo*.

neodymium *Nd*, neon, *Ne*, neptunium *Np*, nickel *Ni*, niobium *Nb*, nitrogen *N*, nobelium *No*, osmium *Os*, oxygen *O*, palladium *Pd*, phosphorus *P*, platinum *Pt*, plutonium *Pu*, polonium *Po*, potassium *K*, praseodymium *Pr*, promethium *Pm*, protactinium *Pa*, radium *Ra*, radon *Rn*, rhenium *Re*, rhodium *Rh*, rubidium *Rb*, ruthenium *Ru*.

samarium *Sm*, scandium *Sc*, selenium *Se*, silicon *Si*, silver *Ag*, sodium *Na*, strontium *Sr*, sulphur *S*, tantalum *Ta*, technetium *Tc*, tellurium *Te*, terbium *Tb*, thallium *Tl*, thorium *Th*, thulium, *Tm*, tin *Sn*, titanium *Ti*, tungsten *W*, uranium *U*, vanadium *V*, xenon *Xe*, ytterbium *Yb*, yttrium *Y*, zinc *Zn*, zirconium *Zr*.

---

chemist noun 1 OTHER SCIENTISTS: SEE **scientist**.
2 *I went to the chemist's for some medicine.* [*old-fashioned*] apothecary, [*American*] drug-store, pharmacist.

chemistry noun OTHER SCIENCES: SEE **science**.

cheque, cheque-card nouns [*American*] check, SEE **money**.

chequered adjective 1 *a chequered pattern.* check, criss-cross, in squares, like a chessboard, patchwork, tartan, tessellated.
2 *a chequered career.* SEE **changeable**.

cherish verb *I cherish the present you gave me.* be fond of, care for, foster, keep safe, look after, love, nourish, nurse, prize, protect, treasure, value.

cherry adjective SEE **red**.

cherub noun SEE **angel**.

cherubic adjective SEE **angelic**.

chess noun CHESSMEN: bishop, castle or rook, knight, king, queen, pawn.
TERMS USED IN CHESS: castle, check, checkmate, mate, move, stalemate, take.

chest noun 1 *a tool chest.* box, case, casket, coffer, crate, strongbox, trunk.
2 *a person's chest.* breast, rib-cage.
RELATED ADJECTIVE: pectoral.

chestnut adjective SEE **brown** adjective.

chevron noun SEE **badge**.

chew verb *to chew food.* bite, champ, crunch, SEE **eat**, gnaw, masticate, munch, nibble.

chewy adjective 1 *chewy toffee.* elastic, flexible, [*formal*] malleable, pliant, springy, sticky, stiff.
OPPOSITES: SEE **brittle**.
2 *chewy meat.* gristly, leathery, rubbery, tough.
OPPOSITES: SEE **tender**.

chic adjective SEE **elegant, fashionable**.

chicanery noun SEE **trickery**.

chick noun SEE **bird**.

chicken noun bantam, broiler, chick, cockerel, fowl, hen, pullet, rooster.

chicken verb **to chicken out** SEE **withdraw**.

chicken-feed noun SEE **small (small amount)**.

chicken-hearted adjective SEE **cowardly**.

chide verb SEE **scold**.

chief adjective 1 *the chief guest.* first, greatest, highest, major, most honoured, most important, principal.
OPPOSITES: SEE **unimportant**.
2 *the chief cook.* arch (*the arch enemy*), head, in charge, leading, most experienced, oldest, senior, supreme, top, unequalled, unrivalled.
OPPOSITES: SEE **junior**.
3 *the chief facts.* basic, cardinal, central, dominant, especial, essential, foremost, fundamental, high-priority, indispensable, key, main, necessary, outstanding, overriding, paramount, predominant, primary, prime, salient, significant, substantial, uppermost, vital, weighty.
OPPOSITES: SEE **unimportant**.

chief noun *Who's the chief around here?* administrator, authority-figure, [*informal*] bigwig, [*informal*] boss, captain, chairperson, chieftain, commander, commanding officer, commissioner, controller, director, employer, executive, foreman, [*informal*] gaffer, [*American*] godfather [*= chief criminal*], governor, head, leader, manager, master, mistress, officer, organizer, overseer, owner, president, principal, proprietor, responsible person, [*uncomplimentary*] ring-leader, ruler, superintendent, supervisor, [*informal*] supremo.
OPPOSITES: SEE **employee**.

chiefly adverb especially, essentially, generally, mainly, mostly, predominantly, primarily, principally, usually.

chieftain noun SEE **chief** noun.

child noun 1 *a growing child.* [*informal*] babe, baby, [*Scottish*] bairn, [*informal, from Italian*] bambino, boy, [*uncomplimentary*] brat, girl, [*uncomplimentary*] guttersnipe, infant, [*formal*] juvenile, [*informal*] kid, [*formal*] minor, [*informal*] nipper, offspring, toddler, [*informal*] tot, [*uncomplimentary*] urchin, youngster, youth.
2 *a child of wealthy parents.* daughter, descendant, heir, issue, offspring, progeny, son.
expert in children's illnesses paediatrician.

childbirth noun SEE **birth**.

childhood noun adolescence, babyhood, boyhood, girlhood, infancy, minority, schooldays, [*informal*] your teens, youth.

childish adjective [*Childish* is a word used by adults to describe behaviour or qualities they disapprove of, whereas *childlike* is used to describe qualities people generally approve of.] *It's childish to make rude noises.* babyish, foolish, immature, infantile, juvenile, puerile, silly.
OPPOSITES: SEE **mature**.

childlike adjective [See note under *childish*.] *a childlike trust in people's goodness.* artless, frank, guileless, ingenuous, innocent, naïve, natural, simple, trustful, unaffected, unsophisticated.
OPPOSITES: SEE **artful**.

chill adjective SEE **chilly**.

chill noun *The chill penetrated to our bones.* SEE **cold** noun.

chill verb **1** *The wind chilled us to the bone.* cool, freeze, make cold.
OPPOSITES: SEE **warm** verb.
2 *to chill food.* keep cold, refrigerate.

chilly adjective **1** *a chilly evening.* cold, cool, crisp, fresh, frosty, icy, [*informal*] nippy, [*informal*] parky, raw, sharp, wintry.
OPPOSITES: SEE **warm** adjective.
2 *a chilly greeting.* aloof, cool, dispassionate, frigid, hostile, ill-disposed, remote, reserved, [*informal*] standoffish, unforthcoming, unfriendly, unresponsive, unsympathetic, unwelcoming.
OPPOSITES: SEE **friendly**.

chime noun, verb SEE **bell**.

chimney noun flue, funnel, smokestack.

chimpanzee noun SEE **monkey**.

china noun crockery, earthenware, porcelain, SEE **pottery**.

chink noun **1** *a chink in the wall.* cleft, crack, crevice, cut, fissure, gap, opening, rift, slit, slot, space, split.
2 *the chink of glasses.* VARIOUS SOUNDS: SEE **sound** noun.

chip noun **1** *I knocked a chip off the cup.* bit, flake, fleck, fragment, piece, scrap, shaving, shiver, slice, sliver, splinter, wedge.
2 *I noticed a chip in the cup.* crack, damage, flaw, gash, nick, notch, scratch, snick.

chip verb *I chipped the cup.* break, crack, damage, gash, nick, notch, scratch, splinter.

chipboard noun OTHER KINDS OF WOODEN MATERIAL: SEE **wood**.

Several English words, including *chiropodist* and *chiropractor*, are related to Greek *kheir = hand.*

---

chiropodist noun pedicurist.

chiropractor noun manipulator, [*male*] masseur, [*female*] masseuse, osteopath, physiotherapist.

chirp noun, verb VARIOUS SOUNDS: SEE **sound** noun.

chirpy adjective SEE **cheerful**.

chirrup noun, verb VARIOUS SOUNDS: SEE **sound** noun.

chisel verb SEE **cut** verb.

chit noun SEE **note** noun.

chit-chat noun SEE **talk** noun.

chivalrous adjective *a chivalrous knight.* bold, brave, chivalric, courageous, courteous, courtly, gallant, generous, gentlemanly, heroic, honourable, knightly, noble, polite, respectable, true, trustworthy, valiant, valorous, worthy.
OPPOSITES: SEE **cowardly**, **dishonourable**, **rude**.

chivvy verb SEE **urge** verb.

chlorinate verb SEE **disinfect**.

chloroform noun SEE **anaesthetic**.

chock noun *a chock of wood.* block, chunk, lump, piece, slab, wedge, [*informal*] wodge.

chocolate adjective SEE **brown** adjective.

chocolate noun OTHER SWEETS: SEE **sweet** noun (**sweets**).

choice adjective SEE **excellent**.

choice noun **1** *The choice was between two good candidates.* alternative, choosing, dilemma, need to choose, option.
2 *The older candidate was our choice.* decision, election, liking, nomination, pick, preference, say, vote.
3 *The greengrocer has a good choice of vegetables.* array, assortment, diversity, miscellany, mixture, range, selection, variety.

choir noun choral society, chorus, vocal ensemble.
OTHER MUSICAL GROUPS: SEE **music**.

choke verb **1** *This collar is choking me.* asphyxiate, smother, stifle, strangle, suffocate, throttle.
2 *The firemen choked in the smoke.* gag, gasp, retch, suffocate.
3 *The roads were choked with traffic.* block, [*informal*] bung up, clog, close, congest, fill, jam, obstruct, smother, stop up.

choleric adjective SEE **angry**.

choose verb **1** *They chose a new leader. I chose a green anorak.* adopt, appoint, decide on, distinguish, draw lots for, elect, fix on, identify, isolate, name, nominate, opt for, pick out, [*informal*] plump for, select, settle on, show a preference for, single out, vote for.
2 *I chose to do it myself.* decide, determine, prefer, resolve.

choosy adjective SEE **fussy**.

chop verb *to chop wood.* cleave, SEE **cut** verb, hack, hew, slash, split.
to chop down cut down, fell.

to chop off amputate, detach, dock, lop, lop off, sever.
to chop up cut up, dice, divide, mince, share out, subdivide.
to chop and change SEE **change** verb.

chopper noun **1** axe, cleaver.
OTHER TOOLS: SEE **tool**.
2 helicopter.

choppy adjective *a choppy sea.* rippled, roughish, ruffled, turbulent, uneven, wavy.
OPPOSITES: SEE **smooth**.

chore noun *chores around the house.* boring work (SEE **boring**), burden, drudgery, duty, errand, job, task, work.

choreography noun SEE **dance** noun.

chorister noun SEE **singer**.

chortle verb SEE **laugh**.

chorus noun **1** choir, choral society, vocal ensemble.
OTHER MUSICAL GROUPS: SEE **music**.
2 *We all sang the chorus.* refrain, response.
in chorus SEE **together**.

christen verb *Tony was christened Antony.* baptize, dub, name.

Christmas noun the festive season, Noel, [*informal*] Xmas, Yule, Yuletide.

Several English words, including *chromatic* and *monochrome,* are related to Greek *khroma = colour.*

---

chromatic adjective **1** SEE **colourful**.
OPPOSITE: monochrome.
2 *the chromatic scale.* semitone.
OPPOSITE: diatonic.

chrome noun chromium.
chrome yellow SEE **yellow**.

Several English words, including *chronic, chronological, chronometer,* etc., are related to Greek *khronos = time.*

---

chronic adjective **1** *a chronic illness.* ceaseless, constant, continual, continuous, deep-rooted, everlasting, habitual, incessant, incurable, ineradicable, ingrained, lifelong, lingering, permanent, persistent, unending.
OPPOSITES: SEE **acute, temporary**.
2 [*informal*] *His driving is chronic!* SEE **bad**.

chronicle noun *a chronicle of events.* account, annals, diary, history, journal, narrative, record, saga, story.

chronological adjective *chronological order.* consecutive, sequential.

chronology noun calendar, dating, diary, order, schedule, sequence, timetable, timing.

chronometer noun clock, timepiece, watch.

chrysalis noun STAGES OF INSECT LIFE: SEE **insect**.

chubby adjective *a chubby figure.* buxom, dumpy, SEE **fat** adjective, plump, podgy, portly, rotund, round, stout, tubby.

chuck verb [*informal*] *Stop chucking rubbish in the water.* cast, ditch, dump, fling, heave, hurl, jettison, lob, pitch, shy, sling, throw, toss.
to chuck away, to chuck out discard, dispose of, reject, scrap, throw away.

chuckle verb SEE **laugh** verb.

chuffed adjective SEE **pleased**.

chug verb VARIOUS SOUNDS: SEE **sound** noun.

chum noun SEE **friend**.

chummy adjective SEE **friendly**.

chump noun SEE **idiot**.

chunk noun *a chunk of cheese. a chunk of wood.* bar, block, brick, chuck, [*informal*] dollop, hunk, lump, mass, piece, portion, slab, wad, wedge, [*informal*] wodge.

church noun

CHURCH BUILDINGS: abbey, basilica, cathedral, chapel, convent, monastery, nunnery, parish church, priory.

PARTS OF A CHURCH: aisle, belfry, buttress, chancel, chapel, cloister, crypt, dome, gargoyle, nave, porch, precinct, sacristy, sanctuary, spire, steeple, tower, transept, vestry.

THINGS YOU FIND IN A CHURCH: altar, Bible, candle, communion-table, crucifix, font, hymn-book, lectern, memorial tablet, pew, prayer-book, pulpit.

WORDS TO DO WITH CHURCH: Advent, angel, Ascension Day, Ash Wednesday, baptism, benediction, christening, Christmas, communion, confirmation, Easter, Good Friday, gospel, hymn, incense, Lent, martyr, mass, Nativity, New Testament, Old Testament, Palm Sunday, patron saint, Pentecost, prayer, preaching, psalm, requiem, Resurrection, sabbath, sacrament, saint, scripture, sermon, service, Whitsun, worship.

PEOPLE CONNECTED WITH CHURCH: archbishop, bishop, cardinal, chaplain, choirboy, choirgirl, churchwarden, clergyman, cleric, congregation, curate, deacon, deaconess, elder, evangelist, friar, layman, minister, missionary, monk, non-conformist, nun, padre, parson, pastor, Pope, preacher, prelate, priest, rector, sexton, sidesman, verger, vicar.

---

churchyard noun burial-ground, cemetery, graveyard.

churlish adjective SEE **rude**.

churn verb SEE **agitate**.

chute noun *a water-chute.* incline, ramp, slide, slope.

chutney noun pickle, relish.

ciao interjection SEE **goodbye**.

cinder noun *a cinder from a fire.* ash, clinker, ember.

cinder-track noun SEE **racecourse**.

cine-camera noun SEE **camera**.

cinema noun films, [*informal*] the movies, the pictures.

cipher noun SEE **character, code**.

circle noun **1** *a perfect circle.* ring.
2 *a large circle of friends.* association, band, body, clique, club, company, fellowship, fraternity, gang, SEE **group** noun, party, set, society.

LINES AND SHAPES IN RELATION TO A CIRCLE: arc, chord, diameter, radius, sector, segment, tangent.

VARIOUS CIRCULAR SHAPES OR MOVEMENTS: band, belt, circlet, circuit, circulation, circumference, circumnavigation, coil, cordon, curl, curve, cycle, disc, ellipse, girdle, globe, gyration, hoop, lap, loop, orb, orbit, oval, revolution, rotation, round, sphere, spiral, tour, turn, wheel, whirl, whorl.

---

circle verb **1** VARIOUS WAYS TO MAKE A CIRCLE OR TO MOVE IN A CIRCLE: circulate, circumnavigate, circumscribe, coil, compass, corkscrew, curl, curve, encircle, girdle, gyrate, hem in, loop, orbit, pirouette, pivot, reel, revolve, ring, rotate, spin, spiral, surround, swirl, swivel, tour, wheel, whirl, wind.
2 *The plane circled before landing.* go round, turn, wheel.
3 *Trees circled the lawn.* encircle, enclose, encompass, girdle, hem in, ring, skirt, surround.

circuit noun **1** SEE **circle** noun.
2 *a racing circuit.* SEE **racecourse**.
3 *I completed one circuit in record time.* lap, orbit, revolution.
4 *We made a circuit of the antique shops.* journey round, tour of.

circuitous adjective *a circuitous route.* curving, devious, indirect, labyrinthine, meandering, oblique, rambling, roundabout, serpentine, tortuous, twisting, winding, zigzag.
OPPOSITES: SEE **direct** adjective.

circular adjective **1** *a circular shape.* elliptical, oval, round.
2 *a circular argument.* cyclic, repeating, repetitive.

circular noun *an advertising circular.* advertisement, leaflet, letter, notice, pamphlet.

circulate verb **1** *I circulated round the room to speak to my friends.* SEE **circle** verb, go round, move about.
2 *We circulated a notice about our sale.* [*formal*] disseminate, distribute, issue, [*formal*] promulgate, publicize, publish, send round, spread about.

circulation noun **1** *the circulation of the blood.* flow, movement, pumping, recycling.
2 *the circulation of information.* broadcasting, dissemination, distribution, spread, transmission.
3 *the circulation of a newspaper.* distribution, sales-figures.

circumference noun *It's a mile round the circumference of the field.* border, boundary, circuit, edge, exterior, fringe, limit, margin, outline, outside, perimeter, periphery, rim, verge.

circumlocution noun SEE **verbiage**.

circumnavigate verb SEE **travel** verb.

circumscribe verb SEE **restrict**.

circumspect adjective SEE **cautious**.

circumstances noun [*usually plural*] *Don't jump to conclusions before you know the circumstances.* background, causes, conditions, considerations, context, contingencies, details, facts, factors, influences, particulars, position, situation, surroundings.

circumstantial adjective *circumstantial evidence.* conjectural, unprovable.
OPPOSITES: SEE **provable**.

circumvent verb SEE **evade**.

circus noun big top.

WORDS TO DO WITH A CIRCUS: acrobat, clown, contortionist, juggler, liontamer, ring, ringmaster, tightrope, trainer, trapeze, trapeze-artist.

---

cirrus noun SEE **cloud** noun.

cistern noun *a water cistern.* reservoir, tank.
OTHER CONTAINERS: SEE **container**.

citadel noun acropolis, bastion, castle, fort, fortification, fortress, garrison, stronghold, tower.

cite verb *She cited several authorities to support her case.* adduce, advance, [*informal*] bring up, enumerate, mention, name, quote, [*informal*] reel off, refer to, specify.

citizen noun *the citizens of a town or country.* [*old-fashioned*] burgess, commoner, denizen, householder, inhabitant, national, native, passport-holder, ratepayer, resident, subject, taxpayer, voter.

citrus fruit noun VARIOUS CITRUS FRUITS: clementine, grapefruit, lemon, lime, mandarin, orange, satsuma, tangerine.

city noun *London is a large city.* conurbation, metropolis, town.
RELATED ADJECTIVE: urban.

civil adjective **1** *I know you're angry, but try to be civil.* affable, civilized, considerate, courteous, obliging, SEE **polite**, respectful, well-bred, well-mannered.
OPPOSITES: SEE **impolite**.
2 *civil defence. civil liberties.* communal, national, public, social, state.
civil engineering SEE **engineering**.
civil rights freedom, human rights, legal rights, liberty, political rights.
civil servant administrator, bureaucrat, mandarin.

civilian adjective, noun
OPPOSITE: military.

civility noun SEE **politeness**.

civilization noun *the civilization of the ancient Egyptians.* achievements, attainments, culture, organization, refinement, sophistication, urbanity, urbanization.

civilize verb *Could we civilize monkeys?* cultivate, educate, enlighten, humanize, improve, make better, organize, refine, socialize, urbanize.

civilized adjective *a civilized nation. civilized behaviour.* cultivated, cultured, democratic, developed, educated, enlightened, orderly, polite, sophisticated, urbane, well-behaved, well-run.
OPPOSITES: SEE **uncivilized**.

clad adjective SEE **clothed**.

cladding noun SEE **covering**.

claim verb **1** *I claimed my reward.* ask for, collect, demand, exact, insist on, request, require, take.
2 *He claims that he's an expert.* affirm, allege, argue, assert, attest, contend, declare, insist, maintain, pretend, profess, state.

clairvoyant adjective *I could foretell the future if I had clairvoyant powers.* extrasensory, oracular, prophetic, psychic, telepathic.

clairvoyant noun fortune-teller, oracle, prophet, seer, sibyl, soothsayer.

clamber verb *We clambered over the rocks.* climb, crawl, move awkwardly, scramble.

clammy adjective *a clammy atmosphere. clammy hands.* damp, dank, humid, moist, muggy, slimy, sticky, sweaty.

clamour noun *The starlings made a clamour.* babel, commotion, din, hubbub, hullabaloo, noise, outcry, racket, row, screeching, shouting, storm (*a storm of protest*), uproar.

clamour verb *They clamoured for attention.* call out, cry out, exclaim, shout, yell.

clamp verb SEE **fasten**.

clan noun *a Scottish clan.* family, house, tribe.

clandestine adjective SEE **secret** adjective.

clang noun, verb, **clangour** noun VARIOUS SOUNDS: SEE **sound** noun.

clank noun, verb VARIOUS SOUNDS: SEE **sound** noun.

clannish adjective *a clannish family.* cliquish, close, close-knit, insular, isolated, narrow, united.

clap noun **1** *a clap of thunder.* SEE **sound** noun.
2 *a clap on the shoulder.* SEE **hit** noun.

clap verb **1** *We clapped her performance.* applaud.
2 *He clapped me on the shoulder.* SEE **hit** verb, pat, slap, smack.

claptrap noun SEE **nonsense**.

clarify verb **1** *Clarify what you want us to do.* define, elucidate, explain, gloss, illuminate, make clear, throw light on.
OPPOSITES: SEE **confuse**.
2 *I passed the wine through a filter to clarify it.* cleanse, clear, filter, purify, refine.

clarion adjective SEE **clear** adjective, **loud**.

clash noun **1** *the clash of cymbals.* SEE **sound** noun.
2 *a clash between enemies.* SEE **conflict** noun.

clash verb **1** *The cymbals clashed.* VARIOUS SOUNDS: SEE **sound** noun.
2 *The rival gangs clashed. The colours clash.* SEE **conflict** verb.

3 *My interview clashes with my dentist's appointment.* SEE **coincide.**

clasp noun 1 *a gold clasp.* brooch, buckle, catch, clip, fastener, fastening, hasp, hook, pin.

2 *a loving clasp.* cuddle, embrace, grasp, grip, hold, hug.

clasp verb 1 *to clasp things together.* SEE **fasten.**

2 *to clasp someone in your arms.* cling to, clutch, embrace, enfold, grasp, grip, hold, hug, squeeze.

3 *to clasp your hands.* hold together, wring.

clasp-knife noun SEE **knife** noun.

class noun 1 *in a class of its own.* category, classification, division, genre, genus, grade, group, kind, league, order, quality, rank, set, sort, species, sphere, type.

2 *social class.* caste, degree, grouping, standing, station, status.

TERMS SOMETIMES USED TO LABEL SOCIAL CLASSES: aristocracy, bourgeoisie, commoners, the commons, gentry, lower class, middle class, nobility, proletariat, ruling class, serfs, upper class, upper-middle class, the workers, working class.

---

3 *a class in a school.* band, form, group, set, stream.

class verb SEE **classify.**

classic adjective [It is useful to distinguish between *classic = excellent or typical of its kind,* and *classical = of the ancient Greeks and Romans,* or *classical = having an elegant style like that associated with classical times.*]

1 *a classic goal.* admirable, consummate, copybook, excellent, exceptional, exemplary, fine, first-class, first-rate, flawless, SEE **good**, ideal, [*informal*] immaculate, masterly, memorable, model, perfect, superlative, supreme, [*informal*] vintage.

OPPOSITES: SEE **commonplace.**

2 *classic works of literature.* abiding, ageless, deathless, enduring, established, immortal, lasting, time-honoured, undying.

OPPOSITES: SEE **ephemeral.**

3 *a classic case of chicken-pox.* archetypal, characteristic, regular, standard, typical, usual.

OPPOSITES: SEE **unusual.**

classic noun *This book is a classic!* masterpiece, model.

classical adjective [See note under *classic.*]

1 *classical civilizations.* ancient, Attic, Greek, Hellenic, Latin, Roman.

OPPOSITES: SEE **modern.**

2 *a classical style of architecture.* austere, dignified, elegant, pure, restrained, simple, symmetrical, well-proportioned.

OPPOSITES: SEE **exuberant.**

3 *classical music.* established, harmonious, highbrow.

OPPOSITES: SEE **modern, popular.**

classification noun *the classification of knowledge.* categorization, SEE **class** noun, codification, ordering, organization, systematization, tabulation, taxonomy.

classified adjective *classified information.* confidential, [*informal*] hush-hush, private, restricted, secret, sensitive, top secret.

classify verb *We classified the plants according to the shape of their leaves.* arrange, catalogue, categorize, class, grade, group, order, organize, [*informal*] pigeon-hole, put into sets, sort, systematize, tabulate.

classy adjective SEE **stylish.**

clatter noun, verb VARIOUS SOUNDS: SEE **sound** noun.

clause noun 1 *a clause in a legal document.* article, condition, item, paragraph, part, passage, provision, proviso, section, subsection.

2 *a clause in a sentence.* LINGUISTIC TERMS: SEE **language.**

claw noun *a bird's claws.* nail, talon.

claw verb *The animal clawed at its attacker.* graze, injure, lacerate, maul, rip, scrape, scratch, tear.

clean adjective 1 *a clean floor. clean clothes.* dirt-free, hygienic, immaculate, laundered, perfect, polished, sanitary, scrubbed, spotless, tidy, unsoiled, unstained, washed, wholesome.

OPPOSITES: SEE **dirty** adjective.

2 *clean water.* clarified, clear, decontaminated, distilled, fresh, pure, purified, sterilized, unadulterated, unpolluted.

OPPOSITES: SEE **impure.**

3 *clean paper.* blank, new, plain, uncreased, unmarked, untouched, unused.

OPPOSITES: SEE **used.**

4 *a clean edge. a clean incision.* neat, regular, smooth, straight, tidy.

OPPOSITES: SEE **jagged, ragged.**

5 *a clean fight.* chivalrous, fair, honest, honourable, sporting, sportsmanlike.

OPPOSITES: SEE **dishonourable.**

6 [*informal*] *a clean joke. clean thoughts.* chaste, decent, good, innocent, moral, respectable, upright, virtuous.

OPPOSITES: SEE **indecent.**

to make a clean breast (of) SEE **confess.**

clean verb VARIOUS WAYS TO CLEAN THINGS: bath, bathe, brush, buff, cleanse, decontaminate, deodorize, disinfect, dry-clean, dust, filter, flush, groom, hoover, launder, mop, polish, purge, purify, rinse, sand-blast, sanitize, scour, scrape, scrub, shampoo, shower, soap, sponge, spring-clean, spruce up, sterilize, swab, sweep, swill, vacuum, wash, wipe, wring out.
OPPOSITES: SEE **contaminate, dirty** verb.

cleanse verb SEE **clean** verb.

clean-shaven adjective beardless, shaved, shaven, shorn, smooth.
OPPOSITES: SEE **shaggy**.

clear adjective **1** *clear water.* clean, colourless, crystalline, glassy, limpid, pellucid, pure, transparent.
OPPOSITES: SEE **opaque**.
2 *a clear sky.* bright, cloudless, sunny, starlit, unclouded.
OPPOSITES: SEE **cloudy**.
3 *a clear conscience.* blameless, easy, guiltless, innocent, quiet, satisfied, sinless, undisturbed, untarnished, untroubled, unworried.
OPPOSITES: SEE **troubled**.
4 *a clear outline. a clear signal. clear handwriting.* bold, clean, definite, distinct, explicit, focused, legible, obvious, plain, positive, recognizable, sharp, simple, unambiguous, unmistakable, visible, well-defined.
OPPOSITES: SEE **indistinct**.
5 *a clear sound.* audible, clarion (*a clarion call*), distinct, penetrating, sharp.
OPPOSITES: SEE **muffled**.
6 *a clear explanation.* clear-cut, coherent, comprehensible, intelligible, lucid, perspicuous, unambiguous, understandable, unequivocal, well-presented.
OPPOSITES: SEE **confused**.
7 *a clear case of cheating.* apparent, blatant, conspicuous, evident, glaring, indisputable, manifest, noticeable, obvious, palpable, perceptible, plain, pronounced, straightforward, unconcealed, undisguised.
OPPOSITES: SEE **disputable**.
8 *a clear road. a clear space.* empty, free, open, passable, uncluttered, uncrowded, unhampered, unhindered, unimpeded, unobstructed.
OPPOSITES: SEE **congested**.

clear verb **1** *The fog cleared.* disappear, evaporate, fade, melt away, vanish.
2 *Wait for the water to clear. The weather cleared.* become clear, brighten, clarify, lighten, uncloud.
3 *I cleared the misty windows.* clean, make clean, make transparent, polish, wipe.
4 *I cleared the weeds from my garden.* disentangle, eliminate, get rid of, remove, strip.
5 *She cleared the blocked drainpipe.* clean out, free, loosen, open up, unblock, unclog.
6 *The court cleared him of all blame.* absolve, acquit, [*formal*] exculpate, excuse, exonerate, free, [*informal*] let off, liberate, release, vindicate.
7 *If the alarm goes, clear the building.* empty, evacuate.
8 *The horse cleared the fence.* bound over, jump, leap over, pass over, spring over, vault.
to clear away SEE **remove**.
to clear off SEE **depart**.
to clear up 1 *Clear up the mess.* clean, remove, put right, put straight, tidy.
2 *I asked her to clear up a difficulty.* answer, clarify, elucidate, explain, make clear, resolve, solve.

clear-cut adjective *Her proposal was clear-cut.* clear, coherent, definite, distinct, explicit, intelligible, lucid, plain, positive, precise, specific, straightforward, unambiguous, understandable, unequivocal, well-defined, well-presented.

clearing noun *a clearing in the forest.* gap, glade, opening, space.

clearway noun SEE **road**.

cleavage noun SEE **split** noun.

cleave verb SEE **cut** verb.

cleaver noun axe, chopper, knife.

cleft noun SEE **split** noun.

clemency noun SEE **mercy**.

clement adjective *clement weather.* balmy, calm, favourable, gentle, mild, peaceful, pleasant, temperate, warm.

clench verb **1** *to clench your teeth. to clench your fist.* clamp up, close tightly, double up, grit (your teeth), squeeze tightly.
2 *to clench something in your hand.* clasp, grasp, grip, hold.

clergyman noun VARIOUS CLERGYMEN: archbishop, bishop, canon, cardinal, chaplain, cleric, curate, deacon, deaconess, dean, evangelist, minister, ordained person, padre, parson, pastor, preacher, prelate, priest, rector, vicar.
OPPOSITES: SEE **layman**.

cleric noun SEE **clergyman**.

clerical adjective **1** *clerical work.* office, secretarial.
2 [= *of clerics, of clergymen*] *clerical duties.* ecclesiastical, pastoral, priestly, spiritual.

clerk noun VARIOUS PEOPLE DOING CLERICAL WORK: assistant, bookkeeper, computer operator, copyist, filing clerk, office boy, office girl, office worker, [*informal*] pen-pusher, receptionist, recorder, scribe, secretary, shorthand-typist, stenographer, typist, word-processor operator.

clever adjective *a clever child. a clever idea.* able, academic, accomplished, acute, adroit, apt, artful, artistic, astute, brainy, bright, brilliant, canny, capable, [*uncomplimentary*] crafty, [*uncomplimentary*] cunning, [*informal*] cute, [*informal*] deep (*She's a deep one!*), deft, dextrous, discerning, expert, gifted, [*informal*] handy, imaginative, ingenious, intellectual, intelligent, inventive, judicious, keen, knowing, knowledgeable, precocious, quick, quick-witted, rational, resourceful, sagacious, sensible, sharp, shrewd, skilful, skilled, [*uncomplimentary*] slick, smart, subtle, talented, [*uncomplimentary*] wily, wise, witty.
OPPOSITES: SEE **stupid, unskilful**.
a clever person [*informal*] egghead, expert, genius, [*uncomplimentary*] know-all, [*sexist*] mastermind, prodigy, sage, virtuoso [=*a brilliant performer*], wizard.

cleverness noun ability, acuteness, astuteness, brilliance, [*uncomplimentary*] cunning, expertise, ingenuity, intellect, intelligence, mastery, quickness, sagacity, sharpness, shrewdness, skill, subtlety, talent, wisdom, wit.
OPPOSITES: SEE **stupidity**.

cliché noun *He talks uninterestingly in boring clichés.* banality, commonplace, familiar phrase, hackneyed expression, platitude, well-worn phrase.

client noun *a client of the bank.* [*plural*] clientele [=*clients*], consumer, customer, patron, user.

clientele plural noun SEE **client**.

cliff noun bluff, crag, escarpment, precipice, rock-face, sheer drop.

climate noun **1** SEE **weather** noun.
2 *a climate of opinion.* ambience, atmosphere, disposition, environment, feeling, mood, spirit, temper, trend.

climax noun **1** *The music built up to a climax.* crisis, culmination, head, highlight, high point, peak, summit.
OPPOSITES: SEE **bathos**.
2 *a sexual climax.* orgasm.

climb noun *a steep climb.* ascent, gradient, hill, incline, rise, slope.

climb verb **1** *She climbed the rope.* ascend, clamber up, go up, mount, move up, scale, swarm up.
2 *The plane climbed steeply.* defy gravity, levitate, lift off, soar, take off.
3 *The road climbs steeply.* incline, rise, slope up.
4 *They climbed the mountain.* conquer, reach the top of.
to climb down SEE **descend, retreat** verb.

climber noun **1** mountaineer, rock-climber.
2 CLIMBING PLANTS INCLUDE: clematis, creeper, honeysuckle, hops, ivy, runner bean, vine.

clinch verb *to clinch a deal.* agree, close, conclude, confirm, decide, make certain of, ratify, settle, shake hands on, sign, verify.

cling verb **1** *Ivy clings to the wall.* adhere, fasten on, stick.
2 *The baby clung to its mother.* clasp, clutch, embrace, grasp, hug.

clinic noun health centre, infirmary, medical centre, sick-bay, surgery.

clinical adjective SEE **unemotional**.

clinker noun *clinker from a furnace.* ash, burnt remains, cinders, embers.

clip noun **1** *a paper clip.* VARIOUS FASTENERS: SEE **fastener**.
2 *a clip from a film.* excerpt, extract, fragment, passage, quotation, section, trailer.
3 [*infomal*] *a clip on the ear*. SEE **hit** noun.

clip verb **1** *to clip papers together.* SEE **fasten**, pin, staple.
2 *to clip a hedge.* crop, SEE **cut** verb, dock, prune, shear, snip, trim.
3 *to clip someone on the ear.* SEE **hit** verb.

clique noun SEE **group** noun.

cloak noun **1** *She wrapped a cloak around her.* cape, coat, cope, mantle, wrap.
2 *The thief operated under the cloak of darkness.* SEE **cover** noun.

clobber verb SEE **defeat** verb, **hit** verb.

clock noun **1** INSTRUMENTS USED TO MEASURE TIME: alarm-clock, chronometer, digital clock, grandfather clock, hour-glass, pendulum clock, sundial, watch.
2 *The car had only 1000 miles on the clock.* SEE **dial**.

clod noun SEE **lump** noun.

clog noun SEE **shoe**.

clog verb *The drain was clogged with leaves.* block, [*informal*] bung up, choke, close, congest, dam, fill, jam, obstruct, plug, stop up.

cloistered adjective SEE **secluded**.

clone noun SEE **copy** noun, **twin** noun.

close adjective **1** *a close position.* adjacent, adjoining, at hand, handy (for), near,

neighbouring, point-blank (*point-blank range*).
OPPOSITES: SEE **distant**.
2 *a close relationship.* affectionate, attached, dear, devoted, familiar, fond, friendly, intimate, loving, [*informal*] thick.
OPPOSITES: SEE **unfriendly**.
3 *a close comparison.* alike, analogous, comparable, compatible, corresponding, related, resembling, similar.
OPPOSITES: SEE **dissimilar**.
4 *a close crowd.* compact, congested, cramped, crowded, dense, [*informal*] jam-packed, packed, thick.
OPPOSITES: SEE **thin** adjective.
5 *a close examination.* attentive, careful, concentrated, detailed, minute, painstaking, precise, rigorous, searching, thorough.
OPPOSITES: SEE **cursory**.
6 *close about her private life.* confidential, private, reserved, reticent, secretive, taciturn.
OPPOSITES: SEE **open** adjective.
7 *close with money.* illiberal, mean, [*informal*] mingy, miserly, niggardly, parsimonious, penurious, stingy, tight, tight-fisted, ungenerous.
OPPOSITES: SEE **generous**.
8 *a close atmosphere.* airless, fuggy, humid, muggy, oppressive, stifling, stuffy, suffocating, sweltering, unventilated, warm.
OPPOSITES: SEE **airy**.

close noun 1 *By the close of business, the shop had taken £1000.* cessation, completion, conclusion, culmination, end, finish, stop, termination.
2 *the close of a piece of music.* cadence, coda, finale.
3 *the close of a play.* curtain, denouement, ending.

close verb 1 *Close the door.* bolt, fasten, lock, seal, secure, shut.
2 *The road was closed.* bar, barricade, block, obstruct, stop up.
3 *We closed the party with "Auld lang syne".* complete, conclude, culminate, discontinue, end, finish, stop, terminate, [*informal*] wind up.
4 *Close the gap.* fill, join up, make smaller, reduce, shorten.

closet noun SEE **cupboard**.

clot noun 1 *a clot of blood.* [*formal*] embolism [=*obstruction of an artery or vein*], lump, mass, thrombosis [=*clot of blood within the body*].
2 [*informal*] *He's a silly clot!* SEE **idiot**.

clot verb *When you cut yourself, blood clots and forms a scab.* coagulate, coalesce, congeal, curdle, make lumps, set, solidify, stiffen, thicken.

cloth noun *cloth to make clothes and curtains.* fabric, material, stuff, textile.

SOME KINDS OF CLOTH: astrakhan, bouclé, brocade, broderie anglaise, buckram, calico, cambric, candlewick, canvas, cashmere, cheesecloth, chenille, chiffon, chintz, corduroy, cotton, crepe, cretonne, damask, denim, dimity, drill, drugget.

elastic, felt, flannel, flannelette, gaberdine, gauze, georgette, gingham, hessian, holland, lace, lamé, lawn, linen, lint, mohair, moiré, moquette, muslin, nankeen, nylon, oilcloth, oilskin, organdie, organza, patchwork, piqué, plaid, plissé, plush, polycotton, polyester, poplin.

rayon, sackcloth, sacking, sailcloth, sarsenet, sateen, satin, satinette, seersucker, serge, silk, stockinet, taffeta, tapestry, tartan, terry, ticking, tulle, tussore, tweed, velour, velvet, velveteen, viscose, voile, winceyette, wool, worsted.

---

clothe verb *She always clothes her children nicely.* array, attire, cover, deck, drape, dress, garb, outfit, robe, swathe, wrap up.
OPPOSITES: SEE **strip** verb.
to clothe yourself in don, dress in, put on, wear.

clothed adjective *warmly clothed.* [*old-fashioned*] apparelled, attired, clad, dressed, fitted out, [*informal*] turned out (*well turned out*), wrapped up.

clothes noun apparel, attire, [*informal*] clobber, clothing, costume, dress, finery [=*best clothes*], garb, garments, [*informal*] gear, [*informal*] get-up, outfit, [*old-fashioned*] raiment, [*informal*] rig-out, trousseau [=*a bride's clothes*], underclothes, uniform, vestments [=*priest's clothes*], wardrobe, wear (*leisure wear*), weeds (*widow's weeds*).
RELATED ADJECTIVE: sartorial.

VARIOUS GARMENTS: anorak, apron, belt, bib, blazer, blouse, bodice, breeches, caftan, cagoule, cape, cardigan, cassock, chemise, chuddar, cloak, coat, cravat, crinoline, culottes, cummerbund, décolletage, doublet, dress, dressing-gown, duffel coat, dungarees, frock.

gaiters, garter, gauntlet, glove, gown, greatcoat, gym-slip, habit (*a monk's habit*), SEE **hat**, housecoat, jacket, jeans, jerkin, jersey, jodhpurs, jumper, kilt, knickers, leg-warmers, leotard, livery, loincloth, lounge suit.

mackintosh, mantle, miniskirt, mitten, muffler, necktie, négligé, night-clothes, night-dress, oilskins, overalls, overcoat, pants, parka, pinafore, poncho, pullover, pyjamas, raincoat, robe, rompers.

sari, sarong, scarf, shawl, shirt, SEE **shoe**, shorts, singlet, skirt, slacks, smock, sock, sou'wester, spats, stocking, stole, suit, surplice, sweater, sweatshirt, tail-coat, tie, tights, trousers, trunks, t-shirt, tunic, tutu, SEE **underclothes**, uniform, waistcoat, wet-suit, wind-cheater, wrap, yashmak.

PARTS OF A GARMENT: bodice, buttonhole, collar, cuff, hem, lapel, pocket, sleeve.

---

clothing noun SEE **clothes**.

cloud noun **1** KINDS OF CLOUD: altocumulus, altostratus, cirrocumulus, cirrostratus, cirrus, cumulonimbus, cumulus, mackerel sky, nimbostratus, rain cloud, storm cloud, stratocumulus, stratus.
2 *a cloud of steam.* billow, haze, mass, mist, puff.

cloud verb *Mist clouded our view.* blur, conceal, cover, darken, dull, eclipse, enshroud, hide, mantle, mist up, obfuscate, obscure, screen, shroud, veil.

cloudburst noun SEE **rain**.

cloudless adjective *a cloudless sky.* bright, clear, starlit, sunny, unclouded.
OPPOSITES: SEE **cloudy**.

cloudy adjective **1** *a cloudy sky.* dark, dismal, dull, gloomy, grey, leaden, lowering, overcast, sullen, sunless.
OPPOSITES: SEE **cloudless**.
2 *cloudy windows.* blurred, blurry, dim, misty, opaque, steamy, unclear.
3 *cloudy liquid.* hazy, milky, muddy, murky.
OPPOSITES: SEE **transparent**.

clout noun, verb SEE **hit** noun, verb.

clown noun buffoon, comedian, comic, fool, jester, joker.

cloying adjective sweet, syrupy.
OPPOSITES: SEE **refreshing**.

club noun **1** *a club to hit someone with.* bat, baton, bludgeon, cosh, cudgel, stick, truncheon.
2 *a football club. a book club.* association, circle, company, group, league, order, organization, party, set, society, union.

club verb *to club someone to death.* SEE **hit** verb.
to club together SEE **combine**.

clubbable adjective SEE **sociable**.

clue noun *I don't know the answer—give me a clue.* hint, idea, indication, inkling, key, lead, pointer, sign, suggestion, tip.

clump noun *a clump of daffodils. a clump of trees.* bunch, bundle, cluster, collection, SEE **group** noun, mass, shock (*a shock of hair*), thicket, tuft.

clumsy adjective **1** *clumsy movements. a clumsy person.* awkward, blundering, bumbling, bungling, fumbling, gangling, gawky, graceless, [*informal*] ham-fisted, heavy-handed, hulking, inelegant, lumbering, maladroit, shambling, uncoordinated, ungainly, ungraceful, unskilful.
OPPOSITES: SEE **dainty, skilful**.
2 *a clumsy raft.* amateurish, badly made, bulky, cumbersome, heavy, inconvenient, inelegant, large, ponderous, rough, shapeless, unmanageable, unwieldy.
OPPOSITES: SEE **neat**.
3 *He made a clumsy remark about her illness.* boorish, gauche, ill-judged, inappropriate, indelicate, indiscreet, inept, insensitive, tactless, uncouth, undiplomatic, unsubtle, unsuitable.
OPPOSITES: SEE **tactful**.
a clumsy person botcher, bungler, [*informal*] butterfingers, fumbler.

cluster noun *a cluster of trees. a cluster of people.* assembly, batch, bunch, clump, collection, crowd, gathering, SEE **group** noun, knot.

clutch noun **1** [*usually plural*] *He had us in his clutches.* clasp, control, evil embrace, grasp, grip, hold, possession, power.
2 *a clutch of eggs.* SEE **group** noun.

clutch verb *He clutched the rope.* catch, clasp, cling to, grab, grasp, grip, hang on to, hold on to, seize, snatch.

clutter noun *We'll have to clear up all this clutter.* confusion, disorder, jumble, junk, litter, lumber, mess, mix-up, muddle, odds and ends, rubbish, untidiness.

clutter verb *Her belongings clutter up my bedroom.* be scattered about, fill, lie about, litter, make untidy, [*informal*] mess up, muddle, strew.

coach noun **1** *a motor coach.* bus, [*old-fashioned*] charabanc.
OTHER VEHICLES: SEE **vehicle**.
2 *a football coach.* instructor, teacher, trainer.

coach verb *to coach a football team.* instruct, prepare, teach, train, tutor.

coagulate verb clot, congeal, curdle, [*informal*] jell, solidify, stiffen, thicken.

coal noun anthracite, coke.
OTHER FUELS: SEE **fuel** noun.

coalesce verb SEE **combine**.

coalition noun SEE **combination**.

coarse adjective **1** *coarse cloth. coarse sand.* bristly, gritty, hairy, harsh, lumpy, rough, scratchy, sharp, stony.
OPPOSITES: SEE **soft**.
2 *coarse language.* bawdy, blasphemous, boorish, common, crude, earthy, foul, immodest, impolite, improper, impure, indecent, indelicate, offensive, ribald, rude, smutty, uncouth, unrefined, vulgar.
OPPOSITES: SEE **polite**.

coast noun beach, coastline, seaboard, sea-shore, seaside, shore.

coast verb *to coast down a hill on a bike.* cruise, drift, free-wheel, glide, sail.

coastal adjective *a coastal town.* maritime, nautical, naval, seaside.

coastline noun SEE **coast** noun.

coat noun **1** KINDS OF COAT YOU CAN WEAR: anorak, blazer, cagoule, cardigan, dinner-jacket, doublet, duffel coat, greatcoat, jacket, jerkin, mackintosh, overcoat, raincoat, tail-coat, tunic, tuxedo, waistcoat, wind-cheater.
OTHER GARMENTS: SEE **clothes**.
2 *an animal's coat.* fleece, fur, hair, hide, pelt, skin.
3 *a coat of paint.* coating, cover, covering, film, finish, glaze, layer, membrane, patina, sheet, veneer, wash.
coat of arms badge, crest, emblem, heraldic device, shield.

coat verb SEE **cover** verb.

coax verb *We coaxed the animal back into its cage.* allure, beguile, cajole, decoy, entice, induce, inveigle, persuade, tempt, wheedle.

cobble noun pebble, stone.

cobble verb *to cobble something together.* botch, knock up, make, mend, patch up, put together.

cobbled adjective *a cobbled street.* OTHER SURFACES: SEE **road**.

cobbler noun shoemaker, shoe-mender, shoe-repairer.

cock noun SEE **bird**.

cockerel noun SEE **chicken** noun.

cocksure adjective SEE **confident**.

cocktail noun OTHER DRINKS: SEE **drink** noun.

cocky adjective SEE **bumptious**.

cocoon noun SEE **wrapping**.

coda noun SEE **end** noun.

coddle verb *to coddle a baby.* SEE **pamper**.

code noun **1** *The Highway Code. a code of conduct.* etiquette, laws, manners, regulations, rule-book, rules, system.
2 *a message in code.* cipher, Morse code, secret language, semaphore, sign-system, signals.

codger noun SEE **man** noun.

codicil noun SEE **appendix**.

codify verb SEE **systematize**.

coeducational adjective *a coeducational school.* mixed.

coerce verb *I was coerced into joining the gang.* bludgeon, browbeat, bully, compel, constrain, dragoon, force, frighten, intimidate, press-gang, pressurize, terrorize.

coercion noun *We prefer you to work voluntarily rather than by coercion.* browbeating, brute force, bullying, compulsion, conscription [*into the armed services*], constraint, duress, force, intimidation, physical force, pressure, [*informal*] strong-arm tactics, threats.

coffee noun KINDS OF COFFEE: black coffee, café au lait, espresso, Irish coffee, white coffee.

coffer noun *coffers full of money.* box, cabinet, case, casket, chest, crate, trunk.

coffin noun sarcophagus.

cog noun tooth.

cogent adjective *a cogent argument.* compelling, conclusive, convincing, effective, forceful, forcible, indisputable, irresistible, persuasive, potent, powerful, rational, strong, unanswerable, weighty, well-argued.

cogitate verb SEE **think**.

Cognac noun brandy.

cognate adjective SEE **related**.

cognition noun SEE **understanding**.

cognizant adjective SEE **aware**.

cog-wheel noun gearwheel, toothed wheel.

cohabit verb live together.

cohere verb *When you squeeze a handful of snow, the flakes cohere to make a snowball.* bind, cake, cling together, coalesce, combine, consolidate, fuse, hang together, hold together, join, stick together, unite.

coherent adjective *a coherent argument. coherent speech.* articulate, clear, cohering, cohesive, connected, consistent, convincing, intelligible, logical, lucid,

orderly, organized, rational, reasonable, reasoned, sound, structured, systematic, understandable, well-structured.
OPPOSITES: SEE **incoherent**.

cohesive adjective SEE **coherent**.

cohort noun SEE **armed services**.

coiffure noun SEE **hair-style**.

coil noun VARIOUS COILED SHAPES OR MOVEMENTS: circle, convolution, corkscrew, curl, helix, kink, loop, ring, roll, screw, spiral, twirl, twist, vortex, whirl, whorl.
the coil SEE **contraception**.

coil verb *The sailor coiled the rope. The snake coiled round a branch.* bend, curl, entwine, loop, roll, snake, spiral, turn, twine, twirl, twist, wind, writhe.

coin noun *a fifty pence coin.* bit, piece.
coins *I haven't any coins, only notes.* change, coppers, loose change, silver, small change.
SEE ALSO **money**.
collector of coins numismatist.

coin verb **1** *It's a serious offence to coin money.* forge, make, mint, mould, stamp.
2 *We coined a new name for our group.* conceive, concoct, create, devise, dream up, fabricate, hatch, introduce, invent, make up, originate, produce, think up.

coincide verb **1** *My birthday coincides with a bank holiday.* clash, coexist, fall together, happen together, synchronize.
2 *Our answers coincided.* accord, agree, be identical, be in unison, be the same, concur, correspond, harmonize, match, square, tally.

coincidence noun *We met by coincidence.* accident, chance, fluke, luck.

coincidental adjective SEE **chance** adjective.

coitus noun SEE **sex**.

cold adjective **1** *cold weather. a cold wind. a cold place.* arctic, biting, bitter, bleak, chill, chilly, cool, crisp, cutting, draughty, freezing, fresh, frosty, glacial, icy, inclement, keen, [*informal*] nippy, numbing, [*informal*] parky, penetrating, perishing, piercing, polar, raw, shivery, Siberian, snowy, unheated, wintry.
OPPOSITES: SEE **hot**.
2 *cold hands.* blue with cold, chilled, dead, frostbitten, frozen, numbed, shivering, shivery.
OPPOSITES: SEE **warm** adjective.
3 *a cold attitude. a cold heart.* aloof, callous, cold-blooded, cool, cruel, distant, frigid, hard, hard-hearted, heartless, indifferent, inhospitable, inhuman, insensitive, passionless, phlegmatic, reserved, standoffish, stony, uncaring, unconcerned, undemonstrative, unemotional, unenthusiastic, unfeeling, unfriendly, unkind, unresponsive, unsympathetic.
OPPOSITES: SEE **kind** adjective, **passionate**.

cold noun **1** *Our cat doesn't like the cold.* chill, coldness, coolness, freshness, iciness, low temperature, wintriness.
OPPOSITES: SEE **heat** noun.
to feel the cold freeze, quiver, shake, shiver, shudder, suffer from hypothermia, tremble.
2 *She's got a nasty cold.* chill, cough.
SYMPTOMS OF A COLD: catarrh, coughing, runny nose, sneezing, sniffing, snuffling.

cold-blooded adjective [*Cold-blooded* properly refers to animals whose body temperature varies with the temperature of their surroundings, but it is often used to describe *inhuman* aspects of human behaviour or character.] *a cold-blooded killing.* barbaric, brutal, callous, cold, cold-hearted, SEE **cruel**, dispassionate, hard-hearted, heartless, impassive, inhuman, insensitive, merciless, pitiless, ruthless, savage, unemotional, unfeeling.
OPPOSITES: SEE **humane**.

cold-hearted adjective SEE **cold-blooded**.

cold-shoulder verb SEE **ostracize**.

colic noun stomach ache, [*informal*] tummy ache.

collaborate verb **1** *The work gets done more quickly when we collaborate.* band together, [*uncomplimentary*] collude, [*uncomplimentary*] connive, co-operate, join forces, [*informal*] pull together, team up, work together.
2 *to collaborate with an enemy.* be a collaborator, join the opposition, [*informal*] rat, turn traitor.

collaboration noun *collaboration between partners.* association, [*uncomplimentary*] collusion, [*uncomplimentary*] connivance, concerted effort, co-operation, partnership, tandem, team-work.

collaborator noun **1** *I need a collaborator to help me.* accomplice (*in wrongdoing*), ally, assistant, associate, co-author, colleague, confederate, fellow worker, helper, helpmate, partner, [*joking*] partner-in-crime.
2 *a collaborator with the enemy.* blackleg, [*informal*] Judas, quisling, [*informal*] scab, traitor, turncoat.

collage noun SEE **picture**.

collapse noun *An earthquake caused the collapse of the hotel.* break-up, cave-in, destruction, downfall, end, fall, ruin, ruination, subsidence, wreck.

collapse verb **1** *Many buildings collapsed in the earthquake.* buckle, cave in, crumble, crumple, disintegrate, fall apart, fall in, fold up, give in, [*informal*] go west, sink, subside, tumble down.
2 *People collapsed in the heat.* be ill, [*informal*] bite the dust, faint, fall down, founder, [*informal*] go under.
3 *Ice-cream sales collapsed in the cold weather.* become less, crash, deteriorate, drop, fail, slump, worsen.

collapsible adjective *a tripod with collapsible legs.* adjustable, folding, retractable, telescopic.

collar verb SEE **capture**.

collate verb SEE **arrange**.

colleague noun SEE **collaborator**, **fellow**.

collect verb **1** *Squirrels collect nuts.* accumulate, agglomerate, aggregate, amass, bring together, garner, gather, harvest, heap, hoard, lay up, pile up, put by, reserve, save, scrape together, stockpile, store.
2 *A crowd collected to watch the fire.* assemble, cluster, come together, congregate, convene, converge, crowd, forgather, group, muster, rally round.
OPPOSITES: SEE **disperse**.
3 *We collected a large sum for charity.* be given, raise, secure, take.
4 *I collected the bread from the baker's.* acquire, bring, fetch, get, obtain.

collected adjective SEE **calm** adjective.

collection noun **1** accumulation, array, assortment, cluster, conglomeration, heap, hoard, mass, pile, set, stack.

VARIOUS COLLECTIONS OF PEOPLE AND THINGS: anthology (*of poems, etc.*), arsenal (*of weapons*), assembly (*of people*), batch (*of cakes, etc.*), company, congregation (*of worshippers*), crowd, gathering, SEE **group** noun, library (*of books*), stockpile (*of weapons*).

---

2 *a collection for charity.* [*old-fashioned*] alms-giving, flag-day, free-will offering, offertory, voluntary contributions, [*informal*] whip-round.

collective adjective *a collective decision.* combined, common, composite, co-operative, corporate, democratic, group, joint, shared, unified, united.
OPPOSITES: SEE **individual** adjective.

college noun academy, conservatory, institute, polytechnic, school (*art school, etc.*), university.

collide verb **to collide with** *The car collided with the gate-post.* bump into, cannon into, crash into, SEE **hit** verb, knock, meet, run into, slam into, smash into, strike, touch.

collier noun coal-miner, miner.

colliery noun coal-mine, mine.

collision noun *a collision on the motorway.* accident, bump, clash, crash, head-on collision, impact, knock, pile-up, scrape, smash.

colloquial adjective *colloquial language.* chatty, conversational, everyday, informal, slangy, [*formal*] vernacular.
OPPOSITES: SEE **formal**.

colloquy noun SEE **conversation**.

collude verb SEE **connive**.

collusion noun SEE **conspiracy**.

collywobbles noun **1** [*slang*] *I had collywobbles after eating too much fruit.* [*informal*] belly-ache, stomach-ache, [*informal*] tummy-ache.
2 [*slang*] *I had collywobbles before my interview.* SEE **nervous (to be nervous)**.

colonist noun *Some of the early colonists were cruel to the native population.* colonizer, explorer, pioneer, settler.
OPPOSITES: SEE **native** noun.

colonize verb *to colonize a territory.* found a colony in, move into, occupy, people, populate, settle in, subjugate.

colony noun **1** *At one time Britain had colonies all over the world.* dependency, dominion, possession, protectorate, province, settlement, territory.
2 *a colony of ants.* SEE **group** noun.

coloration noun SEE **colour** noun.

colossal adjective *A colossal statue towered above us.* SEE **big**, elephantine, enormous, gargantuan, giant, gigantic, huge, immense, mammoth, massive, mighty, monstrous, monumental, prodigious, titanic, towering, vast.
OPPOSITES: SEE **small**.

colour noun **1** coloration, colouring, hue, shade, tincture, tinge, tint, tone.

SUBSTANCES WHICH GIVE COLOUR: cochineal, colourant, colouring, cosmetics, dye, make-up, SEE **paint** noun, pigment, pigmentation, stain, tincture, woad.

VARIOUS COLOURS: amber, azure, beige, black, blue, brindled, bronze, brown, buff, carroty, cherry, chestnut, chocolate, cobalt, cream, crimson, dun, fawn, gilt, gold, golden, green, grey, indigo, ivory, jet-black, khaki, lavender, maroon, mauve, navy blue, ochre, olive, orange, pink, puce, purple, red, rosy, russet, sandy, scarlet, silver, tan, tawny, turquoise, vermilion, violet, white, yellow.

---

2 *colour in your cheeks.* bloom, blush, flush, glow, rosiness, ruddiness.
colours *the colours of a regiment.* banner, ensign, flag, standard.

colour verb **1** *to colour a picture.* colourwash, dye, paint, shade, stain, tinge, tint.
2 *His fair skin colours easily.* blush, bronze, brown, burn, flush, redden, tan.
OPPOSITES: SEE **fade**.
3 *An umpire shouldn't let her prejudices colour her decisions.* affect, bias, distort, impinge on, influence, pervert, prejudice, slant, sway.

colourful adjective **1** *colourful flowers. a colourful scene.* bright, brilliant, chromatic, gaudy, iridescent, multicoloured, psychedelic, showy, vibrant.
OPPOSITES: SEE **colourless**, **pale** adjective.
2 *a colourful description.* exciting, florid, graphic, picturesque, rich, stimulating, striking, telling, vivid.
OPPOSITES: SEE **dull** adjective, **plain** adjective.
3 *a colourful personality.* dashing, distinctive, dynamic, SEE **eccentric**, energetic, flamboyant, flashy, glamorous, interesting, lively, publicity-seeking, unusual, vigorous.
OPPOSITES: SEE **restrained**.

colouring noun SEE **colour** noun.

colourless adjective **1** *a colourless substance.* albino, black, faded, grey, monochrome, neutral, SEE **pale** adjective, [*informal*] washed-out, white.
2 *a colourless personality. a colourless scene.* boring, characterless, dingy, dismal, dowdy, drab, dreary, dull, insipid, lacklustre, shabby, tame, uninteresting, vacuous, vapid.
OPPOSITES: SEE **colourful**.

colt noun SEE **horse**.

column noun **1** *columns supporting a roof.* pilaster, pile, pillar, pole, post, prop, shaft, support, upright.
2 *I write a column in a local newspaper.* article, feature, leader, leading article, piece.
3 *a column of figures. a column of writing.* vertical division, vertical section.
4 *a column of soldiers.* cavalcade, file, line, procession, queue, rank, row, string, train.

columnist noun SEE **journalist**.

coma noun SEE **unconsciousness**.

comatose adjective SEE **unconscious**.

comb verb **1** *to comb your hair.* arrange, groom, neaten, smarten up, spruce up, tidy, untangle.
2 *I combed the house in search of my pen.* hunt through, ransack, rummage through, scour, search thoroughly.

combat noun *a fierce combat.* action, battle, bout, clash, conflict, contest, duel, encounter, engagement, fight, SEE **martial (martial arts)**, skirmish, struggle, war, warfare.

combat verb *to combat crime.* battle against, contend against, contest, counter, defy, face up to, fight, grapple with, oppose, resist, stand up to, strive against, struggle against, tackle, withstand.

combatant noun SEE **fighter**.

combination noun *a combination of things. a combination of people.* aggregate, alliance, alloy, amalgam, amalgamation, association, blend, coalition, compound, concoction, concurrence, confederacy, confederation, conjunction, consortium, conspiracy, federation, fusion, link-up, marriage, merger, mix, mixture, partnership, syndicate, synthesis, unification, union.

combine verb **1** *to combine resources.* add together, amalgamate, bind, blend, bring together, compound, fuse, integrate, intertwine, interweave, join, link, [*informal*] lump together, marry, merge, mingle, mix, pool, put together, synthesize, unify, unite.
2 *to combine as a team.* associate, band together, club together, coalesce, connect, co-operate, gang together, join forces, team up.

combustible adjective *Don't smoke near combustible materials.* flammable, inflammable.
OPPOSITE: incombustible.

combustion noun SEE **fire** noun.

come verb **1** *Visitors are coming tomorrow.* appear, arrive, visit.
2 *Spring came suddenly this year.* advance, draw near, materialize, occur.
3 *Tell me when we come to my station.* approach, arrive at, get to, near, reach.
to come about SEE **happen**.
to come across SEE **find**.
to come clean SEE **confess**.
to come out with SEE **say**.
to come round SEE **recover**.
to come up SEE **arise**.
to come upon SEE **find**.

come-back noun SEE **retort** noun.

comedian noun buffoon, clown, comic, SEE **entertainer**, fool, humorist, jester, joker, wag.

come-down noun SEE **anticlimax**.

comedy noun buffoonery, clowning, facetiousness, farce, hilarity, humour, jesting, joking, satire, slapstick, wit. SEE ALSO **entertainment**.

comestibles noun SEE **food**.

comet noun ASTRONOMICAL TERMS: SEE **astronomy**.

comfort noun **1** *to live in comfort.* affluence, contentment, cosiness, ease, luxury, opulence, relaxation, well-being.
2 *We tried to give the injured woman some comfort.* aid, cheer, consolation, encouragement, help, moral support, reassurance, relief, solace, succour, sympathy.
OPPOSITES: SEE **discomfort**.

comfort verb *He was upset, so we tried to comfort him.* assuage, calm, cheer up, console, ease, encourage, gladden, hearten, help, reassure, relieve, solace, soothe, succour, sympathize with.

comfortable adjective **1** *a comfortable chair. a comfortable place to rest.* [*informal*] comfy, convenient, cosy, easy, padded, reassuring, relaxing, roomy, snug, soft, upholstered, warm.
2 *comfortable clothes.* informal, loose-fitting, well-fitting, well-made.
3 *a comfortable life-style.* affluent, agreeable, contented, happy, homely, luxurious, pleasant, prosperous, relaxed, restful, serene, well-off.
OPPOSITES: SEE **uncomfortable**.

comfy adjective SEE **comfortable**.

comic adjective *a comic situation. comic remarks.* absurd, amusing, comical, diverting, droll, facetious, farcical, funny, hilarious, humorous, hysterical, jocular, joking, laughable, ludicrous, [*informal*] priceless, [*informal*] rich (*That's rich!*), ridiculous, SEE **sarcastic**, sardonic, satirical, side-splitting, silly, uproarious, waggish, witty.

comic noun **1** *A comic sang songs and made us laugh.* SEE **comedian**.
2 *She bought a comic to read on the train.* SEE **magazine**.

command noun **1** *Do you always obey commands?* behest, bidding, commandment (*the Ten Commandments*), decree, directive, edict, injunction, instruction, order, requirement, ultimatum, writ.
2 *She has command of the whole expedition.* authority (over), charge, control, direction, government, management, power (over), rule (over), supervision, sway (over).

command verb **1** *He commanded us to stop.* adjure, bid, charge, compel, decree, demand, direct, enjoin, instruct, ordain, order, require.
2 *A captain commands his ship.* administer, be in charge of, control, direct, govern, head, lead, manage, reign over, rule, supervise.

commandant noun SEE **officer**.

commandeer verb *The police commandeered a passing car to help in the emergency.* appropriate, confiscate, hijack, impound, requisition, seize, sequester, take over.

commander noun captain, SEE **chief** noun, commanding-officer, general, head, leader, officer-in-charge.

commandment noun SEE **command** noun.

commando noun SEE **armed services**.

commemorate verb *a ceremony to commemorate those who died in war.* be a memorial to, be a reminder of, celebrate, honour, keep alive the memory of, pay your respects to, pay tribute to, remember, salute, solemnize.

commence verb SEE **begin**.

commend verb *The boss commended our effort.* acclaim, applaud, approve of, compliment, congratulate, eulogize, extol, praise, recommend.
OPPOSITES: SEE **criticize**.

commendable adjective SEE **praiseworthy**.

commensurate adjective SEE **comparable, proportionate**.

comment verb **1** *I heard several comments about the way we played.* animadversion [=*hostile comment*], criticism, mention, observation, opinion, reference, remark, statement.
2 *Teachers write comments on pupils' work.* annotation, footnote, gloss, note.

comment verb *I commented that the weather had been bad.* explain, interject, interpose, mention, note, observe, remark, say.

commentary noun **1** *a commentary on a football match.* account, broadcast, description, report.
2 *We wrote a commentary on the novel we were studying.* analysis, criticism, critique, discourse, elucidation, explanation, interpretation, notes, review, treatise.

commentator noun *a radio commentator.* announcer, broadcaster, journalist, reporter.

commerce noun *A healthy economy depends on commerce.* business, buying and selling, dealings, financial transactions, marketing, merchandising, trade, trading, traffic.

commercial adjective **1** *commercial dealings.* business, economic, financial, mercantile.
2 *a commercial success.* financially successful, monetary, money-making, pecuniary, profitable, profit-making.

commercial noun *a TV commercial.* [*informal*] ad, [*informal*] advert, advertisement, [*informal*] break (*commercial break*), [*informal*] plug.

commercialize verb [*Commercialize* can mean *to make commercial or profitable*, but it can also mean *to debase or spoil something by making it commercial*: e.g. *Christmas has become commercialized.*] SEE **debase**.

commiserate verb *We commiserated with the losers.* comfort, condole, console, express sympathy for, feel for, SEE **sympathize**.
OPPOSITES: SEE **congratulate**.

commission noun **1** *a commission in the armed services.* appointment, promotion, warrant.
VARIOUS RANKS: SEE **rank** noun.
2 *a commission to paint a portrait.* booking, order, request.
3 *a commission to investigate a complaint.* SEE **committee**.
4 *a salesperson's commission on a sale.* allowance, [*informal*] cut, fee, percentage, [*informal*] rake-off, reward.

commissioner noun SEE **official** noun.

commit verb **1** *to commit a crime.* be guilty of, carry out, do, enact, execute, perform, perpetrate.
2 *to commit valuables to someone's safekeeping.* consign, deliver, deposit, entrust, give, hand over.
to commit yourself *I committed myself to help with the jumble sale.* contract, covenant, guarantee, pledge, promise, undertake, vow.

commitment noun **1** *The builder had a commitment to finish the work on time.* assurance, duty, guarantee, liability, pledge, promise, undertaking, vow, word.
2 *The Green party has a commitment to conservation.* adherence, dedication, determination, involvement, loyalty.
3 *I checked my diary to see if I had any commitments.* appointment, arrangement, engagement.

committed adjective *a committed member of a political party.* active, ardent, [*informal*] card-carrying, dedicated, devoted, earnest, enthusiastic, fervent, firm, keen, passionate, resolute, single-minded, staunch, unwavering, whole-hearted, zealous.
OPPOSITES: SEE **apathetic**.

committee noun GROUPS WHICH MAKE DECISIONS, ETC.: advisory group, assembly, board, cabinet, caucus, commission, convention, council, discussion group, junta, jury, panel, parliament, quango, synod, think-tank, working party.
SEE ALSO **meeting**.

commodious adjective SEE **roomy**.

commodity noun SEE **product**.

common adjective **1** *common knowledge.* accepted, collective, communal, general, joint, mutual, open, popular, public, shared, universal.
OPPOSITES: SEE **individual** adjective.
2 *a common happening.* average, [*informal*] common or garden, SEE **commonplace**, conventional, customary, daily, everyday, familiar, frequent, habitual, normal, ordinary, popular, prevalent, regular, routine, [*informal*] run-of-the-mill, standard, traditional, typical, unsurprising, usual, well-known, widespread.
OPPOSITES: SEE **uncommon**.
3 [*informal*] *common behaviour.* boorish, churlish, coarse, crude, disreputable, ill-bred, loutish, low, plebeian, rude, uncouth, unrefined, vulgar, [*informal*] yobbish.
OPPOSITES: SEE **refined**.
4 *of common birth.* lowly.
OPPOSITES: SEE **aristocratic**.

common noun *We play football on the common.* heath, park.

commoners noun SEE **class** noun.

commonplace adjective *a commonplace event. a commonplace remark.* banal, boring, SEE **common** adjective, familiar, forgettable, hackneyed, humdrum, mediocre, obvious, ordinary, pedestrian, plain, platitudinous, predictable, routine, standard, trite, undistinguished, unexceptional, unexciting, unremarkable, unsurprising.
OPPOSITES: SEE **distinguished**, **memorable**.
a commonplace remark banality, cliché, platitude, truism.

commons noun SEE **class** noun.

commonsense adjective SEE **sensible**.

commonwealth noun SEE **country**.

commotion noun *a commotion in the street.* [*informal*] ado, agitation, [*informal*] bedlam, [*informal*] brouhaha, bother, brawl, [*informal*] bust-up, chaos, clamour, confusion, contretemps, din, disorder, disturbance, excitement, ferment, flurry, fracas, fray, furore, fuss, hubbub, hullabaloo, hurly-burly, incident, [*informal*] kerfuffle, noise, [*informal*] palaver, pandemonium, [*informal*] punch-up, quarrel, racket, riot, row, rumpus, [*informal*] shemozzle, sensation, [*informal*] stir, [*informal*] to-do, tumult, turbulence, turmoil, unrest, upheaval, uproar, upset.

communal adjective *communal washing facilities.* collective, common, general, joint, mutual, open, public, shared.
OPPOSITES: SEE **private**.

commune noun SEE **community**.

commune verb SEE **communicate**.

communicate verb **1** *to communicate information.* advise, announce, broadcast, convey, declare, disclose, disseminate, divulge, express, impart, indicate, inform, intimate, make known, mention, [*in computing*] network, notify, pass on, proclaim, promulgate, publish, put across, relay, report, reveal, say, show, speak, spread, state, write.
2 *to communicate with other people.* commune, confer, contact [=*communicate with*], converse, correspond, discuss, get in touch, interrelate, make contact, speak, talk, write (to).
3 *to communicate a disease.* give, infect someone with, pass on, spread, transfer, transmit.
4 *This passage communicates with the kitchen.* be connected, lead (to).

communication noun *Animals have various methods of communication.* communicating, communion, contact, [*old-fashioned*] intercourse, understanding one another.

METHODS OF HUMAN COMMUNICATION: announcement, bulletin, cable, SEE **card**, communiqué, computer, conversation, correspondence, dialogue, directive, dispatch, document, FAX, gossip, [*informal*] grapevine, information, intelligence, intercom, intimation, SEE **letter**, the media [SEE BELOW], [*informal*] memo, memorandum, message, news, note, notice, proclamation, radar, report, rumour, satellite, signal, speaking, statement, talk, telegram, telegraph, telephone, teleprinter, transmission, walkie-talkie, wire, word, writing.

THE MASS MEDIA: advertising, broadcasting, cable television, newspapers, the press, radio, telecommunications, television.

---

communicative adjective *a communicative person.* frank, informative, open, out-going, sociable, SEE **talkative**.
OPPOSITES: SEE **secretive**.

communion noun SEE **communication, fellowship**.

communiqué noun SEE **communication**.

communism, communist nouns POLITICAL TERMS: SEE **politics**.

community noun *Most people like to live in a community.* colony, commonwealth, commune, country, SEE **group** noun, kibbutz, nation, society, state.

commute verb **1** *to commute a prison sentence.* adjust, alter, curtail, decrease, lessen, lighten, mitigate, reduce, shorten.
2 *to commute into the city every day.* SEE **travel** verb.

compact adjective **1** *compact soil.* close-packed, compacted, compressed, dense, firm, heavy, solid, tight-packed.
OPPOSITES: SEE **loose**.
2 *a compact encyclopaedia.* abbreviated, abridged, brief, compendious, compressed, concentrated, condensed, short, small, succinct, terse.
OPPOSITES: SEE **diffuse** adjective.
3 *a compact tool-box.* handy, neat, portable, small.
OPPOSITES: SEE **large, spacious**.
compact disc OTHER RECORDS: SEE **record**.

compact noun SEE **agreement**.

companion noun *He took a companion with him.* accomplice, assistant, associate, colleague, comrade, confederate, confidant, consort, [*informal*] crony, escort, fellow, follower, SEE **friend**, SEE **helper**, [*informal*] henchman, mate, partner, stalwart.

companionable adjective SEE **friendly**.

company noun **1** *We enjoy other people's company.* companionship, fellowship, friendship, society.
2 [*informal*] *We've got company coming on Sunday.* callers, guests, visitors.
3 *a company of friends.* assemblage, band, body, circle, community, coterie, crew, crowd, entourage, gang, gathering, throng, troop.
4 *a theatrical company.* association, club, ensemble, group, society, troupe.
5 *a trading company.* business, cartel, concern, conglomerate, consortium, corporation, establishment, firm, house, line, organization, partnership, [*informal*] set-up, syndicate, union.

6 *a company of soldiers.* SEE **armed services.**

comparable adjective *I got better quality at a comparable price. The work she does is not comparable to yours.* analogous, cognate, commensurate, compatible, corresponding, equal, equivalent, parallel, proportionate, related, similar.
OPPOSITES: SEE **dissimilar**. [Usually *incomparable* is NOT the opposite of *comparable.*]

comparative adjective *Once she was poor, but now she lives in comparative luxury.* relative.

compare verb **1** *Compare these sets of figures.* check, contrast, correlate, draw parallels between, juxtapose, make connections between, match, parallel, relate, set side by side, weigh.
2 *You can't compare the two teams.* equate, liken.
3 *Their team cannot compare with ours.* compete with, emulate, equal, match, rival, vie with.

comparison noun analogy, contrast, correlation, difference, distinction, juxtaposition, likeness, parallel, resemblance, similarity.

compartment noun *a compartment to keep belongings in. a compartment to sleep in.* alcove, area, bay, berth, booth, cell, chamber, [*informal*] cubby-hole, cubicle, division, kiosk, locker, niche, nook, pigeon-hole, section, space, subdivision.

compassion noun SEE **mercy, sympathy.**

compatible adjective **1** *People who live together must be compatible.* SEE **friendly**, harmonious, like-minded.
2 *The work he did was not compatible with his terms of employment.* accordant, congruent, consistent, consonant, matching, reconcilable.
OPPOSITES: SEE **incompatible.**
to be compatible with SEE **match** verb.

compatriot noun fellow citizen.

compel verb *You can't compel me to join in.* bind, SEE **bully** verb, coerce, constrain, dragoon, drive, exact, force, impel, make, necessitate, oblige, order, press, press-gang, pressurize, require, [*informal*] shanghai, urge.
to be compelled *They'll be compelled to use the motorway if they want to get here for tea.* be bound, be certain, be obliged, have, must, be sure.

compelling adjective SEE **irresistible.**

compendium noun *a compendium of information.* condensation, digest, handbook, summary.

compensate verb *to compensate someone for damage.* atone, [*informal*] cough up, [*formal*] indemnify, make amends, make reparation, make up, offset, pay back, pay compensation [SEE **compensation**], recompense, redress, reimburse, repay.

compensation noun *How much compensation did they get?* amends, damages, [*formal*] indemnity, recompense, refund, reimbursement, reparation, repayment, restitution.

compère noun *the compere of a TV programme.* anchor-man, announcer, disc jockey, host, hostess, linkman, Master of Ceremonies, MC, presenter.

compete verb *to compete in a sport.* be a contestant, enter, participate, perform, take part, take up the challenge. [Also use verbs appropriate to the particular sport: *jump, race, swim, throw*, etc.]
to compete against be in competition with [SEE **competition**], challenge, conflict with, contend against, emulate, SEE **fight** verb, oppose, rival, strive against, struggle with, undercut, vie with.

competent adjective *a competent builder. a competent performance.* able, acceptable, accomplished, adept, adequate, capable, clever, effective, effectual, efficient, experienced, expert, fit, [*informal*] handy, practical, proficient, qualified, satisfactory, skilful, skilled, trained, workmanlike.
OPPOSITES: SEE **incompetent.**

competition noun **1** *The competition between contestants was fierce.* competitiveness, conflict, contention, emulation, rivalry, struggle.
2 *a football competition. a prize competition.* challenge, championship, contest, event, game, heat, match, quiz, race, rally, series, tournament, trial.

competitive adjective **1** *competitive games.* aggressive, antagonistic, combative, contentious, cut-throat, hard-fought, keen, lively, sporting, well-fought.
OPPOSITES: SEE **co-operative.**
2 *competitive prices.* average, comparable with others, fair, moderate, reasonable, similar to others.
OPPOSITES: SEE **exorbitant.**

competitor noun *the competitors in a quiz.* adversary, antagonist, candidate, challenger, contender, contestant, entrant, finalist, opponent, participant, rival.

compile verb *to compile a magazine.* arrange, assemble, collect together, compose, edit, gather together, marshal, organize, put together.

complacent adjective [Do not confuse with *complaisant*.] *You can't be complacent when the job is only half-finished.* confident, contented, pleased with yourself, self-congratulatory, self-righteous, self-satisfied, smug, unconcerned, untroubled.
OPPOSITES: SEE **anxious**.

complain verb *We complained about the awful service.* [*informal*] beef, [*slang*] bind, carp, cavil, find fault (with), fuss, [*informal*] gripe, [*informal*] grouch, grouse, grumble, lament, moan, object, protest, whine, [*informal*] whinge.
OPPOSITES: SEE **approve (approve of)**.
to complain about cast aspersions on, censure, condemn, criticize, decry, disparage, [*informal*] knock, [*informal*] slate.
OPPOSITES: SEE **praise** verb.

complaint noun **1** *We had complaints about the noise.* accusation, [*informal*] beef, charge, condemnation, criticism, grievance, [*informal*] gripe, grouse, grumble, moan, objection, protest, stricture, whine, whinge.
2 *Flu is a common complaint in winter.* affliction, ailment, disease, disorder, SEE **illness**, indisposition, infection, malady, malaise, sickness, upset.

complaisant adjective [Do not confuse with *complacent*.] *She's always helpful and complaisant.* accommodating, acquiescent, amenable, biddable, compliant, co-operative, deferential, docile, obedient, obliging, pliant, polite, submissive, tractable, willing.
OPPOSITES: SEE **obstinate**.

complement noun [Do not confuse with *compliment*.] *The ship carried its full complement of passengers.* aggregate, capacity, quota, sum, total.

complement verb [Do not confuse with *compliment*.] *Her guitar-playing complemented his singing perfectly.* complete, make complete, make perfect, make whole, top up.

complete adjective **1** *the complete story.* comprehensive, entire, exhaustive, full, intact, total, unabbreviated, unabridged, unedited, unexpurgated, whole.
2 *a complete job of work.* accomplished, achieved, completed, concluded, ended, faultless, finished, perfect.
OPPOSITES: SEE **incomplete**.
3 *complete disaster. complete rubbish.* absolute, arrant, downright, extreme, [*informal*] out-and-out, outright, pure, rank, sheer, thorough, thoroughgoing, total, unmitigated, unmixed, unqualified, utter, [*informal*] wholesale.
OPPOSITES: SEE **qualified**.

complete verb **1** *to complete a job of work.* accomplish, achieve, carry out, clinch, close, conclude, do, end, finalize, finish, fulfil, perfect, perform, round off, terminate, [*informal*] wind up.
2 *to complete a questionnaire.* answer, fill in.

complex adjective *a complex substance. a complex task.* complicated, composite, compound, convoluted, elaborate, [*informal*] fiddly, heterogeneous, intricate, involved, manifold, mixed, multifarious, multiple, multiplex, sophisticated.
OPPOSITES: SEE **simple**.

complexion noun *a healthy complexion.* appearance, colour, colouring, look, pigmentation, skin, texture.
WORDS TO DESCRIBE COMPLEXIONS: black, brown, clear, dark, fair, freckled, pasty, ruddy, sickly, spotty, swarthy, tanned, white.

compliant adjective SEE **obedient**.

complicate verb *Don't complicate things by asking for food that's not on the menu.* compound, confuse, elaborate, make complicated (SEE **complicated**), mix up, muddle, tangle.
OPPOSITES: SEE **simplify**.

complicated adjective *a complicated task. a complicated plan.* complex, convoluted, difficult, elaborate, entangled, hard, intricate, involved, knotty (*a knotty problem*), perplexing, problematical, sophisticated, tangled, tortuous, [*informal*] tricky, twisted, twisting.
OPPOSITES: SEE **straightforward**.

complication noun *I thought the job was easy, but then I found a complication.* complexity, confusion, difficulty, [*informal*] mix-up, problem, ramification, setback, snag, tangle.

complicity noun SEE **involvement**.

compliment noun [Do not confuse with *complement*.] [*often plural*] *Give our compliments to the chef.* accolade, admiration, appreciation, approval, commendation, congratulations, [*formal*] encomium, [*formal*] eulogy, [*formal or joking*] felicitations, flattery, honour, [*formal*] panegyric, plaudits, praise, testimonial, tribute.
OPPOSITES: SEE **insult** noun.

compliment verb [Do not confuse with *complement*.] *to compliment someone on their performance.* applaud, commend, congratulate, [*informal*] crack up, eulogize, extol, [*formal*] felicitate, give credit, [*formal*] laud, praise, salute, speak highly of.
OPPOSITES: SEE **criticize, insult** verb.

complimentary adjective **1** *complimentary remarks.* admiring, appreciative, approving, commendatory, congratulatory, eulogistic, favourable, flattering, fulsome, generous, laudatory, rapturous, supportive.
OPPOSITES: SEE **critical, insulting.**
2 *complimentary tickets.* free, [*informal*] give-away, gratis.

comply verb **to comply with** *I complied with the rules.* accede to, acquiesce in, agree to, assent to, conform to, consent to, defer to, fall in with, follow, fulfil, obey, observe, perform, satisfy, submit to, yield to.
OPPOSITES: SEE **defy.**

component noun *components of a car.* bit, constituent part, element, essential part, ingredient, item, part, piece, [*informal*] spare, spare part, unit.

compose verb **1** *The village was composed of small huts.* build, compile, constitute, construct, fashion, form, frame, make, put together.
2 *Mozart composed a lot of music.* arrange, create, devise, imagine, make up, produce, write.
3 *Have a cup of tea and compose yourself.* calm, control, pacify, quieten, soothe, tranquillize.
to be composed of *A hockey team is composed of 11 players.* comprehend, consist of, comprise, contain, embody, embrace, include, incorporate, involve.

composed adjective SEE **calm** adjective.

composer noun OTHER WRITERS: SEE **writer.**

composite adjective SEE **complex.**

composition noun **1** *the composition of a team. the composition of a chemical.* constitution, content, establishment, formation, formulation, [*informal*] make-up, structure.
2 *a musical composition.* [*formal*] opus, piece, work.
VARIOUS COMPOSITIONS: SEE **music.**

compos mentis SEE **sane.**

composure noun SEE **tranquillity.**

compound noun **1** *a chemical compound.* alloy, amalgam, blend, combination, composite, composition, fusion, synthesis.
SEE ALSO **mixture**: but note that in chemical terms *compound* and *mixture* are not the same.
2 *a compound for animals.* [*American*] corral, enclosure, pen, run.

compound verb **1** *to compound substances.* SEE **combine.**
2 *The bad weather compounded our difficulties.* SEE **aggravate, complicate.**

comprehend verb *Can you comprehend what I'm saying?* appreciate, conceive, discern, fathom, follow, grasp, know, perceive, realize, see, [*informal*] twig, understand.

comprehensible adjective *a comprehensible explanation.* clear, easy, intelligible, lucid, meaningful, plain, self-explanatory, simple, straightforward, understandable.
OPPOSITES: SEE **incomprehensible.**

comprehension noun SEE **understanding.**

comprehensive adjective *a comprehensive account of a subject.* all-embracing, broad, catholic, compendious, complete, detailed, encyclopaedic, exhaustive, extensive, full, inclusive, thorough, total, universal, wide-ranging.
OPPOSITES: SEE **selective.**
comprehensive school OTHER SCHOOLS: SEE **school.**

compress verb *to compress ideas into a few words. to compress things into a small space.* abbreviate, abridge, compact, concentrate, condense, constrict, contract, cram, crush, flatten, [*informal*] jam, précis, press, shorten, squash, squeeze, stuff, summarize, telescope, truncate.
OPPOSITES: SEE **expand.**

compressed adjective *a compressed account of my life.* abbreviated, abridged, compact, compendious, concise, condensed, shortened, summarized, telescoped, truncated.

comprise verb *This album comprises the best hits of the year.* be composed of, consist of, contain, cover, embody, embrace, include, incorporate, involve.

compromise noun *The two sides reached a compromise.* bargain, concession, [*informal*] give-and-take, [*informal*] halfway house, middle course, middle way, settlement.

compromise verb **1** *The two sides compromised.* concede a point, go to arbitration, make concessions, meet halfway, negotiate a settlement, reach a formula, settle, [*informal*] split the difference, strike a balance.
2 *He compromised his reputation by getting involved in a scandal.* discredit, dishonour, imperil, jeopardize, prejudice, risk, undermine, weaken.

compromising adjective *a compromising situation.* damaging, discreditable, disgraceful, dishonourable, embarrassing, ignoble, improper, questionable, scandalous, unworthy.

compulsion noun **1** *Slaves work by compulsion, not by choice.* being compelled,

coercion, duress (*under duress*), force, necessity, restriction, restraint.
2 *an irresistible compulsion to eat.* addiction, drive, habit, impulse, pressure, urge.
OPPOSITES: SEE **option**.

compulsive adjective **1** *a compulsive urge.* besetting, compelling, driving, instinctive, involuntary, irresistible, overpowering, overwhelming, powerful, uncontrollable, urgent.
2 *a compulsive eater.* addicted, habitual, incorrigible, incurable, obsessive, persistent.

compulsory adjective *The wearing of seat-belts is compulsory.* binding, de rigueur, imperative, imposed, incumbent, inescapable, mandatory, obligatory, official, required, stipulated, unavoidable.
OPPOSITES: SEE **optional**.

compunction noun SEE **conscience**.

compute verb *to compute figures.* add up, assess, calculate, count, estimate, evaluate, measure, reckon, total, work out.

computer noun mainframe, [*informal*] micro, microcomputer, mini-computer, personal computer, PC, word-processor.

SOME TERMS USED IN COMPUTING: bit, byte, chip, cursor, data, database, data-processing, desk-top publishing, [*adjective*] digital, disc, disc-drive, firmware, floppy-disc, hard copy, hard disc, hardware, input, interface, joystick, keyboard, machine-code, [*adjective*] machine-readable, memory, menu, micro, microchip, micro-processor, monitor, mouse, network, output, printer, printout, processor, program, retrieval, robotics, silicon chip, software, spreadsheet, terminal, VDU, window, word-processing.

---

comrade noun SEE **companion**.

con noun, verb SEE **cheat** noun, verb.

concatenation noun SEE **sequence**.

concave adjective SEE **curved**, dished.
OPPOSITE: convex.

conceal verb blot out, bury, camouflage, cloak, cover up, disguise, envelop, hide, hush up, keep dark, keep quiet, keep secret, mask, obscure, screen, suppress, veil.
OPPOSITES: SEE **reveal**.

concealed adjective camouflaged, cloaked, disguised, furtive, hidden, SEE **invisible**, secret, unobtrusive.
OPPOSITES: SEE **obvious, visible**.

concede verb **1** *I conceded that I was wrong.* acknowledge, admit, agree, allow, confess, grant, make a concession, own, profess, recognize.
2 *After a long fight he conceded.* capitulate, [*informal*] cave in, cede, [*informal*] give in, resign, submit, surrender, yield.

conceit noun SEE **pride**.

conceited adjective arrogant, [*informal*] bigheaded, boastful, bumptious, [*informal*] cocky, egocentric, egotistic, egotistical, haughty, [*informal*] high and mighty, immodest, overweening, pleased with yourself, proud, self-satisfied, [*informal*] snooty, [*informal*] stuck-up, [*informal*] swollen-headed, supercilious, vain, vainglorious.
OPPOSITES: SEE **modest**.
conceited person SEE **show-off**.

conceivable adjective SEE **credible**.

conceive verb **1** *to conceive a baby.* become pregnant.
2 *to conceive an idea.* [*informal*] bring up, conjure up, create, design, devise, [*informal*] dream up, envisage, form, formulate, germinate, hatch, imagine, invent, make-up, originate, plan, produce, realize, suggest, think up, visualize, work out.

concentrate noun *fruit-juice concentrate.* distillation, essence, extract.

concentrate verb **1** *Please concentrate on your work.* apply yourself (to), attend (to), be absorbed (in), be attentive (to), engross yourself (in), focus (on), think (about), work hard (at).
OPPOSITE: be inattentive (SEE **inattentive**).
2 *The crowds concentrated in the middle of town.* accumulate, centre, cluster, collect, congregate, converge, crowd, gather, mass.
OPPOSITES: SEE **disperse**.
3 *to concentrate a liquid.* condense, reduce, thicken.
OPPOSITES: SEE **dilute** verb.

concentrated adjective **1** *concentrated fruit-juice.* condensed, evaporated, strong, undiluted.
OPPOSITES: SEE **dilute** adjective.
2 *concentrated effort.* all-out, committed, hard, intense, intensive, thorough.
OPPOSITES: SEE **half-hearted**.

concept noun SEE **idea**.

conception noun **1** *She has no conception of how difficult it is.* SEE **idea**.
2 *the conception of a baby.* begetting, beginning, conceiving, fathering, fertilization, impregnation.

concern noun **1** *concern for others.* attention, care, consideration, heed, interest, involvement, responsibility, solicitude.

2 *It's no concern of theirs.* affair, business, matter.
3 *a matter of great concern to us all.* anxiety, burden, cause of distress [SEE **distress**], fear, worry.
4 *a business concern.* company, corporation, enterprise, establishment, firm, organization.

concern verb *Road safety concerns us all.* affect, be important to, be relevant to, interest, involve, matter to, [*formal*] pertain to, refer to, relate to.

concerned adjective [The meaning of *concerned* varies according to whether the word comes before or after the noun it describes: compare the examples given here.] 1 *The concerned parents asked for news of their children.* SEE **anxious**, bothered, caring, distressed, disturbed, fearful, solicitous, touched, troubled, unhappy, upset, worried.
OPPOSITES: unconcerned, SEE **callous**.
2 *If you want the truth, talk to the people concerned.* connected, implicated, interested, involved, relevant, referred to.
OPPOSITES: uninvolved, SEE **detached**.

concerning preposition *information concerning our holiday.* about, apropos of, germane to, involving, re, regarding, relating to, relevant to, with reference to, with regard to.

concert noun VARIOUS ENTERTAINMENTS: SEE **entertainment**.

concerted adjective *a concerted effort.* collaborative, collective, combined, cooperative, joint, mutual, shared, united.

concession noun *If you're under 16 you get a concession.* adjustment, allowance, reduction.
to make a concession SEE **concede**.

conciliate verb SEE **pacify, reconcile**.

conciliation noun SEE **negotiation, reconciliation**.

conciliator noun SEE **peacemaker**.

concise adjective *a concise dictionary. a concise account.* abbreviated, abridged, brief, compact, compendious, compressed, concentrated, condensed, laconic, pithy, short, small, succinct, terse.
OPPOSITES: SEE **diffuse** adjective.

conclave noun SEE **meeting**.

conclude verb 1 *The concert concluded with an encore.* cease, close, complete, culminate, end, finish, round off, stop, terminate.
2 *When you didn't arrive, we concluded that the car had broken down.* assume, decide, deduce, gather, infer, judge, reckon, suppose, surmise, SEE **think**.

conclusion noun 1 *the conclusion of a journey. the conclusion of a concert.* close, completion, culmination, end, finale, finish, peroration, rounding-off, termination.
2 *Now that you've heard the evidence, what's your conclusion?* answer, assumption, belief, decision, deduction, inference, interpretation, judgement, opinion, outcome, resolution, result, solution, upshot, verdict.

conclusive adjective *conclusive evidence.* convincing, decisive, definite, persuasive, unambiguous, unanswerable, unequivocal.
OPPOSITES: SEE **inconclusive**.

concoct verb *to concoct excuses. to concoct something to eat.* SEE **cook** verb, cook up, contrive, counterfeit, devise, fabricate, feign, formulate, hatch, invent, make up, plan, prepare, put together, think up.

concomitant adjective SEE **accompanying**.

concord noun SEE **harmony**.

concordat noun SEE **agreement**.

concrete adjective *concrete evidence.* actual, definite, existing, factual, firm, material, objective, palpable, physical, real, solid, substantial, tactile, tangible, touchable, visible.
OPPOSITES: SEE **abstract** adjective.

concretion noun SEE **mass** noun.

concubine noun SEE **lover**.

concur verb 1 *The doctor concurs with my diagnosis.* accede, accord, agree, assent.
2 *Our opinions often concur.* coincide, come together, harmonize, meet, unite.

concurrent adjective *You can't attend two concurrent events!* coexisting, coinciding, concomitant, contemporaneous, contemporary, overlapping, parallel, simultaneous, synchronous.

condemn verb 1 *We condemn violence. We condemn criminals.* blame, castigate, censure, criticize, damn, decry, denounce, deplore, disapprove of, disparage, rebuke, reprehend, reprove, revile, [*informal*] slam, [*informal*] slate, upbraid.
OPPOSITES: SEE **commend**.
2 *They were condemned by the evidence. The judge condemned them.* convict, find guilty, judge, pass judgement, prove guilty, punish, sentence.
OPPOSITES: SEE **acquit**.

condense verb 1 *to condense a book.* abbreviate, abridge, compress, contract, curtail, précis, reduce, shorten, summarize, synopsize.

OPPOSITES: SEE **expand**.
2 *to condense a liquid.* concentrate, distil, reduce, solidify, thicken.
OPPOSITES: SEE **dilute** verb.
3 *Steam condenses on a cold window.* become liquid, form condensation [SEE **condensation**].
OPPOSITES: SEE **evaporate**.

condensation noun *condensation on the windows.* haze, mist, [*formal*] precipitation, [*informal*] steam, water-drops.

condescend verb [*often joking*] *Would you condescend to accompany me?* deign, lower yourself, stoop.

condescending adjective *a condescending attitude.* disdainful, haughty, imperious, lofty, patronizing, [*informal*] snooty, supercilious, superior.

condiment noun *condiments to flavour food.* garnish, relish, seasoning.
CONDIMENTS INCLUDE: chutney, mustard, pepper, pickle, salt, spices.

condition noun 1 *in good condition, in bad condition.* case, circumstance, fettle (*in fine fettle*), fitness, health, [*informal*] nick, order, shape, situation, state, [*informal*] trim.
2 *a medical condition.* SEE **illness**.
3 *conditions of membership.* limitation, obligation, proviso, qualification, requirement, restriction, stipulation, terms.

conditional adjective *a conditional agreement. conditional surrender.* dependent, limited, provisional, qualified, restricted, safeguarded, [*informal*] with strings attached.
OPPOSITES: SEE **unconditional**.

condolences noun SEE **sympathy**.

condom noun SEE **contraception**.

condone verb *Do you condone his sin?* allow, connive at, disregard, endorse, excuse, forgive, ignore, let someone off, overlook, pardon, tolerate.
OPPOSITE: be unforgiving.

conducive adjective *Warm, wet weather is conducive to the growth of weeds.* advantageous, beneficial, encouraging, favourable, helpful, supportive.
to be conducive to SEE **encourage**.

conduct noun 1 *good conduct.* actions, attitude, bearing, behaviour, demeanour, manner, ways.
2 *the conduct of the nation's affairs.* administration, control, direction, discharge, handling, leading, management, organization, running, supervision.

conduct verb 1 *The curator conducted us round the museum.* accompany, convey, escort, guide, lead, pilot, steer, take, usher.
2 *The chairman conducted the meeting well.* administer, be in charge of, chair, command, control, direct, govern, handle, head, lead, look after, manage, organize, oversee, preside over, regulate, rule, run, superintend, supervise.
to conduct yourself *Didn't we conduct ourselves well!* act, behave, carry on.

conduit noun SEE **channel** noun.

cone noun VARIOUS SHAPES: SEE **shape** noun.

confectioners noun sweet-shop.

confectionery noun SEE **sweet** noun (**sweets**).

confederate noun SEE **ally**.

confederation noun SEE **alliance**.

confer verb 1 *to confer an honour on someone.* accord, award, bestow, give, grant, honour with, impart, invest, present.
2 *You may not confer with each other during the exam!* compare notes, consult, converse, debate, deliberate, discourse, discuss, exchange ideas, [*informal*] put your heads together, seek advice, talk, talk things over.

conference noun consultation, convention, council, deliberation, discussion, SEE **meeting**, symposium.

confess verb *to confess guilt.* acknowledge, admit (to), be truthful (about), [*informal*] come clean (about), concede, [*informal*] make a clean breast (of), own up (to), SEE **reveal**, unbosom yourself, unburden yourself.

confession noun *a confession of guilt.* acknowledgement, admission, declaration, disclosure, profession, revelation.

confidant, confidante nouns SEE **friend**.

confide verb **to confide in** consult, have confidence in, open your heart to, speak confidentially to, [*informal*] spill the beans to, [*informal*] tell all to, tell secrets to, trust, unbosom yourself to.

confidence noun 1 *to face the future with confidence.* certainty, credence, faith, hope, optimism, positiveness, reliance, trust.
OPPOSITES: SEE **doubt** noun.
2 *I wish I had her confidence.* aplomb, assurance, boldness, composure, conviction, firmness, nerve, panache, self-assurance, self-confidence, self-possession, self-reliance, spirit, verve.
OPPOSITES: SEE **diffidence**.
confidence trick SEE **deception**.
to have confidence in SEE **trust** verb.

confident adjective **1** *confident of success.* certain, convinced, hopeful, optimistic, positive, sanguine, sure, trusting.
OPPOSITES: SEE **doubtful**.
2 *a confident person.* assertive, assured, bold, [*uncomplimentary*] cocksure, composed, definite, fearless, secure, self-assured, self-confident, self-possessed, self-reliant, unafraid.
OPPOSITES: SEE **diffident**.

confidential adjective **1** *confidential information.* classified, [*informal*] hush-hush, intimate, [*informal*] off the record, personal, private, restricted, secret, suppressed, top secret.
OPPOSITES: unclassified, SEE **public** adjective.
2 *a confidential secretary.* personal, private, trusted.

configuration noun SEE **shape** noun.

confine verb *The police confined the home supporters at one end of the ground.* bind, cage, circumscribe, constrain, [*informal*] coop up, cordon off, cramp, curb, detain, enclose, gaol, hem in, [*informal*] hold down, immure, imprison, incarcerate, intern, isolate, keep, limit, localize, restrain, restrict, rope off, shut in, shut up, surround, wall up.
OPPOSITES: SEE **free** verb.

confinement noun **1** *confinement in prison.* SEE **imprisonment**.
2 = *childbirth.* SEE **birth**.

confines plural noun SEE **boundary**.

confirm verb **1** *The strange events confirmed his belief in the supernatural.* authenticate, back up, bear out, corroborate, demonstrate, endorse, establish, fortify, give credence to, justify, lend force to, prove, reinforce, settle, show, strengthen, substantiate, support, underline, vindicate, witness to.
OPPOSITES: SEE **disprove**.
2 *We shook hands to confirm the deal.* [*informal*] clinch, formalize, guarantee, make legal, make official, ratify, validate, verify.
OPPOSITES: SEE **cancel**.

confiscate verb *The police confiscated his air gun.* appropriate, impound, remove, seize, sequester, take away, take possession of.

conflagration noun SEE **fire** noun.

conflict noun **1** *conflict between rivals.* antagonism, antipathy, contention, difference, disagreement, discord, dissention, friction, hostility, opposition, strife, unrest, variance (*to be at variance*).
2 *conflict on the battlefield.* action, battle, brawl, brush, clash, combat, confrontation, contest, encounter, engagement, feud, fight, quarrel, [*informal*] set-to, skirmish, struggle, war, warfare.

conflict verb **1** *Her account of events conflicts with mine.* [*informal*] be at odds, be at variance, be incompatible, clash, compete, contend, contradict, contrast, differ, disagree, oppose each other.
2 SEE **fight** verb, **quarrel** verb.

conflicting adjective *conflicting views.* SEE **incompatible**.

conform verb *The club has strict rules and will throw you out if you don't conform.* acquiesce, be good, behave conventionally, comply, [*informal*] do what you are told, fit in, [*informal*] keep in step, obey, [*informal*] see eye to eye, [*informal*] toe the line.
to conform to *to conform to the rules.* abide by, accord with, agree with, be in accordance with, coincide with, comply with, concur with, correspond to, fit in with, follow, harmonize with, keep to, match, obey, square with, submit to, suit.
OPPOSITES: SEE **differ**, **disobey**.

conformist noun conventional person [SEE **conventional**], traditionalist, yes-man.
OPPOSITES: SEE **rebel** noun.

conformity noun *Military discipline requires conformity from all soldiers.* complaisance, compliance, conventionality, obedience, orthodoxy, submission, uniformity.

confound verb SEE **amaze**.

confront verb **1** *to confront your enemies.* accost, argue with, attack, brave, challenge, defy, face up to, oppose, resist, stand up to, take on, withstand.
OPPOSITES: SEE **avoid**.
2 *to confront someone unexpectedly.* encounter, face, meet.

confuse verb **1** *Don't confuse the system.* disarrange, disorder, jumble, mingle, mix up, muddle, tangle.
2 *The complicated rules confused us.* agitate, baffle, bemuse, bewilder, confound, disconcert, disorientate, distract, [*informal*] flummox, fluster, mislead, mystify, perplex, puzzle, [*informal*] rattle.
3 *I confuse the twins.* fail to distinguish, muddle.

confused adjective **1** *a confused argument.* aimless, chaotic, disconnected, disjointed, disordered, disorderly, disorganized, garbled, [*informal*] higgledy-piggledy, incoherent, irrational, jumbled, misleading, mixed up, muddled, muddle-headed, obscure, rambling, [*informal*] topsy-turvy, unclear, unsound, woolly.

OPPOSITES: SEE **orderly**.
2 *a confused state of mind*. addled, addle-headed, baffled, bewildered, dazed, disorientated, distracted, flustered, fuddled, [*informal*] in a tizzy, inebriated, muddle-headed, [*informal*] muzzy, nonplussed, perplexed, puzzled.
OPPOSITES: SEE **sane**.

confusion noun 1 [*informal*] ado, anarchy, bedlam, bother, chaos, clutter, commotion, confusion, din, disorder, disorganization, disturbance, fuss, hubbub, hullabaloo, jumble, maelstrom, [*informal*] mayhem, mêlée, mess, [*informal*] mix-up, muddle, pandemonium, racket, riot, rumpus, shambles, tumult, turbulence, turmoil, upheaval, uproar, welter, whirl.
2 *I saw the confusion on their faces*. bemusement, bewilderment, disorientation, distraction, mystification, perplexity, puzzlement.

confute verb SEE **disprove**.

congeal verb *Blood congeals to form a clot. Water congeals to ice*. clot, coagulate, coalesce, condense, curdle, freeze, harden, [*informal*] jell, set, solidify, stiffen, thicken.

congenial adjective *congenial company. congenial surroundings*. acceptable, agreeable, amicable, companionable, compatible, SEE **friendly**, genial, kindly, SEE **pleasant**, suitable, sympathetic, understanding, well-suited.
OPPOSITES: SEE **uncongenial**.

congenital adjective *congenital deafness*. hereditary, inborn, inbred, inherent, inherited, innate, natural.

congested adjective *a congested road. a congested space*. blocked, clogged, crowded, full, jammed, obstructed, overcrowded, stuffed.
OPPOSITES: SEE **clear** adjective.

conglomeration noun SEE **mass** noun.

congratulate verb *We congratulated the winners*. applaud, SEE **compliment** verb, felicitate, praise.
OPPOSITES: SEE **commiserate**, **reprimand** verb.

congratulations noun SEE **compliment** noun.

congregate verb *On summer evenings, we congregate in the park*. accumulate, assemble, cluster, collect, come together, convene, converge (on), crowd, forgather, gather, get together, group, mass, meet, muster, rally, rendezvous, swarm, throng.

congregation noun SEE **group** noun.

congress noun SEE **assembly**.

congruent adjective SEE **identical**.

conical adjective cone-shaped, pointed.

conifer noun VARIOUS TREES: SEE **tree**.
RELATED ADJECTIVE: coniferous.

conjectural adjective SEE **hypothetical**.

conjecture noun, verb SEE **guess** noun, verb.

conjugal adjective SEE **marital**.

conjunction noun *a conjunction of events*. SEE **combination**.

conjure verb *The wizard conjured stones to move*. bewitch, charm, compel, enchant, invoke, raise, rouse, summon.
SEE ALSO **magic** noun (**to do magic**).
to conjure up SEE **produce** verb.

conjuring noun *The entertainer didn't fool us with his conjuring*. illusions, legerdemain, SEE **magic** noun, sleight of hand, tricks, wizardry.

conjuror noun SEE **entertainer**, illusionist, magician.

connect verb 1 *to connect things together*. attach, combine, couple, engage, fasten, fix, interlock, join, link, tie.
OPPOSITES: SEE **disconnect**.
2 *to connect ideas in your mind*. associate, bracket together, compare, make a connection between, put together, relate, tie up.
OPPOSITES: SEE **dissociate**.

connection noun *I don't see the connection*. affinity, association, bond, coherence, contact, correlation, correspondence, interrelationship, join, link, relationship, [*informal*] tie-up, unity.
OPPOSITES: SEE **separation**.

connive verb **to connive at** SEE **condone**.

connoisseur noun SEE **expert** noun.

connotation noun *What are the connotations of the word "food"?* association, implication, insinuation, reverberation, suggested meaning, undertone.
COMPARE: denotation.

connote verb *The word "food" may connote "greed"*. have connotations of [SEE **connotation**], imply, suggest.
COMPARE: denote.

connubial adjective SEE **marital**.

conquer verb 1 *to conquer a territory*. annex, capture, occupy, overrun, possess, quell, seize, subject, subjugate, take, win.
2 *to conquer an opponent*. beat, best, checkmate, crush, defeat, get the better of, humble, [*informal*] lick, master, outdo, overcome, overpower, overthrow, overwhelm, rout, silence, subdue, succeed against, [*informal*] thrash, triumph over, vanquish, worst.

3 *to conquer a mountain.* climb, reach the top of.

conqueror noun SEE **winner**.

conquest noun *the conquest of a territory.* annexation, appropriation, capture, defeat, invasion, occupation, overthrow, subjection, subjugation, [*informal*] takeover, triumph (over), victory (over), win (against).

consanguinity noun SEE **relationship**.

conscience noun *Vegetarians have a conscience about eating animals.* compunction, ethics, misgivings, morals, principles, qualms, reservations, scruples, standards.

conscience-stricken adjective SEE **ashamed**.

conscientious adjective *a conscientious worker.* accurate, attentive, careful, diligent, dutiful, exact, hard-working, honest, meticulous, painstaking, particular (*She's particular about details*), punctilious, responsible, scrupulous, serious, thorough.
OPPOSITES: SEE **careless**.

conscious adjective 1 *In spite of the knock on his head, he remained conscious.* alert, awake, aware, compos mentis, sensible.
OPPOSITES: SEE **unconscious**.
2 *a conscious act. a conscious foul.* calculated, deliberate, intended, intentional, knowing, planned, premeditated, self-conscious, studied, voluntary, waking, wilful.
OPPOSITES: SEE **accidental**.

conscript noun SEE **soldier**.

conscript verb SEE **enlist**.

consecrate verb 1 *They consecrated a temple to their god.* dedicate, devote, hallow, make sacred, sanctify.
OPPOSITES: SEE **desecrate**.
2 *to consecrate a king.* SEE **enthrone**.

consecrated adjective *The churchyard is consecrated ground.* blessed, hallowed, holy, religious, revered, sacred, sanctified.
OPPOSITES: SEE **accursed**.

consecutive adjective *She was away for three consecutive days.* continuous, following, one after the other, running (*three days running*), sequential, succeeding, successive.

consensus, consent nouns SEE **agreement**.

consent verb *They consented to come with us.* agree, undertake.
OPPOSITES: SEE **refuse** verb.
to consent to *She consented to my request.* allow, approve of, authorize, comply with, concede, grant, permit.

consequence noun 1 *The flood was a consequence of all that snow.* aftermath, by-product, corollary, effect, end, [*informal*] follow-up, issue, outcome, repercussion, result, sequel, side-effect, upshot.
2 *The loss of one penny is of no consequence.* account, concern, importance, moment, note, significance, value, weight.

consequent adjective *consequent effects.* consequential, ensuing, following, resultant, resulting, subsequent.

conservation noun *the conservation of the environment.* careful management, economy, maintenance, preservation, protection, safeguarding, saving, upkeep.
OPPOSITES: SEE **destruction**.

conservationist noun ecologist, environmentalist, [*informal*] green, preservationist.

conservative adjective 1 *conservative ideas.* conventional, die-hard, hidebound, moderate, narrow-minded, old-fashioned, reactionary, sober, traditional, unadventurous.
OPPOSITES: SEE **progressive**.
2 *a conservative estimate.* cautious, moderate, reasonable, understated, unexaggerated.
OPPOSITES: SEE **extreme** adjective.
3 *conservative politics.* right-of-centre, right-wing, Tory.
POLITICAL TERMS: SEE **politics**.

conservative noun conformist, die-hard, reactionary, [*political*] right-winger, [*political*] Tory, traditionalist.
POLITICAL TERMS: SEE **politics**.

conservatory noun glass-house, greenhouse, hothouse.

conserve noun *apricot conserve.* SEE **jam** noun.

conserve verb *to conserve energy.* be economical with, hold in reserve, keep, look after, maintain, preserve, protect, safeguard, save, store up, use sparingly.
OPPOSITES: SEE **waste** verb.

consider verb 1 *to consider a problem.* cogitate, contemplate, deliberate, discuss, examine, meditate on, mull over, muse, ponder, reflect on, ruminate, study, think about, [*informal*] turn over, weigh up.
2 *I consider that he was right.* believe, deem, judge, reckon.

considerable adjective *a considerable amount of rain. a considerable margin.* appreciable, big, biggish, comfortable, fairly important, fairly large, noteworthy, noticeable, perceptible, reasonable, respectable, significant, sizeable,

substantial, [*informal*] tidy (*a tidy amount*), tolerable, worthwhile.
OPPOSITES: SEE **negligible**.

considerate adjective *It was considerate to lend your umbrella.* altruistic, attentive, caring, charitable, friendly, gracious, helpful, kind, kind-hearted, obliging, polite, sensitive, solicitous, sympathetic, tactful, thoughtful, unselfish.
OPPOSITES: SEE **selfish**.

consign verb *to consign something to its proper place.* commit, convey, deliver, devote, entrust, give, hand over, pass on, relegate, send, ship, transfer.

consignment noun *a consignment of goods.* batch, cargo, delivery, load, lorry-load, shipment, van-load.

consist verb **to consist of** *What does this fruit salad consist of? What does the job consist of?* add up to, amount to, be composed of, be made of, comprise, contain, embody, include, incorporate, involve.

consistent adjective **1** *a consistent player. a consistent temperature.* constant, dependable, faithful, predictable, regular, reliable, stable, steady, unchanging, unfailing, uniform, unvarying.
2 *His story is consistent with hers.* accordant, compatible, congruous, consonant, in accordance, in agreement, in harmony, of a piece.
OPPOSITES: SEE **inconsistent**.

consolation noun *Music can give you consolation when you're depressed.* cheer, comfort, ease, encouragement, help, relief, solace, succour, support.
consolation prize prize for runner-up, second prize.

console verb *to console someone who is unhappy.* calm, cheer, comfort, ease, encourage, hearten, relieve, solace, soothe, sympathize with.

consolidate verb *This season she consolidated her reputation as our best athlete.* make secure, make strong, reinforce, stabilize, strengthen.
OPPOSITES: SEE **weaken**.

consonant adjective SEE **consistent**.

consort noun OTHER ROYAL FIGURES: SEE **royal**.

consort verb **to consort with** *to consort with criminals.* accompany, associate with, befriend, be friends with, be seen with, fraternize with, [*informal*] gang up with, keep company with, mix with.

consortium noun SEE **group** noun.

conspicuous adjective *a conspicuous landmark. a conspicuous mistake.* apparent, blatant, clear, discernible, dominant, evident, flagrant, glaring, impressive, manifest, notable, noticeable, obvious, patent, perceptible, prominent, pronounced, self-evident, showy, striking, unconcealed, unmistakable, visible.
OPPOSITES: SEE **inconspicuous**.

conspiracy noun *a conspiracy to defraud.* cabal, collusion, [*informal*] frame-up, insider dealing, intrigue, [*often joking*] machinations, plot, [*informal*] racket, scheme, treason.

conspirator noun plotter, schemer, traitor, [*informal*] wheeler-dealer.

conspire verb *Several men conspired to defraud the company.* be in league, collude, combine, co-operate, hatch a plot, have designs, intrigue, plot, scheme.

constable noun SEE **policeman**.

constant adjective **1** *a constant cough. a constant rhythm.* ceaseless, chronic, consistent, continual, continuous, endless, eternal, everlasting, fixed, incessant, invariable, never-ending, non-stop, permanent, perpetual, persistent, predictable, regular, relentless, repeated, stable, steady, sustained, unbroken, unchanging, unending, unflagging, uniform, uninterrupted, unremitting, unvarying, unwavering.
OPPOSITES: SEE **changeable**, **irregular**.
2 *a constant friend.* dedicated, dependable, determined, devoted, faithful, firm, loyal, reliable, staunch, steadfast, true, trustworthy, trusty.
OPPOSITES: SEE **fickle**, **unreliable**.

constellation noun ASTRONOMICAL TERMS: SEE **astronomy**.

consternation noun SEE **dismay** noun.

constituent noun SEE **part** noun.

constitute verb **1** *In soccer, eleven players constitute a team.* compose, comprise, form, make up.
2 *We constituted a committee to organize a jumble sale.* appoint, bring together, create, establish, found, inaugurate, make, set up.

constitution noun **1** *the constitution of a committee.* SEE **composition**.
2 *the country's constitution.* SEE **government**.

constrain verb SEE **compel**.

constraint noun SEE **compulsion**.

constrict verb SEE **tighten**.

constriction noun *a constriction in the throat.* SEE **blockage**, narrowing, pressure, [*formal*] stricture, tightness.

construct verb *to construct a shelter.* assemble, build, create, engineer, erect, [*formal*] fabricate, fashion, fit together, form, [*informal*] knock together, make, manufacture, pitch (*a tent*), produce, put together, put up, set up.
OPPOSITES: SEE **demolish**.

construction noun **1** *The construction of a shelter took an hour.* assembly, building, creation, erecting, erection, manufacture, production, putting-up, setting-up.
2 *The shelter was a flimsy construction.* building, edifice, erection, structure.

constructive adjective *a constructive suggestion.* advantageous, beneficial, co-operative, creative, helpful, positive, practical, useful, valuable, worthwhile.
OPPOSITES: SEE **destructive**.

construe verb SEE **interpret**.

consul noun SEE **official** noun.

consult verb *Please consult me before you do anything.* ask, confer (with), debate (with), discuss (with), exchange views (with), [*informal*] put your heads together (with), question, refer (to), seek advice (from), speak (to).

consume verb **1** *to consume food.* devour, digest, eat, [*informal*] gobble up, [*informal*] guzzle, swallow.
2 *to consume your energy. to consume your savings.* absorb, deplete, drain, eat into, employ, exhaust, expend, swallow up, use up, utilize.

consumer noun *Shops try to give consumers what they want.* buyer, customer, purchaser, shopper.

consuming adjective *a consuming passion.* SEE **irresistible, powerful**.

consummate adjective *a consummate artist.* SEE **skilful**.

consummate verb **to consummate marriage** SEE **sex**.

contact noun **1** *an electrical contact.* connection, join, touch, union.
2 *contact between people.* SEE **communication, meeting**.

contact verb *I'll contact you when I have some news.* approach, call, call on, communicate with, correspond with, [*informal*] drop a line to, get hold of, get in touch with, notify, phone, ring, speak to, talk to.

contagion noun SEE **illness**.

contagious adjective *a contagious disease.* catching, communicable, infectious, spreading, transmittable.
OPPOSITE: non-infectious.

contain verb **1** *This box contains odds and ends. This book contains helpful information.* be composed of, comprise, consist of, embody, embrace, hold, include, incorporate, involve.
2 *Please contain your enthusiasm!* check, control, curb, hold back, keep back, limit, repress, restrain, stifle.

container noun holder, receptacle, repository, vessel.

SOME CONTAINERS: bag, barrel, basin, basket, bath, beaker, billy-can, bin, SEE **bottle**, bowl, box, briefcase, bucket, butt, caddy, can, canister, carton, cartridge, case, cask, casket, casserole, cauldron, chest, churn, cistern, coffer, coffin, crate, creel, cup.

decanter, dish, drum, dustbin, envelope, flask, glass, goblet, hamper, handbag, haversack, hod, hogshead, holdall, holster, jar, jerry-can, jug, keg, kettle, knapsack, luggage, money-box, mould, mug, pail, pan, pannier, pitcher, pocket, portmanteau, pot, pouch, punnet, purse.

rucksack, sachet, sack, satchel, saucepan, scuttle, skip, suitcase, tank, tankard, tea-chest, teapot, test tube, thermos, tin, trough, trunk, tub, tumbler, urn, vacuum flask, vase, vat, wallet, water-butt, watering-can, wine-glass.

---

contaminate verb *Chemicals contaminated the water.* adulterate, defile, foul, infect, poison, pollute, soil, taint.
OPPOSITES: SEE **purify**.

contemplate verb **1** *We contemplated the view.* eye, gaze at, look at, observe, regard, stare at, survey, view, watch.
2 *We contemplated what to do next.* cogitate, consider, deliberate, examine, mull over, plan, reflect on, study, think about, work out.
3 *I contemplate taking a holiday soon.* envisage, expect, intend, propose.
4 *She sat quietly and contemplated.* [*informal*] day-dream, meditate, muse, ponder, reflect, ruminate, think.

contemplative adjective *a contemplative mood.* SEE **thoughtful**.

contemporaneous adjective SEE **contemporary**.

contemporary adjective **1** [= *belonging to the same time as other things you are referring to*] *contemporary events.* coinciding, concurrent, contemporaneous, simultaneous, synchronous, topical.
COMPARE: earlier, later.
2 [= *belonging to the present time*] *contemporary music.* current, fashionable, the

latest, modern, newest, present-day, [*informal*] trendy, up-to-date, [*informal*] with-it.
OPPOSITES: SEE **old**.

contempt noun *Our contempt for their bad behaviour was obvious.* derision, detestation, disdain, disgust, dislike, disparagement, disrespect, SEE **hatred**, loathing, ridicule, scorn.
OPPOSITES: SEE **admiration**.
to feel contempt for SEE **despise**.

contemptible adjective *a contemptible crime.* base, beneath contempt, despicable, detestable, discreditable, disgraceful, dishonourable, disreputable, hateful, ignominious, inferior, loathsome, [*informal*] low-down, mean, odious, pitiful, [*informal*] shabby, shameful, worthless, wretched.
OPPOSITES: SEE **admirable**.

contemptuous adjective *a contemptuous sneer.* arrogant, condescending, derisive, disdainful, dismissive, disrespectful, haughty, [*informal*] holier-than-thou, insolent, insulting, jeering, patronizing, sarcastic, scathing, scornful, sneering, [*informal*] snooty, supercilious, withering.
OPPOSITES: SEE **admiring**.
to be contemptuous (of) SEE **denigrate**, **sneer**.

contend verb **1** *We had to contend with strong opposition.* compete, contest, dispute, SEE **fight** verb, grapple, oppose, SEE **quarrel** verb, rival, strive, struggle, vie.
2 *I contended that I was right.* affirm, allege, argue, assert, claim, declare, maintain.
to contend with *We had a lot to contend with.* cope with, deal with, manage, organize, put up with, sort out.

content adjective SEE **contented**.

content noun **1** *Butter has a high fat content.* constituent, element, ingredient, part.
2 *She smiled with content.* SEE **contentment**.

content verb SEE **satisfy**.

contented adjective *a contented expression.* cheerful, comfortable, complacent, content, fulfilled, gratified, SEE **happy**, peaceful, pleased, relaxed, satisfied, serene, smiling, smug, uncomplaining, untroubled, well-fed.
OPPOSITES: SEE **dissatisfied**.

contention noun SEE **argument**.

contentious adjective **1** *a contentious crowd of objectors.* SEE **quarrelsome**.
2 *a contentious problem.* SEE **controversial**.

contentment noun *a smile of contentment.* comfort, content, contentedness, ease, fulfilment, SEE **happiness**, relaxation, satisfaction, serenity, smugness, tranquillity, well-being.
OPPOSITES: SEE **dissatisfaction**.

contest noun *a sporting contest.* bout, challenge, championship, [*informal*] clash, combat, competition, conflict, confrontation, duel, encounter, SEE **fight** noun, game, match, [*informal*] set-to, struggle, tournament, trial.

contest verb **1** *to contest a title.* compete for, contend for, fight for [SEE **fight** verb], [*informal*] make a bid for, strive for, struggle for, take up the challenge of, vie for.
2 *to contest a decision.* argue against, challenge, debate, dispute, doubt, oppose, query, question, refute, resist.

contestant noun *a contestant in a competition.* candidate, competitor, contender, entrant, participant, player.

context noun *Words only have meaning if you put them in a context.* background, frame of reference, framework, milieu, position, situation, surroundings.

contiguous adjective SEE **adjoining**.

continental quilt noun duvet, eiderdown.

contingency noun *Be prepared for all contingencies.* SEE **accident**.

contingent noun SEE **group** noun.

continual adjective *a continual process of change. continual bickering.* constant, continuing, SEE **continuous**, endless, eternal, everlasting, frequent, interminable, lasting, limitless, ongoing, perennial, permanent, perpetual, persistent, recurrent, regular, relentless, repeated, unending, unremitting.
OPPOSITES: SEE **occasional**, **temporary**.

continuance noun SEE **continuation**.

continuation noun **1** *the continuation of a journey.* carrying on, continuance, continuing, extension, maintenance, prolongation, protraction, resumption.
2 *a continuation of a book.* addition, appendix, postscript, sequel, supplement.

continue verb **1** *We continued the search while it was light.* carry on, keep going, keep up, persevere with, proceed with, prolong, pursue, [*informal*] stick at, sustain.
2 *We'll continue work after lunch.* recommence, restart, resume.
3 *This rain can't continue for long.* carry on, endure, go on, keep on, last, linger, live on, persist, remain, stay, survive.

4 *Continue the line to the edge of the paper.* extend, lengthen.

continuous adjective *continuous bad weather. exhausted by continuous effort.* ceaseless, chronic (*chronic illness*), SEE **continual**, incessant, never-ending, non-stop, [*informal*] round-the-clock, [*informal*] solid (*I worked for 3 solid hours*), sustained, unbroken, unceasing, uninterrupted.

contort verb SEE **twist** verb.

contour noun *the contours of the countryside.* curve, form, outline, relief, shape.

contraband noun *smugglers' contraband.* booty, illegal imports, loot.

contraception noun birth-control, family planning.
VARIOUS METHODS OF BIRTH-CONTROL: cap, coil, condom, contraceptive pill, [*informal*] the pill, rhythm method, spermicide, sterilization, vasectomy.

contract noun *a business contract.* agreement, bargain, bond, commitment, compact, concordat, covenant, deal, indenture, lease, pact, settlement, treaty, understanding, undertaking.

contract verb **1** *Most substances contract as they cool.* become denser, become smaller, close up, condense, decrease, diminish, draw together, dwindle, fall away, lessen, narrow, reduce, shrink, shrivel, slim down, thin out, wither.
OPPOSITES: SEE **expand**.
2 *A local firm contracted to build our extension.* agree, arrange, close a deal, covenant, negotiate a deal, promise, sign an agreement, undertake.
3 *She contracted a mysterious illness.* become infected by, catch, develop, get.

contraction noun **1** *Contraction of the timbers left gaps in the fence.* diminution, narrowing, shortening, shrinkage, shrivelling.
2 *"Jim" is a contraction of "James".* abbreviation, diminutive, shortened form.

contractual adjective *a contractual obligation.* agreed, binding, formal, formalized, legally enforceable, signed and sealed, unbreakable.

contradict verb *It's considered rude to contradict other people's views.* challenge, confute, controvert, disagree with, dispute, gainsay, impugn, oppose, speak against.
OPPOSITES: SEE **confirm**.

contradictory adjective *contradictory opinions.* antithetical, conflicting, contrary, discrepant, different, incompatible, inconsistent, irreconcilable, opposed, opposite.
OPPOSITES: SEE **consistent**.

contraption noun apparatus, contrivance, device, gadget, invention, machine, mechanism.

contrary adjective **1** [pronounced *con*trary] *She spoke for the motion, and I put the contrary view.* contradictory, conflicting, converse, different, opposed, opposite, other, reverse.
OPPOSITES: SEE **similar**.
2 [pronounced *con*trary] *contrary winds.* adverse, hostile, inimical, opposing, unfavourable, unhelpful.
OPPOSITES: SEE **favourable**.
3 [pronounced con*trary*] *a contrary child.* awkward, cantankerous, defiant, difficult, disobedient, disobliging, intractable, obstinate, perverse, rebellious, [*informal*] stroppy, stubborn, uncooperative, wayward, wilful.
OPPOSITES: SEE **co-operative**.

contrast noun *a contrast between two things.* antithesis, comparison, difference, differentiation, disparity, dissimilarity, distinction, divergence, foil (*act as a foil to*), opposition.
OPPOSITES: SEE **similarity**.

contrast verb **1** *The teacher contrasted the work of the two students.* compare, differentiate between, discriminate between, distinguish between, emphasize differences between, make a distinction between, set one against the other.
2 *His style contrasts with mine.* be set off (by), clash (with), deviate (from), differ (from).

contrasting adjective *contrasting colours. contrasting opinions.* antithetical, clashing, conflicting, different, dissimilar, incompatible, opposite.
OPPOSITES: SEE **similar**.

contretemps noun SEE **mishap**.

contribute verb *to contribute money to charity.* bestow, donate, [*informal*] fork out, give, provide, put up, sponsor (*to sponsor an event or a person*), subscribe, supply.
to contribute to *Good weather contributed to our enjoyment.* add to, encourage, SEE **help** verb, reinforce, support.

contribution noun **1** *a contribution to charity.* donation, fee, gift, grant, [*informal*] handout, offering, payment, sponsorship, subscription.
2 *The weather made an important contribution to our enjoyment.* addition, encouragement, SEE **help** noun, input, support.

contributor noun **1** *a contributor to charity.* backer, benefactor, donor, giver, helper, patron, sponsor, subscriber, supporter.

2 *a contributor to a magazine.* columnist, correspondent, free-lance, journalist, reporter, writer.

contrite adjective SEE **penitent.**

contrivance noun SEE **device.**

contrive verb 1 *We contrived to get there in spite of a bus strike.* SEE **manage.**
2 *He contrived a way to do it.* SEE **plan** verb.

control noun *Who is in control? A teacher needs good control in the classroom.* administration, authority, charge, command, direction, discipline, government, guidance, influence, jurisdiction, management, mastery, orderliness, organization, oversight, power, regulation, restraint, rule, strictness, supervision, supremacy.
to gain control of annex, seize, steal, take over, usurp, win.
to have control of SEE **control** verb.

control verb 1 *The government controls the country's affairs. Managers control the workforce.* administer, [*informal*] be at the helm of, be in charge of, [*informal*] boss, command, conduct, cope with, deal with, direct, dominate, engineer, govern, guide, handle, have control of, lead, look after, manage, manipulate, order about, oversee, regiment, regulate, rule, run, superintend, supervise.
2 *They built a dam to control the floods.* check, confine, contain, curb, hold back, keep in check, master, repress, restrain, subdue, suppress.

controversial adjective *a controversial decision.* arguable, contentious, controvertible, debatable, disputable, doubtful, [*formal*] polemical, problematical, questionable.
OPPOSITES: SEE **straightforward.**

controversy noun *controversy about the building of a motorway.* altercation, argument, contention, debate, disagreement, dispute, dissension, issue, [*formal*] polemic, quarrel, war of words, wrangle.

controvert verb SEE **contradict.**

contumely noun SEE **insult** noun.

contusion noun SEE **bruise** noun.

conundrum noun SEE **riddle** noun.

conurbation noun SEE **town.**

convalesce verb *to convalesce after an illness.* get better, improve, make progress, mend, recover, recuperate, regain strength.

convalescent adjective *convalescent after an operation.* getting better, improving, making progress, [*informal*] on the mend, recovering, recuperating.
convalescent home SEE **hospital.**

convector noun SEE **fire** noun.

convene verb 1 *The chairman convened a meeting.* bring together, call, [*formal*] convoke, summon.
2 *The meeting convened at two o'clock.* SEE **assemble.**

convenient adjective *a convenient shop. a convenient tool. a convenient moment.* accessible, appropriate, at hand, available, handy, helpful, labour-saving, nearby, neat, opportune, suitable, timely, usable, useful.
OPPOSITES: SEE **inconvenient.**

convention noun 1 *a convention of business people.* SEE **assembly.**
2 *a human rights convention.* SEE **agreement.**
3 *It's a convention to give presents at Christmas.* custom, etiquette, formality, matter of form, practice, rule, tradition.

conventional adjective 1 *conventional behaviour. conventional ideas.* accepted, accustomed, common, commonplace, correct, customary, decorous, everyday, expected, habitual, mainstream, normal, ordinary, orthodox, prevalent, regular, routine, [*informal*] run-of-the-mill, standard, straight, traditional, unsurprising, usual.
OPPOSITES: SEE **unconventional.**
2 [*uncomplimentary*] *Don't be so conventional!* bourgeois, conservative, formal, hackneyed, hidebound, pedestrian, rigid, stereotyped, [*informal*] stuffy, unadventurous, unimaginative, unoriginal.
OPPOSITES: SEE **independent.**

converge verb *Motorways converge in one mile.* coincide, combine, come together, join, meet, merge.
OPPOSITES: SEE **disperse, diverge.**

conversant adjective SEE **knowledgeable.**

conversation noun [*informal*] chat, [*informal*] chin-wag, [*formal*] colloquy, communication, [*formal*] conference, dialogue, discourse, discussion, exchange of views, gossip, [*informal*] heart-to-heart, [*formal*] intercourse, [*informal*] natter, phone-call, [*informal*] powwow, SEE **talk** noun, tête-à-tête.

converse adjective SEE **opposite** adjective.

converse verb [=*have a conversation*] SEE **talk** verb.

convert verb 1 *We converted the attic to a games-room.* SEE **adapt.**
2 *She converted me to a new way of thinking.* change, change someone's mind, convince, persuade, re-educate, reform, regenerate, rehabilitate, save (=*convert to Christianity*), win over.

convertible noun SEE **car**.

convex adjective bulging, SEE **curved**, domed.
OPPOSITE: concave.

convey verb **1** *to convey goods.* bear, bring, carry, conduct, deliver, export, ferry, fetch, forward, import, move, send, shift, ship, take, transfer, transport.
2 *What does his message convey to you?* communicate, disclose, impart, imply, indicate, mean, reveal, signify, tell.

conveyance noun SEE **vehicle**.

convict noun *Convicts were transported to Australia.* condemned person, criminal, culprit, felon, malefactor, prisoner, wrongdoer.

convict verb *to convict someone of a crime.* condemn, declare guilty, prove guilty, sentence.
OPPOSITES: SEE **acquit**.

conviction noun **1** *He spoke with conviction.* assurance, certainty, confidence, firmness.
2 *She has strong religious convictions.* belief, creed, faith, opinion, persuasion, principle, tenet, view.

convince verb *He convinced the jury. He convinced them that he was innocent.* assure, [*informal*] bring round, convert, persuade, prove to, reassure, satisfy, sway, win over.

convincing adjective *convincing evidence.* conclusive, decisive, definite, persuasive, unambiguous, unarguable, unequivocal.
OPPOSITES: SEE **inconclusive**.

convivial adjective SEE **sociable**.

convocation noun SEE **assembly**.

convoke verb SEE **summon**.

convoluted adjective SEE **complicated**.

convolution noun SEE **coil** noun.

convoy noun *a convoy of ships.* armada, fleet, SEE **group** noun.

convulsion noun **1** *The doctor treated him for convulsions.* attack, fit, involuntary movement, paroxysm, seizure, spasm.
2 *a volcanic convulsion.* disturbance, eruption, outburst, tremor, turbulence, upheaval.

convulsive adjective *convulsive movements.* jerky, shaking, spasmodic, [*informal*] twitchy, uncontrolled, uncoordinated, violent, wrenching.

cook noun chef.

cook verb *to cook a meal.* concoct, heat up, make, prepare, warm up.
RELATED ADJECTIVES: culinary, gastronomic, SEE **taste** verb.
to cook something up SEE **plot** verb.

WAYS TO COOK FOOD: bake, barbecue, boil, braise, brew, broil, casserole, coddle (*eggs*), fry, grill, pickle, poach, roast, sauté, scramble (*eggs*), simmer, steam, stew, toast.

OTHER THINGS TO DO IN COOKING: baste, blend, chop, grate, freeze, infuse, knead, mix, peel, sieve, sift, stir, whisk.

SOME COOKING UTENSILS: baking-tin, basin, billy-can, blender, bowl, breadboard, breadknife, carving knife, casserole, cauldron, chafing dish, chip-pan, coffee grinder, colander, corkscrew, SEE **crockery**, SEE **cutlery**, deep-fat-fryer, dish, food-processor, frying-pan, jug, kettle, ladle, liquidizer, microwave, mincer, mixer, pan, pepper-mill, percolator, plate, pot, pressure-cooker, rolling-pin, rôtisserie, salt-cellar, saucepan, scales, skewer, spatula, spit, strainer, timer, tin-opener, toaster, whisk, wok, wooden spoon.

OTHER KITCHEN EQUIPMENT: SEE **kitchen**.

---

cooker noun SEE **stove**.

cooking noun baking, catering, cookery, cuisine.

cool adjective **1** *cool weather.* chilly, SEE **cold** adjective, coldish.
2 *a cool drink.* chilled, iced, refreshing.
OPPOSITES: SEE **hot**.
3 *a cool reaction to danger.* SEE **brave**, calm, collected, composed, dignified, elegant, [*informal*] laid-back, level-headed, quiet, relaxed, self-possessed, sensible, serene, unflustered, unruffled, urbane.
OPPOSITES: SEE **frantic**.
4 *cool feelings.* aloof, apathetic, dispassionate, distant, frigid, half-hearted, indifferent, lukewarm, negative, offhand, reserved, [*informal*] stand-offish, unconcerned, unemotional, unenthusiastic, unfriendly, unresponsive, unwelcoming.
OPPOSITES: SEE **passionate**.
5 *a cool request for £1000.* bold, cheeky, impertinent, impudent, shameless, tactless.

cool verb **1** *to cool food.* allow to get cold, chill, freeze, ice, lower the temperature of, refrigerate.
OPPOSITES: SEE **heat** verb.
2 *to cool someone's enthusiasm.* abate, allay, assuage, calm, dampen, lessen, moderate, [*informal*] pour cold water on, quiet, temper.
OPPOSITES: SEE **inflame**.

coolie noun SEE **worker**.

coomb noun SEE **valley**.

coop noun *a chicken coop*. SEE **enclosure**.

coop verb **to coop up** SEE **confine**.

co-operate verb *We need two people to co-operate on this job*. aid each other, assist each other, collaborate, combine, conspire (=*co-operate in wrongdoing*), help each other, [*informal*] join forces, [*informal*] pitch in, [*informal*] play ball, [*informal*] pull together, support each other, work as a team, work together.
OPPOSITES: SEE **compete**.

co-operation noun aid, assistance, collaboration, co-operative effort [SEE **co-operative**], co-ordination, help, joint action, team-work.
OPPOSITES: SEE **competition**.

co-operative adjective **1** *As everyone was co-operative, we finished early*. accommodating, comradely, constructive, hard-working, helpful to each other, keen, obliging, supportive, united, willing, working as a team.
OPPOSITES: SEE **competitive**, **unco-operative**.
2 *a co-operative effort*, collective, combined, communal, concerted, co-ordinated, corporate, joint, shared.
OPPOSITES: SEE **individual** adjective.

co-opt verb SEE **appoint**.

co-ordinate verb SEE **organize**.

cop noun SEE **policeman**.

cope verb *Shall I help you, or can you cope?* carry on, get by, make do, manage, survive, win through.
to cope with *She coped with her illness cheerfully*. contend with, deal with, endure, handle, look after, suffer, tolerate.

copier noun SEE **reprographics**.

copious adjective *copious supplies of food*. abundant, ample, bountiful, extravagant, generous, great, huge, inexhaustible, large, lavish, liberal, luxuriant, overflowing, plentiful, profuse, unsparing, unstinting.
OPPOSITES: SEE **scarce**.

copperplate noun SEE **handwriting**.

coppice, copse nouns *a coppice of birch trees*. SEE **wood**.

copulate verb SEE **mate** verb.

copy noun **1** *a copy of a letter. a copy of a work of art*. carbon-copy, clone, counterfeit, double, duplicate, facsimile, fake, forgery, imitation, likeness, model, pattern, photocopy, print, replica, representation, reproduction, tracing, transcript, twin, Xerox.
2 *a copy of a book*. edition, volume.
SEE ALSO **book** noun.

copy verb **1** *to copy a work of art. to copy someone's ideas*. borrow, counterfeit, crib, duplicate, emulate, follow, forge, imitate, photocopy, plagiarize, print, repeat, reproduce, simulate, transcribe, xerox.
2 *to copy someone's voice or mannerisms*. ape, imitate, impersonate, mimic, parrot.

coquette noun (=*a flirtatious person*). SEE **flirtatious**.

coquettish adjective SEE **flirtatious**.

coral reef SEE **island**.

cord noun *a length of cord*. cable, catgut, lace, line, rope, strand, string, twine, wire.

cordial adjective SEE **friendly**.

cordial noun SEE **drink** noun.

cordon noun *a cordon of policemen*. barrier, chain, fence, line, ring, row.

cordon verb **to cordon off** SEE **isolate**.

corduroy noun KINDS OF CLOTH: SEE **cloth**.
corduroys SEE **trousers**.

core noun **1** *the core of an apple. the core of the earth*. centre, heart, inside, middle, nucleus.
2 *the core of a problem*. central issue, crux, essence, kernel, [*slang*] nitty-gritty, nub.

cork noun *a cork in a bottle*. bung, plug, stopper.

corkscrew noun SEE **spiral** noun.

corn noun *a field of corn*. SEE **cereal**.

corner noun **1** *a corner where lines or surfaces meet*. angle, crook (*the crook of your arm*), joint.
2 *a quiet corner*. hideaway, hiding-place, hole, niche, nook, recess, retreat.
3 *the corner of the road*. bend, crossroads, intersection, junction, turn, turning.

corner verb *After a chase, they cornered him*. capture, catch, trap.

corner-stone noun SEE **foundation**.

cornucopia noun SEE **plenty**.

corny adjective SEE **hackneyed**.

corollary noun SEE **consequence**.

coronation noun enthronement, crowning.

coroner noun SEE **official** noun.

coronet noun crown, diadem, tiara.

corporal adjective SEE **physical**.
corporal punishment SEE **punishment**.

corporate adjective SEE **collective**.

corporation noun 1 *a business corporation.* company, concern, enterprise, firm, organization.
2 *the city corporation.* council, local government.

corps noun SEE **armed services.**

corpse noun body, cadaver, carcass, remains, skeleton.

corpulent adjective SEE **fat** adjective.

corral noun SEE **enclosure.**

correct adjective 1 *the correct time. correct information.* accurate, authentic, exact, factual, faithful, faultless, flawless, genuine, precise, reliable, right, strict, true.
OPPOSITES: SEE **inaccurate, wrong.**
2 *the correct thing to do.* acceptable, appropriate, fitting, just, normal, proper, regular, standard, suitable, tactful, unexceptionable, well-mannered.
OPPOSITES: SEE **inappropriate, wrong.**

correct verb 1 *to correct a fault.* adjust, alter, cure, [*informal*] debug (*to debug a computer system*), put right, rectify, redress, remedy, repair.
2 *to correct pupils' homework.* assess, mark.
3 *to correct a wrongdoer.* SEE **rebuke.**

correlate verb SEE **compare.**

correlative adjective SEE **corresponding.**

correspond verb 1 *Her story corresponds with mine.* accord, agree, be consistent, coincide, concur, conform, correlate, fit, harmonize, match, parallel, square, tally.
2 *I corresponded with a girl in Paris.* communicate with, send letters to, write to.

correspondence noun *A secretary deals with his boss's correspondence.* letters, memoranda, [*informal*] memos, messages, notes, writings.

correspondent noun SEE **writer.**

corresponding adjective *When I got a more responsible job I expected a corresponding rise in pay.* analogous, appropriate, commensurate, complementary, correlative, equivalent, matching, parallel, reciprocal, related, similar.

corridor noun hall, passage, passageway.

corroborate verb SEE **support** verb.

corrode verb 1 *Acid may corrode metal.* consume, eat away, erode, oxidize, rot, rust, tarnish.
2 *Many metals corrode.* crumble, deteriorate, disintegrate, tarnish.

corrugated adjective *a corrugated surface.* creased, [*informal*] crinkly, [*formal*] fluted, furrowed, lined, puckered, ribbed, ridged, wrinkled.

corrupt adjective 1 *a corrupt judge. corrupt practices.* [*informal*] bent, bribable, criminal, crooked, dishonest, dishonourable, false, fraudulent, unethical, unprincipled, unscrupulous, unsound, untrustworthy.
2 *corrupt behaviour. a corrupt individual.* debauched, decadent, degenerate, depraved, [*informal*] dirty, dissolute, evil, immoral, iniquitous, low, perverted, profligate, rotten, sinful, venal, vicious, wicked.
OPPOSITES: SEE **honest.**

corrupt verb 1 *to corrupt an official. to corrupt the course of justice.* bribe, divert, [*informal*] fix, influence, pervert, suborn, subvert.
2 *to corrupt the innocent.* debauch, deprave, lead astray, make corrupt [SEE **corrupt** adjective], tempt, seduce.

corsage noun SEE **bouquet.**

cortège noun cavalcade, SEE **funeral,** parade, procession.

cosh verb SEE **hit** verb.

cosmetics noun make-up, toiletries.

VARIOUS COSMETICS: cream, deodorant, eye-shadow, lipstick, lotion, mascara, nail varnish, perfume, powder, scent, talc, talcum powder.

Several English words, including *cosmic*, *cosmopolitan*, and *cosmos*, are related to Greek *kosmos = world*.

---

cosmic adjective *cosmic space.* boundless, endless, infinite, limitless, universal.

cosmonaut noun astronaut, space-traveller.

cosmopolitan adjective *Big cities usually have a cosmopolitan atmosphere.* international, multicultural, sophisticated, urbane.
OPPOSITES: SEE **provincial.**

cosmos noun galaxy, universe.

cosset verb SEE **pamper.**

cost noun *the cost of a ticket.* amount, charge, expenditure, expense, fare, figure, outlay, payment, price, rate, value.

cost verb *This watch costs £10.* be valued at, be worth, fetch, go for, realize, sell for, [*informal*] set you back.

costermonger noun [*old-fashioned*] barrow-boy, market-trader, SEE **seller**, street-trader.

costly adjective SEE **expensive**.

costume noun *actors' costumes.* [*formal*] apparel, attire, SEE **clothes**, clothing, dress, fancy-dress, garb, garments, [*informal*] get-up, livery, outfit, period dress, [*old-fashioned*] raiment, robes, uniform, vestments.

cosy adjective *a cosy room. a cosy atmosphere.* comfortable, [*informal*] comfy, homely, intimate, reassuring, relaxing, restful, secure, snug, soft, warm.
OPPOSITES: SEE **uncomfortable**.

cot noun SEE **bed**.

coterie noun SEE **group** noun.

cottage noun SEE **house** noun.

cotton noun **1** KINDS OF CLOTH: SEE **cloth**.
2 *cotton to sew on a button.* thread.

couch noun SEE **seat** noun.

couchette noun SEE **bed**.

council noun **1** *a council of war.* SEE **assembly**.
2 *the town council.* corporation.
council house SEE **house** noun.

councillor noun [Do not confuse with *counsellor*.] member of the council, official.

counsel noun [Do not confuse with *council*.] **1** *counsel for the defence.* SEE **lawyer**.
2 *She gave me good counsel.* SEE **advice**.

counsel verb *The careers officer counselled me about a possible career.* advise, give help, guide, have a discussion with, listen to your views.

counsellor noun [Do not confuse with *councillor*.] adviser.

count verb **1** *Count your money.* add up, calculate, check, compute, enumerate, estimate, figure out, keep account of, [*informal*] notch up, number, reckon, score, take stock of, tell, total, [*informal*] tot up, work out.
2 *It's taking part that counts, not winning.* be important, have significance, matter, signify.
to count on *You can count on my support.* bank on, believe in, depend on, expect, have faith in, rely on, swear by, trust.

countenance noun *a sad countenance.* air, appearance, aspect, demeanour, expression, face, features, look, visage.

countenance verb *They would not countenance our suggestion.* SEE **approve**.

counter noun **1** *a counter in a shop or café.* bar, sales-point, service-point.
2 *You play ludo with counters.* disc, token.

counteract verb *a treatment to counteract poison.* act against, be an antidote to, cancel out, SEE **counterbalance**, fight against, foil, invalidate, militate against, negate, neutralize, offset, oppose, resist, thwart, withstand, work against.

counter-attack noun, verb SEE **attack** noun, verb.

counterbalance verb *Their strength in defence counterbalances our strength in attack.* balance, compensate for, SEE **counteract**, counterpoise, counterweight, equalize.

counterblast noun SEE **response**.

counter-espionage noun SEE **spying**.

counterfeit adjective *counterfeit money. a counterfeit work of art.* artificial, bogus, copied, ersatz, fake, false, feigned, forged, fraudulent, imitation, pastiche, phoney, [*childish*] pretend, sham, simulated, spurious.
OPPOSITES: SEE **genuine**.

counterfeit verb **1** *to counterfeit money.* copy, fake, forge.
2 *to counterfeit an illness.* feign, imitate, pretend, sham, simulate.

countermand verb SEE **cancel**.

counterpart noun *The sales manager phoned his counterpart in the rival firm.* corresponding person or thing, equivalent, match, opposite number, parallel person or thing.

counter-productive adjective *Our attempt to help her was counter-productive.* negative, worse than useless.

countless adjective *countless stars. a countless number.* endless, immeasurable, incalculable, infinite, innumerable, many, measureless, myriad, numberless, numerous, unnumbered, untold.
OPPOSITES: SEE **finite**.

country noun **1** *the countries of the world.* canton, commonwealth, domain, empire, kingdom, land, nation, people, principality, realm, state, territory.
POLITICAL SYSTEMS FOUND IN VARIOUS COUNTRIES: democracy, dictatorship, monarchy, republic.
2 *There's some attractive country near here.* countryside, green belt, landscape, scenery.
RELATED ADJECTIVES: SEE **rural**.

countryside noun SEE **country**.

county noun [*old-fashioned*] shire.

coup, coup d'état nouns SEE **revolution**.

coupé noun SEE **car**.

couple noun SEE **pair** noun.

couple verb **1** *to couple two things together.* combine, connect, fasten, hitch, join, link, match, pair, unite, yoke.
2 *to couple sexually.* SEE **mate** verb.

coupon noun *Save ten coupons and get a free mug.* tear-off slip, ticket, token, voucher.

courage noun audacity, boldness, [*informal*] bottle, bravery, daring, dauntlessness, determination, fearlessness, fibre (*moral fibre*), firmness, fortitude, gallantry, [*informal*] grit, [*informal*] guts, heroism, indomitability, intrepidity, mettle, [*informal*] nerve, [*informal*] pluck, prowess, resolution, spirit, [*slang*] spunk, [*formal*] stoicism, valour.
OPPOSITES: SEE **cowardice**.

courageous adjective audacious, bold, brave, cool, daring, dauntless, determined, fearless, gallant, game, heroic, indomitable, intrepid, lion-hearted, noble, plucky, resolute, spirited, stalwart, stoical, tough, unafraid, uncomplaining, undaunted, unshrinking, valiant, valorous.
OPPOSITES: SEE **cowardly**.

courier noun **1** *A courier delivers packages.* carrier, messenger, runner.
2 *A courier helps tourists.* guide, representative.

course noun **1** *a normal course of events.* advance, continuation, development, movement, passage, passing, progress, progression, succession.
2 *a ship's course.* bearings, direction, path, route, way.
3 *a course of treatment at hospital.* programme, schedule, sequence, series.
4 *a course in college.* curriculum, syllabus.
5 *a golf course.* links.
6 *a racecourse.* SEE **racecourse**.
7 *a course of a meal.* SEE **meal**.
of course SEE **undoubtedly**.

course verb SEE **flow** verb, **hunt** verb.

court noun **1** SEE **courtyard**.
2 *a monarch's court.* entourage, followers, palace, retinue.
3 *a court of law.* [*old-fashioned*] assizes, bench, court martial, high court, lawcourt, magistrates' court.
LEGAL TERMS: SEE **law**.

court verb **1** *to court attention.* [*informal*] ask for (*She's just asking for attention*), attract, invite, provoke, seek, solicit.
2 [*old-fashioned*] *to court a boyfriend or girlfriend.* date, [*informal*] go out with, make advances to, make love to [SEE **love** noun], try to win, woo.

courteous adjective SEE **polite**.

courtesan noun SEE **prostitute** noun.

courtesy noun SEE **politeness**.

courtier noun [*old-fashioned*] *a king's courtiers.* attendant, follower, lady, lord, noble, page, steward.

courtyard noun court, enclosure, forecourt, patio, [*informal*] quad, quadrangle, yard.

cousin noun MEMBERS OF A FAMILY: SEE **family**.

couturier noun SEE **designer**.

cove noun SEE **bay**.

coven noun SEE **group** noun.

covenant noun SEE **agreement**.

covenant verb SEE **agree**.

cover noun **1** *a cover to keep the rain off.* canopy, cloak, clothes, clothing, coat, SEE **covering**, roof, screen, shield, tarpaulin.
2 *a jam-pot cover.* cap, lid, top.
3 *a cover for papers or a book.* binding, case, dust-jacket, envelope, file, folder, portfolio, wrapper.
4 *cover from a storm.* hiding-place, refuge, sanctuary, shelter.
5 *A helicopter gave them cover from the air.* defence, guard, protection, support.
6 *the cover of an assumed identity.* camouflage, concealment, cover-up, deception, disguise, façade, front, mask, pretence, veneer.

cover verb **1** *A cloth covered the table. Cloud covers the hills. Fresh paint will cover the graffiti.* blot out, bury, camouflage, cap, carpet, cloak, clothe, cloud, coat, conceal, curtain, disguise, drape, dress, encase, enclose, enshroud, envelop, face, hide, hood, mantle, mask, obscure, overlay, overspread, plaster, protect, screen, shade, sheathe, shield, shroud, spread over, surface, tile, veil, veneer, wrap up.
2 *Will £10 cover your expenses?* be enough for, match, meet, pay for, suffice for.
3 *An encyclopedia covers many subjects.* comprise, contain, deal with, embrace, encompass, include, incorporate, involve, treat.

covering noun *a light covering of snow.* blanket, cap, carpet, casing, cladding, cloak, coating, cocoon, cover, facing, film, layer, mantle, pall, sheath, sheet, shroud, skin, surface, tarpaulin, veil, veneer, wrapping.

coverlet noun SEE **bedclothes**.

covert adjective SEE **secret** adjective.

cover-up noun SEE **deception**.

covet verb SEE **desire** verb.

covetous adjective SEE **greedy**.

covey noun SEE **group** noun.

cow noun SEE **cattle**.

cow verb SEE **frighten**.

coward noun [*informal*] chicken, deserter, runaway.
OPPOSITES: SEE **hero**.

cowardice noun cowardliness, desertion, evasion, faint-heartedness, SEE **fear** noun, [*informal*] funk, shirking, spinelessness, timidity.
OPPOSITES: SEE **heroism**.

cowardly adjective *a cowardly person. a cowardly action.* abject, afraid, base, chicken-hearted, cowering, craven, dastardly, faint-hearted, fearful, [*informal*] gutless, [*old-fashioned*] lily-livered, pusillanimous, spineless, submissive, timid, timorous, unheroic, [*informal*] yellow.
OPPOSITES: SEE **brave**.
to be cowardly [*informal*] chicken out, cower, desert, [*informal*] funk it, run away.

cowed adjective SEE **afraid**.

cower verb *The naughty dog cowered in a corner.* cringe, crouch, flinch, grovel, hide, quail, shiver, shrink, skulk, tremble.

cox, coxswain nouns SEE **sailor**.

coy adjective *Don't be coy: come and be introduced.* bashful, coquettish, demure, diffident, embarrassed, modest, reserved, retiring, self-conscious, sheepish, shy, timid.
OPPOSITES: SEE **forward** adjective.

crabbed adjective SEE **bad-tempered**.

crack noun **1** *the crack of a whip.* VARIOUS SOUNDS: SEE **sound** noun.
2 *a crack on the head.* SEE **hit** noun.
3 [*informal*] *a witty crack.* SEE **joke** noun.
4 *a crack in a cup. a crack in a rock.* break, chink, chip, cleavage, cleft, cranny, craze, crevice, fissure, flaw, fracture, gap, opening, rift, split.

crack verb **1** *The whip cracked.* VARIOUS SOUNDS: SEE **sound** noun.
2 *to crack a cup. to crack a nut.* break, chip, fracture, snap, splinter, split.
3 *to crack a code. to crack a problem.* SEE **solve**.
to crack up [*informal*] SEE **disintegrate**, **praise** verb.

crackle noun, verb VARIOUS SOUNDS: SEE **sound** noun.

crackpot noun SEE **madman**.

cradle noun *a baby's cradle.* SEE **bed**.

cradle verb *to cradle someone in your arms.* SEE **hold** verb.

craft noun **1** *the craft of thatching.* art, handicraft, job, skilled work, technique, trade.
VARIOUS CRAFTS: SEE **art**.
2 *I admired the thatcher's craft.* SEE **craftsmanship**.
3 *He wins by craft rather than by honest effort.* SEE **deceit**.
4 *All sorts of craft were in the harbour.* SEE **vessel**.

craftsman noun SEE **artist**.

craftsmanship noun artistry, cleverness, craft, dexterity, expertise, handiwork, knack, [*informal*] know-how, SEE **skill**, workmanship.

crafty adjective *a crafty deception.* artful, astute, calculating, canny, clever, cunning, deceitful, designing, devious, [*informal*] dodgy, [*informal*] foxy, SEE **furtive**, guileful, ingenious, knowing, machiavellian, scheming, shrewd, sly, [*informal*] sneaky, tricky, wily.
OPPOSITES: SEE **innocent**, **straightforward**.
a crafty person SEE **cheat** noun.

crag noun *a steep crag.* bluff, cliff, precipice, rock.

craggy adjective *a craggy pinnacle.* jagged, rocky, rough, rugged, steep, uneven.

cram verb **1** *to cram into a confined space.* compress, crowd, crush, fill, force, jam, overcrowd, overfill, pack, press, squeeze, stuff.
2 *to cram for an examination.* SEE **study** verb.

cramp verb *Your presence cramps my style.* SEE **restrict**.

cramped adjective *cramped accommodation.* crowded, narrow, restricted, tight, uncomfortable.
OPPOSITES: SEE **roomy**.

crane noun *a crane for loading freight.* davit, derrick, hoist.

crane verb *to crane your neck.* SEE **stretch** verb.

cranium noun skull.

crank noun SEE **eccentric** noun.

cranky adjective SEE **eccentric** adjective.

cranny noun *a cranny in a rock.* SEE **crack** noun.

crash noun **1** *a loud crash.* VARIOUS SOUNDS: SEE **sound** noun.
2 *a rail crash. a crash on the motorway.* accident, bump, collision, derailment, SEE **disaster**, impact, knock, pile-up, smash, wreck.
3 *a crash on the stockmarket.* collapse, depression, fall.

crash verb **1** *to crash into someone.* bump, collide, SEE **hit** verb, knock, lurch, pitch, smash.
2 *to crash to the ground.* collapse, fall, plunge, topple.

crash-dive noun, verb SEE **dive** noun, verb.

crash-helmet noun KINDS OF HEAD-GEAR: SEE **hat.**

crass adjective SEE **stupid.**

crate noun *We packed our belongings in crates.* box, carton, case, packing-case, tea-chest.

crater noun *The explosion left a crater.* abyss, cavity, chasm, hole, hollow, opening, pit.

cravat noun necktie.

crave verb SEE **desire** verb.

craven adjective SEE **cowardly.**

craving noun SEE **desire** noun.

crawl verb **1** *I crawled along a narrow ledge.* clamber, creep, edge, inch, slither, wriggle.
2 [*informal*] *She got high marks because she crawled to the teacher.* SEE **obsequious (to be obsequious).**

craze noun *the latest craze.* diversion, enthusiasm, fad, fashion, infatuation, mania, novelty, obsession, passion, pastime, rage, trend, vogue.

crazed adjective SEE **crazy.**

crazy adjective **1** *The dog went crazy when it was stung by a wasp.* berserk, crazed, delirious, demented, deranged, frantic, frenzied, hysterical, insane, lunatic, SEE **mad,** [*informal*] potty, [*informal*] scatty, unbalanced, unhinged, wild.
OPPOSITES: SEE **sane.**
2 *a crazy comedy.* absurd, confused, daft, eccentric, farcical, foolish, idiot, illogical, irrational, ludicrous, nonsensical, preposterous, ridiculous, senseless, silly, stupid, unreasonable, weird, zany.
OPPOSITES: SEE **sensible, straight.**
3 [*informal*] *crazy about snooker.* SEE **enthusiastic.**

creak noun, verb VARIOUS SOUNDS: SEE **sound** noun.

creamy adjective *a creamy liquid.* milky, oily, rich, smooth, thick, velvety.

crease noun *a crease in a piece of cloth.* corrugation, crinkle, fold, furrow, groove, line, pleat, pucker, ridge, ruck, tuck, wrinkle.

crease verb *to crease a piece of paper.* crimp, crinkle, crumple, crush, fold, furrow, pleat, pucker, ridge, ruck, rumple, wrinkle.

create verb *to create something new. to create trouble.* [*old-fashioned*] beget, SEE **begin,** be the creator of [SEE **creator**], breed, bring about, bring into existence, build, cause, conceive, concoct, constitute, construct, design, devise, engender, establish, form, found, generate, give rise to, hatch, institute, invent, make, make up, manufacture, occasion, originate, produce, set up, shape, think up.
OPPOSITES: SEE **destroy.**
to create a work of art compose, draw, embroider, engrave, model, paint, print, sculpt, sketch, throw (*pottery*), weave, write.
OTHER WORDS TO DO WITH ART: SEE **art.**

creation noun **1** *the creation of the world.* beginning, birth, building, conception, constitution, construction, establishing, formation, foundation, generation, genesis, inception, institution, making, origin, procreation, production, shaping.
OPPOSITES: SEE **destruction.**
2 *The dress is her own creation.* achievement, brainchild, concept, effort, handiwork, invention, product, work of art.

creative adjective *a creative imagination.* artistic, clever, fecund, fertile, imaginative, inspired, inventive, original, positive, productive, resourceful, talented.
OPPOSITES: SEE **destructive.**

creator noun **1** *the creator of an empire. the creator of a TV programme.* architect, begetter, builder, designer, deviser, discoverer, initiator, inventor, maker, manufacturer, originator, parent, producer.
2 *the creator of a work of art.* artist, author, composer, craftsman, painter, photographer, potter, sculptor, smith, weaver, writer.
3 *the Creator.* SEE **god.**

creature noun animal, beast, being, brute, mortal being.
VARIOUS SPECIES: SEE **animal** noun, **bird, fish, insect, reptile, snake.**

crèche noun SEE **nursery.**

Several English words, including *credentials, credible, credulous,* etc., are related to Latin *credere = to believe.*

---

credentials noun *You must show your credentials before they'll let you in.* authorization, documents, identity card, licence, passport, permit, proof of identity, warrant.

credible adjective [Do not confuse with *creditable.*] *The report about Martian visitors is not credible.* believable, conceivable, convincing, imaginable, likely,

persuasive, plausible, possible, reasonable, tenable, thinkable, trustworthy.
OPPOSITES: SEE **incredible**.

credit noun **1** *Her success brought credit to the school.* approval, commendation, distinction, esteem, fame, glory, honour, [*informal*] kudos, merit, praise, prestige, recognition, reputation, status.
OPPOSITES: SEE **dishonour**.
2 *a credit balance at the bank.* plus, positive.
OPPOSITE: debit [SEE **debt**].
3 *to buy on credit.* SEE **loan** noun.
credit card SEE **money**.
in credit [*informal*] in the black, solvent.

credit verb **1** *You won't credit her far-fetched story.* accept, believe, [*informal*] buy, count on, depend on, endorse, have faith in, reckon on, rely on, subscribe to, [*informal*] swallow, swear by, trust.
OPPOSITES: SEE **disbelieve**.
2 *I credited you with more sense.* attribute to, ascribe to, assign to, attach to.
3 *The bank credited £10 to my account.* add, enter.
OPPOSITES: SEE **debit**.

creditable adjective [Do not confuse with *credible.*] *a creditable performance.* admirable, commendable, estimable, excellent, good, honourable, laudable, meritorious, praiseworthy, respectable, well thought of, worthy.
OPPOSITES: SEE **unworthy**.

credulous adjective *You must be credulous if she fooled you with that story.* easily taken in, [*informal*] green, gullible, innocent, naïve, [*informal*] soft, trusting, unsuspecting.
OPPOSITES: SEE **sceptical**.

creed noun *a religious creed.* beliefs, convictions, doctrine, dogma, faith, principles, tenets.

creek noun SEE **bay**, estuary, inlet.

creep verb **1** *to creep along the ground.* crawl, edge, inch, move slowly, slink, slither, worm, wriggle, writhe.
2 *to creep quietly past.* move quietly, slip, sneak, steal, tiptoe.

creeper noun *Creepers had grown over the ruin.* SEE **climber**.

creepy adjective *creepy noises in the dark.* disturbing, eerie, frightening, ghostly, hair-raising, macabre, ominous, scary, sinister, spine-chilling, [*informal*] spooky, supernatural, threatening, uncanny, unearthly, weird.
OPPOSITES: SEE **natural, reassuring**.

cremate verb SEE **burn** verb.

cremation noun SEE **funeral**.

crenellated adjective SEE **indented**.

creosote noun wood-preservative.

crescent adjective *a crescent moon.* bow-shaped, curved.

crest noun **1** *a crest on a bird's head.* comb, plume, tuft.
2 *the crest of a hill.* apex, brow, crown, head, peak, ridge, summit, top.
3 *the school crest.* badge, emblem, insignia, seal, sign, symbol.

crestfallen adjective SEE **downcast**.

cretin noun SEE **idiot**.

crevasse noun [Do not confuse with *crevice.*] *a crevasse in a glacier.* SEE **chasm**.

crevice noun [Do not confuse with *crevasse.*] *a crevice in a wall.* SEE **crack** noun.

crew noun *a ship's crew.* SEE **group** noun.

crib noun *a baby's crib.* SEE **bed**, cot, cradle.

crib verb *to crib in a test.* cheat, copy, plagiarize.

crick noun *a crick in the neck.* SEE **pain** noun.

cricket noun CRICKETING TERMS: bail, batsman, bowler, boundary, cricketer, fielder, fieldsman, innings, lbw, maiden over, over, pad, run, slip, stump, test match, umpire, wicket, wicket-keeper.

crime noun *The law punishes crime.* delinquency, dishonesty, [*old-fashioned*] felony, illegality, law-breaking, misconduct, misdeed, misdemeanour, offence, racket, sin, transgression of the law, wrongdoing.

VARIOUS CRIMES: abduction, arson, blackmail, burglary, extortion, hijacking, hold-up, hooliganism, kidnapping, manslaughter, misappropriation, mugging, murder, pilfering, poaching, rape, robbery, shop-lifting, smuggling, stealing, theft, vandalism.

---

criminal adjective *a criminal act.* [*informal*] bent, corrupt, [*informal*] crooked, [*formal*] culpable, dishonest, felonious, illegal, illicit, indictable, nefarious, [*informal*] shady, unlawful, SEE **wrong** adjective.
OPPOSITES: SEE **lawful**.

criminal noun *The law punishes criminals.* convict, [*informal*] crook, culprit, delinquent, felon, hooligan, law-breaker, [*formal*] malefactor, offender, outlaw, recidivist, [*old-fashioned*] transgressor, villain, wrongdoer.

VARIOUS CRIMINALS: assassin, bandit, blackmailer, brigand, buccaneer, burglar, desperado, gangster, gunman, highwayman, hijacker, kidnapper, mugger, murderer, outlaw, pickpocket, pirate, poacher, racketeer, rapist, receiver, robber, shop-lifter, smuggler, swindler, terrorist, thief, thug, vandal.

crimson adjective SEE **red**.

cringe verb *to cringe in fear*. blench, cower, crouch, dodge, duck, flinch, grovel, quail, quiver, recoil, shrink back, shy away, tremble, wince.

crinkle noun, verb SEE **crease** noun, verb.

cripple noun SEE **disabled (disabled person)**.

cripple verb **1** *to cripple a person*. disable, dislocate (*a joint*), fracture (*a bone*), hamper, hamstring, incapacitate, lame, maim, mutilate, paralyse, weaken.
2 *to cripple a machine*. damage, make useless, put out of action, sabotage, spoil.

crippled adjective **1** *a crippled person*. deformed, SEE **disabled**, handicapped, hurt, incapacitated, injured, invalid, lame, maimed, mutilated, paralysed.
2 *a crippled vehicle*. damaged, immobilized, out of action, sabotaged, useless.

crisis noun **1** *the crisis of a story*. climax.
2 *We had a crisis when we found a gas leak*. danger, difficulty, emergency, predicament, problem.

crisp adjective **1** *crisp biscuits*. brittle, crackly, crispy, crunchy, fragile, hard and dry.
OPPOSITES: SEE **soft**.
2 *a crisp winter morning*. SEE **cold** adjective.
3 *a crisp manner*. SEE **brisk**.

criss-cross adjective SEE **chequered**.

criterion noun SEE **measure** noun, touchstone.

critic noun **1** *a music critic*. analyst, authority, commentator, judge, pundit, reviewer.
2 *a critic of the government*. attacker, detractor.

critical adjective **1** *Critical* can mean either (a) *unfavourable* (*a critical review of the dreadful new LP*) or (b) *showing careful judgement* (*a critical analysis of Shakespeare's plays*). (a) = *unfavourable*. captious, censorious, criticizing [SEE **criticize**], deprecatory, derogatory, fault-finding, hypercritical, [*informal*] nit-picking, scathing, slighting, uncomplimentary, unfavourable.
OPPOSITES: SEE **complimentary**.
(b) = *showing careful judgement*. analytical, discerning, discriminating, intelligent, judicious, perceptive.
OPPOSITES: SEE **imperceptive**.
2 *a critical decision*. crucial, SEE **dangerous**, decisive, important, key, momentous, vital.
OPPOSITES: SEE **unimportant**.

criticism noun **1** *unfair criticism of our behaviour*. censure, diatribe, disapproval, disparagement, judgement, reprimand, reproach, stricture, tirade, verbal attack.
2 *literary criticism*. analysis, appraisal, appreciation, assessment, commentary, critique, elucidation, evaluation, notice (*a favourable notice in the papers*), [*informal*] puff [= *a flattering notice*], review.

criticize verb **1** *She criticized us for being noisy. She criticized our efforts*. belittle, berate, blame, carp, [*informal*] cast aspersions on, castigate, censure, [*old-fashioned*] chide, condemn, decry, disapprove of, disparage, fault, find fault with, [*informal*] flay, impugn, [*informal*] knock, [*informal*] lash, [*informal*] pan, [*informal*] pick holes in, [*informal*] pitch into, [*informal*] rap, rate, rebuke, reprimand, satirize, scold, [*informal*] slam, [*informal*] slate, snipe at.
OPPOSITES: SEE **praise** verb.
2 *to criticize an author's work*. analyse, appraise, assess, evaluate, judge, review.

critique noun SEE **criticism**.

croak noun, verb VARIOUS SOUNDS: SEE **sound** noun.

crock, crocks nouns SEE **crockery**.

crockery noun ceramics, china, crocks, dishes, earthenware, porcelain, pottery, tableware.

VARIOUS ITEMS OF CROCKERY: basin, bowl, coffee-cup, coffee-pot, cup, dinner plate, dish, jug, milk-jug, mug, plate, [*American*] platter, pot, sauceboat, saucer, serving dish, side plate, soup bowl, sugar-bowl, teacup, teapot, [*old-fashioned*] trencher, tureen.
VARIOUS COOKING UTENSILS: SEE **cook**.

crocodile noun alligator.

croft noun SEE **farm** noun.

croissant noun SEE **bread**.

crony noun SEE **friend**.

crook noun **1** *the crook of your arm*. angle, bend, corner, hook.

2 [*informal*] *The cops got the crooks.* SEE **criminal** noun.

crooked adjective 1 *The picture hangs crooked.* angled, askew, awry, lopsided, offcentre.
2 *a crooked road. a crooked tree.* bent, bowed, curved, curving, deformed, misshapen, tortuous, twisted, twisty, winding, zigzag.
3 *a crooked salesman.* SEE **criminal** adjective.

croon verb SEE **sing**.

crop noun *a crop of fruit.* gathering, harvest, produce, sowing, vintage, yield.

crop verb 1 *Animals crop grass.* bite off, browse, eat, graze, nibble.
2 *A barber crops hair.* clip, SEE **cut** verb, shear, snip, trim.
to crop up *A difficulty cropped up.* appear, arise, come up, emerge, happen, occur, spring up, turn up.

cropper noun **to come a cropper** SEE **fall** verb.

crosier noun SEE **staff** noun.

cross adjective *She's always cross when she comes in from work.* SEE **angry**, annoyed, bad-tempered, cantankerous, crotchety, [*informal*] grumpy, ill-tempered, irascible, irate, irritable, peevish, short-tempered, testy, tetchy, upset, vexed.
OPPOSITES: SEE **even-tempered**.

cross noun 1 *marked with a cross.* intersecting lines, X.
RELATED ADJECTIVE [=*cross-shaped*]: cruciform.
2 *a cross I have to bear.* affliction, burden, difficulty, grief, misfortune, problem, sorrow, trial, tribulation, trouble, worry.
3 *a cross between two breeds. a cross between soup and stew.* amalgam, blend, combination, cross-breed, half-way house, hybrid, mixture, mongrel [=*a cross between two breeds of dog*].

cross verb 1 *lines which cross.* criss-cross, intersect, intertwine, meet, zigzag.
2 *to cross a river.* bridge, ford, go across, pass over, span, traverse.
3 *The trains crossed at high speed.* pass.
4 *Don't cross him when he's in a temper.* annoy, block, frustrate, hinder, impede, interfere with, oppose, stand in the way of, thwart.
to cross out SEE **cancel**.
to cross swords SEE **quarrel** verb.

cross-breed noun hybrid, mongrel.

cross-check verb SEE **check** verb.

cross-examine verb *to cross-examine a witness.* SEE **question** verb.

cross-eyed adjective [*informal*] boss-eyed, squinting.

crossing noun *a sea crossing.* SEE **journey** noun.

CROSSINGS OVER A RIVER, ROAD, RAILWAY, ETC.: bridge, causeway, flyover, ford, level-crossing, overpass, pedestrian crossing, pelican crossing, subway, stepping-stones, underpass, zebra crossing.

---

crosspatch noun SEE **angry (angry person)**.

cross-question verb SEE **question** verb.

cross-reference noun SEE **note** noun.

crossroads noun interchange, intersection, junction.

crotchety adjective SEE **cross** adjective.

crouch verb *They crouched in the bushes.* bend, bow, cower, cringe, duck, kneel, squat, stoop.

crow verb 1 *The cock crows every morning.*
VARIOUS SOUNDS: SEE **sound** noun.
2 *to crow about an achievement.* SEE **boast** verb.

crowd noun 1 *a crowd of people.* army, assembly, bunch, circle, cluster, collection, company, crush, flock, gathering, SEE **group** noun, horde, host, mass, mob, multitude, pack, rabble, swarm, throng.
2 *a football crowd.* audience, gate, spectators.

crowd verb *We crowded together. They crowded us into a small room.* assemble, bundle, compress, congregate, cram, crush, flock, gather, herd, huddle, jostle, mass, muster, overcrowd, pack, [*informal*] pile, press, push, squeeze, swarm, throng.

crowded adjective *a crowded room.* congested, cramped, full, jammed, jostling, overcrowded, overflowing, packed, swarming, teeming, thronging.
OPPOSITES: SEE **empty** adjective.

crown noun 1 *a monarch's crown.* coronet, diadem, tiara.
2 *the crown of a hill.* apex, brow, crown, head, peak, ridge, summit, top.

crown verb 1 *to crown a monarch.* anoint, appoint, enthrone, install.
2 *to crown your efforts with success.* cap, complete, conclude, consummate, finish off, perfect, round off, top.

crowning adjective *her crowning achievement.* culminating, deserved, final, highest, hoped for, perfect, successful, supreme, top, ultimate.

crowning noun *the crowning of a monarch.* coronation, enthronement.

crucial adjective *a crucial decision. a crucial part of an argument.* central, critical, decisive, important, major, momentous, pivotal, serious.
OPPOSITES: SEE **peripheral**.

crucifix noun cross, [*old-fashioned*] rood.

crude adjective **1** *crude oil.* natural, raw, unprocessed, unrefined.
OPPOSITES: SEE **refined**.
2 *crude workmanship.* amateurish, awkward, bungling, clumsy, inartistic, incompetent, inelegant, inept, makeshift, primitive, rough, rudimentary, unpolished, unrefined, unskilful, unworkmanlike.
OPPOSITES: SEE **dainty, skilful**.
3 *crude language.* SEE **indecent**.

cruel adjective **1** *a cruel action. a cruel person.* atrocious, barbaric, barbarous, beastly, blood-thirsty, bloody, brutal, callous, cold-blooded, diabolical, ferocious, fierce, flinty, grim, hard, hard-hearted, harsh, heartless, hellish, implacable, inexorable, inhuman, inhumane, malevolent, merciless, murderous, pitiless, relentless, remorseless, ruthless, sadistic, savage, spiteful, stern, stony-hearted, tyrannical, unfeeling, unjust, unkind, unmerciful, unrelenting, vengeful, vicious, violent.
OPPOSITES: SEE **kind** adjective.
2 *cruel disappointment.* SEE **severe**.

cruise noun *a sea cruise.* SEE **journey** noun.

cruise verb SEE **travel** verb.

crumb noun *a crumb of bread.* bit, fragment, grain, morsel, particle, scrap, shred, speck.

crumble verb **1** *Rotten wood crumbles.* break up, decay, decompose, deteriorate, disintegrate, fall apart, [*of rubber*] perish.
2 *He crumbled the cake onto his plate.* break into pieces, crush, fragment, grind, pound, powder, pulverize.

crumbly adjective *crumbly soil.* friable, granular, powdery.
OPPOSITES: SEE **solid, sticky**.

crumple verb *Don't crumple your clothes!* crease, crush, dent, fold, pucker, rumple, wrinkle.

crunch verb **1** *The dog crunched up a bone.* break, champ, chew, crush, grind, masticate, munch, scrunch, smash, squash.
2 *Footsteps crunched on the gravel.* VARIOUS SOUNDS: SEE **sound** noun.

crusade noun *a crusade against drugs.* campaign, drive, movement, struggle, war.

crush noun *I couldn't fight my way through the crush.* congestion, SEE **crowd** noun, jam.

crush verb **1** *to crush a finger in the door.* break, bruise, crumple, crunch, grind, SEE **injure**, mangle, mash, pound, press, pulp, pulverize, smash, squash, squeeze.
2 *to crush your opponents.* conquer, defeat, humiliate, mortify, overcome, overpower, overthrow, overwhelm, quash, quell, rout, subdue, thrash, vanquish.

crust noun *the crust of a loaf. the crust of the earth.* coat, coating, covering, incrustation, outer layer, outside, rind, scab, shell, skin, surface.

crustacean noun CRUSTACEANS INCLUDE: crab, lobster, shrimp.

crusty adjective **1** *a crusty loaf.* crisp.
2 *a crusty manner.* SEE **gruff**.

crutch noun *a crutch for a lame person.* prop, support.

crux noun *the crux of a problem.* centre, core, crucial issue, essence, heart, nub.

cry noun *a bird's cry. a cry of pain.* battle-cry, bellow, call, caterwaul, [*formal*] ejaculation, exclamation, hoot, howl, outcry, roar, scream, screech, shout, shriek, yell, yelp.

cry verb **1** *It was so sad it made me cry.* blubber, grizzle, shed tears, snivel, sob, wail, weep, whimper, whinge.
2 *Who cried out?* bawl, bellow, call, caterwaul, clamour, exclaim, roar, scream, screech, shout, shriek, yell, yelp.
to cry off SEE **withdraw**.

crypt noun *a church crypt.* basement, cellar, undercroft, vault.

cryptic adjective *a cryptic message.* coded, concealed, enigmatic, hidden, mysterious, obscure, occult, perplexing, puzzling, secret, unclear, unintelligible, veiled.
OPPOSITES: SEE **intelligible, plain** adjective.

crystal noun glass, mineral.
RELATED ADJECTIVE: crystalline.

crystalline adjective SEE **transparent**.

cub noun YOUNG ANIMALS: SEE **young** adjective.

cubby-hole noun SEE **compartment**.

cube noun cuboid, hexahedron.
RELATED ADJECTIVES: cubical, cuboidal.
OTHER SHAPES: SEE **shape** noun.

cubicle noun *changing cubicles at the swimming baths.* SEE **compartment**.

cuddle verb *to cuddle a baby.* caress, clasp lovingly, dandle, embrace, fondle, hold closely, huddle against, hug, kiss, nestle against, nurse, pet, snuggle against.

cudgel noun *armed with cudgels*. baton, bludgeon, cane, club, cosh, stick, truncheon.

cudgel verb *The attackers cudgelled him unconscious*. batter, beat, bludgeon, cane, [*informal*] clobber, cosh, SEE **hit** verb, pound, pummel, thrash, thump, [*informal*] thwack.

cue noun *Don't miss your cue to speak*. hint, prompt, reminder, sign, signal.

cuff noun PARTS OF A GARMENT: SEE **clothes**.
off-the-cuff SEE **impromptu**.

cuff verb SEE **hit** verb.

cuisine noun SEE **cooking**.

cul-de-sac noun SEE **road**.

culinary adjective *culinary skill*. to do with cooking.

cull verb 1 *to cull flowers*. SEE **pick** verb.
2 *to cull animals*. SEE **kill**.

culminate verb *The gala culminated in a firework display*. build up to, climax, close, conclude, end, finish, reach a finale, rise to a peak, terminate.

culottes noun SEE **trousers**.

culpable adjective *culpable negligence*. blameworthy, criminal, SEE **deliberate** adjective, guilty, knowing, liable, punishable, reprehensible, wrong.
OPPOSITES: SEE **innocent**.

culprit noun *They punished the culprit*. SEE **criminal** noun, delinquent, felon, malefactor, miscreant, offender, trouble-maker, wrongdoer.

cult noun 1 *a religious cult*. SEE **denomination**.
2 *The new pop-idol inspired a cult*. craze, enthusiasts [SEE **enthusiast**], fan-club, fashion, following, party, school, trend, vogue.

cultivate verb 1 *to cultivate land*. dig, farm, fertilize, hoe, manure, mulch, plough, prepare, rake, till, turn, work.
2 *to cultivate crops*. grow, plant, produce, raise, sow, take cuttings, tend.
3 *to cultivate good relations with your neighbours*. court, develop, encourage, foster, further, improve, promote, pursue, try to achieve.

cultivated adjective 1 *a cultivated way of speaking*. SEE **cultured**.
2 *cultivated land*. agricultural, farmed, farming, planted, prepared, tilled.

cultivation noun *the cultivation of the land*. agriculture, agronomy, culture, farming, gardening, horticulture, husbandry.

cultural adjective *The festival included sporting and cultural events*. aesthetic, artistic, civilized, civilizing, educational, elevating, enlightening, highbrow, improving, intellectual.
OPPOSITES: SEE **lowbrow**.

culture noun 1 *a nation's culture*. art, background, civilization, customs, education, learning, traditions.
2 *the culture of rare plants*. breeding, SEE **cultivation**, growing, nurturing.

cultured adjective *a cultured person*. artistic, civilized, cultivated, educated, erudite, highbrow, knowledgeable, scholarly, well-bred, well-educated, well-read.
OPPOSITES: SEE **ignorant**.

culvert noun SEE **drain** noun.

cumbersome adjective SEE **clumsy**.

cummerbund noun SEE **belt** noun.

cumulative adjective *the cumulative effect of something*. accumulating, building up, developing.

cunning adjective 1 *a cunning deception*. artful, SEE **crafty**, devious, dodgy, guileful, insidious, knowing, machiavellian, sly, subtle, tricky, wily.
2 *a cunning way to do something*. adroit, astute, SEE **clever**, ingenious, skilful.

cunning noun 1 [*uncomplimentary*] *Foxes have a reputation for cunning*. artfulness, chicanery, craftiness, deceit, deception, deviousness, duplicity, guile, slyness, trickery.
2 *The inventor showed great cunning in solving the problem*. cleverness, expertise, ingenuity.

cup noun 1 THINGS TO DRINK FROM: beaker, bowl, chalice, glass, goblet, mug, tankard, teacup, tumbler, wineglass.
2 *a cup presented on sports day*. award, prize, trophy.

cupboard noun VARIOUS KINDS OF CUPBOARD: cabinet, chiffonier, closet, dresser, filing-cabinet, food-cupboard, larder, locker, sideboard, wardrobe.
OTHER FURNITURE: SEE **furniture**.

cupidity noun SEE **greed**.

cur noun SEE **dog** noun.

curable adjective *a curable disease*. operable, remediable, treatable.
OPPOSITES: SEE **incurable**.

curate noun SEE **clergyman**.

curator noun *the curator of a museum*. archivist, SEE **custodian**.

curb verb *to curb someone's enthusiasm*. bridle, check, contain, control, deter, hamper, hinder, hold back, impede,

inhibit, limit, moderate, repress, restrain, restrict, subdue, suppress.
OPPOSITES: SEE **encourage, urge** verb.

curdle verb *Milk curdles.* clot, coagulate, congeal, go lumpy, go sour, thicken.
to curdle your blood SEE **frighten**.

cure noun **1** *a cure for a cold.* antidote, corrective, medicine, nostrum, palliative, panacea [=*a cure for everything*], prescription, remedy, restorative, solution, therapy, treatment.
2 *Her unexpected cure amazed the doctors.* SEE **recovery**.

cure verb **1** *The pill cured my headache.* alleviate, counteract, ease, heal, help, palliate, relieve, remedy, treat.
OPPOSITES: SEE **aggravate**.
2 *I cured the fault in the car.* correct, [*informal*] fix, mend, put right, rectify, repair, solve.

curfew noun SEE **restriction**.

curio noun SEE **antique** noun.

curiosity noun *I couldn't restrain my curiosity.* inquisitiveness, interest, meddling, nosiness, prying.

curious adjective **1** *curious questions.* inquiring, inquisitive, interested, [*informal*] nosy, prying, puzzled.
OPPOSITES: incurious, SEE **indifferent**.
to be curious SEE **pry**.
2 *a curious smell.* abnormal, bizarre, extraordinary, funny, mysterious, odd, peculiar, puzzling, queer, rare, strange, surprising, unconventional, unexpected, unusual.
OPPOSITES: SEE **normal**.

curl noun VARIOUS CURLED SHAPES: bend, SEE **circle** noun, coil, curve, kink, loop, ringlet, scroll, spiral, swirl, turn, twist, wave, whorl.

curl verb **1** *The snake curled round a branch.* bend, SEE **circle** verb. coil, corkscrew, curve, entwine, loop, spiral, turn, twine, twist, wind, wreathe, writhe.
2 *to curl your hair.* crimp, frizz, perm.

curly adjective *curly hair.* crimped, curled, curling, frizzy, fuzzy, kinky, permed, wavy.
OPPOSITES: SEE **straight**.

currency noun SEE **money**.

current adjective **1** *current fashions.* contemporary, fashionable, modern, prevailing, prevalent, [*informal*] trendy, up-to-date.
OPPOSITES: SEE **old-fashioned**.
2 *a current passport.* usable, valid.
OPPOSITES: SEE **out-of-date**.
3 *the current government.* existing, extant, present, reigning.

current noun *a current of air or water.* course, draught, drift, flow, jet, river, stream, tide.

curriculum noun *the school curriculum.* course, programme of study, syllabus.

curry verb **to curry favour** SEE **flatter**.

curse noun **1** *I let out a curse.* blasphemy, exclamation, expletive, imprecation, malediction, oath, obscenity, profanity, swearword.
OPPOSITES: SEE **blessing**.
2 *Pollution is a curse in modern society.* SEE **evil** noun.

curse verb *I cursed when I hit my finger.* blaspheme, damn, fulminate, swear, utter curses [SEE **curse** noun].
OPPOSITES: SEE **bless**.

cursed adjective SEE **hateful**.

cursory adjective *a cursory inspection.* brief, careless, casual, desultory, fleeting, hasty, hurried, perfunctory, quick, slapdash, superficial.
OPPOSITES: SEE **thorough**.

curt adjective *a curt answer.* abrupt, brief, brusque, gruff, laconic, monosyllabic, offhand, rude, sharp, short, succinct, tart, terse, uncommunicative, ungracious.
OPPOSITES: SEE **expansive**.

curtail verb *to curtail a debate.* abbreviate, abridge, break off, contract, cut short, decrease, [*informal*] dock, guillotine, halt, lessen, lop, prune, reduce, restrict, shorten, stop, terminate, trim, truncate.
OPPOSITES: SEE **extend**.

curtain noun *Close the curtains.* blind, drape, drapery, hanging, screen.

curtain verb *to curtain the windows.* drape, SEE **hide** verb, mask, screen, shroud, veil.

curtsy verb bend the knee, bow, genuflect (*before an altar*), salaam.

curve noun arc, arch, bend, bow, bulge, camber, SEE **circle** noun, convolution, corkscrew, crescent, curl, curvature, cycloid, loop, meander, spiral, swirl, trajectory, turn, twist, undulation, whorl.

curve verb arc, arch, bend, bow, bulge, SEE **circle** verb, coil, corkscrew, curl, loop, meander, spiral, swerve, swirl, turn, twist, wind.

curved adjective arched, bent, bowed, bulging, cambered, coiled, concave, convex, convoluted, crescent, crooked, curled, [*formal*] curvilinear, curving, curvy, looped, meandering, rounded, serpentine, shaped, sinuous, snaking, spiral, sweeping, swelling, tortuous, turned, twisted, undulating, whorled, winding.

cushion noun bean-bag, bolster, hassock, headrest, pad, pillow.

cushion verb *to cushion the impact of a collision.* absorb, bolster, deaden, lessen, mitigate, muffle, protect from, reduce the effect of, soften, support.

cushy adjective SEE **easy**.

custodian noun *the custodian of a museum.* caretaker, curator, guardian, keeper, overseer, superintendent, warden, warder, [*informal*] watch-dog, watchman.

custody noun **1** *The animals were left in my custody.* care, charge, guardianship, keeping, observation, possession, preservation, protection, safe-keeping.
2 *He was kept in police custody.* captivity, confinement, detention, imprisonment, incarceration, remand [*on remand = in custody*].

custom noun **1** *It's our custom to give presents at Christmas.* convention, etiquette, fashion, form, formality, habit, institution, manner, observance, policy, practice, procedure, routine, tradition, way.
2 *The shop offers discounts to attract custom.* business, buyers, customers, patronage, support, trade.

customary adjective *It was customary to give a tip to the waiter.* accepted, accustomed, common, conventional, established, expected, fashionable, general, habitual, normal, ordinary, popular, prevailing, regular, routine, traditional, typical, usual, wonted.
OPPOSITES: SEE **unusual**.

customer noun *a shop's customers.* buyer, client, consumer, patron, purchaser, shopper.
OPPOSITES: SEE **seller**.

customs noun *You may have to pay customs on imports.* SEE **tax** noun.
customs officer SEE **official** noun.

cut noun **1** *a cut on the finger. a cut in a piece of wood.* gash, graze, groove, [*formal*] incision, SEE **injury**, [*formal*] laceration, nick, notch, rent, rip, slash, slice, slit, snick, snip, split, stab, tear, wound.
2 *a cut in prices.* cut-back, decrease, fall, lowering, reduction, saving.

cut verb **1** VARIOUS WAYS TO CUT THINGS: amputate (*a limb*), axe, carve, chip, chisel, chop, cleave, clip, crop, dissect, dock, engrave (*an inscription on something*), fell (*a tree*), gash, gouge, grate (*into small pieces*), graze, guillotine, hack, hew, incise, lacerate, lop, mince, mow (*grass*), nick, notch, pare (*skin off fruit*), pierce, poll, pollard (*a tree*), prune (*a growing plant*), reap (*corn*), saw, scalp, score, sever, shave, shear, shred, slash, slice, slit, snick, snip, split, stab, trim, whittle (*wood with a knife*), wound.
TOOLS FOR CUTTING: SEE **cutter**.
2 *to cut a long story.* abbreviate, abridge, bowdlerize, censor, condense, curtail, digest, edit, précis, shorten, summarize, truncate.
3 *to cut expenditure.* SEE **reduce**.
cut and dried SEE **definite**.
to cut in, to cut someone off *to cut in when someone is talking. to cut someone off on the phone.* SEE **interrupt**.
to cut short *to cut your holiday short.* SEE **curtail**.

cute adjective SEE **attractive, clever**.

cutlass noun SEE **sword**.

cutlery noun [*informal*] eating irons.

ITEMS OF CUTLERY: breadknife, butter knife, carving knife, cheese knife, dessert-spoon, fish knife, fish fork, fork, knife, ladle, salad servers, spoon, steak knife, tablespoon, teaspoon.

---

cut-price adjective SEE **cheap**.

cutter noun **1** VARIOUS SHIPS: SEE **vessel**.
2 VARIOUS TOOLS FOR CUTTING: axe, bill-hook, chisel, chopper, clippers, guillotine, SEE **knife** noun, lawnmower, SEE **saw**, scalpel, scissors, scythe, secateurs, shears, sickle.

cutthroat adjective *cutthroat competition.* SEE **merciless**.
cutthroat razor SEE **razor**.

cutthroat noun *a murderous cutthroat.* SEE **killer**.

cutting adjective *cutting remarks.* acute, biting, caustic, SEE **hurtful**, incisive, keen, mordant, sarcastic, satirical, sharp, trenchant.

cutting noun *a newspaper cutting.* SEE **extract** noun.

cycle noun **1** *a cycle of events.* circle, repetition, revolution, rotation, round, sequence, series.
2 *A cycle is a cheap form of transport.*
KINDS OF CYCLE: bicycle, [*informal*] bike, moped, [*informal*] motor bike, motor cycle, penny-farthing, scooter, tandem, tricycle.

cycle verb SEE **travel** verb.

cyclic adjective *a cyclic process.* circular, recurring, repeating, repetitive, rotating.

cyclone noun SEE **storm** noun.

cyclostyle verb SEE **reprographics**.

cylinder noun OTHER SHAPES: SEE **shape** noun.

cynical adjective *a cynical outlook.* doubting, [*informal*] hard, misanthropic, negative, pessimistic, questioning, sceptical, sneering.
OPPOSITES: SEE **optimistic**.

cynicism noun SEE **doubt** noun.

cyst noun SEE **growth**.

D

dab verb SEE **touch** verb.

dabble verb **1** *to dabble in water.* dip, paddle, splash, wet.
2 *to dabble in a hobby.* potter about, work casually.

dabbler noun *a dabbler in astrology.* amateur, dilettante, potterer.
OPPOSITES: SEE **expert** noun.

daddy-long-legs noun crane-fly.

daffodil noun narcissus.

daft adjective SEE **silly**.

dagger noun [*old-fashioned*] dirk, SEE **knife** noun, stiletto.

daily adjective *a daily occurrence.* diurnal, everyday, SEE **regular**.

dainty adjective **1** *dainty embroidery.* charming, delicate, exquisite, fine, meticulous, neat, nice, pretty, skilful.
OPPOSITES: SEE **clumsy, crude**.
2 *a dainty eater.* choosy, discriminating, fastidious, finicky, fussy, well-mannered.
OPPOSITES: SEE **gross**.

dais noun SEE **platform**.

dale noun SEE **valley**.

dally verb *Don't dally: we must move on.* dawdle, delay, [*informal*] dilly-dally, hang about, idle, linger, loaf, loiter, play about, procrastinate, saunter, [*old-fashioned*] tarry, waste time.

dam noun *a dam across a river.* bank, barrage, barrier, dike, embankment, wall, weir.

dam verb *to dam the flow of a river.* block, check, hold back, obstruct, restrict, stanch, stem, stop.

damage noun *Did the accident cause any damage?* destruction, devastation, harm, havoc, hurt, SEE **injury**, loss, mutilation, sabotage.

damage verb **1** *A gale damaged the tree. Frost can damage water-pipes.* break, buckle, burst, [*informal*] bust, crack, SEE **destroy**, [*informal*] do a mischief to, fracture, harm, hurt, impair, injure, mutilate, [*informal*] play havoc with, ruin, rupture, strain, warp, weaken, wound, wreck.
2 *Someone damaged the paintwork.* blemish, chip, deface, disfigure, flaw, mar, mark, sabotage, scar, scratch, spoil, vandalize.
3 *Corrosion damaged the engine.* cripple, disable, immobilize, incapacitate, make inoperative, make useless.

damaged adjective *damaged goods.* broken, faulty, flawed, hurt, injured, misused, shop-soiled, unsound.
OPPOSITES: SEE **undamaged**.

damages noun *to pay damages to someone.* SEE **compensation**.

damaging adjective *the damaging effects of war.* calamitous, deleterious, destructive, detrimental, disadvantageous, evil, harmful, injurious, negative, pernicious, prejudicial, ruinous, unfavourable.
OPPOSITES: SEE **helpful**.

dame noun *a pantomime dame.* SEE **woman**.

damn verb SEE **condemn, curse** verb.

damnable adjective SEE **hateful**.

damnation noun doom, everlasting fire, hell, perdition, ruin.
OPPOSITES: SEE **salvation**.

damp adjective **1** *damp clothes. a damp room.* clammy, dank, dripping, moist, perspiring, soggy, sticky, sweaty, unaired, unventilated, wet.
2 *damp weather.* dewy, drizzly, foggy, humid, misty, muggy, raining, wet.
OPPOSITES: SEE **dry** adjective.

damp, dampen verbs **1** *to damp a cloth.* SEE **moisten**.
2 *to damp someone's enthusiasm.* SEE **discourage**.

damsel noun SEE **girl**.

dance noun **1** choreography, dancing.
RELATED ADJECTIVE: choreographic.
2 *We went to a dance.* ball, barn-dance, [*Scottish & Irish*] ceilidh, [*informal*] disco, discothèque, [*informal*] hop, [*informal*] knees-up, party, SEE **social** noun, square dance.

KINDS OF DANCING: aerobics, ballet, ballroom dancing, break-dancing, country dancing, disco dancing, flamenco dancing, folk dancing, Latin American dancing, limbo dancing, morris dancing, old-time dancing, tap-dancing.

VARIOUS DANCES: bolero, cancan, conga, fandango, fling, foxtrot, gavotte, hornpipe, jig, mazurka, minuet, polka, polonaise, quadrille, quickstep, reel, rumba, square dance, tango, waltz.

---

dance verb *We danced all night. I danced for joy.* caper, cavort, frisk, frolic, gambol, hop about, jig about, jive, jump about, leap, prance, rock, skip, [*joking*] trip the light fantastic, whirl.

dancer noun ballerina.

dandle verb SEE **nurse** verb.

danger noun **1** *a danger of frost.* chance, liability, possibility, risk, threat.
2 *He faced the danger bravely.* crisis, distress, hazard, insecurity, jeopardy, menace, peril, pitfall, trouble, uncertainty.
OPPOSITES: SEE **safety**.

dangerous adjective **1** *dangerous driving. a dangerous situation.* alarming, breakneck (*speed*), [*informal*] chancy, critical, explosive (*an explosive situation*), grave, [*slang*] hairy, hazardous, insecure, menacing, [*informal*] nasty, perilous, precarious, reckless (*driving*), risky, uncertain, unsafe.
OPPOSITES: SEE **safe**.
2 *dangerous lions. dangerous criminals.* desperate, SEE **ruthless**, treacherous, unmanageable, unpredictable, violent, volatile, wild.
OPPOSITES: SEE **tame** adjective.
3 *dangerous chemicals.* destructive, harmful, noxious, toxic.
OPPOSITES: SEE **harmless**.

dangle verb *A rope dangled above my head.* be suspended, droop, flap, hang, sway, swing, trail, wave about.

dank adjective *a dank atmosphere.* chilly, clammy, damp, moist, unaired.

dapper adjective SEE **smart** adjective.

dappled adjective *dappled with patches of light.* blotchy, brindled, dotted, flecked, freckled, marbled, motley, mottled, particoloured, patchy, pied, speckled, spotted, stippled, streaked, varicoloured, variegated.

dare verb **1** *Would you dare to make a parachute jump?* gamble, have the courage, risk, take a chance, venture.
2 *He dared me to jump.* challenge, defy, provoke, taunt.

daredevil noun SEE **daring** (**daring person**).

daring adjective *a daring explorer. a daring feat.* adventurous, audacious, bold, SEE **brave**, brazen, [*informal*] cool, dauntless, fearless, hardy, intrepid, plucky, reckless, unafraid, valiant, venturesome.
OPPOSITES: SEE **timid**.
a daring person adventurer, [*informal*] daredevil, hero, stunt man.

dark adjective **1** *a dark room. a dark sky.* black, blackish, cheerless, clouded, coal-black, dim, dingy, dismal, drab, dull, dusky, funereal, gloomy, glowering, glum, grim, inky, moonless, murky, overcast, pitch-black, pitch-dark, [*poetic*] sable, shadowy, shady, sombre, starless, sullen, sunless, unilluminated, unlit.
OPPOSITES: SEE **bright**.
2 *dark colours.* dense, heavy, strong.
OPPOSITES: SEE **pale** adjective.
3 *a dark complexion.* black, brown, brunette [=*dark-haired*], dark-skinned, dusky, swarthy, tanned.
OPPOSITES: SEE **blond, pale** adjective.
4 *a dark secret.* SEE **hidden**.

darken verb **1** *The sky darkened.* become overcast, cloud over.
2 *Clouds darkened the sky.* blacken, dim, eclipse, obscure, overshadow, shade.
OPPOSITES: SEE **brighten**.

darling adjective SEE **dear**.

darling noun beloved, dear, dearest, love, loved one, sweetheart.

darn verb *to darn socks.* SEE **mend**, sew up, stitch up.

dart noun arrow, bolt, missile, shaft.

dart verb *to dart about.* bound, SEE **dash** verb, fling, flit, fly, hurtle, leap, move suddenly, shoot, spring, [*informal*] whiz, [*informal*] zip.

dash noun **1** *a dash to the finishing-post.* chase, race, run, rush, sprint, spurt.
2 [=*punctuation mark*] hyphen.

dash verb **1** *to dash home.* bolt, chase, dart, fly, hasten, hurry, move quickly, race, run, rush, speed, sprint, tear, [*informal*] zoom.
2 *to dash your foot against a rock.* SEE **hit** verb, knock, smash, strike.

dashboard noun facia, instrument panel.

dashing adjective *a dashing figure.* SEE **lively, smart** adjective.

dastardly adjective SEE **cowardly**.

data noun [*Data* is a plural word. We don't say *Have you a data?* but *Have you any data?* It is, however, often used with a singular verb: *The data is in a computer file* rather than *The data are ...*] details, evidence, facts, figures, information, statistics.

date noun **1** *the date of my birthday.* SEE **time**.

2 *a date with a friend.* appointment, assignation, engagement, fixture, meeting, rendezvous.

dated adjective *a dated style.* SEE **old-fashioned.**

daub verb *to daub paint.* SEE **smear.**

daughter noun FAMILY RELATIONSHIPS: SEE **family.**

daunt verb *I was daunted by the size of the task.* alarm, depress, deter, discourage, dishearten, dismay, SEE **frighten**, intimidate, overawe, put off, unnerve.
OPPOSITES: SEE **encourage.**

daunting adjective *a daunting task.* SEE **arduous.**

dauntless adjective SEE **brave.**

davit noun SEE **crane** noun.

dawdle verb *Don't dawdle: we haven't got all day.* be slow, dally, delay, [*informal*] dilly-dally, hang about, idle, lag behind, linger, loaf about, loiter, move slowly, straggle, [*informal*] take your time, trail behind.
OPPOSITES: SEE **hurry** verb.

dawn noun **1** daybreak, first light, [*informal*] peep of day, sunrise.
OPPOSITES: SEE **dusk.**
2 *the dawn of a new age.* SEE **beginning.**

day noun **1** *There are seven days in a week.* twenty-four hours.
RELATED ADJECTIVES: SEE **daily.**
VARIOUS TIMES OF THE DAY: afternoon, dawn, daybreak, dusk, evening, [*poetic*] eventide, gloaming, midday, midnight, morning, night, nightfall, noon, sunrise, sunset, twilight.
2 *Most people are awake during the day.* daylight, daytime, light.
OPPOSITE: night.
3 *Things were different in grandad's day.* age, epoch, era, period, time.

daybreak noun SEE **dawn.**

day-dream noun *a day-dream about being rich and famous.* dream, fantasy, hope, illusion, meditation, pipe-dream, reverie, vision, wool-gathering.

day-dream verb dream, fantasize, imagine, meditate.

daylight noun SEE **day, light** noun.

daze verb *The blow dazed him.* SEE **stun.**

dazzle verb SEE **light** noun [**to give light**].

deacon, deaconess nouns SEE **clergyman.**

dead adjective **1** *a dead animal. a dead body.* cold, dead and buried, deceased, departed, inanimate, inert, killed, late (*the late king*), lifeless, perished, rigid, stiff.
OPPOSITES: SEE **alive, living.**
2 *a dead language. a dead species.* died out, extinct, obsolete.
OPPOSITES: SEE **existing.**
3 *dead with cold.* deadened, insensitive, numb, paralysed, without feeling.
OPPOSITES: SEE **sensitive.**
4 *a dead battery. a dead engine.* burnt out, defunct, flat, inoperative, not going, not working, no use, out of order, unresponsive, used up, useless, worn out.
OPPOSITES: SEE **operational.**
5 *The party was dead until Frank arrived.* boring, dull, moribund, slow, uninteresting.
OPPOSITES: SEE **lively.**
6 *the dead centre.* SEE **exact** adjective.
a dead person body, cadaver, carcass, corpse, [*informal*] goner, mortal remains, [*slang*] stiff.

deaden verb **1** *to deaden a sound. to deaden a blow.* check, cushion, damp, hush, lessen, muffle, mute, quieten, reduce, smother, soften, stifle, suppress, weaken.
OPPOSITES: SEE **amplify, sharpen.**
2 *to deaden a pain. to deaden feeling.* alleviate, anaesthetize, blunt, desensitize, dull, numb, paralyse.
OPPOSITES: SEE **aggravate, intensify.**

deadline noun *the deadline for competition entries.* latest time, time-limit.

deadlock noun *Negotiations reached deadlock.* halt, impasse, stalemate, standstill, stop.
OPPOSITES: SEE **progress** noun.

deadly adjective *a deadly illness. deadly poison.* dangerous, destructive, fatal, SEE **harmful**, lethal, mortal, noxious, terminal.
OPPOSITES: SEE **harmless.**

deadpan adjective SEE **expressionless.**

deaf adjective hard of hearing.
OTHER HANDICAPS: SEE **handicap.**

deafen verb *The noise deafened us.* make deaf, overwhelm.

deafening adjective *a deafening roar.* SEE **loud.**

deal noun **1** *a business deal.* agreement, arrangement, bargain, contract, pact, settlement, transaction, understanding.
2 *a great deal of trouble.* amount, quantity, volume.

deal verb **1** *to deal cards.* allot, apportion, assign, dispense, distribute, divide, [*informal*] dole out, give out, share out.
2 *to deal someone a blow on the head.* administer, apply, deliver, give, inflict, mete out.
3 *to deal in stocks and shares.* buy and sell, do business, trade, traffic.

to deal with 1 *I'll deal with this problem.* attend to, come to grips with, control, cope with, get over, grapple with, handle, look after, manage, overcome, see to, SEE **solve**, sort out, surmount, tackle, take action on.
2 *I want a book that deals with insects.* be concerned with, cover, explain, treat.

dealer noun *a car dealer. a dealer in antiques.* merchant, retailer, shopkeeper, stockist, supplier, trader, tradesman, wholesaler.

dean noun SEE **clergyman**.

dear adjective **1** *dear friends.* beloved, close, darling, intimate, SEE **lovable**, loved, valued.
OPPOSITES: SEE **hateful**.
2 *dear goods.* costly, exorbitant, expensive, over-priced, [*informal*] pricey.
OPPOSITES: SEE **cheap**.

dear noun *He's a dear!* SEE **darling**.

dearth noun *a sad dearth of talent.* SEE **scarcity**.

death noun **1** *We mourn the death of a friend.* [*formal*] decease, demise, dying [SEE **die** verb], end, loss, passing.
2 *The accident resulted in several deaths.* casualty, fatality.
to put to death SEE **execute**.

deathless adjective SEE **immortal**.

débâcle noun SEE **disaster**.

debar verb *debarred from driving.* SEE **ban** verb.

debase verb *They debased that lovely music by using it in an advert.* commercialize, degrade, demean, depreciate, devalue, lower the tone of, pollute, reduce the value of, ruin, soil, spoil, sully, vulgarize.

debatable adjective *a debatable question.* arguable, contentious, controversial, controvertible, disputable, doubtful, dubious, moot (*a moot point*), open to question, problematical, questionable, uncertain.
OPPOSITES: SEE **certain**, **straightforward**.

debate noun *a debate about animal rights.* SEE **argument**, conference, consultation, controversy, deliberation, [*formal*] dialectic, discussion, [*formal*] disputation, dispute, [*formal*] polemic.

debate verb *We debated the pros and cons of the matter.* argue, consider, deliberate, discuss, dispute, [*informal*] mull over, question, reflect on, weigh up.

debauch verb SEE **seduce**.

debauched adjective SEE **immoral**.

debilitate verb SEE **weaken**.

debility noun SEE **weakness**.

debit verb *The bank debited £10 from my account.* cancel, remove, subtract, take away.
OPPOSITES: SEE **credit** verb.

debonair adjective SEE **carefree**.

debrief verb SEE **question** verb.

debris noun *debris from a crashed aircraft.* bits, detritus, flotsam [=*floating debris*], fragments, litter, pieces, remains, rubbish, rubble, ruins, waste, wreckage.

debt noun **1** *Can you pay off your debt?* account, arrears, bill, debit, dues, score (*I have a score to settle*), what you owe.
2 *I owe you a great debt for your kindness.* duty, indebtedness, obligation.
in debt bankrupt, insolvent, SEE **poor**.

debtor noun bankrupt, defaulter.

début noun SEE **performance**.

débutante noun SEE **girl**.

decade noun PERIODS OF TIME: SEE **time** noun.

decadent adjective *a decadent society.* SEE **corrupt** adjective, declining, degenerate, immoral.
OPPOSITES: SEE **moral** adjective.

decamp verb SEE **depart**.

decant verb SEE **pour**.

decanter noun OTHER CONTAINERS: SEE **container**.

decapitate verb behead, SEE **kill**.

decay verb **1** *Dead plants and animals decay.* break down, decompose, degenerate, fester, go bad, moulder, putrefy, rot, shrivel, waste away, wither.
OPPOSITES: SEE **grow**.
2 *Most substances decay in time.* corrode, crumble, deteriorate, disintegrate, dissolve, fall apart, oxidize, perish, spoil.

deceased adjective SEE **dead**.

deceit noun *We saw through his deceit.* artifice, bluff, cheating, chicanery, [*informal*] con, craftiness, cunning, deceitfulness, deception, dishonesty, dissimulation, double-dealing, duplicity, feint, [*informal*] fiddle, fraud, guile, hoax, imposture, insincerity, lie, lying, misrepresentation, pretence, ruse, sham, stratagem, subterfuge, swindle, treachery, trick, trickery, underhandedness, untruthfulness, wile.
OPPOSITES: SEE **honesty**.

deceitful adjective *a deceitful person. a deceitful trick.* cheating, crafty, cunning, deceiving, deceptive, designing, dishonest, double-dealing, false, fraudulent, furtive, hypocritical, insincere, lying, secretive, shifty, sneaky, treacherous, [*informal*] tricky, [*informal*] two-faced,

underhand, unfaithful, untrustworthy, wily.
OPPOSITES: SEE **honest**.

deceive verb *I had no intention to deceive. His disguise deceived me.* [*informal*] bamboozle, be an impostor, beguile, betray, blind, bluff, cheat, [*informal*] con, defraud, delude, [*informal*] diddle, double-cross, dupe, fool, [*informal*] fox, [*informal*] have on, hoax, hoodwink [*informal*] kid, [*informal*] lead on, lie, mislead, mystify, [*informal*] outsmart, outwit, pretend, swindle, [*informal*] take for a ride, [*informal*] take in, trick.

decelerate verb brake, decrease speed, go slower, lose speed, slow down.
OPPOSITES: SEE **accelerate**.

decent adjective **1** *decent behaviour. decent language.* acceptable, appropriate, becoming, befitting, chaste, courteous, decorous, delicate, fitting, honourable, modest, polite, presentable, proper, pure, respectable, seemly, sensitive, suitable.
OPPOSITES: SEE **indecent**.
2 [*informal*] *a decent meal.* agreeable, SEE **good**, nice, pleasant, satisfactory.
OPPOSITES: SEE **bad**.

decentralize verb SEE **disperse**.

deception noun *I was taken in by the deception.* bluff, cheat, cheating, chicanery, [*informal*] con, confidence trick, cover-up, craftiness, cunning, deceit, deceitfulness, dishonesty, dissimulation, double-dealing, duplicity, fake, feint, [*informal*] fiddle, fraud, hoax, imposture, lie, lying, misrepresentation, pretence, ruse, sham, stratagem, subterfuge, swindle, treachery, trick, trickery, underhandedness, untruthfulness, wile.

deceptive adjective *a deceptive argument. deceptive appearances.* delusive, fallacious, false, fraudulent, illusory, insincere, misleading, specious, spurious, treacherous, unreliable.
OPPOSITES: SEE **genuine**.

decide verb *Please decide what to do.* adjudicate, choose, conclude, determine, elect, fix on, judge, make up your mind, opt for, pick, resolve, select, settle.

decided adjective SEE **definite**.

Several English words, including *decathlon, decimal, decimate,* etc., are related to Latin *decem = ten.*

---

decimal adjective metric.

decimate verb [Originally *decimate* meant *to kill one in ten.* Now it usually means *to kill a large number.*] SEE **destroy**.

decipher verb SEE **decode**.

decision noun *The judge announced his decision.* conclusion, findings, judgement, outcome, result, ruling, verdict.

decisive adjective **1** *decisive evidence.* conclusive, convincing, crucial, final, influential, positive, significant.
OPPOSITES: SEE **inconclusive**.
2 *a decisive person. decisive action.* decided, SEE **definite**, determined, firm, forceful, forthright, incisive, resolute, strong-minded, unhesitating.
OPPOSITES: SEE **hesitant**.

deck noun *the deck of a ship.* floor, level.

deck verb SEE **decorate**.

declaim verb SEE **speak**.

declamation noun SEE **speech**.

declaration noun *a formal declaration of intentions.* affirmation, announcement, assertion, avowal, confirmation, deposition, disclosure, edict, manifesto, proclamation, profession, pronouncement, protestation, revelation, statement, testimony.

declare verb *He declared that he would never steal again.* affirm, announce, assert, attest, avow, certify, claim, confirm, contend, disclose, emphasize, insist, maintain, make known, proclaim, profess, pronounce, protest, report, reveal, SEE **say**, show, state, swear, testify, witness.

decline noun *a decline in productivity. a decline in population.* decrease, degeneration, deterioration, downturn, drop, fall, falling off, loss, recession, reduction, slump, worsening.

decline verb **1** *to decline an invitation.* forgo, refuse, reject, turn down.
OPPOSITES: SEE **accept**.
2 *His health declined.* decrease, degenerate, deteriorate, die away, diminish, drop away, dwindle, ebb, fail, fall off, flag, lessen, sink, wane, weaken, wilt, worsen.
OPPOSITES: SEE **improve**.

declivity noun SEE **slope** noun.

decoction noun SEE **extract** noun.

decode verb *to decode a cryptic message.* [*informal*] crack, decipher, explain, figure out, interpret, make out, read, solve, understand, unscramble.
OPPOSITES: SEE **encode**.

decompose verb SEE **decay**.

decontaminate verb SEE **purify**.

décor noun *Do you like the new décor in our lounge?* colour scheme, decorations, design, furnishings, interior design, style.

decorate verb **1** *to decorate a room with flowers.* adorn, array, beautify, [*old-fashioned*] bedeck, deck, embellish, festoon, garnish, make beautiful, ornament, [*uncomplimentary*] prettify, [*uncomplimentary*] tart up.
2 *to decorate a room with a new colour-scheme.* colour, [*informal*] do up, paint, paper, refurbish, renovate, wallpaper.
3 *to decorate someone for bravery.* give a medal to, honour, reward.

decoration **1** *beautiful decorations.* accessory, adornment, arabesque, elaboration, embellishment, embroidery, filigree, finery, flourish, frill, ornament, ornamentation, tracery, [*plural*] trappings, trimming.
2 *a decoration for bravery.* award, badge, medal, ribbon, star.

decorative adjective *decorative details.* elaborate, fancy, non-functional, ornamental, ornate.
OPPOSITES: SEE **functional**.

decorator noun painter.

decorous adjective *decorous behaviour.* appropriate, becoming, befitting, correct, SEE **decent**, dignified, fitting, presentable, proper, refined, respectable, sedate, staid, suitable, well-behaved.
OPPOSITES: SEE **unbecoming**.

decorum noun *He behaved with great decorum.* decency, dignity, etiquette, good manners, gravity, modesty, politeness, propriety, respectability, seemliness.

decoy noun bait, enticement, lure, red herring, stool-pigeon.

decoy verb attract, bait, draw, entice, inveigle, lead, lure, seduce, tempt.

decrease noun *a decrease in wages.* contraction, cut, cut-back, decline, diminuendo [*=decrease in loudness*], downturn, drop, fall, falling off, reduction.
OPPOSITES: SEE **increase** noun.

decrease verb **1** *We decreased speed.* abate, curtail, cut, lessen, lower, reduce, slacken.
2 *Our speed decreased.* contract, decline, die away, diminish, dwindle, fall off, lessen, peter out, shrink, slim down, subside, [*informal*] tail off, taper off, wane.
OPPOSITES: SEE **increase** verb.

decree noun *an official decree.* act, command, declaration, edict, fiat, law, order, ordinance, proclamation, regulation, ruling, statute.

decree verb *The government decrees what we must pay in taxes.* command, decide, declare, determine, dictate, direct, ordain, order, prescribe, proclaim, pronounce, rule.

decrepit adjective *a decrepit old car.* battered, broken down, derelict, dilapidated, feeble, frail, infirm, SEE **old**, ramshackle, tumbledown, weak, worn out.

decry verb SEE **criticize**.

dedicate verb **1** *The church is dedicated to St Paul.* consecrate, hallow, sanctify, set apart.
2 *I dedicate my poem to my father's memory.* address, inscribe.
3 *He dedicates himself to his work.* commit, devote, give (yourself) completely, pledge.

dedicated adjective *dedicated fans.* committed, devoted, enthusiastic, faithful, keen, loyal, single-minded, zealous.

dedication noun **1** *I admire her dedication to the job.* adherence, allegiance, commitment, devotion, faithfulness, loyalty, single-mindedness.
2 *the dedication in a book.* inscription.

deduce verb *The policeman deduced that I was involved.* conclude, draw the conclusion, extrapolate, gather, infer, [*informal*] put two and two together, reason, work out.

deduct verb *to deduct tax from your pay.* [*informal*] knock off, subtract, take away.
OPPOSITES: SEE **add**.

deduction noun **1** [In this sense, *deduction* is related to the verb *deduct.*] *a deduction off your bill.* allowance, decrease, discount, reduction, subtraction.
2 [In this sense, *deduction* is related to the verb *deduce.*] *My deduction was correct.* conclusion, inference, reasoning.

deed noun **1** *a heroic deed.* achievement, act, action, adventure, effort, endeavour, enterprise, exploit, feat, performance, stunt, undertaking.
2 *the deeds of a house.* contract, documents, [*formal*] indenture, papers, records, [*formal*] title.

deem verb SEE **judge** verb.

deep adjective **1** *a deep pit.* bottomless, fathomless, unfathomable, unplumbed.
2 *deep feelings.* earnest, extreme, genuine, heartfelt, intense, serious, sincere.
OPPOSITES: SEE **shallow**.
3 *deep in thought.* absorbed, concentrating, engrossed, immersed, lost, preoccupied, rapt, thoughtful.

4 *a deep subject.* abstruse, arcane, SEE **difficult**, esoteric, intellectual, learned, obscure, profound, recondite.
OPPOSITES: SEE **easy**.
5 *deep sleep.* heavy, sound.
OPPOSITES: SEE **light** adjective.
6 *a deep colour.* dark, rich, strong, vivid.
OPPOSITES: SEE **pale** adjective.
7 *a deep voice.* bass, booming, growling, low, low-pitched, resonant, reverberating, sonorous.
OPPOSITES: SEE **high**.

deepen verb SEE **intensify**.

deer noun DEER AND SIMILAR ANIMALS: antelope, [*male*] buck, caribou, chamois, [*female*] doe, elk, fallow deer, gazelle, gnu, [*male*] hart, [*female*] hind, impala, moose, reindeer, roe, [*male*] roebuck, [*male*] stag, wildebeest.
OTHER ANIMALS: SEE **animal** noun.

deface verb *Vandals defaced the statue.* damage, disfigure, injure, mar, mutilate, spoil, vandalize.

defamation noun SEE **slander** noun.

defamatory adjective SEE **slanderous**.

defame verb SEE **slander** verb.

default verb SEE **wrong (to do wrong)**.

defeat noun *a humiliating defeat.* beating, conquest, downfall, [*informal*] drubbing, failure, humiliation, [*informal*] licking, overthrow, [*informal*] put-down, rebuff, repulse, reverse, rout, setback, subjugation, thrashing, trouncing.
OPPOSITES: SEE **victory**.

defeat verb *to defeat an opponent.* beat, best, checkmate, [*informal*] clobber, confound, conquer, crush, [*informal*] flatten, foil, frustrate, get the better of, [*informal*] lay low, [*informal*] lick, master, outdo, outvote, outwit, overcome, overpower, overthrow, overwhelm, put down, quell, repulse, rout, ruin, [*informal*] smash, subdue, subjugate, suppress, [*informal*] thrash, thwart, triumph over, trounce, vanquish, win a victory over.
to be defeated SEE **lose**.

defeated adjective *the defeated team.* beaten, bottom, last, losing, unsuccessful, vanquished.
OPPOSITES: SEE **winning**.

defecate verb SEE **excrete**.

defect noun *a defect in a piece of work.* blemish, bug (*in a computer program*), deficiency, error, failing, fault, flaw, imperfection, inadequacy, lack, mark, mistake, shortcoming, spot, stain, want, weakness.

defect verb *The traitor defected to the enemy.* desert, go over.

defective adjective SEE **faulty**.

defence noun **1** *What was the accused woman's defence?* alibi, apology, case, excuse, explanation, justification, plea, testimony, vindication.
2 *a defence against attack.* SEE **barricade**, cover, deterrence, fortification, guard, protection, rampart, safeguard, security, shelter, shield.

defenceless adjective SEE **helpless**.

defend verb **1** *to defend yourself against attackers.* cover, fortify, guard, keep safe, preserve, protect, safeguard, screen, secure, shelter, shield, [*informal*] stick up for.
OPPOSITES: SEE **attack** verb.
2 *He defended himself in court.* champion, justify, plead for, speak up for, stand up for, support, uphold, vindicate.
OPPOSITES: SEE **accuse**.

defendant noun accused, appellant, offender, prisoner.

defensible adjective *a defensible argument.* SEE **justifiable**.

defensive adjective **1** *a defensive style of play.* cautious, defending, protective, wary, watchful.
OPPOSITES: SEE **aggressive**.
2 *defensive remarks.* apologetic, faint-hearted, self-justifying.
OPPOSITES: SEE **assertive**.

defer verb **1** *We deferred the remaining business until next week.* adjourn, delay, hold over, postpone, prorogue (*parliament*), put off, [*informal*] shelve, suspend.
2 *I deferred to her superior experience.* SEE **yield**.

deference noun SEE **respect** noun.

deferential adjective SEE **respectful**.

defiant adjective *a defiant attitude.* aggressive, challenging, disobedient, insolent, insubordinate, mutinous, obstinate, rebellious, recalcitrant, refractory, stubborn, truculent, unco-operative, unyielding.
OPPOSITES: SEE **co-operative**.

deficient adjective *Their diet is deficient in vitamins.* defective, imperfect, inadequate, incomplete, insufficient, lacking, meagre, scanty, scarce, short, unsatisfactory, wanting, weak.
OPPOSITES: SEE **adequate, excessive**.

deficit noun *The company had a deficit in their accounts.* loss, shortfall.
OPPOSITES: SEE **excess**.

defile noun *a mountain defile.* SEE **pass** noun.

defile verb *I felt defiled by the filth.* contaminate, corrupt, degrade, desecrate, dirty, dishonour, infect, make dirty [SEE **dirty** adjective], poison, pollute, soil, stain, sully, taint, tarnish.

define verb **1** *A thesaurus simply lists words, whereas a dictionary defines them.* clarify, explain, formulate, give the meaning of, interpret.
2 *The fence defines the extent of our land.* bound, be the boundary of, circumscribe, demarcate, determine, limit, mark out, outline.

definite adjective **1** *definite opinions. a definite manner.* assured, categorical, certain, clear-cut, confident, cut-and-dried, decided, determined, emphatic, exact, explicit, fixed, incisive, particular, precise, settled, specific, sure, unambiguous, unequivocal.
OPPOSITES: SEE **indefinite**.
2 *definite signs of improvement.* apparent, clear, discernible, distinct, marked, noticeable, obvious, perceptible, plain, positive, pronounced, unmistakable.
OPPOSITES: SEE **imperceptible**.

definitely adverb *I'll definitely come tomorrow.* beyond doubt, certainly, doubtless, for certain, indubitably, positively, surely, unquestionably, without doubt, without fail.

definition noun **1** *a dictionary definition.* elucidation, explanation, interpretation.
2 *the definition of a photograph.* clarity, clearness, focus, precision, sharpness.

definitive adjective [Do not confuse with *definite*.] *the definitive account of someone's life.* agreed, authoritative, conclusive, correct, final, last (*He's written the last word on the subject*), official, permanent, reliable, settled, standard.
OPPOSITES: SEE **provisional**.

deflate verb **1** *to deflate a tyre.* let down.
OPPOSITE: inflate.
2 *to deflate your pride.* SEE **humble** verb.

deflect verb *to deflect a blow.* avert, divert, fend off, head off, intercept, parry, prevent, turn aside, ward off.

defoliate verb SEE **strip** verb.

deform verb SEE **distort**.

deformed adjective *a deformed tree.* bent, buckled, contorted, SEE **crippled**, crooked, defaced, disfigured, distorted, gnarled, grotesque, malformed, mangled, misshapen, mutilated, twisted, ugly, warped.

deformity noun malformation.

defraud verb SEE **cheat** verb, [*informal*] diddle, embezzle, [*informal*] fleece, rob, swindle.

defray verb *I've enough money to defray expenses.* cover, foot (*foot the bill*), meet, pay, refund, repay, settle.

defrost verb de-ice, warm, unfreeze.

deft adjective *deft movements.* adept, adroit, agile, clever, dextrous, expert, handy, neat [*informal*] nifty, nimble, proficient, quick, skilful.
OPPOSITES: SEE **clumsy**.

defunct adjective SEE **dead**.

defuse verb SEE **safe (to make safe)**.

defy verb **1** *to defy someone in authority.* confront, disobey, face up to, flout, refuse to obey, resist, stand up to, withstand.
OPPOSITES: SEE **obey**.
2 *I defy you to produce evidence.* challenge, dare.
3 *The jammed door defied my attempts to open it.* baffle, beat, defeat, elude, foil, frustrate, repel, resist, thwart, withstand.

degenerate adjective *degenerate behaviour.* SEE **immoral**.

degenerate verb *His behaviour degenerated.* become worse, decline, deteriorate, regress, retrogress, sink, slip, weaken, worsen.
OPPOSITES: SEE **improve**.

degrade verb *Bad living conditions degrade people.* brutalize, cheapen, corrupt, debase, dehumanize, demean, deprave, desensitize, harden, humiliate, lower, make uncivilized.

degrading adjective *a degrading experience.* brutalizing, cheapening, corrupting, dehumanizing, demeaning, depraving, dishonourable, humiliating, ignoble, lowering, shameful, undignified, unworthy.
OPPOSITES: SEE **uplifting**.

degree noun **1** *a high degree of skill.* calibre, extent, grade, intensity, level, measure, order, standard.
2 *of high degree. of low degree.* class, position, rank, standing, station, status.
3 *a polytechnic degree.* SEE **qualification**.

dehumanize verb SEE **degrade**.

dehydrate verb *Take care not to dehydrate in the heat.* desiccate, dry out, dry up.

de-ice verb *to de-ice the windscreen.* clear, defrost, unfreeze.

deify verb idolize, treat as a god, venerate, worship.

deign verb *He doesn't deign to talk to unimportant people like me.* condescend, demean yourself, lower yourself, stoop.

deity noun *pagan deities.* divinity, god, goddess, godhead, idol, immortal, power, spirit.

dejected adjective *a dejected mood.* SEE **depressed.**

delay noun *a delay in proceedings.* check, filibuster, hitch, hold-up, moratorium, pause, postponement, set-back, wait.

delay verb **1** *The fog delayed the traffic.* bog down, cause a delay, check, detain, halt, hinder, hold up, impede, keep back, keep waiting, make late, obstruct, retard, set back, slow down, stop.
2 *to delay a meeting.* defer, hold over, postpone, put back, put off, suspend.
3 *You'll lose your chance if you delay.* be late, [*informal*] bide your time, dawdle, [*informal*] dilly-dally, hang back, hesitate, lag, linger, loiter, pause, [*informal*] play for time, procrastinate, stall, [*old-fashioned*] tarry, temporize, wait.

delectable adjective SEE **delicious.**

delegate noun *a delegate at a conference.* agent, ambassador, envoy, legate, messenger, representative, spokesperson.

delegate verb *They delegated me to speak on their behalf.* appoint, assign, authorize, charge, commission, depute, empower, entrust, mandate, nominate.

delegation noun *a delegation to pass on our complaints.* commission, deputation, mission, representative group.

delete verb *to delete someone from a list.* blot out, cancel, cross out, edit out, efface, erase, expunge, obliterate, remove, rub out, strike out, wipe out.

deleterious adjective SEE **damaging.**

deliberate adjective **1** *deliberate insults.* calculated, conscious, contrived, culpable, intended, intentional, knowing, organized, planned, pre-arranged, premeditated, prepared, studied, wilful.
OPPOSITES: SEE **unplanned.**
2 *deliberate movements.* careful, cautious, circumspect, considered, methodical, painstaking, slow, thoughtful, unhurried.
OPPOSITES: SEE **hasty.**

deliberate verb SEE **discuss, think.**

deliberation noun SEE **discussion, thought.**

delicacy noun **1** *We admired the delicacy of the craftsmanship.* accuracy, care, cleverness, daintiness, exquisiteness, fineness, fragility, intricacy, precision.
2 *She described the unpleasant details with great delicacy.* discrimination, finesse, sensitivity, subtlety, tact.
3 *The table was loaded with delicacies.* rarity, speciality, treat.

delicate adjective **1** *delicate material. delicate plants.* dainty, diaphanous, easily damaged, fine, flimsy, fragile, frail, gauzy, slender, tender.
OPPOSITES: SEE **strong.**
2 *a delicate touch.* gentle, feathery, light, soft.
OPPOSITES: SEE **clumsy.**
3 *delicate workmanship.* accurate, careful, clever, deft, exquisite, intricate, precise, skilled.
OPPOSITES: SEE **crude.**
4 *a delicate flavour. delicate colours.* faint, gentle, mild, muted, pale, slight, subtle.
OPPOSITES: SEE **harsh.**
5 *delicate machinery.* complex, easily broken, fragile, intricate, sensitive.
OPPOSITES: SEE **robust.**
6 *a delicate constitution.* feeble, puny, sickly, unhealthy, weak.
OPPOSITES: SEE **healthy.**
7 *a delicate problem.* awkward, confidential, embarrassing, private, problematical, prudish, ticklish, touchy.
OPPOSITES: SEE **straightforward.**
8 *a delicate treatment of a problem.* considerate, diplomatic, discreet, judicious, prudent, sensitive, tactful.
OPPOSITES: SEE **tactless.**

delicious adjective *delicious food.* appetizing, choice, delectable, enjoyable, luscious, [*informal*] mouth-watering, palatable, savoury, [*informal*] scrumptious, succulent, tasty.
OPPOSITES: SEE **unpleasant.**

delight noun *A hot bath is a great delight.* bliss, ecstasy, enchantment, enjoyment, [*formal*] felicity, gratification, happiness, joy, paradise, pleasure, rapture.

delight verb *The music delighted us.* amuse, bewitch, captivate, charm, cheer, divert, enchant, enrapture, entertain, enthral, entrance, fascinate, gladden, please, ravish, thrill, transport.
OPPOSITES: SEE **dismay** verb.

delighted verb SEE **pleased.**

delightful adjective SEE **pleasant.**

delineate verb SEE **describe.**

delineation noun SEE **description.**

delinquency noun SEE **crime.**

delinquent noun *a juvenile delinquent.* criminal, culprit, defaulter, hooligan, law-breaker, miscreant, offender, [*informal*] tear-away, vandal, wrongdoer, young offender.

deliquesce verb SEE **dissolve, melt.**

delirious adjective *delirious with joy.* [*informal*] beside yourself, crazy, demented, deranged, SEE **drunk**, ecstatic,

excited, feverish, frantic, frenzied, hysterical, irrational, light-headed, SEE **mad**, wild.
OPPOSITES: SEE **sane, sober**.

delirium noun ecstasy, SEE **excitement**, fever, hysteria, SEE **madness**.

deliver verb **1** *to deliver letters or goods to an address.* bear, bring, convey, distribute, give out, hand over, make over, present, supply, take round, transfer, transport, turn over.
2 *to deliver a lecture.* give, make, read, SEE **speak**.
3 *to deliver a blow.* aim, deal, SEE **hit** verb, launch, strike, throw (*a punch*).
4 *to deliver someone from slavery.* SEE **rescue** verb.

deliverance noun SEE **rescue** noun.

delivery noun **1** *a delivery of vegetables.* batch, consignment, distribution, shipment.
2 *the delivery of a message.* conveyance, dispatch, transmission.

dell noun SEE **valley**.

delude verb SEE **deceive**.

deluge noun *We got soaked in the deluge.* downpour, flood, inundation, rainfall, rainstorm, rush, spate.

deluge verb *They deluged me with questions.* drown, engulf, flood, inundate, overwhelm, submerge, swamp.

delusion noun *a misleading delusion.* deception, dream, fantasy, hallucination, illusion, mirage, misconception, mistake.

delusive adjective SEE **deceptive**.

delve verb *to delve into the past.* burrow, dig, explore, investigate, probe, research, search.

demagogue noun SEE **agitator, leader**.

demand noun *The manager agreed to the workers' demands.* claim, command, desire, expectation, importunity, insistence, need, order, request, requirement, requisition, want.

demand verb **1** *I demanded a refund.* call for, claim, command, exact, expect, insist on, order, request, require, requisition, want.
2 *"What do you want?" she demanded.* SEE **ask**.

demanding adjective **1** *a demanding child.* SEE **importunate**.
2 *a demanding task.* SEE **difficult**.

demarcation noun SEE **boundary**.

demean verb *She demeans herself by doing his dirty work.* abase, cheapen, debase, degrade, disgrace, humble, humiliate, lower, make (yourself) cheap, [*informal*] put (yourself) down, sacrifice (your) pride, undervalue.

demeanour noun SEE **attitude, behaviour**.

demented noun SEE **crazy**.

demerit noun SEE **fault** noun.

demesne noun SEE **territory**.

demise noun SEE **death, end** noun.

demo noun SEE **demonstration**.

demobilize verb *After the war the soldiers were demobilized.* disband, dismiss, release, return to civilian life.

democracy noun POLITICAL TERMS: SEE **politics**.

democratic adjective *democratic government.* chosen, elected, elective, popular, representative.
OPPOSITES: SEE **undemocratic**.

demolish verb *to demolish old buildings.* break down, bulldoze, SEE **destroy**, dismantle, flatten, knock down, level, pull down, raze, tear down, undo, wreck.
OPPOSITES: SEE **build**.

demon noun devil, fiend, goblin, imp, spirit.

demonstrable adjective *a demonstrable fact.* certain, clear, evident, incontrovertible, irrefutable, palpable, positive, provable, undeniable, verifiable.

demonstrate verb **1** *to demonstrate how to do something.* describe, display, embody, establish, exemplify, exhibit, explain, expound, illustrate, indicate, manifest, prove, represent, show, substantiate, teach, typify.
2 *to demonstrate in the streets.* lobby, march, parade, picket, protest.

demonstration noun **1** *a demonstration of how to do something.* confirmation, description, display, evidence, exhibition, experiment, expression, illustration, indication, manifestation, presentation, proof, representation, show, test, trial.
2 *a political demonstration.* [*informal*] demo, march, parade, picket, protest, rally, sit-in, vigil.

demonstrative adjective *a demonstrative person.* affectionate, effusive, emotional, fulsome, loving, open, uninhibited, unreserved, unrestrained.
OPPOSITES: SEE **reserved**.

demoralize verb SEE **discourage**.

demote verb *The boss demoted her to a less responsible position.* downgrade, put down, reduce, relegate.
OPPOSITES: SEE **promote**.

demur verb SEE **object** verb.

demure adjective *a demure expression.* bashful, coy, diffident, modest, prim, quiet, reserved, reticent, retiring, sedate, shy, sober, staid.
OPPOSITES: SEE **bumptious**.

den noun *a den in the garden.* hide-away, hide-out, hiding-place, hole, lair, private place, retreat, sanctuary, secret place, shelter.

denial noun *The jury didn't believe his denial of guilt.* abnegation, disclaimer, negation, rejection, renunciation, repudiation.
OPPOSITES: SEE **admission**.

denigrate verb *It was unkind to denigrate her achievement.* be contemptuous of, belittle, blacken the reputation of, criticize, decry, disparage, impugn, malign, [*informal*] run down, sneer at, speak slightingly of, traduce, vilify.
OPPOSITES: SEE **praise** verb.

denizen noun SEE **inhabitant**.

denomination noun **1** *a Christian denomination.* church, communion, creed, cult, persuasion, sect.

VARIOUS CHRISTIAN DENOMINATIONS: Anglican, Baptist, Congregational, Episcopalian, Lutheran, Methodist, Moravian, Orthodox, Presbyterian, Protestant, Revivalist, Roman Catholic, United Reformed.
COMPARE: ecumenical.

---

2 *I need coins of the right denomination for the slot machine.* category, class, designation, size, type, value.

denote verb *What does this word denote?* be the sign for, express, indicate, SEE **mean** verb, signify, stand for.
COMPARE: connote.

denouement noun [Literally, *denouement* means *untying a knot.*] *the denouement of the plot of a play.* climax, SEE **end** noun, [*informal*] pay-off, resolution, solution, [*informal*] sorting out, [*informal*] tidying up, unravelling.

denounce verb *to denounce a traitor. to denounce wickedness.* accuse, attack verbally, blame, brand, censure, complain about, condemn, declaim against, decry, fulminate against, [*informal*] hold forth against, inform against, inveigh against, report, reveal, stigmatize, [*informal*] tell of.
OPPOSITES: SEE **praise** verb.

dense adjective **1** *dense fog. a dense liquid.* concentrated, heavy, opaque, thick, viscous.
OPPOSITES: SEE **thin** adjective.
2 *a dense crowd. dense undergrowth.* compact, close, impenetrable, [*informal*] jam-packed, lush, massed, packed, solid.
OPPOSITES: SEE **sparse**.
3 *a dense pupil.* crass, dim, dull, foolish, obtuse, slow, stupid, [*informal*] thick, unintelligent.
OPPOSITES: SEE **clever**.

dent noun *a dent in a flat surface.* concavity, depression, dimple, dint, dip, hollow, indentation, pit.

dent verb *I dented the car.* bend, buckle, crumple, knock in, push in.

Several English words, including *dental, dentist, denture, indented*, etc., are related to Latin *dens, dentis* = *tooth*.

---

dental adjective to do with teeth.

dentist noun OTHERS WHO LOOK AFTER OUR HEALTH: SEE **medicine**.

denture noun false teeth, plate, SEE **tooth**.

denude verb *to denude a hillside of vegetation.* bare, defoliate, deforest, expose, make naked, remove, strip, unclothe, uncover.
OPPOSITES: SEE **clothe**.

denunciation noun *We were amazed to hear the witness's denunciation of the accused.* accusation, censure, condemnation, denouncing, incrimination, invective, stigmatization, verbal attack.
OPPOSITES: SEE **praise** noun.

deny verb **1** *to deny an accusation.* contradict, disagree with, disclaim, disown, dispute, oppose, rebuff, refute, reject, repudiate.
OPPOSITES: SEE **acknowledge**.
2 *Her indulgent parents don't deny her anything.* begrudge, deprive of, refuse.
OPPOSITES: SEE **give**.
to deny yourself SEE **abstain, fast** verb.

deodorant noun anti-perspirant.
OTHER TOILETRIES: SEE **cosmetics**.

deodorize verb air, freshen up, purify, refresh, sweeten, ventilate.

depart verb **1** *to depart on a journey.* begin a journey, [*informal*] clear off, decamp, disappear, embark, emigrate, escape, exit, go away, leave, make off, [*informal*] make tracks, migrate, [*informal*] push off, quit, retire, retreat, [*slang*] scram, set off, set out, start, take your leave, vanish, withdraw.
OPPOSITES: SEE **arrive**.
2 *to depart from your script.* deviate, digress, diverge, stray from.
OPPOSITE: stick to.

departed adjective SEE **dead**.

department noun **1** *a government department. a department in a large shop.* branch, division, office, part, section, sector, subdivision, unit.
2 [*informal*] *Ask someone else—it's not my department.* area, domain, field, function, job, line, province, responsibility, specialism, sphere.

departure noun disappearance, embarkation, escape, exit, exodus, going, retirement, retreat, withdrawal.
OPPOSITES: SEE **arrival**.

depend verb **to depend on 1** *My success will depend on good luck.* be dependent on [SEE **dependent**], hinge on, rest on.
2 *I depend on you to be good.* bank on, count on, need, rely on, trust.

dependable adjective *a dependable worker.* conscientious, consistent, faithful, honest, regular, reliable, safe, sound, steady, true, trustworthy, unfailing.
OPPOSITES: SEE **unreliable**.

dependence noun **1** *dependence on others.* confidence (in), need (for), reliance (upon), trust (in).
2 *dependence on drugs.* SEE **addiction**.

dependent adjective [Do not confuse with noun *dependant* = *a person who depends on your support.*] **dependent on 1** *Everything is dependent on the weather.* conditional on, connected with, controlled by, determined by, liable to, relative to, subject to, vulnerable to.
OPPOSITES: SEE **independent (of)**.
2 *dependent on drugs.* addicted to, enslaved by, [*informal*] hooked on, reliant on.

depict verb *to depict a scene.* delineate, describe, draw, illustrate, narrate, outline, paint, picture, portray, represent, reproduce, show, sketch.

deplete verb *The holiday has depleted our savings.* consume, cut, decrease, drain, lessen, reduce, use up.
OPPOSITES: SEE **increase** verb.

deplorable adjective *deplorable behaviour.* SEE **bad**, blameworthy, discreditable, disgraceful, disreputable, lamentable, regrettable, reprehensible, scandalous, shameful, shocking, unfortunate, unworthy.
OPPOSITES: SEE **praiseworthy**.

deplore verb **1** *We deplore suffering.* grieve for, lament, mourn, regret.
2 *We deplore vandalism.* SEE **condemn**, deprecate, disapprove of.

deploy verb *The boss deployed the workers effectively.* arrange, bring into action, distribute, manage, position, use systematically, utilize.

deport verb *They used to deport people for minor crimes.* banish, exile, expatriate, expel, remove, send abroad.

deportment noun SEE **bearing**.

depose verb *to depose a monarch.* demote, dethrone, dismiss, displace, get rid of, oust, remove, [*informal*] topple.
OPPOSITES: SEE **enthrone**.

deposit noun **1** *a deposit on a car.* down-payment, initial payment, part-payment, payment, retainer, security, stake.
2 *a deposit in the bottom of a container.* accumulation, dregs, layer, lees, precipitate, sediment, silt, sludge.

deposit verb **1** *Deposit the dirty plates by the hatch.* [*informal*] dump, lay down, leave, [*informal*] park, place, put down, set down.
2 *I deposited my money in the bank.* bank, pay in, save.
3 *The flood deposited a layer of mud.* precipitate.

depository noun SEE **depot**.

depot noun **1** *a stores depot.* arsenal [= *arms depot*], base, cache, depository, dump, hoard, store, storehouse.
2 *a bus depot.* garage, headquarters, station, terminus.

deprave verb *Do sadistic films deprave the viewers?* brutalize, corrupt, debase, degrade, influence, pervert.

depraved adjective *a depraved person. depraved behaviour.* SEE **bad**, corrupt, degenerate, dissolute, evil, immoral, lewd, perverted, profligate, reprobate, sinful, vicious, vile, wicked.
OPPOSITES: SEE **moral** adjective.

deprecate verb SEE **deplore**.

deprecatory adjective SEE **critical**.

depreciate verb [Do not confuse with *deprecate*.] *The value of antiques is not likely to depreciate.* become less, decrease, deflate, drop, fall, go down, lessen, lower, reduce, slump, weaken.
OPPOSITES: SEE **appreciate**.

depredation noun SEE **pillage** noun.

depress verb **1** *The weather depressed us.* discourage, dishearten, dispirit, enervate, grieve, lower the spirits of, make sad [SEE **sad**], sadden, tire, upset, weary.
OPPOSITES: SEE **cheer** verb.
2 *Bad news depresses the stock market.* bring down, deflate, make less active, push down, undermine, weaken.
OPPOSITES: SEE **boost** verb.

depressed adjective broken-hearted, crestfallen, dejected, desolate, despairing, despondent, disappointed, disconsolate, discouraged, disheartened, dismal, dismayed, dispirited, doleful, [*informal*] down, downcast, downhearted, friendless, gloomy, glum, hopeless, [*informal*] in the doldrums, [*informal*] in the dumps, languishing, [*informal*] low, melancholy, miserable, morose, pessimistic, sad, suicidal, unhappy, weary, woebegone, wretched.
OPPOSITES: SEE **cheerful**.
depressed person depressive.

depressing adjective SEE **sad**.

depression noun **1** *a mood of depression.* [*informal*] blues, dejection, desolation, despair, despondency, doldrums (*in the doldrums*), gloom, glumness, heaviness, hopelessness, low spirits, melancholy, misery, pessimism, sadness, unhappiness, weariness.
OPPOSITES: SEE **cheerfulness**.
2 *an economic depression.* decline, hard times, recession, slump.
OPPOSITES: SEE **boom** noun.
3 *a meteorological depression.* area of low pressure, cyclone, low.
OPPOSITE: anticyclone.
4 *a depression in the ground.* cavity, concavity, dent, dimple, dip, excavation, hole, hollow, indentation, pit, rut, sunken area.
OPPOSITES: SEE **bump** noun.

deprive verb **to deprive of** deny, dispossess of, prevent from using, refuse, rob of, starve of, strip of, take away.

deprived adjective *deprived families.* disadvantaged, needy, SEE **poor**.

deputation noun SEE **delegation**.

depute verb SEE **appoint**.

deputize verb **to deputize for** *I deputized for the manager when she was ill.* act as deputy for [SEE **deputy**], cover for, do the job of, replace, represent, stand in for, substitute for, take over from, understudy [= *deputize for an actor*].

deputy noun *The mayor was ill, so his deputy conducted the ceremony.* agent, assistant, delegate, [*informal*] fill-in, locum, proxy, relief, representative, reserve, replacement, second-in-command, [*informal*] stand-in, substitute, supply, surrogate, understudy, [*informal*] vice [and words with prefix *vice-*, e.g. *vice-captain*, etc.].

derailment noun SEE **accident**.

deranged adjective SEE **mad**.

derelict adjective *derelict buildings.* abandoned, broken down, decrepit, deserted, desolate, dilapidated, forlorn, forsaken, neglected, ruined, tumbledown.

dereliction noun SEE **neglect** noun.

deride verb SEE **mock** verb.

de rigueur SEE **customary**.

derision noun SEE **scorn** noun.

derisive adjective *derisive laughter.* SEE **scornful**.

derisory adjective *I rejected her derisory offer without hesitation.* SEE **laughable**.

derivation noun SEE **origin**.

derivative adjective *Their music seemed very derivative.* SEE **imitative**.

derive verb **1** *I derive pleasure from my garden.* acquire, gain, get, obtain, receive.
2 *He derived his ideas from a text book.* borrow, collect, crib, draw, glean, [*informal*] lift, pick up, procure, take.
to be derived *This word is derived from Latin.* arise, come, descend, develop, originate, proceed, spring, stem.

derogatory adjective SEE **uncomplimentary**.

derrick noun SEE **crane** noun.

descant verb SEE **sing**.

descend verb **1** *to descend a hill. to descend by parachute.* come down, climb down, drop down, fall down [SEE **fall** verb], go down, move down, sink down.
2 *The hill descends gradually.* dip, drop, fall, incline, slant, slope.
OPPOSITES: SEE **ascend**.
to be descended *She's descended from a French family.* come, originate, proceed, spring, stem.
to descend from *to descend from a bus.* alight from, disembark from, dismount from, get off.
to descend on *Bandits descended on the camp. Our friends descended on us at Christmas.* SEE **attack** verb, **visit** verb.

descendant noun *a descendant of a Victorian scientist.* heir, successor.
descendants children, family, issue, line, lineage, offspring, posterity, progeny, [*formal*] scion.
OPPOSITES: SEE **ancestor**.

descent noun **1** *a steep descent.* declivity, dip, drop, fall, incline, slant, slope, way down.
OPPOSITES: SEE **ascent**.
2 *aristocratic descent.* ancestry, background, blood, derivation, extraction, family, pedigree, genealogy, heredity, lineage, origin, parentage, stock, strain.

describe verb **1** *An eyewitness described what happened.* delineate, depict, detail, explain, express, narrate, outline,

recount, relate, report, sketch, tell about.
2 *The novelist describes her as a tyrant.* characterize, portray, present, represent, speak of.
3 *to describe a circle.* draw, mark out, trace.

description noun **1** *a vivid description.* account, characterization, commentary, delineation, depiction, explanation, narration, outline, portrait, portrayal, report, representation, sketch, story, word-picture.
2 *I haven't seen anything of that description.* SEE **kind** noun.

descriptive adjective *descriptive writing.* colourful, detailed, explanatory, expressive, graphic, illustrative, pictorial, vivid.

desecrate verb *to desecrate a holy place.* abuse, contaminate, debase, defile, pollute, profane, treat blasphemously or disrespectfully or irreverently, vandalize, violate.
OPPOSITES: SEE **bless, revere**.

desert adjective **1** *desert conditions.* arid, barren, dry, infertile, sterile, uncultivated, waterless, wild.
OPPOSITES: SEE **fertile**.
2 *a desert island.* desolate, isolated, lonely, solitary, unfrequented, uninhabited.
OPPOSITES: SEE **inhabited**.

desert noun wasteland, wilderness.

desert verb **1** *to desert your friends.* abandon, betray, forsake, give up, jilt, [*informal*] leave in the lurch, maroon (*maroon someone on an island*), [*informal*] rat on, renounce, strand, [*informal*] walk out on, [*informal*] wash your hands of.
2 *to desert a sinking ship.* abandon, leave, quit, vacate.
3 *The soldiers deserted.* abscond, decamp, defect, go absent, run away.

deserter noun *a deserter from the army. a deserter from a cause.* absentee, apostate, backslider, betrayer, defector, disloyal person [SEE **disloyal**], fugitive, outlaw, renegade, runaway, traitor, truant (*from school*), turncoat.

deserve verb *to deserve a reward.* be good enough for, be worthy of, earn, justify, merit, rate, warrant.

deserving adjective *a deserving winner. a deserving cause.* admirable, commendable, creditable, good, laudable, meritorious, praiseworthy, worth supporting, worthy.
OPPOSITES: SEE **unworthy**.

desiccate verb SEE **dry** verb.

design noun **1** *a design for a new car.* blueprint, drawing, model, pattern, plan, prototype, sketch.
2 *an old design.* model, style, type, version.
3 *a jazzy design of dots and lines.* arrangement, composition, configuration, pattern.
4 *I wandered about without any design.* aim, end, goal, intention, object, objective, purpose, scheme.
to have designs SEE **plot** verb.

design verb *Architects design buildings. We designed this book to help you find words.* conceive, construct, contrive, create, devise, draft, draw, draw up, fashion, intend, invent, make, plan, plot, project, propose, scheme, sketch.

designer noun author, contriver, creator, deviser, inventor, originator.

DESIGNERS OF VARIOUS PRODUCTS: architect, artist, couturier, fashion designer, graphic designer, hair stylist, interior designer, stage designer.

---

designate verb SEE **appoint**.

designation noun SEE **title** noun.

designing adjective SEE **crafty**.

desirable adjective SEE **attractive, sexy**.

desire noun **1** *a desire to do good.* ache, ambition, craving, fancy, hankering, [*informal*] itch, longing, urge, want, wish, yearning, [*informal*] yen.
2 *desire for food or drink.* appetite, gluttony, hunger, thirst.
3 *desire for money.* avarice, covetousness, cupidity, greed, miserliness, rapacity.
4 *sexual desire.* ardour, lasciviousness, libido, love, lust, passion.
5 [*formal*] *It is the king's desire that you attend.* entreaty, petition, request, wish.

desire verb *What do you most desire?* ache for, covet, crave, fancy, hanker after, [*informal*] have a yen for, hunger for, [*informal*] itch for, like, long for, lust after, need, pine for, prefer, [*informal*] set your heart on, thirst for, want, wish for, yearn for.
2 [*formal or old-fashioned*] *He desired me to step inside.* SEE **ask**, beg, entreat, importune, petition, request.

desist verb SEE **cease**.

desk noun bureau, lectern, writing-table.
OTHER FURNITURE: SEE **furniture**.

desolate adjective **1** *a desolate place.* abandoned, bare, barren, benighted,

bleak, cheerless, depressing, deserted, dismal, dreary, empty, forsaken, gloomy, [*informal*] god-forsaken, inhospitable, isolated, lonely, remote, unfrequented, uninhabited, wild, windswept.
OPPOSITES: SEE **idyllic**.
2 *He was desolate when his dog died.* bereft, companionless, dejected, SEE **depressed**, disconsolate, distressed, forlorn, forsaken, inconsolable, lonely, melancholy, neglected, sad, solitary, wretched.
OPPOSITES: SEE **cheerful**.

despair noun *a state of despair.* anguish, dejection, depression, desperation, despondency, gloom, hopelessness, melancholy, SEE **misery**, pessimism, wretchedness.
OPPOSITES: SEE **hope** noun.

despair verb give up, [*informal*] lose heart, lose hope.
OPPOSITES: SEE **hope** verb.

desperado noun bandit, brigand, SEE **criminal** noun, cutthroat, gangster, gunman, outlaw, ruffian, thug.

desperate adjective 1 *The starving refugees were desperate.* beyond hope, despairing, hopeless, inconsolable.
2 *a desperate situation.* acute, bad, critical, drastic, grave, irretrievable, serious, severe, urgent.
3 *desperate criminals.* dangerous, impetuous, reckless, violent, wild.

despicable adjective SEE **contemptible**.

despise verb be contemptuous of, condemn, deride, disapprove of, disdain, feel contempt for, SEE **hate** verb, have a low opinion of, look down on, [*informal*] put down, scorn, sneer at, spurn, undervalue.
OPPOSITES: SEE **admire**.

despondent adjective SEE **depressed**.

despot noun SEE **dictator**.

despotic adjective SEE **dictatorial**.

dessert noun [*informal*] afters, fruit, pudding, sweet.
OTHER COURSES: SEE **meal**.

dessert-spoon noun SEE **cutlery**.

destination noun *the destination of a journey.* goal, objective, purpose, target, terminus.

destined adjective 1 *My plans were destined to fail.* bound, certain, doomed, fated.
2 *I foresaw the destined outcome.* inescapable, inevitable, intended, ordained, predestined, predetermined, preordained, unavoidable.

destiny noun chance, doom, fate, fortune, karma, kismet, lot (*Accept your lot*), luck, providence.

destitute adjective *destitute beggars.* bankrupt, deprived, down-and-out, homeless, impecunious, impoverished, indigent, insolvent, needy, penniless, SEE **poor**, poverty-stricken, [*informal*] skint.
OPPOSITES: SEE **wealthy**.
destitute people beggars, down-and-outs, [*informal*] the have-nots, paupers, the poor, tramps, vagrants.

destroy verb abolish, annihilate, blast, break down, crush, decimate [see note under *decimate*], SEE **defeat** verb, demolish, devastate, devour, dismantle, eliminate, SEE **end** verb, eradicate, erase, exterminate, extinguish, extirpate, finish off, flatten, get rid of, SEE **kill**, knock down, lay waste (to), level, liquidate, make useless, pull down, put out of existence, raze, ruin, sabotage, scuttle, shatter, smash, stamp out, undo, uproot, vaporize, wipe out, wreck.
OPPOSITES: SEE **create**.

destruction noun *We deplore the destruction of wildlife.* annihilation, damage, decimation [see note under *decimate*], demolition, depredation, devastation, elimination, end, eradication, erasure, extermination, extinction, extirpation, havoc, holocaust, SEE **killing**, liquidation, overthrow, pulling down, ruin, shattering, smashing, undoing, uprooting, wiping out, wrecking.
OPPOSITES: SEE **conservation**, **creation**.

destructive adjective *a destructive storm. destructive criticism.* adverse, antagonistic, baleful, baneful, calamitous, catastrophic, damaging, dangerous, deadly, deleterious, detrimental, devastating, disastrous, fatal, harmful, injurious, internecine, lethal, malignant, negative, pernicious, pestilential, ruinous, violent.
OPPOSITES: SEE **constructive**.

desultory adjective SEE **disjointed**.

detach verb *to detach one thing from another.* cut loose, cut off, disconnect, disengage, disentangle, divide, free, isolate, part, release, remove, segregate, separate, sever, take off, tear off, uncouple, undo, unfasten, unfix, unhitch.
OPPOSITES: SEE **attach**.

detachable adjective *a detachable hood.* loose, removable, separable, separate.
OPPOSITES: SEE **integral**.

detached adjective 1 *a detached house.* free-standing, separate, unconnected.
COMPARE: semi-detached, terraced.

2 *a detached point of view.* aloof, cool, disinterested, dispassionate, impartial, impassive, independent, neutral, non-partisan, non-party, objective, unbiased, uncommitted, unconcerned, unemotional, uninvolved, unprejudiced.
OPPOSITES: SEE **committed**.

detail noun *Her account was accurate in every detail.* aspect, circumstance, complexity, complication, fact, factor, feature, ingredient, intricacy, item, [*plural*] minutiae, nicety, particular, point, refinement, respect, specific.

detail verb 1 *She detailed the relevant facts.* SEE **describe**.
2 *I was detailed to do the job.* SEE **assign**.

detailed adjective *a detailed description.* complete, complex, [*uncomplimentary*] fussy, giving all details, [*uncomplimentary*] hair-splitting, intricate, minute, specific.
OPPOSITES: SEE **general**.

detain verb 1 *The police detained the suspect.* arrest, capture, confine, gaol, hold, hold in custody, imprison, intern, restrain.
OPPOSITES: SEE **release** verb.
2 *What detained you? Who detained you?* buttonhole, delay, hinder, hold up, impede, keep, keep waiting, prevent, retard, slow, stop, waylay.

detainee noun SEE **prisoner**.

detect verb *to detect a fault.* become aware of, diagnose, discern, discover, expose, feel, [*informal*] ferret out, find, hear, identify, note, notice, observe, perceive, recognize, reveal, scent, see, sense, sight, smell, sniff out, spot, spy, taste, track down, uncover, unearth, unmask.

detective noun investigator, SEE **policeman**, [*informal*] private eye, sleuth.

détente noun SEE **reconciliation**.

detention noun SEE **imprisonment**.

deter verb *How can we deter the wretched starlings?* check, daunt, discourage, dismay, dissuade, frighten off, hinder, impede, intimidate, obstruct, prevent, put off, repel, send away, stop, [*informal*] turn off, warn off.
OPPOSITES: SEE **encourage**.

detergent noun cleaner, soap, washing-powder, washing-up liquid.

deteriorate verb *His work deteriorated. The buildings deteriorated.* crumble, decay, decline, degenerate, depreciate, disintegrate, fall off, get worse, [*informal*] go downhill, lapse, relapse, slip, weaken, worsen.
OPPOSITES: SEE **improve**.

determinate adjective SEE **limited**.

determination noun *Marathon runners show great determination.* [*informal*] backbone, commitment, courage, dedication, doggedness, drive, firmness, fortitude, [*informal*] grit, [*informal*] guts, perseverance, persistence, pertinacity, resolution, resolve, single-mindedness, spirit, steadfastness, [*uncomplimentary*] stubbornness, tenacity, will-power.

determine verb 1 *to determine a number.* SEE **calculate**.
2 *to determine the cause of an accident.* SEE **decide**.

determined adjective 1 *He's determined he will succeed.* adamant, bent (*on succeeding*), certain, convinced, decided, definite, firm, insistent, intent (*on succeeding*), resolved, sure.
OPPOSITES: SEE **doubtful**.
2 *a determined woman.* assertive, decisive, dogged, [*uncomplimentary*] obstinate, persistent, pertinacious, purposeful, resolute, single-minded, steadfast, strong-minded, strong-willed, [*uncomplimentary*] stubborn, sworn (*sworn enemies*), tenacious, tough, unwavering.
OPPOSITES: SEE **irresolute**.

deterrent noun *I put a net over my strawberries as a deterrent to the birds.* barrier, caution, check, curb, difficulty, discouragement, disincentive, dissuasion, hindrance, impediment, obstacle, restraint, threat, [*informal*] turn-off, warning.
OPPOSITES: SEE **encouragement**.

detest verb SEE **hate** verb.

detestable adjective SEE **hateful**.

dethrone verb SEE **depose**.

detonate verb *to detonate a bomb.* SEE **explode**.

detour noun *I wasted time making a detour.* deviation, diversion, indirect route, roundabout route.
to make a detour SEE **deviate**.

detract verb **to detract from** *Damage detracts from the value of an antique.* SEE **reduce**.

detractor noun SEE **critic**.

detriment noun SEE **harm** noun.

detrimental adjective SEE **harmful**.

detritus noun SEE **debris**.

devalue verb SEE **reduce**.

devastate verb 1 *A hurricane devastated the town.* damage severely, demolish, destroy, flatten, lay waste, level, overwhelm, ravage, raze, ruin, wreck.

2 [*informal*] *We were devastated by the bad news.* SEE **dismay** verb.

develop verb 1 *People develop. Plans develop.* advance, age, evolve, get better, grow, flourish, improve, mature, move on, progress, ripen.
OPPOSITES: SEE **regress**.
2 *A storm developed.* arise, [*informal*] blow up, come into existence, [*informal*] get up, work up.
3 *She developed a cold. He developed a posh accent.* acquire, contract, cultivate, evolve, foster, get, pick up.
4 *Develop your ideas.* amplify, augment, elaborate, enlarge on.
5 *Our business will develop next year.* branch out, build up, diversify, enlarge, expand, extend, increase, swell.

development noun 1 *the development of science. the development of trade.* advance, betterment, enlargement, evolution, expansion, extension, [*informal*] forward march, furtherance, growth, improvement, increase, progress, promotion, regeneration, reinforcement, spread.
2 [*informal*] *We'll let you know of any developments.* change, gain, happening, incident, occurrence, outcome, result, upshot.
3 *The land is earmarked for industrial development.* building, conversion, exploitation, use.

deviant adjective *deviant behaviour.* SEE **abnormal**.

deviate verb *to deviate from the usual path.* depart, digress, diverge, err, go astray, go round, make a detour, stray, swerve, turn aside, vary, veer, wander.

deviation noun SEE **abnormality**, **detour**.

device noun 1 *a clever device for opening wine-bottles.* apparatus, appliance, contraption, contrivance, gadget, implement, instrument, invention, machine, tool, utensil.
2 *a device to distract our attention.* dodge, expedient, gambit, gimmick, manœuvre, plan, ploy, ruse, scheme, stratagem, stunt, tactic, trick, wile.
3 *a heraldic device.* badge, crest, design, figure, logo, motif, shield, sign, symbol, token.

devil noun the Adversary, demon, the Evil One, fiend, imp, Lucifer, Satan, spirit.

devilish adjective demoniac, demoniacal, diabolic, diabolical, SEE **evil** adjective, fiendish, hellish, infernal, satanic, wicked.
OPPOSITES: SEE **angelic**.

devilment, **devilry** nouns SEE **mischief**.

devious adjective 1 *a devious route.* circuitous, crooked, deviating, indirect, periphrastic, rambling, roundabout, tortuous, wandering, winding.
OPPOSITES: SEE **direct** adjective.
2 *a devious person. a devious explanation.* calculating, cunning, deceitful, SEE **dishonest**, evasive, insincere, misleading, scheming, [*informal*] slippery (*a slippery customer*), sly, sneaky, treacherous, underhand, wily.
OPPOSITES: SEE **straightforward**.

devise verb *to devise a plan.* conceive, concoct, contrive, design, engineer, form, formulate, imagine, invent, make up, plan, plot, prepare, project, scheme, think out, think up.

devoted adjective SEE **loyal**.

devotee noun SEE **enthusiast**.

devotion noun SEE **love** noun, **piety**.

devotional adjective SEE **religious**.

devour verb 1 *to devour food.* SEE **eat**.
2 *Fire devoured the forest.* SEE **destroy**.

devout adjective SEE **pious**.

dew noun SEE **moisture**.

dexterity noun SEE **skill**.

dextrous adjective SEE **skilful**.

Diabolical and *diabolism* are related to Latin *diabolus=devil.* Compare French *diable.*

---

diabolical adjective 1 *diabolical cruelty.* SEE **devilish**.
2 [*informal*] *a diabolical standard of driving.* SEE **bad**.

diadem noun coronet, crown, tiara.
OTHER FORMS OF HEAD-DRESS: SEE **hat**.

diagnose verb *to diagnose an illness.* detect, determine, distinguish, find, identify, isolate, name, pinpoint, recognize.

diagnosis noun *What's the doctor's diagnosis?* analysis, conclusion, explanation, identification, interpretation, opinion, pronouncement, verdict.

diagram noun *an explanatory diagram.* chart, drawing, figure, flow-chart, graph, illustration, outline, picture, plan, representation, sketch, table.

dial noun *the dials on a dashboard.* clock, digital display, face, instrument, pointer, speedometer.

dial verb *to dial a number.* call, phone, ring, telephone.

dialect noun *a London dialect. a local dialect.* accent, brogue, idiom, jargon, language, patois, pronunciation, register, speech, tongue, vernacular.

dialectic noun SEE **reasoning**.

dialogue noun *a dialogue between two people.* [*informal*] chat, [*informal*] chinwag, [*formal*] colloquy, conversation, debate, discourse, discussion, duologue, exchange, interchange, [*old-fashioned*] intercourse, [*formal*] oral communication, talk.

diameter noun SEE **circle** noun.
RELATED ADJECTIVE: diametrical.

diamond noun OTHER PRECIOUS STONES: SEE **jewel**.
a diamond shape lozenge, rhombus.

diaper noun *a baby's diaper.* nappy.

diaphanous adjective *diaphanous fabric.* airy, SEE **delicate**, filmy, fine, gauzy, light, see-through, sheer, thin, translucent.
OPPOSITES: SEE **opaque, thick**.
diaphanous fabric gauze, net, veil.

diarrhoea noun dysentery, [*informal*] gippy tummy, [*informal*] holiday tummy, looseness of the bowels, [*informal*] the runs, [*informal*] the trots.
OTHER COMPLAINTS: SEE **illness**.

diary noun *a daily diary of events.* appointment book, chronicle, engagement book, journal, log, record.

diatonic adjective *a diatonic melody.*
COMPARE: atonal, chromatic.
OTHER MUSICAL TERMS: SEE **music**.

diatribe noun SEE **censure** noun.

dice verb *to dice with death.* SEE **gamble** verb.

dicey adjective SEE **risky**.

dichotomy noun *an odd dichotomy in his attitude.* ambivalence, divergence, division, doubleness, duality, split.

dictate verb **1** *I dictated while he wrote it down.* read aloud, speak slowly.
2 *Should parents dictate what their children do?* command, decree, direct, enforce, give orders, impose, [*informal*] lay down the law, make the rules, ordain, order, prescribe, state categorically.

dictator noun autocrat, [*informal*] Big Brother, despot, SEE **ruler**, tyrant.

dictatorial adjective *a dictatorial ruler.* absolute, authoritarian, autocratic, [*informal*] bossy, despotic, dogmatic, dominant, domineering, illiberal, imperious, intolerant, oppressive, overbearing, repressive, totalitarian, tyrannical, undemocratic.
OPPOSITES: SEE **democratic**.

dictatorship noun POLITICAL TERMS: SEE **politics**.

diction noun **1** *a poet's diction.* SEE **vocabulary**.
2 *unclear diction.* SEE **pronunciation**.

dictionary noun VARIOUS WORD-LISTS: concordance, glossary, lexicon, thesaurus, vocabulary, wordbook.

dictum noun SEE **saying**.

didactic adjective **1** *a didactic story.* SEE **instructive**.
2 *a didactic manner.* lecturing, pedagogic, pedantic.

diddle verb SEE **cheat** verb.

die verb **1** *All mortal creatures die.* [*informal*] bite the dust, [*informal*] breathe your last, cease to exist, come to the end, [*formal*] decease, depart, [*formal*] expire, fall (*to fall in war*), [*informal*] give up the ghost, pass away, [*slang*] kick the bucket, pass away, [*informal*] peg out, perish, [*slang*] snuff it, starve [=*die of hunger*].
2 *The flowers died.* droop, fade, wilt, wither.
3 *The flames died.* become less, decline, decrease, disappear, dwindle, ebb, end, fail, fizzle out, go out, languish, lessen, peter out, stop, subside, vanish, wane, weaken.
4 [*informal*] *I'm dying to meet you.* SEE **long** verb.

die-hard noun SEE **conservative** noun.

diet noun **1** *a healthy diet.* fare, SEE **food**, nourishment, nutriment, nutrition.
2 *a slimmer's diet.* abstinence, fast, rations, self-denial.
SPECIAL DIETS: vegan, vegetarian.

differ verb **1** *My feelings differ from yours.* be different, contrast (with), deviate, diverge, vary.
OPPOSITES: SEE **conform**.
2 *We differed about where to go.* argue, be at odds with each other, clash, conflict, contradict each other, disagree, dispute, dissent, fall out, oppose each other, quarrel, take issue with each other.
OPPOSITES: SEE **agree**.

difference noun **1** *a difference in price. a difference in meaning.* comparison, contrast, differential, differentiation, discrepancy, disparity, dissimilarity, distinction, diversity, incompatibility, incongruity, inconsistency, nuance, unlikeness, variety.
OPPOSITES: SEE **similarity**.
2 *a difference in our plans.* alteration, change, development, deviation, modification, variation.

3 *a difference of opinion.* argument, clash, conflict, controversy, debate, disagreement, disharmony, dispute, dissent, quarrel, strife, tiff, wrangle.
OPPOSITES: SEE **agreement**.

different adjective **1** *different colours. different opinions.* assorted, clashing, conflicting, contradictory, contrasting, deviating, discordant, discrepant, disparate, dissimilar, distinguishable, divergent, diverse, heterogeneous, ill-matched, incompatible, inconsistent, miscellaneous, mixed, multifarious, numerous, opposed, opposite, [*informal*] poles apart, several, sundry, unlike, varied, various.
OPPOSITES: SEE **identical**, **similar**.
2 *I'm always getting different ideas.* altered, changed, changing, fresh, new, original, revolutionary.
OPPOSITES: SEE **unchanging**.
3 *It's different to have jam with fried potatoes.* abnormal, anomalous, atypical, bizarre, eccentric, extraordinary, irregular, strange, uncommon, unconventional, unorthodox, unusual.
OPPOSITES: SEE **conventional**.
4 *Everyone's handwriting is different.* distinct, distinctive, individual, particular, peculiar, personal, separate, singular, special, specific, unique.
OPPOSITES: SEE **indistinguishable**.

differentiate verb SEE **distinguish**.

difficult adjective **1** *a difficult problem.* abstruse, advanced, baffling, complex, complicated, deep, [*informal*] dodgy, enigmatic, hard, intractable, intricate, involved, [*informal*] knotty, [*informal*] nasty, obscure, perplexing, problematical, thorny, ticklish, tricky,
OPPOSITES: SEE **easy**, **straightforward**.
2 *a difficult climb. a difficult task.* arduous, awkward, burdensome, challenging, demanding, exacting, exhausting, formidable, gruelling, heavy, herculean, [*informal*] killing, laborious, onerous, punishing, rigorous, severe, strenuous, taxing, tough, uphill.
OPPOSITES: SEE **easy**, **light** adjective.
3 *difficult neighbours. a difficult child.* annoying, disruptive, fussy, headstrong, intractable, obstinate, obstreperous, refractory, stubborn, tiresome, troublesome, trying, uncooperative, unfriendly, unhelpful, unresponsive, unruly.
OPPOSITES: SEE **tractable**.

difficulty noun *a difficulty to overcome.* adversity, challenge, complication, dilemma, embarrassment, enigma, [*informal*] fix (*I'm in a bit of a fix*), [*informal*] hang-up, hardship, [*informal*] hiccup, hindrance, hurdle, impediment, jam, obstacle, perplexity, plight, predicament, problem, puzzle, quandary, snag, [*informal*] spot (*I'm in a bit of spot*), [*informal*] stumbling-block, tribulation, trouble, [*informal*] vexed question.

diffident adjective *a diffident manner.* backward, bashful, coy, distrustful, doubtful, fearful, hesitant, hesitating, inhibited, insecure, introvert, meek, modest, nervous, private, reluctant, reserved, retiring, self-effacing, sheepish, shrinking, shy, tentative, timid, timorous, unadventurous, unassuming, underconfident, unsure, withdrawn.
OPPOSITES: SEE **confident**.

diffuse adjective *a diffuse piece of writing.* digressive, discursive, long-winded, loose, meandering, prolix, rambling, vague, verbose, [*informal*] waffly, wandering, wordy.
OPPOSITES: SEE **concise**.

diffuse verb SEE **spread** verb.

dig verb **1** *to dig a hole.* burrow, delve, excavate, gouge out, hollow out, mine, quarry, scoop, tunnel.
2 *to dig the garden.* cultivate, fork over, [*informal*] grub up, till, trench, turn over.
3 *to dig out information.* find, probe, research, search.
4 *to dig someone in the back.* jab, nudge, poke, prod, punch, shove, thrust.
to dig up disinter, exhume.

digest noun *a digest of the latest research.* SEE **summary** noun.

digest verb **1** *to digest food.* absorb, assimilate, dissolve, SEE **eat**, [*formal*] ingest, process, utilize.
2 *to digest information.* consider, ponder, study, take in, understand.

digit noun **1** *Add up the digits.* figure, integer, number, numeral.
2 *We have five digits on each hand and foot.* finger, toe.

dignified adjective *dignified behaviour. a dignified ceremony.* becoming, calm, decorous, elegant, formal, grave, imposing, impressive, majestic, noble, proper, refined, sedate, serious, sober, solemn, stately, tasteful, upright.
OPPOSITES: SEE **undignified**.

dignify verb SEE **honour** verb.

dignitary noun *The dignitaries entered in procession.* important person, [*informal*] VIP, worthy.

dignity noun *They behaved with dignity.* calmness, decorum, eminence, formality, glory, grandeur, gravity, greatness, honour, importance, majesty, nobility, pride, propriety, respectability, seriousness, solemnity, stateliness.

digress verb *to digress from your subject.* depart, deviate, diverge, go off at a tangent, ramble, stray, veer, wander.

digs noun SEE **lodgings**.

dike noun [Note that the two senses of *dike* are almost opposite in meaning.]
1 *a dike to drain the marsh.* channel, conduit, ditch, watercourse, waterway.
2 *a dike to prevent flooding.* dam, earthworks, embankment, wall.

dilapidated adjective *a dilapidated building.* broken down, crumbling, decayed, decrepit, derelict, falling down, in disrepair, in ruins, neglected, ramshackle, rickety, ruined, [*informal*] run-down, tottering, tumbledown, uncared for.
OPPOSITE: well-maintained.

dilate verb SEE **enlarge**.

dilatory adjective SEE **slow** adjective.

dilemma noun *caught in a dilemma.* [*informal*] catch-22, difficulty, doubt, embarrassment, [*informal*] fix, [*informal*] jam, [*informal*] mess, [*informal*] pickle, plight, predicament, problem, quandary, [*informal*] spot (*I'm in a bit of a spot*).

dilettante noun amateur, dabbler.

diligent adjective *a diligent worker.* assiduous, busy, careful, conscientious, devoted, earnest, energetic, hardworking, indefatigable, industrious, painstaking, persevering, persistent, pertinacious, scrupulous, sedulous, studious, thorough, tireless.
OPPOSITES: SEE **lazy**.

dilly-dally verb SEE **dawdle**.

dilute adjective *dilute acid.* adulterated, diluted, thin, watered down, weak.
OPPOSITES: SEE **concentrated**.

dilute verb *You dilute orange squash with water.* adulterate, make less concentrated, reduce the strength of, thin, water down, weaken.
OPPOSITES: SEE **concentrate**.

dim adjective 1 *a dim outline in the mist.* bleary, blurred, cloudy, dark, dingy, dull, faint, foggy, fuzzy, gloomy, grey, hazy, indistinct, misty, murky, obscure, pale, shadowy, unclear, vague.
OPPOSITES: SEE **bright**, **clear** adjective.
2 [*informal*] *You are dim if you can't understand that!* SEE **stupid**.
to take a dim view SEE **disapprove**.

dim verb 1 *Cloud dimmed the sky.* blacken, cloud, darken, dull, make dim, mask, obscure.
2 *The lights dimmed.* become dim, fade, go out, lose brightness, lower.
OPPOSITES: SEE **brighten**.

dimension noun SEE **measurement**.

dimensions *a room of large dimensions.* capacity, extent, magnitude, proportions, scale, scope, size.

diminish verb 1 *Our enthusiasm diminished as time went on.* become less, contract, decline, decrease, depreciate, dwindle, lessen, peter out, reduce, shrink, shrivel, subside, wane.
OPPOSITES: SEE **increase**.
2 *Don't diminish the importance of his contribution.* belittle, demean, devalue, minimize, undervalue.
OPPOSITES: SEE **exaggerate**.

diminutive adjective SEE **small**.

dimple noun SEE **hollow** noun.

din noun *a deafening din.* clamour, clatter, commotion, crash, hubbub, hullabaloo, noise, outcry, pandemonium, racket, row, rumpus, shouting, tumult, uproar.

dine verb SEE **eat**.

dinghy noun OTHER BOATS: SEE **vessel**.

dingo noun SEE **dog** noun.

dingy adjective *dingy colours. a dingy room.* colourless, dark, depressing, dim, dirty, discoloured, dismal, drab, dreary, dull, faded, gloomy, grimy, murky, old, seedy, shabby, soiled, worn.
OPPOSITES: SEE **bright**, **fresh**.

dining-room noun cafeteria, carvery, refectory, restaurant.
OTHER ROOMS IN A HOUSE: SEE **room**.

dinky adjective SEE **small**.

dinner noun banquet, feast, SEE **meal**.

dint noun SEE **dent** noun.

dip noun 1 *a dip in the sea.* bathe, dive, immersion, plunge, soaking, swim.
to take a dip SEE **bathe** verb.
2 *a dip in the ground.* concavity, declivity, dent, depression, fall, hole, hollow, incline, slope.

dip verb 1 *to dip something in liquid.* douse, drop, duck, dunk, immerse, lower, plunge, submerge.
2 *to dip down.* descend, dive, go down, slope down, slump, subside.

diploma noun *a life-saving diploma.* award, certificate, SEE **qualification**.

diplomacy noun *She showed great diplomacy in ending the dispute.* delicacy, discretion, finesse, skill, tact, tactfulness.

diplomat noun 1 ambassador, consul, government representative, negotiator, politician.
2 [used loosely] *Being a diplomat, she smoothed over their differences.* diplomatic person [SEE **diplomatic**], peacemaker, tactician.

diplomatic adjective *a diplomatic reply.* careful, considerate, delicate, discreet, judicious, polite, politic, prudent, sensitive, subtle, tactful, thoughtful, understanding.
OPPOSITES: SEE **tactless**.

dipsomaniac noun alcoholic, drinker, drunkard, toper.

dire adjective **1** *a dire calamity,* SEE **dreadful**.
2 *a dire warning.* SEE **ominous**.
3 *dire need.* SEE **urgent**.

direct adjective **1** *a direct route.* nonstop, shortest, straight, undeviating, unswerving.
OPPOSITES: SEE **indirect**.
2 *a direct answer.* blunt, candid, explicit, frank, honest, outspoken, plain, point-blank, sincere, straightforward, unambiguous, uncomplicated, unequivocal.
OPPOSITES: SEE **evasive**.
3 *direct opposites. a direct contradiction.* absolute, categorical, complete, decided, diametrical, exact, head-on, [*informal*] out-and-out, utter.

direct verb **1** *to direct someone to the station.* guide, indicate the way, point, route, show the way, tell the way.
2 *to direct a letter.* address.
3 *to direct an attack on someone.* aim, point, target, train (on), turn (on).
4 *to direct a project.* administer, be in charge of, command, conduct (*an orchestra*), control, govern, handle, lead, manage, mastermind, oversee, produce (*a play*), regulate, rule, run, stage-manage, superintend, supervise, take charge of.
5 *He directed us to begin.* advise, bid, charge, command, enjoin, instruct, order, tell.

direction noun **1** *Which direction did he take?* aim, approach, bearing (*compass-bearing*), course, orientation, path, point of the compass, road, route, tack, track, way.
PRINCIPAL COMPASS-BEARINGS: east, north, north-east, north-west, south, south-east, south-west, west.
2 [*usually plural*] *The kit comes with directions for assembly.* guidance, guidelines, instructions, orders, plans.

directive noun SEE **command** noun.

director noun SEE **chief** noun.

directorate noun SEE **board** noun.

directory noun *a telephone directory.* catalogue, index, list, register.
OTHER KINDS OF BOOK: SEE **book** noun.

dirge noun lament, mournful song [SEE **mournful**].
OTHER SONGS: SEE **song**.

dirk noun SEE **dagger**.

dirt noun **1** *Clean up the dirt.* dust, filth, garbage, grime, impurity, mess, mire, muck, pollution, refuse, rubbish, slime, sludge, smut, stain, tarnish.
2 *Chickens scratched about in the dirt.* clay, earth, loam, mud, soil.

dirty adjective **1** *a dirty room. dirty clothes.* black, dingy, dusty, filthy, foul, grimy, grubby, marked, messy, mucky, muddy, nasty, scruffy, shabby, smeary, soiled, sooty, sordid, squalid, stained, sullied, tarnished, travel-stained, uncared for, unclean, unwashed.
OPPOSITES: SEE **clean** adjective.
2 *dirty water.* cloudy, impure, muddy, murky, polluted, untreated.
OPPOSITES: SEE **pure**.
3 *dirty tactics.* SEE **corrupt** adjective. dishonest, illegal, [*informal*] low-down, mean, rough, treacherous, unfair, ungentlemanly, unsporting.
OPPOSITES: SEE **honest, sporting**.
4 *dirty language.* coarse, crude, improper, indecent, SEE **obscene**, offensive, rude, smutty, vulgar.
OPPOSITES: SEE **decent**.

dirty verb *Try not to dirty your clothes.* SEE **defile**, foul, make dirty [SEE **dirty** adjective], mark, [*informal*] mess up, smear, smudge, soil, spatter, spot, stain, streak, sully, tarnish.
OPPOSITES: SEE **clean** verb.

disability noun *a physical disability.* affliction, complaint, disablement, handicap, impairment, incapacity, infirmity, weakness.

disable verb **1** *The accident temporarily disabled her.* cripple, debilitate, enfeeble, [*informal*] hamstring, handicap, immobilize, impair, incapacitate, injure, lame, maim, paralyse, weaken.
2 *The storm disabled the generators.* damage, make useless, put out of action, stop working.

disabled adjective *a disabled person.* bedridden, crippled, deformed, handicapped, having a disability, immobilized, incapacitated, infirm, lame, limbless, maimed, mutilated, paralysed, paraplegic, weak, weakened.
disabled person amputee, cripple, invalid, paraplegic.

disabuse verb SEE **disillusion**.

disadvantage noun *It's a disadvantage to be small if you play basketball.* drawback, handicap, hardship, hindrance, impediment, inconvenience, liability, [*informal*] minus, nuisance, privation, snag, trouble, weakness.

disadvantaged adjective SEE **handicapped**.

disaffected adjective SEE **dissatisfied**.

disagree verb argue, bicker, clash, conflict, differ, dissent, fall out, quarrel, squabble, wrangle.
OPPOSITES: SEE **agree**.
to disagree with 1 *He disagrees with everything I say.* argue with, be at variance with, contradict, counter, deviate from, dissent from, object to, oppose, take issue with.
2 *Onions disagree with me.* SEE **upset**.

disagreeable adjective SEE **unpleasant**.

disagreement noun *There was a disagreement between them.* altercation, argument, clash, conflict, controversy, debate, difference of opinion, disharmony, dispute, dissension, dissent, divergence, inconsistency, lack of sympathy, misunderstanding, opposition, quarrel, squabble, [*informal*] tiff, variance, wrangle.
OPPOSITES: SEE **agreement**.

disallow verb *to disallow a goal.* cancel, dismiss, refuse, reject, veto.
OPPOSITES: SEE **allow**.

disappear verb **1** *The fog disappeared.* become invisible [SEE **invisible**], cease to exist, clear, disperse, dissolve, dwindle, ebb, evaporate, fade, melt away, recede, vanish, wane.
2 *He disappeared round the corner.* depart, escape, flee, fly, go, pass, run away, walk away, withdraw.
OPPOSITES: SEE **appear**.

disappoint verb *The weather disappointed us.* be worse than expected, chagrin, [*informal*] dash (a person's) hopes, disillusion, dismay, displease, fail to satisfy, frustrate, [*informal*] let down, upset, thwart, vex.
OPPOSITES: SEE **delight** verb, **satisfy**.

disappointed adjective *a disappointed man.* crestfallen, dejected, discontented, disenchanted, disgruntled, disillusioned, dissatisfied, downcast, downhearted, frustrated, let down, SEE **sad**, unhappy.
OPPOSITES: SEE **contented**.

disapprobation noun SEE **disapproval**.

disapproval noun *Her frown showed her disapproval.* anger, censure, condemnation, criticism, disapprobation, disfavour, dislike, displeasure, dissatisfaction, hostility, reprimand, reproach.
OPPOSITES: SEE **approval**.

disapprove verb **to disapprove of** *They all disapprove of smoking.* be displeased by, blame, censure, condemn, criticize, denounce, deplore, deprecate, dislike, disparage, frown on, jeer at [SEE **jeer**], look askance at, make unwelcome, object to, regret, reject, take exception to, [*informal*] take a dim view of.
OPPOSITES: SEE **approve**.

disapproving adjective *a disapproving look.* [*informal*] black (*I gave him a black look*), censorious, critical, deprecatory, disparaging, reproachful, slighting, unfavourable, unfriendly.
OPPOSITES: SEE **favourable**.

disarm verb **1** *to disarm your opponent.* make powerless, take weapons away from.
2 *to disarm after a war.* demobilize, disband your troops.

disarming adjective SEE **charming**.

disarray noun SEE **disorder**.

disaster noun **1** *a sudden disaster.* accident, blow, calamity, cataclysm, catastrophe, crash, misadventure, mischance, misfortune, mishap, reverse, tragedy.

VARIOUS DISASTERS: air-crash, avalanche, derailment, earthquake, epidemic, fire, flood, hurricane, landslide, plague, road accident, shipwreck, tidal wave, tornado, volcanic eruption.

---

2 [*informal*] *Our play was a disaster.* débâcle, failure, fiasco, [*informal*] flop, [*informal*] mess-up, [*informal*] wash-out.
OPPOSITES: SEE **success**.

disastrous adjective *a disastrous fire. a disastrous failure.* SEE **bad**, calamitous, cataclysmic, catastrophic, crippling, destructive, devastating, dire, dreadful, fatal, ruinous, terrible, tragic.
OPPOSITES: SEE **successful**.

disband verb SEE **disperse**.

disbelief noun distrust, doubt, incredulity, mistrust, scepticism, suspicion.
OPPOSITES: SEE **belief**.

disbelieve verb *Don't think I disbelieve your story.* be sceptical of, discount, discredit, doubt, have no faith in, mistrust, reject, suspect.
OPPOSITES: SEE **believe**.

disbelieving adjective SEE **incredulous**.

disc noun **1** circle, counter, plate, token.
2 *a recorded disc.* album, compact disc, digital recording, LP, SEE **record** noun, single.
3 *a computer disc.* diskette, floppy disc, hard disc.
disc jockey OTHER BROADCASTERS: SEE **broadcaster**.

discard verb *I discarded some old clothes.* cast off, [*informal*] chuck away, dispense with, dispose of, [*informal*] ditch, dump, eliminate, get rid of, jettison, reject, scrap, shed, throw away.

discern verb *We discerned a change in the weather.* become aware of, be sensitive to, detect, discover, discriminate, distinguish, make out, mark, notice, observe, perceive, recognize, see, spy.

discernible adjective *a discernible change in the weather.* SEE **noticeable**.

discerning adjective *a discerning judge.* SEE **perceptive**.

discharge noun *discharge from a wound.* emission, pus, secretion, suppuration.

discharge verb **1** *The chimney discharged thick smoke.* belch, eject, emit, expel, exude, give off, give out, pour out, produce, release, secrete, send out.
2 *to discharge a gun.* detonate, explode, fire, let off, shoot.
3 *to discharge an employee from a job.* dismiss, fire, make redundant, remove, sack, throw out.
4 *to discharge a prisoner.* absolve, acquit, allow to leave, clear, dismiss, excuse, exonerate, free, let off, liberate, pardon, release.

disciple noun *The great teacher had many disciples.* acolyte, admirer, apostle, devotee, follower, pupil, student, supporter.

disciplinarian noun *a strict disciplinarian.* authoritarian, autocrat, despot, [*informal*] hard-liner, [*informal*] hard taskmaster, martinet, [*informal*] slave-driver, [*informal*] stickler (*a stickler for good manners*), tyrant.
OPPOSITE: libertarian.

discipline noun *firm discipline.* control, management, obedience, order, orderliness, self-control, strictness, system, training.

discipline verb **1** *You must discipline a young dog.* break in, control, drill, educate, instruct, restrain, train.
2 *We disciplined those who disobeyed.* chasten, chastise, correct, penalize, punish, reprimand, reprove, scold.

disciplined adjective *a disciplined army.* SEE **obedient**, orderly, well-behaved, well-trained.
OPPOSITES: SEE **undisciplined**.

disclaim verb *to disclaim responsibility.* deny, disown, forswear, reject, renounce, repudiate.
OPPOSITES: SEE **acknowledge**.

disclose verb SEE **reveal**.

disco noun SEE **dance** noun.

discolour verb *Spilt acid discoloured the floor.* bleach, SEE **dirty** verb, fade, mark, spoil the colour of, stain, tarnish, tinge.

discomfit verb SEE **disconcert**.

discomfort noun *the discomfort of a hard chair.* ache, distress, hardship, irritation, pain, soreness, uncomfortableness, uneasiness.
OPPOSITES: SEE **comfort** noun.

discompose verb SEE **disturb**.

disconcert verb *Bright light disconcerted her.* agitate, bewilder, confuse, discomfit, disturb, fluster, nonplus, perplex, [*informal*] put off (*It puts me off*), [*informal*] rattle, ruffle, throw off balance, trouble, unsettle, upset, worry.
OPPOSITES: SEE **reassure**.

disconcerting adjective *The play was spoiled by a lot of disconcerting noise.* distracting, disturbing, offputting, unsettling, upsetting, worrying.
OPPOSITES: SEE **reassuring**.

disconnect verb *to disconnect a telephone.* break off, cut off, detach, disengage, sever, take away, uncouple, unhitch, unplug.

disconnected adjective *a disconnected argument.* SEE **disjointed**.

disconsolate adjective SEE **sad**.

discontented adjective SEE **dissatisfied**.

discontinue verb SEE **end** verb.

discord noun **1** *discord between friends.* argument, clash, conflict, contention, difference of opinion, disagreement, disharmony, dispute, friction, SEE **quarrel** noun.
OPPOSITES: SEE **agreement**.
2 *discords in music.* cacophony, discordant sound [SEE **discordant**], jangle, SEE **noise**.
OPPOSITES: SEE **harmony**.

discordant adjective **1** *discordant sounds.* atonal, cacophanous, clashing, dissonant, grating, grinding, harsh, jangling, jarring, shrill, strident, tuneless, unmusical.
OPPOSITES: SEE **harmonious**.
2 *discordant opinions. a discordant voice.* conflicting, contrary, differing, disagreeing, incompatible, inconsistent, opposite, SEE **quarrelsome**.
OPPOSITE: assenting [SEE **assent** verb].

discount noun *a discount on the full price.* abatement, allowance, concession, cut, deduction, [*informal*] mark-down, rebate, reduction.

discount verb *We discounted his unlikely story.* disbelieve, disregard, ignore, overlook, reject.

discourage verb **1** *The threat of violence discouraged us.* cow, damp (*It damped our*

enthusiasm), dampen, daunt, demoralize, depress, disenchant, dishearten, dismay, dispirit, frighten, hinder, inhibit, intimidate, [*informal*] put down, [*informal*] put off, scare, [*informal*] throw cold water on, unman, unnerve.
2 *How can we discourage vandals?* check, deflect, deter, dissuade, prevent, put an end to, repress, restrain, stop.
OPPOSITES: SEE **encourage**.

discouragement noun *The loud music was a discouragement to conversation.* constraint, [*informal*] damper, deterrent, disincentive, hindrance, impediment, obstacle, restraint, setback.
OPPOSITES: SEE **encouragement**.

discouraging adjective *discouraging advice.* daunting, demoralizing, depressing, dispiriting.

discourse noun KINDS OF DISCOURSE: SEE **conversation**, disquisition, dissertation, essay, literature, monograph, paper, speech, thesis, treatise.
VARIOUS KINDS OF WRITING: SEE **writing**.

discourse verb *He discoursed on his pet topic.* SEE **speak**.

discourteous adjective SEE **rude**.

discover verb *We discovered a secret spot. I discovered some new facts.* ascertain, come across, detect, [*informal*] dig up, [*informal*] dredge up, explore, find, hit on, identify, learn, light upon, locate, notice, observe, perceive, recognize, reveal, search out, see, spot, [*slang*] sus out, track down, uncover, unearth.
OPPOSITES: SEE **hide** verb.

discoverer noun *the discoverer of penicillin. discoverers of new lands.* creator, explorer, finder, initiator, inventor, originator, pioneer, traveller.

discovery noun *a new discovery.* breakthrough, disclosure, exploration, [*informal*] find, innovation, invention, revelation.

discredit verb **1** *to discredit someone.* attack, defame, disgrace, dishonour, ruin the reputation of, slander, slur, smear, vilify.
2 *to discredit someone's story.* challenge, disbelieve, dispute, [*informal*] explode, prove false, refuse to believe, show up.

discreditable adjective SEE **shameful**.

discreet adjective [Do not confuse with *discrete.*] *I asked a few discreet questions.* careful, cautious, circumspect, considerate, delicate, diplomatic, guarded, judicious, polite, politic, prudent, sensitive, tactful, thoughtful, wary.
OPPOSITES: SEE **indiscreet**.

discrepancy noun *a discrepancy between two versions of a story.* conflict, SEE **difference**, disparity, dissimilarity, divergence, incompatibility, incongruity, inconsistency.
OPPOSITES: SEE **similarity**.

discrete adjective [Do not confuse with *discreet.*] SEE **distinct**.

discretion noun *Handle confidential matters with discretion.* SEE **diplomacy**, good sense, judgement, maturity, prudence, responsibility, sensitivity, tact, wisdom.
OPPOSITES: SEE **tactlessness**.

discriminate verb **1** *Can you discriminate between butter and margarine?* differentiate, distinguish, make a distinction, tell apart.
2 *It's wrong to discriminate against people because of their religion, colour, or sex.* be biased, be intolerant, be prejudiced, show discrimination [SEE **discrimination**].

discriminating adjective *a discriminating judge of wine.* choosy, critical, discerning, fastidious, [*uncomplimentary*] fussy, particular, perceptive, selective.
OPPOSITES: SEE **undiscriminating**.

discrimination noun **1** *She shows discrimination in her choice of music.* discernment, good taste, insight, judgement, perceptiveness, refinement, selectivity, subtlety, taste.
2 *racial discrimination. positive discrimination.* bias, bigotry, chauvinism, favouritism, intolerance, male chauvinism, prejudice, racialism, racism, sexism, unfairness.
OPPOSITES: SEE **impartiality**.

discursive adjective *a discursive essay.* SEE **rambling**.

discuss verb *to discuss a problem.* argue about, confer about, consider, consult about, debate, deliberate, examine, [*informal*] put heads together about, talk about, [*informal*] weigh up the pros and cons of, write about.

discussion noun *a lively discussion.* argument, SEE **conference**, consideration, consultation, conversation, debate, deliberation, dialogue, discourse, examination, exchange of views, symposium, talk.

disdain noun, verb SEE **scorn** noun, verb.

disdainful adjective SEE **scornful**.

disease noun *suffering from a disease.* SEE **illness**.

diseased adjective SEE **ill**.

disembark verb *to disembark from a ship.* alight, go ashore, land.
OPPOSITES: SEE **embark**.

disembodied adjective *a disembodied voice.* bodiless, SEE **ghostly**, immaterial, incorporeal, insubstantial, intangible, unreal.

disembowel verb SEE **kill**.

disenchant verb SEE **disillusion**.

disengage verb SEE **detach**.

disentangle verb **1** *to disentangle a knot.* sort out, straighten, undo, unknot, unravel, untangle, untie, untwist.
OPPOSITES: SEE **entangle**.
2 *The fish disentangled itself from the net.* disengage, extricate, free, liberate, release, rescue, separate.
OPPOSITES: SEE **enmesh**.

disfavour noun SEE **disapproval**.

disfigure verb *He was disfigured in a fire.* damage, deface, deform, make ugly [SEE **ugly**], mar, mutilate, scar, spoil.
OPPOSITES: SEE **beautify**.

disgorge verb SEE **pour**.

disgrace noun **1** *He never got over the disgrace of his court-case.* blot on your name, [*formal*] contumely, degradation, discredit, dishonour, embarrassment, humiliation, ignominy, opprobrium, scandal, shame, slur, stain, stigma.
2 [*informal*] *The way he treats his dog is a disgrace!* SEE **outrage**.

disgraceful adjective *disgraceful behaviour.* SEE **bad**.

disgruntled adjective SEE **dissatisfied**.

disguise noun *I didn't recognize him in that disguise.* camouflage, cloak, costume, cover, fancy dress, front, [*informal*] get-up, impersonation, make-up, mask, pretence, smoke-screen.

disguise verb **1** *to disguise your looks.* blend into the background, camouflage, dress up, make inconspicuous, mask, screen, shroud, veil.
2 *to disguise your feelings.* conceal, cover up, falsify, gloss over, hide, misrepresent.
to disguise yourself as counterfeit, dress up as, imitate, impersonate, mimic, pretend to be, [*informal*] take off.

disgust noun *I couldn't hide my disgust at the rotten food.* abhorrence, antipathy, aversion, contempt, detestation, dislike, distaste, hatred, loathing, nausea, repugnance, repulsion, revulsion.
OPPOSITES: SEE **liking**.

disgust verb *The rotten food disgusted me.* appal, be distasteful to, displease, horrify, nauseate, offend, outrage, put off, repel, revolt, shock, sicken, [*informal*] turn your stomach.
OPPOSITES: SEE **please**.

disgusting adjective *disgusting food, disgusting cruelty.* loathsome, nauseating, offensive, repugnant, repulsive, revolting, sickening, SEE **unpleasant**.

dish noun **1** *an earthenware dish.* basin, bowl, casserole, SEE **container**, plate, [*old-fashioned*] platter, tureen.
2 *Stew is a nutritious dish.* concoction, food, item on the menu, recipe.

dish verb [*informal*] *to dish someone's chances.* SEE **spoil**.
to dish out SEE **distribute**.
to dish up SEE **serve**.

disharmony noun SEE **discord**.

dishearten verb *The feeble applause disheartened us.* depress, deter, SEE **discourage**, dismay, put off, sadden.
OPPOSITES: SEE **encourage**.

disheartened adjective SEE **depressed**.

dishevelled adjective *dishevelled hair.* bedraggled, disarranged, disordered, messy, ruffled, rumpled, [*informal*] scruffy, slovenly, tangled, tousled, uncombed, unkempt, untidy.
OPPOSITES: SEE **neat**.

dishonest adjective *a dishonest deal. a dishonest salesman.* [*informal*] bent, cheating, corrupt, criminal, crooked, deceitful, deceiving, devious, disreputable, fair, false, fraudulent, immoral, insincere, lying, mendacious, misleading, [*formal*] perfidious, [*informal*] shady, [*informal*] slippery, specious, swindling, thieving, [*informal*] underhand, unethical, unprincipled, unscrupulous, untrustworthy, untruthful.
OPPOSITES: SEE **honest**.

dishonesty noun corruption, crookedness, deceit, deviousness, falsity, immorality, insincerity, mendacity, perfidy, speciousness.
OPPOSITES: SEE **honesty**.

dishonour noun *There's no dishonour in losing.* blot on your reputation, degradation, discredit, disgrace, humiliation, ignominy, indignity, [*formal*] opprobrium, reproach, scandal, shame, slur, stain, stigma.
OPPOSITES: SEE **honour** noun.

dishonourable adjective *dishonourable behaviour.* base, blameworthy, compromising, SEE **corrupt** adjective, despicable, discreditable, disgraceful, disgusting, dishonest, disreputable, ignoble, ignominious, improper, infamous, mean, outrageous, reprehensible, scandalous, shabby, shameful, shameless, treacherous, unchivalrous, unethical, unprincipled, unscrupulous, untrustworthy, unworthy, wicked.
OPPOSITES: SEE **honourable**.

dishy adjective SEE **sexy**.

disillusion verb *They became disillusioned about the glory of war.* disabuse, disappoint, disenchant, SEE **enlighten**, reveal the truth to, undeceive.
OPPOSITES: SEE **deceive**.

disincentive noun SEE **discouragement**.

disinclined adjective SEE **unwilling**.

disinfect verb *to disinfect a wound.* cauterize, chlorinate (*water*), clean, cleanse, decontaminate, fumigate (*a room*), purify, sanitize, sterilize.
OPPOSITES: SEE **infect**.

disinfectant noun antiseptic, carbolic, cleaner, germicide.

disingenuous adjective SEE **insincere**.

disinherit verb *to disinherit an heir.* cut off, cut you out of a will, deprive you of your inheritance or birthright.

disintegrate verb *The wreck disintegrated. The team disintegrated when the captain quitted.* become disunited, break into pieces, break up, crack up, crumble, decay, decompose, degenerate, deteriorate, fall apart, lose coherence, rot, shatter, smash up, splinter.

disinter verb *to disinter a body.* dig up, exhume, unbury, unearth.
OPPOSITES: SEE **bury**.

disinterested adjective SEE **unbiased**. [Don't use *disinterested* as a synonym for *uninterested. A disinterested referee* is not *an uninterested referee.*]

disjoin verb SEE **separate** verb.

disjointed adjective *a disjointed story.* aimless, broken up, confused, desultory, disconnected, dislocated, disordered, disunited, incoherent, jumbled, loose, mixed up, muddled, rambling, unconnected, uncoordinated, wandering.
OPPOSITES: SEE **coherent**.

dislike noun *I tried to hide my dislike of the food.* antagonism (to), antipathy (to), aversion (to), contempt (for), detestation, disapproval, disgust (for), distaste (for), SEE **hatred**, loathing, revulsion (from).
OPPOSITES: SEE **liking**.

dislike verb *I dislike shopping.* avoid, despise, detest, disapprove of, feel dislike [SEE **dislike** noun], SEE **hate** verb, loathe, scorn, [*informal*] take against.
OPPOSITES: SEE **like**.

dislocate verb *to dislocate your shoulder.* disengage, disjoint, displace, misplace, [*informal*] put out, put out of joint.

dislodge verb SEE **displace**.

disloyal adjective *a disloyal ally.* faithless, false, insincere, perfidious, seditious, subversive, treacherous, treasonable, [*informal*] two-faced, unfaithful, unreliable, untrustworthy.
OPPOSITES: SEE **loyal**.
disloyal person SEE **deserter**.

disloyalty noun *We couldn't forgive his disloyalty.* betrayal, double-dealing, duplicity, faithlessness, falseness, inconstancy, infidelity, perfidy, treachery, treason, unfaithfulness.
OPPOSITES: SEE **loyalty**.

dismal adjective **1** *dismal surroundings.* SEE **gloomy**.
2 [*informal*] *a dismal performance.* SEE **feeble**.

dismantle verb *to dismantle a building or machine.* demolish, knock down, strike, strip down, take apart, take down.
OPPOSITES: SEE **assemble**.

dismay noun *We listened with dismay to the bad news.* agitation, alarm, anxiety, apprehension, astonishment, consternation, depression, disappointment, discouragement, distress, dread, SEE **fear** noun, gloom, horror, pessimism, surprise.

dismay verb *The bad news dismayed us.* alarm, appal, daunt, depress, devastate, disappoint, discourage, disgust, dishearten, dispirit, distress, SEE **frighten**, horrify, scare, shock, unnerve.
OPPOSITES: SEE **encourage**.

dismember verb *to dismember a body.* amputate (*limbs*), cut up, disjoint, divide, remove the limbs of.

dismiss verb **1** *to dismiss a class.* free, let go, release, send away.
2 *to dismiss employees.* [*informal*] axe, banish, [*formal*] cashier, disband, discharge, [*informal*] fire, give notice to, [*informal*] give them their cards, [*informal*] give the push to, lay off, make redundant, sack, [*informal*] send packing.
3 *to dismiss an idea.* discard, discount, disregard, drop, get rid of, give up, [*informal*] pooh-pooh, reject, repudiate, set aside, shelve, wave aside.

dismount verb *to dismount from a horse.* alight, descend, get off.

disobedient adjective *a disobedient dog. a disobedient class.* badly behaved, contrary, defiant, disorderly, disruptive, fractious, headstrong, insubordinate, intractable, mutinous, SEE **naughty**, obstinate, obstreperous, perverse, rebellious, recalcitrant, refractory, riotous, self-willed, stubborn, uncontrollable,

undisciplined, ungovernable, unmanageable, unruly, wayward, wild, wilful.
OPPOSITES: SEE **obedient**.

disobey verb **1** *to disobey the rules.* break, contravene, defy, disregard, flout, ignore, infringe, rebel against, resist, transgress, violate.
2 *Soldiers must never disobey.* be disobedient, mutiny, protest, rebel, revolt, rise up, strike.
OPPOSITES: SEE **obey**.

disorder noun **1** *disorder in the streets.* anarchy, brawl, clamour, commotion, disorderliness, disturbance, fighting, fracas, fuss, hubbub, lawlessness, quarrelling, rioting, rumpus, tumult, uproar.
OPPOSITES: SEE **peace**.
2 *the disorder on my desk.* chaos, confusion, disarray, disorganization, jumble, mess, muddle, shambles, untidiness.
OPPOSITES: SEE **tidiness**.

disorderly adjective **1** *a disorderly class.* SEE **disobedient**.
2 *disorderly work.* SEE **disorganized**.

disorganized adjective *disorganized work.* careless, chaotic, confused, disorderly, haphazard, illogical, jumbled, messy, muddled, scatter-brained, [*informal*] slapdash, [*informal*] slipshod, [*informal*] sloppy, slovenly, unmethodical, unplanned, unstructured, unsystematic, untidy.
OPPOSITES: SEE **neat, systematic**.

disorientate verb SEE **confuse**.

disown verb *I'll disown you if you misbehave.* cast off, disclaim knowledge of, renounce, repudiate.

disparage verb SEE **criticize**.

disparaging adjective SEE **uncomplimentary**.

disparate adjective SEE **different**.

disparity noun SEE **difference**.

dispassionate adjective *a dispassionate look at a problem.* calm, cool, SEE **impartial**, level-headed, unemotional.
OPPOSITES: SEE **emotional**.

dispatch noun *A messenger brought dispatches.* bulletin, communiqué, letter, message, report.

dispatch verb **1** *to dispatch a parcel.* consign, convey, forward, post, send, transmit.
2 *to dispatch a wounded animal.* dispose of, finish off, SEE **kill**, put an end to.

dispel verb SEE **disperse**.

dispensable adjective SEE **inessential**.

dispensary noun pharmacy.

dispense verb **1** *to dispense charity.* allocate, allot, apportion, deal out, distribute, dole out, give out, mete out, provide, share.
2 *to dispense medicine.* make up, prepare, supply.
to dispense with *We dispensed with the formalities.* abolish, cancel, dispose of, do without, get rid of, jettison, make unnecessary, relinquish, remove.

dispenser noun chemist, pharmacist.

disperse verb **1** *to disperse a crowd.* break up, disband, dismiss, dispel, dissipate, divide up, drive away, send away, send in different directions, separate.
2 *The crowd dispersed.* disappear, dissolve, melt away, scatter, spread out, vanish.
OPPOSITES: SEE **collect**.
3 *The company dispersed its workforce throughout the country.* decentralize, devolve, distribute, spread.
OPPOSITES: SEE **centralize**.

dispirited adjective SEE **depressed**.

displace verb **1** *Vibration displaced part of the mechanism.* disarrange, dislocate, dislodge, disturb, misplace, move, put out of place, shift.
2 *Newcomers displace older players.* crowd out, depose, dispossess, oust, replace, succeed, supersede, supplant.

display noun *a gymnastics display.* demonstration, exhibition, pageant, parade, presentation, show, spectacle.

display verb *to display your knowledge.* air, demonstrate, disclose, exhibit, flaunt, flourish, give evidence of, parade, present, produce, put on show, reveal, show, show off, vaunt.
OPPOSITES: SEE **hide** verb.

displease verb SEE **annoy**.

displeasure noun SEE **annoyance**.

disport verb **to disport yourself** SEE **play** verb.

disposable adjective **1** *disposable income.* at your disposal, available, usable.
2 *a disposable razor.* expendable, replaceable, [*informal*] throwaway.

dispose verb *A general disposes his troops for battle.* arrange, array, group, place, position, set out
to dispose of *to dispose of rubbish.* deal with, destroy, discard, dump, get rid of, give away, jettison, scrap, sell, throw away.
to be disposed to *Are you disposed to lend me £100?* be inclined to, be liable to, be likely to, be ready to, be willing to.

disposition noun **1** *the disposition of troops.* SEE **arrangement**.

2 *a friendly disposition.* SEE **character**.

dispossess verb SEE **deprive**.

disproportionate adjective *Little jobs can use up a disproportionate amount of time.* excessive, inordinate, unbalanced, uneven, unreasonable.
OPPOSITES: SEE **proportionate**.

disprove verb *to disprove an allegation.* confute, controvert, discredit, [*informal*] explode, invalidate, negate, rebut, refute, show to be wrong.
OPPOSITES: SEE **prove**.

disputable adjective SEE **debatable**.

dispute noun *a dispute between rivals.* SEE **debate** noun, **quarrel** noun.

dispute verb **1** *We disputed the rights and wrongs of the affair.* SEE **debate** verb.
2 *No one disputed the referee's decision.* argue against, challenge, contest, contradict, controvert, deny, doubt, impugn, oppose, quarrel with, question.
OPPOSITES: SEE **accept**.

disqualify verb *to disqualify someone from driving.* debar, declare ineligible [SEE **ineligible**], preclude, prohibit.

disquiet noun SEE **anxiety**.

disquisition noun SEE **discourse** noun.

disregard verb **1** *to disregard advice.* brush aside, despise, discount, dismiss, disobey, disparage, [*informal*] fly in the face of, forget, ignore, [*informal*] make light of, neglect, overlook, pay no attention to, [*informal*] pooh-pooh, reject, shrug off, slight, snub, turn a blind eye to.
OPPOSITES: SEE **heed**.
2 *I disregarded the boring parts of the book.* exclude, leave out, miss out, omit, pass over, skip.

disrepair noun *buildings in a sad state of disrepair.* bad condition, collapse, decay, dilapidation, neglect, ruin, shabbiness.
OPPOSITES: SEE **renovation**.

disreputable adjective **1** *a disreputable firm.* dishonest, dishonourable, [*informal*] dodgy, dubious, infamous, questionable, [*informal*] shady, suspect, suspicious, unreliable, unsound, untrustworthy.
OPPOSITES: SEE **reputable**.
2 *a disreputable appearance.* raffish, unconventional.
OPPOSITES: SEE **respectable**.

disrespectful adjective SEE **rude**.

disrobe verb SEE **undress**.

disrupt verb *A fire-practice disrupted work.* break the routine of, break up, confuse, dislocate, disturb, interfere with, interrupt, intrude on, spoil, throw into disorder, unsettle, upset.

disruptive adjective *disruptive pupils.* SEE **unruly**.

dissatisfaction noun *I expressed dissatisfaction at the poor service.* annoyance, chagrin, disappointment, discontentment, dismay, displeasure, disquiet, exasperation, frustration, irritation, mortification, regret, unhappiness.
OPPOSITES: SEE **satisfaction**.

dissatisfied adjective *dissatisfied customers.* disaffected, disappointed, discontented, disgruntled, displeased, [*informal*] fed up, frustrated, unfulfilled, SEE **unhappy**, unsatisfied.
OPPOSITES: SEE **satisfied**.

dissect verb SEE **analyse, cut** verb.

dissemble verb SEE **pretend**.

disseminate verb SEE **spread** verb.

dissension, dissent nouns SEE **disagreement**.

dissent verb SEE **disagree**.

dissertation noun SEE **discourse** noun.

disservice noun SEE **harm** noun.

dissident noun [*uncomplimentary*] agitator, dissenter, independent thinker, non-conformer, protester, [*uncomplimentary*] rebel, [*informal*] refusenik.
OPPPOSITE: conformist.

dissimilar adjective *dissimilar clothes. dissimilar personalities.* contrasting, different, disparate, distinct, distinguishable, divergent, diverse, heterogeneous, incompatible, opposite, unlike, unrelated, various.
OPPOSITES: SEE **similar**.

dissimulation noun SEE **pretence**.

dissipate verb **1** *to dissipate your energy.* SEE **disperse**.
2 *to dissipate your wealth.* SEE **squander**.

dissipated adjective SEE **immoral**.

dissociate verb *The editor dissociated herself from the views in the article.* back away, cut off, detach, distance, divorce, isolate, SEE **separate** verb.
OPPOSITES: SEE **associate**.

dissolute adjective SEE **immoral**.

dissolve verb **1** [It's useful to note a distinction between *dissolve = disperse in a liquid* (*Sugar dissolves in tea*) and *melt = become liquid by heating* (*Ice melts*).] become liquid, deliquesce, diffuse, disappear, disintegrate, disperse, liquefy.
2 *to dissolve a partnership.* break up, bring to an end, cancel, dismiss, divorce, end, sever, split up, suspend, terminate, [*informal*] wind up.

dissonant adjective SEE **discordant**.

dissuade verb **to dissuade from** advise against, argue (someone) out of, deter from, discourage from, persuade (someone) not to, put off, remonstrate (with someone) against, warn against.
OPPOSITES: SEE **persuade**.

distance noun **1** *the distance between two points.* breadth, extent, gap, [*informal*] haul (*a long haul*), interval, journey, length, measurement, mileage, range, reach, separation, space, span, stretch, width.
2 *He keeps his distance.* aloofness, coolness, isolation, remoteness, separation, [*informal*] standoffishness, unfriendliness.
OPPOSITE: closeness.

distance verb *to distance yourself from someone.* be unfriendly (with), keep away, keep your distance, remove, separate, set yourself apart, stay away.
OPPOSITES: SEE **involve**.

distant adjective **1** *distant places.* far, faraway, far-flung, [*informal*] god-forsaken, inaccessible, outlying, out-of-the-way, remote.
OPPOSITES: SEE **close** adjective.
2 *a distant manner.* aloof, cool, formal, haughty, reserved, reticent, unenthusiastic, unfriendly, withdrawn.
OPPOSITES: SEE **friendly**.

distasteful adjective SEE **unpleasant**.

distend verb SEE **swell**.

distended adjective SEE **swollen**.

distil verb *to distil water. to distil spirit from wine.* extract, purify, refine, vaporize and condense.

distilled adjective *distilled water.* pure, purified, refined, vaporized and condensed.

distinct adjective **1** [See note under *distinctive.*] *distinct footprints in the mud. a distinct sound.* apparent, clear, clear-cut, definite, evident, noticeable, obvious, patent, plain, recognizable, sharp, unambiguous, unmistakable, visible, well-defined.
OPPOSITES: SEE **indistinct**.
2 *Organize your ideas into distinct sections.* contrasting, detached, different, discrete, dissimilar, distinguishable, individual, separate, special, unconnected.

distinction noun **1** *I can't see any distinction between the twins.* contrast, difference, differentiation, discrimination, dissimilarity, distinctiveness, individuality, particularity, peculiarity.
OPPOSITES: SEE **similarity**.
2 *I had the distinction of being first home.* celebrity, credit, eminence, excellence, fame, glory, greatness, honour, importance, merit, prestige, renown, reputation, superiority.

distinctive adjective [Do not confuse with *distinct. Distinct handwriting* is *clear writing*; *distinctive handwriting* is *writing you don't confuse with someone else's.*] characteristic, different, distinguishing, idiosyncratic, individual, inimitable, original, peculiar, personal, singular, special, striking, typical, uncommon, unique.

distinguish verb **1** *Can you distinguish between butter and margarine?* SEE **choose**, decide, differentiate, discriminate, judge, make a distinction, separate, tell apart.
2 *In the dark we couldn't distinguish who she was.* ascertain, determine, discern, know, make out, perceive, pick out, recognize, see, single out, tell.

distinguished adjective **1** *distinguished work.* acclaimed, conspicuously good, SEE **excellent**, exceptional, first-rate, outstanding.
OPPOSITES: undistinguished, SEE **ordinary**.
2 *a distinguished actor.* celebrated, eminent, famed, famous, foremost, great, illustrious, important, leading, notable, noted, prominent, renowned, well-known.
OPPOSITES: SEE **unknown**.

distort verb **1** *to distort a shape.* bend, buckle, contort, deform, twist, warp, wrench.
2 *to distort the truth.* exaggerate, falsify, garble, misrepresent, pervert, slant, twist.

distorted adjective *a distorted account of what happened.* biased, coloured, false, one-sided, perverted, prejudiced, slanted, twisted.

distract verb *Don't distract the driver.* bewilder, confuse, disconcert, divert, harass, perplex, puzzle, sidetrack, trouble, worry.

distracted adjective *distracted with grief.* SEE **sad**.

distraction noun **1** *The TV is a distraction when I'm working.* bewilderment, cause of confusion, SEE **distress** noun, interference, interruption, upset.
2 *He's always looking for some new distraction.* amusement, diversion, enjoyment, entertainment, fun, interest, pastime, pleasure, recreation.
3 *The ants tormented me to distraction.* delirium, frenzy, insanity, madness.

distraught adjective SEE **agitated, sad.**

distress noun *It was painful to see her distress.* adversity, affliction, anguish, anxiety, danger, desolation, difficulty, discomfort, dismay, fright, grief, heartache, misery, pain, poverty, privation, sadness, sorrow, suffering, torment, tribulation, trouble, worry, wretchedness.

distress verb *The bad news distressed us.* afflict, alarm, bother, [*informal*] cut up, dismay, disturb, frighten, grieve, harrow, hurt, make miserable, pain, perplex, perturb, sadden, scare, shake, shock, terrify, torment, torture, trouble, upset, worry, wound.
OPPOSITES: SEE **comfort** verb.

distribute verb **1** *They distributed free samples.* allocate, allot, assign, circulate, deal out, deliver, [*informal*] dish out, dispense, dispose of, divide out, [*informal*] dole out, give out, hand round, issue, mete out, share out, take round.
2 *Distribute the seeds evenly.* arrange, disperse, disseminate, scatter, spread, strew.

district noun *a rural district. an urban district.* area, community, locality, neighbourhood, parish, part, province, quarter (*of a town*), region, sector, vicinity, ward, zone.

distrust verb *I distrust dogs that bark.* be sceptical about, be wary of, disbelieve, doubt, have misgivings about, have qualms about, mistrust, question, suspect.
OPPOSITES: SEE **trust** verb.

distrustful adjective SEE **suspicious.**

disturb verb **1** *Don't disturb her if she's asleep.* agitate, alarm, annoy, bother, discompose, disrupt, distract, distress, excite, fluster, frighten, perturb, pester, ruffle, scare, shake, startle, stir up, trouble, unsettle, upset, worry.
2 *Don't disturb the papers on my desk.* confuse, disorder, [*informal*] mess about with, move, muddle, rearrange, reorganize.

disturbance noun *a disturbance in the street.* SEE **commotion.**

disunited adjective *The committee was disunited on the main issue.* divided, polarized, split.
OPPOSITES: SEE **united.**

disunity noun difference of opinion, disagreement, division, polarization.
OPPOSITES: SEE **solidarity.**

disused adjective *a disused railway line.* abandoned, closed, dead, discarded, discontinued, idle, neglected, obsolete, superannuated, unused, withdrawn.
OPPOSITES: SEE **operational.**

ditch noun *a drainage ditch.* aqueduct, channel, dike, drain, gully, gutter, moat, trench, watercourse.

ditch verb [*informal*] *We ditched the idea.* SEE **abandon.**

dither verb SEE **hesitate.**

ditty noun SEE **song.**

diurnal adjective daily.

divan noun SEE **bed.**

dive verb *to dive into water. to dive down.* crash-dive, descend, dip, drop, fall, go diving [SEE **diving**], go under, jump, leap, nosedive, pitch, plummet, plunge, sink, submerge, subside, swoop.

diver noun frogman, scuba-diver.

diverge noun **1** *to diverge from the path.* branch, deviate, divide, fork, go off at a tangent, part, radiate, separate, split.
2 *Our views diverge.* SEE **differ.**

diverse adjective SEE **various.**

diversify verb *The shop has diversified into a wider range of goods.* branch out, expand, spread out.

diversion noun **1** *a traffic diversion.* detour, deviation.
2 *We organized diversions for the guests.* amusement, distraction, entertainment, game, hobby, pastime, play, recreation, relaxation, sport.

diversity noun SEE **variety.**

divert verb **1** *They diverted the plane to another airport.* change direction, redirect, re-route, shunt (*a train*), switch.
2 *She diverted us with funny stories.* amuse, cheer up, delight, distract, entertain, keep happy, recreate, regale.

diverting adjective SEE **funny.**

divest verb SEE **strip** verb.

divide verb **1** *The path divides. We divided into two groups.* branch, break up, diverge, fork, move apart, part, polarize, split.
OPPOSITES: SEE **converge.**
2 *We divided the food between us.* allocate, allot, apportion, deal out, dispense, distribute, give out, halve, parcel out, pass round, share out.
OPPOSITES: SEE **gather.**
3 *I divided the potatoes according to size.* arrange, categorize, classify, grade, group, sort out, separate, subdivide.
OPPOSITES: SEE **mix.**

dividend noun interest, SEE **money.**

dividers noun compasses.

divine adjective *divine beings.* angelic, celestial, god-like, heavenly, holy, immortal, mystical, religious, sacred, spiritual, superhuman, supernatural, transcendental.

divine verb SEE **guess** verb.

diving noun deep-sea diving, scuba diving, snorkelling, subaqua swimming.

divinity noun **1** SEE **god**.
2 *the study of divinity.* religion, religious studies, theology.

division noun **1** *the division of land into building plots.* allocation, apportionment, cutting up, dividing, partition, splitting.
2 *a division of opinion.* disagreement, discord, disunity, feud, SEE **quarrel** noun, rupture, schism (*in the church*), split.
3 *a box with divisions for various tools.* compartment, part, section, segment.
4 *a division between two rooms or territories.* boundary, demarcation, divider, dividing wall, fence, partition, screen.
5 *a division of an organization.* branch, department, section, subdivision, unit.

divorce noun *Their marriage ended in divorce.* annulment, [*informal*] break-up, [*formal*] decree nisi, separation, [*informal*] split-up.

divorce verb SEE **separate** verb.
to be divorced annul a marriage, dissolve a marriage, part, separate, [*informal*] split up.

divulge verb SEE **reveal**.

dizziness noun faintness, giddiness, vertigo.

dizzy adjective *I feel dizzy when I look from a height.* bewildered, confused, dazed, faint, giddy, light-headed, muddled, reeling, shaky, swimming, unsteady.

do verb [The verb *do* can mean many things. The words given here are only a few of the synonyms you could use.] **1** *to do a job.* accomplish, achieve, carry out, commit, complete, execute, finish, fulfil, organize, perform, undertake.
2 *to do the garden.* arrange, attend to, cope with, deal with, handle, look after, manage, work at.
3 *to do sums.* answer, give your mind to, puzzle out, solve, think out, work out.
4 *to do good.* bring about, cause, effect, implement, initiate, instigate, produce, result in.
5 *Will £10 do?* be acceptable, be enough, be satisfactory, be sufficient, be suitable, satisfy, serve, suffice.
6 *Do as you like.* act, behave, conduct yourself, perform.
7 [*informal*] *The rotten cheat did me!* SEE **swindle** verb.
to do away with SEE **abolish**.
to do up SEE **decorate, fasten**.

docile adjective *a docile animal.* SEE **obedient**.

dock noun PLACES WHERE SHIPS UNLOAD, ETC.: berth, boat-yard, dockyard, dry-dock, harbour, haven, jetty, landing-stage, marina, pier, port, quay, slipway, wharf.

dock verb **1** *We can't land until the ship docks.* anchor, berth, drop anchor, moor, tie up.
2 *to dock a dog's tail.* SEE **cut** verb.
3 *to dock someone's wages.* SEE **reduce**.

docker noun stevedore.

docket noun SEE **label** noun.

doctor noun general practitioner, [*informal*] GP, medical officer or MO, medical practitioner, physician, [*uncomplimentary*] quack, surgeon.
OTHERS WHO LOOK AFTER OUR HEALTH: SEE **medicine**.

doctrinaire adjective SEE **dogmatic**.

doctrine noun *religious doctrines.* axiom, belief, conviction, creed, dogma, maxim, orthodoxy, precept, principle, teaching, tenet.

document noun VARIOUS DOCUMENTS: certificate, charter, deed, diploma, form, instrument, legal document, licence, manuscript or MS, passport, policy (*insurance policy*), print-out, record, typescript, visa, warrant, will.

documentary adjective **1** *documentary evidence.* authenticated, recorded, written.
2 *a documentary film.* factual, non-fiction.

doddery adjective SEE **old**.

dodge noun *a clever dodge.* device, knack, manœuvre, ploy, ruse, scheme, stratagem, trick, [*informal*] wheeze.

dodge verb **1** *to dodge a snowball.* avoid, duck, elude, evade, fend off, move out of the way of, swerve away from, turn away from, veer away from.
2 *to dodge work.* shirk, [*informal*] skive, [*informal*] wriggle out of.
3 *to dodge a question.* equivocate, fudge, hedge, side-step.

dodgems noun bumper cars.

dodgy adjective **1** [*informal*] *a dodgy customer.* SEE **cunning**.
2 [*informal*] *a dodgy problem.* SEE **difficult**.

dog noun bitch, [*childish*] bow-wow, [*uncomplimentary*] cur, dingo, hound, mongrel, pedigree, pup, puppy, whelp.
RELATED ADJECTIVES: canine, doglike.

SOME BREEDS OF DOG: Alsatian, basset, beagle, bloodhound, borzoi, boxer, bulldog, bull-terrier, cairn terrier, chihuahua, chow, cocker spaniel, collie, corgi, dachshund, Dalmatian, foxhound, fox-terrier, Great Dane, greyhound, husky, Labrador, mastiff, Pekingese or Pekinese, Pomeranian, poodle, pug, retriever, Rottweiler, setter, sheepdog, spaniel, terrier, whippet.

dog verb SEE **follow**.

dogfight noun SEE **battle** noun.

dogged adjective SEE **determined**.

doggerel noun SEE **poem**.

dogma noun *religious dogma.* article of faith, belief, conviction, creed, doctrine, orthodoxy, precept, principle, teaching, tenet, truth.

dogmatic adjective *You won't argue him out of his dogmatic position.* assertive, authoritarian, authoritative, categorical, certain, dictatorial, doctrinaire, [*informal*] hard-line, hidebound, imperious, SEE **inflexible**, intolerant, legalistic, narrow-minded, obdurate, obstinate, opinionated, pontifical, positive.
OPPOSITES: SEE **open-minded**.

dogsbody noun SEE **servant**.

doldrums noun **in the doldrums** SEE **depressed**.

dole noun [*informal*] *living on the dole.* benefit, income support, social security, unemployment benefit.
on the dole SEE **unemployed**.

dole verb **to dole out** SEE **distribute**.

doleful adjective SEE **sad**.

doll noun cuddly toy, [*childish*] dolly, figure, [*racist*] golliwog, marionette, puppet, rag doll.

dollop noun SEE **mass** noun.

dolorous adjective SEE **sad**.

dolt noun SEE **idiot**.

domain noun **1** [*old-fashioned*] *the king's domain.* SEE **country**.
2 *the domain of science.* area, concern, field, speciality, sphere.

dome noun convex roof, cupola.

domed adjective SEE **convex**.

Several English words, including *domestic, domesticity,* and *domicile,* are related to Latin *domus = home.*

domestic adjective **1** *domestic arrangements.* family, household, in the home [SEE **home**], private.
OPPOSITES: SEE **public** adjective.
2 *domestic air services.* inland, internal, national.
OPPOSITES: SEE **foreign**.
3 *domestic animals.* SEE **domesticated**.
domestic science home economics.

domesticated adjective *domesticated animals.* house-trained, tame, tamed, trained.
OPPOSITES: SEE **wild**.

domesticity noun *a simple life of domesticity.* family life, home-making, housekeeping, staying at home.

domicile noun SEE **residence**.

dominant adjective **1** *a dominant influence. the dominant issues.* chief, commanding, dominating, influential, leading, main, major, powerful, predominant, presiding, prevailing, primary, principal, ruling, supreme, uppermost.
2 *a dominant feature in the landscape.* biggest, SEE **conspicuous**, eye-catching, highest, imposing, largest, obvious, outstanding, tallest, widespread.

dominate verb **1** *The captain dominated the game.* be the dominant person in [SEE **dominant**], control, direct, govern, influence, lead, manage, master, monopolize, rule, take control of, tyrannize.
2 *A castle dominates our town.* be the dominant thing in [SEE **dominant**], dwarf, look down on, overshadow, tower over.

domineering adjective *a domineering person.* SEE **tyrannical**.

dominion noun SEE **territory**.

don noun *an Oxford don.* SEE **lecturer**.

don verb *to don a disguise.* clothe yourself in, dress in, put on, wear.

donate verb SEE **give**.

donation noun SEE **gift**.

donkey noun jackass, [*informal*] jenny.

donkey-work noun SEE **work** noun.

donor noun *a donor to a charity.* benefactor, contributor, giver, philanthropist, provider, sponsor.
OPPOSITES: SEE **recipient**.

doodle verb SEE **draw** verb, scribble.

doom noun **1** *It is his doom to suffer.* SEE **fate**.
2 *She faced her doom bravely.* SEE **end** noun.

doomed adjective **1** *All mortals are doomed to die.* condemned, fated, intended.

2 *The voyage was doomed from the start.* accursed, bedevilled, hopeless, ill-fated, ill-starred, luckless.

doomsday noun apocalypse, end of the world, judgement day.

door noun barrier, doorway, [*informal*] SEE **entrance** noun, SEE **exit**, French window, gate, gateway, opening, portal, postern, revolving door, swing door.

dope noun **1** [*informal*] *addicted to dope.* SEE **drug** noun.
2 [*informal*] *You silly dope!* SEE **idiot**.

dope verb *to dope a horse.* SEE **drug** verb.

dopey adjective SEE **silly, sleepy**.

Several English words, including *dormant* and *dormitory,* are related to Latin *dormire* = *to sleep.*

---

dormant adjective **1** *Many living things are dormant in winter.* asleep, comatose, hibernating, resting, sleeping.
OPPOSITES: SEE **awake**.
2 *a dormant illness. a dormant volcano.* inactive, inert, latent, passive, quiescent, quiet.
OPPOSITES: SEE **active**.

dormitory noun bedroom, sleeping-quarters.
OTHER ROOMS: SEE **room**.

dose noun *a dose of medicine.* dosage, measure, portion, prescribed amount, quantity.

dose verb SEE **drug** verb.

doss verb SEE **sleep** verb.

dossier noun *a secret dossier.* file, folder, records, set of documents.

dot noun *Join up the dots.* full stop, mark, point, speck, spot.

dot verb *Sheep dot the hillside.* fleck, mark with dots, punctuate, scatter with dots, speckle, spot.

dotage noun SEE **old (old age)**.

dote verb SEE **love** verb.

dotty adjective SEE **silly**.

double adjective *a double railway-track.* doubled, dual, [*in music*] duple, duplicated, paired, twin, twofold.
double Dutch SEE **nonsense**.
double glazing SEE **window**.

double noun *I saw your double in town.* clone, copy, duplicate, [*informal*] look-alike, [*informal*] spitting image, twin.

double verb *We must double our efforts.* duplicate, increase, multiply by two, reduplicate, repeat.
to double back backtrack, do a U-turn, retrace your steps, return, turn back.
to double up *She doubled up with pain.* bend over, collapse, crumple up, fold over, fold up.

double-cross verb SEE **betray**.

double-decker noun SEE **bus**.

doublet noun SEE **coat** noun.

doubt noun **1** *I had my doubts.* agnosticism [= *religious doubts*], anxiety, cynicism, disbelief, distrust, fear, hesitation, incredulity, indecision, misgiving, mistrust, qualm, reservation, scepticism, suspicion, worry.
OPPOSITE: SEE **confidence**.
2 *There's some doubt about the arrangements.* ambiguity, confusion, difficulty, dilemma, perplexity, problem, query, question, uncertainty.
OPPOSITES: SEE **certainty**.

doubt verb **1** *I doubt whether he can afford it.* be dubious about, feel uncertain about [SEE **uncertain**], hesitate, lack confidence.
OPPOSITE: be confident [SEE **confident**].
2 *I doubt her honesty.* be sceptical about, disbelieve, distrust, fear, mistrust, query, question, suspect.
OPPOSITES: SEE **trust** verb.

doubtful adjective **1** *I'm doubtful about her honesty.* agnostic, cynical, disbelieving, distrustful, dubious, hesitant, incredulous, sceptical, suspicious, uncertain, unclear, unconvinced, undecided, unsure.
OPPOSITES: SEE **certain**.
2 *a doubtful decision.* ambiguous, debatable, dubious, equivocal, [*informal*] iffy, inconclusive, problematical, questionable, suspect, vague, worrying.
OPPOSITES: SEE **clear** adjective, **indisputable**.
3 *a doubtful ally.* irresolute, uncommitted, unreliable, untrustworthy, vacillating, wavering.
OPPOSITES: SEE **dependable**.

douche noun shower.

dour adjective SEE **stern** adjective.

douse verb **1** *to douse with water.* SEE **drench**.
2 *to douse a light.* SEE **extinguish**.

dovetail verb SEE **fit** verb.

dowager noun SEE **woman**.

dowdy adjective *dowdy clothes.* colourless, dingy, drab, dull, [*informal*] frumpish, old-fashioned, shabby, [*informal*] sloppy, slovenly, [*informal*] tatty, unattractive, unstylish.
OPPOSITES: SEE **smart** adjective, **stylish**.

down adjective *You seem down today.* SEE **depressed**.

down noun *pillows filled with down.* feathers, fluff, fluffy material.

downcast adjective SEE **depressed**.

downfall noun SEE **ruin** noun.

downgrade verb SEE **demote**.

downhearted adjective SEE **depressed**.

downhill adjective SEE **downward**.

downpour noun SEE **rain** noun.

downright adjective *a downright lie.* SEE **categorical**.

downs noun SEE **hill**.

downstairs adjective *a downstairs room.* ground-floor, lower.

down-trodden adjective SEE **oppressed**.

downturn noun SEE **decline** noun.

downward adjective *a downward path.* descending, downhill, easy, falling, going down, slanting, sloping.
OPPOSITES: SEE **upward**.

downy adjective *downy material.* feathery, fleecy, fluffy, furry, fuzzy, soft, velvety, woolly.

dowry noun SEE **money**.

doze verb SEE **sleep** verb.

drab adjective *drab colours.* cheerless, colourless, dingy, dismal, dowdy, dreary, dull, flat, gloomy, grey, grimy, lacklustre, shabby, sombre, unattractive, uninteresting.
OPPOSITES: SEE **bright**.

Draconian adjective SEE **harsh**.

draft noun [Don't confuse with *draught.*]
1 *a draft of an essay.* first version, notes, outline, plan, rough version, sketch.
2 *a bank draft.* cheque, order, postal order.

draft verb **1** *to draft an essay.* outline, plan, prepare, sketch out, work out, write a draft of.
2 *to draft someone into the army.* SEE **conscript** verb.

drag verb **1** *The tractor dragged a load of logs.* draw, haul, lug, pull, tow, trail, tug.
OPPOSITES: SEE **push**.
2 *Time drags if you're bored.* be boring, crawl, creep, go slowly, linger, loiter, lose momentum, move slowly, pass slowly.
OPPOSITE: pass quickly.

dragon noun OTHER LEGENDARY CREATURES: SEE **legend**.

dragoon verb SEE **compel**.

drain noun *a drain to take away water.* channel, conduit, culvert, dike, ditch, SEE **drainage**, drainpipe, duct, gutter, outlet, pipe, sewer, trench, watercourse.

drain verb **1** *to drain marshland.* dry, dry out, remove water from.
2 *to drain oil from an engine.* bleed, clear, draw off, empty, remove, take off, tap.
3 *The water drained through the sieve.* leak out, ooze, seep, strain, trickle.
4 *The exercise drained my energy.* consume, deplete, SEE **exhaust** verb, sap, spend, use up.

drainage noun *mains drainage.* sanitation, sewage system, sewers, waste disposal.

drake noun SEE **duck** noun.

drama noun **1** *theatrical drama.* acting, dramatics, histrionics, improvisation, SEE **literature**, melodrama, play, show, stagecraft, SEE **theatre**, theatricals.
2 *a real-life drama.* action, crisis, SEE **excitement**, suspense, turmoil.

dramatic adjective **1** *a dramatic performance.* SEE **theatrical**.
2 *a dramatic rescue.* SEE **exciting**.

dramatist noun playwright.
OTHER WRITERS: SEE **writer**.

dramatization noun *dramatization of a novel.* screenplay, script, stage or TV version.

dramatize verb **1** *to dramatize a novel for TV.* adapt, make into a play, rewrite, write a dramatization [SEE **dramatization**].
2 *Don't dramatize a quite ordinary event.* exaggerate, make too much of, overdo, overstate.

drape verb SEE **cover** verb.

drastic adjective *a drastic remedy.* desperate, dire, extreme, harsh, severe.

draught noun [Don't confuse with *draft.*] **1** *a draught of air.* breeze, current, movement, puff, wind.
2 *a draught of ale.* drink, pull, swallow.

draughtsman, draughtswoman nouns OTHER ARTISTS AND CRAFTSMEN: SEE **artist**.

draughty adjective SEE **cold** adjective, **windy**.

draw noun *a prize draw.* competition, lottery, raffle.

draw verb **1** *The horse drew the cart.* drag, haul, lug, pull, tow, tug.
2 *to draw a big crowd.* allure, attract, bring in, coax, entice, invite, lure, persuade, pull in, win over.
3 *to draw a tooth. to draw money from a bank. to draw a sword.* extract, remove, take out, unsheathe (*a sword*), withdraw.
4 *to draw names from a hat.* choose, pick, select.

5 *to draw a diagram.* depict, doodle, map out, mark out, outline, paint, pen, pencil, portray, represent, sketch, trace.
6 *to draw a conclusion.* arrive at, come to, deduce, formulate, infer, work out.
7 *The two teams drew 1–1.* be equal, finish equal, tie.
to draw out *to draw out chewing-gum. to draw out a conversation.* elongate, extend, lengthen, make longer, prolong, stretch.
to draw up 1 *The bus drew up.* brake, halt, pull up, stop.
2 *The lawyer drew up a contract.* compose, make, prepare, write out.
3 *I drew myself up.* make yourself tall, stand erect, stand straight, stand upright, straighten up.

drawback noun SEE **disadvantage**.

drawers noun [*old-fashioned*] bloomers, briefs, knickers, panties, pants, underpants.

drawing noun cartoon, design, graphics, illustration, outline, SEE **picture** noun, sketch.

drawing-room noun living-room, lounge, sitting-room.
OTHER ROOMS: SEE **room**.

drawl verb SEE **speak**.

drawn adjective *She looked drawn.* SEE **strained**.

dray noun SEE **cart**.

dread noun, verb SEE **fear** noun, verb.

dreadful adjective **1** *a dreadful accident.* alarming, appalling, awful, dire, distressing, fearful, frightening, frightful, ghastly, grisly, gruesome, harrowing, horrible, horrifying, indescribable, monstrous, shocking, terrible, tragic, unspeakable, upsetting.
2 [*informal*] *dreadful weather.* SEE **bad**.

dream noun **1** *Odd things happen in dreams.* delusion, fantasy, hallucination, illusion, nightmare, reverie, trance, vision.
2 *a dream of fame and riches.* ambition, aspiration, day-dream, ideal, pipe-dream, wish.

dream verb *I dreamed I could fly.* day-dream, fancy, fantasize, hallucinate, have a vision, imagine, think.
to dream up SEE **invent**.

dreary adjective SEE **boring, gloomy**.

dredge verb **to dredge up** SEE **discover**.

dregs noun *dregs at the bottom of a cup.* deposit, grounds (*of coffee*), lees (*of wine*), remains, sediment.

drench verb *The rain drenched us.* douse, drown, flood, inundate, saturate, soak, souse, steep, wet thoroughly.

dress noun **1** *formal dress.* apparel, attire, SEE **clothes**, clothing, costume, garb, garments, [*informal*] gear, outfit, [*old-fashioned*] raiment.
2 *a woman's dress.* frock, gown, robe, shift.

dress verb **1** *Dad dressed the children.* attire, clothe, cover, provide clothes for, put clothes on.
OPPOSITES: SEE **undress**.
2 *A nurse dressed my wound.* attend to, bandage, bind up, care for, put a dressing on, tend, treat.

dresser noun SEE **cupboard**.

dressing 1 *a dressing on a wound.* bandage, compress, plaster, poultice.
2 *salad dressing.* French dressing, mayonnaise.

dressing-gown noun housecoat, négligé.

dressmaker noun couturier, seamstress.

dribble verb **1** *He dribbled over his food.* drool, slaver, slobber.
2 *Rain dribbled down the window.* drip, flow, leak, ooze, run, seep, trickle.

drier noun airer, spin-drier, tumble-drier, wringer.

drift noun **1** *a drift of snow.* accumulation, bank, heap, mound, pile, ridge.
2 *the drift of a speech.* SEE **gist**.

drift verb **1** *The boat drifted downstream.* be carried, coast, float, move slowly.
2 *We had nowhere to go, so we drifted about.* meander, move casually, ramble, stray, walk aimlessly, wander.
3 *The snow drifted.* accumulate, gather, make drifts, pile up.

drill noun **1** *military drill.* discipline, exercise, instruction, practice, [*slang*] square-bashing, training.
2 [*informal*] *You know the drill.* SEE **routine**.
3 *Sow the seeds in a drill.* SEE **furrow**.

drill verb **1** *to drill through something.* bore, penetrate, perforate, pierce.
2 *to drill soldiers.* discipline, exercise, instruct, rehearse, train.

drink noun alcohol, beverage, [*informal*] bevvy, [*informal*] booze, [*joking*] grog, [*informal*] gulp, liquor, [*informal*] nightcap, [*informal*] nip, [*often plural*] refreshment, sip, swallow, swig, [*joking*] tipple (*What's your tipple?*).

SOME NON-ALCOHOLIC DRINKS: barley-water, cocoa, coffee, cordial, juice, lemonade, lime-juice, milk, mineral water, nectar, orangeade, pop, sherbet, soda-water, squash, tea, water.

SOME ALCOHOLIC DRINKS: ale, beer, bourbon, brandy, champagne, chartreuse, cider, cocktail, Cognac, crème de menthe, gin, Kirsch, lager, mead, perry, [*informal*] plonk, port, punch, rum, schnapps, shandy, sherry, vermouth, vodka, whisky, wine.

CONTAINERS YOU DRINK FROM: beaker, cup, glass, goblet, mug, tankard, tumbler, wine-glass.

---

drink verb [*informal*] booze, gulp, guzzle, [*formal*] imbibe, [*informal*] knock back, lap, partake of, [*old-fashioned*] quaff, sip, suck, swallow, swig, [*informal*] swill.

drip noun *a drip of oil.* bead, dribble, drop, leak, splash, spot, sprinkling, trickle.

drip verb *Water dripped into the basin.* dribble, drizzle, drop, fall in drips, leak, plop, splash, sprinkle, trickle, weep.

dripping noun SEE **fat** noun.

drive noun **1** *a drive in the country.* excursion, jaunt, journey, outing, ride, run, trip.
2 *the drive to succeed.* ambition, determination, energy, enterprise, enthusiasm, initiative, keenness, motivation, persistence, [*informal*] push, zeal.
3 *a publicity drive.* campaign, crusade, effort.

drive verb **1** *to drive a spade into the ground.* bang, dig, hammer, hit, impel, knock, plunge, prod, push, ram, sink, stab, strike, thrust.
2 *to drive someone to take action.* coerce, compel, constrain, force, oblige, press, urge.
3 *to drive a car. to drive sheep.* control, direct, guide, handle, herd, manage, pilot, propel, send, steer.
to drive out SEE **expel**.

drivel noun SEE **nonsense**.

driver noun chauffeur, motorist.

drizzle noun SEE **rain** noun.

droll adjective SEE **funny**.

dromedary noun camel.

drone noun VARIOUS SOUNDS: SEE **sound** noun.

droop verb *The flag drooped.* be limp, bend, dangle, fall, flop, hang, sag, slump, wilt, wither.

drop noun **1** *a drop of liquid.* bead, blob, bubble, dab, drip, droplet, globule, pearl, spot, tear.
2 *a drop of whisky.* dash, [*informal*] nip, small quantity, [*informal*] tot.
3 *a drop of 2 metres.* descent, dive, fall, plunge, SEE **precipice**.
4 *a drop in prices.* cut, decrease, reduction, slump.
OPPOSITES: SEE **rise** noun.

drop verb **1** *to drop to the ground.* collapse, descend, dip, dive, fall, go down, jump down, lower, nosedive, plummet, [*informal*] plump, plunge, sink, slump, subside, swoop, tumble.
2 *to drop someone from a team.* eliminate, exclude, leave out, omit.
3 *to drop a friend.* abandon, desert, [*informal*] dump, forsake, give up, jilt, leave, reject.
4 *to drop a plan.* discard, scrap, shed.
to drop behind SEE **lag**.
to drop in on SEE **visit** verb.
to drop off SEE **sleep** verb.

droppings noun SEE **excreta**.

dross noun SEE **rubbish**.

drown verb **1** *The flood drowned everything in the area.* SEE **flood** verb, **kill**.
2 *The music drowned our conversation.* be louder than, overpower, overwhelm, silence.

drowse verb SEE **sleep** verb.

drowsy adjective SEE **sleepy**.

drubbing noun SEE **defeat** noun.

drudge noun SEE **servant**.

drudgery noun SEE **work** noun.

drug noun **1** *a medicinal drug.* cure, medicament, medication, medicine, painkiller, [*old-fashioned*] physic, remedy, sedative, stimulant, tonic, tranquillizer, treatment.
2 *an addictive drug.* [*informal*] dope, narcotic, opiate.

VARIOUS DRUGS: barbiturate, caffeine, cannabis, cocaine, digitalis, hashish, heroin, insulin, laudanum, marijuana, morphia, nicotine, opium, phenobarbitone, quinine.

---

drug verb anaesthetize, [*informal*] dope, dose, give a drug to, [*informal*] knock out, medicate, poison, stupefy, treat.

Druid noun SEE **priest**.

drum noun **1** VARIOUS DRUMS: bass-drum, bongo-drums, kettledrum, side-drum, snare-drum, tambour, tenor-drum, [*plural*] timpani, tom-tom.
OTHER PERCUSSION INSTRUMENTS: SEE **percussion**.
2 *a drum of oil.* SEE **barrel**.

drunk adjective *The revellers got drunk.* delirious, fuddled, inebriated, intoxicated, over-excited, riotous, uncontrollable, unruly.

SOME OF THE MANY SLANG SYNONYMS ARE: blotto, boozed-up, canned, legless, merry, paralytic, pickled, plastered, sozzled, tiddly, tight, tipsy.
OPPOSITES: SEE **sober**.

drunkard noun alcoholic, [*informal*] boozer, dipsomaniac, drunk, [*informal*] tippler, toper, [*slang*] wino.
OPPOSITES: SEE **teetotaller**.

drunken adjective *drunken revellers.* [*informal*] boozy, SEE **drunk**, inebriate, inebriated, intoxicated.
OPPOSITES: SEE **sober, teetotal**.

dry adjective **1** *dry desert.* arid, barren, dehydrated, desiccated, moistureless, parched, thirsty, waterless.
OPPOSITES: SEE **wet** adjective.
2 *dry wine.* OPPOSITE: sweet.
3 *a dry book.* boring, dreary, dull, tedious, tiresome, uninteresting.
OPPOSITES: SEE **interesting**.
4 *a dry sense of humour.* [*informal*] deadpan, droll, expressionless, laconic, lugubrious, unsmiling.
OPPOSITES: SEE **lively**.

dry verb [Also **to dry out, to dry up**] become dry, dehumidify, dehydrate, desiccate, go hard, make dry, parch, shrivel, towel (*to towel yourself dry*), wilt, wither.
OPPOSITES: SEE **wet** verb.

dryness noun *the dryness of the desert.* aridity, barrenness, drought, thirst.

Several English words, including *dual, duel, duet, duologue, duplicate,* etc., are related to Latin *duo = two.*

---

dual adjective *dual controls.* binary, coupled, double, duplicate, linked, paired, twin.
dual carriageway SEE **road**.

dub verb **1** SEE **name** verb.
2 *to dub a sound track.* add, re-record, superimpose.

dubious adjective **1** *I was dubious about her honesty.* SEE **doubtful**.
2 *a dubious character.* [*informal*] fishy, [*informal*] shady, suspect, suspicious, unreliable, untrustworthy.

duck noun drake, duckling.

duck verb **1** *I ducked when he threw a stone.* avoid, bend, bob down, crouch, dip down, dodge, evade, sidestep, stoop, swerve, take evasive action.
2 *They ducked me in the pool.* immerse, plunge, push under, submerge.

duct noun SEE **channel** noun.

ductile adjective *ductile substances.* flexible, malleable, plastic, pliable, pliant, tractable, yielding.
OPPOSITES: SEE **brittle**.

dud adjective SEE **useless**.

dudgeon noun **in high dudgeon** SEE **indignant**.

due adjective **1** *Subscriptions are now due.* in arrears, outstanding, owed, owing, payable, unpaid.
2 *I gave the matter due consideration.* adequate, appropriate, decent, deserved, fitting, just, mature, merited, proper, requisite, right, rightful, sufficient, suitable, well-earned.
3 *Is the bus due?* expected, scheduled.

due noun *Give him his due.* deserts, entitlement, merits, reward, rights.
dues SEE **fee**.

duel noun, verb SEE **fight** noun, verb.

duet noun duo.

duffer noun SEE **idiot**.

dug-out noun canoe.

dulcet adjective SEE **sweet** adjective.

dull adjective **1** *dull colours.* dim, dingy, dowdy, drab, dreary, faded, flat, gloomy, lacklustre, lifeless, matt (*matt paint*), plain, shabby, sombre, subdued.
OPPOSITES: SEE **bright**.
2 *a dull sky.* cloudy, dismal, grey, heavy, leaden, murky, overcast, sullen, sunless.
OPPOSITES: SEE **clear** adjective.
3 *a dull sound.* deadened, indistinct, muffled, muted.
OPPOSITES: SEE **distinct**.
4 *a dull pupil.* dense, dim, dim-witted, obtuse, slow, SEE **stupid**, [*informal*] thick, unimaginative, unintelligent, unresponsive.
OPPOSITES: SEE **clever**.
5 *a dull edge to a knife.* blunt, blunted, unsharpened.
OPPOSITES: SEE **sharp**.
6 *a dull conversation.* boring, commonplace, dry, monotonous, prosaic, stodgy, tame, tedious, unexciting, uninteresting.
OPPOSITES: SEE **interesting**.

dull verb **1** *to dull a sound.* SEE **muffle**.
2 *to dull a pain.* SEE **relieve**.

dumb adjective **1** *dumb with amazement.* inarticulate, [*informal*] mum, mute, silent, speechless, tongue-tied, unable to speak.
2 [*informal*] *He's too dumb to understand.* SEE **stupid**.

dumbfounded adjective SEE **amazed**.

dummy noun **1** *The revolver was a dummy.* copy, counterfeit, duplicate, imitation, model, sham, substitute, toy.
2 *a ventriloquist's dummy.* doll, figure, manikin, puppet.
3 *a baby's dummy.* teat.
dummy run SEE **practice.**

dump noun **1** *a rubbish dump.* junk yard, rubbish-heap, tip.
2 *an ammunition dump.* cache, depot, hoard, store.

dump verb **1** *to dump rubbish.* discard, dispose of, [*informal*] ditch, get rid of, jettison, reject, scrap, throw away.
2 [*informal*] *Dump your things on the table.* deposit, drop, empty out, let fall, offload, [*informal*] park, place, put down, throw down, tip, unload.

dumps noun **in the dumps** SEE **depressed.**

dumpy adjective SEE **fat** adjective.

dun adjective SEE **brown** adjective.

dunce noun SEE **fool** noun.

dune noun *dunes behind the beach.* drift, hillock, hummock, mound, sand-dune.

dung noun SEE **excreta,** manure, muck.

dungeon noun [*old-fashioned*] gaol, lock-up, pit, prison, underground chamber, vault.

dunk verb SEE **dip** verb.

duo noun SEE **pair** noun.

duologue noun SEE **dialogue.**

dupe verb SEE **trick** verb.

duple adjective SEE **double** adjective.

duplicate adjective *a duplicate key.* alternative, copied, corresponding, identical, matching, second, twin.

duplicate noun *a duplicate of an original document.* carbon copy, clone, copy, double, facsimile, imitation, likeness, photocopy, photostat, replica, reproduction, twin, Xerox.

duplicate verb **1** *to duplicate documents.* copy, photocopy, print, reproduce, Xerox.
2 *If you both do it, you duplicate the work.* do again, double, repeat.

duplicator noun SEE **reprographics.**

duplicity noun SEE **deceit.**

durable adjective SEE **lasting.**

duration noun SEE **time** noun.

duress noun SEE **force** noun.

dusk noun evening, gloaming, gloom, sundown, sunset, twilight.
OPPOSITES: SEE **dawn.**

dusky adjective SEE **dark.**

dust noun *chalk dust.* dirt, grime, grit, particles, powder.

dust verb SEE **clean** verb.

dust-jacket noun SEE **cover** noun.

dusty adjective **1** *a dusty substance. dusty soil.* chalky, crumbly, dry, fine, friable, gritty, powdery, sandy, sooty.
OPPOSITES: SEE **solid, wet** adjective.
2 *a dusty room.* dirty, filthy, grimy, grubby, mucky, uncleaned, unswept.
OPPOSITE: SEE **clean** adjective.

dutiful adjective *a dutiful worker.* careful, compliant, conscientious, devoted, diligent, faithful, hard-working, loyal, obedient, punctilious, reliable, responsible, scrupulous, thorough, trustworthy.
OPPOSITES: SEE **irresponsible.**

duty noun **1** *a sense of duty towards your employer.* allegiance, faithfulness, loyalty, obedience, obligation, responsibility, service.
2 *household duties.* assignment, business, [*informal*] chore, function, job, office, role, task, work.
3 *customs duty.* charge, customs, dues, levy, tariff, tax, toll.

duvet noun SEE **bedclothes.**

dwarf adjective SEE **small.**

dwarf noun midget, pigmy.

dwarf verb *The elephant dwarfed the tortoise.* dominate, look bigger than, overshadow, tower over.

dwell verb **to dwell in** SEE **inhabit.**

dwelling noun SEE **house** noun.

dwindle verb SEE **decrease** verb.

dye noun, verb SEE **colour** noun, verb.

dying adjective declining, fading, moribund.
OPPOSITES: SEE **thriving.**

Several English words, including *dynamic, dynamite,* and *dynamo,* are related to Greek *dunamis* = *power.*

---

dynamic adjective *a dynamic leader.* active, committed, driving, energetic, enterprising, enthusiastic, forceful, [*informal*] go-ahead, [*uncomplimentary*] go-getting, highly motivated, lively, powerful, pushful, [*uncomplimentary*] pushy, spirited, vigorous.
OPPOSITES: SEE **apathetic.**

dynamite noun SEE **explosive** noun.

dynamo noun generator.

dynasty noun SEE **family.**

dyspepsia noun indigestion.

dyspeptic adjective SEE **irritable.**

E

eager adjective *an eager pupil. eager to hear the news.* agog, anxious (*anxious to please*), ardent, avid, bursting, committed, [*formal*] desirous, earnest, enthusiastic, excited, fervent, impatient, intent, interested, keen, [*informal*] keyed up, motivated, passionate, [*informal*] raring (*raring to go*), voracious, zealous.
OPPOSITES: SEE **apathetic**.

eagerness noun *I began the work with great eagerness.* alacrity, ardour, commitment, desire, earnestness, enthusiasm, excitement, fervour, impatience, intentness, interest, keenness, longing, motivation, passion, thirst (*thirst for knowledge*), zeal.

ear noun ear-drum, lobe.
RELATED ADJECTIVE [= *of hearing*]: aural.

early adjective **1** *early flowers.* advanced, first, forward.
OPPOSITES: SEE **late**.
COMPARE: punctual.
2 *an early baby.* premature.
OPPOSITES: SEE **overdue**.
3 *early civilizations. an early computer.* ancient, antiquated, SEE **old**, primitive.
OPPOSITES: SEE **advanced, recent**.

earliest adjective SEE **first**.

earmark verb SEE **reserve** verb.

earn verb **1** *to earn money.* [*informal*] bring in, [*informal*] clear (*He clears £300 a week*), fetch in, get, [*informal*] gross, make, net, obtain, realize, receive, [*informal*] take home, work for.
2 *to earn success.* attain, deserve, gain, merit, warrant, win.

earnest adjective **1** *an earnest request.* grave, heartfelt, impassioned, serious, sincere, solemn, thoughtful, well-meant.
OPPOSITES: SEE **casual, flippant**.
2 *an earnest worker.* committed, conscientious, determined, devoted, diligent, eager, hard-working, industrious, involved, purposeful.
OPPOSITES: SEE **casual, half-hearted**.

earnings noun SEE **pay** noun.

earth noun **1** *the planet Earth.* SEE **planet**.
2 *fertile earth.* clay, dirt, ground, humus, land, loam, soil, topsoil.

earthenware noun [*formal*] ceramics, china, crockery, [*informal*] crocks, porcelain, pots, pottery.

earthly adjective [Do not confuse with *earthy*.] *earthly pleasures.* human, materialistic, mundane, SEE **physical**, secular, temporal.
OPPOSITES: SEE **spiritual**.

earthquake noun quake, shock, tremor, upheaval.
RELATED ADJECTIVE: seismic.

earthy adjective [Do not confuse with *earthly*.] *an earthy sense of humour.* SEE **bawdy**.

ease noun **1** *The plumber did the job with ease.* dexterity, easiness, effortlessness, facility, nonchalance, simplicity, skill, speed, straightforwardness.
OPPOSITES: SEE **difficulty**.
2 *Now she's retired and leads a life of ease.* aplomb, calmness, comfort, composure, contentment, enjoyment, happiness, leisure, luxury, peace, quiet, relaxation, repose, rest, serenity, tranquillity.
OPPOSITES: SEE **stress** noun.

ease verb **1** *to ease pain.* allay, alleviate, assuage, calm, comfort, lessen, lighten, mitigate, moderate, pacify, quell, quieten, relieve, soothe, tranquillize.
OPPOSITES: SEE **aggravate**.
2 *to ease pressure or tension.* decrease, reduce, relax, slacken, take off.
OPPOSITES: SEE **increase** verb.
3 *to ease something into position.* edge, guide, inch, manœuvre, move gradually, slide, slip.
to ease off *The rain eased off.* SEE **lessen**.

easy adjective **1** *easy work.* [*informal*] cushy, effortless, light, painless, pleasant, undemanding.
OPPOSITES: SEE **difficult, heavy**.
2 *an easy machine to use. easy instructions to follow.* clear, elementary, facile, foolproof, [*informal*] idiot-proof, manageable, plain, simple, straightforward, uncomplicated, understandable, user-friendly.
OPPOSITES: SEE **complicated, difficult**.
3 *an easy person to get on with.* accommodating, affable, amenable, docile, SEE **easy-going**, friendly, informal, natural, open, tolerant, unexacting.
OPPOSITES: SEE **difficult, intolerant**.
4 *an easy life. easy conditions.* carefree, comfortable, contented, cosy, leisurely, peaceful, relaxed, relaxing, restful, serene, soft, tranquil, unhurried, untroubled.
OPPOSITES: SEE **stressful**.
free and easy SEE **easygoing**.

easygoing adjective *an easygoing attitude.* calm, carefree, SEE **casual**, cheerful, even-tempered, [*informal*] free and easy, genial, [*informal*] happy-go-lucky, indulgent, informal, [*informal*] laid-back, lax, lenient, liberal, nonchalant, patient, permissive, placid, relaxed, tolerant, unexcitable, unruffled.
OPPOSITES: SEE **strict, tense** adjective.

eat verb *to eat food.* consume, devour, digest, feed on, [*formal*] ingest, live on, [*old-fashioned*] partake of, swallow, take.

VARIOUS WAYS TO EAT: bite, bolt, champ, chew, crunch, gnaw, gobble, gorge yourself, gormandize, graze, gulp, guzzle, [*informal*] make a pig of yourself, [*formal*] masticate, munch, nibble, overeat, peck, [*informal*] scoff, [*informal*] slurp, [*informal*] stuff yourself, taste, [*informal*] tuck in, [*informal*] wolf it down.

TO EAT AT A PARTICULAR MEAL: banquet, breakfast, dine, feast, lunch, [*old-fashioned*] sup.

THINGS TO EAT: SEE **food**.

---

to eat away. *The river ate the bank away.* crumble, erode, wear away.
to eat into *Acid can eat into metal.* cause to decay, corrode, oxidize, rot, rust.

eatable adjective *Is the food eatable?* digestible, edible, fit to eat, good, palatable, safe to eat, wholesome.
OPPOSITES: SEE **inedible**.

eaves noun *the eaves of a roof.* edge, overhang.

eavesdrop verb SEE **listen**.

ebb verb **1** *The tide ebbed.* fall, flow back, go down, recede, retreat.
2 *Her strength ebbed.* SEE **weaken**.

ebullient adjective SEE **exuberant**.

eccentric adjective **1** *eccentric behaviour.* aberrant, abnormal, absurd, bizarre, cranky, curious, freakish, [*informal*] funny, grotesque, idiosyncratic, ludicrous, SEE **mad**, odd, outlandish, out of the ordinary, peculiar, preposterous, queer, quirky, ridiculous, singular, strange, unconventional, unusual, [*informal*] way-out, [*informal*] weird, [*informal*] zany.
OPPOSITES: SEE **conventional**.
2 *eccentric circles.* irregular, off-centre.
COMPARE: concentric.

eccentric noun [All these synonyms are used *informally*] character (*She's a bit of a character*), crackpot, crank, freak, oddity, weirdie, weirdo.

echo verb **1** *The sound echoed across the valley.* resound, reverberate, ring, sound again.
2 *The parrot echoed what I said.* ape, copy, imitate, mimic, reiterate, repeat, reproduce, say again.

eclectic adjective *eclectic tastes.* SEE **catholic**.

eclipse verb **1** *to eclipse a light.* block out, blot out, cloud, cover, darken, extinguish, obscure, veil.
2 *to eclipse someone else's achievement.* dim, excel, outdo, outshine, overshadow, put into the shade, surpass.

economic adjective [=*to do with economics.* Don't confuse with *economical.*] *economic affairs.* budgetary, business, financial, fiscal, monetary, money-making, trading.

economical adjective [=*to do with saving money.* Don't confuse with *economic.*]
1 *Cycling is more economical than going by bus.* careful, cost-effective, [*uncomplimentary*] SEE **miserly**, parsimonious, prudent, sparing, thrifty.
OPPOSITES: SEE **wasteful**.
2 *Beans make an economical meal.* cheap, [*informal*] cheese-paring, frugal, inexpensive, low-priced, reasonable.
OPPOSITES: SEE **expensive**.

economize verb *If you're poor you have to economize.* be economical [SEE **economical**], cut back, save, [*informal*] scrimp, skimp, spend less, [*informal*] tighten your belt.
OPPOSITES: SEE **squander**.

economy noun **1** *economy in the use of your money.* frugality, [*uncomplimentary*] meanness, [*uncomplimentary*] miserliness, parsimony, providence, prudence, thrift.
OPPOSITE: wastefulness.
2 *I cancelled the holiday as an economy.* cut (*a cut in expenditure*), saving.
3 *the national economy.* budget, economic affairs [SEE **economic**], wealth.

ecstasy noun *an ecstasy of pleasure.* bliss, SEE **delight** noun, delirium, elation, enthusiasm, euphoria, exaltation, fervour, frenzy, trance, [*old-fashioned*] transport.

ecstatic adjective *an ecstatic welcome.* blissful, delighted, delirious, elated, enraptured, enthusiastic, euphoric, exultant, fervent, frenzied, gleeful, SEE **happy**, joyful, overjoyed, [*informal*] over the moon, rapturous.

eddy noun *an eddy in the water.* circular movement, swirl, vortex, whirl, whirlpool.

eddy verb *The water eddied between the rocks.* move in circles, swirl, whirl.

edge noun **1** *the edge of a knife.* acuteness, keenness, sharpness.
2 *the edge of a cup.* brim, brink, lip, rim.
3 *the edge of an area.* border, boundary, circumference, frame, kerb (*of a street*), limit, margin, outline, outlying parts,

outskirts (*of a town*), perimeter, periphery, side, suburbs (*of a town*), verge.
4 *the edge of a dress.* edging, fringe, hem, selvage.

edge verb **1** *I edged the dress with lace.* bind, border, fringe, hem, make an edge for, trim.
2 *We edged away.* creep, inch, move stealthily, sidle, slink, steal.

edgy adjective SEE **nervous**.

edible adjective *I don't think conkers are edible.* digestible, eatable, fit to eat, good to eat, palatable, safe to eat, wholesome.
OPPOSITES: SEE **inedible**.

edict noun SEE **order** noun.

edifice noun SEE **building**.

edify verb SEE **educate**.

edit verb *to edit a film, book, etc.* adapt, alter, assemble, compile, get ready, modify, organize, prepare, put together, supervise the production of.

VARIOUS WAYS TO EDIT A PIECE OF WRITING, ETC.: abridge, amend, annotate, bowdlerize, censor, condense, correct, cut, dub (*sound*), emend, format, polish, proof-read, rearrange, rephrase, revise, rewrite, select, shorten, splice (*film*).

---

edition noun **1** *a Christmas edition of a magazine.* copy, issue, number.
2 *a first edition of a book.* impression, printing, publication, version.

educate verb *to educate people about hygiene. to educate students.* bring up, civilize, coach, counsel, discipline, drill, edify, guide, improve, indoctrinate, inform, instruct, lecture, rear, school, teach, train, tutor.

educated adjective *an educated person.* civilized, cultivated, cultured, enlightened, erudite, informed, knowledgeable, learned, literate, numerate, sophisticated, well-bred, well-read.

education noun coaching, curriculum, enlightenment, guidance, indoctrination, instruction, schooling, syllabus, teaching, training, tuition.

PLACES WHERE YOU ARE EDUCATED: academy, college, conservatory, kindergarten, play-group, polytechnic, SEE **school**, sixth-form college, tertiary college, university.
PEOPLE WHO EDUCATE: coach, counsellor, demonstrator, don, governess, guru, headteacher, instructor, lecturer, pedagogue, professor, SEE **teacher**, trainer, tutor.

---

eel noun elver [=*young eel*].

eerie adjective *eerie sounds in the night.* creepy, SEE **frightening**, ghostly, mysterious, [*informal*] scary, [*informal*] spooky, strange, uncanny, unearthly, unnatural, weird.

efface verb SEE **obliterate**.

effect noun **1** *One effect of overeating may be obesity.* aftermath, consequence, impact, influence, issue, outcome, repercussion, result, sequel, upshot.
2 *The rosy lighting gave an effect of warmth.* feeling, illusion, impression, sense.
to put into effect SEE **effect** verb.

effect verb [Do not confuse with *affect*.] *to effect changes.* achieve, bring about, bring in, carry out, cause, create, [*formal*] effectuate, enforce, execute, implement, initiate, make, put into effect.

effective adjective **1** *an effective cure for colds.* effectual, [*formal*] efficacious, efficient, potent, powerful, real, strong, worthwhile.
2 *an effective goalkeeper.* able, capable, competent, impressive, productive, proficient, successful, useful.
3 *an effective argument.* cogent, compelling, convincing, meaningful, persuasive, striking, telling.
OPPOSITES: SEE **ineffective**.

effectual adjective SEE **effective**.

effectuate verb SEE **effect** verb.

effeminate adjective [*Effeminate* and its synonyms have sexist overtones, and are usually uncomplimentary. Compare *feminine*.] *effeminate behaviour.* camp, effete, girlish, [*informal*] pansy, [*informal*] sissy, unmanly, weak, womanish.
OPPOSITES: SEE **manly**.

effervesce verb boil, bubble, ferment, fizz, foam, froth, sparkle.

effervescent adjective *effervescent drinks.* bubbling, bubbly, carbonated, fizzy, foaming, sparkling.

effete adjective SEE **effeminate**, **feeble**.

efficacious adjective SEE **efficient**.

efficient adjective *an efficient worker. an efficient use of resources.* able, capable, competent, cost-effective, economic, effective, effectual, efficacious, impressive, productive, proficient, successful, thrifty, useful.
OPPOSITES: SEE **inefficient**.

effigy noun SEE **sculpture** noun.

effluent noun SEE **sewage**.

effort noun **1** *strenuous effort.* diligence, endeavour, exertion, industry, labour, pains, strain, stress, striving, struggle, toil, [*old-fashioned*] travail, trouble, work.
2 *a real effort to win.* attempt, endeavour, go, try.
3 *She congratulated us on a good effort.* accomplishment, achievement, feat, job, outcome, product, production, result.

effortless adjective SEE **easy**.

effrontery noun SEE **insolence**.

effusion noun SEE **flow** noun.

effusive adjective SEE **demonstrative**.

egalitarian adjective *egalitarian views.* democratic, populist.
OPPOSITES: SEE **élitist**.

egg verb **to egg on** SEE **encourage**.

egghead noun SEE **intellectual** noun.

egocentric adjective SEE **selfish**.

egoism noun egocentricity, self-centredness, self-importance, selfishness, self-love, self-regard.

egotism noun SEE **pride**.

egotistical adjective SEE **conceited**.

egregious adjective SEE **bad**.

egress noun SEE **exit** noun.

eiderdown noun duvet, quilt.
OTHER BEDCLOTHES: SEE **bedclothes**.

ejaculate verb **1** SEE **speak**.
2 SEE **eject**.

eject verb **1** *to eject someone from a building or country.* banish, [*informal*] boot out, deport, discharge, dismiss, drive out, evict, exile, expel, get rid of, [*informal*] kick out, oust, remove, sack, send out, throw out, turn out.
2 *to eject smoke or liquid.* belch, discharge, disgorge, ejaculate [= *eject semen*], emit, spew, spout, vomit.

eke verb **to eke out** *to eke out a food supply.* economize on, ration, spin out, stretch out, supplement.

elaborate adjective **1** *an elaborate plan.* complex, complicated, detailed, intricate, involved, thorough, well worked out.
2 *elaborate carvings.* baroque, decorative, fancy, fantastic, fussy, grotesque, intricate, ornamental, ornate, rococo, showy.
OPPOSITES: SEE **simple**.

elaborate verb *to elaborate a simple story.* add to, amplify, complicate, decorate, develop, embellish, expand, expatiate on, fill out, give details of, improve on, ornament.
OPPOSITES: SEE **simplify**.

elapse verb *Many days elapsed before we met again.* go by, lapse, pass.

elastic adjective *elastic material.* bendy, ductile, flexible, plastic, pliable, pliant, rubbery, [*informal*] springy, [*informal*] stretchy, yielding.
OPPOSITES: SEE **brittle, rigid**.

elated adjective SEE **ecstatic**.

elder noun SEE **official** noun.

elderly adjective SEE **old**.

elect adjective [Note: *elect* goes *after* the noun it describes.] *the president elect.* [also going *after* the noun] designate, to be; [going *before* the noun] chosen, elected [SEE **elect** verb], prospective.

elect verb *to elect a leader.* adopt, appoint, choose, name, nominate, opt for, pick, select, vote for.

election noun *the election of a leader.* ballot, choice, poll, selection, vote.

electioneering noun campaigning.

electorate noun constituents, electors, voters.

electric adjective **1** *an electric motor.* SEE **electrical**.
2 *an electric performance.* SEE **electrifying**.

electrical adjective *electrical equipment.* battery-operated, electric, mains-operated.

SOME ITEMS OF ELECTRICAL EQUIPMENT: accumulator, adaptor, battery, bell, bulb, cable, capacitor, charger, circuit, dynamo, electric heater, electric motor, electrode, electromagnet, electrometer, electrophorus, electroscope, element, flex, fuse, generator, insulation, lead, light, meter, plug, power-point, socket, switch, terminal, torch, transformer, wiring.

---

electrician noun electrical engineer.

electricity noun *Is the electricity on?* current, power, power supply.

electrifying adjective *an electrifying performance.* amazing, astonishing, astounding, electric, exciting, hair-raising, stimulating, thrilling.

electrocute verb SEE **kill**.

elegant adjective *an elegant building. elegant clothes.* artistic, SEE **beautiful**, chic, courtly, dignified, fashionable, graceful, gracious, handsome, modish, noble, [*informal*] posh, refined, smart, sophisticated, splendid, stately, stylish, tasteful.
OPPOSITES: SEE **inelegant**.

elegy noun dirge, lament, requiem.

element noun **1** *an element of truth in her story.* component, constituent, factor, feature, fragment, hint, ingredient, part, small amount, trace.
2 *Ducks are in their element swimming in a pond.* domain, environment, habitat, sphere.
elements 1 *We battled against the elements.* SEE **weather** noun.
2 *the elements of a subject.* SEE **rudiments.**
3 CHEMICAL ELEMENTS: SEE **chemical.**

elementary adjective *an elementary problem.* basic, early, SEE **easy**, first (*the first stages*), fundamental, initial, primary, principal, rudimentary, simple, straightforward, uncomplicated.
OPPOSITES: SEE **advanced, complex.**

elephantine adjective SEE **large.**

elevate verb SEE **raise.**

elevated adjective SEE **high.**

elevator noun hoist, lift.

elicit verb [Do not confuse with *illicit.*] *to elicit information.* derive, draw out, extort, extract, SEE **obtain.**

eligible adjective *eligible to apply for a job.* acceptable, allowed, appropriate, authorized, competent, equipped, fit, proper, qualified, suitable, worthy.
OPPOSITES: SEE **ineligible.**

eliminate verb **1** *to eliminate mistakes. to eliminate ants from your garden.* abolish, annihilate, delete, destroy, dispense with, do away with, eject, end, eradicate, exterminate, finish off, get rid of, SEE **kill**, put an end to, remove, stamp out.
2 *Our team was eliminated from the competition.* cut out, drop, exclude, knock out, leave out, omit, reject.

élite noun *These experienced workers are the élite of their profession.* aristocracy, the best, first-class people, flower, meritocracy, nobility, top people.

élitist adjective SEE **snobbish.**

elixir noun SEE **essence, remedy** noun.

elocution noun SEE **speech.**

elongate verb SEE **lengthen.**

elope verb SEE **run** verb (**to run away**).

eloquent adjective [See note at *loquacious.*] *an eloquent speaker.* articulate, expressive, fluent, forceful, [*uncomplimentary*] glib, moving, persuasive, plausible, powerful, unfaltering.
OPPOSITES: SEE **inarticulate.**

elucidate verb SEE **clarify, explain.**

elude verb *to elude capture.* avoid, circumvent, dodge, escape, evade, foil, get away from.

elusive adjective **1** *an elusive criminal.* [*informal*] always on the move, evasive, fugitive, hard to find.
2 *The poem's meaning is elusive.* ambiguous, baffling, deceptive, hard to pin down, indefinable, puzzling, shifting.

emaciated adjective *emaciated bodies.* anorectic, bony, cadaverous, gaunt, haggard, skeletal, skinny, starved, SEE **thin** adjective, undernourished, wasted away.

emanate verb SEE **originate.**

emancipate verb *to emancipate slaves.* deliver from slavery, discharge, enfranchise, free, give rights to, liberate, release, set free.
OPPOSITES: SEE **enslave.**

emasculate verb SEE **weaken.**

embalm verb SEE **preserve** verb.

embankment noun bank, causeway, dam, earthwork, mound, rampart.

embargo noun SEE **ban** noun.

embark verb **1** *to embark on a ship.* board, depart, go aboard, leave, set out.
OPPOSITES: SEE **disembark.**
2 *to embark on a project.* begin, commence, start, undertake.

embarrass verb *They embarrassed me by telling everyone my secret.* chagrin, confuse, disconcert, disgrace, distress, fluster, humiliate, make (someone) blush, make (someone) feel embarrassed [SEE **embarrassed**], mortify, [*informal*] put (someone) on the spot, shame, upset.

embarrassed adjective *an embarrassed silence.* abashed, ashamed, awkward, bashful, confused, disconcerted, distressed, flustered, humiliated, mortified, [*informal*] red in the face, self-conscious, shamed, shy, uncomfortable, upset.

embarrassing adjective *an embarrassing mistake.* awkward, disconcerting, distressing, humiliating, shameful, touchy, tricky, uncomfortable, uneasy, upsetting.

embassy noun *a foreign embassy.* consulate, delegation, legation, mission.

embed verb SEE **fix** verb, **insert.**

embellish verb SEE **ornament** verb.

embers noun ashes, cinders, coals.

embezzle verb *to embezzle funds.* appropriate, misappropriate, SEE **steal**, take fraudulently.

embezzlement noun *embezzlement of funds.* appropriation, fraud, misappropriation, stealing, theft.

embittered adjective *embittered by failure.* bitter, disillusioned, envious, resentful, sour.

emblazon verb SEE **ornament** verb.

emblem noun *The olive branch is an emblem of peace.* badge, crest, device, image, insignia, mark, regalia, seal, sign, symbol, token.

embody verb SEE **include**.

embolden verb SEE **encourage**.

embolism noun *a pulmonary embolism.* clot, obstruction, thrombosis.

emboss verb SEE **ornament** verb.

embrace verb **1** *She embraced him lovingly.* clasp, cling to, cuddle, enfold, fondle, grasp, hold, hug, kiss, snuggle up to.
2 *She's quick to embrace new ideas.* accept, espouse, receive, take on, welcome.
3 *The syllabus embraces all aspects of the subject.* bring together, comprise, embody, enclose, gather together, include, incorporate, involve, take in.

embrasure noun SEE **window**.

embrocation noun liniment, lotion, ointment, salve.

embroider verb SEE **ornament** verb.

embroidery noun needlework, sewing, tapestry.

embroil verb *Don't get embroiled in an argument.* SEE **involve**.

embryo noun foetus.

embryonic adjective *an embryonic organism. an embryonic idea.* early, immature, just beginning, rudimentary, underdeveloped, undeveloped, unformed.

emend verb SEE **alter**.

emerge verb *He didn't emerge from his bedroom until noon.* SEE **appear**, arise, come out, [*old-fashioned*] issue forth, [*informal*] pop up, surface.

emergency noun *She always keeps calm in an emergency.* crisis, danger, difficulty, predicament, serious situation.

emigrant noun OPPOSITE: immigrant.

emigrate verb *to emigrate to another country.* leave, quit, set out, SEE **travel** verb.

eminent adjective **1** *an eminent actor.* august, celebrated, distinguished, esteemed, familiar, famous, great, illustrious, important, notable, noteworthy, renowned, well-known.
OPPOSITES: SEE **unknown**.
2 *an eminent landmark.* conspicuous, elevated, high, noticeable, obvious, outstanding, prominent, visible.
OPPOSITES: SEE **inconspicuous**.

emit verb *Chimneys emit smoke. Transmitters emit radio signals.* belch, discharge, eject, exhale, expel, give off, give out, issue, radiate, send out, spew out, transmit.
OPPOSITES: SEE **absorb, receive**.

emollient adjective *an emollient cream.* softening, soothing.

emolument noun SEE **pay** noun.

emotion noun *His voice was full of emotion.* agitation, excitement, feeling, fervour, passion, sentiment, warmth.
SEE ALSO **anger** noun, **love** noun, etc.

emotional adjective *an emotional farewell. an emotional speech.* demonstrative, SEE **emotive**, fervent, fiery, heated, impassioned, intense, moving, passionate, romantic, touching, warm-hearted.
SEE ALSO **angry, loving**, etc.
OPPOSITES: SEE **unemotional**.

emotive adjective *emotive language.* affecting, biased, SEE **emotional**, inflammatory, loaded, moving, pathetic, poignant, prejudiced, provocative, sentimental, stirring, subjective, tear-jerking, touching.
OPPOSITES: SEE **dispassionate, objective** adjective.

empathy noun SEE **understanding**.

emperor noun SEE **ruler**.

emphasis noun *She put special emphasis on certain words.* accent, attention, force, importance, intensity, priority, prominence, strength, stress, urgency, weight.

emphasize verb *She emphasized the important points.* accent, accentuate, dwell on, focus on, foreground, give emphasis to, highlight, impress, insist on, [*informal*] play up, [*informal*] press home, spotlight, stress, underline.

emphatic adjective *an emphatic denial.* SEE **categorical**.

empire noun SEE **country**.

empirical adjective *empirical knowledge.* gained through experience, observed, practical.
OPPOSITES: SEE **theoretical**.

employ verb **1** *to employ workers.* engage, give work to, have on your payroll, hire, pay, take on, use the services of.
2 *to employ modern methods.* apply, use, utilize.

employed adjective active, busy, earning, engaged, hired, involved, occupied, working.
OPPOSITES: SEE **unemployed**.

employee noun [*old-fashioned*] hand, [*informal*] underling, worker.
employees staff, workforce.

employer noun boss, chief, [*informal*] gaffer, head, manager, owner, taskmaster. [An employer can be a business rather than an individual: SEE **company**.]

employment noun *What's her employment?* business, calling, craft, job, line, living, occupation, profession, trade, vocation, work.

emporium noun SEE **shop**.

empower verb SEE **authorize**.

empty adjective **1** *empty space. an empty room. an empty van.* bare, blank, clean, clear, deserted, desolate, forsaken, hollow, unfilled, unfurnished, uninhabited, unladen, unoccupied, unused, vacant, void.
OPPOSITES: SEE **full**.
2 *empty threats. empty compliments.* futile, idle, impotent, ineffective, insincere, meaningless, pointless, purposeless, senseless, silly, unreal, worthless.
OPPOSITES: SEE **effective**.

empty verb *Empty your cup. Empty the building.* clear, drain, evacuate, exhaust, pour out, unload, vacate, void.
OPPOSITES: SEE **fill**.

emulate verb SEE **rival** verb.

enable verb **1** *The extra money enabled us to have a holiday.* aid, assist, equip, help, make it possible, provide the means.
2 *A passport enables you to travel to certain countries.* allow, authorize, empower, entitle, license, permit, qualify, sanction.
OPPOSITES: SEE **prevent**.

enact verb **1** *to enact a law.* SEE **pass** verb. **2** *to enact a play.* SEE **perform**.

enamoured adjective SEE **love** noun (**in love**).

encampment noun *a military encampment.* camp, camping-ground, campsite.

encase verb SEE **enclose**.

enchant verb *The ballet enchanted us.* allure, bewitch, captivate, charm, delight, enrapture, enthral, entrance, fascinate, spellbind.

enchantment noun SEE **delight** noun, **magic** noun.

encircle verb SEE **enclose**.

enclave noun SEE **territory**.

enclose verb **1** *to enclose animals within a fence.* cage, confine, cordon off, encircle, encompass, envelop, fence in, hedge in, hem in, imprison, pen, restrict, ring, shut in, surround, wall in.
2 *to enclose something in an envelope, box, etc.* box, case, cocoon, conceal, contain, cover, encase, enfold, insert, package, parcel up, secure, sheathe, wrap.

enclosed adjective *an enclosed space.* confined, contained, encircled, fenced, limited, restricted, shut in, surrounded, walled.
OPPOSITES: SEE **open** adjective.

enclosure noun **1** *an enclosure for animals.* arena, cage, compound, coop, corral, court, courtyard, farmyard, field, fold, paddock, pen, pound, ring, run, sheepfold, stockade, sty.
2 *an enclosure in an envelope.* contents, inclusion, insertion.

encode verb OPPOSITES: SEE **decode**.

encomium noun SEE **praise** noun.

encompass verb SEE **enclose, include**.

encore noun *She sang an encore.* extra item, repeat performance.

encounter noun **1** *a friendly encounter.* meeting.
2 *a violent encounter.* battle, brush (*a brush with the authorities*), clash, collision, confrontation, dispute, SEE **fight** noun, struggle.

encounter verb *I encountered fierce opposition.* clash with, come upon, confront, contend with, [*informal*] cross swords with, face, grapple with, happen upon, have an encounter with, meet, [*informal*] run into.

encourage verb **1** *We encouraged our team.* abet, animate, applaud, cheer, [*informal*] egg on, embolden, give hope to, hearten, incite, inspire, rally, reassure, rouse, spur on, support.
2 *Advertising encourages sales.* aid, be conducive to, be an incentive to, boost, engender, foster, further, generate, help, increase, induce, promote, stimulate.
3 *Encourage people to stop smoking.* advocate, invite, persuade, prompt, urge.
OPPOSITES: SEE **discourage**.

encouragement noun *We need a little encouragement.* applause, approval, boost, cheer, incentive, inspiration, reassurance, [*informal*] shot in the arm, stimulation, support.

encouraging adjective *encouraging news.* auspicious, cheering, comforting, favourable, heartening, hopeful, optimistic, promising, reassuring.

encroach verb *to encroach on someone's territory.* enter, impinge, SEE **intrude**, invade, trespass, violate.

encrust verb SEE **cake** verb.

encumber verb SEE **hamper** verb.

encyclopaedic adjective *Her encyclopaedic knowledge amazes me.* SEE **comprehensive**.

end noun 1 *the end of the garden.* boundary, edge, limit.
2 *the end of an event.* cessation, close, coda (*of a piece of music*), completion, conclusion, culmination, curtain (*of a play*), denouement (*of a plot*), ending, finale, finish, [*informal*] pay-off, resolution.
3 *the end of a journey.* destination, expiration, home, termination, terminus.
4 *the end of a queue.* back, rear, tail.
5 *the end of a walking-stick.* ferrule, point, tip.
6 *the end of life.* SEE **death**, demise, destiny, destruction, doom, extinction, fate, passing, ruin.
7 *an end in view.* aim, aspiration, consequence, design, effect, intention, objective, outcome, plan, purpose, result, upshot.

end verb 1 *to end your work.* break off, bring to an end, complete, conclude, cut off, discontinue, [*informal*] drop, halt, put an end to, [*informal*] round off.
2 *to end a life.* abolish, destroy, eliminate, exterminate, [*informal*] get rid of, SEE **kill**, [*informal*] put an end to, ruin, scotch (*to scotch a rumour*).
3 *When does term end?* break up, cease, close, come to an end, culminate, expire, finish, reach a climax, stop, terminate.

endanger verb *Bad driving endangers others.* expose to risk, imperil, jeopardize, put at risk, threaten.
OPPOSITES: SEE **protect**.

endearing adjective *endearing ways.* appealing, attractive, charming, disarming, enchanting, engaging, lovable, sweet, winning.
OPPOSITES: SEE **repulsive**.

endeavour verb SEE **try** verb.

endless adjective 1 *endless space.* boundless, everlasting, immeasurable, infinite, limitless, measureless, never-ending, unbounded, unlimited.
2 *an endless afterlife.* eternal, immortal, undying.
3 *an endless supply.* ceaseless, constant, continual, continuous, everlasting, incessant, inexhaustible, interminable, perpetual, persistent, unbroken, unending, unfailing, uninterrupted.

endorse verb 1 *to endorse a cheque.* sign.
2 *to endorse someone's opinion.* agree with, approve of, condone, SEE **confirm**, subscribe to.

endow verb SEE **provide**.

endowment noun SEE **money**.

endurance noun *The big climb was a test of endurance.* ability to endure [SEE **endure**], determination, fortitude, patience, perseverance, persistence, pertinacity, resolution, stamina, staying-power, strength, tenacity.

endure verb 1 *to endure pain. to endure a storm.* bear, cope with, experience, go through, put up with, stand, [*informal*] stick, [*informal*] stomach, submit to, suffer, tolerate, undergo, weather, withstand.
2 *Life on earth will endure for a long time yet.* carry on, continue, exist, last, live on, persevere, persist, prevail, remain, stay, survive.

enduring adjective *an enduring friendship.* SEE **lasting**.

enemy noun adversary, antagonist, assailant, attacker, competitor, foe, opponent, opposition, the other side, rival, [*informal*] them (*us and them*).
OPPOSITES: SEE **ally** noun, **friend**.

energetic adjective *an energetic person. an energetic game.* active, animated, brisk, dynamic, enthusiastic, fast, forceful, hard-working, high-powered, indefatigable, lively, powerful, quick-moving, spirited, strenuous, tireless, unflagging, vigorous.
OPPOSITES: SEE **lethargic**.

energy noun 1 *She has tremendous energy.* animation, drive, dynamism, enthusiasm, fire, force, [*informal*] get-up-and-go, [*informal*] go (*She's got lots of go*), life, liveliness, might, spirit, stamina, strength, verve, vigour, [*informal*] vim, vitality, vivacity, zeal, zest.
OPPOSITES: SEE **lethargy**.
2 *Industry needs a reliable supply of energy.* fuel, power.

enervate verb SEE **tire**.

enfeeble verb SEE **weaken**.

enfold verb SEE **embrace, enclose**.

enforce verb *to enforce the rules.* administer, apply, carry out, execute, implement, impose, inflict, insist on, put into effect.
OPPOSITES: SEE **waive**.

enfranchise verb SEE **emancipate**.

engage verb 1 *to engage workers.* SEE **employ**.
2 *to engage to do something.* SEE **promise** verb.
3 *to engage someone in conversation.* SEE **occupy**.
4 *Cog-wheels engage.* bite, fit together, interlock.

engaged adjective 1 *engaged to be married.* [*formal*] affianced, betrothed, [*old-*

fashioned] promised, [*informal*] unavailable.
OPPOSITES: SEE **unattached**.
2 *engaged in your work.* absorbed, active, busy, committed, employed, engrossed, immersed, involved, occupied, preoccupied, tied up.
OPPOSITES: SEE **idle**.
3 *an engaged telephone-line. an engaged lavatory.* being used, busy, occupied, unavailable.
OPPOSITES: SEE **available**.

engagement 1 *The couple announced their engagement.* betrothal, promise to marry, [*old-fashioned*] troth.
2 *a business engagement.* appointment, arrangement, commitment, date, fixture, meeting, obligation.
3 *a military engagement.* SEE **battle** noun.

engaging adjective SEE **attractive**.

engender verb SEE **generate**.

engine noun 1 KINDS OF ENGINE: diesel engine, electric motor, internal-combustion engine, jet engine, outboard-motor, steam-engine, turbine, turbo-jet, turbo-prop.
2 *a railway engine.* locomotive.

engineer verb SEE **construct, devise**.

engineering noun There are many branches of *engineering*, including: aeronautical, chemical, civil, computer, electrical, electronic, manufacturing, marine, mechanical, plant.

engrave verb SEE **cut** verb, etch.

engraving noun SEE **picture** noun.

engross verb SEE **occupy**.

engulf verb SEE **submerge, surround**.

enhance verb SEE **improve**.

enigma noun SEE **puzzle** noun.

enigmatic adjective SEE **puzzling**.

enjoin verb SEE **command** verb.

enjoy verb 1 *We enjoy outings. I enjoyed her paintings.* admire, appreciate, be pleased by, delight in, indulge in, like, love, luxuriate in, rejoice in, relish, revel in, savour, take pleasure from or in.
2 *Visitors can enjoy the college facilities.* benefit from, experience, have, take advantage of, use.
to enjoy yourself celebrate, [*informal*] gad about, [*informal*] have a fling, have a good time.

enjoyable adjective *an enjoyable party. enjoyable food.* agreeable, amusing, SEE **delicious**, delightful, gratifying, likeable, [*informal*] nice, pleasant, pleasurable, rewarding, satisfying.
OPPOSITES: SEE **unpleasant**.

enlarge verb amplify (*sound*), augment, blow up (*a tyre, a photograph*), broaden (*the river broadened*), build up, develop, dilate (*the pupil of an eye*), diversify (*your interests*), elaborate (*a story or argument*), elongate, expand, extend, fill out, get bigger, grow, increase, inflate (*a balloon, a tyre*), lengthen, magnify, make bigger, multiply, stretch, swell, wax (*the moon waxes and wanes*), widen.
OPPOSITES: SEE **decrease** verb, **shrink**.

enlargement noun SEE **photograph** noun.

enlighten verb SEE **illuminate, inform**.

enlist verb 1 *to enlist troops.* conscript, engage, enrol, muster, recruit.
2 *The men enlisted in the army.* enrol, enter, join up, register, sign on, volunteer.
3 *to enlist someone's help.* SEE **obtain**.

enliven verb SEE **animate** verb.

enmesh verb SEE **tangle** verb.

enmity noun SEE **hostility**.

enormity noun 1 *the enormity of the crime.* SEE **wickedness**.
2 *the enormity of the problem.* SEE **seriousness**.

enormous adjective SEE **big**, colossal, elephantine, gargantuan, giant, gigantic, huge, hulking, immense, [*informal*] jumbo, mammoth, massive, mighty, monstrous, mountainous, titanic, towering, tremendous, vast.
OPPOSITES: SEE **small**.

enough adjective *enough food.* adequate, ample, as much as necessary, sufficient.

enquire verb ask, beg, demand, entreat, implore, inquire, query, question, quiz, request.
to enquire about [*informal*] go into, have an investigation into [SEE **investigation**], investigate, probe, research, scrutinize.

enquiry noun SEE **investigation**.

enrage verb SEE **anger** verb.

enrapture verb SEE **delight** verb.

enrich verb SEE **improve**.

enrobe verb SEE **dress** verb.

enrol verb SEE **enlist**.

ensconce verb SEE **establish**.

ensemble noun 1 GROUPS OF MUSICIANS: SEE **music**.
2 *She wore a new ensemble.* SEE **outfit**.

enshroud verb SEE **cover** verb.

ensign noun SEE **flag** noun.

enslave verb disenfranchise, dominate, make slaves of, subject, subjugate, take away the rights of.
OPPOSITES: SEE **emancipate**.

ensnare verb SEE **trap** verb.

ensue verb SEE **follow**.

ensure verb [Do not confuse with *insure.*] *Ensure that you lock the door.* confirm, guarantee, make certain, make sure, secure.

entail verb *What does the operation entail?* SEE **involve**.

entangle verb SEE **tangle** verb.

entente noun SEE **agreement**.

enter verb **1** *to enter a room.* arrive at, come in, go in, move into.
OPPOSITES: SEE **leave** verb.
2 *The bullet entered his leg.* cut into, dig into, penetrate, pierce, push into.
3 *to enter a competition.* engage in, enlist in, enrol in, [*informal*] go in for, join, participate in, sign up for, take part in, take up, volunteer for.
OPPOSITES: SEE **resign**, **withdraw**.
4 *to enter a name on a list.* add, inscribe, insert, note down, put down, record, register, set down, sign, write.
OPPOSITES: SEE **remove**.
to enter into *They entered into negotiations.* SEE **begin**.

enterprise noun **1** *a bold enterprise.* adventure, business, effort, endeavour, operation, project, undertaking, venture.
2 *She shows enterprise.* SEE **initiative**.

enterprising adjective *Some enterprising girls organized a sponsored walk.* adventurous, ambitious, bold, courageous, daring, eager, energetic, enthusiastic, [*informal*] go-ahead, hard-working, imaginative, industrious, intrepid, keen, pushful, [*uncomplimentary*] pushy, resourceful, spirited, venturesome.
OPPOSITES: SEE **unadventurous**.

entertain verb **1** *to entertain someone with stories.* amuse, cheer up, delight, divert, keep amused, make laugh, occupy, please, regale, [*informal*] tickle.
OPPOSITES: SEE **bore** verb.
2 *to entertain friends at Christmas.* accommodate, be the host or hostess to, cater for, give hospitality to, [*informal*] put up, receive, welcome.
3 *She wouldn't entertain the idea.* accept, agree to, approve, consent to, consider, contemplate, take seriously.

entertainer noun performer.

VARIOUS ENTERTAINERS: acrobat, actor, actress, ballerina, broadcaster, busker, clown, comedian, comic, compère, conjuror, contortionist, co-star, dancer, disc jockey, DJ, jester, juggler, lion-tamer, magician, matador, minstrel, musician, question-master, singer, star, stunt man, superstar, toreador, trapeze artist, trouper, ventriloquist.

---

entertaining adjective SEE **amusing**.

entertainment noun amusement, distraction, diversion, enjoyment, fun, night-life, pastime, play, pleasure, recreation, sport.

VARIOUS KINDS OF ENTERTAINMENT: aerobatics, air-show, ballet, bullfight, cabaret, casino, ceilidh, cinema, circus, comedy, concert, dance, disco, discothèque, drama, fair, firework display, flower show, gymkhana, motor show, SEE **music**, musical, night-club, opera, pageant, pantomime, play, radio, recital, recitation, revue, rodeo, show, son et lumière, SEE **sport**, tap-dancing, tattoo, television, theatre, variety show, waxworks, zoo.

---

enthral verb SEE **captivate**.

enthralling adjective SEE **exciting**.

enthrone verb *to enthrone a king or queen.* anoint, consecrate, crown, make a king or queen, place on the throne.
OPPOSITES: SEE **depose**.

enthuse verb SEE **enthusiastic (be enthusiastic)**.

enthusiasm noun **1** *To be successful you need enthusiasm.* ambition, ardour, commitment, drive, eagerness, excitement, fervour, keenness, panache, spirit, verve, zeal, zest.
OPPOSITES: SEE **apathy**.
2 *Her current enthusiasm is judo.* craze, [*informal*] fad, diversion, hobby, interest, passion, pastime.

enthusiast noun *a pop music enthusiast.* addict, admirer, aficionado, [*informal*] buff, devotee, fan, fanatic, [*informal*] fiend, [*informal*] freak, lover, supporter.

enthusiastic adjective *an enthusiastic supporter.* ardent, avid, [*informal*] crazy, delight, devoted, eager, earnest, ebullient, energetic, excited, exuberant, fervent, fervid, hearty, impassioned, keen, lively, [*informal*] mad keen, optimistic, passionate, positive, rapturous, raring (*raring to go*), spirited, unstinting, vigorous, wholehearted, zealous.
OPPOSITES: SEE **apathetic**.
to be enthusiastic enthuse, get excited, [*informal*] go into raptures, [*informal*] go overboard, rave.

entice verb SEE **lure** verb.

entire adjective SEE **whole**.

entitle verb **1** *The voucher entitles you to a refund. Her success entitles her to feel proud.* accredit, allow, authorize, empower, enable, justify, license, permit, warrant.
2 *What did you entitle your story?* call, christen, designate, dub, name, style, title.

entitlement noun *an entitlement to an inheritance.* claim, ownership, prerogative, right, title.

entity noun SEE **thing**.

entomb verb SEE **bury**.

entourage noun *the president's entourage.* attendants, SEE **company**, court (*a royal court*), escort, followers, [*informal*] hangers-on, [*old-fashioned*] retainers, retinue, staff.

entrails noun *an animal's entrails.* bowels, guts, [*informal*] innards, inner organs, [*informal*] insides, intestines, [*formal*] viscera.

entrance noun **1** *You pay at the entrance,* access, door, doorway, entry, gate, gateway, [*formal*] ingress, opening, portal, turnstile, way in.
OPPOSITES: SEE **exit** noun.
2 *I looked up at their entrance.* SEE **arrival**.
entrance hall ante-room, foyer, lobby, porch, vestibule.

entrance verb *The music entranced us.* SEE **delight** verb.

entrant noun *an entrant in a competition.* applicant, candidate, competitor, contender, contestant, entry, participant, player, rival.

entreat verb SEE **request** verb.

entreaty noun SEE **request** noun.

entrench verb SEE **establish**.

entrepreneur noun SEE **businessman**.

entrust verb *They entrusted me with the money.* put in charge of, trust.

entry noun **1** *Please don't block the entry.* SEE **entrance** noun.
2 *an entry in a diary.* insertion, item, jotting, note, record.
3 *an entry in a competition.* SEE **entrant**.

entwine verb SEE **interweave, tangle** verb.

enumerate verb SEE **count** verb, **mention**.

enunciate verb SEE **pronounce**.

envelop verb SEE **cover** verb, **wrap** verb.

envelope noun cover, sheath, wrapper, wrapping.

enviable adjective *an enviable salary.* attractive, desirable, favourable.

envious adjective *envious of her success.* begrudging, bitter, covetous, dissatisfied, [*informal*] green with envy, grudging, jaundiced, jealous, resentful.

environment noun *a natural environment.* conditions, context, habitat, location, setting, situation, surroundings, territory.

environs noun SEE **area**.

envisage noun SEE **visualize**.

envoy noun SEE **messenger**.

envy noun *feelings of envy.* bitterness, covetousness, cupidity, dissatisfaction, ill-will, jealousy, resentment.

envy verb *He envies her success.* begrudge, grudge, resent.

ephemeral adjective *Most newspapers are of ephemeral interest.* brief, evanescent, fleeting, impermanent, momentary, passing, short-lived, temporary, transient, transitory.
OPPOSITES: SEE **eternal, lasting**.

epic noun KINDS OF LITERATURE: SEE **literature**.

epicure noun SEE **gourmet**.

epicurean adjective SEE **hedonistic**.

epidemic noun *an epidemic of measles.* outbreak, plague.

epidermis noun SEE **skin** noun.

epigram noun SEE **saying**.

epilogue noun afterword, postscript.
OTHER PARTS OF A BOOK: SEE **book** noun.
OPPOSITES: SEE **prelude**.

episode noun **1** *a happy episode in my life.* SEE **event**.
2 *an episode of a serial.* chapter, instalment, part, passage, scene, section.

epistle noun SEE **letter**.

epitaph noun *an epitaph on a tombstone.* inscription.

epithet noun description, designation, name, [*informal*] tag, title.

epitome noun *She's the epitome of kindness.* embodiment, essence, personification, quintessence, representation, type.

epoch noun SEE **period**.

epoch-making adjective SEE **important**.

Many English words, including *equable, equal, equate, equilateral*, etc., are related to Latin *aequus* = *even.*

Don't confuse these with words such as *equestrian* and *equine* which are related to Latin *equus* = *horse.*

---

equable adjective SEE **calm** adjective.

equal adjective **1** *equal opportunities. equal quantities.* corresponding, egalitarian, equivalent, even, fair, identical, level, like, matched, matching, proportionate, the same, symmetrical, uniform.
2 *Is she equal to the job?* SEE **capable**.

equality noun *equality of opportunity.* balance, correspondence, evenhandedness, fairness, parity, similarity, uniformity.

equalize verb *to equalize scores.* balance, even up, level, make equal, match, [*informal*] square.

equanimity noun SEE **calmness**.

equate verb *You can't equate wealth and happiness.* assume to be equal, compare, juxtapose, liken, match, parallel, set side by side.

equerry noun SEE **official** noun.

equilateral adjective equal-sided.

equilibrium noun SEE **balance** noun.

equinox noun OPPOSITE: solstice.

equip verb *to equip workers with tools. to equip a room with furniture.* arm (*troops*), fit out, furnish, [*informal*] kit out, provide, stock, supply.

equipment noun *equipment you need for a job.* accoutrements, apparatus, furnishings, [*informal*] gear, [*informal*] hardware, implements, instruments, kit, machinery, materials, outfit, paraphernalia, plant, [*informal*] rig, [*informal*] stuff, supplies, tackle, [*informal*] things, tools.

equipoise noun SEE **balance** noun.

equitable adjective *an equitable reward.* SEE **just** adjective.

equities noun investments.

equivalent adjective SEE **equal**.

equivocal adjective SEE **ambiguous**.

equivocate verb SEE **quibble** verb.

era noun SEE **period**.

eradicate, erase verbs SEE **remove**.

erect adjective *an erect posture.* SEE **upright**.

erect verb *to erect a tent. to erect a flag pole.* build, construct, elevate, lift up, make upright [SEE **upright**], pitch (*a tent*), put up, raise, set up.

erection noun SEE **construction**.

erode verb *Water erodes the topsoil.* corrode, destroy, eat away, grind down, wear away.

erotic adjective SEE **amorous**.

err verb SEE **misbehave, miscalculate**.

errand noun *an errand to the shops.* assignment, job, journey, mission, task, trip.

erratic adjective *an erratic performance.* capricious, changeable, fickle, fitful, fluctuating, inconsistent, irregular, shifting, spasmodic, sporadic, uneven, unpredictable, unreliable, unstable, unsteady, variable, wandering, wayward.
OPPOSITES: SEE **consistent**.

erroneous adjective SEE **wrong** adjective.

error noun *factual errors. a fatal error on the motorway.* [*informal*] bloomer, blunder, [*informal*] boob, fallacy, falsehood, fault, flaw, [*informal*] howler, inaccuracy, inconsistency, inexactitude, lapse, misapprehension, miscalculation, misconception, mistake, misunderstanding, omission, oversight, sin, [*informal*] slip-up, [*formal*] solecism, transgression, [*old-fashioned*] trespass, wrongdoing.

erudite adjective SEE **learned**.

erupt verb *Smoke erupted from the volcano.* be discharged, be omitted, belch, break out, burst out, explode, gush, issue, pour out, shoot out, spew, spout, spurt, vomit.

eruption noun *an eruption of laughter. a volcanic eruption.* burst, explosion, outbreak, outburst.

escalate verb *Fighting escalated as more people joined in.* become worse, build up, expand, grow, increase, intensify, multiply, rise, spiral, step up.

escalator noun lift, moving staircase.

escapade noun *a childish escapade.* adventure, exploit, [*informal*] lark, mischief, practical joke, prank, scrape, stunt.

escape noun **1** *an escape from gaol.* bolt, break-out, flight, flit, get-away, retreat, running away.
2 *an escape of gas.* discharge, emission, leak, leakage, seepage.
3 *an escape from reality.* avoidance, distraction, diversion, escapism, evasion, relaxation, relief.

escape verb **1** *The prisoner escaped.* abscond, bolt, break free, break out, [*informal*] do a bunk, elope, flee, get away, [*informal*] give someone the slip, run away, [*slang*] scarper, slip away, [*informal*] slip the net.
2 *Oil escaped from a crack.* discharge, drain, leak, ooze, pour out, run out, seep.

3 *She always escapes the nasty jobs.* avoid, dodge, duck, evade, get away from, shirk.
4 *His name escapes me.* baffle, be forgotten by, elude.

escapism noun day-dreaming, fantasy, pretence, unreality, wishful thinking.

eschew verb SEE **avoid**.

escort noun 1 *a protective escort.* bodyguard, convoy, guard, guide, pilot.
2 *escorts to the queen.* attendant, entourage, retinue, train.
3 *an escort at a dance.* chaperon, companion, partner.

escort verb *to escort someone to a party. to escort a prisoner.* accompany, chaperon, guard, [*informal*] keep an eye on, [*informal*] keep tabs on, look after, protect, stay with, usher, watch.

escutcheon noun SEE **shield** noun.

esoteric adjective *esoteric knowledge.* SEE **obscure** adjective, **specialized**.

espalier noun VARIOUS TREES: SEE **tree**.

especial adjective SEE **special**.

espionage noun SEE **spying**.

esplanade noun SEE **path**.

espouse verb *to espouse a cause.* SEE **support** verb.

espy verb SEE **see**.

essay noun KINDS OF WRITING: SEE **writing**.

essay verb SEE **try** verb.

essayist noun VARIOUS WRITERS: SEE **writer**.

essence noun 1 *the essence of a problem. the essence of someone's personality.* centre, character, core, crux, essential quality [SEE **essential**], heart, kernel, life, meaning, nature, pith, quintessence, soul, spirit.
2 *peppermint essence.* concentrate, decoction, elixir, extract, fragrance, perfume, scent, tincture.

essential adjective 1 *essential information for travellers.* basic, chief, crucial, elementary, fundamental, important, indispensable, irreplaceable, key, main, necessary, primary, principal, requisite, vital.
OPPOSITES: SEE **inessential**.
2 *essential features.* characteristic, inherent, innate, intrinsic, quintessential.

establish verb 1 *to establish a business.* base, begin, construct, create, found, inaugurate, initiate, institute, introduce, organize, originate, set up, start.
2 *to establish yourself as leader.* confirm, ensconce, entrench, install, secure, settle.
3 *to establish the facts.* agree, authenticate, certify, confirm, corroborate, decide, demonstrate, fix, prove, ratify, show to be true, substantiate, verify.

established adjective *an established business. an established favourite on TV. established habits.* accepted, confirmed, deep-rooted, deep-seated, entrenched, fixed, indelible, ineradicable, ingrained, long-lasting, long-standing, permanent, proved, proven, recognized, reliable, respected, rooted, secure, settled, traditional, well-known, well-tried.
OPPOSITES: SEE **new**, **untried**.

establishment noun 1 *the establishment of a new club.* composition, constitution, creation, formation, foundation, inauguration, inception, institution, introduction.
2 *a well-run establishment.* business, concern, factory, household, shop.

estate noun 1 *a housing estate.* area, development.
2 *an estate left in a will.* assets, effects, fortune, goods, inheritance, lands, possessions, property, wealth.

estate car noun SEE **car**.

esteem noun *held in high esteem.* admiration, credit, estimation, favour, honour, regard, respect, reverence, veneration.

esteem verb SEE **respect** verb.

estimable adjective SEE **admirable**.

estimate noun 1 *What's your estimate of the situation?* appraisal, assessment, conjecture, estimation, evaluation, guess, judgement, opinion, surmise.
2 *an estimate of what a job will cost.* calculation, [*informal*] guesstimate, price, quotation, reckoning, specification, valuation.

estimate verb *to estimate how much something will cost.* appraise, assess, calculate, compute, conjecture, consider, count up, evaluate, gauge, guess, judge, project, reckon, surmise, think out, weigh up, work out.

estimation noun *I respect her estimation of the situation.* appraisal, appreciation, assessment, calculation, computation, consideration, estimate, evaluation, judgement, opinion, rating, view.

estrange verb SEE **antagonize**.

estuary noun *a river estuary.* arm of the sea, creek, [*Scottish*] firth, fjord, inlet, [*Scottish*] loch, mouth.

etch verb SEE **engrave.**

etching noun SEE **picture** noun.

eternal adjective **1** *eternal life.* deathless, endless, everlasting, heavenly, immeasurable, immortal, infinite, lasting, limitless, measureless, timeless, unchanging, undying, unending, unlimited.
OPPOSITES: SEE **ephemeral, transitory.**
2 [*informal*] *I'm sick of your eternal quarrelling.* ceaseless, constant, continual, frequent, incessant, interminable, never-ending, non-stop, perennial, permanent, perpetual, persistent, recurrent, relentless, repeated, unceasing, unremitting.
OPPOSITES: SEE **occasional, temporary.**

eternity noun *an eternity in heaven.* afterlife, eternal life [SEE **eternal**], immortality, infinity, perpetuity.

ether noun SEE **anaesthetic.**

ethical adjective *an ethical problem.* SEE **moral** adjective.

ethics noun SEE **morality.**

ethnic adjective *ethnic music.* cultural, folk, national, racial, traditional, tribal.

ethos noun SEE **belief, morality.**

etiolate verb SEE **pale** verb.

etiquette noun *It's polite to observe correct etiquette.* ceremony, civility, conventions, courtesy, decency, decorum, formalities, manners, politeness, propriety, protocol, rules of behaviour, standards of behaviour.

Eucharist noun Communion, Holy Communion, Lord's Supper, Mass.

eulogize verb SEE **praise** verb.

eulogy noun SEE **praise** noun.

eunuch noun SEE **man.**

euphemistic adjective *euphemistic language.* SEE **indirect.**

euphony noun SEE **harmony.**

euphoria noun SEE **happiness.**

euthanasia noun SEE **killing** noun.

evacuate verb **1** *to evacuate people from a building or an area.* clear, move out, remove, send away.
2 *to evacuate a building or an area.* abandon, decamp from, desert, empty, forsake, leave, quit, relinquish, vacate, withdraw from.
to evacuate the bowels SEE **excrete.**

evade verb *to evade your responsibilities.* avoid, [*informal*] chicken out of, circumvent, dodge, duck, elude, escape from, fend off, shirk, shun, sidestep, [*informal*] skive, steer clear of, turn your back on.
OPPOSITES: SEE **accept.**

evaluate verb SEE **assess.**

evanescent adjective SEE **fleeting.**

evangelist noun SEE **preacher.**

evangelize verb SEE **preach.**

evaporate verb *Dew evaporates in the morning.* disappear, disperse, dissipate, dissolve, dry up, melt away, vanish, vaporize.
OPPOSITES: SEE **condense.**

evasive adjective *an evasive answer.* ambiguous, deceptive, devious, disingenuous, equivocal, inconclusive, indecisive, indirect, misleading, noncommittal, oblique, prevaricating, shifty, uninformative.
OPPOSITES: SEE **straightforward.**

even adjective **1** *an even surface.* flat, flush, horizontal, level, smooth, straight, true, unbroken, unruffled.
OPPOSITES: SEE **rough.**
2 *an even temper.* SEE **even-tempered.**
3 *the even ticking of a clock.* balanced, consistent, equalized, metrical, monotonous, proportional, regular, rhythmical, steady, symmetrical, unvarying.
OPPOSITES: SEE **irregular.**
4 *even scores.* equal, identical, level, the same.
OPPOSITES: SEE **unequal.**
to get even SEE **retaliate.**

even verb **to even out** *I evened out the wrinkled carpet.* flatten, level, smooth, straighten.
to even up *The next goal evened up the scores.* balance, equalize, level, [*informal*] square.

evening noun dusk, [*poetic*] eventide, [*poetic*] gloaming, nightfall, sundown, sunset, twilight.

evensong noun CHURCH SERVICES: SEE **service.**

event noun **1** *an unexpected event.* affair, business, chance, circumstance, contingency, episode, eventuality, experience, happening, incident, occurrence.
2 *a special event.* activity, ceremony, entertainment, function, occasion.
3 *a sporting event.* bout, championship, competition, contest, engagement, fixture, game, match, meeting, tournament.

even-tempered adjective *an even-tempered character.* calm, composed, cool, equable, even, impassive, imperturbable, peaceable, peaceful, placid, reliable, serene, stable, steady, tranquil, unexcitable.
OPPOSITES: SEE **excitable.**

eventual adjective *the eventual result.* concluding, consequent, ensuing, final, last, overall, resulting, ultimate.

eventuate verb SEE **result** verb.

evergreen noun VARIOUS TREES: SEE **tree.**

everlasting adjective SEE **eternal.**

evermore adverb always, eternally, for ever, unceasingly.

everyday adjective *an everyday happening.* SEE **ordinary, usual.**

everywhere adverb RELATED ADJECTIVE: ubiquitous.

evict verb *to evict a tenant.* [*formal*] dispossess, eject, expel, [*slang*] give (someone) the boot, [*informal*] kick out, oust, put out, remove, throw out, [*informal*] turf out, turn out.

evidence noun *legal evidence. scientific evidence.* confirmation, corroboration, data, demonstration, documentation, facts, grounds, information, proof, sign, statistics, substantiation, testimony.
to give evidence SEE **testify.**

evident adjective *It's evident that he doesn't like work.* apparent, certain, clear, discernible, manifest, noticeable, obvious, palpable, patent, perceptible, plain, self-explanatory, unambiguous, undeniable, unmistakable, visible.
OPPOSITES: SEE **unclear.**

evil adjective **1** *an evil deed. an evil person.* amoral, atrocious, SEE **bad**, base, black-hearted, blasphemous, corrupt, criminal, cruel, dark (*dark deeds*), depraved, devilish, diabolical, dishonest, fiendish, foul, harmful, hateful, heinous, hellish, immoral, impious, infamous, iniquitous, irreligious, machiavellian, malevolent, malicious, malignant, nefarious, pernicious, perverted, reprobate, satanic, sinful, sinister, treacherous, ungodly, unprincipled, unrighteous, vicious, vile, villainous, wicked, wrong.
OPPOSITES: SEE **good.**
2 *an evil smell. an evil mood.* foul, nasty, pestilential, poisonous, troublesome, SEE **unpleasant**, unspeakable, vile.
OPPOSITES: SEE **pleasant.**

evil noun **1** *the fight against evil.* amorality, blasphemy, corruption, SEE **crime**, criminality, cruelty, depravity, dishonesty, fiendishness, heinousness, immorality, impiety, iniquity, [*old-fashioned*] knavery, malevolence, malice, mischief, pain, sin, sinfulness, suffering, treachery, turpitude, ungodliness, unrighteousness, vice, viciousness, villainy, wickedness, wrongdoing.
2 *Pollution is one of the evils of our world.* affliction, bane, calamity, catastrophe, curse, disaster, enormity, harm, ill, misfortune, sin, wrong.

evince verb *to evince interest.* SEE **show** verb.

eviscerate verb SEE **kill.**

evocative adjective *an evocative description.* atmospheric, convincing, descriptive, emotive, graphic, imaginative, provoking, realistic, stimulating, suggestive, vivid.

evoke verb *to evoke a response.* arouse, awaken, call up, conjure up, elicit, excite, inspire, kindle, produce, provoke, raise, stimulate, stir up, suggest, summon up.

evolution noun *the evolution of life. the evolution of an idea.* development, emergence, growth, improvement, maturing, progress, unfolding.

evolve verb *Animals evolved from simple forms of life.* derive, descend, develop, emerge, grow, improve, mature, modify gradually, progress.

ewe noun SEE **sheep.**

ewer noun SEE **jug.**

exacerbate verb SEE **worsen.**

exact adjective **1** *exact measurements.* accurate, correct, dead (*the dead centre*), faultless, meticulous, precise, right, specific, [*informal*] spot-on, strict.
2 *an exact account.* detailed, faithful, scrupulous, true, truthful, veracious.
3 *an exact copy.* flawless, identical, indistinguishable, perfect.
OPPOSITES: SEE **approximate** adjective, **wrong** adjective.

exact verb *to exact payment.* claim, demand, extort, extract, get, impose, insist on, obtain, require.

exacting adjective *an exacting task.* SEE **difficult.**

exaggerate verb **1** *to exaggerate a difficulty.* amplify, enlarge, inflate, magnify, make too much of, maximize, overdo, over-emphasize, overestimate, overstate, [*informal*] pile it on, [*informal*] play up.
OPPOSITES: SEE **underestimate.**
2 *to exaggerate someone's mannerisms.* burlesque, caricature, overact, parody, [*informal*] take off.

exaggerated adjective *exaggerated mannerisms.* burlesque, [*informal*] camp, SEE **excessive**, extravagant, hyperbolical, inflated, overdone, [*informal*] over the top.

exalt verb SEE **praise** verb, **raise.**

exalted adjective *an exalted rank.* SEE **high.**

examination noun **1** *an examination of our finances.* analysis, appraisal, audit,

[*informal*] post-mortem, review, scrutiny, study, survey.
2 *a school examination.* assessment, catechism [=*questions and answers about religious knowledge*], exam, oral [=*oral examination*], paper, test, viva or [*Latin*] viva voce.
3 *a medical examination.* [*informal*] check-up, inspection, investigation, probe, scan.
4 *an examination by the police.* cross-examination, enquiry, inquiry, inquisition, interrogation, questioning, trial.

examine verb 1 *to examine evidence.* analyse, appraise, audit (*accounts*), check, [*informal*] check out, explore, inquire into, inspect, investigate, probe, scrutinize, sift, sort out, study, [*slang*] sus out, test, vet, weigh up.
2 *to examine a witness.* catechize, cross-examine, cross-question, [*informal*] grill, interrogate, question.

example noun 1 *Give an example of what you mean.* case, illustration, instance, occurrence, sample, specimen.
2 *She's an example to us all.* ideal, lesson, model, paragon, pattern, prototype.
to make an example of SEE **punish**.

exasperate verb SEE **anger** verb, **annoy**.

excavate verb SEE **dig**.

exceed verb *to exceed the speed limit. to exceed a particular number.* beat, better, excel, go over, outdo, outnumber, outstrip, pass, surpass, top.

exceedingly adverb *exceedingly good cake.* amazingly, especially, exceptionally, excessively, extraordinarily, extremely, outstandingly, specially, unusually, very.

excel verb 1 *Their team excelled ours in every event.* beat, better, do better than, eclipse, exceed, outclass, outdo, outshine, surpass, top.
2 *She's a good all-round player, but she excels in tennis.* be excellent [SEE **excellent**], do best, shine, stand out.

excellent adjective *an excellent player. excellent food.* [*informal*] ace, [*informal*] brilliant, [*old-fashioned*] capital, champion, choice, [*slang*] cracking, distinguished, esteemed, estimable, exceptional, extraordinary, [*informal*] fabulous, [*informal*] fantastic, fine, first-class, first-rate, SEE **good**, gorgeous, great, high-class, impressive, magnificent, marvellous, notable, outstanding, remarkable, [*informal*] smashing, splendid, sterling, [*informal*] stunning, [*informal*] super, superb, superlative, supreme, surpassing, [*informal*] tip-top, [*informal*] top-notch, top-ranking, [*informal*] tremendous, unequalled, wonderful.
OPPOSITES: SEE **bad, mediocre**.

except verb SEE **exclude**.

exception noun 1 *an exception from a list.* exclusion, omission, rejection.
2 *an exception from what is normal.* abnormality, anomaly, departure, deviation, eccentricity, freak, irregularity, oddity, peculiarity, quirk, rarity.
to take exception SEE **object** verb.

exceptional adjective 1 *exceptional weather. an exceptional stroke of bad luck.* aberrant, abnormal, anomalous, atypical, curious, deviant, eccentric, extraordinary, memorable, notable, odd, peculiar, phenomenal, quirky, rare, remarkable, singular, special, strange, surprising, uncommon, unconventional, unexpected, unheard of, unparalleled, unprecedented, unpredictable, unusual.
OPPOSITES: SEE **normal**.
2 *an exceptional performance.* SEE **excellent**.

excerpt noun *We read excerpts from '1984'.* [*formal*] citation, clip, extract, fragment, highlight, part, passage, quotation, section, selection.

excess noun 1 *an excess of food.* abundance, glut, over-indulgence, superabundance, superfluity, surfeit.
OPPOSITES: SEE **scarcity**.
2 *an excess of income over expenditure.* profit, surplus.
OPPOSITES: SEE **deficit**.
3 *We were shocked by their excesses.* SEE **extravagance**.

excessive adjective 1 *excessive zeal.* disproportionate, exaggerated, extreme, fanatical, SEE **great**, immoderate, inordinate, intemperate, needless, overdone, profuse, undue, unnecessary.
2 *excessive amounts of food.* extravagant, SEE **huge**, prodigal, profligate, superfluous, unneeded, wasteful.
OPPOSITES: SEE **inadequate, moderate** adjective.
3 *excessive prices.* SEE **exorbitant**, extortionate, unrealistic, unreasonable.
OPPOSITES: SEE **low** adjective.

exchange noun 1 *an exchange of prisoners.* replacement, substitution, [*informal*] swap, switch.
2 *exchange of goods.* bargain, barter, deal, trade-in, traffic.
an exchange of views SEE **conversation**.

exchange verb *to exchange one thing for another.* barter, change, convert (*convert pounds into dollars*), interchange, reciprocate, replace, substitute, [*informal*] swap or swop, switch, trade, trade in, traffic.
to exchange words SEE **talk** verb.

excise noun SEE **tax** noun.

excise verb SEE **remove**.

excitable adjective *an excitable crowd.* [*informal*] bubbly, chattery, emotional, SEE **excited**, explosive, fiery, highly strung, hot-tempered, irrepressible, lively, SEE **nervous**, passionate, quick-tempered, restive, temperamental, unstable, volatile.
OPPOSITES: SEE **subdued**.

excite verb **1** *The smell of food excited the animals.* agitate, animate, discompose, disturb, electrify, exhilarate, [*informal*] get going, inflame, intoxicate, make excited [SEE **excited**], move, provoke, rouse, stimulate, stir up, thrill, titillate, [*informal*] turn on, upset.
OPPOSITES: SEE **calm** verb.
2 *My idea excited some interest.* activate, arouse, awaken, cause, elicit, encourage, engender, evoke, fire, generate, incite, motivate, produce, set off, whet (*whet the appetite*).

excited adjective *an excited crowd. an excited reaction.* agitated, animated, aroused, boisterous, delirious, disturbed, SEE **eager**, elated, enthusiastic, SEE **excitable**, exuberant, feverish, frantic, frenzied, heated, [*informal*] het up, hysterical, impassioned, lively, moved, nervous, overwrought, restless, roused, spirited, stimulated, stirred, thrilled, vivacious, wild, [*informal*] worked up.
OPPOSITES: SEE **apathetic**.

excitement noun **1** *feelings of excitement.* agitation, animation, delirium, discomposure, eagerness, enthusiasm, heat (*the heat of the moment*), intensity, [*informal*] kicks, passion, stimulation, suspense, tension, thrill.
2 *A crowd watched the excitement.* action, activity, adventure, SEE **commotion**, drama, furore, fuss, unrest.

exciting adjective *an exciting discovery.* amazing, cliff-hanging, dramatic, electrifying, enthralling, eventful, exhilarating, fast-moving, gripping, hair-raising, inspiring, interesting, intoxicating, moving, [*informal*] nail-biting, provocative, rousing, sensational, stimulating, stirring, suspenseful, thrilling, titillating.
OPPOSITES: SEE **boring**.

exclaim verb call, cry out, [*old-fashioned*] ejaculate, SEE **say**, shout, utter an exclamation [SEE **exclamation**], [*formal*] vociferate, [*informal*] yell.

exclamation noun call, cry, [*old-fashioned*] ejaculation, expletive, interjection, oath, shout, swear word.

exclude verb *to exclude someone from a conversation. to exclude illegal imports.* ban, banish, bar, blacklist, debar, disallow, disown, eject, except, excommunicate (*from the church*), expel, forbid, [*formal*] interdict, keep out, leave out, lock out, omit, ostracize, oust, outlaw, prohibit, proscribe, put an embargo on, refuse, reject, SEE **remove**, repudiate, rule out, shut out, veto.
OPPOSITES: SEE **include**.

exclusive adjective **1** *an exclusive contract.* limiting, restrictive, sole, unique, unshared.
2 *an exclusive club.* classy, closed, fashionable, [*informal*] members only, [*slang*] posh, private, select, selective, snobbish, [*informal*] trendy, [*informal*] up-market.

excommunicate verb SEE **exclude**.

excrement noun SEE **excreta**.

excrescence noun SEE **growth**.

excreta noun droppings, dung, excrement, faeces, manure, sewage, waste matter.

excrete verb defecate, eliminate waste matter, evacuate the bowels, go to the lavatory, relieve yourself.

excruciating adjective SEE **painful**.

exculpate verb SEE **excuse** verb.

excursion noun *an excursion to the seaside.* expedition, jaunt, journey, outing, ramble, tour, trip.

excusable adjective SEE **forgivable**.

excuse noun *a feeble excuse.* alibi, defence, explanation, extenuation, justification, mitigation, plea, pretext, reason, vindication.

excuse verb **1** *to excuse bad behaviour.* condone, explain, forgive, ignore, justify, overlook, pardon, sanction, tolerate, vindicate.
2 *The judge excused the prisoner.* absolve, acquit, discharge, [*formal*] exculpate, exonerate, free, let off, liberate, release.

execrable adjective SEE **bad**.

execrate verb SEE **hate** verb.

execute verb **1** *to execute a manœuvre.* accomplish, achieve, carry out, complete, do, effect, enact, finish, implement, perform.
2 *to execute a criminal.* SEE **kill**, SEE **punish**, put to death.
METHODS USED TO EXECUTE PEOPLE: behead, burn, crucify, decapitate, electrocute, garotte, gas, guillotine, hang, lynch, shoot, stone.

executioner noun hangman, SEE **killer**.

executive noun SEE **manager**.

exemplary adjective *exemplary behaviour.* SEE **admirable**, faultless, flawless, ideal, model, perfect, unexceptionable.

exemplify verb SEE **demonstrate**.

exempt adjective *exempt from paying tax.* excepted, excluded, excused, free, immune, let off, released, spared.
OPPOSITES: SEE **liable**.

exercise noun 1 *Exercise helps to keep you fit.* action, activity, aerobics, effort, exertion, games, gymnastics, PE, sport, [*informal*] work-out.
2 *army exercises. exercises on the piano.* discipline, drill, manœuvre, operation, practice, training.
exercise book jotter, notebook, pad.

exercise verb 1 *to exercise self-control. to exercise power.* apply, bring to bear, display, employ, exert, expend, show, use, utilize, wield.
2 *to exercise your body.* discipline, drill, exert, jog, keep fit, practise, train, [*informal*] work out.
3 *A problem exercised me.* SEE **worry** verb.

exert verb *to exert your authority.* SEE **exercise** verb.

exertion noun SEE **effort**.

exhale verb SEE **breathe**.

exhaust noun *exhaust from a car.* discharge, emission, fumes, gases, smoke.

exhaust verb 1 *to exhaust your resources. to exhaust your energy.* consume, deplete, drain, dry up, empty, finish off, sap, spend, use up, void.
2 *to exhaust yourself.* SEE **tire**.

exhausted adjective 1 *an exhausted oil-well.* drained, dry, empty, finished, used up.
2 *exhausted after a hard game.* breathless, [*informal*] done in, fatigued, gasping, [*slang*] knackered, panting, puffed out, [*informal*] shattered, SEE **tired**, weary, [*informal*] whacked, worn out.

exhausting adjective *exhausting work.* arduous, backbreaking, crippling, demanding, difficult, fatiguing, gruelling, hard, laborious, punishing, sapping, severe, strenuous, taxing, tiring, wearying.
OPPOSITES: SEE **refreshing**.

exhaustion noun debility, fatigue, tiredness, weakness, weariness.

exhaustive adjective *an exhaustive search.* all-out, careful, SEE **comprehensive**, intensive, meticulous, thorough.

exhibit verb 1 *to exhibit paintings.* arrange, display, present, put up, set up, show.
2 *to exhibit your knowledge.* air, demonstrate, [*uncomplimentary*] flaunt, indicate, manifest, [*uncomplimentary*] parade, reveal, [*uncomplimentary*] show off.
OPPOSITES: SEE **hide** verb.

exhibition noun *an art exhibition.* demonstration, display, presentation, show.

exhibitionist noun extrovert, [*informal*] show-off.

exhilarating adjective SEE **exciting**.

exhilaration noun SEE **happiness**.

exhort verb SEE **urge** verb.

exhortation noun *an exhortation to do better.* advice, SEE **encouragement**, lecture, [*informal*] pep talk, sermon.

exhume verb dig up, disinter.

exigent adjective SEE **urgent**.

exiguous adjective SEE **small**.

exile noun 1 *Exile can be a harsh punishment.* banishment, deportation, expatriation, expulsion.
2 *an exile from your own country.* exiled person, deportee, émigré, expatriate, outcast, refugee, wanderer.

exile verb *to exile someone.* banish, deport, drive out, eject, expatriate, expel, send away.

exist verb 1 *Do dragons exist?* be, be in existence, occur.
2 *We can't exist without food.* continue, endure, hold out, keep going, last, live, remain alive, subsist, survive.

existence noun 1 *I don't believe in the existence of ghosts.* actuality, being, life, living, reality.
2 *We depend on the environment for our existence.* continuance, survival.
in existence SEE **existing**.

existing adjective *existing species.* actual, alive, continuing, corporeal, current, enduring, existent, extant, factual, in existence, living, material, ongoing, present, real, remaining, surviving.
OPPOSITES: SEE **non-existent**.

Exit is a Latin word = *he or she goes out.* *Exeunt* is the plural = *they go out.*

---

exit noun 1 *Pass through the exit.* barrier, SEE **door**, doorway, egress, gate, gateway, opening, portal, way out.
2 *We made a hurried exit.* SEE **departure**.

exit verb SEE **depart**.

exodus noun SEE **departure**.

exonerate verb SEE **excuse** verb.

exorbitant adjective *exorbitant prices.* excessive, expensive, extortionate, extravagant, high, outrageous, overpriced, prohibitive, [*informal*] sky-high, [*informal*] steep, [*informal*] stiff, [*informal*] swingeing, top, unrealistic, unreasonable.
OPPOSITES: SEE **competitive**, **low** adjective.

exorcise verb SEE **expel**.

exotic adjective **1** *exotic places.* alien, different, exciting, faraway, foreign, remote, romantic, unfamiliar, wonderful.
OPPOSITES: SEE **familiar**.
2 *exotic food.* colourful, different, extraordinary, foreign-looking, novel, outlandish, peculiar, strange, striking, unfamiliar, unusual.
OPPOSITES: SEE **ordinary**.

expand verb **1** *to expand a business. to expand a story.* amplify, augment, broaden, build up, develop, diversify, elaborate, enlarge, extend, fill out, increase, make bigger, make longer.
OPPOSITES: SEE **reduce**.
2 *Metal expands in the heat.* become bigger, dilate, grow, increase, lengthen, open out, stretch, swell, thicken, widen.
OPPOSITES: SEE **contract** verb.

expanse noun *an expanse of water or land.* area, breadth, extent, range, sheet, stretch, sweep, surface, tract.

expansive adjective *an expansive talker.* affable, communicative, friendly, genial, open, outgoing, sociable, SEE **talkative**, well-disposed.
OPPOSITES: SEE **curt**, **unfriendly**.

expect verb **1** *We expected 100 guests.* anticipate, await, bank on, bargain for, count on, envisage, forecast, foresee, hope for, imagine, look forward to, predict, prophesy, reckon on, wait for.
2 *We expect good behaviour.* consider necessary, demand, insist on, rely on, require, want.
3 *I expect he missed the bus.* assume, believe, SEE **guess** verb, judge, presume, presuppose, think.

expected adjective *an expected increase in prices.* awaited, forecast, foreseen, planned, predictable, predicted, unsurprising.
OPPOSITES: SEE **unexpected**.

expectant adjective SEE **pregnant**.

expecting adjective SEE **pregnant**.

expectorant noun cough-mixture, linctus.

expedient adjective *It was expedient to retire gracefully.* advantageous, advisable, appropriate, convenient, desirable, helpful, judicious, opportune, politic, practical, pragmatic, profitable, prudent, sensible, suitable, to your advantage, useful, worthwhile.

expedient noun *His tantrum was simply an expedient to get his own way.* contrivance, device, [*informal*] dodge, manœuvre, means, measure, method, [*informal*] ploy, resort, ruse, scheme, stratagem, tactics.

expedite verb SEE **hurry** verb.

expedition noun *an expedition to foreign parts.* crusade, exploration, SEE **journey** noun, mission, pilgrimage, quest, raid, safari, voyage.

expeditious adjective SEE **quick**.

expel verb **1** *to expel a pupil from a school.* ban, banish, cast out, [*informal*] chuck out, dismiss, drive out, eject, evict (*from your home*), exile (*from your country*), exorcise (*evil spirits*), oust, remove, send away, throw out, [*informal*] turf out.
2 *to expel exhaust fumes.* belch, discharge, emit, exhale, give out, send out, spew out.

expend verb SEE **use** verb.

expendable adjective *expendable materials.* disposable, replaceable, [*informal*] throwaway.
OPPOSITE: reusable.

expenditure noun SEE **expense**.
OPPOSITE: income.

expense noun *the expense of running a car.* charges, cost, expenditure, outgoings, outlay, overheads, payment, price, spending.

expensive adjective *expensive presents.* costly, dear, SEE **exorbitant**, extravagant, generous (*a generous gift*), high-priced, [*informal*] pricey, [*informal*] steep, [*informal*] up-market.
OPPOSITES: SEE **cheap**.

experience noun **1** *You learn by experience.* [*informal*] doing it, familiarity, involvement, observation, participation, practice, taking part.
2 *They want someone with experience.* [*informal*] know-how, knowledge, skill, understanding.
3 *a frightening experience.* adventure, event, happening, incident, occurrence, ordeal.

experienced adjective **1** *an experienced worker.* expert, knowledgeable, practised, professional, qualified, skilled, specialized, trained, well-versed.
OPPOSITES: SEE **inexperienced**.
2 *an experienced man of the world.* knowing, sophisticated, wise, worldly-wise.
OPPOSITES: SEE **innocent**.
an experienced person SEE **expert** noun, [*informal*] old hand, veteran.

experiment noun **1** *scientific experiments.* demonstration, investigation, practical, proof, research, test.
2 *The new bus-service is an experiment.* trial, try-out, venture.

experiment verb *to experiment in a laboratory.* do an experiment, investigate, make tests, research, test, try out.

experimental adjective **1** *experimental evidence.* based on experiments, empirical, proved, tested.
2 *an experimental bus-service.* being tested, exploratory, on trial, pilot, provisional, tentative, trial.

expert adjective *an expert craftsman.* able, [*informal*] ace, [*informal*] brilliant, capable, SEE **clever**, competent, [*informal*] crack, experienced, knowledgeable, master (*a master craftsman*), masterly, practised, professional, proficient, qualified, skilful, skilled, specialized, trained, well-versed.
OPPOSITES: SEE **amateurish, unskilful.**

expert noun *an expert in her subject.* [*informal*] ace, authority, connoisseur, [*informal*] dab hand, genius, [*uncomplimentary*] know-all, master, professional, pundit, specialist, virtuoso [= *an expert musician*], [*uncomplimentary*] wiseacre, [*informal*] wizard.
OPPOSITES: SEE **amateur, ignoramus.**

expertise noun SEE **skill.**

expiate verb *to expiate a crime.* SEE **atone.**

expire verb **1** *The animal expired.* SEE **die.**
2 *My licence expired.* become invalid, come to an end, finish, [*informal*] run out.

explain verb **1** *to explain a problem.* clarify, clear up, decipher, decode, demonstrate, disentangle, elucidate, expound, gloss, illustrate, interpret, resolve, simplify, solve, [*informal*] sort out, spell out, teach, translate, unravel.
2 *to explain a mistake.* account for, excuse, give reasons for, justify, make excuses for, rationalize, vindicate.

explanation noun **1** *an explanation of what happened.* account, clarification, definition, demonstration, description, elucidation, [*formal*] exegesis, explication, exposition, illustration, interpretation, meaning, significance.
2 *the explanation for a mistake.* cause, justification, motivation, motive, reason, vindication.
3 *an explanation beneath a diagram.* caption, gloss, key, legend, rubric.

explanatory adjective *explanatory remarks.* descriptive, expository, helpful, illuminating, illustrative, interpretive.

expletive noun SEE **exclamation.**

explicable adjective *an explicable failure.* accountable, explainable, intelligible, justifiable, straightforward, understandable.
OPPOSITES: SEE **inexplicable.**

explicit adjective *explicit criticism.* clear, definite, detailed, direct, exact, express, frank, graphic, open, outspoken, patent, plain, positive, precise, put into words, said, specific, [*informal*] spelt out, spoken, straightforward, unambiguous, unconcealed, unequivocal, unhidden, unreserved.
OPPOSITES: SEE **implicit.**

explode verb **1** *to explode with a bang.* backfire, blast, blow up, burst, detonate, erupt, go off, make an explosion, set off, shatter.
2 *to explode a theory.* destroy, discredit, disprove, put an end to, rebut, refute.

exploit noun *heroic exploits.* SEE **deed.**

exploit verb **1** *to exploit an advantage.* build on, capitalize on, [*informal*] cash in on, develop, make use of, profit by, work on, use, utilize.
2 *to exploit your employees.* [*informal*] bleed, enslave, ill-treat, impose on, keep down, manipulate, [*informal*] milk, misuse, oppress, [*informal*] rip off, [*informal*] squeeze dry, take advantage of, treat unfairly, withhold rights from.

explore verb **1** *to explore unknown lands.* break new ground, probe, prospect, reconnoitre, scout, search, survey, tour, travel through.
2 *to explore a problem.* analyse, examine, inspect, investigate, look into, research, scrutinize.

explosion noun *a loud explosion.* bang, blast, burst, clap (*of thunder*), crack, detonation, discharge (*of a gun*), eruption (*of a volcano, of noise*), outburst (*of laughter*), report.

explosive adjective *explosive substances. an explosive situation.* SEE **dangerous**, highly charged, liable to explode, sensitive, unstable, volatile.
OPPOSITES: SEE **stable.**

explosive noun EXPLOSIVES INCLUDE: cordite, dynamite, gelignite, gunpowder, TNT.

exponent noun **1** *a talented exponent of jazz.* executant, interpreter, performer, player.
2 *an exponent of a new theory.* advocate, champion, defender, expounder, presenter, propagandist, proponent, supporter, upholder.

export verb *to export goods.* SEE **convey.**

exports noun SEE **goods.**

expose verb SEE **reveal, uncover**.

expostulate verb SEE **protest** verb.

expound verb SEE **explain**.

express adjective **1** *It was his express wish.* SEE **explicit**.
2 *an express train.* SEE **fast** adjective.

express verb *to express ideas.* air, SEE **communicate**, give vent to, phrase, put into words, release, vent, ventilate, word.

expression noun **1** *a verbal expression.* cliché, formula, phrase, phraseology, remark, SEE **saying**, statement, term, turn of phrase, wording.
2 *a facial expression.* air, appearance, aspect, countenance, face, look, mien.

VARIOUS FACIAL EXPRESSIONS: beam, frown, glare, glower, grimace, grin, laugh, leer, long face, poker-face, pout, scowl, smile, smirk, sneer, wince, yawn.

---

3 *She reads with expression.* emotion, feeling, intensity, sensibility, sensitivity, sympathy, understanding.

expressionless adjective *an expressionless face.* blank, [*informal*] dead-pan, emotionless, empty, glassy (*a glassy stare*), impassive, inscrutable, poker-faced, straight-faced, uncommunicative, wooden.
2 *an expressionless voice.* boring, dull, flat, monotonous, uninspiring, unmodulated, unvarying.
OPPOSITES: SEE **expressive**.

expressive adjective **1** *an expressive look.* meaningful, mobile, revealing, sensitive, significant, striking, suggestive, telling.
2 *an expressive voice.* articulate, eloquent, lively, modulated, varied.
OPPOSITES: SEE **expressionless**.

expunge verb SEE **delete**.

expurgate verb SEE **censor**.

exquisite adjective SEE **delicate**.

extant adjective SEE **existing**.

extempore adjective SEE **impromptu**.

extemporize verb SEE **improvise**.

extend verb **1** *to extend a meeting.* draw out, keep going, lengthen, make longer, prolong, protract, [*informal*] spin out.
OPPOSITES: SEE **shorten**.
2 *to extend a deadline.* defer, delay, postpone, put back, put off.
3 *to extend your hand.* give, hold out, offer, present, proffer, put out, raise, reach out, stick out, stretch out.
4 *to extend a business.* add to, build up, develop, enlarge, expand, increase, widen the scope of.
5 *The garden extends to the fence.* continue, go, reach, spread, stretch.

extension noun **1** *an extension to a building.* SEE **addition**.
2 *an extension of a deadline.* delay, postponement.

extensive adjective SEE **large**.

extent noun **1** *The map shows the extent of the estate.* area, bounds, breadth, dimensions, distance, expanse, length, limit, measurement, reach, space, spread, width.
2 *After the storm we saw the extent of the damage.* amount, degree, magnitude, measure, proportions, quantity, range, scope, size.

extenuating adjective *extenuating circumstances.* SEE **mitigating**.

exterior adjective SEE **outside** adjective.

exterior noun SEE **outside** noun.

exterminate verb SEE **destroy**.

extermination noun SEE **destruction**.

external adjective SEE **outside** adjective.

extinct adjective **1** *an extinct volcano.* extinguished, inactive.
OPPOSITES: SEE **active**.
2 *extinct species.* dead, defunct, died out, exterminated, vanished.
OPPOSITES: SEE **existing**.

extinguish verb *to extinguish a fire.* damp down, douse, put out, quench, slake, smother, snuff (*a candle*).
OPPOSITES: SEE **light** verb.

extirpate verb SEE **destroy**.

extol verb SEE **praise** verb.

extort verb *to extort money from someone.* bully, exact, extract, force, obtain by force [SEE **obtain**].

extortionate adjective SEE **exorbitant**.

extra adjective *extra supplies.* added, additional, excess, further, more, other, reserve, spare, supplementary, surplus, unneeded, unused, unwanted.
2 *extra staff.* ancillary, auxiliary, supernumerary, temporary.

extract noun **1** *beef extract.* concentrate, decoction, distillation, essence.
2 *an extract from a newspaper.* [*formal*] citation, [*informal*] clip, clipping, cutting, excerpt, passage, quotation, selection.

extract verb **1** *to extract a tooth.* draw out, pull out, remove, take out, withdraw.
2 *to extract information from a book.* derive, gather, SEE **obtain**, quote, select.

extraordinary adjective *an extraordinary story. extraordinary behaviour.* abnormal, amazing, bizarre, curious, exceptional, fantastic, [*informal*] funny, incredible, marvellous, miraculous, mysterious, mystical, notable, noteworthy, odd, outstanding, peculiar, [*informal*] phenomenal, queer, rare, remarkable, singular, special, strange, striking, stupendous, surprising, [*informal*] unbelievable, uncommon, unheard of, unimaginable, unique, unusual, [*informal*] weird, wonderful.
OPPOSITES: SEE **ordinary**.

extrapolate verb SEE **deduce**.

extra-terrestrial adjective SEE **alien** adjective.

extravagance noun *I disapproved of their extravagance.* excess, improvidence, lavishness, over-indulgence, prodigality, wastefulness.

extravagant adjective *an extravagant waste of money.* excessive, SEE **expensive**, [*informal*] fancy, grandiose, improvident, lavish, outrageous, pretentious, prodigal, profligate, profuse, reckless, self-indulgent, [*informal*] showy, spendthrift, uneconomical, unreasonable, unthrifty, wasteful.
OPPOSITES: SEE **economical**.
an extravagant person SEE **spendthrift**.

extravaganza noun SEE **show** noun.

extreme adjective **1** *extreme cold. extreme care.* acute, drastic, excessive, greatest, intensest, maximum, severest, utmost.
2 *the extreme edge of the field.* farthest, furthest, furthermost, outermost, ultimate.
3 *extreme opinions.* absolute, avant-garde, exaggerated, extravagant, fanatical, [*informal*] hard-line, immoderate, intemperate, intransigent, militant, obsessive, outrageous, uncompromising, [*informal*] way-out, zealous.
4 *an extreme disaster.* SEE **complete** adjective.

extreme noun *from one extreme to the other.* edge, end, extremity, limit, maximum or minimum, opposite, pole, top or bottom, ultimate.

extremist noun SEE **fanatic**.

extremity noun SEE **extreme** noun.

extricate verb SEE **disentangle**.

extrovert noun [*uncomplimentary*] exhibitionist, good mixer, socializer.
OPPOSITES: SEE **introvert**.

extroverted adjective active, confident, outgoing, positive, SEE **sociable**.
OPPOSITES: SEE **introverted**.

extrude verb SEE **squeeze (to squeeze out)**.

exuberant adjective **1** *an exuberant mood.* animated, boisterous, [*informal*] bubbly, buoyant, cheerful, eager, ebullient, effervescent, elated, energetic, enthusiastic, excited, exhilarated, high-spirited, irrepressible, lively, spirited, sprightly, vivacious.
OPPOSITES: SEE **apathetic**.
2 *an exuberant style of decoration.* baroque, exaggerated, highly decorated, ornate, overdone, rich, rococo.
OPPOSITES: SEE **classical**.
3 *exuberant growth.* abundant, copious, lush, luxuriant, overflowing, profuse, rank, teeming.
OPPOSITES: SEE **sparse**.

exude verb SEE **discharge** verb.

exult verb SEE **rejoice**.

exultant adjective SEE **joyful**.

eye noun PARTS OF THE EYE: cornea, eyeball, eyebrow, eyelash, eyelid, iris, pupil, retina, white.
RELATED ADJECTIVES: optical, ophthalmic.
to keep an eye open SEE **look** verb.

eye verb SEE **look** verb **(to look at)**.

eyelet noun SEE **hole**.

eye-opener noun SEE **surprise** noun.

eyepiece noun SEE **lens**.

eyesight noun *good eyesight.* vision.
WORDS TO DESCRIBE EYESIGHT: astigmatic, long-sighted, myopic, short-sighted.

eyesore noun SEE **blemish**.

eye-witness noun *Eye-witnesses described the accident.* bystander, looker-on, observer, onlooker, spectator, watcher, witness.

F

fable noun SEE **story**.

fabled adjective SEE **legendary**.

fabric noun cloth, material, stuff, textile.
VARIOUS FABRICS: SEE **cloth**.

fabricate verb **1** *to fabricate a building.* SEE **construct**.
2 *to fabricate a story.* SEE **invent**.

fabulous adjective **1** *fabulous monsters.* SEE **legendary**.
2 [*informal*] *a fabulous party.* SEE **excellent**.

façade noun SEE **face** noun.

face noun **1** *a person's face.* air, appearance, countenance, SEE **expression**, features, look, [*slang*] mug, [*old-fashioned*] physiognomy, visage.
2 *the face of a building.* aspect (*a house with a southern aspect*), exterior, façade, front, outside.
3 *A cube has six faces.* facet, side, surface.

face verb **1** *to face one another.* be opposite to, front, look towards, overlook.
2 *to face danger.* come to terms with, confront, cope with, defy, encounter, experience, face up to, meet, oppose, square up to, stand up to, tackle.
3 *to face a wall with plaster.* SEE **cover** verb.

face-lift noun SEE **improvement**.

facet noun SEE **face** noun.

facetious adjective SEE **amusing**.

facia noun dashboard, instrument-panel.

Several English words, including *facile*, *facilitate*, and *facility*, are related to Latin *facilis* = *easy*. Compare French *facile*.

---

facile adjective **1** [*uncomplimentary*] *a facile solution to a problem.* cheap, easy, effortless, hasty, obvious, quick, simple, superficial, unconsidered.
OPPOSITES: SEE **thorough**.
2 [*uncomplimentary*] *a facile talker.* fluent, glib, insincere, plausible, shallow, slick, [*informal*] smooth.
OPPOSITES: SEE **profound**.

facilitate verb SEE **help** verb.

facility noun **1** *The facility with which he did the job surprised us.* SEE **ease** noun.
2 *The crèche is a useful facility for working parents.* amenity, convenience, help, provision, resource, service.

facing noun SEE **covering**.

facsimile noun SEE **reproduction**.

fact noun *a known fact.* actuality, certainty, fait accompli, reality, truth.
OPPOSITES: SEE **fiction**.
the facts circumstances, data, details, evidence, information, particulars, statistics

faction noun SEE **party**.

factitious adjective SEE **artificial**.

factor noun *The judge took every factor into account.* aspect, cause, circumstance, component, consideration, contingency, detail, determinant, element, fact, influence, item, parameter, particular.

factory noun PLACES WHERE THINGS ARE MANUFACTURED: assembly line, forge, foundry, manufacturing plant, mill, refinery, shop-floor, workshop.

factotum noun SEE **servant**.

factual adjective **1** *factual information.* accurate, circumstantial, SEE **correct** adjective, demonstrable, empirical, objective, provable, true, well-documented.
OPPOSITES: SEE **false**.
2 *a factual film.* biographical, documentary, historical, real-life, true.
OPPOSITES: SEE **fictional**.
3 *a strictly factual account.* matter-of-fact, plain, prosaic, realistic, unadorned, unemotional, unimaginative.
OPPOSITES: SEE **unrealistic**.

faculty noun **1** *the faculty of sight.* capability, capacity, power.
2 *a faculty for learning languages.* SEE **ability**.

fad noun SEE **craze**.

faddy adjective SEE **fussy**.

fade verb **1** *Sunlight fades the curtains.* blanch, bleach, discolour, whiten.
OPPOSITES: SEE **brighten**.
2 *Daylight faded.* decline, decrease, dim, diminish, disappear, dwindle, evanesce, fail, melt away, pale, vanish, wane, weaken.
OPPOSITES: SEE **increase** verb.
3 *The flowers faded.* droop, flag, perish, shrivel, wilt, wither.
OPPOSITES: SEE **bloom** verb.

faeces noun SEE **excreta**.

fagged adjective SEE **tired**.

fail verb **1** *The engine failed.* break down, [*informal*] conk out, cut out, give out, give up, [*informal*] miss out, stop working.
OPPOSITES: SEE **succeed**.
2 *The attempt failed. The business failed.* be unsuccessful, close down, come to an end, [*informal*] come to grief, [*informal*] crash, fall through, [*informal*] flop, fold, fold up, founder, go bankrupt, [*informal*] go bust, go out of business, meet with disaster, miscarry, misfire, peter out, stop trading.
OPPOSITES: SEE **succeed**.
3 *The light failed.* decline, diminish, disappear, dwindle, fade, get worse, melt away, vanish, wane, weaken.
OPPOSITES: SEE **improve**.
4 *Don't fail to phone!* forget, neglect, omit.
OPPOSITES: SEE **remember**.
5 *She's upset: she thinks she failed us.* disappoint, [*informal*] let down.
OPPOSITES: SEE **please**.

failing noun SEE **weakness**.

failure noun **1** *a power failure.* breakdown, collapse, crash, stoppage.
2 *The attempt ended in failure.* defeat, disappointment, downfall, disaster, fiasco, [*informal*] flop, [*informal*] wash-out.
OPPOSITES: SEE **success**.

faint adjective **1** *a faint picture. faint colours.* blurred, dim, faded, hazy, ill-defined, indistinct, misty, pale, pastel (*pastel colours*), shadowy, unclear, vague.
OPPOSITES: SEE **clear** adjective.
2 *a faint smell.* delicate, slight.
OPPOSITES: SEE **strong**.
3 *a faint sound.* distant, hushed, low, muffled, muted, soft, subdued, thin, weak.
OPPOSITES: SEE **clear** adjective.
4 *to feel faint.* dizzy, exhausted, feeble, giddy, light-headed, unsteady, weak, [*informal*] woozy.

faint verb become unconscious, black out, collapse, [*informal*] flake out, pass out, swoon.

faint-hearted adjective SEE **timid**.

fair adjective **1** *fair hair.* blond, blonde, flaxen, golden, light, yellow.
2 [*old-fashioned*] *a fair maiden.* SEE **beautiful**.
3 *fair weather.* bright, clear, clement, cloudless, dry, favourable, fine, pleasant, sunny.
4 *a fair referee, a fair decision.* disinterested, even-handed, fair-minded, honest, honourable, impartial, just, lawful, legitimate, non-partisan, open-minded, proper, right, unbiased, unprejudiced, upright.
5 *a fair performance.* acceptable, adequate, average, indifferent, mediocre, middling, moderate, ordinary, passable, reasonable, respectable, satisfactory, [*informal*] so-so, tolerable.

fair noun **1** *the fun of the fair.* amusement park, carnival, fun-fair, gala.
2 *a Christmas fair.* bazaar, festival, fête, market, sale.
3 *a craft fair.* exhibition, show.

fairly adverb *fairly good.* moderately, pretty, quite, rather, reasonably, somewhat, tolerably, up to a point.

fairness noun SEE **impartiality**.

fairy noun OTHER LEGENDARY CREATURES: SEE **legend**.

fairy-tale noun SEE **story**.

fait accompli noun SEE **fact**.

faith noun **1** *faith that something will happen.* belief, confidence, trust.
2 *religious faith.* conviction, creed, devotion, SEE **religion**.
OPPOSITES: SEE **disbelief, doubt** noun.

faithful adjective **1** *a faithful companion.* close, consistent, constant, dependable, devoted, dutiful, loyal, reliable, staunch, trusty, trustworthy, unswerving.
2 *a faithful account of what happened.* accurate, exact, precise, SEE **true**.

faithless adjective SEE **disloyal**.

fake adjective *a fake antique.* artificial, bogus, counterfeit, ersatz, false, fictitious, forged, imitation, [*slang*] phoney, sham, simulated, synthetic, unreal.
OPPOSITES: SEE **genuine**.

fake noun **1** *The picture was a fake.* copy, duplicate, forgery, hoax, imitation, replica, reproduction, sham, simulation.
2 *The so-called expert was a fake.* charlatan, cheat, fraud, impostor, [*slang*] phoney, quack [= *fake doctor*].

fake verb *to fake a posh accent.* affect, copy, counterfeit, SEE **falsify**. feign, forge, fudge, imitate, pretend, put on, reproduce, sham, simulate.

fall noun **1** *a fall in prices.* collapse, crash, decline, decrease, descent, dip, dive, drop, lowering, plunge, reduction, slant, slope, tumble.
2 *the fall of a besieged town.* capitulation, defeat, surrender.

fall verb **1** *He fell off the wall.* collapse, [*informal*] come a cropper, crash down, dive, drop down, founder, keel over, overbalance, pitch, plummet, plunge, slump, stumble, topple, tumble.
2 *Silence fell.* come, come about, happen, occur, settle.
3 *The curtains fell in thick folds.* be suspended, cascade, dangle, dip down, hang.
4 *The water-level fell.* become lower, decline, decrease, diminish, dwindle, ebb, go down, lessen, sink, subside.
5 *The road falls to sea-level.* SEE **descend**.
6 *Millions fell in the war.* SEE **die**.
7 *The besieged town fell.* SEE **surrender** verb.
to fall out SEE **quarrel** verb.
to fall through SEE **fail**.

fallacious adjective SEE **false**.

fallacy noun SEE **error**.

fallible adjective *We're fallible, so we make mistakes.* erring, frail, human, imperfect, liable to make mistakes, uncertain, unpredictable, unreliable, weak.
OPPOSITES: SEE **infallible**.

fallow adjective *fallow land.* dormant, resting, uncultivated, unplanted, unsown, unused.

false adjective **1** *a false idea.* deceptive, erroneous, fallacious, inaccurate, incorrect, inexact, invalid, misleading, mistaken, spurious, unsound, untrue, wrong.
OPPOSITES: SEE **correct** adjective.
2 *a false friend.* deceitful, dishonest, disloyal, double-dealing, double-faced, faithless, lying, treacherous, unfaithful, unreliable, untrustworthy.
OPPOSITES: SEE **trustworthy**.
3 *false documents.* artificial, bogus, concocted, counterfeit, fake, fictitious, imitation, invented, made-up, mock, [*slang*] phoney, pretended, sham, simulated, synthetic, trumped-up, unfounded, unreal.
OPPOSITES: SEE **authentic**.
a false name SEE **pseudonym**.
false teeth dentures, plate.

falsehood noun SEE **lie** noun.

falsify verb *to falsify the facts.* alter, [*informal*] cook (*cook the books*), distort, exaggerate, SEE **fake** verb, misrepresent, oversimplify, pervert, slant, tamper with, tell lies about, twist.

falter verb **1** *to falter in the face of danger.* become weaker, flag, flinch, hesitate, hold back, lose confidence, pause, quail, stagger, stumble, totter, vacillate, waver.
OPPOSITES: SEE **persevere**.
2 *to falter in your speech.* stammer, stutter.

faltering adjective SEE **hesitant**.

fame noun *a superstar's fame.* celebrity, credit, distinction, eminence, glory, honour, importance, [*informal*] kudos, name, prestige, prominence, public esteem, renown, reputation, repute, [*informal*] stardom.

famed adjective SEE **famous**.

familiar adjective **1** *a familiar sight.* accustomed, common, conventional, customary, everyday, frequent, mundane, normal, ordinary, regular, routine, stock (*a stock reply*), usual, well-known.
OPPOSITES: SEE **strange**, unfamiliar.
2 *a familiar relationship. familiar language.* [*informal*] chatty, close, confidential, [*informal*] free-and-easy, SEE **friendly**, informal, intimate, near, relaxed, unceremonious.
OPPOSITES: SEE **formal**.
familiar with *Are you familiar with this music?* acquainted with, [*informal*] at home with, aware of, conscious of, expert in, informed about, knowledgeable about, trained in, versed in.

familiarize verb *Familiarize the new employee with our routine.* introduce (to), make familiar (with), teach.

family noun **1** [=*children of the same parents*] brood, [*informal*] flesh and blood (*our own flesh and blood*), generation, litter (*a litter of puppies*).
2 [=*the wider set of relations*] clan, kindred, [*old-fashioned*] kith and kin, relations, relatives, tribe.
3 [=*the line from which a person is descended*] *the royal family.* ancestry, blood, clan, dynasty, extraction, forebears, genealogy, house (*a royal house*), line, lineage, pedigree, race, strain.
RELATED ADJECTIVE: genealogical.

MEMBERS OF A FAMILY: adopted child, ancestor, aunt, brother, child, cousin, [*informal*] dad or daddy, daughter, descendant, divorcee, father, [*male*] fiancé, [*female*] fiancée, forefather, foster-child, foster-parent, godchild, godparent, grandchild, grandparent, guardian, husband, [*informal or American*] junior, kinsman or kinswoman, [*old-fashioned*] mater, mother, [*informal*] mum or mummy, nephew, next-of-kin, niece, offspring, orphan, parent, [*old-fashioned*] pater, quadruplet, quintuplet, relation, relative, sextuplet, sibling, sister, son, step-child, step-parent, triplet, twin, uncle, ward, widow, widower, wife.

---

famine noun *The drought caused widespread famine.* dearth, hunger, malnutrition, scarcity, shortage, starvation, want.
OPPOSITES: SEE **plenty**.

famished, famishing adjectives SEE **hungry**.

famous adjective *a famous person.* acclaimed, celebrated, distinguished, eminent, famed, great, historic, honoured, illustrious, important, legendary, lionized, notable, noted, outstanding, prominent, proverbial, renowned, time-honoured, well-known, world-famous.
OPPOSITES: SEE **unknown**.
famous person SEE **celebrity**.

fan noun **1** *an air-conditioning fan.* blower, extractor, propeller, ventilator.
2 *a pop music fan* SEE **fanatic**.

fanatic noun **1** *a pop music fanatic.* addict, admirer, aficionado, devotee, enthusiast, [*informal*] fan, [*informal*] fiend, follower, [*informal*] freak, lover, supporter.
2 *a political fanatic.* activist, adherent, bigot, extremist, fanatical supporter [SEE **fanatical**], militant, zealot.

fanatical adjective *fanatical political views.* bigoted, extreme, fervent, immoderate, irrational, militant, obsessive, over-enthusiastic, passionate, rabid, single-minded, zealous.
OPPOSITES: SEE **moderate** adjective.

fanciful adjective *a fanciful idea.* SEE **unrealistic.**

fancy adjective *fancy patterns.* SEE **decorative.**

fancy noun **1** *a poet's fancy.* SEE **imagination.**
2 *a fancy to do something.* SEE **whim.**

fancy verb **1** *I fancied I saw pink elephants.* SEE **imagine.**
2 *What do you fancy to eat?* SEE **desire** verb.

fanfare noun MUSICAL COMPOSITIONS: SEE **music.**

fang noun SEE **tooth.**

fanlight noun SEE **window.**

fantasize verb SEE **day-dream** verb.

fantastic adjective **1** *fantastic decoration.* absurd, elaborate, exaggerated, extravagant, fanciful, grotesque, ostentatious, quaint, rococo.
OPPOSITES: SEE **plain** adjective.
2 *a fantastic story about dragons.* amazing, extraordinary, fabulous, far-fetched, imaginative, implausible, incredible, odd, remarkable, strange, unbelievable, unlikely, unrealistic, weird.
OPPOSITES: SEE **realistic.**
3 [*informal*] *We had a fantastic time.* SEE **excellent.**

fantasy noun *a fantasy about the future.* day-dream, delusion, dream, fancy, hallucination, illusion, invention, make-believe, reverie, vision.
OPPOSITES: SEE **reality.**

far adjective *far places.* SEE **distant.**

farce noun SEE **comedy.**

farcical adjective SEE **comic** adjective.

fare noun *the train fare to London.* charge, cost, fee, payment, price.

farewell adjective *a farewell speech.* goodbye, last, leaving, parting, valedictory.

farewell noun *a sad farewell.* SEE **goodbye,** [*informal*] send-off, valediction.

far-fetched adjective SEE **unlikely.**

far-reaching adjective *far-reaching effects.* SEE **influential.**

farm noun [*old-fashioned*] grange.

KINDS OF FARM: arable farm, croft, dairy farm, fish farm, fruit farm, livestock farm, organic farm, plantation, poultry farm, ranch, smallholding.

FARM BUILDINGS, ETC.: barn, barn-yard, byre, cowshed, dairy, Dutch barn, farmhouse, farmstead, farmyard, granary, haystack, milking parlour, outhouse, pigsty, rick, shed, silo, stable, sty.

FARMING EQUIPMENT: baler, combine harvester, cultivator, drill, harrow, harvester, hay fork, hoe, irrigation system, manure spreader, mower, planter, plough, scythe, tedder, tractor, trailer.

FARM WORKERS: [*American*] cowboy, [*old-fashioned*] dairymaid, farm manager, farm worker, labourer, [*old-fashioned*] land-girl, shepherd, stock-breeder, [*old-fashioned*] swineherd, [*old-fashioned*] yeoman.

CROPS GROWN ON FARMS: barley, cereals, corn, fodder, SEE **fruit,** maize, oats, potatoes, rape, rye, sugar-beet, sweet corn, SEE **vegetable,** wheat.

FARM ANIMALS: SEE **cattle,** chicken, cow, duck, fatstock, goat, goose, hen, horse, lamb, livestock, pig, SEE **poultry,** sheep, turkey.

---

farming noun agriculture, [*formal*] agronomy, crofting, husbandry.
RELATED ADJECTIVES: agricultural.

farrago noun SEE **jumble** noun.

farrier noun blacksmith, smith.

farrow verb SEE **birth (to give birth).**

fascinate verb **1** *He fascinated us with his tales.* attract, beguile, bewitch, captivate, charm, delight, enchant, engross, enthral, entrance, interest, rivet, spellbind.
2 *Some snakes fascinate their prey.* allure, entice, hypnotize, mesmerize.

fascinating adjective SEE **attractive.**

fascism noun POLITICAL TERMS: SEE **politics.**

fashion noun **1** *He behaved in a strange fashion.* manner, method, mode, way.
2 *the latest fashion in clothes.* convention, craze, cut, [*informal*] fad, line, look, pattern, rage (*it's all the rage*), style, taste, trend, vogue.

fashionable adjective *fashionable clothes.* chic, contemporary, current, elegant, [*informal*] in (*the in thing*), the latest, modern, modish, popular, smart, [*informal*] snazzy, sophisticated, stylish, tasteful, [*informal*] trendy, up-to-date, [*informal*] with it.
OPPOSITES: SEE **unfashionable.**

fast adjective **1** *a fast pace.* breakneck, brisk, expeditious, express (*express delivery*), hasty, headlong, high-speed, hurried, lively, [*informal*] nippy, precipitate, quick, rapid, smart, [*informal*] spanking, speedy, supersonic, swift, unhesitating.
OPPOSITES: SEE **slow** adjective.
2 *Make the rope fast.* attached, fastened, firm, immobile, immovable, secure, tight.
OPPOSITES: SEE **loose** adjective.
3 *fast colours.* fixed, indelible, lasting, permanent, stable.
OPPOSITES: SEE **impermanent**.
4 *fast living.* SEE **immoral**.

fast adverb *travelling fast.* at full tilt, briskly, in no time, post-haste, quickly, rapidly, swiftly.

fast verb *to fast on a holy day.* abstain, deny yourself, diet, go hungry, go without food, starve.
OPPOSITE: indulge yourself [SEE **indulge**].

fasten verb affix, anchor, attach, batten, bind, bolt, buckle, button, chain, clamp, clasp, cling, close, connect, couple, do up (*do up a button*), fix, grip, hitch, hook, knot, join, lace, lash, latch on, link, lock, moor (*a boat*), nail, padlock, paste, pin, rivet (*metal plates*), rope, seal, secure, solder, staple, SEE **stick** verb, strap, tack, tape, tether (*an animal*), tie, unite, weld (*metal*).
OPPOSITES: SEE **undo**.

THINGS USED FOR FASTENING: anchor, bolt, buckle, button, catch, chain, clamp, clasp, clip, dowel, dowel-pin, drawing-pin, SEE **glue** noun, hasp, hook, knot, lace, latch, lock, mooring, nail, padlock, painter, peg, pin, rivet, rope, safety-pin, screw, seal, Sellotape, solder, staple, strap, string, tack, tape, tether, tie, toggle, velcro, wedge, zip.

---

fastener, **fastening** nouns connection, connector, coupling, link, linkage.

fastidious adjective *a fastidious eater.* choosy, dainty, discriminating, finicky, fussy, particular, [*informal*] pernickety, selective, squeamish.

fat adjective **1** *a fat figure.* chubby, corpulent, dumpy, SEE **enormous**, flabby, fleshy, gross, heavy, obese, overweight, paunchy, plump, podgy, portly, pot-bellied, pudgy, rotund, round, solid, squat, stocky, stout, tubby.
OPPOSITES: SEE **thin** adjective.
2 *fat meat.* fatty, greasy, oily.
OPPOSITE: lean.
3 *a fat book.* bulky, thick, weighty.

fat noun KINDS OF FAT: [*formal*] adipose tissue, blubber, butter, dripping, grease, lard, margarine, oil, suet.

fatal adjective **1** *a fatal dose.* deadly, lethal.
2 *a fatal illness.* final, incurable, malignant, mortal, terminal.
3 *a fatal mistake.* calamitous, destructive, disastrous, vital.

fatality noun *The accident resulted in fatalities.* casualty, death, loss.

fate noun **1** *Fate was kind to him.* chance, destiny, doom, fortune, karma, kismet, luck, nemesis, predestination, providence, the stars.
2 *He met a terrible fate.* death, demise, end.

fated adjective *I was fated to miss that train.* certain, destined, doomed, foreordained, intended, predestined, predetermined, preordained, sure.

fateful adjective *a fateful decision.* SEE **momentous**.

fat-head noun SEE **idiot**.

father noun [*informal*] dad or daddy, parent, [*old-fashioned*] pater.

fathom verb *I can't fathom what he's getting at.* SEE **understand**.

fatigue noun *overcome with fatigue.* debility, exhaustion, feebleness, lethargy, tiredness, weakness, weariness.

fatigue verb SEE **tire**.

fatstock noun farm animals, livestock.

fatten verb *to fatten cattle.* build up, feed up, make fat.

fatty adjective *fatty food.* fat, greasy, oily.

fatuous adjective *fatuous jokes.* SEE **silly**.

fault noun **1** *a fault in the engine.* blemish, defect, deficiency, failure, flaw, imperfection, malfunction, snag, weakness.
2 *a fault in your reasoning.* error, fallacy, inaccuracy, miscalculation, mistake.
3 *The mistake was my fault.* blunder, [*informal*] boob, demerit, failing, guilt, indiscretion, lapse, misconduct, misdeed, negligence, offence, omission, oversight, responsibility, shortcoming, sin, slip, [*informal*] transgression, [*old-fashioned*] trespass, wrongdoing.

fault verb *I can't fault his work.* SEE **criticize**.

faultless adjective SEE **perfect** adjective.

faulty adjective *faulty goods, a faulty argument.* broken, damaged, defective, deficient, flawed, illogical, imperfect, inaccurate, incomplete, incorrect,

inoperative, invalid, not working, out of order, unusable, useless.
OPPOSITES: SEE **perfect** adjective.

fauna noun animal-life, wildlife.
VARIOUS ANIMALS: SEE **animal** noun.

faux pas SEE **mistake** noun.

favour noun **1** *She shows favour towards her friends.* acceptance, approval, bias, favouritism, friendliness, goodwill, grace, liking, preference, support.
2 *He did me a favour.* benefit, courtesy, gift, good deed, good turn, indulgence, kindness, service.

favour verb **1** *She favours the original plan.* approve of, be in sympathy with, champion, choose, commend, esteem, [*informal*] fancy, [*informal*] go for, like, opt for, prefer, show favour to [SEE **favour** noun], think well of, value.
OPPOSITES: SEE **dislike** verb.
2 *The wind favoured our team.* abet, back, be advantageous to, befriend, SEE **help** verb, support.
OPPOSITES: SEE **hinder**.

favourable adjective **1** *a favourable wind. favourable comments.* advantageous, approving, auspicious, beneficial, benign, complimentary, encouraging, following (*a following wind*), friendly, generous, helpful, kind, positive, promising, propitious, reassuring, supportive, sympathetic, understanding, well-disposed.
OPPOSITES: SEE **unfavourable**.
2 *a favourable reputation.* agreeable, desirable, enviable, good, pleasing, satisfactory.
OPPOSITES: SEE **undesirable**.

favourite adjective *a favourable toy.* best, chosen, dearest, esteemed, liked, popular, preferred, well-liked.

favourite noun **1** *mother's favourite* [*informal*] apple of (someone's) eye, darling, idol, pet.
2 *the favourite in a race.* likely winner.

favouritism noun SEE **bias** noun.

fawn verb SEE **flatter**.

fealty noun SEE **loyalty**.

fear noun *trembling with fear.* alarm, anxiety, apprehension, awe, concern, consternation, cowardice, dismay, doubt, dread, faint-heartedness, foreboding, fright, [*informal*] funk, horror, misgiving, panic, [*formal*] phobia, qualm, suspicion, terror, timidity, trepidation, uneasiness, worry.
VARIOUS KINDS OF FEAR: SEE **phobia**.
OPPOSITES: SEE **courage**.

fear verb *to fear the worst.* be afraid of [SEE **afraid**], dread, suspect, tremble at, worry about.

fearful adjective **1** *fearful about the future.* SEE **afraid**.
2 *a fearful sight.* SEE **frightening**.

fearless adjective SEE **courageous**.

fearsome adjective SEE **frightening**.

feasible adjective **1** *a feasible plan.* achievable, attainable, possible, practicable, practical, realizable, viable, workable.
OPPOSITES: SEE **impractical**.
2 *a feasible excuse.* acceptable, credible, likely, plausible, reasonable.
OPPOSITES: SEE **implausible**.

feast noun SEE **meal**.

feat noun *a daring feat.* accomplishment, achievement, act, action, attainment, deed, exploit, performance.

feather noun plume, quill.
feathers down, plumage.

feather-brained adjective SEE **silly**.

feathery adjective downy, fluffy, light, wispy.

feature noun **1** *The crime had some unusual features.* aspect, characteristic, circumstance, detail, facet, peculiarity, point, quality, trait.
2 *a feature in a newspaper.* article, column, item, piece, report, story.
features *a person's features.* countenance, expression, face, lineaments, look, [*formal*] physiognomy.

feature verb *The play featured a new actor.* focus on, give prominence to, highlight, present, promote, show up, [*informal*] spotlight, [*informal*] star.

feckless adjective SEE **ineffective**.

fecund adjective SEE **fertile**.

federate verb SEE **unite**.

federation noun SEE **group** noun.

fee noun *a club membership fee. legal fees.* charge, cost, dues, fare, payment, price, remuneration, subscription, sum, terms, toll.

feeble adjective **1** *feeble after illness.* debilitated, delicate, exhausted, faint, frail, helpless, ill, inadequate, ineffective, listless, poorly, powerless, puny, sickly, useless, weak.
OPPOSITES: SEE **strong**.
2 *a feeble character.* effete, feckless, hesitant, incompetent, indecisive, ineffectual, irresolute, [*informal*] namby-pamby, spineless, vacillating, weedy, [*informal*] wishy-washy.
OPPOSITES: SEE **decisive**.
3 *a feeble excuse.* flimsy, lame, paltry, poor, tame, thin, unconvincing, weak.
OPPOSITES: SEE **convincing**.

feed verb **1** *to feed your children.* cater for, give food to, nourish, provide for, provision, strengthen, suckle.
2 *We fed well.* dine, eat, fare.
to feed on SEE **eat**.

feel verb **1** *to feel the texture of something.* caress, finger, fondle, handle, hold, manipulate, maul, [*informal*] paw, stroke, touch.
2 *to feel your way in the dark.* explore, fumble, grope.
3 *to feel the cold.* be aware of, be conscious of, detect, experience, know, notice, perceive, sense, suffer, undergo.
4 *It feels cold.* appear, give the feeling of [SEE **feeling**], seem.
5 *I feel it's time to go.* believe, consider, deem, have a feeling [SEE **feeling**], judge, think.

feeling noun **1** *a feeling in my leg.* sensation, sense of touch, sensitivity.
2 *feelings of love. feelings of hate.* ardour, emotion, fervour, passion, sentiment, warmth.
3 *a feeling that something is wrong.* attitude, belief, consciousness, guess, hunch, idea, impression, instinct, intuition, notion, opinion, perception, thought, view.
4 *a feeling for music.* fondness, responsiveness, sensibility, sympathy, understanding.
5 [*informal*], *a Christmassy feeling.* aura, atmosphere, mood, tone, [*informal*] vibrations.

feign verb SEE **pretend**.

feint noun SEE **pretence**.

felicitate verb SEE **congratulate**.

felicitous adjective SEE **appropriate** adjective.

felicity noun SEE **happiness**.

feline adjective cat-like.

fell noun SEE **hill**.

fell verb **1** *to fell an opponent.* bring down, flatten, [*informal*] floor, knock down, prostrate.
2 *to fell trees.* chop down, cut down.

fellow noun SEE **man** noun.

fellowship noun SEE **friendship**, **society**.

felon noun SEE **criminal** noun.

felony noun SEE **crime**.

female adjective, noun SEE **feminine**.
RELATED ADJECTIVE: gynaecological.
OPPOSITES: SEE **male**.

FEMALE PEOPLE: aunt, [*old-fashioned*] damsel, daughter, [*old-fashioned*] débutante, fiancée, girl, girlfriend, grandmother, lady, [*informal*] lass, lesbian, [*old-fashioned*] maid, [*old-fashioned*] maiden, [*old-fashioned*] mistress, mother, niece, sister, spinster, [*old-fashioned or insulting*] wench, wife, woman.

FEMALE CREATURES: bitch, cow, doe, ewe, hen, lioness, mare, nanny-goat, sow, tigress, vixen.

---

feminine adjective *feminine behaviour. feminine clothes.* [*of males*] effeminate, female, [*uncomplimentary*] girlish, ladylike, womanly.
OPPOSITES: SEE **masculine**.

fen noun bog, lowland, marsh, morass, quagmire, slough, swamp.

fence noun *a garden fence.* barricade, barrier, fencing, hedge, hurdle, obstacle, paling, palisade, railing, rampart, stockade, wall, wire.

fence verb **1** *to fence someone in.* circumscribe, confine, coop up, encircle, enclose, hedge in, immure, pen, surround, wall in.
2 *to fence with foils.* SEE **fight** verb.

fend verb **to fend for** care for, [*informal*] do for, look after.
to fend off SEE **repel**.

ferment noun *a state of ferment.* agitation, SEE **commotion**.

ferment verb *fermenting wine.* bubble, effervesce, [*informal*] fizz, foam, seethe, work.

ferocious adjective SEE **fierce**.

ferret verb **to ferret about** SEE **search** verb.

ferrous adjective iron.

ferry noun VARIOUS VESSELS: SEE **vessel**.

ferry verb *to ferry passengers.* SEE **convey**, drive, ship, shuttle, take across, taxi, transport.

fertile adjective **1** *a fertile garden.* abundant, fecund, flourishing, fruitful, lush, luxuriant, productive, prolific, rich, teeming, well-manured.
OPPOSITES: SEE **barren**.
2 *a fertile egg.* fertilized [SEE **fertilize**].
OPPOSITES: SEE **sterile**.

fertilize verb **1** *to fertilize flowers or eggs.* impregnate, inseminate, pollinate.
2 *to fertilize the soil.* add fertilizer to, cultivate, dress, enrich, feed, make fertile, manure, mulch, top-dress.

fertilizer noun compost, dressing, dung, manure, mulch.

fervent adjective *a fervent supporter.* ardent, avid, committed, devout, eager, earnest, enthusiastic, excited, fanatical, fervid, fiery, impassioned, keen, passionate, spirited, vehement, vigorous, warm, wholehearted, zealous.

fervour noun *The fervour of her speech showed she felt strongly.* ardour, eagerness, energy, enthusiasm, excitement, fervency, fire, heat, intensity, keenness, passion, sparkle, spirit, vehemence, vigour, warmth, zeal.

fester verb *The wound festered.* become infected, become inflamed, become poisoned, decay, discharge, gather, go bad, go septic, putrefy, suppurate, ulcerate.

festival noun *a bank-holiday festival.* anniversary, carnival, celebration, commemoration, fair, feast, festivity, fête, fiesta, gala, holiday, jamboree, jubilee, merry-making.

festive adjective *a festive occasion.* cheerful, cheery, convivial, gay, gleeful, happy, jolly, jovial, joyful, joyous, lighthearted, merry, uproarious.

festivities noun *Christmas festivities.* celebrations, entertainment, feasting, SEE **festival**, festive occasion [SEE **festive**], [*informal*] jollification, party, revelry, revels.

festoon verb SEE **decorate**.

fetch verb 1 *to fetch things from the shops.* bear, bring, call for, carry, collect, convey, get, import, obtain, pick up, retrieve, transfer, transport.
2 *How much would our car fetch?* be bought for, bring in, earn, go for, make, produce, raise, realize, sell for.

fetching adjective SEE **attractive**.

fête noun SEE **festival**.

fetid, foetid adjective SEE **smelly**.

fetish noun SEE **obsession**.

fetter noun, verb SEE **chain** noun, verb.

fettle noun SEE **condition**.

feud noun *a feud between two families.* animosity, antagonism, conflict, dispute, enmity, hostility, SEE **quarrel** noun, rivalry, strife, vendetta.

feud verb SEE **quarrel** verb.

fever noun delirium, feverishness, high temperature.
RELATED ADJECTIVE: febrile.

feverish adjective 1 *a feverish illness.* burning, febrile, fevered, flushed, hot, inflamed, trembling.
2 *feverish activity.* agitated, excited, frantic, frenetic, frenzied, hectic, hurried, impatient, restless.

few adjective *We have few buses on Sunday.* [*informal*] few and far between, inadequate, infrequent, rare, scarce, sparse, sporadic, [*informal*] thin on the ground, uncommon.
OPPOSITES: SEE **many**.

fiasco noun SEE **failure**.

fiat noun SEE **decree** noun.

fib noun, verb SEE **lie** noun, verb.

fibre noun 1 *woven fibres.* filament, hair, strand, thread.
2 *moral fibre.* backbone, SEE **courage**, determination, spirit, tenacity, toughness.

fickle adjective *They have no use for fickle supporters.* changeable, changing, disloyal, erratic, faithless, inconsistent, inconstant, mutable, treacherous, unfaithful, unpredictable, unreliable, unstable, [*informal*] up and down, vacillating, variable, volatile.
OPPOSITES: SEE **constant, stable**.

fiction noun 1 *a work of fiction.* VARIOUS KINDS OF WRITING: SEE **writing**.
2 *Her account was a fiction from start to finish.* concoction, deception, fabrication, fantasy, figment of the imagination, flight of fancy, invention, SEE **lie** noun, [*informal*] tall story.
OPPOSITES: SEE **fact**.

fictional adjective *a fictional story.* fabulous, fanciful, imaginary, invented, legendary, made-up, make-believe, mythical.
OPPOSITES: SEE **factual**.

fictitious adjective *a fictitious name.* apocryphal, assumed, SEE **fake** adjective, false, deceitful, fraudulent, imagined, invented, spurious, unreal, untrue.
OPPOSITES: SEE **genuine, true**.

fiddle noun 1 violin.
2 [*slang*] *a financial fiddle.* SEE **cheat** noun.

fiddle verb 1 *to fiddle with the knobs on the TV.* SEE **fidget**.
2 [*informal*] *to fiddle the accounts.* SEE **cheat** verb.

fiddling adjective *fiddling details.* SEE **trivial**.

fiddly adjective [*informal*] *a fiddly job.* SEE **intricate**.

fidelity noun SEE **loyalty**.

fidget verb *It annoys me when you fidget!* be restless, [*informal*] fiddle about, fret, frisk about, jerk about, [*informal*] jiggle, [*informal*] mess about, move restlessly, [*informal*] play about, twitch, worry.

fidgety adjective *fidgety movements.* agitated, frisky, impatient, jittery, jumpy, nervous, on edge, restive, restless, twitchy, uneasy.
OPPOSITES: SEE **calm** adjective.

field noun **1** *a farm field.* enclosure, [*poetic*] glebe, green, [*old-fashioned & poetic*] mead, meadow, paddock, pasture.
2 *a games field.* arena, ground, pitch, playing-field, recreation ground, stadium.
3 *Electronics isn't my field.* area, [*informal*] department, domain, province, sphere, subject, territory.

field-glasses noun binoculars.
OTHER OPTICAL INSTRUMENTS: SEE **optical.**

fiend noun **1** *a wicked fiend.* demon, devil, evil spirit, goblin, hobgoblin, imp, Satan, spirit.
2 *a cruel fiend.* SEE **savage** noun.

fiendish adjective SEE **evil** adjective, **fierce.**

fierce adjective **1** *a fierce attack. fierce animals.* angry, barbaric, barbarous, blood-thirsty, bloody, brutal, cold-blooded, cruel, dangerous, fearsome, ferocious, fiendish, homicidal, inhuman, merciless, murderous, pitiless, ruthless, sadistic, savage, untamed, vicious, violent, wild.
OPPOSITES: SEE **humane, kind** adjective.
2 *fierce opposition.* active, aggressive, competitive, eager, heated, furious, intense, keen, passionate, relentless, strong, unrelenting.
OPPOSITES: SEE **gentle.**
3 *a fierce fire.* SEE **fiery.**

fiery adjective **1** *a fiery furnace.* ablaze, aflame, blazing, burning, flaming, fierce, glowing, heated, hot, raging, red, red-hot.
2 *a fiery temper.* angry, ardent, choleric, excitable, fervent, furious, hot-headed, intense, irritable, livid, mad, passionate, violent.

fight noun action, affray, attack, battle, bout, brawl, [*informal*] brush, [*informal*] bust-up, clash, combat, competition, conflict, confrontation, contest, counter-attack, dispute, dogfight, duel, [*informal*] dust-up, encounter, engagement, feud, [*old-fashioned*] fisticuffs, fracas, fray, [*informal*] free-for-all, hostilities, joust, SEE **martial (martial arts)**, match, mêlée, [*informal*] punch-up, SEE **quarrel** noun, raid, riot, rivalry, row, scramble, scrap, scrimmage, scuffle, [*informal*] set-to, skirmish, squabble, strife, struggle, tussle, war, wrangle.

fight verb **1** *to fight against an enemy.* attack, battle, box, brawl, [*informal*] brush, clash, compete, conflict, contend, do battle, duel, engage, exchange blows, fence, feud, grapple, have a fight [SEE **fight** noun], joust, quarrel, row, scrap, scuffle, skirmish, spar, squabble, stand up (to), strive, struggle, [*old-fashioned*] tilt, tussle, wage war, wrestle.
2 *to fight a decision.* campaign against, contest, defy, oppose, protest against, resist, take a stand against.

fighter noun aggressor, antagonist, attacker, belligerent, campaigner, combatant, contender, contestant, defender.

VARIOUS FIGHTERS: archer, boxer, [*informal*] brawler, champion, duellist, freedom-fighter, gladiator, guerrilla, gunman, knight, marine, marksman, mercenary, partisan, prize-fighter, pugilist, sniper, SEE **soldier**, swordsman, terrorist, warrior, wrestler.

---

figment noun *a figment of the imagination.* SEE **invention.**

figurative adjective *figurative language.* allegorical, metaphorical, poetic, symbolic.
OPPOSITES: SEE **literal.**

figure noun **1** *the figures 1 to 10.* amount, digit, integer, number, numeral, value.
figures *She's good at figures.* accounts, mathematics, statistics, sums.
2 *a diagrammatic figure.* diagram, drawing, graph, illustration, outline, representation.
3 *a plump figure.* body, build, form, physique, shape, silhouette.
4 *a bronze figure.* SEE **sculpture** noun.
5 *a well-known figure.* SEE **personality.**
figure of speech conceit, emblem, image, [*informal*] manner of speaking, trope.

COMMON FIGURES OF SPEECH: alliteration, anacoluthon, antithesis, assonance, climax, ellipsis, hendiadys, hyperbole, irony, litotes, meiosis, metaphor, metonymy, onomatopoeia, oxymoron, parenthesis, personification, simile, synecdoche, zeugma.

---

figure verb *Macbeth figures in a Shakespeare play.* SEE **appear.**
to figure out 1 *to figure out an answer.* add up, calculate, compute, count, reckon, total, [*informal*] tot up, work out.
2 *to figure out what something means.* comprehend, fathom, make out, puzzle out, reason out, see, understand.

figurine noun SEE **sculpture** noun.

filament noun SEE **fibre.**

filch verb SEE **steal.**

file noun **1** *a file for papers.* binder, box-file, cover, document-case, dossier, folder, portfolio, ring-binder.
2 *single file.* column, line, procession, queue, rank, row, stream, string, train.

file verb **1** *to file rough edges off something.* SEE **smooth** verb.
2 *to file documents.* enter, organize, pigeon-hole, put away, store.
3 *to file through a door.* march, parade, proceed in a line, stream, troop.

filibuster verb SEE **delay** verb.

fill verb **1** *to fill a container.* cram, flood (*with liquid*), inflate (*with air*), load, pack, refill, replenish, [*informal*] stuff, [*informal*] top up.
OPPOSITES: SEE **empty** verb.
2 *to fill a gap.* block, [*informal*] bung up, clog, close up, crowd, jam, obstruct, plug, seal, stop up.
OPPOSITES: SEE **clear** verb.
3 *to fill a need.* fulfil, furnish, meet, provide, satisfy, supply.
4 *to fill a post.* hold, occupy, take up.
to fill out *His figure filled out after his illness.* enlarge, expand, get bigger, make bigger, swell.

filling noun *the filling in a cushion.* contents, insides, padding, stuffing.

filling-station noun garage, petrol station.

fillip noun SEE **impetus.**

filly noun SEE **horse.**

film noun **1** *a film of oil.* coat, coating, covering, layer, membrane, sheet, skin, slick, tissue, veil.
2 *a cinema film.* [*old-fashioned*] flick, motion picture, movie, picture, video.

KINDS OF FILM: cartoon, comedy, documentary, epic, feature, horror film, short, western.

---

filter noun gauze, membrane, mesh, screen, sieve, strainer.

filter verb *to filter a liquid.* clarify, filtrate, percolate, purify, screen, sieve, strain.

filth noun *Clean up this filth!* dirt, SEE **excreta**, garbage, grime, SEE **impurity**, muck, mud, pollution, refuse, scum, sewage, slime, sludge.

filthy adjective **1** *filthy shoes. a filthy room.* caked, dirty, disgusting, dusty, foul, grimy, grubby, impure, messy, mucky, muddy, nasty, slimy, smelly, soiled, sooty, sordid, squalid, stinking, uncleaned, unwashed.
OPPOSITES: SEE **clean** adjective.
2 *filthy language.* SEE **obscene.**

final adjective *the final moments of a game.* clinching, closing, concluding, conclusive, decisive, dying, eventual, last, terminal, terminating, ultimate.
OPPOSITES: SEE **introductory.**

finale noun SEE **conclusion.**

finalize verb SEE **complete** verb.

finance noun *He works in finance.* accounting, banking, business, commerce, investment, stocks and shares.
finances *What's the state of your finances?* assets, bank account, budget, funds, income, money, resources, wealth.

finance verb *The bank helped to finance our business.* back, fund, invest in, pay for, provide money for, sponsor, subsidize, support, underwrite.

financial adjective *financial affairs.* economic, fiscal, monetary, pecuniary.

financier noun SEE **businessman.**

find verb **1** *to find something new.* acquire, arrive at, become aware of, chance upon, come across, come upon, dig up, discover, encounter, expose, [*informal*] ferret out, happen on, hit on, learn, light on, locate, meet, note, notice, observe, reach, recognize, spot, stumble on, uncover, unearth.
2 *to find something that was lost.* get back, recover, rediscover, regain, retrieve, trace, track down.
3 *to find a fault.* detect, diagnose, identify.
4 *He found me a job.* give, pass on, procure, provide, supply.

findings noun *The judge announced his findings.* conclusion, decision, judgement, verdict.

fine adjective **1** *a fine performance.* admirable, commendable, excellent, first-class, SEE **good.**
2 *fine weather.* bright, clear, cloudless, fair, pleasant, sunny.
3 *fine thread. fine china.* delicate, flimsy, fragile, narrow, slender, slim, thin.
4 *fine sand.* minute, powdery.
5 *fine embroidery.* beautiful, dainty, delicate, exquisite, skilful.
6 *a fine distinction.* discriminating, fine-drawn, subtle.

fine noun *a parking fine.* charge, penalty.
OTHER PUNISHMENTS: SEE **punishment.**

finesse noun SEE **delicacy.**

finger noun digit, fingertip, index finger, little finger, middle finger, ring finger.

finger verb SEE **touch** verb.

finicky adjective SEE **fastidious.**

finish noun **1** *the finish of a race.* cessation, close, completion, conclusion, culmination, end, ending, finale, resolution, result, termination.
2 *a shiny finish on the metalwork.* appearance, gloss, lustre, polish, shine, smoothness, surface, texture.
3 *Their performance lacked finish.* completeness, perfection, polish.

finish verb **1** *to finish a job.* accomplish, achieve, break off, bring to an end, cease, complete, conclude, discontinue, end, finalize, halt, perfect, reach the end of, round off, sign off, stop, terminate, [*informal*] wind up.
2 *to finish your rations.* consume, drink up, eat up, empty, exhaust, expend, get through, [*informal*] polish off, [*informal*] say goodbye to, use up.
3 [*informal*] *The effort finished me.* exhaust, tire out, wear out.
to finish off annihilate, destroy, dispatch, exterminate, SEE **kill**.

finite adjective *finite resources. a finite number.* calculable, definable, defined, fixed, known, limited, measurable, numbered, restricted.
OPPOSITES: SEE **infinite**.

fire noun **1** blaze, burning, combustion, conflagration, flames, holocaust, inferno, pyre.
2 *a fire in the lounge.* fireplace, grate, hearth.

KINDS OF FIRE OR HEATING APPARATUS: boiler, bonfire, brazier, central heating, convector, electric fire, SEE **fireworks**, forge, furnace, gas fire, immersion-heater, incinerator, kiln, oven, radiator, stove.

---

fire verb **1** *The vandals fired a barn.* burn, ignite, kindle, light, put a light to, set alight, set fire to.
2 *to fire pottery.* bake, heat.
3 *to fire your imagination.* animate, enliven, excite, incite, inflame, inspire, rouse, stimulate, stir.
4 *to fire a gun or missile.* detonate, discharge, explode, launch, let off, set off, shoot, trigger off.
5 *to fire someone from a job.* dismiss, make redundant, sack, throw out.
to fire at *I fired at the target.* aim at, bombard, [*informal*] let fly at, shell, shoot at.

firearm noun SEE **gun**.

firelight noun SEE **light** noun.

fireman noun fire-fighter.

fireplace noun SEE **fire** noun.

fireproof adjective *fireproof material.* flameproof, incombustible, non-flammable.
OPPOSITES: SEE **inflammable**.

fire-raiser noun arsonist, pyromaniac.

firewood noun kindling.

fireworks noun pyrotechnics.
VARIOUS FIREWORKS: banger, Catherine wheel, cracker, rocket, Roman candle, sparkler, squib.

firing noun SEE **gunfire**.

firm adjective **1** *firm ground.* compact, compressed, congealed, dense, hard, rigid, solid, stable, stiff, unyielding.
OPPOSITES: SEE **soft**.
2 *a firm fit.* anchored, fast, fixed, immovable, secure, steady, tight.
3 *firm convictions.* adamant, decided, determined, dogged, obstinate, persistent, resolute, unshakeable, unwavering.
4 *a firm arrangement.* agreed, settled, unchangeable.
5 *a firm friend.* constant, dependable, devoted, faithful, loyal, reliable.

firm noun *a business firm.* business, company, concern, corporation, establishment, organization.

first adjective **1** *first signs of spring.* earliest, foremost, initial, leading, soonest.
2 *the first thing to consider.* basic, cardinal, chief, fundamental, key, main, paramount, predominant, primary, prime, principal, uppermost.
3 *first steps in arithmetic.* elementary, introductory, preliminary, rudimentary.
4 *the first version of something.* archetypal, eldest, embryonic, oldest, original, primeval.
5 *the first authority on a subject.* dominant, foremost, head, highest, outstanding, prime, top.
first aid SEE **treatment**.
first name Christian name, forename, given name, personal name.

first-class, first-rate adjectives SEE **excellent**.

first-hand adjective *first-hand knowledge.* direct, empirical, personal.

fiscal adjective SEE **financial**.

fish noun OTHER CREATURES: SEE **animal** noun.

VARIOUS FISH: brill, brisling, carp, catfish, chub, cod, coelacanth, conger, cuttlefish, dab, dace, eel, flounder, goldfish, grayling, gudgeon, haddock, hake, halibut, herring, jellyfish, lamprey, ling, mackerel, minnow, mullet, perch, pike, pilchard, piranha, plaice, roach, salmon, sardine, sawfish, shark, skate, sole, sprat, squid, starfish, stickleback, sturgeon, swordfish, [*informal*] tiddler, trout, tuna, turbot, whitebait, whiting.

PARTS OF A FISH: dorsal fin, fin, gills, roe, scales, tail.

---

fish verb angle, go fishing [SEE **fishing**], trawl.

fisher noun angler, fisherman, trawlerman.

fishing noun angling, trawling.
RELATED ADJECTIVE: piscatorial.
fishing tackle gaff, line, net, rod.

fish-tank noun aquarium.

fishy adjective SEE **suspicious**.

fissure noun SEE **split** noun.

fist noun *a clenched fist.* hand, knuckles.

fisticuffs noun SEE **fight** noun.

fit adjective **1** *The house isn't fit to live in.* adapted, adequate, equipped, good enough, satisfactory, sound.
OPPOSITES: SEE **unfit**.
2 *Her rude song isn't fit for your ears!* apposite, appropriate, apt, becoming, befitting, decent, fitting, proper, right, seemly, suitable.
OPPOSITES: SEE **inappropriate**.
3 *Are you fit to play?* able, capable, competent, in good form, healthy, prepared, ready, strong, well enough.
OPPOSITES: SEE **ill**.

fit noun *a fit of coughing.* attack, bout, convulsion, eruption, explosion, outbreak, outburst, paroxysm, seizure, spasm, spell.

fit verb **1** *My jeans don't fit me.* be the right shape and size for.
2 *Fit the pieces together.* arrange, assemble, build, construct, dovetail, install, interlock, join, match, position, put in place, put together.
3 *Wear clothes to fit the occasion.* accord with, become, be fitting for [SEE **fitting**], conform with, correspond with or to, go with, harmonize with, suit.

fitful adjective SEE **spasmodic**.

fitting adjective *a fitting memorial.* apposite, appropriate, apt, becoming, befitting, decent, due, fitting, proper, right, seemly, suitable, timely.
OPPOSITES: SEE **inappropriate**.

fix noun *I got into a fix.* corner, difficulty, dilemma, [*informal*] hole, [*informal*] jam, mess, plight, predicament, problem, quandary.

fix verb **1** *to fix something into place.* attach, bind, connect, embed, SEE **fasten**, implant, install, join, link, make firm, plant, position, secure, stabilize, stick.
2 *to fix a price. to fix a time.* agree, appoint, arrange, arrive at, confirm, decide, establish, finalize, name, ordain, settle, sort out, specify.
3 [*informal*] *to fix a broken window.* make good, mend, put right, repair.

fixative noun SEE **glue** noun.

fixture noun *a home fixture.* date, engagement, game, match, meeting.

fizz verb bubble, effervesce, fizzle, foam, froth, hiss, sizzle.

fizzy adjective *fizzy drinks.* bubbly, effervescent, foaming, sparkling.
OPPOSITE: still.

flabbergasted adjective SEE **surprised**.

flabby adjective [*informal*] *flabby muscles.* SEE **fat** adjective, feeble, flaccid, floppy, limp, loose, out of condition, slack, weak.
OPPOSITES: SEE **firm** adjective.

flaccid adjective SEE **flabby**.

flag noun *decorated with flags.* banner, bunting, colours, ensign, pennant, pennon, standard, streamer.

flag verb **1** *Our interest flagged.* SEE **decline** verb.
2 *The police flagged me down.* SEE **signal** verb.

flagellate verb SEE **whip** verb.

flagrant adjective SEE **obvious**.

flail verb SEE **beat** verb.
to flail about SEE **wave** verb.

flair noun SEE **talent**.

flake noun *flakes of old paint. flakes of flint.* bit, chip, leaf, scale, shaving, slice, splinter, wafer.

flamboyant adjective SEE **showy**.

flame noun SEE **fire** noun.

flame verb blaze, SEE **burn** verb, flare.

flammable adjective SEE **inflammable**.

flap verb *The sail flapped in the wind.* beat, flutter, sway, swing, thrash about, wag, wave about.

flare verb blaze, SEE **burn** verb, erupt, flame.
to flare up SEE **angry (to become angry)**.

flash verb **1** *Lights flashed on and off.* flicker, glare, glint, SEE **light** noun **(to give light)**, sparkle, twinkle.

flashlight noun SEE **torch**.

flashy adjective SEE **showy**.

flask noun SEE **bottle** noun.

flat adjective **1** *The snooker-table must be flat.* horizontal, level, levelled.

OPPOSITES: SEE **vertical**.
2 *lying flat in bed.* outstretched, prone, prostrate, recumbent, spread-eagled, spread out, supine.
OPPOSITES: SEE **upright**.
3 *a flat sea.* calm, even, smooth, unbroken, unruffled.
OPPOSITES: SEE **uneven**.
4 *a flat voice.* boring, dry, dull, insipid, lacklustre, lifeless, monotonous, spiritless, tedious, unexciting, uninteresting, unmodulated, unvarying.
OPPOSITES: SEE **lively**.
5 *a flat tyre.* blown out, burst, deflated, punctured.
OPPOSITE: inflated.

flat noun *living in a flat.* apartment, bedsitter, flatlet, maisonette, penthouse.

flatten verb *to flatten a rough surface.* even out, iron out, level out, press, roll, smooth.
2 *They flattened the flowers.* compress, crush, demolish, SEE **destroy**, devastate, level, raze, run over, squash, trample.
3 [*informal*] *He flattened his opponent.* SEE **defeat** verb, fell, floor, knock down, prostrate.

flatter verb 1 be flattering to [SEE **flattering**], [*informal*] butter up, compliment, curry favour with, fawn on, humour, [*informal*] play up to, praise, [*slang*] suck up to, [*informal*] toady to.
OPPOSITES: SEE **insult** verb.

flatterer noun [*informal*] crawler, [*informal*] creep, groveller, lackey, sycophant, [*informal*] toady, [*informal*] yes-man.

flattering adjective *flattering remarks.* adulatory, complimentary, effusive, fawning, fulsome, ingratiating, insincere, mealy-mouthed, obsequious, servile, sycophantic, unctuous.
OPPOSITES: SEE **insulting, sincere**.

flattery noun adulation, blandishments, [*informal*] blarney, fawning, [*informal*] flannel, insincerity, obsequiousness, servility, [*informal*] soft soap, sycophancy, unctuousness.

flatulence noun SEE **indigestion**.

flaunt verb SEE **display** verb.

flavour noun 1 *the flavour of food.* SEE **taste** noun.
2 *a film with an oriental flavour.* atmosphere, character, characteristic, feel, feeling, property, quality, style.

flavour verb *I flavoured the meat with herbs.* season, spice.

flavouring noun *peppermint flavouring.* additive, essence, extract, seasoning.

flaw noun *a flaw in someone's work. a flaw in a piece of china.* SEE **blemish**, break, chip, crack, error, fallacy, imperfection, inaccuracy, mistake, shortcoming, slip, split, weakness.

flawed adjective SEE **imperfect**.

flawless adjective SEE **perfect** adjective.

flaxen adjective *flaxen hair.* SEE **fair** adjective.

flay verb SEE **strip** verb.

fleck noun SEE **speck**.

flecked adjective SEE **speckled**.

fledgeling noun BIRDS: SEE **bird**.

flee verb *to flee from invaders.* abscond, [*informal*] beat a retreat, bolt, clear off, disappear, escape, fly, hurry off, make off, retreat, run away, [*slang*] scarper, [*informal*] take to your heels, vanish, withdraw.

fleece noun down, SEE **hair**, wool.

fleece verb SEE **defraud**.

fleet adjective SEE **swift** adjective.

fleet noun *a fleet of ships.* armada, convoy, flotilla, navy, squadron, task force.

fleeting adjective *a fleeting moment.* SEE **brief** adjective, ephemeral, evanescent, impermanent, momentary, mutable, passing, short-lived, transitory.
OPPOSITES: SEE **lasting**.

flesh noun *an animal's flesh.* carrion [=*dead flesh*], fat, meat, muscle, tissue.
flesh and blood 1 *The pain was more than flesh and blood could stand.* the body, human nature, physical nature.
2 *Your children are your flesh and blood.* SEE **family**.

flex noun *a flex for an electric iron.* cable, lead, wire.

flex verb SEE **bend** verb.

flexible adjective 1 *flexible wire.* bendable, [*informal*] bendy, floppy, limp, pliable, soft, springy, supple, whippy.
OPPOSITES: SEE **brittle, rigid**.
2 *flexible arrangements.* adjustable, alterable, fluid, mutable, open, provisional, variable.
OPPOSITES: SEE **immutable**.
3 *a flexible person.* accommodating, adaptable, amenable, compliant, open-minded, responsive, tractable, willing to please.
OPPOSITES: SEE **inflexible**.

flick verb SEE **hit** verb.

flicker verb *The candles flickered.* blink, flutter, glimmer, SEE **light** noun (**to give light**), quiver, tremble, twinkle, waver.

flight noun 1 *the flight of a missile.* SEE **journey**, trajectory.

2 *a flight from danger.* SEE **escape** noun.

flimsy adjective **1** *the flimsy wings of a butterfly.* brittle, delicate, fine, fragile, frail, insubstantial, light, slight, thin.
OPPOSITES: SEE **substantial**.
2 *a flimsy structure.* decrepit, gimcrack, loose, makeshift, rickety, shaky, tottering, weak, wobbly.
OPPOSITES: SEE **sturdy**.
3 *a flimsy argument.* feeble, implausible, superficial, trivial, unconvincing, unsatisfactory.
OPPOSITES: SEE **convincing**.

flinch verb *to flinch in alarm.* blench, cower, cringe, dodge, draw back, duck, falter, jerk away, jump, quail, quake, recoil, shrink back, shy away, start, swerve, wince.
to flinch from *to flinch from your duty.* avoid, evade, shirk, shrink from.

fling verb SEE **throw** verb.

flinty adjective SEE **hard**.

flip verb SEE **hit** verb.

flippant adjective SEE **frivolous**.

flipper noun SEE **limb**.

flirt noun [*woman*] coquette, [*man*] philanderer, [*informal*] tease.

flirt verb SEE **love** noun (**to make love**).

flirtatious adjective amorous, coquettish, flirty, [*uncomplimentary*] promiscuous, teasing.

flit verb SEE **move** verb.

float verb **1** *to float on water.* bob, drift, sail, swim.
2 *to float in the air.* glide, hang, hover, waft.
3 *to float a ship.* launch.
OPPOSITES: SEE **sink** verb.

flock noun SEE **group** noun.

floe noun ice, iceberg.

flog verb beat, birch, cane, flagellate, flay, SEE **hit** verb, lash, scourge, thrash, [*slang*] wallop, whack, whip.

flood noun **1** *a flood of water.* deluge, downpour, flash-flood, inundation, overflow, rush, spate, tide, torrent.
OPPOSITES: drought, trickle.
2 *a flood of imports.* excess, large quantity, plethora, superfluity.
OPPOSITES: SEE **scarcity**.

flood verb *The river flooded the town.* cover, drown, engulf, fill up, immerse, inundate, overflow, overwhelm, sink, submerge, swamp.

floodlights noun SEE **light** noun.

floor noun **1** deck, floorboards.
FLOOR COVERINGS: carpet, lino, linoleum, mat, matting, parquet, rug, tiles.
2 *first floor. top floor.* deck, level, storey, tier.

flop verb **1** *The seedlings flopped in the heat.* collapse, dangle, droop, drop, fall, flag, hang down, sag, slump, wilt.
2 *The business flopped.* SEE **fail**.

floppy adjective *floppy lettuce leaves.* droopy, flabby, SEE **flexible**, hanging loose, limp, pliable, soft.
OPPOSITES: SEE **crisp, rigid**.

flora noun botany, plant-life, plants, vegetation.

florid adjective **1** *florid decoration.* SEE **ornate**.
2 *a florid complexion.* SEE **ruddy**.

florist noun flower-shop.

flotilla noun SEE **fleet** noun.

flotsam noun SEE **wreckage**.
flotsam and jetsam SEE **junk**.

flounce verb *She flounced out of the room.* SEE **move** verb.

flounder verb **1** *to flounder in mud.* flail, fumble, grope, move clumsily, stagger, struggle, stumble, tumble, wallow.
2 *to flounder through a speech.* falter, get confused, make mistakes, talk aimlessly.

flourish noun SEE **gesture** noun.

flourish verb **1** *The plants flourished after the rain. Trade flourished in the sales.* be fruitful, be successful, bloom, blossom, boom, burgeon, develop, do well, flower, grow, increase, [*informal*] perk up, progress, prosper, strengthen, succeed, thrive.
OPPOSITES: SEE **fail, wilt**.
2 *He flourished his umbrella.* brandish, flaunt, gesture with, shake, swing, twirl, wag, wave.

flout verb *to flout the rules.* SEE **disobey**.

flow noun *a steady flow.* cascade, course, current, drift, ebb (*the ebb and flow of the tide*), effusion, flood, gush, outpouring, spate, spurt, stream, tide, trickle.

flow verb *Liquids flow.* bleed, cascade, course, dribble, drift, drip, ebb, flood, flush, glide, gush, issue, leak, move in a flow [SEE **flow** noun], ooze, overflow, pour, ripple, roll, run, seep, spill, spring, spurt, squirt, stream, trickle, well, well up.

flower noun *flowers in the garden.* bloom, blossom, floret, petal.
a bunch of flowers arrangement, bouquet, garland, posy, spray, wreath.

VARIOUS FLOWERS: begonia, bluebell, buttercup, campanula, campion, candytuft, carnation, catkin, celandine, chrysanthemum, coltsfoot, columbine, cornflower, cowslip, crocus, crowfoot, cyclamen, daffodil, dahlia, daisy, dandelion.

forget-me-not, foxglove, freesia, geranium, gladiolus, gypsophila, harebell, hollyhock, hyacinth, iris, jonquil, kingcup, lilac, lily, lupin, marguerite, marigold, montbretia, nasturtium, orchid.

pansy, pelargonium, peony, periwinkle, petunia, phlox, pink, polyanthus, poppy, primrose, rhododendron, rose, saxifrage, scabious, scarlet pimpernel, snowdrop, speedwell, sunflower, tulip, violet, wallflower, water-lily.

PARTS OF A FLOWER: axil, bract, calyx, carpel, corolla, perianth, pistil, pollen, sepal, stamen, whorl.

---

flower verb *Most plants flower in the summer.* bloom, blossom, [*poetic*] blow, SEE **flourish** verb, have flowers, open out.

flowery adjective *a flowery style of writing.* SEE **ornate**.

fluctuate verb SEE **vary**.

flue noun chimney.

fluent adjective *a fluent speaker.* articulate, effortless, eloquent, [*uncomplimentary*] facile, flowing, [*uncomplimentary*] glib, natural, polished, ready, smooth, voluble, unhesitating.
OPPOSITES: SEE **hesitant**.

fluff noun down, dust, floss, fuzz, thistledown.

fluff verb *to fluff a pillow.* make fluffy, shake, soften.

fluffy adjective *fluffy toys.* downy, feathery, fibrous, fleecy, furry, fuzzy, hairy, silky, soft, velvety, woolly.

fluid adjective **1** *a fluid substance.* aqueous, flowing, gaseous, liquefied, liquid, melted, molten, running, [*informal*] runny, sloppy, watery.
OPPOSITES: SEE **solid**.
2 *fluid movements.* SEE **graceful**.
3 *a fluid situation.* SEE **flexible**.

fluid noun *bodily fluids.* fluid substance [SEE **fluid** adjective], gas, liquid, plasma.

fluke noun *a lucky fluke.* accident, chance, stroke of good luck.

flummox verb SEE **baffle**.

flunkey noun SEE **servant**.

fluorescent adjective SEE **glowing**.

flurry noun *a flurry of activity.* SEE **commotion**.

flush adjective SEE **level** adjective.
flush with money SEE **wealthy**.

flush verb **1** *to flush with embarrassment.* blush, colour, glow, go red, redden.
2 *to flush a lavatory.* cleanse, [*informal*] pull the plug, rinse out, wash out.
3 *to flush a bird from its hiding-place.* chase out, drive out, expel, send up.

fluster verb SEE **confuse**.

flutter verb bat (*your eyelids*), flap, flicker, flit, move agitatedly, palpitate, quiver, tremble, vibrate.

flux noun SEE **instability**.

fly noun VARIOUS INSECTS: SEE **insect**.

fly verb **1** *Most birds fly.* ascend, flit, glide, hover, rise, soar, stay in the air, swoop, take wing.
2 *to fly an aircraft.* aviate, pilot, take off (in), travel (in).
3 *to fly a flag.* display, flap, flutter, hang up, hoist, raise, show, wave.
to fly at SEE **attack** verb.
to fly in the face of SEE **disregard**.
to fly off the handle SEE **angry** (**to become angry**).

flying adjective *a flying machine.* aeronautical, airborne, airworthy, gliding, hovering, soaring, winged.

flying noun [*formal*] aeronautics, airtravel, [*old-fashioned*] aviation, flight, [*informal*] jetting.
flying saucer spaceship, UFO.

flyover noun bridge, overpass, viaduct.

foal noun SEE **horse**.

foal verb SEE **birth** (**to give birth**).

foam noun **1** bubbles, effervescence, froth, head (*on beer*), lather, scum, spume, suds.
2 *a mattress made of foam.* sponge, spongy rubber.

foam verb *What makes the water foam?* boil, bubble, effervesce, fizz, froth, lather, make foam [SEE **foam** noun].

focus noun **1** *Get the camera into focus.* clarity, correct adjustment, sharpness.
2 *The cathedral is the main focus for tourism.* centre, core, focal point, heart, hub, pivot.

focus verb *to focus a camera.* adjust the lens.
to focus on *Focus on the main problem.* aim at, centre on, concentrate on, direct attention to, fix attention on, home in on, look at, spotlight, think about.

fodder noun *cattle fodder.* feed, food, forage, hay, provender, silage.

foe noun SEE **enemy**.

foetus noun embryo.

fog noun *fog on the motorway.* bad visibility, cloud, foggy conditions [SEE **foggy**], haze, mist, smog.

foggy adjective *foggy weather. a foggy picture.* blurry, clouded, dim, hazy, indistinct, misty, murky, obscure.
OPPOSITES: SEE **clear** adjective.

fogy, fogey noun *an old fogy.* SEE **old-fashioned (old-fashioned person).**

foible noun SEE **peculiarity.**

foil noun **1** *The thin comedian is a foil to his fat partner.* SEE **contrast** noun.
2 *fighting with foils.* SEE **sword.**

foil verb *The security officer foiled the thieves.* baffle, block, check, frustrate, halt, hamper, hinder, obstruct, outwit, prevent, stop, thwart.

foist verb *He foisted a load of bad fruit on us.* get rid of, impose, offload, palm off.

fold noun **1** *a fold in paper or cloth.* bend, corrugation, crease, furrow, hollow, knife-edge, line, pleat, wrinkle.
2 *a fold for sheep.* SEE **enclosure.**

fold verb **1** *to fold in two.* bend, crease, crinkle, double over, jack-knife, overlap, pleat, tuck in, turn over.
2 *to fold in your arms.* clasp, embrace, enclose, enfold, entwine, envelop, hold close, hug, wrap.
3 *to fold an umbrella.* close, collapse, let down, put down.
4 *The business folded.* SEE **fail.**

folder noun *a folder for papers.* SEE **cover** noun, portfolio.

foliage, folio nouns SEE **leaf.**

folk noun SEE **person.**

folklore noun SEE **tradition.**

follow verb **1** *Follow that car! He follows her everywhere.* accompany, chase, dog, escort, go after, hound, hunt, keep pace with, pursue, shadow, stalk, [*informal*] tag along with, tail, track, trail.
OPPOSITES: SEE **abandon.**
2 *James I followed Elizabeth I.* come after, replace, succeed, supersede, supplant, take the place of.
OPPOSITES: SEE **precede.**
3 *Follow the rules.* attend to, comply with, heed, keep to, obey, observe, pay attention to, take notice of.
OPPOSITES: SEE **ignore.**
4 *Try to follow what I say.* comprehend, grasp, keep up with, understand.
5 *Do you follow snooker?* be a fan of, keep abreast of, know about, support, take an interest in.
6 *It's sunny now, but it doesn't follow that it'll be fine tonight.* be inevitable, come about, ensue, happen, have the consequence, mean, result.

follower noun SEE **disciple.**

following adjective *the following day.* coming, consequent, ensuing, future, later, next, resulting, subsequent, succeeding.
OPPOSITES: SEE **foregoing.**

folly noun SEE **stupidity.**

foment verb *to foment trouble.* See **stimulate.**

fond adjective **1** *a fond kiss.* SEE **loving.**
2 *a fond hope.* SEE **silly.**
fond of *She's fond of him* SEE **love** noun **(in love with).**

fondle verb SEE **caress** verb.

food noun [*old-fashioned*] comestibles, cooking, cuisine, delicacies, diet, [*informal*] eatables, [*informal*] eats, fare, feed (*chicken feed*), fodder (*cattle fodder*), foodstuff, forage (*forage for horses*), [*informal*] grub, SEE **meal**, meat (*meat and drink*), nourishment, [*especially = plant food*] nutriments, [*joking*] provender, provisions, rations, recipe, refreshments, sustenance, swill (*pig-swill*), [*old-fashioned*] tuck, [*old-fashioned*] viands, [*old-fashioned*] victuals.
RELATED ADJECTIVES: cordon bleu, culinary, gastronomic, gourmet.

CONSTITUENTS OF FOOD: carbohydrate, cholesterol, fibre, protein, roughage, vitamin.

VARIOUS FOODS: bacon, batter, beans, biryani, SEE **biscuit**, blancmange, bran, bread, broth, SEE **cake** noun, caviare, SEE **cereal**, charlotte, cheese, cheesecake, chilli, chips, chop suey, chupatti, chutney, coleslaw, cornflakes, cornflour, cream, crisps, croquette, crouton, crumpet, curry, custard.

doughnut, dumplings, egg, SEE **fat** noun, SEE **fish** noun, flan, flour, fondue, fricassee, fritter, SEE **fruit**, ghee, gherkin, glucose, goulash, greens, gruel, haggis, hash, health foods, honey, hot-pot, ice-cream, icing, jam, jelly, junket, kebab, kedgeree, kipper, kosher food.

lasagne, lentils, macaroni, malt, marmalade, SEE **meat**, milk, mincemeat, mince pies, moussaka, mousse, muesli, noodles, SEE **nut**, oatmeal, omelette, paella, pancake, pasta, pastry, pasty, pâté, pie, pikelet, pizza, porridge, pudding, quiche, rice, risotto, rissole, roly-poly, rusk.

sago, SEE **salad**, sandwich, sauerkraut, sausage, sausage-roll, scampi, schnitzel, seafood, semolina, smorgasbord, sorbet, soufflé, soup, soya beans, spaghetti, stew, stock, sundae, syllabub, syrup, tandoori, tapioca, tart, toast, treacle, trifle, truffle, SEE **vegetable**, vegetarian food, waffle, wholemeal flour, yam, yeast, yogurt or yoghurt.

CONDIMENTS, FLAVOURINGS, ETC.: chutney, colouring, dressing, garlic, gravy, herbs, ketchup, marinade, mayonnaise, mustard, pepper, pickle, preservative, relish, salt, sauce, seasoning, spice, stuffing, sugar, vanilla, vinegar.

---

fool noun **1** *I am a fool!* [All the synonyms given are normally used *informally*.] ass, blockhead, booby, buffoon, dimwit, dope, dunce, dunderhead, dupe, fathead, half-wit, SEE **idiot**, ignoramus, mug, muggins, mutt, ninny, nit, nitwit, silly person [SEE **silly**], simpleton, sucker, twerp, wally.
2 [*old-fashioned*] *a fool in the king's court.* clown, comic, coxcomb, entertainer, jester.

fool verb *to fool someone with a trick.* [*informal*] bamboozle, bluff, cheat, [*informal*] con, deceive, delude, dupe, [*informal*] have on, hoax, hoodwink, [*informal*] kid, mislead, [*informal*] string along, swindle, take in, trick.
to fool about SEE **misbehave, play** verb.

foolhardy adjective SEE **rash** adjective.

foolish adjective SEE **stupid**.

foolishness noun SEE **stupidity**.

foolproof adjective SEE **simple**.

foot noun **1** *an animal's foot.* claw, hoof, paw, trotter.
2 *the foot of a mountain.* SEE **base** noun.
3 *a metrical foot.* SEE **verse**.

football noun American football, Association football, Rugby football, [*informal*] rugger, [*informal*] soccer.

foothill noun SEE **hill**.

footing noun SEE **base** noun, **basis**.

footling adjective SEE **trivial**.

footloose adjective SEE **independent**.

footman noun SEE **servant**.

footnote noun annotation, note.

footpath noun SEE **path**.

footprint noun footmark, spoor (*of an animal*), track.

footslog noun SEE **walk** verb.

footsore adjective SEE **tired**.

footstep noun footfall, tread.

footwear noun boot, [*mountaineering*] crampon, SEE **shoe**, sock, stocking.

forage noun SEE **food**.

foray noun SEE **attack** noun.

forbear verb SEE **refrain** verb.

forbearance noun SEE **patience**.

forbearing adjective SEE **patient** adjective.

forbid verb *to forbid smoking.* ban, bar, deny (*He denied me the chance*), deter, disallow, exclude, make illegal, outlaw, preclude, prevent, prohibit, proscribe, refuse, rule out, say no to, stop, veto.
OPPOSITES: SEE **allow**.

forbidden adjective **1** *Games are forbidden.* against the law, banned, barred, disallowed, SEE **illegal**, outlawed, prohibited, proscribed, taboo, unlawful, wrong.
OPPOSITES: SEE **permissible**.
2 *This is a forbidden area.* closed, out of bounds, restricted, secret.

forbidding adjective *forbidding storm clouds.* gloomy, grim, menacing, ominous, stern, threatening, SEE **unfriendly**, uninviting, unwelcoming.
OPPOSITES: SEE **friendly**.

force noun **1** *We used force to open the door.* drive, effort, energy, might, power, pressure, strength, vehemence, vigour, weight.
2 *the force of an explosion.* effect, impact, intensity, momentum, shock.
3 *a military force.* army, body, SEE **group** noun, troops.
3 *They took over by force.* aggression, brunt (*We bore the brunt of the attack*), coercion, compulsion, constraint, duress, violence.
4 *I could see the force of her argument.* cogency, effectiveness, persuasiveness, rightness, validity.

force verb **1** *You can't force me to do it.* [*informal*] bulldoze, coerce, compel, constrain, drive, impel, impose on, make, oblige, order, press-gang, pressurize.
2 *We had to force the door.* break open, burst open, prise open, smash, use force on, wrench.
3 *They forced the change on us.* impose, inflict.

forceful adjective SEE **powerful**.

forceps noun pincers, tongs, tweezers.

ford noun river-crossing, water-splash.

ford verb *to ford a river.* SEE **cross** verb, drive through, ride through, wade across.

fore adjective SEE **front** adjective.

forebear noun SEE **ancestor**.

forebode verb SEE **foretell**.

foreboding noun *a foreboding that something is wrong.* anxiety, augury, dread, fear, feeling, intuition, misgiving, omen, portent, premonition, presentiment, warning, worry.

forecast noun *a weather forecast.* augury, expectation, outlook, prediction, prognosis, prognostication, projection, prophecy.

forecast verb SEE **foretell.**

forecourt noun SEE **courtyard.**

forefather noun SEE **ancestor.**

forefront noun *in the forefront of fashion.* avant-garde, front, lead, vanguard, the very front.

foregoing adjective *the foregoing remarks.* above, aforementioned, aforesaid, earlier, just mentioned, preceding, previous.
OPPOSITES: SEE **following.**

foregone adjective **foregone conclusion** SEE **certainty.**

foreground noun *the foreground of a picture.* forefront, front, nearest part.
OPPOSITES: SEE **background.**

forehead noun brow.
PARTS OF YOUR HEAD: SEE **head** noun.

foreign adjective **1** *foreign places.* distant, exotic, far-away, outlandish, remote, strange, unfamiliar, unknown.
OPPOSITES: SEE **familiar, native.**
2 *foreign tourists.* alien, external, immigrant, incoming, international, outside, overseas, visiting.
OPPOSITES: SEE **domestic.**
3 *foreign goods.* imported.
OPPOSITE: indigenous.
4 *Cruelty is foreign to her.* uncharacteristic (of), unnatural (to), untypical (of).
OPPOSITES: SEE **natural.**
5 *a foreign body in his eye.* extraneous, unwanted.

foreigner noun alien, immigrant, newcomer, outsider, overseas visitor, stranger.
OPPOSITES: SEE **native** noun.

foreknowledge noun SEE **forewarning.**

foreland noun SEE **promontory.**

foreman, forewoman nouns boss, SEE **chief** noun, controller, [*of a jury*] spokesman, superintendent, supervisor.

foremost adjective SEE **chief** adjective.

forename noun SEE **name** noun.

forerunner noun SEE **predecessor.**

foresee verb *I foresaw what would happen.* anticipate, envisage, expect, forecast, foretell, have a foretaste of, predict, prognosticate, prophesy.

foreshadow verb SEE **foretell.**

foresight noun *She commended my foresight in bringing an umbrella.* anticipation, caution, farsightedness, forethought, looking ahead, perspicacity, planning, preparation, prudence, readiness.

forest noun coppice, copse, jungle, plantation, trees, woodland, woods.
RELATED ADJECTIVES: arboreal, silvan.

forestall verb SEE **prevent.**

foretaste noun *a foretaste of things to come.* example, SEE **forewarning,** preview, sample, specimen, trailer, [*informal*] try-out.

foretell verb *The omens foretold what would happen.* augur, [*old-fashioned*] bode, forebode, forecast, foreshadow, forewarn, give a foretaste of, herald, portend, presage, prognosticate, prophesy, signify.

forethought noun SEE **foresight.**

forewarning noun *I had no forewarning of trouble.* advance warning, augury, foreknowledge, foretaste, indication, omen, premonition, [*informal*] tip-off.

forewoman noun SEE **foreman.**

foreword noun introduction, prologue.
OTHER PARTS OF A BOOK: SEE **book** noun.

forfeit noun *He had to pay a forfeit.* damages, fine, penalty.

forfeit verb *Because he broke the rules, he forfeited his winnings.* abandon, give up, let go, lose, pay up, relinquish, renounce, surrender.

forgather verb SEE **gather.**

forge noun *a blacksmith's forge.* furnace, smithy, workshop.

forge verb **1** *to forge metal.* beat into shape, cast, hammer out, mould, shape, work.
2 *to forge money.* coin, copy, counterfeit, fake, falsify, imitate, make illegally.
to forge ahead SEE **advance** verb.

forgery noun *The painting was a forgery.* copy, counterfeit, [*informal*] dud, fake, fraud, imitation, [*informal*] phoney, replica, reproduction.

forget verb **1** *I forget things.* be forgetful [SEE **forgetful**], be oblivious (of), disregard, fail to remember, ignore, leave out, lose track (of), miss out, neglect, omit, overlook, skip, suffer from amnesia, unlearn.
OPPOSITES: SEE **remember.**
2 *I forgot my money.* abandon, be without, leave behind.
OPPOSITES: SEE **bring.**

forgetful adjective absent-minded, [*formal*] amnesiac, careless, inattentive, neglectful, negligent, oblivious, unconscious, unmindful, unreliable, vague, [*informal*] woolly-minded.

forgetfulness noun absent-mindedness, [*formal*] amnesia, negligence, oblivion, unconsciousness.

forgivable adjective *a forgivable lapse.* allowable, excusable, justifiable, negligible, pardonable, petty, understandable, venial (*a venial sin*).
OPPOSITES: SEE **unforgivable**.

forgive verb **1** *to forgive a person for doing wrong.* [*formal*] absolve, [*formal*] exculpate, excuse, exonerate, let off, pardon, spare.
2 *to forgive a crime.* condone, overlook.

forgiveness noun absolution, exoneration, mercy, pardon.
OPPOSITES: SEE **retribution**.

forgiving adjective *a forgiving nature.* SEE **kind** adjective, merciful, tolerant, understanding.
OPPOSITES: SEE **vengeful**.

forgo verb SEE **abandon**.

fork verb **1** *to fork the garden.* SEE **dig**.
2 *The road forks.* SEE **divide**.
to fork out SEE **pay** verb.

forked adjective *a forked stick.* branched, divided, split, V-shaped.

forlorn adjective SEE **friendless, sad**.

form noun **1** *human form.* anatomy, body, build, figure, frame, outline, physique, shape, silhouette.
2 *What form did it take?* appearance, arrangement, cast, character, configuration, design, format, framework, genre, guise, kind, manifestation, manner, model, mould, nature, pattern, plan, semblance, sort, species, structure, style, system, type, variety.
3 *your form in school.* class, group, level, set, stream, tutor-group.
4 [*informal*] *It's good form to shake hands.* behaviour, convention, custom, etiquette, fashion, manners, practice.
5 *an application form.* document, paper.
6 *an athlete's form.* condition, fettle (*in fine fettle*), fitness, health, performance, spirits.
7 [*old-fashioned*] *a form to sit on.* bench, seat.

form verb **1** *A sculptor forms her material.* cast, construct, design, forge, give form to, model, mould, shape.
2 *We formed a society.* bring into existence, bring together, constitute, create, establish, found, make, organize, produce.
3 *They form a good team.* act as, compose, comprise, make up, serve as.
4 *Icicles formed under the bridge.* appear, come into existence, develop, grow, materialize, take shape.

formal adjective **1** *a formal occasion. formal behaviour.* aloof, ceremonial, ceremonious, conventional, cool, correct, dignified, [*informal*] dressed-up, official, orthodox. [*informal*] posh, [*uncomplimentary*] pretentious, proper, reserved, ritualized, solemn, sophisticated, stately, [*informal*] starchy, stiff, stiff-necked, unbending, unfriendly.
2 *formal language.* academic, impersonal, legal, official, precise, specialist, stilted, technical.
3 *a formal design.* calculated, geometrical, orderly, regular, rigid, symmetrical.
OPPOSITES: SEE **informal**.

formality noun SEE **ceremony**.

former adjective earlier, opening, SEE **previous**.
OPPOSITES: SEE **latter**.

formidable adjective *a formidable task.* SEE **difficult**.

formula noun **1** *a verbal formula.* form of words, ritual, rubric, spell, wording.
2 *a formula for success.* blueprint, method, prescription, procedure, recipe, rule, way.

formulate verb *to formulate a plan.* create, define, devise, evolve, express clearly, form, invent, plan, set out in detail, specify, systematize, work out.

fornicate verb SEE **sex (to have sexual intercourse)**.

forsake verb SEE **abandon, renounce**.

forswear verb SEE **renounce**.

fort noun camp, castle, citadel, fortification, fortress, garrison, stronghold, tower.

forthcoming adjective SEE **future** adjective.

forthright adjective *forthright views.* blunt, candid, direct, SEE **frank**, outspoken, plain-speaking, straightforward, unequivocal.
OPPOSITES: SEE **cautious**.

fortification noun SEE **fort**.

fortify verb **1** *to fortify a town.* defend, garrison, protect, reinforce, secure against attack.
OPPOSITE: demilitarize.
2 *to fortify yourself for difficulties ahead.* boost, cheer, encourage, hearten, invigorate, lift the morale of, reassure, stiffen the resolve of, strengthen, support, sustain.
OPPOSITES: SEE **weaken**.

fortitude noun SEE **courage**.

fortress noun SEE **fort**.

fortuitous adjective SEE **accidental**.

fortunate adjective SEE **lucky**.

fortune noun **1** *good fortune. bad fortune.* accident, chance, destiny, fate, kismet, luck, providence.

2 *He left his fortune to a charity.* affluence, assets, estate, inheritance, millions, [*informal*] pile (*She made a pile*), possessions, property, prosperity, riches, treasure, wealth.

fortune-teller noun crystal-gazer, palmist, prophet, soothsayer.

forward adjective **1** *a forward movement.* front, frontal, leading, onward, progressive.
OPPOSITES: SEE **backward**.
2 *forward planning.* advance, early, forward-looking, future.
OPPOSITE: retrospective.
3 [*uncomplimentary*] *too forward for his age.* assertive, bold, brazen, cheeky, familiar, [*informal*] fresh, impertinent, impudent, insolent, over-confident, precocious, presumptuous, pushful, [*informal*] pushy, shameless, uninhibited.
OPPOSITES: SEE **diffident**.

forward verb **1** *to forward a letter.* post on, re-address, send on.
2 *to forward goods.* dispatch, expedite, freight, send, ship, transmit, transport.
3 *to forward someone's career.* accelerate, advance, encourage, facilitate, foster, hasten, SEE **help** verb, help along, [*informal*] lend a helping hand to, promote, speed up, support.
OPPOSITES: SEE **hinder**.

fossilize verb ossify, petrify, turn into a fossil.

foster verb **1** *to foster a happy atmosphere.* cultivate, encourage, promote, stimulate.
2 *to foster a child.* adopt, bring up, care for, look after, nourish, nurse, raise, rear, take care of. [The legal meaning of *adopt* and *foster* is not the same.]

foster-child, foster-parent nouns SEE **family**.

foul adjective **1** *a foul mess. foul air.* contaminated, SEE **dirty** adjective, disagreeable, disgusting, filthy, hateful, impure, infected, loathsome, nasty, nauseating, noisome, obnoxious, offensive, polluted, putrid, repulsive, revolting, rotten, smelly, squalid, stinking, unclean, SEE **unpleasant**, vile.
OPPOSITES: SEE **pure**.
2 *a foul crime.* abhorrent, abominable, atrocious, SEE **cruel**, evil, monstrous, villainous, wicked.
3 *foul language.* abusive, blasphemous, coarse, common, crude, improper, indecent, insulting, SEE **obscene**, offensive, rude, uncouth, vulgar.
4 *foul weather.* foggy, rainy, rough, stormy, violent, windy.
5 *a foul tackle.* against the rules, illegal, prohibited, unfair.

foul verb *Chemicals fouled the drains.* SEE **contaminate**.
to foul up SEE **muddle** verb.

found verb **1** *to found a business.* begin, create, endow, establish, fund, [*informal*] get going, inaugurate, initiate, institute, organize, provide money for, raise, set up, start.
2 *a building founded on solid rock.* base, build, construct, erect.

foundation noun **1** *the foundation of a new association.* beginning, establishment, inauguration, initiation, institution, setting up, starting.
2 *the foundation of a building.* base, basis, bottom, cornerstone, foot, footing, substructure, underpinning.
3 [*plural*] *the foundations of science.* basic principles [SEE **principle**], elements, essentials, fundamentals, origins, rudiments.

founder verb SEE **fall** verb, **sink** verb.

foundling noun orphan, stray, waif.

foundry noun SEE **factory**.

fountain noun *a fountain of water.* fount, jet, spout, spray, spring, well.

fowl noun bird, chicken, hen.

fox noun [*female*] vixen.

fox verb SEE **deceive**.

foxy adjective SEE **crafty**.

foyer noun ante-room, entrance, entrance hall, hall, lobby, reception.

fracas noun SEE **commotion**.

Several English words, including *fraction, fracture, fragile, fragment*, etc., are related to Latin *frangere* = *to break*.

---

fraction noun *I could afford only a fraction of the amount.* division, part, portion, section, subdivision.

fractional adjective *a fractional amount.* SEE **small**.

fractious adjective SEE **irritable**.

fracture noun *a fracture in a bone.* break, breakage, chip, cleft, crack, fissure, gap, opening, rent, rift, split.

fracture verb *to fracture a bone.* break, cause a fracture in, chip, crack, split, suffer a fracture in.

fragile adjective *Egg-shell is fragile.* breakable, brittle, SEE **delicate**, easily damaged, feeble, frail, insubstantial, slight, thin, weak.
OPPOSITES: SEE **strong**.

fragment noun **1** *a fragment of broken pottery.* atom, bit, chip, crumb, part, particle, piece, remnant, scrap, shiver, shred, sliver, snippet, speck.
2 [*plural*] *smashed into fragments.* debris, shivers, [*informal*] smithereens.

fragment verb SEE **break** verb.

fragmentary adjective *fragmentary evidence.* [*informal*] bitty, broken, disintegrated, disjointed, fragmented, in bits, incoherent, incomplete, in fragments [SEE **fragment** noun], partial, scattered, scrappy, uncoordinated.
OPPOSITES: SEE **complete** adjective.

fragrance noun SEE **smell** noun.

fragrant adjective SEE **smelling**.

frail adjective **1** *a frail person.* delicate, feeble, SEE **ill**, infirm, [*uncomplimentary*] puny, slight, unsteady, vulnerable, weak, [*uncomplimentary*] weedy.
2 *a frail structure.* flimsy, SEE **fragile**, insubstantial, rickety, unsound.
OPPOSITES: SEE **strong**.

frame noun **1** *the frame of a building.* bodywork, construction, framework, scaffolding, shell, skeleton, structure.
2 *a frame for a picture.* border, case, casing, edge, edging, mount, mounting.
a frame of mind SEE **attitude**.

frame verb **1** *to frame a picture.* enclose, mount, surround.
2 *to frame a letter.* SEE **compose**.

framework noun bare bones, frame, outline, plan, shell, skeleton, structure, trellis.

franchise noun SEE **right** noun.

frank adjective *a frank reply, a frank discussion.* blunt, candid, direct, downright, explicit, forthright, genuine, [*informal*] heart-to-heart, honest, ingenuous, [*informal*] no-nonsense, open, outright, outspoken, plain, plainspoken, revealing, serious, sincere, straight from the heart, straightforward, to the point, trustworthy, truthful, unconcealed, undisguised, unreserved.
OPPOSITES: SEE **insincere**.

frankfurter noun SEE **sausage**.

frantic adjective *frantic activity. frantic with worry.* berserk, [*informal*] beside yourself, crazy, delirious, demented, deranged, desperate, distraught, excitable, feverish, [*informal*] fraught, frenetic, frenzied, furious, hectic, hysterical, mad, overwrought, rabid, uncontrollable, violent, wild, worked up.
OPPOSITES: SEE **calm** adjective.

fraternal adjective *fraternal love.* brotherly.

fraternity noun SEE **society**.

fraternize verb SEE **associate** verb.

fraud noun **1** *His fraud landed him in gaol.* chicanery, [*informal*] con-trick, deceit, deception, dishonesty, double-dealing, duplicity, forgery, imposture, [*informal*] sharp practice, swindling, trickery.
2 *The "special offer" was a fraud.* cheat, counterfeit, fake, hoax, pretence, [*informal*] put-up job, ruse, sham, swindle, trick.
3 *The salesman was a fraud.* charlatan, cheat, [*informal*] con-man, hoaxer, impostor, [*slang*] phoney, [*informal*] quack, swindler.

fraudulent adjective *a fraudulent business deal.* bogus, cheating, corrupt, counterfeit, criminal, [*informal*] crooked, deceitful, devious, [*informal*] dirty, dishonest, false, illegal, lying, [*slang*] phoney, sham, specious, swindling, underhand, unscrupulous.
OPPOSITES: SEE **honest**.

fraught adjective [*informal*] *You seem a bit fraught.* SEE **anxious**.

fray noun SEE **fight** noun.

frayed *a frayed collar.* rough at the edges, tattered, threadbare, untidy, worn.

freak adjective *freak weather conditions.* aberrant, abnormal, atypical, exceptional, extraordinary, odd, peculiar, queer, unaccountable, unforeseeable, unpredictable, unusual.
OPPOSITES: SEE **normal**.

freak noun **1** *a freak of Nature.* aberration, abnormality, abortion, anomaly, irregularity, monster, monstrosity, mutant, oddity, quirk, sport, variant.
2 [*informal*] *a keep-fit freak.* SEE **fanatic**.

freckle noun SEE **spot** noun.

free adjective **1** *free to come and go.* able, allowed, at leisure, at liberty, disengaged, idle, loose, not working, permitted, uncommitted, unconstrained, unfixed, unrestrained, unrestricted, untrammelled.
OPPOSITE: restricted.
2 *free from slavery.* emancipated, liberated, released.
OPPOSITE: enslaved.
3 *a free country.* democratic, independent, self-governing, sovereign.
OPPOSITES: SEE **occupied, totalitarian**.
4 *a free gift.* complimentary, gratis, without charge.
5 *Is the bathroom free?* available, open, unoccupied, vacant.
OPPOSITES: SEE **engaged**.

6 *free with your money.* bounteous, casual, generous, lavish, liberal, ready, unstinting, willing.
OPPOSITES: SEE **mean** adjective.
free and easy SEE **informal**.
free-lance independent, self-employed.

free verb **1** *to free someone from prison.* deliver, emancipate, liberate, loose, make free, ransom, release, rescue, save, set free, turn loose, unchain, unfetter, unleash, unlock, unloose.
OPPOSITES: SEE **confine**.
2 *to free an accused person.* absolve, acquit, clear, discharge, [*formal*] exculpate, exonerate, let go, let off, pardon, prove innocent, relieve, spare.
OPPOSITES: SEE **condemn**.
3 *to free tangled ropes.* clear, disengage, disentangle, extricate, loose, undo, unknot, untangle, untie.
OPPOSITES: SEE **tangle** verb.

freedom noun *freedom to do as you please.* autonomy, discretion, independence, latitude, leeway, liberty, licence, opportunity, privilege, scope.
OPPOSITES: SEE **repression, restriction**.

free-for-all noun SEE **fight** noun.

free-standing adjective SEE **separate** adjective.

freeway noun SEE **road**.

free-wheel verb *to free-wheel downhill.* coast, drift, glide, ride.

freeze verb **1** *Water freezes at 0°C.* become ice, become solid, congeal, ice over.
2 *The wind froze us to the bone.* chill, cool, make cold, numb.
3 *to freeze food.* chill, deep-freeze, dry-freeze, refrigerate.
4 *to freeze prices.* fix, hold, keep as they are, peg.

freezing adjective SEE **cold** adjective.

freight noun *Some aircraft carry freight.* cargo, consignment, goods, load, merchandise, shipment.

frenetic, frenzied adjectives SEE **frantic**.

frenzy noun *a frenzy of excitement.* delirium, fit, fury, hysteria, insanity, lunacy, madness, mania, outburst, paroxysm, passion.

frequent adjective **1** *frequent trains. frequent headaches.* constant, continual, countless, incessant, many, numerous, recurrent, recurring, regular, repeated.
2 *a frequent visitor.* common, customary, familiar, habitual, ordinary, persistent, regular.
OPPOSITES: SEE **infrequent, rare**.

frequent verb SEE **haunt**.

fresco noun mural, SEE **picture** noun.

fresh adjective **1** *fresh evidence. fresh ideas. fresh bread.* additional, different, extra, just arrived, new, recent, unfamiliar, up-to-date.
OPPOSITES: SEE **stale**.
2 *fresh water.* clear, drinkable, potable, pure, refreshing, sweet, uncontaminated.
OPPOSITES: SEE **salty**.
3 *fresh air. a fresh atmosphere.* airy, bracing, breezy, circulating, clean, cool, draughty, invigorating, unpolluted, ventilated.
OPPOSITES: SEE **stuffy**.
4 *fresh food.* healthy, natural, newly gathered, raw, unprocessed, untreated, wholesome.
OPPOSITES: SEE **preserved**.
5 *fresh sheets on the bed.* clean, crisp, laundered, untouched, unused, washed-and-ironed.
OPPOSITES: SEE **dirty** adjective.
6 *fresh colours. fresh paint.* bright, clean, glowing, just painted, renewed, restored, sparkling, unfaded, vivid.
OPPOSITES: SEE **dingy**.
7 *fresh after a shower.* alert, energetic, healthy, invigorated, lively, [*informal*] perky, rested, revived, sprightly, spry, tingling, vigorous, vital.
OPPOSITES: SEE **weary** adjective.

fret verb SEE **worry** verb.

fretful adjective SEE **anxious**.

friable adjective SEE **crumbly**.

friar noun mendicant, monk.

friction noun **1** *Bike brakes work by friction against the wheel.* abrasion, chafing, resistance, rubbing, scraping.
2 *There was some friction between the two sides.* SEE **conflict** noun.

fried adjective *fried potatoes.* sauté.

friend noun acquaintance, ally, associate, [*informal*] buddy, [*informal*] chum, companion, comrade, [*male*] confidant, [*female*] confidante, [*informal*] crony, SEE **lover**, [*informal*] mate, [*informal*] pal, partner, pen-friend, playfellow, playmate, supporter, well-wisher.
OPPOSITES: SEE **enemy**.
to be friends associate, consort, fraternize, [*informal*] go around, [*informal*] hob-nob, keep company, mix.
to make friends with befriend, [*informal*] chat up, [*informal*] gang up with, get to know, make the acquaintance of, [*informal*] pal up with.

friendless adjective *a friendless person.* abandoned, alienated, alone, deserted, estranged, forlorn, forsaken, isolated, lonely, ostracized, shunned, shut out, solitary, unattached, unloved.

friendliness noun goodwill, hospitality, kindness, sociability, warmth.

friendly adjective *a friendly person. a friendly welcome.* affable, affectionate, agreeable, amiable, amicable, approachable, attached, benevolent, benign, [*informal*] chummy, civil, close, companionable, compatible, comradely, conciliatory, congenial, convivial, cordial, expansive, SEE **familiar**, favourable, genial, good-natured, gracious, helpful, hospitable, intimate, kind, kind-hearted, likeable, SEE **loving**, [*informal*] matey, neighbourly, outgoing, [*informal*] pally, sociable, sympathetic, tender, [*informal*] thick (*They're very thick with each other*), warm, welcoming, well-disposed.
OPPOSITES: SEE **unfriendly**.

friendship noun *She values our friendship.* affection, alliance, amity, association, attachment, camaraderie, closeness, comradeship, familiarity, fellowship, fondness, friendliness, goodwill, harmony, hospitality, SEE **love** noun, rapport, relationship.
OPPOSITES: SEE **hostility**.

frieze noun *a decorative frieze.* border, edging.

fright noun **1** *The explosion gave them a fright.* jolt, scare, shock, surprise.
2 *You could see the fright in their faces.* alarm, consternation, dismay, dread, fear, horror, panic, terror, trepidation.

frighten verb *The hooligans frightened the passers-by.* alarm, appal, browbeat, bully, cow, curdle the blood of, daunt, dismay, horrify, intimidate, make afraid, menace, persecute, [*informal*] petrify, [*informal*] put the wind up, scare, shake, shock, startle, terrify, terrorize, threaten, unnerve.
OPPOSITES: SEE **reassure**.

frightened adjective afraid, alarmed, apprehensive, [*informal*] chicken, cowed, dismayed, fearful, horror-struck, intimidated, panicky, panic-stricken, [*informal*] petrified, scared, terrified, terror-stricken, trembling, unnerved, [*informal*] windy.

frightening adjective alarming, appalling, awful, blood-curdling, [*informal*] creepy, dire, dreadful, eerie, fearful, fearsome, formidable, frightful, ghastly, ghostly, grim, hair-raising, horrific, horrifying, intimidating, menacing, scary, sinister, spine-chilling, [*informal*] spooky, terrifying, traumatic, uncanny, unnerving, upsetting, weird, worrying.

frightful adjective **1** *a frightful accident.* SEE **frightening**, grisly, gruesome, harrowing, hideous, horrible, horrid, macabre, shocking, terrible.
2 [*informal*] *frightful weather.* SEE **bad**.

frigid adjective SEE **cold**.

frill noun SEE **fringe**.

fringe noun **1** *a fringe round the edge of a curtain.* border, edging, flounce, frill, gathering, trimming, valance.
2 *the fringe of a town.* borders, edge, limits, margin, outskirts, periphery.

frippery noun SEE **ornament** noun.

frisk verb **1** *to frisk about.* SEE **frolic**.
2 [*informal*] *to frisk a suspect.* SEE **search** verb.

frisky adjective frolicsome, high-spirited, jaunty, lively, perky, playful, skittish, spirited, sprightly.

fritter verb *to fritter your money.* SEE **waste** verb.

frivolity noun *We enjoy a bit of frivolity on holiday.* facetiousness, fun, fun-and-games, gaiety, joking, levity, light-heartedness, nonsense, playing about, silliness, triviality.

frivolous adjective. *frivolous questions. frivolous behaviour.* facetious, flighty, flippant, foolish, jocular, joking, petty, pointless, ridiculous, shallow, silly, stupid, superficial, trifling, trivial, unimportant, unserious, vacuous, worthless.
OPPOSITES: SEE **serious**.

frizzy adjective SEE **curly**.

frock noun dress, gown, robe.

frogman noun diver.

frolic verb caper, cavort, dance, frisk about, gambol, have fun, hop about, jump about, lark around, leap about, play about, prance, rollick, romp, skip, sport.

frond noun SEE **leaf**.

front adjective *the front row.* first, foremost, leading, most advanced.
OPPOSITES: SEE **back** adjective.

front noun **1** bow (*of a ship*), façade (*of a house*), face, facing, forefront, foreground (*of a picture*), frontage (*of a building*), head, nose, van, vanguard (*of an army*).
OPPOSITES: SEE **back** noun.
2 *Troops were sent to the front.* battle area, danger zone, front line.
3 *His cheerfulness was only a front.* appearance, blind, [*informal*] cover-up, disguise, mask, pretence, show.

frontal adjective *a frontal attack.* direct, facing, head-on, oncoming, straight.

frontier noun *a national frontier.* border, borderline, boundary, limit.

frosty adjective SEE **cold** adjective.

froth noun bubbles, effervescence, foam, head (*on beer*), lather, scum, spume, suds.

frown noun VARIOUS EXPRESSIONS: SEE **expression.**

frown verb [*informal*] give a dirty look, glare, glower, grimace, knit your brow, look sullen, lour, lower, scowl.
to frown on SEE **disapprove.**

frozen adjective SEE **cold** adjective, **icy.**

frugal adjective SEE **economical.**

fruit noun berry.

VARIOUS FRUITS: apple, apricot, avocado, banana, bilberry, blackberry, cherry, citrus fruit, coconut, crab-apple, cranberry, currant, damson, date, fig, gooseberry, grape, grapefruit, greengage, guava, hip, kiwi fruit, lemon, lime, litchi or lichee, loganberry, mango, medlar, melon, mulberry, nectarine, olive, orange, papaw or pawpaw, peach, pear, pineapple, plum, pomegranate, prune, quince, raisin, raspberry, rhubarb, satsuma, sloe, strawberry, sultana, tangerine, tomato, ugli.

---

fruitful adjective **1** *a fruitful crop. a fruitful garden.* abundant, copious, fertile, flourishing, lush, plenteous, productive, profuse, prolific, rich.
OPPOSITES: SEE **unproductive.**
2 *a fruitful search.* effective, gainful, profitable, rewarding, successful, useful, worthwhile.
OPPOSITES: SEE **fruitless.**

fruitless adjective *a fruitless search.* abortive, disappointing, futile, pointless, profitless, unavailing, unfruitful, unproductive, unprofitable, unrewarding, unsuccessful, useless, vain.
OPPOSITES: SEE **fruitful.**

frumpish adjective SEE **dowdy.**

frustrate verb *The police frustrated an attempted robbery.* baffle, baulk, block, check, defeat, discourage, foil, halt, hinder, inhibit, prevent, [*informal*] scotch, stop, thwart.
OPPOSITES: SEE **fulfil.**

frustrated adjective inhibited, loveless, lovesick, thwarted.

fry verb sauté.
OTHER WAYS TO COOK: SEE **cook** verb.

fuddled adjective *fuddled with alcohol.* confused, SEE **drunk,** flustered, hazy, mixed up, muddled, stupefied.
OPPOSITE: clear-headed.

fudge verb SEE **fake** verb.

fuel noun KINDS OF FUEL: anthracite, butane, Calor Gas, charcoal, coal, coke, derv, diesel, electricity, gas, gasoline, logs, methylated spirit, nuclear fuel, oil, paraffin, peat, petrol, propane.

fuel verb *to fuel a fire. to fuel someone's anger.* encourage, feed, inflame, keep going, nourish, put fuel on, stoke up, supply with fuel.

fuggy adjective [*informal*] *a fuggy room.* SEE **stuffy.**

fugitive noun *a fugitive from justice.* deserter, escapee, escaper, refugee, renegade, runaway.

fulfil verb **1** *to fulfil an ambition.* accomplish, achieve, bring about, carry out, complete, effect, make it come true, perform, realize.
2 *to fulfil certain requirements.* answer, comply with, conform to, execute, implement, meet, respond to, satisfy.
OPPOSITES: SEE **frustrate.**

full adjective **1** *a full cup. a full cinema.* brimming, bursting, [*informal*] chock-a-block, [*informal*] chock-full, congested, crammed, crowded, filled, jammed, [*informal*] jam-packed, overflowing, packed, stuffed, topped-up, well-filled, well-stocked.
OPPOSITES: SEE **empty** adjective.
2 *a full stomach.* gorged, replete, sated, satiated, satisfied, well-fed.
OPPOSITES: SEE **hungry.**
3 *the full story. a full investigation.* complete, comprehensive, detailed, entire, exhaustive, total, unabridged, uncensored, uncut, unedited, unexpurgated, whole.
OPPOSITES: SEE **incomplete.**
4 *full price. full speed.* greatest, highest, maximum, top.
OPPOSITES: SEE **minimum.**
5 *a full figure.* ample, buxom, generous, SEE **fat** adjective, large, plump, rounded.
OPPOSITES: SEE **slight** adjective.
6 *a full skirt.* baggy, broad, voluminous, wide.
OPPOSITE: close-fitting.

full-blooded adjective SEE **vigorous.**

full-grown adjective adult, grown-up, mature, ready, ripe.

fulminate verb SEE **protest** verb.

fulsome adjective SEE **flattering.**

fumble verb *He fumbled the ball.* grope at, handle awkwardly, mishandle.

fume verb 1 *fuming chimneys.* emit fumes, smoke.
2 *He was fuming because he'd missed the bus.* SEE **angry (to be angry)**.

fumes plural noun exhaust, fog, gases, pollution, smog, smoke, vapour.

fumigate verb SEE **disinfect**.

fun noun amusement, diversion, enjoyment, entertainment, SEE **frivolity**, games, horseplay, jokes, joking, [*joking*] jollification, laughter, merriment, merrymaking, pastimes, play, pleasure, recreation, romp, [*informal*] skylarking, sport, teasing, tomfoolery.
to make fun of SEE **mock** verb.

function noun 1 *the function of the police.* SEE **job**.
2 *an official function.* SEE **event**.

function verb *The computer doesn't function.* SEE **work** verb.

functional adjective *The machine doesn't look elegant—it's purely functional.* practical, serviceable, useful, utilitarian.
OPPOSITES: SEE **decorative**.

functionary noun SEE **official** noun.

fund noun 1 *a charitable fund.* [*often plural*] *He invested all his funds.* capital, endowment, SEE **money**, reserves, resources, riches, savings, wealth.
2 *a fund of jokes. a fund of wisdom.* hoard, [*informal*] kitty, mine, pool, reservoir, stock, store, supply, treasure-house.

fundamental adjective *fundamental principles.* axiomatic, basic, SEE **elementary**, essential, important, key, main, necessary, primary, prime, principal, underlying.
OPPOSITES: SEE **advanced, inessential**.

funeral noun burial, cremation, interment, [*informal*] obsequies, Requiem Mass, wake.

WORDS TO DO WITH FUNERALS: bier, catafalque, cemetery, churchyard, cinerary urn, coffin, cortège, cremation, crematorium, grave, graveyard, hearse, memorial, mortuary, mourner, mourning, pall, sarcophagus, tomb, undertaker, wreath.

---

funereal adjective dark, depressing, dismal, gloomy, grave, mournful, SEE **sad**, sepulchral, solemn, sombre.
OPPOSITES: SEE **cheerful, lively**.

fun-fair noun

ENTERTAINMENTS AT A FUN-FAIR: amusements, big-dipper, big-wheel, dodgems, merry-go-round, ride, rifle-range, roundabout, side-show, shooting-gallery, switchback.

---

fungus noun mould, mushroom, toadstool.

funk noun SEE **fear** noun.

funnel noun *a funnel on a steam-ship.* chimney, smoke-stack.

funnel verb *to funnel something into an opening.* channel, direct, filter, pour.

funny adjective 1 *a funny joke.* absurd, amusing, comic, comical, diverting, droll, entertaining, facetious, farcical, hilarious, humorous, hysterical, ironic, jocular, [*informal*] killing, laughable, ludicrous, [*informal*] priceless, ridiculous, risible, sarcastic, satirical, [*informal*] side-splitting, silly, uproarious, witty.
OPPOSITES: SEE **serious**.
2 [*informal*] a funny pain. SEE **peculiar**.

funny-bone noun elbow.

fur noun bristles, coat, down, fleece, hair, hide, pelt, skin, wool.

furious adjective 1 *a furious bull. a furious temper.* SEE **angry**, boiling, enraged, fuming, incensed, infuriated, irate, livid, mad, raging, savage, wrathful.
2 *furious activity.* agitated, frantic, frenzied, intense, tempestuous, tumultuous, turbulent, violent, wild.
OPPOSITES: SEE **calm** adjective.

furl verb SEE **roll** verb.

furnace noun SEE **fire** noun.

furnish verb 1 *to furnish a room.* equip, fit out, fit up.
2 *to furnish someone with information.* give, grant, provide, supply.

furnishings noun SEE **furniture**.

furniture noun antiques, effects, equipment, fittings, furnishings, household goods, [*informal*] moveables, possessions.

ITEMS OF FURNITURE: armchair, bed, bench, bookcase, bunk, bureau, cabinet, chair, chest of drawers, chesterfield, chiffonier, commode, cot, couch, cradle, cupboard, cushion, desk, divan, drawer, dresser, dressing-table, easel, fender, filing-cabinet, fireplace, mantelpiece, ottoman, overmantel, pelmet, pew, pouffe, rocking-chair, seat, settee, sideboard, sofa, stool, suite, table, trestle-table, wardrobe, workbench.

---

furore noun SEE **commotion**.

furrow noun channel, corrugation, crease, ditch, drill *(for seeds)*, fluting, groove, hollow, line, rut, trench, wrinkle.

furrowed adjective 1 *a furrowed brow.* creased, frowning, lined, worried, wrinkled.
2 *a furrowed surface.* corrugated, fluted, grooved, ploughed, ribbed, ridged, rutted.
OPPOSITES: SEE **smooth** adjective.

furry adjective *furry animals.* bristly, downy, feathery, fleecy, fuzzy, hairy, woolly.

further adjective *further information.* additional, extra, fresh, more, new, supplementary.

furthermore adverb additionally, also, besides, moreover, too.

furtive adjective *a furtive look.* concealed, conspirational, covert, SEE **crafty**, deceitful, disguised, hidden, mysterious, secretive, shifty, sly, [*informal*] sneaky, stealthy, surreptitious, underhand, untrustworthy.
OPPOSITES: SEE **blatant**.

fury noun *the fury of a storm.* SEE **anger** noun, ferocity, fierceness, force, intensity, madness, power, rage, savagery, tempestuousness, turbulence, vehemence, violence, wrath.

fuse verb *to fuse substances together.* amalgamate, blend, combine, compound, join, meld, melt, merge, solder, unite, weld.

fusillade noun *a fusillade of gunfire.* barrage, burst, firing, outburst, salvo, volley.

fuss noun SEE **commotion**.

fuss verb *Please don't fuss!* agitate, bother, complain, [*informal*] create, fidget, [*informal*] flap, [*informal*] get worked up, grumble, make a commotion [SEE **commotion**], worry.

fussy adjective 1 *fussy about food.* carping, choosy, difficult, discriminating, [*informal*] faddy, fastidious, [*informal*] finicky, hard to please, niggling, [*informal*] nit-picking, particular, [*informal*] pernickety, scrupulous, squeamish.
2 *fussy decorations.* complicated, detailed, elaborate, overdone.

fusty adjective 1 *a fusty atmosphere.* SEE **stuffy**.
2 *fusty ideas.* SEE **old-fashioned**.

futile adjective *a futile attempt to achieve the impossible.* abortive, absurd, empty, foolish, forlorn, fruitless, ineffective, ineffectual, pointless, profitless, silly, sterile, unavailing, unproductive, unprofitable, unsuccessful, useless, vain *(a vain attempt)*, wasted, worthless.
OPPOSITES: SEE **fruitful**.

futility noun *the futility of unrealistic ambitions.* absurdity, aimlessness, emptiness, hollowness, ineffectiveness, pointlessness, uselessness, vanity, wasted effort.

future adjective *future events.* approaching, awaited, coming, destined, expected, forthcoming, impending, intended, planned, prospective.
OPPOSITES: SEE **past** adjective.

future noun *a bright future.* expectations, outlook, prospects, time to come.

futuristic adjective SEE **advanced**.

fuzz noun down, floss, fluff, hair.

fuzzy adjective 1 *a fuzzy beard.* downy, feathery, fleecy, fluffy, frizzy, woolly.
2 *a fuzzy picture.* bleary, blurred, cloudy, dim, faint, hazy, ill-defined, indistinct, misty, out of focus, shadowy, unclear, unfocused, vague.
OPPOSITES: SEE **clear** adjective.

G

gabble verb babble, chatter, jabber, mutter, prattle, [*informal*] rattle on, SEE **speak**.

gad verb **to gad about** SEE **enjoy (to enjoy yourself)**.

gadget noun *a gadget for opening tins.* appliance, contraption, contrivance, device, implement, instrument, invention, machine, tool, utensil.

gaff noun SEE **fishing (fishing tackle)**.

gaffe noun SEE **mistake** noun.

gaffer noun SEE **chief** noun.

gag noun SEE **joke** noun.

gag verb *to gag someone.* keep quiet, muzzle, prevent from speaking, silence, stifle, suppress.

gaggle noun SEE **group** noun.

gaiety noun SEE **cheerfulness**.

gain noun [*often plural*] *We counted our gains.* achievement, acquisition, advantage, asset, attainment, benefit, dividend, earnings, income, increase, proceeds, profit, return, winnings, yield.
OPPOSITES: SEE **loss**.

gain verb 1 *What do you gain by fighting?* achieve, acquire, bring in, capture,

earn, get, make, net, obtain, pick up, procure, profit, realize, receive, win.
OPPOSITES: SEE **lose**.
2 *The explorers gained their objective.* arrive at, attain, get to, reach, secure.

gainful adjective SEE **profitable**.

gainsay verb SEE **contradict**.

gait noun SEE **walk** noun.

gala noun carnival, celebration, fair, festival, festivity, fête, [*informal*] jamboree, party.

galaxy noun **1** Milky Way, solar system, universe.
2 *a galaxy of famous people.* SEE **group** noun.

gale noun SEE **wind** noun.

gall verb SEE **sore** adjective **(to make sore)**.

gallant adjective *a gallant knight.* attentive, SEE **brave**, chivalrous, courageous, courteous, dashing, fearless, gentlemanly, heroic, honourable, intrepid, magnanimous, noble, polite, valiant.
OPPOSITES: SEE **cowardly, rude**.

gallery noun *the gallery in a theatre.* balcony, circle, [*informal*] the gods, upstairs.

galley noun *a galley in a ship.* kitchen.

galling adjective SEE **annoying**.

gallivant verb SEE **enjoy (to enjoy yourself), travel** verb.

gallop verb SEE **run** verb.

gallows noun *sent to the gallows.* gibbet, scaffold.

galvanize verb *to galvanize someone into action.* SEE **stimulate**.

gambit noun SEE **move** noun.

gamble verb bet, game, [*informal*] have a flutter, risk money, speculate, [*informal*] take a chance, take risks, [*informal*] try your luck, venture, wager.

WAYS OF GAMBLING: backing horses, bingo, cards, dice, drawing lots, lottery, pools, raffle, sweepstake, wager.

PEOPLE WHO GAMBLE: better, gambler, punter, speculator.

PEOPLE WHO SUPERVISE GAMBLING: croupier, bookmaker, turf accountant.

---

gambol verb SEE **frolic**.

game adjective **1** *a game fighter.* SEE **brave**.
2 *game for anything.* SEE **willing**.
3 *a game leg.* SEE **lame**.

game noun **1** *It's just a game.* amusement, diversion, entertainment, frolic, fun, jest, joke, [*informal*] lark, [*informal*] messing about, pastime, play, playing, recreation, romp, sport.
2 *Shall we play a game?* competition, contest, match, tournament.

SOME GAMES OFTEN PLAYED INDOORS: backgammon, bagatelle, billiards, bingo, cards, charades, chess, crossword puzzle, darts, dice, dominoes, draughts, hoopla, jigsaw puzzle, lotto, ludo, mahjong, marbles, ping-pong, pool, skittles, snooker, solitaire, spelling-bee, table-tennis, tiddly-winks, tombola.

SOME CHILDREN'S GAMES PLAYED OUT OF DOORS: ball, conkers, hide-and-seek, hopscotch, leapfrog, roller-skating, seesaw, skate-boarding, skating, sledging, sliding, tag.

OTHER OUTDOOR GAMES: SEE **sport**.

---

3 *hunting for game.* animals, game-birds, prey.
to give the game away SEE **reveal**.

game verb SEE **gamble**.

gammon noun bacon, ham.

gammy adjective SEE **lame**.

gamut noun SEE **range** noun.

gang noun SEE **group** noun.

gang verb **to gang together** SEE **combine**.

gangling adjective SEE **lanky**.

gangster noun bandit, brigand, criminal, crook, desperado, gunman, mugger, robber, ruffian, thug, tough.

gaol noun [The spellings *gaol* and *jail* are both acceptable. *Gaol* is more common in British official documents; *jail* is more common in America.] borstal, cell, custody, dungeon, guardhouse, jail, [*American*] penitentiary, prison.
OTHER PUNISHMENTS: SEE **punishment**.

gaol verb *He was gaoled for fraud.* confine, detain, imprison, incarcerate, intern, [*informal*] send down, send to prison, [*informal*] shut away, shut up.

gaoler noun guard, prison officer, [*slang*] screw, warder.

gap noun **1** *a gap in a wall.* breach, break, chink, cleft, crack, cranny, crevice, hole, SEE **opening**, rift, space, void.
2 *a gap between events.* breathing-space, discontinuity, hiatus, interlude, intermission, interval, lacuna, lapse, lull, pause, recess, respite, rest.
3 *a gap to be measured.* difference, disparity, distance, interval, space.

gape verb **1** *A chasm gaped.* SEE **open** verb.
2 *He gaped in surprise.* SEE **stare**.

garage noun car-port, filling-station, petrol station, service station.

garb noun SEE **clothes**.

garbage noun SEE **rubbish**.

garbled adjective *a garbled message.* SEE **confused**.

garden noun allotment, patch, plot, yard.
gardens grounds, park.

PARTS OF A GARDEN: arbour, bed, border, compost heap, flower bed, greenhouse, hedge, herbaceous border, hothouse, lawn, orchard, patio, pergola, pond, rockery, rock garden, rose garden, shrubbery, terrace, vegetable garden, walled garden, water garden, window-box.

GARDEN TOOLS AND EQUIPMENT: bill-hook, broom, cloche, cultivator, dibber, fork, hedge-trimmer, hoe, hose, lawn aerator, lawnmower, lawn-rake, mattock, pruning-knife, rake, riddle, secateurs, shears, shovel, sickle, sieve, spade, sprayer, sprinkler, trowel, watering-can, wheelbarrow.

SOME GARDENING ACTIVITIES: cultivation, digging, hedge-cutting, hoeing, lawn-mowing, manuring, mulching, planting, pricking-out, pruning, raking, thinning-out, transplanting, watering, weeding.

RELATED ADJECTIVE: horticultural.

---

gardener noun horticulturist.

gardening noun cultivation, horticulture.

gargantuan adjective SEE **large**.

gargle noun mouthwash.

garish adjective SEE **gaudy**.

garment noun SEE **clothes**.

garner verb SEE **gather**.

garnish verb SEE **decorate**.

garret noun attic.

garrison noun **1** *A garrison of troops defended the town.* contingent, detachment, force, unit.
2 *The enemy took the garrison.* barracks, camp, citadel, fort, fortification, fortress, station, stronghold.

garrotte verb WAYS TO KILL: SEE **kill**.

garrulous adjective SEE **talkative**.

gas noun **1** *poisonous gas.* exhaust, fumes, vapour.
2 *cooking by gas.* OTHER FUELS: SEE **fuel**.

SOME GASES: carbon dioxide, carbon monoxide, coal gas, helium, hydrogen, laughing-gas, methane, natural gas, nitrogen, nitrous oxide, oxygen, ozone, sulphur dioxide, tear-gas.

---

gas verb WAYS TO KILL: SEE **kill**.

gasbag noun SEE **talkative (talkative person)**.

gash noun, verb SEE **cut** noun, verb.

gasoline noun [*informal*] gas, petrol.

gasp verb **1** *The smoke made them gasp.* blow, breathe with difficulty, choke, gulp, pant, puff, wheeze.
2 *He gasped his message.* SEE **speak**.

gasping adjective breathless, exhausted, puffed, tired out.

gate noun barrier, door, entrance, entry, exit, gateway, kissing-gate, [*poetic*] portal, portcullis, turnstile, way in, way out, wicket, wicket-gate.

gateau noun OTHER CAKES: SEE **cake** noun.

gatecrash verb SEE **intrude**.

gateway noun SEE **gate**.

gather verb **1** *to gather in a pile or crowd.* accumulate, amass, assemble, bring together, build up, cluster, collect, come together, concentrate, congregate, convene, crowd, flock together, forgather, get together, group, grow, herd, marshal, mass, meet, mobilize, muster, round up, swarm round, throng.
OPPOSITES: SEE **divide**, **scatter**.
2 *to gather a harvest.* cull, garner, get in, glean, harvest, heap up, hoard, pick, pick up, pile up, pluck, reap, stockpile, store up.
3 *I gather you've been ill.* conclude, deduce, guess, infer, learn, surmise, understand.

gathering noun *a gathering of people.* assembly, function, [*informal*] get-together, SEE **group** noun, meeting, party, social.

gauche adjective SEE **gawky**, **tactless**.

gaudy adjective [*uncomplimentary*] *gaudy colours.* bright, flamboyant, flashy, garish, loud (*loud colours*), lurid, ostentatious, showy, startling, tasteless, tawdry, vivid, vulgar.
OPPOSITES: SEE **tasteful**.

gauge noun *the gauge of a railway.* measurement, size, span, standard, width.

gauge verb SEE **estimate** verb, **measure** verb.

gaunt adjective **1** *gaunt after an illness.* bony, cadaverous, emaciated, haggard,

hollow-eyed, lank, lean, pinched, skeletal, skinny, starving, thin, wasted away.
OPPOSITES: SEE **healthy, plump**.
2 *a gaunt ruin.* bare, bleak, desolate, forbidding, grim.

gauntlet noun SEE **glove**.

gavel noun SEE **hammer** noun.

gawky adjective *gawky movements.* awkward, blundering, clumsy, gangling, gauche, inept, lumbering, maladroit, uncoordinated, ungainly, ungraceful, unskilful.
OPPOSITES: SEE **graceful**.

gay adjective 1 *gay colours. gay laughter.* animated, bright, carefree, cheerful, colourful, festive, fun-loving, SEE **happy**, jolly, jovial, joyful, light-hearted, lively, merry, sparkling, sunny, vivacious.
2 homosexual, lesbian, [*impolite*] queer.

gaze verb SEE **look** verb.

gazebo noun summer-house.

gazette noun SEE **newspaper**.

gear noun *camping gear.* accessories, apparatus, baggage, belongings, SEE **clothes**, equipment, [*informal*] get-up, harness, instruments, kit, luggage, paraphernalia, rig, stuff, tackle, things.

geezer noun SEE **person**.

gel verb SEE **harden**.

geld verb SEE **castrate**.

gelding noun SEE **horse**.

gem noun SEE **jewel**.

gender noun SEE **sex**.

genealogy noun SEE **descent**, family tree.

general adjective 1 *a general problem. our general experience.* accustomed, collective, common, communal, comprehensive, conventional, customary, everyday, familiar, global, habitual, normal, ordinary, popular, prevailing, regular, shared, typical, universal, usual, widespread.
OPPOSITES: SEE **local, special**.
3 *a general idea of where we are going.* approximate, broad, ill-defined, imprecise, indefinite, in outline, loose, unclear, unspecific, vague.
OPPOSITES: SEE **particular, specific**.
general practitioner SEE **doctor**.

generalize verb *to generalize about something.* be vague, draw general conclusions, speak in general terms.

generally adverb as a rule, broadly, chiefly, commonly, in the main, mainly, mostly, normally, on the whole, predominantly, principally, usually.

Several English words, including *generate, genesis, genetics,* and *genital,* are related to Latin *generare = beget,* and Greek *gen- = be produced.*

---

generate verb *to generate business.* beget, breed, bring about, cause, create, engender, give rise to, make, produce, propagate, [*informal*] whip up.

generation noun age-group, SEE **family**.

generosity noun bounty, largess, liberality, munificence, philanthropy.

generous adjective 1 *a generous sponsor.* bounteous, bountiful, charitable, [*informal*] free (*free with her money*), liberal, munificent, [*informal*] open-handed, philanthropic, unsparing, unstinting.
OPPOSITES: SEE **mean** adjective.
2 *a generous gift.* SEE **expensive**, princely, valuable.
OPPOSITES: SEE **worthless**.
3 *generous portions of food.* abundant, ample, bounteous, copious, SEE **large**, lavish, liberal, plentiful, sizeable, substantial, unstinting.
OPPOSITES: SEE **scanty**.
4 *a generous attitude.* benevolent, big-hearted, forgiving, impartial, kind, magnanimous, open, public-spirited, unmercenary, unprejudiced, unselfish.
OPPOSITES: SEE **selfish**.

genesis noun SEE **beginning**.

genial adjective *a genial welcome.* cheerful, easygoing, SEE **friendly**, good-natured, happy, jolly, kindly, pleasant, relaxed, sunny, warm, warm-hearted.
OPPOSITES: SEE **austere, unfriendly**.

genitals noun [*informal*] private parts, pudenda, sexual organs.

genius noun 1 *He has a genius for maths.* aptitude, bent, flair, gift, intellect, knack, talent.
2 *He's a mathematical genius.* academic, [*informal*] egg-head, expert, intellectual, [*uncomplimentary*] know-all, mastermind, thinker.

genre noun SEE **kind** noun.

genteel adjective SEE **polite**.

gentility noun SEE **manners (good manners)**.

gentle adjective 1 *a gentle person.* amiable, biddable, compassionate, docile, easygoing, good-tempered, harmless, humane, kind, kindly, lenient, loving, meek, merciful, mild, moderate, obedient, pacific, passive, peace-loving, pleasant, quiet, soft-hearted, sweet-tempered, sympathetic, tame, tender.
OPPOSITES: SEE **violent**.

2 *gentle music. a gentle voice.* low, muted, peaceful, quiet, reassuring, relaxing, soft, soothing.
OPPOSITES: SEE **harsh**.
3 *a gentle wind.* balmy, delicate, faint, light, soft, warm.
OPPOSITES: SEE **strong**.
4 *a gentle hint.* indirect, polite, subtle, tactful.
OPPOSITES: SEE **tactless**.
5 *a gentle hill.* gradual, hardly noticeable, imperceptible, moderate, slight, steady.
OPPOSITES: SEE **steep** adjective.

gentleman noun SEE **man** noun.

gentlemanly adjective SEE **polite**.

gentry noun SEE **class** noun.

genuflect verb *to genuflect before an altar.* bend the knee, bob, bow, kneel.

genuine adjective **1** *a genuine antique.* actual, authentic, authenticated, bona fide, legitimate, original, real, sterling.
OPPOSITES: SEE **fake** adjective.
2 *genuine feelings.* devout, earnest, frank, heartfelt, honest, sincere, true, unaffected, unfeigned.
OPPOSITES: SEE **insincere**.

genus noun SEE **kind** noun.

geography noun

MAJOR GEOGRAPHICAL AREAS: Antarctic, Arctic, the continents (Africa, Antarctica, Asia, Australasia, Europe, North America, South America), the oceans (Antarctic, Arctic, Atlantic, Indian, Pacific), the polar regions (North Pole, South Pole), the tropics.

EVERYDAY GEOGRAPHICAL TERMS: archipelago, bay, canyon, cape, capital, city, climate, continent, contour, conurbation, country, county, creek, dale, delta, downs, east, equator, estate, estuary, fells, fen, fjord, geyser, glacier, glen, gulf, hamlet, heath, hemisphere, highlands, hill.
industry, inlet, island, isthmus, lagoon, lake, land, latitude, longitude, mainland, north, oasis, parish, pass, peninsula, plain, plateau, pole, prairie, province, reef, relief map, river, sea, south, strait, subtropics, suburb, town, tributary, tropics, valley, village, volcano, west, world.

---

geometry noun SEE **mathematics**.

geriatric adjective SEE **old**.

germ noun **1** *the germ of a new organism. the germ of a new idea.* beginning, embryo, genesis, cause, nucleus, origin, seed.
2 *Germs can cause illness.* [*plural*] bacteria, [*informal*] bug, microbe, microorganism, virus.

germane adjective SEE **relevant**.

germinate verb *Seeds germinate in the right conditions.* begin to grow, bud, develop, grow, root, shoot, spring up, sprout, start growing, take root.

gestation noun SEE **pregnancy**.

gesticulate verb SEE **gesture** verb.

gesture noun *an eloquent gesture.* action, flourish, gesticulation, indication, motion, movement, sign, signal.

gesture verb make a gesture, sign, signal.

VARIOUS WAYS TO GESTURE: beckon, bow, gesticulate, motion, nod, point, salute, shake your head, shrug, smile, wave, wink.

---

get verb [*Get* can mean many things. We also use *get* in many phrases, the meanings of which depend on their context. For example, *to get on* could mean: *make progress* (*Get on with your work*); *step on a bus* (*Get on before it goes*); *be friendly* (*They get on with each other*); or *become older* (*Grandad is getting on*). All we can do here is to give a few synonyms for some of the main senses of *get*.]
1 *What can I get for £10?* acquire, be given, buy, come into possession of, gain, get hold of, obtain, procure, purchase, receive.
2 *Try to get him on the phone.* contact, get in touch with, speak to.
3 *Go and get the ball.* bring, fetch, pick up, retrieve.
4 *She got a prize.* earn, take, win.
5 *I got a cold.* catch, contract, develop, suffer from.
6 *They got the thieves.* apprehend, arrest, capture, catch.
7 *Get someone to help.* cause, persuade.
8 *I'll get tea.* make ready, prepare.
9 *I get what you mean.* comprehend, follow, grasp, understand.
10 *When did you get here?* arrive, reach.
11 *How can I get home?* come, go, travel.
12 *It got cold.* become, grow, turn.

getaway noun SEE **escape** noun.

gewgaw noun SEE **ornament** noun.

ghastly adjective *a ghastly mistake.* SEE **frightful**.

ghetto noun SEE **town**.

ghost noun apparition, [*informal*] bogy, ghostly apparition [SEE **ghostly**], hallucination, illusion, phantasm, phantom, poltergeist, shade, shadow, spectre, SEE

spirit, [*informal*] spook, vision, visitant, wraith.
to give up the ghost SEE **die**.

ghostly adjective *a ghostly noise.* creepy, disembodied, eerie, frightening, illusory, phantasmal, scary, spectral, [*informal*] spooky, supernatural, uncanny, unearthly, weird.

ghoul noun SEE **spirit**.

ghoulish adjective SEE **gruesome**.

giant adjective *a giant statue.* colossal, elephantine, enormous, gargantuan, gigantic, huge, immense, [*informal*] jumbo, [*informal*] king-size, SEE **large**, mammoth, massive, mighty, monstrous, prodigious, titanic, vast.
OPPOSITES: SEE **small**.

giant noun colossus, Goliath, giant person (SEE **giant** adjective], leviathan, monster, ogre, Titan, [*informal*] whopper.

gibber verb SEE **talk** verb.

gibberish noun SEE **nonsense**.

gibbet noun SEE **gallows**.

gibbon noun SEE **monkey**.

gibe verb SEE **jeer**.

giblets noun *giblets of a chicken.* insides, offal.

giddiness noun dizziness, faintness, unsteadiness, vertigo.

giddy adjective *a giddy feeling.* dizzy, faint, light-headed, reeling, silly, spinning, unbalanced, unsteady.

gift noun **1** *a birthday gift. a gift to charity.* bonus, bounty, contribution, donation, grant, gratuity, offering, present, tip.
2 *a gift for gymnastics.* ability, aptitude, bent, capability, capacity, flair, genius, knack, talent.

gifted adjective SEE **talented**.

gigantic adjective SEE **giant** adjective.

giggle verb SEE **laugh**, snigger, titter.

gild verb SEE **paint** verb.

gilt adjective gilded, gold-coloured, golden.

gimcrack adjective *gimcrack ornaments.* cheap, [*informal*] cheap and nasty, flimsy, rubbishy, shoddy, tawdry, trashy, trumpery, useless, worthless.

gimmick noun *a publicity gimmick.* device, ploy, stratagem, stunt, trick.

gingerly adjective *a gingerly approach.* SEE **cautious**.

girder noun *a framework of girders.* bar, beam, joist, rafter, RSJ.

girdle noun band, belt, corset, waistband.

girdle verb SEE **surround**.

girl noun [*old-fashioned*] damsel, daughter, débutante, hoyden, lass, [*old-fashioned*] maid, [*old-fashioned*] maiden, schoolgirl, tomboy, virgin, [*old-fashioned or sexist*] wench, SEE **woman**.

girth noun circumference, measurement round.

gist noun *the gist of a message.* direction, drift, essence, general sense, main idea, meaning, nub, point, significance.

give verb **1** *to give money. to give praise.* accord, allocate, allot, allow, apportion, assign, award, bestow, confer, contribute, deal out, [*informal*] dish out, distribute, [*informal*] dole out, donate, endow, entrust, [*informal*] fork out, furnish, give away, give out, grant, hand over, lend, let (someone) have, offer, pass over, pay, present, provide, ration out, render, share out, supply.
OPPOSITES: SEE **take**.
2 *to give information.* deliver, display, express, impart, issue, notify, publish, put across, put into words, reveal, set out, show, tell, transmit.
3 *to give a shout.* let out, utter, voice.
4 *to give punishment.* administer, impose, inflict, mete out.
5 *to give medicine.* dispense, dose with, give out, prescribe.
6 *to give a party.* arrange, organize, provide, put on, run, set up.
7 *to give out heat.* cause, create, emit, engender, generate, give off, produce, release, send out, throw out.
8 *to give under pressure.* be flexible, bend, buckle, distort, give way, warp, yield.
to give away *to give away secrets* SEE **betray**.
to give in *to give in after a fight.* SEE **surrender**.
to give up *to give up smoking.* SEE **abandon**.

glacial adjective SEE **icy**.

glacier noun SEE **ice**.

glad adjective SEE **pleased**.

gladden verb SEE **please**.

glade noun *a forest glade.* clearing, space.

glamorize verb idealize, romanticize.

glamorous adjective **1** *a glamorous film-star.* SEE **beautiful**.
2 *a glamorous life in show-business.* alluring, colourful, dazzling, enviable, exciting, fascinating, glittering, prestigious, smart, spectacular, wealthy.

glamour noun **1** SEE **beauty**.
2 *the glamour of show-business.* allure, appeal, attraction, excitement, fascination, glitter, high-life, lustre, magic.

glance noun, verb SEE **look** noun, verb.

glare noun **1** *an angry glare.* SEE **expression.**
2 *the glare from a fire.* SEE **light** noun.

glaring adjective SEE **bright, obvious.**

glass noun **1** *window glass.* double glazing, glazing, pane, plate-glass.
2 *a glass of water.* beaker, goblet, tumbler, wine-glass.
glasses VARIOUS OPTICAL INSTRUMENTS: bifocals, binoculars, contact-lenses, eye-glass, field-glasses, goggles, lorgnette, magnifying glass, monocle, opera-glasses, pince-nez, reading glasses, spectacles, sun-glasses, telescope.

glasshouse noun conservatory, greenhouse, hothouse, orangery, vinery.

glasspaper sandpaper.

glassy adjective **1** *a glassy stare.* SEE **expressionless.**
2 *a glassy surface.* glazed, shiny, vitreous.

gleam noun, verb SEE **light** noun.

gleaming adjective SEE **bright.**

glean verb SEE **gather.**

glebe noun SEE **field.**

glee noun SEE **joy.**

gleeful adjective SEE **joyful, triumphant.**

glen noun SEE **valley.**

glib adjective *a glib talker.* articulate, facile, fluent, insincere, plausible, quick, ready, slick, smooth, superficial, SEE **talkative.**
OPPOSITES: SEE **inarticulate, sincere.**

glide verb **1** *to glide across ice or snow.* coast, glissade, move smoothly, skate, ski, skid, skim, slide, slip.
2 *to glide through the air.* drift, float, fly, hang, hover, sail, soar.

glider noun SEE **aircraft.**

glimmer noun, verb SEE **light** noun.

glimpse noun *a quick glimpse.* glance, look, peep, sight, [*informal*] squint, view.

glimpse verb *I glimpsed someone moving between the trees.* discern, distinguish, espy, get a glimpse of, make out, notice, observe, see briefly, sight, spot, spy.

glint noun, verb, **glisten** verb, **glitter** noun, verb SEE **light** noun.

glittering adjective *a glittering occasion.* brilliant, colourful, glamorous, resplendent, scintillating, sparkling, SEE **splendid.**

gloaming noun SEE **evening.**

gloat verb *to gloat over a victim.* boast, brag, [*informal*] crow, exult, rejoice, [*informal*] rub it in, show off, triumph.

global adjective SEE **universal.**

globe noun **1** *the shape of a globe.* ball, orb, sphere.
2 *the globe we live on.* earth, planet, world.

globe-trotter noun SEE **traveller.**

globular adjective SEE **spherical.**

globule noun SEE **drop** noun.

gloom noun **1** *We could hardly see in the gloom.* cloudiness, dimness, dullness, dusk, murk, obscurity, semi-darkness, shade, shadow, twilight.
2 *a feeling of gloom.* SEE **depression.**

gloomy adjective **1** *a gloomy house. gloomy weather.* cheerless, cloudy, dark, depressing, dim, dingy, dismal, dreary, dull, glum, SEE **grim**, heavy, joyless, murky, overcast, shadowy, sombre.
OPPOSITES: SEE **bright.**
2 *a gloomy person.* SEE **depressed**, lugubrious, mournful, saturnine.

glorify verb SEE **praise** verb.

glorious adjective **1** *a glorious victory.* bringing glory [SEE **glory**], celebrated, distinguished, famous, heroic, illustrious, noble, noted, renowned, triumphant.
OPPOSITES: SEE **humiliating.**
2 *a glorious sunset.* beautiful, bright, brilliant, dazzling, excellent, fine, gorgeous, grand, impressive, lovely, magnificent, majestic, marvellous, resplendent, spectacular, splendid, [*informal*] super, superb, wonderful.

glory noun **1** *the glory of winning an Olympic medal.* credit, distinction, fame, honour, [*informal*] kudos, praise, prestige, success, triumph.
2 *glory to God.* adoration, homage, praise, thanksgiving, veneration, worship.
3 *the glory of the sunrise.* SEE **beauty**, brightness, brilliance, grandeur, magnificence, majesty, radiance, splendour.

gloss noun *I polished the table to a high gloss.* brightness, brilliance, burnish, lustre, polish, sheen, shine, varnish.

gloss verb **to gloss over** SEE **disguise** verb.

glossary noun dictionary, phrase-book, vocabulary, word-list.

glossy adjective *a glossy surface.* bright, burnished, glassy, glazed, gleaming, lustrous, polished, reflective, shiny, silky, sleek, smooth.
OPPOSITES: SEE **dull** adjective.

glove noun gauntlet, mitt, mitten.

glow noun **1** *the glow of a light bulb.* SEE **light** noun.

2 *the glow of a fire.* burning, fieriness, heat, incandescence, red-heat, redness.
3 *a glow in your cheeks.* blush, flush, rosiness, warmth.
4 *a glow of excitement.* ardour, enthusiasm, fervour, passion.

glow verb SEE **light** noun **(to give light)**.

glower verb frown, glare, lour, lower, scowl, stare angrily.
FACIAL EXPRESSIONS: SEE **expression**.

glowing adjective **1** *a glowing light.* bright, fluorescent, hot, incandescent, luminous, phosphorescent, radiant, red, red-hot, white-hot.
2 *a glowing recommendation.* complimentary, enthusiastic, fervent, passionate, warm.

glue noun [In addition to the words given here, there are many kinds of glue with proprietary names.] adhesive, cement, fixative, gum, paste, sealant, size, wallpaper-paste.

glue verb *to glue things together.* affix, bond, cement, fasten, fix, gum, paste, seal, stick.

gluey adjective SEE **sticky**.

glum adjective SEE **gloomy**.

glut noun *a glut of fruit.* abundance, excess, plenty, superfluity, surfeit, surplus.
OPPOSITES: SEE **scarcity**.

gluttonous adjective SEE **greedy**.

gnarled adjective *a gnarled old tree.* contorted, distorted, knobbly, knotted, lumpy, rough, rugged, twisted.

gnash verb *to gnash your teeth.* SEE **grind**.

gnaw verb *to gnaw a bone.* bite, chew, SEE **eat**.

go verb **1** *Let's go!* advance, begin, be off, commence, decamp, depart, disappear, embark, escape, get away, get going, get moving, get out, get under way, leave, move, [*informal*] nip along, pass along, pass on, proceed, retire, retreat, SEE **run** verb, set off, set out, [*informal*] shove off, start, take your leave, SEE **travel** verb, SEE **walk** verb, [*old-fashioned*] wend, withdraw.
2 *How far does this road go?* extend, lead, reach, stretch.
3 *The car won't go.* act, function, operate, perform, run, work.
4 *The firework went bang.* give off, make, produce, sound.
5 *Time goes quickly.* elapse, lapse, pass.
6 *Milk soon goes sour.* become, grow, turn.
7 *The butter goes in the fridge.* belong, feel at home, have your proper place.
8 *The light goes in the evening.* die, disappear, fade, fail, give way, vanish.
to go away SEE **depart**.
to go down SEE **sink** verb.
to go in for 1 *I go in for foreign food.* SEE **like** verb.
2 *They go in for competitions.* SEE **enter**.
to go into *Don't go into details.* SEE **investigate**.
to go off *A bomb went off.* SEE **explode**.
to go on *How long can you go on?* SEE **continue**.
to go through *She went through a nasty illness.* SEE **suffer**.
to go to *I want to go to America.* SEE **visit** verb.
to go with 1 *Will you go with me?* SEE **accompany**.
2 *What goes with blue?* SEE **match** verb.
to go without *They went without food.* SEE **abstain**.

goad verb *to goad someone to do something.* badger, [*informal*] chivvy, egg on, [*informal*] hassle, needle, prick, prod, prompt, spur, SEE **stimulate**, urge.

go-ahead adjective SEE **ambitious**.

goal noun *a goal in life.* aim, ambition, aspiration, design, end, intention, object, objective, purpose, target.

goat noun billy-goat, kid, nanny-goat.

gob noun SEE **mouth**.

gobble verb *to gobble food.* bolt, devour, SEE **eat**, gulp, guzzle.

gobbledegook noun SEE **nonsense**.

go-between noun agent, broker, envoy, intermediary, mediator, messenger, middleman.
to act as a go-between SEE **mediate**.

goblet noun SEE **cup**.

god, goddess nouns the Almighty, the Creator, deity, divinity, godhead.
the gods the immortals, pantheon, the powers above.
RELIGIOUS TERMS: SEE **religion**.

godless adjective SEE **irreligious**.

godly adjective SEE **religious**.

godsend noun *Her gift of money was a godsend.* blessing, miracle, stroke of good luck, windfall.

go-getting adjective SEE **ambitious**.

goggle verb gape, gawp, SEE **look** verb, stare.
goggles noun SEE **glass (glasses)**.

going-over noun **1** [*informal*] *I gave the car a going-over.* SEE **inspection**.
2 [*informal*] *The boss gave him a right going-over.* SEE **reprimand** noun.

golden adjective gilded, gilt, yellow.

goldsmith noun jeweller.

golliwog noun SEE **doll**.

gondolier noun SEE **boatman**.

good adjective [We apply the word *good* to anything we like or approve of. The number of possible synonyms, therefore, is virtually unlimited. We give here some of the more common words which express approval.]
1 [= *good* in a general sense] acceptable, admirable, agreeable, appropriate, approved of, champion, commendable, delightful, enjoyable, esteemed, SEE **excellent**, [*informal*] fabulous, fair, [*informal*] fantastic, fine, gratifying, happy, [*informal*] incredible, lovely, marvellous, nice, outstanding, perfect, [*informal*] phenomenal, pleasant, pleasing, praiseworthy, proper, remarkable, right, satisfactory, [*informal*] sensational, sound, splendid, [*informal*] super, superb, suitable, useful, valid, valuable, wonderful, worthy.
2 *a good person. a good deed.* angelic, benevolent, caring, charitable, chaste, considerate, decent, dependable, dutiful, ethical, friendly, helpful, holy, honest, honourable, humane, incorruptible, innocent, just, SEE **kind** adjective, law-abiding, loyal, merciful, moral, noble, obedient, personable, pure, reliable, religious, righteous, saintly, sound, [*informal*] straight, thoughtful, true, trustworthy, upright, virtuous, well-behaved, well-mannered, worthy.
3 *a good musician. a good worker.* able, accomplished, capable, SEE **clever**, conscientious, efficient, gifted, proficient, skilful, skilled, talented.
4 *good work.* competent, correct, creditable, efficient, meritorious, neat, orderly, presentable, professional, thorough, well-done.
5 *good food.* delicious, eatable, nourishing, nutritious, tasty, well-cooked, wholesome.
6 *a good book.* classic, exciting, great, interesting, readable, well-written.
a good person [*informal*] angel, [*informal*] jewel, philanthropist, [*informal*] saint, Samaritan, worthy.

goodbye interjection [Several terms we use when saying goodbye are from foreign languages. Generally, they are used informally.] adieu, adios, arrivederci, auf Wiedersehen, au revoir, bon voyage, ciao, cheerio, farewell, so long.
OPPOSITES: SEE **greeting**.

good-for-nothing adjective SEE **worthless**.

good-humoured adjective SEE **good-tempered**.

good-looking adjective SEE **handsome**.

good-natured adjective SEE **good-tempered**.

goods noun SEE **freight**.

good-tempered adjective accommodating, amenable, benevolent, benign, cheerful, considerate, cordial, friendly, good-humoured, good-natured, helpful, in a good mood, SEE **kind** adjective, obliging, patient, pleasant, relaxed, sympathetic, thoughtful, willing.
OPPOSITES: SEE **bad-tempered**.

goodwill noun SEE **friendliness**.

goody-goody adjective SEE **virtuous**.

gooey adjective SEE **sticky**.

goose noun gander, gosling.

gore noun *covered in gore.* blood.

gore verb *gored by a bull.* SEE **wound** verb.

gorge noun SEE **valley**.

gorge verb **to gorge yourself** SEE **eat**.

gorgeous adjective SEE **beautiful, magnificent**.

gormandize verb SEE **eat**.

gormless adjective SEE **stupid**.

gory adjective *a gory wound. a gory battle.* bloodstained, bloody, grisly, gruesome, savage.

gospel noun *preaching the gospel.* creed, doctrine, good news, good tidings, message, religion, revelation, teaching, testament.

gossamer noun cobweb, flimsy material, gauze.

gossip noun **1** *Don't listen to gossip.* casual talk, chatter, hearsay, prattle, rumour, scandal, [*informal*] tattle, [*informal*] tittle-tattle.
2 *Don't listen to him—he's a real gossip.* busybody, Nosy Parker, scandalmonger, SEE **talkative (talkative person)**, tell-tale.

gossip verb *They just stood gossiping.* chat, chatter, [*informal*] natter, prattle, spread scandal, SEE **talk** verb, [*informal*] tattle, tell tales, [*informal*] tittle-tattle.

gouge verb *to gouge out a hole.* chisel, SEE **cut** verb, dig, hollow, scoop.

goulash noun hash, stew.

gourmand noun SEE **greedy (greedy person)**.

gourmet noun connoisseur, epicure, gastronome.

govern verb **1** *to govern a country.* administer, be in charge of, command, conduct the affairs of, control, direct, guide, head, lead, look after, manage, oversee, preside over, reign, rule, run, steer, superintend, supervise.
2 *to govern your temper.* bridle, curb, check, control, discipline, keep in

check, keep under control, master, regulate, restrain, tame.

governess noun SEE **teacher**.

government noun *Any country needs strong government.* administration, bureaucracy, conduct of state affairs, constitution, control, direction, management, regime, regulation, rule, sovereignty, supervision, surveillance.

GROUPS INVOLVED IN GOVERNMENT: Cabinet, constituency, electorate, [*informal*] the Establishment, junta, local authority, ministry, parliament, [*informal*] the powers that be, regime, senate, state.

TYPES OF REGIME: commonwealth, democracy, dictatorship, empire, federation, kingdom, monarchy, oligarchy, republic.

PEOPLE INVOLVED IN GOVERNMENT OR PUBLIC ADMINISTRATION: ambassador, chancellor, Chancellor of the Exchequer, civil servant, consul, councillor, diplomat, elected representative, mayor, Member of Parliament, minister, politician, premier, president, prime minister, SEE **royalty**, Secretary of State (*Home Secretary, Foreign Secretary*, etc.), senator, statesman, stateswoman, viceroy.

---

governor noun SEE **chief** noun.

gown noun dress, frock.

grab verb *Grab what you can.* [*informal*] bag, capture, catch, clutch, [*informal*] collar, get hold of, grasp, hold, [*informal*] nab, pluck, seize, snap up, snatch.

grace noun **1** *grace of movement.* attractiveness, beauty, charm, ease, elegance, fluidity, gracefulness, loveliness, poise, refinement, softness, tastefulness.
2 *God's grace.* beneficence, benevolence, compassion, favour, forgiveness, goodness, graciousness, kindness, love, mercy.
3 *grace before dinner.* blessing, giving thanks, prayer.

graceful adjective **1** *graceful movements.* agile, balletic, deft, easy, flowing, fluid, natural, nimble, pliant, smooth, supple.
OPPOSITES: SEE **clumsy**.
2 *a graceful figure.* attractive, beautiful, dignified, elegant, slim, slender, willowy.
OPPOSITES: SEE **bony, fat** adjective.

graceless adjective **1** *graceless movements.* SEE **clumsy**.
2 *graceless manners.* SEE **rude**.

gracious adjective **1** *a gracious lady.* affable, agreeable, charitable, compassionate, courteous, dignified, elegant, friendly, good-natured, SEE **kind** adjective, pleasant, polite, with grace.
2 *a gracious judge.* SEE **merciful**.
3 *gracious living.* SEE **affluent**.

grade noun **1** *top grade meat.* class, condition, quality, standard.
2 *The examiner re-marked the work and put it up a grade.* category, level, mark, notch, point, position, rank, rung, step.

grade verb **1** *They grade eggs according to size.* arrange, categorize, classify, differentiate, group, range, sort.
2 *Teachers grade students' work.* assess, evaluate, mark, rank, rate.

gradient noun *a steep gradient.* ascent, bank, declivity, hill, incline, rise, slope.

gradual adjective *a gradual increase in prices. a gradual slope.* continuous, even, gentle, leisurely, moderate, slow, steady, unhurried, unspectacular.
OPPOSITES: SEE **steep** adjective, **sudden**.

graduate verb **1** *to graduate at a college or university.* become a graduate, be successful, get a degree, pass, qualify.
2 *to graduate a measuring-rod.* calibrate, divide into graded sections, mark off, mark with a scale.

graffiti plural noun SEE **picture** noun.

graft verb *to graft a bud onto a rose-bush.* implant, insert, join, splice.

grain noun **1** *the grain harvest.* SEE **cereal**.
2 *a grain of sand. a tiny grain.* bit, crumb, fragment, granule, iota, jot, mite, morsel, particle, seed, speck.
RELATED ADJECTIVE: granular.

grammar noun syntax.
LINGUISTIC TERMS: SEE **language**.

grammar school OTHER SCHOOLS: SEE **school**.

gramophone noun SEE **audio equipment**.

grand adjective **1** *a grand occasion. a grand house.* SEE **big**, dignified, glorious, great, important, imposing, impressive, lordly, magnificent, majestic, noble, opulent, [*uncomplimentary*] ostentatious, palatial, posh, [*uncomplimentary*] pretentious, regal, royal, splendid, stately, sumptuous, superb.
OPPOSITES: SEE **modest**.
2 [*often uncomplimentary*] *They're too grand for us.* aristocratic, august, eminent, SEE **grandiose**, haughty, [*informal*] high-and-mighty, patronizing, pompous, upper class, [*informal*] upper crust.
OPPOSITES: SEE **ordinary**.
3 *grand ideas.* SEE **unrealistic**.

grandchild noun granddaughter, grandson.
FAMILY RELATIONSHIPS: SEE **family**.

grandee noun SEE **aristocrat**.

grandeur noun SEE **splendour**.

grandiloquent adjective *grandiloquent language.* bombastic, elaborate, flowery, SEE **grandiose**, high-flown, inflated, ornate, poetic, pompous, rhetorical, turgid.
OPPOSITES: SEE **simple**.

grandiose adjective [*uncomplimentary*] *grandiose ideas.* affected, exaggerated, extravagant, flamboyant, SEE **grand**, SEE **grandiloquent**, ostentatious, [*informal*] over the top, pretentious, showy.
OPPOSITES: SEE **unpretentious**.

grandparent noun [*informal*] gran, [*informal*] grandad, grandfather, grandmother, [*informal*] grandpa, [*informal*] granny.
FAMILY RELATIONSHIPS: SEE **family**.

grant noun *a grant of money.* allocation, allowance, annuity, award, benefaction, bursary, donation, expenses, gift, honorarium, investment, loan, scholarship, sponsorship, subsidy.

grant verb **1** *to grant someone a sum of money.* allocate, allow, allot, award, confer, donate, give, pay, provide.
2 *She granted that I was right.* accept, acknowledge, admit, agree, concede, vouchsafe.

granular adjective *a granular substance.* crumbly, grainy, granulated, gritty, in grains, rough, sandy.
OPPOSITES: SEE **solid**.

granule noun SEE **grain**.

graph noun chart, column-graph, diagram, grid, pie chart, table.

graphic adjective *a graphic description.* SEE **vivid**.

graphics noun SEE **art**.

grapnel noun anchor, hook.

grapple verb **to grapple with 1** *to grapple with an intruder.* SEE **fight** verb, lay hold of, struggle with, tackle, wrestle with.
2 *to grapple with a problem.* attend to, come to grips with, contend with, cope with, deal with, engage with, get involved with, handle, [*informal*] have a go at, manage, try to solve.
OPPOSITES: SEE **avoid**.

grasp verb **1** *to grasp something in your hands.* catch, clasp, clutch, get hold of, grab, grapple with, grip, hang on to, hold, seize, snatch.
2 *to grasp an idea.* apprehend, comprehend, [*informal*] cotton on to, follow, learn, master, realize, take in, understand.
able to grasp prehensile.

grasping adjective *a grasping miser.* SEE **greedy**.

grass noun PLANTS RELATED TO GRASS: bamboo, esparto grass, pampas grass, sugar cane.

AREAS OF GRASS: downland, field, grassland, green, lawn, meadow, pasture, playing-field, prairie, recreation ground, savannah, steppe, [*poetic*] sward, turf, veld, village green.

---

grasshopper noun cicada, cricket.

grassy adjective grass-covered, green, turfed.

grate noun *a fire in the grate.* fireplace, hearth.

grate verb **1** *to grate cheese.* SEE **cut** verb, shred.
2 *a grating noise.* VARIOUS SOUNDS: SEE **sound** noun.
3 *His manner grates on me.* SEE **annoy**.

grateful adjective *grateful for the gift.* appreciative, indebted, obliged, thankful.
OPPOSITES: SEE **ungrateful**.

gratify verb SEE **please**.

grating noun *iron grating over a drain.* bars, grid, grille, lattice-work.

gratis adjective complimentary, free, without charge.

gratitude noun SEE **thanks**.

gratuitous adjective *gratuitous insults.* groundless, inappropriate, needless, unasked for, uncalled for, undeserved, unjustifiable, unmerited, unnecessary, unprovoked, unsolicited, unwarranted.
OPPOSITES: SEE **justifiable**.

gratuity noun *a gratuity at Christmas.* bonus, [*informal*] perk, present, recompense, reward, tip.

Several English words, including *aggravate, grave* (adjective), and *gravity,* are related to Latin *gravis = heavy, serious.*

---

grave adjective **1** *a grave decision.* crucial, SEE **important**, momentous, pressing, serious, significant, urgent, vital, weighty.
OPPOSITES: SEE **unimportant**.
2 *a grave illness.* acute, critical, dangerous, major, serious, severe, terminal, threatening, worrying.
OPPOSITES: SEE **slight** adjective.

3 *a grave offence.* criminal, indictable, punishable.
OPPOSITES: SEE **minor**.
4 *a grave expression.* dignified, earnest, gloomy, grim, long-faced, pensive, SEE **sad**, sedate, serious, severe, sober, solemn, sombre, subdued, thoughtful, unsmiling.
OPPOSITES: SEE **happy**.

grave noun *graves where people are buried.* barrow, burial-place, SEE **gravestone**, mausoleum, sepulchre, tomb, tumulus, vault.

gravel noun grit, pebbles, shingle, stones.

gravestone noun headstone, memorial, monument, tombstone.

graveyard noun burial-ground, cemetery, churchyard.

gravitate verb *We all gravitated towards the food.* be attracted to, descend on, head for, make for, move towards.

gravity noun **1** *the gravity of an illness.* acuteness, danger, importance, magnitude, momentousness, seriousness, severity.
2 *the gravity of a state occasion.* ceremony, dignity, earnestness, pomp, sedateness, sobriety, solemnity.
3 *the force of gravity.* gravitation, heaviness, ponderousness, pull, weight.

graze noun *a graze on the knee.* abrasion, laceration, raw spot.

graze verb **1** *grazing cattle.* SEE **eat**.
2 *to graze your knee.* [*formal*] abrade, chafe, scrape, scratch, SEE **wound** verb.

grease noun SEE **fat** noun, lubrication, oil.

greasy adjective **1** *greasy fingers.* fatty, oily, slippery, smeary.
2 *a greasy manner.* fawning, flattering, fulsome, grovelling, ingratiating, [*informal*] smarmy, sycophantic, unctuous.

great adjective **1** *a great mountain. a great ocean.* SEE **big**, colossal, enormous, extensive, huge, immense, large, tremendous.
2 *great pain. great difficulties.* acute, excessive, extreme, intense, SEE **severe**.
3 *a great event.* grand, SEE **important**, large-scale, momentous, serious, significant, spectacular.
4 *a great piece of music.* brilliant, classic, SEE **excellent**, [*informal*] fabulous, famous, [*informal*] fantastic, fine, first-rate, outstanding, wonderful.
5 *a great athlete.* able, celebrated, distinguished, eminent, SEE **famous**, gifted, notable, noted, prominent, renowned, talented, well-known.
6 *a great friend.* SEE **chief** adjective, close, devoted, main, valued.
7 *a great reader.* active, assiduous, SEE **enthusiastic**, frequent, keen.
8 [*informal*] *a great day out.* SEE **good**.
OPPOSITES: SEE **insignificant, small**.

greatcoat noun SEE **coat** noun, overcoat.

greed noun **1** *greed for food.* appetite, craving, gluttony, gormandizing, greediness, hunger, intemperance, insatiability, overeating, ravenousness, self-indulgence, voraciousness, voracity.
2 *greed for possessions.* acquisitiveness, avarice, covetousness, cupidity, desire, rapacity, self-interest, selfishness.

greedy adjective **1** *greedy for food.* famished, gluttonous, gormandizing, hungry, insatiable, intemperate, omnivorous, [*informal*] piggish, ravenous, self-indulgent, starving, voracious.
OPPOSITES: SEE **abstemious**.
2 *greedy for possessions.* acquisitive, avaricious, avid, covetous, desirous, eager, grasping, miserly, [*informal*] money-grabbing, rapacious, selfish.
OPPOSITES: SEE **unselfish**.
a greedy person glutton, [*joking*] good trencherman, gormandizer, gourmand, [*informal*] greedy-guts, guzzler, [*informal*] pig.
to be greedy gobble your food, gorge yourself, gormandize, guzzle, indulge yourself, [*informal*] make a pig of yourself, overeat.

green adjective, noun greenish, verdant.
SHADES OF GREEN: emerald, grass-green, jade, khaki, lime, olive, pea-green, turquoise.
OTHER COLOURS: SEE **colour** noun.
green light SEE **permission**.

greenery noun foliage, leaves, plants, vegetation.

greenhorn noun SEE **inexperienced (inexperienced person)**.

greenhouse noun SEE **glasshouse**.

greet verb *to greet visitors.* acknowledge, give a greeting to, hail, receive, salute, say (greeting) to [SEE **greeting**], welcome.

greeting noun salutation, welcome.
OPPOSITES: SEE **goodbye**.

VARIOUS WORDS OF GREETING: good day, good morning (afternoon, evening), hallo, hello, hullo, how do you do, welcome.

GREETINGS USED ON SPECIAL OCCASIONS: condolences, congratulations, felicitations, happy anniversary (birthday,

Christmas, etc.), many happy returns, sympathies, well done.

gregarious adjective SEE **sociable**.

gremlin noun SEE **mishap**.

grey adjective *grey hair. grey skies.* ashen, blackish, greying, grizzled, grizzly, hoary, leaden, silver, silvery, slate-grey, whitish.

grid noun 1 *an iron grid.* framework, grating, grille, lattice.
2 *Draw the plan on a grid.* graph paper, network of lines, pattern of intersecting lines, squares.

grief noun *the grief of bereavement.* affliction, anguish, desolation, distress, heartache, heartbreak, misery, mourning, pain, regret, remorse, sadness, sorrow, suffering, tragedy, [*informal*] trials and tribulations, unhappiness, woe.
OPPOSITES: SEE **happiness**.
to come to grief SEE **fail**.

grievance noun SEE **complaint**.

grieve verb 1 *The uncalled-for criticism grieved her.* afflict, cause grief to [SEE **grief**], depress, dismay, distress, hurt, pain, sadden, upset, wound.
OPPOSITES: SEE **delight** verb.
2 *He grieved terribly when his dog died.* feel grief [SEE **grief**], [*informal*] eat your heart out, fret, go into mourning, lament, mope, mourn, suffer, wail, weep.
OPPOSITES: SEE **rejoice**.

grievous adjective 1 *a grievous loss.* causing grief [SEE **grief**], SEE **sad**.
2 *a grievous disaster.* SEE **serious**.

grill noun grid, gridiron, toaster.

grill verb 1 *to grill bacon.* SEE **cook** verb.
2 *to grill a suspect.* SEE **question** verb.

grille noun *a grille over a window.* bars, grating, grid, lattice-work.

grim adjective 1 *a grim expression.* bad-tempered, cruel, dour, fearsome, fierce, forbidding, frightful, ghastly, gloomy, grisly, gruesome, harsh, hideous, horrible, [*informal*] horrid, menacing, merciless, ominous, relentless, severe, stark, stern, sullen, surly, terrible, threatening, unattractive, unfriendly, unrelenting.
2 *grim weather.* SEE **gloomy**.
OPPOSITES: SEE **cheerful, pleasant**.

grimace noun FACIAL EXPRESSIONS: SEE **expression**.

grime noun SEE **dirt**.

grimy adjective *grimy windows.* SEE **dirty** adjective.

grin noun FACIAL EXPRESSIONS: SEE **expression**.

grin verb beam, SEE **laugh**, smile.

grind verb 1 *to grind coffee, corn, etc.* crush, granulate, grate, mill, pound, powder, pulverize.
2 *to grind your teeth.* gnash, rub together.
3 *to grind a knife.* polish, sharpen, whet.
4 *to grind away. to grind down.* abrade, eat away, erode, file, sand, sandpaper, scrape, smooth, wear away.
5 *to grind people down.* SEE **oppress**.
6 *to grind away at a job.* labour, slave, sweat, toil, SEE **work** verb.

grindstone noun SEE **sharpener**.
to keep your nose to the grindstone SEE **work** verb.

grip noun *a firm grip.* clasp, clutch, control, grasp, hand-clasp, hold, purchase, stranglehold.
to come to grips with SEE **deal** verb (**to deal with**).

grip verb 1 *to grip someone's hand.* clasp, clutch, get a grip of [SEE **grip** noun], grab, grasp, hold, seize, take hold of.
2 *to grip someone's attention.* absorb, compel, engross, enthral, fascinate, rivet, spellbind.

gripe verb SEE **complain**.

grisly adjective [Don't confuse with *gristly*.] *a grisly accident.* SEE **gruesome**.

gristle noun *gristle in meat.* cartilage, gristly meat [SEE **gristly**].

gristly adjective [Don't confuse with *grisly*.] *gristly meat.* leathery, rubbery, tough, unchewable, uneatable.

grit noun 1 *grit in my eye.* dust, gravel, sand.
2 [*informal*] *grit in facing danger.* SEE **courage**.

grit verb 1 *to grit your teeth.* SEE **clench**.
2 *to grit the road.* salt, sand, treat.

gritty adjective *something gritty in the food.* abrasive, dusty, grainy, granular, gravelly, harsh, rough, sandy.

grizzle verb SEE **cry** verb.

grizzled, grizzly adjectives SEE **grey**.

groan verb *to groan with pain.* cry out, moan, sigh, wail.

groggy adjective SEE **ill**.

groom noun 1 [=*person who looks after horse*] ostler, stable-lad, stable-man.
2 [=*man on his wedding day*] bridegroom, husband.

groom verb 1 *to groom a horse. to groom yourself.* brush, clean, make neat, preen, smarten up, spruce up, tidy, [*informal*] titivate.
2 *to groom someone for a job.* coach, educate, get ready, prepare, train up.

groove noun *a groove in a surface.* channel, cut, fluting, furrow, gutter, indentation, rut, score, scratch, slot, track.

grope verb *to grope in the dark. to grope for an answer.* cast about, feel about, flounder, fumble, search blindly.

gross adjective 1 *a gross figure.* SEE **fat** adjective.
2 *gross manners.* SEE **vulgar**.
3 *gross injustice.* SEE **obvious**.
4 *gross income.* SEE **total** adjective.

grotesque adjective *grotesque carvings.* absurd, bizarre, deformed, distorted, fantastic, ludicrous, macabre, malformed, misshapen. monstrous, preposterous, ridiculous, strange, ugly, unnatural, weird.

grotto noun cave, cavern, underground chamber.

grouch verb SEE **complain**.

ground noun 1 *the ground someone owns.* area, land, property, terrain.
2 *fertile ground.* clay, earth, loam, soil.
3 *the grounds of a building.* campus, estate, gardens, park, playing-fields, surroundings.
4 *a sports ground.* arena, field, pitch, stadium.
5 *If you accuse someone, be sure of your ground.* argument, basis, case, cause, evidence, foundation, proof, reason.

ground verb 1 *to ground a ship.* beach, run ashore, shipwreck, strand, wreck.
OPPOSITES: SEE **float** verb.
2 *to ground an aircraft.* keep on the ground, prevent from flying.
OPPOSITES: SEE **fly** verb.
3 *On what facts do you ground your argument?* SEE **base** verb.

grounding noun *a thorough grounding in maths.* SEE **teaching**.

groundless adjective *a groundless accusation.* baseless, false, gratuitous, imaginary, irrational, needless, uncalled for, unfounded, unjustified, unproven, unreasonable, unsubstantiated, unsupported, unwarranted.
OPPOSITES: SEE **justifiable**.

groundsheet noun SEE **waterproof** noun.

group noun

VARIOUS GROUPS OF PEOPLE: alliance, assembly, association, band, bevy (*of women*), body, brotherhood, [*informal*] bunch, cadre, cartel, caste, caucus, circle (*of friends*), clan, class, [*uncomplimentary*] clique, club, cohort (*of soldiers*), colony, committee, community, company, conclave (*of cardinals*), congregation (*of worshippers*), consortium, contingent, coterie, coven (*of witches*), crew, crowd, delegation, faction (*a break-away faction*), family, federation, force (*of invaders*), fraternity, gang, gathering, guild (*of workers*), horde, host, knot, league, meeting, [*uncomplimentary*] mob, multitude, organization, party, phalanx (*of soldiers*), picket (*of strikers*), platoon, posse (*of law-enforcers*), [*uncomplimentary*] rabble, ring (*of criminals*), sect, [*uncomplimentary*] shower, sisterhood, society, squad, squadron, swarm, team, throng, troop (*of soldiers*), troupe (*of actors*), union.

GROUPS OF ANIMALS, THINGS, ETC.: accumulation, assortment, batch, battery (*of guns*), brood (*of chicks*), bunch, bundle, category, class, clump (*of trees*), cluster, clutch (*of eggs*), collection, combination, conglomeration, constellation (*of stars*), convoy (*of ships*), covey (*of birds*), fleet (*of ships*), flock (*of birds or sheep*), gaggle (*of geese*), galaxy (*of stars*), herd (*of animals*), hoard, host, litter (*of pigs*), mass, pack (*of wolves*), pride (*of lions*), school, set, shoal (*of fish*), species.
groups of musicians: SEE **music**.

---

group verb 1 *to group things together.* arrange, assemble, bring together, categorize, classify, collect, deploy, gather, herd, marshal, order, organize, put into groups [SEE **group** noun], set out, sort.
2 *to group around a leader.* associate, band, cluster, come together, congregate, crowd, flock, gather, get together, herd, make groups [SEE **group** noun], swarm, team up, throng.

grouse verb SEE **complain**.

grove noun *a grove of trees.* SEE **wood**.

grovel verb *Don't grovel—stick up for yourself!* abase yourself, be humble, cower, [*informal*] creep, cringe, demean yourself, [*informal*] kowtow, prostrate yourself, snivel, [*informal*] toady.

grow verb 1 *Plants grow well in springtime.* become bigger, burgeon, come to life, develop, emerge, evolve, fill out, flourish, germinate, get bigger, increase in size, lengthen, live, make progress, mature, multiply, mushroom, proliferate, put on growth, spread, spring up, sprout, survive, swell, thicken up, thrive.
OPPOSITES: SEE **die**.
2 *I grow roses.* cultivate, farm, help along, nurture, produce, propagate, raise.
OPPOSITES: SEE **kill**.

3 *Her business grew. Her confidence grew.* augment, build up, develop, enlarge, expand, extend, improve, increase, progress, prosper.
OPPOSITES: SEE **shrink**.
4 *She grew more confident.* become, turn.
to grow up become adult, mature.

growl verb snarl.

grown-up adjective adult, fully grown, mature, well-developed.

growth noun **1** *the growth of children.* advance, development, education, getting bigger, growing, maturation, maturing, progress.
2 *the growth of wealth.* accretion, augmentation, enlargement, expansion, improvement, increase, prosperity, success.
3 *growth in the garden.* crop, plants, vegetation.
4 *a growth on the body.* cancer, cyst, excrescence, lump, swelling, tumour.

groyne noun breakwater.

grub noun **1** *a grub in an apple.* caterpillar, larva, maggot.
2 [*informal*] *pub grub.* SEE **food**.

grub verb *to grub up the soil.* SEE **dig**.

grubby adjective *grubby clothes.* SEE **dirty** adjective.

grudge noun *a grudge against someone.* SEE **resentment**.

grudge verb SEE **resent**.

grudging adjective *grudging admiration.* cautious, envious, guarded, half-hearted, hesitant, jealous, reluctant, resentful, secret, unenthusiastic, ungracious, unkind, unwilling.
OPPOSITES: SEE **enthusiastic**.

gruel noun porridge.

gruelling adjective *a gruelling climb.* arduous, backbreaking, demanding, difficult, exhausting, fatiguing, hard, laborious, punishing, severe, stiff, strenuous, taxing, tiring, tough, uphill, wearying.
OPPOSITES: SEE **easy**.

gruesome adjective *a gruesome accident.* appalling, awful, bloody, disgusting, dreadful, fearful, frightful, ghastly, ghoulish, gory, grim, grisly, hair-raising, hideous, horrible, [*informal*] horrid, horrifying, macabre, revolting, sickening, terrible.

gruff adjective **1** *a gruff voice.* harsh, hoarse, husky, rough.
2 *a gruff manner.* SEE **bad-tempered**.

grumble verb SEE **complain**.

grumpy adjective SEE **bad-tempered**.

grunt verb VARIOUS SOUNDS: SEE **sound** noun.

guarantee noun assurance, oath, pledge, promise, surety, warranty.

guarantee verb **1** *to guarantee that a thing works.* assure, certify, give a guarantee, pledge, promise, swear, vouch, vow.
2 *This ticket guarantees your seat.* ensure, make sure of, secure.

guard noun *a prison guard.* custodian, escort, lookout, patrol, security-officer, sentinel, sentry, warder, watchman.
on your guard SEE **alert** adjective.
to stand guard over SEE **guard** verb.

guard verb *A mother guards her young. A warder guards prisoners.* be on guard over, care for, defend, keep safe, keep watch on, look after, mind, oversee, patrol, police, preserve, prevent from escaping, protect, safeguard, secure, shelter, shield, stand guard over, supervise, tend, watch, watch over.
OPPOSITES: SEE **abandon**.

guarded adjective *a guarded remark.* SEE **cautious**.

guardian noun **1** *the guardian of a child.* adoptive parent, foster-parent.
2 *a guardian of public morals.* custodian, defender, keeper, minder, preserver, protector, trustee, warden, warder.

guardsman noun SEE **soldier**.

guerrilla noun SEE **fighter**.

guess noun *a guess about the future.* assumption, conjecture, estimate, feeling, [*informal*] guesstimate, guesswork, hunch, hypothesis, intuition, opinion, prediction, [*informal*] shot in the dark, speculation, supposition, surmise, suspicion, theory.

guess verb *I guess it will cost a lot.* assume, conjecture, divine, estimate, expect, feel, have a hunch, have a theory, [*informal*] hazard a guess, hypothesize, imagine, judge, make a guess [SEE **guess** noun], predict, speculate, suppose, surmise, suspect, think likely.

guesstimate, guesswork nouns SEE **guess** noun.

guest noun **1** *guests at home.* caller, company, visitor.
2 *hotel guests.* boarder, customer, lodger, resident, tenant.

guest-house noun SEE **accommodation**.

guffaw verb SEE **laugh**.

guidance noun *He was new to the job and needed guidance.* advice, briefing, counselling, direction, guidelines, guiding, help, instruction, [*informal*] spoon-feeding, [*informal*] taking by the hand, teaching, tips.

guide noun **1** *a guide who shows the way.* courier, escort, leader, pilot.
2 *maps and guides from the bookshop.* atlas, directory, gazetteer, guidebook, handbook.

guide verb **1** *to guide someone on a journey.* conduct, direct, escort, lead, manœuvre, navigate, pilot, steer, supervise.
2 *to guide someone in her studies.* advise, brief, counsel, direct, educate, give guidance to [SEE **guidance**], help along, influence, [*informal*] take by the hand, teach, train.
OPPOSITES: SEE **mislead**.

guidelines noun SEE **guidance**.

guile noun SEE **cunning** noun.

guileful adjective SEE **cunning** adjective.

guillotine verb **1** *to guillotine a criminal.* behead, decapitate, SEE **execute**.
2 *to guillotine paper.* SEE **cut** verb.
3 *to guillotine a debate.* SEE **curtail**.

guilt noun **1** *The evidence proved his guilt.* blame, blameworthiness, criminality, culpability, fault, guiltiness, liability, responsibility, sinfulness, wickedness.
OPPOSITES: SEE **innocence**.
2 *a look of guilt on her face.* bad conscience, contrition, dishonour, guilty feelings, penitence, regret, remorse, self-accusation, self-reproach, shame.
OPPOSITES: SEE **virtue**.

guiltless adjective *a guiltless conscience.* above suspicion, blameless, clear, faultless, free, honourable, immaculate, innocent, irreproachable, pure, sinless, untarnished, untroubled, virtuous.
OPPOSITES: SEE **guilty**.

guilty adjective **1** *guilty of wrongdoing.* at fault, blamable, blameworthy, culpable, in the wrong, liable, reprehensible, responsible.
OPPOSITES: SEE **innocent**.
2 *a guilty look.* ashamed, conscience-stricken, contrite, penitent, regretful, remorseful, repentant, shamefaced, sheepish, sorry.
OPPOSITES: SEE **guiltless**.

guise noun SEE **pretence**.

gulf noun **1** *the Gulf of Mexico.* bay.
2 *a deep gulf.* SEE **chasm**.

gullet noun throat.

gullible adjective *He's so gullible he'll believe anything.* credulous, easily taken in, [*informal*] green, impressionable, innocent, naïve, suggestible, trusting, unsuspecting.

gully noun SEE **channel** noun.

gulp verb *to gulp food or drink.* SEE **drink** verb, **eat**.

gum noun *a pot of gum.* SEE **glue** noun.

gummed adjective *gummed paper.* adhesive, gluey, sticky.

gummy adjective SEE **sticky**.

gumption noun [*informal*] *Use your gumption.* common sense, initiative, judgement, [*informal*] nous, sense, wisdom.

gun noun [*plural*] artillery, firearm.

VARIOUS GUNS: airgun, automatic, blunderbuss, cannon, machine-gun, mortar, musket, pistol, revolver, rifle, shot-gun, small-arms, sub-machine-gun, tommy-gun.

PARTS OF A GUN: barrel, bolt, breach, butt, magazine, muzzle, sights, trigger.

---

gun verb **to gun down** SEE **shoot** verb.

gunfire noun cannonade, firing, gunshots, salvo.

gunman noun assassin, bandit, criminal, desperado, SEE **fighter**, gangster, killer, murderer, sniper, terrorist.

gunner noun SEE **soldier**.

gunpowder noun SEE **explosive** noun.

gunship noun SEE **aircraft**.

gunshot noun SEE **gunfire**.

gurgle verb VARIOUS SOUNDS: SEE **sound** noun.

guru noun leader, SEE **teacher**.

gush noun *a gush of liquid.* burst, cascade, eruption, flood, flow, jet, outpouring, overflow, rush, spout, spurt, squirt, stream, tide, torrent.

gush verb *Liquid gushed out.* come in a gush, cascade, flood, flow quickly, overflow, pour, run, rush, spout, spurt, squirt, stream, well up.
OPPOSITES: SEE **trickle**.

gusher noun oil well.

gust noun SEE **wind** noun.

gusto noun *The musicians played with gusto.* enjoyment, SEE **liveliness**, spirit, verve, zest.

gusty adjective SEE **windy**.

gut adjective *a gut feeling.* SEE **instinctive**.

gut noun [*often plural, informal*] *a pain in the guts.* belly, bowels, entrails, [*informal*] innards, insides, intestines, stomach.
guts [*informal*] *She had guts.* SEE **courage**.

gut verb **1** *to gut an animal.* clean, disembowel, draw, remove the guts of.

2 *to gut a building.* clear, empty, ransack, remove the contents of, strip.

gutless adjective SEE **cowardly.**

gutter noun *a gutter to carry away water.* channel, conduit, ditch, drain, duct, guttering, sewer, sluice, trench, trough.

guttural adjective *a guttural voice.* SEE **throaty.**

guy verb SEE **imitate, ridicule** verb.

guzzle verb SEE **drink** verb, **eat.**

gymnasium noun gym, sports-hall.

gymnastics noun VARIOUS SPORTS: SEE **sport.**

gypsy noun nomad, Romany, traveller, wanderer.

gyrate verb circle, pirouette, revolve, rotate, spin, spiral, turn, twirl, wheel, whirl.

H

habit noun **1** *the habit of shaking hands.* convention, custom, practice, routine, rule, [*old-fashioned*] wont.
2 *the habit of scratching your head.* manner, mannerism, propensity, quirk, tendency, way.
3 *the habit of smoking.* addiction, compulsion, confirmed habit, craving, dependence, fixation, obsession, vice.
to have a compulsive habit be addicted, be a slave, [*informal*] be hooked.
to have a habit of be accustomed to, be used to, do habitually [SEE **habitual**], practice.

Several English words, including *habitable, habitat, habitation,* and *inhabit,* are related to Latin *habitare = to inhabit.* Compare French *habiter.*

---

habitable adjective *a habitable building.* in good repair, inhabitable, usable.
OPPOSITE: uninhabitable.

habitation noun SEE **home.**

habitual adjective **1** *my habitual route to work.* accustomed, common, conventional, customary, expected, familiar, fixed, frequent, natural, normal, ordinary, predictable, regular, routine, standard, traditional, typical, usual, [*old-fashioned*] wonted.
OPPOSITES: SEE **abnormal.**
2 *a habitual weakness.* addictive, besetting, chronic, established, ineradicable, ingrained, obsessive, persistent, recurrent.
3 *a habitual smoker.* addicted, conditioned, confirmed, dependent, [*informal*] hooked, inveterate, persistent.
OPPOSITES: SEE **occasional.**

habituate verb SEE **accustom.**

habitué noun SEE **regular** noun.

hack noun **1** SEE **horse.**
2 SEE **writer.**

hack verb SEE **cut** verb.

hackneyed adjective *hackneyed language.* banal, clichéd, cliché-ridden, commonplace, conventional, [*informal*] corny, familiar, feeble, obvious, overused, pedestrian, platitudinous, predictable, stale, stereotyped, stock, threadbare, tired, trite, uninspired, unoriginal.
OPPOSITES: SEE **exciting, new.**

Hades noun SEE **hell.**

Several English words, including *haemophilia, haemorrhage,* and *haemorrhoid,* are related to Greek *haima = blood.*

---

haemorrhage noun bleeding, internal bleeding.

haemorrhoids noun piles.

haft noun SEE **handle** noun.

hag noun SEE **woman.**

haggard adjective *haggard with exhaustion.* [*informal*] all skin and bone, careworn, drawn, emaciated, exhausted, gaunt, hollow-eyed, pinched, shrunken, thin, tired out, ugly, unhealthy, wasted, withered, worn out, [*informal*] worried to death.
OPPOSITES: SEE **healthy.**

haggle verb *to haggle over the price.* argue, bargain, barter, discuss terms, negotiate, SEE **quarrel** verb, wrangle.

hail verb SEE **greet.**

hair noun **1** *hair on an animal's skin.* bristles, fleece, fur, mane.
2 *hair on your head.* curls, hank, locks, [*informal*] mop, shock, tresses.

WORDS TO DESCRIBE THE COLOUR OF HAIR: auburn, [*male*] blond, [*female*] blonde, brunette, [*informal*] carotty, dark, fair, flaxen, ginger, SEE **grey**, grizzled, mousy, platinum blonde, redhead.
VARIOUS HAIR-STYLES: SEE **hair-style.**

---

hairdresser noun barber, [*male*] coiffeur, [*female*] coiffeuse, hair-stylist.

hairless adjective bald, bare, clean-shaven, naked, shaved, shaven, smooth.
OPPOSITES: SEE **hairy**.

hairpin adjective *a hairpin bend.* acute, sharp, V-shaped.

hair-raising adjective SEE **frightening**.

hair-splitting SEE **fussy**.

hair-style noun coiffure, cut, hair-cut, [*informal*] hair-do, style.

VARIOUS HAIR-STYLES: bob, crew-cut, dreadlocks, fringe, Mohican, [*informal*] perm, permanent wave, pigtail, plaits, pony-tail, quiff, short back and sides, sideboards, sideburns, tonsure, top-knot.

FALSE HAIR: hair-piece, toupee, wig.

---

hairy adjective *hairy skin.* bearded, bristly, downy, feathery, fleecy, furry, fuzzy, hirsute, long-haired, shaggy, stubbly, woolly.
OPPOSITES: SEE **hairless**.

hale adjective SEE **healthy**.

half-baked adjective SEE **silly**.

half-caste noun half-breed, mulatto, person of mixed race.

half-hearted adjective *half-hearted about her work.* apathetic, cool, easily distracted, feeble, indifferent, ineffective, lackadaisical, listless, lukewarm, passive, perfunctory, uncommitted, unenthusiastic, unreliable, wavering, weak, [*informal*] wishy-washy.
OPPOSITES: SEE **committed**.

half-wit noun SEE **idiot**.

hall noun **1** *the village hall.* assembly hall, auditorium, concert-hall, theatre.
2 *Wait in the hall.* corridor, entrance-hall, foyer, hallway, lobby, passage, vestibule.

hallmark noun SEE **characteristic** noun.

hallowed adjective *hallowed ground.* blessed, consecrated, dedicated, holy, honoured, revered, reverenced, sacred, sacrosanct, worshipped.
OPPOSITE: desecrated [SEE **desecrate**].

hallucinate verb day-dream, dream, fantasize, [*informal*] have a trip, have hallucinations, [*informal*] see things, see visions.

hallucination noun apparition, day-dream, delusion, dream, fantasy, figment of the imagination, illusion, mirage, vision.

halo noun SEE **light** noun.

halt noun **1** *a halt in our progress.* break, interruption, pause, standstill, stop, stoppage.
2 *a railway halt.* platform, station.

halt verb **1** *A traffic-jam halted traffic.* arrest, block, check, curb, impede, obstruct, stop.
2 *Traffic halts at a red light.* come to a halt, come to rest, draw up, pull up, stop, wait.
3 *Work halted when the whistle went.* break off, cease, end, terminate.
OPPOSITES: SEE **start** verb.

halter noun SEE **harness** noun.

halting adjective *halting speech. halting progress.* erratic, faltering, hesitant, irregular, stammering, stumbling, stuttering, uncertain, underconfident, unsure.
OPPOSITES: SEE **fluent**.

halve verb *to halve your income.* bisect, cut by half, cut in half, decrease, divide into halves, lessen, reduce by half, share equally, split in two.

halyard noun SEE **rope** noun.

ham noun SEE **meat**.

ham verb [*informal*] *The actor hammed up the part dreadfully.* act exaggeratedly, [*informal*] camp it up, overact, overdo, overdramatize, [*informal*] send it up.

hamlet noun settlement, village.

hammer noun mallet, sledge-hammer.
to put under the hammer SEE **sell**.

hammer verb *to hammer on the door.* bash, batter, beat, SEE **hit** verb, knock, strike.

hammock noun SEE **bed**.

hamper noun *a picnic hamper.* SEE **basket**.

hamper verb **1** *Bad weather hampered the work.* curb, curtail, foil, hold up, interfere with, obstruct, prevent, restrict, thwart.
2 *My wellingtons hampered me when I ran.* encumber, entangle, fetter, frustrate, handicap, hinder, hold back, impede, restrain, shackle, slow down, trammel.
OPPOSITES: SEE **help** verb.

hamstring verb SEE **cripple** verb.

hand noun **1** *a human hand.* fist, palm.
RELATED ADJECTIVE: manual.
2 *hands on a clock.* pointer.
3 [*old-fashioned*] *factory hands.* SEE **worker**.
at hand, on hand, to hand available, close by, present, waiting, within reach.
to give a hand SEE **help** verb.

hand verb *to hand something to someone.* convey, deliver, give, offer, pass, present, submit.

to hand down *to hand down property.* bequeath, leave as a legacy, pass down, pass on, will.
to hand over 1 *to hand over money.* donate, [*informal*] fork out, give up, pay, surrender, tender.
2 *to hand over a prisoner.* deliver up, extradite, release, [*informal*] turn over.
to hand round *to hand round the drinks.* circulate, deal out, distribute, give out, pass round, share.

handbag noun bag, purse.

handbook noun guide, instruction book, manual.

handicap noun **1** *Luggage is a handicap when you run for a train.* difficulty, disadvantage, drawback, encumbrance, hindrance, inconvenience, [*informal*] minus, nuisance, obstacle, problem, restriction, shortcoming, stumbling-block.
OPPOSITES: SEE **advantage**.
2 *Blindness is a handicap.* defect, disability, impairment, impediment, limitation.

handicap verb *A strong wind handicapped the athletes.* be a handicap to [SEE **handicap** noun], burden, create problems for, disadvantage, encumber, hamper, hinder, hold back, impede, limit, restrict, retard.
OPPOSITES: SEE **help** verb.

handicapped adjective *handicapped people.* disabled, disadvantaged.

SOME WAYS IN WHICH YOU CAN BE HANDICAPPED: autistic, crippled, deaf, disabled, dumb, dyslexic, impaired hearing or sight, lame, limbless, maimed, mute, paralysed, paraplegic, retarded, slow.

---

handicraft noun SEE **art**.

handkerchief noun [*informal*] hanky, tissue.

handiwork noun *Is this your handiwork?* achievement, creation, doing, invention, production, responsibility, work.

handle noun *Hold it by the handle.* grip, haft, hand-grip, helve, hilt (*of a sword*), knob, stock (*of a rifle*).

handle verb **1** *Take care how you handle small animals.* feel, finger, fondle, grasp, hold, [*informal*] maul, [*informal*] paw, stroke, touch, treat.
2 *to handle a rowdy class. to handle a situation.* conduct, control, cope with, deal with, guide, look after, manage, manipulate, supervise.
3 *The car handles well.* manœuvre, operate, respond, steer, work.
4 *We don't handle second-hand goods.* deal in, do trade in, sell, stock, touch, traffic in.

handsome adjective **1** *a handsome man.* attractive, comely, good-looking, personable.
2 *handsome furniture.* admirable, beautiful, elegant, tasteful, well-made.
OPPOSITES: SEE **ugly**.
3 *a handsome gift. a handsome gesture.* big, big-hearted, bountiful, generous, gracious, large, liberal, magnanimous, munificent, sizeable, unselfish, valuable.
OPPOSITES: SEE **mean** adjective.

handwriting noun SEE **writing**.

handy adjective **1** *a handy tool.* convenient, easy to use, helpful, manageable, practical, serviceable, useful, well-designed, worth having.
OPPOSITES: SEE **awkward**.
2 *Keep your tools handy.* accessible, available, close at hand, easy to reach, get-at-able, nearby, reachable, ready.
OPPOSITES: SEE **inaccessible**.
3 *She's handy with tools.* adept, capable, clever, competent, practical, proficient, skilful.
OPPOSITES: SEE **incompetent**.

handyman noun maintenance man, odd-job man.

hang verb **1** *A flag hangs from a flagpole.* be hanging [SEE **hanging**], dangle, droop, swing, trail down.
2 *to hang washing on a line. to hang pictures on a wall.* attach, fasten, fix, peg up, pin up, stick up, suspend.
3 *Smoke hung in the air.* drift, float, hover.
4 *to hang criminals.* SEE **execute**.
to hang about *Don't hang about in the cold.* dally, dawdle, linger, loiter.
to hang back *You'll lose your chance if you hang back.* hesitate, pause, wait.
to hang on *Try to hang on until help comes.* carry on, continue, endure, hold on, keep going, persevere, persist, stay with it, stick it out, wait.
to hang on to *Hang on to the rope.* catch, grasp, hold, keep, retain, seize.

hangdog adjective *a hangdog expression.* SEE **shamefaced**.

hang-glider noun SEE **aircraft**.

hanging adjective dangling, drooping, flopping, pendent, pendulous, swinging loose, suspended.

hangings noun *hangings on the wall.* draperies, drapes, tapestries.

hangman noun executioner.

hang-up noun SEE **inhibition**.

hank noun *a hank of wool.* coil, length, loop, piece, skein.

hanker verb **to hanker after** SEE **desire** verb.

haphazard adjective *The organization was haphazard.* accidental, arbitrary, chaotic, confusing, disorderly, SEE **disorganized**, [*informal*] higgledy-piggledy, [*informal*] hit-or-miss, random, unplanned.
OPPOSITES: SEE **orderly**.

hapless adjective SEE **unlucky**.

happen verb *Did anything interesting happen?* arise, befall, [*old-fashioned*] betide, chance, come about, crop up, emerge, follow, materialize, occur, result, take place, [*informal, sometimes regarded as incorrect*] transpire.
to happen on SEE **find** verb.

happening noun *an unexpected happening.* accident, affair, chance, circumstance, event, incident, occasion, occurrence, phenomenon.

happiness noun bliss, cheer, SEE **cheerfulness**, contentment, delight, ecstasy, elation, euphoria, exhilaration, exuberance. felicity, gaiety, gladness, heaven, high spirits, joy, jubilation, light-heartedness, merriment, pleasure, pride, rapture, well-being.
OPPOSITES: SEE **sorrow** noun.

happy adjective **1** *a happy person. a happy event.* beatific, blessed, blissful, [*poetic*] blithe, SEE **cheerful**, contented, delighted, ecstatic, elated, exultant, felicitous, festive, gay, glad, gleeful, good-humoured, halcyon (*halcyon days*), heavenly, idyllic, jolly, joyful, joyous, laughing, light-hearted, lively, merry, overjoyed, [*informal*] over-the-moon, pleased, proud, radiant, rapturous, relaxed, [*informal*] starry-eyed, thrilled.
OPPOSITES: SEE **unhappy**.
2 *a happy accident.* advantageous, convenient, favourable, fortunate, lucky, opportune, propitious, timely, well-timed.
OPPOSITES: SEE **unlucky**.

happy-go-lucky adjective SEE **carefree**.

harangue noun SEE **speech**.

harangue verb SEE **speak**.

harass verb *Dogs mustn't harass the sheep.* annoy, badger, bait, bother, disturb, harry, [*informal*] hassle, hound, make harassed [SEE **harassed**], molest, persecute, pester, [*informal*] plague, torment, trouble, vex, worry.

harassed adjective *a harassed look.* [*informal*] at the end of your tether, careworn, distraught, distressed, exhausted, frayed, [*informal*] hassled, irritated, pressured, strained, stressed, tired, troubled, vexed, weary, worn out, worried.
OPPOSITES: SEE **carefree**.

harbinger noun SEE **herald** noun.

harbour noun *ships tied up in the harbour.* anchorage, dock, haven, jetty, landing-stage, marina, moorings, pier, port, quay, shelter, wharf.

harbour verb **1** *to harbour criminals.* conceal, give asylum to, give refuge to, give sanctuary to, hide, protect, shelter, shield.
2 *to harbour a grudge.* cherish, cling on to, hold on to, keep in mind, maintain, nurture, retain.

hard adjective **1** *hard concrete. hard ground.* compact, dense, firm, flinty, impenetrable, inflexible, rigid, rocky, solid, stony, unyielding.
OPPOSITES: SEE **soft**.
2 *hard work.* arduous, back-breaking, exhausting, fatiguing, formidable, gruelling, harsh, heavy, laborious, rigorous, severe, stiff, strenuous, tiring, tough, uphill, wearying.
OPPOSITES: SEE **easy**.
3 *a hard problem.* baffling, complex, complicated, confusing, difficult, intricate, involved, knotty, perplexing, puzzling, [*informal*] thorny.
OPPOSITES: SEE **simple**.
4 *a hard heart. hard feelings.* acrimonious, SEE **angry**, callous, cruel, harsh, heartless, hostile, inflexible, intolerant, merciless, pitiless, rancorous, resentful, ruthless, severe, stern, strict, unbending, unfeeling, unfriendly, unkind.
OPPOSITES: SEE **kind** adjective.
5 *a hard blow.* forceful, heavy, powerful, strong, violent.
OPPOSITES: SEE **light** adjective.
6 *a hard time.* calamitous, disagreeable, intolerable, painful, unhappy, unpleasant.
OPPOSITES: SEE **pleasant**.
hard of hearing deaf.
hard up SEE **poor**.

hard-boiled adjective SEE **callous**.

harden verb VARIOUS WAYS SUBSTANCES HARDEN: bake, cake, clot, coagulate, congeal, freeze, gel, jell, ossify, petrify, set, solidify, stiffen, toughen.
OPPOSITES: SEE **soften**.

hard-headed adjective SEE **businesslike**.

hard-hearted adjective SEE **cruel**.

hardly adverb *hardly visible.* barely, faintly, only just, scarcely, with difficulty.

hardship noun *financial hardship.* adversity, affliction, austerity, destitution, difficulty, misery, misfortune, need, privation, suffering, [*informal*] trials and tribulations, trouble, unhappiness, want.

hardware noun equipment, implements, instruments, machinery, tools.
VARIOUS TOOLS: SEE **tool**.

hard-wearing adjective *hard-wearing clothes.* durable, lasting, stout, strong, sturdy, tough, well-made.
OPPOSITES: SEE **flimsy**.

hardy adjective **1** *a hardy constitution. hardy plants.* fit, healthy, hearty, resilient, robust, rugged, strong, sturdy, tough, vigorous.
OPPOSITES: SEE **tender**.
2 *hardy exploits.* SEE **daring**.

hare noun [*male*] buck, [*female*] doe, [*young*] leveret.

hare-brained adjective SEE **silly**.

harelip noun SEE **deformity**.

harem noun seraglio.

hark verb SEE **listen**.

harlot noun SEE **prostitute** noun.

harm noun *Did the storm cause any harm?* damage, detriment, disservice, SEE **evil** noun, havoc, hurt, inconvenience, injury, loss, mischief, pain, unhappiness, [*informal*] upset, wrong.
OPPOSITES: SEE **benefit** noun.

harm verb *His captors didn't harm him. Chemicals might harm the soil.* be harmful to [SEE **harmful**], damage, hurt, ill-treat, impair, injure, maltreat, misuse, ruin, spoil, wound.
OPPOSITES: SEE **benefit** verb.

harmful adjective *a harmful habit. harmful chemicals.* bad, damaging, dangerous, deadly, deleterious, destructive, detrimental, evil, hurtful, injurious, malign, noxious, pernicious, poisonous, prejudicial, unhealthy, unpleasant, unwholesome.
OPPOSITES: SEE **beneficial, harmless**.

harmless adjective *harmless animals. a harmless habit.* acceptable, innocent, innocuous, inoffensive, mild, non-addictive, non-toxic, safe, unobjectionable.
OPPOSITES: SEE **harmful**.

harmonious adjective **1** *a harmonious group of friends.* amicable, compatible, congenial, co-operative, friendly, integrated, like-minded, sympathetic.
OPPOSITES: SEE **quarrelsome**.
2 *harmonious music.* concordant, [*informal*] easy on the ear, euphonious, harmonizing, melodious, musical, sweet-sounding, tonal, tuneful.
OPPOSITES: SEE **discordant**.

harmonize verb *I'd like the colours to harmonize.* be in harmony [SEE **harmony**], blend, co-ordinate, correspond, go together, match, suit each other, tally, tone in.

harmony noun **1** *living in harmony.* accord, agreement, amity, compatibility, conformity, co-operation, friendliness, goodwill, like-mindedness, peace, rapport, sympathy, understanding.
2 *musical harmony.* assonance, chords, concord, consonance, euphony, tunefulness.
OPPOSITES: SEE **discord**.

harness noun *a horse's harness.* equipment, [*informal*] gear, straps, tackle.

PARTS OF A HORSE'S HARNESS: bit, blinker, bridle, collar, crupper, girth, halter, headstall, noseband, pommel, rein, saddle, spurs, stirrups, trace.

---

harness verb **1** *to harness a horse.* saddle.
2 *to harness the forces of nature.* control, domesticate, exploit, keep under control, make use of, mobilize, tame, use, utilize.

harp verb **to harp on** *He harps on about his hobby.* be obsessive, dwell (*I won't dwell on that subject*), keep talking, SEE **talk** verb, talk boringly.

harpoon noun spear.

harridan noun SEE **woman**.

harry verb SEE **harass**.

harsh adjective **1** *a harsh voice.* croaking, disagreeable, discordant, dissonant, grating, guttural, irritating, jarring, rasping, raucous, rough, shrill, stertorous, strident, unpleasant.
OPPOSITES: SEE **gentle**.
2 *harsh colours. harsh light.* bright, brilliant, dazzling, gaudy, glaring, lurid.
OPPOSITES: SEE **subdued**.
3 *a harsh smell. harsh flavours.* acrid, bitter, unpleasant.
OPPOSITES: SEE **mellow**.
4 *harsh conditions.* arduous, austere, comfortless, difficult, hard, severe, stressful, tough.
OPPOSITES: SEE **easy**.
5 *a harsh texture.* abrasive, bristly, coarse, hairy, rough, scratchy.
OPPOSITES: SEE **smooth** adjective.

6 *harsh criticism.* abusive, bitter, sharp, unkind, unsympathetic.
OPPOSITES: SEE **sympathetic**.
7 *a harsh judge. harsh punishment.* brutal, cruel, Draconian, hard-hearted, merciless, pitiless, severe, stern, strict, unforgiving, unrelenting.
OPPOSITES: SEE **lenient**.

hart noun SEE **deer**.

harum-scarum adjective SEE **reckless**.

harvest noun *a corn harvest.* crop, gathering in, produce, reaping, return, yield.

harvest verb *to harvest the corn.* bring in, collect, garner, gather, mow, pick, reap, take in.

hash noun goulash, stew.
to make a hash of SEE **bungle**.

hasp noun SEE **fastener**.

hassle noun [*informal*] *I don't want any hassle.* altercation, argument, bother, confusion, difficulty, disagreement, disturbance, fighting, fuss, harassment, inconvenience, making difficulties, nuisance, persecution, problem, SEE **quarrelling**, struggle, trouble, upset.
OPPOSITE: peace and quiet [SEE **peace**].

hassle verb *Don't hassle me.* SEE **harass**.

haste noun dispatch, hurry, impetuosity, precipitateness, quickness, rush, SEE **speed** noun, urgency.

hasty adjective **1** *a hasty exit. a hasty decision.* abrupt, fast, foolhardy, headlong, hot-headed, hurried, ill-considered, impetuous, impulsive, [*informal*] pell-mell, precipitate, quick, rapid, rash, reckless, speedy, sudden, summary (*summary justice*), swift.
OPPOSITES: SEE **leisurely**.
2 *hasty work.* brief, careless, cursory, hurried, perfunctory, rushed, short, slapdash, superficial, thoughtless.
OPPOSITES: SEE **careful**.

hat noun head-dress.

VARIOUS HEAD-DRESSES: Balaclava, bearskin, beret, biretta, boater, bonnet, bowler, busby, cap, coronet, crash-helmet, crown, deerstalker, diadem, fez, fillet, headband, helmet, hood, mitre, skull-cap, sombrero, sou'wester, stetson, sun-hat, tiara, top hat, toque, trilby, turban, wig, wimple, yarmulka.

---

hatch verb **1** *to hatch eggs.* brood, incubate.
2 *to hatch a plot.* conceive, concoct, contrive, [*informal*] cook up, devise, [*informal*] dream up, invent, plan, plot, scheme, think up.

hate noun *What's your pet hate?* abomination, aversion, bête noire, dislike, SEE **hatred**, loathing.

hate verb *We hate cruelty. He hates spiders.* abhor, abominate, [*informal*] can't bear, [*informal*] can't stand, deplore, despise, detest, dislike, execrate, fear, feel hostility towards, find intolerable, loathe, recoil from, resent, scorn.
OPPOSITES: SEE **like** verb, **love** verb.

hateful adjective *a hateful sin.* abhorrent, abominable, accursed, awful, contemptible, cursed, [*informal*] damnable, despicable, detestable, disgusting, execrable, foul, hated, heinous, horrible, loathsome, obnoxious, odious, offensive, repellent, repugnant, repulsive, revolting, SEE **unpleasant**, vile.
OPPOSITES: SEE **lovable**.

hatred noun *He made his hatred obvious.* animosity, antagonism, antipathy, aversion, contempt, detestation, dislike, enmity, execration, hate, hostility, ill-will, intolerance, loathing, misanthropy, odium, repugnance, revulsion.
OPPOSITES: SEE **love** noun.

haughty adjective *a haughty manner.* arrogant, boastful, bumptious, cavalier, [*informal*] cocky, condescending, disdainful, [*informal*] high-and-mighty, [*informal*] hoity-toity, imperious, lofty, lordly, offhand, pompous, presumptuous, pretentious, proud, self-important, snobbish, [*informal*] snooty, [*informal*] stuck-up, supercilious, superior.
OPPOSITES: SEE **modest**.

haul noun *a long haul.* SEE **distance** noun.

haul verb *to haul a sledge.* convey, drag, draw, heave, [*informal*] lug, move, pull, tow, trail, tug.

haulage noun *road haulage.* SEE **transport** noun.

haunt verb **1** *to haunt a place.* frequent, [*informal*] hang around, keep returning to, loiter about, visit frequently.
2 *to haunt the imagination.* linger in, obsess, prey on.

have verb [*Have* has many meanings. These are only some of the synonyms you can use.] **1** *I have my own radio.* be in possession of, keep, own, possess.
2 *Our house has six rooms.* consist of, contain, embody, hold, include, incorporate, involve.
3 *They had fun. I had a bad time.* endure, enjoy, experience, feel, go through, know, live through, put up with, suffer, tolerate, undergo.
4 *They all had presents.* accept, acquire, be given, gain, get, obtain, procure, receive.

5 *The thieves had everything.* remove, retain, secure, steal, take.
6 *She had the last toffee.* consume, eat.
7 *We had visitors yesterday.* be host to, entertain, put up.
to have on *Don't believe him—he's having you on.* SEE **hoax** verb.
to have to *I'll have to pay for the damage.* be compelled to, be forced to, have an obligation to, must, need to, ought, should.
to have up *The police had her up for speeding.* SEE **arrest**.

haven noun **1** *a haven for ships.* SEE **harbour** noun.
2 *The climbers found haven in a mountain hut.* asylum, refuge, retreat, safety, sanctuary, shelter.

haversack noun bag, knapsack, rucksack.

havoc noun *The explosion caused havoc.* SEE **carnage**, chaos, confusion, damage, destruction, devastation, disorder, disruption, [*informal*] mayhem, ruin, waste, wreckage.

hawk verb SEE **sell**.

hawser noun SEE **rope** noun.

hay noun fodder, forage.

haystack noun rick.

haywire adjective SEE **chaotic**.

hazard noun *a hazard to traffic.* SEE **risk** noun.

hazard verb SEE **risk** verb.

hazardous adjective *a hazardous journey.* chancy, dangerous, [*informal*] dicey, perilous, precarious, risky, uncertain, unpredictable, unsafe.
OPPOSITES: SEE **safe**.

haze noun cloud, film, fog, mist, steam, vapour.

hazy adjective **1** *a hazy view.* SEE **misty**.
2 *a hazy understanding.* SEE **vague**.

head adjective SEE **chief** adjective.

head noun **1** PARTS OF YOUR HEAD: brain, brow, cheek, chin, cranium, crown, dimple, ear, eye, forehead, gums, hair, jaw, jowl, lip, mouth, nose, nostril, scalp, skull, teeth, temple, tongue.
OTHER PARTS OF YOUR BODY: SEE **body**.
2 *a head for mathematics.* ability, brains, capacity, imagination, intellect, intelligence, mind, understanding.
3 *the head of a mountain.* apex, crown, highest point, summit, top, vertex.
4 *the head of an organization.* boss, SEE **chief** noun, director, employer, leader, manager, ruler.
5 *the head of a school.* headmaster, headmistress, headteacher, principal.
6 *the head of a river.* SEE **source**.
off your head SEE **mad**.
to lose your head SEE **panic** verb.
to put heads together SEE **consult**.

head verb **1** *to head an expedition.* be in charge of, command, control, direct, govern, guide, lead, manage, rule, run, superintend, supervise.
2 *to head a ball.* SEE **hit** verb.
3 *to head for home.* aim, go, make, set out, start, steer, turn.
to head off SEE **deflect**.

headache noun **1** migraine, neuralgia.
2 [*informal*] *Parking can be a headache.* SEE **problem**.

head-dress, headgear nouns SEE **hat**.

heading noun *the heading of a leaflet.* caption, headline, rubric, title.

headlamp noun SEE **light** noun.

headland noun SEE **promontory**.

headlight noun SEE **light** noun.

headline noun *a newspaper headline.* caption, heading, title.

headlong adjective SEE **hasty**.

headquarters noun **1** *the headquarters of an expedition.* base, depot, HQ.
2 *the headquarters of a business.* head office, main office.

headstone noun SEE **gravestone**.

headstrong adjective SEE **obstinate**.

headway noun SEE **progress** noun.

heady adjective SEE **intoxicating**.

heal verb **1** *Wounds heal in time.* get better, knit, mend, recover, unite.
2 *to heal the sick.* cure, make better, remedy, restore, treat.

health noun **1** *your state of health.* condition, constitution, fettle (*in fine fettle*), form (*feeling a bit off-form*), shape (*in good shape*).
2 *We value health.* fitness, robustness, strength, vigour, well-being.

VARIOUS MEDICAL TREATMENTS, ETC.: SEE **medicine**.

VARIOUS ILLNESSES, ETC.: SEE **ill, illness**.

---

healthy adjective **1** *a healthy animal. in a healthy condition.* active, [*informal*] blooming, fine, fit, flourishing, good, [*informal*] hale-and-hearty, hearty, [*informal*] in fine fettle, in good shape, lively, perky, robust, sound, strong, sturdy, vigorous, well.
OPPOSITES: SEE **ill**.
2 *healthy surroundings.* bracing, health-giving, hygienic, invigorating, salubrious, sanitary, wholesome.
OPPOSITES: SEE **unhealthy**.

heap noun *a heap of rubbish.* SEE **collection**, mass, mound, mountain, pile, stack.
heaps SEE **plenty**.

heap verb *We heaped up the rubbish.* bank, SEE **collect**, mass, pile, stack.

hear verb **1** *to hear a sound.* catch, listen to [SEE **listen**], overhear, pick up.
2 *to hear evidence in a lawcourt.* examine, investigate, judge, try.
3 *to hear news.* be told, discover, find out, gather, learn, receive.
RELATED ADJECTIVES: auditory, aural.

hearing noun *a court hearing.* case, inquest, inquiry, trial.

hearsay noun SEE **rumour** noun.

heart noun **1** OTHER PARTS OF YOUR BODY: SEE **body**.
RELATED ADJECTIVE [= *of the heart*]: cardiac.
2 *the heart of a forest. the heart of a problem.* centre, core, crux, focus, hub, inside, kernel, middle, nub, nucleus.
3 *Have you no heart?* affection, compassion, feeling, humanity, kindness, love, sympathy, tenderness, understanding.
heart attack cardiac arrest, heart failure.
heart specialist cardiologist.
heart to heart SEE **frank**.
to set your heart on SEE **want** verb.

heartache, heartbreak nouns SEE **sorrow** noun.

heartbreaking adjective distressing, grievous, heartrending, pitiful, SEE **sad**, tragic.

heartbroken adjective broken-hearted, dejected, desolate, despairing, dispirited, grieved, inconsolable, miserable, SEE **sad**, [*informal*] shattered.

heartburn noun indigestion.

hearten verb SEE **encourage**.

heartfelt adjective SEE **sincere**.

hearth noun fireplace, grate.

heartless adjective *heartless cruelty.* cold, SEE **cruel**, icy, steely, stony, unemotional.

heart-searching noun self-examination, self-questioning, thought.

hearty adjective **1** *a hearty welcome.* enthusiastic, sincere, warm.
2 *a hearty appetite.* big, healthy, robust, strong, vigorous.

heat noun **1** *the heat of a fire.* [*formal*] calorific value, fieriness, glow, hotness, incandescence, warmth.
2 *the heat of summer.* closeness, heatwave, high temperatures, hot weather [SEE **hot**], sultriness, warmth.
OPPOSITES: SEE **cold** noun.
3 *the heat of the moment.* ardour, SEE **excitement**, fervour, feverishness, violence.
RELATED ADJECTIVE: thermal.

heat verb VERBS SIGNIFYING TO BE HOT, BECOME HOT, OR MAKE HOT: bake, blister, boil, burn, cook, [*informal*] frizzle, fry, grill, SEE **inflame**, make hot [SEE **hot**], melt, reheat, roast, scald, scorch, simmer, sizzle, smoulder, steam, stew, swelter, toast, warm up.
OPPOSITES: SEE **cool** verb.

heated adjective **1** *heated food.* SEE **hot**.
2 *a heated argument.* SEE **angry, excited**.

heath noun common land, moor, moorland, open country, wasteland.

heathen adjective *heathen beliefs.* atheistic, barbaric, godless, idolatrous, infidel, irreligious, pagan, Philistine, savage, unenlightened.

heave verb *to heave sacks onto a lorry.* drag, draw, haul, hoist, lift, lug, pull, raise, SEE **throw**, tow, tug.
to heave into sight SEE **appear**.
to heave up SEE **vomit**.

heaven noun **1** after-life, Elysium, eternal rest, next world, nirvana, paradise.
OPPOSITES: SEE **hell**.
2 [*informal*] *It's heaven to have a hot bath.* bliss, contentment, delight, ecstasy, felicity, happiness, joy, pleasure, rapture.
the heavens SEE **sky**.

heavenly adjective *heavenly music.* angelic, beautiful, blissful, celestial, delightful, divine, exquisite, lovely, [*informal*] out of this world, SEE **pleasant**, wonderful.
OPPOSITES: SEE **devilish, unpleasant**.

heavy adjective **1** *a heavy load.* SEE **big**, bulky, burdensome, hefty, immovable, large, leaden, massive, ponderous, unwieldy, weighty.
2 *heavy work.* arduous, demanding, difficult, hard, exhausting, laborious, onerous, strenuous, tough.
3 *heavy rain.* concentrated, dense, penetrating, pervasive, severe, torrential.
4 *a heavy crop. heavy with fruit.* abundant, copious, laden, loaded, profuse, thick.
5 *a heavy heart.* burdened, depressed, gloomy, miserable, SEE **sad**, sorrowful.
6 [*informal*] *a heavy lecture.* deep, dull, intellectual, intense, serious, tedious, wearisome.
OPPOSITES: SEE **light** adjective.

heavy-hearted adjective SEE **sad**.

heckle verb *to heckle a speaker.* barrack, disrupt, harass, interrupt, shout down.

hectic adjective *hectic activity.* animated, boisterous, brisk, bustling, busy, chaotic, excited, feverish, frantic, frenetic, frenzied, hurried, lively, mad, restless, riotous, rumbustious, [*informal*] rushed off your feet, turbulent, wild.
OPPOSITES: SEE **leisurely**.

hector verb SEE **intimidate**.

hedge noun barrier, fence, hedgerow, screen.

hedge verb *When I asked for an answer, he hedged.* [*informal*] beat about the bush, be evasive, equivocate, [*informal*] hum and haw, quibble, stall, temporize, waffle.
to hedge in circumscribe, confine, encircle, enclose, fence in, hem in, pen, restrict, shield, surround.

hedonist noun epicurean, hedonistic person [SEE **hedonistic**], pleasure-lover, sybarite.
OPPOSITE: SEE **puritan**.

hedonistic adjective epicurean, extravagant, intemperate, luxurious, pleasure-loving, self-indulgent, sensual, sybaritic, voluptuous.
OPPOSITES: SEE **puritanical**.

heed verb *to heed a warning.* attend to, concern yourself about, consider, follow, keep to, listen to, mark, mind, note, notice, obey, observe, pay attention to, regard, take notice of.
OPPOSITES: SEE **disregard**.

heedful adjective *heedful of people's needs.* attentive, careful, concerned, considerate, mindful, observant, sympathetic, taking notice, vigilant, watchful.
OPPOSITES: SEE **heedless**.

heedless adjective *heedless of other people.* careless, inattentive, inconsiderate, neglectful, thoughtless, uncaring, unconcerned, unobservant, unsympathetic.
OPPOSITES: SEE **heedful**.
heedless of danger SEE **reckless**.

heel verb **1** *to heel a ball.* SEE **kick** verb.
2 *to heel to one side.* lean, list, slope, tilt.

hefty adjective *a hefty man.* beefy, big, brawny, bulky, burly, heavy, heavyweight, hulking, husky, large, mighty, muscular, powerful, robust, solid, [*informal*] strapping (*a strapping lad*), strong, tough.
OPPOSITES: SEE **slight** adjective.

height noun **1** *the height of a mountain.* altitude, elevation, tallness, vertical measurement.
2 [*often plural*] *scaling mountainous heights.* SEE **top** noun.

heighten verb **1** *to heighten the level of something.* build up, elevate, lift up, make higher, raise.
OPPOSITES: SEE **lower**.
2 *to heighten your enjoyment.* add to, augment, boost, enhance, improve, increase, intensify, magnify, maximize, sharpen, strengthen.
OPPOSITES: SEE **lessen**.

heinous adjective SEE **wicked**.

heir, heiress nouns beneficiary, inheritor, successor.

helix noun SEE **spiral** noun.

hell noun eternal punishment, Hades, infernal regions, lower regions, nether world, underworld.
OPPOSITES: SEE **heaven**.

hellish adjective SEE **devilish**.

helm noun *the helm of a ship.* tiller, wheel.
to be at the helm SEE **control** verb.

helmet noun FORMS OF HEAD-DRESS: SEE **hat**.

helmsman noun boatman, cox, pilot, steersman.

help noun *Give me some help.* advice, aid, assistance, avail (*It was of no avail*), backing, benefit, boost, collaboration, contribution, co-operation, friendship, guidance, moral support, relief, succour, support.
OPPOSITES: SEE **hindrance**.

help verb **1** *Help each other. Can I help?* advise, aid, aid and abet, assist, back, befriend, be helpful (to) [SEE **helpful**], boost, collaborate, contribute (to), co-operate, facilitate, forward, further the interests of, [*informal*] give a hand (to), profit, promote, [*informal*] rally round, serve, side (with), [*informal*] spoon-feed, stand by, succour, support, take pity on.
OPPOSITES: SEE **hinder**.
2 *Some medicine might help your cough.* alleviate, benefit, cure, ease, improve, lessen, make easier, relieve, remedy.
OPPOSITES: SEE **aggravate**.
3 *I can't help coughing.* SEE **avoid, prevent**.

helper noun abettor, ally, assistant, collaborator, colleague, deputy, helpmate, partner, [*informal*] right-hand man, second, supporter, [*informal*] willing hands.

helpful adjective **1** *a helpful person.* accommodating, benevolent, caring, considerate, constructive, co-operative, favourable, friendly, helping (*a helping hand*), kind, neighbourly, obliging,

practical, supportive, sympathetic, thoughtful.
OPPOSITES: SEE **unhelpful**.
2 *a helpful suggestion.* advantageous, beneficial, informative, instructive, profitable, valuable, useful, worthwhile.
OPPOSITES: SEE **worthless**.
3 *a helpful tool.* SEE **handy**.

helping adjective *a helping hand.* SEE **helpful**.

helping noun *a helping of food.* amount, plateful, portion, ration, serving, share.

helpless adjective 1 *a helpless invalid.* defenceless, dependent, destitute, feeble, SEE **handicapped**, impotent, incapable, infirm, powerless, unprotected, vulnerable, weak, [*uncomplimentary*] weedy.
OPPOSITES: SEE **independent**.
2 *a helpless ship.* aground, crippled, drifting, stranded, without power.

hem noun *the hem of a skirt.* border, edge, fringe, hemline.

hem verb **to hem in** SEE **surround**.

hen noun SEE **chicken**.

henchman noun SEE **supporter**.

henpeck verb SEE **nag** verb.

herald noun 1 [*old-fashioned*] *the king's herald.* announcer, courier, messenger, town crier.
2 *The cuckoo is the herald of spring.* forerunner, harbinger, omen, precursor, sign.

herald verb *The thunder heralded a change in the weather.* advertise, announce, SEE **foretell**, indicate, make known, proclaim, promise, publicize.

heraldic adjective **heraldic device** badge, coat of arms, crest, emblem, escutcheon, insignia, shield.

heraldry noun heraldic devices [SEE **heraldic**].

Several English words, including *herb, herbaceous, herbicide,* and *herbivorous,* are related to Latin *herba = grass.*

---

herb noun culinary herb.

VARIOUS HERBS: angelica, anise, balm, balsam, basil, borage, camomile, caraway, chervil, chicory, chive, coriander, cumin, dill, fennel, fenugreek, hyssop, liquorice, lovage, marjoram, mint, oregano, parsley, peppermint, rosemary, rue, sage, savory, spearmint, tansy, tarragon, thyme, wintergreen.

---

herbicide noun SEE **poison** noun.

herbivorous adjective *herbivorous animals.* grass-eating, plant-eating, vegetarian.
COMPARE: carnivorous, omnivorous.

herculean adjective 1 *herculean strength.* SEE **strong**.
2 *a herculean task.* SEE **difficult**.

herd noun, verb SEE **group** noun, verb.

hereditary adjective 1 *a hereditary title.* bequeathed, family (*the family name*), handed down, inherited, passed on.
2 *a hereditary disease. hereditary characteristics.* congenital, constitutional, inborn, inbred, inherent, innate, native, natural, transmissible, transmittable.
OPPOSITE: **acquired**.

heresy noun *guilty of heresy.* blasphemy, rebellion, [*informal*] stepping out of line, unorthodox thinking.
OPPOSITES: SEE **orthodoxy**.

heretic noun apostate, blasphemer, dissenter, free-thinker, iconoclast, nonconformist, rebel, renegade, unorthodox thinker.
OPPOSITES: SEE **conformist**.

heritage noun *our national heritage.* birthright, culture, history, inheritance, legacy, past, tradition.

hermaphrodite noun SEE **sex**.

hermetic adjective *a hermetic closure.* airtight, sealed, watertight.

hermit noun monk, recluse, solitary person.

hernia noun rupture.

hero, heroine nouns celebrity, champion, conqueror, daredevil, idol, protagonist [= *leading character in a play*], star, superman, [*informal*] superstar, victor, winner.

heroic adjective *heroic efforts, heroic rescuers.* adventurous, bold, brave, chivalrous, courageous, daring, dauntless, doughty, epic, fearless, gallant, herculean, intrepid, lion-hearted, noble, selfless, stout-hearted, superhuman, unafraid, valiant, valorous.
OPPOSITES: SEE **cowardly**.

heroine noun SEE **hero**.

hero-worship verb SEE **admire**.

hesitant adjective *a hesitant speaker.* cautious, diffident, dithering, faltering, half-hearted, halting, hesitating, indecisive, irresolute, nervous, [*informal*] shilly-shallying, shy, tentative, timid, uncertain, uncommitted, undecided,

underconfident, unsure, vacillating, wary, wavering.
OPPOSITES: SEE **decisive, fluent.**

hesitate verb *I hesitated before jumping into the water.* be hesitant [SEE **hesitant**], delay, dither, falter, halt, hang back, [*informal*] hum and haw, pause, put it off, [*informal*] shilly-shally, shrink back, think twice, vacillate, wait, waver.

hesitation noun caution, indecision, irresolution, nervousness, [*informal*] shilly-shallying, uncertainty, vacillation.

heterogeneous adjective SEE **mixed.**

heterosexual adjective SEE **sex.**

hew verb SEE **cut** verb.

hiatus noun SEE **gap.**

hibernate verb SEE **sleep** verb.

hibernating adjective *a hibernating animal.* asleep, dormant, inactive.

hidden adjective **1** *hidden from view.* concealed, covered, enclosed, invisible, out of sight, private, shrouded, [*informal*] under wraps, unseen, veiled.
OPPOSITES: SEE **visible.**
2 *a hidden meaning.* abstruse, coded, covert, cryptic, dark, implicit, mysterious, mystical, obscure, occult, recondite, secret, unclear.
OPPOSITES: SEE **obvious.**

hide noun *an animal's hide.* fur, leather, pelt, skin.

hide verb **1** *to hide something from view. to hide your feelings.* blot out, bury, camouflage, censor, cloak, conceal, cover, curtain, disguise, eclipse, enclose, mask, obscure, put away, put out of sight, screen, secrete, shelter, shroud, suppress, veil, withhold.
OPPOSITES: SEE **display** verb.
2 *to hide from someone.* disguise yourself, go into hiding, [*informal*] go to ground, keep yourself hidden [SEE **hidden**], [*informal*] lie low, lurk, shut yourself away, take cover.

hideaway noun SEE **hiding-place.**

hide-bound adjective SEE **narrow-minded.**

hideous adjective *a hideous wound.* appalling, disgusting, dreadful, frightful, ghastly, grim, grisly, gruesome, macabre, odious, repulsive, revolting, shocking, sickening, terrible, SEE **ugly.**
OPPOSITES: SEE **beautiful.**

hide-out noun SEE **hiding-place.**

hiding noun **to give someone a hiding** SEE **punish.**
to go into hiding SEE **hide** verb.

hiding-place noun den, hide, hideaway, [*informal*] hide-out, [*informal*] hidy-hole, lair, refuge, sanctuary.

hierarchy noun *The Principal comes at the top of the college hierarchy.* grading, ladder, [*informal*] pecking-order, ranking, scale, sequence, series, social order, system.

hieroglyphics noun SEE **writing.**

hi-fi noun SEE **audio equipment.**

higgledy-piggledy adjective SEE **haphazard.**

high adjective **1** *a high building. a high altitude.* elevated, extending upwards, high-rise, lofty, raised, soaring, tall, towering.
OPPOSITES: SEE **deep, low** adjective.
2 *high in rank.* aristocratic, chief, distinguished, eminent, exalted, important, leading, powerful, prominent, royal, top, upper.
3 *high prices.* dear, excessive, exorbitant, expensive, extravagant, unreasonable.
4 *a high wind.* exceptional, extreme, great, intense, stormy, strong.
5 *a high reputation.* favourable, good, noble, respected, virtuous.
6 *a high sound.* high-pitched, piercing, sharp, shrill, soprano, treble.
high and dry SEE **stranded.**
high and mighty SEE **arrogant.**
high living SEE **luxury.**

highbrow adjective **1** *highbrow literature.* classic, cultural, deep, educational, improving, intellectually demanding, serious.
2 *highbrow music.* classical.
3 *a highbrow person.* academic, bookish, brainy, cultured, intellectual, [*uncomplimentary*] pretentious, sophisticated.
OPPOSITES: SEE **lowbrow.**

high-class adjective SEE **excellent.**

high-falutin adjective SEE **pompous.**

high-fidelity SEE **audio equipment.**

high-handed adjective SEE **arrogant.**

highlight noun *the highlight of the evening.* best moment, climax, high spot, peak, top point.

highly-strung adjective SEE **nervous.**

high-minded adjective SEE **moral** adjective.

high-powered adjective SEE **powerful.**

high-priced adjective SEE **expensive.**

high-speed adjective SEE **fast** adjective.

high-spirited adjective SEE **lively.**

highway noun SEE **road.**

highwayman noun bandit, brigand, SEE **criminal**, robber, thief.

hijack noun, verb SEE **crime**.

hijacker noun SEE **criminal** noun.

hike verb *to hike across the moors.* ramble, tramp, trek, SEE **walk** verb.

hilarious adjective **1** *a hilarious party.* SEE **merry**.
2 *a hilarious joke.* SEE **funny**.

hill noun **1** elevation, eminence, foothill, height, hillock, hillside, hummock, knoll, mound, mount, mountain, peak, prominence, ridge, summit.
Words for *hill* used in particular geographical areas: brae, down, fell, [*plural*] Highlands, pike, stack, tor, wold.
2 *a steep hill in the road.* ascent, gradient, incline, rise, slope.

hilt noun SEE **handle** noun.

hind, hinder, hindmost adjectives SEE **back** adjective.

hind noun SEE **deer**.

hinder verb *Snowdrifts hindered our progress.* arrest, bar, be a hindrance to [SEE **hindrance**], check, curb, delay, deter, endanger, frustrate, get in the way of, hamper, handicap, hit, hold back, hold up, impede, keep back, limit, obstruct, oppose, prevent, restrain, restrict, retard, sabotage, slow down, slow up, stand in the way of, stop, thwart.
OPPOSITES: SEE **help** verb.

hindrance noun *Our heavy shoes were more of a hindrance than a help.* bar, burden, check, deterrent, difficulty, disadvantage, [*informal*] drag, drawback, encumbrance, handicap, impediment, inconvenience, limitation, obstacle, obstruction, restraint, restriction, stumbling-block.
OPPOSITES: SEE **help** noun.

hinge noun *the hinge of a door.* articulation, joint, pivot.

hinge verb *Everything hinges on your decision.* depend, hang, rest, revolve, turn.

hint noun *I don't know the answer: give me a hint.* allusion, clue, idea, implication, indication, inkling, innuendo, insinuation, pointer, sign, suggestion, tip, [*informal*] tip-off.

hint verb *She hinted that we'd get a surprise.* give a hint [SEE **hint** noun], imply, indicate, insinuate, suggest, tip (someone) off.

hire verb *to hire a bus. to hire a hall for a party.* book, charter, engage, lease, pay for the use of, rent, take on.
to hire out lease out, let, rent out, take payment for the use of.

hirsute adjective SEE **hairy**.

hiss verb **1** VARIOUS SOUNDS: SEE **sound** noun.
2 *to hiss someone's performance.* SEE **jeer**.

hissing adjective *a hissing sound.* sibilant.

historian noun antiquarian, archivist, chronicler.

historic adjective [Note the difference in meaning between *historic* and *historical.*] *a historic battle.* celebrated, eminent, epoch-making, famed, famous, important, momentous, notable, outstanding, remarkable, renowned, significant, well-known.
OPPOSITES: SEE **unimportant**.

historical adjective [See note under *historic.*] *a historical event.* actual, authentic, documented, real, real-life, true, verifiable.
OPPOSITES: SEE **fictitious**.

history noun **1** *Are you interested in history?* bygone days, heritage, historical events [SEE **historical**], the past.
2 *I enjoy reading history.* annals, chronicles, records.

histrionic adjective actorish, dramatic, theatrical.

hit noun **1** *a hit on the head. a hit with a cricket bat.* [Many of these words are normally *informal.*] bang, bash, belt, biff, blow, buffet, bump, clap, clip, clonk, clout, collision, crack, crash, cuff, drive, flick, flip, hammering, impact, jab, kick, knock, nudge, pat, poke, prod, punch, rap, shot, slap, slog, slosh, slug, smack, smash, smite, sock, stab, stroke, swipe, tap, thump, wallop, whack.
2 *The new record was an instant hit.* success, triumph, [*informal*] winner.

hit verb **1** VARIOUS WAYS TO HIT THINGS: [Many of these words are normally *informal.*] bang, bash, baste, batter, beat, belt, biff, birch, buffet, bump, butt, cane, clap, clip, clobber, clock, clonk, clout, club, collide with, cosh, crack, crash into, cudgel, cuff, dash, deliver a blow, drive (*a ball with a golf-club*), elbow, flagellate, flail, flick, flip, flog, hammer, head (*a football*), jab, jar, jog, kick, knee, knock, lam, lambaste or lambast, lash, nudge, pat, poke, pound, prod, pummel, punch, punt, putt (*a golf-ball*), ram, rap, scourge, slam, slap, slog, slosh, slug, smack, smash, smite, sock, spank, stab, strike, stub (*your toe*), swat, swipe, tan, tap, thrash, thump, thwack, wallop, whack, wham, whip.

2 *The drought hit the farmers.* affect, attack, bring disaster to, damage, do harm to, harm, have an effect on, SEE **hinder**, hurt, make suffer, ruin.
to hit back SEE **retaliate**.
to hit on SEE **discover**.

hitch noun SEE **delay** noun.

hitch verb **1** *to hitch a trailer to a car.* SEE **fasten**.
2 SEE **hitch-hike**.

hitch-hike verb beg a lift, hitch, thumb a lift.

hive noun apiary, beehive.

hive verb **to hive off** SEE **separate** verb.

hoard noun *a hoard of treasure.* cache, heap, pile, stockpile, store, supply, treasure-trove.

hoard verb *Squirrels hoard nuts.* accumulate, amass, be miserly with, collect, gather, keep, lay up, mass, pile up, put by, save, stockpile, store, treasure.
OPPOSITES: SEE **squander**, **use** verb.

hoarding noun *a roadside hoarding.* advertisement, board, display, fence, panel.

hoarse adjective *a hoarse voice.* croaking, grating, gravelly, growling, gruff, harsh, husky, rasping, raucous, rough, throaty.

hoary adjective **1** *hoary hair.* SEE **grey**.
2 *a hoary joke.* SEE **old**.

hoax noun *The alarm was a hoax.* cheat, [*informal*] con, deception, fake, fraud, imposture, joke, [*informal*] leg-pull, practical joke, spoof, swindle, trick.

hoax verb *to hoax someone.* bluff, [*informal*] con, deceive, delude, dupe, fool, [*informal*] have on, hoodwink, lead on, mislead, [*informal*] pull someone's leg, swindle, [*informal*] take for a ride, take in, SEE **tease**, trick.

hoaxer noun SEE **cheat** noun, [*informal*] con-man, impostor, joker, practical joker, trickster.

hobble verb limp, totter, SEE **walk** verb.

hobby noun *a spare-time hobby.* amateur interest, diversion, interest, pastime, pursuit, recreation, relaxation.

hobby-horse noun SEE **obsession**.

hob-nob verb SEE **friend (to be friends)**.

hocus-pocus noun SEE **trickery**.

hog noun SEE **pig**.

hoi polloi noun SEE **people** noun.

hoist noun block-and-tackle, crane, davit, jack, lift, pulley, winch, windlass.

hoist verb *to hoist crates onto a ship.* heave, lift, lift with a hoist, pull up, raise, winch up.

hoity-toity adjective SEE **haughty**.

hold noun **1** *a firm hold on something.* clasp, clutch, grasp, grip, purchase.
2 *The blackmailer had a hold over him.* authority, control, dominance, influence, power, sway.
3 *the hold of a ship.* cargo-space.

hold verb **1** *to hold in your arms or in your hand.* bear, carry, catch, clasp, cling to, clutch, cradle, embrace, enfold, grasp, grip, hang on to, have, hug, keep, possess, retain, seize, support, take.
2 *to hold a suspect.* arrest, confine, detain, imprison, keep in custody.
3 *to hold a position. to hold an opinion.* continue, keep up, maintain, occupy, preserve, retain, stick to.
4 *to hold a party.* celebrate, conduct, convene, have, organize.
5 *The jug holds one litre.* contain, enclose, have a capacity of, include.
6 *Will this fine weather hold?* be unaltered, carry on, last, persist, remain unchanged, stay.
to hold back *to hold back tears.* block, check, control, curb, delay, halt, keep back, repress, restrain, retain, stifle, stop, suppress, withhold.
to hold out 1 *to hold out your hand.* extend, offer, reach out, stick out, stretch out.
2 *to hold out against opposition.* be resolute, carry on, endure, hang on, keep going, last, persevere, persist, resist, stand fast.
to hold up *to hold up traffic.* delay, detain, hinder, impede, obstruct, retard, slow down.

holdall noun SEE **luggage**.

hold-up noun **1** *a hold-up at a bank.* SEE **crime**.
2 *a hold-up on a journey.* SEE **delay** noun.

hole noun **1** *a hole in the ground.* abyss, burrow, cave, cavern, cavity, chamber, chasm, crater, depression, excavation, fault, fissure, hollow, pit, pocket, pothole, shaft, tunnel.
2 *a hole in a fence. a hole in a piece of paper.* aperture, breach, break, chink, crack, cut, eyelet, gap, gash, leak, opening, orifice, perforation, puncture, slit, split, tear, vent.

holiday noun *a holiday from school or from work.* bank holiday, break, day off, half-term, leave, rest, sabbatical, time off, vacation.

SOME KINDS OF HOLIDAY: busman's holiday, camping, caravanning, cruise, honeymoon, pony-trekking, safari, seaside holiday, tour, travelling, trip.

HOLIDAY ACCOMMODATION: apartment, boarding-house, camp-site, flat, guest-house, hostel, hotel, inn, motel, self-catering, villa.

---

holiness noun devotion, divinity, faith, godliness, piety, [*uncomplimentary*] religiosity, sacredness, saintliness, [*uncomplimentary*] sanctimoniousness, sanctity, venerability.

hollow adjective **1** *a hollow space.* cavernous, concave, deep, empty, unfilled, vacant.
OPPOSITES: SEE **solid.**
2 *a hollow victory. a hollow laugh.* cynical, false, futile, insincere, insubstantial, SEE **meaningless,** pointless, valueless, worthless.
OPPOSITES: SEE **meaningful.**

hollow noun *a hollow in a surface.* bowl, cavity, concavity, crater, dent, depression, dimple, dip, dint, dish, hole, indentation, SEE **valley.**

hollow verb **to hollow out** burrow, dig, excavate, gouge, scoop.

holocaust noun annihilation, conflagration, SEE **destruction,** inferno, massacre, pogrom.

holy adjective **1** *a holy shrine.* blessed, consecrated, divine, hallowed, heavenly, revered, sacred, sacrosanct, venerable.
2 *holy pilgrims.* dedicated, devoted, devout, faithful, godly, pious, pure, religious, righteous, saintly, [*uncomplimentary*] sanctimonious.
OPPOSITES: SEE **irreligious.**

homage noun **to pay homage to** SEE **honour** verb.

home noun **1** [= *where I live*] [*old-fashioned*] abode, accommodation, [*formal*] domicile, dwelling, dwelling-place, [*formal*] habitation, SEE **house** noun, household, lodging, residence.
2 [= *where I come from*] birthplace, native land.
3 *a home for the sick or elderly.* [*old-fashioned*] almshouse, convalescent home, hospice, institution, nursing-home.
4 *an animal's home.* habitat, territory.
home help SEE **servant.**

homecoming noun SEE **return** noun.

homeless adjective *homeless families.* abandoned, destitute, down-and-out, evicted, forsaken, itinerant, nomadic, outcast, unhoused, wandering.
homeless people beggars, the destitute, the poor, tramps, vagrants.

homely adjective *a homely atmosphere.* comfortable, congenial, cosy, easy-going, familiar, friendly, informal, intimate, natural, relaxed, simple, unaffected, unpretentious, unsophisticated.
OPPOSITES: SEE **formal, sophisticated.**

home-made adjective *home-made clothes.* amateur, [*informal*] DIY or do-it-yourself.
OPPOSITES: SEE **manufactured.**

homesick adjective SEE **sad.**

homework noun assignments, [*informal*] prep, preparation, private study, SEE **work** noun.

homicidal adjective SEE **murderous.**

homicide noun SEE **murder** noun.

homily noun SEE **sermon.**

The prefix *homo-* in words like *homogeneous* and *homosexual* comes from Greek *homos = same.*

---

homogeneous adjective *a homogeneous group.* alike, comparable, compatible, consistent, identical, matching, similar, uniform, unvarying.
OPPOSITES: heterogeneous, SEE **mixed.**

homosexual adjective [*informal*] camp, gay, lesbian, [*uncomplimentary*] queer.
OPPOSITE: heterosexual.

hone noun SEE **sharpener.**

hone verb SEE **sharpen.**

honest adjective *an honest worker. an honest answer.* above-board, blunt, candid, conscientious, direct, equitable, fair, forthright, frank, genuine, good, honourable, impartial, incorruptible, just, law-abiding, legal, legitimate, moral, [*informal*] on the level, open, outspoken, plain, pure, reliable, respectable, scrupulous, sincere, square (*a square deal*), straight, straightforward, trustworthy, trusty, truthful, unbiased, unequivocal, unprejudiced, upright, veracious, virtuous.
OPPOSITES: SEE **dishonest.**
to be honest [*informal*] come clean, [*informal*] put your cards on the table, tell the truth.

honesty noun **1** *I didn't doubt his honesty.* fairness, goodness, integrity, morality, probity, rectitude, reliability, scrupulousness, sense of justice, trustworthiness, truthfulness, uprightness, veracity, virtue.
2 *I was surprised by the honesty of his comments.* bluntness, candour, directness, frankness, outspokenness, plainness, sincerity, straightforwardness.
OPPOSITES: SEE **dishonesty.**

honeymoon noun SEE **holiday**.

honorarium noun SEE **payment**.

honorary adjective *an honorary title. an honorary post.* nominal, unofficial, unpaid.

honour noun **1** *She brought honour to the family.* acclaim, accolade, compliment, credit, esteem, fame, good name, [*informal*] kudos, regard, renown, reputation, repute, respect, reverence, veneration.
2 *I had the honour of making a speech.* distinction, duty, importance, privilege.
3 *a sense of honour.* decency, dignity, honesty, integrity, loyalty, morality, nobility, principle, rectitude, righteousness, sincerity, uprightness, virtue.

honour verb *On Remembrance Sunday we honour those who died.* acclaim, admire, applaud, celebrate, commemorate, commend, dignify, esteem, give credit to, glorify, pay homage to, pay respects to, pay tribute to, praise, remember, respect, revere, reverence, show respect to, sing the praises of, value, venerate, worship.

honourable adjective *an honourable action. an honourable person.* admirable, chivalrous, creditable, decent, estimable, ethical, fair, good, high-minded, SEE **honest**, irreproachable, just, law-abiding, loyal, moral, noble, principled, proper, reputable, respectable, respected, righteous, sincere, [*informal*] straight, trustworthy, trusty, upright, venerable, virtuous, worthy.
OPPOSITES: SEE **dishonourable**.

hood noun SEE **hat**.

hoodlum noun SEE **hooligan**.

hoodwink verb SEE **deceive**.

hoof noun SEE **foot**.

hook noun barb, crook, SEE **fastener**, peg (*to hang a coat on*).

hook verb **1** *to hook a fish.* capture, catch, take.
2 *to hook a trailer to a car.* SEE **fasten**.

hooligan noun bully, SEE **criminal** noun, delinquent, hoodlum, lout, mugger, rough, ruffian, [*informal*] tearaway, thug, tough, trouble-maker, vandal, [*informal*] yob.

hoop noun band, circle, girdle, loop, ring.

hoot noun, verb VARIOUS SOUNDS: SEE **sound** noun.

hooter noun horn, siren, whistle.

Hoover verb SEE **clean** verb.

hop verb bound, caper, dance, jump, leap, limp, prance, skip, spring.

hope noun **1** *His hope is to become a professional.* ambition, aspiration, desire, dream, wish.
2 *There's hope of better weather tomorrow.* assumption, expectation, likelihood, optimism, prospect.
OPPOSITES: SEE **despair** noun.

hope verb *I hope that I'll win.* [*informal*] anticipate, be hopeful [SEE **hopeful**], believe, desire, expect, have faith, have hope [SEE **hope** noun], trust, wish.
OPPOSITES: SEE **despair** verb.

hopeful adjective **1** *in a hopeful mood.* confident, expectant, optimistic, positive, sanguine.
OPPOSITES: SEE **pessimistic**.
2 *hopeful signs of success.* auspicious, cheering, encouraging, favourable, heartening, promising, propitious, reassuring.
OPPOSITES: SEE **discouraging**.

hopefully adverb **1** *The hungry dog looked hopefully at the food.* confidently, expectantly, optimistically, with hope.
2 [*informal*] *Hopefully, I'll be fit to play.* all being well, most likely, probably. [Many people think that this is a wrong use of *hopefully*.]

hopeless adjective **1** *hopeless refugees.* beyond hope, demoralized, despairing, desperate, disconsolate, pessimistic, wretched.
2 *a hopeless situation.* daunting, depressing, impossible, incurable, irremediable, irreparable, irreversible.
OPPOSITES: SEE **hopeful**.
3 [*informal*] *a hopeless footballer.* SEE **bad**, feeble, inadequate, incompetent, inefficient, poor, useless, weak, worthless.
OPPOSITES: SEE **competent**.

horde noun *hordes of children from other schools.* band, crowd, gang, SEE **group** noun, mob, swarm, throng, tribe.

horizon noun skyline.

horizontal adjective *a horizontal line.* flat, level, lying down.
OPPOSITES: SEE **vertical**.

horn noun *an animal's horns.* antler.

horoscope noun astrological diagram, [*informal*] your stars, zodiac.

horrendous adjective SEE **horrific**.

Horrible and *horrid* often describe things that are not really important (*horrible food; horrid weather*), whereas *horrific* and *horrifying* describe things that really horrify you (*horrific injuries; horrifying cruelty*).

---

horrible adjective [*informal*] *horrible weather. horrible people.* awful, beastly, disagreeable, dreadful, ghastly, hateful, horrid, loathsome, nasty, objectionable, odious, offensive, revolting, terrible, unkind, SEE **unpleasant**.
OPPOSITES: SEE **pleasant**.

horrid adjective SEE **horrible**.

horrific *a horrific accident.* appalling, atrocious, blood-curdling, disgusting, dreadful, frightening, frightful, grisly, gruesome, hair-raising, harrowing, horrendous, horrifying, nauseating, shocking, sickening, spine-chilling, unacceptable, unnerving, unthinkable.

horrified adjective *horrified onlookers.* aghast, appalled, disgusted, frightened, horror-stricken, horror-struck, shocked, sickened, stunned, unnerved.

horrify verb *The accident horrified us.* alarm, appal, disgust, frighten, harrow, nauseate, scare, shock, sicken, terrify, unnerve.

horrifying adjective SEE **horrific**.

horror noun **1** *a feeling of horror. a horror of spiders.* abhorrence, antipathy, aversion, detestation, disgust, dislike, dismay, dread, fear, loathing, panic, repugnance, revulsion, terror.
2 *I saw the full horror of the disaster.* awfulness, frightfulness, ghastliness, gruesomeness, hideousness.

horror-stricken, horror-struck adjectives SEE **horrified**.

hors-d'œuvre noun OTHER COURSES: SEE **meal**.

horse noun bronco, carthorse, [*old-fashioned*] charger, cob, colt, filly, foal, [*childish*] gee-gee, gelding, hack, hunter, [*old-fashioned*] jade, mare, mount, mule, mustang, [*informal*] nag, [*old-fashioned*] palfrey, piebald, pony, race-horse, roan, skewbald, stallion, steed, warhorse.
RELATED ADJECTIVES: equestrian, equine.
OTHER ANIMALS: SEE **animal** noun.
to ride a horse amble, canter, gallop, trot.

horseman, horsewoman nouns cavalryman, equestrian, jockey, rider.

horseplay noun SEE **misbehaviour**.

horticulture noun cultivation, gardening.

hose noun **1** hosiery, panti-hose, socks, stockings, tights.
2 *a water hose.* hose-pipe, pipe, tube.

hosiery noun SEE **hose**.

hospice noun SEE **home, hospital**.

hospitable adjective SEE **sociable**.

hospital noun clinic, convalescent home, hospice, infirmary, nursing home, sanatorium.

hospitality noun **1** *I gave her hospitality for the night.* accommodation, catering, entertainment.
2 *They thanked us for our hospitality.* SEE **friendliness**, sociability, welcome.

host noun **1** *a host of people.* SEE **group** noun.
2 *the host of a TV programme.* SEE **compère**.

hostage noun captive, prisoner.

hostel noun SEE **accommodation**.

hostile adjective **1** *a hostile crowd.* aggressive, SEE **angry**, antagonistic, antipathetic, attacking, averse, bellicose, belligerent, confrontational, ill-disposed, inhospitable, inimical, malevolent, pugnacious, resentful, unfriendly, unwelcoming, warlike.
OPPOSITES: SEE **friendly**.
2 *hostile weather conditions.* adverse, bad, contrary, opposing, unfavourable, unhelpful, unpropitious.
OPPOSITES: SEE **favourable**.

hostility noun *hostility between enemies.* aggression, animosity, antagonism, antipathy, aversion, bad feeling, belligerence, confrontation, detestation, dislike, enmity, estrangement, hate, hatred, ill will, imcompatibility, malevolence, malice, opposition, pugnacity, resentment, unfriendliness.
OPPOSITES: SEE **friendship**.

hot adjective **1** *hot weather. a hot iron.* baking, blistering, boiling, burning, fiery, flaming, oppressive, piping hot (*piping hot food*), red-hot, roasting, scalding, scorching, searing, sizzling, steamy, stifling, sultry, summery, sweltering, thermal (*a thermal spring*), torrid, tropical, warm.
OPPOSITES: SEE **cold** adjective.
2 *a hot temper. in hot pursuit.* angry, eager, emotional, excited, feverish, fierce, heated, hotheaded, impatient, impetuous, intense, passionate, violent.
OPPOSITES: SEE **calm** adjective.
3 *a hot taste.* acrid, biting, gingery, peppery, piquant, pungent, spicy, strong.
OPPOSITES: SEE **mild**.
hot under the collar SEE **angry**.

hotchpotch noun SEE **jumble** noun.

hotel noun SEE **accommodation**.

hotheaded adjective SEE **impetuous**.

hothouse noun SEE **glasshouse**.

hot-tempered adjective SEE **bad-tempered**.

hound noun SEE **dog** noun.

hound verb SEE **pursue**.

hour noun OTHER UNITS OF TIME: SEE **time** noun.

house noun *a house to live in.* abode, [*formal*] domicile, dwelling, dwelling-place, [*formal*] habitation, home, household, lodging, place (*Come to my place*), quarters, residence.

KINDS OF HOUSE: SEE **accommodation**, apartment, bungalow, chalet, cottage, council house, croft, detached house, farmhouse, flat, grange, hovel, homestead, hut, igloo, lodge, maisonette, manor, manse, mansion, penthouse, [*informal*] prefab, public house, rectory, semi-detached house, shack, shanty, terraced house, thatched house, vicarage, villa.

ROOMS IN A HOUSE: SEE **room**.

---

house verb *to house someone.* accommodate, billet, board, [*formal*] domicile, keep, lodge, place, [*informal*] put up, quarter, shelter, take in.

housebreaker noun SEE **burglar**.

household noun establishment, family, home, ménage, [*informal*] set-up.

housekeeper, housemaid nouns SEE **servant**.

house-trained adjective *house-trained animals.* clean in the house, domesticated, tame.

housewife noun SEE **woman**.

housework noun SEE **work** noun.

hovel noun cottage, SEE **house** noun, hut, shack, shanty, shed.

hover verb **1** *to hover in the air.* drift, float, flutter, fly, hang.
2 *to hover about.* be indecisive, dally, dither, [*informal*] hang about, hesitate, linger, loiter, pause, wait about, vacillate, waver.

hovercraft noun OTHER VESSELS: SEE **vessel**.

howl verb VARIOUS SOUNDS: SEE **sound** noun.

howler noun *silly howlers in an exam.* SEE **mistake** noun.

hoyden noun SEE **girl**.

hub noun *the hub of a wheel. a hub of activity.* axis, centre, focal point, heart, middle, pivot.

hubbub noun SEE **commotion**.

huddle verb **1** *to huddle in a corner.* cluster, converge, crowd, flock, gather, heap, herd, jumble, pile, press, squeeze, swarm, throng.
OPPOSITES: SEE **scatter**.
2 *to huddle together to keep warm.* cuddle, curl up, nestle, snuggle.

hue noun SEE **colour** noun, complexion, dye, nuance, shade, tincture, tinge, tint, tone.
hue and cry SEE **pursuit**.

huff noun SEE **annoyance**.

huffy adjective SEE **annoyed**.

hug verb *to hug baby.* clasp, cling to, crush, cuddle, embrace, enfold, fold in your arms, hold close, nurse, squeeze, snuggle against.

huge adjective *Elephants are huge animals. The bank handles huge sums of money.* SEE **big**, colossal, enormous, giant, gigantic, great, [*informal*] hulking, immeasurable, immense, imposing, impressive, incalculable, [*informal*] jumbo-sized, large, majestic, mammoth, massive, mighty, [*informal*] monster, monstrous, monumental, mountainous, prodigious, stupendous, titanic, towering, [*informal*] tremendous, vast, weighty, [*informal*] whopping.
OPPOSITES: SEE **small**.

hulk noun **1** *the hulk of an old ship.* body, carcass, frame, hull, shell, wreck.
2 *a clumsy hulk.* clumsy person, lout, lump, oaf.

hulking adjective [*informal*] *a hulking great parcel.* awkward, bulky, clumsy, cumbersome, heavy, SEE **huge**, ungainly, unwieldy.

hull noun *the hull of a ship.* body, framework.

hullabaloo noun SEE **commotion**.

hullo interjection SEE **greeting**.

hum verb buzz, drone, murmur, purr, sing, SEE **sound** noun, vibrate, whirr.
to hum and haw SEE **hesitate**.

human adjective **1** *the human race.* anthropoid, mortal.
2 *human feelings.* altruistic, SEE **humane**, kind, merciful, philanthropic, rational, reasonable, sympathetic.
OPPOSITES: SEE **inhuman**.
human beings folk, humanity, mankind, men and women, mortals, people [SEE **person**].

humane adjective *Is it humane to kill animals for food?* benevolent, charitable, civilized, compassionate, feeling, forgiving, good, human, humanitarian, kind, kind-hearted, loving, magnanimous, merciful, pitying, sympathetic, tender, understanding, unselfish, warm-hearted.
OPPOSITES: SEE **inhumane**.

humanism noun RELIGIONS: SEE **religion**.

humanitarian adjective SEE **humane**.

humanity noun 1 SEE **human (human beings)**.
2 SEE **mercy**.

humanize verb *We hoped that education would humanize our brutal instincts.* civilize, domesticate, educate, make more human [SEE **human**], refine, soften, tame.
OPPOSITES: SEE **dehumanize**.

humble adjective 1 *humble behaviour.* deferential, docile, meek, [*uncomplimentary*] obsequious, polite, respectful, self-effacing, [*uncomplimentary*] servile, submissive, unassertive, unassuming, unpretentious.
OPPOSITES: SEE **proud**.
2 *a humble life-style. humble origins.* commonplace, insignificant, low, lowly, mean, modest, obscure, ordinary, plebeian, poor, simple, undistinguished, unimportant, unremarkable.
OPPOSITES: SEE **important**.

humble verb SEE **humiliate**.

humdrum adjective SEE **ordinary**.

humid adjective *humid weather.* clammy, damp, dank, moist, muggy, steamy, sticky, sultry, sweaty.

humiliate verb *They humiliated us by winning 14–0.* abase, abash, break (someone's) spirit, bring down, chagrin, chasten, crush, deflate, degrade, demean, discredit, disgrace, embarrass, humble, make ashamed, make (someone) feel humble [SEE **humble** adjective], mortify, [*informal*] put (someone) in their place, shame, [*informal*] take down a peg.

humiliating adjective *a humiliating defeat.* chastening, crushing, degrading, demeaning, discreditable, dishonourable, embarrassing, humbling, ignominious, inglorious, mortifying, shaming, undignified.
OPPOSITES: SEE **glorious**.

humiliation noun chagrin, degradation, dishonour, embarrassment, ignominy, indignity, mortification, shame.

humility noun deference, humbleness, lowliness, meekness, modesty, self-effacement, unpretentiousness.
OPPOSITES: SEE **pride**.

hummock noun SEE **hill**.

humorist noun SEE **comedian**.

humorous adjective SEE **funny**.

humour noun 1 *Her humour makes me laugh.* badinage, banter, comedy, facetiousness, jesting, jocularity, jokes, joking, quips, raillery, repartee, [*informal*] sense of fun, wit, witticisms, wittiness.
2 *You're in a good humour!* disposition, frame of mind, mood, spirits, state of mind, temper.

hump noun *a hump in the road.* bulge, bump, curve, knob, lump, mound, protuberance, rise, swelling.

hump verb 1 *The cat humped its back.* arch, bend, curl, curve, hunch, raise.
2 *He humped the sack onto his shoulders.* hoist, lift, raise, shoulder.

humpback noun hunchback, round shoulders, stoop.

humus noun compost, soil.

hunch noun *I have a hunch that they won't come.* feeling, guess, idea, impression, inkling, intuition, suspicion.

hunch verb *to hunch your shoulders.* arch, bend, curl, curve, huddle, hump, shrug.

hunchback noun SEE **humpback**.

hunger noun 1 *a hunger for food.* appetite, craving, SEE **desire** noun, greed, ravenousness.
2 *Hunger kills millions of people.* deprivation, famine, lack of food, malnutrition, starvation.

hungry adjective aching, avid, covetous, eager, famished, famishing, greedy, longing, peckish, ravenous, starved, starving, underfed, undernourished, voracious.

hunk noun SEE **lump** noun.

hunt noun *a hunt for prey.* chase, SEE **hunting**, pursuit, quest, search.

hunt verb 1 *to hunt animals.* chase, course, ferret, hound, poach, pursue, stalk, track down, trail.
2 *to hunt for something you've lost.* ferret out, look for, rummage, search for, seek.

hunter noun huntsman, predator, trapper.

hunting noun KINDS OF HUNTING: beagling, deer-stalking, falconry, fox-hunting, hawking, SEE **hunt** noun, whaling.

hurdle noun 1 *The runners cleared the first hurdle.* barricade, barrier, fence, hedge, jump, obstacle, wall.
2 *There are many hurdles to overcome in life.* difficulty, handicap, hindrance, obstruction, problem, snag, stumbling block.

hurl verb *to hurl something into the air.* cast, catapult, chuck, dash, fire, fling, heave, launch, pelt, pitch, project, shy, sling, throw, toss.

hurly-burly noun SEE **activity**.

hurricane noun cyclone, SEE **storm** noun, tornado, typhoon, whirlwind.

hurried adjective *a hurried decision.* SEE **hasty**.

hurry noun SEE **haste**.

hurry verb **1** *to hurry home.* [*informal*] belt, chase, dash, dispatch, [*informal*] fly, [*informal*] get a move on, hasten, hurtle, hustle, move quickly, rush, speed.
OPPOSITE: go slowly.
2 *If you want to finish, you must hurry.* [*informal*] buck up, [*informal*] shift, [*informal*] step on it, work faster.
OPPOSITES: SEE **dawdle**.
3 *to hurry a process.* accelerate, expedite, quicken, speed up.
OPPOSITES: SEE **delay** verb.

hurt verb **1** *Where do you hurt?* ache, be painful [SEE **painful**], smart, sting, suffer pain [SEE **pain** noun], throb, tingle.
2 *Did they hurt you?* abuse, afflict, agonize, bruise, cause pain to [SEE **pain** noun], cripple, cut, damage, disable, harm, injure, maim, misuse, torture, wound.
3 *The insult hurt her.* be hurtful to [SEE **hurtful**], distress, grieve, pain, torment, upset.

hurtful adjective *hurtful remarks,* biting, cruel, cutting, damaging, derogatory, distressing, hard to bear, harmful, injurious, malicious, nasty, painful, sarcastic, scathing, spiteful, uncharitable, unkind, upsetting, vicious, wounding.
OPPOSITES: SEE **kind** adjective.

hurtle verb *to hurtle along. to hurtle earthwards.* charge, chase, dash, fly, plunge, race, rush, shoot, speed, tear.

husband noun spouse.
FAMILY RELATIONSHIPS: SEE **family**.

husbandry noun agriculture, cultivation, farming.

hush interjection be quiet! be silent! [*informal*] hold your tongue! [*informal*] shut up! silence!

hush noun SEE **silence** noun.

hush verb **to hush up** *to hush up the facts.* conceal, cover up, hide, keep quiet, keep secret, stifle, suppress.

hush-hush adjective SEE **secret** adjective.

husk noun *the husk of a seed.* covering, shell.

husky adjective **1** *a husky voice.* SEE **hoarse**.
2 *a big, husky fellow.* SEE **hefty**.

husky noun *a team of huskies.* SEE **dog** noun.

hussy noun SEE **woman**.

hustle verb *to hustle someone along.* bustle, force, hasten, hurry, jostle, push, rush, shove.

hut noun cabin, den, hovel, lean-to, shack, shanty, shed, shelter.

hutch noun SEE **cage**.

hybrid noun *a hybrid of two species.* amalgam, combination, composite, compound, cross, cross-breed, mixture, mongrel.

hydrant noun SEE **pipe** noun.

hydraulic adjective water-powered.

hygiene noun cleanliness, health, sanitariness, sanitation, wholesomeness.

hygienic adjective *hygienic conditions in hospital.* aseptic, clean, disinfected, germ-free, healthy, pure, salubrious, sanitary, sterilized, unpolluted, wholesome.
OPPOSITES: SEE **unhealthy**.

hyperbole noun exaggeration, overstatement.

hypercritical adjective [Do not confuse with *hypocritical.*] SEE **critical**.

hypermarket noun SEE **shop**.

hypersensitive adjective SEE **sensitive**.

hyphen noun dash.

hypnotic adjective *a hypnotic rhythm.* fascinating, irresistible, magnetic, mesmeric, mesmerizing, sleep-inducing, soothing, soporific, spellbinding.

hypnotism noun hypnosis, magnetism, suggestion.

hypnotize verb bewitch, captivate, dominate, entrance, fascinate, gain power over, magnetize, mesmerize, [*informal*] put to sleep, [*informal*] stupefy.

hypochondriac noun valetudinarian, [*informal*] worrier.

hypocrisy noun *the hypocrisy of people who say one thing and do another.* cant, deceit, deception, double-talk, duplicity, falsity, [*informal*] humbug, inconsistency, insincerity.

hypocritical adjective [Do not confuse with *hypercritical.*] *It's hypocritical to say one thing and do another.* deceptive, false, inconsistent, insincere, [*informal*] phoney, [*informal*] two-faced.

hypothesis noun *an unproved hypothesis.* conjecture, guess, premise, proposition, supposition, theory, [*formal*] thesis.

hypothetical adjective *a hypothetical problem.* academic, conjectural, imaginary, putative, speculative, supposed, suppositional, theoretical, unreal.

hysteria noun *uncontrollable hysteria in the crowd.* frenzy, hysterics, madness, mania, panic.

hysterical adjective 1 *hysterical fans.* berserk, crazed, delirious, demented, distraught, frantic, frenzied, mad, raving, uncontrollable, wild.
2 [*informal*] *a hysterical joke.* comic, crazy, SEE **funny**, hilarious, [*informal*] killing, ridiculous, [*informal*] side-splitting, uproarious.

I

ice noun 1 FORMS OF ICE: black ice, floe, frost, glacier, iceberg, ice-rink, icicle, rime.
2 *a vanilla ice.* ice-cream.

icon noun SEE **picture** noun.

iconoclast noun SEE **rebel** noun.

icy adjective 1 *icy weather.* arctic, SEE **cold** adjective, freezing, frosty.
2 *icy roads.* frozen, glacial, glassy, greasy, slippery, [*informal*] slippy.

idea noun 1 *a philosophical idea.* abstraction, attitude, belief, concept, conception, conjecture, conviction, hypothesis, notion, opinion, theory, view.
2 *the main idea of a poem.* intention, meaning, point, thought.
3 *I have an idea!* brainwave, fancy, guess, inspiration, plan, proposal, scheme, suggestion.
4 *The sample gives an idea of what to expect.* clue, guidelines, impression, inkling, intimation, model, pattern, perception, vision.

ideal adjective 1 *ideal conditions.* best, classic, excellent, faultless, model, optimum, perfect, suitable.
2 *an ideal world.* hypothetical, imaginary, unattainable, unreal, Utopian, visionary.

ideal noun 1 *an ideal worth imitating.* SEE **model** noun.
2 *a person of high ideals.* SEE **principle**.

idealistic adjective *I don't think her idealistic plans will ever materialize.* high-minded, over-optimistic, quixotic, romantic, starry-eyed, unrealistic.
OPPOSITES: SEE **realistic**.

idealize verb *People idealize their heroes.* deify, glamorize, glorify, [*informal*] put on a pedestal, romanticize, worship.

identical adjective *identical twins. identical in appearance.* alike, congruent (*congruent triangles*), corresponding, duplicate, equal, indistinguishable, interchangeable, matching, the same, similar, twin.
OPPOSITES: SEE **different**.

identifiable adjective *an identifiable accent.* detectable, discernible, distinctive, distinguishable, familiar, known, named, noticeable, perceptible, recognizable, unmistakable.
OPPOSITES: SEE **unidentifiable**.

identify verb 1 *to identify a suspect.* name, pick out, recognize, single out.
2 *to identify an illness.* detect, diagnose, discover, distinguish, pinpoint, [*informal*] put a name to, spot.
to identify with *to identify with a character in a story.* emphathize with, feel for, [*informal*] put yourself in the shoes of, relate to.

identikit noun SEE **picture** noun.

identity noun 1 *Can you prove your identity?* [*informal*] ID, name, nature.
2 *Prisoners sometimes lose their sense of identity.* character, individuality, personality, selfhood, uniqueness.

ideology noun *political ideology.* economic theories, ideas, philosophy, political theories, principles, set of beliefs, underlying attitudes.

idiom noun *It's hard to understand the colloquial idioms of a foreign language.* choice of words, expression, manner of speaking, phrase, phraseology, phrasing, turn of phrase, usage.

idiomatic adjective *idiomatic expressions.* colloquial, natural, well-phrased.

idiosyncrasy noun *Most of us have a few funny idiosyncrasies.* characteristic, eccentricity, feature, habit, mannerism, oddity, peculiarity, quirk, trait.

idiosyncratic adjective *idiosyncratic behaviour.* characteristic, distinctive, eccentric, individual, odd, peculiar, personal, quirky, singular, unique.
OPPOSITES: SEE **common** adjective.

idiot noun [These words are used *informally* and are usually insulting.] ass, blockhead, bonehead, booby, chump, clot, cretin, dimwit, dolt, dope, duffer, dumbell, dummy, dunce, dunderhead, fat-head, fool, half-wit, ignoramus, imbecile, moron, nincompoop, ninny, nitwit, simpleton, twerp, twit.

idiotic adjective SEE **stupid**.

idle adjective 1 *The machines lay idle during the strike.* dormant, inactive, inoperative, in retirement, not working, redundant, retired, unemployed, unoccupied, unproductive, unused.
OPPOSITES: SEE **busy, working**.

2 *He lost his job because he was idle.* apathetic, good-for-nothing, indolent, lackadaisical, lazy, shiftless, slothful, slow, sluggish, torpid, uncommitted, work-shy.
OPPOSITES: SEE **keen.**
3 *idle speculation.* casual, frivolous, futile, pointless, worthless.
OPPOSITES: SEE **serious.**
an idle person [*informal*] good-for-nothing, idler, [*informal*] layabout, [*informal*] lazybones, loafer, malingerer, shirker, [*informal*] skiver, slacker, sluggard, wastrel.

idle verb **to idle about** be lazy [SEE **lazy**], dawdle, do nothing, [*informal*] hang about, [*informal*] kill time, laze, loaf, lounge about, potter, slack, stagnate, take it easy, vegetate.
OPPOSITES: SEE **work** verb.

idol noun **1** *a pagan idol.* deity, god, icon, image, statue.
2 *a pop idol.* favourite, hero, [*informal*] pin-up, star, [*informal*] superstar.

idolatry noun SEE **worship** noun.

idolize verb SEE **worship** verb.

idyllic adjective *an idyllic scene.* charming, delightful, happy, idealized, lovely, pastoral, peaceful, perfect, unspoiled.
OPPOSITES: SEE **desolate.**

ignite verb *The central-heating boiler won't ignite.* burn, catch fire, fire, kindle, light, set alight, set on fire, spark off.

ignoble adjective *ignoble motives.* base, churlish, cowardly, despicable, disgraceful, dishonourable, infamous, low, mean, selfish, shabby, uncharitable, unchivalrous, unworthy.
OPPOSITES: SEE **noble** adjective.

ignominious adjective *ignominious defeat.* SEE **humiliating.**

ignoramus noun SEE **idiot**, ignorant person [SEE **ignorant**].

ignorance noun *ignorance of the facts.* inexperience, innocence, lack of information, unawareness, unconsciousness, unfamiliarity.
OPPOSITES: SEE **knowledge.**

ignorant adjective **1** *ignorant of the facts.* [*informal*] clueless, ill-informed, innocent, lacking knowledge, unacquainted, unaware, unconscious, unfamiliar (with), uninformed.
OPPOSITES: SEE **knowledgeable.**
2 *You'd be ignorant if you didn't go to school.* illiterate, uncultivated, uneducated, unenlightened, unlettered, unscholarly.
OPPOSITES: SEE **educated.**
3 [*informal*] *He's just plain ignorant!* SEE **stupid.**

ignore verb *to ignore a warning. to ignore your friends.* disobey, disregard, leave out, miss out, neglect, omit, overlook, pass over, [*informal*] shut your eyes to, skip, slight, take no notice of, [*informal*] turn a blind eye to.

ill adjective **1** ailing, bedridden, bilious, [*informal*] dicky, diseased, feeble, frail, [*informal*] funny (*feeling a bit funny*), [*informal*] groggy, indisposed, infected, infirm, nauseated, nauseous, [*informal*] off-colour, [*informal*] out of sorts, pasty, poorly, queasy, queer, [*informal*] seedy, sick, sickly, suffering, [*informal*] under the weather, unhealthy, unwell, weak.
OPPOSITES: SEE **healthy.**
2 *ill effects.* SEE **bad**, damaging, detrimental, evil, harmful, injurious, unfavourable, unfortunate, unlucky.
OPPOSITES: SEE **good.**
ill people the infirm, invalids, patients, the sick, sufferers, victims.
ill will SEE **hostility.**
to be ill ail, languish, sicken.

ill-bred adjective SEE **rude.**

illegal adjective *illegal activities. illegal trade.* actionable, against the law, banned, black-market, criminal, forbidden, SEE **illegitimate**, illicit, invalid, irregular, outlawed, prohibited, proscribed, unauthorized, unconstitutional, unlawful, unlicensed, wrong.
OPPOSITES: SEE **legal.**

illegible adjective *illegible writing.* SEE **bad**, indecipherable, indistinct, obscure, unclear, unreadable.
OPPOSITES: SEE **legible.**

illegitimate adjective **1** *an illegitimate course of action.* against the rules, SEE **illegal**, improper, inadmissible, incorrect, invalid, unauthorized, unjustifiable, unreasonable, unwarranted.
OPPOSITES: SEE **legitimate.**
2 *an illegitimate child.* bastard, [*old-fashioned*] born out of wedlock, natural.

illicit adjective SEE **illegal.**

ill-fated adjective SEE **unlucky.**

ill-favoured adjective SEE **ugly.**

ill-humoured adjective SEE **bad-tempered.**

illiberal adjective *illiberal views.* SEE **prejudiced.**

illiterate adjective *He is illiterate because he never went to school.* ignorant, unable to read, uneducated.
OPPOSITES: SEE **literate.**

ill-judged adjective SEE **mistaken.**

ill-mannered adjective SEE **rude.**

ill-natured adjective SEE **unkind**.

illness noun *suffering from an illness.* abnormality, affliction, ailment, attack, blight. [*informal*] bug, complaint, condition, contagion, disability, disease, disorder, epidemic, health problem, indisposition, infection, infirmity, malady, malaise, pestilence, plague, sickness, [*informal*] trouble, [*informal*] turn (*He had a nasty turn*), [*informal*] upset, weakness, SEE **wound** noun.

VARIOUS ILLNESSES OR COMPLAINTS: abscess, acne, allergy, amnesia, anaemia, appendicitis, arthritis, asthma, bedsore, beriberi, bilious attack, blister, boil, bronchitis, brucellosis, bubonic plague, bunion, cancer, caries, catalepsy, cataract, catarrh, chicken-pox, chilblains, chill, cholera, claustrophobia, cold, colic, coma, concussion, conjunctivitis, constipation, convulsion, corns, coronary thrombosis, cough, cramp, croup, cystitis.

dandruff, delirium, dermatitis, diabetes, diarrhoea, diphtheria, dipsomania, dropsy, dysentery, dyspepsia, dystrophy, ear-ache, eczema, embolism, enteritis, epilepsy, fever, fits, flu, frostbite, gangrene, gastric flu, glandular fever, goitre, gonorrhoea, gout, gumboil, haemophilia, haemorrhage, haemorrhoids, hay fever, headache, hernia, hypothermia.

impetigo, indigestion, inflammation, influenza, insomnia, jaundice, laryngitis, leprosy, leukaemia, lockjaw, lumbago, malaria, measles, melancholia, meningitis, mental illness, migraine, mongolism, multiple sclerosis, mumps, neuralgia, neuritis, neurosis, paralysis, paratyphoid, pellagra, peritonitis, phobia, piles, plague, pleurisy, pneumonia, polio or poliomyelitis, psychosis, quinsy.

rabies, rheumatism, rickets, ringworm, rupture, scabies, scarlet fever, schizophrenia, sciatica, sclerosis, scrofula, scurvy, sea-sickness, seizure, shingles, silicosis, smallpox, spastic, spina bifida, stomach-ache, stroke, sty, sunstroke, syphilis, tetanus, thrombosis, tonsillitis, toothache, tuberculosis, typhoid, typhus, ulcer, verruca, wart, whooping-cough.

---

illogical adjective *an illogical argument.* absurd, fallacious, inconsequential, inconsistent, invalid, irrational, senseless, SEE **silly**, unreasonable, unsound.
OPPOSITES: SEE **logical**.

ill-omened, ill-starred adjectives SEE **unlucky**.

ill-tempered adjective SEE **bad-tempered**.

ill-treat verb SEE **mistreat**.

illuminate verb **1** *to illuminate a place with lights.* brighten, decorate with lights, light up, make brighter.
2 *to illuminate a problem.* clarify, clear up, elucidate, enlighten, explain, throw light on.

ill-use verb SEE **mistreat**.

illusion noun *an optical illusion.* apparition, conjuring trick, day-dream, deception, delusion, dream, fancy, fantasy, figment of the imagination, hallucination, mirage.

illusionist noun conjuror, magician.

illusory adjective *illusory pleasures.* deceptive, deluding, delusive, false, illusive, SEE **imaginary**, misleading, sham, unreal, untrue.
OPPOSITES: SEE **real**.

illustrate verb **1** *to illustrate a book.* adorn, decorate, illuminate.
2 *to illustrate a story.* depict, draw pictures of, picture, portray.
3 *to illustrate how to do something.* demonstrate, elucidate, exemplify, explain, show.

illustration noun **1** *illustrations in a picture-book.* decoration, depiction, diagram, drawing, photograph, picture, sketch.
2 *This thesaurus gives illustrations of how words are used.* case, demonstration, example, instance, specimen.

illustrious adjective SEE **famous**.

image noun **1** *an image in a mirror. an image on a screen.* imitation, likeness, SEE **picture** noun, projection, reflection.
2 *The temple contained the god's image.* carving, effigy, figure, icon, idol, representation, statue.
3 [*informal*] *She's the image of her mother.* counterpart, double, likeness, spitting-image, twin.

imaginable adjective SEE **credible**.

imaginary adjective *The unicorn is an imaginary beast.* fabulous, fanciful, fictional, fictitious, hypothetical, SEE **illusory**, imagined, insubstantial, invented, legendary, made up, mythical, mythological, non-existent, supposed, unreal, visionary.
OPPOSITES: SEE **real**.

imagination noun *Use your imagination.* artistry, cleverness, creativity, fancy, ingenuity, insight, inspiration, inventiveness, originality, resourcefulness, sensitivity, thought, vision.

imaginative adjective *imaginative paintings. an imaginative story.* artistic, attractive, beautiful, clever, creative, fanciful, ingenious, inspired, inventive, original, poetic, resourceful, sensitive, thoughtful, unusual, visionary, vivid.
OPPOSITES: SEE **unimaginative**.

imagine verb **1** *Imagine you're on a desert island. Imagine what it would be like.* conceive, conjure up, create, dream up, envisage, fancy, fantasize, invent, make believe, make up, picture, pretend, see, think up, visualize.
2 *I imagine you'd like a drink.* assume, believe, conjecture, guess, infer, presume, suppose, surmise, [*informal*] take it.

imbalance noun SEE **bias, inequality**.

imbecile noun SEE **idiot**.

imbibe verb SEE **drink** verb.

imitate verb **1** *to imitate someone's mannerisms. to imitate another person.* ape, caricature, disguise yourself as, echo, guy, impersonate, masquerade as, mimic, parody, parrot, pose as, pretend to be, send up, take off, travesty.
2 *to imitate someone else's example.* copy, emulate, follow, match, model yourself on.
3 *to imitate the sound of the sea.* counterfeit, duplicate, reproduce, simulate.

imitation adjective *The actors carried imitation guns.* artificial, copied, counterfeit, dummy, ersatz, mock, model, sham, simulated.
OPPOSITES: SEE **real**.

imitation noun *an imitation of the real thing.* copy, counterfeit, dummy, duplicate, duplication, fake, forgery, impersonation, impression, likeness, [*informal*] mock-up, model, parody, reflection, replica, reproduction, sham, simulation, [*informal*] take-off, toy, travesty.

imitative adjective *imitative behaviour. an imitative style.* conventional, copied, derivative, fake, mock, plagiarized, traditional, unimaginative, unoriginal.
OPPOSITES: SEE **inventive**.

immaculate adjective SEE **perfect** adjective.

immanent adjective [Do not confuse with *imminent*.] SEE **inherent**.

immaterial adjective SEE **unimportant**.

immature adjective *immature behaviour. an immature person.* adolescent, babyish, backward, callow, childish, [*informal*] green, inexperienced, infantile, juvenile, puerile, undeveloped, [*of fruit*] unripe, young, youthful.
OPPOSITES: SEE **mature**.

immeasurable adjective SEE **infinite**.

immediate adjective **1** *immediate action.* direct, instant, instantaneous, present, pressing, prompt, quick, speedy, swift, top-priority, unhesitating, urgent.
OPPOSITES: delayed, low-priority.
2 *our immediate neighbours.* adjacent, close, closest, near, nearest, neighbouring, next.
OPPOSITES: SEE **remote**.

immediately adverb at once, directly, forthwith, instantly, now, promptly, [*informal*] right away, straight away, unhesitatingly.

immense adjective SEE **huge**.

immerse verb *to immerse something in water.* bathe, dip, drench, drown, duck, dunk, lower, plunge, submerge.

immersed adjective *immersed in your work.* absorbed, busy, engrossed, interested, involved, occupied, preoccupied, wrapped up.

immersion noun *immersion in water.* baptism, dipping, ducking, plunge, submersion.
immersion heater SEE **fire** noun.

immigrant noun incomer, newcomer, settler.

immigrate verb move in, settle.

imminent adjective [Do not confuse with *immanent*.] *imminent disaster.* about to happen, approaching, close, coming, foreseeable, impending, looming, near, threatening.

immobile adjective **1** *immobile in deep mud.* fast, firm, fixed, immobilized, immovable, motionless, paralysed, secure, solid, static, stationary, still, stuck, unmoving.
2 *immobile features.* frozen, inexpressive, inflexible, rigid.
OPPOSITES: SEE **mobile**.

immobilize verb *to immobilize a vehicle.* cripple, damage, disable, make immobile (SEE **immobile**], paralyse, put out of action, stop.

immoderate adjective SEE **excessive**.

immodest adjective SEE **indecent**.

immoral adjective *immoral behaviour.* abandoned, SEE **bad**, base, conscienceless, corrupt, debauched, degenerate, depraved, dishonest, dissipated, dissolute, evil, [*informal*] fast (*fast living*), impure, SEE **indecent**, licentious, loose, low, profligate, promiscuous, sinful, unchaste, unethical, unprincipled,

unscrupulous, vicious, villainous, wanton, SEE **wicked**, wrong.
OPPOSITES: SEE **moral** adjective.
COMPARE: amoral.
an immoral person blackguard, cheat, degenerate, liar, libertine, profligate, rake, reprobate, SEE **scoundrel**, sinner, villain, wrongdoer.

immorality noun dishonesty, misbehaviour, misconduct, unscrupulousness, SEE **wickedness**.
COMPARE: amorality, morality.

immortal adjective *immortal souls. an immortal work of art.* ageless, deathless, endless, eternal, everlasting, perpetual, timeless, unchanging, undying.
OPPOSITES: SEE **mortal**.

immortality noun *the immortality of a work of art.* agelessness, endless life, permanence, timelessness.

immortalize verb *to immortalize someone's memory.* commemorate, deify, enshrine, keep alive, make immortal, make permanent, perpetuate.

immovable adjective SEE **immobile**.

immune adjective *immune to disease.* exempt (from), free (from), immunized (against), inoculated (against), invulnerable, protected (from), resistant, safe (from), unaffected (by), vaccinated (against).

immunize verb inoculate, vaccinate.

immunization noun inoculation, vaccination.

immure verb SEE **imprison**.

immutable adjective *immutable truths.* constant, dependable, enduring, eternal, fixed, invariable, lasting, permanent, perpetual, reliable, settled, stable, unalterable, unchangeable.
OPPOSITES: SEE **changeable**.

imp noun SEE **spirit**.

impact noun **1** *Was the car damaged in the impact?* bang, blow, bump, collision, concussion, contact, crash, knock, smash.
2 *The tragedy had a strong impact on us.* effect, force, impression, influence, repercussions, shock.

impair verb SEE **damage** verb.

impale verb SEE **pierce**.

impart verb SEE **give**.

impartial adjective *an impartial referee.* balanced, detached, disinterested, dispassionate, equitable, even-handed, fair, fair-minded, just, neutral, non-partisan, objective, open-minded, unbiased, uninvolved, unprejudiced.
OPPOSITES: SEE **biased**.

impartiality noun balance, detachment, disinterest, fairness, justice, lack of bias, neutrality, objectivity, open-mindedness.
OPPOSITES: SEE **bias**.

impassable adjective *an impassable road.* blocked, closed, obstructed, unusable.

impasse noun SEE **deadlock**.

impassioned adjective SEE **passionate**.

impassive adjective SEE **unemotional**.

impatient adjective **1** *impatient to start.* anxious, eager, keen, impetuous, precipitate, [*informal*] raring (*raring to go*).
OPPOSITES: SEE **apathetic**.
2 *impatient because of the delay.* agitated, chafing, edgy, fidgety, fretful, irritable, nervous, restless, uneasy.
OPPOSITES: SEE **calm** adjective, **patient** adjective.
3 *an impatient manner.* abrupt, brusque, curt, hasty, intolerant, quick-tempered, snappy, testy.
OPPOSITES: SEE **easygoing**, **patient** adjective.

impeach verb SEE **accuse**.

impeccable adjective SEE **perfect** adjective.

impecunious adjective SEE **poor**.

impede verb SEE **hinder**.

impediment noun **1** SEE **hindrance**.
2 *a speech impediment.* SEE **handicap** noun.

impel verb SEE **propel**, **urge** verb.

impending adjective SEE **imminent**.

impenetrable adjective **1** *impenetrable forest.* dense, impassable, solid, thick.
2 *impenetrable by water.* SEE **impermeable**.

impenitent adjective SEE **unrepentant**.

imperative adjective SEE **necessary**.

imperceptible adjective *imperceptible movement. imperceptible sounds.* faint, gradual, inaudible, infinitesimal, insignificant, invisible, microscopic, minute, negligible, slight, small, subtle, tiny, undetectable, unnoticeable.
OPPOSITES: SEE **noticeable**.

imperfect adjective *imperfect goods. an imperfect success.* broken, damaged, defective, deficient, faulty, flawed, incomplete, incorrect, marred, partial, shop-soiled, spoilt, unfinished, with imperfections.
OPPOSITES: SEE **perfect** adjective.

imperfection noun *a performance with obvious imperfections.* blemish, damage,

defect, deficiency, failing, fault, flaw, inadequacy, shortcoming, weakness.
OPPOSITES: SEE **perfection**.

imperial adjective SEE **majestic**.

imperil verb SEE **endanger**.

imperious adjective SEE **bossy**.

impermanent adjective *an impermanent relationship.* destructible, ephemeral, evanescent, fleeting, momentary, passing, short-lived, temporary, transient, transitory, unstable.
OPPOSITES: SEE **permanent**.

impermeable adjective *impermeable by water.* hermetic, impenetrable, impervious, non-porous, waterproof, water-repellent, watertight.
OPPOSITES: SEE **porous**.

impersonal adjective *an impersonal manner.* aloof, businesslike, cold, cool, correct, detached, distant, formal, hard, inhuman, official, remote, unapproachable, unemotional, unfriendly, unsympathetic, without emotion.
OPPOSITES: SEE **friendly**.

impersonate verb SEE **imitate**.

impertinent adjective *impertinent remarks.* bold, brazen, cheeky, [*informal*] cocky, [*informal*] cool (*He's a cool customer!*), discourteous, disrespectful, forward, fresh (*Don't get fresh with me!*), impolite, impudent, insolent, insubordinate, insulting, irreverent, pert, SEE **rude**, saucy.
OPPOSITES: SEE **respectful**.

imperturbable adjective SEE **calm** adjective.

impervious adjective **1** *impervious to damp.* SEE **impermeable**.
2 *impervious to criticism.* SEE **resistant**.

impetuous adjective *an impetuous dash for freedom.* careless, eager, hasty, headlong, hot-headed, impulsive, incautious, precipitate, quick, rash, reckless, speedy, thoughtless, spontaneous, [*informal*] tearing (*in a tearing hurry*), unplanned, unpremeditated, unthinking, violent.
OPPOSITES: SEE **cautious**.

impetus noun *Hot weather gives an impetus to swimwear sales.* boost, drive, energy, fillip, force, impulse, incentive, momentum, motivation, power, push, spur, stimulus.

impiety noun blasphemy, godlessness, irreverence, profanity, sacrilege, sinfulness, ungodliness, unrighteousness, wickedness.
OPPOSITES: SEE **piety**.

impinge verb SEE **encroach**.

impious adjective blasphemous, godless, sacrilegious, SEE **wicked**.

implacable adjective SEE **relentless**.

implant verb SEE **insert**.

implausible adjective *an implausible excuse.* far-fetched, feeble, improbable, suspect, unconvincing, unlikely, unreasonable, weak.
OPPOSITES: SEE **plausible**.

implement noun *gardening implements.* appliance, device, gadget, instrument, tool, utensil.

implement verb *to implement a plan.* bring about, carry out, effect, enforce, execute, fulfil, perform, put into practice, realize, try out.

implicate verb *The evidence clearly implicated him in the crime.* associate, connect, embroil, entangle, incriminate, inculpate, involve, show involvement in.

implication noun **1** *What was the implication of her comments?* hidden meaning, hint, innuendo, insinuation, overtone, significance.
2 *He was suspected of implication in the crime.* association, connection, entanglement, involvement.

implicit adjective **1** *implicit criticism.* hinted at, implied, indirect, insinuated, tacit, understood, unexpressed, unsaid, unspoken, unstated, unvoiced.
OPPOSITES: SEE **explicit**.
2 *implicit faith in her competence.* SEE **absolute**.

implore verb SEE **ask**.

imply verb *to imply something without saying it directly.* hint, indicate, insinuate, intimate, mean, point to, suggest.

impolite adjective SEE **rude**.

imponderable adjective *imponderable questions.* SEE **profound**.

import verb *to import goods.* bring in, buy in, SEE **convey**, introduce, ship in.
OPPOSITE: export.

important adjective **1** *important facts. an important event.* basic, big, cardinal, central, chief, epoch-making, essential, foremost, fundamental, historic, key, main, major, momentous, newsworthy, noteworthy, once in a lifetime, outstanding, pressing, primary, principal, rare, salient, serious, significant, strategic, urgent, valuable, weighty.
2 *an important person.* celebrated, distinguished, eminent, famous, great, high-ranking, influential, known, leading, notable, powerful, pre-eminent, prominent, renowned, well-known.
OPPOSITES: SEE **unimportant**.

to be important be significant, count, have influence, matter, signify, stand out, take first place.
an important person SEE **celebrity**, mogul, [*informal*] somebody, VIP.

importunate adjective *importunate requests.* demanding, impatient, insistent, persistent, pressing, relentless, urgent, unremitting.

importune verb *He's for ever importuning me for money.* SEE **ask**, badger, harass, hound, pester, plague, plead with, press, solicit, urge.

impose verb *to impose a penalty.* charge with, decree, dictate, enforce, exact, fix, inflict, insist on, introduce, lay, levy, prescribe, set.
to impose on *I don't want to impose on you.* burden, encumber, place a burden on, [*informal*] saddle, take advantage of.

imposing adjective *an imposing castle.* big, dignified, distinguished, grand, grandiose, great, important, impressive, magnificent, majestic, splendid, stately, striking.

impossibility noun hopelessness, impracticability, unlikelihood.
OPPOSITES: SEE **possibility**.

impossible adjective *an impossible task.* hopeless, impracticable, impractical, inconceivable, insoluble, insurmountable, out of the question, overwhelming, unachievable, unattainable, unimaginable, unobtainable, unviable, unworkable.
OPPOSITES: SEE **possible**.

impostor, imposture nouns SEE **cheat** noun.

impotence noun *His impotence to help made him despair.* feebleness, inability, inadequacy, incapacity, ineffectuality, powerlessness, weakness.

impotent adjective *impotent to help.* feeble, helpless, inadequate, incapable, incompetent, ineffective, ineffectual, powerless, unable, weak.
OPPOSITES: SEE **powerful**.

impound verb *to impound someone's property.* SEE **confiscate**.

impoverished adjective SEE **poor**.

impracticable adjective SEE **impractical**.

impractical adjective *an impractical suggestion.* academic, idealistic, SEE **impossible**, impracticable, inconvenient, not feasible, romantic, theoretical, unachievable, unrealistic, unworkable.
OPPOSITES: SEE **practical**.

imprecation noun SEE **curse** noun.

imprecise adjective **1** *imprecise measurements.* approximate, estimated, guessed, inaccurate, inexact, unscientific.
2 *imprecise wording.* ambiguous, SEE **careless**, ill-defined, inexplicit, loose, [*informal*] sloppy, undefined, vague, [*informal*] waffling, [*informal*] woolly.
OPPOSITES: SEE **precise**.

impregnable adjective *an impregnable castle.* impenetrable, invincible, invulnerable, safe, secure, strong, unassailable, unconquerable.
OPPOSITES: SEE **vulnerable**.

impregnate verb SEE **fertilize**.

impress verb **1** *Her hard work impressed me.* affect, be memorable to, excite, influence, inspire, leave its mark on, move, [*informal*] stick in the mind of, stir.
2 *She impressed on us the need for caution.* SEE **emphasize**.

impression noun **1** *The film made a big impression on me.* effect, impact, influence, mark.
2 *I had the impression you were bored.* belief, consciousness, conviction, fancy, feeling, hunch, idea, notion, opinion, sense, suspicion, view.
3 *Granny has clear impressions of her childhood.* memory, recollection.
4 *Our feet left impressions in the snow.* dent, hollow, imprint, indentation, mark, print, stamp.
5 *a new impression of a book.* edition, printing, reprint.

impressionable adjective *impressionable young children.* easily influenced, gullible, inexperienced, naïve, receptive, suggestible, susceptible.
OPPOSITES: SEE **knowing**.

impressive adjective *an impressive win. an impressive building.* affecting, SEE **big**, grand, great, important, imposing, magnificent, majestic, memorable, moving, powerful, remarkable, splendid, stately, stirring, striking, touching.
OPPOSITES: SEE **insignificant**.

imprint verb SEE **print** verb.

imprison verb *to imprison a criminal.* cage, commit to prison, confine, detain, gaol, immure, incarcerate, intern, jail, keep in custody, keep under house arrest, [*informal*] keep under lock and key, lock up, [*informal*] put away, [*informal*] send down, shut up.
OPPOSITES: SEE **free** verb.

imprisonment noun confinement, custody, detention, duress (*under duress*), gaol, house arrest, incarceration, internment, restraint.

improbable adjective *an improbable story.* doubtful, far-fetched, implausible, incredible, preposterous, questionable, unbelievable, unconvincing, unexpected, unlikely.
OPPOSITES: SEE **probable**.

impromptu adjective *impromptu remarks.* [*informal*] ad-lib, extempore, extemporized, improvised, offhand, [*informal*] off the cuff, spontaneous, unplanned, unpremeditated, unprepared, unrehearsed, unscripted.
OPPOSITES: SEE **rehearsed**.

improper adjective **1** *an improper course of action.* ill-timed, inappropriate, incorrect, inopportune, out of place, uncalled for, unsuitable, unwarranted, SEE **wrong** adjective.
2 *improper language.* SEE **indecent**.
OPPOSITES: SEE **proper**.

impropriety noun *I was surprised by the impropriety of his remarks.* bad manners, inappropriateness, indecency, indelicacy, insensitivity, obscenity, rudeness, vulgarity, unseemliness.
OPPOSITES: SEE **propriety**.

improve verb **1** *Her work improved.* advance, develop, get better, move on, progress.
2 *Has he improved since his illness?* get better, [*informal*] pick up, rally, recover, recuperate, strengthen, [*informal*] turn the corner.
OPPOSITES: SEE **decline** verb, **deteriorate**.
3 *The new job improved my finances.* ameliorate, better, enhance, enrich, make better.
4 *Improve your manners!* amend, correct, mend, rectify, refine, reform, revise.
OPPOSITES: SEE **worsen**.
5 *We received a grant to improve our house.* bring up to date, extend, modernize, rebuild, renovate, touch up.

improvement noun **1** *an improvement in behaviour.* advance, amelioration, betterment, correction, development, enhancement, gain, progress, rally, recovery, reformation, upturn.
2 *improvements to our house.* alteration, extension, [*informal*] face-lift, modernization, modification, renovation.

improvident adjective SEE **wasteful**.

improvise verb **1** *to improvise music.* [*informal*] ad-lib, extemporize, make up, perform impromptu [SEE **impromptu**], [*informal*] play it by ear, vamp.
2 *to improvise a meal.* concoct, invent, make do, [*informal*] throw together.

imprudent adjective [Don't confuse with *impudent.*] SEE **unwise**.

impudence noun SEE **cheek**.

impudent adjective [Don't confuse with *imprudent.*] SEE **cheeky**.

impugn verb *to impugn someone's integrity.* SEE **question** verb.

impulse noun **1** *What was the impulse behind your decision?* drive, force, impetus, motive, pressure, push, stimulus, thrust.
2 *a sudden impulse to do something.* caprice, desire, instinct, urge, whim.

impulsive adjective *an impulsive action.* automatic, hare-brained, hasty, headlong, hot-headed, impetuous, impromptu, instinctive, intuitive, involuntary, madcap, precipitate, rash, reckless, spontaneous, sudden, thoughtless, unconscious, unplanned, unpremeditated, unthinking, wild.
OPPOSITES: SEE **deliberate** adjective.

impure adjective **1** *impure water.* adulterated, contaminated, defiled, dirty, SEE **filthy**, foul, infected, polluted, tainted, unclean, unwholesome.
2 *impure thoughts.* SEE **indecent**.

impurity noun *impurities in water.* contamination, dirt, SEE **filth**, foreign body, infection, pollution, taint.

impute verb SEE **attribute** verb.

inaccessible adjective *an inaccessible spot.* cut off, godforsaken, hard to find, inconvenient, isolated, lonely, outlying, out of reach, out-of-the-way, remote, solitary, unfrequented, [*informal*] unget-at-able, unreachable.
OPPOSITES: SEE **accessible**.

inaccuracy noun SEE **mistake** noun.

inaccurate adjective *inaccurate maths. an inaccurate statement.* erroneous, false, faulty, imperfect, imprecise, incorrect, inexact, misleading, mistaken, unfaithful, unreliable, unsound, untrue, vague, wrong.
OPPOSITES: SEE **accurate**.

inactive adjective *Hedgehogs are inactive in winter.* asleep, dormant, hibernating, idle, immobile, inanimate, inert, languid, lazy, lethargic, out of action, passive, quiet, sedentary, sleepy, slow, sluggish, somnolent, torpid, unemployed, unoccupied, vegetating.
OPPOSITES: SEE **active**.

inadequate adjective *an inadequate supply. inadequate preparation.* deficient, imperfect, ineffective, insufficient, little, meagre, niggardly, [*informal*] pathetic, scanty, [*informal*] skimpy, sparse, unsatisfactory.
OPPOSITES: SEE **adequate**.

inadmissible adjective *inadmissible evidence.* SEE **unacceptable.**

inadvertent adjective SEE **unintentional.**

inadvisable adjective *an inadvisable course of action.* foolish, ill-advised, imprudent, misguided, silly, unwise.
OPPOSITES: SEE **advisable.**

inalienable adjective *an inalienable right.* SEE **absolute.**

inane adjective SEE **silly.**

inanimate adjective dead, dormant, inactive, insentient, lifeless, unconscious.
OPPOSITES: SEE **animate** adjective.

inapplicable adjective SEE **inappropriate.**

inappropriate adjective *an inappropriate gift. inappropriate comments.* ill-judged, ill-suited, ill-timed, improper, inapplicable, inapposite, incongruous, incorrect, inopportune, irrelevant, out of place, tactless, tasteless, unbecoming, unfit, unseasonable, unseemly, unsuitable, untimely, wrong.
OPPOSITES: SEE **appropriate.**

inarticulate adjective *an inarticulate speaker.* dumb, faltering, halting, hesitant, SEE **incoherent**, mumbling, mute, shy, silent, speechless, stammering, stuttering, tongue-tied, unclear, unintelligible.
OPPOSITES: SEE **articulate** adjective.

inartistic adjective SEE **unimaginative.**

inattentive adjective *an inattentive driver.* absent-minded, careless, daydreaming, dreaming, heedless, lacking concentration, negligent, preoccupied, unobservant, vague, wandering.
OPPOSITES: SEE **alert** adjective.

inaudible adjective *inaudible sounds.* faint, indistinct, low, muffled, mumbled, muted, quiet, silent, unclear, undetectable, unidentifiable, weak.
OPPOSITES: SEE **audible.**

inaugural adjective SEE **opening** adjective.

inaugurate verb SEE **open** verb.

inauspicious adjective SEE **unfavourable.**

inborn, inbred adjectives SEE **hereditary.**

incalculable adjective SEE **infinite.**

incandescent adjective SEE **glowing.**

incantation noun SEE **spell** noun.

incapable adjective **1** *incapable of doing things for himself.* clumsy, helpless, impotent, inadequate, incompetent, ineffective, ineffectual, inept, stupid, unable, useless, weak.
OPPOSITES: SEE **capable.**
2 [*informal*] *incapable after a couple of drinks.* SEE **drunk.**

incapacitate verb SEE **disable.**

incarcerate verb SEE **imprison.**

incarnate verb SEE **personify.**

incarnation noun SEE **personification.**

incautious adjective SEE **careless.**

incendiary noun **1** [= *an incendiary bomb*] OTHER WEAPONS: SEE **weapons.**
2 arsonist, fireraiser, pyromaniac.

incense verb SEE **anger** verb.

incentive noun *an incentive to work.* bait, [*informal*] carrot, encouragement, inducement, motivation, reward, stimulus, [*informal*] sweetener.

inception noun SEE **beginning.**

incessant adjective *an incessant rhythm. incessant demands.* ceaseless, chronic, constant, continual, continuous, endless, eternal, everlasting, interminable, never-ending, non-stop, perennial, permanent, perpetual, persistent, relentless, unbroken, unceasing, unending, unremitting.
OPPOSITES: SEE **occasional, temporary.**

inch verb *to inch forward.* SEE **creep.**

incident noun **1** *an amusing incident.* affair, circumstance, event, happening, occasion, occurrence.
2 *a nasty incident.* accident, SEE **commotion**, confrontation, disturbance, fight, scene.

incidental adjective *Let's discuss the main point, not incidental issues.* attendant, SEE **chance** adjective, inessential, minor, odd, random, secondary, subordinate, subsidiary.
OPPOSITES: SEE **essential.**

incinerate verb SEE **burn** verb.

incinerator noun SEE **fire** noun.

incipient adjective *an incipient disease.* beginning, developing, early, embryonic, growing, new, rudimentary, starting.
OPPOSITES: SEE **established.**

incise verb SEE **cut** verb.

incision noun SEE **cut** noun.

incisive adjective **1** *an incisive way of dealing with things.* SEE **decisive.**
2 *incisive wit.* SEE **cutting** adjective.

incite verb *to incite violence.* SEE **provoke.**

inclement adjective *inclement weather.* WORDS TO DESCRIBE WEATHER: SEE **weather** noun.

inclination noun *an inclination to doze off.* bent, bias, disposition, fondness, habit, instinct, leaning, liking, partiality, penchant, predilection, predisposition, preference, proclivity, propensity, readiness, tendency, trend, willingness.

incline noun SEE **slope** noun.

incline verb *to incline at an angle.* bend, lean, slant, slope, tilt, tip, veer.
to be inclined *I'm inclined to doze off after lunch.* be disposed, be in the habit (of), be liable, have an inclination [SEE **inclination**], like, prefer.

include verb **1** *The programme includes some new songs.* blend in, combine, comprise, consist of, contain, embody, encompass, incorporate, involve, make room for, mix, subsume, take in.
2 *The price includes transport.* add in, allow for, cover, take into account.
OPPOSITES: SEE **exclude**.

incognito adjective or adverb *to travel incognito.* anonymous(ly), disguised, under a pseudonym, unknown, unnamed, unrecognized.

incoherent adjective *incoherent messages. an incoherent speaker.* confused, disconnected, disjointed, disordered, disorganized, garbled, illogical, SEE **inarticulate**, inconsistent, jumbled, mixed up, muddled, rambling, unclear, unconnected, unintelligible, unstructured, unsystematic.
OPPOSITES: SEE **coherent**.

incombustible adjective fireproof, fire-resistant, flameproof, non-flammable.
OPPOSITES: SEE **combustible**.

income noun earnings, interest, SEE **money**, pay, pension, profits, receipts, revenue, salary, takings, wages.
OPPOSITES: SEE **expenditure**.

incoming adjective **1** *an incoming aircraft.* approaching, arriving, coming, landing, next, returning.
2 *the incoming tide.* flowing, rising.
OPPOSITES: SEE **outgoing**.

incommode verb SEE **inconvenience** verb.

incommunicado adjective *a prisoner held incommunicado.* cut off, isolated, silent, solitary, without communication.

incomparable adjective *incomparable beauty.* SEE **unequalled**.

incompatible adjective *The two accounts are incompatible.* at variance, clashing, conflicting, contradictory, contrasting, different, discrepant, incongruous, inconsistent, irreconcilable.
OPPOSITES: SEE **compatible**.

incompetent adjective *incompetent workers.* bungling, feckless, helpless, [*informal*] hopeless, inadequate, incapable, ineffective, ineffectual, inefficient, inexperienced, inexpert, stupid, unacceptable, unfit, unqualified, unsatisfactory, unskilful, untrained, useless.
OPPOSITES: SEE **competent**.

incomplete adjective **1** *an incomplete story.* abbreviated, abridged, [*informal*] bitty, edited, expurgated, partial, selective, shortened.
2 *incomplete work.* deficient, faulty, imperfect, insufficient, unfinished, unpolished, wanting.
OPPOSITES: SEE **complete** adjective.

incomprehensible adjective *an incomprehensible message.* baffling, beyond your comprehension, cryptic, enigmatic, illegible, impenetrable, indecipherable, meaningless, mysterious, obscure, opaque, perplexing, puzzling, strange, too difficult, unclear, unfathomable, unintelligible.
OPPOSITES: SEE **comprehensible**.

inconceivable *The distances in the universe are inconceivable.* implausible, impossible to understand, incredible, [*informal*] mind-boggling, staggering, unbelievable, undreamed of, unimaginable, unthinkable.
OPPOSITES: SEE **credible**.

inconclusive adjective *inconclusive evidence.* ambiguous, equivocal, indecisive, indefinite, open, uncertain, unconvincing.
OPPOSITES: SEE **conclusive**.

incongruous adjective *an absurdly incongruous couple.* clashing, conflicting, contrasting, discordant, ill-matched, ill-suited, inappropriate, incompatible, inconsistent, irreconcilable, odd, out of place, uncoordinated, unsuited.
OPPOSITES: SEE **matching**.

inconsequential adjective **1** *an inconsequential argument.* SEE **illogical**.
2 *an inconsequential event.* SEE **unimportant**.

inconsiderable adjective *an inconsiderable sum of money.* SEE **negligible**.

inconsiderate adjective *an inconsiderate remark. inconsiderate neighbours.* careless, cruel, insensitive, negligent, rude, self-centred, selfish, tactless, thoughtless, uncaring, unconcerned, unfriendly, unhelpful, unkind, unsympathetic, unthinking.
OPPOSITES: SEE **considerate**.

inconsistent adjective **1** *He is inconsistent in his views.* capricious, changeable,

erratic, fickle, inconstant, patchy, unpredictable, unreliable, unstable, [*informal*] up-and-down, variable.
2 *The stories of the two witnesses are inconsistent.* SEE **incompatible.**
OPPOSITES: SEE **consistent.**

inconsolable adjective SEE **heartbroken.**

inconspicuous adjective *an inconspicuous worker. an inconspicuous act of bravery.* camouflaged, hidden, insignificant, invisible, modest, ordinary, out of sight, plain, restrained, retiring, self-effacing, unassuming, unobtrusive.
OPPOSITES: SEE **conspicuous.**

inconstant adjective SEE **changeable.**

incontestable adjective SEE **indisputable.**

incontinent adjective enuretic, unable to control yourself, uncontrolled.

incontrovertible adjective SEE **indisputable.**

inconvenience noun *the inconvenience of having to change buses.* annoyance, bother, disadvantage, disruption, drawback, encumbrance, hindrance, irritation, nuisance, trouble.

inconvenience verb *Does the noise of the TV inconvenience you?* annoy, be an inconvenience [SEE **inconvenience** noun], bother, disturb, incommode, irritate, [*informal*] put you out, trouble.

inconvenient adjective *an inconvenient moment.* annoying, awkward, bothersome, cumbersome, difficult, embarrassing, inopportune, irritating, tiresome, troublesome, unsuitable, untimely, untoward, unwieldy.
OPPOSITES: SEE **convenient.**

incorporate verb SEE **include.**

incorporeal adjective *incorporeal voices.* disembodied, ethereal, ghostly, impalpable, insubstantial, intangible, spectral, unreal.
OPPOSITES: SEE **physical.**

incorrect adjective SEE **wrong** adjective.

incorrigible adjective *an incorrigible thief.* committed, confirmed, hardened, hopeless, impenitent, incurable, inveterate, SEE **irredeemable**, shameless, unreformable, unrepentant.
OPPOSITES: SEE **penitent.**

incorruptible adjective *an incorruptible judge.* SEE **good**, honest, honourable, just, moral, sound, [*informal*] straight, true, trustworthy, unbribable, upright.
OPPOSITES: SEE **corrupt** adjective.

increase noun *an increase in the size, length, intensity, etc., of something.* addition, amplification, augmentation, boost, build-up, crescendo, development, enlargement, escalation, expansion, extension, gain, growth, increment, inflation, intensification, proliferation, rise, upsurge, upturn.
OPPOSITES: SEE **decrease** noun.

increase verb **1** *to increase the size, length, intensity, etc., of something.* add to, amplify, augment, boost, build up, develop, enlarge, expand, extend, lengthen, magnify, make greater, maximize, multiply, prolong, put up, raise, [*informal*] step up, strengthen, stretch, swell.
2 *My responsibilities have increased.* escalate, gain (*in size, etc.*), get greater, grow, intensify, proliferate, [*informal*] snowball, spread, [*poetic*] wax.
OPPOSITES: SEE **decrease** verb.

incredible adjective *an incredible story.* extraordinary, far-fetched, implausible, improbable, inconceivable, miraculous, surprising, unbelievable, unconvincing, unimaginable, unlikely, untenable, unthinkable.
OPPOSITES: SEE **credible.**

incredulous adjective *She was incredulous when told she'd won.* disbelieving, distrustful, dubious, questioning, sceptical, suspicious, uncertain, unconvinced.
OPPOSITES: SEE **credulous.**

increment noun SEE **increase** noun.

incriminate verb *to incriminate someone in wrongdoing.* accuse, blame, embroil, implicate, inculpate, involve.
OPPOSITES: SEE **excuse** verb.

incrustation noun SEE **crust.**

incubate verb *Birds incubate eggs.* bring on, brood on, develop, hatch.

inculcate verb SEE **teach.**

inculpate verb SEE **incriminate.**

incumbent adjective SEE **compulsory.**

incur verb *to incur a fine.* [*informal*] be on the receiving end of, bring upon yourself, earn, get, provoke, run up, suffer.

incurable adjective **1** *incurable illness.* fatal, hopeless, inoperable, irreparable, terminal, untreatable.
OPPOSITES: SEE **curable.**
2 *an incurable romantic.* SEE **incorrigible.**

incurious adjective SEE **indifferent.**

incursion noun SEE **raid** noun.

indebted adjective *I'm indebted to you.* [*old-fashioned*] beholden, grateful, obliged, thankful, under an obligation.

indecent adjective *indecent behaviour. indecent language.* [*informal*] blue, coarse, crude, dirty, immodest, impolite,

improper, impure, indecorous, indelicate, insensitive, naughty, SEE **obscene**, offensive, risqué, rude, [*informal*] sexy, [*informal*] smutty, suggestive, tasteless, titillating, unbecoming, unprintable, unrepeatable, unseemly, vulgar.
OPPOSITES: SEE **decent**.

indecipherable adjective SEE **illegible**.

indecision noun SEE **hesitation**.

indecisive adjective SEE **hesitant**.

indecorous adjective *indecorous language.* churlish, ill-bred, inappropriate, SEE **indecent**, rough, tasteless, unbecoming, uncouth, undignified, unseemly, vulgar.
OPPOSITES: SEE **decorous**.

indefatigable adjective SEE **tireless**.

indefensible adjective *Her silly behaviour puts her in an indefensible position.* unjustifiable, unpardonable, untenable, vulnerable, weak.

indefinable adjective SEE **indescribable**.

indefinite adjective ambiguous, confused, equivocal, evasive, general, ill-defined, imprecise, inexact, [*informal*] leaving it open, neutral, uncertain, unclear, undefined, unsettled, unspecific, unspecified, unsure, vague.
OPPOSITES: SEE **definite**.

indelible adjective **1** *indelible ink.* fast, fixed, ineradicable, ingrained, lasting, permanent.
2 *indelible memories.* unforgettable.
OPPOSITE: erasable.

indelicate adjective SEE **indecent**.

indemnify verb SEE **insure**.

indentation noun *an indentation in a surface.* cut, dent, depression, dimple, dip, hollow, nick, notch, serration.

indented adjective *the indented line of the battlements.* crenellated, dented, notched, serrated, toothed, zigzag.

indenture noun SEE **contract** noun.

independence noun *We value independence.* autonomy, being independent [SEE **independent**], freedom, individualism, liberty, nonconformity, self-government.
OPPOSITES: SEE **dependence**.

independent adjective **1** *an independent country.* autonomous, liberated, neutral, nonaligned, self-determining, self-governing, sovereign.
2 *an independent individual.* carefree, [*informal*] foot-loose, free, individualistic, private, self-reliant, separate, unconventional, untrammelled, without ties.
OPPOSITES: SEE **dependent**.
3 *an independent opinion.* SEE **unbiased**.

indescribable adjective *indescribable beauty.* beyond words, indefinable, ineffable, inexpressible, leaving you speechless, stunning, unspeakable, unutterable.
OPPOSITES: SEE **ordinary, prosaic**.

indestructible adjective **1** *indestructible materials.* durable, lasting, permanent, solid, strong, tough, toughened, unbreakable.
OPPOSITES: SEE **impermanent**.
2 *the indestructible spirit of humankind.* enduring, eternal, everlasting, immortal, imperishable.
OPPOSITES: SEE **mortal**.

indeterminate adjective SEE **uncertain**.

index noun *a library index.* alphabetical list, catalogue, directory, register.

indiarubber noun eraser, rubber.

indicate verb **1** *Indicate where you are going.* describe, display, give an indication of [SEE **indication**], intimate, make known, manifest, point out, reveal, say, show, specify.
2 *A red light indicates danger.* be an indication of [SEE **indication**], betoken, communicate, convey, denote, express, mean, register, signal, signify, spell, stand for, symbolize.

indication noun *He gave no indication of his feelings.* clue, evidence, hint, inkling, intimation, omen, portent, sign, signal, suggestion, symptom, token, warning.

indicative adjective *A high temperature is indicative of illness.* meaningful, significant, suggestive, symptomatic.

indicator noun *The indicators showed that the machine was working normally.* clock, dial, display, gauge, index, instrument, marker, meter, pointer, screen, sign, signal, trafficator.

indict verb SEE **accuse**.

indictable adjective *an indictable offence.* SEE **criminal** adjective.

indictment noun SEE **accusation**.

indifferent adjective [Note: *indifferent* is NOT the opposite of *different*.]
1 *I was indifferent about the result.* aloof, apathetic, blasé, bored, casual, cold, cool, detached, disinterested, dispassionate, half-hearted, incurious, neutral, nonchalant, not bothered, uncaring, unconcerned, unemotional, unenthusiastic, unexcited, unimpressed, uninterested, uninvolved, unmoved.
OPPOSITES: SEE **concerned, enthusiastic**.
2 *The food was indifferent.* commonplace, fair, mediocre, middling, moderate, [*informal*] nothing to write home about, SEE **ordinary**, unexciting.
OPPOSITES: SEE **excellent**.

indigenous adjective *indigenous plants.* SEE **native** adjective.

indigent adjective SEE **poor**.

indigestion noun dyspepsia, flatulence, heartburn.

indignant adjective *We were indignant about the way they treated us.* [*informal*] aerated, SEE **angry**, annoyed, cross, disgruntled, exasperated, furious, heated, infuriated, [*informal*] in high dudgeon, irate, irritated, livid, mad, [*informal*] peeved, provoked, [*informal*] put out, riled, sore, upset, vexed.

indignation noun SEE **anger** noun.

indignity noun SEE **humiliation**.

indigo noun SEE **blue** adjective.

indirect adjective **1** *an indirect route.* [*informal*] all round the houses, circuitous, devious, long, meandering, rambling, roundabout, tortuous, winding, zigzag.
2 *an indirect insult.* ambiguous, backhanded, circumlocutory, disguised, equivocal, euphemistic, SEE **evasive**, implicit, implied, oblique.
OPPOSITES: SEE **direct** adjective.

indiscreet adjective *indiscreet remarks.* careless, ill-advised, ill-considered, ill-judged, impolite, impolitic, incautious, injudicious, tactless, undiplomatic, unguarded, unthinking, unwise.
OPPOSITES: SEE **discreet**.

indiscriminate adjective *indiscriminate attacks. indiscriminate praise.* aimless, desultory, general, haphazard, [*informal*] hit or miss, imperceptive, miscellaneous, mixed, random, uncritical, undifferentiated, undiscriminating, uninformed, unselective, unsystematic, wholesale.
OPPOSITES: SEE **selective**.

indispensable adjective *indispensable equipment.* basic, central, crucial, essential, imperative, key, necessary, needed, required, requisite, vital.
OPPOSITES: SEE **unnecessary**.

indisposed adjective SEE **ill**.

indisposition noun SEE **illness**.

indisputable adjective *indisputable facts.* accepted, acknowledged, axiomatic, certain, clear, evident, incontestable, incontrovertible, indubitable, irrefutable, positive, proved, proven, self-evident, sure, unanswerable, unarguable, undeniable, undisputed, undoubted, unimpeachable, unquestionable.
OPPOSITES: SEE **debatable**.

indissoluble adjective SEE **lasting**.

indistinct adjective **1** *an indistinct image.* bleary, blurred, confused, dim, faint, fuzzy, hazy, ill-defined, indefinite, misty, obscure, shadowy, unclear, vague.
2 *indistinct sounds.* deadened, dull, indistinguishable, muffled, mumbled, slurred, unintelligible.
OPPOSITES: SEE **distinct**.

indistinguishable adjective *indistinguishable twins.* identical, interchangeable, the same, twin.
OPPOSITES: SEE **different**.

individual adjective *an individual style.* characteristic, different, distinct, distinctive, exclusive, idiosyncratic, particular, peculiar, personal, private, separate, singular, special, specific, unique.
OPPOSITES: SEE **collective**.

individual noun *Who was that odd individual?* SEE **person**.

indoctrinate verb *to indoctrinate someone with political propaganda.* brainwash, instruct, re-educate, SEE **teach**, train.

indolent adjective SEE **lazy**.

indomitable adjective *indomitable courage.* SEE **brave**, invincible, persistent, resolute, staunch, steadfast, [*uncomplimentary*] stubborn, unbreakable, unconquerable, unyielding.

indubitable adjective SEE **indisputable**.

induce verb **1** *We couldn't induce her to come out.* coax, encourage, incite, influence, persuade, prevail on, [*informal*] talk (someone) into, tempt.
OPPOSITES: SEE **dissuade**.
2 *What induced your cold?* bring on, cause, engender, generate, give rise to, lead to, occasion, produce, provoke.

inducement noun SEE **incentive**.

indulge verb *Older people sometimes indulge children.* be indulgent to [SEE **indulgent**], cosset, favour, give in to, gratify the whims of, humour, mollycoddle, pamper, pander to, spoil, [*informal*] spoon-feed, treat.
OPPOSITES: SEE **deprive**.
to indulge in SEE **enjoy**.
to indulge yourself be self-indulgent, drink (eat, etc.) too much, overdo it, overeat, spoil yourself.

indulgent adjective *indulgent grandparents.* compliant, easygoing, fond, forbearing, forgiving, genial, kind, lenient, liberal, overgenerous, patient, permissive, tolerant.
OPPOSITES: SEE **strict**.

industrial adjective *an industrial area.* industrialized, manufacturing.

industrialist noun businessman, magnate, manufacturer, tycoon.

industrious adjective *an industrious worker.* assiduous, busy, conscientious, diligent, earnest, energetic, enterprising, hard-working, involved, keen, laborious, persistent, productive, sedulous, tireless, zealous.
OPPOSITES: SEE **lazy**.

industry noun **1** *There's a lot of industry in this town.* business, commerce, manufacturing, trade.
2 *We admired the industry of the volunteers.* activity, application, commitment, determination, diligence, effort, energy, hard work, industriousness, keenness, labour, perseverance, persistence, tirelessness, toil, zeal.
OPPOSITES: SEE **laziness**.

inebriated adjective SEE **drunk**.

inedible adjective *inedible food.* bad for you, harmful, indigestible, nauseating, [*informal*] off (*This meat is off*), poisonous, rotten, tough, uneatable, unpalatable, unwholesome.
OPPOSITES: SEE **edible**.

ineducable adjective incorrigible, SEE **stupid**, unresponsive, unteachable.
OPPOSITES: SEE **responsive**.

ineffable adjective SEE **indescribable**.

ineffective adjective **1** *ineffective efforts.* fruitless, futile, [*informal*] hopeless, inept, unconvincing, unproductive, unsuccessful, useless, vain, worthless.
2 *an ineffective salesman.* feckless, feeble, idle, impotent, inadequate, incapable, incompetent, ineffectual, inefficient, powerless, shiftless, unenterprising, weak.
OPPOSITES: SEE **effective**.

ineffectual adjective SEE **ineffective**.

inefficient adjective **1** *an inefficient worker.* SEE **ineffective**.
2 *inefficient use of resources.* extravagant, prodigal, uneconomic, wasteful.
OPPOSITES: SEE **efficient**.

inelegant adjective *inelegant movements. inelegant style.* awkward, clumsy, crude, gauche, graceless, inartistic, rough, SEE **ugly**, uncouth, ungainly, unpolished, unskilful, unsophisticated, unstylish.
OPPOSITES: SEE **elegant**.

ineligible adjective *ineligible for a job.* disqualified, inappropriate, [*informal*] out of the running, [*informal*] ruled out, unacceptable, unfit, unsuitable.
OPPOSITES: SEE **eligible**.

inept adjective *an inept attempt to put things right.* bungling, clumsy, SEE **inappropriate**, incompetent, maladroit.

inequality noun *inequalities between rich and poor.* difference, disparity, dissimilarity, imbalance.
OPPOSITES: SEE **equality**.

inequitable adjective SEE **unjust**.

ineradicable adjective SEE **indelible**.

inert adjective SEE **lifeless**.

inertia noun *The cheering crowd roused us from our inertia.* apathy, deadness, idleness, immobility, inactivity, indolence, lassitude, laziness, lethargy, listlessness, numbness, passivity, sluggishness, torpor.
OPPOSITES: SEE **liveliness**.

inescapable adjective SEE **unavoidable**.

inessential adjective *Leave inessential equipment behind.* dispensable, expendable, minor, needless, non-essential, optional, ornamental, secondary, spare, superfluous, unimportant, unnecessary.
OPPOSITES: SEE **essential**.

inestimable adjective SEE **infinite**.

inevitable adjective *inevitable disaster.* SEE **unavoidable**.

inexact adjective SEE **imprecise**.

inexcusable adjective SEE **unforgivable**.

inexhaustible adjective SEE **infinite**.

inexorable adjective SEE **relentless**.

inexpensive adjective SEE **cheap**, cut-price, low-priced, reasonable.
OPPOSITES: SEE **expensive**.

inexperienced adjective *an inexperienced recruit.* callow, [*informal*] green, immature, inexpert, naïve, new, probationary, raw, unaccustomed, unskilled, unsophisticated, untried, [*informal*] wet behind the ears, young.
OPPOSITES: SEE **experienced**.
an inexperienced person apprentice, beginner, [*informal*] greenhorn, learner, novice, starter, tiro, trainee.

inexpert adjective SEE **unskilful**.

inexplicable adjective *an inexplicable mystery.* baffling, enigmatic, incomprehensible, insoluble, mysterious, mystifying, puzzling, strange, unaccountable, unfathomable, unsolvable.
OPPOSITES: SEE **explicable**.

inexpressible adjective SEE **indescribable**.

infallible adjective *an infallible method.* certain, dependable, foolproof, perfect,

predictable, reliable, sound, sure, trustworthy, unbeatable.
OPPOSITES: SEE **fallible**.

infamous adjective [Note: *infamous* is NOT the opposite of *famous*.] *an infamous crime.* SEE **notorious**.

infant noun baby, SEE **child**, [*informal*] toddler.

infantile adjective [*uncomplimentary*] *infantile behaviour.* adolescent, babyish, childish, immature, juvenile, puerile, SEE **silly**.
OPPOSITES: SEE **mature**.

infantry noun SEE **armed services**.

infatuated adjective besotted, [*informal*] head over heels, in love [SEE **love** noun], obsessed, [*informal*] smitten.

infatuation noun [*informal*] crush, SEE **love** noun, obsession, passion.

infect verb **1** *to infect the water supply. to infect a wound.* blight, contaminate, defile, make infected [SEE **infected**], poison, pollute, spoil, taint.
2 *to infect someone with your laughter.* affect, influence, inspire, touch.

infected adjective *an infected wound.* blighted, contaminated, festering, inflamed, poisoned, polluted, putrid, septic, tainted.

infection noun **1** *The infection spread rapidly.* blight, contagion, contamination, epidemic, pestilence, pollution, virus.
2 *He's off work with some sort of infection.* SEE **illness**.

infectious adjective *infectious diseases.* catching, communicable, contagious, spreading, transmissible, transmittable.

infer verb [Note: *infer* and *imply* are NOT synonyms.] *I infer from what you say that you are unhappy?* assume, conclude, deduce, extrapolate, gather, guess, reach the conclusion, understand, work out.

inferior adjective **1** *inferior rank.* junior, lesser, lower, menial, secondary, second-class, servile, subordinate, subsidiary.
2 *inferior quality.* SEE **bad**, cheap, indifferent, mediocre, poor, shoddy, tawdry, [*informal*] tinny.

inferior noun *The boss is too aloof from her inferiors.* SEE **subordinate** noun.

infernal adjective SEE **devilish**.

inferno noun SEE **fire** noun.

infertile adjective SEE **barren**.

infested adjective *infested with mice.* alive, crawling, overrun, plagued, ravaged, swarming, teeming, verminous.

infidelity noun **1** *infidelity to a leader.* SEE **disloyalty**.
2 *infidelity to a wife or husband.* adultery, unfaithfulness.

infiltrate verb *to infiltrate the enemy's camp.* enter secretly, insinuate, intrude, penetrate.

infiltrator noun SEE **spy** noun.

infinite adjective *infinite numbers. infinite patience.* boundless, countless, endless, everlasting, SEE **huge**, immeasurable, immense, incalculable, inestimable, inexhaustible, interminable, limitless, never-ending, numberless, uncountable, undefined, unending, unfathomable, unlimited, unnumbered, untold.
OPPOSITES: SEE **finite**.

infinitesimal adjective SEE **tiny**.

infinity noun endlessness, eternity, infinite amount (distance, quantity, etc.) [SEE **infinite**], infinitude, perpetuity, space.

infirm adjective *Infirm people may need our help.* bedridden, crippled, elderly, feeble, frail, SEE **ill**, lame, old, poorly, senile, sickly, unwell, weak.
OPPOSITES: SEE **healthy**.

infirmary noun SEE **hospital**.

infirmity noun SEE **illness**.

inflame verb *to inflame violent feelings.* SEE **anger** verb, arouse, encourage, excite, fire, foment, ignite, kindle, madden, provoke, rouse, stimulate.
OPPOSITES: SEE **cool** verb.

inflamed adjective **1** *an inflamed wound.* festering, infected, poisoned, red, septic, swollen.
2 *inflamed passions.* angry, enraged, excited, feverish, fiery, heated, hot, passionate, roused.

inflammable adjective [Note: *inflammable* is NOT the opposite of *flammable*.] *inflammable chemicals.* burnable, combustible, flammable, volatile.
OPPOSITES: SEE **incombustible**.

inflammation noun *an inflammation of the skin.* abscess, boil, infection, redness, sore, soreness.

inflate verb **1** *to inflate a tyre.* blow up, dilate, distend, puff up, pump up, swell.
2 *to inflate the importance of something.* SEE **exaggerate**.

inflection noun *an inflection in someone's voice.* SEE **tone** noun.

inflexible adjective **1** *inflexible materials.* firm, hard, hardened, immovable, rigid, solid, stiff, unbending, unyielding.
2 *an inflexible attitude.* entrenched, immutable, intractable, intransigent, obdurate, obstinate, resolute, strict, stubborn, unaccommodating, unalterable, uncompromising, unhelpful.
OPPOSITES: SEE **flexible**.

inflict verb *to inflict punishment or pain.* administer, apply, deal out, enforce, force, impose, mete out, perpetrate, wreak.

influence noun *Our trainer had a strong influence on the team.* authority, control, direction, dominance, effect, guidance, impact, power, pressure, pull.

influence verb **1** *Our trainer influenced the way we played.* affect, change, control, determine, direct, dominate, exert an influence on [SEE **influence** noun], guide, impinge on, impress, manipulate, modify, motivate, move, persuade, prompt, stir, sway.
2 *Don't try to influence the referee.* bias, bribe, corrupt, lead astray, prejudice, suborn, tempt.

influential adjective **1** *an influential person.* authoritative, dominant, important, leading, powerful.
2 *an influential idea.* compelling, convincing, effective, far-reaching, moving, persuasive, significant, telling.
OPPOSITES: SEE **unimportant**.

influx noun *an influx of imports.* flood, flow, inflow, inundation, invasion, rush, stream.

inform verb *to inform someone of the facts.* advise, apprise, enlighten, [*informal*] fill in, give information to, instruct, leak, notify, [*informal*] put in the picture, teach, tell, tip off.
to inform against *to inform against a wanted man.* accuse, betray, complain about, denounce, give information about, [*informal*] grass on, incriminate, inculpate, report, [*informal*] sneak on, [*informal*] split on, [*informal*] tell of, [*informal*] tell tales about.

informal adjective **1** *an informal greeting. informal clothes. an informal party.* approachable, casual, comfortable, cosy, easy, easygoing, everyday, familiar, free and easy, friendly, homely, natural, ordinary, relaxed, simple, unceremonious, unofficial, unpretentious, unsophisticated.
2 *informal language.* chatty, colloquial, personal, slangy.
3 *an informal design.* asymmetrical, flexible, fluid, intuitive, irregular, spontaneous.
OPPOSITES: SEE **formal**.

information noun **1** *information about what is happening.* announcement, briefing, bulletin, communication, enlightenment, facts, instruction, message, news, report, statement, [*old-fashioned*] tidings, [*informal*] tip-off.
2 *information gathered for a purpose.* data, database, dossier, evidence, intelligence, knowledge, statistics.

informative adjective *an informative booklet.* communicative, enlightening, factual, giving information, helpful, illuminating, instructive, revealing, useful.
OPPOSITES: SEE **evasive**.

informed adjective SEE **knowledgeable**.

informer noun informant, spy, tell-tale.

infrequent adjective *an infrequent guest. infrequent buses.* exceptional, intermittent, irregular, occasional, [*informal*] once in a blue moon, rare, spasmodic, uncommon, unusual.
OPPOSITES: SEE **frequent** adjective.

infringe verb *to infringe the law.* SEE **violate**.

infuriate verb SEE **anger** verb.

infuse verb SEE **instil**.

ingenious adjective [Don't confuse with *ingenuous.*] *an ingenious plan.* artful, astute, brilliant, clever, complex, crafty, creative, cunning, imaginative, inspired, intricate, inventive, original, resourceful, shrewd, skilful, subtle.
OPPOSITES: SEE **unimaginative**.

ingenuous adjective [Don't confuse with *ingenious.*] *an ingenuous beginner.* artless, childlike, frank, guileless, honest, innocent, naïve, open, plain, simple, trusting, uncomplicated, unsophisticated.
OPPOSITES: SEE **sophisticated**.

ingest verb SEE **eat**.

inglorious adjective SEE **shameful**.

ingot noun *a gold ingot.* lump, nugget.

ingrained adjective SEE **established**.

ingratiate verb **to ingratiate yourself with** be obsequious to [SEE **obsequious**], [*informal*] crawl to, curry favour with, fawn on, flatter, get on the right side of, [*informal*] lick the boots of, [*informal*] suck up to, [*informal*] toady to.

ingratitude noun ungratefulness.
OPPOSITES: SEE **thanks**.

ingredient noun component, constituent, element, part.

inhabit verb *to inhabit a place.* [*old-fashioned*] abide in, dwell in, live in, make your home in, occupy, people, populate, possess, reside in, settle in, set up home in.

inhabited adjective *an inhabited island.* colonized, lived-in, occupied, peopled, populated, settled.
OPPOSITES: SEE **uninhabited**.

inhabitant noun citizen, [*old-fashioned*] denizen, dweller, inmate, native, occupant, occupier, [*plural*] population, resident, settler, tenant, [*plural*] townsfolk, [*plural*] townspeople.

inhale verb *to inhale smoke.* breathe in.

inherent adjective *inherent qualities.* congenital, essential, fundamental, hereditary, immanent, inborn, inbred, ingrained, intrinsic, native, natural.
OPPOSITE: acquired.

inherit verb *to inherit property.* be the inheritor of [SEE **inheritor**], be left, [*informal*] come into, receive as an inheritance [SEE **inheritance**], succeed to.

inheritance noun *a small inheritance from uncle's will.* bequest, estate, fortune, heritage, legacy.

inherited adjective *an inherited title.* family, hereditary, passed down.
OPPOSITE: acquired.

inheritor noun *the inheritor of an estate.* beneficiary, heir, heiress, [*formal*] legatee, recipient, successor.

inhibit verb *to inhibit someone from doing something.* SEE **restrain**.

inhibited adjective *too inhibited to join the fun.* bashful, diffident, formal, frustrated, full of inhibitions [SEE **inhibition**], guarded, [*informal*] prim and proper, repressed, reserved, self-conscious, shy, tense, undemonstrative, unemotional, [*informal*] uptight.
OPPOSITES: SEE **uninhibited**.

inhibition noun **1** [*usually plural*] *Try to overcome your inhibitions.* diffidence, [*informal*] hang-ups, repression, reserve, self-consciousness, shyness.
2 *There's no inhibition on your freedom here.* bar, barrier, check, impediment, interference, restraint.

inhospitable adjective **1** *an inhospitable person.* SEE **unfriendly**.
2 *an inhospitable place.* SEE **desolate**.

inhuman adjective *inhuman feelings.* barbaric, barbarous, bestial, blood-thirsty, brutish, cruel, diabolical, fiendish, heartless, SEE **inhumane**, merciless, pitiless, ruthless, savage, unkind, unnatural.
OPPOSITES: SEE **human**.

inhumane adjective *inhumane treatment of animals.* cold-hearted, cruel, hard, heartless, inconsiderate, SEE **inhuman**, insensitive, uncaring, uncharitable, uncivilized, unfeeling, unkind, unsympathetic.
OPPOSITES: SEE **humane**.

inimical adjective SEE **hostile**.

inimitable adjective *an inimitable style.* SEE **distinctive**.

iniquitous adjective SEE **wicked**.

initial adjective *an initial payment. an initial reaction.* beginning, commencing, earliest, first, inaugural, introductory, opening, original, preliminary, starting.
OPPOSITES: SEE **final**.

initiate verb *to initiate negotiations.* SEE **begin**.

initiative verb *Show some initiative.* ambition, drive, dynamism, enterprise, [*informal*] get-up-and-go, inventiveness, lead, leadership, originality, resourcefulness.
to take the initiative SEE **begin**.

inject verb *to inject into a vein.* insert, introduce, make an injection.

injection noun *The nurse gave me an injection.* [*informal*] fix, inoculation, [*informal*] jab, vaccination.

injudicious adjective SEE **unwise**.

injunction noun SEE **command** noun.

injure verb break, crush, cut, damage, deface, disfigure, harm, hurt, ill-treat, mar, ruin, spoil, vandalize, SEE **wound** verb.

injurious adjective SEE **harmful**.

injury noun damage, harm, hurt, mischief (*did him a mischief*), SEE **wound** noun.

injustice noun *The injustice of the decision angered me.* bias, discrimination, dishonesty, favouritism, illegality, inequality, inequity, oppression, partiality, prejudice, unfairness, unlawfulness, wrongness.
OPPOSITES: SEE **justice**.

inkling noun *I'd no inkling he was coming.* SEE **hint** noun.

inlet noun SEE **bay**.

inmate noun SEE **inhabitant**.

inn noun [*old-fashioned*] hostelry, hotel, [*informal*] local, pub, tavern.

innards noun SEE **entrails**.

innate adjective SEE **hereditary**.

inner adjective *inner walls. inner feelings.* central, concealed, hidden, innermost, inside, interior, internal, intimate, inward, mental, middle, private, secret.
OPPOSITES: SEE **outer**.

innocent adjective **1** *The trial proved he was innocent.* blameless, free from blame, guiltless.
OPPOSITES: SEE **guilty**.
2 *innocent babes.* angelic, chaste, faultless, [*informal*] green, harmless, honest, incorrupt, inexperienced, ingenuous, inoffensive, naïve, pure, righteous, simple-minded, sinless, spotless, untainted, virtuous.
OPPOSITES: SEE **corrupt** adjective, **experienced**.

innocuous adjective SEE **harmless**.

innovation noun *We propose to introduce some innovations next year.* change, departure, new feature, novelty, reform, revolution.

innovator noun discoverer, experimenter, inventor, pioneer, reformer, revolutionary.

innuendo noun SEE **hint** noun.

innumerable adjective *innumerable stars.* countless, SEE **infinite**, many, numberless, uncountable, untold.

inoculate verb SEE **immunize**.

inoculation noun SEE **immunization**.

inoffensive adjective SEE **harmless**.

inoperable adjective SEE **incurable**.

inoperative adjective SEE **idle** adjective.

inopportune adjective SEE **inconvenient**.

inordinate adjective SEE **excessive**.

inorganic adjective *inorganic fertilizers.* artificial, chemical, dead, inanimate, unnatural.
OPPOSITES: SEE **organic**.

input noun SEE **contribution**.

inquest noun **1** *an inquest to determine how someone died.* hearing, inquiry.
2 [*informal*] *an inquest into why we lost the game.* discussion, exploration, investigation, [*informal*] post-mortem, probe, review.

inquire verb SEE **ask**.

inquiring adjective *an inquiring mind.* SEE **inquisitive**.

inquiry, inquisition nouns SEE **investigation**.

inquisitive adjective *I want to know simply because I'm inquisitive!* curious, inquiring, interested, interfering, meddling, nosy, probing, prying, questioning, sceptical, snooping.
to be inquisitive SEE **pry**.
an inquisitive person SEE **busybody**.

inroad noun SEE **invasion**.

insalubrious adjective SEE **unhealthy**.

insane adjective SEE **mad**.

insanitary adjective SEE **unhealthy**.

insanity noun SEE **madness**.

insatiable adjective SEE **greedy**.

inscribe verb SEE **write**.

inscription noun *the inscription on a memorial.* engraving, epigraph, superscription, wording, writing.

inscrutable adjective SEE **baffling**.

insect noun [*informal*] creepy-crawly.

VARIOUS INSECTS: ant, aphid, bee, beetle, black-beetle, blackfly, bluebottle, bumble-bee, butterfly, cicada, cockchafer, cockroach, Colorado beetle, crane-fly, cricket, daddy-long-legs, damsel-fly, dragonfly, earwig, firefly, fly, glow-worm, gnat, grasshopper, hornet, ladybird, locust, mantis, mayfly, midge, mosquito, moth, sawfly, termite, tsetse-fly, wasp, weevil.

OTHER FORMS OF AN INSECT: caterpillar, chrysalis, grub, larva, maggot.

There are many crawling creatures commonly called *insects* which, strictly speaking, are not insects: e.g. arachnid, centipede, earthworm, mite, slug, spider, woodlouse, worm.

---

insecticide noun pesticide, SEE **poison** noun.

insecure adjective **1** *an insecure foothold.* SEE **dangerous**, loose, precarious, rocky, shaky, uncertain, unsafe, unstable, unsteady, unsupported, weak, wobbly.
2 *an insecure feeling.* SEE **anxious**, exposed, underconfident, vulnerable.
OPPOSITES: SEE **secure** adjective.

inseminate verb SEE **fertilize**.

insensible adjective *insensible after a hit on the head.* [*informal*] dead to the world, inert, knocked out, [*informal*] out, senseless, unaware, unconscious.
OPPOSITES: SEE **conscious**.

insensitive adjective **1** *It's insensitive to joke about people's misfortunes.* callous, SEE **cruel**, imperceptive, obtuse, tactless, [*informal*] thick-skinned, thoughtless, uncaring, unfeeling, unsympathetic.
OPPOSITES: SEE **tactful**.
2 *an insensitive spot on your skin.* anaesthetized, dead, numb, unresponsive, without feeling.
OPPOSITES: SEE **sensitive**.

inseparable adjective always together, attached, indissoluble, indivisible, integral.

insert verb *to insert a wedge. to insert papers in a file.* drive in, embed, implant, interleave (*pages in a book*), introduce, [*informal*] pop in, push in, put in, tuck in.

inside adjective *the inside walls of a house.* indoor, inner, innermost, interior, internal.
OPPOSITES: SEE **outside** adjective.

inside noun bowels (*the bowels of the earth*), centre, contents, core, heart, indoors, interior, middle.
OPPOSITES: SEE **outside** noun.
insides *an animal's insides.* SEE **entrails**.

insidious adjective *insidious propaganda.* SEE **cunning**, furtive, pervasive, secretive, stealthy, subtle, surreptitious, underhand.

insight noun SEE **intelligence, understanding**.

insignia noun SEE **symbol**.

insignificant adjective inconsiderable, irrelevant, lightweight, meaningless, negligible, small, trivial, SEE **unimportant**, unimpressive, valueless, worthless.
OPPOSITES: SEE **significant**.

insincere adjective *insincere compliments.* deceitful, deceptive, devious, dishonest, disingenuous, false, feigned, flattering, hollow, hypocritical, lying, [*informal*] mealy-mouthed, mendacious, [*informal*] phoney, pretended, [*informal*] put on, sycophantic, [*informal*] two-faced, untrue.
OPPOSITES: SEE **sincere**.

insinuate verb *He insinuated that I was lying.* SEE **imply**.

insipid adjective SEE **bland**.

insist verb *He insisted he was innocent.* assert, aver, declare, emphasize, maintain, state, stress, swear, take an oath, vow.
to insist on *She insists on obedience.* command, demand, enforce, [*informal*] put your foot down, require, stipulate.

insistent adjective *an insistent rhythm. insistent requests.* assertive, demanding, emphatic, forceful, importunate, peremptory, persistent, relentless, repeated, unrelenting, unremitting, urgent.

insolence noun *Teachers don't like insolence from pupils.* arrogance, boldness, [*informal*] cheek, defiance, disrespect, effrontery, forwardness, impertinence, impudence, incivility, insubordination, [*informal*] lip, presumptuousness, rudeness, [*informal*] sauce.
OPPOSITES: SEE **politeness**.

insolent adjective *an insolent stare.* arrogant, bold, brazen, [*informal*] cheeky, contemptuous, disdainful, disrespectful, forward, impertinent, impolite, impudent, insulting, presumptuous, rude, saucy, shameless, sneering, uncivil.
OPPOSITES: SEE **polite**.

insoluble *an insoluble problem.* baffling, enigmatic, incomprehensible, inexplicable, mysterious, mystifying, puzzling, strange, unaccountable, unanswerable, unfathomable, unsolvable.
OPPOSITES: SEE **soluble**.

insolvent adjective SEE **bankrupt**.

insomnia noun sleeplessness.

inspect verb *to inspect damage. to inspect someone's work.* check, examine, [*informal*] give it the once over, investigate, make an inspection of, scrutinize, study, survey, vet.

inspection noun check, check-up, examination, [*informal*] going-over, investigation, review, scrutiny, survey.

inspector noun **1** *An inspector checked the standard of work.* controller, examiner, investigator, official, scrutineer, superintendent, supervisor, tester.
2 *a police inspector.* SEE **policeman**.

inspiration noun **1** *the inspiration behind a poem.* creativity, enthusiasm, genius, imagination, influence, motivation, muse, spur, stimulus.
2 *I had a sudden inspiration.* brainwave, idea, thought.

inspire verb *The crowd inspired us to play well.* animate, arouse, [*informal*] egg on, encourage, enthuse, galvanize, influence, motivate, prompt, reassure, spur, stimulate, stir, support.

instability noun *emotional instability. instability in prices.* capriciousness, change, changeableness, fickleness, fluctuation, flux, impermanence, inconstancy, insecurity, mutability, precariousness, shakiness, transience, uncertainty, unpredictability, unreliability, unsteadiness, [*informal*] ups-and-downs, vacillation, variability, variations, weakness.
OPPOSITES: SEE **stability**.

install verb **1** *to install central heating.* establish, fix, introduce, put in, set up.
2 *He installed himself in the best chair.* ensconce, place, plant, position, situate, station.
OPPOSITES: SEE **remove**.

instalment noun **1** *We pay for the TV in instalments.* payment, rent, rental.
2 *an instalment of a serial.* chapter, episode, part.

instance noun *Give me an instance of what you mean.* case, example, illustration, occurrence, sample.

instant adjective *an instant reply.* direct, fast, immediate, instantaneous, prompt, quick, rapid, speedy, swift, unhesitating, urgent.

instant noun *The shooting star was gone in an instant.* flash, moment, point of time, second, split second, [*informal*] tick, [*informal*] twinkling.

instantaneous adjective SEE **instant** adjective.

instigate verb *to instigate a riot.* activate, begin, be the instigator of [SEE **instigator**], bring about, cause, encourage, foment, generate, incite, initiate, inspire, kindle, prompt, provoke, set up, start, stimulate, stir up, urge, [*informal*] whip up.

instigator noun *the instigator of a riot.* agitator, fomenter, inciter, initiator, inspirer, leader, mischief-maker, provoker, ringleader, trouble-maker.

instil verb *to instil knowledge into pupils' minds.* [*informal*] din into, implant, inculcate, indoctrinate, infuse, inject, insinuate, introduce.

instinct noun *People do some things by instinct.* feel, feeling, guesswork, hunch, impulse, inclination, instinctive urge [SEE **instinctive**], intuition, presentiment, sixth-sense, tendency, urge.

instinctive adjective *an instinctive reaction.* automatic, [*informal*] gut (*gut feeling*), impulsive, inborn, inherent, innate, intuitive, involuntary, natural, reflex, spontaneous, unconscious, unreasoning, unthinking.
OPPOSITES: SEE **deliberate** adjective.

institute noun SEE **institution**.

institute verb *to institute a new set of rules.* begin, create, establish, fix, found, inaugurate, initiate, introduce, launch, open, originate, set up, start.

institution 1 *the institution of a new set of rules.* creation, establishing, formation, founding, inauguration, inception, initiation, introduction, launching, opening, setting up.
2 *an institution for blind people.* academy, college, establishment, foundation, home, hospital, institute, SEE **organization**, school, [*informal*] set-up.
3 *Sunday dinner is a regular institution in our house.* convention, custom, habit, practice, ritual, routine, tradition.

instruct verb 1 *The teacher instructed us in a new technique.* SEE **teach**.
2 *He instructed us to wait.* SEE **command** verb.

instruction noun 1 *He gave us instruction in the use of the equipment.* SEE **teaching**.
2 *Obey instructions!* SEE **command** noun.

instructive adjective *an instructive book.* didactic, edifying, educational, enlightening, helpful, illuminating, improving, informative, revealing.

instructor noun SEE **teacher**.

instrument noun *surgical instruments. mathematical instruments.* apparatus, appliance, contraption, device, equipment, gadget, implement, machine, mechanism, tool, utensil.
MUSICAL INSTRUMENTS: SEE **music**.

instrumental adjective *I was instrumental in getting things changed.* active, contributory, helpful, influential, useful.

insubordinate adjective *Many teachers dislike insubordinate children.* defiant, disobedient, SEE **impertinent**, insurgent, mutinous, rebellious, riotous, seditious, undisciplined, unruly.
OPPOSITES: SEE **obedient**.

insubstantial adjective SEE **flimsy**.

insufferable adjective SEE **intolerable**.

insufficient adjective *insufficient supplies.* deficient, inadequate, meagre, poor, scanty, scarce, short, sparse, unsatisfactory.
OPPOSITES: SEE **excessive**, **sufficient**.

Several English words, including *insular, insulate,* and *peninsula,* are related to Latin *insula = island.*

---

insular adjective *Having lived in one place all his life, his views are insular.* closed, limited, narrow, narrow-minded, parochial, provincial.
OPPOSITES: SEE **open-minded**.

insulate verb *to insulate water-pipes.* cocoon, cover, enclose, isolate, lag, protect, surround, wrap up.
OPPOSITES: SEE **bare** verb.

insult noun *I was offended by his insults.* abuse, cheek, contumely, impudence, insulting behaviour [SEE **insulting**], rudeness, slander, slight, snub.
OPPOSITES: SEE **compliment** noun.

insult verb abuse, affront, be insulting to [SEE **insulting**], [*informal*] call someone names, [*informal*] cock a snook at, mock, offend, outrage, patronize, revile, slander, slight, sneer at, snub, [*informal*] thumb your nose at, vilify.
OPPOSITES: SEE **compliment** verb.

insulting adjective *insulting remarks.* abusive, condescending, contemptuous, disparaging, insolent, mocking, offensive, patronizing, SEE **rude**, scornful, scurrilous, slanderous, [*informal*] snide.
OPPOSITES: SEE **complimentary**.

insuperable adjective *insuperable difficulties.* SEE **impossible**, insurmountable, overwhelming, unconquerable.

insupportable adjective SEE **intolerable**.

insurance noun *an insurance against loss or accident.* assurance, cover, indemnity, policy, protection, security.

insure verb *to insure yourself against loss or accident.* cover, indemnify, protect, take out insurance.

insurgent adjective SEE **rebellious**.

insurmountable adjective SEE **insuperable**.

insurrection noun SEE **rebellion**.

intact adjective SEE **undamaged**.

intangible adjective. *The scent of flowers is an intangible quality.* abstract, airy, disembodied, elusive, ethereal, impalpable, incorporeal, indefinite, insubstantial, invisible, unreal, vague.
OPPOSITES: SEE **tangible**.

integer noun SEE **number** noun.

integral adjective **1** *The boiler is an integral part of the heating system.* constituent, essential, indispensable, intrinsic, irreplaceable, necessary, requisite.
OPPOSITES: SEE **detachable**.
2 *The equipment is supplied as an integral unit.* complete, full, indivisible, whole.

integrate verb *We tried to integrate the two groups.* amalgamate, blend, bring together, combine, consolidate, desegregate, fuse, harmonize, join, merge, mix, put together, unify, unite, weld.
OPPOSITES: SEE **separate** verb.

integration noun SEE **union**.

integrity noun *You can trust his integrity.* fidelity, goodness, SEE **honesty**, honour, incorruptibility, loyalty, morality, principle, reliability, righteousness, sincerity, uprightness, virtue.
OPPOSITES: SEE **dishonesty**.

intellect noun SEE **intelligence**.

intellectual adjective **1** *an intellectual student.* academic, [*informal*] bookish, cerebral, cultured, highbrow, SEE **intelligent**, scholarly, studious, thoughtful.
2 *an intellectual book.* cultural, deep, difficult, educational, highbrow, improving, thought-provoking.

intellectual noun *The prof is a true intellectual.* [*informal*] egg-head, genius, highbrow, intellectual person [SEE **intellectual** adjective], member of the intelligentsia, thinker.

intelligence noun **1** *Use your intelligence!* ability, acumen, [*informal*] brains, brightness, brilliance, capacity, cleverness, discernment, genius, insight, intellect, judgement, mind, [*informal*] nous, perceptiveness, quickness, reason, sense, understanding, wisdom, wit (*He didn't have the wit to ask*), wits.
2 *They received intelligence of an impending invasion.* data, facts, information, knowledge, news, notification, report, [*informal*] tip-off, warning.
3 *Our intelligence discovered the enemy's position.* espionage, secret service, spies.

intelligent adjective *an intelligent student. intelligent work.* able, acute, alert, astute, brainy, bright, brilliant, clever, discerning, intellectual, knowing, penetrating, perceptive, perspicacious, profound, quick, rational, sagacious, sharp, shrewd, [*informal*] smart, trenchant, wise, [*informal*] with it.
OPPOSITES: SEE **stupid**.

intelligible adjective *an intelligible message.* clear, comprehensible, decipherable, legible, logical, lucid, meaningful, plain, straightforward, unambiguous, understandable.
OPPOSITES: SEE **incomprehensible**.

intemperate adjective *an intemperate drinker.* SEE **excessive**.

intend verb **1** *What do you intend to do?* aim, aspire, contemplate, design, have in mind, mean, plan, plot, propose, purpose, scheme.
2 *The gift was intended to please you.* design, destine, put forward, set up.

intense adjective **1** *intense pain.* acute, agonizing, extreme, fierce, great, keen, severe, sharp, strong, violent.
OPPOSITES: SEE **slight** adjective.
2 *intense emotions.* ardent, burning, deep, eager, earnest, fanatical, impassioned, passionate, powerful, profound, serious, towering, vehement.
OPPOSITES: SEE **cool** adjective.
3 *an intense person.* SEE **emotional**.

intensify verb *The heat intensified. They intensified the pressure.* add to, aggravate, become greater, boost, build up, deepen, emphasize, escalate, fire, fuel, heighten, increase, magnify, make greater, quicken, raise, redouble, reinforce, sharpen, [*informal*] step up, strengthen.
OPPOSITES: SEE **reduce, soften**.

intensive adjective *intensive effort. intensive enquiries.* [*informal*] all-out, concentrated, detailed, exhaustive, high-powered, thorough, unremitting.

intent adjective *intent on what you're doing.* absorbed, attentive (to), committed (to), concentrating, determined, eager, engrossed, keen, occupied, preoccupied, set, steadfast, watchful.

intent noun *The prosecution had to prove intent to kill.* SEE **intention**.

intention noun *What is your intention?* aim, ambition, design, end, goal, intent, object, objective, plan, point, purpose, target.

intentional adjective *an intentional foul.* calculated, conscious, deliberate, designed, intended, planned, pre-arranged, premeditated, wilful.
OPPOSITES: SEE **unintentional**.

inter verb SEE **bury**.

The prefix *inter-* is related to Latin *inter = among, between.* The verb *inter* and the noun *interment,* however, are related to a different Latin word, *terra = earth.*

---

interaction noun *the interaction of two influences.* effect on each other, exchange, [*informal*] give and take, interplay, reciprocal effect, [*informal*] to and fro.

intercede verb SEE **intervene**.

intercept verb *I intercepted the messenger before he delivered the message.* ambush, block, catch, check, cut off, deflect, head off, interrupt, obstruct, stop, thwart, trap.

interchange noun **1** *a motorway interchange.* crossroads, intersection, junction.
2 *an interchange of ideas.* exchange, [*informal*] swap.

intercom noun SEE **communication**.

intercourse noun **sexual intercourse** SEE **sex**.

interdict verb SEE **prohibit**.

interest noun **1** *Did he show any interest?* attention, attentiveness, care, commitment, concern, curiosity, involvement, notice, regard.
2 *The information was of no interest.* consequence, importance, moment, note, significance, value.
2 *What are your main interests?* activity, diversion, hobby, pastime, preoccupation, pursuit, relaxation.

interest verb *Astronomy interests me.* appeal to, arouse the curiosity of, attract, capture the imagination of, concern, divert, engage, engross, entertain, SEE **excite**, fascinate, intrigue, involve, stimulate, [*informal*] turn on.
OPPOSITES: SEE **bore**.

interested adjective **1** *an interested listener. interested in your work.* absorbed, attentive, curious, engrossed, enthusiastic, excited, fascinated, intent, keen, preoccupied, responsive.
OPPOSITES: SEE **uninterested**.
2 *Don't consult the owner of the damaged car: she's an interested party.* SEE **biased**, concerned, involved, partial.
OPPOSITES: SEE **disinterested**.
to be interested in SEE **like** verb.

interesting adjective [Things and experiences can be *interesting* in many ways. Only some of the possible synonyms are given here.] *an interesting problem. interesting conversation.* absorbing, challenging, curious, engaging, engrossing, entertaining, exciting, fascinating, important, intriguing, piquant, [*often ironic*] riveting, stimulating, unpredictable, unusual, varied.
OPPOSITES: SEE **boring**.

interface noun *the interface between two regions or systems.* SEE **boundary**, meeting-point.

interfere verb *to interfere in someone's affairs.* be a busybody, butt in, interrupt, intervene, intrude, meddle, molest, obtrude, [*informal*] poke your nose in, pry, snoop, tamper.
to interfere with *to interfere with the smooth running of something.* block, get in the way of, hamper, hinder, impede, obstruct.

interfering adjective *an interfering busybody.* curious, meddlesome, nosy, prying, snooping.

interim adjective *The test isn't finished, but we've produced an interim report.* half-time, halfway, provisional, temporary.

interior adjective, noun SEE **inside** adjective, noun.

interject verb SEE **interpose**.

interlink verb SEE **link** verb.

interlock verb SEE **engage**.

interloper noun SEE **intruder**.

interlude noun SEE **interval**.

intermediary noun SEE **go-between**.

intermediate adjective *an intermediate position.* average, [*informal*] betwixt and between, half-way, mean, medial, median, middle, midway, [*informal*] neither one thing nor the other, neutral, [*informal*] sitting on the fence, transitional.

interment noun [Do not confuse with *internment.*] SEE **funeral.**

interminable adjective SEE **ceaseless.**

intermingle verb SEE **mix.**

intermission noun SEE **interval.**

intermittent adjective *an intermittent fault in a machine.* fitful, irregular, occasional, [*informal*] on and off, periodic, recurrent, spasmodic, sporadic.
OPPOSITES: SEE **continual.**

intern verb SEE **imprison.**

internal adjective *the internal parts of something.* inner, inside, interior, intimate, private.
OPPOSITES: SEE **external.**

international adjective *international travel.* global, inter-continental, worldwide.

internecine adjective SEE **destructive.**

internee noun SEE **captive** noun.

internment noun [Do not confuse with *interment.*] SEE **captivity.**

inter-planetary adjective SEE **space** adjective.

interplay noun SEE **interaction.**

interpolate verb SEE **interpose.**

interpose verb *to interpose remarks in a conversation.* add, contribute, insert, interject, interlard, interpolate, introduce, put in, throw in.

interpret verb *Can you interpret this old writing?* clarify, construe, decipher, decode, elucidate, explain, expound, gloss, make clear, paraphrase, render (*into another language*), rephrase, reword, translate, understand.

interpretation noun *What's your interpretation of her behaviour?* definition, explanation, gloss, reading, understanding, version.

interpreter noun linguist, translator.

interrogate verb SEE **question** verb.

interrogative, interrogatory adjectives asking, inquiring, inquisitive, investigatory, questioning.

interrupt verb **1** *Interrupt if you have any questions.* [*informal*] barge in, break in, butt in, cut in, heckle, intervene, punctuate (*He punctuated the lecture with questions*).
2 *A fire alarm interrupted work.* break in on, break off, call a halt to, cause an interruption in [SEE **interruption**], cut (someone) off, cut short, disrupt, disturb, hold up, stop, suspend.
3 *The new houses interrupt our view.* get in the way of, interfere with, intrude upon, obstruct, spoil.

interruption noun *an interruption in service.* break, check, disruption, division, gap, halt, hiatus, pause, stop, suspension.

intersect verb *motorways intersect.* bisect each other, converge, criss-cross, cross, divide, meet, pass across each other.

intersection noun *a motorway intersection.* crossroads, interchange, junction.

intersperse verb SEE **scatter.**

interstellar adjective SEE **space** adjective.

intertwine verb SEE **interweave.**

interval noun **1** *an interval between events, places, etc.* break, [*informal*] breather, breathing-space, delay, distance, gap, hiatus, lapse, lull, opening, pause, respite, rest, space, wait.
2 *an interval in a play or concert.* adjournment, interlude, intermission, recess.

intervene verb **1** *A week intervened before I saw her again.* come between, happen, intrude, occur.
2 *to intervene in a quarrel.* arbitrate, butt in, intercede, interfere, interrupt, mediate, [*informal*] step in.

interview noun *an interview for a job.* audience, formal discussion, meeting, questioning.

interview verb *A reporter interviewed eyewitnesses.* ask questions, examine, interrogate, question.

interweave verb *The lines interweave in a complex pattern.* criss-cross, entwine, interlace, intertwine, knit, tangle, weave together.

intestines noun bowels, entrails, innards, insides.

intimate adjective **1** *an intimate relationship.* affectionate, close, familiar, SEE **friendly**, informal, loving, sexual.
2 *intimate details.* confidential, detailed, exhaustive, personal, private, secret.

intimate verb SEE **indicate.**

intimidate verb *The strong often intimidate the weak.* browbeat, bully, coerce, cow, daunt, frighten, hector, make afraid, menace, persecute, scare, terrify, terrorize, threaten.

intolerable adjective *intolerable pain.* excruciating, impossible, insufferable, insupportable, unbearable, unendurable.
OPPOSITES: SEE **tolerable.**

intolerant adjective *intolerant of other people's views.* bigoted, chauvinistic, dogmatic, illiberal, narrow-minded, opinionated, prejudiced, racialist, racist, sexist.
OPPOSITES: SEE **tolerant.**

intonation noun *an unusual intonation in her voice.* accent, inflection, sound, tone.

intone verb SEE **sing, speak.**

intoxicant noun SEE **alcohol.**

intoxicated adjective SEE **drunk.**

intoxicating adjective **1** *intoxicating drink.* SEE **alcoholic.**
2 *an intoxicating experience.* exciting, heady, stimulating.

intractable, intransigent adjectives SEE **stubborn.**

intrepid adjective SEE **courageous.**

intricate adjective *intricate machinery. intricate negotiations.* complex, complicated, convoluted, delicate, detailed, elaborate, [*informal*] fiddly, involved, sophisticated, tangled, tortuous.
OPPOSITES: SEE **simple.**

intrigue noun *a political intrigue.* SEE **plot** noun.

intrigue verb **1** *to intrigue against the state.* SEE **plot** verb.
2 *Science intrigues me.* SEE **interest** verb.

intrinsic adjective *The brooch has little intrinsic value.* basic, essential, fundamental, inborn, in-built, inherent, native, natural, proper, real.

introduce verb **1** *to introduce someone to a friend.* acquaint, make known, present.
2 *to introduce a radio programme.* announce, give an introduction to, lead into, preface.
3 *to introduce something new.* add, SEE **begin**, bring in, bring out, broach, create, establish, initiate, offer, pioneer, set up, start.

introduction noun **1** *an introduction to a book or song.* foreword, [*informal*] intro, introductory part [SEE **introductory**], [*informal*] lead-in, opening, overture, preamble, preface, prelude, prologue.
2 *the introduction of a new bus service.* SEE **beginning.**

introductory adjective *an introductory offer. introductory chapters of a book.* early, first, inaugural, initial, opening, prefatory, preliminary, preparatory, starting.
OPPOSITES: SEE **final.**

introspective adjective SEE **introverted.**

introverted adjective *an introverted character.* contemplative, introspective, inward-looking, meditative, pensive, quiet, reserved, retiring, self-contained, shy, thoughtful, unsociable, withdrawn.
OPPOSITES: SEE **extroverted.**

intrude verb *to intrude on a private conversation.* break in, butt in, eavesdrop, encroach, gatecrash, interfere, interrupt, intervene, join uninvited.

intruder noun **1** *intruders at a party.* eavesdropper, gatecrasher, infiltrator, interloper, snooper, [*informal*] uninvited guest.
2 *an intruder on your property.* burglar, housebreaker, invader, prowler, raider, robber, thief, trespasser.

intuition noun SEE **instinct.**

intuitive adjective SEE **instinctive.**

inundate verb SEE **flood** verb.

inure verb SEE **accustom.**

invade verb *to invade enemy territory.* SEE **attack** verb, descend on, encroach on, enter, impinge on, infest, infringe, march into, occupy, overrun, penetrate, raid, subdue, violate.

invalid adjective **1** *an invalid passport.* false, null and void, out-of-date, unacceptable, unusable, void, worthless.
2 *an invalid argument.* fallacious, illogical, incorrect, irrational, unconvincing, unfounded, unreasonable, unscientific, unsound, untrue.
OPPOSITES: SEE **valid.**

invalid noun *an invalid who spends most of the time in bed.* patient, sufferer.

invaluable adjective [Note: *invaluable* is NOT the opposite of *valuable.*] *Your help was invaluable.* incalculable, inestimable, precious, priceless, useful, SEE **valuable.**
OPPOSITES: SEE **worthless.**

invariable adjective *an invariable rule.* certain, constant, eternal, even, immutable, inflexible, permanent, predictable, reliable, rigid, solid, stable, steady, unalterable, unchangeable, unchanging, unvarying.
OPPOSITES: SEE **variable.**

invasion noun **1** *an invasion by an enemy.* SEE **attack** noun, encroachment, incursion, inroad, onslaught, raid, violation.
2 *an invasion of ants.* colony, flood, horde, infestation, spate, stream, swarm, throng.

invasive adjective *invasive weeds in the garden.* burgeoning, colonizing, increasing, mushrooming, profuse, proliferating, relentless, unstoppable.

invective noun SEE **abuse** noun.

inveigh verb **to inveigh against** SEE **abuse** verb.

inveigle verb SEE **lure** verb.

invent verb *to invent something new.* be the inventor of [SEE **inventor**], coin [= *to invent a new word*], conceive, concoct, construct, contrive, [*informal*] cook up, create, design, devise, discover, [*informal*] dream up, fabricate, imagine, improvise, make up, originate, plan, put together, think up, trump up (*to trump up charges against someone*).

invention noun **1** *The system is my own invention.* brainchild, coinage, contrivance, creation, design, discovery, figment (*of the imagination*).
2 *She let us see her new invention.* contraption, device, gadget.
3 *His work is full of lively invention.* creativity, genius, imagination, ingenuity, inspiration, inventiveness, originality.
4 *Her story was pure invention.* deceit, fabrication, fantasy, fiction, lies.

inventive adjective *an inventive mind. inventive work.* creative, enterprising, fertile, imaginative, ingenious, innovative, inspired, original, resourceful.
OPPOSITES: SEE **imitative.**

inventor noun *the inventor of something new.* architect, author, [*informal*] boffin, creator, designer, discoverer, maker, originator.

inventory noun SEE **catalogue.**

inverse adjective *in inverse proportion.* opposite, reversed, transposed.

invert verb capsize, overturn, reverse, turn upside down, upset.

invertebrate adjective VARIOUS ANIMALS: SEE **animal** noun.

invest verb *to invest money.* buy stocks and shares, put to work, save, use profitably.
to invest in *I invested in a new washing-machine.* SEE **buy.**

investigate verb *to investigate a crime or a problem.* consider, examine, explore, follow up, gather evidence about, [*informal*] go into, inquire into, look into, probe, research, scrutinize, study, [*informal*] sus out.

investigation noun *an investigation into a crime or problem.* enquiry, examination, inquiry, inquisition, inspection, [*informal*] post-mortem, [*informal*] probe, research, scrutiny, study, survey.

investiture noun *the investiture of a bishop.* installation, robing.

investment noun SEE **money.**

inveterate adjective *an inveterate smoker.* SEE **habitual.**

invidious adjective *invidious comparisons.* discriminatory, objectionable, offensive, undesirable, unjust, unwarranted.

invigilate verb SEE **supervise.**

invigorate verb SEE **animate** verb.

invigorating adjective *an invigorating cold shower.* bracing, enlivening, exhilarating, fresh, health-giving, healthy, refreshing, rejuvenating, revitalizing, stimulating.
OPPOSITES: SEE **soporific, wearying.**

invincible adjective *an invincible army.* indestructible, indomitable, invulnerable, strong, unbeatable, unconquerable.

invisible adjective *an invisible repair.* concealed, covered, disguised, hidden, imperceptible, inconspicuous, obscured, out of sight, secret, undetectable, unnoticeable, unnoticed, unseen.
OPPOSITES: SEE **visible.**

invite verb **1** *We invite you to join in.* ask, encourage, request, summon, urge.
2 *Shops want to invite our custom.* attract, entice, solicit, tempt.

inviting adjective SEE **attractive.**

invocation noun SEE **prayer.**

invoice noun *an invoice showing goods supplied.* account, bill, list, statement.

invoke verb *to invoke someone's help.* appeal to, call for, cry out for, entreat, implore, pray for, solicit, supplicate.

involuntary adjective *Blinking is an involuntary movement.* automatic, conditioned, impulsive, instinctive, reflex, spontaneous, unconscious, unintentional, unthinking.
OPPOSITES: SEE **deliberate** adjective.

involve verb **1** *What does your job involve?* comprise, contain, embrace, entail, hold, include, incorporate, take in.
2 *Conserving resources involves us all.* affect, concern, interest, touch.
3 *Don't involve me in your dubious activities!* embroil, implicate, include, incriminate, inculpate, mix up.

involved adjective **1** *an involved problem.* complex, complicated, confusing, convoluted, difficult, elaborate, intricate, [*informal*] knotty, tangled.
OPPOSITES: SEE **straightforward.**
2 *involved in your work.* active, busy, caught up, committed, concerned, dedicated, employed, keen, occupied.
OPPOSITES: uninvolved, SEE **detached.**

involvement noun **1** *involvement in sport.* activity, interest, participation.
2 *involvement with criminals.* association, complicity, entanglement, partnership.

invulnerable adjective *The dangerous drivers are those who think they're invulnerable.* indestructible, SEE **invincible**, protected, safe, secure, unwoundable.
OPPOSITES: SEE **vulnerable**.

iota noun SEE **particle**.

Several English words, including *irascible, irate,* and *ire,* are related to Latin *ira=anger.*

---

irascible adjective SEE **irritable**.

irate adjective SEE **angry**.

ire noun SEE **anger** noun.

iridescent adjective SEE **colourful**.

irk verb SEE **annoy**.

irksome adjective SEE **annoying**.

iron noun cast iron, steel.
RELATED ADJECTIVE: ferrous.
irons *convicts in irons.* chains, fetters, manacles, shackles.

iron verb *to iron the washing.* flatten, press, smooth.

ironic adjective *I was being ironic when I said their dreadful play was brilliant.* derisive, double-edged, ironical, mocking, sarcastic, satirical, wry.

ironmongers noun hardware store.

irony noun *I don't think they saw the irony in my comments.* double meaning, hidden meaning, sarcasm, satire.

irrational adjective *irrational behaviour. irrational argument.* absurd, arbitrary, biased, crazy, emotional, emotive, illogical, insane, mad, nonsensical, prejudiced, senseless, SEE **silly**, subjective, unintelligent, unreasonable, unreasoning, unsound, unthinking, wild.
OPPOSITES: SEE **rational**.

irreconcilable adjective SEE **incompatible**.

irredeemable adjective *an irredeemable sinner.* beyond redemption, impenitent, SEE **incorrigible**, irretrievable, lost, shameless, unsaveable, wicked.
OPPOSITES: SEE **penitent**.

irrefutable adjective SEE **indisputable**.

irregular adjective **1** *irregular intervals. an irregular rhythm.* erratic, fitful, fluctuating, haphazard, intermittent, occasional, random, spasmodic, sporadic, unequal, unpredictable, unpunctual, variable, varying, wavering.
2 *irregular behaviour. an irregular procedure.* abnormal, anomalous, eccentric, exceptional, extraordinary, illegal, improper, odd, peculiar, quirky, unconventional, unofficial, unplanned, unscheduled, unusual.
3 *an irregular surface.* broken, bumpy, jagged, lumpy, patchy, pitted, ragged, rough, uneven, up and down.
OPPOSITES: SEE **regular**.

irrelevant adjective *Omit irrelevant details.* extraneous, immaterial, inapplicable, inappropriate, inessential, pointless, unconnected, unnecessary, unrelated.
OPPOSITES: SEE **relevant**.

irreligious adjective *If you don't go to church, you aren't necessarily irreligious.* agnostic, atheistic, godless, heathen, humanist, impious, irreverent, pagan, uncommitted, ungodly, unrighteous, wicked.
OPPOSITES: SEE **religious**.

irreparable adjective *irreparable damage.* hopeless, incurable, irrecoverable, irremediable, irretrievable, irreversible, lasting, permanent, unalterable.
OPPOSITE: reparable.

irreplaceable adjective *an irreplaceable work of art.* inimitable, priceless, SEE **rare**, unique.
OPPOSITES: SEE **common** adjective.

irrepressible adjective *irrepressible high spirits.* boisterous, bouncy, ebullient, SEE **lively**, resilient, uncontrollable, ungovernable, uninhibited, unstoppable, vigorous.
OPPOSITES: SEE **sluggish**.

irresistible adjective *an irresistible temptation.* compelling, inescapable, inexorable, not to be denied, overpowering, overwhelming, persuasive, SEE **powerful**, seductive, unavoidable.

irresolute adjective *irresolute about what to choose.* doubtful, fickle, flexible, [*informal*] hedging your bets, SEE **hesitant**, indecisive, open to compromise, tentative, undecided, vacillating, wavering, weak, weak-willed.
OPPOSITES: SEE **resolute**.

irresponsible adjective *irresponsible driving.* careless, conscienceless, feckless, immature, immoral, inconsiderate, negligent, rash, reckless, selfish, shiftless, thoughtless, unethical, unreliable, unthinking, untrustworthy.
OPPOSITES: SEE **responsible**.

irreverent adjective *irreverent behaviour in church.* blasphemous, disrespectful,

impious, profane, SEE **rude**, sacrilegious.
OPPOSITES: SEE **reverent**.

irreversible adjective **1** *an irreversible decision.* SEE **irrevocable**.
2 *irreversible damage.* SEE **irreparable**.

irrevocable adjective *an irrevocable decision.* binding, final, fixed, hard and fast, immutable, irreversible, settled, unalterable, unchangeable.
OPPOSITE: reversible.

irrigate verb *to irrigate the desert.* flood, inundate, supply water to, water.

irritable adjective *an irritable mood. an irritable person.* SEE **angry**, bad-tempered, cantankerous, choleric, cross, crotchety, dyspeptic, easily annoyed, edgy, fractious, grumpy, ill-tempered, impatient, irascible, oversensitive, peevish, pettish, petulant, [*informal*] prickly, querulous, [*informal*] ratty, short-tempered, snappy, testy, tetchy, touchy, waspish.
OPPOSITES: SEE **even-tempered**.

irritant noun SEE **annoyance**.

irritate verb **1** *Rudeness irritates me.* SEE **annoy**.
2 *These spots irritate.* cause irritation, itch, tickle, tingle.

irritation noun **1** *Our neighbours' noise is a continual irritation.* SEE **annoyance**.
2 *My rash causes an irritation.* itch, pain, tickling, tingling.

island noun atoll, coral reef, isle, islet.
RELATED ADJECTIVE: insular.
group of islands archipelago.

isolate verb **1** *The police isolated the trouble-makers.* cordon off, cut off, keep apart, segregate, separate, single out.
2 *The hospital isolated the infectious patients.* place apart, quarantine, set apart.

isolated adjective **1** *an isolated farmhouse.* deserted, desolate, [*informal*] godforsaken, inaccessible, lonely, [*informal*] off the beaten track, outlying, out of the way, private, remote, secluded, sequestered, solitary, unfrequented.
OPPOSITES: SEE **accessible**.
2 *an isolated case of cheating.* abnormal, exceptional, single, uncommon, unique, untypical, unusual.
OPPOSITES: SEE **common** adjective.

issue noun **1** *political issues.* affair, argument, controversy, dispute, matter, point, problem, question, subject, topic.
2 *an issue of a magazine.* copy, edition, instalment, number, printing, publication.
3 *We awaited the issue of the election.* consequence, effect, end, impact, outcome, repercussions, result, upshot.
4 *The duke died without issue.* SEE **offspring**.

issue verb **1** *Smoke issued from the chimney.* appear, come out, emerge, erupt, flow out, gush, leak, rise, spring.
2 *He issued a formal statement.* bring out, circulate, distribute, give out, print, produce, promulgate, publicize, publish, put out, release, send out, supply.

itch noun **1** *an itch in my foot.* irritation, need to scratch, tickle, tingling.
2 *an itch to do something.* ache, desire, hankering, impatience, impulse, longing, lust, need, restlessness, urge, wish, yearning, [*informal*] yen.

itch verb **1** *My skin itches.* be irritated, tickle, tingle.
2 [*informal*] *We itched to be off.* SEE **want** verb.

item noun **1** *items in a sale. an item on a list.* article, bit, component, contribution, entry, ingredient, lot (*in an auction*), object, single thing, thing.
2 *an item in a newspaper.* account, article, feature, piece, report.

itemize verb SEE **list** verb.

itinerant adjective SEE **travelling**.

itinerary noun SEE **route**.

J

jab verb *to jab someone in the ribs.* elbow, SEE **hit** verb, nudge, poke, prod, stab, thrust.

jabber verb SEE **talk** verb.

jack verb **to jack up** SEE **lift** verb.

jackass noun SEE **donkey**.

jacket noun **1** OTHER COATS: SEE **coat** noun.
2 *a jacket for a book, an insulating jacket.* casing, coat, cover, covering, envelope, folder, sheath, skin, wrapper, wrapping.

jack-knife noun SEE **knife** noun.

jack-knife verb SEE **fold** verb.

jackpot noun SEE **prize** noun.

jaded adjective *jaded by lack of success.* bored, [*informal*] done in, exhausted, [*informal*] fagged, fatigued, [*informal*] fed up, listless, spent, tired out, weary.
OPPOSITES: SEE **lively**.

jagged adjective *a jagged edge.* angular, barbed, broken, indented, irregular,

ragged, rough, serrated, sharp, snagged, spiky, toothed, uneven, zigzag.
OPPOSITES: SEE **even** adjective.

jail SEE **gaol**.

jalopy noun SEE **car**.

jam noun **1** *a jam on the motorway.* blockage, bottleneck, crowd, crush, press, squeeze, throng, traffic jam.
2 *Help me out of a jam!* difficulty, dilemma, embarrassment, [*informal*] fix, [*informal*] hole, [*informal*] hot water, plight, predicament, quandary, tight corner, trouble.
3 *bread and jam.* conserve, jelly, marmalade, preserve.

jam verb **1** *They jammed us into a minibus.* cram, crowd, crush, pack, ram, squash, squeeze, stuff.
2 *Cars jammed the street.* block, [*informal*] bung up, congest, fill, obstruct, overcrowd, stop up.
3 *Jam the door open.* prop, stick, wedge.

jamboree noun SEE **celebration**.

jangle verb VARIOUS SOUNDS: SEE **sound** noun.

janitor noun SEE **caretaker**.

jar noun *a glass jar.* carafe, SEE **container**, crock, flagon, glass, jug, mug, pitcher, pot, urn, vessel.

jar verb **1** *The nasty noise jarred on me.* SEE **annoy**, grate, grind, [*informal*] jangle.
2 *The impact of the collision jarred me.* jerk, jolt, [*informal*] rattle, shake, shock, upset.

jargon noun *I can't understand the technical jargon.* cant, dialect, idiom, language, slang.

jarring adjective *a jarring noise.* annoying, disagreeable, discordant, grating, grinding, harsh, [*informal*] jangling, raucous, unpleasant.

jaundiced adjective SEE **jealous**.

jaunt noun *to go on a pleasure jaunt.* excursion, expedition, SEE **journey** noun, outing, tour, trip.

jaunty adjective *a jaunty tune,* alert, breezy, bright, carefree, [*informal*] cheeky, debonair, frisky, lively, perky, sprightly.

jaw noun chin, mouth.

jazz noun KINDS OF MUSIC: SEE **music**.

jazzy adjective **1** *jazzy music.* animated, lively, rhythmic, spirited, swinging, syncopated, vivacious.
2 *jazzy colours.* bold, clashing, contrasting, flashy, gaudy, loud.

jealous adjective **1** *He's jealous because I won.* bitter, covetous, envious, [*informal*] green-eyed, grudging, jaundiced, resentful.
2 *He's jealous of his reputation.* careful, possessive, protective, vigilant, watchful.

jeans noun SEE **trousers**.

jeer verb **to jeer at** *It's unkind to jeer at the losers.* barrack, boo, disapprove of, hiss, gibe at, heckle, [*informal*] knock, laugh at, make fun of, mock, ridicule, scoff at, sneer at, taunt.
OPPOSITES: SEE **cheer** verb.

jell verb SEE **harden**.

jelly noun RELATED ADJECTIVE: gelatinous.

jeopardize verb SEE **endanger**.

jeopardy noun SEE **danger**.

jerk verb *Jerk the rope when you are ready.* jog, jolt, move suddenly, pluck, pull, tug, tweak, twist, twitch, wrench, [*informal*] yank.

jerkin noun VARIOUS COATS: SEE **coat** noun.

jerky adjective *jerky movements.* bouncy, bumpy, convulsive, erratic, fitful, jolting, jumpy, rough, shaky, spasmodic, [*informal*] stopping and starting, twitchy, uncontrolled, uneven.
OPPOSITES: SEE **steady** adjective.

jerry-built adjective SEE **shoddy**.

jest noun, verb SEE **joke** noun, verb.

jester noun *the king's jester.* buffoon, clown, comedian, comic, SEE **entertainer**, fool, joker.

jet adjective SEE **black** adjective.

jet noun **1** *a jet of water.* flow, fountain, gush, rush, spout, spray, spurt, squirt, stream.
2 *Direct the jet at the fire.* nozzle, sprinkler.
3 *to fly by jet.* VARIOUS AIRCRAFT: SEE **aircraft**.

jettison verb SEE **discard**.

jetty noun *A boat tied up at the jetty.* breakwater, groyne, landing-stage, mole, pier, quay, wharf.

Jew noun WORDS TO DO WITH JEWISH RELIGION: bar mitzvah, kosher food, Passover, rabbi, sabbath, scripture, synagogue, Yom Kippur.
OTHER RELIGIOUS TERMS: SEE **religion**.

jewel noun gem, gemstone, precious stone.
VARIOUS JEWELS: SEE **jewellery**.

jeweller noun goldsmith.

jewellery noun gems, jewels, ornaments, [*informal*] sparklers, treasure.

ITEMS OF JEWELLERY: bangle, beads, bracelet, brooch, chain, charm, clasp, cufflinks, ear-ring, locket, necklace, pendant, pin, ring, signet-ring, tie-pin, watch-chain.

JEWELS AND JEWELLERY STONES: amber, cairngorm, carnelian or cornelian, coral, diamond, emerald, garnet, ivory, jade, jasper, jet, lapis lazuli, moonstone, onyx, opal, pearl, rhinestone, ruby, sapphire, topaz, turquoise.

METALS USED TO MAKE JEWELLERY: gold, platinum, silver.

---

jib verb SEE **refuse** verb.

jiffy noun SEE **moment**.

jig noun VARIOUS DANCES: SEE **dance** noun.

jiggery-pokery noun SEE **trickery**.

jiggle verb SEE **fidget**.

jilt verb SEE **abandon**.

jingle noun SEE **song**.

jingle verb *coins jingling in his pocket.* chink, clink, jangle, ring, tinkle. VARIOUS SOUNDS: SEE **sound** noun.

jingoism noun SEE **patriotism**.

jinx noun SEE **curse** noun.

jittery adjective SEE **nervous**.

jive verb SEE **dance** verb.

job noun **1** *a well-paid job.* business, calling, career, employment, livelihood, occupation, position, post, profession, sinecure, trade, vocation, work.
2 *jobs in the house.* activity, assignment, chore, duty, errand, function, housework, pursuit, responsibility, role, stint, task, work.

SOME JOBS PEOPLE DO: accountant, actuary, air hostess, architect, SEE **artist**, astronaut, astronomer, banker, barber, barmaid or barman, barrister, beautician, blacksmith, bookmaker, bookseller, brewer, bricklayer, broadcaster, builder, butler, cameraman, caretaker, carpenter, cashier, caterer, chauffeur, chef, chimney-sweep, cleaner, clergyman, clerk, coastguard, cobbler, commentator, composer, compositor, conductor, constable, cook, courier, croupier, curator.

decorator, dentist, designer, detective, dietician, diver, driver, docker, doctor, draughtsman, dressmaker, dustman, editor, electrician, engineer, SEE **entertainer**, estate agent, executive, farmer, farrier, fireman, fitter, forester, frogman, gamekeeper, gardener, glazier, groom, groundsman, gunsmith, hairdresser, handyman, hotelier, industrialist, interpreter, joiner, journalist.

labourer, lawyer, lecturer, lexicographer, librarian, lifeguard, lighterman, linguist, locksmith, longshoreman, lumberjack, machinist, manicurist, mannequin, manufacturer, mason, [*male*] masseur, [*female*] masseuse, mechanic, metallurgist, midwife, milkman, miller, milliner, miner, model, musician [SEE **music**], naturalist, night-watchman, nurse, nurseryman.

office worker, optician, parson, pathologist, pharmacist, photographer, platelayer, physiotherapist, pilot, plasterer, ploughman, plumber, policeman, politician, porter, postman, postmaster, postmistress, printer, probation officer, professor, programmer, projectionist, psychiatrist, psychologist, publisher, radiographer, radiologist, railwayman, receptionist, reporter.

saddler, sailor, salesperson, SEE **scientist**, secretary, shepherd, shoemaker, SEE **shopkeeper**, signalman, social worker, soldier, solicitor, stableman, steeplejack, stevedore, steward, stewardess, stockbroker, stoker, stonemason, stunt man, surgeon, surveyor, tailor, taxidermist, teacher, technician, telephonist, teller, test-pilot, traffic warden, translator, treasurer, typist, undertaker, [*male*] usher, [*female*] usherette, vet, [*male*] waiter, [*female*] waitress, warehouseman, woodman.

---

jobless adjective SEE **unemployed**.

jockey noun rider.

jockey verb *to jockey for position.* SEE **manœuvre** verb.

jocular adjective SEE **merry**.

jocund adjective SEE **joyful**.

jog verb **1** *to jog someone's elbow.* SEE **hit** verb, jar, jerk, jolt, knock, nudge.
2 *to jog someone's memory.* prompt, refresh, remind, set off, stimulate, stir.
3 *to jog round the park.* exercise, run, trot.

joggle verb SEE **shake**.

join noun *I can't see the join.* connection, joint, knot, link, mend, seam.

join verb **1** *to join things together.* add, amalgamate, attach, combine, connect, couple, dock, dovetail, SEE **fasten**, fit, fix, knit, link, marry, merge, put together, splice, tack on, unite, yoke.

2 *Two rivers join here.* come together, converge, meet.
OPPOSITES: SEE **separate** verb.
3 *to join a crowd.* follow, go with, [*informal*] latch on to, tag along with.
4 *to join a youth club.* affiliate with, become a member of, enlist in, enrol in, participate in, register for, sign up for, volunteer for.
OPPOSITES: SEE **leave** verb.

joiner noun carpenter.

joint adjective *a joint effort.* collective, combined, common, communal, concerted, co-operative, general, mutual, shared, united.
OPPOSITES: SEE **individual** adjective.

joint noun JOINTS IN YOUR BODY: ankle, elbow, hip, knee, knuckle, shoulder, vertebra, wrist.

joist noun beam, girder, rafter.

joke noun *an amusing joke.* [*informal*] crack, funny story, [*informal*] gag, [*old-fashioned*] jape, jest, pleasantry, pun, quip, wisecrack, witticism.

joke verb be facetious, clown, jest, have a laugh, make jokes [SEE **joke** noun].

joker noun SEE **jester**.

jollification noun SEE **merrymaking**.

jollity noun SEE **merriment**.

jolly adjective SEE **joyful, merry**.

jolt verb 1 *The car jolted over the rough track.* bounce, bump, jar, jerk, jog, shake, twitch.
2 *The noise jolted us into action.* astonish, disturb, nonplus, shock, startle, surprise.

jostle verb *The crowd jostled us.* crowd in on, hustle, press, push, shove.

jot verb *to jot down some notes.* SEE **write**.

jotter noun exercise book, notebook, pad.

journey noun 1 *a trade journal.* gazette, magazine, monthly, newspaper, paper, periodical, publication, weekly.
2 *the journal of a voyage.* account, chronicle, diary, log, record.

journalist noun *a newspaper journalist.* columnist, contributor, correspondent, reporter, writer.

journey noun itinerary, peregrination, route, travels, trip.

KINDS OF JOURNEY: crossing (*sea crossing*), cruise, drive, excursion, expedition, flight, hike, jaunt, joy-ride, mission, odyssey, outing, passage (*a sea passage*), pilgrimage, ramble, ride, run, safari, sail, tour, trek, voyage, walk, wanderings.
SEE ALSO **travel** noun.

---

journey verb go on a journey [SEE **journey** noun], SEE **travel** verb.

joust noun, verb SEE **fight** noun, verb.

jovial adjective SEE **joyful**.

jowl noun PARTS OF YOUR HEAD: SEE **head** noun.

joy noun bliss, cheerfulness, delight, ecstasy, elation, euphoria, exaltation, exultation, felicity, gaiety, gladness, glee, happiness, hilarity, joyfulness, jubilation, mirth, pleasure, rapture, rejoicing, triumph.
OPPOSITES: SEE **sorrow** noun.

joyful adjective *a joyful occasion, a joyful welcome.* cheerful, delighted, ecstatic, elated, enraptured, euphoric, exultant, gay, glad, gleeful, happy, jocund, jolly, jovial, joyous, jubilant, merry, overjoyed, pleased, rapturous, rejoicing, triumphant.
OPPOSITES: SEE **sad**.

joyless adjective SEE **sad**.

joyous, jubilant adjectives SEE **joyful**.

jubilee noun anniversary, celebration, commemoration, festival.

judge noun 1 *a judge at a sporting event.* adjudicator, arbiter, arbitrator, referee, umpire.
2 *a judge in a lawcourt.* SEE **law**.
3 *a good judge of wines.* connoisseur, critic, expert.

judge verb 1 *to judge someone in a lawcourt.* condemn, convict, examine, pronounce judgement on [SEE **judgement**], punish, sentence, try.
2 *The umpire judged that the ball was out.* adjudicate, conclude, decide, decree, deem, determine, pass judgement, rule.
3 *to judge others. to judge a work of art.* appraise, assess, criticize, evaluate, give your opinion of, rebuke, scold, sit in judgement on.
4 *I judged that the eggs would be cooked.* believe, consider, estimate, gauge, guess, reckon, suppose.

judgement noun 1 *The court pronounced its judgement.* arbitration, award, conclusion, conviction, decision, decree, [*old-fashioned*] doom, finding, outcome, penalty, punishment, result, ruling, verdict.
2 *Use your judgement.* acumen, common sense, discernment, discretion, discrimination, expertise, good sense, SEE **intelligence**, reason, wisdom.

3 *In my judgement, he was driving too fast.* assessment, belief, estimation, evaluation, idea, impression, mind, notion, opinion, point of view, valuation.

judicial adjective [Do not confuse with *judicious.*] *a judicial decision.* legal, official.

judicious adjective [Do not confuse with *judicial.*] *a judicious change of policy.* appropriate, astute, SEE **clever**, diplomatic, expedient, politic, prudent, sensible, shrewd, thoughtful, well judged, wise.

judo noun SEE **martial (martial arts)**.

jug noun carafe, SEE **container**, ewer, flagon, jar, pitcher, vessel.

juggle verb *He juggled the figures to make it seem that he'd made a profit.* alter, [*informal*] cook, [*informal*] doctor, falsify, [*informal*] fix, manipulate, move about, rearrange.

juice noun *the juice of an orange.* SEE **drink** noun, fluid, liquid, sap.

juicy adjective *juicy fruit.* full of juice, lush, moist, soft, [*informal*] squelchy, succulent, wet.
OPPOSITES: SEE **dry** adjective.

jumble noun *a jumble of odds and ends.* chaos, clutter, confusion, disorder, farrago, hotchpotch, mess, muddle.
jumble sale SEE **sale**.

jumble verb *Don't jumble the papers I've just sorted.* confuse, disarrange, [*informal*] mess up, mix up, muddle, shuffle, tangle.
OPPOSITES: SEE **organize**.

jumbo noun VARIOUS AIRCRAFT: SEE **aircraft**.

jump noun 1 *a jump in the air.* bounce, bound, hop, leap, pounce, skip, spring, vault.
JUMPS IN ATHLETICS: high jump, long jump, pole vault, triple jump.
2 *The horse easily cleared the last jump.* ditch, fence, gap, gate, hurdle, obstacle.
3 *a jump in prices.* SEE **rise** noun.

jump verb 1 *to jump in the air.* bounce, bound, hop, leap, skip, spring.
2 *to jump a fence.* clear, hurdle, vault.
3 *to jump about.* caper, dance, frisk, frolic, gambol, prance.
4 *The cat jumped on the mouse.* SEE **attack** verb, pounce.
5 *I jumped the boring chapters.* SEE **omit**.
6 *The bang made me jump.* SEE **flinch**.
7 *Prices jumped.* SEE **rise** verb.

jumpy adjective SEE **nervous**.

junction noun *a road junction. a junction between two routes.* confluence (*of two rivers*), corner, crossroads, interchange, intersection, joining, meeting, T-junction.

juncture noun SEE **moment**.

jungle noun *a jungle of vegetation.* forest, tangle, undergrowth, woods.

junior adjective *junior rank.* inferior, lesser, lower, minor, secondary, subordinate, subsidiary, younger.
OPPOSITES: SEE **senior**.

junk noun *a lot of old junk.* clutter, debris, flotsam-and-jetsam, garbage, litter, lumber, oddments, odds and ends, refuse, rubbish, rummage, scrap, trash, waste.

junketing noun SEE **merrymaking**.

junkie noun SEE **addict**.

junta noun SEE **government**.

jurisdiction noun SEE **authority**.

jurisprudence noun law.
LEGAL TERMS: SEE **law**.

just adjective *a just punishment. a just decision,* apt, deserved, equitable, ethical, even-handed, fair, fair-minded, honest, impartial, justified, lawful, legal, legitimate, merited, proper, reasonable, rightful, right-minded, unbiased, unprejudiced, upright.
OPPOSITES: SEE **unjust**.

justice noun 1 *Justice demands that women and men should be paid the same.* equity, fairness, honesty, impartiality, integrity, legality, right.
OPPOSITES: SEE **injustice**.
2 *Lawcourts exist to administer justice.* the law, legal proceedings, punishment, retribution, vengeance.

justifiable adjective *a justifiable course of action.* acceptable, allowable, defensible, excusable, forgivable, justified, lawful, legitimate, pardonable, permissible, reasonable, understandable, warranted.
OPPOSITES: SEE **unjustifiable**.

justify verb *Don't try to justify his wickedness.* condone, defend, [*informal*] exculpate, excuse, exonerate, explain, explain away, forgive, pardon, support, uphold, vindicate, warrant (*Nothing can warrant such cruelty*).

jut verb *The mantelpiece juts over the fireplace.* extend, overhand, poke out, project, protrude, stick out.

juvenile adjective 1 [*uncomplimentary*] *juvenile behaviour.* babyish, childish, immature, infantile, puerile.
OPPOSITES: SEE **mature**.
2 *juvenile novels.* adolescent, young, youthful.

juxtapose verb *When you juxtapose the two, you can see the difference.* SEE **compare.**

K

kaleidoscopic adjective *a kaleidoscopic effect.* brightly coloured, changing, fluctuating, multicoloured, shifting, variegated.

karate noun SEE **martial (martial arts).**

karma noun SEE **fate.**

kayak noun canoe.

keel verb **to keel over** SEE **capsize**, collapse, lean, tilt.

keen adjective **1** *a keen cutting-edge.* piercing, pointed, razor-sharp, sharp, sharpened.
OPPOSITES: SEE **blunt** adjective.
2 *a keen wit.* biting, cutting, incisive, lively, mordant, satirical, scathing, shrewd, sophisticated.
OPPOSITES: SEE **dull** adjective.
3 *keen eyesight.* acute, clear, perceptive, sensitive.
OPPOSITES: SEE **dim** adjective.
4 *a keen wind.* bitter, cold, extreme, icy, intense, penetrating, severe.
OPPOSITES: SEE **mild.**
5 *keen prices.* competitive, low, rock-bottom.
OPPOSITES: SEE **exorbitant.**
6 *a keen pupil.* ambitious, anxious, assiduous, avid, bright, clever, committed, diligent, eager, enthusiastic, fervent, industrious, intelligent, intent, interested, motivated, quick, zealous.
OPPOSITES: SEE **apathetic.**

keep noun *the keep of a castle.* SEE **castle.**

keep verb **1** *to keep something safe. to keep it for later.* conserve, guard, hang on to, hold, preserve, protect, put aside, put away, retain, safeguard, save, store, stow away, withhold.
OPPOSITES: SEE **lose, use** verb.
2 *to keep looking for something.* carry on, continue, do again and again, do for a long time, keep on, persevere in, persist in.
OPPOSITES: SEE **abandon.**
3 *to keep a pet. to keep a shop.* be responsible for, care for, cherish, foster, guard, have, have charge of, look after, manage, mind, own, tend, watch over.
4 *to keep a family.* feed, maintain, pay for, provide for, support.
5 *to keep your birthday.* celebrate, commemorate, mark, observe, [*formal*] solemnize.
6 *How long does milk keep?* be preserved, be usable, last, stay good.
7 *I won't keep you.* block, check, curb, delay, detain, deter, get in the way of, hamper, hinder, hold up, impede, obstruct, prevent, restrain, retard.
to keep an eye open SEE **watch** verb.
to keep still linger, remain, stay.
to keep to *Keep to the rules!* abide by, adhere to, be ruled by, conform to, honour, obey, recognize, submit to.

keeper noun *the keeper of a museum.* curator, custodian, gaoler, guard, guardian, warden, warder.

keepsake noun memento, souvenir.

keg noun SEE **barrel.**

kerb noun SEE **edge** noun.

kerfuffle noun SEE **commotion.**

kernel noun core, heart, middle, nut.

ketchup noun relish, sauce.

kettle noun VARIOUS CONTAINERS: SEE **container.**

kettledrums noun timpani.
OTHER DRUMS: SEE **drum.**

key noun **1** *the key to a problem.* answer, clue, indicator, pointer, secret, solution.
2 *a key to a map.* explanation, glossary, guide, index.

keyboard noun KEYBOARD INSTRUMENTS: accordion, celesta, clavichord, clavier, harmonium, harpsichord, organ, piano, spinet, virginals.
OTHER MUSICAL TERMS: SEE **music.**

keynote noun *the keynote of a speech.* core, emphasis, gist, heart, message, theme.

kibbutz noun SEE **settlement.**

kick noun **1** *a kick at the ball.* SEE **hit** noun.
2 *It gave me a kick to see my story in print.* SEE **thrill** noun.

kick verb **1** *to kick a ball.* boot, heel, SEE **hit** verb, punt.
2 [*informal*] *to kick a habit.* SEE **cease.**

kid verb [*informal*] *Don't try to kid me!* bluff, SEE **deceive**, fool, hoodwink, lie to.

kidnap verb abduct, carry off, run away with, seize, snatch.

kidney noun RELATED ADJECTIVE: renal.

kill verb annihilate, assassinate, be guilty of the killing of [SEE **killing** noun], be the killer of [SEE **killer**], [*informal*] bump off, butcher, cull [=*kill animals* *selectively*], decimate [see note under *decimate*], destroy, [*informal*] dispatch, [*informal*] do away with, execute, exterminate, [*informal*] finish off, [*informal*] knock off, liquidate, martyr, massacre, murder, put down, put to death, slaughter, slay, take life.

WAYS TO KILL: behead, brain, choke, crucify, decapitate, disembowel, drown, electrocute, eviscerate, garrotte, gas, guillotine, hang, knife, lynch, poison, pole-axe, shoot, smother, stab, starve, stifle, stone, strangle, suffocate, throttle.

---

killer noun assassin, butcher, cut-throat, destroyer, executioner, exterminator, gunman, murderer, slayer.

killing adjective [*informal*] *a killing joke.* SEE **funny**.

killing noun annihilation, assassination, bloodshed, butchery, carnage, decimation [see note under *decimate*], destruction, elimination, eradication, euthanasia, execution, extermination, extinction, fratricide, genocide, homicide, infanticide, liquidation, manslaughter, martyrdom, massacre, matricide, murder, parricide, patricide, pogrom, regicide, slaughter, suicide.

kiln noun SEE **fire** noun.

kin noun SEE **family**.

kind adjective *a kind action. a kind person. a kind remark.* accommodating, affectionate, agreeable, altruistic, amenable, amiable, attentive, avuncular, beneficent, benevolent, benign, bountiful, brotherly, caring, charitable, comforting, compassionate, considerate, cordial, courteous, encouraging, fatherly, favourable, friendly, generous, genial, gentle, good-natured, good-tempered, gracious, helpful, hospitable, humane, indulgent, kind-hearted, kindly, lenient, loving, merciful, mild, motherly, neighbourly, nice, obliging, patient, philanthropic, pleasant, polite, public-spirited, sensitive, sisterly, soft-hearted, sweet, sympathetic, tactful, tender, thoughtful, understanding, unselfish, warm-hearted, well-intentioned, well-meaning, well-meant.
OPPOSITES: SEE **unkind**.

kind noun *a kind of dog. a kind of food. a kind of book.* brand, breed, category, class, description, family, form, genre, genus, make, nature, race, set, sort, species, style, type, variety.

kindle verb **1** *to kindle a fire.* burn, fire, ignite, light, set fire to.
2 *to kindle strong emotions.* SEE **arouse**.

kindling noun firewood.

kindly adjective SEE **kind** adjective.

kindred noun SEE **family**.

king noun SEE **ruler**.

kingdom noun SEE **country**, monarchy, realm.

kingly adjective SEE **regal**.

kink noun *a kink in a rope.* bend, coil, knot, loop, tangle, twist.

kinsman, **kinswoman** nouns SEE **family**.

kiosk noun **1** *a newspaper kiosk.* bookstall, booth, news-stand, stall.
2 *a telephone kiosk.* telephone box.

kip verb SEE **sleep** verb.

kismet noun SEE **fate**.

kiss verb caress, embrace, SEE **touch** verb.

kit noun *games kit. a wine-making kit. a soldier's kit.* apparatus, baggage, effects, equipment, gear, [*informal*] impedimenta, luggage, outfit, paraphernalia, rig, tackle, tools.

kitchen, **kitchenette** nouns OTHER ROOMS: SEE **room**.

SOME KITCHEN EQUIPMENT: blender, cooker, SEE **crockery**, SEE **cutlery**, deep-freeze, dish rack, dishwasher, draining-board, extractor-fan, food-processor, freezer, fridge, grill, kettle, liquidizer, microwave-oven, mincer, mixer, oven, pantry, percolator, range, refrigerator, scales, sink, stove, thermos, toaster, tray, vacuum flask.

COOKING UTENSILS: SEE **cook**.

---

kith noun **kith and kin** SEE **family**.

kitsch adjective SEE **tasteless**.

kitten noun SEE **cat**.

kitty noun SEE **fund**.

knack noun *a knack for making friends. a knack for mending machines.* ability, adroitness, art, bent, dexterity, expertise, flair, genius, gift, skill, talent, trick.

knackered adjective SEE **exhausted**.

knapsack noun backpack, haversack, rucksack.

knave noun SEE **scoundrel**.

knead verb *to knead dough.* manipulate, massage, pound, press, pummel, squeeze, work.

kneel verb bend, bow, crouch, fall to your knees, genuflect, stoop.

knell noun SEE **bell**.

knickerbockers noun SEE **trousers.**

knickers noun [*old-fashioned*] bloomers, boxer-shorts, briefs, drawers, panties, pants, shorts, trunks, underpants.

knife noun KINDS OF KNIFE: butter-knife, carving-knife, clasp-knife, cleaver, dagger, flick-knife, machete, penknife, pocket-knife, scalpel, sheathknife.
OTHER CUTLERY: SEE **cutlery.**

knife verb *to knife someone.* SEE **kill**, slash, stab, wound.

knight noun SEE **fighter**, horseman, warrior.

knit verb **1** *to knit a pullover.* crochet, weave.
2 *to knit together.* bind, combine, connect, fasten, interweave, knot, mend, tie, unite.
to knit your brow SEE **frown** verb.

knob noun **1** *a door knob.* handle.
2 boss, bulge, bump, lump, projection, protuberance, swelling.

knock verb **1** *to knock against something.* [*informal*] bash, buffet, bump, SEE **hit** verb, rap, smack, [*old-fashioned*] smite, strike, tap, thump.
2 *to knock someone's work.* SEE **criticize.**
to knock off *to knock off work.* SEE **cease.**
to knock out *to knock someone out.* make unconscious [SEE **unconscious**].

knock-out noun SEE **victory.**

knoll noun SEE **hill.**

knot noun **1** *a knot in a rope.* VARIOUS KNOTS: bow, bowline, clovehitch, grannyknot, hitch, noose, reef-knot, sheephank, slipknot.
2 *a knot of people.* SEE **group** noun.

knot verb *to knot ropes together.* bind, do up (*do up your shoelace*), entangle, entwine, SEE **fasten**, join, knit, lash, link, tie, unite.
OPPOSITES: SEE **untie.**

know verb **1** *to know facts. to know how to do something.* comprehend, have experience of, have in mind, remember, understand.
2 *to know that you are right.* be certain, have confidence.
3 *to know what something is. to know who someone is.* discern, distinguish, identify, make out, perceive, realize, recognize, see.
4 *to know a person.* be acquainted with, be familiar with, be a friend of.

know-all noun expert, pundit, [*informal*] show-off, wiseacre.

know-how noun SEE **knowledge.**

knowing adjective *Her knowing smile showed that she understood.* artful, astute, aware, clever, crafty, cunning, discerning, experienced, expressive, intelligent, meaningful, perceptive, shrewd, sly, well-informed, wily.
OPPOSITES: SEE **innocent.**

knowledge noun **1** *An encyclopaedia contains a lot of knowledge.* data, facts, information, learning, scholarship, science.
2 *She's got enough knowledge to do the job.* ability, awareness, background, competence, education, experience, familiarity, grasp, [*informal*] know-how, learning, lore, skill, talent, technique, training, understanding, wisdom.
OPPOSITES: SEE **ignorance.**

knowledgeable adjective *knowledgeable about antiques.* aware, conversant, educated, erudite, experienced, familiar (with), informed, learned, scholarly, versed (in), well-informed.
OPPOSITES: SEE **ignorant.**

knuckleduster noun cosh.
OTHER WEAPONS: SEE **weapon.**

kowtow verb SEE **grovel.**

kung fu noun SEE **martial (martial arts).**

L

label noun *a label on a parcel.* docket, marker, sticker, tag, ticket.

label verb *We labelled him as a troublemaker.* brand, call, categorize, class, classify, define, describe, identify, mark, name, stamp.

laborious adjective *a laborious climb. laborious effort.* arduous, back-breaking, difficult, exhausting, fatiguing, gruelling, hard, heavy, onerous, stiff, strenuous, tiresome, tough, uphill, wearisome.
OPPOSITES: SEE **easy.**

labour noun **1** *You deserve a reward for your labour.* [*informal*] donkey-work, drudgery, effort, exertion, industry, [*informal*] pains, toil, SEE **work** noun.
2 *Because of increased orders, the firm took on extra labour.* employees, [*old-fashioned*] hands, workers, workforce.
3 [=*giving birth to a baby*] childbirth, contractions, delivery, labour pains, [*old-fashioned*] travail.
the Labour Party POLITICAL TERMS: SEE **politics.**

labour verb drudge, exert yourself, [*informal*] slave away, [*informal*] sweat, toil, SEE **work** verb, work hard.

labourer noun SEE **worker**.

labour-saving adjective *labour-saving tools.* convenient, handy, helpful, time-saving.

labyrinth noun *a labyrinth of corridors.* complex, jungle, maze, network, tangle.

lace noun **1** *lace curtains.* filigree, net, tatting.
VARIOUS FABRICS: SEE **cloth**.
2 *a lace for your shoe.* cord, string, thong.

lace verb SEE **fasten**.

lacerate verb *to lacerate your skin.* claw, graze, mangle, rip, scrape, scratch, tear, SEE **wound** verb.

lachrymose adjective SEE **tearful**.

lack noun *a lack of food. a lack of self-confidence.* absence, dearth, deprivation, famine, need, paucity, privation, scarcity, shortage, want.
OPPOSITES: SEE **plenty**.

lack verb *The game lacked excitement.* be deficient in, be short of, be without, miss, need, require, want.

lackadaisical adjective SEE **apathetic**.

lackey noun SEE **servant**.

lacking adjective **1** *lacking in courage.* defective, deficient, inadequate, short, unsatisfactory, wanting, weak.
2 [*informal*] *He's a bit lacking.* SEE **stupid**.

laconic adjective SEE **terse**.

lacquer noun SEE **paint** noun.

lad noun SEE **boy**.

ladder noun fire-escape, step-ladder, steps.

laden adjective *laden with shopping.* burdened, fraught, full, hampered, loaded, oppressed, weighed down.

lading noun SEE **cargo**.

lady noun SEE **woman**.

ladylike adjective *ladylike behaviour.* dainty, genteel, modest, SEE **polite**, posh, prim and proper, [*uncomplimentary*] prissy, refined, respectable, well-bred.

lag verb **1** *to lag behind.* [*informal*] bring up the rear, come last, dally, dawdle, drop behind, fall behind, go too slow, hang about, idle, linger, loiter, saunter, straggle, trail.
2 *to lag water-pipes.* insulate, wrap up.

lager noun ale, beer.

lagoon noun SEE **lake**.

laid-back adjective SEE **easygoing**.

lair noun *an animal's lair.* den, hide-out, hiding-place, refuge, retreat, shelter.

lake noun boating-lake, lagoon, lido, (*Scottish*) loch, mere, pond, pool, reservoir, sea, tarn, water.

lam verb SEE **hit** verb.

lamb noun SEE **sheep**.

lama noun SEE **priest**.

lambast, lambaste verb SEE **hit** verb.

lame adjective **1** *a lame person.* crippled, disabled, SEE **handicapped**, incapacitated, maimed.
2 *a lame leg.* dragging, game (*a game leg*), [*informal*] gammy, injured, limping, stiff.
3 *a lame excuse.* feeble, flimsy, inadequate, poor, tame, thin, unconvincing, weak.
to be lame SEE **limp** verb.

lame verb *The accident temporarily lamed him.* cripple, disable, incapacitate, make limp [SEE **limp** verb], maim.

lament noun *a lament for the dead.* dirge, elegy, lamentation, monody, requiem, threnody.

lament verb *to lament the passing of someone or something.* bemoan, bewail, complain about, deplore, express your sorrow about, grieve about, mourn, regret, shed tears for, wail, weep.

lamentable adjective SEE **regrettable**.

lamentation noun *the lamentation of mourners at a funeral.* complaints, grief, SEE **lament** noun, mourning, regrets, tears, wailing, weeping.

laminated adjective *laminated chipboard.* coated, covered, layered, veneered.

lamp noun SEE **light** noun.

lampoon verb SEE **ridicule** verb.

lance noun javelin, spear, SEE **weapon**.

land noun **1** *Surveyors mapped out the lie of the land.* geography, landscape, terrain, topography.
2 *your native land.* country, nation, region, state, territory.
3 *land to grow things on.* farmland, earth, ground, soil.
4 *land belonging to a person.* estate, grounds, property.
5 *The sailors came to land.* coast, landfall, shore, [*joking*] terra firma.

land verb *to land from an aircraft, ship, or vehicle.* alight, arrive, berth, come ashore, disembark, dock, end a journey, get down, reach landfall, touch down.

landing noun **1** *the landing of an aircraft or spacecraft.* re-entry, return, touch-down.

2 *the landing of passengers.* SEE **arrival**, disembarkation.

landing-stage noun berth, dock, harbour, jetty, landing, quay, wharf.

landing-strip noun SEE **airfield**.

landlady, landlord nouns 1 *the landlady or landlord of a pub.* hotelier, [*old-fashioned*] innkeeper, licensee, publican.
2 *the landlady or landlord of rented property.* landowner, letter, owner, proprietor.

landmark noun 1 *a landmark in the countryside.* feature, high point, visible feature.
2 *a landmark in history.* milestone, new era, turning point.

landscape noun *a painting of a landscape.* countryside, outlook, panorama, prospect, rural scene, scene, scenery, view, vista.

landslide adjective *a landslide victory.* SEE **overwhelming**.

landslide noun avalanche, landslip.

lane noun SEE **road**.

language noun 1 *the language we speak. foreign languages.* [*informal*] lingo, speech, tongue.
2 *language of particular people or of particular situations.* argot, cant, colloquialism, dialect, formal language, idiolect, idiom, informal language, jargon, journalese, lingua franca, patois, register, slang, vernacular.
3 *a computer language.* code, system of signs.

EVERYDAY LINGUISTIC TERMS: accent, active verb or voice, adjective, adverb, clause, conjunction, consonant, grammar, indicative mood, noun, paragraph, passive verb or voice, phrase, plural, predicate, prefix, preposition, pronoun, SEE **punctuation**, sentence, singular, subject, subjunctive mood, suffix, syllable, synonym, syntax, tense, verb, vocabulary, vowel, word.

ASPECTS OF THE STUDY OF LANGUAGE: etymology, lexicography, linguistics, orthography, philology, phonetics, psycholinguistics, semantics, semiotics, sociolinguistics.

---

languid adjective [*uncomplimentary*] *His languid manner annoys me when there's work to be done.* apathetic, [*informal*] droopy, feeble, inactive, inert, lackadaisical, lazy, lethargic, slow, sluggish, torpid, unenthusiastic, weak.
OPPOSITES: SEE **energetic**.

languish verb *He languished after his dog died. Our project languished during the holidays.* become languid [SEE **languid**], decline, flag, lose momentum, mope, pine, slow down, stagnate, suffer, sulk, waste away, weaken, wither.
OPPOSITES: SEE **flourish** verb.

lank adjective 1 [*uncomplimentary*] *lank hair.* drooping, lifeless, limp, long, straight, thin.
2 *a lank figure.* SEE **lanky**.

lanky adjective [*uncomplimentary*] *a lanky figure.* angular, awkward, bony, gangling, gaunt, lank, lean, long, scraggy, scrawny, skinny, tall, thin, ungraceful, weedy.
OPPOSITES: SEE **graceful, sturdy**.

lantern noun SEE **light** noun.

lap noun 1 *Sit on my lap.* knees, thighs.
2 *a lap of a racetrack.* circle, circuit, course, orbit.

lap verb SEE **drink** verb.

lapse noun 1 *a lapse of memory. a lapse in behaviour.* backsliding, error, fault, flaw, mistake, relapse, shortcoming, slip, temporary failure, weakness.
2 *a lapse in a training programme.* break, gap, interruption, interval, lull, pause.

lapse verb 1 *to lapse from your normal standard of work.* decline, deteriorate, drop, fall, slide, slip.
2 *My membership has lapsed.* become invalid [SEE **invalid** adjective], expire, finish, run out, stop.

larceny noun SEE **stealing**.

larder noun food cupboard, pantry.

large adjective [The meaning of *large* is relative. You can speak of *a large ant* and *a small elephant*, but you are not really confused about which is larger in size! The words listed here are just some of the many words which can mean *larger than average for its kind.*] above average, abundant, ample, big, bold (*bold handwriting*), broad, bulky, capacious, colossal, commodious, considerable, copious, elephantine, enormous, extensive, [*informal*] fat (*a fat increase*), formidable, gargantuan, generous, giant, gigantic, grand, great, heavy, hefty, high, huge, [*informal*] hulking, immeasurable, immense, impressive, incalculable, infinite, [*informal*] jumbo, [*informal*] king-sized, large, largish, lofty, long, mammoth, massive, mighty, [*informal*] monstrous, monumental, mountainous, outsize, overgrown, oversized, prodigious, [*informal*] roomy, sizeable, spacious, substantial, swingeing (*a swingeing increase*), tall, thick, [*informal*] thumping,

[*informal*] tidy (*a tidy sum*), titanic, towering, tremendous, vast, voluminous, weighty, [*informal*] whacking, [*informal*] whopping, wide.
OPPOSITES: SEE **small**.

largess noun SEE **generosity**.

lariat noun lasso, SEE **rope** noun.

larva noun caterpillar, grub, maggot.

larynx noun throat, vocal cords.

lasagne noun SEE **pasta**.

lascivious adjective SEE **lustful**.

laser noun SEE **light** noun.

lash noun SEE **whip** noun.

lash verb **1** *to lash with a whip.* SEE **whip** verb.
2 *to lash with your tongue.* SEE **criticize**.
3 *to lash with rope.* SEE **fasten**.

lass noun SEE **girl**.

lassitude noun SEE **tiredness**.

lasso noun lariat, SEE **rope** noun.

last adjective **1** *last in the queue.* furthest, hindmost.
OPPOSITES: SEE **first**.
2 *Z is the last letter of the alphabet.* closing, concluding, final, terminal, terminating, ultimate.
OPPOSITES: SEE **initial**.
3 *What was his last record called?* latest, most recent.
OPPOSITES: SEE **next**.

last verb *I hope the fine weather lasts.* carry on, continue, endure, hold, hold out, keep on, linger, live, persist, remain, stay, survive, wear (*These jeans have worn well*).

lasting adjective *a lasting friendship.* abiding, continuing, durable, enduring, indestructible, indissoluble, lifelong, long-lasting, long-lived, long-standing, permament, stable, unchanging, undying, unending.
OPPOSITES: SEE **temporary**.

last-minute adjective *a last-minute dash for the bus.* belated, eleventh-hour, late.
OPPOSITES: SEE **early**.

latch noun *the latch on a door.* bolt, catch, SEE **fastener**, lock.

late adjective **1** *The bus is late.* behindhand, belated, delayed, dilatory, overdue, slow, tardy, unpunctual.
OPPOSITES: SEE **early**.
2 *the late king.* dead, deceased, departed, former.

lately adverb latterly, recently.

latent adjective *latent talent.* dormant, hidden, invisible, potential, undeveloped, undiscovered.

later adjective SEE **following**.

lateral adjective *lateral shoots on a plant.* side, sideways.

lather noun *soapy lather.* bubbles, foam, froth, suds.

latitude noun *He gives his students latitude to express themselves.* [*informal*] elbow-room, freedom, leeway, liberty, room, scope, space.

latrine noun SEE **lavatory**.

latter adjective *The latter part of the speech became tedious.* closing, concluding, last, later, recent, second.
OPPOSITES: SEE **former**.

lattice noun *honeysuckle growing over a lattice.* criss-cross, framework, grid, mesh, trellis.

laud verb SEE **praise** verb.

laudable adjective SEE **praiseworthy**.

laudanum noun opium.

laudatory adjective SEE **complimentary**.

laugh verb WAYS TO EXPRESS AMUSEMENT: beam, burst into laughter [SEE **laughter**], chortle, chuckle, giggle, grin, guffaw, simper, smile, smirk, sneer, snigger, titter.
to laugh at SEE **ridicule** verb.

laughable adjective *The play was a tragedy, but the acting was laughable.* absurd, derisory, SEE **funny**, ludicrous, preposterous, ridiculous.

laughing-stock noun *His eccentric ways made him a laughing-stock.* butt, figure of fun, victim.

laughter noun *Their performance caused a lot of laughter.* chuckling, giggling, guffaws, hilarity, [*informal*] hysterics, laughing, laughs, merriment, mirth, sniggering, tittering.

launch noun **1** *a seagoing launch.* VARIOUS VESSELS: SEE **vessel**.
2 *the launch of a rocket.* blast-off, launching.

launch verb **1** *to launch a ship.* float.
2 *to launch a rocket.* blast off, fire, propel, send off, set off.
3 *to launch a new business.* begin, embark on, establish, found, inaugurate, initiate, open, set up, start.

launder verb *to launder clothes.* clean, wash.

laundry noun *to do the laundry.* washing.

lavatory noun cloakroom, convenience, latrine, [*informal*] loo, [*childish*] potty, [*old-fashioned*] privy, public convenience, toilet, urinal, water-closet, WC.

lavish adjective *a lavish supply of food.* abundant, bountiful, copious, extravagant, exuberant, generous, liberal, luxuriant, luxurious, munificent, opulent,

plentiful, prodigal, sumptuous, unstinting, wasteful.
OPPOSITES: SEE **economical**.

law noun **1** *the laws of the land.* act, bill [=*draft of a proposed law*], commandment, decree, edict, order, pronouncement, statute.
2 *the laws of a game.* code, principle, regulation, rule.
3 *a court of law.* justice, litigation.
RELATED ADJECTIVES: legal, litigious.

EVENTS IN A COURT OF LAW: action, case, court martial, hearing, inquest, lawsuit, litigation, proceedings, suit, trial.

PEOPLE INVOLVED IN LEGAL AFFAIRS: accused, advocate, attorney, bailiff, barrister, clerk, coroner, counsel for the defence, counsel for the prosecution, defendant, judge, juror, lawyer, magistrate, plaintiff, police, prosecutor, solicitor, usher, witness.

SOME EVERYDAY LEGAL TERMS: accusation, arrest, bail, the bar, the bench, charge, court, dock, evidence, judgement, jurisprudence, lawcourt, litigant, notary public, plea, probate, SEE **punishment**, remand, sentence, statute, sue, summons, testimony, tort, verdict.

---

law-abiding adjective *law-abiding citizens.* compliant, decent, disciplined, good, honest, obedient, orderly, peaceable, peaceful, respectable, well-behaved.
OPPOSITES: SEE **lawless**.

lawful adjective **1** *It isn't lawful to steal.* allowable, allowed, authorized, just, permissible, permitted, right.
2 *Who's the lawful owner of this car?* documented, legal, legitimate, prescribed, proper, recognized, regular, rightful, valid.
OPPOSITES: SEE **illegal**.

lawless adjective *a lawless mob.* anarchic, anarchical, badly behaved, chaotic, disobedient, disorderly, ill-disciplined, insubordinate, mutinous, rebellious, riotous, rowdy, seditious, turbulent, uncontrolled, undisciplined, ungoverned, unrestrained, unruly, wild.
OPPOSITES: SEE **law-abiding**.

lawlessness noun *lawlessness in the streets.* anarchy, chaos, disobedience, disorder, mob-rule, rebellion, rioting.
OPPOSITES: SEE **order** noun.

lawn noun green, mown grass.

lawsuit, lawyer nouns SEE **law**.

lax adjective *lax morals. lax discipline.* careless, casual, SEE **easygoing**, lenient, loose, neglectful, negligent, permissive, remiss, slack, unreliable, vague.
OPPOSITES: SEE **strict**.

laxative noun aperient, enema, purgative.

lay verb **1** *Lay your work on the table. Lay the paint on thickly.* apply, arrange, deposit, leave, place, position, put down, rest, set down, set out, spread.
2 *Don't lay all the blame on her.* ascribe, assign, burden, impose, plant, [*informal*] saddle.
3 *We laid secret plans.* concoct, create, design, establish, organize, plan, set up.
[*Lay* is also past tense of the verb *to lie*: *I lay down yesterday evening for a rest.* It is often used wrongly as present tense. Do NOT say *Let's lay down and have a rest* but *Let's lie . . .*]
to lay bare SEE **reveal**.
to lay down the law SEE **dictate**.
to lay into someone SEE **attack** verb.
to lay someone low SEE **defeat** verb.
to lay someone off SEE **dismiss**.
to lay off something SEE **cease**.
to lay to rest SEE **bury**.
to lay up SEE **store** verb.
to lay waste SEE **destroy**.

layabout noun SEE **loafer**.

layer noun **1** *a layer of paint.* coat, coating, covering, film, sheet, skin, surface, thickness.
2 *a layer of rock.* seam, stratum, substratum.
in layers laminated, layered, sandwiched, stratified.

layer verb *to layer plants.* SEE **propagate**.

layman noun **1** *A layman shouldn't do electrical work.* amateur, untrained person.
OPPOSITES: SEE **professional**.
2 *laymen of the church.* layperson, member of the congregation, parishioner, unordained person.
OPPOSITES: SEE **clergyman**.

layout noun SEE **arrangement**.

laze verb *to laze in the sun.* be lazy [SEE **lazy**], do nothing, lie about, loaf, lounge, relax, sit about, unwind.

laziness noun dilatoriness, idleness, inactivity, indolence, lethargy, loafing, lounging about, sloth, slowness, sluggishness.
OPPOSITES: SEE **industry**.

lazy adjective **1** *a lazy worker.* easily pleased, idle, inactive, indolent, languid, lethargic, listless, shiftless, [*informal*] skiving, slack, slothful, slow, sluggish, torpid, unenterprising, work-shy.
OPPOSITES: SEE **industrious**.

2 *a lazy holiday.* peaceful, quiet, relaxing.
OPPOSITES: SEE **energetic**.
to be lazy idle, laze, loaf, malinger, shirk, [*informal*] skive.
a lazy person [*informal*] good-for-nothing, malingerer, [*informal*] skiver, slacker, sluggard.

lead noun **1** [pronounced *led*] *lead pipes.* METALS: SEE **metal**.
2 [pronounced *leed*] *We looked to the captain for a lead.* direction, example, guidance, leadership.
3 [*informal*] *The police hoped for a lead on the crime.* clue, hint, line, tip, tip-off.
4 *She was in the lead from the start.* first place, front position, spearhead, vanguard.
5 *the lead in a play or film.* chief part, starring role, title role.
6 *an electrical lead.* cable, flex, wire.
7 *a dog's lead.* chain, leash, strap.

lead verb **1** *to lead someone in a certain direction.* conduct, draw, escort, guide, influence, pilot, steer, usher.
OPPOSITES: SEE **follow**.
2 *to lead an expedition.* be in charge of, command, direct, govern, head, manage, preside over, rule, supervise.
3 *to lead in a race.* be in front, be in the lead, head the field.

leaden adjective *leaden skies.* SEE **grey**.

leader noun **1** LEADERS IN VARIOUS SITUATIONS: ayatollah, boss, captain, chief, chieftain, commander, conductor, courier, demagogue, director, figure-head, godfather, guide, head, patriarch, premier, prime minister, principal, ringleader, SEE **ruler**, superior, [*informal*] supremo.
2 *a leader in a newspaper.* editorial, leading article.

leading adjective *a leading figure in politics.* SEE **chief** adjective, dominant, foremost, important, inspiring, outstanding, prominent, well-known.

leaf noun **1** *leaves of a plant.* blade (*of grass*), foliage, frond, greenery.
2 *leaves in a book.* folio, page, sheet.

leaflet noun *an advertising leaflet.* booklet, brochure, circular, handout, pamphlet.

league noun *a football league.* SEE **group** noun.
to be in league with SEE **conspire**.

leak noun *a leak in a bucket.* crack, drip, hole, opening, perforation, puncture.

leak verb **1** *to leak water or oil.* drip, escape, exude, ooze, percolate, seep, spill, trickle.
2 *to leak secrets.* disclose, divulge, give away, let out, make known, pass on, reveal.

leaky adjective cracked, dripping, holed, perforated, punctured.
OPPOSITES: SEE **watertight**.

lean adjective **1** *a lean figure.* bony, emaciated, gaunt, lanky, skinny, slender, slim, spare, thin, wiry.
OPPOSITES: SEE **fat** adjective.
2 *lean meat.* OPPOSITE: fatty.

lean verb **1** *to lean to one side.* bank, heel over, incline, list, loll, slant, slope, tilt, tip.
2 *to lean against the fence.* prop yourself up, recline, rest, support yourself.

leaning noun *a leaning towards science. a leaning towards vegetarianism.* bent, bias, inclination, instinct, liking, partiality, penchant, predilection, preference, propensity, readiness, taste, tendency, trend.

leap verb **1** *to leap in the air.* bound, clear (*clear a fence*), jump, leap-frog, spring, vault.
2 *to leap on someone.* ambush, attack, pounce.
3 *to leap for joy.* caper, cavort, dance, frisk, gambol, hop, prance.

learn verb *At school, you learn facts and skills.* acquire, assimilate, become aware of, be taught [SEE **teach**], discover, find out, gain, gain understanding of, gather, grasp, master, memorize, [*informal*] mug up, pick up, remember, study, [*informal*] swot up.

learned adjective *a learned professor.* academic, clever, cultured, educated, erudite, highbrow, intellectual, SEE **knowledgeable**, scholarly.

learner noun apprentice, beginner, cadet, L-driver, novice, pupil, scholar, starter, student, trainee, tiro.

learning noun *a person of great learning.* culture, education, erudition, information, knowledge, scholarship, wisdom.

lease noun SEE **contract** noun.

lease verb SEE **rent** verb.

leash noun *a dog's leash.* chain, lead, strap.

least adjective *the least amount. least in importance. least in number.* fewest, lowest, minimum, negligible, poorest, slightest, smallest, tiniest.

leather noun chamois, hide, skin, suede.

leathery adjective SEE **tough**.

leave noun **1** *Will you give me leave to speak?* authorization, liberty, permission.

2 *leave from the army.* absence, free time, holiday, sabbatical, time off, vacation.
to take your leave SEE **leave** verb.

leave verb **1** *I have to leave.* depart, go away, go out, [*informal*] pull out, run away, say goodbye, set off, take your leave, withdraw.
OPPOSITES: SEE **arrive, enter.**
2 *The rats left the sinking ship.* abandon, desert, evacuate, forsake, vacate.
3 *I left my job.* [*informal*] chuck in, give up, quit, relinquish, resign from, retire from, [*informal*] walk out of.
4 *Leave it where it is.* allow (it) to stay, let (it) alone, [*informal*] let (it) be.
5 *She left me some money in her will.* bequeath, hand down, will.
6 *Leave the milk bottles by the front door.* deposit, place, position, put down, set down.
7 *Leave the arrangements to me.* consign, entrust, refer.
8 *to leave the stage.* exeunt [= *they go out*], exit [= *she or he goes out*].
to leave off SEE **stop** verb.
to leave out SEE **omit.**

leaven verb SEE **lighten.**

lecherous adjective SEE **lustful.**

lectern noun reading-desk.

lecture noun **1** *a lecture on science.* address, discourse, lesson, speech, talk.
2 *a lecture on bad manners.* SEE **reprimand** noun.

lecture verb **1** *I lecture at a polytechnic.* be a lecturer [SEE **lecturer**], teach.
2 *He lectured on an interesting topic.* discourse, give a lecture, [*informal*] hold forth, speak, talk formally.
3 *She lectured us on our bad manners.* SEE **reprimand** verb.

lecturer noun *a college lecturer.* don, fellow, instructor, professor, speaker, teacher, tutor.

ledge noun projection, ridge, shelf, sill, step, window-sill.

lee noun SEE **shelter** noun.

leer noun, verb FACIAL EXPRESSIONS: SEE **expression.**

lees noun SEE **sediment.**

leeward adjective SEE **sheltered.**

leeway noun SEE **latitude.**

left adjective, noun **1** *on the left side.* left-hand, port [= *left side of a ship when you face the bow*].
2 *the left in politics.* communist, Labour, leftist, left-wing, liberal, Marxist, progressive, radical, revolutionary, socialist.
OPPOSITES: SEE **right** adjective, noun.

leg noun **1** lower limb, [*informal*] pin (*unsteady on his pins*), shank.
PARTS OF YOUR LEG: ankle, calf, foot, hock, knee, shin, thigh.
WORDS TO DESCRIBE PEOPLE'S LEGS: bandy, bandy-legged, bow-legged, knock-kneed.
2 *a leg of a table.* prop, support, upright.
3 *a leg of a journey.* lap, part, section, stage.
to pull someone's leg SEE **hoax** verb.

legacy noun *a legacy bequeathed in a will.* bequest, endowment, estate, inheritance.

legal adjective **1** *legal proceedings.* judicial.
2 *I'm the legal owner of my car.* above-board, allowable, allowed, authorized, constitutional, lawful, legalized, legitimate, licensed, permissible, permitted, regular, rightful, valid.
OPPOSITES: SEE **illegal.**

legalize verb *They won't ever legalize the drugs trade.* allow, legitimize, license, make legal [SEE **legal**], normalize, permit, regularize.
OPPOSITES: SEE **ban** verb.

legate noun SEE **ambassador.**

legend noun SEE **story.**

CREATURES YOU READ ABOUT IN LEGENDS: brownie, centaur, chimera, dragon, dwarf, elf, fairy, faun, giant, gnome, goblin, griffin, imp, leprechaun, leviathan, mermaid, monster, nymph, ogre, phoenix, pixie, troll, unicorn, vampire, werewolf, witch, wizard.

---

legendary adjective **1** *Unicorns are legendary beasts.* apocryphal, fabled, fabulous, fictional, fictitious, invented, made-up, mythical, non-existent, storybook.
OPPOSITES: SEE **real.**
2 *Presley is a legendary name in the pop world.* SEE **famous.**

legible adjective *legible handwriting.* clear, decipherable, distinct, intelligible, neat, plain, readable.
OPPOSITES: SEE **illegible.**

legitimate adjective **1** *The solicitor said it was legitimate to sell the house.* SEE **legal.**
OPPOSITES: SEE **illegal.**
2 *Do you believe it's legitimate to copy his ideas?* ethical, just, justifiable, moral, proper, reasonable, right.
OPPOSITES: SEE **immoral.**
3 *a legitimate child* = *a child born within a legal marriage.*
OPPOSITES: SEE **illegitimate.**

legitimize verb SEE **legalize**.

leg-pull noun SEE **hoax** noun.

leisure noun *Most people enjoy their leisure.* ease, holiday time, liberty, recreation, relaxation, rest, spare time, time off.

leisurely adjective *a leisurely walk.* easy, gentle, lingering, peaceful, relaxed, relaxing, restful, SEE **slow** adjective, unhurried.
OPPOSITES: SEE **brisk**.

lend verb *to lend money.* advance, loan.
OPPOSITES: SEE **borrow**.

length noun **1** *the length of a piece of string.* distance, extent, measurement, stretch.
2 *the length of a piece of music.* duration, period, time.

lengthen verb *The days lengthen in spring. You can lengthen the ladder if you need to.* draw out, enlarge, elongate, expand, extend, get longer, increase, make longer, prolong, pull out, stretch.
OPPOSITES: SEE **shorten**.

lengthy adjective SEE **long** adjective.

lenient adjective *a lenient teacher.* easy-going, forgiving, indulgent, kind, merciful, mild, soft, soft-hearted, tolerant.
OPPOSITES: SEE **strict**.

lens adjective SEE **optical instruments**.

lesbian adjective, noun SEE **homosexual**.

lesion noun SEE **wound** noun.

lessen verb **1** *The ointment will lessen the pain.* assuage, cut, deaden, decrease, lower, make less, minimize, mitigate, reduce, tone down.
2 *The pain lessened.* abate, become less, decline, decrease, die away, diminish, dwindle, ease off, moderate, slacken, subside, tail off, weaken.
OPPOSITES: SEE **increase** verb.

less adjective fewer, smaller.
OPPOSITES: SEE **more**.

lesson noun **1** *Pupils are expected to attend lessons.* class, lecture, seminar, tutorial.
2 *Let that be a lesson to you!* example, moral, SEE **reprimand** noun, warning.
to teach someone a lesson SEE **reprimand** verb.

let verb **1** *You let it happen. Let him have it.* agree to, allow, consent to, give permission to, permit.
OPPOSITES: SEE **forbid, object** verb.
2 *a house to let.* hire, lease, rent.
to let alone, to let be *Let the poor creature alone!* allow to stay, leave, leave untouched.
to let go, to let loose *to let prisoners go. to let animals loose.* free, liberate, release.
to let off *to let off fireworks.* detonate, discharge, explode, fire, set off.
to let someone off *to let an accused person off.* acquit, excuse, exonerate.

let-down noun *After all the publicity, the film was a bit of a let-down.* anti-climax, disappointment, [*informal*] wash-out.

lethal adjective *a lethal dose of a drug.* deadly, fatal, mortal, poisonous.

lethargic adjective *The fumes made us feel lethargic.* apathetic, inactive, languid, lazy, listless, SEE **sleepy**, slow, sluggish, torpid.
OPPOSITES: SEE **energetic**.

lethargy noun apathy, laziness, listlessness, slowness, sluggishness, torpor.

letter noun **1** *the letters of the alphabet.* character, consonant, vowel.
2 *a letter to a friend.* [*old-fashioned*] billet-doux, card, SEE **communication**, [*formal*] dispatch, [*formal or joking*] epistle, message, [*joking*] missive, note, postcard.
letters correspondence, mail, post.

letter-box noun pillar-box, post-box.

level adjective **1** *a level surface.* even, flat, flush, horizontal, plane, regular, smooth, uniform.
OPPOSITES: SEE **uneven**.
2 *level scores.* balanced, equal, even, matching, [*informal*] neck-and-neck, the same.

level noun **1** *floods at a dangerous level. prices at a high level.* altitude, depth, height, value.
2 *the first level of an exam.* grade, stage, standard.
3 *promotion to a higher level.* degree, echelon, plane, position, rank, [*informal*] rung on the ladder, standing, status.
4 *rooms on the ground level.* floor, storey.

level verb **1** *We levelled the ground to make a lawn.* bulldoze, even out, flatten, rake, smooth.
2 *An earthquake levelled the town.* demolish, destroy, devastate, knock down, lay low, raze.

level-headed adjective SEE **sensible**.

lever verb *to lever open a box.* force, prise, wrench.

levitate verb SEE **rise** verb.

levity noun SEE **frivolity**.

levy noun SEE **tax** noun.

lewd adjective SEE **obscene**.

lexicon noun dictionary, glossary, vocabulary.

liable adjective **1** *The drunken driver was held to be liable for the accident.* accountable, answerable, responsible.
2 *I'm liable to fall asleep in the evenings.* disposed, inclined, likely, predisposed, prone, ready, willing.
OPPOSITES: SEE **unlikely**.

liaise verb SEE **mediate**.

liaison noun **1** *liaison between business interests.* communication, co-operation, liaising, links, mediation.
2 *a liaison between a man and a woman.* SEE **love** noun **(love affair)**.

liar noun deceiver, [*informal*] fibber, [*formal*] perjurer, [*informal*] story-teller.

libel noun, verb SEE **slander** noun, verb. [A *libel* is a slander published in a book, newspaper, etc.]

libellous adjective SEE **slanderous**.

liberal adjective **1** *a liberal supply of food.* abundant, ample, bounteous, bountiful, copious, generous, lavish, munificent, plentiful, unstinting
OPPOSITES: SEE **mean** adjective.
2 *liberal attitudes.* broad-minded, charitable, easygoing, enlightened, fair-minded, humanitarian, indulgent, lenient, magnanimous, permissive, tolerant, unbiased, unprejudiced.
OPPOSITES: SEE **narrow-minded**.
3 *liberal political views.* progressive, radical.
OPPOSITES: SEE **conservative** adjective.
The Liberal Party POLITICAL TERMS: SEE **politics**.

liberalize verb *to liberalize the laws on drinking.* make more liberal, relax, soften.

liberate verb *to liberate prisoners.* discharge, emancipate, free, let out, loose, ransom, release, rescue, save, set free, untie.
OPPOSITES: SEE **enslave, imprison**.

libertine noun SEE **immoral (immoral person)**.

liberty noun *liberty from slavery. liberty to do what you want.* emancipation, freedom, independence, liberation, release.
at liberty SEE **free** adjective.
civil liberties privileges, rights.

libido noun SEE **lust**.

licence noun **1** *a TV licence.* certificate, document, permit, warrant.
2 *licence to do as you please.* SEE **permission**.

license verb **1** *The authorities license certain shops to sell tobacco.* allow, authorize, empower, entitle, give a licence to, permit.
2 *to license a car.* buy a licence for, make legal.

licentious adjective SEE **lustful**.

lick verb **1** *to lick a lollipop.* suck.
2 [*informal*] *to lick the opposition.* SEE **defeat** verb.

lid noun *the lid of a container.* cap, cover, covering, top.

lie noun *His lies didn't fool us.* deceit, dishonesty, disinformation, fabrication, falsehood, falsification, [*informal*] fib, fiction, invention, untruth.
OPPOSITES: SEE **truth**.

lie verb **1** *to lie in order to deceive.* be economical with the truth, bluff, SEE **deceive**, falsify the facts, [*informal*] fib, perjure yourself.
2 *to lie on a bed.* be horizontal, be prone [= *lie face downwards*], be supine [= *lie face upwards*], lean back, lounge, recline, repose, rest, sprawl, stretch out.
3 *The house lies in a valley.* be, be found, be located, be situated, exist.
to lie low SEE **hide** verb.

life noun **1** *life on earth.* being, existence.
2 *full of life.* activity, animation, energy, [*informal*] go, liveliness, spirit, sprightliness, verve, vigour, vitality, vivacity, zest.
3 *a life of Elvis Presley.* autobiography, biography, story.

lifeless adjective **1** *a lifeless body.* comatose, dead, deceased, inanimate, inert, killed, motionless, unconscious.
OPPOSITES: SEE **living** adjective.
2 *lifeless desert.* arid, bare, barren, sterile.
OPPOSITES: SEE **fertile**.
3 *a lifeless performance.* apathetic, boring, flat, lack-lustre, lethargic, slow, unexciting.
OPPOSITES: SEE **animated**.

lifelike adjective *a lifelike image.* authentic, convincing, natural, photographic, realistic, true-to-life.
OPPOSITES: SEE **unrealistic**.

lifelong adjective SEE **lasting**.

lift noun elevator, escalator, hoist.

lift verb **1** *to lift into the air.* buoy up, carry, elevate, hoist, jack up, pick up, pull up, raise, rear.
2 *The plane lifted off the ground.* ascend, rise, soar.
3 [*informal*] *to lift someone else's property.* SEE **steal**.

light adjective **1** *light to carry.* lightweight, SEE **portable**, underweight, weightless.
OPPOSITES: SEE **heavy**.

2 *a light and airy room.* SEE **bright**, illuminated, lit-up, well-lit.
OPPOSITES; SEE **dark.**
[The adjective *light* has many other senses. We refer you to entries where you can find synonyms for some of the common ones.]
3 *light work.* SEE **easy.**
4 *light wind.* SEE **gentle.**
5 *a light touch.* SEE **delicate.**
6 *light colours.* SEE **pale** adjective.
7 *a light heart.* SEE **cheerful.**
8 *light traffic.* SEE **sparse.**

light noun *a shining light.* beam, blaze, brightness, brilliance, effulgence, flare, flash, fluorescence, glare, gleam, glint, glitter, glow, halo, illumination, incandescence, luminosity, lustre, phosphorescence, radiance, ray, reflection, shine, sparkle, twinkle.
to give light, to reflect light be bright, be luminous, be phosphorescent, blaze, blink, burn, coruscate, dazzle, flash, flicker, glare, gleam, glimmer, glint, glisten, glitter, glow, radiate, reflect, scintillate, shimmer, shine, spark, sparkle, twinkle.

KINDS OF LIGHT: daylight, electric light, firelight, floodlight, half-light, moonlight, starlight, sunlight, torchlight, twilight.

THINGS WHICH GIVE LIGHT: arc light, beacon, bulb, candelabra, candle, chandelier, fire, fluorescent lamp, headlamp, headlight, illuminations, lamp, lantern, laser, lighter, lighthouse, lightship, match, moon, neon light, pilot light, searchlight, spotlight, standard lamp, star, street light, strobe or stroboscope, sun, torch, traffic lights.

---

light verb **1** *to light a fire.* begin to burn, fire, ignite, kindle, set alight, set fire to, put a match to, switch on.
OPPOSITES: SEE **quench.**
2 *The bonfire lit the sky.* brighten, cast light on, floodlight, illuminate, irradiate, lighten, light up, shed light on, shine on.
OPPOSITES: SEE **obscure** verb.

lighten verb **1** *The bonfire lightened the sky.* SEE **light** verb.
2 *to lighten someone's burden.* SEE **ease** verb.

light-fingered adjective SEE **thieving** adjective.

light-headed adjective SEE **dizzy.**

light-hearted adjective SEE **cheerful.**

lighthouse noun beacon, light, lightship, warning-light.

lightweight adjective SEE **insignificant.**

like adjective SEE **similar.**

like verb *to like a person. to like food.* admire, appreciate, approve of, be interested in, be fond of, be partial to, be pleased by, delight in, enjoy, find pleasant, [*informal*] go in for, have a high regard for, SEE **love** verb, prefer, relish, [*informal*] take to, welcome.
I (you, she, etc.) would like fancy, SEE **want** verb, wish for.
OPPOSITES: SEE **dislike** verb.

likeable adjective *a likeable person.* attractive, charming, congenial, endearing, SEE **friendly**, lovable, nice, personable, pleasant, pleasing.
OPPOSITES: SEE **hateful.**

likelihood noun *Is there any likelihood of a change in the weather?* chance, hope, possibility, probability, prospect.

likely adjective **1** *a likely result.* anticipated, expected, feasible, foreseeable, plausible, possible, predictable, probable, reasonable, unsurprising.
2 *a likely candidate for election.* appropriate, convincing, credible, favourite, fitting, hopeful, qualified, suitable, [*informal*] tipped to win.
3 *He's likely to be late.* apt, disposed, inclined, liable, prone, willing.
OPPOSITES: SEE **unlikely.**

like-minded adjective SEE **compatible.**

liken verb SEE **compare.**

likeness noun **1** *The photo is a good likeness of her.* copy, depiction, image, picture, portrait, replica, representation, reproduction, study.
2 *There's a strong likeness between the two sisters.* affinity, compatibility, congruity, correspondence, resemblance, similarity.
OPPOSITES: SEE **difference.**

liking noun *a liking for classical music. a liking for sweet things.* affection, fondness, inclination, love, partiality, penchant, predilection, preference, propensity, [*informal*] soft spot, taste, weakness (*Chocolate is one of my weaknesses*).
OPPOSITES: SEE **dislike** noun.

lilliputian adjective SEE **small.**

lilting adjective *lilting music.* attractive, dance-like, light, pleasant, song-like, tuneful.

limb noun *limbs of an animal. a limb of a tree.* appendage, member, offshoot, projection.
VARIOUS LIMBS: arm, bough, branch, flipper, foreleg, forelimb, leg, wing.

limber adjective SEE **lithe.**

limber verb **to limber up** exercise, get ready, loosen up, prepare, warm up.

limbo noun **in limbo** *Neither party accepted her, so she was in limbo.* abandoned, forgotten, left out, neglected, neither one thing nor the other, unattached.
limbo dancing SEE **dance** noun.

limelight noun SEE **publicity**.

limit noun **1** *the limit of a territory.* border, boundary, bounds, brink, confines, edge, end, extent, extreme point, frontier, perimeter.
2 *a speed-limit. a limit on numbers.* ceiling, curb, cut-off point, deadline [=*a time-limit*], limitation, maximum, restraint, restriction, threshold.

limit verb *to limit someone's freedom. to limit numbers.* check, circumscribe, confine, control, curb, fix, put a limit on, ration, restrain, restrict.

limitation noun **1** *a limitation on numbers.* SEE **limit** noun.
2 *I know my limitations.* defect, deficiency, inadequacy, weakness.

limited adjective *limited funds. limited space.* circumscribed, controlled, cramped, defined, determinate, finite, fixed, inadequate, insufficient, narrow, rationed, reduced, restricted, short, small, unsatisfactory.
OPPOSITES: SEE **limitless**.

limitless adjective *limitless funds. limitless opportunities.* boundless, countless, endless, incalculable, inexhaustible, infinite, never-ending, renewable, unbounded, unending, unimaginable, unlimited, vast.
OPPOSITES: SEE **limited**.

limousine noun SEE **car**.

limp adjective *limp lettuce.* [*informal*] bendy, drooping, flabby, flexible, [*informal*] floppy, pliable, sagging, slack, soft, weak, wilting, yielding.
OPPOSITES: SEE **rigid**.

limp verb be lame, falter, hobble, hop, SEE **walk** verb.

limpid adjective SEE **transparent**.

linctus noun cough mixture, expectorant.

line noun **1** *a dirty line round the bath. a line drawn on paper.* band, borderline, boundary, contour, contour line, dash, mark, streak, striation, strip, stripe, stroke, trail.
2 *lines on a person's face.* crease, furrow, groove, score, wrinkle.
3 *Hold the end of this line.* cable, cord, flex, hawser, lead, rope, string, thread, wire.
4 *a line of cars. a line of police.* chain, column, cordon, crocodile, file, procession, queue, rank, row, series.
5 *a railway line.* branch, mainline, route, service, track.

line verb *to line a garment with fabric. to line a dish with pastry.* cover the inside, encase, insert a lining [SEE **lining**], reinforce.
to line up *They lined up in rows.* [*military command*] fall in, form a line, queue.

lineage noun SEE **ancestry**.

lineaments noun SEE **feature** noun.

liner noun VARIOUS SHIPS: SEE **vessel**.

linger verb **1** *The smell of burning lingered.* continue, endure, hang about, last, persist, remain, stay, survive.
OPPOSITES: SEE **disappear**.
2 *Don't linger outside in this cold weather.* dally, dawdle, delay, hang about, hover, idle, lag, loiter, stay behind, wait about.
OPPOSITES: SEE **hurry** verb.

lingerie noun SEE **underclothes**.

linguist noun interpreter, translator.

linguistic adjective LINGUISTIC TERMS: SEE **language**.

liniment noun cream, embrocation, lotion, ointment, salve.

lining noun *the lining of a garment. a lining of a container.* inner coat, inner layer, interfacing, liner, padding.

link noun **1** *a link between two things.* bond, connection, connector, coupling, SEE **fastener**, join, joint, linkage, tie, yoke.
2 *links between nations. a link between two groups.* alliance, association, communication, liaison, partnership, relationship, [*informal*] tie-up, twinning, union.

link verb **1** *to link one object with another.* amalgamate, attach, connect, couple, SEE **fasten**, interlink, join, merge, network (*networked microcomputers*), twin (*an English town twinned with a French town*), unite, yoke.
OPPOSITES: SEE **isolate, separate** verb.
2 *to link one idea with another.* associate, compare, make a link, relate, see a link.

linkage noun SEE **link** noun.

lion noun king of beasts, lioness.
RELATED ADJECTIVE: leonine.
OTHER ANIMALS: SEE **animal** noun.

lionize verb SEE **worship** verb.

lip noun *the lip of a cup.* brim, brink, edge, rim.

liquefy verb *Ice liquefies at 0°C.* become liquid, dissolve, SEE **liquidize**, melt, run, thaw.
OPPOSITES: SEE **solidify**.

liqueur noun DRINKS: SEE **drink** noun.

liquid adjective *a liquid substance.* aqueous, flowing, fluid, molten, running, [*informal*] runny, sloppy, [*informal*] sloshy, thin, watery, wet.
OPPOSITES: SEE **solid**.

liquid noun *He can only consume liquids.* fluid, liquid substance [SEE **liquid** adjective].

liquidate verb [Do not confuse with *liquidize.*] *to liquidate your enemy.* annihilate, destroy, [*informal*] do away with, [*informal*] get rid of, SEE **kill**, remove, silence, wipe out.

liquidize verb [Do not confuse with *liquidate.*] *to liquidize vegetables to make soup.* SEE **liquefy**, make into liquid, pulp.

liquor noun alcohol, spirits, strong drink.
DRINKS: SEE **drink** noun.

lisp verb SEE **speak**.

lissom adjective SEE **lithe**.

list noun *a list of names.* catalogue, column, directory, file, index, inventory, listing, register, roll, shopping-list, table.

list verb **1** *to list your possessions.* catalogue, file, index, itemize, make a list of [SEE **list** noun], record, register, tabulate, write down.
2 *to list to one side.* heel, incline, lean, slope, tilt, tip.

listen verb *Did you listen to what I said?* attend to, concentrate on, [*old-fashioned*] hark, hear, heed, eavesdrop, lend an ear to, overhear, pay attention to, take notice of.

listless adjective *listless in the heat.* apathetic, enervated, feeble, heavy, lackadaisical, languid, lazy, lethargic, lifeless, sluggish, tired, torpid, unenthusiastic, uninterested, weak, weary.
OPPOSITES: SEE **lively**.

litany noun SEE **prayer**.

literal adjective [Do not confuse with *literary.*] *the literal meaning of something.* close, plain, prosaic, strict, unimaginative, word for word.

literary adjective **1** *literary writing.* highly regarded, imaginative, ornate, polished, recognized as literature, [*uncomplimentary*] self-conscious, sophisticated, stylish.
2 *literary tastes.* cultured, educated, erudite, literate, refined, well-read, widely read.
a literary person [*informal*] bookworm, critic, reader, scholar, SEE **writer**.

literate adjective **1** *a literate person.* able to read and write, SEE **educated**.
2 *literate writing.* accurate, correct, properly spelt, readable, well-written.

literature noun **1** *literature about local tourist attractions.* brochures, handouts, leaflets, pamphlets, papers.
2 *English literature.* books, writings.

KINDS OF LITERATURE: autobiography, biography, children's literature, comedy, crime fiction, criticism, drama, epic, essay, fantasy, fiction, folk-tale, journalism, myth and legend, novels, parody, poetry, prose, romance, satire, science fiction, tragedy, tragi-comedy.

OTHER KINDS OF WRITING: SEE **writing**.

---

lithe adjective *a lithe gymnast.* agile, flexible, limber, lissom, loose-jointed, pliant, supple.

litigation noun LEGAL TERMS: SEE **law**.

litter noun **1** *Clear up the litter.* bits and pieces, clutter, debris, garbage, jumble, junk, mess, odds and ends, refuse, rubbish, trash, waste.
2 *a litter of puppies.* SEE **family**.

litter verb *to litter a room with papers.* clutter, fill with litter [SEE **litter** noun], make untidy, [*informal*] mess up, scatter, strew.

little adjective SEE **small**.

liturgy noun SEE **service** noun.

live adjective **1** *live animals.* SEE **living**.
2 *a live fire.* SEE **burning**.
3 *a live volcano.* active, functioning.
4 *a live issue.* contemporary, current, important, pressing, relevant, topical, vital.

live verb **1** *Will these plants live through the winter?* continue, exist, flourish, last, remain, stay alive, survive.
OPPOSITES: SEE **die**.
2 *I can live on £20 a week.* [*informal*] get along, keep going, make a living, pay the bills, subsist.
to live in *I live in a flat.* dwell in, inhabit, occupy, reside in.
to live on *What do polar bears live on?* eat, feed on.

livelihood noun SEE **living** noun, **work** noun.

liveliness noun activity, animation, boisterousness, bustle, dynamism, energy, enthusiasm, exuberance, [*informal*] go, gusto, high spirits, spirit, sprightliness, verve, vigour, vitality, vivacity, zeal.
OPPOSITES: SEE **inertia**, **tiredness**.

lively adjective *lively kittens. a lively party. a lively expression.* active, agile, alert, animated, boisterous, bubbly, bustling, busy, cheerful, colourful, dashing, energetic, enthusiastic, exciting, expressive, exuberant, frisky, gay, SEE **happy**, high-spirited, irrepressible, jaunty, jolly, merry, nimble, [*informal*] perky, playful, quick, spirited, sprightly, stimulating, vigorous, vital, vivacious, [*informal*] zippy.
OPPOSITES: SEE **apathetic, tired.**

liven verb SEE **animate** verb.

livery noun uniform.

livestock noun cattle, farm animals.

livid adjective **1** *a livid colour.* bluish-grey.
2 *livid with anger.* SEE **angry.**

living adjective *living creatures.* SEE **active**, alive, animate, breathing, existing, live, sentient, surviving, vigorous, vital.
OPPOSITES: SEE **dead, extinct.**

living noun *She makes a living from painting.* income, livelihood, occupation, subsistence, way of life.

living-room drawing-room, lounge, sitting-room.
OTHER ROOMS: SEE **room.**

lizard noun RELATED ADJECTIVE: saurian.

load noun **1** *a load of goods.* cargo, consignment, freight, [*formal*] lading, lorry-load, shipment, van-load.
2 *a heavy load of responsibility.* burden, millstone, onus, weight.

load verb **1** *We loaded the luggage into the car.* fill, heap, pack, pile, ply, stow.
2 *They loaded me with their shopping.* burden, encumber, weigh down.

loaded adjective **1** *loaded with gifts.* burdened, inundated, laden, piled high, weighed down.
2 *a loaded argument.* biased, distorted, emotive, one-sided, partial, prejudiced, unfair.
3 [*informal*] *He can afford it—he's loaded!* SEE **wealthy.**

loaf noun SEE **bread.**

loaf verb *to loaf about.* SEE **lounge** verb.

loafer noun idler, [*informal*] good-for-nothing, layabout, [*informal*] lazybones, lounger, shirker, [*informal*] skiver, wastrel.

loam noun *Plant the seeds in good loam.* SEE **soil** noun.

loan noun *I need a loan to buy a car.* advance, credit, mortgage.

loan verb *Can you loan me 50p?* SEE **lend.**

loath adjective SEE **unwilling.**

loathe verb *Our dog loathes cats.* SEE **hate** verb.

loathing noun SEE **hatred.**

loathsome adjective SEE **hateful.**

lob verb *to lob a ball in the air.* bowl, cast, chuck, fling, loft, pitch, shy, sling, throw, toss.

lobby noun **1** *Wait for me in the lobby.* ante-room, entrance hall, foyer, hall, hallway, porch, vestibule.
2 *the environmental lobby. the road-users lobby.* campaign, campaigners, pressure-group, supporters.

lobby verb *to lobby your MP.* persuade, petition, pressurize, try to influence, urge.

local adjective **1** *local amenities.* nearby, neighbourhood, neighbouring, serving the locality [SEE **locality**].
2 *a matter of local interest.* community, limited, narrow, parochial, particular, provincial, regional.
OPPOSITES: SEE **general, national.**

local noun **1** [*informal*] *the local.* SEE **pub.**
2 *If you want to know the way, ask one of the locals.* inhabitant, person from the locality [SEE **locality**], resident.

locality noun *There are good shops in our locality.* area, catchment area, community, district, location, neighbourhood, parish, region, residential area, town, vicinity, zone.

localize verb *The authorities tried to localize the epidemic.* concentrate, confine, contain, enclose, keep within bounds, limit, narrow down, pin down, restrict.
OPPOSITES: SEE **spread** verb.

locate verb **1** *I located the book I wanted in the library.* detect, discover, find, identify, [*informal*] run to earth, search out, track down, unearth.
OPPOSITES: SEE **lose.**
2 *They located the new offices in the middle of town.* build, establish, find a place for, found, place, position, put, set up, site, situate, station.

location noun **1** *Can you find the location on the map?* locale, SEE **locality**, place, point, position, site, situation, spot, venue, whereabouts.
2 *The film was shot in real locations.* background, scene, setting.

loch noun SEE **lake.**

lock noun **1** *a lock on a door.* bolt, catch, clasp, SEE **fastening**, latch, padlock.
2 *a lock of hair.* SEE **hair.**

lock verb *to lock a door.* bolt, close, SEE **fasten**, seal, secure, shut.
to lock in, to lock up SEE **imprison.**
to lock out SEE **exclude.**

locker noun SEE **cupboard**.
locomotive noun engine.
locum noun SEE **deputy** noun.
locus noun SEE **position** noun.
lodestar noun SEE **star**.
lodge noun SEE **house** noun.
lodge verb **1** *to lodge homeless families in a hostel.* accommodate, billet, board, SEE **house** verb, put up.
2 *to lodge in a motel.* reside, stay.
3 *to lodge a complaint.* file, make formally, put on record, register, submit.
lodger noun *a lodger in a guest-house.* boarder, guest, inmate, paying guest, resident, tenant.
lodgings noun accommodation, apartments, billet, boarding-house, [*informal*] digs, lodging-house, [*informal*] pad, quarters, rooms, [*informal*] squat, temporary home.
loft noun attic.
lofty adjective *a lofty spire.* SEE **high**.
log noun **1** *logs to burn.* timber, wood.
2 *the log of a voyage.* account, diary, journal, record.
loggerheads adjective **to be at loggerheads** SEE **quarrel** verb.
logic noun *I admired the logic of his argument.* clarity, logical thinking [SEE **logical**], rationality, reasoning, sense, validity.
logical adjective *a logical argument.* clear, cogent, coherent, consistent, intelligent, methodical, rational, reasonable, sensible, sound, systematic, valid.
OPPOSITES: SEE **illogical**.
logistics noun SEE **organization**.
logo noun SEE **symbol**.
loiter verb *We'll be left behind if we loiter.* be slow, dally, dawdle, hang back, linger, [*informal*] loaf about, [*informal*] mess about, skulk, [*informal*] stand about, straggle.
loll verb SEE **lean** verb.
lone adjective *a lone walker on the hills. a lone voice.* isolated, SEE **lonely**, separate, single, solitary, solo, unaccompanied.
lonely adjective **1** *I was lonely while my friends were away.* alone, forlorn, friendless, lonesome, neglected, SEE **sad**, solitary.
2 *a lonely farmhouse. a lonely road.* abandoned, desolate, distant, far-away, forsaken, isolated, [*informal*] off the beaten track, out of the way, remote, secluded, unfrequented, uninhabited.
loner noun hermit, outsider, recluse.
lonesome adjective SEE **lonely**.
long adjective *a long piece of rope. a long wait.* drawn out, elongated, endless, extended, extensive, interminable, lasting, lengthy, longish, prolonged, protracted, slow, stretched, time-consuming, unending.
a long face SEE **expression**.
long verb **to long for** [*informal*] be dying for (*I'm dying for a drink*), desire, fancy, hanker after, have a longing for [SEE **longing**], hunger after, [*informal*] itch for, lust after, pine for, thirst for, want, wish for, yearn for.
longevity noun long life, old age.
longing noun appetite, craving, desire, hunger, [*informal*] itch, need, thirst, urge, wish, yearning, [*informal*] yen.
longitudinal adjective lengthwise, longways.
long-lasting, long-lived adjectives SEE **lasting**.
long-playing record noun album, LP, SEE **record** noun.
long-standing adjective SEE **lasting**.
long-suffering adjective SEE **patient** adjective.
long-winded adjective *a long-winded speaker.* boring, diffuse, dreary, dry, garrulous, lengthy, long, rambling, tedious, uninteresting, verbose, wordy.
loo noun SEE **lavatory**.
look noun **1** *Give me a look. Take a look.* glance, glimpse, observation, peek, peep, sight, [*informal*] squint, view.
2 *She has a friendly look.* [*often plural*] *He's vain about his looks.* air, appearance, aspect, bearing, complexion, countenance, demeanour, expression, face, manner, mien.
look verb **1 to look at** behold, [*informal*] cast your eye over, consider, contemplate, examine, eye, gape at, [*informal*] gawp at, gaze at, glance at, glimpse, goggle at, inspect, observe, ogle, peek at, peep at, peer at, read, regard, scan, scrutinize, see, skim through (*I'll just skim through the book*), squint at, stare at, study, survey, take a look at, take note of, view, watch.
2 *Our house looks south.* face, overlook.
3 *You look pleased.* appear, seem.
to look after SEE **care** verb (**to care for**).
to look down on SEE **despise**.
to look for SEE **seek**.
to look into SEE **investigate**.
to look out *If you don't look out, you'll get wet.* be vigilant, beware, keep an eye open, keep an eye out, pay attention, watch out.
to look up to SEE **admire**.

looking-glass noun mirror.

look-out noun guard, sentinel, sentry, watchman.

loom verb *A castle loomed on the skyline.* appear, arise, dominate, emerge, materialize, rise, stand out, stick up, threaten, tower.

loony adjective SEE **mad**.

loop noun *a loop in a rope.* bend, circle, coil, curl, hoop, kink, noose, ring, turn, twist.

loop verb *Loop the rope round the post.* bend, coil, curl, entwine, make a loop [SEE **loop** noun], turn, twist, wind.

loophole noun *a loophole in the law.* escape, [*informal*] get-out, [*informal*] let-out.

loose adjective **1** *loose stones. loose wires.* detachable, detached, disconnected, insecure, loosened, movable, shaky, unattached, unfastened, unsteady, untied, wobbly.
2 *loose animals.* at large, free, roaming, uncaged, unconfined, unrestricted.
OPPOSITES: SEE **secure** adjective.
3 *loose clothing.* baggy, [*informal*] floppy, loose-fitting, slack, unbuttoned.
OPPOSITES: SEE **tight**.
4 *a loose agreement. a loose translation.* diffuse, general, ill-defined, imprecise, inexact, informal, vague.
OPPOSITES: SEE **precise**.
5 *loose behaviour.* SEE **immoral**.

loose verb *to loose an animal from its cage.* SEE **free** verb.

loosen verb **1** *Loosen the knots.* ease off, free, let go, loose, make loose, relax, release, slacken, undo, unfasten, unloose, untie.
2 *Check that the knots haven't loosened.* become loose, come adrift, open up.
OPPOSITES: SEE **tighten**.

loot noun *thieves' loot.* booty, contraband, haul, [*informal*] ill-gotten gains, plunder, prize, spoils, [*informal*] swag, takings.

loot verb *Rioters looted the shops.* pillage, plunder, raid, ransack, rifle, rob, steal from.

lop verb *to lop off a branch.* SEE **cut** verb.

lope verb SEE **walk** verb.

lopsided adjective *The lopsided load on the lorry looked dangerous.* askew, asymmetrical, [*informal*] cock-eyed, crooked, tilting, unbalanced, uneven.

Several English words, including *colloquial, eloquent,* and *loquacious,* are related to Latin *loqui = to speak.*

---

loquacious adjective SEE **talkative**.

lord noun noble, peer, [*old-fashioned*] thane.
VARIOUS TITLES: SEE **title** noun.

lordly adjective SEE **bossy**.

lore noun SEE **knowledge**.

lorry noun VARIOUS VEHICLES: SEE **vehicle**.

lose verb **1** *to lose something or someone.* be deprived of, be unable to find, cease to have, drop, find yourself without, forfeit, forget, leave behind, mislay, misplace, miss, stray from, suffer the loss of [SEE **loss**].
OPPOSITES: SEE **find, gain** verb.
2 *to lose in a game or race.* be defeated, capitulate, [*informal*] come to grief, fail, get beaten, [*informal*] get thrashed, suffer defeat.
OPPOSITES: SEE **win**.

loser noun the defeated, runner-up, the vanquished.
OPPOSITES: SEE **winner**.

losing adjective *the losing side.* bottom, defeated, last, unsuccessful, vanquished.
OPPOSITES: SEE **winning**.

loss noun bereavement, damage, defeat, deficit, deprivation, destruction, disappearance, failure, forfeiture, impairment, privation.
OPPOSITES: SEE **gain** noun.
losses *losses in battle.* casualties, deaths, death toll, fatalities.

lost adjective **1** *lost property. lost animals.* abandoned, disappeared, gone, irrecoverable, left behind, mislaid, misplaced, strayed, untraceable, vanished.
2 *lost in thought.* absorbed, day-dreaming, dreamy, distracted, engrossed, preoccupied, rapt.
3 *lost souls.* corrupt, damned, SEE **wicked**.

lot noun **1 a lot of, lots of** *a lot of food. lots of money.* SEE **plenty**.
2 the lot *Give her the lot.* all, everything.
3 *a lot in an auction sale.* SEE **item**.
to draw lots SEE **choose, gamble** verb.

lotion noun balm, cream, embrocation, liniment, ointment, salve.

lottery noun gamble.

loud adjective **1** *loud noise.* audible, blaring, booming, clamorous, clarion (*a clarion call*), deafening, ear-splitting, echoing, fortissimo, high, noisy, penetrating, piercing, raucous, resounding, reverberating, rowdy, shrieking, shrill,

stentorian, strident, thundering, thunderous, uproarious, vociferous.
OPPOSITES: SEE **quiet**.
2 *loud colours.* SEE **gaudy**.

lounge noun drawing-room, living-room, sitting-room.
OTHER ROOMS: SEE **room**.

lounge verb *to lounge about. to lounge in a chair.* be idle, be lazy, dawdle, hang about, idle, [*informal*] kill time, laze, loaf, lie around, loiter, [*informal*] loll about, [*informal*] mess about, [*informal*] mooch about, relax, [*informal*] skive, slouch, slump, sprawl, stand about, take it easy, waste time.

lour verb SEE **frown** verb.

lousy adjective [*slang*] *What lousy weather!* SEE **nasty**.

lout noun *ill-mannered lout.* boor, churl, rude person [SEE **rude**], oaf, [*informal*] yob.

loutish adjective *loutish behaviour.* SEE **rude**.

lovable adjective *Teddy bears are lovable toys.* adorable, appealing, attractive, charming, cuddly, enchanting, endearing, engaging, likeable, lovely, pleasing, taking, winning.
OPPOSITES: SEE **hateful**.

love noun **1** *Giving flowers is one way to show your love.* admiration, adoration, affection, ardour, desire, devotion, fondness, friendship, infatuation, liking, passion.
2 *My dearest love.* beloved, darling, dear, dearest, loved one, SEE **lover**.
in love with devoted to, enamoured with, fond of, infatuated with.
to make love court, flirt, have sexual intercourse [SEE **sex**], philander, woo.
love affair affair, courtship, intrigue, liaison, relationship, romance.
RELATED ADJECTIVES: amatory, erotic.

love verb **1** *to love someone.* admire, adore, be charmed by, be in love with [SEE **love** noun (**in love with**)], care for, cherish, desire, dote on, fancy, feel love for [SEE **love** noun], have a passion for, idolize, lust after, treasure, value, want, worship.
OPPOSITES: SEE **hate** verb.
2 *I love fish and chips.* SEE **like** verb.

loved adjective *loved ones.* adored, beloved, darling, dear, idolized, valued.

loveless adjective *a loveless relationship.* cold, frigid, heartless, passionless, undemonstrative, unfeeling, unloving, unresponsive.
OPPOSITES: SEE **loving**.

lovely adjective *a lovely day. lovely flowers.* appealing, attractive, SEE **beautiful**, charming, delightful, enjoyable, fine, nice, pleasant, pretty, sweet.
OPPOSITES: SEE **nasty**.

love-making noun courting, courtship, kissing, petting, SEE **sex**, wooing.

lover noun [*old-fashioned*] admirer, boyfriend, companion, concubine, [*male*] fiancé, [*female*] fiancée, [*old-fashioned*] follower, friend, gigolo, girlfriend, mistress, [*old-fashioned*] paramour, suitor, sweetheart, valentine, wooer.

lovesick adjective frustrated, languishing, lovelorn, pining.

loving adjective *loving kisses. a loving nature.* affectionate, amorous, ardent, demonstrative, devoted, doting, fatherly, fond, SEE **friendly**, kind, maternal, motherly, passionate, paternal, tender, warm.
OPPOSITES: SEE **loveless**.

low adjective **1** *low land.* flat, low-lying, sunken.
OPPOSITES: SEE **high**.
2 *a low position.* abject, base, degraded, humble, inferior, junior, lower, lowly, menial, modest, servile.
OPPOSITES: SEE **superior**.
3 *low behaviour.* churlish, coarse, common, cowardly, crude, [*old-fashioned*] dastardly, disreputable, ignoble, SEE **immoral**, mean, nasty, vulgar, wicked.
OPPOSITES: SEE **noble**.
4 *low whispers.* muffled, muted, pianissimo, quiet, soft, subdued.
OPPOSITES: SEE **loud**.
5 *a low note.* bass, deep.
OPPOSITES: SEE **high**.
a low point nadir, trough.
in low spirits SEE **sad**.

low verb *Cows were lowing.* VARIOUS SOUNDS: SEE **sound** noun.

lowbrow adjective **1** *lowbrow literature.* easy, popular, [*uncomplimentary*] rubbish, simple, straightforward, [*uncomplimentary*] trashy, undemanding.
2 *lowbrow music.* pop, popular.
3 *a lowbrow person.* ordinary, simple, [*uncomplimentary*] uncultured, unpretentious, unsophisticated.
OPPOSITES: SEE **highbrow**.

lower verb **1** *to lower a flag.* dip, drop, haul down, let down, take down.
2 *to lower prices.* bring down, cut, decrease, lessen, reduce, [*informal*] slash.
3 *to lower the volume.* abate, quieten, tone down, turn down.
OPPOSITES: SEE **raise**.
4 *He's too high-and-mighty to lower himself by coming out with us.* degrade, demean, discredit, disgrace, humiliate, stoop.

lowly adjective *a lowly position in life.* base, humble, insignificant, low, lowborn, meek, modest.

loyal adjective *a loyal supporter.* constant, dependable, devoted, dutiful, faithful, honest, patriotic, reliable, sincere, staunch, steadfast, true, trustworthy, trusty, unswerving.
OPPOSITES: SEE **disloyal**.

loyalty noun allegiance, constancy, dependability, devotion, faithfulness, fealty, fidelity, honesty, patriotism, reliability, staunchness, steadfastness, trustworthiness.
OPPOSITES: SEE **disloyalty**.

lozenge noun **1** *a lozenge to suck.* cough sweet, pastille.
2 *in the shape of a lozenge.* diamond, rhombus.

LP SEE **long-playing record**.

lubricate verb grease, oil.

lucid adjective *a lucid explanation.* SEE **clear** adjective.

luck noun **1** *I found my watch by luck.* accident, [*informal*] break (*a lucky break*), chance, coincidence, destiny, fate, [*informal*] fluke, fortune.
2 *I had a bit of luck today.* good fortune, happiness, prosperity, success.

luckless adjective SEE **unlucky**.

lucky adjective **1** *a lucky discovery.* accidental, chance, [*informal*] fluky, fortuitous, providential, timely, unintended, unintentional, unplanned, welcome.
OPPOSITES: SEE **intentional**.
2 *a lucky person.* favoured, fortunate, SEE **happy**, successful.
3 *3 is my lucky number.* auspicious.
OPPOSITES: SEE **unlucky**.

lucrative adjective SEE **profitable**.

lucre noun SEE **money**.

ludicrous adjective SEE **ridiculous**.

lug verb SEE **carry**.

luggage noun baggage, bags, belongings, boxes, cases, impedimenta, paraphernalia, things.

ITEMS OF LUGGAGE: bag, basket, box, briefcase, case, chest, hamper, handbag, hand luggage, haversack, holdall, knapsack, pannier, [*old-fashioned*] portmanteau, purse, rucksack, satchel, suitcase, trunk, wallet.

---

lugubrious adjective SEE **mournful**.

lukewarm adjective **1** *lukewarm water.* tepid, warm.
2 *a lukewarm response.* apathetic, cool, half-hearted, unenthusiastic.

lull noun *a lull in a storm.* break, calm, gap, interval, [*informal*] let-up, pause, respite, rest, silence.

lull verb *to lull someone to sleep.* calm, hush, pacify, quell, quieten, soothe, subdue, tranquillize.

lumber noun **1** *cutting lumber in the forest.* timber, wood.
2 *We cleared the lumber out of the garage.* bits and pieces, clutter, jumble, junk, odds and ends, rubbish, trash.

lumber verb **1** [*informal*] *They lumbered me with the clearing up.* SEE **burden** verb.
2 *A rhinoceros lumbered towards them.* blunder, move clumsily, shamble, trudge.

luminous adjective *a luminous dial.* glowing, luminescent, lustrous, phosphorescent, shining.

lump noun **1** *a lump of chocolate. a lump of soap.* ball, bar, bit, block, cake, chunk, clod, clot, [*informal*] dollop, gobbet, hunk, ingot, mass, nugget, piece, slab, [*informal*] wodge.
2 *a lump on the head.* bulge, bump, hump, knob, node, nodule, protrusion, protuberance, spot, swelling, tumour.

lump verb **to lump together** SEE **combine**.
to lump it SEE **tolerate**.

lunacy noun SEE **madness**.

lunatic adjective SEE **mad**.

lunatic noun SEE **madman**.

lunch, luncheon nouns OTHER MEALS: SEE **meal**.

lung noun RELATED ADJECTIVE: pulmonary.

lunge verb **1** *to lunge with a sword.* jab, stab, strike, thrust.
2 *to lunge after someone.* charge, dash, dive, lurch, pounce, rush, throw yourself.

lurch noun **to leave in the lurch** SEE **abandon**.

lurch verb *to lurch from side to side.* heave, lean, list, lunge, pitch, plunge, reel, roll, stagger, stumble, sway, totter, wallow.

lure verb *to lure someone into a trap.* allure, attract, bait, coax, decoy, draw, entice, inveigle, invite, lead on, persuade, seduce, tempt.

lurid adjective **1** *lurid colours.* SEE **gaudy**.
2 *lurid details.* SEE **sensational**.

lurk verb *to lurk in wait for prey.* crouch, hide, lie in wait, lie low, skulk, wait.

luscious adjective *luscious peaches.* appetizing, delicious, juicy, succulent, sweet, tasty.

lush adjective **1** *lush grass.* SEE **luxuriant**.
2 *lush surroundings.* SEE **luxurious**.

lust noun **1** *sexual lust.* carnality, lasciviousness, lechery, libido, licentiousness, passion, sensuality.
2 *a lust for power.* appetite, craving, desire, greed, itch, hunger, longing.

lustful adjective carnal, lascivious, lecherous, libidinous, licentious, passionate, [*informal*] randy, sensual, SEE **sexy**.

lustrous adjective SEE **bright**.

lusty adjective SEE **vigorous**.

luxuriant adjective *luxuriant growth.* abundant, ample, copious, dense, exuberant, fertile, flourishing, green, lush, opulent, plenteous, plentiful, profuse, prolific, rich, teeming, thick, thriving, verdant.
OPPOSITES: SEE **barren, sparse**.

luxuriate verb **to luxuriate in** SEE **enjoy**.

luxurious adjective *luxurious surroundings.* comfortable, costly, expensive, grand, hedonistic, lavish, lush, magnificent, [*informal*] plush, rich, self-indulgent, splendid, sumptuous, voluptuous.
OPPOSITES: SEE **spartan**.

luxury noun *a life of luxury.* affluence, comfort, ease, enjoyment, extravagance, hedonism, high living, indulgence, pleasure, relaxation, self-indulgence, splendour, sumptuousness, voluptuousness.

lying adjective *a lying witness.* crooked, deceitful, dishonest, double-dealing, false, inaccurate, insincere, mendacious, perfidious, unreliable, untrustworthy, untruthful.
OPPOSITES: SEE **truthful**.

lying noun deceit, dishonesty, falsehood, mendacity, [*formal*] perjury.

lynch verb SEE **kill**.

lyric noun *the lyric of a song.* SEE **poem**, words.

lyrical adjective *a lyrical tune. a lyrical description.* emotional, expressive, inspired, poetic, song-like.

M

mac noun SEE **mackintosh**.

macabre adjective *He takes a macabre interest in graveyards.* eerie, ghoulish, SEE **gruesome**, morbid, sick, unhealthy, weird.

macaroni noun SEE **pasta**.

machiavellian adjective SEE **crafty, wicked**.

machinations noun SEE **scheme** noun.

machine noun apparatus, appliance, contraption, contrivance, device, engine, gadget, instrument, SEE **machinery**, mechanism, robot, tool.

machinery noun **1** *machinery in a factory.* equipment, gear, machines [SEE **machine**], plant.
2 *machinery for electing a new leader.* constitution, method, organization, procedure, structure, system.

macho noun SEE **manly**.

mackintosh noun anorak, cape, mac, raincoat, sou'wester, waterproof.
OTHER COATS: SEE **coat** noun.

mad adjective **1** [Many of these words are used informally. Though they may be used jokingly, they are often offensive.] *a mad person. mad behaviour.* batty, berserk, bonkers, certified, crackers, crazed, crazy, daft, delirious, demented, deranged, disordered, dotty, eccentric, fanatical, frantic, frenzied, hysterical, insane, irrational, loony, lunatic, maniacal, manic, mental, mentally unstable, moonstruck, [*Latin*] non compos mentis, nutty, off your head, off your rocker, out of your mind, possessed, potty, [*formal*] psychotic, queer in the head, round the bend, round the twist, screwy, touched, unbalanced, unhinged, unstable, up the pole, wild.
OPPOSITES: SEE **sane**.
2 *a mad sense of humour.* SEE **absurd**.
3 *mad with rage.* SEE **angry**.
4 *mad about snooker.* SEE **enthusiastic**.
a mad person SEE **madman, madwoman**.
to be mad [*informal*] have a screw loose, rave.

madam, madame nouns SEE **title** noun, **woman**.

madcap adjective SEE **impulsive**.

madden verb *The noise maddened me.* anger, craze, derange, enrage, exasperate, incense, inflame, infuriate, irritate, make mad [SEE **mad**], provoke, [*informal*] send round the bend, unhinge, vex.

madhouse noun SEE **asylum**.

madman, madwoman nouns [Though these words may be used jokingly, they are often offensive.] [*informal*] crackpot, [*informal*] crank, eccentric, lunatic, mad person [SEE **mad**], maniac, [*informal*] mental case, [*informal*] nutcase, [*informal*] nutter, [*formal*] psychopath, [*formal*] psychotic.

madness noun delirium, derangement, eccentricity, frenzy, hysteria, insanity, lunacy, mania, mental illness, psychosis.

maelstrom noun SEE **confusion**, vortex, whirlpool.

maestro noun VARIOUS MUSICIANS: SEE **music**.

magazine noun **1** *a magazine to read.* comic, journal, monthly, newspaper, pamphlet, paper, periodical, publication, quarterly, weekly.
2 *a magazine of weapons.* ammunition dump, arsenal, storehouse.

maggot noun caterpillar, grub, larva.

magic adjective *a magic trick.* conjuring, magical, miraculous, supernatural.

magic noun **1** *magic performed by witches.* black magic, charms, enchantment, hocus-pocus, incantation, [*informal*] mumbo-jumbo, necromancy, occultism, sorcery, spell, voodoo, witchcraft, witchery, wizardry.
2 *magic performed by a conjuror.* conjuring, illusion, legerdemain, sleight of hand, trick, trickery.
to do magic bewitch, cast spells, charm, conjure, enchant, work miracles.

magician noun conjuror, enchanter, enchantress, SEE **entertainer**, illusionist, sorcerer, [*old-fashioned*] warlock, witch, witch-doctor, wizard.

magisterial adjective SEE **bossy**.

magistrate noun LEGAL TERMS: SEE **law**.

magnanimous adjective SEE **generous**.

magnate noun SEE **businessman**.

magnetic adjective *a magnetic personality.* alluring, SEE **attractive**, captivating, charismatic, charming, compelling, fascinating, hypnotic, irresistible, seductive.
OPPOSITES: SEE **repulsive**.

magnetism noun *personal magnetism.* allure, appeal, attractiveness, charisma, charm, fascination, lure, power, seductiveness.

magnetize verb SEE **attract**.

magnificent adjective *a magnificent palace. magnificent mountain scenery.* SEE **beautiful**, excellent, glorious, gorgeous, grand, grandiose, imposing, impressive, majestic, marvellous, noble, opulent, [*informal*] posh, regal, spectacular, splendid, stately, sumptuous, superb, wonderful.
OPPOSITES: SEE **ordinary, paltry**.

magnify verb **1** *to magnify an image.* amplify, augment, [*informal*] blow up, enlarge, expand, increase, intensify, make larger.
OPPOSITES: SEE **reduce**.
2 *to magnify difficulties.* [*informal*] blow up out of all proportion, dramatize, exaggerate, inflate, make too much of, maximize, overdo, overestimate, overstate.
OPPOSITES: SEE **minimize**.
magnifying glass SEE **optical** (**optical instruments**).

magnitude noun SEE **size**.

maid noun SEE **girl, servant**.

maiden noun SEE **girl**.

mail noun **1** *The postman brings the mail.* correspondence, letters, parcels, post.
2 *chain-mail.* armour, protection.

mail verb *The shop mailed the book to me.* dispatch, forward, post, send.

maim verb *He was maimed in an accident.* cripple, disable, handicap, injure, mutilate, SEE **wound** verb.

main adjective *the main ingredients. the main point of a story.* basic, biggest, cardinal, central, chief, crucial, dominant, essential, foremost, fundamental, greatest, important, largest, leading, major, outstanding, predominant, preeminent, prevailing, primary, prime, principal, special, supreme, top (*the top attraction*).
OPPOSITES: SEE **unimportant**.

mainly adverb chiefly, especially, generally, in the main, largely, mostly, normally, on the whole, predominantly, primarily, principally, usually.

mainstream adjective SEE **conventional, orthodox**.

maintain verb **1** *to maintain a constant speed.* carry on, continue, hold to, keep up, retain, stick to.
2 *to maintain a car in good order.* keep in good condition, look after, preserve, service, take care of.
3 *to maintain a family.* feed, keep, pay for, provide for, support.
4 *to maintain that you are innocent.* affirm, allege, argue, assert, aver, claim, contend, declare, insist, proclaim, profess, state, uphold.

maintenance noun **1** *the maintenance of a house or a car.* care, conservation, looking after, preservation, repairs, servicing, upkeep.
2 *He pays maintenance to his ex-wife.* alimony, allowance, subsistence.

maisonette noun SEE **house** noun.

maize noun corn on the cob, sweetcorn.
OTHER CEREALS: SEE **cereal**.

majestic adjective *a majestic palace.* august, awe-inspiring, awesome, dignified, distinguished, grand, imperial, imposing, impressive, kingly, lordly, magnificent, monumental, noble, pompous, princely, regal, royal, SEE **splendid**, stately.

majesty noun **1** *the majesty of the mountains.* SEE **splendour**.
2 *His Majesty the King.* SEE **royalty**.

major adjective *major roadworks. a major city, a major operation.* bigger, chief, considerable, extensive, great, greater, important, key, large, larger, leading, outstanding, principal, serious, significant.
OPPOSITES: SEE **minor**.

majority noun **1** *The majority voted to go back to work.* bulk, greater number, preponderance.
2 *the age of majority.* adulthood, coming of age, manhood, maturity, womanhood.
OPPOSITES: SEE **minority**.
to be in the majority be greater, dominate, outnumber, predominate, preponderate, prevail.

make noun *What make is your car?* brand, kind, model, sort, type, variety.

make verb **1** *to make furniture. to make a success of something.* assemble, beget, bring about, build, compose, constitute, construct, create, do, engender, erect, execute, fabricate, fashion, forge, form, generate, invent, make up, manufacture, mass-produce, originate, produce, think up.
[*Make* is used in many other senses. We give only a selection of them here.]
2 *to make a cake.* SEE **cook** verb.
3 *to make clothes.* knit, [*informal*] run up, sew, weave.
4 *to make a sculpture.* carve, cast, model, mould, shape.
5 *to make a speech.* deliver, pronounce, speak, utter.
6 *to make someone captain.* appoint, elect, nominate, ordain.
7 *to make a P into a B.* alter, change, convert, modify, transform, turn.
8 *to make a fortune.* earn, gain, get, obtain, receive.
9 *to make a good games player.* become, change into, grow into, turn into.
10 *to make your objective.* accomplish, achieve, arrive at, attain, catch, get to, reach, win.
11 *2 and 2 make 4.* add up to, amount to, come to, total.
12 *to make rules.* agree, arrange, codify, establish, decide on, draw up, fix, write.
13 *to make someone happy.* cause to become, render.
14 *to make trouble.* bring about, carry out, cause, give rise to, provoke, result in.
15 *to make someone do something.* coerce, compel, constrain, force, induce, oblige, order, pressurize, prevail on, require.
to make amends SEE **compensate**.
to make believe SEE **imagine**.
to make fun of, to make jokes about SEE **ridicule**.
to make good SEE **prosper**.
to make love SEE **love** noun (**make love**).
to make off SEE **depart**.
to make off with SEE **steal**.
to make out, to make sense of SEE **understand**.
to make up SEE **invent**.
to make up for SEE **compensate**.
to make up your mind SEE **decide**.

make-believe adjective *a make-believe story.* fanciful, fantasy, feigned, imaginary, made-up, mock, [*childish*] pretend, pretended, sham, simulated, unreal.

maker noun architect, author, builder, creator, manufacturer, originator, producer.

makeshift adjective SEE **temporary**.

make-up noun SEE **cosmetics**.

A number of English words, including *maladjusted, malefactor, malevolent, malnutrition*, etc., are related to Latin *male- = badly, evilly, ill.* Contrast words beginning *bene-*, such as *benefactor, benevolent*, etc.

---

maladjusted adjective *a maladjusted child.* disturbed, muddled, neurotic, unbalanced.

maladroit adjective SEE **clumsy**.

malady, malaise nouns SEE **illness**.

malcontent noun SEE **rebel** noun.

male adjective *male characteristics.* SEE **manly, masculine**.
OPPOSITES: SEE **female**.
MALE HUMAN BEINGS: SEE **boy, man**.
MALE CREATURES: SEE **animal** noun.

malediction noun SEE **curse** noun.

malefactor noun SEE **wrongdoer**.

malevolent adjective SEE **malicious**.

malformation noun SEE **deformity**.

malfunction noun SEE **fault** noun.

malice noun animosity, [*informal*] bitchiness, bitterness, [*informal*] cattiness, enmity, hatred, hostility, ill-will, malevolence, maliciousness, malignity, nastiness, rancour, spite, spitefulness, vengefulness, venom, viciousness, vindictiveness.

malicious adjective *malicious remarks.* [*informal*] bitchy, bitter, [*informal*] catty, evil, evil-minded, hateful, ill-natured, malevolent, malignant, mischievous, nasty, rancorous, revengeful, sly, spiteful, vengeful, venomous, vicious, villainous, vindictive, wicked.
OPPOSITES: SEE **benevolent, kind** adjective.

malignant adjective **1** *a malignant disease.* dangerous, destructive, harmful, injurious, poisonous, spreading, [*informal*] terminal, uncontrollable, virulent.
OPPOSITE: benign.
2 *malignant intentions.* SEE **malicious**.

malinger verb SEE **shirk**.

malleable adjective *a malleable substance.* ductile, plastic, pliable, soft, tractable, workable.
OPPOSITES: SEE **brittle**.

mallet noun hammer.

malnutrition noun famine, hunger, starvation, under-nourishment.

malpractice noun SEE **wrongdoing**.

maltreat verb SEE **harm** verb.

mammal noun VARIOUS ANIMALS: SEE **animal**.

mammoth adjective SEE **large**.

man noun **1** =*human beings of either sex.* SEE **mankind**.
2 =*male human being.* bachelor, boy, [informal] bloke, boyfriend, [*informal*] bridegroom, chap, [*informal*] codger, father, fellow, gentleman, groom, [*informal*] guy, husband, lad, lover, male, son, [*joking*] squire, widower.

man verb *to man an undertaking. to man a ship.* provide men for, provide staff for, staff.

manacle noun, verb SEE **chain** noun, verb.

manage verb **1** *to manage a business. to manage a crowd.* administer, be in charge of, be the manager of [SEE **manager**], command, conduct, control, cope with, deal with, direct, dominate, govern, handle, lead, look after, manipulate, mastermind, operate, oversee, preside over, regulate, rule, run, superintend, supervise, take control of, take over.
2 *How much work can you manage before dinner?* accomplish, achieve, bring about, carry out, contrive, do, finish, perform, succeed in, undertake.
3 *If you can't pay it all, pay what you can manage.* afford, spare.

manageable adjective **1** *a manageable size. a manageable quantity.* acceptable, convenient, easy to manage [SEE **manage**], governable, handy, neat, reasonable.
OPPOSITES: SEE **awkward**.
2 *a manageable horse. a manageable crowd.* amenable, disciplined, docile, SEE **obedient**, tractable.
OPPOSITES: SEE **disobedient**.

manager noun administrator, boss, SEE **chief**, controller, director, executive, governor, head, organizer, overseer, proprietor, ruler, superintendent, supervisor.

mandarin noun SEE **official** noun.

mandate noun SEE **authority**.

mandatory adjective SEE **compulsory**.

mangle verb *He was off work because he'd mangled his hand in a machine.* crush, cut, damage, disfigure, injure, lacerate, maim, maul, mutilate, squash, tear, SEE **wound** verb.

mangy adjective *a mangy animal.* dirty, scabby, scruffy, [*informal*] tatty, unkempt.

manhandle verb **1** *We manhandled the piano up the stairs.* carry, haul, heave, hump, lift, manœuvre, move, pull, push.
2 *The muggers manhandled him.* [*informal*] beat up, knock about, maltreat, mistreat, misuse, [*informal*] rough up, treat roughly.

mania noun *a mania for collecting things.* craze, enthusiasm, fad, fetish, frenzy, hysteria, infatuation, insanity, lunacy, madness, obsession, passion, preoccupation.

maniac noun *a raving maniac.* SEE **madman**.

maniacal, manic adjectives SEE **mad**.

manifest adjective SEE **clear** adjective.

manifesto noun *a party manifesto.* declaration, policy, statement.

manipulate verb **1** *to manipulate a crowd. to manipulate election results.* control,

engineer, guide, handle, influence, manage, steer.
2 *to manipulate an injured person's leg.* feel, massage, rub.

mankind noun human beings, humanity, the human race, man, men and women, people [SEE **person**].
RELATED ADJECTIVE: anthropological.

manly adjective [*Manly* as a term of approval may have sexist overtones.] SEE **brave**, heroic, [*uncomplimentary*] macho, male, mannish, masculine, strong, swashbuckling, vigorous, virile.
OPPOSITES: SEE **effeminate**.

man-made adjective *man-made substances.* artificial, imitation, manufactured, simulated, synthetic, unnatural.
OPPOSITES: SEE **natural**.

mannequin noun SEE **model** noun.

manner noun 1 *She does things in a professional manner.* fashion, means, method, mode, procedure, process, style, way.
2 *I don't like his cheeky manner.* air, attitude, bearing, behaviour, character, conduct, demeanour, disposition, look, mien.
3 *We've tried all manner of things.* genre, kind, sort, type, variety.
good manners good behaviour, breeding, civility, conduct, courtesy, etiquette, gentility, politeness, refinement.

mannerism noun *an annoying mannerism.* characteristic, habit, idiosyncrasy, peculiarity, quirk, trait.

manœuvre noun 1 *Getting the car into the drive is a tricky manœuvre.* move, operation.
2 *It was a clever manœuvre to take his bishop.* dodge, gambit, move, plan, plot, ploy, ruse, scheme, stratagem, strategy, tactics, trick.
manœuvres *army manœuvres,* exercise, movement, operation, training.

manœuvre verb *to manœuvre something into position.* engineer, guide, jockey, manipulate, move, navigate, negotiate, pilot, steer.

manor, manor-house nouns SEE **mansion**.

manservant noun VARIOUS SERVANTS: SEE **servant**.

mansion noun castle, château, manor, manor-house, palace, stately home, villa.
OTHER HOUSES: SEE **house** noun.

manslaughter noun SEE **killing** noun.

mantle noun cape, cloak, hood, shroud, wrap.

mantrap noun SEE **trap** noun.

manual adjective *manual work.* by hand, physical.

manual noun KINDS OF BOOK: SEE **book** noun.

manufacture verb *to manufacture goods in a factory.* assemble, build, fabricate, make, mass-produce, prefabricate, process, [*informal*] turn out.

manufactured adjective 1 *manufactured goods.* factory-made, mass-produced.
OPPOSITES: SEE **home-made**.
2 *manufactured substances.* artificial, man-made, synthetic.
OPPOSITES: SEE **natural**.

manufacturer noun factory-owner, industrialist, producer.

manure noun compost, dung, fertilizer, [*informal*] muck.

manuscript noun SEE **book** noun, document, papers, script.

many adjective abundant, copious, countless, frequent, innumerable, multifarious, numberless, numerous, profuse, [*informal*] umpteen, untold, various.
OPPOSITES: SEE **few**.

map noun chart, diagram, plan.
a book of maps atlas, roadbook.
the drawing of maps cartography.

map verb *to map an area.* chart, survey.
to map out *to map out your future.* SEE **plan** verb.

mar verb SEE **spoil**.

marauder noun bandit, buccaneer, invader, pirate, plunderer, raider.

march noun 1 *The band played a march.* MUSICAL COMPOSITIONS: SEE **music**.
2 *the march of time.* SEE **progress** noun.

march verb *Soldiers marched into town.* file, parade, stride, troop, SEE **walk** verb.

mare noun SEE **horse**.

margin noun *the margin of a piece of paper. the margin of a lake.* border, boundary, SEE **edge** noun, frieze, perimeter, side, verge.

marginal adjective *of marginal importance.* borderline, doubtful, minimal, negligible, peripheral, small, unimportant.

marina noun SEE **harbour** noun.

marine adjective SEE **sea** adjective.

marine noun SEE **soldier**.

mariner noun sailor, seafarer, seaman.

marionette noun SEE **doll**.

mark noun 1 *dirty marks. marks on your skin.* blemish, blot, blotch, dot, finger-mark, [*plural*] graffiti, marking, print, scar, scratch, scribble, smear, smudge, smut, [*informal*] splotch, SEE **spot** noun,

stain, [*formal*] stigma (*plural* stigmata), streak, trace, vestige.
2 *a mark of respect. a mark of good breeding.* characteristic, emblem, feature, hallmark, indication, sign, symbol, token.
3 *a manufacturer's mark.* badge, brand, device, label, seal, stamp, standard.

mark verb **1** *to mark a surface.* blemish, blot, brand, bruise, damage, deface, dirty, disfigure, draw on, make a mark on [SEE **mark** noun], mar, scar, scratch, scrawl over, scribble on, smudge, spot, stain, stamp, streak, tattoo, write on.
2 *to mark students' work.* appraise, assess, correct, evaluate, grade.
3 *Mark what I say.* attend to, heed, listen to, mind, note, notice, observe, take note of, [*informal*] take to heart, watch.

marked adjective SEE **noticeable**.

market noun auction, bazaar, fair, sale.

market verb *His firm markets furniture.* SEE **advertise**, retail, sell, [*informal*] tout, trade, trade in.

marketable adjective *marketable goods.* in demand, merchantable, saleable, sellable.

marking noun SEE **mark** noun.

marksman noun [*informal*] crack shot, gunman, sharpshooter, sniper.

marl noun SEE **soil** noun.

maroon verb *to maroon someone on an island.* abandon, cast away, desert, forsake, isolate, leave, put ashore, strand.
a marooned person castaway.

marquee noun SEE **tent**.

marriage noun **1** *They celebrated 25 years of marriage.* matrimony, partnership, union, wedlock.
2 *Today is the anniversary of their marriage.* [*old-fashioned*] espousal, match, nuptials, wedding.
VARIOUS STATES OF MARRIAGE: bigamy, monogamy, polyandry, polygamy.
COMPARE: bachelorhood, celibacy, divorce, separation, spinsterhood, widowhood.
RELATED ADJECTIVES: conjugal, marital, matrimonial, nuptial.

marriageable adjective adult, mature, nubile.

marry verb **1** *to marry a husband or wife.* espouse, [*informal*] get hitched, join in matrimony, [*informal*] tie the knot, wed.
2 *to marry two things together.* SEE **unite**.

marsh noun bog, fen, marshland, mire, morass, mud, mudflats, quagmire, quicksands, saltings, saltmarsh, [*old-fashioned*] slough, swamp, wetland.

marshal noun SEE **official** noun, **rank** noun.

marshal verb *to marshal troops. to marshal your thoughts.* arrange, assemble, collect, deploy, draw up, gather, group, line up, muster, organize, set out.

marshy adjective SEE **swampy**.

martial adjective **1** *a martial figure.* aggressive, bellicose, belligerent, militant, pugnacious, warlike.
OPPOSITES: SEE **peaceable**.
2 *martial law.* military.
OPPOSITE: civil.
martial arts judo, karate, kung fu, taekwondo.

martinet noun SEE **disciplinarian**.

martyr verb SEE **kill**.

martyrdom noun SEE **killing** noun.

marvel noun *the marvel of space travel.* miracle, wonder.

marvel verb **to marvel at** *We marvelled at their skill.* admire, applaud, be amazed by, be astonished by, be surprised by, gape at, SEE **praise** verb, wonder at.

marvellous adjective **1** *a marvellous scientific discovery. marvellous works of art.* admirable, amazing, astonishing, excellent, extraordinary, [*informal*] fabulous, [*informal*] fantastic, glorious, incredible, magnificent, miraculous, phenomenal, praiseworthy, remarkable, sensational, spectacular, splendid, [*informal*] super, superb, surprising, unbelievable, wonderful, wondrous.
OPPOSITES; SEE **ordinary**.
2 [*informal*] *We had a marvellous time.* SEE **good**.

Marxism noun POLITICAL TERMS: SEE **politics**.

masculine adjective [*Masculine* and its synonyms may have sexist overtones, and therefore should be used with care.] *a masculine appearance. masculine behaviour.* boyish, [*informal*] butch, dynamic, gentlemanly, heroic, [*uncomplimentary*] macho, male, manly, mannish, muscular, powerful, strong, vigorous, virile.
OPPOSITES: SEE **feminine**.

mash verb *to mash something to a pulp.* beat, crush, grind, mangle, pound, pulp, pulverize, smash, squash.

mask noun *a mask to cover your face.* camouflage, cover, disguise, façade, front, screen, shield, veil, visor.

mask verb *We planted a tree to mask the ugly building.* blot out, camouflage, cloak, conceal, cover, disguise, hide, obscure, screen, shield, shroud, veil.

masonry noun bricks, brickwork, stone, stonework.

masquerade noun SEE **pretence**.

mass adjective *a mass revolt.* comprehensive, general, large-scale, popular, universal, wholesale, widespread.
the mass media SEE **communication**.

mass noun **1** *a mass of rubbish.* accumulation, body, bulk, [*informal*] chunk, concretion, conglomeration, [*informal*] dollop, heap, [*informal*] hunk, [*informal*] load, lot, lump, mound, pile, quantity, stack.
2 *a mass of people.* SEE **group** noun.
3 *We go to Mass on Sundays.* SEE **service** noun.

mass verb *to mass together.* SEE **gather**.

massacre noun SEE **killing** noun.

massacre verb SEE **kill**.

massage verb *The trainer massaged my injured leg.* knead, manipulate, rub.

massive adjective SEE **huge**.

mast noun aerial, flagpole, maypole, pylon, transmitter.

master noun **1** *the master of a dog.* keeper, owner, person in charge, proprietor.
2 *a schoolmaster.* SEE **teacher**.
3 *the master of a ship.* captain.
4 *a master at chess.* [*informal*] ace, expert, genius, mastermind, virtuoso.

master verb [Some people regard the verb *master* as sexist.] **1** *to master the rules.* acquire, [*informal*] get off by heart, [*informal*] get the hang of, grasp, learn, understand.
2 *to master a wild horse.* break in, bridle, conquer, control, curb, defeat, dominate, [*informal*] get the better of, govern, manage, overcome, overpower, quell, regulate, rule, subdue, subjugate, suppress, tame, triumph over, vanquish.

masterful adjective [Do not confuse with *masterly*.] *a masterful personality.* SEE **bossy**.

masterly adjective [Do not confuse with *masterful*.] *masterly control of the ball.* SEE **expert** adjective.

mastermind noun **1** *the mastermind behind an undertaking.* architect, brains, creator, engineer, inventor, manager, originator, planner, prime mover.
2 [*informal*] *Ask the mastermind!* [*informal*] egghead, expert, genius, intellectual, master.

mastermind verb *She masterminded the whole operation.* be the mastermind behind [SEE **mastermind** noun], carry through, direct, execute, SEE **manage**, organize, plan.

masterpiece noun *This piece of music is the composer's masterpiece.* best work, chef-d'œuvre, classic, [*informal*] hit, pièce de résistance.

mastery noun **1** *mastery over other people.* SEE **control** noun.
2 *Her mastery in several foreign languages amazed us.* SEE **cleverness**.

masticate verb SEE **chew**.

mat noun carpet, floor-covering, matting, rug.

match noun **1** *It was an exciting match on Saturday.* competition, contest, game, test match, tie, tournament.
2 *The jacket and tie are a good match.* combination, complement, counterpart, double, equivalent, fit, pair, similarity, tally, twin.
3 *a love match.* friendship, marriage, partnership, relationship, union.

match verb **1** *The tie matches my shirt.* agree with, be compatible with, be the same colour (style, etc.) as, be similar to, blend with, coincide with, combine with, compare with, correspond to, fit with, go with, harmonize with, marry with, tally with, tone in with.
OPPOSITES: SEE **contrast** verb.
2 *We'll match you with a suitable partner.* ally, combine, couple, fit, join, link up, mate, put together, team.

matching adjective *a blue shirt with matching tie.* alike, appropriate, comparable, compatible, co-ordinating, corresponding, equal, equivalent, harmonizing, identical, similar, toning, twin.
OPPOSITES: SEE **incongruous**.

matchless adjective SEE **unequalled**.

mate noun **1** *a plumber's mate.* assistant, collaborator, colleague, helper, partner.
2 *a mate for life.* husband, spouse, wife.
3 [*informal*] *He's a mate of mine.* SEE **friend**.

mate verb *Many birds mate in the springtime.* become partners, copulate, couple, have intercourse, [*informal*] have sex [SEE **sex**], marry, unite, wed.

material noun **1** *material to make a shirt.* SEE **cloth**, fabric, textile.
2 *material for a story.* content, data, facts, ideas, information, matter, notes, subject matter.
3 *material to make a patio.* building materials, stuff, substances, things.
VARIOUS BUILDING MATERIALS: SEE **building**.

materialize verb *A shape materialized out of the fog.* SEE **appear**.

maternal adjective *maternal love.* motherly.

maternity noun motherhood, pregnancy.

matey adjective SEE **friendly**.

mathematics noun [*informal*] maths, number work.

BRANCHES OF MATHEMATICS: algebra, arithmetic, calculus, geometry, statistics, trigonometry.

EVERYDAY MATHEMATICAL TERMS; addition, angle, area, binary system, concentric, congruence, cosine, decimal, fraction, decimal point, diagonal, diameter, division, equation, equilateral, exponent, factor, fraction, function, graph, index (*plural* indices), locus, logarithm, matrix, mensuration, minus, multiplication, negative number, parallel, percentage, perpendicular, plus, positive number, radius, ratio, right angle, SEE **shape** noun, sine, subtraction, sum, symmetry, tangent, tessellation, theorem.

MATHEMATICAL INSTRUMENTS: compasses, dividers, protractor, ruler, set-square.

---

matriarch noun SEE **woman**.

matrimony noun SEE **marriage**.

matron noun SEE **woman**.

matt adjective SEE **dull** adjective.

matted adjective *matted hair.* knotted, tangled, uncombed, unkempt.

matter noun **1** *mind over matter. colouring matter.* body, material, stuff, substance.
2 *poisonous matter in a wound.* discharge, pus, suppuration.
3 *The manager will deal with this matter.* affair, business, concern, incident, issue, situation, subject, thing, topic.
4 *What's the matter with the car?* difficulty, problem, trouble, upset, worry, wrong (*What's wrong?*).

matter verb *Will it matter if I'm late?* be important, count, make a difference, signify.

matter-of-fact adjective *a matter-of-fact description.* [*informal*] dead-pan, down to earth, SEE **factual**, mechanical, prosaic, to the point, unadorned, unemotional, unimaginative.
OPPOSITES: SEE **emotional**, **imaginative**.

matting noun SEE **mat**.

mature adjective **1** *mature for her age.* adult, advanced, full-grown, grown-up, nubile, well-developed.
OPPOSITES: SEE **immature**.
2 *mature fruit.* mellow, ready, ripe.
OPPOSITES: SEE **unripe**.

maudlin adjective SEE **sentimental**.

maul verb *The lion mauled the keeper.* claw, injure, [*informal*] knock about, lacerate, mangle, manhandle, mutilate, paw, treat roughly, SEE **wound** verb.

maunder verb *to maunder on boringly.* SEE **talk** verb.

mausoleum noun SEE **tomb**.

maverick noun SEE **rebel** noun.

mawkish adjective SEE **sentimental**.

maxim noun SEE **saying**.

maximize verb **1** *to maximize your profits.* SEE **increase** verb.
2 *to maximize your problems.* SEE **exaggerate**.
OPPOSITE: **minimize**.

maximum adjective *maximum size. maximum speed.* biggest, full, fullest, greatest, highest, largest, most, supreme, top.
OPPOSITES: SEE **minimum** adjective.

maximum noun *Temperatures usually reach their maximum after noon.* ceiling, highest point, peak, top, upper limit, zenith.
OPPOSITES: SEE **minimum** noun.

maybe adverb conceivably, perhaps, possibly.
OPPOSITES: SEE **definitely**.

mayhem noun SEE **confusion**.

mayor, mayoress nouns SEE **official** noun.

maze noun *a maze of corridors.* confusion, labyrinth, network, tangle, web.

meadow noun field, [*poetic*] mead, paddock, pasture.

meagre adjective SEE **scanty**.

meal noun [*informal*] blow-out, repast, [*informal*] spread.

VARIOUS MEALS: banquet, barbecue, breakfast, buffet, dinner, [*informal*] elevenses, feast, high tea, lunch, luncheon, picnic, snack, supper, takeaway, tea, tea-break, [*old-fashioned*] tiffin.

COURSES OF A MEAL: [*informal*] afters, dessert, [*formal*] entrée, hors-d'œuvres, main course, pudding, starter, sweet.

---

mealy-mouthed adjective SEE **flattering**.

mean adjective **1** *too mean to give a donation.* beggarly, [*informal*] cheese-paring, close, close-fisted, [*informal*] mingy, miserly, niggardly, parsimonious, [*informal*] penny-pinching, selfish, sparing, [*informal*] stingy, [*informal*] tight, tight-fisted.
OPPOSITES: SEE **generous**.
2 *a mean trick.* base, callous, churlish, contemptible, cruel, despicable, hard-hearted, malicious, nasty, shabby, shameful, [*informal*] sneaky, spiteful, unkind, vicious.
OPPOSITES: SEE **kind** adjective.
3 [*old-fashioned*] *a mean dwelling.* humble, inferior, insignificant, lowly, SEE **poor**, squalid, wretched.
OPPOSITES: SEE **superior**.
4 *mean temperature.* SEE **average** adjective.

mean verb **1** *What does that sign mean?* betoken, communicate, connote, convey, denote, express, hint at, imply, indicate, portend, presage, say, signify, spell out, stand for, suggest, symbolize.
2 *I mean to work harder.* aim, desire, intend, plan, propose, purpose, want, wish.
3 *The job means working long hours.* entail, involve, necessitate.

meander verb SEE **wander**.

meandering adjective SEE **roundabout** adjective.

meaning adjective *a meaning glance.* SEE **meaningful**.

meaning noun **1** *the meaning of a word.* connotation, definition, denotation, force, sense, signification.
2 *the meaning of a poem. the meaning of someone's behaviour.* explanation, gist, implication, interpretation, message, point, purport, purpose, significance, thrust.

meaningful adjective *a meaningful glance. meaningful discussions.* eloquent, expressive, meaning, pointed, positive, pregnant, significant, suggestive, warning, worthwhile.
OPPOSITES: SEE **meaningless**.

meaningless adjective **1** *meaningless compliments.* empty, flattering, hollow, insincere, sycophantic, worthless.
2 *a meaningless message.* absurd, coded, incoherent, incomprehensible, inconsequential, nonsensical, pointless, senseless.
OPPOSITES: SEE **meaningful**.

means noun **1** *the means to do something. a means to an end.* ability, capacity, channel, course, fashion, machinery, manner, medium, method, mode, process, way.
2 *the means to pay for something. private means.* affluence, capital, finances, funds, income, money, resources, riches, wealth, [*informal*] wherewithal.

measly adjective [*slang*] *a measly spoonful of pudding.* SEE **scanty**.

measurable adjective *a measurable amount.* appreciable, considerable, perceptible, quantifiable, reasonable, significant.
OPPOSITES: SEE **negligible**.

measure noun **1** *full measure.* amount, capacity, distance, extent, length, magnitude, measurement, quantity, ration, size, unit, way.
2 *a measure of someone's ability.* criterion, standard, test, touchstone, yardstick.
3 *measures to curb crime.* act, action, bill, expedient, law, means, procedure, step.

UNITS USED IN MEASURING:
BREADTH, DEPTH, DISTANCE, GAUGE, HEIGHT, LENGTH, WIDTH: centimetre, cubit, fathom, foot, furlong, inch, kilometre, light-year, metre, millimetre, parsec, yard.

AREA: acre, hectare, square centimetres (metres, etc.).

TIME: century, day, decade, hour, microsecond, millennium, minute, month, second, week, year.

CAPACITY, VOLUME: bushel, cubic centimetres (inches, etc.), gallon, hogshead, litre, millilitre, pint, quart.

WEIGHT: carat, drachm, gram, hundredweight, kilo or kilogram, megaton, megatonne, milligram, ounce, pound, stone, ton, tonne.

SPEED, VELOCITY: kilometres per hour, knot, Mach number, miles per hour, [*informal*] ton.

QUANTITY: century [= *100*], dozen, gross, score.

TEMPERATURE: degree Celsius, degree centigrade, degree Fahrenheit.

INFORMAL MEASUREMENTS: armful, cupful, handful, mouthful, pinch, plateful, spoonful.

---

measure verb *He measured its size.* assess, calculate, calibrate, compute, determine, gauge, judge, mark-out, plumb (*to plumb the depths of water*), quantify, survey, take measurements of, weigh.
to measure out *She measured out their daily ration.* allot, apportion, deal out, dispense, distribute, [*informal*] dole out, ration out, share out.

measured adjective *a measured rhythm.* SEE **regular**.

measurement noun **1** *the measurements of a room.* dimensions, extent, SEE **measure** noun, size.
2 *The children did some work on measurement in maths.* mensuration.

meat noun flesh.

KINDS OF MEAT: bacon, beef, chicken, game, gammon, ham, lamb, mutton, offal, oxtail, pork, poultry, tripe, turkey, veal, venison.

VARIOUS CUTS OR JOINTS OF MEAT: breast, brisket, chine, chops, chuck, cutlet, fillet, flank, leg, loin, oxtail, rib, rump, scrag, shoulder, silverside, sirloin, spare-rib, steak, topside, trotter.

KINDS OF PROCESSED MEAT: brawn, burger, corned beef, hamburger, mince, pasty, pâté, pie, potted meat, rissole, salted meat, sausage.

---

mechanic noun *a motor mechanic.* engineer, technician.

mechanical adjective **1** *a mechanical process.* automated, automatic, machine-driven, technological.
OPPOSITE: manual.
2 *a mechanical response.* cold, inhuman, lifeless, matter-of-fact, perfunctory, routine, soulless, unconscious, unemotional, unfeeling, unimaginative, unthinking.
OPPOSITES: SEE **thoughtful**.

mechanism noun SEE **machine**.

mechanize verb *to mechanize a production line.* automate, bring up to date, equip with machines, modernize.

medal noun award, decoration, honour, medallion, prize, reward, trophy.

medallist noun champion, victor, winner.

meddle verb SEE **interfere**.

meddlesome adjective SEE **interfering**.

media noun SEE **communication**.

medial, median adjectives SEE **middle** adjective.

mediate verb *to mediate in a dispute.* act as mediator [SEE **mediator**], arbitrate, intercede, liaise, negotiate.

mediator noun arbitrator, broker, go-between, intermediary, negotiator, peacemaker, referee, umpire.

medicinal adjective *a medicinal ointment.* healing, medical, restorative, therapeutic.

medicine noun **1** *the study of medicine.* healing, surgery, therapeutics, treatment of diseases.
2 *medicine from the chemist's.* cure, dose, drug, medicament, medication, [*uncomplimentary*] nostrum, prescription, remedy, treatment.

SOME BRANCHES OF MEDICAL PRACTICE: anaesthesiology (*anaesthetics*), audiometrics (*hearing*), chiropody (*feet*), dentistry (*teeth*), dermatology (*skin*), dietetics (*diet*), family practice, general practice, geriatrics (*old age*), gynaecology (*women's illnesses*), homeopathy, immunology (*resistance to infection*), neurology (*nerves*), neurosurgery, obstetrics (*childbirth*), ophthalmology (*eyes*), orthopaedics (*bones & muscles*), osteopathy, paediatrics (*children*), pathology, plastic surgery, preventive or preventative medicine, psychiatry (*mind*), radiology (*X-rays*), surgery, SEE **therapy**.

PEOPLE WHO LOOK AFTER OUR HEALTH: acupuncturist, anaesthetist, audiometrician, chiropodist, chiropractor, dentist, dermatologist, dietician, doctor, general practitioner, gynaecologist, homeopath, hygienist, hypnotherapist, [*male*] masseur, [*female*] masseuse, medical practitioner, midwife, neurologist, nurse, obstetrician, oculist, optician, osteopath, paediatrician, physician, physiotherapist, plastic surgeon, psychiatrist, radiographer, sister, surgeon.

PLACES WHERE YOU GET MEDICAL TREATMENT: clinic, dispensary, health centre, health farm, hospital, infirmary, intensive-care unit, nursing home, operating theatre, outpatients' department, sick-bay, surgery, ward.

VARIOUS MEDICINES, ETC.: anaesthetic, antibiotic, antidote, antiseptic, aspirin, capsule, embrocation, gargle, herbs, inhaler, iodine, linctus, lotion, lozenge, manipulation, massage, morphia, narcotic, ointment, pastille, penicillin, [*informal*] the pill, sedative, suppository, tablet, tonic, tranquillizer.

OTHER MEDICAL TERMS: bandage, biopsy, dressing, first aid, forceps, hypodermic syringe, immunization, injection, inoculation, lint, plaster, poultice, scalpel, sling, splint, stethoscope, stretcher, syringe, thermometer, transfusion, transplant, tweezers, X-ray.

WORDS TO DO WITH ILLNESS: SEE **ill**, **illness**.

---

mediocre adjective *mediocre work.* amateurish, average, commonplace, fair, indifferent, inferior, middling, moderate, [*informal*] neither one thing nor the other, [*informal*] nothing special, ordinary, passable, pedestrian, poorish, second-rate, [*informal*] so-so, undistinguished, unexciting, uninspired, unremarkable, weakish.

meditation noun contemplation, prayer, reflection, yoga.

meditate verb *to meditate in silence.* brood, cogitate, consider, contemplate, deliberate, mull things over, muse, ponder, pray, reflect, ruminate, think.

meditative adjective SEE **thoughtful**.

medium adjective average, intermediate, mean, middle, middling, midway, moderate, normal, ordinary, usual.

medium noun **1** *a happy medium.* average, compromise, mean, middle, midpoint,
2 *This artist's favourite medium is watercolour.* form, means, method, vehicle, way.
3 *a medium who claims to communicate with the dead.* clairvoyant, seer, spiritualist.
the media [*Media* is plural, so we should speak not of *a media*, but of *the media.*] SEE **communication**.
mass media broadcasting, magazines, newspapers, the press, radio, television.

medley noun SEE **mixture**.

meek adjective *meek acceptance of defeat.* acquiescent, compliant, docile, forbearing, gentle, humble, long-suffering, lowly, mild, modest, obedient, patient, quiet, resigned, soft, spineless, tame, unassuming, unprotesting, weak.
OPPOSITES: SEE **aggressive**.

meet verb **1** *I met my friend in town.* [*informal*] bump into, chance upon, come across, confront, contact, encounter, face, happen on, have a meeting with [SEE **meeting**], [*informal*] run across, [*informal*] run into, see.
2 *I'll meet you at the station.* come and fetch, greet, [*informal*] pick up, welcome.
3 *We all met in the hall.* assemble, collect, come together, congregate, convene, forgather, gather, have a meeting [SEE **meeting**], muster, rally.
4 *Two roads meet here.* come together, connect, converge, cross, intersect, join, link up, merge, unite.
5 *We met their demands.* acquiesce in, agree to, comply with, fulfil, [*informal*] measure up to, satisfy.

meeting noun **1** *a business meeting.* assembly, audience (*an audience with the king*), board meeting, briefing, cabinet meeting, committee, conclave, conference, congregation, congress, convention, council, discussion group, forum, gathering, [*informal*] powwow, prayer meeting, rally, seminar, service (*in church*), synod (*of the church*).
2 *a chance meeting.* confrontation, contact, encounter.
3 *an arranged meeting with someone.* appointment, assignation, date, engagement, [*informal*] get-together, rendezvous, [*old-fashioned*] tryst.
4 *the meeting of two routes.* confluence (*of rivers*), convergence, crossing, crossroads, intersection, junction.

The prefix *mega-* is related to Greek *megas = great, large.*

---

megalomania noun SEE **pride**.

megaphone noun amplifier, loudhailer.

melancholia noun depression.

melancholy adjective *a melancholy look on her face. a melancholy scene.* cheerless, dejected, depressed, depressing, despondent, dispirited, dispiriting, [*informal*] down, down-hearted, gloomy, joyless, lifeless, low, lugubrious, melancholic, miserable, moody, mournful, sad, sombre, sorrowful, unhappy, woebegone, woeful.
OPPOSITES: SEE **cheerful**.

mélange noun SEE **mixture**.

mêlée noun SEE **confusion, fight** noun.

mellifluous adjective SEE **tuneful**.

mellow adjective **1** *a mellow taste.* mature, mild, pleasant, rich, ripe, smooth, sweet.
2 *mellow light. mellow sounds. mellow surroundings.* agreeable, comforting, genial, gentle, happy, kindly, peaceful, reassuring, soft, subdued, warm.
OPPOSITES: SEE **harsh**.

melodious adjective SEE **tuneful**.

melody noun air, strain, theme, tune.

melt verb *The sun's warmth melts the snow.* deliquesce, liquefy, soften, thaw, unfreeze.
to melt away *The crowd melted away.* dematerialize, disappear, disperse, dissolve, dwindle, evaporate, fade, pass away, vanish.

member noun **1** *a member of a club.* associate, fellow.
2 *the members of your body.* SEE **limb.**
to be a member SEE **belong.**

membrane noun SEE **skin** noun.

memento noun SEE **souvenir.**

memo noun SEE **communication.**

memoir, memoirs nouns autobiography, SEE **biography,** recollections.

memorable adjective **1** *a memorable occasion.* distinguished, SEE **extraordinary,** impressive, indelible, ineradicable, outstanding, remarkable, striking, unforgettable.
2 *a memorable tune.* [*informal*] catchy, haunting.
OPPOSITES: SEE **commonplace.**

memorandum noun SEE **communication.**

memorial noun cairn, cenotaph, gravestone, headstone, monument, plaque, tablet, SEE **tomb.**

memorize noun *to memorize facts.* commit to memory, [*informal*] get off by heart, SEE **learn,** learn by rote, learn parrot-fashion, remember.

memory noun **1** *a bad memory.* ability to remember, recall, retention.
2 *happy memories of our holiday.* impression, recollection, remembrance, reminder, reminiscence, souvenir.
3 *The memory of people we loved is always with us.* fame, name, reputation.

menace noun *a menace to society.* SEE **threat.**

menace verb SEE **threaten.**

menacing adjective SEE **threatening.**

ménage noun [*informal*] domestic set-up, family, household.

menagerie noun zoo.
VARIOUS ANIMALS: SEE **animal** noun.

mend verb **1** *to mend the car. to mend clothes.* fix, put right, rectify, renew, renovate, repair, restore.
WAYS TO MEND THINGS: beat out (*to beat out dents*), darn, patch, replace parts, sew up, solder, stitch up, touch up, weld.
2 *to mend your ways.* amend, correct, cure, improve, make better, reform, revise.
3 *The wound mended quickly.* get better, heal, recover, recuperate.

mendacious adjective SEE **lying.**

mendicant noun SEE **beggar.**

menial adjective *menial jobs.* base, boring, degrading, demeaning, humble, lowly, mean, servile, slavish, subservient, unskilled, unworthy.

menial noun SEE **servant.**

menstruate verb have a period.

mensuration noun measuring, measurement.

mental adjective **1** *mental arithmetic. mental effort.* abstract, cerebral, intellectual, rational, theoretical.
2 *a mental condition.* emotional, psychological, subjective, temperamental.
3 [*informal*] *He must be mental.* SEE **mad.**

mentality noun *a criminal mentality.* attitude, character, disposition, frame of mind, [*informal*] make-up, outlook, personality, predisposition, propensity, psychology, way of thinking.

mention verb **1** *to mention something casually.* allude to, comment on, disclose, hint at, [*informal*] let drop, let out, refer to, reveal, speak about, touch on.
2 *The speaker mentioned all the prize-winners.* acknowledge, cite, draw attention to, enumerate, make known, name, point out.
3 *I mentioned that I might go out.* observe, remark, say.

mentor noun SEE **adviser.**

menu noun bill of fare, tariff.

mercenary noun SEE **fighter, soldier.**

merchandise noun commodities, goods, things for sale.

merchandise verb SEE **advertise, sell.**

merchant noun *a timber merchant,* dealer, retailer, salesman, shopkeeper, stockist, supplier, trader, tradesman, wholesaler.

merciful adjective *a merciful judge. merciful treatment.* benevolent, charitable, clement, compassionate, forbearing, forgiving, generous, gracious, humane, humanitarian, kind, lenient, liberal, mild, pitying, [*uncomplimentary*] soft, sympathetic, tender-hearted, tolerant.
OPPOSITES: SEE **merciless.**

merciless adjective *a merciless judge. merciless punishment.* barbaric, callous, cruel, cut-throat, hard, hard-hearted, harsh, heartless, inexorable, inhuman, inhumane, intolerant, pitiless, relentless, remorseless, ruthless, savage, severe, stern, strict, unfeeling, unforgiving, unkind, unrelenting, unremitting, vicious.
OPPOSITES: SEE **merciful.**

mercurial adjective SEE **changeable.**

mercury noun quicksilver.

mercy noun *The attackers showed no mercy.* charity, clemency, compassion, feeling, forbearance, forgiveness,

grace, humanity, kindness, leniency, love, pity, sympathy, understanding.
OPPOSITES: SEE **cruelty**.

merge verb **1** *to merge two schools.* amalgamate, blend, combine, come together, confederate, fuse, integrate, join together, link up, mingle, mix, put together, unite.
2 *motorways merge.* converge, join, meet.
OPPOSITES: SEE **separate** verb.

merit noun **1** *Your work has some merit.* asset, excellence, goodness, importance, quality, strength, talent, value, virtue, worth.
2 *a certificate of merit.* credit, distinction.

merit verb *Her performance merited first prize.* be entitled to, deserve, earn, incur, justify, rate, warrant.

meritorious adjective SEE **praiseworthy**.

merriment noun *What's all the merriment about?* amusement, gaiety, hilarity, jocularity, joking, jollity, joviality, laughter, levity, light-heartedness, liveliness, SEE **merrymaking**, mirth, vivacity.

merry adjective *a merry tune.* bright, carefree, cheerful, [*informal*] chirpy, festive, fun-loving, gay, glad, SEE **happy**, hilarious, jocular, jolly, jovial, joyful, joyous, light-hearted, lively, rollicking, spirited, vivacious.
OPPOSITES: SEE **serious**.

merry-go-round noun carousel, roundabout.

merrymaking noun *Come and join in the merrymaking.* carousing, celebration, conviviality, festivity, frolic, fun, [*informal*] fun and games, [*joking*] jollification, [*informal*] junketing, merriment, SEE **party**, revelry, roistering, sociability, [*old-fashioned*] wassailing.

mesh noun *a mesh of intersecting lines.* lattice, net, netting, network, tangle, tracery, web.

mesmerize verb SEE **hypnotize**.

mess noun **1** *Clear up this mess.* chaos, clutter, SEE **confusion**, SEE **dirt**, disorder, jumble, litter, muddle, [*informal*] shambles, untidiness.
2 *I made a mess of it!* [*informal*] botch, failure, [*informal*] hash, [*informal*] mix-up.
3 *I got into a mess.* difficulty, dilemma, [*informal*] fix, [*informal*] jam, plight, predicament, problem.
to make a mess of SEE **bungle, muddle** verb.

mess verb **to mess about** [*informal*] *Stop messing about and start work!* amuse yourself, loaf, loiter, lounge about [SEE **lounge** verb], [*informal*] monkey about, [*informal*] muck about, play about.
to mess up SEE **muddle** verb.
to mess up a job SEE **bungle**.

message noun announcement, bulletin, cable, SEE **communication**, communiqué, dispatch, letter, memo, memorandum, note, notice, report, statement.

messenger noun bearer, carrier, courier, dispatch-rider, [*formal*] emissary, [*formal*] envoy, go-between, [*poetic*] harbinger, herald, postman, runner.

messy adjective *a messy appearance.* blowzy, careless, chaotic, cluttered, SEE **dirty**, dishevelled, disorderly, filthy, grubby, mucky, muddled, [*informal*] shambolic, slapdash, sloppy, slovenly, unkempt, untidy.
OPPOSITES: SEE **neat**.

metal noun **a lump of metal** ingot, nugget.

METALLIC ELEMENTS: aluminium, barium, beryllium, bismuth, cadmium, calcium, chromium, cobalt, copper, gold, iridium, iron, lead, lithium, magnesium, manganese, mercury, molybdenum, nickel, platinum, potassium, silver, sodium, strontium, tin, titanium, tungsten, uranium, zinc.

SOME METAL ALLOYS: brass, bronze, gunmetal, pewter, solder, steel.

---

metallic adjective **1** *a metallic sheen.* gleaming, lustrous, shiny.
2 *a metallic sound.* clanking, clinking, ringing.

metamorphose verb SEE **change** verb.

metamorphosis noun SEE **change** noun.

metaphor noun SEE **figure** noun **(figures of speech)**.

metaphysics noun SEE **philosophy**.

mete verb **to mete out** SEE **distribute**.

meteor, meteorite nouns ASTRONOMICAL TERMS: SEE **astronomy**.

meter verb SEE **measure** verb.

method noun **1** *a method of doing something.* fashion, [*informal*] knack, manner, means, mode, plan, procedure, process, recipe, scheme, style, technique, trick, way.
2 *method behind the chaos.* arrangement, design, order, orderliness, organization, pattern, routine, system.

methodical adjective *a methodical worker.* businesslike, careful, deliberate, disciplined, logical, meticulous,

neat, orderly, organized, painstaking, precise, rational, regular, structured, systematic, tidy.
OPPOSITES: SEE **arbitrary, careless.**

meticulous adjective SEE **scrupulous.**

metric adjective *the metric system of weights and measures.* decimal.
OPPOSITE: imperial.

metrical adjective SEE **rhythmic.**

metricate verb decimalize, make metric.

metropolis noun SEE **city.**

mettle noun SEE **courage.**

mezzanine noun landing.

miasma noun fog, reek, smell, stench, vapour.

The prefix *micro-* is related to Greek *mikros=small.*

---

micro noun SEE **computer.**

microbe noun SEE **micro-organism.**

microlight noun SEE **aircraft.**

micro-organism noun bacillus, [*plural*] bacteria, [*informal*] bug, germ, microbe, virus.

microphone noun SEE **audio equipment.**

microscope noun SEE **optical (optical instruments).**

microscopic adjective SEE **tiny.**

microwave-oven noun KITCHEN EQUIPMENT: SEE **kitchen.**

midday noun lunchtime, noon.
OTHER TIMES OF DAY: SEE **time** noun.

midden noun dung-heap, dunghill, manure-heap.

middle adjective *the middle stump.* central, half-way, inner, inside, intermediate, intervening, mean, medial, median, middle-of-the-road, midway, neutral.

middle noun *the middle of the earth. the middle of the road.* centre, core, crown (*of the road*), focus, heart, hub, inside, middle position [SEE **middle** adjective], midpoint, midst (*in the midst of the confusion*), nucleus.

middleman noun *the middleman in business.* agent, broker, distributor.

middle-of-the-road adjective SEE **moderate** adjective.

middling adjective *a middling performance.* average, fair, [*informal*] fair to middling, indifferent, mediocre, moderate, modest, [*informal*] nothing to write home about, ordinary, passable, run-of-the-mill, [*informal*] so-so, unremarkable.
OPPOSITES: SEE **outstanding.**

midge noun SEE **insect.**

midget adjective SEE **small.**

midget noun dwarf, pygmy.

midshipman noun SEE **sailor.**

midst noun SEE **middle** noun.

midwife noun obstetrician.

mien noun SEE **look** noun.

miffed adjective SEE **annoyed.**

might noun *I banged at the door with all my might.* energy, force, power, strength, vigour.

mighty adjective *a mighty blow. a mighty figure.* big, enormous, forceful, great, hefty, SEE **huge**, muscular, powerful, strong, vigorous.
OPPOSITES: SEE **weak.**

migraine noun headache.

migrate verb SEE **travel** verb.

migration noun SEE **travel** noun.

mild adjective **1** *a mild person.* amiable, docile, easygoing, forbearing, gentle, good-tempered, harmless, indulgent, kind, lenient, SEE **merciful**, placid, [*uncomplimentary*] soft, soft-hearted, understanding.
2 *mild weather.* balmy, calm, clement, peaceful, pleasant, temperate, warm.
OPPOSITES: SEE **severe.**
3 *a mild flavour.* bland, delicate, faint, mellow, subtle.
OPPOSITES: SEE **strong.**

mildew noun fungus, mould.

mildness noun *the mildness of someone's manner. the mildness of a punishment.* amiability, clemency, docility, forbearance, gentleness, kindness, leniency, moderation, softness, tenderness.
OPPOSITES: SEE **asperity.**

milieu noun SEE **surroundings.**

militant adjective [Do not confuse with *militaristic* or *military.*] *militant political views.* active, aggressive, assertive, attacking, positive.

militant noun *a political militant.* activist, extremist, [*informal*] hawk, partisan.

militaristic adjective [Do not confuse with *militant.*] belligerent, combative, fond of fighting, hostile, pugnacious, warlike.
OPPOSITES: SEE **peaceable.**

military adjective **1** *military might. military personnel.* armed, belligerent, enlisted, uniformed, warlike.
OPPOSITE: civilian.

2 *military law.* martial.
OPPOSITE: civil.

militate verb **to militate against** SEE **counteract**.

militia noun SEE **armed forces**.

milk noun KINDS OF MILK: condensed, dried, evaporated, long-life, pasteurized, skimmed, UHT.

FOODS MADE FROM MILK: butter, cheese, cream, curds, custard, dairy products, junket, milk pudding, yoghurt.

---

milk verb *to milk someone of all they have.* SEE **exploit** verb.

milksop noun SEE **weakling**.

milky adjective *a milky liquid.* chalky, cloudy, misty, opaque, whitish.
OPPOSITES: SEE **clear** adjective.

mill noun 1 *a steel mill.* factory, processing plant, works, workshop.
2 *a mill for grinding corn.* water-mill, windmill.
3 *a pepper-mill.* grinder.

mill verb *to mill corn.* SEE **grind**.
to mill about move aimlessly, swarm, throng.

millionaire noun SEE **rich (rich person)**.

millstone noun *a millstone round my neck.* SEE **burden** noun.

mime noun SEE **theatre**.

mimic noun impersonator, impressionist.

mimic verb *Children often mimic their teachers.* ape, caricature, copy, do impressions of, echo, imitate, impersonate, look like, parody, parrot, pretend to be, simulate, sound like, [*informal*] take off.

minatory adjective SEE **threatening**.

mince verb 1 *to mince food.* SEE **cut** verb.
2 *to mince along the street.* SEE **walk** verb.

mincer noun blender, food-processor, mincing machine.

mind noun 1 *Use your mind!* brain, cleverness, [*informal*] grey matter, head, intellect, intelligence, judgement, memory, mental power, psyche, rationality, reasoning, remembrance, sense, thinking, understanding, wits.
RELATED ADJECTIVES: mental, psychological.
2 *He's changed his mind.* belief, intention, opinion, outlook, point of view, view, way of thinking, wishes.

mind verb 1 *Mind my things while I'm swimming.* attend to, care for, guard, keep an eye on, look after, watch.
2 *Mind the step.* be careful about, beware of, heed, look out for, note, remember, take notice of, watch out for.
3 *We won't mind if you're late.* be resentful, bother, care, complain, disapprove, grumble, object, take offence, worry.

mindful adjective SEE **careful**.

mindless adjective SEE **stupid**.

mine noun 1 *a coal-mine.* colliery, excavation, pit, quarry, shaft, tunnel, working.
2 *a land-mine.* WEAPONS: SEE **weapons**.

mine verb *to mine gold.* dig for, excavate, extract, quarry, remove.

miner noun coal-miner, collier.

mineral noun *minerals quarried out of the ground.* metal, ore, rock.

mingle verb *People mingled happily at the carnival.* associate, blend, circulate, combine, get together, intermingle, merge, mix, move about, [*informal*] rub shoulders, socialize.

mingy adjective SEE **mean** adjective.

The prefix *mini-* and words like *miniature, minimize, minimum*, etc. are related to Latin *minimus = least, smallest.*

---

miniature adjective SEE **tiny**.

miniature noun SEE **painting**.

minibus, minicab nouns VEHICLES: SEE **vehicle**.

minimal adjective *Modern cars require minimal servicing.* SEE **minimum** adjective, negligible, slightest.

minimize verb 1 *They banned smoking to minimize the danger of fire.* SEE **reduce**.
2 *He always minimizes the difficulties.* gloss over, make light of, play down, SEE **underestimate**.
OPPOSITES: SEE **maximize**.

minimum adjective *minimum wages. minimum temperature.* bottom, least, littlest, lowest, minimal, [*informal*] rock bottom, slightest, smallest.
OPPOSITES: SEE **maximum** adjective.

minimum noun *Keep expenses to the minimum.* lowest level, minimum amount (quantity, etc.) [SEE **minimum** adjective], nadir.
OPPOSITES: SEE **maximum** noun.

minion noun SEE **assistant**.

minister noun 1 *a government minister.* SEE **government**.
2 *a minister of the church.* SEE **clergyman**.

minister verb *to minister to the sick.* SEE **attend (attend to)**.

minor adjective *a minor accident. a minor official.* inconsequential, inferior, insignificant, lesser, little, petty, secondary, SEE **small**, subordinate, trivial, unimportant.
OPPOSITES: SEE **major** adjective.

minority noun *Only a minority voted to strike.* lesser number, smaller number.
to be in a minority be outnumbered, lose.

minster noun SEE **church**.

minstrel noun bard, entertainer, musician, singer, troubadour.

mint adjective *in mint condition.* brand-new, first-class, fresh, immaculate, new, perfect, unblemished, unmarked, unused.

mint noun **1** *a mint of money.* fortune, heap, [*informal*] packet, pile, stack, unlimited supply, vast amount.
2 *strong-smelling mint.* SEE **herb**.

mint verb *to mint coins.* cast, coin, forge, make, manufacture, stamp out, strike.

minuscule, minute adjectives SEE **tiny**.

minute noun *minutes of a meeting.* SEE **record** noun.

minutiae noun SEE **detail** noun.

miracle noun *the miracle of birth.* marvel, miraculous event [SEE **miraculous**], mystery, wonder.

miraculous adjective *a miraculous cure.* amazing, astonishing, extraordinary, incredible, inexplicable, magic, marvellous, mysterious, preternatural, supernatural, unaccountable, unbelievable, wonderful.

mirage noun *a mirage in the desert.* delusion, hallucination, illusion, vision.

mire noun *sinking in the mire.* bog, SEE **dirt**, marsh, morass, mud, ooze, quagmire, quicksand, slime, swamp.

mirror noun looking-glass, reflector.

mirror verb SEE **reflect**.

mirth noun SEE **merriment**.

The prefix *mis-* usually gives the sense of *bad, wrong* or *badly, wrongly*.

---

misadventure noun *death by misadventure.* accident, calamity, catastrophe, disaster, ill fortune, mischance, misfortune, mishap.

misanthropic adjective *a misanthropic attitude towards your fellow human beings.* cynical, mean, nasty, surly, unfriendly, unpleasant, unsociable.
OPPOSITES: SEE **philanthropic**.

misappropriate verb SEE **misuse** verb.

misbehave verb behave badly, be mischievous [SEE **mischievous**], be a nuisance, [*informal*] blot your copybook, [*informal*] carry on, commit an offence, default, disobey, do wrong, err, fool about, make mischief, [*informal*] mess about, [*informal*] muck about, offend, [*informal*] play up, sin, transgress.

misbehaviour noun delinquency, disobedience, horseplay, indiscipline, insubordination, mischief, mischief-making, misconduct, naughtiness, rudeness, sin, vandalism, wrongdoing.

miscalculate verb [*informal*] boob, err, [*informal*] get it wrong, go wrong, make a mistake [SEE **mistake** noun], misjudge, [*informal*] slip up.

miscalculation noun SEE **mistake** noun.

miscarriage noun **1** *miscarriage of a baby.* abortion, premature birth, termination of pregnancy.
2 *a miscarriage of justice.* breakdown, error, failure, SEE **mistake** noun, perversion.

miscarry verb **1** *to miscarry in pregnancy.* [*informal*] lose the baby, suffer a miscarriage [SEE **miscarriage**].
2 *The project miscarried.* break down, come to nothing, fail, fall through, go wrong, misfire.
OPPOSITES: SEE **succeed**.

miscellaneous adjective *miscellaneous odds and ends.* assorted, different, diverse, heterogeneous, mixed, motley (*a motley crowd*), multifarious, sundry, varied, various.
OPPOSITES: SEE **identical**.

miscellany noun SEE **mixture**.

mischief noun **1** *Don't get into mischief.* devilment, [*joking*] devilry, escapade, misbehaviour, misconduct, [*informal*] monkey business, naughtiness, prank, scrape, trouble.
2 *Did you come to any mischief?* damage, harm, hurt, injury, misfortune.
to make mischief SEE **misbehave**.

mischievous adjective *mischievous children.* annoying, badly behaved, boisterous, disobedient, fractious, full of mischief [SEE **mischief**], impish, lively, naughty, playful, [*informal*] puckish, roguish, uncontrollable, [*informal*] up to no good, wicked.
a mischievous person imp, rascal, rogue, scamp.

misconception noun SEE **misunderstanding**.

misconduct noun SEE **misbehaviour**.

miscreant noun SEE **wrongdoer**.

miser noun hoarder, miserly person [SEE **miserly**], [*informal*] skinflint.
OPPOSITES: SEE **spendthrift**.

miserable adjective **1** *miserable after hearing bad news.* broken-hearted, dejected, depressed, desolate, despondent, disconsolate, distressed, doleful, [*informal*] down, downcast, down-hearted, forlorn, gloomy, glum, grief-stricken, heartbroken, joyless, lonely, melancholy, moping, mournful, SEE **sad**, tearful, uneasy, unfortunate, unhappy, unlucky, woebegone, wretched.
OPPOSITES: SEE **happy**.
2 *miserable living conditions.* abject, destitute, disgraceful, distressing, heartbreaking, hopeless, impoverished, inhuman, pathetic, pitiable, pitiful, SEE **poor**, sordid, soul-destroying, squalid, uncivilized, uncomfortable, vile, worthless, wretched.
OPPOSITES: SEE **affluent**.
3 *miserable weather.* SEE **bad**, cheerless, depressing, dismal, dreary, grey.
OPPOSITES: SEE **bright**.
4 *He's a miserable old so-and-so!* churlish, cross, disagreeable, discontented, [*informal*] grumpy, ill-natured, mean, miserly, morose, sulky, sullen, surly, unfriendly, unhelpful.
OPPOSITES: SEE **cheerful**.

miserly adjective avaricious, [*informal*] close, [*informal*] close-fisted, covetous, economical, grasping, mean, mercenary, mingy, niggardly, parsimonious, penny-pinching, stingy, [*informal*] tight, [*informal*] tight-fisted.
OPPOSITES: SEE **generous**.

misery noun **1** *You could see the misery on their faces.* anguish, bitterness, depression, despair, distress, gloom, grief, heartache, heartbreak, melancholy, sadness, sorrow, suffering, unhappiness, wretchedness.
2 *a life of misery.* adversity, affliction, deprivation, destitution, hardship, misfortune, need, oppression, penury, poverty, privation, squalor, tribulation, want.

misfire verb *The plan misfired.* abort, fail, fall through, [*informal*] flop, founder, go wrong, miscarry.
OPPOSITES: SEE **succeed**.

misfortune noun *We had the misfortune of breaking down.* accident, adversity, affliction, bad luck, bane (*the bane of my life*), calamity, catastrophe, disappointment, disaster, hardship, misadventure, mischance, mishap, reverse, setback, tragedy, trouble, vicissitude.
OPPOSITES: SEE **luck**.

misgiving noun SEE **anxiety**.

misguided adjective SEE **mistaken**.

mishap noun SEE **accident**.

misinform verb SEE **mislead**.

misjudge verb *to misjudge a situation.* get wrong, guess wrongly, [*informal*] jump to the wrong conclusion about, make a mistake about, miscalculate, misinterpret, SEE **misunderstand**, overestimate, underestimate, undervalue.

mislay verb *I mislaid my purse.* SEE **lose**.

mislead verb *Don't try to mislead us!* bluff, confuse, deceive, delude, fool, give misleading information to [SEE **misleading**], give a wrong impression to, hoax, hoodwink, [*informal*] kid, [*informal*] lead up the garden path, lie to, misinform, [*informal*] take for a ride, take in, trick.

misleading adjective *misleading directions.* ambiguous, confusing, deceptive, dishonest, distorted, equivocal, evasive, fallacious, false, SEE **lying**, muddling, puzzling, specious, spurious, unreliable, unsound, wrong.

mismanage verb SEE **bungle**.

misplace verb SEE **lose**, put in the wrong place.

misprint noun SEE **mistake** noun.

misrepresent verb SEE **falsify**.

miss verb **1** *to miss a bus.* be too late for, let go, lose.
2 *to miss a target.* be wide of, fail to hit, fall short of.
3 *to miss an appointment.* avoid, be absent from, forget, play truant from, [*informal*] skip, [*informal*] skive off.
4 *to miss someone who is absent.* grieve for, lament, long for, need, pine for, want, yearn for.
to miss something out SEE **omit**.

missal noun prayer-book.

misshapen adjective *a misshapen tree-trunk.* crooked, deformed, disfigured, distorted, grotesque, malformed, monstrous, twisted, ugly, warped.
OPPOSITE: SEE **perfect** adjective.

missile noun VARIOUS MISSILES: arrow, bomb, brickbat, bullet, dart, grenade, projectile, rocket, shell, shot, torpedo.
VARIOUS WEAPONS: SEE **weapons**.

missing adjective *missing children.* absent, disappeared, lost, mislaid, straying, unaccounted for.

mission noun **1** *a mission into the unknown.* expedition, exploration, journey, sortie, voyage.
2 *a mission to help the starving.* SEE **campaign**.

missionary noun SEE **preacher**.

missive noun SEE **letter**.

mist noun **1** *mist in the air.* cloud, drizzle, fog, haze, vapour.
2 *mist on the windows.* condensation, film, steam.

mistake noun [*informal*] bloomer, blunder, [*informal*] boob, [*informal*] clanger, error, faux pas, gaffe, [*informal*] howler, inaccuracy, indiscretion, lapse, miscalculation, miscarriage (*of justice*), misjudgement, misprint, misspelling, misunderstanding, omission, oversight, slip, slip-up, [*formal*] solecism.

mistake verb *I mistook your message.* confuse, get wrong, [*informal*] get the wrong end of the stick, misconstrue, misinterpret, misjudge, misread, misunderstand, mix up.

mistaken adjective *a mistaken decision.* erroneous, ill-judged, inappropriate, incorrect, inexact, misguided, misinformed, unfounded, unjust, unsound, SEE **wrong** adjective.

mistimed adjective *mistimed publicity. a mistimed visit.* badly timed, early, inconvenient, inopportune, late, unseasonable, untimely.

mistreat verb *to mistreat animals.* abuse, batter, harm, hurt, ill-treat, ill-use, [*informal*] knock about, misuse.

mistress noun **1** *the mistress of a dog.* keeper, owner, person in charge, proprietor.
2 [*mostly old-fashioned*] *a man's mistress.* SEE **lover**.

mistrust verb *I mistrust his judgement.* be sceptical about, be wary of, disbelieve, distrust, doubt, fear, have misgivings about, question, suspect.
OPPOSITES: SEE **trust** verb.

misty adjective *misty windows. a misty view.* bleary, blurred, blurry, clouded, cloudy, dim, faint, foggy, fuzzy, hazy, indistinct, opaque, shadowy, smoky, steamy, unclear, vague.
OPPOSITES: SEE **clear** adjective.

misunderstand verb *to misunderstand a message.* get wrong, [*informal*] get the wrong end of the stick, have a misunderstanding about [SEE **misunderstanding**], misconstrue, mishear, misinterpret, SEE **misjudge**, misread, miss the point, mistake, mistranslate.
OPPOSITES: SEE **understand**.

misunderstanding noun **1** *a misunderstanding of the problem.* error, failure of understanding, misapprehension, misconception, misinterpretation, misjudgement, mistake, [*informal*] mix-up.
2 *a misunderstanding with someone.* argument, [*informal*] contretemps, difference of opinion, disagreement, dispute, SEE **quarrel** noun.

misuse noun *You won't get your money back if it's damaged through misuse.* abuse, careless use, ill-treatment, ill-use, maltreatment, mishandling, mistreatment.

misuse verb **1** *Someone misused my tape-recorder.* damage, harm, mishandle, treat carelessly.
2 *He misused his dog shamefully.* abuse, batter, hurt, ill-treat, injure, [*informal*] knock about, mistreat, treat badly.
3 *She misused the club funds.* fritter away, misappropriate, squander, use wrongly, waste.

mitigate verb *to mitigate the effect of something.* SEE **lessen**.

mitigating adjective *mitigating circumstances.* extenuating, justifying, qualifying.

mix verb **1** *Mix the ingredients together. Oil and water won't mix.* amalgamate, blend, coalesce, combine, compound, confuse, diffuse, emulsify, fuse, homogenize, integrate, intermingle, join, jumble up, make a mixture [SEE **mixture**], meld, merge, mingle, mix up, muddle, put together, shuffle (*cards or papers*), unite.
OPPOSITES: SEE **separate** verb.
2 *He mixed with the wrong crowd.* SEE **socialize**.

mixed adjective **1** *mixed biscuits.* assorted, different, diverse, heterogeneous, miscellaneous, muddled, varied, various.
2 *a mixed team.* amalgamated, combined, composite, integrated, hybrid, joint, united.
3 *mixed feelings.* ambiguous, ambivalent, confused, equivocal, uncertain.

mixture noun *a mixture of ingredients.* alloy (*of metals*), amalgam, association, assortment, blend, collection, combination, composite, compound, concoction, conglomeration, emulsion (*of a solid in a liquid*), fusion, [*informal*] hotchpotch, hybrid [*=a mixture of species or varieties*], jumble, medley, mélange, miscellany, mix, mongrel [*=a mixture of breeds*], pot-pourri, suspension (*of a solid in a liquid*), variety.

mnemonic noun SEE **reminder**.

moan verb **1** VARIOUS SOUNDS: SEE **sound** noun.
2 *We moaned about the food.* SEE **complain**.

moat noun SEE **ditch** noun.

mob noun *an angry mob.* [*informal*] bunch, crowd, gang, SEE **group** noun, herd, horde, pack, rabble, riot, [*informal*] shower, swarm, throng.

mob verb *to mob a pop idol.* besiege, crowd round, hem in, jostle, surround, swarm round, throng round.

mobile adjective **1** *a mobile caravan.* itinerant, movable, portable, travelling.
2 *It didn't take me long to get mobile after my accident.* able to move, active, agile, independent, moving about, [*informal*] on the go, [*informal*] up and about.
3 *mobile features.* changeable, changing, expressive, flexible, fluid, shifting.
OPPOSITES: SEE **immobile, static.**

mobilize verb *to mobilize support.* activate, assemble, call up, enlist, gather, get together, levy, marshal, muster, organize, rally, stir up, summon.

mock adjective *mock cream.* SEE **imitation** adjective.

mock verb *They mocked my pathetic attempts.* deride, disparage, insult, jeer at, lampoon, laugh at, make fun of, parody, poke fun at, ridicule, satirize, scoff at, scorn, [*informal*] send up, sneer at, taunt, tease, travesty.

mockery noun *a mockery of the truth.* lampoon, parody, satire, [*informal*] send-up, travesty.

mocking adjective *mocking insults.* contemptuous, derisive, disparaging, disrespectful, insulting, irreverent, rude, sarcastic, satirical, scornful, taunting, teasing, uncomplimentary, unkind.
OPPOSITES: SEE **respectful.**

mock-up noun SEE **model** noun.

mode noun SEE **method.**

model adjective **1** *a model railway.* SEE **imitation** adjective, **toy** adjective.
2 *a model pupil.* SEE **ideal** adjective.

model noun **1** *scale models.* copy, dummy, effigy, image, imitation, miniature, replica, representation, toy.
2 *a model of a futuristic car.* archetype, [*informal*] mock-up, paradigm, pattern, prototype.
3 *a model of good behaviour.* byword, example, ideal, paragon, yardstick.
4 *an out-of-date model.* design, mark, type, version.
5 *a fashion model.* mannequin.

model verb **1** *to model something in clay.* SEE **sculpture** verb.
2 *I modelled the characters on my own family.* base.

moderate adjective **1** *moderate prices. moderate opinions. a moderate drinker.* average, cautious, deliberate, fair, medium, middle, [*informal*] middle-of-the-road, middling, modest, normal, ordinary, rational, reasonable, respectable, sensible, sober, steady, temperate, usual.
2 *a moderate wind.* gentle, light, mild.
OPPOSITES: SEE **excessive, extreme** adjective.

moderate verb **1** *The storm moderated.* abate, become less extreme, decline, decrease, die down, ease off, subside.
2 *Please moderate the noise.* check, curb, keep down, lessen, make less extreme, mitigate, modify, modulate, regulate, restrain, subdue, temper, tone down.

moderately adverb *moderately good.* fairly, passably, [*informal*] pretty, quite, rather, reasonably, somewhat, to some extent.

moderation noun *He always showed moderation in his drinking.* caution, reasonableness, sobriety, temperance.

modern adjective *modern music. modern architecture.* advanced, avant-garde, contemporary, current, fashionable, forward-looking, futuristic, the latest, new, [*uncomplimentary*] newfangled, novel, present, present-day, progressive, recent, stylish, [*informal*] trendy, up-to-date, up-to-the-minute, [*informal*] with it.
OPPOSITES: SEE **old.**

modernize verb *to modernize an old house.* [*informal*] do up, improve, make modern [SEE **modern**], rebuild, refurbish, regenerate, renovate, update.

modest adjective **1** *modest about your success.* humble, lowly, meek, quiet, reserved, reticent, unassuming, unpretentious.
OPPOSITES: SEE **conceited.**
2 *modest about getting undressed.* bashful, coy, demure, shamefaced, shy.
3 *a modest dress.* chaste, decent, discreet, plain, proper, seemly, simple.
OPPOSITES: SEE **indecent.**
4 *a modest sum of money.* SEE **moderate** adjective.

modesty noun **1** *modesty about your success.* humbleness, humility, reserve, reticence, self-effacement.
2 *modesty about getting undressed.* bashfulness, coyness, demureness, shyness.

modicum noun SEE **small (small amount).**

modify verb *to modify the design of something.* adapt, adjust, alter, change, convert, improve, SEE **moderate** verb, redesign, re-organize, revise, transform, vary.

modish adjective SEE **fashionable.**

modulate verb *to modulate your voice.* adjust, change, change the tone of, SEE **moderate** verb, regulate, tone down.

module noun SEE **unit**.

mogul noun SEE **important (important person)**.

moist adjective affected by moisture [SEE **moisture**], clammy, damp, dank, dewy, humid [*informal*] muggy, rainy, [*informal*] runny, steamy, watery, SEE **wet** adjective.
OPPOSITES: SEE **dry** adjective.

moisten verb damp, dampen, humidify, make moist [SEE **moist**], moisturize, soak, wet.
OPPOSITES: SEE **dry** verb.

moisture noun condensation, damp, dampness, dankness, dew, humidity, liquid, [*formal*] precipitation, steam, vapour, water, wet, wetness.

moisturize verb SEE **moisten**.

molar noun SEE **tooth**.

mole noun **1** *a mole on the skin.* SEE **spot** noun.
2 *a mole built into the sea.* SEE **breakwater**.
3 [*informal*] *a mole working for the government.* agent, secret agent, spy.

molecule noun SEE **particle**.

molest verb *Hooligans molested the bystanders.* abuse, annoy, assault, attack, badger, bother, harass, harry, hassle, interfere with, irritate, manhandle, mistreat, persecute, pester, set on, tease, torment, vex, worry.

mollify verb SEE **soothe**.

mollycoddle verb SEE **pamper**.

molten adjective *molten metal.* liquefied, liquid, melted.

moment noun **1** *over in a moment.* flash, instant, [*informal*] jiffy, minute, second, split second, [*informal*] tick, [*informal*] trice, [*informal*] twinkling of an eye.
2 *an important moment.* juncture, occasion, opportunity, point in time, time.

momentary adjective *a momentary lapse of memory.* brief, ephemeral, fleeting, passing, quick, short, temporary, transient, transitory.
OPPOSITES: SEE **permanent**.

momentous adjective *a momentous decision.* critical, crucial, decisive, epoch-making, fateful, historic, SEE **important**, significant.
OPPOSITES: SEE **unimportant**.

momentum noun SEE **impetus**.

monarch noun SEE **ruler**.

monarchy noun kingdom, realm.
FORMS OF GOVERNMENT: SEE **government**.

monastery noun SEE **church**.

monaural adjective SEE **monophonic**.

money noun [*informal*] bread, currency, [*informal*] dough, finances, [*informal*] lolly, [*old-fashioned*] lucre, riches, wealth, [*informal*] the wherewithal.
RELATED ADJECTIVES: financial, monetary, pecuniary.

FORMS IN WHICH YOU CAN SPEND MONEY: bank-notes, cash, change, cheque, coins, coppers, credit card, credit transfer, notes, pennies, silver, sterling, traveller's cheque.

EVERYDAY TERMS FOR MONEY YOU OWE, OWN, PAY, OR RECEIVE: arrears, assets, capital, damages, debt, dividend, dowry, dues, duty, earnings, endowment, estate, expenditure, fortune, funds, grant, income, interest, investments, loan, mortgage, [*informal*] nest-egg, outgoings, patrimony, pay, pension, pocket-money, proceeds, profits, remittance, resources, revenue, salary, savings, takings, tax, wages, winnings.

---

money-box noun cash-box, coffer, piggy-bank, safe, till.

moneyed adjective SEE **wealthy**.

money-grubbing adjective SEE **greedy**.

mongolism noun Down's syndrome.

mongrel noun cross-breed, hybrid.

monitor noun *a TV monitor.* screen, set, television, TV, VDU [=*visual display unit*].

monk noun brother, friar, hermit.

monkey noun SOME KINDS OF MONKEY: ape, baboon, chimpanzee, gibbon, gorilla, marmoset, orang-utan.
RELATED ADJECTIVE: simian.
OTHER ANIMALS: SEE **animal** noun.

monkey verb to **monkey about** SEE **mess** verb (**to mess about**).

The prefix *mono-* or *mon-* in words such as *monarchy, monaural, monogamy,* etc. is related to Greek *monos* = *alone, single.*

---

mono adjective SEE **monophonic**.

monochrome adjective *monochrome pictures.* black and white.
OPPOSITES: coloured, in colour.

monocle noun SEE **glass (glasses)**.

monogamy noun SEE **marriage**.

monogram noun SEE **symbol**.

monograph noun SEE **writing**.

monolith noun SEE **stone** noun.

monologue noun SEE **speech**.

monophonic adjective monaural, [*informal*] mono.
OPPOSITES: stereo, stereophonic.

monopolize verb *to monopolize a conversation.* control, [*informal*] corner, have a monopoly of, [*informal*] hog, keep for yourself, shut others out of, take over.
OPPOSITES: SEE **share** verb.

monotonous adjective *a monotonous voice. a monotonous landscape.* boring, dreary, dull, featureless, flat, level, repetitive, tedious, toneless, unchanging, uneventful, unexciting, uniform, uninteresting, unvarying, wearisome.
OPPOSITES: SEE **interesting**.

monsoon noun SEE **wind** noun.

monster adjective *a monster birthday cake.* SEE **huge**.

monster noun *a frightening monster.* abortion, beast, brute, freak, giant, monstrosity, monstrous creature or thing [SEE **monstrous**], mutant, ogre.
OTHER LEGENDARY CREATURES: SEE **legend**.

monstrosity noun SEE **monster** noun.

monstrous adjective **1** *a creature of monstrous size.* SEE **big**, colossal, elephantine, enormous, gargantuan, giant, gigantic, great, huge, hulking, immense, mammoth, mighty, titanic, towering, vast.
2 *a monstrous crime.* abhorrent, atrocious, cruel, dreadful, evil, gross, gruesome, heinous, hideous, [*informal*] horrendous, horrible, horrifying, inhuman, obscene, outrageous, repulsive, shocking, terrible, villainous, wicked.

montage noun SEE **picture** noun.

monument noun *a monument to the dead. an ancient monument.* cairn, cenotaph, cross, gravestone, headstone, mausoleum, memorial, obelisk, pillar, prehistoric remains [SEE **prehistoric**], relic, reminder, shrine, tomb, tombstone.

monumental adjective **1** *a monumental plaque.* commemorative, memorial.
2 *of monumental size.* awe-inspiring, awesome, grand, SEE **huge**, impressive.

moo verb VARIOUS SOUNDS: SEE **sound** noun.

mooch verb SEE **walk** verb.

mood noun **1** *in a good mood. in a bad mood.* disposition, humour, spirit, state of mind, temper, vein.
2 *the mood of a piece of music.* atmosphere, feeling, tone.
WORDS TO DESCRIBE VARIOUS MOODS: SEE **angry**, **happy**, **sad**, etc.

moody adjective bad-tempered, capricious, changeable, cross, depressed, depressive, disgruntled, erratic, gloomy, grumpy, irritable, melancholy, miserable, morose, peevish, short-tempered, snappy, sulky, sullen, temperamental, [*informal*] touchy, unpredictable, unstable, volatile.

moon noun ASTRONOMICAL TERMS: SEE **astronomy**.
RELATED ADJECTIVE: lunar.

moon verb *to moon about.* SEE **mope**.

moonlight noun SEE **light** noun.

moor noun *a windswept moor.* fell, heath, moorland.

moor verb *to moor a boat.* anchor, berth, SEE **fasten**, secure, tie up.

moot adjective *a moot point.* SEE **debatable**.

moot verb *to moot an idea.* SEE **suggest**.

mop verb *to mop up.* SEE **clean** verb.

mope verb *He moped about because he wasn't invited to the party.* be sad [SEE **sad**], brood, despair, grieve, languish, [*informal*] moon, pine, sulk.

moral adjective **1** *a moral person. moral principles.* blameless, chaste, decent, ethical, good, high-minded, honest, honourable, incorruptible, innocent, irreproachable, just, law-abiding, noble, principled, pure, responsible, right, righteous, sinless, trustworthy, truthful, upright, virtuous.
2 *a moral tale.* cautionary, didactic, moralistic, moralizing.
OPPOSITES: SEE **immoral**.
a moral tale cautionary tale, fable, parable.

moral noun *What's the moral of the story?* lesson, meaning, message, precept, principle.
morals SEE **morality**.

morale noun *The team's morale is high.* cheerfulness, confidence, [*informal*] heart, mood, self-confidence, self-esteem, spirit, state of mind.

morality noun *I question the morality of some kinds of advertising.* conduct, decency, ethics, ethos, goodness, honesty, ideals, integrity, morals, principles, scruples, standards, uprightness, virtue.
OPPOSITES: SEE **immorality**.

moralize verb lecture, philosophize, pontificate, preach, sermonize.

morass noun SEE **marsh**.

moratorium noun SEE **ban** noun, **delay** noun.

morbid adjective *a morbid account of her death.* brooding, ghoulish, gloomy, grim, macabre, melancholy, morose,

pessimistic, [*informal*] sick, unhappy, unhealthy, unpleasant, unwholesome.
OPPOSITES: SEE **cheerful**.

mordant adjective *mordant criticism.* SEE **sharp**.

more adjective added, additional, extra, further, increased, new, other, renewed, supplementary.
OPPOSITES: SEE **less**.

moreover adverb also, besides, further, furthermore, too.

morgue noun mortuary.

moribund adjective SEE **dying**.

morning noun TIMES OF THE DAY: SEE **day**.
RELATED ADJECTIVE: matutinal.

moron noun SEE **idiot**.

moronic adjective SEE **stupid**.

morose adjective *a morose expression.* bad-tempered, churlish, depressed, gloomy, glum, grim, humourless, ill-natured, melancholy, moody, mournful, pessimistic, SEE **sad**, saturnine, sour, sulky, sullen, surly, taciturn, unhappy, unsociable.
OPPOSITES: SEE **cheerful**.

morsel noun *a morsel of food.* bite, crumb, fragment, mouthful, nibble, piece, scrap, small amount [SEE **small**], taste, titbit.

mortal adjective **1** *mortal beings.* earthly, ephemeral, human, passing, transient.
OPPOSITES: SEE **immortal**.
2 *a mortal sickness.* deadly, fatal, lethal, terminal.
3 *mortal enemies.* deadly, implacable, irreconcilable, remorseless, sworn (*sworn enemy*), unrelenting.

mortal noun *We are mortals, not gods.* human being, mortal creature [SEE **mortal** adjective], SEE **person**.

mortality noun **1** *We aren't gods: we must accept our mortality.* corruptibility, humanity, impermanence, transience.
OPPOSITES: SEE **immortality**.
2 *There is high mortality among young birds.* death-rate, dying, fatalities, loss of life.
OPPOSITES: SEE **survival**.

mortgage noun SEE **loan**.

mortify verb SEE **humiliate**.

mortuary noun morgue.

mosaic noun VARIOUS PICTURES: SEE **picture** noun.

mostly adverb chiefly, commonly, generally, largely, mainly, normally, predominantly, primarily, principally, typically, usually.

motel noun SEE **accommodation**.

moth-eaten adjective *a moth-eaten appearance.* antiquated, decrepit, mangy, SEE **old**, ragged, shabby, [*informal*] tatty.

mother noun **1** [*informal*] ma or mamma, [*old-fashioned*] mater, [*informal*] mum or mummy, parent.

mother verb *He likes to mother the toddlers.* care for, cherish, comfort, cuddle, fuss over, love, nurse, pamper, protect.

motherly adjective *a motherly person.* caring, kind, SEE **loving**, maternal, protective.

motif noun *a floral motif on the curtains.* design, device, ornament, pattern, SEE **symbol**, theme.

motion noun SEE **movement**.

motion verb *She motioned him to sit down.* SEE **gesture** verb.

motionless adjective *motionless statues. motionless waters.* at rest, calm, frozen, immobile, inanimate, inert, lifeless, paralysed, peaceful, resting, stagnant, static, stationary, still, stock-still, unmoving.
OPPOSITES: SEE **moving**.

motivate verb *What motivated her to do such a thing?* arouse, be the motivation of [SEE **motivation**], encourage, incite, induce, inspire, move, persuade, prompt, provoke, push, spur, stimulate, stir, urge.

motivation noun *the motivation behind someone's achievement.* drive, encouragement, impulse, incentive, inducement, inspiration, instigation, SEE **motive**, provocation, push, spur, stimulus.

motive noun *the motive for a crime.* aim, cause, grounds, intention, SEE **motivation**, object, purpose, rationale, reason, thinking.

motley adjective SEE **miscellaneous**.

motor noun *an electric motor.* engine.
a motor boat BOATS: SEE **vessel**.
a motor car VEHICLES: SEE **vehicle**.

motor verb *We motored into town.* drive, go by car, SEE **travel** verb.

motorist noun SEE **traveller**.

motorway noun VARIOUS ROADS: SEE **road**.

mottled adjective SEE **dappled**.

motto noun SEE **saying**.

mould noun *mould on cheese.* fungus, growth, mildew.

mould verb *to mould clay.* cast, fashion, form, model, [*informal*] sculpt, shape.

moulder verb SEE **decay**.

mouldy adjective *a mouldy smell.* damp, decaying, fusty, mildewed, musty, rotten, stale.

mound noun *a mound of rubbish.* SEE **pile** noun.

mount noun SEE **mountain**.

mount verb **1** *to mount the stairs. to mount into the air.* ascend, climb, go up, rise, soar.
OPPOSITES: SEE **descend**.
2 *to mount a horse.* get astride, get on, jump onto.
OPPOSITES: SEE **dismount**.
3 *My savings mounted. The excitement mounted.* accumulate, get bigger, grow, increase, intensify, multiply, pile up, swell.
OPPOSITES: SEE **decrease** verb.
4 *to mount a picture. to mount an exhibition.* display, frame, install, put in place, set up.

mountain noun **1** [*poetic*] alp, arête, [*Scottish*] ben, eminence, height, hill, mound, mount, peak, range, ridge, sierra, summit, volcano.
2 [*informal*] *a mountain of business to get through.* SEE **pile** noun.

mountaineer noun climber.

mountaineering noun climbing, rock-climbing.

mountainous adjective **1** *mountainous slopes.* alpine, daunting, high, hilly, precipitous, rocky, rugged, steep, towering.
2 *mountainous waves.* SEE **huge**.

mountebank noun SEE **swindler**.

mourn verb *He mourned for his dead dog.* bewail, fret, go into mourning, grieve, lament, mope, pine, wail, weep.
OPPOSITES: SEE **rejoice**.

mourner noun WORDS TO DO WITH FUNERALS: SEE **funeral**.

mournful adjective *a mournful cry. a mournful occasion.* dismal, distressed, distressing, doleful, funereal, gloomy, grief-stricken, grieving, heartbreaking, heartbroken, lamenting, lugubrious, melancholy, plaintive, plangent, SEE **sad**, sorrowful, tearful, tragic, unhappy, woeful.
OPPOSITES: SEE **cheerful**.

moustache noun whiskers.

mousy adjective SEE **timid**.

mouth noun **1** [*slang*] gob, jaws, lips, palate.
RELATED ADJECTIVE: oral.
2 *the mouth of a cave. the mouth of a bottle.* aperture, doorway, entrance, exit, gateway, opening, orifice, outlet.
3 *the mouth of a river.* estuary, outlet.

mouth verb *to mouth curses.* articulate, form, pronounce, SEE **say**.

mouthful noun *a mouthful of food.* bite, gobbet, gulp, morsel, spoonful, swallow, taste.

mouth-organ noun harmonica.

movable adjective *movable furniture.* adjustable, detachable, mobile, portable, transferable, transportable.
OPPOSITES: SEE **immobile**.

move noun **1** *What will the criminal's next move be?* act, action, deed, gambit, manœuvre, measure, movement, ploy, [*informal*] shift, step, stratagem, [*informal*] tack, tactic.
2 *It's your move next.* chance, go, opportunity, turn.

move verb [Many words can be used as synonyms of *move*. We give some of the commoner ones.]
1 *to move about.* be agitated, be astir, budge, change places, change position, fidget, flap, roll, shake, shift, stir, swing, toss, tremble, turn, twist, twitch, wag, [*informal*] waggle, wave, [*informal*] wiggle.
2 *to move along.* cruise, fly, jog, journey, make headway, make progress, march, pass, proceed, SEE **travel** verb, **walk** verb.
3 *to move along quickly.* bolt, canter, career, dart, dash, flit, flounce, fly, gallop, hasten, hurry, hurtle, hustle, [*informal*] nip, race, run, rush, shoot, speed, stampede, streak, tear (*We tore home*), [*informal*] zip, [*informal*] zoom.
4 *to move along slowly.* amble, crawl, dawdle, drift, stroll.
5 *to move along gracefully.* dance, flow, glide, skate, skim, slide, slip, sweep.
6 *to move along awkwardly.* dodder, falter, flounder, lumber, lurch, pitch, shuffle, stagger, stumble, sway, totter, trip, trundle.
7 *to move along stealthily.* crawl, creep, edge, slink, slither.
8 *to move things from one place to another.* carry, export, import, shift, ship, relocate, transfer, transplant, transport, transpose.
9 *to move someone to do something.* encourage, impel, influence, inspire, persuade, prompt, stimulate, urge.
10 *to move someone's feelings.* affect, arouse, enrage, fire, impassion, rouse, stir, touch.
11 *I wonder when they will move on our application.* act, do something, make a move [SEE **move** noun], take action.

to move away budge, depart, go, leave, migrate, quit, start.
to move back back off, retreat, reverse, withdraw.
to move down descend, drop, fall, lower, sink, swoop.
to move in enter, penetrate.
to move round circulate, revolve, roll, rotate, spin, tour, turn, twirl, twist, wheel, whirl.
to move towards advance, approach, come, proceed, progress.
to move up arise, ascend, climb, mount, rise.

movement noun 1 *Animals are capable of movement.* action, activity, SEE **gesture** noun, motion, SEE **move** noun.
2 *Has there been any movement in their attitude?* change, development, evolution, progress, shift, trend.
3 *a political movement.* campaign, crusade, group, organization, party.
4 *military movements.* exercise, operation.

movie noun SEE **film**.

moving adjective 1 *a moving object.* active, alive, astir, dynamic, mobile, movable, on the move, travelling, under way.
OPPOSITES: SEE **motionless**.
2 *a moving story.* affecting, emotional, emotive, heart-warming, inspiring, pathetic, poignant, [*uncomplimentary*] sentimental, stirring, [*informal*] tear-jerking, touching.
OPPOSITES: SEE **unemotional**.

mow verb *to mow the grass.* clip, SEE **cut** verb, trim.

Mr, Mrs, Ms VARIOUS TITLES: SEE **title** noun.

muck noun dirt, dung, filth, grime, manure, mire, mud, ooze, rubbish, sewage, slime, sludge.

mucky adjective dirty, filthy, foul, grimy, grubby, messy, muddy, soiled, sordid, squalid.
OPPOSITES: SEE **clean** adjective.

mucus noun phlegm, slime.

mud noun clay, dirt, mire, muck, ooze, silt, slime, sludge, slurry, soil.

muddle noun 1 *There was a muddle over the arrangements.* bewilderment, confusion, misunderstanding, [*informal*] mix-up.
2 *My room is in a muddle.* clutter, disorder, jumble, mess, [*informal*] shambles, tangle, untidiness.

muddle verb 1 *You muddle me when you talk fast.* bewilder, confuse, disorientate, mislead, perplex, puzzle.
OPPOSITES: SEE **clarify**.
2 *Don't muddle the clothes in the drawer.* disarrange, disorder, disorganize, [*informal*] foul up, jumble, make a mess of, [*informal*] mess up, mix up, shuffle, tangle.
OPPOSITES: SEE **tidy** verb.

muddled, muddle-headed adjectives SEE **confused**.

muddy adjective 1 *muddy shoes.* caked, dirty, filthy, messy, mucky, soiled.
OPPOSITES: SEE **clean** adjective.
2 *muddy ground.* boggy, marshy, sloppy, sodden, soft, spongy, waterlogged, SEE **wet** adjective.
OPPOSITES: SEE **firm** adjective, **dry** adjective.
3 *muddy water.* cloudy, impure, misty, opaque.
OPPOSITES: SEE **clear** adjective.

muff verb SEE **bungle**.

muffle verb 1 *to muffle yourself up in cold weather.* cover, enclose, envelop, swathe, wrap up.
2 *to muffle a noise.* dampen, deaden, disguise, dull, make muffled [SEE **muffled**], mask, mute, quieten, silence, soften, stifle, suppress.

muffled adjective *a muffled sound.* deadened, dull, fuzzy, indistinct, muted, unclear, woolly.
OPPOSITE: SEE **clear** adjective.

muffler noun scarf.

mug noun 1 *a mug to drink from.* beaker, cup, [*old-fashioned*] flagon, tankard.
2 [*slang*] *a mug who is easily fooled.* SEE **fool** noun.

mug verb assault, attack, beat up, jump on, molest, rob, set on, steal from.
to mug up SEE **learn**.

mugger noun attacker, SEE **criminal** noun, hooligan, robber, ruffian, thief, thug.

mugging noun attack, robbery, street crime.
OTHER CRIMES: SEE **crime**.

muggins noun SEE **fool** noun.

muggy adjective *muggy weather.* clammy, close, damp, humid, moist, oppressive, steamy, sticky, stuffy, sultry, warm.

mulct verb SEE **rob**.

mule noun SEE **horse**.

mulish adjective SEE **stubborn**.

mull verb **to mull over** SEE **think**.

The prefix *multi-* and words such as *multifarious, multiply*, and *multitude* are related to Latin *multus = much, many*.

---

multifarious adjective SEE **various**.

multiple adjective *a multiple crash on the motorway. multiple injuries.* complex, compound, double [= × *2*], involving many, numerous, plural, quadruple [= × *4*], quintuple [= × *5*], triple [= × *3*].

multiplicity noun *The accident was due to a multiplicity of causes.* abundance, array, complex, diversity, number, plurality, profusion, variety.

multiply verb **1** double [= *multiply by 2*], quadruple [× *4*], quintuple [× *5*], triple [× *3*], [*informal*] times.
MATHEMATICAL TERMS: SEE **mathematics**.
2 *Mice multiply quickly.* become numerous, breed, increase, proliferate, propagate, reproduce, spread.

multitude noun *a multitude of people. a multitude of things to do.* SEE **crowd** noun, host, large number, legion, lots, mass, myriad, swarm, throng.

multitudinous adjective SEE **numerous**.

mum adjective *Keep mum!* SEE **silent**.

mum noun SEE **mother** noun.

mumble verb SEE **talk** verb.

mumbo-jumbo noun SEE **magic** noun.

mummify verb embalm, SEE **preserve** verb.

mummy noun **1** SEE **mother** noun.
2 *an Egyptian mummy.* SEE **body**.

munch verb bite, chew, chomp, crunch, SEE **eat**, gnaw.

mundane adjective *It was hard to return to mundane matters after such excitement.* banal, common, commonplace, down-to-earth, dull, everyday, familiar, human, material, SEE **ordinary**, physical, practical, quotidian, routine, worldly.
OPPOSITES: SEE **extraordinary**, **spiritual**.

municipal adjective *municipal government. municipal affairs.* borough, city, civic, community, district, local, public, urban.
OPPOSITES: SEE **national**.

munificent adjective SEE **generous**.

munitions noun SEE **weapons**.

mural noun fresco, wall-painting.
VARIOUS PICTURES: SEE **picture** noun.

murder noun assassination, fratricide, homicide, infanticide, SEE **killing** noun, matricide, parricide, patricide, regicide.

murder verb assassinate, SEE **kill**.

murderer noun assassin, SEE **killer**.

murderous adjective *murderous bandits.* barbarous, bloodthirsty, brutal, cruel, dangerous, deadly, ferocious, fierce, homicidal, pitiless, ruthless, savage, vicious, violent.

murky adjective *murky water. murky light.* cloudy, dark, dim, dull, foggy, gloomy, grey, misty, muddy, obscure, sombre.
OPPOSITES: SEE **clear** adjective.

murmur noun, verb SEE **sound** noun, **talk** verb.

muscle noun PARTS OF YOUR BODY: SEE **body**.

muscular adjective *a muscular wrestler.* athletic, [*informal*] beefy, brawny, burly, hefty, [*informal*] hulking, husky, powerful, robust, sinewy, [*informal*] strapping, strong, sturdy, tough, well-built, well-developed, wiry.
OPPOSITES: SEE **feeble**.

muse verb SEE **think**.

mush noun SEE **pulp** noun.

mushroom noun SEE **fungus**.

mushroom verb SEE **grow**.

mushy adjective SEE **soft**.

music noun harmony, pleasant sound.

KINDS OF MUSIC: chamber music, choral music, classical music, dance music, disco music, folk-music, instrumental music, jazz, orchestral music, plainsong, pop music, ragtime, reggae, rock, soul, swing.

VARIOUS MUSICAL COMPOSITIONS: anthem, ballad, blues, cadenza, calypso, canon, cantata, canticle, carol, chant, concerto, SEE **dance** noun, dirge, duet, étude, fanfare, fugue, hymn, improvisation, intermezzo, lullaby, march, musical, nocturne, nonet, octet, opera, operetta, oratorio, overture, prelude, quartet, quintet, rhapsody, rondo, scherzo, sea shanty, septet, sextet, sonata, SEE **song**, spiritual, symphony, toccata, trio.

FAMILIES OF MUSICAL INSTRUMENTS: brass, keyboard, percussion, strings, woodwind.

MUSICAL INSTRUMENTS: accordion, bagpipes, banjo, barrel organ, bassoon, bugle, castanets, cello, clarinet, clavichord, concertina, cor anglais, cornet, cymbals, double-bass, drum, dulcimer, euphonium, fiddle, fife, flute, French horn, glockenspiel, gong, guitar.

harmonica, harmonium, harp, harpsichord, horn, hurdy-gurdy, kettledrum, keyboard, lute, lyre, mouth-organ, oboe, organ, piano, piccolo, pipes, recorder, saxophone, sitar, spinet, synthesizer, tambourine, timpani, tomtom, triangle, trombone, trumpet, tuba, tubular bells, ukulele, viol, viola, violin, virginals, xylophone, zither.

VARIOUS MUSICIANS: accompanist, bass, bugler, cellist, clarinettist, composer, conductor, contralto, drummer, fiddler, flautist, guitarist, harpist, instrumentalist, maestro, minstrel, oboist, organist, percussionist, pianist, piper, singer, soloist, soprano, tenor, timpanist, treble, trombonist, trumpeter, violinist, virtuoso, vocalist.

GROUPS OF MUSICIANS: band, choir, chorus, consort, duet, duo, ensemble, group, nonet, octet, orchestra, quartet, quintet, septet, sextet, trio.

OTHER EVERYDAY MUSICAL TERMS: baton, chord, chromatic scale, clef, counterpoint (adjective contrapuntal), crotchet, diatonic scale, discord, flat, harmony, key, melody, metronome marking, minim, natural, note, octave, pentatonic scale, pitch, polyphony, quaver, rhythm, scale, semibreve, semiquaver, semitone, sharp, stave, tempo, theme, time signature, tone, tune, unison.

---

musical adjective *musical sounds.* euphonious, harmonious, lyrical, melodious, pleasant, sweet-sounding, tuneful. OPPOSITES: SEE **cacophonous**.

musician noun performer, player. VARIOUS MUSICIANS: SEE ABOVE.

musky adjective SEE **smelling**.

muster verb *Can we muster a team for Saturday?* assemble, call together, collect, convene, gather, get together, group, marshal, mobilize, rally, round up, summon.

musty adjective *a musty smell.* airless, damp, dank, fusty, mildewed, mouldy, smelly, stale, stuffy, unventilated.

mutable adjective SEE **changeable**.

mutant noun abortion, deviant, freak, monster, monstrosity, sport.

mutate verb SEE **change** verb, undergo mutation (SEE **mutation**).

mutation noun *a genetic mutation.* alteration, change, deviance, evolution, metamorphosis, modification, transformation, variation.

mute adjective dumb, silent, speechless, tongue-tied, voiceless.

mutilate verb *The soldier was horribly mutilated in the explosion.* cripple, damage, disable, disfigure, injure, lame, maim, mangle, SEE **wound** verb.

mutineer noun SEE **rebel** noun.

mutinous adjective *a mutinous crew.* SEE **rebellious**.

mutiny noun *a mutiny on board ship.* SEE **rebellion**.

mutiny verb SEE **rebel** verb.

mutt noun SEE **fool** noun.

mutter verb SEE **talk** verb.

mutual adjective *friends with mutual interests.* common, joint, reciprocal, reciprocated, shared.

muzzle noun *an animal's muzzle.* jaws, mouth, nose, snout.

muzzle verb *to muzzle someone.* censor, gag, restrain, silence, stifle, suppress.

muzzy adjective *muzzy in the head.* blurred, SEE **confused**, dazed, hazy, muddled.

myopic adjective short-sighted.

myriad noun SEE **multitude**.

mysterious adjective *a mysterious illness. mysterious powers.* arcane, baffling, curious, enigmatic, incomprehensible, inexplicable, insoluble, magical, miraculous, SEE **mystical**, mystifying, obscure, perplexing, puzzling, secret, strange, uncanny, unexplained, unfathomable, unknown, weird.
OPPOSITES: SEE **straightforward**.

mystery noun **1** *an insoluble mystery.* enigma, miracle, mysterious happening [SEE **mysterious**], problem, puzzle, riddle, secret.
2 *I like reading a good mystery.* SEE **thriller**.

mystic noun SEE **visionary** noun.

mystical adjective *a mystical experience.* abnormal, metaphysical, SEE **mysterious**, occult, religious, spiritual, supernatural.
OPPOSITES: SEE **mundane**.

mystify verb baffle, bamboozle, bewilder, perplex, SEE **puzzle** verb.

mythical adjective *mythical monsters.* fabled, fabulous, fanciful, fictional, imaginary, invented, legendary, make-believe, mythological, non-existent, unreal.
OPPOSITES: SEE **real**.

mythological adjective SEE **mythical**.

N

nab verb SEE **capture**.

nadir noun bottom, lowest point.
OPPOSITES: SEE **zenith**.

naevus noun birthmark, mole, SEE **spot** noun.

nag noun SEE **horse**.

nag verb *to nag about jobs to be done.* badger, [*informal*] go on (*Stop going on about it!*), [*informal*] henpeck, keep complaining, pester, [*informal*] plague, scold.

nail noun *an iron nail.* pin, stud, tack.

nail verb OTHER WAYS TO FASTEN THINGS: SEE **fasten**.

naïve adjective *too naïve to succeed in politics.* artless, childlike, credulous, [*informal*] green, guileless, gullible, inexperienced, ingenuous, innocent, open, simple, simple-minded, [*uncomplimentary*] stupid, unsophisticated, unwary.
OPPOSITES: SEE **knowing**.

naked adjective bare, denuded, disrobed, exposed, nude, stark naked, stripped, unclothed, uncovered, undressed.
OPPOSITES: SEE **clothed**.

namby-pamby adjective SEE **feeble**.

name noun **1** *a person's name.* alias [= *assumed name*], [*formal*] appellation, Christian name, first name, forename, given name, [*informal*] handle, identity, nickname, nom de plume, pen name, personal name, pseudonym, sobriquet, surname.
2 *the name of a book.* title.
to call someone names SEE **insult** verb.

name verb **1** *His parents named him Antony.* baptize, call, christen, dub, style.
2 *What did you name your story?* entitle, label.
3 *They named me as captain.* appoint, choose, designate, elect, nominate, select, single out, specify.

named adjective *named varieties of flowers.* identified, known, specific, specified.

nameless adjective **1** *nameless heroes.* anonymous, unheard of, unidentified, unnamed.
2 *nameless horrors.* SEE **unspeakable**.

nanny noun governess, nurse.

nanny-goat noun SEE **goat**.

nap noun SEE **sleep** noun.
to take a nap SEE **sleep** verb.

napkin noun *a table-napkin.* serviette.

nappy noun *a baby's nappy.* diaper.

narrate verb *to narrate a story.* chronicle, describe, recount, relate, report, tell.

narration noun *Whose voice was doing the narration?* account, commentary, description, reading, relation, story-telling, voice-over.

narrative noun *a narrative of events.* account, chronicle, history, story, tale, [*informal*] yarn.

narrow adjective **1** *a narrow line.* fine, slender, slim, thin.
2 *a narrow space.* close, confined, constricting, cramped, enclosed, limited, [*old-fashioned*] strait.
OPPOSITES: SEE **wide**.
3 *a narrow outlook.* SEE **narrow-minded**.

narrow-minded adjective *a narrow-minded outlook.* biased, bigoted, conservative, hidebound, illiberal, inflexible, insular, intolerant, narrow, old-fashioned, parochial, petty, prejudiced, prim, prudish, rigid, small-minded, straight, straight-laced.
OPPOSITES: SEE **broad-minded**.

nasty adjective [The meaning of *nasty* is vague: it can refer to almost anything you don't like. The number of synonyms is virtually limitless, so we give just some of the commoner ones here, and refer you to some of the places where you may find more.] SEE **bad** (*a nasty person*), beastly, SEE **dangerous** (*a nasty weapon*), SEE **difficult** (*a nasty problem*), SEE **dirty** (*a nasty mess*), disagreeable, disgusting, distasteful, foul, hateful, horrible, loathsome, [*slang*] lousy, SEE **objectionable** (*a nasty smell*), obnoxious, SEE **obscene** (*a nasty film*), [*informal*] off-putting, repulsive, revolting, SEE **severe** (*a nasty illness*), sickening, SEE **unkind** (*nasty to animals*), SEE **unpleasant**.
OPPOSITES: SEE **nice**.

Several words, including *nation, native, nativity, post-natal,* etc., are related to Latin *natus* = *born*.

---

nation noun **1** *The nation mourned when the king died.* community, people, population, society.
2 *the nations of the world.* civilization, country, land, power, race, state, superpower.

national adjective **1** *national customs.* ethnic, popular, racial.
2 *a national emergency.* countrywide, general, nationwide, state, widespread.
OPPOSITES: SEE **local** adjective.

national noun *British nationals.* citizen, native, resident, subject.

nationalism noun [*uncomplimentary*] chauvinism, [*uncomplimentary*] jingoism, patriotism, [*uncomplimentary*] xenophobia.

nationalistic adjective *nationalistic feelings.* [*uncomplimentary*] chauvinist or chauvinistic, [*uncomplimentary*] jingoistic, loyal, patriotic, [*uncomplimentary*] xenophobic.

native adjective **1** *native inhabitants.* aboriginal, indigenous, local, original.
2 *native wit.* congenital, hereditary, inborn, inbred, inherent, inherited, innate, natural.

native noun **1** *a native of the USA.* citizen, life-long resident.
2 *The early invaders fought the natives.* aborigine, native inhabitant [SEE **native** adjective]. [Do not use *savage* or *uncivilized person* as synonyms for *native.*]

nativity noun birth.
The Nativity birth of Christ, Christmas.

natter noun, verb SEE **talk** noun, verb.

natty adjective SEE **smart** adjective.

natural adjective **1** *the natural world.* normal, ordinary, predictable, regular, usual.
2 *natural feelings.* healthy, hereditary, human, inborn, inherited, innate, instinctive, intuitive, kind, maternal, native, paternal, proper, right.
3 *natural behaviour.* artless, authentic, genuine, sincere, spontaneous, unaffected, uncorrupted, unselfconscious, unsurprising.
4 *natural resources.* crude (*crude oil*), found in nature, raw, unadulterated, unprocessed, unrefined.
5 *a natural leader.* born, congenital, untaught.
OPPOSITES: SEE **unnatural.**
natural history biology, nature study.

nature noun **1** *A naturalist loves nature.* countryside, natural environment, natural history, wildlife.
2 *He has a kind nature.* character, disposition, make-up, manner, personality, temperament.
3 *I collect coins, medals, and things of that nature.* description, kind, sort, species, type, variety.

naturist noun nudist.

naught noun SEE **nothing.**

naughty adjective **1** *naughty children.* SEE **bad**, badly-behaved, bad-mannered, boisterous, contrary, delinquent, disobedient, fractious, headstrong, impish, impolite, incorrigible, insubordinate, intractable, mischievous, obstinate, perverse, playful, rascally, rebellious, rude, self-willed, stubborn, troublesome, uncontrollable, ungovernable, unmanageable, unruly, wayward, wicked, wilful.
OPPOSITES: SEE **well-behaved.**
2 [*childish*] *naughty words. naughty jokes.* cheeky, improper, SEE **obscene**, ribald, risqué, shocking, [*informal*] smutty, vulgar.
OPPOSITES: SEE **proper.**
to be naughty SEE **misbehave.**

nausea noun SEE **sickness.**

nauseate verb SEE **sicken.**

nauseating, nauseous adjectives SEE **sickening.**

nautical adjective *nautical dress.* marine, maritime, naval, of sailors, seafaring, seagoing.

naval adjective *naval warfare.* marine, maritime, nautical, of the navy.

navel noun [*informal*] tummy-button, [*formal*] umbilicus.

navigate verb **1** *to navigate a ship.* captain, direct, drive, guide, handle, manœuvre, pilot, sail, steer.
2 [*informal*] *Who's going to navigate?* map-read.

navvy noun SEE **worker.**

navy noun armada, convoy, fleet, flotilla.
navy blue SEE **blue** adjective.
RANKS IN THE NAVY: SEE **rank** noun.

near adjective **1** *near neighbours.* adjacent, adjoining, bordering, close, connected, nearby, neighbouring, next-door.
2 *My birthday is near.* approaching, coming, forthcoming, imminent, impending, [*informal*] round the corner.
3 *near friends.* close, dear, familiar, intimate, related.
OPPOSITES: SEE **distant.**

nearby adjective SEE **near.**

nearly adverb *It's nearly dinner time.* about, almost, approaching, approximately, around, not quite, practically, roughly, virtually.

neat adjective **1** *a neat room.* clean, orderly, [*informal*] shipshape, [*informal*] spick and span, straight, tidy, uncluttered, well-kept.
2 *neat clothes.* dainty, elegant, pretty, smart, spruce, trim.
3 *a neat person. a neat job.* accurate, adroit, deft, expert, houseproud (*a houseproud person*), methodical, meticulous, precise, skilful.
OPPOSITES: SEE **untidy.**

neaten verb SEE **tidy** verb.

neatness noun SEE **tidiness.**

nebulous adjective SEE **vague**.

necessary adjective *necessary repairs.* compulsory, essential, imperative, important, indispensable, inescapable, inevitable, mandatory, needed, needful, obligatory, required, requisite, unavoidable, vital.
OPPOSITES: SEE **unnecessary**.

necessitate verb SEE **compel**.

necessity noun **1** *Is it a necessity, or can we do without it?* compulsion, essential, inevitability, [*informal*] must (*It's a must!*), need, obligation, requirement, [*Latin*] sine qua non.
2 *Necessity compelled them to steal.* beggary, destitution, hardship, need, penury, poverty, privation, shortage, suffering, want.

neck noun cervix, nape, throat.
RELATED ADJECTIVE: cervical.

necktie noun cravat, tie.

need noun **1** SEE **necessity**.
2 *There's a great need for more shops in our area.* call, demand, requirement.

need verb **1** *We need £10.* be short of, lack, miss, require, want.
2 *We need your support.* crave, depend on, rely on.

needful adjective SEE **necessary**.

needle noun *injection with a needle.* hypodermic, syringe.

needle verb SEE **annoy**.

needless adjective SEE **unnecessary**.

needlework noun SEE **sewing**.

needy adjective SEE **poor**.

ne'er-do-well noun SEE **rascal**.

nefarious adjective SEE **wicked**.

negate verb SEE **nullify**.

negative adjective *a negative attitude.* antagonistic, contradictory, destructive, dissenting, grudging, nullifying, obstructive, opposing, pessimistic, rejecting, saying "no", uncooperative, unenthusiastic, unwilling.
OPPOSITES: SEE **positive**.
a negative reply SEE **refusal**.

neglect noun *guilty of neglect.* carelessness, dereliction of duty, inattention, indifference, negligence, slackness.

neglect verb *Don't neglect your work.* disregard, forget, ignore, leave alone, let slide, miss, omit, overlook, pay no attention to, shirk, skip.

neglected adjective **1** *neglected by friends. feeling neglected.* abandoned, disregarded, forlorn, [*informal*] in limbo, overlooked, unappreciated, unloved.
2 *a neglected garden.* derelict, overgrown, uncared for, untended, unweeded.

négligé noun dressing-gown.

negligent adjective *negligent work. a negligent attitude.* careless, forgetful, inattentive, inconsiderate, indifferent, irresponsible, lax, offhand, reckless, remiss, slack, sloppy, slovenly, thoughtless, uncaring, unthinking.
OPPOSITE: SEE **careful**.

negligible adjective *a negligible amount.* imperceptible, inconsiderable, insignificant, slight, small, SEE **tiny**, trifling, trivial, unimportant.
OPPOSITES: SEE **considerable**.

negotiate verb *to negotiate a price, to negotiate with an enemy.* arbitrate, bargain, confer, discuss terms, enter into negotiation [SEE **negotiation**], haggle, make arrangements, mediate, parley.

negotiation noun arbitration, bargaining, conciliation, debate, diplomacy, discussion, mediation, transaction.

negotiator noun ambassador, arbitrator, broker, conciliator, diplomat, go-between, intermediary, mediator.

neigh verb whinny.

neighbourhood noun *Are there many shops in your neighbourhood?* area, community, district, environs, locality, place, region, surroundings, vicinity, zone.

neighbouring adjective *The cats from the neighbouring houses come to our garden.* adjacent, adjoining, attached, bordering, close, closest, connecting, near, nearby, nearest, next-door.

neighbourly adjective SEE **friendly**.

nemesis noun SEE **fate**.

nephew noun FAMILY RELATIONSHIPS: SEE **family**.

nepotism noun SEE **bias** noun.

nerve noun **1** *the nerves in your body.*
RELATED ADJECTIVE: neural.
2 [*informal*] *That steeplejack has some nerve!* SEE **courage**.
3 [*informal*] *She's got a nerve, taking my pen!* SEE **cheek**.

nervous adjective *I get nervous before an exam.* afraid, agitated, anxious, apprehensive, edgy, excitable, fearful, fidgety, flustered, highly-strung, insecure, [*informal*] jittery, jumpy, [*informal*] nervy, neurotic, on edge, restless, shaky, shy, strained, tense, timid, [*informal*] touchy, [*informal*] twitchy, uneasy, [*informal*] uptight, worried.
OPPOSITES: SEE **calm** adjective.

to be nervous fret, [*informal*] have the collywobbles, [*informal*] have the willies, worry.

nervy adjective SEE **nervous**.

nest-egg noun SEE **money**.

nestle verb *to nestle up against someone.* cuddle, curl up, huddle, lie comfortably, nuzzle, snuggle.

nestling noun chick, fledgeling, young bird.

net noun *a fish net.* mesh, netting, SEE **network**.

net verb **1** *to net a fish.* SEE **catch** verb, enmesh, trammel.
2 *to net a big salary.* accumulate, bring in, clear, earn, get, make, receive.

nether adjective inferior, lower.

netting noun SEE **network**.

nettle verb SEE **annoy**.

network noun **1** *a network of lines.* criss-cross pattern, grid, labyrinth, lattice, maze, mesh, net, netting, tracery, web.
2 *a railway network.* complex, organization, system.

neurosis noun abnormality, anxiety, depression, mental condition, obsession, phobia.

neurotic adjective *Don't get neurotic about things that worry you.* anxious, distraught, disturbed, maladjusted, mentally unbalanced, nervous, obsessive, overwrought, unstable.

neuter adjective *neuter gender.* ambiguous, ambivalent, indeterminate, neither one thing nor the other, uncertain.
COMPARE: feminine, hermaphrodite, masculine.

neuter verb *to neuter an animal.* castrate, [*informal*] doctor, geld, spay, sterilize.

neutral adjective **1** *a neutral referee.* detached, disinterested, dispassionate, fair, impartial, indifferent, non-aligned, non-partisan, objective, unbiased, uninvolved, unprejudiced.
OPPOSITES: SEE **prejudiced**.
2 *neutral colours.* characterless, colourless, dull, indefinite, indeterminate, intermediate, middle.
OPPOSITES: SEE **distinctive**.

neutralize verb *Alkalis neutralize acids.* cancel out, counteract, counterbalance, invalidate, make ineffective, negate, nullify, offset.

never-ending adjective SEE **continual**.

new adjective **1** *a new banknote.* brand-new, clean, fresh, mint, unused.
2 *a new invention. new music.* advanced, contemporary, current, latest, modern, modernistic, [*uncomplimentary*] newfangled, novel, original, recent, revolutionary, [*informal*] trendy, up-to-date.
3 *new evidence. a new problem.* added, additional, changed, different, extra, just arrived, more, supplementary, unaccustomed, unexpected, unfamiliar, unknown.
OPPOSITES: SEE **old**.

newcomer noun *Get to know the newcomers.* arrival, beginner, immigrant, new boy, new girl, outsider, settler, stranger.

newfangled adjective SEE **new**.

news noun *news from abroad. news of a special event.* advice, announcement, bulletin, communiqué, dispatch, headlines, information, intelligence, [*informal*] latest (*What's the latest?*), message, newscast, newsletter, notice, press-release, proclamation, report, rumour, statement, [*old-fashioned*] tidings, word.

newsagent noun paper-shop.

newspaper noun [*informal*] daily, gazette, journal, paper, periodical, [*uncomplimentary*] rag, tabloid.
OTHER MEDIA: SEE **communication**.

newsworthy adjective SEE **significant**.

next adjective **1** *the next street.* adjacent, adjoining, closest, nearest, neighbouring.
OPPOSITES: SEE **distant**.
2 *the next bus.* following, soonest, subsequent, succeeding.
OPPOSITES: SEE **previous**.

next-door adjective SEE **neighbouring**.

next-of-kin noun SEE **relation**.

nibble verb SEE **eat**.

nice adjective **1** *nice food. a nice view. a nice person.* [In this sense, the meaning of *nice* is vague: it can refer to almost anything you like. The number of synonyms is virtually limitless, so we give just some of the commoner ones here, and refer you to some of the places where you may find more.] acceptable, agreeable, amiable, attractive, SEE **beautiful**, SEE **delicious**, delightful, SEE **friendly**, SEE **good**, gratifying, SEE **kind** adjective, likeable, SEE **pleasant**, pleasing, satisfactory, welcome.
OPPOSITES: SEE **nasty**.
2 *a nice calculation. a nice distinction.* accurate, careful, delicate, discriminating, exact, fine, meticulous, precise, punctilious, scrupulous.
OPPOSITES: SEE **careless**.
3 *nice table-manners.* dainty, elegant, fastidious, [*uncomplimentary*] fussy, particular, [*informal*] pernickety, polished, refined, well-mannered.
OPPOSITES: SEE **inelegant**.

niche noun SEE **recess**.

nick verb **1** *to nick your finger.* SEE **cut** verb.
2 [*informal*] *to nick money.* SEE **steal**.

nickname noun alias, SEE **name** noun, sobriquet.

niece noun FAMILY RELATIONSHIPS: SEE **family**.

night noun TIMES OF THE DAY: SEE **day**.
RELATED ADJECTIVE: nocturnal.

night-cap noun DRINKS: SEE **drink** noun.

night-clothes noun night-dress, night-gown, [*informal*] nightie, [*old-fashioned*] night-shirt, pyjamas.

night-club noun VARIOUS ENTERTAINMENTS: SEE **entertainment**.

night-dress, night-gown nouns SEE **night-clothes**.

nightmare noun SEE **dream** noun.

night-shirt noun SEE **night-clothes**.

nil noun SEE **nothing**.

nimble adjective *nimble movements.* acrobatic, active, agile, brisk, deft, dextrous, lively, [*informal*] nippy, quick, quick-moving, sprightly, spry, swift.

nincompoop, ninny nouns SEE **idiot**.

nip noun SEE **drink** noun.

nip verb **1** *The teeth nipped my leg.* bite, clip, pinch, snag, snap at, squeeze.
2 [*informal*] *I nipped along to the shops.* SEE **go**.
to nip something in the bud SEE **stop** verb.

nipper noun SEE **child**.

nippy adjective **1** [*informal*] *a nippy car.* fast, SEE **nimble**, quick, rapid, speedy.
2 [*informal*] *nippy weather.* SEE **cold** adjective.

nirvana noun SEE **heaven**.

nit-picking adjective [*informal*] *nit-picking objections.* SEE **fussy**.

nitty-gritty noun SEE **reality**.

nitwit noun SEE **idiot**.

nobble verb **1** [*informal*] *to nobble a race-horse.* get at, hamper, incapacitate, interfere with, tamper with.
2 [*informal*] *to nobble a criminal.* SEE **catch** verb.

nobility noun **1** *nobility of character.* dignity, greatness, integrity, magnanimity, morality, nobleness, uprightness, virtue, worthiness.
2 *the nobility.* aristocracy, gentry, nobles [SEE **noble** noun], peerage.

noble adjective **1** *a noble family.* aristocratic, [*informal*] blue-blooded, courtly, élite, gentle, high-born, princely, royal, thoroughbred, titled, upper-class.
OPPOSITES: SEE **common** adjective.
2 *a noble deed.* brave, chivalrous, courageous, gallant, glorious, heroic, honourable, magnanimous, upright, virtuous, worthy.
OPPOSITES: SEE **ignoble**.
3 *a noble edifice.* dignified, distinguished, elegant, grand, great, imposing, impressive, magnificent, majestic, SEE **splendid**, stately.
OPPOSITES: SEE **insignificant**.

noble noun aristocrat, grandee, lady, lord, nobleman, noblewoman, peer, peeress.
VARIOUS NOBLE TITLES: SEE **title** noun.

nobody noun *He's a nobody.* nonentity.

nod verb *to nod your head.* bend, bob, bow, SEE **gesture** verb.
to nod off SEE **sleep** verb.

node, nodule nouns SEE **lump** noun.

noggin noun SEE **drink** noun.

noise noun *a dreadful noise.* babble, [*informal*] ballyhoo, [*informal*] bedlam, blare, cacophony, clamour, clatter, commotion, din, discord, fracas, hubbub, hullabaloo, outcry, pandemonium, racket, row, rumpus, screaming, screeching, shrieking, shouting, tumult, uproar, yelling.
OPPOSITES: SEE **silence** noun.
VARIOUS WAYS TO MAKE NOISE: SEE **sound** noun.

noiseless adjective SEE **silent**.

noisome adjective SEE **objectionable**.

noisy adjective *a noisy class of children. noisy traffic.* blaring, boisterous, booming, cacophonous, chattering, clamorous, deafening, ear-splitting, fortissimo, loud, raucous, resounding, reverberating, rowdy, screaming, screeching, shrieking, shrill, strident, talkative, thunderous, tumultuous, uproarious, vociferous.
OPPOSITES: SEE **silent**.

nomad noun *a wandering nomad.* SEE **traveller**.

nomadic adjective SEE **travelling**.

nom de plume *She writes under a nom de plume.* alias, assumed name, pen name, pseudonym.

nominal adjective **1** *He's the nominal head, but his deputy does the work.* formal, in name only, ostensible, supposed, theoretical.
2 *If we pay a nominal sum, the dog is ours.* minimal, small, token.

nominate verb *We nominated him as captain.* appoint, choose, elect, name, select.

non-aligned adjective SEE **neutral**.

nonchalant adjective SEE **casual**.

non-committal adjective SEE **cautious**.

nonconformist noun SEE **rebel** noun.
a nonconformist church SEE **church**.

nondescript adjective SEE **ordinary**.

nonentity noun nobody.

non-existent adjective *Unicorns are non-existent.* fictitious, hypothetical, imaginary, imagined, legendary, made-up, mythical, unreal.
OPPOSITES: SEE **existing**.

non-fiction noun SEE **writing**.

non-flammable adjective SEE **non-inflammable**.

non-inflammable adjective *non-inflammable material.* fireproof, fire-resistant, flameproof, incombustible, non-flammable.
OPPOSITES: SEE **inflammable**.

non-partisan adjective SEE **unbiased**.

nonplussed adjective SEE **amazed**.

non-resident adjective *non-resident guests.* casual, living out, passing, transient, visiting.
OPPOSITES: SEE **resident** adjective.

nonsense noun **1** *She's talking nonsense.* [Most of these synonyms are used *informally.*] balderdash, bilge, boloney, bosh, bunk, bunkum, claptrap, codswallop, double Dutch, drivel, fiddlesticks, gibberish, gobbledegook, piffle, poppycock, rot, rubbish, stuff and nonsense, tommy-rot, tripe, twaddle.
2 *I thought from the start that her plan was a nonsense.* absurdity, inanity, mistake, nonsensical idea [SEE **nonsensical**].

nonsensical adjective absurd, crazy, fatuous, foolish, inane, incomprehensible, illogical, impractical, irrational, laughable, ludicrous, meaningless, ridiculous, senseless, SEE **silly**, stupid, unreasonable.
OPPOSITES: SEE **sensible**.

non-stop adjective **1** *a non-stop train.* direct, express, fast.
OPPOSITE: stopping.
2 *non-stop chattering.* SEE **continual**.

noodles noun SEE **pasta**.

nook noun SEE **recess**.

noon noun midday.
OTHER TIMES OF THE DAY: SEE **day**.

noose noun *a noose in a rope.* collar, halter, loop.

norm noun SEE **standard** noun.

normal adjective **1** *normal temperature. a normal kind of day.* accepted, accustomed, average, common, commonplace, conventional, customary, established, everyday, familiar, habitual, natural, ordinary, predictable, prosaic, quotidian, regular, routine, [*informal*] run-of-the-mill, standard, typical, unsurprising, usual.
2 *a normal person.* balanced, healthy, rational, reasonable, sane, [*informal*] straight, well-adjusted.
OPPOSITES: SEE **abnormal**.

normalize verb *to normalize relationships after a quarrel.* legalize, regularize, return to normal.

north noun GEOGRAPHICAL TERMS: SEE **geography**.

nose noun **1** nostrils, [*formal*] proboscis, snout,
RELATED ADJECTIVE: nasal.
ADJECTIVES DESCRIBING TYPES OF NOSE: aquiline, retroussé, Roman, snub.
2 *the nose of a boat*, bow, front, prow.

nose verb *to nose into a space. to nose into the traffic.* enter cautiously, insinuate, yourself, intrude, nudge your way in, penetrate, probe, push, shove.
to nose about *He was nosing about in my room!* interfere, look, meddle, pry, search, snoop.

nosedive verb SEE **plunge**.

nostalgia noun *nostalgia for the past.* longing, memory, nostalgic feeling [SEE **nostalgic**], pining, regret, reminiscence, sentiment, sentimentality, yearning.

nostalgic adjective *nostalgic feelings about your childhood.* emotional, maudlin, regretful, romantic, sentimental, wistful, yearning.

nostrum noun SEE **remedy** noun.

nosy adjective SEE **inquisitive**.

notability noun SEE **celebrity**.

notable adjective *a notable example of something. a notable visitor.* celebrated, conspicuous, distinguished, eminent, evident, extraordinary, famous, important, impressive, memorable, noted, noteworthy, noticeable, obvious, outstanding, pre-eminent, prominent, rare, remarkable, renowned, striking, uncommon, unusual, well-known.
OPPOSITES: SEE **ordinary**.

notary public LEGAL TERMS: SEE **law**.

notation noun SEE **writing**.

notch noun, verb SEE **cut** noun, verb.

note noun **1** *I wrote her a note.* billet-doux, chit, communication, [*joking*] epistle, jotting, letter, [*informal*] memo, memorandum, message.

2 *a note in a textbook.* annotation, cross-reference, explanation, footnote, gloss.
3 *an angry note in her voice.* feeling, quality, sound, tone.
4 *a £5 note.* bill, banknote.
OTHER FORMS OF MONEY: SEE **money**.
to take note of SEE **notice** verb.

note verb **1** *to note what is happening.* SEE **notice** verb.
2 *to note something on paper.* enter, jot down, record, scribble, write down.

notebook noun diary, exercise-book, jotter, writing-book.

notecase noun pocket-book, wallet.

noted adjective SEE **famous**.

notepaper noun SEE **paper** noun.

noteworthy adjective SEE **remarkable**.

nothing noun [*cricket*] duck, [*tennis*] love, [*football*] nil, [*old-fashioned*] naught, nought, zero.

notice noun **1** *Didn't you see the notice?* advertisement, announcement, handbill, handout, intimation, leaflet, message, note, placard, poster, sign, warning.
2 *She didn't take any notice of the signs.* cognizance, heed, note, regard, warning.
to give someone notice SEE **dismiss**.
to take notice SEE **notice** verb.

notice verb *to notice what is happening.* detect, discern, discover, feel, find, heed, mark, mind (*Mind what I say*), note, observe, pay attention to, register, remark, see, spy, take note of, take notice of [SEE **notice** noun].

noticeable adjective *a noticeable improvement in the weather. a noticeable foreign accent.* appreciable, audible, clear, conspicuous, detectable, discernible, distinct, important, manifest, marked, measurable, notable, obtrusive, obvious, perceptible, plain, prominent, pronounced, salient, significant, striking, unmistakable, visible.
OPPOSITES: SEE **imperceptible**.

notify verb *If you see anything suspicious, notify the police.* acquaint, advise, alert, inform, make known to, report to, tell, warn.

notion noun *I had a notion that you were on holiday. He has strange notions about religion.* apprehension, belief, concept, fancy, hypothesis, idea, impression, opinion, sentiment, theory, thought, understanding, view.

notional adjective SEE **theoretical**.

notorious adjective *a notorious criminal.* disreputable, famous, flagrant, known, infamous, obvious, outrageous, overt, patent, scandalous, shocking, talked about, undisguised, undisputed, well-known, wicked.

nought noun SEE **nothing**.

nourish verb *Food nourishes us.* feed, maintain, strengthen, support, sustain.

nourishing adjective *nourishing food.* beneficial, good for you, health-giving, nutritious, sustaining, wholesome.

nourishment noun diet, food, goodness, nutrient, nutriment, nutrition, sustenance.

nous noun SEE **sense** noun.

nouveau riche noun SEE **upstart**.

novel adjective *a novel way of doing something.* different, fresh, imaginative, innovative, new, odd, original, rare, singular, startling, strange, surprising, uncommon, unconventional, unfamiliar, unusual.
OPPOSITES: SEE **familiar**.

novel noun *I like to read a novel.* fiction, novelette, romance, story.
OTHER KINDS OF WRITING: SEE **writing**.

novelist noun author, story-teller.
OTHER WRITERS: SEE **writer**.

novelty noun **1** *The novelty will soon wear off.* freshness, newness, oddity, originality, strangeness, surprise, unfamiliarity.
2 *novelties sold in holiday resorts.* curiosity, gimmick, knick-knack, souvenir, trinket.

novice noun SEE **beginner**.

now adverb at present, here and now, immediately, nowadays, straight away.

noxious adjective *noxious fumes.* corrosive, foul, SEE **harmful**, nasty, noisome, objectionable, poisonous, polluting, sulphureous, sulphurous, unpleasant, unwholesome.

nozzle noun spout.

nuance noun SEE **difference**.

nub noun *the nub of the problem.* centre, core, crux, essence, gist, heart, kernel, nucleus, point.

nubile adjective [*often sexist*] *a nubile young woman.* attractive, buxom, marriageable, mature, [*informal*] sexy, voluptuous, well-developed.
OPPOSITES: SEE **immature**.

nucleus noun centre, core, heart, middle.

nude adjective SEE **naked**.

nudge verb *to nudge someone with your elbow.* bump, SEE **hit** verb, jog, jolt, poke, prod, shove, touch.

nudist noun naturist.

nugget noun *a nugget of gold.* ingot, SEE **lump** noun.

nuisance noun *That dog's a nuisance.* annoyance, bother, inconvenience, irritation, [*informal*] pain, pest, plague, trouble, vexation, worry.

nullify verb *to nullify an agreement.* abolish, annul, SEE **cancel**, do away with, invalidate, negate, neutralize, repeal, rescind, revoke, stultify.

numb adjective *My leg's gone numb.* anaesthetized, [*informal*] asleep, cold, dead, deadened, frozen, immobile, insensitive, paralysed, suffering from pins and needles.
OPPOSITES: SEE **sensitive**.

numb verb *The cold numbs my hands. The dentist's injection numbed my mouth.* anaesthetize, deaden, desensitize, freeze, immobilize, make numb, paralyse.

number noun **1** *numbers written on paper.* digit, figure, integer, numeral, unit.
RELATED ADJECTIVE: numerical.
2 *a large number.* aggregate, amount, collection, crowd, multitude, quantity, sum, total.
3 *a musical number.* item, piece, song.
4 *a special number of a magazine.* copy, edition, impression, issue, printing, publication.

number verb *The crowd numbered a thousand.* add up to, total, work out at.

numberless adjective SEE **numerous**.

numeral noun digit, figure, integer, number.

numerate adjective SEE **educated**.

numerous adjective *a numerous crowd. numerous people.* abundant, copious, countless, innumerable, many, multitudinous, numberless, plentiful, plenty of, several, uncountable, untold.
OPPOSITES: SEE **few**, **small**.

nun noun abbess, mother-superior, prioress, sister.

nunnery noun convent.
OTHER RELIGIOUS INSTITUTIONS: SEE **church**.

nuptials plural noun marriage, wedding.

nurse noun **1** *a medical nurse.* district-nurse, [*old-fashioned*] matron, sister.
2 *a child's nurse.* nanny, nursemaid.

nurse verb **1** *to nurse a sick person.* care for, look after, tend, treat.
2 *to nurse a baby.* breast-feed, feed, suckle.
3 *to nurse someone in your arms.* cherish, cradle, cuddle, dandle, hold, hug, mother.

nursery noun **1** *a nursery for young children.* crèche, kindergarten, nursery school.
2 *a nursery for growing plants.* garden centre, market garden.

nurseryman noun market gardener.

nursing home noun SEE **hospital**.

nurture verb *to nurture the young. to nurture tender plants.* bring up, cultivate, educate, feed, look after, nourish, nurse, rear, tend, train.

nut noun kernel.

KINDS OF NUT: almond, brazil, cashew, chestnut, cob-nut, coconut, filbert, hazel, peanut, pecan, pistachio, walnut.

---

nutrient noun *Provide plants with their proper nutrients.* fertilizer, SEE **nourishment**.

nutriment noun SEE **nourishment**.

nutritious adjective SEE **nourishing**.

nutty adjective SEE **mad**.

nuzzle verb SEE **touch** verb.

O

oaf noun SEE **lout**.

oafish adjective SEE **rude**.

oar noun paddle.

oarsman noun boatman, rower.

oasis noun **1** *an oasis in the desert.* spring, watering-hole, well.
2 *an oasis of peace.* haven, refuge, retreat.

oath noun **1** *to swear an oath.* assurance, guarantee, pledge, promise, undertaking, vow, word of honour.
2 *a terrible oath.* blasphemy, curse, exclamation, expletive, imprecation, profanity, swear-word.

obdurate adjective SEE **stubborn**.

obedient adjective *obedient servants. obedient animals.* acquiescent, amenable, biddable, compliant, deferential, disciplined, docile, dutiful, law-abiding, manageable, submissive, subservient, tamed, tractable, well-behaved, well-trained.
OPPOSITES: SEE **disobedient**.

obelisk noun SEE **monument**.

obese adjective SEE **fat** adjective.

obey verb **1** *Obey the rules.* abide by, adhere to, be ruled by, carry out, comply with, conform to, execute, follow, heed, implement, keep to, mind, observe, submit to.
2 *Soldiers are trained to obey.* acquiesce, be obedient [SEE **obedient**], conform, do what you are told, submit, take orders.
OPPOSITES: SEE **disobey**.

object noun **1** *What's that object you've found?* article, body, item, thing.
2 *What is the object of this exercise?* aim, end, goal, intent, intention, objective, point, purpose, target.

object verb *She objected to the smell. He objected against the plan.* argue, be opposed, carp, complain, demur, disapprove, dispute, dissent, expostulate, [*slang*] grouse, grumble, make an objection [SEE **objection**], mind, moan, protest, quibble, raise questions, remonstrate, take exception (to).
OPPOSITES: SEE **accept, agree**.

objection noun *The secretary noted our objection.* challenge, complaint, disapproval, opposition, outcry, protest, query, question, quibble, remonstration.

objectionable adjective *an objectionable smell.* abhorrent, detestable, disagreeable, disgusting, dislikeable, displeasing, distasteful, foul, hateful, insufferable, intolerable, loathsome, nasty, nauseating, noisome, obnoxious, odious, offensive, [*informal*] offputting, repellent, repugnant, revolting, sickening, unacceptable, undesirable, SEE **unpleasant**, unwanted.
OPPOSITES: SEE **acceptable**.

objective adjective *objective evidence. an objective account.* detached, disinterested, dispassionate, empirical, existing, factual, impartial, impersonal, observable, outward-looking, rational, real, scientific, unbiased, unemotional, unprejudiced.
OPPOSITES: SEE **subjective**.

objective noun *The objective is to get the ball into the net. Our objective was the top of the hill.* aim, ambition, aspiration, design, destination, end, goal, intent, intention, object, point, purpose, target.

objet d'art noun SEE **art (work of art)**.

obligation noun *an obligation to pay taxes.* commitment, compulsion, duty, liability, need, requirement, responsibility.
OPPOSITES: SEE **option**.

oblige verb *to oblige someone to do something.* coerce, compel, constrain, force, make, require.

obliged adjective **1** *He's obliged to come.* bound, certain, compelled, constrained, forced, required, sure.
2 *I'm obliged to you for your kindness.* appreciative, grateful, gratified, indebted, thankful.

obliging adjective *Thank you for being so obliging.* accommodating, agreeable, civil, considerate, co-operative, courteous, friendly, helpful, kind, neighbourly, polite, thoughtful, willing.
OPPOSITES: SEE **unhelpful**.

oblique adjective **1** *an oblique line.* angled, diagonal, inclined, slanting, sloping, tilted.
2 *an oblique insult.* backhanded, circumlocutory, SEE **evasive**, implicit, indirect, roundabout.
OPPOSITES: SEE **direct** adjective.

obliterate verb *to obliterate your tracks.* blot out, cancel, cover over, delete, destroy, efface, eradicate, erase, expunge, extirpate, leave no trace of, rub out, wipe out.

oblivion noun **1** *Most of this composer's music has fallen into oblivion.* disregard, extinction, neglect, obscurity.
2 *After the accident I was in a state of oblivion.* amnesia, coma, forgetfulness, ignorance, insensibility, obliviousness, unawareness, unconsciousness.

oblivious adjective *oblivious of what is going on.* forgetful, heedless, ignorant, insensible (to), insensitive (to), unacquainted (with), unaware, unconscious, uninformed (about), unmindful, unresponsive (to).
OPPOSITES: SEE **aware**.

oblong noun rectangle.
OTHER SHAPES: SEE **shape** noun.

obnoxious adjective SEE **objectionable**.

obscene adjective *obscene language. obscene books.* bawdy, [*informal*] blue, coarse, corrupting, crude, depraved, dirty, disgusting, filthy, foul, gross, immodest, immoral, improper, impure, indecent, indecorous, indelicate, [*informal*] kinky, lewd, nasty, SEE **objectionable**, offensive, outrageous, perverted, pornographic, prurient, repulsive, rude, salacious, scurrilous, shameless, shocking, [*informal*] sick, smutty, suggestive, vile, vulgar.
OPPOSITES: SEE **decent**.

obscenity noun **1** *the obscenity of war. the obscenity of pornography.* abomination, blasphemy, coarseness, dirtiness, evil, filth, foulness, immorality, impropriety, indecency, lewdness, licentiousness, offensiveness, outrage, pornography, profanity, vileness.

2 *His language was full of obscenities.* SEE **swearword**.

obscure adjective 1 *an obscure shape in the mist.* blurred, clouded, concealed, covered, dark, dim, hidden, inconspicuous, indefinable, indistinct, masked, misty, murky, shadowy, shady, shrouded, unclear, unlit, unrecognizable, vague, veiled.
OPPOSITES: SEE **clear** adjective.
2 *an obscure poet.* forgotten, minor, undistinguished, unheard of, unimportant, unknown.
OPPOSITES: SEE **famous**.
3 *an obscure joke.* arcane, complex, cryptic, enigmatic, esoteric, incomprehensible, puzzling, recherché, recondite.
OPPOSITES: SEE **obvious**.

obscure verb *Mist obscured the view. The complications obscured the main point.* block out, blur, cloud, conceal, cover, darken, disguise, eclipse, envelop, hide, make obscure [SEE **obscure** adjective], mask, screen, shade, shroud, veil.
OPPOSITES: SEE **clarify**.

obsequies noun SEE **funeral**.

obsequious adjective *obsequious flattery.* abject, cringing, deferential, fawning, flattering, [*informal*] greasy, grovelling, ingratiating, menial, [*informal*] oily, servile, [*informal*] smarmy, subservient, sycophantic, unctuous.
to be obsequious [*informal*] crawl, fawn, flatter, grovel, [*informal*] suck up (to), [*informal*] toady.

observant adjective *an observant sentry.* alert, astute, attentive, aware, careful, eagle-eyed, heedful, perceptive, percipient, quick, sharp-eyed, shrewd, vigilant, watchful.
OPPOSITES: SEE **inattentive**.

observation noun 1 *an astronomer's observation of the stars.* attention (to), examination, inspection, monitoring, scrutiny, study, surveillance, watching.
2 *Have you any observations?* comment, opinion, reaction, reflection, remark, response, statement, thought, utterance.

observe verb 1 *to observe an eclipse. to observe someone's behaviour.* contemplate, detect, discern, [*informal*] keep an eye on, look at, monitor, note, notice, perceive, regard, scrutinize, see, spot, spy, stare at, study, view, watch, witness.
2 *to observe the rules.* abide by, adhere to, comply with, conform to, follow, heed, honour, keep, obey, pay attention to, respect.
3 *to observe Christmas.* celebrate, commemorate, keep, remember, solemnize.
4 *I observed that it was a nice day.* comment, declare, explain, make an observation [SEE **observation**], mention, reflect, remark, say.

observer noun bystander, commentator, eye-witness, onlooker, spectator, viewer, watcher, witness.

obsess verb *His hobby obsessed him.* become an obsession with [SEE **obsession**], consume, dominate, grip, haunt, monopolize, plague, possess, rule, take hold of.

obsession noun *Don't let your hobby become an obsession.* addiction, [*informal*] bee in your bonnet, fetish, fixation, [*informal*] hobby-horse, infatuation, mania, passion, preoccupation.

obsessive adjective *an obsessive interest in something.* addictive, compulsive, consuming, dominating.

obsolescent adjective *an obsolescent design.* [*Obsolescent* does not mean *obsolete* but *becoming obsolete.*] ageing or aging, dying out, going out of use, losing popularity, moribund, [*informal*] on the way out, waning.

obsolete adjective *an obsolete design.* anachronistic, antiquated, antique, archaic, dated, dead, discarded, disused, extinct, old-fashioned, outdated, out-of-date, outmoded, primitive, superannuated, superseded, unfashionable.
OPPOSITES: SEE **current** adjective.

obstacle noun *an obstacle to be got over.* bar, barricade, barrier, block, blockage, check, difficulty, hindrance, hurdle, impediment, obstruction, problem, snag, [*informal*] stumbling-block.

obstetrician noun midwife.

obstinate adjective *an obstinate refusal to co-operate.* defiant, determined, dogged, firm, headstrong, inflexible, intractable, intransigent, [*informal*] mulish, obdurate, persistent, perverse, [*informal*] pig-headed, refractory, rigid, self-willed, [*informal*] stiff-necked, stubborn, tenacious, unreasonable, unyielding, wilful, wrong-headed.
OPPOSITES: SEE **amenable**.

obstreperous adjective *a class of obstreperous children.* awkward, boisterous, disorderly, irrepressible, naughty, SEE **noisy**, rough, rowdy, [*informal*] stroppy, unmanageable, unruly.
OPPOSITES: SEE **well-behaved**.

obstruct verb *to obstruct progress.* bar, block, check, curb, deter, frustrate, halt, hamper, hinder, hold up, impede, inhibit, interfere with, interrupt,

[*formal*] occlude, prevent, restrict, retard, slow down, [*informal*] stonewall, stop, [*informal*] stymie, thwart.
OPPOSITE: SEE **help** verb.

obstruction noun SEE **obstacle**.

obstructive adjective SEE **uncooperative**.

obtain verb **1** *to obtain what you want.* acquire, attain, be given, bring, buy, come by, come into possession of, earn, elicit, enlist (*She enlisted my help*), extort, extract, find, gain, get, get hold of, [*informal*] lay hands on, [*informal*] pick up, procure, purchase, receive, secure, win.
2 *The old rules still obtain.* be in force, be in use, be valid, exist, prevail, stand.

obtrude verb SEE **interfere**.

obtrusive adjective *The factory is an obtrusive eyesore.* blatant, conspicuous, inescapable, interfering, intrusive, SEE **obvious**, out of place, prominent, ugly, unwanted, unwelcome.
OPPOSITES: unobtrusive, SEE **inconspicuous**.

obtuse adjective SEE **stupid**.

obverse noun *the obverse of a coin.* face, front, head.
OPPOSITE: reverse.

obviate verb *to obviate the need for something.* avert, forestall, make unnecessary, preclude, prevent, remove, take away.

obvious adjective *an obvious accent. an obvious landmark. obvious favouritism.* blatant, clear, conspicuous, distinct, evident, eyecatching, flagrant, glaring, gross (*gross negligence*), inescapable, intrusive, notable, noticeable, obtrusive, open, patent, perceptible, plain, prominent, pronounced, recognizable, self-evident, unconcealed, undisguised, undisputed, unmistakable, visible.
OPPOSITES: SEE **hidden**.

occasion noun **1** *A party should be a happy occasion.* affair, celebration, ceremony, event, happening, incident, occurrence.
2 *If I can find the right occasion, I'll tell him.* chance, moment, opportunity, time.
3 *There was no occasion for rudeness.* cause, excuse, justification, need, reason.

occasional adjective *occasional showers. occasional moments of enthusiasm.* casual, desultory, fitful, infrequent, intermittent, irregular, odd, [*informal*] once in a while, periodic, rare, scattered, spasmodic, sporadic, uncommon, unpredictable.
OPPOSITES: SEE **frequent** adjective, **regular**.

occlude verb SEE **obstruct**.

occult adjective *occult powers.* SEE **supernatural**.

occult noun **the occult** black magic, diabolism, sorcery, the supernatural, witchcraft.

occupant noun **1** *the occupant of a house.* householder, inhabitant, occupier, resident, tenant.
2 *the occupant of a position.* incumbent.

occupation noun **1** *the occupation of a house.* lease, occupancy, possession, residency, tenancy, tenure, use.
2 *the occupation of a foreign country.* colonization, conquest, invasion, seizure, subjugation, [*informal*] take-over, usurpation.
3 *a full-time occupation.* business, calling, employment, job, [*informal*] line, post, profession, trade, vocation, work.
VARIOUS OCCUPATIONS: SEE **job**.
4 *a leisure occupation.* activity, hobby, pastime, pursuit.

occupied adjective **1** *occupied in your work.* absorbed, active, busy, engaged, engrossed, [*informal*] hard at it, involved.
2 *an occupied house.* inhabited, lived-in, tenanted.
3 *an occupied country.* conquered, defeated, overrun, subjugated.

occupy verb **1** *We occupy a council house.* dwell in, inhabit, live in, reside in.
2 *Troops occupied the town.* capture, conquer, garrison, invade, overrun, possess, take over, take possession of.
3 *The garden occupies her spare time.* absorb, engage, engross, fill, monopolize, preoccupy, take up, use, utilize.

occur verb *Earthquakes don't often occur in this part of the world.* appear, arise, befall, be found, come about, come into being, crop up, develop, exist, happen, manifest itself, materialize, [*informal*] show up, take place, [*informal*] turn up.

occurrence noun *an unusual occurrence.* affair, case, circumstance, development, event, happening, incident, manifestation, occasion, phenomenon, proceeding.

ocean noun SEE **sea**.

octogenarian noun SEE **old (old person)**.

odd adjective **1** *odd numbers.* uneven.
OPPOSITE: even.
2 *an odd sock.* left over, remaining, single, spare, unmatched.
3 *odd jobs.* casual, irregular, miscellaneous, occasional, random, varied, various.

4 *odd behaviour.* abnormal, atypical, bizarre, [*informal*] cranky, curious, eccentric, freak, funny, incongruous, inexplicable, [*informal*] kinky, peculiar, puzzling, queer, singular, strange, uncharacteristic, uncommon, unconventional, unusual, weird.
OPPOSITES: SEE **normal**.

oddity noun 1 *I noticed the oddity of his behaviour.* SEE **strangeness**.
2 *From his weird behaviour, he seems a bit of an oddity.* SEE **eccentric** noun.

oddment noun *oddments left over from a jumble sale.* bit, [*plural*] bits and pieces, fragment, leftover, [*plural*] odds and ends, offcut, remnant, scrap, unwanted piece.

odious adjective SEE **hateful**.

odium noun SEE **hatred**.

odorous adjective SEE **smelling**.

odour noun SEE **smell** noun.

odourless adjective deodorized, unscented.

odyssey noun SEE **journey** noun.

off-beat adjective SEE **unconventional**.

off-colour adjective SEE **ill**.

offcut noun SEE **oddment**.

offence noun 1 *a criminal offence.* crime, fault, infringement, misdeed, misdemeanour, outrage, peccadillo, sin, transgression, trespass, wrong, wrongdoing.
2 *The bad language caused offence to our neighbours.* anger, annoyance, disgust, displeasure, hard feelings, indignation, irritation, resentment, [*informal*] upset.
to give offence SEE **offend**.

offend verb 1 *to offend someone.* affront, anger, annoy, cause offence [SEE **offence**], disgust, displease, give offence (to), insult, irritate, make angry, outrage, pain, provoke, rile, sicken, upset, vex.
to be offended be annoyed, [*informal*] take umbrage.
2 *to offend against the law.* do wrong, transgress, violate.

offender noun criminal, culprit, delinquent, guilty party, malefactor, miscreant, sinner, transgressor, wrongdoer.

offensive adjective *offensive behaviour. offensive language.* abusive, aggressive, annoying, antisocial, coarse, detestable, disagreeable, disgusting, displeasing, disrespectful, embarrassing, foul, impolite, improper, indecent, insulting, loathsome, nasty, nauseating, objectionable, obnoxious, SEE **obscene**, [*informal*] offputting, revolting, rude, sickening, unpleasant, vile, vulgar.
OPPOSITES: SEE **pleasant**.

offer noun *He made me an offer.* bid, proposal, proposition, suggestion, tender.

offer verb 1 *He offered me a cup of tea. The bank offered me a loan.* be willing to provide, extend, give the opportunity of, hold out, make available, make an offer of [SEE **offer** noun], proffer, put forward, suggest.
2 *She offered to come with me.* propose, [*informal*] show willing, volunteer.

offering noun *an offering in church.* contribution, donation, gift, offertory, sacrifice.

offhand adjective 1 *an offhand manner.* aloof, SEE **casual**, curt, offhanded, perfunctory, unceremonious, uncooperative, uninterested.
2 *I can't think of anything offhand.* SEE **impromptu**.

office noun 1 *the manager's office.* bureau, room, workroom.

OFFICE EQUIPMENT INCLUDES: answering machine, calculator, computer, copier, desk, diary, dictating machine, duplicator, file, filing cabinet, intercom, photocopier, stapler, stationery, switchboard, telephone, typewriter, word-processor.

OFFICE WORKERS INCLUDE: cashier, clerk, filing clerk, office-boy, office-girl, office junior, receptionist, secretary, shorthand-typist, stenographer, telephonist, typist, word-processor operator.

---

2 *The office of prime minister is a responsible one.* appointment, duty, function, occupation, place, position, post, responsibility, situation, work.

officer noun 1 *an officer in the armed services.* adjutant, aide-de-camp, CO, commandant, commanding officer.
VARIOUS RANKS: SEE **rank** noun.
2 *an officer of an organization.* SEE **official** noun.
3 *a police officer.* constable, policeman, policewoman.

official adjective *an official document. an official organization.* accredited, approved, authentic, authoritative, authorized, bona fide, certified, formal, legitimate, licensed, proper, trustworthy.

official noun *We spoke to an official of the organization.* agent, authorized person, [*uncomplimentary*] bureaucrat, SEE **chief** noun, executive, [*often uncomplimentary*] functionary, [*often uncomplimentary*] mandarin, officer, organizer, representative, responsible person.

TITLES OF VARIOUS OFFICIALS: bailiff, captain, clerk of the court, commander, commanding officer, commissioner, consul, customs officer, director, elder (*of the church*), equerry, governor, manager, managing director, marshal, mayor, mayoress, monitor, ombudsman, overseer, prefect, president, principal, proctor, proprietor, registrar, sheriff, steward, superintendent, supervisor, usher.

---

officiate verb *to officiate at a ceremony.* be in charge, be responsible, have official authority, manage, preside.

officious adjective *an officious car-park attendant.* SEE **bossy**, bumptious, [*informal*] cocky, impertinent, interfering, meddling, over-zealous, [*informal*] pushy, self-important.

offload verb SEE **unload.**

offputting adjective SEE **disconcerting.**

offset verb SEE **balance** verb.

offshoot noun *an unexpected offshoot of my research.* branch, by-product, [*informal*] development, spin-off, subsidiary product.

offspring noun [*Offspring* can refer either to one (*singular*) or to *many* (*plural*).]
Singular: baby, child, descendant, heir, successor.
Plural: brood, family, fry, issue, litter, progeny, seed, spawn, young.

often adverb again and again, constantly, frequently, generally, many times, regularly, repeatedly, time after time.

ogle verb SEE **look** verb.

ogre noun giant, monster.
LEGENDARY CREATURES: SEE **legend.**

oil noun SEE **fat** noun, **fuel** noun.

oil verb *to oil your bike.* grease, lubricate.

oily adjective **1** *oily food.* fat, fatty, greasy.
2 *an oily manner.* SEE **obsequious.**

ointment noun *an ointment for the skin.* balm, cream, embrocation, emollient, liniment, lotion, paste, salve, unguent.

old adjective **1** *old buildings. an old car.* ancient, [*joking*] antediluvian, antiquated, antique, crumbling, decayed, decaying, decrepit, dilapidated, early, historic, medieval, obsolete, prehistoric, primitive, quaint, ruined, [*joking*] superannuated, venerable, veteran, vintage.
2 *old times.* bygone, forgotten, former, immemorial (*from time immemorial*), [*old-fashioned*] olden, past, prehistoric, previous, primeval, remote.
3 *old people.* aged, [*informal*] doddery, elderly, [*formal*] geriatric, grey-haired, hoary, [*informal*] in your dotage, oldish, [*informal*] past it, senile.
4 *old clothes.* moth-eaten, SEE **old-fashioned**, ragged, scruffy, shabby, worn, worn-out.
5 *old bread. old news.* dry, stale.
6 *old bus-tickets.* cancelled, expired, invalid, used.
7 *an old hand at the game.* experienced, expert, familiar, long-established, mature, practised, skilled, well-established.
OPPOSITES: SEE **new, recent, young.**
old age decrepitude [*informal*] dotage, senility.
an old person centenarian, [*uncomplimentary*] fogy or fogey, nonagenarian, octogenarian, pensioner, septuagenarian.
medical treatment of old people geriatrics.

old-fashioned adjective **1** *old-fashioned ways.* anachronistic, antiquated, archaic, backward-looking, conventional, dated, fusty, hackneyed, obsolete, old, outdated, out-of-date, out-of-touch, outmoded, passé, reactionary, time-honoured, traditional, unfashionable.
OPPOSITES: SEE **modern.**
old-fashioned person [*informal*] fogy or fogey, [*informal*] fuddy-duddy, [*informal*] square.
2 *old-fashioned morals.* narrow-minded, prim, proper, prudish.
OPPOSITES: SEE **advanced.**

ombudsman noun SEE **official** noun.

omen noun *an omen of disaster.* augury, auspice, foreboding, indication, portent, premonition, presage, prognostication, sign, warning.
to be an omen of SEE **foretell.**

ominous adjective *ominous signs of disaster.* baleful, dire, fateful, forbidding, grim, inauspicious, menacing, portentous, sinister, threatening, unlucky, unpropitious.
OPPOSITES: SEE **auspicious.**

omission noun *an unfortunate omission.* exclusion, gap, oversight.

omit verb **1** *to omit facts from a report.* cut, drop, edit out, eliminate, exclude, ignore, jump, leave out, miss out, overlook, pass over, reject, skip.

2 *to omit to do something.* fail, forget, neglect.

The prefix *omni-* is related to Latin *omnis = all.*

---

omnibus adjective *an omnibus edition.* compendious, eclectic, encyclopaedic, inclusive, varied, wide-ranging.

omnipotent adjective all-powerful, almighty, supreme.

oncoming adjective *oncoming traffic.* advancing, approaching, looming.

onerous adjective SEE **burdensome**.

one-sided adjective **1** *a one-sided referee.* SEE **prejudiced**.
2 *a one-sided match.* SEE **uneven**.

ongoing adjective SEE **continual**.

onlooker noun SEE **observer**.

onset noun SEE **beginning**.

onslaught noun SEE **attack** noun.

onus noun SEE **burden** noun.

oodles noun SEE **plenty**.

ooze noun SEE **mud**.

ooze verb SEE **seep**.

opaque adjective *The diver couldn't see through the opaque water.* cloudy, dark, dull, filmy, hazy, impenetrable, muddy, murky, obscure, turbid, unclear.
OPPOSITES: SEE **clear** adjective.

open adjective **1** *an open door. an open mouth.* ajar, gaping, unfastened, unlocked, wide, wide-open, yawning.
2 *open to the public.* accessible, available, exposed, public, revealed.
OPPOSITES: SEE **shut** adjective.
3 *open space. the open road.* broad, clear, empty, extensive, uncrowded, unfenced, unobstructed, unrestricted.
OPPOSITES: SEE **enclosed**.
4 *an open nature. an open face.* artless, communicative, frank, honest, SEE **open-minded**, sincere, straightforward.
OPPOSITES: SEE **deceitful**.
5 *open defiance.* barefaced, blatant, candid, conspicuous, evident, flagrant, obvious, outspoken, overt, plain, unconcealed, undisguised, visible.
OPPOSITE: SEE **concealed**.
6 *an open question.* arguable, debatable, unanswered, undecided, unresolved.

open verb **1** *to open a door, bottle, letter, etc.* unblock, unbolt, unclose, uncork, undo, unfasten, unfold, unfurl, unlock, unroll, unseal, unwrap.
2 *The door opened. Her mouth opened.* become open [SEE **open** adjective], gape, yawn.
3 *to open a campaign. to open a new shop.* begin, commence, establish, [*informal*] get going, inaugurate, initiate, launch, set up, start.
OPPOSITES: **close** verb.

open-air adjective SEE **outdoor**.

open-handed adjective SEE **generous**.

opening adjective *the opening item in a concert.* first, inaugural, initial, introductory.
OPPOSITES: SEE **final**.

opening noun **1** *an opening in a fence.* aperture, breach, break, chink, crack, cut, door, doorway, fissure, gap, gash, gate, gateway, hatch, hole, leak, mouth, orifice, outlet, rent, rift, slit, slot, space, split, tear, vent.
2 *the opening of a concert. the opening of a new era.* beginning, birth, commencement, dawn, inauguration, inception, initiation, launch, outset, start.
3 *The job provides a good opening for someone with initiative.* [*informal*] break, chance, opportunity.

open-minded adjective SEE **unbiased**.

opera noun grand opera, light opera, musical, operetta.

operable adjective *an operable illness.* curable, treatable.

opera-glasses noun SEE **optical** (**optical instruments**).

operate verb **1** *The device operates in all weathers.* act, function, go, perform, run, work.
2 *Can you operate this machine?* deal with, drive, handle, manage, use, work.
3 *The surgeon operated to remove her appendix.* do an operation, perform surgery.

operation noun **1** *a military operation. a business operation.* action, activity, campaign, effort, enterprise, exercise, manœuvre, movement, procedure, proceeding, process, transaction, undertaking.
2 *a surgical operation.* biopsy, surgery, transplant.

operational adjective *Is the new machinery operational yet?* functioning, going, operating, usable, working.

operative adjective [*informal*] *When I say "come quickly", the operative word is "quickly".* crucial, effective, important, key, principal, relevant, significant.

operative, operator nouns SEE **worker**.

operetta noun SEE **opera**.

opiate noun drug, narcotic, sedative, tranquillizer.

opinion noun *I've got my own opinion.* assessment, attitude, belief, comment, conclusion, conjecture, conviction, estimate, feeling, guess, idea, impression, judgement, notion, perception, point of view, theory, thought, view.

opinionated adjective SEE **stubborn**.

opponent noun *an opponent in a debate.* adversary, antagonist, challenger, competitor, contestant, enemy, foe, opposer, opposition, rival.
OPPOSITES: SEE **ally** noun.

opportune adjective *an opportune moment.* advantageous, appropriate, auspicious, convenient, favourable, lucky, propitious, right, suitable, timely.
OPPOSITES: SEE **inconvenient**.

opportunity noun *The weekend is a good opportunity for shopping.* [*informal*] break, chance, moment, occasion, opening, time.

oppose verb *to oppose someone's ideas. to oppose an enemy.* argue with, attack, be opposed to [SEE **opposed**], challenge, combat, compete against, confront, contest, contradict, controvert, counter, counter-attack, defy, disapprove of, face, fight, obstruct, [*informal*] pit your wits against, quarrel with, resist, rival, stand up to, [*informal*] take a stand against, withstand.
OPPOSITES: SEE **support** verb.

opposed adjective *I'm opposed to the idea.* against, antagonistic, antipathetic, hostile, inimical, SEE **opposite** adjective, unsympathetic.

opposite adjective **1** *the opposite view. the opposite theory.* antithetical, conflicting, contradictory, contrary, contrasting, converse, different, incompatible, SEE **opposed**, opposing, reverse.
2 *the opposite side of the road. your opposite number.* corresponding, equivalent, facing, matching, similar.

opposite noun *She says one thing and does the opposite.* antithesis, contrary, converse, reverse.

opposition noun **1** *We didn't expect so much opposition.* antagonism, competition, disapproval, resistance, scepticism, unfriendliness.
OPPOSITES: SEE **support** noun.
2 *We underestimated the strength of the opposition.* SEE **opponent**.

oppress verb *The factory owners oppressed their workers.* abuse, afflict, crush, depress, enslave, exploit, grind down, [*informal*] keep under, persecute, subdue, subjugate, SEE **terrorize**, [*informal*] trample on, tyrannize.

oppressed adjective *oppressed sections of the community.* abused, browbeaten, crushed, disadvantaged, downtrodden, enslaved, exploited, maltreated, misused, persecuted, subjugated.
OPPOSITES: SEE **privileged**.

oppressive adjective **1** *an oppressive ruler.* brutal, cruel, despotic, harsh, repressive, severe, tyrannical, unjust.
2 *oppressive weather.* airless, close, heavy, hot, humid, muggy, stifling, stuffy, sultry.

opprobrium noun SEE **disgrace** noun.

opt verb SEE **choose**.

optical adjective VARIOUS OPTICAL INSTRUMENTS: bifocals, binoculars, field-glasses, glasses, lens, magnifier, magnifying glass, microscope, monocle, opera-glasses, periscope, spectacles, sun-glasses, telescope.

Several English words, including *optimism* and *optimum*, are related to Latin *optimus = best*. Compare *pessimism*, which is related to Latin *pessimus = worst*.

---

optimism noun cheerfulness, confidence, hope, positiveness.
OPPOSITES: SEE **pessimism**.

optimistic adjective *optimistic about our chances.* buoyant, cheerful, confident, expectant, hopeful, positive, sanguine.
OPPOSITES: SEE **pessimistic**.

optimum adjective *the optimum value of something.* best, highest, ideal, maximum, perfect, top.
OPPOSITE: worst.

option noun *You had the option of staying or leaving.* alternative, choice, possibility.
OPPOSITES: SEE **compulsion**.

optional adjective *optional extras.* discretionary, dispensable, elective, inessential, possible, unnecessary, voluntary.
OPPOSITES: SEE **compulsory**.

opulent adjective SEE **rich**.

oracle noun SEE **prophet**.

oral adjective *an oral report.* by mouth, said, spoken, unwritten, verbal.
OPPOSITE: written.

oration noun SEE **speech**.

orator noun SEE **speaker**.

oratory noun *I admire the oratory of some politicians.* eloquence, rhetoric, speaking, speechmaking.

orb noun SEE **sphere**.

orbit noun *the orbit of a spacecraft.* circuit, course, path, revolution, trajectory.

orbit verb *to orbit the earth.* circle, travel round.

orbital adjective *an orbital route.* circular, encircling.

orchestra noun GROUPS OF MUSICIANS: SEE **music**.

orchestrate verb **1** *to orchestrate music.* arrange, compose.
2 *to orchestrate a demonstration.* SEE **organize**.

ordain verb *to ordain that something shall happen.* SEE **command** verb.

ordeal noun *a painful ordeal.* difficulty, experience, [*informal*] nightmare, suffering, test, torture, trial, tribulation, trouble.

order noun **1** *alphabetical order. chronological order.* arrangement, array, classification, [*informal*] line-up, pattern, progression, sequence, series, succession.
2 *We restored order after the party.* neatness, system, tidiness.
3 *The army restored order after the riot.* calm, control, discipline, good behaviour, government, harmony, law and order, obedience, orderliness, organization, peace, quiet, rule.
OPPOSITES: SEE **disorder**.
4 *Keep your car in good order.* condition, state.
5 *The boss gives the orders.* command, decree, directive, edict, injunction, instruction.
6 *an order for a new carpet. an order for work to be done.* application, booking, commission, demand, mandate, request, requisition, reservation.
7 *an order of monks. a chivalric order.* brotherhood, community, fraternity, SEE **group** noun, society.
to put things in order SEE **arrange**.

order verb **1** *to order things properly.* SEE **arrange**.
2 *She ordered us to be quiet.* [*old-fashioned*] bid, charge, command, compel, decree, direct, enjoin, instruct, ordain, require.
3 *He ordered a new magazine.* apply for, book, requisition, reserve.

orderly adjective **1** *orderly work.* careful, methodical, neat, organized, systematic, tidy, well-arranged, well-organized, well-prepared.
2 *orderly behaviour. an orderly crowd.* civilized, controlled, decorous, disciplined, law-abiding, peaceable, restrained, well-behaved.
OPPOSITES: SEE **disorderly**.

ordinance noun SEE **decree** noun.

ordinary adjective *ordinary people. ordinary behaviour.* accustomed, average, common, commonplace, conventional, customary, established, everyday, familiar, habitual, humble, [*informal*] humdrum, indifferent, mediocre, medium, middling, moderate, modest, mundane, nondescript, normal, orthodox, pedestrian, plain, prosaic, quotidian, reasonable, regular, routine, [*informal*] run-of-the-mill, satisfactory, simple, standard, stock (*a stock reply*), typical, undistinguished, unexceptional, unexciting, unimpressive, uninteresting, unsurprising, usual, well-known, workaday.
OPPOSITES: SEE **exceptional**.

ordnance noun WEAPONS: SEE **weapons**.

ore noun SEE **rock** noun.

organ noun **1** *a church organ.* KEYBOARD INSTRUMENTS: SEE **keyboard**.
2 *organs of the body.* PARTS OF THE BODY: SEE **body**.

organic adjective **1** *an organic substance.* animate, biological, growing, live, living, natural.
OPPOSITES: SEE **inorganic**.
2 *an organic whole.* evolving, integrated, organized, structured, systematic.

organism noun *a living organism.* animal, cell, creature, living thing, plant.

organization noun **1** *Who was responsible for the organization of the outing?* arrangement, co-ordination, logistics, organizing, planning, regimentation, [*informal*] running.
2 *a business organization. a charitable organization.* alliance, association, body, business, club, company, concern, confederation, consortium, corporation, federation, firm, group, institute, institution, league, network, [*informal*] outfit, party, society, syndicate, union.

organize verb **1** *to organize into groups.* arrange, classify, group, put in order, rearrange, regiment, sort, sort out, structure, systematize, tidy up.
OPPOSITES: SEE **jumble** verb.
2 *to organize a party. to organize a demonstration.* co-ordinate, create, establish, make arrangements for, mobilize, orchestrate, plan, run, [*informal*] see to, set up.

organized adjective *an organized argument. organized effort.* careful, clear, efficient, logical, methodical, neat, orderly, planned, regimented, scientific, structured, systematic, tidy, well-arranged, well-presented, well-run.
OPPOSITES: SEE **disorganized**.

orgy noun Bacchanalia, [*informal*] binge, party, revelry, Saturnalia.

orient verb SEE **orientate**.

oriental adjective *oriental nations.* Asiatic, eastern, far-eastern.

orientate verb *to orientate yourself to a new situation.* acclimatize, accustom, adapt, adjust, familiarize, orient, position.

orifice noun hole, mouth, SEE **opening**.

origin noun **1** *the origin of life on earth. the origin of a rumour.* basis, beginning, birth, cause, commencement, creation, derivation, foundation, genesis, inauguration, inception, provenance, root, source, start.
OPPOSITES: SEE **end** noun.
2 *a millionaire of humble origin.* ancestry, background, descent, extraction, family, parentage, pedigree, start in life, stock.

original adjective **1** *the original inhabitants of a country.* aboriginal, archetypal, earliest, first, initial, native, primal, primitive, primordial.
OPPOSITES: SEE **recent**.
2 *an original idea. an original story.* creative, first-hand, fresh, imaginative, innovative, inspired, inventive, new, novel, resourceful, thoughtful, unconventional, unfamiliar, unique, unusual.
OPPOSITES: SEE **unoriginal**.
3 *an original work of art.* authentic, genuine, real, unique.
OPPOSITES: SEE **fake** adjective.

originate verb **1** *Where did the idea originate?* arise, be born, begin, commence, crop up, emanate, emerge, start.
2 *Who originated the idea?* be the inventor of, conceive, create, design, discover, give birth to, inaugurate, initiate, inspire, institute, introduce, invent, launch, pioneer.

ornament noun accessory, adornment, bauble, decoration, embellishment, filigree, frill, frippery, garnish, gewgaw, SEE **jewel**, tracery, trimming, trinket.

ornament verb adorn, beautify, deck, decorate, dress up, embellish, emblazon, emboss, embroider, festoon, garnish, [*uncomplimentary*] prettify, trim.

ornamental adjective attractive, decorative, fancy, [*uncomplimentary*] flashy, pretty, showy.

ornate adjective *ornate decorations.* [*formal*] baroque, decorated, elaborate, fancy, florid, flowery, fussy, ornamented, [*formal*] rococo.
OPPOSITES: SEE **plain** adjective.

ornithology noun bird-watching.

orphan noun foundling, stray, waif.
FAMILY RELATIONSHIPS: SEE **family**.

orthodox adjective *orthodox beliefs. the orthodox way to do something.* accepted, approved, conformist, conventional, customary, established, mainstream, normal, official, ordinary, regular, standard, traditional, usual, well-established.
OPPOSITES: unorthodox, SEE **unconventional**.

orthodoxy noun compliance, conformity, conventionality, submission.

oscillate verb fluctuate, move to and fro, [*informal*] see-saw, swing, vacillate, vary, vibrate.

ossify verb SEE **harden**.

ostensible adjective *The ostensible reason wasn't the real reason.* alleged, apparent, offered, outward, pretended, professed, [*informal*] put-on, reputed, specious, supposed, visible.
OPPOSITES: SEE **real**.

ostentation noun *I don't like the ostentation of their expensive life-style.* affectation, display, exhibitionism, flamboyance, [*informal*] flashiness, pretentiousness, self-advertisement, show, showing off, [*informal*] swank.
OPPOSITES: SEE **modesty**.

ostracize verb *to ostracize someone you don't like.* avoid, [*informal*] black, blackball, blacklist, boycott, cast out, cold-shoulder, [*informal*] cut, [*informal*] cut dead, [*formal*] excommunicate, exile, expel, reject, [*informal*] send to Coventry, shut out.
OPPOSITES: SEE **friend (make friends with)**.

oust verb banish, eject, expel, [*informal*] kick out, remove, unseat.

out-and-out adjective SEE **complete** adjective.

outboard motor noun SEE **engine**.

outbreak noun *an outbreak of measles. an outbreak of vandalism.* epidemic, [*informal*] flare-up, SEE **outburst**, plague, rash, upsurge.

outburst noun *an outburst of laughter.* attack, eruption, explosion, fit, paroxysm, spasm, surge.

outcast noun *an outcast from society.* castaway, exile, outlaw, outsider, pariah, refugee, untouchable.

outclass verb SEE **beat** verb, **surpass**.

outcome noun SEE **result** noun.

outcry noun SEE **protest** noun.

outdated adjective SEE **obsolete**.

outdistance verb SEE **beat** verb.

outdo verb SEE **beat** verb, **surpass**.

outdoor adjective *an outdoor party.* alfresco, open-air, outside.

outer adjective **1** *outer clothing.* exterior, external, outside, outward, superficial, surface.
2 *outer regions.* distant, further, outlying, peripheral, remote.
OPPOSITES: SEE **inner**.

outfit noun **1** *a complete water-skiing outfit.* SEE **equipment**.
2 *a new outfit of clothes.* costume, ensemble, [*informal*] get-up, suit, [*informal*] turn-out.

outgoing adjective **1** *an outgoing personality.* SEE **sociable**.
2 *the outgoing president.* ex-, former, last, past, retiring.
3 *the outgoing tide.* ebbing, falling, retreating.
OPPOSITES: SEE **incoming**.

outgoings noun SEE **expense**.

outhouse noun shed.

outing noun *an outing to the seaside.* excursion, expedition, jaunt, picnic, tour, trip.

outlandish adjective SEE **strange**.

outlast verb SEE **survive**.

outlaw noun *outlaws hiding in the mountains.* bandit, brigand, criminal, deserter, desperado, fugitive, marauder, outcast, renegade, robber.

outlaw verb SEE **prohibit**.

outlay noun SEE **expense**.

outlet noun *an outlet for waste water.* channel, duct, exit, mouth, opening, orifice, vent, way out.

outline noun **1** *an outline of a scheme.* [*informal*] bare bones, diagram, framework, plan, rough idea, skeleton, sketch, summary.
2 *the outline of someone passing the window.* figure, form, profile, shadow, shape, silhouette.

outline verb *to outline your plans.* delineate, draft, give an outline of [SEE **outline** noun], rough out, sketch, summarize.

outlive verb SEE **survive**.

outlook noun **1** *the outlook from my window.* aspect, panorama, prospect, scene, sight, vantage-point, view, vista.
2 *a person's mental outlook.* attitude, frame of mind, point of view, standpoint, viewpoint.
3 *the weather outlook.* expectations, forecast, [*informal*] look-out, prediction, prognosis.

outlying adjective *outlying areas.* distant, far-flung, far-off, outer, remote.
OPPOSITES: SEE **central**.

outmoded adjective SEE **old-fashioned**.

outnumber verb SEE **exceed**.

out-of-date adjective SEE **old-fashioned**.

outpace verb SEE **beat** verb.

output noun *the output of a factory.* production, yield.

outrage noun **1** *The way he treats his pets is an outrage.* atrocity, crime, disgrace, outrageous act [SEE **outrageous**], scandal, sensation.
2 *You can imagine our outrage when we heard what he'd done.* anger, disgust, fury, horror, indignation, resentment, revulsion, sense of shock.

outrageous adjective *outrageous behaviour. outrageous prices.* abominable, atrocious, beastly, bestial, criminal, disgraceful, disgusting, excessive, execrable, extortionate, extravagant, immoderate, infamous, iniquitous, monstrous, nefarious, notorious, offensive, preposterous, revolting, scandalous, shocking, unreasonable, unspeakable, unthinkable, vile, villainous, wicked.
OPPOSITES: SEE **reasonable**.

outright adjective *an outright villain.* SEE **complete** adjective.

outrun verb SEE **beat** verb.

outset noun SEE **beginning**.

outshine verb SEE **surpass**.

outside adjective **1** *outside walls.* exterior, external, outer, outward, superficial, surface, visible.
2 *outside interference.* alien, extraneous, foreign.
OPPOSITES: SEE **inside** adjective.
3 *an outside chance.* SEE **remote**.

outside noun *the outside of a house.* exterior, façade, shell, skin, surface.
OPPOSITES: SEE **inside** noun.

outsider noun *Make outsiders feel welcome.* alien, foreigner, immigrant, interloper, intruder, newcomer, non-resident, outcast, stranger, visitor.
OPPOSITES: SEE **member**, **resident** noun.

outsize adjective SEE **large**, overgrown, oversized.

outskirts plural noun *the outskirts of the town.* edge, fringe, margin, outer areas, periphery, purlieus, suburbs.
OPPOSITES: SEE **centre**.

outspoken adjective SEE **frank**.

outspread adjective SEE **wide**.

outstanding adjective **1** *an outstanding player. an outstanding feature.* above the rest, celebrated, conspicuous, distinguished, dominant, eminent, excellent, exceptional, extraordinary, great, important, impressive, memorable, notable, noteworthy, noticeable, predominant, pre-eminent, prominent, remarkable, singular, special, striking, unrivalled, well-known.
OPPOSITES: SEE **ordinary**.
2 *outstanding bills.* due, overdue, owing, unpaid, unsettled.

outstrip verb SEE **surpass**.

outvote verb SEE **defeat** verb.

outward adjective *outward appearances.* apparent, evident, exterior, external, noticeable, obvious, ostensible, outer, outside, superficial, surface, visible.

outweigh verb SEE **cancel (cancel out)**.

outwit verb *The fox outwitted the hounds.* cheat, SEE **deceive**, dupe, fool, hoax, hoodwink, [*informal*] outsmart, [*informal*] take in, trick.

oval adjective egg-shaped, elliptical, ovoid.
OTHER SHAPES: SEE **shape** noun.

ovation noun SEE **applause**.

oven noun cooker, stove.

overact verb SEE **exaggerate**.

overall adjective *the overall impression given by something.* SEE **total** adjective.

overbalance verb SEE **fall** verb.

overbearing adjective SEE **arrogant, tyrannical**.

overcast adjective *an overcast sky.* black, cloudy, dark, dismal, dull, gloomy, grey, leaden, lowering, stormy, threatening.

overcoat noun greatcoat, mackintosh, top-coat, trench-coat.
OTHER CLOTHES: SEE **clothes**.

overcome adjective *overcome by the heat.* beaten, [*informal*] done in, SEE **exhausted**, prostrate.

overcome verb **1** *to overcome an opponent.* SEE **defeat** verb.
2 *to overcome a problem.* SEE **deal** verb **(deal with)**.

overcrowded adjective *an overcrowded room.* congested, crammed, filled to capacity, full, jammed, overloaded, packed.

overdo verb do excessively, SEE **exaggerate**.

overdue adjective **1** *The train is overdue.* belated, delayed, late, slow, tardy, unpunctual.
OPPOSITES: SEE **early**.
2 *The gas bill is overdue.* outstanding, owing, unpaid.

overeat verb be greedy [SEE **greedy**], eat too much, gorge yourself, gormandize, [*informal*] guzzle, indulge yourself, [*informal*] make a pig of yourself.

overeating noun excess, gluttony, self-indulgence.
OPPOSITES: SEE **starvation**.

overestimate verb SEE **exaggerate**.

overflow verb *The lavatory cistern overflowed.* brim over, flood, pour over, run over, spill, well up.

overgrown adjective **1** *an overgrown schoolboy.* SEE **large**, outsize, oversized.
2 *an overgrown garden.* rank, tangled, uncut, unkempt, untidy, untrimmed, unweeded, weedy, wild.

overhang verb SEE **jut**.

overhaul verb **1** *to overhaul an engine.* check over, examine, inspect, renovate, repair, restore, service.
2 *The express overhauled a goods train.* SEE **overtake**.

overhead adjective *an overhead walkway.* aerial, elevated, high, overhanging, raised.

overheads noun SEE **expense**.

overhear verb *to overhear a conversation.* eavesdrop on, listen in to.

overjoyed adjective SEE **pleased**.

overload verb SEE **burden** verb.

overlook verb **1** *to overlook someone's wrongdoing.* condone, disregard, excuse, forget, ignore, leave out, let pass, miss, neglect, omit, pardon, pass over, pay no attention to, [*informal*] turn a blind eye to.
2 *My window overlooks the pie factory.* face, front, have a view of, look at, look on to.

overpass noun SEE **bridge** noun.

overpower verb *to overpower an attacker.* SEE **subdue**.

overpowering adjective *an overpowering urge.* compelling, irrepressible, irresistible, overwhelming, powerful, uncontrollable.

override, overrule verbs SEE **cancel**.

overrun verb SEE **invade**.

overseas adjective *overseas travel.* foreign.

overseas adverb *to travel overseas.* abroad.

oversee verb SEE **supervise**.

overseer noun SEE **supervisor**

overshadow verb SEE **dominate**.

oversight noun *It wasn't deliberate—just an oversight.* SEE **error**.

oversimplify verb SEE **falsify**.

oversized adjective SEE **large**, outsize, overgrown.

overstate verb SEE **exaggerate**.

overt adjective *overt hostility.* blatant, SEE **obvious**, open, plain, unconcealed, undisguised.
OPPOSITES: SEE **secret** adjective.

overtake verb *Overtake the car in front.* catch up with, leave behind, outdistance, outpace, outstrip, overhaul, pass.

overthrow noun, verb SEE **defeat** noun, verb.

overtire verb SEE **tire**.

overtone noun *The word "witchcraft" has sinister overtones.* association, connotation, implication, reverberation, suggestion.

overturn verb **1** *The boat overturned.* capsize, keel over, tip over, turn over, turn turtle.
2 *The cat overturned the milk.* knock over, spill, tip over, topple, upset.

overweight adjective SEE **fat** adjective.

overwhelm verb **1** *to overwhelm the opposition.* SEE **defeat** verb.
2 *A tidal-wave overwhelmed the town.* SEE **submerge**.

overwhelming adjective *an overwhelming victory.* crushing, devastating, SEE **great**, landslide, overpowering.

overwrought adjective SEE **excited**.

ovoid adjective egg-shaped, elliptical, oval.

owe verb **to owe money** be in debt, have debts.

owing adjective *I'll pay whatever is owing.* due, outstanding, overdue, owed, payable, unpaid, unsettled.
owing to because of, caused by, thanks to.

own verb *We own our house.* be the owner of, have, hold, possess.
to own up acknowledge your guilt, admit, [*informal*] come clean, confess, [*informal*] make a clean breast of it, [*informal*] tell all.

owner noun *the owner of property.* freeholder, landlady, landlord, possessor, proprietor.

ox noun SEE **cattle**.
RELATED ADJECTIVE: bovine.

P

pace noun **1** *Move forward two paces.* step, stride.
2 *The front runner set a quick pace.* gait, [*informal*] lick, movement, quickness, rate, speed, velocity.

pace verb SEE **walk** verb.

pacific adjective SEE **peaceable**.

pacifism noun non-violence.
OPPOSITE: militarism.

pacify verb *to pacify an angry person. to pacify someone's anger.* appease, assuage, calm, conciliate, humour, mollify, placate, propitiate, quell, quieten, soothe, subdue, tame, tranquillize.
OPPOSITES: SEE **anger** verb.

pack noun **1** *a pack of goods.* bale, box, bundle, package, packet, parcel.
2 *a pack to carry on your back.* back-pack, haversack, kitbag, knapsack, rucksack.
3 *a pack of wolves.* SEE **group** noun.

pack verb **1** *to pack things in a box.* bundle, fill, load, package, put, put together, store, stow, wrap up.
2 *to pack things tightly. to pack people into a minibus.* compress, cram, crowd, huddle, jam, overcrowd, press, ram, squeeze, stuff, wedge.

package, packet nouns SEE **pack** noun.

pact noun *a pact with the enemy.* agreement, alliance, armistice, arrangement, bargain, compact, contract, covenant, deal, entente, league, peace, settlement, treaty, truce, understanding.

pad noun **1** *a pad to kneel on.* cushion, hassock, kneeler, padding, pillow, wad.
2 *a writing-pad.* jotter, notebook.

pad verb **1** *to pad something with soft material.* cover, fill, line, pack, protect, stuff, upholster.
2 *to pad along quietly.* SEE **walk** verb.

padding noun **1** *padding in an armchair.* filling, protection, upholstery, stuffing, wadding.
2 *padding in an essay.* prolixity, verbiage, verbosity, [*informal*] waffle, wordiness.

paddle noun oar, scull.

paddle verb **1** *to paddle a boat.* propel, row, scull.
2 *to paddle in the sea.* dabble, splash about, wade.

paddock noun enclosure, field, meadow, pasture.

paddy noun *to be in a paddy.* SEE **angry** **(be angry)**.

padlock noun SEE **fastening**, lock.

padlock verb OTHER WAYS TO FASTEN THINGS: SEE **fasten**.

padre noun SEE **clergyman**.

pagan adjective *pagan tribes.* atheistic, godless, heathen, idolatrous, irreligious, unchristian.

pagan noun *Missionaries wished to convert the pagans.* atheist, heathen, infidel, savage, unbeliever.

page noun **1** *a page of a book.* folio, leaf, sheet, side.
2 *a page serving at court.* OTHER SERVANTS: SEE **servant**.

pageant noun *a historical pageant.* display, parade, procession, spectacle, tableau.

pageantry noun *the pageantry of a royal wedding.* ceremony, display, formality, grandeur, magnificence, pomp, ritual, show, spectacle, splendour.

pail noun bucket.
OTHER CONTAINERS: SEE **container**.

pain noun ache, affliction, agony, anguish, cramp, crick (*in the neck*), discomfort, distress, headache, hurt, irritation, ordeal, pang, smart, soreness, spasm, stab, sting, suffering, tenderness, throb, throes (*throes of childbirth*), toothache, torment, torture, twinge.
to suffer pain SEE **hurt** verb.

pain verb SEE **hurt** verb.

pained adjective *a pained expression.* distressed, grieved, hurt, offended.

painful adjective **1** *painful torture.* agonizing, cruel, excruciating, severe.
2 *a painful wound.* aching, [*informal*] achy, hurting, inflamed, raw, smarting, sore, [*informal*] splitting (*a splitting headache*), tender.
3 *a painful experience.* distressing, hard to bear, harrowing, hurtful, nasty, [*informal*] traumatic, trying, unpleasant, upsetting.
4 *a painful decision.* difficult, hard, laborious, troublesome.
OPPOSITES: SEE **painless**.
to be painful SEE **hurt** verb.

pain-killer noun anaesthetic, analgesic, anodyne, sedative.

painless adjective *a painless visit to the dentist. a painless decision.* comfortable, easy, effortless, pain-free, simple, trouble-free, undemanding.
OPPOSITES: SEE **painful**.

painstaking adjective SEE **careful**.

paint noun colour, colouring, pigment, tint.
KINDS OF PAINT: distemper, emulsion, enamel, gloss paint, lacquer, matt paint, oil-colour, oil-paint, pastel, primer, stain, tempera, undercoat, varnish, water-colour, whitewash.

paint verb **1** *to paint a wall. to paint a toy.* apply paint to, coat with paint, colour, cover with paint, decorate, enamel, gild, lacquer, redecorate, varnish, whitewash.
2 *to paint a picture.* delineate, depict, describe, portray, represent.

painter noun **1** *a house painter.* decorator.
2 *a painter of pictures.* SEE **artist**.

painting noun KINDS OF PAINTED PICTURE: fresco, landscape, miniature, mural, oil-painting, portrait, still-life, water-colour.
OTHER KINDS OF PICTURE: SEE **picture** noun.

pair noun *a pair of friends. working as a pair.* brace, couple, duet, duo, mates, partners, partnership, set of two, twins, twosome.

pair verb SEE **couple** verb.

pal noun SEE **friend**.

palace noun castle, château, mansion, official residence, stately home.
RELATED ADJECTIVE: palatial.

palatable adjective *palatable food.* acceptable, agreeable, appetizing, easy to take, eatable, edible, nice to eat, pleasant, tasty.
OPPOSITES: SEE **unpalatable**.

palatial adjective SEE **grand**.

palaver noun SEE **commotion**.

pale adjective **1** *a pale face.* anaemic, ashen, bloodless, colourless, drained, etiolated, ill-looking, pallid, pasty, [*informal*] peaky, sallow, sickly, unhealthy, wan, [*informal*] washed-out, [*informal*] whey-faced, white, whitish.
OPPOSITES: SEE **ruddy**.
2 *pale colours.* bleached, dim, faded, faint, light, pastel, subtle, weak.
OPPOSITES: SEE **bright**.

pale verb *He paled when he heard the bad news. Plants pale through lack of light.* become pale, blanch, etiolate, fade, lighten, lose colour, whiten.

palfrey noun SEE **horse**.

paling noun fence, fencing, palisade, railing, stockade.

palisade noun SEE **paling**.

pall noun **1** *a pall on a coffin.* mantle, shroud, veil.
2 *a pall of smoke.* SEE **covering**.

pall verb *The novelty soon began to pall.* become boring, become uninteresting, weary.

pallet, palliasse nouns SEE **bed**.

palliate verb SEE **alleviate**.

palliative adjective *a palliative treatment.* alleviating [SEE **alleviate**], calming, reassuring, sedative, soothing.

palliative noun *The medicine she took was only a palliative, not a real cure.* SEE **pain-killer**, sedative, tranquillizer.

pallid adjective SEE **pale** adjective.

pally adjective SEE **friendly**.

palm noun *the palm of your hand.* SEE **hand** noun.

palmer noun SEE **pilgrim**.

palmist noun SEE **fortune-teller**.

palpable adjective SEE **tangible**.

palpitate verb SEE **pulsate**.

palsied adjective SEE **paralysed**.

palsy noun SEE **paralysis**.

paltry adjective SEE **worthless**.

pamper verb *to pamper your pet.* coddle, cosset, humour, indulge, mollycoddle, over-indulge, pet, spoil, spoon-feed.

pamphlet noun *a pamphlet about road safety.* booklet, brochure, catalogue, folder, handout, leaflet, tract.

pan noun COOKING UTENSILS: SEE **cook** verb.

pan verb SEE **criticize**.

panacea noun SEE **remedy** noun.

panache noun *We were bowled over by the panache of her performance.* SEE **confidence**, enthusiasm, flourish, spirit, style, verve, zest.

pandemonium noun SEE **uproar**.

pander verb **to pander to** *to pander to low tastes.* cater for, fulfil, gratify, indulge, please, provide, satisfy.

pane noun glass, sheet of glass, window.

panegyric noun SEE **praise** noun.

panel noun **1** *a wooden panel.* insert, rectangle, rectangular piece.
panels panelling, wainscot.
2 *a panel of experts.* committee, group, jury, team.
member of a panel expert, panellist, pundit.

pang noun SEE **pain** noun.

panic noun *If a fire starts, we don't want any panic!* alarm, consternation, SEE **fear** noun, [*informal*] flap, horror, hysteria, stampede, terror.

panic verb *Don't panic!* become panic-stricken [SEE **panic-stricken**], [*informal*] flap, [*informal*] go to pieces, [*informal*] lose your head, over-react, stampede.

panicky adjective SEE **panic-stricken**.

panic-stricken adjective alarmed, disorientated, frantic, SEE **frightened**, horrified, hysterical, overexcited, panicky, terror-stricken, undisciplined, unnerved.
OPPOSITES: SEE **cool** adjective.

pannier noun basket.

panoply noun SEE **array** noun.

panorama noun *a beautiful panorama across the valley.* landscape, perspective, prospect, scene, view, vista.

panoramic adjective SEE **wide**.

pant verb *to pant because you've been running.* breathe quickly, gasp, puff, wheeze.

panting adjective *panting after running for the bus.* breathless, exhausted, gasping, out of breath, puffed, tired out, winded.

panties noun SEE **pants**.

pantry noun food cupboard, larder.

pants noun **1** briefs, knickers, panties, shorts, trunks, underpants.
OTHER UNDERCLOTHES: SEE **underclothes**.
2 SEE **trousers**.

pap noun SEE **pulp** noun.

paper noun **1** *a piece of paper.* folio, leaf, sheet.

KINDS OF PAPER: card, cardboard, cartridge paper, manila, notepaper, papyrus, parchment, postcard, stationery, tissue-paper, toilet-paper, tracing-paper, vellum, wallpaper, wrapping-paper, writing-paper.

PAPER SIZES: A4 (A1, A2, etc.), foolscap, quarto.

---

2 *I keep important papers in a file.* certificates, deeds, documents, forms, records.
3 *a daily paper.* SEE **newspaper**.
4 *a scientific paper.* article, dissertation, essay, monograph, thesis, treatise.

paper verb *to paper a room.* decorate.

paperback noun KINDS OF BOOK: SEE **book** noun.

papoose noun SEE **baby**.

papyrus noun SEE **paper** noun.

parable noun KINDS OF STORY: SEE **story**.

parade noun *a military parade. a fancy dress parade.* cavalcade, ceremony, column, display, march-past, motorcade, pageant, procession, review, show.

parade verb **1** *to parade in front of the judges.* assemble, file past, form up, line

up, make a procession, march past, present yourself, process.
2 *to parade up and down.* SEE **walk** verb.
3 *to parade your virtues.* SEE **display** verb.

paradigm noun SEE **model** noun.

paradise noun SEE **delight** noun, Eden, Elysium, heaven, nirvana, Utopia.

paradox noun absurdity, anomaly, contradiction, self-contradiction.

paradoxical adjective *It seems paradoxical to make weapons in order to maintain peace.* absurd, anomalous, conflicting, contradictory, illogical, incongruous, self-contradictory.

paragon noun SEE **model** noun.

paragraph noun LINGUISTIC TERMS: SEE **language**.

parakeet noun parrot.

parallel adjective 1 *parallel lines.* equidistant.
2 *a parallel example. parallel events.* analogous, corresponding, matching, SEE **similar**.

parallel noun *I saw a parallel between her situation and mine.* analogy, comparison, correspondence, likeness, match, resemblance, similarity.

paralyse verb *The shock paralysed him.* anaesthetize, cripple, deaden, desensitize, freeze, immobilize, incapacitate, lame, numb, petrify, stun.

paralysed adjective *a paralysed person. paralysed limbs.* crippled, desensitized, disabled, SEE **handicapped**, immobile, immovable, incapacitated, lame, numb, palsied, paralytic, paraplegic, rigid, unusable, useless.

paralysis noun immobility, palsy, paraplegia.

paralytic adjective 1 SEE **paralysed**.
2 SEE **drunk**.

paramount adjective SEE **supreme**.

paramour noun SEE **lover**.

parapet noun battlement, fortification, rampart.

paraphernalia noun *Can you move all your paraphernalia out of the way?* baggage, belongings, effects, equipment, gear, impedimenta, [*informal*] odds and ends, stuff, tackle, things.

paraphrase verb *to paraphrase something in simpler language.* interpret, rephrase, reword, rewrite, translate.

paraplegia noun SEE **paralysis**.

paraplegic adjective SEE **paralysed**.

parasol noun sunshade, umbrella.

paratroops noun SEE **armed services**.

parboil verb SEE **cook** verb.

parcel noun bale, bundle, carton, pack, package, packet.

parcel verb **to parcel out** SEE **divide**.

parch verb SEE **dry** verb.

parched adjective 1 *Plants won't grow in parched ground.* arid, baked, barren, dehydrated, dry, lifeless, scorched, sterile, waterless.
2 *I'm parched!* gasping, thirsty.

parchment noun SEE **paper** noun.

pardon noun *pardon for a condemned criminal.* absolution, amnesty, discharge, forgiveness, mercy, reprieve.

pardon verb *to pardon a condemned person.* absolve, condone, [*formal*] exculpate, excuse, exonerate, forgive, free, let off, overlook, release, reprieve, set free, spare.

pardonable adjective *a pardonable mistake.* allowable, excusable, forgivable, justifiable, minor, negligible, petty, understandable, venial (*a venial sin*).
OPPOSITES: SEE **unforgivable**.

pare verb 1 *to pare an apple.* peel, skin.
2 *to pare something down.* clip, SEE **cut** verb, prune, reduce, trim.

parent noun FAMILY RELATIONSHIPS: SEE **family**.

parentage noun SEE **ancestry**.

parenthesis noun aside, interpolation.

pariah noun SEE **outcast**.

parity noun SEE **equality**.

park noun KINDS OF PARK: amusement park, arboretum, botanical gardens, car-park, estate, nature reserve, parkland, public gardens, recreation ground, safari park, theme park.

park verb *to park a car.* leave, place, position, station.
to park yourself SEE **settle**.

parky adjective SEE **cold** adjective.

parlance noun SEE **phraseology**.

parley verb SEE **negotiate**.

parliament noun assembly, conclave, congress, convocation, council, SEE **government**, the Houses of Parliament, legislature, senate.

parliamentarian noun SEE **politician**.

parlour noun VARIOUS ROOMS: SEE **room**.

parochial adjective SEE **local** adjective.

parody noun caricature, SEE **imitation**, satire, [*informal*] send-up, [*informal*] take-off, travesty.
OTHER KINDS OF WRITING: SEE **writing**.

parody verb ape, caricature, guy, SEE **imitate**, satirize, [*informal*] send up, [*informal*] take off, travesty.

paroxysm noun SEE **spasm**.

parrot noun parakeet.

parry verb *to parry a blow.* avert, block, deflect, evade, fend off, push away, repel, repulse, stave off, ward off.

parsimonious adjective SEE **stingy**.

parson noun SEE **clergyman**.

parsonage noun rectory, vicarage.
OTHER HOUSES: SEE **house** noun.

part noun **1** *a part of a whole.* bit, branch, component, constituent, department, division, element, fraction, fragment, ingredient, particle, piece, portion, ramification, scrap, section, sector, segment, share, single item, subdivision, unit.
2 *a part of a book or TV programme.* chapter, episode.
3 *a part of a town or country.* area, district, neighbourhood, quarter, region, sector.
4 *parts of your body.* limb, member, organ.
PARTS OF THE BODY: SEE **body**.
5 *a part in a play.* cameo, character, role.

part verb **1** *to part a child from its parents. to part a branch from the trunk.* cut off, detach, disconnect, divide, separate, sever, split, sunder.
OPPOSITES: SEE **join** verb.
2 *to part from someone.* depart, go away, leave, quit, say goodbye, split up, take your leave, withdraw.
to part with SEE **relinquish**.

partake verb SEE **participate**.

partial adjective **1** *Our play was only a partial success.* imperfect, incomplete, limited, unfinished.
OPPOSITES: SEE **complete** adjective.
2 *a partial referee.* SEE **prejudiced**.
to be partial to *I'm partial to a drink at bedtime.* appreciate, be fond of, be keen on, enjoy, [*informal*] go for, like.

participate verb *to participate in a game.* assist, be active, be involved, co-operate, engage, help, join in, partake, share, take part.

participation noun *participation in sport. participation in a crime.* assistance, complicity, contribution, co-operation, involvement, partnership, sharing.

particle noun **1** *a particle of food.* bit, crumb, drop, fragment, grain, iota, jot, morsel, piece, scrap, shred, sliver, speck.
2 *a particle of matter.* atom, electron, molecule, neutron.

particoloured adjective SEE **dappled**.

particular adjective **1** *I recognized his particular way of talking.* distinct, individual, peculiar, personal, singular, specific, uncommon, unique, unmistakable.
OPPOSITES: SEE **general**.
2 *I made a particular effort.* exceptional, important, notable, outstanding, special, unusual.
OPPOSITES: SEE **ordinary**.
3 *The cat's particular about food.* choosy, discriminating, fastidious, finicky, fussy, meticulous, nice, pernickety, selective.
OPPOSITES: SEE **undiscriminating**.

particulars plural noun *Give me the particulars.* circumstances, details, facts, information, [*slang*] low-down.

particularize verb SEE **specify**.

parting noun *We were sad when it came to parting.* departure, going, leave-taking, leaving, saying goodbye [SEE **goodbye**], separation, splitting up.

partisan adjective SEE **prejudiced**.

partisan noun SEE **fighter**.

partition noun **1** *the partition of a country after a war.* division.
2 *a partition between two parts of a room.* barrier, panel, room-divider, screen, wall.

partition verb *to partition a country.* divide, parcel out, separate off, share out, split up, subdivide.

partner noun **1** *a business partner.* accomplice, ally, assistant, [*joking*] bedfellow, collaborator, colleague, companion, confederate, helper.
2 *a marriage partner.* consort, husband, mate, spouse, wife.

partnership noun **1** *a business partnership.* affiliation, alliance, combination, company, co-operative, syndicate.
2 *partnership in crime.* association, collaboration, complicity, co-operation.
3 *a marriage partnership.* marriage, relationship, union.

parturition noun SEE **birth**.

party noun **1** *a Christmas party.* celebration, [*informal*] do, festivity, function, gathering, [*informal*] get-together, [*joking*] jollification, merrymaking, [*informal*] rave-up.

VARIOUS KINDS OF PARTY: ball, banquet, barbecue, birthday party, ceilidh, Christmas party, dance, [*informal*] disco, discothèque, feast, [*informal*] hen-party, house-warming, orgy, picnic, reception, reunion, social, [*informal*] stag-party, tea-party, wedding.

---

2 *a political party.* alliance, association, cabal, [*informal*] camp (*He went over to their camp*), coalition, faction, SEE **group** noun, league.

pass noun 1 *a mountain pass.* canyon, defile, gap, gorge, ravine, valley, way through.
2 *a bus pass.* authority, authorization, licence, permission, permit, ticket, warrant.

pass verb 1 *We watched the traffic pass.* go by, move on, move past, proceed, progress, [*informal*] thread your way.
2 *Try to pass the car in front.* go beyond, outstrip, overhaul, overtake.
3 *The time passed slowly.* elapse, lapse, [*informal*] tick by.
4 *The pain passed.* disappear, fade, go away, vanish.
5 *Pass the books round.* circulate, deal out, deliver, give, hand over, offer, present, share, submit, supply, transfer.
6 *They passed a law. The judge passed sentence.* agree, approve, authorize, confirm, decree, enact, establish, ordain, pronounce, ratify, validate.
7 *I pass!* [*informal*] give in, opt out, say nothing, waive your rights.
to pass away SEE **die**.
to pass out SEE **faint** verb.
to pass over SEE **ignore**.

passable adjective 1 *a passable standard of work.* acceptable, adequate, all right, fair, mediocre, middling, moderate, ordinary, satisfactory, [*informal*] so-so, tolerable.
OPPOSITES: SEE **unacceptable**.
2 *The road is passable again.* clear, navigable, open, traversable, unblocked, usable.
OPPOSITES: SEE **impassable**.

passage noun 1 *the passage of time.* advance, moving on, passing, progress, progression.
2 *a sea passage.* crossing, SEE **journey** noun, voyage.
3 *a secret passage.* corridor, passageway, thoroughfare, tube, tunnel, way through.
4 *Wait in the passage!* entrance, hall, hallway, lobby, vestibule.
5 *a passage of a book.* episode, excerpt, extract, paragraph, piece, quotation, scene, section.

passé adjective SEE **old-fashioned**.

passenger noun commuter, rider, SEE **traveller**.

passer-by noun bystander, onlooker, witness.

passing adjective SEE **temporary**.

passion noun *a passion for adventure.* appetite, ardour, commitment, craving, desire, drive, eagerness, emotion, enthusiasm, fervour, frenzy, greed, [*informal*] heat (*in the heat of the moment*), infatuation, love, lust, obsession, strong feeling, thirst, urge, zeal, zest.

passionate adjective *passionate feelings.* ardent, avid, burning, committed, greedy, eager, emotional, enthusiastic, excited, fervent, fiery, frenzied, hot, impassioned, inflamed, intense, lustful, obsessive, sexy, strong, urgent, vehement, violent, zealous.
OPPOSITES: SEE **apathetic**.

passive adjective *a passive response.* compliant, docile, impassive, inactive, long-suffering, non-violent, patient, resigned, submissive, unresisting.
OPPOSITES: SEE **active**.

passport noun SEE **document**, pass, permit, visa.

past adjective *past events.* bygone, earlier, ended, finished, former, gone, [*informal*] over and done with, previous.
OPPOSITES: SEE **future** adjective.
past it SEE **old**.

past noun *In the past, things were different.* antiquity, days gone by, history, old days, olden days, past times [SEE **past** adjective].
OPPOSITES: SEE **future** noun.

pasta noun KINDS OF PASTA: cannelloni, lasagne, macaroni, noodles, ravioli, spaghetti, tagliatelle, vermicelli.
OTHER FOODS: SEE **food**.

paste noun 1 *adhesive paste.* adhesive, fixative, glue, gum.
2 *fish-paste.* pâté, spread.

paste verb *to paste wallpaper.* SEE **fasten**, glue, gum.

pastel adjective *pastel colours.* SEE **pale** adjective.

pastel noun SEE **paint** noun.

pasteurize verb SEE **sterilize**.

pastiche noun *a pastiche of various styles.* blend, composite, [*informal*] hodgepodge or hotchpotch, medley, mixture, motley collection, patchwork, selection.

pastille noun *a cough pastille.* lozenge.

pastime noun *What's your favourite pastime?* activity, amusement, diversion, entertainment, game, hobby, occupation, recreation, relaxation, sport.
VARIOUS SPORTS AND GAMES: SEE **game** noun, **sport**.

Several English words, including *pastor, pastoral,* and *pasture,* are related to Latin *pastor* = *shepherd.*

---

pastor noun SEE **clergyman.**

pastoral adjective 1 *a pastoral scene.* agrarian, bucolic, country, farming, idyllic, outdoor, peaceful, rural, rustic. OPPOSITES: SEE **urban.**
2 *a clergyman's pastoral duties.* caring, ecclesiastical, parochial, ministerial, priestly.

pasture noun *pasture for sheep or cattle.* field, grassland, grazing, [*old-fashioned, poetic*] mead, meadow, paddock, pasturage.

pasty adjective *a pasty complexion.* SEE **pale** adjective.

pasty noun *a meat pasty.* SEE **pie.**

pat verb *to pat with your hand.* caress, dab, slap, tap, SEE **touch** verb.

patch noun *a patch on your jeans.* mend, repair.

patch verb *to patch a hole.* cover, darn, fix, mend, reinforce, repair, sew up, stitch up.

patchy adjective 1 *patchy fog. patchy success.* [*informal*] bitty, changeable, changing, erratic, inconsistent, irregular, uneven, unpredictable, variable, varied, varying.
2 *patchy colours.* SEE **dappled.**
OPPOSITES: SEE **uniform** adjective.

patent adjective *a patent lie.* SEE **obvious.**

paternal adjective [Compare with *paternalistic.*] *paternal love.* fatherly.

paternalistic adjective [Compare with *paternal.*] *a paternalistic attitude.* SEE **patronizing.**

path noun alley, bridle-path, bridle-way, esplanade, footpath, footway, SEE **road**, route, pathway, pavement, [*American*] sidewalk, towpath, track, trail, walk, walkway, way.

pathetic adjective 1 *a pathetic farewell.* affecting, distressing, heartrending, lamentable, moving, piteous, pitiable, pitiful, poignant, SEE **sad**, touching, tragic.
2 [*informal*] *He's a pathetic goalkeeper.* SEE **inadequate.**

pathos noun *The pathos of the situation brought tears to our eyes.* emotion, feeling, pity, poignancy, sadness, tragedy.

patience noun *I waited with great patience.* calmness, composure, endurance, equanimity, forbearance, fortitude, long-suffering, perseverance, persistence, resignation, restraint, self-control, stoicism, toleration.

patient adjective 1 *patient suffering. a patient animal.* accommodating, calm, composed, docile, easygoing, even-tempered, forbearing, long-suffering, mild, philosophical, quiet, resigned, self-possessed, serene, stoical, submissive, tolerant, uncomplaining.
2 *patient effort. a patient worker.* determined, diligent, persevering, persistent, steady, unhurried, untiring.
OPPOSITES: SEE **impatient.**

patient noun *a hospital patient.* case, invalid, outpatient, sufferer.

patio noun courtyard, paved area, terrace.

patois noun SEE **dialect.**

patriarch noun *the patriarch of a tribe.* father, head, SEE **leader.**

patrician adjective SEE **aristocratic.**

patrimony noun SEE **money.**

patriot noun [*uncomplimentary*] chauvinist, loyalist, nationalist.

patriotic adjective *a patriotic person.* [*uncomplimentary*] chauvinistic, [*uncomplimentary*] jingoistic, loyal, nationalistic, [*uncomplimentary*] xenophobic.

patriotism noun [*uncomplimentary*] chauvinism, [*uncomplimentary*] jingoism, loyalty, nationalism, [*uncomplimentary*] xenophobia.

patrol noun 1 *on patrol.* guard, policing, sentry-duty, surveillance, watch.
2 *a night-patrol.* guard, look-out, sentinel, sentry, watchman.
patrol car panda car, police car.

patrol verb *Police patrolled the area all night.* be on patrol [SEE **patrol** noun], guard, inspect, keep a look-out, police, tour, walk the beat.

patron noun 1 *a patron of the arts.* [*informal*] angel, backer, benefactor, champion, defender, helper, sponsor, subscriber, supporter.
2 *a patron of a shop or restaurant.* client, customer, frequenter, [*informal*] regular, shopper.

patronage noun *We give our patronage to local shops.* backing, business, custom, help, sponsorship, SEE **support** noun, trade.

patronize verb 1 *I patronize the local shops.* back, be a patron of [SEE **patron**], encourage, frequent, give patronage to [SEE **patronage**], shop at, support.
2 *to patronize someone.* be patronizing towards [SEE **patronizing**], talk down to.

patronizing adjective *a patronizing attitude.* condescending, disdainful, haughty, lofty, paternalistic, snobbish, supercilious, superior.

patter noun *a comedian's patter.* WAYS OF TALKING: SEE **talk** verb.

patter verb VARIOUS SOUNDS: SEE **sound** noun.

pattern noun **1** *patterns on wallpaper.* arrangement, decoration, design, device, figuration, figure, motif, ornamentation, shape, tessellation.
2 *a pattern to copy.* archetype, criterion, example, guide, model, norm, original, precedent, prototype, sample, specimen, standard.

patty noun SEE **pie**.

paucity noun SEE **lack** noun.

paunch noun SEE **belly**.

pauper noun SEE **poor (poor person)**.

pause noun *a pause to get our breath back.* break, [*informal*] breather, check, delay, gap, halt, interlude, intermission, interruption, interval, lull, respite, rest, stand-still, stop, stoppage, suspension, wait.

pause verb *She paused uncertainly. We'll pause for a rest.* break off, delay, halt, hang back, have a pause [SEE **pause** noun], hesitate, rest, stop, [*informal*] take a break, wait.

pave verb *to pave a path.* asphalt, concrete, cover with paving [SEE **paving**], flag, [*informal*] make up, surface, tile.

pavement noun SEE **path**.

paving noun VARIOUS KINDS OF PAVING: cobbles, concrete, crazy-paving, flagstones, paving-stones, setts, tiles.

paw noun *an animal's paw.* foot.

paw verb *to paw the ground.* SEE **touch** verb.

pay noun *How much pay do you get?* earnings, emoluments, fee, [*formal*] honorarium, income, SEE **payment**, reimbursement, salary, stipend, wages.

pay verb **1** *Did you pay a lot for your bike?* [*informal*] cough up, [*informal*] fork out, give, hand over, proffer, spend.
2 *They pay her a good wage.* grant, remunerate.
3 *I'll pay my debts.* clear, [*informal*] foot, meet, pay off, pay up, settle.
4 *He paid me for the glass he broke.* bear the cost of, compensate, indemnify, pay back, recompense, refund, reimburse, repay.
5 *Crime doesn't pay.* be profitable [SEE **profitable**].
6 *She'll pay for her mistake!* SEE **suffer**.
to pay back *to pay someone back for an insult, injury, etc.* SEE **retaliate**.
to pay the penalty for *to pay the penalty for wrongdoing.* SEE **atone**.

payment noun *monthly payments.* charge, cost, expenditure, figure, outgoings, outlay, price, rate, remittance.
OPPOSITES: SEE **income**.

KINDS OF PAYMENT: advance, alimony, allowance, commission, compensation, contribution, deposit, donation, fare, fee, fine, instalment, loan, SEE **pay** noun, pocket-money, premium, ransom, reward, royalty, [*informal*] sub, subscription, subsistence, supplement (*a supplement for first-class travel*), surcharge, tip, toll, wage.

---

peace noun **1** *After the war, there was a period of peace.* accord, agreement, amity, conciliation, concord, friendliness, harmony, order.
OPPOSITES: SEE **war**.
2 *The two sides signed a peace.* alliance, armistice, cease-fire, pact, treaty, truce.
OPPOSITE: declaration of war.
3 *the peace of the countryside. peace of mind.* calmness, peace and quiet, peacefulness, placidity, quiet, repose, serenity, silence, stillness, tranquillity.
OPPOSITES: SEE **activity, anxiety, noise**.

peaceable adjective *a peaceable community.* amicable, conciliatory, co-operative, friendly, gentle, harmonious, mild, non-violent, pacific, SEE **peaceful**, peace-loving, placid, understanding.
OPPOSITES: SEE **quarrelsome**.

peaceful adjective *a peaceful evening. peaceful music.* balmy, calm, easy, gentle, pacific, SEE **peaceable**, placid, pleasant, quiet, relaxing, restful, serene, slow-moving, soothing, still, tranquil, undisturbed, unruffled, untroubled.
OPPOSITES: SEE **noisy, troubled**.

peacemaker noun arbitrator, conciliator, intercessor, mediator,

peak noun **1** *the peak of a mountain.* apex, brow, cap, crest, crown, pinnacle, point, summit, tip, top.
2 *snowy peaks.* SEE **mountain**.
3 *the peak of her career.* acme, climax, crisis, culmination, height, highest point, zenith.

peaky adjective SEE **pale** adjective.

peal noun *a peal of bells.* carillon, chime, ringing.

peal verb *The bells pealed.* chime, ring, toll.
OTHER SOUNDS: SEE **sound** noun.

peasant noun **1** *Peasants working on the land.* SEE **worker**.
2 [*uncomplimentary*] bumpkin, churl, rustic, serf, yokel.

pebbles noun cobbles, gravel, stones.

peckish adjective SEE **hungry**.

peculiar adjective **1** *There's a peculiar person snooping around. That's a peculiar way to do it.* abnormal, bizarre, curious, eccentric, funny, odd, outlandish, out of the ordinary, quaint, queer, quirky, surprising, strange, uncommon, unconventional, unusual, weird.
OPPOSITES: SEE **ordinary**.
2 *I recognized her peculiar way of writing.* characteristic, different, distinctive, identifiable, idiosyncratic, individual, particular, personal, private, special, singular, unique.
OPPOSITES: SEE **common** adjective.

peculiarity noun *We all have our peculiarities.* abnormality, characteristic, eccentricity, foible, idiosyncrasy, mannerism, oddity, peculiar feature [SEE **peculiar**], quirk, singularity, speciality, trait, uniqueness.

pecuniary adjective SEE **financial**.

pedagogue noun SEE **teacher**.

A number of English words such as *pedal, pedestal, pedestrian* are related to Latin *pes, pedis=foot.*

---

pedal verb SEE **travel** verb.

pedantic adjective **1** *a pedantic use of long words.* academic, bookish, formal, humourless, learned, old-fashioned, pompous, scholarly, schoolmasterly, stilted.
OPPOSITES: SEE **informal**.
2 *pedantic observance of the rules.* inflexible, [*informal*] nit-picking, precise, strict, unimaginative.
OPPOSITES: SEE **flexible**.

peddle verb SEE **sell**.

pedestal noun SEE **base** noun.

pedestrian adjective **1** *a pedestrian precinct.* pedestrianized, traffic-free.
2 *a pedestrian performance.* SEE **ordinary**.

pedestrian noun foot-traveller, walker.

pedigree adjective *a pedigree animal.* pure-bred, thoroughbred.

pedigree noun *a dog's pedigree.* ancestry, descent, SEE **family**, family history, line.

pedlar noun *a pedlar of cheap goods.* [*old-fashioned*] chapman, door-to-door salesman, hawker, seller, street-trader, vendor.

peek noun, verb SEE **look** noun, verb.

peel noun *orange peel.* rind, skin.

peel verb *to peel an orange. to peel off a covering.* denude, pare, skin, strip.

peep noun, verb SEE **look** noun, verb.
peep of day SEE **dawn**.

peer verb SEE **look** verb.

peer, peeress nouns aristocrat, noble, nobleman, noblewoman, titled person.
OPPOSITE: commoner.

TITLES OF BRITISH PEERS: baron, baroness, duchess, duke, earl, lady, lord, marchioness, marquis or marquess, viscount, viscountess.

OTHER TITLES: SEE **title** noun.

---

peers 1 *the peers of the land.* the aristocracy, the nobility, the peerage.
OPPOSITE: the commons.
2 *She's quite at ease with her peers.* equals, fellows.

peerless adjective SEE **unequalled**.

peeved adjective SEE **annoyed**.

peevish adjective SEE **irritable**.

peewit noun lapwing, plover.

peg noun SEE **fastener**.

peg verb SEE **fasten**.

pejorative adjective SEE **uncomplimentary**.

pelargonium noun geranium.

pellet noun ball, pill.

pell-mell adjective, adverb SEE **hasty**.

pellucid adjective SEE **clear** adjective.

pelt noun SEE **skin** noun.

pelt verb *to pelt someone with missiles.* assail, bombard, shower, SEE **throw**.

pen noun **1** *a pen for animals.* SEE **enclosure**.
2 *a pen to write with.* ball-point, biro, felt-tipped pen, fountain pen.
OTHER WRITING IMPLEMENTS: SEE **write**.
pen-name SEE **pseudonym**.

pen verb SEE **write**.

penal adjective **penal servitude** SEE **punishment**.

penalize verb SEE **punish**.

penalty noun SEE **punishment**.
to pay the penalty for SEE **atone**.

penance noun **to do penance for** SEE **atone**.

penchant noun SEE **inclination**.

pendent adjective *the pendent branches of a willow.* dangling, hanging, loose, pendulous, suspended, swinging, trailing.

pending adjective *There's an inquiry pending.* about to happen, forthcoming, imminent, impending, [*informal*] in the offing, undecided, waiting.

pendulous adjective SEE **pendent**.

pendulum noun SEE **clock**.

penetrate verb 1 *The drill can penetrate concrete.* bore through, make a hole in, pierce, puncture.
2 *We penetrated their defences.* enter, get through, infiltrate, probe.
3 *Damp had penetrated the brick-work.* impregnate, permeate, pervade, seep into.

penetrating adjective 1 *a penetrating analysis.* SEE **intelligent**.
2 *a penetrating scream.* SEE **loud**.

penitent adjective *penitent about his mistake.* apologetic, conscience-stricken, contrite, regretful, remorseful, repentant, sorry.
OPPOSITES: impenitent, SEE **unrepentant**.

pen-name noun SEE **pseudonym**.

pennant noun SEE **flag** noun.

penniless adjective SEE **poor**.

pennon noun SEE **flag** noun.

penny-pinching adjective SEE **stingy**.

pension noun SEE **money**.

pensioner noun SEE **old (old person)**.

pensive adjective SEE **thoughtful**.

A number of English words beginning *penta-* are related to Greek *pente=five*.

---

pentagon noun SEE **shape** noun.

pentagram noun SEE **star**.

pentathlon noun ATHLETIC SPORTS: SEE **athletics**.

penthouse noun SEE **house** noun.

penumbra noun SEE **shadow** noun.

penurious adjective SEE **poor**.

penury noun SEE **poverty**.

people noun 1 *Do you like being with other people?* folk, [*uncomplimentary*] hoi polloi, human beings, humanity, humans, individuals, mankind, mortals, persons.
2 *In an election, the people decide who will govern.* citizens, common people, community, electorate, nation, populace, population, the public, society.
3 *After living abroad for a time, he returned to his people.* clan, family, kith and kin, nation, race, relatives, tribe.

people verb *a strange world peopled by monsters.* colonize, fill, inhabit, occupy, overrun, populate, settle.

pep verb **to pep up** SEE **animate** verb.
pep talk SEE **exhortation**.

pepper verb SEE **sprinkle**.

peppery adjective *a peppery taste.* hot, spicy.

perambulate verb SEE **walk** verb.

perambulator noun baby-carriage, pram, push-chair.

perceive verb 1 *I perceived a shape on the horizon.* become aware of, catch sight of, detect, discern, distinguish, make out, notice, observe, recognize, see, spot.
2 *I began to perceive what she meant.* apprehend, comprehend, deduce, feel, gather, grasp, know, realize, sense, understand.

perceptible adjective *a perceptible drop in temperature. perceptible anger in his voice.* appreciable, audible, detectable, distinct, evident, marked, noticeable, observable, obvious, palpable, perceivable, recognizable, visible.
OPPOSITES: SEE **imperceptible**.

perception noun *What is your perception of the problem? Ears and eyes are organs of perception.* apprehension, awareness, cognition, comprehension, consciousness, discernment, insight, observation, recognition, sensation, sense, understanding, view.

perceptive adjective [Do not confuse with *perceptible*.] *a perceptive judge of character.* acute, alert, astute, aware, clever, discriminating, discerning, SEE **intelligent**, observant, penetrating, percipient, perspicacious, responsive, sensitive, sharp, sharp-eyed, shrewd, sympathetic, understanding.

perch noun *a bird's perch.* resting-place, roost.

perch verb *to perch on a fence.* balance, rest, roost, settle, sit.

percipient adjective SEE **perceptive**.

percolate verb SEE **filter** verb.

percussion noun [*uncomplimentary*] kitchen department.

PERCUSSION INSTRUMENTS INCLUDE: castanets, celesta or celeste, chime bars, cymbals, SEE **drum**, glockenspiel, gong, kettledrum, maracas, rattle, tambourine, [*plural*] timpani, triangle, tubular bells, vibraphone, wood block, xylophone.

OTHER MUSICAL INSTRUMENTS: SEE **music**.

---

perdition noun damnation, doom, hell, ruination.

peregrination noun SEE **journey** noun.

peremptory adjective SEE **bossy**.

perennial adjective SEE **continual**.

perfect adjective **1** *a perfect example of something.* complete, excellent, faultless, finished, flawless, ideal, mint (*in mint condition*), unbeatable, undamaged, unexceptionable, whole.
2 *Nobody is perfect.* blameless, irreproachable, pure, spotless.
3 *a perfect fit. a perfect copy.* accurate, correct, exact, faithful, immaculate, impeccable, precise, tailor-made.
OPPOSITES: SEE **imperfect**.
4 [*informal*] *perfect chaos.* SEE **absolute**.

perfect verb *to perfect your plans.* bring to fruition, carry through, complete, consummate, finish, fulfil, make perfect [SEE **perfect** adjective], realize, [*informal*] see through (*When I've started a thing I like to see it through*).

perfection noun **1** *the perfection of a lovely jewel.* beauty, completeness, excellence, ideal, precision, wholeness.
2 *the perfection of our plans.* accomplishment, achievement, completion, consummation, end, fruition, fulfilment, realization.

perfectionist noun idealist, purist, [*informal*] stickler.

perfidious adjective SEE **treacherous**.

perforate verb *to perforate something with a pin.* bore through, drill, penetrate, pierce, prick, puncture.

perform verb **1** *to perform your duty.* accomplish, achieve, bring about, carry out, commit, complete, discharge, do, execute, finish, fulfil.
2 *to perform on the stage.* act, appear, dance, enact, play, present, produce, put on (*to put on a play*), render, represent, serenade, sing, take part.

performance noun **1** *a performance by actors or musicians.* acting, concert, début [= *a first performance*], impersonation, interpretation, matinée, play, playing, portrayal, première, presentation, preview, production, rendition, representation, show, sketch, turn.
MUSICAL TERMS: SEE **music**.
THEATRICAL TERMS: SEE **theatre**.
2 *a poor performance by our team.* achievement, behaviour, conduct, exhibition, exploit, feat.
3 *He put on a bit of a performance.* act, deception, play-acting, pretence.

performer noun actor, actress, artist, artiste, player, singer, star, [*informal*] superstar, trouper.
VARIOUS ENTERTAINERS: SEE **entertainer**.

perfume noun *the perfume of roses.* aroma, fragrance, odour, scent, SEE **smell** noun, whiff.
VARIOUS COSMETICS: SEE **cosmetics**.

perfunctory adjective *perfunctory applause.* apathetic, brief, cursory, dutiful, half-hearted, hurried, inattentive, indifferent, mechanical, offhand, routine, superficial, uncaring, unenthusiastic, uninterested, uninvolved.
OPPOSITES: SEE **enthusiastic**.

perhaps adverb conceivably, maybe, possibly.
OPPOSITES: SEE **definitely**.

peril noun SEE **danger**.

perilous adjective SEE **dangerous**.

The prefix *peri-* in words like *perimeter, peripatetic, periphery, periphrasis,* and *periscope* is from Greek *peri = around, about.*

---

perimeter noun *the perimeter of a field.* border, borderline, boundary, bounds, circumference, confines, edge, fringe, frontier, margin, periphery.

period noun *a period of history. a period spent doing something.* age, epoch, era, interval, phase, season, session, spell, stage, stint, stretch, term, SEE **time** noun, while.

periodic adjective SEE **occasional**.

periodical noun SEE **magazine**.

peripatetic adjective SEE **travelling**.

peripheral adjective **1** *peripheral areas of town.* distant, on the perimeter [SEE **perimeter**], outer, outermost, outlying.
2 *Don't waste time on peripheral details.* borderline, inessential, irrelevant, marginal, minor, secondary, unimportant, unnecessary.
OPPOSITES: SEE **central**.

periphery noun SEE **perimeter**.

periphrasis noun SEE **verbosity**.

perish verb **1** *Many birds perished in the cold weather.* be destroyed, be killed, die, expire, fall, pass away.
2 *There was a leak where the rubber hose had perished.* crumble away, decay, decompose, disintegrate, go bad, rot.

perishable adjective *perishable goods.* biodegradable (*biodegradable plastic*), destructible, liable to perish [SEE **perish**], unstable.
OPPOSITES: SEE **lasting**.

perjure verb **to perjure yourself** SEE **lie** verb.

perjury noun SEE **lying** noun.

perk noun [*informal*] *Are there any perks that go with your job?* SEE **perquisite**.

perky adjective SEE **lively**.

permanent adjective *a permanent job. a permanent relationship. a permanent problem.* abiding, chronic, constant, continual, continuous, durable, enduring, everlasting, fixed, immutable, incessant, incurable, indestructible, ineradicable, irreparable (*irreparable damage*), irreversible (*an irreversible decision*), lasting, lifelong, long-lasting, neverending, perennial, perpetual, persistent, stable, steady, unalterable, unchanging, unending.
OPPOSITES: SEE **temporary**.

permeable adjective SEE **porous**.

permeate verb *The smell permeated the house.* filter through, flow through, impregnate, penetrate, percolate, pervade, saturate, spread through.

permissible adjective *Is it permissible to smoke?* acceptable, admissible, allowable, allowed, lawful, legal, legitimate, permitted, proper, right, sanctioned, valid.
OPPOSITES: SEE **forbidden**.

permission noun *We had her permission to leave.* agreement, approval, assent, authority, authorization, consent, dispensation, [*informal*] go-ahead, [*informal*] green light, leave, licence, SEE **permit** noun, [*informal*] rubber stamp, sanction.

permissive adjective SEE **tolerant**.

permit noun *a permit to fish in the lake.* authorization, charter, licence, order, pass, passport, ticket, visa, warrant.

permit verb **1** *We don't permit smoking in the house.* agree to, allow, approve of, authorize, consent to, endorse, give permission for [SEE **permission**], license, [*old-fashioned*] suffer, tolerate.
2 *Will you permit me to speak?* give an opportunity, make it possible.

permutation noun SEE **variation**.

pernicious adjective SEE **harmful**.

pernickety adjective SEE **fussy**.

peroration noun SEE **conclusion**.

perpendicular adjective at right angles, upright, vertical.

perpetrate verb *to perpetrate a crime.* SEE **commit**.

perpetual adjective *the perpetual cycle of life and death. a baby's perpetual crying for attention.* abiding, ceaseless, chronic, constant, continual, continuous, endless, eternal, everlasting, frequent, immortal, incessant, interminable, lasting, long-lasting, neverending, non-stop, ongoing, perennial, permanent, persistent, protracted, recurrent, recurring, repeated, unceasing, unchanging, unending, unfailing, unremitting.
OPPOSITES: SEE **brief** adjective, **temporary**.

perpetuate verb SEE **preserve** verb.

perplex verb *The mystery perplexed us.* baffle, bewilder, confound, confuse, disconcert, muddle, mystify, puzzle, [*informal*] stump, [*informal*] throw, worry.

perquisite noun *She gets various perquisites in addition to her wages.* benefit, bonus, extra, fringe benefit, gratuity, [*informal*] perk, tip.

persecute verb *to persecute people for their religious beliefs.* badger, bother, bully, discriminate against, harass, hound, ill-treat, intimidate, maltreat, martyr, molest, oppress, pester, [*informal*] put the screws on, terrorize, torment, torture, tyrannize, victimize, worry.

persevere verb *If you persevere you'll succeed in the end.* be diligent, be steadfast [SEE **steadfast**], carry on, continue, endure, [*informal*] hang on, [*informal*] keep at it, keep going, persist, [*informal*] plug away, [*informal*] soldier on, stand firm, [*informal*] stick at it.
OPPOSITES: SEE **cease, falter**.

persiflage noun SEE **banter**.

persist verb **1** *If you persist, you'll succeed in the end.* SEE **persevere**.
2 *How long will this snow persist?* go on, keep on, last, linger, remain.
OPPOSITES: SEE **cease**.

persistent adjective **1** *a persistent cold. persistent rumours.* ceaseless, chronic, constant, continual, continuous, endless, eternal, everlasting, incessant, interminable, lasting, long-lasting, neverending, obstinate, permanent, perpetual, persisting, recurrent, recurring, repeated, unending, unrelenting, unrelieved, unremitting.
OPPOSITES: SEE **intermittent, short-lived**.
2 *a persistent worker.* assiduous, determined, dogged, hard-working, indefatigable, patient, persevering, pertinacious, relentless, resolute, steadfast, steady, stubborn, tenacious, tireless, unflagging, untiring, unwavering, zealous.
OPPOSITES: SEE **lazy**.

person noun adolescent, adult, baby, being, [*informal*] body, character, SEE **child**, [*joking*] customer (*a difficult customer*), figure, human, human being, individual, infant, SEE **man** noun, personage, soul, [*informal*] type, SEE **woman**. SEE ALSO **people**.

persona noun *On stage, the actor adopts a fictitious persona.* character, image, personality, role.

personable adjective SEE **good-looking**.

personal adjective 1 *personal characteristics.* distinct, distinctive, idiosyncratic, individual, inimitable, particular, peculiar, private, special, unique, your own.
OPPOSITES: SEE **general**.
2 *personal information.* confidential, intimate, private, secret.
OPPOSITES: SEE **public** adjective.
3 *personal remarks.* critical, derogatory, disparaging, insulting, offensive, pejorative, SEE **rude**, slighting.

personality noun 1 *She has an attractive personality.* character, disposition, identity, individuality, [*informal*] make-up, nature, [*formal*] psyche, temperament.
2 *She has great personality.* attractiveness, charisma, charm, magnetism.
3 *a show-business personality.* big name, celebrity, figure (*a well-known figure in show-business*), star, [*informal*] superstar.

personification noun *Santa Claus is the personification of Christmas.* allegorical representation, embodiment, epitome, human likeness, incarnation, living image, manifestation.

personify verb *Santa Claus personifies the spirit of Christmas.* allegorize, be the personification of [SEE **personification**], embody, epitomize, give a human shape to, incarnate, personalize, represent, symbolize.

personnel noun *the personnel who work in a factory.* employees, manpower, people, staff, work-force, workers.

perspective noun *Birds see a garden from a different perspective.* angle, outlook, point of view, slant, view, viewpoint.

perspicacious adjective *a perspicacious criticism.* SEE **perceptive**.

perspicuous adjective *a perspicuous explanation.* SEE **clear** adjective.

perspire verb sweat.

persuade verb *I persuaded him to accept my terms.* bring round, cajole, coax, convert, convince, entice, induce, influence, inveigle, prevail upon, talk into, tempt, urge, use persuasion [SEE **persuasion**], wheedle (into), win over.
OPPOSITES: SEE **dissuade**.

persuasion noun 1 *It took a lot of persuasion to convince him.* argument, blandishment, cajolery, brainwashing, conditioning, enticement, exhortation, persuading [SEE **persuade**], propaganda, reasoning.
2 *What is your religious persuasion?* SEE **belief**.

persuasive adjective *a persuasive argument.* cogent, compelling, convincing, credible, effective, eloquent, forceful, influential, logical, plausible, reasonable, sound, strong, telling, valid, watertight.
OPPOSITES: SEE **unconvincing**.

pert adjective SEE **cheeky**.

pertain verb *Will the same conditions pertain next year?* appertain, apply, be relevant [SEE **relevant**].

pertinacious adjective SEE **persistent**.

pertinent adjective SEE **relevant**.

perturb verb *The bad news perturbed us.* agitate, alarm, bother, disconcert, distress, disturb, frighten, make anxious [SEE **anxious**], scare, shake, trouble, unsettle, upset, vex, worry.
OPPOSITES: SEE **reassure**.

peruse verb SEE **read**.

pervade verb *The smell pervaded the whole building.* affect, diffuse, fill, filter through, flow through, impregnate, penetrate, percolate, permeate, saturate, spread through, suffuse.

pervasive adjective *a pervasive smell.* general, inescapable, insidious, permeating, pervading, prevalent, rife, ubiquitous, universal, widespread.

perverse adjective *It's perverse of him to buy hot dogs when we want ice-cream.* contradictory, contrary, disobedient, fractious, headstrong, illogical, inappropriate, intractable, intransigent, obdurate, obstinate, [*informal*] pigheaded, rebellious, refractory, stubborn, tiresome, uncooperative, unhelpful, unreasonable, wayward, wilful, wrong-headed.
OPPOSITES: SEE **helpful, reasonable**.

perversion noun 1 *perversion of the truth.* corruption, distortion, falsification, misrepresentation, misuse, twisting.
2 *sexual perversion.* abnormality, depravity, deviance, deviation, immorality, impropriety, [*informal*] kinkiness, unnaturalness, vice, wickedness.

pervert noun *a sexual pervert.* deviant, perverted person [SEE **perverted**].

pervert verb 1 *to pervert the course of justice.* bend, distort, divert, perjure, subvert, twist, undermine.
2 *to pervert a witness.* bribe, corrupt, lead astray.

perverted adjective *perverted behaviour. perverted sexual practices.* abnormal, corrupt, debauched, depraved, deviant, eccentric, immoral, improper, [*informal*] kinky, SEE **obscene**, sick, twisted, unnatural, warped, wicked, wrong.
OPPOSITES: SEE **natural**.

pessimism noun [See note preceding *optimism*.] *pessimism about the future.* cynicism, despair, despondency, fatalism, gloom, hopelessness, negativeness, resignation, unhappiness.
OPPOSITES: SEE **optimism**.

pessimistic adjective *pessimistic about our chances.* cynical, defeatist, despairing, despondent, fatalistic, gloomy, hopeless, melancholy, morbid, negative, resigned, unhappy.
OPPOSITES: SEE **optimistic**.

pest noun **1** *Don't be a pest!* annoyance, bother, curse, irritation, nuisance, [*informal*] pain in the neck, trial, vexation.
2 *garden pests.* [*informal*] bug, [*informal*] creepy-crawly, insect, parasite, [*plural*] vermin.

pester noun *Don't pester me while I'm busy!* annoy, badger, bait, besiege, bother, harass, harry, [*informal*] hassle, molest, nag, plague, torment, trouble, worry.

pesticide noun SEE **poison** noun.

pestiferous adjective SEE **troublesome**.

pestilence noun SEE **illness**.

pestilential adjective SEE **troublesome**.

pet noun **1** CREATURES COMMONLY KEPT AS PETS: budgerigar, canary, cat, dog, ferret, fish, gerbil, goldfish, guinea-pig, hamster, mouse, parrot, pigeon, rabbit, rat, tortoise.
OTHER ANIMALS: SEE **animal** noun.
2 [*informal*] *teacher's pet.* darling, favourite.

pet verb *Our dog loves you to pet him.* caress, cuddle, fondle, kiss, pat, stroke, SEE **touch** verb.

peter verb **to peter out** SEE **diminish**.

petite adjective SEE **small**.

petition noun *a petition to the government.* appeal, entreaty, list of signatures, plea, request, suit, supplication.

petitioner noun suppliant.

petrify verb SEE **terrify**.

petrol noun [*informal or American*] gas, gasoline.

pettifogging adjective SEE **trivial**.

petting noun SEE **love-making**.

pettish adjective SEE **irritable**.

petty adjective **1** *petty crime.* insignificant, minor, small, trifling, trivial, SEE **unimportant**.
OPPOSITES: SEE **important**.
2 *a petty attitude.* grudging, nit-picking, SEE **small-minded**, ungenerous.
OPPOSITES: SEE **open-minded**.

petulant adjective SEE **irritable**.

pew noun SEE **seat** noun.

phalanx noun SEE **group** noun.

phantasm, phantom nouns SEE **ghost**.

pharmacist noun dispensing chemist.

pharmacy noun *Get your medicine from the pharmacy.* chemists, dispensary, [*American*] drug-store.

phase noun *a phase of your life. a phase of an activity.* development, period, season, spell, stage, step, SEE **time** noun.

phenomenal adjective *The winner of the quiz had a phenomenal memory.* amazing, exceptional, extraordinary, [*informal*] fantastic, incredible, notable, outstanding, remarkable, [*informal*] sensational, singular, unbelievable, unusual, [*informal*] wonderful.
OPPOSITES: SEE **ordinary**.

phenomenon noun **1** *Snow is a common phenomenon in winter.* circumstance, event, fact, happening, incident, occurrence, sight.
2 *They said the six-year old pianist was quite a phenomenon.* curiosity, marvel, phenomenal person or thing [SEE **phenomenal**], prodigy, wonder.

phial noun SEE **bottle** noun.

A number of words like *philander, philanthropic, philosophy* are related to Greek *phileo = to love.* Compare words like *bibliophile* [*= a lover of books*], *Francophile* [*= a lover of French things*], etc.

---

philander verb SEE **love** noun (**to make love**).

philanthropic adjective *She's known for her philanthropic work in the community.* altruistic, beneficent, benevolent, bountiful, caring, charitable, generous, humane, humanitarian, SEE **kind** adjective, munificent.
OPPOSITES: SEE **misanthropic**.

philanthropist noun SEE **benefactor**.

philately noun stamp-collecting.

Philistine adjective *a Philistine attitude to the arts.* SEE **uncivilized**.

philology noun LINGUISTIC TERMS: SEE **language**.

philosopher noun sage, student of philosophy, thinker.

philosophical adjective **1** *a philosophical debate.* abstract, academic, analytical, ideological, intellectual, learned, logical, metaphysical, rational, reasoned, theoretical, thoughtful, wise.
2 *philosophical in defeat.* calm, collected, composed, patient, reasonable, resigned, stoical, unemotional, unruffled.
OPPOSITES: SEE **emotional**.

philosophize verb *He philosophizes instead of actually doing something.* analyse, be philosophical [SEE **philosophical**], moralize, pontificate, preach, rationalize, reason, sermonize, theorize, think things out.

philosophy noun *your philosophy of life.* convictions, ideology, metaphysics, set of beliefs, values, wisdom.

philtre noun SEE **potion**.

phlegm noun mucus, spittle.

phlegmatic adjective *a phlegmatic temperament.* apathetic, cold, cool, frigid, impassive, imperturbable, lethargic, placid, slow, sluggish, stolid, undemonstrative, unemotional, unresponsive.
OPPOSITES: SEE **excitable**.

phobia noun *a phobia about spiders.* anxiety, aversion, dislike, dread, SEE **fear** noun, [*informal*] hang-up, hatred, horror, neurosis, obsession, revulsion.

Phobia is related to Greek *phobos=fear.* There are a number of words for particular fears which end in *-phobia,* such as: acrophobia (*fear of heights*), agoraphobia (*open spaces*), anglophobia (*the English*), arachnephobia (*spiders*), claustrophobia (*enclosed spaces*), hydrophobia (*water*), nyctophobia (*the dark*), photophobia (*light*), xenophobia (*strangers*), zoophobia (*animals*).

---

phone verb *I phoned granny.* call, dial, [*informal*] give a buzz, ring, telephone.

Several English words, including *phone, phonetics, phonograph, telephone,* etc., are related to Greek *phone=sound, voice.*

---

phonetics noun LINGUISTIC TERMS: SEE **language**.

phoney adjective [*slang*] *a phoney Welsh accent.* affected, artificial, assumed, bogus, cheating, counterfeit, faked, false, fictitious, fraudulent, imitation, insincere, pretended, [*informal*] put-on, [*informal*] put-up (*a put-up job*), sham, synthetic, trick, unreal.
OPPOSITES: SEE **real**.

phosphorescent adjective SEE **glowing**.

A number of English words, including *photocopy, photograph, photosynthesis,* etc., are related to Greek *photos=light.*

---

photo noun, verb SEE **photograph** noun, verb.

photocopy verb copy, duplicate, photostat, print off, reproduce, [*informal*] run off.

photograph noun enlargement, exposure, negative, photo, plate, positive, print, shot, slide, [*informal*] snap, snapshot, transparency.
OTHER PICTURES: SEE **picture** noun.

photograph verb *to photograph an event.* shoot, snap, take a picture of [SEE **picture** noun].

photographic adjective **1** *a photographic description.* accurate, exact, faithful, graphic, lifelike, naturalistic, realistic, representational, true to life.
2 *a photographic memory.* pictorial, retentive, visual.

PHOTOGRAPHIC EQUIPMENT INCLUDES: box camera, ciné-camera, dark-room, developer, enlarger, exposure-meter, fixer, light-meter, Polaroid camera, reflex camera, SLR camera, telephoto lens, tripod, zoom lens.

---

photography noun taking photographs.

phrase noun SEE **expression**.

phrase verb SEE **express** verb.

phraseology noun *I liked her neat phraseology.* diction, SEE **expression**, idiom, language, parlance, phrasing, style, turn of phrase, wording.

physical adjective **1** *physical contact.* bodily, carnal, corporal, corporeal.
2 *Ghosts have no physical existence.* earthly, fleshly, material, mortal, palpable, physiological, real, solid, substantial, tangible.
OPPOSITES: SEE **incorporeal**, **spiritual**.

physician noun SEE **doctor**.

physics noun VARIOUS SCIENCES: SEE **science**.

physiognomy noun SEE **face** noun.

physiological adjective anatomical, bodily, physical.

physiology noun anatomy, the body.

physique noun *a person's physique.* body, build, figure, form, frame, muscles, physical condition, shape.

piazza noun concourse, market place, plaza, square.

pick noun **1** *Take your pick.* SEE **choice** noun, election, preference, selection.
2 *the pick of the bunch.* best, cream, élite, favourite, flower, pride.

pick verb **1** *Pick a partner. Pick your representative.* choose, decide on, elect, fix on, make a choice of, name, nominate, opt for, prefer, select, settle on, single out, vote for.
2 *to pick flowers.* collect, cull, cut, gather, harvest, pluck, pull off, take.

picket noun SEE **group** noun.

pickle verb *to pickle onions.* SEE **preserve** verb.

picnic noun SEE **meal**.

pictogram, pictograph nouns SEE **symbol**.

pictorial adjective *a pictorial representation of something.* diagrammatic, graphic, illustrated, representational.

picture noun *a recognizable picture.* delineation, depiction, image, likeness, outline, portrayal, profile, representation.
to take pictures of film, photograph, shoot (*to shoot a film*), video.

KINDS OF PICTURE: abstract, cameo, caricature, cartoon, collage, design, doodle, drawing, engraving, etching, film, fresco, [*plural*] graffiti, [*plural*] graphics, icon, identikit, illustration, landscape, montage, mosaic, mural, oil-painting, old master, painting, photofit, photograph, pin-up, plate (*photographic plate*), portrait, print, reproduction, self-portrait, sketch, slide, [*informal*] snap, snapshot, still life, transfer, transparency, triptych, trompe l'œil, video, vignette.

---

picture verb **1** *Historical scenes were pictured on the wall.* delineate, depict, evoke, illustrate, outline, portray, represent, show.

WAYS TO MAKE A PICTURE: caricature, doodle, draw, engrave, etch, film, paint, photograph, print, sketch, video.

---

2 *Can you picture what the world will be like in 100 years?* conceive, describe, dream up, envisage, imagine, think up, visualize.

picturesque adjective **1** *picturesque scenery.* attractive, SEE **beautiful**, charming, pleasant, pretty, quaint, scenic.
OPPOSITES: SEE **ugly**.
2 *picturesque language.* colourful, descriptive, expressive, graphic, imaginative, poetic, vivid.
OPPOSITES: SEE **prosaic**.

pie noun flan, pasty, patty, quiche, tart, tartlet, turnover, vol-au-vent.

piebald adjective SEE **pied**.

piece noun **1** *a piece of cake. a piece of wood.* bar, bit, bite, block, chip, chunk, crumb, division, [*informal*] dollop, fraction, fragment, grain, helping, hunk, length, lump, morsel, part, particle, portion, quantity, sample, scrap, section, segment, share, shred, slab, slice, snippet, speck, stick, tablet, [*informal*] titbit.
2 *a piece of a machine.* component, constituent, element, spare part, unit.
3 *a piece of music. a piece of writing. a piece of clothing.* article, composition, example, instance, item, number, passage, specimen, work.

piecemeal adverb *to do something piecemeal.* a bit at a time, bit by bit, intermittently, little by little, piece by piece.

pied adjective dappled, flecked, mottled, particoloured, piebald, spotted, variegated.

pied-à-terre noun SEE **accommodation**.

pier noun **1** *Passengers disembark at the pier.* breakwater, SEE **dock** noun, jetty, landing-stage, quay, wharf.
2 *the piers of a bridge. a pier supporting a wall.* buttress, column, pile, pillar, support, upright.

pierce verb bore through, drill through, enter, go through, impale, make a hole in, penetrate, perforate, prick, punch (*punch a hole in a ticket*), puncture, skewer, spike, spit, stab, stick into, transfix, wound.

piercing adjective **1** *a piercing scream.* deafening, high-pitched, SEE **loud**, penetrating, sharp, shrill.
2 *a piercing wind.* SEE **cold** adjective.

piety noun *the piety of the martyrs.* devotion, devoutness, faith, godliness, holiness, piousness, religion, [*uncomplimentary*] religiosity, saintliness, sanctity.
OPPOSITES: SEE **impiety**.

piffle noun SEE **nonsense**.

piffling adjective SEE **trivial**.

pig noun boar, hog, [*childish*] piggy, piglet, runt [=*smallest piglet in a litter*], sow, swine.

pigeon-hole noun SEE **compartment**.

piggy-bank noun money-box.

pigment, pigmentation nouns SEE **colouring.**

pigmy dwarf, midget.

pigsty noun piggery, sty.

pike noun *armed with a pike.* lance, spear. OTHER WEAPONS: SEE **weapons.**

pikelet noun crumpet.

pile noun **1** *a pile of rubbish.* accumulation, heap, hoard, mass, mound, [*informal*] mountain, quantity, stack.
2 *piles driven into the ground.* column, pier, post, support, upright.
piles *suffering from piles.* haemorrhoids.

pile verb *Pile everything in the corner.* accumulate, amass, assemble, bring together, build up, collect, concentrate, gather, heap up, hoard, load, mass, stack up, store.

pilfer verb SEE **steal.**

pilgrim noun *pilgrims to a holy shrine.* [*old-fashioned*] palmer, SEE **traveller.**

pilgrimage noun SEE **journey** noun.

pill noun *Swallow the pills with a little water.* capsule, pellet, tablet.
the pill SEE **contraceptive.**

pillage noun *The invading troops were guilty of rape and pillage.* depredation, despoliation, devastation, looting, plundering, ransacking, robbing, stealing.

pillage verb SEE **plunder** verb.

pillar noun *supporting pillars.* baluster, column, pier, pilaster [=*ornamental pillar*], pile, post, prop, shaft, stanchion, support, upright.

pillar-box noun letter-box, post-box.

pillion noun SEE **seat** noun.

pillory verb SEE **ridicule** verb.

pillow noun bolster, cushion. OTHER BEDDING: SEE **bedclothes.**

pilot adjective *a pilot scheme.* SEE **experimental.**

pilot noun **1** *the pilot of an aircraft.* airman, [*old-fashioned*] aviator, flier.
2 *the pilot of a boat.* coxswain, helmsman, navigator, steersman.

pilot verb *He piloted us back to safety.* conduct, convey, direct, drive, fly, guide, lead, navigate, steer.

pilot-light noun SEE **light** noun.

pimple noun boil, pustule, [*plural*] rash, spot, swelling, [*slang*] zit.

pin noun [*old-fashioned*] bodkin, brooch, clip, drawing-pin, SEE **fastener**, hat-pin, peg, safety-pin, tie-pin.

pin verb SEE **fasten**, pierce, transfix.

pinafore noun apron.

pince-nez noun SEE **glass (glasses).**

pincers noun VARIOUS TOOLS: SEE **tool.**

pinch verb **1** *to pinch something between your fingers.* crush, nip, squeeze, tweak.
2 [*informal*] *to pinch things from other people.* SEE **steal.**

pine verb *The dog pined when its master died.* mope, mourn, sicken, waste away.
to pine for *In winter I pine for warm sunshine!* crave, hanker after, long for, miss, SEE **want** verb, yearn for.

ping verb VARIOUS SOUNDS: SEE **sound** noun.

ping-pong noun table-tennis.

pinion noun [*poetic*] *gliding on outspread pinions.* wing.

pinion verb SEE **restrain.**

pink adjective OTHER COLOURS: SEE **colour** noun.

pinnacle noun **1** *the pinnacle of your career.* acme, apex, climax, height, highest point, peak, summit, top, zenith.
2 *a tower topped with ornate pinnacles.* spire, steeple, turret.

pin-up noun SEE **picture** noun.

pioneer noun **1** *pioneers who opened up new territories.* colonist, discoverer, explorer, settler.
2 *a pioneer of a new technique.* innovator, inventor, originator.

pioneer verb *to pioneer a new idea.* [*informal*]. bring out, develop, discover, experiment with, invent, launch, originate, set up, start.

pious adjective **1** [*complimentary*] *pious worshippers.* dedicated, devout, god-fearing, godly, holy, moral, religious, reverent, saintly, sincere, spiritual. OPPOSITES: SEE **impious.**
2 [*uncomplimentary*] *I hate their pious moralizing.* [*informal*] holier-than-thou, hypocritical, insincere, sanctimonious, self-righteous, self-satisfied, unctuous. OPPOSITES: SEE **sincere.**

pip noun **1** *an orange pip.* seed, stone.
2 *a pip on a dice, officer's uniform, etc.* mark, spot, star.
3 *At the last pip it will be exactly six o'clock.* bleep, blip, stroke.
OTHER SOUNDS: SEE **sound** noun.

pipe noun *a water pipe.* conduit, duct, hose, hydrant, pipeline, piping, tube.
pipes bagpipes.

pipe verb **1** *to pipe something to another place.* carry along a pipe or wire, channel, convey, transmit.
2 *to pipe a tune.* blow, play, sound, whistle.
to pipe down SEE **silent (be silent).**
to pipe up SEE **speak.**

piping adjective *a piping voice.* SEE **shrill.**
piping hot SEE **hot.**

pippin noun apple.

piquant adjective **1** *a piquant taste.* pungent, salty, sharp, spicy, tangy, tart, tasty.
OPPOSITES: SEE **bland**.
2 *a piquant notion.* arresting, exciting, interesting, provocative, stimulating.
OPPOSITES: SEE **banal**.

pique noun SEE **annoyance**.

pirate noun *a pirate on the high seas.* buccaneer, [*old-fashioned*] corsair, marauder, SEE **thief**.

pirate verb *to pirate a video.* SEE **plagiarize**.

pirouette verb SEE **spin**.

pistol noun SEE **gun**.

pit noun **1** *a deep pit.* abyss, chasm, crater, depression, excavation, hole, hollow, pothole.
2 *Miners work in a pit.* coal-mine, colliery, mine, quarry, shaft, working.

pitch noun **1** *black as pitch.* tar.
2 *the pitch of a roof.* angle, gradient, incline, slope, steepness, tilt.
3 *the pitch of a musical note.* height, tuning.
4 *a football pitch.* arena, ground, playing-field, stadium.

pitch verb **1** *to pitch a tent.* erect, put up, raise, set up.
2 *to pitch a stone into a pond.* bowl, [*informal*] bung, cast, [*informal*] chuck, fling, heave, hurl, lob, sling, throw, toss.
3 *to pitch into the water.* dive, drop, fall heavily, plunge, topple.
4 *to pitch about in a storm.* dip up and down, lurch, rock, roll, toss.
to pitch in SEE **co-operate**.
to pitch into SEE **attack** verb.

pitch-black adjective SEE **black** adjective.

pitch-dark adjective SEE **dark**.

pitcher noun SEE **container**, jar, jug, urn.

pitchfork verb SEE **propel**.

Piteous means *deserving pity* (*We wept to hear their piteous cries*). *Pitiable* and *pitiful* may also mean *deserving pity*; but they often mean *deserving contempt* (*We laughed at their pitiful efforts*).

---

piteous adjective *piteous cries for help.* affecting, distressing, heartbreaking, heartrending, miserable, moving, pathetic, pitiable, pitiful, SEE **sad**, touching, wretched.

pitfall noun *I tried to avoid the obvious pitfalls.* catch, danger, difficulty, hazard, snag, trap.

pitiable adjective SEE **piteous**, **pitiful**.

pitiful adjective **1** *pitiful cries for help.* SEE **piteous**.
2 [*uncomplimentary*] *a pitiful attempt to stop the ball.* abject, contemptible, deplorable, hopeless, inadequate, incompetent, laughable, [*informal*] miserable, [*informal*] pathetic, pitiable, ridiculous, useless, worthless.
OPPOSITES: SEE **admirable**.

pitiless adjective *a pitiless attack.* bloodthirsty, callous, cruel, hard, heartless, inexorable, SEE **merciless**, relentless, ruthless, unfeeling, unrelenting, unrelieved, unremitting.
OPPOSITES: SEE **merciful**.

pittance noun SEE **money**.

pitted adjective *a pitted surface.* dented, holey, marked, pock-marked, rough, scarred, uneven.
OPPOSITES: SEE **smooth** adjective.

pity noun *The thugs showed no pity.* charity, clemency, compassion, feeling, forbearance, forgiveness, grace, humanity, kindness, leniency, love, mercy, regret, softness, sympathy, tenderness, understanding, warmth.
OPPOSITES: SEE **cruelty**.
to take pity on SEE **help** verb.

pity verb *I pitied anyone who was out in the storm.* [*informal*] bleed for (*My heart bleeds for them*), commiserate with, [*informal*] feel for, feel or show pity for [SEE **pity** noun], sympathize with, weep for.

pivot noun *turning on a pivot.* axis, axle, centre, fulcrum, hub, point of balance, swivel.

pivot verb SEE **turn** verb.

pivotal adjective SEE **central**.

placard noun *an advertising placard.* advert, advertisement, bill, notice, poster, sign.

placate verb SEE **pacify**.

place noun **1** *a place on a map.* location, point, position, site, situation, [*informal*] spot, [*informal*] whereabouts.
2 *a nice place for a holiday.* area, country, district, locale, locality, neighbourhood, region, SEE **town**, venue, vicinity.
3 *your place in society.* degree, function, grade, SEE **job**, office, position, rank, station, status.
4 *a place to live.* SEE **house** noun.
5 *a place to sit.* SEE **seat** noun.

place verb **1** *Place your things on the table.* arrange, deposit, dispose, [*informal*] dump, lay, leave, locate, plant, position,

put down, rest, set down, settle, situate, stand, station, [*informal*] stick.
2 *The judges placed me third.* grade, position, put in order, rank.
3 *I've heard the tune before, but I can't place it.* identify, locate, put a name to, put into context, recognize.

placid adjective **1** *a placid temperament.* collected, composed, cool, equable, even-tempered, imperturbable, level-headed, mild, phlegmatic, restful, sensible, stable, steady, unexcitable.
OPPOSITES: SEE **excitable**.
2 *a placid sea.* calm, motionless, peaceful, quiet, tranquil, unruffled, untroubled.
OPPOSITES: SEE **stormy**.

plagiarize verb *to plagiarize someone else's ideas.* borrow, copy, [*informal*] crib, imitate, [*informal*] lift, pirate, reproduce, SEE **steal**.

plague noun **1** *bubonic plague.* blight, contagion, epidemic, SEE **illness**, infection, outbreak, pestilence.
2 *a plague of flies.* infestation, invasion, nuisance, scourge, swarm.

plague verb *The flies plagued us. Don't plague me with your questions.* afflict, annoy, be a nuisance to, be a plague to, bother, disturb, irritate, molest, [*informal*] nag, persecute, pester, torment, trouble, vex, worry.

plain adjective **1** *a plain signal.* apparent, audible, certain, clear, comprehensible, definite, distinct, evident, legible, manifest, obvious, unambiguous, unmistakable, visible, well-defined.
OPPOSITES: SEE **unclear**.
2 *plain speech. the plain truth.* basic, blunt, candid, direct, downright, explicit, forthright, frank, honest, informative, outspoken, plain-spoken, prosaic, sincere, straightforward, unadorned, unequivocal, unvarnished.
OPPOSITES: SEE **cryptic**, **evasive**.
3 *a plain appearance. plain cooking.* austere, everyday, frugal, homely, modest, ordinary, simple, unattractive, undecorated, unprepossessing, unpretentious, unremarkable, workaday.
OPPOSITES: SEE **attractive**, **elaborate** adjective.

plain noun *a wide plain.* prairie, savannah, steppe.

plain-spoken SEE **plain** adjective.

plaintiff noun *the plaintiff in a lawsuit.* accuser.
OPPOSITES: SEE **defendant**.
LEGAL TERMS: SEE **law**.

plaintive adjective *a plaintive tune.* doleful, melancholy, mournful, SEE **sad**, sorrowful, wistful.

plan noun **1** *a plan of the town.* [*informal*] bird's-eye view, chart, diagram, drawing, layout, map, representation, sketch-map.
2 *a carefully worked-out plan.* aim, blueprint, course of action, design, idea, intention, method, plot, policy, procedure, programme, project, proposal, proposition, scenario, scheme, strategy.

plan verb **1** *We planned our campaign.* arrange, concoct, contrive, design, devise, draw up a plan of [SEE **plan** noun], formulate, invent, map out, [*informal*] mastermind, organize, outline, plot, prepare, scheme, think out, work out.
2 *What do they plan to do next?* aim, conspire, contemplate, envisage, intend, mean, propose, think of.

plane adjective *a plane surface.* SEE **level** adjective.

plane noun **1** *raised to a higher plane.* SEE **level** noun.
2 [=*aircraft*] OTHER AIRCRAFT: SEE **aircraft**.
3 [=*carpenter's tool*] OTHER TOOLS: SEE **tool**.

planet noun globe, orb, satellite, sphere, world.

PLANETS OF THE SOLAR SYSTEM: Earth, Jupiter, Mars, Mercury, Neptune, Pluto, Saturn, Uranus, Venus.

OTHER ASTRONOMICAL TERMS: SEE **astronomy**.

---

plangent adjective *a plangent cry.* SEE **mournful**.

plank noun beam, board, planking, timber.

planned adjective *Was the meeting planned, or did it happen by chance?* arranged, contrived, SEE **deliberate** adjective, designed, masterminded, organized, premeditated, [*informal*] set up, thought out, worked out.
OPPOSITES: SEE **unplanned**.

planning noun *You should do the planning in advance.* arrangement, design, drafting, forethought, organization, preparation, setting up, thinking out.

plant noun **1 plants** greenery, growth, undergrowth, vegetation.

KINDS OF PLANT: annual, SEE **bulb**, cactus, SEE **cereal**, climber, fern, SEE **flower** noun, SEE **fungus**, grass, SEE **herb**, lichen, moss, perennial, seedling, shrub, SEE **tree**, SEE **vegetable**, water-plant, weed.

PARTS OF A PLANT: bloom, blossom, branch, bud, bulb, corm, SEE **flower** noun, frond, fruit, [*formal*] inflorescence, leaf, [*formal*] panicle, petal, pod, [*formal*] raceme, root, seed, shoot, [*formal*] spadix, stalk, stem, trunk, tuber, twig.

---

2 *industrial plant.* SEE **equipment**.

plant verb *to plant flowers.* set out, sow, transplant.

plantation noun SEE **farm** noun.

plaque noun SEE **memorial**.

plasma noun SEE **fluid** noun.

plaster noun **1** *plaster on a wall.* mortar, stucco.
2 *a plaster to cover a wound.* dressing, sticking-plaster.

plaster verb *to plaster a wall.* coat, cover, daub.

plastic adjective SEE **pliable**.

plastic noun KINDS OF PLASTIC: bakelite, celluloid, polystyrene, polythene, polyurethane, polyvinyl, PVC, vinyl.

plate noun **1** *plates piled with food.* dinner-plate, dish, [*old-fashioned*] platter, side-plate, soup-plate.
OTHER ITEMS OF CROCKERY: SEE **crockery**.
2 *a steel plate. plates of rock.* layer, panel, sheet, slab, stratum.
3 *plates in a book.* illustration, [*informal*] photo, SEE **picture** noun.
4 *a dental plate.* dentures, false teeth.

plate verb *to plate one metal with a layer of another.* anodize, coat, cover, electroplate, galvanize (*with zinc*), gild (*with gold*).

platform 1 *The speakers sat on a platform.* dais, podium, rostrum, stage.
2 *a political platform.* SEE **policy**.

platinum noun OTHER METALS: SEE **metal**.

platitude noun SEE **commonplace (commonplace remark)**.

platitudinous adjective SEE **commonplace**.

platoon noun SEE **armed services**.

platter noun SEE **plate** noun.

plaudits noun SEE **applause**.

plausible adjective *a plausible excuse.* acceptable, believable, conceivable, credible, likely, persuasive, possible, probable, reasonable, tenable.
OPPOSITES: SEE **implausible**.

play noun **1** *We all enjoy play.* amusement, diversion, fun, [*informal*] fun and games, joking, make-believe, playing, pretending, recreation, sport.
VARIOUS GAMES AND SPORTS: SEE **game** noun, **sport**.
2 *a play on TV.* drama, performance, production.
THEATRICAL ENTERTAINMENTS: SEE **theatre**.
3 *play in the moving parts of a machine.* freedom, freedom of movement, latitude, leeway, looseness, tolerance.

play verb **1** *The children went to play.* amuse yourself, caper, disport yourself, fool about, frisk, frolic, gambol, have fun, [*informal*] mess about, romp, sport.
2 *He won't play.* join in, participate, take part.
3 *I played him at snooker.* challenge, compete against, oppose, vie with.
4 *Who played Mary in the nativity play?* act, impersonate, perform, portray, pretend to be, represent, take the part of.
5 *to play the piano.* make music on, perform on, strum.
6 *to play records. to play a tape-recorder.* have on, listen to, operate, put on, switch on.
to play about SEE **fidget**.
to play ball SEE **co-operate**.
to play (it) by ear SEE **improvise**.
to play down SEE **minimize**.
to play for time SEE **delay** verb.
to play up SEE **misbehave**.
to play up to SEE **flatter**.

player noun **1** *the players in a game.* competitor, contestant, sportsman, sportswoman.
2 *players on stage.* actor, actress, entertainer, instrumentalist, musician, performer, soloist, [*joking*] Thespian.
VARIOUS PERFORMERS: SEE **music**, **theatre**.

playful adjective *a playful puppy. playful teasing.* active, cheerful, flirtatious, frisky, good-natured, humorous, impish, [*informal*] jokey, joking, light-hearted, lively, mischievous, puckish, roguish, skittish, spirited, sportive, sprightly, [*informal*] tongue-in-cheek, vivacious, waggish.
OPPOSITES: SEE **serious**.

playground noun play-area, recreation ground, school yard.

play-group noun SEE **school**.

playing-field noun arena, ground, pitch, recreation ground, sports-ground.

playmate noun SEE **friend**.

plaything noun SEE **toy** noun.

playtime noun break.

playwright noun dramatist, script-writer.
OTHER WRITERS: SEE **writer**.

plaza noun SEE **piazza**.

plea noun *a plea for mercy.* appeal, entreaty, invocation, petition, prayer, request, supplication.
LEGAL TERMS: SEE **law**.

plead verb *He pleaded to be let off.* appeal, ask, beg, entreat, implore, importune, petition, request, solicit.

pleasant adjective [*Pleasant* can refer to anything which pleases you, and there are many possible synonyms. We give just some of the commoner ones here.] *pleasant food. pleasant weather. pleasant manners.* acceptable, affable, agreeable, amiable, attractive, balmy, beautiful, charming, cheerful, congenial, decent, delicious, delightful, enjoyable, entertaining, excellent, fine, friendly, genial, gentle, SEE **good**, gratifying, [*informal*] heavenly, hospitable, kind, likeable, lovely, mellow, mild, nice, palatable, peaceful, pleasing, pleasurable, pretty, relaxed, satisfying, soothing, sympathetic, warm, welcome, welcoming.
OPPOSITES: SEE **unpleasant**.

please verb **1** *I did it to please you.* amuse, content, delight, entertain, give pleasure to, gladden, gratify, make happy, satisfy.
2 *Do what you please.* SEE **want** verb.

pleased adjective *a pleased expression.* [*informal*] chuffed, [*uncomplimentary*] complacent, contented, delighted, elated, euphoric, glad, grateful, gratified, SEE **happy**, satisfied, thankful, thrilled.
OPPOSITES: SEE **annoyed**.

pleasing, pleasurable adjectives SEE **pleasant**.

pleasure noun **1** *I get pleasure from my garden.* bliss, comfort, contentment, delight, ecstasy, enjoyment, gladness, gratification, happiness, joy, rapture, satisfaction, solace.
2 *What are your favourite pleasures?* amusement, diversion, entertainment, fun, luxury, recreation, self-indulgence.

pleasure-loving adjective SEE **hedonistic**.

pleat noun *a pleat in a skirt.* crease, flute, fold, gather, tuck.

plebeian adjective SEE **common** adjective.

plebiscite noun ballot, poll, referendum, vote.

pledge noun **1** *a pledge left at a pawnbroker's.* bail, bond, deposit, security, surety.
2 *a pledge of good faith.* assurance, guarantee, oath, pact, promise, undertaking, vow, word.

pledge verb *She pledged to give her support.* agree, commit yourself, contract, give a pledge [SEE **pledge** noun], guarantee, promise, swear, undertake, vow.

plenary adjective *a plenary session of the conference.* full, general, open.

plenipotentiary noun SEE **ambassador**.

plentiful adjective *a plentiful supply of food.* abounding, abundant, ample, bounteous, bountiful, bristling, bumper (*a bumper crop*), copious, generous, inexhaustible, lavish, liberal, overflowing, plenteous, profuse, prolific.
OPPOSITES: SEE **scarce**.
to be plentiful *Fish are plentiful in this part of the river.* abound, flourish, proliferate, swarm, thrive.

plenty noun *plenty to do. plenty in the garden.* abundance, affluence, cornucopia, excess, fertility, flood, fruitfulness, glut, more than enough, [*informal*] oodles, plentifulness, plethora, profusion, prosperity, sufficiency, superabundance, surfeit, surplus, wealth.
OPPOSITES: SEE **scarcity**.
plenty of *plenty of food.* abundant, ample, heaps of, [*informal*] lashings of, [*informal*] loads of, a lot of, lots of, [*informal*] masses of, much, [*informal*] oodles of, piles of, SEE **plentiful**.

pliable adjective **1** *pliable wire.* bendable, [*informal*] bendy, ductile, flexible, plastic, pliant, springy, supple.
2 *a pliable character.* compliant, easily influenced, easily led, easily persuaded, impressionable, responsive, suggestible, tractable.

pliant adjective SEE **pliable**.

plight noun SEE **difficulty**.

plinth noun SEE **base** noun.

plod verb **1** *to plod through mud.* tramp, trudge, SEE **walk** verb.
2 *to plod through your work.* grind on, labour, persevere, SEE **work** verb.

plop noun, verb VARIOUS SOUNDS: SEE **sound** noun.

plot noun **1** *a plot of ground.* allotment, area, estate, garden, lot, parcel, patch, smallholding, tract.
2 *the plot of a novel.* narrative, organization, outline, scenario, story, thread.
3 *a plot against the government.* cabal, conspiracy, intrigue, machination, plan, scheme.

plot verb **1** *to plot a route.* chart, draw, map out, plan, project.

2 *They plotted to rob a bank.* collude, conspire, have designs, intrigue, scheme.
3 *What are you two plotting?* [*informal*] brew, [*informal*] cook up, design, hatch.

plough verb *to plough a field.* cultivate, till, turn over.

ploy noun SEE **trick** noun.

pluck noun SEE **courage**.

pluck verb **1** *to pluck fruit off a tree.* collect, gather, harvest, pick, pull off.
2 *to pluck a chicken.* denude, remove the feathers from, strip.
3 *to pluck something out of someone's hand.* grab, jerk, seize, snatch, tweak, yank.
4 *to pluck the strings of a violin.* play pizzicato, strum, twang.

plucky adjective SEE **brave**.

plug noun **1** *Put a plug in the hole.* bung, cork, stopper.
2 [*informal*] *a plug for a new record.* SEE **advertisement**.

plug verb **1** *to plug a leak.* block up, [*informal*] bung up, close, cork, fill, jam, seal, stop up, stuff up.
2 [*informal*] *to plug a record on radio.* advertise, mention frequently, promote.
to plug away SEE **work** verb.

plumage noun feathers, plumes.

plumb adverb *plumb in the middle.* [*informal*] dead, exactly, precisely, [*informal*] slap.

plumb verb *to plumb the depths.* measure, penetrate, probe, sound.

plumber noun heating-engineer.

plumbing noun pipes, water-supply.

plume noun feather, quill.

plummet verb SEE **plunge**.

plump adjective *a plump figure.* buxom, chubby, dumpy, SEE **fat** adjective, overweight, podgy, portly, pudgy, rotund, round, squat, stout, tubby.
OPPOSITES: SEE **thin** adjective.

plump verb *to plump down.* SEE **drop** verb.
to plump for SEE **choose**.

plunder noun *The robbers escaped with their plunder.* booty, contraband, loot, pickings, prize, spoils, swag, takings.

plunder verb *Rioters plundered the shops.* despoil, loot, pillage, raid, ransack, ravage, rifle, rob, sack, steal from.

plunge verb **1** *She plunged into the water.* dive, drop, fall, hurtle, jump, leap, nose-dive, pitch, plummet, swoop, tumble.
2 *I plunged my hand in the water.* dip, lower, immerse, sink, submerge.
3 *He plunged his spear into the animal's side.* force, push, thrust.

plural adjective OPPOSITE: singular.

plush adjective SEE **luxurious**.

plutocrat noun SEE **wealthy (wealthy person)**.

pneumatic adjective *pneumatic tyres.* air-filled, pumped up.

poach verb **1** *to poach an egg.* SEE **cook** verb.
2 *to poach game.* hunt, steal.

pocket verb *Who'll pocket the profits?* SEE **take**.

pocket-knife noun VARIOUS KNIVES: SEE **knife** noun.

pocket-money noun allowance.

pod noun *a pea-pod.* case, hull, shell.

podgy adjective *a podgy figure.* SEE **plump** adjective.

podium noun SEE **platform**.

poem noun poetry, rhyme, verse.

KINDS OF POEM: ballad, ballade, [*informal*] ditty, doggerel, eclogue, elegy, epic, epithalamium, free-verse, haiku, idyll, [*informal*] jingle, lay, limerick, lyric, nursery-rhyme, pastoral, ode, sonnet.

VERSE FORMS: SEE **verse**.

OTHER KINDS OF WRITING: SEE **writing**.

---

poet noun bard, lyricist, minstrel, rhymer, sonneteer, versifier.
OTHER WRITERS: SEE **writer**.

poetic adjective *poetic language.* emotive, [*uncomplimentary*] flowery, imaginative, lyrical, metrical, poetical.
OPPOSITES: SEE **prosaic**.

poetry noun SEE **poem**.

pogrom noun SEE **killing** noun.

poignant adjective *a poignant moment of farewell.* affecting, distressing, heartbreaking, moving, painful, pathetic, piquant, SEE **sad**, tender, touching.

point noun **1** *the point of a spear.* prong, sharp end, spike, tine, tip.
2 *a point on a map.* location, place, position, site, situation.
3 *a point of time.* instant, juncture, moment, second, stage, time.
4 *a decimal point.* dot, full stop, spot.
5 *the point of a story.* aim, crux, drift, end, essence, gist, goal, idea, intention, meaning, motive, nub, object, objective, purpose, subject, theme, use, usefulness.

6 *Honesty is one of his good points.* aspect, attribute, characteristic, facet, feature, peculiarity, quality, trait.
7 *a point jutting into the sea.* SEE **promontory**.
to the point SEE **relevant**.

point verb 1 *She pointed the way.* draw attention to, indicate, point out, show, signal.
2 *She pointed us in the right direction.* aim, direct, guide, lead, steer.

point-blank adjective 1 *at point-blank range.* SEE **close** adjective.
2 *a point-blank question.* SEE **direct** adjective.

pointed adjective 1 *a pointed stick.* SEE **sharp**.
2 *I didn't like her pointed remarks.* barbed, biting, edged, hinting, hurtful, insinuating, sarcastic, sharp, telling, trenchant.
OPPOSITES: SEE **bland**.

pointless adjective SEE **futile**.

poise noun *She showed considerable poise on her first public appearance.* aplomb, assurance, balance, calmness, composure, coolness, dignity, equilibrium, presence, self-confidence, self-control, serenity, steadiness.

poise verb *He poised himself on a narrow ledge.* balance, be poised [SEE **poised**], keep in balance, support, suspend.

poised adjective 1 *poised on the edge.* balanced, hovering, in equilibrium, steady.
2 *poised to begin.* keyed up, ready, set, waiting.
3 *a poised performer.* assured, calm, composed, cool, dignified, self-confident, suave, urbane.

poison noun toxin, venom.

POISONS INCLUDE: arsenic, cyanide, DDT, digitalin, hemlock, herbicide, insecticide, Paraquat, pesticide, rat-poison, strychnine, weed-killer.

---

poison verb 1 *to poison someone.* SEE **kill**.
2 *Chemicals are poisoning the sea.* contaminate, infect, pollute, taint.
3 *Propaganda can poison people's minds.* corrupt, deprave, pervert, prejudice, subvert, warp.

poisoned adjective *a poisoned wound.* diseased, festering, infected, septic.

poisonous adjective *a poisonous snakebite.* deadly, fatal, lethal, mortal, noxious, toxic, venomous, virulent.

poke verb *to poke with a finger or a stick.* dig, SEE **hit** verb, jab, nudge, prod, stab, stick, thrust.
to poke about SEE **search** verb.
to poke fun at SEE **ridicule** verb.
to poke out SEE **protrude**.

poker-face noun SEE **expression**.

poker-faced adjective SEE **expressionless**.

poky adjective *a poky little room.* confined, cramped, inconvenient, restrictive, SEE **small**, uncomfortable.
OPPOSITES: SEE **spacious**.

polar adjective *polar regions.* antarctic, arctic.

polarize verb *Opinions have polarized into two opposing sides.* diverge, divide, move to opposite positions, separate, split.

pole noun 1 [*plural*] *the poles of the earth.* extremes, opposite ends.
GEOGRAPHICAL TERMS: SEE **geography**.
2 *a long pole.* bar, column, flagpole, mast, post, rod, shaft, spar, staff, stake, stick, stilt.
poles apart SEE **different**.

pole-axe verb SEE **kill**.

polemic noun SEE **argument**.

polemical adjective SEE **controversial**.

police noun [*plural*] *Call the police.* constabulary, [*informal*] the law, police force, policemen [SEE **policeman**].

police verb *to police a football match.* control, keep in order, keep the peace at, monitor, patrol, provide a police presence at, supervise, watch over.

policeman, policewoman nouns [*informal*] bobby, constable, [*informal*] cop, [*informal*] copper, detective, inspector, officer.

policy noun 1 *the library's policy on lost books.* approach, code of conduct, guidelines, [*informal*] line, practice, procedure, protocol, rules, stance, strategy, tactics.
2 *the policy of a political party.* intentions, manifesto, plan of action, platform, programme, proposals.
3 *an insurance policy.* SEE **document**.

polish noun 1 *a lovely polish on the woodwork.* brightness, brilliance, finish, glaze, gloss, lustre, sheen, shine, smoothness, sparkle.
2 *I wish his manners had more polish.* [*informal*] class, elegance, finesse, grace, refinement, sophistication, style, suavity, urbanity.

polish verb *to polish the furniture. to polish the cutlery.* brush up, buff up,

burnish, French-polish, rub down, rub up, shine, wax.
to polish off SEE **finish** verb.

SUBSTANCES USED TO SMOOTH AND POLISH THINGS: beeswax, Carborundum, emery, emery-paper, furniture polish, glasspaper, oil, sandpaper, shellac, varnish, wax.

polished adjective **1** *a polished surface.* bright, burnished, glassy, gleaming, glossy, lustrous, shining, shiny.
2 *polished manners.* cultured, elegant, gracious, perfected, SEE **polite**, [*sometimes uncomplimentary*] posh, refined, sophisticated, suave, urbane.
OPPOSITES: SEE **rough**.

polite adjective *polite behaviour. polite language.* acceptable, attentive, chivalrous, civil, considerate, correct, courteous, cultivated, deferential, diplomatic, discreet, euphemistic, gallant, genteel, gentlemanly, ladylike, obliging, SEE **polished**, respectful, tactful, thoughtful, well-bred, well-mannered, well-spoken.
OPPOSITES: SEE **rude**.

politic adjective SEE **prudent**.

politics noun *In a democracy, everyone should be involved in politics.* diplomacy, government, political affairs, political science, statesmanship.

VARIOUS POLITICAL POSITIONS: activist, anarchist, capitalist, communist, conservative, democrat, fascist, Labour, leftist, left-wing, liberal, Marxist, moderate, monarchist, nationalist, Nazi, parliamentarian, radical, republican, revolutionary, rightist, right-wing, socialist, Tory, [*old-fashioned*] Whig.

VARIOUS POLITICAL SYSTEMS: anarchy, capitalism, communism, democracy, dictatorship, martial law, monarchy, oligarchy, parliamentary democracy, republic.

poll noun **1** *to go to the polls.* ballot, election, vote.
2 *an opinion poll.* census, plebiscite, referendum, survey.

poll verb **1** *Our candidate polled few votes.* receive votes.
2 *to poll a tree.* SEE **pollard**.

pollard verb *to pollard a tree.* SEE **cut** verb, cut the top off, lop, poll, [*informal*] top.

pollinate verb SEE **fertilize**.

pollute verb *Chemicals pollute the rivers.* contaminate, defile, dirty, foul, infect, poison, soil, taint.

poltergeist noun SEE **ghost**.

The prefix *poly-* is related to Greek *polus = much, polloi = many.*

polyglot adjective multilingual.

polygon, polyhedron nouns VARIOUS SHAPES: SEE **shape** noun.

polyphonic adjective *polyphonic music.* contrapuntal.

polytechnic noun SEE **college**.

pomp noun *The coronation was conducted with great pomp.* ceremonial, ceremony, display, formality, grandeur, magnificence, ostentation, pageantry, ritual, show, solemnity, spectacle, splendour.

pompous adjective [*uncomplimentary*] *pompous language. a pompous manner.* affected, arrogant, bombastic, grandiose, haughty, [*informal*] high-faluting, long-winded, ostentatious, pontifical, posh, pretentious, self-important, sententious, showy, snobbish, [*informal*] stuck-up, supercilious.
OPPOSITES: SEE **modest**.

pond noun *a fish pond.* lake, pool, puddle.

ponder verb SEE **think**.

ponderous adjective **1** *a ponderous load.* bulky, burdensome, cumbersome, heavy, hefty, massive, unwieldy, weighty.
OPPOSITES: SEE **light** adjective.
2 *a ponderous style.* dull, heavy-handed, humourless, laboured, lifeless, long-winded, plodding, prolix, slow, stilted, stodgy, tedious, verbose.
OPPOSITES: SEE **lively**.

pong noun, verb SEE **smell** noun, verb.

pontifical adjective SEE **pompous**.

pontificate verb SEE **preach**.

pony noun SEE **horse**.

pooh-pooh verb SEE **dismiss**.

pool noun *a pool of water.* lake, mere, oasis, pond, puddle, swimming-pool, tarn.

pool verb *to pool resources.* SEE **combine**.

poor adjective **1** *Poor people can't afford luxuries.* badly off, bankrupt, beggarly, [*informal*] broke, deprived, destitute, hard up, homeless, impecunious, impoverished, in debt, indigent, needy, penniless, penurious, poverty-stricken, [*informal*] skint, underpaid, underprivileged.
OPPOSITES: SEE **rich**.

2 *poor soil* barren, exhausted, infertile, sterile, unproductive.
OPPOSITES: SEE **fertile**.
3 *a poor yield from the garden.* low, mean, SEE **scanty**, small, sparse, unprofitable, unrewarding.
OPPOSITES: SEE **plentiful**.
4 *goods of poor quality.* bad, cheap, deficient, faulty, imperfect, inadequate, inferior, low-grade, mediocre, paltry, second-rate, shoddy, substandard, unsatisfactory, useless, worthless.
OPPOSITES: SEE **superior**.
5 [*informal*] *The poor animals stood in the rain.* forlorn, hapless, luckless, miserable, pathetic, pitiable, sad, unfortunate, unhappy, unlucky, wretched.
OPPOSITES: SEE **lucky**.
a poor person beggar, down-and-out, pauper, tramp, vagrant, wretch.
poor people the destitute, the homeless.

poorly adjective *I felt poorly.* SEE **ill**.

pop verb *The cork popped.* VARIOUS SOUNDS: SEE **sound** noun.

poppycock noun SEE **nonsense**.

populace noun the masses, the people, the public.

popular adjective *a popular performer. popular styles.* accepted, celebrated, famous, fashionable, favoured, favourite, [*informal*] in (*It's the in thing*), liked, lionized, loved, renowned, sought after, well-known, well-liked.
OPPOSITES: SEE **unpopular**.
popular music pop.
OPPOSITE: classical music.

popularize verb **1** *to popularize a new product.* make popular [SEE **popular**], promote, spread.
2 *to popularize Shakespeare's plays.* make easy, present in a popular way, simplify, [*informal*] tart up.

populate verb *In summer the town is populated mainly by holidaymakers.* colonize, fill, inhabit, live in, occupy, overrun, settle.

population noun *the population of a country.* citizens, community, inhabitants, natives, occupants, SEE **populace**, residents.

populous adjective *a populous area.* crowded, full, overpopulated, packed, swarming, teeming.

porcelain noun SEE **crockery**.

porch noun doorway, entrance, lobby, portico.

pore verb **to pore over** SEE **study** verb.

pornographic adjective SEE **obscene**.

pornography noun SEE **obscenity**.

porous adjective *Porous substances will soak up liquid.* absorbent, cellular, holey, permeable, pervious, spongy.
OPPOSITES: SEE **impermeable**.

port adjective *the port side of a ship.* left-hand (when facing forward).
OPPOSITE: starboard.

port noun *The ship entered port.* anchorage, SEE **dock** noun, dockyard, harbour, haven, marina, sea-port.

portable adjective *a portable tool-box.* compact, convenient, easy to carry, handy, light, lightweight, manageable, mobile, movable, small, transportable.
OPPOSITES: SEE **unwieldy**.

portal noun SEE **door**.

The two meanings of *porter* relate to two different Latin words: *porta* = *door* [compare *portal, portico*]; and *portare* = *to carry* [compare *portable*].

---

porter noun **1** caretaker, door-keeper, doorman, gatekeeper, janitor, security guard.
2 baggage-handler, bearer, carrier.

portfolio noun cover, folder.

porthole noun window.

portico noun SEE **porch**.

portion noun *a small portion of pie.* allocation, allowance, bit, fraction, fragment, helping, measure, part, piece, quantity, quota, ration, section, segment, serving, share, slice.

portly adjective *a portly figure.* SEE **plump**.

portmanteau noun SEE **luggage**.

portrait noun *a portrait of a famous person.* depiction, image, likeness, SEE **picture** noun, portrayal, profile, representation, self-portrait.

portray verb *The book portrays what life was like 1000 years ago.* delineate, depict, describe, evoke, illustrate, SEE **picture** verb, represent, show.

pose noun **1** *The model adopted a suitable pose.* attitude, position.
2 *Don't take his behaviour seriously—it's only a pose.* act, affectation, façade, masquerade, posture, pretence.

pose verb **1** *to pose for a portrait.* model, sit.
2 *to pose in front of your friends.* adopt a pose [SEE **pose** noun], be a poser [SEE **poser**], posture, show off.
3 *to pose a question.* ask, posit, present, put forward, suggest.
to pose as *The burglar posed as the gas man.* impersonate, masquerade as, pass yourself off as, pretend to be.

poser noun **1** [*informal*] *The dilemma presented quite a poser.* SEE **puzzle** noun.
2 [*informal*] *I hate to see posers showing off.* exhibitionist, [*informal*] phoney, poseur, [*informal*] show-off.

posh adjective [*informal*] *a posh party.* [*informal*] classy, elegant, fashionable, formal, lavish, ostentatious, showy, smart, snobbish, stylish, [*informal*] swanky, [*informal*] swish.

position noun **1** *Mark our position on the map.* locality, location, locus, place, point, reference, site, situation, spot, whereabouts.
2 *Having lost my money, I was in an embarrassing position.* circumstances, condition, predicament, state.
3 *I'll get cramp if I don't shift my position.* angle, posture.
4 *A referee adopts a neutral position.* attitude, opinion, outlook, perspective, standpoint, view, viewpoint.
5 *a responsible position in the firm.* appointment, degree, employment, function, grade, job, level, niche, occupation, rank, role, standing, station, status, title.

position verb *The captain positioned her players where she wanted them.* arrange, deploy, dispose, locate, place, put, settle, situate, stand, station.

positive adjective **1** *He was positive that he was right.* affirmative, assured, certain, confident, convinced, decided, definite, emphatic, sure, unequivocal.
2 *I can show you positive evidence.* categorical, clear, conclusive, explicit, firm, incontestable, incontrovertible, irrefutable, real, undeniable.
2 *The counsellor gave me positive advice.* beneficial, constructive, helpful, optimistic, practical, useful, worthwhile.
OPPOSITES: SEE **negative**.

posse noun SEE **group** noun.

possess verb **1** *Do you possess a pen?* be in possession of, have, own.
2 *Foreign invaders possessed the country.* acquire, control, dominate, govern, occupy, rule, seize, take over.

possessions noun assets, belongings, chattels, effects, estate, fortune, goods, property, riches, wealth.

possessive adjective *a possessive nature.* clinging, domineering, jealous, proprietorial, protective, selfish.

possibility noun *a possibility of rain. the possibility of travelling to Mars.* capability, chance, danger, feasibility, likelihood, opportunity, potential, potentiality, practicality, probability, risk.
OPPOSITES: SEE **impossibility**.

possible adjective *a possible outcome. a possible explanation.* achievable, attainable, conceivable, credible, feasible, imaginable, likely, obtainable, plausible, potential, practicable, practical, probable, prospective, viable, workable.
OPPOSITES: SEE **impossible**.

possibly adverb [*informal*] hopefully, maybe, perhaps.

post noun **1** VARIOUS KINDS OF UPRIGHT POST: baluster, bollard, capstan, column, gate-post, leg, newel, pier, pile, pillar, pole, prop, shaft, stake, stanchion, starting-post, strut, support, upright, winning-post.
2 *a sentry's post.* location, place, point, position.
3 *a post in a local business.* appointment, employment, SEE **job**, occupation, office, place, position, situation, work.
4 *Was there any post today?* airmail, cards, delivery, letters, mail, packets, parcels, postcards.

post verb **1** *to post information.* advertise, announce, display, pin up, put up, stick up.
2 *to post a letter.* dispatch, mail, send, transmit.

post-box noun letter-box, pillar-box.

postcard noun SEE **letter**.

poster noun *We put up posters advertising sports day.* advertisement, announcement, bill, display, notice, placard, sign.

posterior adjective SEE **back** adjective.

posterior noun SEE **buttocks**.

posterity noun *What will posterity say about modern architecture?* descendants, future generations, heirs, offspring, successors.

postern noun SEE **door**.

The prefix *post-* in words like *postgraduate, posthumous, post-mortem, postpone*, etc., is from Latin *post* = *after*.

---

postgraduate noun SEE **student**.

post-haste adverb SEE **fast** adverb.

posthumous adjective SEE **belated**.

post-mortem noun **1** *a post-mortem on a dead body.* autopsy.
2 [*informal*] *a post-mortem on last week's disaster.* SEE **investigation**.

postpone verb *to postpone a meeting. to postpone a decision.* adjourn, defer, delay, extend, hold over, put back, put off, [*informal*] put on ice, [*informal*] shelve, stay (*to stay judgement*), suspend.

postscript noun *a postscript to a letter.* [*formal*] addendum, addition, afterthought, codicil (*to a will*), epilogue, [*informal*] PS.

postulate verb assume, hypothesize, posit, propose, suppose, theorize.

posture noun **1** *your physical posture.* bearing, deportment, stance.
2 *a mental posture.* SEE **attitude**.

posy noun *a posy of flowers.* bouquet, bunch, buttonhole, corsage, nosegay, spray.

pot noun *a cooking pot. pots and pans.* basin, bowl, casserole, cauldron, container, crock, crucible, dish, jar, pan, saucepan, teapot, urn, vessel.

pot-bellied adjective SEE **fat** adjective.

potent adjective *a potent drug. a potent smell. a potent influence.* effective, forceful, formidable, influential, intoxicating (*potent drink*), overpowering, overwhelming, powerful, strong.
OPPOSITES: SEE **impotent, weak**.

potentate noun SEE **ruler**.

potential adjective **1** *a potential champion.* budding, embryonic, future, likely, possible, probable, promising, prospective.
OPPOSITES: SEE **established**.
2 *a potential disaster.* imminent, impending, latent, looming, threatening.

pot-hole noun **1** *exploring pot-holes.* SEE **cave** noun.
2 *pot-holes in the road.* SEE **hole**.

pot-holing noun caving.

potion noun *a health-giving potion.* brew, concoction, dose, draught, drug, elixir, liquid, medicine, mixture, philtre, tonic.

pot-pourri noun SEE **mixture**.

potted adjective *a potted version of a story.* SEE **abridged**.

potter noun ARTISTS AND CRAFTSMEN: SEE **artist**.

potter verb **to potter about** SEE **work** verb.

pottery noun ceramics, china, SEE **crockery**, crocks, earthenware, porcelain, stoneware.

potty adjective SEE **mad**.

pouch noun *a pouch to keep money in.* bag, SEE **container**, purse, sack, wallet.

poultry noun KINDS OF POULTRY: bantam, chicken, duck, fowl, goose, guinea-fowl, hen, pullet, turkey.

pounce verb **to pounce on** *The cat pounced on the mouse.* ambush, attack, drop on, jump on, leap on, seize, snatch, spring at, swoop down on.

pound noun **1** *a pound of jam.* SEE **measure** noun.
2 *Lend me a few pounds.* SEE **money**.
3 *a pound for animals.* SEE **enclosure**.

pound verb *I pounded the clay until it was soft.* batter, beat, crush, grind, SEE **hit** verb, knead, mash, pulp, smash.

pour verb **1** *Water poured through the hole.* cascade, course, disgorge, flow, gush, run, spew, spill, spout, stream.
2 *I poured the milk out of the bottle.* decant, serve, tip.

pout noun FACIAL EXPRESSIONS: SEE **expression**.

poverty noun *He was rich, but is now reduced to poverty.* bankruptcy, beggary, dearth, debt, destitution, hardship, indigence, lack, necessity, need, penury, privation, scarcity, shortage, want.
OPPOSITES: SEE **wealth**.

poverty-stricken adjective SEE **poor**.

powder noun dust, particles.

powder verb **1** *to powder a substance in a pestle and mortar.* atomize, crush, grind, pound, pulverize, reduce to powder.
2 *to powder a baby's bottom.* cover with powder, dust, sprinkle.

powdered adjective **1** *powdered coffee. powdered stone.* crushed, granulated, ground, pulverized.
2 *powdered milk.* dehydrated, dried.

powdery adjective *a powdery substance.* chalky, crumbly, disintegrating, dry, dusty, fine, friable, granular, loose, pulverized, sandy.
OPPOSITES: SEE **solid, wet** adjective.

power noun **1** *the power to do something.* ability, capability, competence, energy, faculty, force, might, muscle, skill, strength, talent, vigour.
2 *the power to arrest someone.* authority, privilege, right.
3 *the power of a tyrant.* [*informal*] clout, command, control, domination, influence, omnipotence, oppression, potency, rule, sovereignty, supremacy, sway.
OPPOSITES: SEE **impotence**.

powerful adjective *a powerful machine. a powerful ruler. a powerful argument.* authoritative, cogent, commanding, compelling, consuming, convincing, dominant, dynamic, effective, effectual, energetic, forceful, influential, invincible, irresistible, high-powered, mighty, muscular, omnipotent, overpowering,

overwhelming, persuasive, potent, sovereign, SEE **strong**, vigorous, weighty.
OPPOSITES: SEE **powerless, weak.**

powerless *powerless against the enemy's might.* defenceless, feeble, helpless, impotent, incapable, ineffective, ineffectual, unable, SEE **weak.**
OPPOSITES: SEE **powerful, strong.**

powwow noun SEE **meeting.**

practicable adjective *a practicable plan.* achievable, attainable, feasible, possible, practical, realistic, sensible, viable, workable.
OPPOSITES: impracticable, SEE **impractical.**

practical adjective **1** *practical science.* applied, empirical, experimental.
2 *a practical approach.* businesslike, efficient, down-to-earth, hard-headed, matter-of-fact, [*informal*] no-nonsense, pragmatic, realistic, sensible, utilitarian.
OPPOSITES: SEE **theoretical.**
3 *a practical worker.* accomplished, capable, competent, expert, proficient, skilled.
4 *a practical tool.* convenient, functional, handy, usable, useful.
OPPOSITES: SEE **impractical.**
5 *a practical plan* SEE **practicable.**
a practical joke hoax, prank, trick.

practically adverb *We're practically there.* almost, close to, just about, nearly, virtually.

practice noun **1** *What does the plan mean in practice?* action, actuality, application, effect, operation, reality, use.
2 *We need more practice.* [*informal*] dummy-run, exercise, preparation, rehearsal, [*informal*] run-through, training.
OPPOSITES: SEE **theory.**
3 *Smoking is still a common practice.* custom, habit, routine, tradition.
4 *a doctor's practice.* SEE **business.**

Notice the different spellings of *practice* (noun) and *practise* (verb).

---

practise verb **1** *Keep practising.* do exercises, drill, exercise, prepare, rehearse, train, warm up.
2 *Practise what you preach.* apply, carry out, do, engage in, follow, perform, put into practice.

practitioner noun **medical practitioner** SEE **doctor.**

pragmatic adjective SEE **practical.**

prairie noun grassland, plain.

praise noun **1** *Our praise embarrassed her.* acclamation, accolade, admiration, adulation, applause, approval, commendation, compliment, congratulation, [*formal*] encomium, eulogy, homage, honour, ovation, panegyric, plaudits, testimonial, thanks, tribute.
2 *Give praise to God.* adoration, worship.

praise verb **1** *to praise someone for an achievement. to praise a performance.* acclaim, admire, applaud, cheer, clap, commend, compliment, congratulate, [*informal*] crack up (*They cracked her up as one of our best actresses*), eulogize, exalt, extol, give a good review of, marvel at, offer praise to [SEE **praise** noun], pay tribute to, [*informal*] rave about, recommend, [*informal*] say nice things about, show approval of.
OPPOSITES: SEE **criticize.**
2 *to praise God.* adore, glorify, honour, [*formal*] laud, magnify, worship.
OPPOSITES: SEE **curse** verb.

praiseworthy adjective *a praiseworthy effort.* admirable, commendable, creditable, deserving, SEE **good**, laudable, meritorious, worthy.
OPPOSITES: SEE **deplorable.**

pram noun baby-carriage, [*old-fashioned*] perambulator, push-chair.

prance verb *to prance about.* caper, cavort, dance, frisk, frolic, gambol, jump, leap, play, romp, skip.

prank noun SEE **escapade.**

prattle verb babble, chatter, [*informal*] rattle on, SEE **talk** verb.

pray verb **1** *to pray to God.* call upon, invoke, say prayers, supplicate.
2 SEE **ask.**

prayer noun *a prayer to God.* collect, devotion, entreaty, invocation, litany, meditation, petition, supplication.

prayer-book noun breviary, missal.

preach verb **1** *to preach in church.* deliver a sermon, evangelize, expound, proselytize, spread the Gospel.
2 *He's a fine one to preach about turning up on time!* expatiate, give moral advice, [*informal*] lay down the law, lecture, moralize, pontificate, sermonize, tell others what to do.

preacher noun SEE **clergyman**, crusader, evangelist, minister, missionary, moralist, pastor, revivalist.

The prefix *pre-* is from Latin *prae* = *before.*

---

preamble noun SEE **preface.**

pre-arranged adjective *a pre-arranged meeting.* arranged beforehand, fixed, planned, predetermined, prepared.
OPPOSITES: SEE **unplanned**.

precarious adjective dangerous, insecure, perilous, risky, rocky, shaky, uncertain, unsafe, unstable, unsteady, vulnerable, wobbly.
OPPOSITES: SEE **safe**.

precaution noun *What precautions can you take against flu?* anticipation, defence, insurance, protection, provision, safeguard, safety measure.

precede verb **1** *A flag-bearer preceded the procession.* be in front of, come before, go before, lead.
2 *He preceded his speech with an announcement.* introduce, lead into, preface, prefix, start.
OPPOSITES: SEE **follow**.

precedent noun SEE **pattern**.

precept noun SEE **rule** noun.

preceptor noun SEE **teacher**.

precinct noun SEE **area**.

precious adjective SEE **valuable**.

precipice noun *The climber fell down a precipice.* cliff, crag, drop, escarpment, precipitous face [SEE **precipitous**], rock.

precipitate adjective *a precipitate departure.* SEE **hasty**, **premature**.

precipitate verb *to precipitate a crisis.* bring on, cause, encourage, expedite, further, hasten, induce, occasion, spark off, trigger off.

precipitation noun KINDS OF PRECIPITATION: dew, drizzle, hail, rain, sleet, snow.

precipitous adjective *a precipitous hillside.* abrupt, perpendicular, sharp, sheer, steep, vertical.

précis noun SEE **summary**.

précis verb SEE **summarize**.

precise adjective **1** *the precise time. precise instructions.* accurate, clear-cut, correct, defined, definite, distinct, exact, explicit, fixed, measured, right, specific, unambiguous, unequivocal.
OPPOSITES: SEE **imprecise**.
2 *precise workmanship.* careful, finicky, meticulous, punctilious, scrupulous.
OPPOSITES: SEE **careless**.

preclude verb *Does this agreement preclude changes later on?* debar, exclude, make impossible, pre-empt, prevent, rule out.

precocious adjective *a precocious child.* advanced, SEE **clever**, forward, mature, quick.
OPPOSITES: SEE **backward**.

preconception noun *I had no preconceptions about what to expect.* assumption, expectation, prejudice, presupposition.

precondition noun SEE **prerequisite** noun.

precursor noun SEE **predecessor**.

predator noun hunter.

predatory adjective *predatory animals. predatory bands of robbers.* acquisitive, covetous, greedy, hunting, marauding, pillaging, plundering, preying, rapacious, voracious.

predecessor noun ancestor, antecedent, forebear, forefather, forerunner, precursor.

predestination noun SEE **fate**.

predestined adjective SEE **fated**.

predetermined adjective **1** *Do you believe his death was predetermined?* SEE **fated**.
2 *a predetermined signal.* SEE **pre-arranged**.

predicament *How did you get out of that predicament?* crisis, difficulty, dilemma, embarrassment, emergency, jam, [*informal*] mess, [*informal*] pickle, plight, problem, quandary.

predict verb *to predict the future.* forebode, forecast, foresee, foretell, forewarn, prognosticate, prophesy, tell fortunes.

predictable adjective *a predictable disaster.* certain, expected, foreseeable, likely, probable.
OPPOSITES: SEE **unpredictable**.

predilection noun SEE **preference**.

predispose verb SEE **prejudice** verb.

predisposition noun SEE **inclination**, **prejudice** noun.

predominant adjective SEE **chief** adjective.

predominate verb *Women still predominate in the nursing profession.* be in the majority, dominate, hold sway, outnumber, outweigh, preponderate, prevail.

pre-eminent adjective SEE **outstanding**.

pre-empt verb *We pre-empted any criticism by admitting that we'd done a poor job.* anticipate, forestall.

preen verb **to preen yourself** SEE **groom** verb.

prefab noun SEE **house** noun.

prefabricate verb SEE **manufacture**.

preface noun *the preface to a book.* foreword, introduction, preamble, prelude, prologue.

preface verb *He prefaced his speech with an announcement.* introduce, lead into, precede, prefix, start.

prefatory adjective *prefatory remarks.* SEE **preliminary**.

prefect noun *a school prefect.* monitor. VARIOUS OFFICIALS: SEE **official** noun.

prefer verb *Which style do you prefer?* advocate, [*informal*] back, choose, fancy, favour, [*informal*] go for, incline towards, like, like better, pick out, [*informal*] plump for, recommend, single out, think preferable [SEE **preferable**], vote for, SEE **want** verb.

preferable adjective *Vote for whoever you think is preferable.* advantageous, better, better-liked, desirable, likely, nicer, preferred, recommended, wanted.
OPPOSITES: SEE **objectionable**.

preference noun *a preference for sweet things. What's your preference?* choice, fancy, favouritism, inclination, liking, option, partiality, predilection, wish.
to show a preference for SEE **choose**.

preferential adjective *preferential treatment.* better, biased, favoured, privileged, showing favouritism, special.

preferment noun SEE **promotion**.

prefix noun LINGUISTIC TERMS: SEE **language**.
OPPOSITE: suffix.

prefix verb SEE **precede**.

pregnancy noun gestation.

pregnant adjective **1** *a pregnant woman.* carrying a child, expectant, [*informal*] expecting, [*old-fashioned*] with child.
2 *a pregnant remark.* SEE **meaningful**.
to be pregnant expect a baby.

WORDS TO DO WITH PREGNANCY: abortion, SEE **birth**, conception, gestation, miscarriage, parturition, premature birth.

---

prehensile adjective able to grasp [SEE **grasp**].

prehistoric adjective SEE **old**.
prehistoric remains barrow, dolmen, menhir, standing stones.

prejudice noun *racial prejudice. sexual prejudice.* bias, bigotry, chauvinism, discrimination, dogmatism, fanaticism, favouritism, intolerance, jingoism, narrow-mindedness, partisanship, predisposition, racialism, racism, sexism, unfairness, xenophobia.
OPPOSITES: SEE **tolerance**.

prejudice verb **1** *His dirty appearance prejudiced me against him.* bias, incline, predispose, sway.
2 *Publicity might prejudice the result of the trial.* influence, interfere with, prejudge, sway.
3 *Will a criminal record prejudice your chances of a job?* damage, harm, injure, ruin, spoil, undermine.

prejudiced adjective *a prejudiced attitude. prejudiced remarks.* biased, bigoted, chauvinist, discriminatory, illiberal, intolerant, jingoistic, leading (*a leading question*), loaded, narrow-minded, one-sided, partial, partisan, racist, sexist, tendentious, unfair, xenophobic.
OPPOSITES: SEE **impartial**.
a prejudiced person bigot, chauvinist, fanatic, racist, sexist, zealot.

prejudicial adjective *The news-report was prejudicial to the defendant's case.* damaging, detrimental, harmful, injurious, unfavourable.

prelate noun SEE **clergyman**.

preliminary adjective *We'll go ahead if the preliminary survey is encouraging.* earliest, early, experimental, exploratory, first, inaugural, initial, introductory, opening, prefatory, preparatory, qualifying, (*qualifying rounds of a competition*), tentative, trial.

prelude noun *The first match was an exciting prelude to the series.* beginning, [*informal*] curtain-raiser, introduction, opener, opening, overture, preamble, precursor, preface, preliminary, preparation, prologue, start, starter, [*informal*] warm-up.
OPPOSITES: SEE **epilogue**.

premature adverb *a premature birth. a premature decision.* abortive, before time, early, hasty, precipitate, [*informal*] previous (*You were a bit previous with your congratulations!*), too early, too soon, untimely.
OPPOSITES: SEE **late**.

premeditated adjective *a premeditated crime.* calculated, conscious, considered, deliberate, intended, intentional, planned, pre-arranged, predetermined, pre-planned, wilful.
OPPOSITES: unpremeditated, SEE **impulsive**.

premier noun prime minister.

première noun *the première of a play.* SEE **performance**.

premises noun SEE **building, property**.

premiss noun SEE **assumption**.

premium noun SEE **payment**.

premonition noun *I had a premonition that something nasty would happen.* anxiety, fear, foreboding, forewarning, indication, intuition, misgiving, omen, portent, presentiment, suspicion, warning, worry.

preoccupied adjective **1** *preoccupied in her work.* absorbed, engaged, engrossed, immersed, interested, involved, obsessed, sunk, taken up, wrapped up.
2 *You look preoccupied: what are you thinking of?* absent-minded, day-dreaming, faraway, inattentive, pensive, rapt, thoughtful.

prep noun SEE **homework**.
prep school VARIOUS SCHOOLS: SEE **school**.

preparation noun [*often plural*] *preparations for Christmas.* arrangement(s), getting ready, groundwork, making provision, measure(s), organization.

preparatory adjective *a preparatory meeting to fix an agenda.* SEE **preliminary**.

prepare verb **1** *to prepare dinner. to prepare for visitors.* arrange, SEE **cook** verb, devise, [*informal*] do what's necessary, [*informal*] fix up, get ready, make arrangements for, organize, plan, process, set up.
2 *A teacher has to prepare pupils for exams.* brief, coach, educate, equip, instruct, rehearse, teach, train, tutor.
to prepare yourself *Prepare yourself for a shock.* be prepared, be ready, brace yourself, discipline yourself, steel yourself.

prepared adjective **1** *prepared to go anywhere.* able, equipped, fit, ready, set, trained, willing.
OPPOSITES: SEE **unwilling**.
2 *a prepared statement* SEE **pre-arranged**.

preponderance noun SEE **majority**.

preponderate verb SEE **majority (to be in a majority)**.

prepossessing adjective SEE **attractive**.

preposterous adjective SEE **absurd**.

prerequisite adjective *prerequisite qualifications for entry to college.* compulsory, indispensable, mandatory, necessary, prescribed, required, requisite, specified, stipulated.
OPPOSITES: SEE **optional**.

prerequisite noun *It is a prerequisite of entry to the profession that you pass the exams.* condition, essential, necessity, precondition, qualification, requirement, stipulation.

prerogative noun SEE **right** noun.

prescribe noun **1** *The doctor prescribed medicine.* advise, recommend, suggest.
2 *The boss prescribed our duties.* assign, dictate, fix, impose, lay down, ordain, specify, stipulate.

prescription noun SEE **medicine**.

presence noun **1** *The boss requires your presence.* attendance.
2 *I value the presence of friends when I'm sad.* closeness, companionship, company, nearness, propinquity, proximity.
3 *an actor with a commanding presence.* air, appearance, bearing, demeanour, impressiveness, personality.

present adjective **1** *Is everyone present?* at hand, here, in attendance.
2 *Who's the present champion?* contemporary, current, existing, extant.

present noun **1** *We live in the present, not in the past.* [*informal*] here and now, present time [SEE **present** adjective].
2 *She gave me a present.* contribution, donation, gift, gratuity, offering, tip.

present verb **1** *to present prizes.* award, confer, donate, give, hand over, offer.
2 *to present your work.* demonstrate, display, exhibit, reveal, show.
3 *to present a guest.* introduce, make known.
4 *to present a play.* act, bring out, perform, put on.
to present yourself *Present yourself at the office.* appear at, attend, go to, visit.

presentable adjective *a presentable appearance.* acceptable, clean, decent, neat, passable, proper, respectable, satisfactory, tidy, tolerable, worthy.

presentiment noun SEE **foreboding**.

presently adverb shortly, soon.

preservative noun VARIOUS PRESERVATIVES: alcohol, creosote, salt, sugar.

preserve noun **1** *strawberry preserve.* conserve, jam.
2 *a wildlife preserve.* SEE **reserve** noun.

preserve verb **1** *to preserve peace.* defend, guard, maintain, perpetuate, protect, retain, safeguard, secure, sustain, uphold.
2 *to preserve food. to preserve resources.* conserve, keep, lay up, look after, save, stockpile, store.

WAYS TO PRESERVE FOOD: bottle, can, chill, cure, dehydrate, dry, freeze, freeze-dry, irradiate, jam (*to jam fruit*), pickle, refrigerate, salt, tin.

---

3 *to preserve a dead body.* embalm, mummify.
OPPOSITES: SEE **destroy**.

preserved adjective *preserved food.* bottled, canned, chilled, dehydrated, desiccated, dried, freeze-dried, frozen, irradiated, pickled, refrigerated, salted, tinned.
OPPOSITES: SEE **fresh**.

preside verb *to preside at a meeting.* be in charge, officiate, take charge.
to preside over SEE **govern**.

president noun PEOPLE INVOLVED IN GOVERNMENT: SEE **government**.

press noun *the press.* newspapers, magazines, the media.
FORMS OF COMMUNICATION: SEE **communication**.

press verb **1** *to press things together.* compress, condense, cram, crowd, crush, force, gather, [*informal*] jam, shove, squash, squeeze.
2 *to press a pair of trousers.* flatten, iron, smooth.
3 *Press the bell.* apply pressure to [SEE **pressure**], depress, push.
4 *They pressed me to stay.* beg, bully, coerce, constrain, dragoon, entreat, exhort, implore, importune, [*informal*] lean on, persuade, pressure, pressurize, put pressure on, require, urge.

press-gang verb SEE **compel**.

pressing adjective *pressing business.* SEE **urgent**.

pressure noun **1** *the pressure of a load on your back.* burden, force, heaviness, load, might, power, stress, weight.
2 *air pressure in a tyre.* compression.
3 *the pressure of modern life.* adversity, constraint, difficulty, [*informal*] hassle, hurry, oppression, stress, urgency.

pressurize verb *They pressurized me to stay.* SEE **press** verb.

prestige noun *If we lose again, our prestige will suffer.* credit, esteem, fame, glory, good name, honour, importance, [*informal*] kudos, renown, reputation, standing.

prestigious adjective SEE **reputable**.

presume verb **1** *I presume you want something to eat.* assume, believe, conjecture, guess, hypothesize, imagine, infer, postulate, suppose, surmise, [*informal*] take it for granted, think.
2 *She presumed to tell us what to do.* be presumptuous enough [SEE **presumptuous**], dare, make bold, [*informal*] take the liberty, venture.

presumptuous adjective *It was presumptuous of him to take charge.* arrogant, bold, [*informal*] cheeky, conceited, forward, impertinent, impudent, insolent, over-confident, [*informal*] pushy, shameless, unauthorized, unwarranted.

presuppose verb SEE **assume**.

pretence noun *I saw through her pretence.* act, acting, affectation, charade, counterfeiting, deceit, deception, disguise, dissembling, dissimulation, façade, feigning, feint, guise, hoax, insincerity, invention, lying, make-believe, masquerade, pose, posing, posturing, ruse, sham, show, simulation, subterfuge, trickery, wile.

pretend verb **1** *Don't believe him—he was pretending. I pretended to be someone else.* act, affect, behave insincerely, bluff, counterfeit, deceive, disguise, dissemble, dissimulate, fake, feign, fool, hoax, hoodwink, imitate, impersonate, [*informal*] kid, lie, mislead, play a part, perform, pose, posture, profess, purport, put on an act, sham, simulate, take someone in, trick.
2 *Pretend you're on a desert island.* SEE **imagine**.
3 *I don't pretend that I play well.* SEE **claim** verb.

pretentious adjective *a pretentious show of knowledge.* affected, [*informal*] arty, conceited, grandiose, inflated, ostentatious, [*informal*] over the top, SEE **pompous**, showy.
OPPOSITES: SEE **modest**.

preternatural adjective SEE **supernatural**.

pretext noun SEE **excuse** noun.

prettify verb SEE **beautify**.

pretty adjective *pretty decorations.* appealing, attractive, SEE **beautiful**, charming, [*informal*] cute, dainty, delicate, good-looking, lovely, nice, pleasing, [*uncomplimentary*] pretty-pretty.
OPPOSITES: SEE **ugly**.

pretty adverb [*informal*] *That's pretty good!* fairly, moderately, quite, rather, somewhat, tolerably.
OPPOSITES: SEE **very**.

prevail verb **1** *to prevail over an enemy.* SEE **win**.
2 *After a long argument, common sense prevailed.* SEE **predominate**.

prevailing adjective *the prevailing fashion.* accepted, chief, common, current, dominant, familiar, fashionable, general, influential, main, mainstream, normal, ordinary, orthodox, popular, predominant, prevalent, principal, usual, widespread.
OPPOSITES: SEE **unusual**.

prevalent adjective SEE **prevailing**.

prevaricate verb *Stop prevaricating and say what you think.* [*informal*] beat about the bush, be evasive [SEE **evasive**], cavil, dither, equivocate, hedge, [*informal*] hesitate, hum and haw, quibble, [*informal*] shilly-shally, temporize, vacillate, waver.

prevent verb **1** *to prevent a mishap.* anticipate, avert, avoid, foil, forestall, frustrate, [*informal*] head off, [*informal*] help (*I can't help coughing*), inoculate against (*a disease*), intercept, [*informal*] nip in the bud, pre-empt, stave off, take precautions against, thwart, ward off.
OPPOSITES: SEE **encourage**.
2 *to prevent someone from doing something.* check, curb, deter, hamper, hinder, impede, obstruct, save, stop.
OPPOSITES: SEE **help** verb.

preventative, preventive adjectives *preventive measures.* deterrent, obstructive, precautionary, pre-emptive.

preview noun SEE **performance**.

previous adjective *looking back on previous events.* antecedent, earlier, foregoing, former, preceding, prior.
OPPOSITES: SEE **following**.

prey noun *The lion killed its prey.* quarry, victim.

prey verb **to prey on** *Owls prey on small animals.* eat, feed on, hunt, kill.

price noun **1** *a reasonable price to pay.* amount, charge, cost, [*informal*] damage (*What's the damage?*), expenditure, expense, fare, fee, figure, outlay, payment, rate, sum, terms, toll, valuation, value, worth.
to pay the price for *He paid the price for his crime.* SEE **atone**.

priceless adjective **1** *priceless jewels.* costly, dear, expensive, inestimable, invaluable, irreplaceable, precious, [*informal*] pricey, rare, valuable.
2 [*informal*] *a priceless joke.* SEE **funny**.

prick verb **1** *to prick with a pin.* bore into, jab, perforate, pierce, punch, puncture, stab, sting.
2 *to prick someone into action.* SEE **goad**.

prickle noun **1** *a bush with prickles on.* barb, needle, spike, spine, thorn.
2 *The scream sent a prickle down my spine.* itch, pricking sensation, prickling, tingle, tingling.

prickly adjective **1** *a prickly bush.* bristly, scratchy, sharp, spiky, spiny, thorny.
2 [*informal*] *He's in a prickly mood.* SEE **irritable**.

pride noun **1** *Display your work with pride.* delight, dignity, gratification, happiness, honour, pleasure, satisfaction, self-respect, self-satisfaction.
2 *The new car is her pride and joy.* jewel, treasured possession.
3 [*uncomplimentary*] *Pride goes before a fall.* arrogance, being proud [SEE **proud**], [*informal*] big-headedness, conceit, egotism, haughtiness, megalomania, presumption, self-esteem, self-importance, self-love, smugness, snobbery, vainglory, vanity.
OPPOSITES: SEE **humility**.
4 *a pride of lions.* SEE **group** noun.

priest noun SEE **clergyman**, Druid, lama.

prig noun SEE **self-righteous** (**self-righteous person**).

priggish adjective SEE **self-righteous**.

prim adjective *She's too prim to enjoy rude jokes!* demure, fastidious, SEE **narrow-minded**, [*informal*] prissy, proper, prudish, starchy, strait-laced.
OPPOSITES: SEE **broad-minded**.

A number of words, including *primal, primary, prime, primitive*, etc., are related to Latin *primus=first.*

---

primal adjective **1** *primal forms of life.* earliest, early, first, original, primeval, primitive, primordial.
2 *matters of primal importance.* central, chief, fundamental, major, paramount, principal.

primarily adverb basically, chiefly, especially, firstly, fundamentally, generally, mainly, mostly, predominantly, principally.

primary adjective *Our primary aim was to win.* basic, chief, dominant, first, foremost, fundamental, greatest, important, initial, leading, main, major, outstanding, paramount, prime, principal, supreme, top.
primary school OTHER SCHOOLS: SEE **school**.

prime adjective **1** *Our prime aim was to win.* SEE **primary**.
2 *prime beef. prime grade.* best, first-class, select, top.

prime verb *to prime a pump.* get ready, prepare.

primer noun **1** *primer paint.* SEE **paint** noun.
2 *a Latin primer.* textbook.
OTHER BOOKS: SEE **book** noun.

primeval adjective SEE **primal**, **primitive**.

primitive adjective **1** *primitive tribes.* ancient, barbarian, early, prehistoric, primeval, savage, uncivilized, uncultivated, unsophisticated.
OPPOSITES: SEE **civilized**.

2 *primitive technology.* backward, basic, [*informal*] behind the times, crude, elementary. SEE **obsolete**, rough, rudimentary, simple, undeveloped.
OPPOSITES: SEE **advanced**.

primordial adjective SEE **primal**.

prince, princess OTHER ROYAL RANKS: SEE **royal**.

principal adjective *What's your principal interest in life?* basic, chief, dominant, dominating, first, foremost, fundamental, greatest, highest, important, leading, main, major, outstanding, paramount, pre-eminent, primary, prime, supreme, top.

principal noun *the principal of a college.* SEE **chief** noun.

principality noun SEE **country**.

principle noun **1** *moral principles.* assumption, axiom, belief, doctrine, dogma, ethic, ideal, maxim, precept, proposition, rule, tenet, theory, values.
2 [*plural*] *the basic principles of a subject.* basics, elements, essentials, fundamentals, laws.
3 *a person of principle.* high-mindedness, honesty, honour, ideals, integrity, morality, probity, scruples, standards, uprightness, virtue.

print noun **1** *the print of feet in the sand.* impression, imprint, indentation, mark, stamp.
2 *I like a book with clear print.* characters, fount, lettering, letters, printing, type, typeface.
3 *It's a print, not an original painting.* copy, duplicate, engraving, lithograph, photograph, reproduction.

print verb **1** *to print a book.* issue, publish.
2 *Print your name clearly.* SEE **write**.

prior adjective SEE **previous**.

priority noun *Give priority to traffic on the main road.* greater importance, precedence, right-of-way, seniority.

priory noun abbey, SEE **church**, monastery.

prise, prize verb *to prise off a lid.* force, lever, wrench.

prism noun VARIOUS SHAPES: SEE **shape** noun.

prison noun *sentenced to six months in prison.* Borstal, cell, confinement, custody, detention centre, dungeon, gaol, house of correction, imprisonment, jail, [*American*] penitentiary, reformatory.

prisoner noun captive, convict, detainee, hostage, inmate, internee.

prissy adjective SEE **prim**.

privacy noun *I enjoy the privacy of my own room.* concealment, isolation, quietness, seclusion, secrecy, solitude.

private adjective **1** *private property.* individual, personal, privately owned.
2 *private information.* classified, confidential, intimate, secret.
OPPOSITES: SEE **public** adjective.
3 *a private meeting.* clandestine, closed, restricted.
OPPOSITES: SEE **open** adjective.
4 *a private hideaway.* concealed, hidden, SEE **isolated**, little-known, quiet, secluded, sequestered, solitary, unknown.
OPPOSITES: SEE **popular**.

privation noun SEE **poverty**.

privilege noun *Club members enjoy special privileges.* advantage, benefit, concession, entitlement, licence, right.

privileged adjective *The boss has a privileged position.* advantaged, élite, favoured, powerful, special, superior.
OPPOSITES: SEE **oppressed**.

prize noun *a prize for coming first.* award, jackpot, reward, trophy, winnings.

prize verb **1** *Which of your possessions do you prize most highly?* appreciate, approve of, cherish, esteem, hold dear, like, rate, regard, revere, treasure, value.
OPPOSITES: SEE **disregard**.
2 SEE **prise**.

probable adjective *the probable result.* believable, credible, expected, feasible, likely, plausible, possible, predictable, presumed.
OPPOSITES: SEE **improbable**.

probate noun LEGAL TERMS: SEE **law**.

probation noun **1** *New employees are on probation for three months.* apprenticeship, test, trial period.
2 *The magistrate put her on probation.* VARIOUS PUNISHMENTS: SEE **punishment**.

probationer noun apprentice, beginner, inexperienced worker, learner, novice.

probe noun *a probe into a smuggling racket.* examination, inquiry, investigation, research, scrutiny, study.

probe verb **1** *to probe a wound.* poke, prod.
2 *to probe the depths of the sea.* SEE **explore**, penetrate, plumb (*the depths*).
3 *to probe a problem.* examine, go into, inquire into, investigate, look into, research into, scrutinize, study.

probity noun SEE **honesty**.

problem noun **1** *an intriguing problem to solve.* brainteaser, conundrum, enigma, mystery, poser, puzzle, question, riddle.

2 *a worrying problem to overcome.* burden, complication, difficulty, dilemma, dispute, [*informal*] headache, predicament, quandary, set-back, snag, trouble, worry.

problematic, problematical adjectives *There's no easy solution to such a problematical issue.* complicated, controversial, debatable, difficult, enigmatic, hard to deal with, intractable, puzzling, taxing, worrying.
OPPOSITES: SEE **straightforward.**

proboscis noun SEE **snout.**

procedure noun *What's the procedure for getting a licence?* course of action, formula, method, [*Latin*] modus operandi, plan of action, practice, process, routine, scheme, strategy, system, technique, way.

proceed verb **1** *After a rest, we proceeded.* advance, carry on, continue, follow, go ahead, go on, make progress, move forward, [*informal*] press on, progress.
2 *Great things proceed from small beginnings.* arise, originate, SEE **result** verb.

proceedings noun **1** *legal proceedings.* action, lawsuit.
2 *The secretary writes up the proceedings of the meeting.* [*informal*] doings, minutes, records, report, transactions.
3 [*informal*] *On sports day, a storm ended proceedings.* events, [*informal*] goings-on, happenings, matters, things.

proceeds *proceeds from an OXFAM collection.* earnings, income, SEE **money**, profit, receipts, revenue, takings.

process noun **1** *a manufacturing process.* method, operation, SEE **procedure**, system, technique.
2 *the process of growing up.* course, development, evolution, experience, progression.

process verb **1** *to process crude oil.* alter, change, convert, deal with, make usable, prepare, refine, transform, treat.
2 [*informal*] *A cavalcade processed through town.* SEE **parade** verb.

procession noun cavalcade, column, cortège, line, march, motorcade, pageant, parade.

proclaim verb **1** *to proclaim something publicly.* announce, assert, declare, give out, make known, profess, pronounce.
2 *to proclaim a public holiday.* SEE **decree** verb.

proclivity noun SEE **tendency.**

procrastinate verb *Stop procrastinating and do something.* be indecisive, defer a decision, delay, [*informal*] dilly-dally, dither, [*informal*] drag your feet, [*informal*] hum and haw, [*informal*] play for time, postpone, prevaricate, put things off, [*informal*] shilly-shally, stall, temporize.

procreate verb SEE **reproduce.**

proctor noun SEE **official** noun.

procurable adjective SEE **available.**

procure verb SEE **obtain.**

prod verb *to prod with a stick.* dig, goad, SEE **hit** verb, jab, nudge, poke, push, urge on.

prodigal adjective SEE **wasteful.**

prodigious adjective SEE **amazing.**

prodigy noun *a child prodigy.* curiosity, freak, genius, marvel, phenomenon, rarity, sensation, talent, wonder.

produce noun *garden produce.* crop, harvest, output, products, yield.

produce verb **1** *Can you produce evidence?* advance, bring out, disclose, display, exhibit, furnish, offer, present, put forward, reveal, show, supply, throw up.
2 *A factory produces goods. Farmers produce crops.* cause, compose, conjure up, construct, create, cultivate, develop, fabricate, form, generate, give rise to, grow, invent, make, manufacture, originate, provoke, result in, think up, turn out, yield.
3 *to produce children.* bear, beget, breed, give birth to, raise, rear.
4 *to produce a play.* direct.

producer, production nouns SEE **theatre.**

product noun **1** *What kind of product does this factory make?* artefact, commodity, end-product, goods, merchandise, output, produce, production.
2 *Our plan was the product of much thought.* consequence, effect, fruit, outcome, result, upshot.

productive adjective **1** *productive work.* beneficial, busy, constructive, creative, effective, efficient, gainful (*gainful employment*), profitable, profitmaking, rewarding, useful, valuable, worthwhile.
2 *a productive garden.* fertile, fruitful, lush, prolific.
OPPOSITES: SEE **unproductive.**

profane adjective *profane language.* SEE **blasphemous.**

profess verb **1** *He professed to be the gas man.* allege, claim, make out, pretend, purport.
2 *to profess your faith.* SEE **declare.**

profession noun **1** *Nursing is a worthwhile profession.* business, calling, career, employment, job, line of work, occupation, trade, vocation, work.

2 *a profession of faith.* acknowledgement, confession, declaration, statement, testimony.

professional adjective 1 *professional advice.* competent, efficient, expert, paid, proficient, qualified, skilled, trained.
OPPOSITES: SEE **amateur.**
2 *a professional attitude.* conscientious, dutiful, responsible.
OPPOSITES: SEE **unprofessional.**

professor noun SEE **lecturer.**

proffer verb SEE **offer** verb.

proficient adjective *a proficient worker.* SEE **competent.**

profile noun 1 *the profile of a person's face.* outline, SEE **picture** noun, shape, side view, silhouette.
2 *a profile of a famous personality.* account, biography, [*Latin*] curriculum vitae, sketch, study.

profit noun *a profit on your investment.* advantage, benefit, excess, gain, interest, SEE **money**, return, surplus, yield.

profit verb 1 *It won't profit anyone to get angry.* benefit, further the interests of, SEE **help** verb, pay (*It doesn't pay to get angry*), serve.
2 *Did you profit from the sale?* earn money, gain, make money, receive a profit [SEE **profit** noun].
to profit by or **from** *You can sometimes profit from other people's mistakes.* capitalize on, [*informal*] cash in on, exploit, take advantage of, use.

profitable adjective *profitable employment.* advantageous, beneficial, commercial, fruitful, gainful, lucrative, moneymaking, paying, productive, profitmaking, remunerative, rewarding, useful, valuable, worthwhile.
OPPOSITES: SEE **unprofitable.**

profiteering noun *Profiteering in a time of shortage is wrong.* exploitation, extortion, overcharging.

profligate adjective SEE **wasteful.**

profound adjective 1 *profound sympathy.* deep, heartfelt, intense, sincere.
OPPOSITES: SEE **insincere.**
2 *a profound discussion.* abstruse, erudite, imponderable, intellectual, knowledgeable, learned, philosophical, serious, thoughtful, wise.
OPPOSITES: SEE **facile.**

profuse adjective SEE **plentiful.**

progenitor noun SEE **ancestor.**

progeny noun SEE **offspring.**

prognosis, prognostication nouns SEE **forecast** noun.

program noun COMPUTER TERMS: SEE **computer.**

programme noun 1 *a published programme of events.* agenda, [*informal*] line-up, listing, plan, schedule, timetable.
2 *a television programme.* broadcast, performance, production, transmission.

progress noun 1 *scientific progress.* advance, breakthrough, development, gain, headway, improvement, march (*the march of time*), movement, progression, [*informal*] step forward.
2 *I traced their progress on a map.* journey, route, travels, way.

progress verb *Our plans are progressing.* advance, [*informal*] come on, develop, [*informal*] forge ahead, improve, make progress [SEE **progress** noun], move forward, proceed, prosper.
OPPOSITES: SEE **regress.**

progression noun *a progression of events.* chain, row, sequence, series, string, succession.

progressive adjective 1 *a progressive increase in prices.* accelerating, continuing, continuous, escalating, growing, increasing, ongoing, steady.
OPPOSITES: SEE **erratic.**
2 *progressive ideas.* advanced, avant-garde, contemporary, enterprising, forward-looking, [*informal*] go-ahead, modernistic, radical, revolutionary, up-to-date.
OPPOSITES: SEE **conservative** adjective.

prohibit verb *to prohibit smoking. to prohibit non-members.* ban, bar, censor, [*informal*] cut out, debar, disallow, exclude, forbid, hinder, [*formal*] interdict, make illegal, outlaw, place an embargo on, preclude, prevent, proscribe, restrict, rule out, shut out, stop, veto.
OPPOSITES: SEE **allow.**

prohibitive adjective *prohibitive prices.* discouraging, excessive, SEE **exorbitant**, impossible, out of reach, unreasonable, unthinkable.

project noun 1 *a project to build a bypass.* design, enterprise, idea, plan, proposal, scheme, undertaking, venture.
2 *a history project.* activity, assignment, piece of research, piece of work, task.

project verb 1 *A narrow ledge projects from the cliff.* beetle, bulge, extend, jut out, overhang, protrude, stand out, stick out.
2 *The lighthouse projects a strong beam.* cast, flash, shine, throw out.
3 *Can you project what your profits will be next year?* SEE **estimate** verb.

projectile noun SEE **missile.**

projector noun AUDIO-VISUAL AIDS: SEE **audio-visual**.

proletariat noun working class.
OPPOSITE: bourgeoisie.
TERMS FOR SOCIAL CLASSES: SEE **class** noun.

proliferate verb SEE **multiply**.

prolific adjective *prolific crops. a prolific writer.* abundant, copious, fertile, fruitful, productive, profuse, rich.
OPPOSITES: SEE **unproductive**.

prologue noun SEE **prelude**.

prolong verb *The game was prolonged by injuries.* delay, draw out, extend, increase, lengthen, make longer, protract, [*informal*] spin out, stretch out.
OPPOSITES: SEE **shorten**.

prolonged adjective SEE **long** adjective.

promenade noun SEE **walk** noun.

prominent adjective **1** *prominent teeth.* bulging, jutting out, large, projecting, protruding, sticking out.
2 *a prominent landmark.* conspicuous, eye-catching, noticeable, obtrusive, obvious, pronounced, salient, significant.
OPPOSITES: SEE **inconspicuous**.
3 *a prominent politician.* celebrated, distinguished, eminent, familiar, famous, foremost, important, leading, major, much-publicized, noted, outstanding, recognizable, renowned, well-known.
OPPOSITES: SEE **unknown**.

promiscuous adjective *promiscuous sexual relationships.* casual, haphazard, SEE **immoral**, indiscriminate, random, undiscriminating.
OPPOSITES: SEE **moral** adjective.

promise noun **1** *We had promises of help from many people.* assurance, commitment, [*formal*] covenant, guarantee, oath, pledge, undertaking, vow, word, word of honour.
2 *The young actor shows promise.* latent ability, potential, promising qualities [SEE **promising**], talent.

promise verb **1** *You promised me that you'd pay. She promised to come.* agree, assure, consent, contract, engage, give a promise [SEE **promise** noun], give your word, guarantee, pledge, swear, take an oath, undertake, vow.
2 *The clouds promise rain.* augur, forebode, indicate, presage, prophesy, suggest.

promising adjective *a promising debut. a promising newcomer.* auspicious, budding, encouraging, hopeful, likely, propitious, talented, [*informal*] up-and-coming.

promontory noun cape, foreland, headland, peninsula, point, projection, ridge, spit, spur.

promote verb **1** *to promote someone to a higher rank.* advance, elevate, exalt, give promotion [SEE **promotion**], move up, prefer, raise, upgrade.
2 *A local firm promoted our festival.* back, boost, encourage, help, sponsor, support.
3 *to promote a new product.* advertise, make known, market, [*informal*] plug, popularize, publicize, [*informal*] push, sell.

promoter noun backer, sponsor.

promotion noun **1** *promotion to a higher rank.* advancement, elevation, preferment, rise, upgrading.
2 *the promotion of a new product.* advertising, backing, encouragement, marketing, publicity, selling.

prompt adjective *a prompt reply.* eager, efficient, immediate, instantaneous, on time, punctual, SEE **quick**, unhesitating, willing.
OPPOSITES: SEE **belated**.

prompt verb *If you forget what to say, I'll prompt you.* advise, egg on, encourage, help, incite, inspire, jog the memory, motivate, nudge, persuade, prod, provoke, remind, spur, stimulate, urge.

prone adjective **1** *lying prone on the floor.* face down, on your front, prostrate.
OPPOSITES: SEE **supine**.
2 *She's prone to exaggerate. I'm prone to colds.* apt, disposed, given, inclined, liable, likely, predisposed, susceptible, vulnerable.
OPPOSITES: SEE **immune**.

prong noun *the prong of a fork.* point, spike, spur, tine.

pronounce verb **1** *Try to pronounce the words clearly.* articulate, aspirate, enunciate, say, sound, speak, utter.
2 *The doctor pronounced me fit again.* announce, assert, declare, decree, judge, make known, proclaim.

pronounced adjective *a pronounced limp.* clear, conspicuous, decided, definite, distinct, evident, marked, noticeable, obvious, prominent, striking, unmistakable.

pronunciation noun *The announcer's pronunciation is very clear.* accent, articulation, diction, elocution, enunciation, inflection, intonation.

proof noun *proof of guilt.* confirmation, corroboration, demonstration, evidence, facts, grounds, testimony, verification.

prop noun *a prop to lean on.* buttress, crutch, post, strut, support.

prop verb *to prop a bike against a wall.* lean, rest, stand.
to prop up *to prop up a wall.* buttress, hold up, reinforce, shore up, support.

propaganda noun *government propaganda.* advertising, brain-washing, indoctrination, persuasion, publicity.

propagate verb **1** *to propagate lies.* disseminate, generate, multiply, pass on, produce, proliferate, spread, transmit.
2 *to propagate plants.* breed, grow from seed, increase, layer, reproduce, sow, take cuttings.

propel verb *The crowd propelled me forward. The spacecraft was propelled by a rocket.* drive, force, impel, launch, move, pitchfork (*They pitchforked me into it*), push, send, shoot, spur, thrust, urge.

propeller noun rotor, screw, vane.
PARTS OF AN AIRCRAFT: SEE **aircraft**.

propensity noun SEE **tendency**.

proper adjective **1** *proper language. proper manners.* acceptable, becoming, decent, decorous, delicate, dignified, fitting, formal, genteel, gentlemanly, grave, in good taste, ladylike, modest, orthodox, polite, respectable, sedate, seemly, serious, solemn, suitable, tactful, tasteful.
2 *the proper thing to do. a proper price.* advisable, appropriate, conventional, correct, deserved, fair, fitting, just, lawful, legal, right, usual, valid.
OPPOSITES: SEE **improper**.

property noun **1** *I don't own much property.* assets, belongings, [*formal*] chattels, effects, fortune, goods, patrimony, possessions, riches, wealth.
2 *Keep off! Private property.* buildings, estate, land, premises.
3 *This chemical has unusual properties.* attribute, characteristic, feature, idiosyncrasy, peculiarity, quality, trait.

Notice the difference in spelling between *prophecy* (noun) and *prophesy* (verb).

---

prophecy noun *a prophecy that came true.* augury, forecast, prediction, prognosis, prognostication.

prophesy verb *She prophesied the tragic outcome.* forecast, foresee, foretell, predict, prognosticate.

prophet noun clairvoyant, forecaster, fortune-teller, oracle, seer, soothsayer.

prophetic adjective *a prophetic warning.* apocalyptic, far-seeing, oracular, prophesying.

propinquity noun SEE **proximity**.

propitiate verb SEE **pacify**.

propitious adjective SEE **favourable**.

proportion noun **1** *the proportion of girls to boys in a class.* balance, ratio.
2 *A large proportion of the audience cheered.* fraction, part, piece, quota, section, share.
proportions *a gentleman of large proportions.* dimensions, measurements, size.

proportionate adjective *The cost of the ticket is proportionate to the distance you travel.* commensurate, comparable, corresponding, in proportion, proportional, relative.
OPPOSITES: SEE **disproportionate**.

proposal noun *a proposal to build a supermarket.* bid, motion [*= a proposal made at a meeting*], offer, plan, project, proposition, recommendation, scheme, suggestion.

propose verb **1** *I proposed a change in the rules.* ask for, present, put forward, recommend, submit, suggest.
2 *Our friends propose to visit us.* aim, have in mind, intend, mean, offer, plan, purpose.
3 *They proposed me as a candidate in the election.* nominate, put up.
to propose marriage [*old-fashioned*] ask for someone's hand, get engaged, [*informal*] pop the question.

proposition noun **1** *I don't accept the proposition that the moon is made of cheese.* SEE **statement**.
2 *I made a proposition that we should adjourn the meeting.* SEE **proposal**.

propound verb *to propound a theory.* SEE **suggest**.

proprietor noun *the proprietor of a shop.* boss, manager, owner.

propriety noun *The sensitive matter was handled with great propriety.* appropriateness, correctness, decency, decorum, delicacy, etiquette, good manners, politeness, seemliness, sensitivity, tact.
OPPOSITES: SEE **impropriety**.

prorogue verb SEE **adjourn**.

prosaic adjective *a prosaic statement.* clear, dry, dull, hackneyed, matter-of-fact, ordinary, pedestrian, plain, prosy, simple, straightforward, trite, unimaginative, uninspired, uninspiring, unvarnished.
OPPOSITES: SEE **poetic**.

proscenium noun SEE **stage** noun.

proscribe verb SEE **prohibit**.

prose noun KINDS OF WRITING: SEE **writing**.

prosecute verb *They prosecuted him for dangerous driving.* accuse, bring to trial, charge, institute legal proceedings against, prefer charges against, sue, take legal proceedings against.
LEGAL TERMS: SEE **law**.

prosecution, prosecutor nouns LEGAL TERMS: SEE **law**.

proselytize verb SEE **preach**.

prosody noun *the prosody of a poem.* metre, rhythm, scansion, verse form.
VARIOUS VERSE FORMS: SEE **verse**.

prospect noun **1** *a lovely prospect from the top of the hill.* landscape, outlook, panorama, perspective, scene, sight, spectacle, view, vista.
2 *the prospect of a change in the weather.* chance, expectation, hope, likelihood, possibility, probability, promise.

prospect verb *to prospect for gold.* explore, quest, search, survey.

prospective adjective *prospective changes. a prospective employee.* anticipated, coming, expected, forthcoming, future, imminent, intended, likely, negotiable, possible, potential, probable.

prospectus noun *a college prospectus.* brochure, catalogue, leaflet, manifesto, pamphlet, programme, scheme, syllabus.

prosper verb *to prosper in business.* become prosperous [SEE **prosperous**], be successful, [*informal*] boom, burgeon, do well, flourish, [*informal*] get on, [*informal*] go from strength to strength, grow, make good, progress, strengthen, succeed, thrive.
OPPOSITES: SEE **fail**.

prosperity noun *Will this prosperity last?* affluence, [*informal*] bonanza, [*informal*] boom, growth, plenty, profitability, success, wealth.

prosperous adjective *a prosperous business.* affluent, [*informal*] booming, buoyant, flourishing, moneymaking, profitable, prospering, rich, successful, thriving, wealthy, well-off, well-to-do.
OPPOSITES: SEE **unsuccessful**.

prostitute noun [*old-fashioned*] bawd, call-girl, [*old-fashioned*] courtesan, [*old-fashioned*] harlot, [*old-fashioned*] strumpet, [*informal*] tart, whore.

prostitute verb *to prostitute your talents.* cheapen, debase, devalue, misuse.

prostrate adjective **1** *lying prostrate.* SEE **prone**.
2 *prostrate with grief.* SEE **overcome** adjective.

prostrate verb **to prostrate yourself** SEE **grovel**.

prosy adjective SEE **prosaic**.

protagonist noun *the protagonist of a play.* chief actor, contender, contestant, hero, heroine, leading figure, principal.

protect verb **1** *to protect someone from danger.* defend, escort, guard, harbour, insulate, keep safe, preserve, provide cover (for), safeguard, screen, secure, shield.
2 *Parents protect their young.* care for, cherish, look after, mind, support, watch over.
OPPOSITES: SEE **abandon**.

protection noun *protection from the weather. protection against enemies.* barrier, bulwark, cloak, cover, defence, guard, guardianship, insulation, preservation, safety, screen, security, shelter, shield, tutelage.

protective adjective **1** *a protective cover.* defensive, insulating, protecting, sheltering, shielding.
2 *protective parents.* careful, jealous, paternalistic, possessive, solicitous, watchful.

protector noun benefactor, bodyguard, champion, defender, guard, guardian, patron.

protectorate noun SEE **country**.

protégé noun *The professor took a keen interest in the work of her protégé.* discovery, pupil, student.

protest noun **1** *We made a protest against the referee's decision.* complaint, cry of disapproval, objection, outcry, protestation, remonstrance.
2 *They held a big protest in the square.* [*informal*] demo, demonstration, march, rally.

protest verb **1** *We protested against his decision.* argue, complain, cry out, expostulate, express disapproval, fulminate, grouse, grumble, make a protest [SEE **protest** noun], moan, object, remonstrate.
2 *A big crowd protested in the square.* demonstrate, [*informal*] hold a demo, march.
3 *He protested that he was innocent.* SEE **declare**.

protestation noun SEE **declaration**.

protocol noun **1** *We must observe the correct protocol.* SEE **etiquette**.
2 *The statesmen signed a protocol.* SEE **agreement**.

prototype noun SEE **model** noun.

protracted adjective SEE **long** adjective.

protrude verb *His stomach protrudes above his waistband.* be protruding [SEE **protruding**], bulge, jut out, poke out, project, stand out, stick out, swell.

protruding adjective *a protruding stomach.* bulbous, bulging, projecting, prominent, protuberant, swollen.

protuberant adjective SEE **protruding**.

proud adjective **1** *proud of his new car.* appreciative, delighted (with), happy (with), pleased (with), satisfied (with).
2 *a proud bearing.* dignified, honourable, independent, self-respecting.
3 *He's too proud to mix with the likes of us!* arrogant, boastful, bumptious, [*informal*] cocky, conceited, disdainful, egotistical, grand, haughty, [*informal*] high and mighty, lordly, self-important, snobbish, [*informal*] snooty, [*informal*] stuck-up, [*informal*] toffee-nosed, vain.
OPPOSITES: SEE **humble** adjective.

provable adjective demonstrable, verifiable.

prove verb *to prove a theory.* ascertain, attest, authenticate, [*informal*] bear out, confirm, corroborate, demonstrate, establish, explain, justify, show to be true, substantiate, test, verify.
OPPOSITES: SEE **disprove**.

proven adjective *a player of proven ability.* accepted, authenticated, certified, checked, confirmed, corroborated, demonstrated, established, proved, reliable, tested, tried, trustworthy, undoubted, unquestionable, valid, verified.
OPPOSITES: SEE **doubtful**.

provenance noun SEE **origin**.

provender noun SEE **food**.

proverb noun SEE **saying**.

proverbial adjective *a proverbial remark.* conventional, clichéd, customary, famous, legendary, traditional, well-known.

provide verb *We provide food and clothing for our families.* afford, allot, allow, arrange for, cater, contribute, donate, endow, equip, [*informal*] fork out, furnish, give, grant, lay on, lend, make provision, produce, spare, supply.

providence noun SEE **fate**.

provident adjective SEE **thrifty**.

providential adjective SEE **lucky**.

province noun SEE **district**.

provincial adjective *a provincial area. provincial government.* local, regional.
OPPOSITES: SEE **national** adjective.
2 [*uncomplimentary*] *City dwellers think country folk have provincial attitudes.* bucolic, insular, narrow-minded, parochial, rural, rustic, small-minded, unsophisticated.
OPPOSITES: SEE **cosmopolitan**.

provisional adjective *a provisional agreement.* conditional, interim, stop-gap, temporary, tentative.
OPPOSITES: SEE **permanent**.

provisions noun food, foodstuff, groceries, rations, requirements, stores, subsistence, supplies.

proviso noun SEE **condition**.

provocation noun *The dog won't attack without provocation.* [*informal*] aggravation, cause, challenge, grievance, grounds, incitement, inducement, justification, motivation, reason, taunts, teasing.

provoke verb **1** *If you provoke the dog, it'll bite.* [*informal*] aggravate, anger, annoy, arouse, encourage, enrage, exasperate, goad, incense, incite, inflame, infuriate, insult, irk, irritate, offend, pique, rile, tease, torment, upset, urge on, vex, worry.
OPPOSITES: SEE **pacify**.
2 *His jokes provoked a lot of laughter.* arouse, bring about, cause, elicit, excite, generate, give rise to, induce, inspire, kindle, occasion, produce, promote, prompt, spark off, stimulate, stir up.

prow noun *the prow of a ship.* bow, front.

prowess noun **1** *prowess in battle.* bravery, courage, daring, heroism, spirit, valour.
2 *The dancers showed off their prowess.* ability, accomplishment, adroitness, aptitude, cleverness, competence, excellence, expertise, genius, skill, talent.

prowl verb *to prowl about in the dark.* creep, roam, slink, sneak, steal, SEE **walk** verb.

prowler noun intruder.

proximity noun **1** *We objected to the proximity of the pig-farm.* closeness, nearness, propinquity.
2 *There are several shops in the proximity.* neighbourhood.

prude noun SEE **puritan**.

prudent adjective *It's prudent to keep money in a bank.* advisable, careful, cautious, discreet, economical, far-sighted, politic, proper, sensible, shrewd, thoughtful, thrifty, wise.
OPPOSITES: SEE **unwise**.

prudish adjective *a prudish attitude to sex.* easily shocked, illiberal, intolerant, narrow-minded, old-fashioned, priggish, prim, [*informal*] prissy, proper,

puritanical, shockable, strait-laced, strict.
OPPOSITES: SEE **open-minded**.

prune verb SEE **cut** verb, trim.

pry verb *Don't pry into my affairs.* be curious, be inquisitive, delve, [*informal*] ferret, interfere, meddle, [*informal*] nose about, peer rudely, poke about, [*informal*] snoop, [*informal*] stick your nose in.

prying adjective *We pulled down the blind to keep out prying eyes.* curious, impertinent, inquisitive, interfering, meddlesome, [*informal*] nosy, [*informal*] snooping, spying.
OPPOSITES: SEE **discreet**.

The prefix *pseudo-* is related to Greek *pseudes=false.*

---

pseudonym noun alias, assumed name, false name, [*French*] nom de plume, penname, sobriquet.

A number of English words like *psyche, psychiatry, psychic, psychology* are related to Greek *psukhe=breath, life, soul.*

---

psyche noun SEE **mind** noun, **soul**.

psychiatrist noun OTHER MEDICAL PRACTITIONERS: SEE **medicine**.

psychic adjective *Some people are said to have psychic powers.* clairvoyant, extrasensory, mystic, occult, psychical, supernatural, telepathic.

psychological adjective *a psychological condition.* emotional, mental, subconscious, subjective.
OPPOSITES: SEE **physiological**.

psychopath noun SEE **madman**.

pub noun bar, [*old-fashioned*] hostelry, inn, [*informal*] local, public house, saloon, tavern.

puberty noun *You reach puberty in your teens.* adolescence, growing-up, sexual maturity.

public adjective *a public place. public knowledge.* accessible, common, communal, familiar, general, known, national, open, popular, shared, unconcealed, universal, unrestricted, well-known.
OPPOSITES: SEE **private**.
public house SEE **pub**.
public school VARIOUS SCHOOLS: SEE **school**.

public noun *the public.* citizens, the community, the country, the nation, people, the populace, society, voters.

publication noun **1** *the publication of a book.* appearance, issuing, printing, production.
2 *the publication of secret information.* announcement, broadcasting, disclosure, dissemination, promulgation, reporting.
3 *I bought his latest publication.* KINDS OF PUBLICATION: SEE **book** noun, **magazine, recording**.

publicity noun **1** *Did you see the publicity for our play?* SEE **advertisement**.
2 *Famous people don't always enjoy publicity.* attention, [*informal*] ballyhoo, fame, limelight, notoriety.

publicize verb SEE **advertise**.

public-spirited adjective SEE **unselfish**.

publish verb **1** *to publish a book or magazine.* bring out, circulate, issue, print, produce, release.
2 *to publish secrets.* announce, broadcast, communicate, declare, disclose, disseminate, divulge, [*informal*] leak, make known, make public, proclaim, promulgate, publicize, report, reveal, spread.

pucker verb *to pucker your lips.* compress, crease, purse, screw up, tighten, wrinkle.

puckish adjective SEE **mischievous**.

pudding noun [*informal*] afters, dessert, sweet.
VARIOUS FOODS: SEE **food**.

puddle noun pool.

pudenda plural noun SEE **genitals**.

pudgy adjective SEE **plump**.

puerile adjective SEE **childish**.

puff noun **1** *a puff of wind.* blast, breath, draught, flurry, gust.
2 *a puff of smoke.* cloud, whiff.

puff verb **1** *By the end of the race I was puffing.* blow, breathe heavily, gasp, pant, wheeze.
2 *The sails puffed out.* become inflated, billow, distend, rise, swell.

puffy adjective *puffy eyes.* SEE **swollen**.

pugilist noun SEE **fighter**.

pugnacious adjective *a pugnacious fighter.* aggressive, bellicose, belligerent, combative, excitable, hostile, hot-tempered, militant, quarrelsome, warlike.
OPPOSITES: SEE **placid**.

puke verb SEE **vomit**.

pull verb **1** *A locomotive pulls a train.* drag, draw, haul, lug, tow, trail.
OPPOSITES: SEE **push**.
2 *You nearly pulled my arm off!* jerk, tug, pluck, rip, wrench.
3 *The dentist pulled a tooth.* extract, pull out, remove, take out.
to pull someone's leg SEE **tease**.
to pull out SEE **withdraw**.
to pull round, to pull through SEE **recover**.
to pull together SEE **co-operate**.
to pull up SEE **halt** verb.

pulp noun *fruit pulp. squashed to a pulp.* mash, mush, paste, purée.

pulp verb *to pulp food.* crush, liquidize, mash, pound, pulverize, purée, smash, squash.

pulpit noun SEE **church**.

pulpy adjective SEE **soft**.

pulsar noun ASTRONOMICAL TERMS: SEE **astronomy**.

pulsate verb *A regular rhythm pulsated in our ears.* beat, drum, oscillate, palpitate, quiver, throb, tick, vibrate.

pulse noun *a regular pulse.* beat, drumming, oscillation, pulsation, rhythm, throb, ticking, vibration.

pulverize verb SEE **powder** verb.

pumice noun lava.
VARIOUS ROCKS: SEE **rock** noun.

pummel verb batter, beat, SEE **hit** verb, pound, thump.

pump verb *The fire brigade pumped water out of the cellar.* drain, draw off, empty, force, raise, siphon.

pun noun double meaning, SEE **joke** noun.

punch noun *hot punch.* VARIOUS DRINKS: SEE **drink** noun.

punch verb **1** *to punch someone on the nose.* beat, clout, cuff, SEE **hit** verb, jab, poke, prod, slog, strike, thump.
2 *to punch a hole.* SEE **pierce**.

punch-up noun SEE **fight** noun.

punctilious adjective SEE **conscientious**.

punctual adjective *The bus is punctual today.* in good time, [*informal*] on the dot, on time, prompt.
OPPOSITES: SEE **unpunctual**.

punctuate verb **1** *to punctuate a piece of writing.* insert punctuation [SEE **punctuation**].
2 *His speech was punctuated by cat-calls.* SEE **interrupt**.

punctuation noun PUNCTUATION MARKS: accent, apostrophe, asterisk, bracket, caret, cedilla, colon, comma, dash, exclamation mark, full stop, hyphen, question mark, quotation marks, semicolon, speech marks.

puncture noun **1** *a puncture in a tyre.* burst, hole, leak, pin-prick, rupture.
2 *We had a puncture on the way home.* blow-out, burst tyre, [*informal*] flat, flat tyre.

puncture verb *A nail punctured my tyre.* deflate, let down, SEE **pierce**, rupture.

pundit noun SEE **expert** noun.

pungent adjective SEE **smelling**.

punish verb *to punish someone for wrongdoing.* chasten, chastise, correct, discipline, exact retribution (from), impose or inflict punishment on [SEE **punishment**], [*informal*] make an example of, pay back, penalize, [*informal*] teach (someone) a lesson.

WAYS TO PUNISH PEOPLE: beat, cane, detain, SEE **execute**, exile, fine, flog, gaol or jail, give a hiding (to), imprison, [*old-fashioned*] keelhaul, pillory, put in the stocks, put on probation, scourge, send to prison, spank, torture, whip.

---

punishable adjective *a punishable offence.* actionable, criminal, illegal.

punishing adjective *a punishing session of training.* SEE **strenuous**.

punishment noun chastisement, correction, discipline, penalty, retribution, revenge.
RELATED ADJECTIVE: penal.

VARIOUS PUNISHMENTS: beating, Borstal, the cane, capital punishment, confiscation, corporal punishment, detention, execution [SEE **execute**], fine, flogging, forfeit, gaol or jail, [*informal*] a hiding, imposition, pillory, prison, probation, spanking, the stocks, torture, whipping.

---

punitive adjective *They took punitive measures against the whole gang.* penal, retaliatory, revengeful, vindictive.

punt verb *to punt a ball.* boot, SEE **hit** verb, kick.

punter noun better, gambler, speculator.

puny adjective *a puny child.* SEE **feeble**.

pup noun SEE **dog** noun.

pupa noun chrysalis.

pupil noun **1** *a teacher's pupil.* discipline, follower, learner, protégé, scholar,

schoolboy, schoolchild, schoolgirl, student.
2 *the pupil of your eye.* PARTS OF THE EYE: SEE **eye** noun.

puppet noun doll, dummy, glove-puppet, marionette.

puppy noun SEE **dog** noun.

purchase noun **1** *I put my purchases in a bag.* acquisition, [*informal*] buy (*That was a good buy*), investment.
2 *I can't get enough purchase to prise this lid off.* grasp, hold, leverage.

purchase verb *What can you purchase for £1?* acquire, buy, get, invest in, obtain, pay for, procure, secure.

pure adjective **1** *pure alcohol. pure gold.* authentic, genuine, neat, real, straight, unadulterated, unalloyed, undiluted.
2 *pure food.* eatable, germ-free, hygienic, natural, pasteurized, uncontaminated, untainted, wholesome.
3 *pure water.* clean, clear, distilled, drinkable, fresh, potable, sterile, unpolluted.
OPPOSITES: SEE **impure**.
4 *a pure person.* chaste, good, innocent, irreproachable, modest, moral, sinless, stainless, virginal, virtuous.
OPPOSITES: SEE **immoral**.
5 *pure nonsense. pure genius.* absolute, complete, perfect, sheer, total, true, unmitigated, utter.
6 *pure science.* abstract, theoretical.
OPPOSITES: SEE **applied**.

purée noun, verb SEE **pulp** noun, verb.

purgative noun aperient, enema, laxative.

purgatory noun SEE **torment** noun.

purge verb **1** *to purge your bowels.* clean out, cleanse, empty, purify.
2 *to purge spies from the government.* eradicate, expel, get rid of, remove, root out.

purify verb *to purify water.* clarify, clean, disinfect, distil, filter, make pure [SEE **pure**], refine, sterilize.

puritan noun [*uncomplimentary*] killjoy, moralist, [*uncomplimentary*] prude, puritanical person [SEE **puritanical**], zealot.
OPPOSITES: SEE **hedonist**.

puritanical adjective *a puritanical dislike of self-indulgence.* ascetic, austere, moralistic, narrow-minded, prim, prudish, self-denying, self-disciplined, severe, strait-laced, strict, temperate, unbending.
OPPOSITES: SEE **hedonistic**.

purlieus noun SEE **outskirts**.

purloin verb SEE **steal**.

purport noun *the purport of a message.* SEE **meaning**.

purport verb *She purports to represent the whole group.* SEE **pretend**.

purpose noun **1** *a particular purpose in mind.* aim, ambition, aspiration, design, end, goal, hope, intention, motive, object, objective, outcome, plan, result, target, wish.
2 *a sense of purpose.* determination, devotion, firmness, persistence, resolution, resolve, steadfastness, zeal.
3 *What's the purpose of this gadget?* application, point, use, usefulness, value.

purpose verb SEE **intend**.

purposeful adjective *Her purposeful stare showed she meant business.* calculated, decided, decisive, deliberate, determined, firm, positive, resolute, steadfast, unwavering.
OPPOSITES: SEE **hesitant**.

purposeless adjective *purposeless vandalism.* aimless, gratuitous, pointless, senseless, unnecessary, useless, wanton.
OPPOSITES: SEE **useful**.

purposely adverb consciously, deliberately, intentionally, knowingly, on purpose, wilfully.

purr verb VARIOUS SOUNDS: SEE **sound** noun.

purse noun bag, handbag, pouch, wallet.

pursue verb **1** *Hounds pursue the fox.* chase, follow, go in pursuit of, harry, hound, hunt, run after, seek, shadow, tail, track down.
2 *She's pursuing a career in engineering.* aim for, aspire to, [*informal*] go for, strive for, try for.
3 *I pursue my hobbies at weekends.* carry on, conduct, continue, engage in, follow up, inquire into, investigate, keep up with, persevere in, proceed with.

pursuit noun **1** *The hounds were in pursuit of the fox.* chase, [*informal*] hue and cry, hunt, tracking down, trail.
2 *What are your favourite pursuits?* activity, hobby, interest, occupation, pastime, pleasure.

purvey verb SEE **supply** verb.

purveyor noun SEE **supplier**.

push verb **1** *to push something away from you.* advance, drive, force, hustle, impel, jostle, poke, press, prod, propel, shove, thrust.
OPPOSITES: SEE **pull**.
2 *I pushed my things into a bag.* compress, cram, crowd, crush, insert, jam, pack, put, ram, squash, squeeze.

3 *They pushed him to work even harder.* browbeat, bully, coerce, compel, constrain, dragoon, hurry, importune, [*informal*] lean on, persuade, put pressure on, pressurize, urge.
4 *The firm is pushing its new product hard.* advertise, make known, market, [*informal*] plug, promote, publicize.
to push (someone) around SEE **bully** verb.
to push off SEE **depart.**

push-chair noun SEE **pram.**

pushy adjective SEE **assertive.**

pusillanimous adjective SEE **timid.**

pustule noun SEE **pimple.**

put verb 1 *Put the books on the shelf.* arrange, assign, consign, deploy, deposit, dispose, fix, hang, lay, leave, locate, park, place, [*informal*] plonk, position, rest, set down, situate, stand, station.
2 *to put a question.* express, formulate, frame, phrase, say, state, suggest, utter, voice, word, write.
3 *to put the blame on someone else.* cast, impose, inflict, lay.
to put across *to put your ideas across.* SEE **communicate.**
to put by *to put food by for later.* SEE **save.**
to put down 1 *to put down a rebellion.* SEE **suppress.**
2 *to put down an animal.* SEE **kill.**
to put in *to put in new sparking-plugs.* SEE **insert** verb, **install.**
to put off *to put off a visit.* SEE **postpone.**
to put out *to put out a fire.* SEE **extinguish.**
to put right *to put damage right.* SEE **repair** verb.
to put up 1 *to put up a tent.* SEE **erect** verb.
2 *to put up prices.* SEE **raise.**
3 *to put up guests.* SEE **accommodate.**
to put your foot down SEE **insist.**
to pur your foot in it SEE **blunder** verb.

putative adjective SEE **supposed.**

putrefy verb SEE **rot** verb.

putrid adjective SEE **rotten.**

putt verb SEE **hit** verb, strike, tap.

puzzle noun *Can you solve this puzzle?* brainteaser, difficulty, dilemma, enigma, mystery, [*informal*] poser, problem, quandary, question.
KINDS OF PUZZLE: acrostic, anagram, conundrum, crossword, maze, riddle.

puzzle verb 1 *His coded message puzzled us.* baffle, bewilder, confuse, [*informal*] floor, [*informal*] flummox, mystify, nonplus, perplex, set thinking, stump, worry.
2 *We puzzled over the problem for hours.* SEE **think.**

puzzling adjective *a puzzling problem.* baffling, bewildering, confusing, cryptic, enigmatic, impenetrable, inexplicable, insoluble, [*informal*] mind-boggling, mysterious, mystifying, perplexing, strange, unaccountable, unanswerable, unfathomable.
OPPOSITES: SEE **straightforward.**

pygmy adjective SEE **small.**

pygmy noun dwarf, lilliputian, midget.

pyjamas noun night-clothes.

pyramid noun VARIOUS SHAPES: SEE **shape** noun.

Several English words, including *pyre, pyromaniac,* and *pyrotechnics,* are related to Greek *pur=fire.*

---

pyre noun *a funeral pyre.* SEE **fire** noun.

pyromaniac noun arsonist, fireraiser, incendiary.

pyrotechnics noun firework display, fireworks.

Q

quack noun 1 *That doctor's a quack!* SEE **cheat** noun.
2 *the quack of a duck.* VARIOUS SOUNDS: SEE **sound** noun.

The first syllable of words like *quadrilateral, quadrangle,* and *quadruped* is related to Latin *quattuor=four.*

---

quadrangle noun *a quadrangle surrounded by buildings.* cloisters, courtyard, enclosure, [*informal*] quad, yard.

quadrant, quadrilateral nouns SEE **shape** noun.

quadruped noun VARIOUS ANIMALS: SEE **animal** noun.

quadruple adjective SEE **multiple.**

quadruple verb *Prices quadrupled in ten years.* SEE **multiply.**

quaff verb SEE **drink** verb.

quagmire noun *My wellingtons got stuck in a quagmire.* bog, fen, marsh, mire, morass, mud, quicksand, [*old-fashioned*] slough, swamp.

quail verb *I quailed at the danger.* back away, blench, cower, cringe, falter, flinch, quake, recoil, show fear, shrink, tremble, wince.

quaint adjective *a quaint thatched cottage.* antiquated, antique, charming, curious, fanciful, fantastic, odd, old-fashioned, old-world, picturesque, [*informal*] twee, unusual, whimsical.

quake verb *The buildings quaked when the bomb went off.* convulse, heave, move, quaver, quiver, rock, shake, shiver, shudder, sway, tremble, vibrate, wobble.

qualification noun **1** *the proper qualifications for a job.* ability, certification, competence, eligibility, experience, fitness, [*informal*] know-how, knowledge, quality, skill, suitability, training.
2 *academic qualifications.* Bachelor's degree (*BA, BEd, BEng, BSc, LLB,* etc.), certificate, degree, diploma, doctorate, first degree, Master's degree (*MA, MEng, MPhil, MSc,* etc.), matriculation.
3 *I'd say without qualification that he's our best player.* condition, exception, limitation, proviso, reservation, restriction.

qualified adjective **1** *a qualified electrician.* certificated, chartered, competent, equipped, experienced, graduate, professional, skilled, trained.
OPPOSITES: SEE **amateur** adjective.
2 *qualified applicants for a job.* appropriate, eligible, suitable.
3 *qualified praise.* cautious, conditional, equivocal, guarded, half-hearted, limited, modified, reserved, restricted.
OPPOSITES: SEE **unconditional**.

qualify verb **1** *The driving test qualifies you to drive.* authorize, empower, entitle, equip, fit, permit, sanction.
2 *The first three runners qualify for the final.* become eligible, [*informal*] get through, pass.
3 *He qualified his praise with one criticism.* abate, lessen, limit, moderate, restrain, restrict, soften, temper, weaken.

quality noun **1** *top quality meat.* calibre, class, condition, excellence, grade, rank, sort, standard, value.
2 *She has many good qualities.* attribute, characteristic, feature, peculiarity, property, trait.

qualm noun SEE **anxiety**.

quandary noun *in a quandary.* confusion, SEE **dilemma**, perplexity, uncertainty.

quantify verb SEE **measure** verb.

quantity noun *a quantity of goods. a measurable quantity.* aggregate, amount, bulk, consignment, dosage, dose, expanse, extent, length, load, lot, magnitude, mass, SEE **measure** noun, measurement, number, part (*1 part of sugar to 2 parts of flour*), pinch (*a pinch of salt*), portion, proportion, quantum, sum, total, volume, weight.

An almost infinite number of words indicating *quantity* can be formed using suffixes *-ful* and *-load*: e.g., armful, barrowload, bucketful, busload, cupful, handful, lorryload, mouthful, plateful, pocketful, spadeful, spoonful.

UNITS OF MEASUREMENT: SEE **measure** noun.

---

quantum noun SEE **quantity**.

quarantine noun isolation, segregation.

quarrel noun *a quarrel between rivals.* altercation, argument, bickering, brawl, clash, conflict, confrontation, contention, controversy, difference, disagreement, discord, disharmony, dispute, dissension, division, feud, SEE **fight** noun, [*informal*] hassle, misunderstanding, row, [*informal*] ructions, rupture, [*informal*] scene, schism, [*informal*] slanging match, split, squabble, strife, [*informal*] tiff, vendetta, wrangle.

quarrel verb *Members of the rival teams often quarrel.* argue [*informal*] be at loggerheads, be at odds, bicker, clash, conflict, contend, [*informal*] cross swords, differ, disagree, dissent, fall out, SEE **fight** verb, haggle, have a quarrel [SEE **quarrel** noun], [*informal*] row, squabble, wrangle.
to quarrel with *I can't quarrel with your decision.* complain about, disagree with, dispute, fault, object to, SEE **oppose**, [*informal*] pick holes in, query, question, take exception to.

quarrelsome adjective *a quarrelsome customer.* aggressive, SEE **angry**, argumentative, bad-tempered, belligerent, cantankerous, contentious, cross, defiant, explosive, fractious, impatient, irascible, irritable, petulant, quick-tempered, [*informal*] stroppy, truculent.
OPPOSITES: SEE **peaceable**.

quarry noun **1** *a lion's quarry.* game, kill, prey, victim.
2 *a slate quarry.* excavation, mine, pit, working.

quarry verb *to quarry stone.* dig out, excavate, extract, mine.

quarter noun **1** *the commercial quarter of a city.* area, district, division, locality, neighbourhood, part, sector, vicinity, zone.
2 [*plural*] *soldiers' quarters.* SEE **accommodation**, barracks, billet, housing, living quarters, lodgings.

quarter verb *The troops were quartered in barracks.* accommodate, billet, board, house, lodge, [*informal*] put up, station.

quash verb **1** *to quash a court order.* SEE **abolish**.
2 *to quash a rebellion.* SEE **suppress**.

quatrain noun VERSE FORMS: SEE **verse**.

quaver verb **1** *I quavered when I heard him shout.* falter, quake, quiver, shake, shudder, tremble, waver.
2 *His voice quavered.* pulsate, vibrate.

quay noun *a quay where ships tie up.* berth, dock, harbour, jetty, landing-stage, pier, wharf.

queasy adjective bilious, SEE **ill**, nauseous, [*informal*] poorly, [*informal*] queer, sick, unwell.

queen noun ROYALTY: SEE **royal**.

queer adjective **1** *A queer thing happened.* aberrant, abnormal, anomalous, atypical bizarre, curious, eerie, [*informal*] fishy, SEE **funny**, inexplicable, irrational, mysterious, odd, off-beat, outlandish, peculiar, puzzling, quaint, remarkable, [*informal*] rum, singular, strange, unaccountable, uncanny, uncommon, unconventional, unexpected, unnatural, unorthodox, unusual, weird.
2 [*informal*] *a queer person.* [*informal*] cranky, deviant, eccentric, SEE **mad**, questionable, [*informal*] shady (*a shady customer*), [*informal*] shifty, suspect, suspicious.
3 *I felt queer after eating too much.* SEE **ill**.
4 [= *homosexual*] SEE **homosexual**.

quell verb *to quell a riot.* SEE **suppress**.

quench **1** *to quench a fire.* damp down, douse, extinguish, put out, smother, snuff out.
OPPOSITES: SEE **light** verb.
2 *to quench your thirst.* allay, cool, satisfy, slake.

querulous adjective SEE **irritable**.

query noun, verb SEE **question** noun, verb.

quest noun *a quest for treasure.* crusade, expedition, hunt, mission, search.

question noun **1** *Answer this question.* [*informal*] brainteaser, conundrum, demand, enquiry, inquiry, mystery, [*informal*] poser, problem, puzzle, query, riddle.
2 *There's some question about whether he can play.* argument, controversy, debate, dispute, doubt, misgiving, SEE **objection**, uncertainty.

question verb **1** *They questioned me about the accident.* ask, [*formal*] catechize, cross-examine, cross-question, debrief, examine, [*informal*] grill, interrogate, interview, probe, [*informal*] pump, quiz.
2 *He questioned the referee's decision.* argue over, be sceptical about, challenge, dispute, doubt, enquire about, impugn, inquire about, object to [SEE **object** verb], oppose, quarrel with, query.

questionable adjective *questionable evidence.* arguable, borderline, debatable, disputable, doubtful, dubious, [*informal*] iffy, moot (*a moot point*), suspect, uncertain, unclear, unprovable, unreliable.

questionnaire noun [*formal*] catechism, opinion poll, question sheet, quiz, survey, test.

queue noun *a queue of cars.* column, file, line, line-up, procession, row, string, tail-back.

queue verb *Please queue at the door.* form a queue [SEE **queue** noun], line up, wait in a queue.

quibble noun *a quibble about the wording of a statement.* SEE **objection**.

quibble verb *He quibbled about the price.* carp, cavil, equivocate, SEE **object** verb, [*informal*] split hairs.

quiche noun SEE **pie**.

quick adjective **1** *a quick pace. a quick journey.* breakneck, brisk, expeditious, express (*an express train*), fast, [*old-fashioned*] fleet, hasty, headlong, high-speed, hurried, [*informal*] nippy, precipitate, rapid, [*informal*] smart (*a smart pace*), [*informal*] spanking, speedy, swift.
2 *quick movements.* adroit, agile, animated, brisk, deft, dextrous, lively, nimble, sudden.
OPPOSITES: SEE **slow** adjective.
3 *a quick rest.* brief, fleeting, momentary, passing, perfunctory, short, short-lived, temporary, transitory.
OPPOSITES: SEE **long** adjective.
4 *a quick reply.* abrupt, early, immediate, instant, instantaneous, prompt, punctual, ready, unhesitating.
OPPOSITES: SEE **belated**.
5 *a quick pupil.* acute, alert, apt, astute, bright, clever, intelligent, perceptive, quick-witted, sharp, shrewd, smart.
OPPOSITES: SEE **stupid**.
6 [*old-fashioned*] *the quick and the dead.* SEE **alive**.

quicken verb **1** *Our speed quickened.* accelerate, hasten, hurry, go faster, speed up.
2 *The appearance of a new character quickened our interest.* SEE **arouse**.

quicksand noun SEE **quagmire**.

quicksilver noun mercury.

quick-tempered adjective SEE **quarrelsome.**

quiescent adjective SEE **dormant.**

quiet adjective **1** *a quiet engine.* inaudible, noiseless, silent, soundless.
OPPOSITES: SEE **audible.**
2 *quiet music.* hushed, low, pianissimo, soft.
OPPOSITES: SEE **loud.**
3 *a quiet person. a quiet member of a group.* reserved, retiring, taciturn, uncommunicative, unforthcoming.
OPPOSITES: SEE **talkative.**
4 *a quiet personality. a quiet mood.* composed, contemplative, contented, gentle, introverted, meditative, meek, mild, modest, peaceable, shy, thoughtful.
OPPOSITES: SEE **extroverted.**
5 *quiet weather.* calm, motionless, placid, restful, serene, still, tranquil, untroubled.
OPPOSITES: SEE **turbulent.**
6 *a quiet road. a quiet place for a holiday.* isolated, lonely, peaceful, private, secluded, sequestered, undisturbed, unfrequented.
OPPOSITES: SEE **busy.**

quieten verb **1** *Please quieten the baby!* calm, compose, hush, pacify, soothe, subdue, tranquillize.
2 *A silencer quietens the noise of the engine.* deaden, dull, muffle, mute, reduce the volume of, silence, soften, stifle, suppress, tone down.

quill noun feather, plume.

quilt noun SEE **bedclothes.**

The first syllable of words like *quinquereme, quintet,* and *quintuplet* is related to Latin *quinque=five.*

---

quintessence noun SEE **essence.**

quintuple adjective SEE **multiple.**

quintuple verb SEE **multiply.**

quip noun SEE **joke** noun.

quirk noun SEE **peculiarity.**

quisling noun SEE **traitor.**

quit verb **1** *to quit the house. It's time to quit.* abandon, decamp, depart, desert, forsake, go away, leave, walk out, withdraw.
2 *to quit your job.* abdicate, discontinue, drop, give up, [*informal*] pack it in, relinquish, renounce, repudiate, resign from.
3 [*informal*] *Quit pushing!* cease, leave off, stop.

quite adverb [Take care how you use *quite,* as the two senses are almost opposite.] **1** *Yes, I have quite finished.* absolutely, altogether, completely, entirely, perfectly, totally, utterly, wholly.
2 *It was quite good, but far from perfect.* comparatively, fairly, moderately, [*informal*] pretty, rather, relatively, somewhat.

quits adjective *to be quits with someone.* equal, even, level, repaid, revenged, square.

quiver verb *The leaves quivered in the breeze.* flicker, flutter, oscillate, palpitate, pulsate, quake, quaver, shake, shiver, shudder, tremble, vibrate, wobble.

quixotic adjective *a quixotic act of chivalry.* fanciful, SEE **idealistic.** impractical, unrealistic, unselfish, Utopian.
OPPOSITES: SEE **realistic.**

quiz noun competition, examination, questioning, questionnaire, test.

quiz verb SEE **question** verb.

quizzical adjective *a quizzical smile.* SEE **amused.**

quorum noun *a quorum for a meeting.* minimum number.

quota noun *a daily quota of food.* allocation, allowance, assignment, portion, proportion, ration, share.

quotation noun **1** *a quotation from a book.* [*informal*] citation, [*informal*] clip (*a clip from a TV programme*), cutting (*a cutting from a newspaper*), excerpt, extract, passage, piece, reference.
2 *The garage gave us a quotation for repairing the car.* estimate, likely price, tender.
quotation marks inverted commas, speech marks.

quote verb **1** *to quote what someone has said or written.* cite, instance, mention, produce a quotation from [SEE **quotation**], refer to, repeat, reproduce.
2 *The builder quoted a figure of £10,000 for our extension.* estimate, tender.

R

rabble noun *a noisy rabble.* crowd, gang, SEE **group** noun, herd, horde, mob, swarm, throng.

rabid adjective **1** *a rabid attack.* SEE **frenzied.**
2 *a rabid extremist.* SEE **fanatical.**

rabies noun SEE **illness.**

race noun **1** *a race of people.* clan, ethnic group, nation, people, tribe.
RELATED ADJECTIVES: ethnic, racial.
the study of race ethnology.
2 *the human race.* breed, genus, kind, species, variety.
3 *a running race.* chase, competition, contest, heat, rivalry.

COMPETITIVE RACES: cross-country, horse-race, hurdles, marathon, motor-race, regatta, relay race, road-race, rowing, scramble, speedway, sprint, steeple-chase, stock-car race, swimming, track race.
OTHER SPORTS: SEE **sport**.

---

race verb **1** *I'll race you.* compete with, contest with, have a race with, try to beat.
2 *I raced home because I was late.* career, dash, fly, gallop, hasten, hurry, move fast, run, rush, sprint, tear, zoom.

racecourse, racetrack nouns cinder-track, circuit, dog-track, lap.

racial adjective *racial characteristics.* ethnic, national, tribal.

racialism, racism nouns anti-Semitism, apartheid, bias, bigotry, chauvinism, discrimination, intolerance, prejudice, racial hatred, xenophobia.

racialist, racist adjectives *racist attitudes.* anti-Semitic, biased, bigoted, chauvinist, discriminatory, intolerant, prejudiced.

rack noun *a plate rack. a luggage rack.* frame, framework, shelf, stand, support.

rack verb SEE **torture** verb.
to rack your brains SEE **think**.

racket noun **1** *a tennis racket.* bat, club.
2 [*informal*] *a noisy racket.* SEE **commotion**.
3 [*informal*] *a money-making racket.* SEE **swindle** noun.

racketeer noun SEE **swindler**.

raconteur noun SEE **storyteller**.

racy adjective **1** *a racy style.* SEE **spirited**.
2 *racy jokes.* SEE **bawdy**.

radiant adjective **1** *a radiant light.* SEE **bright**.
2 *a radiant smile.* SEE **beautiful, happy**.

radiate verb *The fire radiates heat.* diffuse, emit, give off, glow, send out, shed, shine, spread, transmit.

radiator noun KINDS OF HEATING: SEE **fire** noun.

radical adjective **1** *a radical inquiry.* basic, drastic, fundamental, thorough.
OPPOSITES: SEE **superficial**.
2 *radical political views.* extreme, extremist, far-reaching, revolutionary, [*uncomplimentary*] subversive.
OPPOSITES: SEE **moderate** adjective.

radio noun receiver, set, [*informal*] transistor, transmitter, [*old-fashioned*] wireless.
OTHER MODES OF COMMUNICATION: SEE **communication**.

radiogram noun SEE **audio equipment**.

radiotherapy noun MEDICAL TREATMENTS: SEE **medicine**.

raffish adjective *a raffish appearance.* SEE **disreputable, tawdry**.

raffle noun KINDS OF GAMBLING: SEE **gamble**.

raft noun KINDS OF BOAT: SEE **vessel**.

rafter noun *rafters in the roof.* beam, girder, joist.

rag noun SEE **rags**.

rage noun SEE **anger** noun.

rage verb SEE **angry (be angry)**.

ragged adjective **1** *ragged clothes.* frayed, in ribbons, old, patched, patchy, rent, ripped, shabby, shaggy, tattered, tatty, threadbare, torn, unkempt, worn out.
2 *a ragged line.* disorganized, erratic, irregular, uneven.

ragout noun SEE **stew** noun.

rags noun [*plural*] bits and pieces, cloths, old clothes, remnants, scraps, shreds, tatters.

raid noun *a raid on an enemy.* assault, attack, blitz, foray, incursion, inroad, invasion, onslaught, sortie, strike, swoop.

raid verb **1** *Police raided the gang's hideaway.* attack, descend on, invade, make a raid on [SEE **raid** noun], pounce on, rush, storm, swoop on.
2 *We raided the larder.* loot, pillage, plunder, ransack, rob, steal from.

raider noun *Raiders swooped down from the mountains.* attacker, brigand, invader, looter, marauder, pillager, pirate, plunderer, ransacker, robber, rustler, thief.

rail noun bar, rod.

railing noun barrier, fence, paling.

raillery noun SEE **teasing**.

railway noun line, permanent way, [*American*] railroad, rails, track.

KINDS OF RAILWAY: branch line, cable railway, funicular, light railway, main line, metro, mineral line, monorail, mountain railway, narrow gauge, rack-and-pinion railway, rapid transit system, siding, standard gauge, tramway, tube, underground railway.

TRAINS AND ROLLING-STOCK: buffet-car, cable-car, carriage, coach, container wagon, diesel, dining-car, DMU, electric train, engine, express, freight train, goods train, goods van, goods wagon, guard's van, Inter-city, locomotive, shunter, sleeper, sleeping-car, steam-engine, steam-train, stopping train, tender, truck, tube-train, underground train, wagon.

PEOPLE WHO WORK ON THE RAILWAY: announcer, booking-clerk, crossing-keeper, driver, engineer, fireman, guard, plate-layer, porter, signalman, station manager, [*old-fashioned*] station-master, steward.

SOME OTHER RAILWAY TERMS: bogie, booking-office, buffer, compartment, corridor, coupling, cutting, footplate, gauge, halt, left-luggage office, level-crossing, luggage, trolley, marshalling yard, platform, points, sidings, signals, signal-box, sleepers, station, terminus, ticket-office, timetable, track, waiting-room.

---

raiment noun SEE **clothes.**

rain noun *Take a mac to keep the rain off.* cloudburst, deluge, downpour, drizzle, [*formal*] precipitation, raindrops, rainfall, rainstorm, shower, squall.

rain verb *It always seems to rain when we go on holiday.* bucket, drizzle, pelt, pour, [*informal*] rain cats and dogs, spit, teem.
METEOROLOGICAL TERMS: SEE **weather** noun.

rainfall noun *annual rainfall.* [*formal*] precipitation.

rainy adjective *a rainy day.* damp, drizzly, pouring, showery, wet.

raise verb **1** *to raise your hand. to raise your head.* hold up, lift, put up, rear.
2 *to raise something to a higher position.* elevate, heave up, hoist, jack up, lift, pick up.
3 *to raise prices. to raise the volume on a radio.* augment, boost, increase, inflate, put up, [*informal*] up.
OPPOSITES: SEE **lower.**
4 *to raise someone to a higher rank.* exalt, prefer, promote, upgrade.
OPPOSITES: SEE **demote.**
5 *to raise a monument.* build, construct, create, erect, set up.
6 *to raise someone's hopes.* activate, arouse, awaken, build up, cause, encourage, engender, enlarge, excite, foment, foster, heighten, incite, kindle, motivate, provoke, rouse, stimulate, uplift.
OPPOSITES: SEE **destroy.**
7 *to raise animals and crops. to raise a family.* breed, bring up, care for, cultivate, educate, grow, look after, nurture, produce, propagate, rear.
8 *to raise money for charity.* collect, get, make, receive.
9 *to raise questions.* advance, broach, instigate, introduce, moot, originate, pose, present, put forward, suggest.
to raise from the dead SEE **resurrect.**
to raise the alarm SEE **warn.**

rake noun **1** *a garden rake.* SEE **tool.**
2 *the rake of a stage.* SEE **slope** noun.
3 [=*immoral person*] SEE **immoral (immoral person).**

rally noun **1** *a political rally.* [*informal*] demo, demonstration, march, meeting, protest.
2 *a motor rally.* SEE **competition.**

rally verb **1** *to rally your supporters.* SEE **assemble.**
2 *to rally after an illness.* SEE **recover.**

ram noun SEE **sheep.**

ram verb *Our car rammed the one in front.* bump, collide with, crash into, SEE **hit** verb, smash into, strike.

ramble noun *a ramble in the country.* hike, SEE **walk** noun.

ramble verb **1** *to ramble in the hills.* hike, roam, rove, stroll, SEE **walk** verb.
2 *to ramble off the point.* digress, drift, maunder, wander.

rambling adjective **1** *a rambling route.* circuitous, indirect, labyrinthine, meandering, roundabout, tortuous, twisting, wandering, winding, zigzag.
OPPOSITES: SEE **direct** adjective.
2 *a rambling speech. a rambling speaker.* aimless, SEE **confused**, disconnected, discursive, disjointed, incoherent, unstructured, verbose, wordy.
OPPOSITES: SEE **coherent.**
3 *a rambling old farmhouse.* asymmetrical, extensive, large, sprawling, straggling.
OPPOSITES: SEE **compact** adjective.

ramification noun *I don't understand all the ramifications of your plan.* branch, complication, consequence, extension, implication, offshoot, result, upshot.

ramp noun SEE **slope** noun.

rampage verb *Hooligans rampaged through the town.* behave violently, go berserk, go wild, race about, run amok, run riot, rush about.

rampant adjective unchecked, unrestrained, wild.

rampart noun PARTS OF A CASTLE: SEE **castle**.

ramshackle adjective *a ramshackle old hut.* broken down, decrepit, dilapidated, rickety, ruined, shaky, tumbledown, unsafe.
OPPOSITES: SEE **solid**.

ranch noun SEE **farm** noun.

rancour noun SEE **animosity**.

random adjective *a random choice.* accidental, aimless, arbitrary, casual, chance, fortuitous, haphazard, indiscriminate, irregular, unconsidered, unplanned, unpremeditated.
OPPOSITES: SEE **deliberate** adjective.

randy adjective SEE **lustful**.

range noun **1** *a range of mountains.* chain, file, line, row, series, string.
2 *a wide range of goods. your range of knowledge.* area, compass, extent, field, gamut, limits, scope, selection, spectrum, variety.
3 *the range of a gun.* distance, limit, reach.
4 [*old-fashioned*] *a kitchen range.* SEE **stove**.

range verb **1** *His trophies were ranged on the shelf.* SEE **arrange**.
2 *Prices range from £10 to £15.* differ, extend, fluctuate, reach, vary.
3 *Sheep range over the hills.* roam, rove, stray, travel, wander.

rangy adjective SEE **thin** adjective.

rank adjective **1** *a rank growth of weeds.* SEE **abundant**.
2 *a rank smell of garbage.* SEE **smelling**.
3 *rank injustice.* SEE **complete** adjective.

rank noun **1** *Line up in single rank.* column, file, formation, line, order, row, series, tier.
2 *a high rank. a low rank.* caste, class, condition, degree, estate, grade, level, position, standing, station, status, title.

RANKS IN THE ARMED SERVICES [within each group, these are listed in descending order of seniority]:

AIR FORCE: Marshal of the RAF, Air Chief Marshal, Air Marshal, Air Vice-Marshal, air commodore, group captain, wing-commander, squadron leader, flight-lieutenant, flying officer, pilot officer; warrant officer, flight sergeant, chief technician, sergeant, corporal, junior technician, senior aircraftman, leading aircraftman, aircraftman.

ARMY: Field Marshal, general, lieutenant general, major general, brigadier, colonel, lieutenant colonel, major, captain, lieutenant, second lieutenant or subaltern; warrant officer, staff sergeant, sergeant, corporal, lance-corporal, private.

NAVY: Admiral of the Fleet, admiral, vice-admiral, rear-admiral, commodore, captain, commander, lieutenant commander, lieutenant, sub-lieutenant; chief petty officer, petty officer, leading rating, able rating, ordinary rating.

---

rankle verb SEE **annoy**.

ransack verb **1** *I ransacked the house looking for my purse.* comb, rummage through, scour, search, [*informal*] turn upside down.
2 *Rioters ransacked the shops.* loot, pillage, plunder, raid, ravage, rob, wreck.

ransom noun SEE **payment**.

rant verb WAYS OF TALKING: SEE **talk** verb.

rap verb *to rap on a door.* SEE **hit** verb, knock, strike, tap.

rapacious adjective SEE **greedy**.

rape noun assault, SEE **crime**, sexual attack.

rape verb [*applied to the action of a man*] *to rape a woman.* assault, defile, force yourself on, [*old-fashioned*] ravish, SEE **sex (have sexual intercourse)**.

rapid adjective *rapid progress.* breakneck, brisk, expeditious, express, fast, hasty, high-speed, headlong, hurried, [*informal*] nippy, precipitate, quick, smooth, speedy, swift, unchecked, uninterrupted.
OPPOSITES: SEE **slow** adjective.

rapids noun *swept along by the rapids.* cataract, current, waterfall, white water.

rapier noun SEE **sword**.

rapport noun SEE **harmony**.

rapscallion noun SEE **rascal**.

rapt adjective SEE **absorbed**.

rapture noun SEE **delight** noun.

rapturous SEE **happy**.

rare adjective **1** *a rare visitor. a rare example of something.* abnormal, curious, exceptional, infrequent, irreplaceable, occasional, odd, peculiar, scarce, singular, special, strange, surprising, uncommon, unusual.
OPPOSITES: SEE **common** adjective.
2 [*informal*] *We had a rare time.* SEE **good**.

rarefied adjective *a rarefied atmosphere.* thin.

raring adjective SEE **enthusiastic**.

rascal noun [*Rascal* and its synonyms are often used informally or jokingly.]

blackguard, SEE **criminal** noun, good-for-nothing, imp, knave, miscreant, ne'er-do-well, rapscallion, rogue, scallywag, scamp, scoundrel, trouble-maker, villain.

rascally adjective SEE **naughty**.

rash adjective *a rash decision.* careless, foolhardy, hare-brained, hasty, headstrong, heedless, hot-headed, hurried, ill-advised, ill-considered, impetuous, imprudent, impulsive, incautious, injudicious, precipitate, reckless, risky, thoughtless, unthinking.
OPPOSITES: SEE **careful**.

rash noun **1** *a rash on your skin.* eruption, spots.
2 [*informal*] *a rash of petty thefts.* SEE **outbreak**.

rasher noun *a rasher of bacon.* slice.

rasp noun file.

rasp verb *to rasp with a file.* SEE **scrape** verb.

rasping adjective *a rasping voice.* croaking, croaky, grating, gravelly, gruff, harsh, hoarse, husky, raucous, rough.

rat verb *to rat on a promise.* SEE **renege**.

rate noun **1** *We set out at a fast rate.* pace, speed, tempo, velocity.
2 *What's a reasonable rate for the job?* amount, charge, cost, fare, fee, figure, SEE **payment**, price, wage.

rate verb **1** *How do you rate our chance of winning?* appraise, assess, consider, estimate, evaluate, judge, measure, prize, put a price on, rank, regard, value, weigh.
2 *We rated him for his incompetence.* SEE **reprimand** verb.

rather adverb **1** *I was rather ill.* fairly, moderately, [*informal*] pretty, quite, relatively, slightly, somewhat.
2 *I'd rather have an apple than an orange.* preferably, sooner.

ratify verb *to ratify an agreement.* SEE **confirm**.

rating noun *Her performance would get a high rating from me.* SEE **class** noun, evaluation, grade, grading, mark, placing, ranking.

ratio noun *The ratio of boys to girls is about 50:50.* balance, correlation, fraction, percentage, proportion, relationship.

ration noun *You've had your ration of sweets!* allocation, allowance, helping, measure, portion, quota, share.
rations *The expedition carried rations to last a month.* food, necessaries, necessities, provisions, stores, supplies.

ration verb SEE *In time of war, the government may ration food supplies.* allocate, allot, apportion, conserve, control, distribute fairly, dole out, give out a ration [SEE **ration** noun], limit, restrict, share equally.

rational adjective *a rational discussion. a rational decision.* balanced, intelligent, judicious, logical, lucid, normal, reasonable, reasoned, sane, sensible, sound, thoughtful, wise.
OPPOSITES: SEE **irrational**.

rationale noun SEE **reason** noun.

rationalize verb **1** *I rationalized the silly arrangement of books in the library.* make rational [SEE **rational**], reorganize, [*informal*] sort out.
2 *I can't rationalize my absurd fear of insects.* be rational about [SEE **rational**], elucidate, explain, justify, think through.

rattle noun, verb VARIOUS SOUNDS: SEE **sound** noun.

ratty adjective SEE **angry**.

raucous adjective *raucous laughter.* harsh, grating, jarring, noisy, rough, shrill, strident.

ravage verb *The invaders ravaged the countryside.* damage, despoil, destroy, devastate, lay waste, loot, pillage, plunder, raid, ransack, ruin, sack, wreck.

rave verb **1** *The head raved about our bad behaviour.* be angry [SEE **angry**], fulminate, fume, rage, rant, roar, storm.
2 *The papers raved about her success.* be enthusiastic [SEE **enthusiastic**].

ravel verb SEE **tangle** verb.

ravenous adjective *The ravenous children ate everything on the table.* famished, gluttonous, greedy, hungry, insatiable, ravening, starved, starving, voracious.

ravine noun *a deep ravine.* SEE **valley**.

ravioli noun SEE **pasta**.

ravish verb **1** SEE **rape** verb.
2 *We were ravished by her beauty.* SEE **delight** verb.

ravishing adjective SEE **beautiful**.

raw adjective **1** *raw food.* fresh, rare (*rare steak*), uncooked, underdone, wet (*wet fish*).
OPPOSITE: cooked.
2 *raw materials.* crude, natural, unprocessed, unrefined, untreated.
OPPOSITE: processed.
3 *a raw place on your skin.* bloody, chafed, grazed, inflamed, painful, red, rough, scraped, scratched, sore, tender, vulnerable.
4 *a raw recruit.* ignorant, SEE **inexperienced**, innocent, new, untrained.

OPPOSITES: SEE **experienced**.
5 *a raw wind.* SEE **cold** adjective.

ray noun 1 *a ray of light.* bar, beam, laser, shaft, stream.
2 *a ray of hope.* gleam, glimmer, hint, indication, sign.

raze verb *Fire razed the building to the ground.* SEE **demolish**.

razor noun cut-throat razor, disposable razor, electric razor, safety razor.

reach noun *The shops are in easy reach.* compass, distance, range, scope.

reach verb 1 *I reached the end. We reached our target.* achieve, arrive at, attain, get to, go as far as, [*informal*] make.
2 *I can't reach the handle.* grasp, get hold of, take, touch.
3 *You can reach me by phone.* communicate with, contact, get in touch with.
to reach out *Reach out your hand.* extend, hold out, put out, raise, stick out, stretch.

The common English prefix *re-* comes from a Latin prefix meaning *again, back.*

---

react verb *How did she react when you asked for money?* act, answer, behave, reply, respond, retort.

reaction noun *a reaction to a question. a reaction to a stimulus.* answer, backlash, [*informal*] come-back, feedback, reflex, rejoinder, reply, response, retort, [*joking*] riposte.

reactionary adjective, noun SEE **conservative** adjective, noun.

read verb 1 *to read a story.* [*informal*] dip into, glance at, interpret, peruse, pore over, scan, skim, study.
2 *I can't read your handwriting.* decipher, decode, make out, understand.

readable adjective 1 *a readable story.* compulsive, enjoyable, entertaining, gripping, interesting, well-written.
OPPOSITES: SEE **boring**.
2 *readable handwriting.* clear, decipherable, legible, neat, plain, understandable.
OPPOSITES: SEE **illegible**.

readily adverb eagerly, easily, gladly, happily, voluntarily, willingly.

reading noun 1 *Take some reading for the train journey.* SEE **book** noun, **magazine**.
2 *What is your reading of her remarks?* SEE **interpretation**.

ready adjective 1 *Dinner is ready.* available, complete, convenient, done, finalized, finished, obtainable, prepared, set up, waiting.
OPPOSITE: unready.
2 *I'm ready to lend a hand.* disposed, eager, fit, [*informal*] game (*game for a laugh*), glad, inclined, keen, [*informal*] keyed up, liable, likely, minded, organized, pleased, poised, predisposed, primed, raring (*raring to go*), willing.
OPPOSITES: SEE **reluctant**.
3 *a ready reply. a ready wit.* acute, alert, facile, immediate, prompt, quick, quick-witted, rapid, sharp, smart, speedy.
OPPOSITES: SEE **slow** adjective.

real adjective 1 *real events. real people.* actual, certain, everyday, existing, factual, ordinary, palpable, SEE **realistic**, tangible, true, verifiable.
OPPOSITES: SEE **imaginary**.
2 *real wood. real gold.* authentic, genuine, natural, pure.
OPPOSITES: SEE **artificial**.
3 *a real work of art.* authenticated, bona fide, legitimate, unquestionable, valid.
OPPOSITES: SEE **imitation** adjective.
4 *a real friend.* dependable, positive, reliable, sound, trustworthy, worthy.
OPPOSITES: SEE **untrustworthy**.
5 *real grief.* heartfelt, honest, sincere, undoubted, unfeigned.
OPPOSITES: SEE **insincere**.

realism noun 1 *realism in a work of art.* authenticity, fidelity, truth to life, verisimilitude.
2 *realism in the way you deal with things.* clear-sightedness, common sense, objectivity, practicality, pragmatism.

realistic adjective 1 *a realistic portrait.* authentic, convincing, faithful, lifelike, natural, recognizable, representational, true to life, truthful.
2 *a realistic plan. a realistic assessment of the situation.* businesslike, clear-sighted, common-sense, down-to-earth, feasible, level-headed, logical, objective, possible, practicable, practical, pragmatic, rational, sensible, unemotional, viable, workable.
3 *realistic prices. realistic wages.* acceptable, adequate, fair, justifiable, moderate, reasonable.
OPPOSITES: SEE **unrealistic**.

reality noun *Stop day-dreaming and face reality.* actuality, certainty, fact, [*informal*] nitty-gritty, the real world [SEE **real**], truth, verity.
OPPOSITES: SEE **fantasy**.

realize verb 1 *I suddenly realized what you meant.* accept, appreciate, apprehend, be aware of, [*informal*] catch on to, comprehend, grasp, know, recognize, see, sense, [*informal*] twig, understand, [*informal*] wake up to.
2 *It'll take years to realize my ambition.* accomplish, achieve, complete, fulfil, implement, obtain, perform.

3 *My old car realized a good price.* [*informal*] bring in, [*informal*] clear, earn, fetch, make, net, obtain, produce.

realm noun SEE **country**, domain, empire, kingdom, monarchy.

reap verb 1 *to reap corn.* SEE **cut** verb, gather in, harvest, mow.
2 *to reap your reward.* collect, get, obtain, receive, win.

reappear verb SEE **return** verb.

reappraisal noun SEE **review** noun.

rear adjective *the rear legs of an animal.* back, end, hind, hinder, hindmost, last, rearmost.
OPPOSITES: SEE **front** adjective.

rear noun 1 *the rear of a train.* back, end, stern (*of a ship*), tail-end.
2 [*informal*] *Our dog nipped the intruder in the rear.* SEE **buttocks**.

rear verb 1 *Parents rear their families. Farmers rear cattle.* breed, bring up, care for, cultivate, feed, look after, nurture, produce, raise, train.
2 *The animal reared its head.* elevate, lift, raise.
3 *They reared a monument to the victims of the earthquake.* SEE **build**.

rearguard noun SEE **armed services**.
OPPOSITE: vanguard.

rearrange verb SEE **change** verb, regroup, reorganize, switch round, swop round, transpose.

rearrangement noun anagram [=*rearrangement of letters*], SEE **change** noun, reorganization, transposition.

reason noun 1 *He had a good reason for his behaviour.* apology, argument, case, cause, excuse, explanation, grounds, incentive, justification, motive, occasion, pretext, rationale, vindication.
2 *Show some reason!* brains, common sense, [*informal*] gumption, intelligence, judgement, mind, [*informal*] nous, rationality, SEE **reasoning**, understanding, wisdom, wit.
3 *She tried to make him see reason.* logic, reasonableness, sanity, sense.

reason verb 1 *I reasoned that it was cheaper to go by bus.* calculate, conclude, consider, deduce, infer, judge, resolve, think, work out.
2 *I reasoned with him, but I couldn't persuade him.* argue, debate, discuss, expostulate, intellectualize, remonstrate, use reason.

reasonable adjective 1 *a reasonable person. reasonable behaviour.* calm, honest, intelligent, rational, realistic, sane, sensible, sincere, sober, thoughtful, unemotional, wise.
OPPOSITES: SEE **irrational**.
2 *a reasonable argument.* believable, credible, defensible, justifiable, logical, plausible, practical, reasoned, sound, tenable, viable.
OPPOSITES: SEE **absurd**.
3 *a reasonable price.* acceptable, average, cheap, fair, inexpensive, moderate, ordinary, proper.
OPPOSITES: SEE **excessive**.

reasoning noun *I don't follow your reasoning.* analysis, argument, case, [*uncomplimentary*] casuistry, deduction, dialectic, hypothesis, line of thought, logic, proof, SEE **reason** noun, [*uncomplimentary*] sophistry, thinking.

reassemble verb SEE **return** verb.

reassure verb *to reassure someone who is worried.* assure, bolster (up), calm, comfort, encourage, give confidence to, hearten, support.
OPPOSITES: SEE **threaten**.

reassuring adjective *a reassuring smile. reassuring signs of success.* calming, caring, comforting, encouraging, favourable, hopeful, promising, supportive, sympathetic, understanding.
OPPOSITES: SEE **threatening**.

rebate noun SEE **refund** noun.

rebel adjective *rebel forces.* breakaway, insubordinate, insurgent, malcontent, mutinous, SEE **rebellious**, revolutionary.

rebel noun *a rebel against authority.* anarchist, apostate, dissenter, heretic, iconoclast, insurgent, malcontent, maverick, mutineer, nonconformist, revolutionary, schismatic.

rebel verb *to rebel against authority.* be a rebel [SEE **rebel** noun], disobey, dissent, fight, [*informal*] kick (against), [*informal*] kick over the traces, mutiny, refuse to obey, revolt, rise up, [*informal*] run riot, [*informal*] take a stand.
OPPOSITES: SEE **obey**.

rebellion noun *rebellion in the ranks.* disobedience, insubordination, insurgency, insurrection, mutiny, rebelliousness, resistance, revolt, revolution, rising, schism, sedition, uprising.

rebellious adjective *rebellious troops. a rebellious class of children.* [*informal*] bolshie, breakaway, defiant, difficult, disaffected, disloyal, disobedient, insubordinate, insurgent, intractable, malcontent, mutinous, quarrelsome, rebel, refractory, resistant, revolting, revolutionary, seditious, uncontrollable, ungovernable, unmanageable, unruly, wild.
OPPOSITES: SEE **obedient**.

rebirth noun SEE **renewal**.

rebound verb 1 *The dart rebounded off the wall.* SEE **bounce**, ricochet, spring back.
2 *His wily plan rebounded on him.* [*informal*] backfire, [*informal*] boomerang, misfire, recoil.

rebuff noun, verb SEE **snub** noun, verb.

rebuild noun *to rebuild a town.* build again, reconstruct, redevelop, regenerate.
2 *to rebuild an old car.* make good, overhaul, reassemble, recondition, recreate, refashion, remake, renew, renovate, repair, restore.

rebuke noun, verb SEE **reprimand** noun, verb.

rebut verb SEE **refute**.

recalcitrant adjective SEE **disobedient**.

recall verb 1 *The garage recalled the faulty cars.* bring back, call in, withdraw.
2 *Try to recall what happened.* SEE **remember**.

recant verb SEE **repudiate**.

recapitulate verb SEE **repeat**.

recapture verb SEE **retrieve**.

recede verb *The flood gradually receded.* decline, ebb, go back, regress, retire, retreat, return, shrink back, slacken, subside.

receipt noun *a receipt for goods bought.* account, acknowledgement, bill, proof of purchase, ticket.
receipts gains, gate (*at a football match*), income, proceeds, profits, takings.

receive verb 1 *to receive payment for something.* accept, acquire, be given, be sent, collect, earn, get, obtain, take.
OPPOSITES: SEE **give**.
2 *to receive an injury.* bear, experience, suffer, sustain, undergo.
OPPOSITES: SEE **inflict**.
3 *to receive visitors.* accommodate, entertain, greet, meet, welcome.

receiver noun *a radio receiver.* apparatus, radio, set, tuner, [*old-fashioned*] wireless.

recent adjective *recent events. recent innovations.* contemporary, current, fresh, modern, new, novel, present-day, up-to-date.
OPPOSITES: SEE **old**.

receptacle noun SEE **container**.

reception noun 1 *They gave us a friendly reception.* greeting, welcome.
2 *a wedding reception.* SEE **party**.

receptive adjective *receptive to new ideas.* amenable, favourable, interested, kindly disposed, open, open-minded, responsive, susceptible, sympathetic, welcoming.

recess noun 1 *a recess in a wall.* alcove, apse, bay, cavity, corner, hollow, indentation, niche, nook.
2 *a recess during a meeting.* adjournment, break, breathing-space, interlude, intermission, interval, respite, rest.

recession noun *an economic recession.* decline, depression, downturn, slump.

recherché adjective SEE **abstruse**.

recidivist noun SEE **criminal** noun.

recipe noun *a recipe for a cake.* directions, instructions, method, procedure.

recipient noun *the recipient of a gift or bequest.* beneficiary, legatee, receiver.
OPPOSITES: SEE **donor**.

reciprocal adjective *reciprocal affection.* corresponding, mutual, returned, shared.

reciprocate verb *Did she reciprocate his love?* exchange, give the same in return, match, requite, return.

recital noun 1 *a piano recital.* concert, performance, programme.
2 *a recital of events.* account, narration, narrative, SEE **recitation**, repetition, story, telling.

recitation noun *a recitation of a poem.* declaiming, delivery, narration, performance, [*old-fashioned*] rendition, speaking, telling.

recite verb *to recite a poem.* articulate, declaim, deliver, narrate, perform, recount, rehearse, relate, repeat, speak, tell.

reckless adjective 1 *reckless driving. reckless extravagance.* brash, careless, [*informal*] crazy, daredevil, foolhardy, [*informal*] harum-scarum, hasty, heedless, imprudent, impulsive, inattentive, incautious, irresponsible, [*informal*] mad, madcap, negligent, rash, thoughtless, unconsidered.
OPPOSITES: SEE **careful**.
2 *reckless criminals.* dangerous, desperate, violent, wild.

reckon verb 1 *I reckoned up how much she owed me.* add up, assess, calculate, compute, count, estimate, evaluate, figure out, gauge, number, total, work out.
2 [*informal*] *I reckon it's going to rain.* SEE **think**.

reckoning noun [*informal*] *The waiter gave me the reckoning.* addition, bill, score, sum, tally, total.

reclaim verb 1 *You can reclaim expenses after your interview.* get back, [*informal*] put in for, recover, regain.

2 *to reclaim derelict land.* make usable, regenerate, reinstate, restore, salvage, save.

recline verb *to recline on a sofa.* lean back, lie, loll, lounge, rest, sprawl, stretch out.

recluse noun *a recluse who never appears in public.* hermit, loner, solitary.

recognizable adjective *a recognizable figure.* distinctive, distinguishable, identifiable, known, undisguised, unmistakable.

recognize verb **1** *to recognize a person. to recognize a landmark.* discern, distinguish, identify, know, name, perceive, pick out, [*informal*] put a name to, recall, recollect, remember, see, spot.
2 *The doctor recognized the symptoms.* detect, diagnose, notice, perceive.
3 *I recognize my shortcomings.* accept, acknowledge, admit to, be aware of, concede, confess, grant, realize, understand.

recoil verb **1** *His wily plan recoiled on him.* SEE **rebound**.
2 *I recoiled when I saw blood.* blench, draw back, falter, flinch, jerk back, quail, shrink, wince.

recollect verb SEE **remember**.

recollection noun *I have no recollection of what happened.* SEE **memory**.

recommend verb **1** *The doctor recommends a complete rest.* advise, counsel, prescribe, propose, suggest, urge.
2 *The critics recommend this film.* advocate, applaud, approve of, commend, [*informal*] plug, praise, speak well of, vouch for.

recompose verb SEE **repay**.

reconcile verb *I managed to reconcile them after their quarrel.* bring together, conciliate, harmonize, placate, reunite.
to be reconciled to *I'm reconciled to doing without a holiday.* SEE **accept**.

recondite adjective SEE **obscure** adjective.

recondition verb SEE **rebuild**.

reconnaissance noun *The troops moved in after a reconnaissance of the area.* examination, exploration, inspection, investigation, observation, reconnoitring [SEE **reconnoitre**], spying, survey.

reconnoitre verb *The troops reconnoitred the area before moving in.* [*informal*] case, examine, explore, gather intelligence, inspect, investigate, patrol, scout, spy, survey.

reconsider verb SEE **review** verb.

reconstitute verb SEE **renew**.

reconstruct verb SEE **rebuild**.

record noun **1** *We kept a record of what we saw.* account, chronicle, diary, dossier, file, journal, log, minute (*minutes of a meeting*), narrative, note, register, report.
2 [*plural*] *historical records.* annals, archives, documents.
3 *a gramophone record.* album, disc, long-playing record, LP, SEE **recording**, single.
4 *Her time in the last race was a school record.* [*informal*] best, [*informal*] highest.

record verb **1** *I recorded what I saw in a notebook.* enter, inscribe, log, minute, note, put down, register, set down, write down.
2 *We recorded our performance on tape.* keep, preserve, tape, tape-record, video.

recorder noun *a tape recorder.* SEE **audio equipment**.

recording noun *Have you heard their latest recording?* performance, release.

KINDS OF RECORDING: audio-tape, cassette, compact disc, digital recording, mono recording, quadraphonic recording, SEE **record** noun, stereo recording, tape, tape-recording, tele-recording, video, video-cassette, video disc, videotape.

---

record-player noun SEE **audio equipment**.

recount verb *He recounted his adventures.* describe, detail, narrate, recite, relate, report, retail, tell.

recoup verb SEE **recover, refund** verb.

recover verb **1** *to recover after an illness.* come round, convalesce, get better, heal, improve, mend, [*informal*] pull round, [*informal*] pull through, rally, recuperate, revive.
2 *to recover something you have lost.* find, get back, make good, recapture, reclaim, recoup, regain, repossess, restore, retrieve, salvage, trace, track down.

recovery noun **1** *recovery from an illness.* convalescence, cure, healing, improvement, recuperation.
2 *the recovery of business after a recession.* revival, upturn.
3 *recovery of something you had lost.* recapture, reclamation, repossession, restoration, retrieval, salvaging.

recreate verb SEE **renew**.

recreation noun *We deserve some recreation after working hard.* amusement, diversion, enjoyment, entertainment,

fun, games, hobby, leisure, pastime, play, pleasure, relaxation.
recreation ground park, playground, playing-field.

recrimination noun *I don't want any recriminations if this goes wrong.* accusation, [*informal*] come-back, retaliation, retort.

recrudescence noun SEE **return** noun.

recruit noun *a recruit in the services. a new recruit to the firm.* apprentice, beginner, conscript, learner, [*informal*] new boy, [*informal*] new girl, new member, novice, tiro, trainee.
OPPOSITES: SEE **veteran** noun.

recruit verb *to recruit new staff.* advertise for, engage, enlist, enrol, mobilize, sign on, take on.

rectangle noun oblong.
VARIOUS SHAPES: SEE **shape** noun.

rectify verb SEE **correct** verb.

rector noun SEE **clergyman**.

recumbent adjective *a recumbent posture.* flat, horizontal, lying down, prone, reclining, supine.
OPPOSITES: SEE **upright**.

recuperate verb SEE **recover**.

recuperating adjective SEE **convalescent**.

recur verb *Go to the dentist if the pain recurs.* come again, persist, reappear, repeat, return.

recurrent adjective *a recurrent illness. recurrent problems.* chronic, SEE **continual**, cyclical, frequent, intermittent, periodic, persistent, recurring, regular, repeated.

recycle verb *to recycle waste.* reclaim, recover, retrieve, re-use, salvage, use again.

red adjective **1** *red in the face.* blushing, embarrassed, flaming, florid, flushed, glowing, inflamed, rosy, rubicund, ruddy.
2 *red eyes.* bloodshot.

VARIOUS SHADES OF RED: auburn, blood-red, brick-red, cardinal red, carmine, carroty, cerise, cherry, crimson, damask, flame-coloured, magenta, maroon, pink, rose, roseate, ruby, scarlet, vermilion, wine-coloured.
OTHER COLOURS: SEE **colour** noun.

---

red herring decoy, distraction, diversion, trick.

red-blooded adjective SEE **vigorous**.

redden verb *His face reddened with embarrassment.* blush, colour, flush, glow.

redecorate verb SEE **renew**.

redeem verb **1** *He redeemed his watch from the pawnbroker's.* buy back, reclaim, recover, re-purchase.
2 *I redeemed some Premium Bonds.* cash in, exchange for cash, trade in.
to redeem yourself *After playing badly for weeks, he redeemed himself by scoring a goal.* SEE **atone**.

redeemer noun SEE **saviour**.

re-deploy verb SEE **reorganize**.

redevelop verb SEE **rebuild, renew**.

red-hot adjective SEE **hot**.

redirect verb *to redirect a letter.* re-address, send on.

redo verb SEE **renew, repeat**.

redolent adjective **1** *redolent of onions.* SEE **smelling**.
2 *redolent of the past.* SEE **reminiscent**.

redouble verb SEE **intensify**.

redoubtable adjective *a redoubtable enemy.* SEE **formidable**.

redress verb SEE **correct** verb.

reduce verb **1** *to reduce the amount or intensity or effect of something.* commute (*to commute a prison sentence*), curtail, cut, cut back, decimate [see note under *decimate*], decrease, detract from, devalue, dilute, diminish, [*informal*] dock (*to dock someone's wages*), halve, impair, lessen, lower, make less, minimize, moderate, narrow, shorten, shrink, [*informal*] slash, slim down, trim, truncate, weaken, whittle.
2 *Our supplies gradually reduced.* become less, contract, dwindle, shrink.
OPPOSITES: SEE **increase** verb.
3 *to reduce liquid by boiling.* concentrate, condense, thicken.
OPPOSITES: SEE **dilute** verb.
4 *to reduce someone to a lower rank. to reduce someone to poverty.* degrade, demote, downgrade, humble, impoverish, move down, put down, ruin.
OPPOSITES: SEE **promote**.

reduction noun **1** *a reduction in amount or intensity or effect.* contraction, cutback, deceleration [= *reduction in speed*], decimation, decline, decrease, diminution, drop, impairment, lessening, limitation, loss, moderation, narrowing, remission, shortening, shrinkage, weakening.
2 *a reduction in price.* concession, cut, depreciation, devaluation, discount, rebate, refund.
OPPOSITES: SEE **increase** noun.

redundant adjective *redundant workers. Omit any redundant words in your essay.* excessive, superfluous, surplus, too many, unnecessary, unwanted.
OPPOSITES: SEE **necessary**.

reduplicate verb SEE **double** verb.

re-echo verb SEE **repeat**.

reek noun, verb SEE **smell** noun, verb.

reel noun *a reel of cotton.* bobbin, spool.

reel verb *I reeled after that knock on the head.* lurch, rock, roll, spin, stagger, stumble, sway, totter, whirl, wobble.

reeling adjective *My head was reeling.* SEE **dizzy**.

re-enter verb SEE **return** verb.

refectory noun cafeteria, dining-room.

refer verb **1** *I won't refer to your mistake.* allude to, cite, comment on, draw attention to, make reference to, mention, quote, speak of, touch on.
2 *They didn't have what I wanted, so they referred me to another shop.* direct, guide, recommend, send.
to refer to *If I can't spell a word, I refer to my dictionary.* consult, go to, look up, turn to.

referee noun adjudicator, arbitrator, judge, umpire.

reference noun **1** *Which book does this reference come from?* allusion, citation, example, illustration, instance, mention, quotation, remark.
2 *When you apply for jobs you need a reference.* recommendation, testimonial.

referendum noun SEE **poll** noun.

refill verb *Refill the tank.* refuel, renew, replenish, top up.

refine verb **1** *to refine raw materials.* clarify, distil, process, purify, treat.
2 *to refine your behaviour.* SEE **improve**.

refined adjective *refined tastes.* civilized, courteous, cultivated, cultured, delicate, dignified, discerning, discriminating, elegant, fastidious, genteel, gentlemanly, ladylike, nice, polished, polite, [*informal*] posh, [*uncomplimentary*] pretentious, [*uncomplimentary*] prissy, sophisticated, subtle, tasteful, [*informal*] upper crust, urbane, well-bred, well brought-up.
OPPOSITES: SEE **vulgar**.
2 *refined oil.* distilled, processed, purified, treated.
OPPOSITES: SEE **crude**.

refinement noun **1** *refinement of manners.* breeding, [*informal*] class (*She's got real class*), courtesy, cultivation, delicacy, discrimination, elegance, finesse, gentility, polish, [*uncomplimentary*] pretentiousness, sophistication, style, subtlety, taste, urbanity.
2 *They've made some refinements in the design of the new model.* alteration, change, improvement, modification.

refit verb SEE **renew**, **repair** verb.

reflect verb **1** *A mirror reflects your image. Cat's-eyes reflect headlights.* mirror, return, send back, shine back, throw back.
2 *Their success reflects their hard work.* bear witness to, correspond to, demonstrate, echo, exhibit, indicate, match, reveal, show.
to reflect on *to reflect on past events.* brood on, [*informal*] chew over, consider, contemplate, meditate on, ponder, remind yourself of, reminisce about, ruminate, talk over, think about.

reflection noun **1** *a reflection in a mirror.* image, likeness.
2 *Their success is a reflection of their hard work.* demonstration, echo, indication, manifestation, result.
3 *Your exam failure is no reflection on your intelligence.* censure, criticism, discredit, reproach, shame, slur.
4 *a quiet time for reflection.* contemplation, deliberation, meditation, pondering, rumination, study, thinking, thought.

reflective adjective **1** *reflective glass.* reflecting, SEE **shiny**.
2 *a reflective mood.* SEE **thoughtful**.

reflector noun Cat's-eyes, looking-glass, mirror, reflective glass, reflective patch.

reflex adjective *a reflex action.* SEE **involuntary**.

reform verb **1** *to reform your behaviour.* amend, become better, change, convert, correct, improve, make better, save.
2 *to reform a political system.* purge, reconstitute, regenerate, remodel, reorganize, revolutionize.

reformatory noun SEE **prison**.

refract verb *to refract light rays.* bend, distort.

refractory adjective SEE **stubborn**.

refrain noun *the refrain of a song.* chorus.

refrain verb **to refrain from** *Please refrain from smoking.* abstain from, avoid, desist from, do without, eschew, forbear, [*informal*] quit, stop.

refresh verb **1** *The drink refreshed us.* cool, freshen, invigorate, quench the thirst of, rejuvenate, renew, restore, revitalize, revive.

2 *Let me refresh your memory.* jog, remind, prod, prompt, stimulate.

refreshing adjective 1 *a refreshing drink. a refreshing shower.* bracing, cool, enlivening, invigorating, restorative, reviving, stimulating, thirst-quenching, tingling.
OPPOSITES: SEE **cloying, exhausting**.
2 *a refreshing change.* different, fresh, interesting, new, novel, original, unexpected, unfamiliar, unforeseen, unpredictable, welcome.
OPPOSITES: SEE **boring**.

refreshments noun drink, [*informal*] eats, food, snack.

refrigerate verb *to refrigerate food.* chill, cool, freeze, keep cold, SEE **preserve** verb.

refuel verb SEE **refill**.

refuge noun *The climbers found refuge from the blizzard.* asylum, [*informal*] bolt-hole, cover, haven, hideout, hiding-place, protection, retreat, safety, sanctuary, security, shelter.

refugee noun displaced person, exile, fugitive, outcast.

refund noun *If you are not satisfied, ask for a refund.* rebate, repayment.

refund verb *to refund expenses.* give back, pay back, recoup, reimburse, repay, return.

refurbish verb SEE **renew**.

refusal noun *Our request was met with a refusal.* [*informal*] brush-off, denial, negative reply, rebuff, rejection.
OPPOSITES: SEE **acceptance**.

refuse noun *Throw away the refuse.* SEE **rubbish**.

refuse verb 1 *to refuse an invitation.* baulk at, decline, give a negative reply to, [*informal*] jib at, reject, say no to, spurn, turn down.
OPPOSITES: SEE **accept**.
2 *to refuse someone their rights.* deny, deprive of, withhold.
OPPOSITES: SEE **grant** verb.

refute verb *to refute an argument.* counter, discredit, disprove, negate, prove wrong, rebut.

regain verb *to regain something you've lost.* be reunited with, find, get back, recapture, reclaim, recoup, recover, repossess, retake, retrieve, return to, win back.

Regal, regalia, regicide, and a number of similar words are related to Latin *rex* = *king* and *regina* = *queen.*

---

regal adjective *a regal figure.* kingly, majestic, noble, princely, queenly, royal, SEE **splendid**, stately.

regale verb SEE **entertain**.

regalia noun SEE **emblem**.

regard noun 1 *I quailed under his stern regard.* gaze, look, scrutiny, stare.
2 *Give due regard to the warnings.* attention, care, concern, consideration, deference, heed, notice, respect, thought.
3 *I have a high regard for her ability.* admiration, affection, esteem, honour, love, respect.

regard verb 1 *to regard something closely.* contemplate, eye, gaze at, look at, observe, scrutinize, stare at, view, watch.
2 *We regard her as our best swimmer.* account, consider, deem, esteem, judge, reckon, respect, think, value.

regardful adjective *under his regardful gaze.* SEE **attentive**.

regarding preposition about, concerning, connected with, involving, on the subject of, with reference to, with regard to.

regardless adjective *regardless of danger.* careless (about), heedless, indifferent (to), neglectful, uncaring (about), unconcerned (about), unmindful.

regenerate verb SEE **renew**.

regent noun VARIOUS RULERS: SEE **ruler**.

regime noun SEE **government, system**.

regiment noun SEE **armed services**.

regiment verb SEE **organize**.

regimented adjective SEE **organized**.

region noun *The Arctic is a cold region.* area, SEE **country**, district, expanse, land, locality, neighbourhood, place, province, quarter, territory, tract, vicinity, zone.

register noun *a register of names and addresses.* catalogue, directory, file, index, ledger, list, record, roll.

register verb 1 *to register as a voter. to register as a member of a club.* enlist, enrol, enter your name, join, sign on.
2 *to register a complaint.* make official, present, record, set down, write down.
3 *Did you register what she was wearing?* keep in mind, make a note of, mark, notice, take account of.
4 *His face registered pleasure.* express, indicate, reveal, show.

registrar noun VARIOUS OFFICIALS: SEE **official** noun.

regress verb *Business tends to regress during a holiday.* backslide, degenerate, deteriorate, fall back, go back, move backwards, retreat, retrogress, revert, slip back.
OPPOSITES: SEE **progress** verb.

regressive adjective SEE **backward**.

regret noun **1** *regret for doing wrong.* compunction, contrition, guilt, penitence, pricking of conscience, remorse, repentance, self-accusation, shame.
2 *regret about someone's loss.* grief, sadness, sorrow, sympathy.

regret verb **1** *I regret that I lost my temper.* be regretful [SEE **regretful**], feel regret [SEE **regret** noun], repent, reproach yourself.
2 *I deeply regret the death of your friend.* be sad about, feel regret about [SEE **regret** noun], grieve over, lament, mourn.

regretful adjective *a regretful smile.* apologetic, ashamed, conscience-stricken, contrite, disappointed, penitent, remorseful, repentant, SEE **sad**, sorry.
OPPOSITES: SEE **happy, unrepentant**.

regrettable adjective *a regrettable accident.* deplorable, disappointing, distressing, lamentable, reprehensible, sad, shameful, undesirable, unfortunate, unhappy, unlucky, unwanted.

regroup verb SEE **rearrange**.

regular adjective **1** *regular intervals. a regular pattern.* consistent, constant, daily, equal, even, fixed, hourly, measured, monthly, ordered, predictable, recurring, repeated, rhythmic, steady, symmetrical, systematic, uniform, unvarying, weekly, yearly.
2 *the regular procedure. our regular postman.* accustomed, common, commonplace, conventional, customary, established, everyday, familiar, frequent, habitual, known, normal, official, ordinary, orthodox, prevailing, proper, routine, scheduled, standard, traditional, typical, usual.
3 *a regular supporter.* dependable, faithful, reliable.
OPPOSITES: SEE **irregular**.

regular noun *She's one of the regulars here.* [*informal*] faithful, frequenter, habitué, regular customer [SEE **regular** adjective], patron.

regularize verb SEE **legalize**.

regulate verb **1** *to regulate the traffic.* control, direct, govern, manage, order, organize, restrict, supervise.
2 *to regulate the temperature.* adjust, alter, change, get right, moderate, vary.

regulation noun *Obey the regulations.* by-law, commandment, decree, directive, edict, law, order, requirement, restriction, rule, statute.

regurgitate verb **1** *to regurgitate food.* SEE **vomit**.
2 [*informal*] *to regurgitate what you have learned.* SEE **repeat**.

rehabilitate verb SEE **reinstate**.

rehash verb SEE **revise**.

rehearsal noun *a rehearsal for a play.* practice, preparation, [*informal*] run-through, [*informal*] try-out.
THEATRICAL TERMS: SEE **theatre**.

rehearse verb *to rehearse a play.* go over, practise, prepare, [*informal*] run over (*Just run over the last scene*), try out.

rehearsed adjective *I'm sure his remarks were rehearsed, not impromptu.* calculated, practised, pre-arranged, premeditated, prepared, thought out.
OPPOSITES: SEE **impromptu**.

reign verb *Which British monarch reigned the longest?* be king, be queen, be on the throne, govern, have power, rule.

rein verb SEE **check** verb.

reincarnation noun *the reincarnation of souls.* rebirth, return to life, [*formal*] transmigration.

reinforce verb **1** *to reinforce a wall.* back up, bolster, buttress, fortify, give strength to, hold up, prop up, stiffen, strengthen, support, toughen.
2 *to reinforce an army.* add to, assist, help, increase the size of, provide reinforcements for, supplement.

reinforcements noun additional troops, auxiliaries, back-up, help, reserves, support.

reinstate verb *The firm reinstated the man who was wrongly dismissed.* recall, rehabilitate, restore, take back, welcome back.
OPPOSITES: SEE **dismiss**.

reject verb **1** *Good shops reject sub-standard goods.* discard, eliminate, exclude, jettison, scrap, send back, throw away, throw out.
2 *It's not nice to reject your friends.* dismiss, disown, [*informal*] drop, jilt, rebuff, renounce, repel, repudiate, repulse, spurn.
3 *to reject an invitation.* decline, refuse, say no to, turn down, veto.
OPPOSITES: SEE **accept**.

rejoice verb *Everyone rejoiced in their team's success.* be happy [SEE **happy**], celebrate, delight, exult, glory, revel, triumph.
OPPOSITES: SEE **grieve**.

rejoin verb SEE **answer** verb.

rejoinder noun SEE **answer** noun.

rejuvenate verb SEE **renew**.

relapse noun *After making some progress, he suffered a relapse.* deterioration, recurrence, set-back.

relapse verb *to relapse after making progress.* degenerate, deteriorate, fall back, have a relapse, regress, revert, slip back, weaken.

relate verb **1** *to relate your adventures.* describe, detail, narrate, recite, recount, rehearse, report, tell.
2 *The police related the two crimes.* associate, compare, connect, consider together, join, link.
3 *I saw a TV programme which related to a book I'd just read.* be relevant [SEE **relevant**], concern, pertain, refer.
4 *The team members relate well to each other.* be friends, fraternize, have a relationship [SEE **relationship**], socialize.

related adjective *related crimes. related businesses. related facts.* affiliated, akin, allied, associated, cognate, comparable, connected, interconnected, joined, linked, parallel, SEE **relative** adjective, similar.
OPPOSITES: SEE **separate** adjective.
FAMILY RELATIONSHIPS: SEE **family**.

relation noun **1** *the relation between two people or things.* SEE **relationship**.
2 *All our relations came to the wedding.* SEE **relative** noun.
3 *the relation of a story.* SEE **narration**.

relationship **1** *the relationship between two people or things.* affinity, association, bond, connection, [*formal*] consanguinity, contrast, correlation, correspondence, kinship, link, parallel, ratio (= *relationship of one number to another*), similarity, tie.
2 *The twins have a close relationship.* attachment, closeness, SEE **friendship**, rapport, understanding.
3 [*informal*] *a sexual relationship.* affair, [*informal*] intrigue, [*informal*] liaison, love affair, romance, sexual relations.
FAMILY RELATIONSHIPS: SEE **family**.

relative adjective **1** *I've had relative good luck recently.* comparative.
2 *The police gathered evidence relative to the crime.* allied, appropriate, associated, cognate, connected, germane, pertinent, related, relevant.
OPPOSITES: SEE **unrelated**.

relative noun *All our relatives came to the wedding.* [*old-fashioned*] kinsman, [*old-fashioned*] kinswoman, [*plural*] kith and kin, member of the family, relation.
FAMILY RELATIONSHIPS: SEE **family**.

relax verb **1** *to relax your grip. to relax the pressure on something.* diminish, ease off, lessen, loosen, moderate, reduce, release, relieve, slacken, soften, unclench, unfasten, weaken.
OPPOSITES: SEE **increase, tighten**.
2 *to relax in front of the TV.* be easy, be relaxed [SEE **relaxed**], feel at home, rest, unbend, unwind.

relaxation noun informality, loosening up, SEE **recreation**, relaxing, rest, unwinding.
OPPOSITES: SEE **tension**.

relaxed adjective *a relaxed atmosphere. a relaxed conversation.* calm, carefree, casual, comfortable, contented, cosy, easygoing, friendly, good-humoured, happy, informal, [*informal*] laid-back, leisurely, light-hearted, nonchalant, reassuring, restful, serene, [*uncomplimentary*] SEE **slack** adjective, tranquil, unconcerned, unhurried, untroubled.
OPPOSITES: SEE **tense** adjective.

relay noun **1** *working in relays.* shift, turn.
2 *a live relay on TV.* broadcast, programme, transmission.
relay race VARIOUS RACES: SEE **race** noun.

relay verb *to relay information.* broadcast, communicate, pass on, send out, spread, transmit, televise.

release verb **1** *to release prisoners.* acquit, allow out, deliver, discharge, dismiss, emancipate, excuse, exonerate, free, let go, let loose, liberate, loose, pardon, rescue, save, set free, set loose, unleash, SEE **unfasten**, untie.
OPPOSITES: SEE **detain**.
2 *to release a missile.* fire off, launch, let fly, let off, send off.
3 *to release information.* circulate, disseminate, distribute, issue, make available, publish, send out.

relegate verb SEE **demote**.

relent verb *He was cross at first, but later he relented.* become more lenient, give in, show pity, soften, weaken, yield.

relentless adjective *a relentless attack. relentless nagging.* SEE **continual**, cruel, fierce, hard-hearted, implacable, incessant, inexorable, merciless, pitiless, remorseless, ruthless, unceasing, uncompromising, unfeeling, unforgiving, unmerciful, unrelieved, unremitting.
OPPOSITES: SEE **temporary**.

relevant adjective *Don't interrupt unless you have something relevant to say.* appertaining, applicable, apposite, appropriate, apropos, apt, connected, essential,

fitting, germane, linked, material, pertinent, related, relative, significant, suitable, to the point.
OPPOSITES: SEE **irrelevant**.

reliable adjective *reliable information. a reliable friend. a reliable car.* certain, consistent, constant, dependable, devoted, efficient, faithful, loyal, predictable, proven, regular, responsible, safe, solid, sound, stable, staunch, steady, sure, trustworthy, unchanging, unfailing.
OPPOSITES: SEE **unreliable**.

reliance noun *Don't put too much reliance on patent medicines.* confidence, dependence, faith, trust.

relic noun *a relic from the past.* memento, reminder, remnant, souvenir, survival, token, vestige.

relief noun *The pills gave some relief from the pain.* abatement, aid, alleviation, assistance, comfort, cure, diversion, ease, easement, help, [*informal*] let-up, mitigation, palliation, relaxation, release, remission, respite, rest.

relieve verb *to relieve pain. to relieve pressure on something.* alleviate, anaesthetize, assuage, bring relief [SEE **relief**], calm, comfort, console, cure, diminish, dull, ease, SEE **help** verb, lessen, lighten, make less, mitigate, moderate, palliate, reduce, relax, soothe.
OPPOSITES: SEE **intensify**.
to relieve your feelings [*informal*] let go, [*informal*] let off steam, show your feelings.

religion noun **1** *the religions of the world.* creed, cult, denomination, faith, sect.
2 *An evangelist preaches religion.* belief, doctrine, dogma, theology.
COMPARE: agnosticism, atheism, humanism.

SOME PRINCIPAL WORLD RELIGIONS: Buddhism, Christianity, Hinduism, Islam, Judaism, Sikhism, Taoism, Zen.
CHRISTIAN DENOMINATIONS: SEE **denomination**.
OTHER RELATED WORDS: SEE **church, clergyman, worship**.

---

religious adjective **1** *a religious service. religious writings.* devotional, divine, holy, sacramental, sacred, scriptural, theological.
OPPOSITES: SEE **secular**.
2 *a religious person.* committed, dedicated, devout, God-fearing, godly, pious, reverent, [*uncomplimentary*] religiose, righteous, [*uncomplimentary*] sanctimonious, spiritual.
OPPOSITES: SEE **irreligious**.
3 *a religious dispute. religious wars.* bigoted, doctrinal, fanatical, sectarian, schismatic.

relinquish verb SEE **surrender**.

relish noun **1** *We tucked into the food with relish.* appetite, delight, enjoyment, enthusiasm, gusto, zest.
2 *Spices add relish to a dish.* flavour, piquancy, savour, tang, taste.

relish verb *She relishes a challenge.* appreciate, delight in, enjoy, like, love, revel in.

relocate verb *They've relocated our bus-stop.* move, reposition.

reluctant adjective *I was reluctant to pay what they demanded.* disinclined, grudging, hesitant, loath, unenthusiastic, SEE **unwilling**.
OPPOSITES: SEE **eager**.

rely verb *You can rely on me to do my best.* [*informal*] bank on, count on, depend on, have confidence in, trust.

remain verb *Only half the audience remained at the end of the concert.* be left, carry on, continue, endure, keep on, linger, live on, persist, stay, survive.

remainder noun *Use what you can now, and keep the remainder for later.* balance, excess, extra, SEE **remains**, remnant, residue, rest, surplus.

remaining adjective abiding, continuing, left over, persisting, residual, surviving, unused.

remains noun **1** *the remains of something that has been used, damaged, or destroyed.* crumbs, debris, dregs, fragments, [*informal*] left-overs, [*informal*] odds and ends, SEE **remainder**, remnants, residue, rubble, ruins, scraps, traces, vestiges, wreckage.
2 *historic remains.* heritage, relics.
3 *the remains of a dead animal.* ashes, body, carcass, corpse.

remake verb SEE **renew**.

remand verb LEGAL TERMS: SEE **law**.

remark noun *The judge made a few remarks about our performance.* comment, mention, observation, opinion, reflection, statement, thought, utterance, word.

remark verb **1** *He remarked that it was a nice day.* comment, declare, mention, note, observe, reflect, say, state.
2 *Did you remark anything unusual?* heed, mark, notice, observe, perceive, see.

remarkable adjective *a remarkable achievement.* amazing, conspicuous, distinguished, exceptional, extraordinary,

important, impressive, notable, noteworthy, out of the ordinary, outstanding, phenomenal, prominent, singular, special, strange, striking, surprising, [*informal*] terrific, [*informal*] tremendous, uncommon, unusual, wonderful.
OPPOSITES: SEE **ordinary**.

remedy noun *a remedy for a cold. a remedy for a problem.* [*informal*] answer, antidote, corrective, cure, elixir, medicine, nostrum, palliative, panacea [=*a cure for everything*], prescription, relief, restorative, solution, therapy, treatment.

remedy verb *I remedied the fault in the car.* alleviate, correct, counteract, cure, [*informal*] fix, heal, help, mend, mitigate, palliate, put right, rectify, redress, relieve, repair, solve, treat.

remember verb **1** *Do you remember Uncle George?* have a memory of, have in mind, recall, recognize, recollect, summon up.
2 *Remember what I say!* keep in mind, learn, memorize, retain.
OPPOSITES: SEE **forget**.
3 *We sat for hours remembering old times.* be nostalgic about, hark back to, recall, reminisce about, review, tell stories about, think back to.
4 *They always go out for a meal to remember their anniversary.* celebrate, commemorate, observe.

remind verb *Remind me to buy potatoes.* give a reminder to [SEE **reminder**], jog the memory, prompt.

reminder noun **1** *a reminder of what you have to do or say.* aide-mémoire, cue, hint, [*informal*] memo, [*formal*] memorandum, mnemonic, nudge, prompt, [*informal*] shopping list.
2 *a reminder of the past.* memento, relic, souvenir.

reminisce verb *to reminisce about the past.* be nostalgic, hark back, recall, remember, review, tell stories, think back.

reminiscence noun *reminiscences of childhood.* account, anecdote, memoir, memory, recollection, remembrance.

reminiscent adjective *scenes reminiscent of the past.* evocative, nostalgic, recalling, redolent, suggestive.

remiss adjective SEE **negligent**.

remission noun SEE **reduction**.

remit verb **1** *to remit a debt.* SEE **cancel**.
2 *to remit money in the post.* SEE **send**.

remittance noun SEE **money**.

remnants noun SEE **remains**.

remodel verb SEE **renew**.

remonstrate verb SEE **protest** verb.

remorse noun *remorse for wrongdoing.* compunction, contrition, grief, guilt, penitence, pricking of conscience, regret, repentance, sadness, self-accusation, shame, sorrow.

remorseful adjective SEE **repentant**.

remorseless adjective SEE **relentless**.

remote adjective **1** *a remote corner of the world.* alien, cut off, desolate, distant, faraway, foreign, godforsaken, hard to find, inaccessible, isolated, lonely, out of reach, outlying, out of the way, secluded, solitary, unfamiliar, unfrequented, [*informal*] unget-at-able, unreachable.
OPPOSITES: SEE **accessible**.
2 *a remote chance of winning.* doubtful, implausible, improbable, negligible, outside, poor, slender, slight, small, unlikely.
OPPOSITES: SEE **likely**.
3 *a remote manner.* aloof, cold, cool, detached, haughty, preoccupied, reserved, standoffish, uninvolved, withdrawn.
OPPOSITES: SEE **friendly**.

removable adjective detachable, separable.
OPPOSITES: SEE **integral**.

removal noun **1** *the removal of furniture from a house.* relocation, taking away, transfer, transportation.
2 *the removal of a tooth.* drawing, extraction, taking out, withdrawal.
3 *the removal of someone from a job or position.* dismissal, displacement, ejection, elimination, eradication, exile, expulsion, ousting, purge, purging.

remove verb **1** *to remove unwanted people or things.* abolish, abstract, amputate (*amputate a limb*), clear away, cut out, delete, depose (*depose a monarch*), detach, disconnect, dismiss, dispense with, displace, eject, eliminate, eradicate, erase, evict (*evict a tenant*), excise, exile, expel, expunge, [*informal*] get rid of, [*informal*] kick out, kill, oust, purge, root out, rub out, send away, separate, strike out (*strike out words in a document*), take out, throw out, turn out, uproot, wash off, wipe (*wipe a recording from a tape*), wipe out.
2 *to remove furniture.* carry away, convey, move, take away, transfer, transport.
3 *to remove a tooth.* draw out, extract, pull out, take out.
4 *to remove clothes.* doff (*to doff a hat*), peel off, strip off, take off.

remunerate verb SEE **pay** verb.

remunerative adjective SEE **profitable**.

renaissance noun SEE **renewal**.

rend verb SEE **tear** verb.

render verb 1 *to render someone a service.* SEE **give**.
2 *to render a song.* SEE **perform**.
3 *to render someone speechless.* SEE **make**.

rendezvous noun *a secret rendezvous.* appointment, assignation, date, engagement, meeting, meeting-place.

rendition noun SEE **performance**.

renegade noun *Faithful supporters were bitter about the renegades.* apostate, backslider, defector, deserter, fugitive, mutineer, outlaw, rebel, runaway, traitor, turncoat.

renege verb **to renege on** *to renege on an agreement.* break, fail to keep, go back on, [*informal*] rat on, repudiate, [*informal*] welsh on (*to welsh on a bet*).

renew verb VARIOUS WAYS TO RENEW OLD THINGS: bring up to date, [*informal*] do up, [*informal*] give a face-lift to, improve, mend, modernize, overhaul, recondition, reconstitute, recreate, redecorate, redesign, redevelop, redo, refit, refresh (*refresh the paintwork*), refurbish, regenerate, reintroduce, rejuvenate, remake, remodel, renovate, repaint, repair, replace, replenish, restore, resume, revamp, revitalize, revive, touch up, transform, update.

renewal noun 1 *the renewal of life in the spring.* reawakening, rebirth, regeneration, renaissance, resumption, resurgence, resurrection, return, revival.
2 *renewal of the paintwork.* SEE **renovation**.
3 *renewal of your passport.* replacement, revalidation, updating.

renounce verb 1 *to renounce violence.* abandon, abjure, declare your opposition to, discard, disown, forsake, forswear, reject, repudiate, spurn.
2 *to renounce the throne.* abdicate, give up, quit, relinquish, resign.

renovation noun *the renovation of an old building.* improvement, modernization, overhaul, reconditioning, redevelopment, refit, refurbishment, renewal, repair, restoration, transformation, updating.

renovate verb SEE **renew**.

renown noun SEE **fame**.

renowned adjective SEE **famous**.

rent noun 1 *I forgot to pay the rent for the TV.* fee, hire, instalment, regular payment, rental.
2 *a rent in my jeans.* SEE **tear** noun.

rent verb *We rented a caravan for our holiday.* charter, hire, lease, let.

rental noun SEE **rent** noun.

reorganize verb *to reorganize a business. to reorganize your time.* rearrange, redeploy, reshuffle, restructure.

repair verb 1 *to repair a damaged car.* [*informal*] fix, mend, overhaul, patch up, put right, rectify, refit, SEE **renew**, service.
2 *to repair clothes.* darn, patch, sew up.

reparation noun **to make reparation** SEE **compensate**.

repartee noun SEE **wit**.

repast noun SEE **meal**.

repatriate verb SEE **return** verb.

repay verb 1 *They repaid my expenses.* compensate, pay back, recompense, refund, reimburse, remunerate, settle.
2 [*uncomplimentary*] *She repaid his insult with interest.* avenge, get even with, [*informal*] get your own back for, reciprocate, requite, retaliate, return, revenge.

repeal verb SEE **cancel**.

repeat verb *to repeat an action or an event or a saying.* do again, duplicate, echo, quote, recapitulate, redo, re-echo, regurgitate, rehearse, reiterate, replay, reproduce, re-run, restate, retell, say again, show again.

repeated adjective SEE **recurrent**.

repel verb 1 *to repel an attack.* check, drive away, fend off, fight off, hold off, parry, push away, rebuff, repulse, ward off.
2 *This oily material repels water.* be impermeable to, exclude, keep out, reject, resist.
OPPOSITES: SEE **attract**.
3 *Her callous attitude repels me.* be repellent to [SEE **repellent**], disgust, nauseate, offend, [*informal*] put off (*Her attitude puts me off*), revolt, sicken, [*informal*] turn off (*Her attitude turns me off*).
OPPOSITES: SEE **delight** verb.

repellent adjective 1 *Tents are made of material which is repellent to water.* impermeable, impervious, resistant, unsusceptible.
2 *a repellent smell.* SEE **repulsive**.

repent verb *to repent your sins.* be repentant about [SEE **repentant**], feel repentance for [SEE **repentance**], regret, reproach yourself for.

repentance noun contrition, guilt, penitence, regret, remorse, self-accusation, self-reproach, sorrow.

repentant adjective *He was repentant when he saw what he'd done.* apologetic, ashamed, conscience-stricken, contrite,

grief-stricken, guilt-ridden, guilty, penitent, regretful, remorseful, sorry.
OPPOSITES: SEE **unrepentant**.

repercussion noun SEE **result** noun.

repertoire, repertory nouns *He has a vast repertoire of stories.* collection, reserve, stock, supply.

repetitive adjective *a repetitive job. a repetitive story.* boring, monotonous, recurrent, repeating, repetitious, tautological, tedious, unchanging, unvaried.

rephrase verb SEE **revise**.

replace verb **1** *Replace the books on the shelf.* put back, reinstate, restore, return.
2 *Who will replace the present prime minister?* be a substitute for, come after, follow, oust, succeed, supersede, supplant, take over from, take the place of.
3 *It's time we replaced those tyres.* change, provide a substitute for, renew.

replacement noun *a replacement for the regular teacher.* [*informal*] fill-in, proxy, stand-in, substitute, successor, understudy [= *replacement for an actor*].

replay verb SEE **repeat**.

replenish verb SEE **refill**.

replete adjective SEE **full**.

replica noun *a replica of a lunar-module. a replica of a document.* clone, copy, duplicate, facsimile, imitation, model, reconstruction, reproduction.

reply noun *a reply to a letter or a question.* acknowledgement, answer, [*informal*] come-back, reaction, rejoinder, response, retort, [*joking*] riposte.

reply verb **to reply to** *to reply to a letter or a question.* acknowledge, answer, counter, give a reply to [SEE **reply** noun], react to, respond to.

report noun **1** *a report in a newspaper. a report on an investigation.* account, announcement, article, communication, communiqué, description, dispatch, narrative, news, record, statement, story, [*informal*] write-up.
2 *the report of a gun.* bang, blast, crack, detonation, explosion, noise.

report verb **1** *I reported the results of my investigation.* announce, circulate, communicate, declare, describe, document, give an account of, notify, present a report on [SEE **report** noun], proclaim, publish, record, recount, reveal, state, tell.
2 *Report to reception when you arrive.* announce yourself, introduce yourself, make yourself known, present yourself.
3 *I reported him to the police.* complain about, SEE **denounce**, inform against, [*informal*] tell of.

reporter noun *a newspaper reporter.* correspondent, journalist.

repose noun *a moment of repose in the midst of activity.* calm, comfort, ease, inactivity, peace, peacefulness, poise, quiet, quietness, relaxation, respite, rest, serenity, stillness, tranquillity.

repository noun SEE **store** noun.

repossess verb SEE **retrieve**.

reprehend verb SEE **reprimand** verb.

reprehensible adjective *reprehensible behaviour.* SEE **bad**, blameworthy, culpable, deplorable, disgraceful, immoral, objectionable, regrettable, remiss, shameful, unworthy, wicked.

represent verb **1** *Our pageant represented scenes from history.* act out, delineate, depict, describe, draw, enact, exhibit, illustrate, paint, picture, portray, show.
2 *Santa Claus represents the spirit of Christmas.* embody, epitomize, exemplify, incarnate, personify, stand for, symbolize.
3 *Our spokesperson represents the views of us all.* be an example of, express, present, speak for.

representation noun *a representation of a goddess.* depiction, figure, icon, image, imitation, likeness, model, picture, portrait, portrayal, resemblance, statue.

representative adjective **1** *representative voters.* average, characteristic, illustrative, normal, typical.
OPPOSITES: SEE **abnormal**.
2 *representative government.* chosen, democratic, elected, elective, popular.
OPPOSITES: SEE **undemocratic**.

representative noun **1** *a representative who speaks for someone else.* delegate [= *a person representing a group*], deputy, proxy, stand-in, substitute.
2 *a sales representative.* agent, [*informal*] rep, salesman, salesperson, saleswoman, [*informal*] traveller.
3 *a government representative.* ambassador, consul, diplomat.

repress verb *to repress your feelings.* [*informal*] bottle up, control, crush, curb, inhibit, keep down, quell, restrain, stifle, suppress.

repressed adjective **1** *a repressed person.* cold, frigid, inhibited, neurotic, unbalanced.
2 *repressed emotions.* [*informal*] bottled up, hidden, latent, subconscious, suppressed, unconscious, unfulfilled.
OPPOSITES: SEE **uninhibited**.

repression noun **1** *political repression.* authoritarianism, censorship, coercion, control, despotism, dictatorship, oppression, subjugation, totalitarianism, tyranny.
OPPOSITES: SEE **freedom**.
2 *repression of a person's feelings.* [*informal*] bottling up, inhibition, suffocation.

repressive adjective *repressive laws.* authoritarian, autocratic, coercive, cruel, despotic, dictatorial, harsh, illiberal, oppressive, restricting, severe, totalitarian, tyrannical, undemocratic, unenlightened.
OPPOSITES: SEE **liberal**.

reprieve verb *to reprieve a condemned prisoner.* forgive, let off, pardon, set free, spare.

reprimand noun *The teacher gave the class a severe reprimand.* admonition, censure, [*informal*] dressing-down, [*informal*] going-over, lecture, lesson, rebuke, reproach, reproof, scolding, [*informal*] talking-to, [*informal*] telling-off, [*informal*] ticking-off, [*informal*] wigging.

reprimand verb *to reprimand a wrongdoer.* admonish, censure, chide, condemn, criticize, disapprove of, give a reprimand to [SEE **reprimand** noun], lecture, [*informal*] rap, rate, rebuke, reprehend, reproach, reprove, scold, [*informal*] slate, [*informal*] take to task, [*informal*] teach (someone) a lesson, [*informal*] tell off, [*informal*] tick off, upbraid.
OPPOSITES: SEE **congratulate**.

reprisal noun *a reprisal against the attackers.* counter-attack, retaliation, retribution, revenge, vengeance.

reproach noun *She gave the naughty child a look of reproach.* blame, disapproval, disgrace, SEE **reprimand** noun, scorn.

reproach verb *to reproach someone you disapprove of.* censure, criticize, SEE **reprimand** verb, show disapproval of, upbraid.
OPPOSITES: SEE **praise** verb.

reproachful adjective *a reproachful frown.* censorious, critical, disapproving, reproving, scornful, withering.

reprobate noun SEE **immoral (immoral person)**.

reproduce verb **1** *to reproduce a document.* copy, counterfeit, duplicate, forge, imitate, mimic, photocopy, print, redo, reissue, SEE **repeat**, reprint, simulate.
2 *to reproduce your own kind.* breed, increase, multiply, procreate, produce offspring, propagate, spawn.

reproduction noun **1** *the reproduction of animals or plants.* breeding, increase, multiplying, procreation, propagation.
2 *a reproduction of an original picture.* copy, duplicate, facsimile, fake, forgery, imitation, likeness, print, replica.

reprographics noun REPROGRAPHIC MACHINES: cyclostyle, duplicator, heat copier, laser printer, photocopier, printer, printing press, spirit copier.
OTHER REPROGRAPHIC PROCESSES: desktop publishing, offset litho, Xerox.

reproof noun SEE **reprimand** noun.

reprove verb SEE **reprimand** verb.

reptile noun

SOME REPTILES: alligator, basilisk, chameleon, crocodile, lizard, salamander, snake, tortoise, turtle.
OTHER ANIMALS: SEE **animal** noun.

---

republic noun SEE **country**.

republican adjective, noun POLITICAL TERMS: SEE **politics**.

repudiate verb **1** *to repudiate an accusation.* deny, disagree with, dispute, rebuff, refute, reject, renounce.
2 *to repudiate an agreement.* disown, go back on, recant, rescind, retract, reverse, revoke.
OPPOSITES: SEE **acknowledge**.

repugnant adjective SEE **repulsive**.

repulse verb SEE **reject**, **repel**.

repulsive adjective *repulsive behaviour. a repulsive appearance.* abhorrent, disagreeable, disgusting, distasteful, foul, hateful, hideous, loathsome, nauseating, objectionable, obnoxious, odious, offensive, [*informal*] off-putting, repellent, repugnant, revolting, sickening, SEE **ugly**, unattractive, unpleasant, unsightly, vile.
OPPOSITES: SEE **attractive**.

reputable adjective *a reputable business.* dependable, esteemed, famous, highly regarded, honoured, prestigious, reliable, respectable, respected, trustworthy, unimpeachable, [*informal*] upmarket, well thought of.
OPPOSITES: SEE **disreputable**.

reputation noun *a good reputation for reliability.* character, fame, name, prestige, recognition, renown, repute, standing.

repute noun SEE **reputation**.

reputed adjective *reputed to be of good quality.* alleged, believed, considered, famed, reckoned, regarded, rumoured, said, supposed, thought.

request noun *He didn't listen to our request.* appeal, application, call, demand, entreaty, petition, plea, prayer, question, requisition, [*formal*] suit, supplication.

request verb *We requested help. He requested to see my licence.* adjure, appeal (for), apply (for), ask, beg, call (for), claim, demand, desire, entreat, implore, importune, invite, [*formal*] petition, pray for, require, requisition, seek, solicit, [*formal*] supplicate.

requiem noun SEE **funeral**.

require verb **1** *We required 3 runs to win.* be short of, depend on, lack, need, want.
2 *The officer required me to show my licence.* command, compel, direct, force, instruct, make, oblige, order, SEE **request** verb.

required adjective *Have you got the required qualifications?* compulsory, essential, imperative, indispensable, mandatory, necessary, needed, obligatory, prescribed, requisite, set, stipulated.
OPPOSITES: SEE **optional**.

requisite adjective SEE **required**.

requisition noun *a requisition for goods.* application, demand, order, request.

requisition verb *to requisition vehicles to deal with an emergency.* appropriate, commandeer, occupy, seize, take over.

reroute verb SEE **divert**.

rescind verb SEE **repeal**.

rescue noun *the rescue of a prisoner. a heroic rescue at sea.* deliverance, liberation, recovery, release, relief, salvage.

rescue verb **1** *to rescue someone from captivity.* deliver, extricate, free, liberate, ransom, release, save, set free.
2 *I rescued my belongings from the flood.* bring away, recover, retrieve, salvage.

research noun *research into the causes of disease.* experimentation, exploration, inquiry, investigation, [*informal*] probe, searching, study.

researcher noun analyst, [*informal*] boffin, investigator, scientist, student.

resemblance noun *the resemblance of twins.* affinity, closeness, correspondence, likeness, similarity, similitude.

resemble verb *Twins usually resemble each other.* be similar to, look like, mirror, [*informal*] take after.

resent verb *to resent someone else's success.* begrudge, be resentful about [SEE **resentful**], dislike, envy, grudge, grumble at, object to, [*informal*] take exception to, [*informal*] take umbrage at.

resentful adjective *resentful feelings about someone else's success.* aggrieved, SEE **angry**, annoyed, bitter, displeased, embittered, envious, grudging, hurt, indignant, jaundiced, jealous, malicious, offended, [*informal*] peeved, [*informal*] put out, spiteful, unfriendly, ungenerous, upset, vexed, vindictive.

resentment noun *feelings of resentment.* SEE **anger** noun, animosity, bitterness, discontent, grudge, hatred, hurt, ill-will, indignation, malevolence, malice, pique, rancour, spite, unfriendliness, vexation, vindictiveness.

reservation noun **1** *a hotel reservation.* booking.
2 *I have reservations about our plan.* condition, doubt, hesitation, misgiving, proviso, qualification, scepticism, scruple.
3 *a wildlife reservation.* SEE **reserve** noun.

reserve noun **1** *a reserve of food.* fund, hoard, reservoir, savings, stock, stockpile, store, supply.
2 *reserves for a game of football.* deputy, [*plural*] reinforcements, replacement, stand-by, [*informal*] stand-in, substitute, understudy.
3 *a wildlife reserve.* enclave, game park, preserve, protected area, reservation, safari-park, sanctuary.
4 *Overcome your reserve and join in.* aloofness, caution, modesty, reluctance, reserved behaviour [SEE **reserved**], reticence, self-consciousness, self-effacement, shyness, timidity.

reserve verb **1** *Reserve some food to eat later.* earmark, hoard, hold back, keep, keep back, preserve, put aside, retain, save, set aside, stockpile, store up.
2 *We reserved seats on the train.* [*informal*] bag, book, order, pay for.

reserved adjective *too reserved to speak up for herself.* aloof, bashful, cautious, cool, demure, diffident, discreet, distant, modest, quiet, restrained, reticent, retiring, secretive, self-conscious, self-effacing, shy, silent, [*uncomplimentary*] standoffish, taciturn, timid, uncommunicative, undemonstrative, unforthcoming, withdrawn.
OPPOSITES: SEE **demonstrative**.

reservoir noun SEE **lake**.

reshuffle verb SEE **reorganize**.

reside verb **to reside in** dwell in, have as a home, inhabit, live in, lodge in, occupy, settle in.

residence noun *your permanent residence.* [*old-fashioned*] abode, address, [*formal*] domicile, dwelling, habitation, home, SEE **house** noun.

resident adjective *The hostel has its own resident staff.* in residence, living-in, permanent.
OPPOSITES: SEE **non-resident**.

resident noun *the residents of an area.* citizen, denizen, inhabitant, [*informal*] local, native.
a temporary resident guest, lodger, occupant, tenant, visitor.

residential adjective *a residential area.* built-up, suburban.
OPPOSITES: commercial, industrial, rural.

residual adjective SEE **remaining**.

residue noun SEE **remainder**.

resign verb *to resign your job.* abdicate, forsake, give up, leave, quit, relinquish, renounce, stand down from, surrender, vacate.
to resign yourself to SEE **accept**.

resigned adjective *resigned about your problems.* calm, [*uncomplimentary*] defeatist, long-suffering, patient, philosophical, reasonable, stoical, submissive.

resilient adjective **1** *Rubber is a resilient material.* bouncy, elastic, firm, plastic, pliable, rubbery, springy, supple.
OPPOSITES: SEE **brittle**.
2 *a resilient person.* adaptable, buoyant, irrepressible, strong, tough, unstoppable.
OPPOSITES: SEE **vulnerable**.

resist verb *to resist arrest. to resist temptation.* avoid, be resistant to [SEE **resistant**], counteract, defy, SEE **fight** verb, oppose, prevent, refuse, stand up to, withstand.

resistant adjective *resistant to heat. resistant to temptation.* hostile, impervious, invulnerable, opposed, repellent, unaffected (by), unresponsive, unsusceptible, unyielding.
OPPOSITES: SEE **susceptible**.

resolute adjective *resolute opposition. resolute courage.* adamant, bold, committed, constant, courageous, decided, decisive, determined, dogged, firm, immovable, [*uncomplimentary*] inflexible, [*uncomplimentary*] obstinate, relentless, resolved, staunch, steadfast, strong-minded, strong-willed, [*uncomplimentary*] stubborn, unbending, undaunted, unflinching, unswerving, unwavering.
OPPOSITES: SEE **irresolute**.

resolution noun **1** *resolution in the face of danger.* boldness, commitment, constancy, courage, devotion, firmness, fortitude, [*uncomplimentary*] obstinacy, perseverance, resolve, staunchness, steadfastness, [*uncomplimentary*] stubbornness, tenacity, will-power.
2 *a resolution passed at a meeting.* decision, motion, statement.
3 *a resolution of all our problems.* answer, settlement, solution.

resolve noun SEE **resolution**.

resolve verb *We resolved to start our own business.* agree, conclude, decide formally, determine, elect, make a firm decision, opt, pass a resolution, settle, undertake, vote.

resonant adjective *a resonant voice. the resonant sound of a gong.* booming, echoing, full, resounding, reverberant, reverberating, rich, ringing, sonorous, vibrant.

resonate verb SEE **resound**.

resort noun **1** *Use violence only as a last resort.* alternative, course of action, expedient, option, recourse, refuge.
2 *a seaside resort.* holiday town, retreat, spa, [*old-fashioned*] watering-place.

resort verb *I don't want to resort to violence.* adopt, [*informal*] fall back on, make use of, turn to, use.

resound verb *Our voices resounded in the cave.* boom, echo, resonate, reverberate, ring, vibrate.

resounding adjective **1** *a resounding clash of cymbals.* SEE **resonant**.
2 [*informal*] *a resounding success.* SEE **great**.

resourceful adjective *a resourceful inventor.* clever, creative, enterprising, imaginative, ingenious, innovative, inspired, inventive, original, talented.
OPPOSITES: SEE **unimaginative**.

resources noun **1** *financial resources.* assets, capital, funds, SEE **money**, reserves, riches, wealth.
2 *natural resources.* materials, raw materials.

respect noun **1** *We remained silent as a sign of respect.* admiration, awe, consideration, deference, esteem, homage, honour, liking, love, regard, reverence, tribute, veneration.
2 *My work isn't perfect in every respect.* aspect, characteristic, detail, facet, feature, particular, point, way.

respect verb *Everyone respects her for her courage.* admire, esteem, honour, pay

homage to, revere, reverence, show respect to [SEE **respect** noun], think well of, value, venerate.
OPPOSITES: SEE **scorn** verb.

respectable adjective **1** *respectable people.* decent, honest, honourable, law-abiding, respected, upright, worthy.
2 *respectable clothes.* clean, modest, presentable, proper.
OPPOSITES: SEE **disreputable.**
3 *He gets a respectable income.* SEE **considerable.**

respectful adjective *a respectful greeting.* civil, courteous, deferential, dutiful, gracious, humble, polite, proper, reverent, reverential, [*uncomplimentary*] servile, subservient.
OPPOSITES: disrespectful, SEE **rude.**

respective adjective *We all returned to our respective homes.* individual, own, particular, personal, several, specific.

respiration noun breathing.

respire verb SEE **breathe.**

respite noun *a respite from your labours.* break, [*informal*] breather, interval, [*informal*] let-up, lull, pause, recess, relaxation, relief, remission, rest.

resplendent adjective *resplendent in her jewels.* bright, SEE **brilliant**, dazzling, glittering, shining, splendid.

respond verb **to respond to** *to respond to a question.* acknowledge, answer, counter, give a response to [SEE **response**], react to, reply to.

response noun *a response to a question.* acknowledgement, answer, [*informal*] come-back, counterblast, feedback, reaction, rejoinder, reply, retort, [*joking*] riposte.

responsible adjective **1** *A teacher is responsible for her class.* accountable, answerable, in charge of.
2 *I was responsible for the damage.* culpable, guilty, liable.
3 *We need a responsible person as treasurer.* concerned, conscientious, dependable, diligent, dutiful, ethical, honest, law-abiding, loyal, mature, moral, reliable, sensible, sober, steady, thinking, thoughtful, trustworthy, unselfish.
OPPOSITES: SEE **irresponsible.**
4 *a responsible job.* burdensome, executive, important.

responsive adjective *a responsive audience. responsive pupils.* alert, alive, aware, impressionable, interested, open, perceptive, receptive, sympathetic, warm-hearted, willing.
OPPOSITES: SEE **uninterested, unsympathetic.**

rest noun **1** *a rest from work. a rest on the sofa.* break, [*informal*] breather, breathing-space, comfort, ease, holiday, idleness, inactivity, interlude, intermission, interval, leisure, [*informal*] lie-down, lull, nap, pause, quiet, relaxation, relief, repose, siesta, time off, vacation.
2 *a rest for a telescope.* base, holder, prop, stand, support.
to come to rest SEE **halt** verb.
the rest SEE **remainder.**

rest verb **1** *to rest on the sofa. to rest from your labours.* be still, doze, have a rest [SEE **rest** noun], idle, laze, lie back, lie down, lounge, nod off, recline, relax, sleep, slumber, snooze, [*informal*] take a nap.
2 *Rest the ladder against the wall.* lean, place, prop, stand, support.
3 *Everything rests on the committee's decision.* depend, hang, hinge, rely, turn.

restaurant noun bistro, brasserie, buffet, café, cafeteria, canteen, carvery, diner, dining-room, eating-place, grill, snack-bar, steak-house.

restful adjective *a restful holiday.* calm, comfortable, leisurely, peaceful, quiet, relaxing, soothing, tranquil, undisturbed, unhurried, untroubled.
OPPOSITES: SEE **exhausting.**

restitution noun *the restitution of someone's rights.* SEE **compensation**, restoration, return.

restive adjective SEE **restless.**

restless adjective **1** *restless animals.* agitated, anxious, edgy, excitable, fidgety, impatient, jittery, jumpy, nervous, restive, worried.
OPPOSITES: SEE **relaxed.**
2 *a restless night.* disturbed, interrupted, sleepless, troubled, uncomfortable, unsettled.
OPPOSITES: SEE **restful.**

restore verb **1** *to restore something you have borrowed.* give back, put back, replace, return.
2 *to restore an old building.* clean, [*informal*] do up, fix, [*informal*] make good, mend, rebuild, recondition, reconstruct, refurbish, renew, renovate, repair, touch up.
3 *to restore good relations with the neighbours.* bring back, re-establish, rehabilitate, reinstate, reintroduce, revive.
4 *to restore someone to health.* cure, nurse, rejuvenate, revitalize.

restrain verb *Please restrain your dog. Restrain your laughter.* bridle, check, confine, control, curb, fetter, govern, handcuff, harness, hold back, inhibit, keep back, keep under control, muzzle, pinion, rein in, repress, restrict, stop, straitjacket, subdue, suppress, tie up.

restrained adjective *In spite of his anger, his remarks were restrained.* calm, controlled, discreet, low-key, mild, moderate, muted, quiet, repressed, reserved, reticent, soft, subdued, temperate, undemonstrative, understated, unemotional.
OPPOSITES: SEE **uninhibited**.

restrict verb **1** *to restrict someone's freedom.* circumscribe, control, cramp, inhibit, limit, regulate.
2 *The prisoners were restricted in their cells.* confine, enclose, imprison, keep, SEE **restrain**, shut.
OPPOSITES: SEE **free** verb.

restriction noun **1** *restrictions on your freedom.* check, constraint, control, curb, curfew, inhibition, limitation, restraint.
2 *a speed restriction.* ban, limit, regulation, rule, stipulation.

result noun **1** *The water shortage is a result of the hot weather.* consequence, effect, end-product, issue, outcome, product, repercussion, sequel, upshot.
2 *the result of a trial.* decision, judgement, verdict.
3 *the result of a game.* score.
4 *the result of a calculation.* answer.

result verb *What resulted from your interview?* arise, come about, culminate, develop, emanate, emerge, ensue, eventuate, follow, happen, issue, occur, proceed, spring, stem, take place, turn out.
to result in *I hope it doesn't result in tears!* achieve, bring about, cause, give rise to, lead to, provoke.

resume verb *to resume after a break.* begin again, carry on, continue, [*informal*] pick up the threads, proceed, recommence, reconvene, re-open, restart.

resumption noun *the resumption of work after a holiday.* continuation, recommencement, re-opening, restarting.

résumé noun SEE **summary** noun.

resurgence noun SEE **renewal**.

resurrect verb *to resurrect an old railway line.* bring back, SEE **renew**, restore, resuscitate, revitalize, revive.
2 *to resurrect from the dead.* bring back to life, raise.

resurrection noun SEE **renewal**.

resuscitate verb SEE **resurrect**.

retail verb **1** *to retail goods.* SEE **sell**.
2 *to retail your adventures.* SEE **recount**.

retain verb **1** *Please retain your ticket.* [*informal*] hang on to, hold, hold back, keep, reserve, save.
OPPOSITES: SEE **surrender**.
2 *Throughout the crisis he retained his composure.* keep control of, maintain, preserve.
OPPOSITES: SEE **lose**.
3 *He retains everything he reads.* keep in mind, learn, memorize, remember.
OPPOSITES: SEE **forget**.

retainer noun SEE **servant**.

retaliate verb *to retaliate against someone who hurt you.* [*informal*] get even (with), [*informal*] get your own back, hit back, make a counter-attack, pay back, repay, revenge yourself, seek retribution, strike back, take revenge.

retaliation noun counter-attack, reprisal, retribution, revenge, vengeance.

retard verb SEE **delay** verb.

retarded adjective *a retarded pupil.* backward, disadvantaged, handicapped, slow, undeveloped.

retch verb SEE **vomit**.

reticent adjective *a reticent person.* SEE **reserved**.

retinue noun attendants, entourage, followers, servants.
VARIOUS SERVANTS: SEE **servant**.

retire verb *to retire from work. to retire from a fight.* give up, leave, quit, resign, SEE **withdraw**.

retiring adjective *a retiring personality.* SEE **reserved**.

retort noun *a sharp retort.* answer, comeback, quip, recrimination, rejoinder, reply, response, retaliation, [*joking*] riposte.

retort verb *He retorted rudely.* answer, counter, react, reply, respond, retaliate, return.

retrace verb **to retrace your steps** SEE **return** verb.

retract verb **1** *A snail can retract its horns.* draw in, pull back, pull in.
2 *to retract an accusation.* abandon, cancel, disclaim, disown, [*informal*] have second thoughts about, recant, renounce, repeal, repudiate, rescind, reverse, revoke, withdraw.

retractable adjective SEE **collapsible**.

retreat noun **1** *We made a quick retreat.* departure, escape, evacuation, exit, flight, withdrawal.
2 *a secluded retreat in the hills.* asylum, den, haven, [*informal*] hide-away, hide-

out, hiding-place, refuge, resort, sanctuary, shelter.

retreat verb **1** *The army retreated.* back away, back down, climb down, depart, fall back, go away, leave, move back, retire, [*informal*] run away, [*informal*] turn tail, withdraw.
2 *The floods retreated.* ebb, flow back, recede, shrink back.

retribution noun *The victim's family sought retribution.* compensation, recompense, redress, reprisal, retaliation, revenge, vengeance.
OPPOSITES: SEE **forgiveness**.

retrieve verb *to retrieve something you lost.* fetch back, find, get back, recapture, recoup, recover, regain, repossess, rescue, restore, return, salvage, save, trace, track down.

The prefix *retro-* is from Latin *retro* = *backwards.*

---

retrograde, retrogressive adjectives *a retrograde step.* SEE **backward**.

retrospective adjective *a retrospective glance.* backward-looking, looking behind.

return noun **1** *We look forward to your return.* arrival, re-entry, homecoming, reappearance.
2 *After the flood there was a slow return to normality.* re-establishment (of), regression, restoration (of), reversion.
3 *We must avoid a return of the problem.* recrudescence, recurrence.
4 *I want a good return on my investment.* gain, income, interest, profit.

return verb **1** *I'll see you when you return.* come back, reappear, reassemble, reconvene, re-enter, retrace your steps.
2 *to return someone or something to their place of origin.* convey, deliver, repatriate, replace, restore, send back.
3 *Things soon returned to their original state.* go back, regress, revert.
4 *The problem may return.* happen again, recur.
5 *Please return the money I lent you.* give back, refund, reimburse, repay.
6 *She returned a witty response.* SEE **answer** verb.

reunion noun VARIOUS KINDS OF PARTY: SEE **party**.

revamp verb SEE **renew**.

reveal verb *to reveal the truth.* announce, bare, betray, communicate, confess, declare, disclose, display, divulge, exhibit, expose, [*informal*] give the game away, lay bare, leak, make known, proclaim, produce, publish, show, show up, [*informal*] spill the beans, tell, uncover, unfold, unmask, unveil.
OPPOSITES: SEE **hide** verb.

revel verb *We were revelling all night.* carouse, celebrate, [*informal*] have a spree, have fun, indulge in revelry [SEE **revelry**], make merry.
to revel in *I revel in the sunshine.* be happy in, delight in, enjoy, love, luxuriate in, rejoice in, relish, take pleasure in.

revelation noun *The revelation of what he'd done amazed me.* announcement, confession, disclosure, discovery, exposé, exposure, news, publication, revealing, unmasking.

revelry noun *The revelry continued all night.* carousing, celebration, conviviality, debauchery, festivity, fun, [*joking*] jollification, [*informal*] junketing, merrymaking, orgy, party, revelling, revels, roistering, [*informal*] spree.

revenge noun *His cruel heart was set on revenge.* reprisal, retaliation, retribution, vengeance, vindictiveness.
to take revenge SEE **revenge** verb.

revenge verb *to revenge a wrong.* avenge, [*informal*] get your own back for, repay, retaliate, take revenge for.
to be revenged be even, [*informal*] be quits.

revenue noun *the revenue from a business.* income, SEE **money**, proceeds, profits, receipts.

reverberate verb SEE **resound**.

reverberation noun *the reverberation of a gong.* echo, resonance, ringing, rumble, vibration.

revere verb *We revere our heroes.* admire, adore, feel reverence for [SEE **reverence**], honour, idolize, pay homage to, praise, respect, reverence, value, venerate, worship.
OPPOSITES: SEE **despise**.

reverence noun *reverence for our heroes.* admiration, adoration, awe, deference, devotion, esteem, homage, praise, respect, veneration, worship.

reverent adjective *reverent worshippers. a reverent silence.* adoring, awed, awestruck, deferential, devout, pious, respectful, reverential, solemn.
OPPOSITES: SEE **irreverent**.

reverie noun SEE **dream** noun.

reverse adjective *the reverse side.* back, contrary, opposite, rear.

reverse noun **1** *He says one thing and does the reverse.* antithesis, contrary, converse, opposite.

2 *We suffered a number of reverses last year.* defeat, failure, SEE **misfortune**, reversal, set-back, [*informal*] upset.

reverse verb 1 *to reverse a sequence.* change, invert, transpose, turn round.
2 *to reverse a car.* back, drive backwards, go backwards, go into reverse.
3 *to reverse a decision.* countermand, negate, overturn, repeal, rescind, retract, revoke, undo.

review noun 1 *a review of the year.* look back, reappraisal, recapitulation, reconsideration, re-examination, report, study, survey.
2 *a book or record review.* appreciation, criticism, critique, notice, [*informal*] write-up.

review verb 1 *to review the evidence.* appraise, assess, consider, evaluate, [*informal*] go over, inspect, recapitulate, reconsider, re-examine, scrutinize, study, survey, [*informal*] weigh up.
2 *to review a book or record.* criticize, write a review of [SEE **review** noun].

revile verb SEE **abuse** verb.

revise verb 1 *to revise your opinions. to revise a draft.* adapt, alter, change, correct, edit, emend, improve, modify, [*informal*] polish up, reconsider, [*informal*] redo, [*informal*] rehash, rephrase, revamp, reword, rewrite, update.
2 *to revise for an exam.* [*informal*] cram, learn, study, [*informal*] swot.

revival noun *a revival of interest in old crafts.* reawakening, rebirth, recovery, renaissance, renewal, restoration, resurgence, resurrection, return, revitalization, upsurge.

revivalist noun SEE **preacher**.

revive verb 1 *He soon revived after his black-out.* awaken, come back to life, [*informal*] come round, [*informal*] come to, rally, recover, rouse.
2 *A cold drink revived us.* bring back to life, [*informal*] cheer up, freshen up, invigorate, refresh, renew, restore, resuscitate, revitalize.
OPPOSITES: SEE **weaken, weary** verb.

revoke verb *to revoke a decree.* SEE **cancel**.

revolt verb 1 *to revolt against authority.* disobey, mutiny, rebel, riot, rise up.
2 *Cruelty to animals revolts us.* SEE **disgust** verb.

revolting adjective *a revolting mess.* SEE **disgusting**.

revolution noun 1 *a political revolution.* civil war, coup, coup d'état, mutiny, SEE **rebellion**, reformation, revolt, rising, uprising.
2 *a revolution of the earth.* circuit, orbit, rotation, turn.
3 *Computers have created an economic revolution.* change, reorganization, reorientation, shift, transformation, [*informal*] turn-about, upheaval, [*informal*] upset, [*informal*] U-turn.

revolutionary adjective *revolutionary ideas.* avant-garde, challenging, experimental, extremist, innovative, new, novel, progressive, radical, seditious, subversive, [*informal*] unheard of, upsetting.
OPPOSITES: SEE **conservative** adjective.

revolutionize verb SEE **transform**.

revolve verb *Wheels revolve. Planets revolve round the sun.* circle, gyrate, orbit, pirouette (*Dancers pirouette*), rotate, spin, swivel, turn, twirl, wheel, whirl.

revolver noun SEE **gun**.

revue noun KINDS OF ENTERTAINMENT: SEE **entertainment**.

revulsion noun *a revulsion against cruelty.* SEE **disgust** noun.

reward noun *a reward for bravery. a reward for hard work.* award, bonus, bounty, compensation, decoration, honour, medal, payment, prize, recompense, remuneration, return.
OPPOSITES: SEE **punishment**.

reward verb 1 *to reward someone for bravery.* decorate, honour.
2 *to reward someone for hard work.* compensate, give a reward to [SEE **reward** noun], recompense, remunerate, repay.
OPPOSITES: SEE **punish**.

rewarding adjective *Nursing is said to be a rewarding job.* fulfilling, gratifying, satisfying, worthwhile.
OPPOSITES: SEE **thankless**.

reword verb *to reword a statement.* paraphrase, rephrase, SEE **revise**.

rewrite verb SEE **revise**.

rhapsody noun MUSICAL TERMS: SEE **music**.

rhetoric noun *a politician's rhetoric.* eloquence, [*uncomplimentary*] grandiloquence, [*uncomplimentary*] magniloquence, oratory, rhetorical language [SEE **rhetorical**].

rhetorical adjective [*nowadays usually uncomplimentary*] *a rhetorical style.* artificial, bombastic, [*informal*] flowery, high-flown, insincere, oratorical, ornate, pretentious, verbose, wordy.
OPPOSITES: SEE **simple**.

rhyme noun SEE **poem**.

rhythm noun *a steady rhythm.* accent, beat, metre, movement, pattern, pulse, tempo, throb.

rhythmic adjective *a rhythmic beat.* metrical, predictable, regular, repeated, steady, throbbing.
OPPOSITES: SEE **irregular**.

ria noun SEE **bay**.

ribald adjective *ribald laughter.* SEE **bawdy**, disrespectful, naughty, rude, vulgar.

ribbon noun **1** *a ribbon for her hair.* braid, head-band, tape.
2 *a ribbon of colour.* band, strip, stripe.
in ribbons SEE **ragged**.

rice noun VARIOUS CEREALS: SEE **cereal**.

rich adjective **1** *a rich industrialist.* affluent, [*informal*] flush, [*informal*] loaded, moneyed, opulent, [*joking*] plutocratic, prosperous, wealthy, [*informal*] well-heeled, well-off, well-to-do.
2 *rich furnishings.* costly, elaborate, expensive, lavish, luxurious, splendid, sumptuous, valuable.
3 *rich agricultural land.* fertile, fruitful, lush, productive.
4 *a rich harvest.* abundant, copious, plenteous, plentiful, prolific, teeming.
5 *rich colours.* deep, full, strong, vivid, warm.
OPPOSITES: SEE **poor**.
a rich person billionaire, capitalist, millionaire, plutocrat, tycoon.

riches noun SEE **wealth**.

rick noun hayrick, haystack.

rick verb *to rick your neck.* SEE **strain** verb.

rickety adjective *a rickety old building.* SEE **unsteady**.

ricochet verb bounce, rebound.

rid verb *to rid the town of rats.* clear, free, purge.
to get rid of dispense with, eject, evict, expel, remove, throw out.

riddle noun **1** *Can you solve this riddle?* conundrum, mystery, [*informal*] poser, problem, puzzle, question.
2 *She sifted the soil in a riddle.* sieve.

riddle verb **1** *to riddle out large bits with a sieve.* filter, screen, sieve, sift, strain.
2 *to riddle something with holes.* [*informal*] pepper, perforate, pierce, puncture.

ride noun *a ride in a car.* SEE **journey** noun.

ride verb **1** *to ride a horse.* control, handle, manage, sit on.
2 *to ride on a bike.* be carried, free-wheel, pedal, SEE **travel** verb.

ridge noun *There's a good view from the ridge.* bank, edge, embankment, escarpment, SEE **hill**.

ridicule noun *We had to put up with the ridicule of local youths.* badinage, banter, derision, jeering, laughter, mockery, raillery, [*informal*] ribbing, sarcasm, satire, scorn, sneers, taunts, teasing.

ridicule verb *Don't ridicule them because of their appearance.* be sarcastic about, be satirical about, caricature, chaff, deride, guy, jeer at, joke about, lampoon, laugh at, make fun of, make jokes about, mock, parody, pillory, [*informal*] poke fun at, [*informal*] rib, scoff at, [*informal*] send up, sneer at, subject (someone) to ridicule [SEE **ridicule** noun], taunt, tease.

ridiculous adjective *a ridiculous comedy. ridiculous behaviour.* absurd, amusing, comic, [*informal*] crazy, [*informal*] daft, eccentric, farcical, foolish, funny, grotesque, hilarious, illogical, irrational, laughable, ludicrous, mad, nonsensical, preposterous, senseless, silly, stupid, unbelievable, unreasonable, weird, [*informal*] zany.
OPPOSITES: SEE **sensible**.

rife adjective *Disease is rife in the area.* abundant, common, endemic, prevalent, widespread.

rifle noun SEE **gun**.

rift noun *a rift in a rock. a rift in a friendship.* breach, break, chink, cleft, crack, division, fracture, gap, opening, separation, split.

rig noun **1** *a ship's rig.* SEE **rigging**.
2 *an oil rig.* platform.
3 [*informal*] *the rig you need for mountaineering.* apparatus, clothes, equipment, gear, kit, outfit, stuff, tackle.

rigging noun *a ship's rigging.* rig, tackle.
PARTS OF A SHIP'S RIGGING: halyard, pulley, rope, sail.

right adjective **1** *the right thing to do.* decent, ethical, fair, honest, honourable, just, law-abiding, lawful, moral, principled, responsible, righteous, upright, virtuous.
2 *the right answer. the right word.* accurate, apposite, appropriate, apt, correct, exact, factual, faultless, fitting, genuine, precise, proper, suitable, true.
3 *Have we come the right way?* best, convenient, good, normal, recommended, sensible, usual.
OPPOSITES: SEE **wrong** adjective.
4 *your right side.* right-hand, starboard [=*right side of a ship when you face the bow*].
5 *right in politics.* conservative, fascist, reactionary, right-wing, Tory.

right noun **1** *the right to free speech.* entitlement, facility, freedom, liberty, prerogative, privilege.

2 *a teacher's right to give orders. a chemist's right to sell medicines.* authority, commission, franchise, influence, licence, position, power.

right verb **1** *to right something which was overturned.* make perpendicular, pick up, set upright, stand upright, straighten.
OPPOSITES: SEE **overturn**.
2 *to right a wrong.* correct, make amends for, put right, rectify, redress, remedy, repair, set right.

righteous adjective *It is not only the righteous who go to church.* blameless, God-fearing, good, guiltless, just, law-abiding, moral, pure, [*uncomplimentary*] SEE **sanctimonious**, upright, virtuous.
OPPOSITES: unrighteous, SEE **sinful**.

rightful adjective *the rightful owner of a car.* authorized, just, lawful, legal, legitimate, licensed, proper, real, true, valid.
OPPOSITES: SEE **illegal**.

rigid adjective **1** *a rigid board. a rigid framework. a rigid expression.* adamant, firm, hard, inflexible, solid, stiff, unbending, wooden.
2 *a rigid disciplinarian.* harsh, intransigent, stern, strict, stubborn, uncompromising, unkind, unyielding.
OPPOSITES: SEE **flexible**.

rigorous adjective **1** *rigorous training.* conscientious, demanding, exacting, hard, painstaking, rigid, stringent, structured, thorough, tough, unsparing.
OPPOSITES: SEE **easygoing**.
2 *a rigorous climate.* extreme, harsh, inclement, inhospitable, severe, unfriendly, unpleasant.
OPPOSITES: SEE **mild**.

rile verb SEE **annoy**.

rill noun SEE **stream** noun.

rim noun *the rim of a cup.* brim, brink, circumference, edge, lip.

rind noun *cheese rind. the rind of an orange.* crust, outer layer, peel, skin.

ring noun **1** *in the shape of a ring.* band, circle, hoop, loop.
OTHER SHAPES: SEE **shape** noun.
2 *a boxing-ring.* arena.
3 *a smuggling ring.* association, band, gang, SEE **group** noun, mob, organization, syndicate.
ring road SEE **road**.

ring verb **1** *The police ringed the area.* circle, encircle, enclose, encompass, surround.
2 *The bell rang.* chime, clang, clink, jangle, peal, ping, resonate, resound, reverberate, sound the knell, tinkle, toll.
3 *Ring me tomorrow evening.* call, [*informal*] give a buzz, phone, ring up, telephone.

ring-leader noun SEE **leader**.

ringlet noun SEE **curl** noun.

ringmaster noun SEE **circus**.

rink noun *an ice-rink.* SEE **arena**.

rinse verb *to rinse in clean water.* bathe, clean, sluice, swill, wash.

riot noun *a riot in the streets.* anarchy, brawl, chaos, commotion, demonstration, disorder, disturbance, hubbub, insurrection, lawlessness, mass protest, mutiny, pandemonium, revolt, rioting, rising, [*informal*] rumpus, [*informal*] shindy, turmoil, unrest, uproar, violence.

riot verb *The discontented crowd rioted.* create a riot [SEE **riot** noun], [*informal*] go wild, mutiny, rampage, rebel, revolt, rise up, run riot.

rioting noun SEE **riot** noun.

riotous adjective *a riotous party.* anarchic, boisterous, disorderly, lawless, mutinous, noisy, rampageous, rebellious, rowdy, uncivilized, uncontrollable, undisciplined, ungovernable, unrestrained, unruly, violent, wild.
OPPOSITES: SEE **orderly**.

rip verb SEE **tear** verb.

ripe adjective *ripe fruit.* mature, mellow, ready to use.

ripen verb *These pears need to ripen.* age, become riper, develop, mature, mellow.

riposte noun SEE **reply** noun.

ripple noun SEE **wave** noun.

ripple verb *Wind rippled the surface of the water.* agitate, disturb, make waves on, ruffle, stir.

rise noun **1** *a rise in the ground.* ascent, bank, climb, elevation, SEE **hill**, incline, ramp, slope.
2 *a rise in wages, temperature, etc.* escalation, increase, increment, jump, leap, upsurge, upswing, upturn, upward movement.

rise verb **1** *to rise into the air.* arise, ascend, climb, fly up, go up, jump, leap, levitate, lift, lift off, mount, soar, spring, take off.
2 *to rise from bed.* get up, stand up.
3 *Prices have risen.* escalate, grow, increase.
4 *A cliff rose above us.* loom, stand out, stick up, tower.

rising noun SEE **revolution**.

risk noun **1** *a risk of frost.* chance, likelihood, possibility.

2 *Starting a business involves financial risk.* danger, gamble, hazard, peril, speculation, uncertainty, venture.

risk verb *He risked his capital starting the business.* chance, dare, gamble, hazard, jeopardize, speculate, venture.

risky adjective *It's risky to cycle on icy roads.* [*informal*] chancy, SEE **dangerous**, hazardous, perilous, precarious, unsafe.
OPPOSITES: SEE **safe**.

rite noun SEE **ritual**.

ritual noun *a religious ritual.* ceremonial, ceremony, formality, liturgy, practice, rite, sacrament, service, solemnity, tradition.

rival noun *sporting rivals.* adversary, challenger, competitor, contender, contestant, enemy, opponent, opposition.

rival verb *The new shop rivals the shop down the road.* be as good as, compare with, compete with, contend with, contest, emulate, equal, match, oppose, struggle with, vie with.
OPPOSITES: SEE **co-operate**.

rivalry noun *rivalry between two teams.* antagonism, competition, competitiveness, opposition.
OPPOSITES: SEE **co-operation**.

river noun rivulet, SEE **stream** noun, waterway.
PARTS OF A RIVER: channel, confluence, delta, estuary, lower reaches, mouth, source, tributary, upper reaches.
RELATED ADJECTIVE: fluvial.
GEOGRAPHICAL TERMS: SEE **geography**.

rivet verb SEE **fasten**.

rivulet noun SEE **stream** noun.

road noun roadway, route, way.

ROADS AND PATHWAYS: alley, arterial road, avenue, boulevard, bridle-path, bridle-way, bypass, by-road, byway, cart-track, causeway, clearway, crescent, cul-de-sac, drive, driveway, dual carriageway, esplanade, footpath, [*American*] freeway, highway, lane, motorway, one-way street, path, pathway, pavement, ring road, service road, side-road, side-street, slip-road, street, thoroughfare, tow-path, track, trail, trunk-road, [*old-fashioned*] turnpike, walk, walkway.

WORDS TO DO WITH ROADS: bridge, camber, flyover, footbridge, ford, hairpin bend, junction, lay-by, level crossing, roadworks, roundabout, service area, service station, signpost, traffic lights, underpass, viaduct, zebra crossing.

SURFACES FOR ROADS AND PATHS: asphalt, cobbles, concrete, crazy paving, flagstones, gravel, paving stones, Tarmac, tiles.

---

roadworthy adjective *a roadworthy vehicle.* safe, usable.

roam verb *Sheep roam over the hills.* meander, prowl, ramble, range, rove, stray, travel, SEE **walk** verb, wander.

roar noun, verb VARIOUS SOUNDS: SEE **sound** noun.

roast verb SEE **cook** verb.

roasting adjective SEE **hot**.

rob verb *to rob a shop. to rob someone in the street.* [*informal*] con, defraud, loot, [*informal*] mug, [*informal*] mulct, pick (someone's) pocket, pilfer from, pillage, plunder, ransack, steal from [SEE **steal**].

robber noun bandit, brigand, burglar, [*informal*] con-man, embezzler, fraud, highwayman, looter, mugger, pickpocket, pirate, shop-lifter, swindler, thief.
OTHER CRIMINALS: SEE **criminal** noun.

robbery noun burglary, confidence trick, embezzlement, fraud, [*informal*] hold-up, larceny, mugging, pillage, plunder, shop-lifting, stealing, [*informal*] stick-up, theft.
OTHER CRIMES: SEE **crime**.

robe noun bath-robe, dress, dressing-gown, frock, gown, habit (*a monk's habit*), house-coat.

robe verb SEE **dress** verb.

robot noun android, automated machine, automaton, bionic man, bionic woman, computerized machine.

robust adjective **1** *a robust physique.* athletic, brawny, hardy, healthy, muscular, powerful, rugged, sound, strong, vigorous.
2 *a robust machine.* durable, serviceable, sturdy, tough.
OPPOSITES: SEE **weak**.

rock noun **1** *a lorry-load of rock.* ore, stone.
2 *We clambered over the rocks.* boulder, crag, outcrop, scree.

PRINCIPAL TYPES OF ROCK: igneous, metamorphic, sedimentary.

SOME KINDS OF ROCK: basalt, chalk, clay, flint, gneiss, granite, gravel, lava, limestone, marble, obsidian, pumice, quartz, sandstone, schist, shale, slate, tufa, tuff.

---

rock verb **1** *to rock to and fro.* move gently, sway, swing.
2 *The ship rocked in the storm.* lurch, pitch, reel, roll, shake, toss, totter.
3 *The nation was rocked by the news.* SEE **amaze** verb, **amazed** adjective.

rockery noun alpine garden, rock-garden.

rocket noun SEE **firework, space** noun, **weapons.**

rocky adjective **1** *rocky terrain.* barren, inhospitable, pebbly, rough, rugged, stony.
2 *a rocky chair.* SEE **unsteady.**

rococo adjective SEE **ornate.**

rod noun bar, baton, cane, dowel, pole, rail, shaft, spoke, staff, stick, strut, wand.

rodent noun VARIOUS ANIMALS: SEE **animal** noun.

roe noun SEE **deer.**

rogue noun *rogues and criminals.* [*old-fashioned*] blackguard, charlatan, cheat, [*informal*] con-man, SEE **criminal** noun, fraud, [*old-fashioned*] knave, mischievous person [SEE **mischievous**], [*informal*] quack, rascal, ruffian, scoundrel, swindler, villain.

roguish adjective SEE **mischievous.**

roistering noun SEE **revelry.**

role noun **1** *an actor's role.* character, part, portrayal.
2 *What's her role in this business?* contribution, duty, function, job, position, post, task.

roll noun **1** *a roll of paper.* cylinder, drum, scroll.
2 *a roll of honour.* catalogue, index, inventory, list, record, register.

roll verb **1** *The wheels began to roll.* gyrate, move round, revolve, rotate, run, spin, turn, twirl, whirl.
2 *to roll up a carpet, a sail, etc.* coil, curl, furl, make into a roll, twist, wind, wrap.
3 *to roll a cricket pitch.* flatten, level out, smooth, use a roller on.
4 *The ship rolled in the storm. A drunk rolled along the street.* lumber, lurch, pitch, reel, rock, stagger, sway, toss, totter, wallow, welter.
to roll in, to roll up SEE **arrive.**

rollicking adjective SEE **boisterous.**

rolling adjective *a rolling sea. rolling hills.* heaving, undulating, up and down, wavy.

romance noun **1** *a historical romance.* KINDS OF WRITING: SEE **writing.**
2 *the romance of travel.* adventure, excitement, fascination, glamour.
3 *Are those two having a romance?* affair, attachment, intrigue, liaison, love affair, relationship.

romantic adjective **1** *a romantic setting for a love affair.* colourful, dream-like, exotic, glamorous, idyllic, picturesque.
2 *a romantic novel.* emotional, escapist, heart-warming, nostalgic, reassuring, sentimental, [*uncomplimentary*] sloppy, tender, unrealistic.
3 *romantic notions of changing the world.* [*informal*] head in the clouds, idealistic, impractical, improbable, quixotic, starry-eyed, unworkable, Utopian, visionary.
OPPOSITES: SEE **realistic.**

romp verb *The children romped in the playground.* caper, cavort, dance, frisk, frolic, leap about, play, prance, run about.

roof noun MATERIALS USED FOR ROOFS: asbestos, corrugated iron, slates, thatch, tiles.

rook verb SEE **swindle** verb.

room noun **1** *Give me more room.* [*informal*] elbow-room, freedom, latitude, leeway, scope, space, territory.
2 *a room in a house.* [*old-fashioned*] chamber.

VARIOUS ROOMS: ante-room, attic, audience chamber, bathroom, bedroom, boudoir, cell, cellar, chapel, classroom, cloakroom, conservatory, corridor, dining-room, dormitory, drawing-room, dressing-room, gallery, guest-room, hall, kitchen, kitchenette, laboratory, landing, larder, laundry, lavatory, library, living-room, loft, lounge, music-room, nursery, office, outhouse, pantry, parlour, passage, play-room, porch, salon, saloon, scullery, sick-room, sitting-room, spare-room, state-room, store-room, studio, study, toilet, utility room, waiting-room, ward, washroom, WC, workroom, workshop.

---

roomy adjective *a roomy car.* SEE **big,** capacious, commodious, large, sizeable, spacious, voluminous.
OPPOSITES: SEE **cramped.**

root noun **1** *the root of a plant.* radicle, rhizome, rootlet, tuber.
2 *the root of a problem.* basis, bottom (*I want to get to the bottom of this*), origin, seat, source, starting-point.

root verb **to root out** SEE **remove, uproot.**

rope noun cable, cord, halyard, hawser, lanyard, lariat, lasso, line, string.

rope verb [= *to fasten with a rope*] bind, hitch, moor, tie.
OTHER WAYS TO FASTEN THINGS: SEE **fasten**.

rosette noun SEE **badge**.

roster noun SEE **rota**.

rostrum noun SEE **platform**.

rot noun **1** *The damp has caused some rot.* corrosion, decay, decomposition, deterioration, disintegration, dry rot, mouldiness, wet rot.
2 [*informal*] *Don't talk rot.* SEE **nonsense**.

rot verb *Most substances eventually rot.* become rotten [SEE **rotten**], corrode, crumble, decay, decompose, degenerate, deteriorate, disintegrate, go bad, perish, putrefy, spoil.

rota noun *a duty rota.* list, roster, schedule, timetable.

rotary adjective *rotary movement.* gyrating, revolving, rotating, rotatory, spinning, turning, twirling, twisting, whirling.

rotate verb *to rotate on an axis.* gyrate, have a rotary movement, pirouette, pivot, reel, revolve, spin, swivel, turn, turn anticlockwise, turn clockwise, twiddle, twirl, twist, wheel, whirl.

rotor noun propeller, screw, vane.
PARTS OF AN AIRCRAFT: SEE **aircraft**.

rotten adjective **1** *rotten wood. rotten ironwork.* corroded, crumbling, decayed, decaying, decomposed, disintegrating, [*of iron, etc.*] rusty, unsound.
2 *rotten food.* foul, mouldering, mouldy, [*informal*] off (*The fish is off*), perished, putrid, smelly, tainted, unfit for consumption.
OPPOSITES: SEE **sound** adjective.
3 *a rotten thing to do.* SEE **bad**.

rough adjective **1** *a rough surface.* broken, bumpy, coarse, craggy, irregular, jagged, pitted, rocky, rugged, stony, uneven.
OPPOSITES: SEE **even** adjective.
2 *rough skin.* bristly, callused, chapped, coarse, hairy, harsh, leathery, scratchy, shaggy, unshaven, wrinkled.
OPPOSITES: SEE **smooth** adjective.
3 *a rough sea.* choppy, stormy, tempestuous, turbulent, violent, wild.
OPPOSITES: SEE **calm** adjective.
4 *a rough voice.* grating, gruff, harsh, hoarse, husky, rasping, raucous, unpleasant.
OPPOSITES: SEE **soft**.
5 *a rough crowd. rough manners.* badly behaved, bluff, blunt, brusque, churlish, ill-bred, impolite, loutish, SEE **rowdy**, rude, surly, [*informal*] ugly, uncivil, uncivilized, undisciplined, unfriendly.
OPPOSITES: SEE **polite**.
6 *rough work.* amateurish, careless, clumsy, crude, hasty, imperfect, inept, [*informal*] rough and ready, unfinished, unpolished, unskilful.
OPPOSITES: SEE **skilful**.
7 *a rough estimate.* approximate, imprecise, inexact, vague.
OPPOSITES: SEE **exact** adjective.

roughage noun dietary fibre.

roughly adverb about, approximately, around, close to, nearly.

round adjective **1** *a round shape.* bulbous, circular, curved, cylindrical, globular, spherical.
2 *a round figure.* ample, SEE **fat** adjective, full, plump, rotund, rounded, well-padded.
round the bend SEE **mad**.
round the clock SEE **continual**.

round noun *a round in a competition.* bout, contest, game, heat, stage.

round verb *to round a corner.* skirt, travel round, turn.
to round off *We rounded the evening off with some songs.* SEE **complete** verb.
to round on *He rounded on me for not supporting his plan.* SEE **attack** verb.
to round up *The farmer rounded up his sheep.* SEE **assemble**.

roundabout adjective *a roundabout route.* circuitous, devious, indirect, long, meandering, rambling, tortuous, twisting, winding.
OPPOSITES: SEE **direct** adjective.

roundabout noun **1** merry-go-round.
2 traffic island.

round-shouldered adjective humpbacked, hunchbacked, stooping.

roundsman noun delivery man, tradesman.

rouse verb **1** *to rouse someone from sleep.* arouse, awaken, call, get up, wake up.
2 *to rouse someone to a frenzy.* agitate, animate, excite, incite, inflame, provoke, stimulate, stir up.

rousing adjective *rousing music.* SEE **exciting**.

rout verb *We routed the opposition.* conquer, crush, SEE **defeat** verb, overwhelm.

route noun *Which route shall we take?* course, direction, itinerary, journey, path, road, way.

routine noun **1** *a normal routine.* course of action, custom, [*informal*] drill (*Follow the usual drill*), habit, method, pattern, practice, procedure, system, way.
2 *The skaters performed their new routine.* act, performance, programme.

rove verb SEE **roam**.

row noun **1** [Rhymes with *crow*.] *Arrange them in a row.* chain, column, cordon, file, line, queue, rank, sequence, series, string.
2 [Rhymes with *cow*.] *I heard his row all down the street.* SEE **noise**, [*informal*] racket, rumpus, tumult, uproar.
3 [Rhymes with *cow*.] *They don't speak to each other since their row.* altercation, argument, controversy, disagreement, dispute, fight, SEE **quarrel** noun, [*informal*] ructions, [*informal*] slanging match, squabble.

row verb **1** [Rhymes with *crow*.] *to row a boat.* move, propel, scull.
2 [Rhymes with *cow*.] [*informal*] *They row about politics.* SEE **quarrel** verb.

rowdy adjective *a rowdy crowd.* badly behaved, boisterous, disorderly, ill-disciplined, irrepressible, lawless, SEE **noisy**, obstreperous, riotous, rough, turbulent, undisciplined, unruly, violent, wild.
OPPOSITES: SEE **quiet**.

rowing-boat noun dinghy, eight, skiff.
VARIOUS BOATS: SEE **vessel**.

royal adjective *a royal palace. by royal command.* imperial, kingly, majestic, princely, queenly, regal, stately.

royalty noun **1** = *royal family*.
2 = *payment to an author.* SEE **payment**.

MEMBERS OF ROYALTY: consort, Her or His Majesty, Her or His Royal Highness, king, monarch, prince, princess, queen, queen mother, regent, sovereign.
OTHER RULERS: SEE **ruler**.

---

rub verb **1** *to rub a sore place and make it better.* caress, knead, massage, smooth, stroke.
2 *to rub a place and damage it.* abrade, chafe, graze, scrape, wear away.
3 *to rub something clean.* polish, scour, scrub, wipe.
to rub out blot out, cancel, delete, erase, expunge, obliterate, remove, wipe out.
to rub up the wrong way SEE **annoy**.

rubber noun *a blackboard rubber.* cleaner, eraser.

rubbery adjective SEE **tough**.

rubbish noun **1** *Throw away that rubbish.* debris, dross, flotsam and jetsam, garbage, junk, leavings, [*informal*] leftovers, litter, lumber, muck, [*informal*] odds and ends, offcuts, refuse, rubble, scrap, trash, waste.
2 *Don't talk rubbish!* SEE **nonsense**.

rubble noun *The building collapsed into a pile of rubble.* broken bricks, debris, fragments, remains, ruins, wreckage.

rubicund adjective SEE **red**.

rubric noun SEE **explanation**.

ruck noun, verb SEE **crease** noun, verb.

rucksack noun bag, haversack, knapsack.

ructions noun SEE **row** noun.

ruddy adjective *a ruddy complexion.* fresh, flushed, glowing, healthy, SEE **red**, sunburnt.

rude noun *rude language. rude behaviour. a rude person.* abrupt, abusive, bad-mannered, bad-tempered, blasphemous, blunt, boorish, brusque, cheeky, churlish, coarse, common, condescending, contemptuous, crude, discourteous, disparaging, disrespectful, foul, graceless, gross, ignorant, ill-bred, ill-mannered, impertinent, impolite, improper, impudent, in bad taste, inconsiderate, indecent, insolent, insulting, loutish, mocking, naughty, oafish, SEE **obscene**, offensive, offhand, patronizing, peremptory, personal (*Don't make personal remarks*), saucy, scurrilous, shameless, tactless, unchivalrous, uncivil, uncomplimentary, uncouth, ungracious, [*old-fashioned*] unmannerly, unprintable, vulgar.
OPPOSITES: SEE **polite**.
to be rude to abuse, SEE **insult** verb, offend, sneer at, snub.

rudeness noun *I'm sick of her rudeness.* abuse, [*informal*] backchat, bad manners, boorishness, [*informal*] cheek, churlishness, condescension, contempt, discourtesy, disrespect, ill-breeding, impertinence, impudence, incivility, insolence, insults, oafishness, tactlessness, uncouthness, vulgarity.

rudiments noun *the rudiments of a subject.* basic principles, basics, elements, essentials, foundations, fundamentals, principles.

rudimentary adjective *He has only a rudimentary knowledge of the subject.* basic, crude, elementary, embryonic, immature, introductory, preliminary, primitive, provisional, undeveloped.
OPPOSITES: SEE **advanced**.

rueful adjective *a rueful expression.* SEE **sorrowful**.

ruffian noun [*informal*] brute, bully, desperado, gangster, hoodlum, hooligan, lout, mugger, SEE **rogue**, scoundrel, thug, [*informal*] tough, villain, [*informal*] yob.

ruffle verb **1** *A breeze ruffled the water.* agitate, disturb, ripple, stir.

2 *She ruffled his hair.* derange, dishevel, [*informal*] mess up, rumple, tousle.
OPPOSITES: SEE **smooth** verb.
3 *Their unexpected rudeness ruffled him.* annoy, disconcert, fluster, irritate, [*informal*] nettle, [*informal*] rattle, unsettle, upset, vex, worry.
OPPOSITES: SEE **calm** verb.

rug noun 1 *a rug to wrap yourself in.* blanket, coverlet.
2 *a rug to go on the floor.* mat, matting.

rugged adjective 1 *rugged mountains.* bumpy, craggy, irregular, jagged, rocky, rough, uneven.
2 *rugged good looks.* burly, husky, muscular, robust, rough, strong, sturdy, tough, unpolished, weather-beaten.

ruin noun 1 *the ruin of a business.* bankruptcy, breakdown, collapse, [*informal*] crash, destruction, downfall, end, failure, fall, ruination, undoing, wreck.
2 [*often plural*] *the ruins of a building.* debris, havoc, remains, rubble, ruined buildings [SEE **ruined**], wreckage.

ruin verb *The storm ruined the flowers.* damage, demolish, destroy, devastate, flatten, overthrow, shatter, spoil, wreck.

ruined adjective *a ruined castle.* crumbling, derelict, dilapidated, fallen down, in ruins, ramshackle, ruinous, tumbledown, uninhabitable, unsafe, wrecked.

ruinous adjective 1 *a ruinous disaster.* apocalyptic, cataclysmic, catastrophic, crushing, destructive, devastating, dire, disastrous, fatal, pernicious, shattering.
2 *The house was in a ruinous condition.* SEE **ruined**.

rule noun 1 *rules of conduct. the rules of a game.* code, convention, custom, law, practice, precept, principle, regulation, routine.
2 *under foreign rule.* administration, authority, command, control, domination, dominion, empire, government, influence, jurisdiction, management, mastery, power, regime, reign, sovereignty, supremacy, sway.

rule verb 1 *to rule a country.* administer, command, control, direct, dominate, govern, lead, manage, reign over, run.
2 *Elizabeth I ruled for many years.* be ruler [SEE **ruler**], reign.
3 *The umpire ruled that the batsman was out.* adjudicate, decide, decree, determine, find, judge, pronounce, resolve.
to rule out SEE **exclude**.

ruler noun VARIOUS RULERS: autocrat, caesar, SEE **chief** noun, demagogue, dictator, doge, emir, emperor, empress, governor, kaiser, king, lord, monarch, potentate, president, prince, princess, queen, rajah, regent, satrap, sovereign, sultan, suzerain, triumvirate [= *three people ruling jointly*], tyrant, tzar, viceroy.

rumble noun, verb VARIOUS SOUNDS: SEE **sound** noun.

ruminate verb SEE **meditate**.

rummage verb SEE **search** verb.

rumour noun *The scandalous story was only a rumour.* gossip, hearsay, prattle, scandal, whisper.

rump noun SEE **buttocks**.

rumple verb SEE **crumple**.

rumpus noun SEE **commotion**.

run noun 1 *a run across the park.* canter, dash, gallop, jog, marathon, race, sprint, trot.
2 *a run in the car.* drive, SEE **journey** noun, joyride, ride, [*informal*] spin.
3 *a run of bad luck.* chain, sequence, series, stretch.
4 *a chicken run.* compound, coop, enclosure, pen.

run verb 1 *We ran as fast as our legs could carry us.* bolt, canter, career, dash, gallop, hare, hurry, jog, race, rush, scamper, scoot, scurry, scuttle, speed, sprint, tear, trot.
2 *The buses don't run on Sundays.* go, operate, ply, provide a service, travel.
3 *The car runs well.* behave, function, perform, work.
4 *Water ran down the wall.* cascade, dribble, flow, gush, leak, pour, spill, stream, trickle.
5 *The government is supposed to run the country's affairs.* administer, conduct, control, direct, govern, look after, maintain, manage, rule, supervise.
to run across SEE **meet**.
to run after SEE **pursue**.
to run away abscond, [*informal*] beat it, bolt, depart, elope, SEE **escape** verb, [*informal*] take to your heels, [*informal*] turn tail.
to run into SEE **collide**.

runaway noun SEE **fugitive**.

runner noun 1 *a runner in a race.* athlete, competitor, entrant, jogger, participant, sprinter.
2 *The commanding officer sent a runner to headquarters.* courier, messenger.
3 *a runner of a plant.* offshoot, shoot, sprout.

running adjective 1 *three days running.* SEE **consecutive**.
2 *running water.* flowing, SEE **liquid** adjective.

runny adjective fluid, free-flowing, liquid, thin, watery.
OPPOSITES: SEE **viscous**.

runt noun SEE **small (small person)**.

runway noun air strip, landing-strip. SEE **airport**.

rupture verb SEE **burst**.

rural adjective *I like to get away from the town into rural surroundings.* agricultural, bucolic, countrified, pastoral, rustic, sylvan.

ruse noun SEE **trick** noun.

rush noun **1** *a rush to get things finished.* haste, hurry, pressure, race, scramble, urgency.
2 *a rush of water.* cataract, flood, gush, spate.
3 *a rush of people or animals.* charge, onslaught, panic, stampede.

rush verb *to rush home. to rush in with good news.* bolt, burst, canter, career, charge, dash, fly, gallop, hare, hasten, hurry, jog, move fast, race, run, scamper, scramble, scurry, scuttle, shoot, speed, sprint, stampede, [*informal*] tear, trot, [*informal*] zoom.

rust verb *Iron rusts.* become rusty [SEE **rusty**], corrode, crumble away, oxidize, rot.

rustic adjective **1** *rustic surroundings.* SEE **rural**.
2 *rustic fencing. rustic simplicity.* artless, clumsy, crude, rough, simple, unpolished, unsophisticated.

rustle verb VARIOUS SOUNDS: SEE **sound** noun.

rusty adjective **1** *rusty iron.* corroded, oxidized, rotten, tarnished.
2 [*informal*] *My French is a bit rusty.* dated, forgotten, unused.

rut noun *a rut in a path.* channel, furrow, groove, indentation, pothole, track, trough.

rutted adjective SEE **uneven**.

ruthless *a ruthless attack. ruthless criminals.* brutal, cruel, dangerous, ferocious, fierce, SEE **pitiless**, vicious, violent.

S

sabbatical noun SEE **holiday**.

sable adjective SEE **black** adjective.

sabotage noun *Terrorists were responsible for the sabotage.* deliberate destruction, disruption, treachery, vandalism, wilful damage, wrecking.

sabotage verb *to sabotage a machine.* cripple, damage, destroy, disable, put out of action, vandalize, wreck.

saboteur noun traitor, vandal, wrecker.

sabre noun SEE **sword**.

sachet noun SEE **container**.

sack noun bag, SEE **container**, pouch.
to get the sack be sacked [SEE **sack** verb], [*informal*] get your cards, lose your job.
to give someone the sack SEE **sack** verb.

sack verb **1** *to sack someone from a job.* [*informal*] axe, discharge, dismiss, [*informal*] fire, give (someone) notice, [*informal*] give (someone) the sack, lay off [= *to discharge temporarily*], make redundant.
2 *to sack a town.* SEE **plunder** verb.

sacred adjective *The Koran is a sacred book.* blessed, consecrated, dedicated, divine, godly, hallowed, holy, religious, revered, sacrosanct, venerated.
OPPOSITES: SEE **secular**.

sacrifice noun *a sacrifice to the gods.* [*formal*] oblation, offering, propitiation, votive offering.

sacrifice verb **1** *I sacrificed my weekend to finish the job.* abandon, forgo, give up, let go, lose, relinquish, surrender.
2 *to sacrifice an animal to the gods.* kill, offer up, slaughter.

sacrilege noun blasphemy, desecration, godlessness, impiety, irreverence, profanity, ungodliness.
OPPOSITES: SEE **piety**.

sacrilegious adjective SEE **blasphemous**.

sacrosanct adjective inviolate, protected, respected, SEE **sacred**, secure, untouchable.

sad adjective **1** *sad faces. sad emotions.* [*informal*] blue, broken-hearted, careworn, cheerless, crestfallen, dejected, depressed, desolate, despairing, desperate, despondent, disappointed, disconsolate, discontented, discouraged, disgruntled, dismal, dispirited, dissatisfied, distracted, distraught, distressed, doleful, dolorous, [*informal*] down, downcast, down-hearted, dreary, forlorn, gloomy, glum, grave, grief-stricken, grieving, grim, guilty, heartbroken, [*informal*] heavy, heavy-hearted, homesick, hopeless, in low spirits, [*informal*] in the doldrums, joyless, lachrymose, lonely, [*informal*] long-faced, [*informal*] low, lugubrious, melancholy, miserable, moody, moping, morose, mournful, pathetic, penitent, pessimistic, piteous, pitiable, pitiful, plaintive, poignant, regretful, rueful, serious, sober, sombre, sorrowful, sorry, tearful, troubled, unhappy,

upset, wistful, woebegone, woeful, wretched.
2 *sad news. a sad event.* calamitous, deplorable, depressing, disastrous, discouraging, distressing, grievous, heartbreaking, heart-rending, lamentable, morbid, moving, painful, regrettable, [*informal*] tear-jerking, touching, tragic, unfortunate, unsatisfactory, unwelcome, upsetting.
OPPOSITES: SEE **happy**.

sadden verb *Our friend's illness saddened us.* [*informal*] break (someone's) heart, depress, disappoint, discourage, dishearten, dismay, dispirit, distress, grieve, make sad [SEE **sad**], upset.
OPPOSITES: SEE **cheer** verb.

sadistic adjective SEE **cruel**.

sadness noun SEE **sorrow** noun.

safari noun SEE **holiday**.

safe adjective **1** *Is your house safe against burglars?* defended, foolproof, guarded, immune, impregnable, invulnerable, protected, secure.
OPPOSITES: SEE **vulnerable**.
2 *We got home safe in spite of the storm.* [*informal*] alive and well, [*informal*] all right, [*informal*] in one piece, intact, sound, undamaged, unharmed, unhurt, uninjured, unscathed.
OPPOSITES: SEE **damaged**.
3 *She's a safe driver.* cautious, circumspect, dependable, reliable, trustworthy.
4 *The dog's quite safe.* docile, friendly, harmless, innocuous, tame.
5 *The water's safe to drink. The food's safe to eat.* drinkable, eatable, good, non-poisonous, non-toxic, potable, pure, uncontaminated, wholesome.
OPPOSITES: SEE **dangerous**.
6 *a safe aircraft or ship.* airworthy. seaworthy.
to make safe defuse (*a bomb*), fasten down, fix, neutralize, secure, sterilize, tie down.

safeguard verb SEE **protect**.

safety noun **1** *The airline does all it can to ensure passengers' safety.* immunity, invulnerability, protection, security.
2 *The nurse assured me of the safety of the drug.* harmlessness, reliability.

safety-belt noun safety-harness, seat-belt.

sag verb *The rope sags in the middle.* be limp, dip, droop, fall, flop, hang down, sink, slump.

saga noun VARIOUS STORIES: SEE **story**.

sagacious, sage adjectives SEE **wise**.

sage noun SEE **wise (wise person)**.

sail noun **1** *the sails of a ship.*
KINDS OF SAIL: foresail, gaffsail, jib, lateen sail, lugsail, mainsail, mizzen, spinnaker, spritsail, topsail.
2 *We went for a sail.* cruise, SEE **journey** noun, sea-passage, voyage.

sail verb **1** *to sail a boat.* captain, navigate, pilot, skipper, steer.
2 *to sail in a boat.* cruise, paddle, punt, row, steam, SEE **travel** verb.

sailor noun mariner, seaman.
VARIOUS SAILORS: able seaman, bargee, boatman, boatswain or bosun, captain, cox or coxswain, [*plural*] crew, helmsman, mate, midshipman, navigator, pilot, rating, rower, yachtsman
RANKS IN THE NAVY: SEE **rank** noun.

saint noun SEE **good (good person)**.

saintly adjective angelic, blessed, SEE **good**, holy, innocent, pure, religious, sinless, virtuous.
OPPOSITES: SEE **devilish**.

sake noun *Do it for my sake.* advantage, behalf, benefit, gain, good, interest, welfare.

salacious adjective SEE **bawdy**.

salad noun

VEGETABLES OFTEN EATEN IN SALADS: beetroot, celery, chicory, cress, cucumber, lettuce, mustard and cress, onion, potato, radish, tomato, watercress.
OTHER VEGETABLES: SEE **vegetable**.

---

salary noun *a salary of £15,000 a year.* earnings, emolument, income, pay, payment, remuneration, stipend, wages.

sale noun KINDS OF SALE: auction, bazaar, closing-down sale, fair, jumble sale, market, winter sales.

salesman, salesperson, saleswoman nouns assistant, auctioneer, representative, shopkeeper.

salient adjective *salient features.* SEE **prominent**.

saline adjective SEE **salt** adjective.

saliva noun [*informal*] dribble, [*informal*] spit, spittle, [*formal*] sputum.

sallow adjective *a sallow complexion.* anaemic, bloodless, colourless, etiolated, pale, pallid, pasty, unhealthy, wan, yellowish.

salon noun SEE **room**.

saloon noun **1** SEE **room**.
2 [= *saloon car*] SEE **car**.

salt adjective *salt water.* brackish, briny, saline, salted, salty, savoury.
OPPOSITES: SEE **fresh.**
salt water brine, saline solution.

salting noun SEE **marsh.**

salty adjective SEE **salt** adjective.

salubrious adjective *The surroundings were not very salubrious.* health-giving, healthy, hygienic, invigorating, nice, pleasant, refreshing, sanitary, wholesome.
OPPOSITES: SEE **unhealthy.**

salutary adjective SEE **beneficial.**

salutation noun SEE **greeting.**

salute verb SEE **greet.**
WAYS TO GESTURE: SEE **gesture** verb.

salvage noun **1** *The salvage of the wreck will take weeks.* reclamation, recovery, rescue, retrieval, saving.
2 *We collect old newspapers and other salvage.* recyclable material, waste.

salvage verb *to salvage waste materials.* conserve, preserve, reclaim, recover, recycle, rescue, retrieve, re-use, save, use again.

salvation noun **1** [*theological*] *the salvation of souls.* redemption, saving.
OPPOSITE: damnation.
2 *When I lost my cash, my credit card was my salvation.* deliverance, escape, help, preservation, rescue, way out.

salve noun SEE **ointment.**

salve verb SEE **soothe.**

salver noun *a silver salver.* tray.

salvo noun *a salvo of guns.* SEE **gunfire.**

Samaritan noun SEE **good (good person).**

same adjective **1** *That's the same person who came yesterday.* actual, identical, selfsame.
2 *Make it the same shape. Come on the same date next year.* analogous, comparable, consistent, corresponding, duplicate, equal, equivalent, indistinguishable, interchangeable, matching, parallel, similar, synonymous [=*having the same meaning*], twin, unaltered, unchanged, uniform, unvaried.
OPPOSITES: SEE **different.**

sample noun *a sample of your work.* demonstration, example, foretaste, free sample, illustration, indication, instance, model, pattern, representative piece, selection, specimen.

sample verb *We sampled the food.* inspect, take a sample of [SEE **sample** noun], taste, test, try.

sanatorium noun SEE **hospital.**

sanctify verb SEE **bless.**

sanctimonious adjective [*uncomplimentary*] *sanctimonious preaching.* holier-than-thou, hypocritical, insincere, moralizing, pious, SEE **righteous,** self-righteous, sententious, [*informal*] smarmy, smug, superior, unctuous.
OPPOSITES: SEE **modest.**

sanction noun SEE **permission.**

sanction verb SEE **authorize.**

sanctity adjective SEE **holiness.**

sanctuary noun *The hunted fox found sanctuary in a wood.* asylum, haven, protection, refuge, retreat, safety, shelter.

sanctum noun holy place, retreat.
PLACES OF WORSHIP: SEE **worship** noun.

sand noun grit.
sands beach, seaside, shore, [*poetic*] strand.

sandal noun VARIOUS SHOES: SEE **shoe.**

sand-dune noun sand-hill.

sandstone noun VARIOUS ROCKS: SEE **rock** noun.

sane adjective *a sane person. a sane decision.* balanced, [*informal*] compos mentis, level-headed, lucid, normal, rational, reasonable, sensible, sound, stable.
OPPOSITES: SEE **mad.**

sang-froid noun SEE **calmness.**

sanguine adjective SEE **optimistic.**

sanitary adjective *sanitary conditions in a hospital.* aseptic, clean, disinfected, germ-free, healthy, hygienic, pure, salubrious, sterilized, uncontaminated, unpolluted.
OPPOSITES: insanitary, SEE **unhealthy.**

sanitation noun *You need proper sanitation on a camp-site.* drainage, drains, lavatories, sanitary arrangements, sewage disposal, sewers.

sap noun *the sap of a tree.* moisture, vital juices.

sap verb *The climb sapped our energy.* SEE **exhaust.**

sapling noun SEE **tree.**

sapper noun SEE **soldier.**

sarcasm noun SEE **ridicule** noun.

sarcastic adjective *sarcastic jokes. a sarcastic manner.* SEE **comic** adjective, contemptuous, cutting, demeaning, derisive, disparaging, hurtful, ironical, mocking, SEE **sardonic,** satirical, scathing, sharp, sneering, taunting, vitriolic, withering.

sarcophagus noun coffin.

sardonic adjective *sardonic humour.* acid, biting, black (*black comedy*), SEE

comic adjective, cynical, heartless, malicious, mordant, SEE **sarcastic**, wry.

sash noun *a sash round the waist.* band, belt, cummerbund, girdle, waistband.

satanic adjective SEE **devilish**.

satchel noun bag, SEE **container**, schoolbag, shoulder-bag.

sate verb SEE **satisfy**.

satellite noun **1** moon, planet.
ASTRONOMICAL TERMS: SEE **astronomy**.
2 *a man-made satellite.* SEE **space** noun.

satiate verb SEE **satisfy**.

satire noun *a satire on human folly.* burlesque, caricature, invective, irony, lampoon, mockery, parody, SEE **ridicule** noun, satirical comedy [SEE **satirical**], [*informal*] send-up, [*informal*] spoof, [*informal*] take-off, travesty.
OTHER KINDS OF WRITING: SEE **writing**.

satirical adjective *a satirical comedy.* SEE **comic** adjective, critical, disparaging, disrespectful, ironic, irreverent, mocking, SEE **sarcastic**.

satirize verb *to satirize someone's faults.* be satirical about [SEE **satirical**], burlesque, caricature, SEE **criticize**, deride, lampoon, laugh at, make fun of, mock, parody, ridicule, [*informal*] send up, [*informal*] take off, travesty.

satisfaction noun *I get satisfaction from my hobby.* comfort, contentment, enjoyment, fulfilment, gratification, happiness, pleasure, pride, self-satisfaction, sense of achievement.
OPPOSITES: SEE **dissatisfaction**.

satisfactory adjective *satisfactory work.* acceptable, adequate, [*informal*] all right, competent, fair, [*informal*] good enough, passable, pleasing, satisfying, sufficient, suitable, tolerable, [*informal*] up to scratch.
OPPOSITES: SEE **unsatisfactory**.

satisfy verb *to satisfy a need. to satisfy someone's curiosity.* appease, assuage, content, fulfil, gratify, make happy, meet, pacify, please, put an end to, quench (*your thirst*), sate, satiate, settle, slake (*your thirst*), supply.
OPPOSITES: SEE **frustrate**.

saturate verb *to saturate a sponge with water.* drench, impregnate, permeate, soak, steep, suffuse, wet.

saturated adjective *saturated with water.* drenched, soaked, sodden, steeped (in), suffused, waterlogged, wringing.

saturnine adjective SEE **gloomy**.

sauce noun KINDS OF SAUCE: bread sauce, cranberry sauce, custard, gravy, horseradish sauce, ketchup, mayonnaise, mint sauce, salad cream.

saucepan noun cauldron, pan, pot, skillet, stockpot.
OTHER CONTAINERS: SEE **container**.

saucer noun OTHER ITEMS OF CROCKERY: SEE **crockery**.

saucy adjective *saucy jokes.* SEE **impudent**.

sauna noun SEE **bath**.

saunter verb SEE **walk** verb.

sausage noun KINDS OF SAUSAGE: [*informal*] banger, chipolata, frankfurter, salami, saveloy.
OTHER KINDS OF MEAT: SEE **meat**.

sauté adjective *sauté potatoes.* fried.

savage adjective **1** *savage tribes.* barbarian, barbaric, cannibal, heathen, pagan, primitive, uncivilized, uncultivated, uneducated.
OPPOSITES: SEE **civilized**.
2 *savage beasts.* fierce, undomesticated, untamed, wild.
OPPOSITES: SEE **domesticated**.
3 *a savage attack.* angry, atrocious, barbarous, beastly, bestial, blistering, blood-thirsty, bloody, brutal, callous, cold-blooded, cruel, diabolical, ferocious, heartless, inhuman, merciless, murderous, pitiless, ruthless, sadistic, unfeeling, vicious, violent.
OPPOSITES: SEE **humane**.

savage noun *a violent savage.* barbarian, beast, brute, cannibal, fiend, savage person [SEE **savage** adjective].

savannah noun SEE **plain** noun.

save verb **1** *to save money.* collect, conserve, hold back, hold on to, hoard, invest, keep, [*informal*] put by, put in a safe place, reserve, retain, scrape together, set aside, [*informal*] stash away, store up, take care of.
OPPOSITES: SEE **squander**.
2 *to save fuel.* be sparing with, economize on, use wisely.
OPPOSITES: SEE **waste** verb.
3 *to save people or property from a wreck.* free, liberate, recover, release, rescue, retrieve, salvage, set free.
4 *to save someone from danger.* defend, guard, keep safe, preserve, protect, safeguard, screen, shield.
5 *I saved him from making a fool of himself.* check, deter, prevent, stop.

saving noun *You can make a saving if you buy in a sale.* cut, discount, economy, reduction.
savings *I put my savings in the bank.*

nest-egg, reserves, resources, riches, wealth.

saviour noun **1** *the saviour of a cause.* champion, defender, guardian, rescuer.
2 [*theological*] *Our Saviour.* Christ, Our Lord, The Messiah, The Redeemer.

savoir-faire noun SEE **knowledge**.

savour noun SEE **taste** noun.

savoury adjective *We often follow the savoury course with a sweet course.* appetizing, piquant, salty, SEE **tasty**.
OPPOSITES: SEE **sweet** adjective.

saw noun chain-saw, hack-saw, jigsaw.
VARIOUS TOOLS: SEE **tool**.

saw verb *to saw logs.* SEE **cut** verb.

say verb *Did you hear what I said?* affirm, allege, announce, answer, articulate, assert, [*informal*] come out with, comment, communicate, convey, declare, disclose, divulge, ejaculate, enunciate, exclaim, express, intimate, maintain, mention, mouth, pronounce, read aloud, recite, rejoin, remark, repeat, reply, report, respond, retort, reveal, speak, state, suggest, SEE **talk** verb, utter.

saying noun *an old Chinese saying.* adage, aphorism, apophthegm, axiom, [*informal*] catch-phrase, catchword, cliché, dictum, epigram, expression, formula, maxim, motto, phrase, precept, proverb, quotation, remark, [*old-fashioned*] saw, slogan, statement, tag, truism, watchword.

scab noun *a scab on a wound.* clot of blood, crust, sore.

scabbard noun *a scabbard for a sword.* sheath.

scaffold noun gallows.

scald verb SEE **heat** verb, **wound** verb.

scale noun **1** *scales on a fish.* flake, plate.
2 *scale in a kettle.* crust, deposit, encrustation, [*informal*] fur.
3 *a scale on a measuring instrument.* [*formal*] calibration, gradation.
4 *the social scale.* hierarchy, ladder, order, ranking, spectrum.
5 *a musical scale.* chromatic scale, diatonic scale, major scale, minor scale, sequence, series.
6 *the scale of a map.* proportion, ratio.
7 *We were amazed by the huge scale of the building.* SEE **size**.
scales *bathroom scales.* balance, weighing-machine.

scale verb *to scale a ladder.* ascend, climb, mount.

scallywag noun SEE **rascal**.

scalp noun SEE **head** noun.

scalpel noun SEE **knife** noun.

scamp noun SEE **rascal**.

scamper verb *to scamper home.* dash, hasten, hurry, run, rush, scuttle.
to scamper about frisk, frolic, gambol, play, romp, run about.

scampi plural noun prawns.

scan verb **1** *to scan the horizon.* examine, eye, gaze at, look at, scrutinize, search, stare at, study, survey, view, watch.
2 *to scan a newspaper.* glance at, read quickly, skim.

scandal noun **1** *It's a scandal when food is wasted.* disgrace, embarrassment, notoriety, outrage, reproach, sensation, shame.
2 *The newspapers shouldn't print such scandal.* calumny, gossip, libel, rumour, slander, [*informal*] tittle-tattle.

scandalize verb SEE **shock** verb.

scandalmonger noun SEE **gossip** noun.

scandalous adjective **1** *a scandalous waste of money.* disgraceful, improper, infamous, notorious, outrageous, shameful, shocking, wicked.
2 *a scandalous lie.* defamatory, libellous, scurrilous, slanderous, untrue.

scansion noun *the scansion of a line of verse.* metre, prosody, rhythm, SEE **verse**.

scanty adjective **1** *a scanty supply of food.* inadequate, insufficient, meagre, mean, [*slang*] measly, [*informal*] mingy, scant, scarce, [*informal*] skimpy, small, sparing, sparse, stingy.
OPPOSITES: SEE **plentiful**.
2 *scanty clothes.* barely adequate, indecent, revealing, [*informal*] see-through, thin.

scapegoat noun whipping-boy.

scar noun *The cut left a scar.* blemish, mark, scab, SEE **wound** noun.

scar verb *The wound scarred his face.* brand, damage, deface, disfigure, leave a scar on, mark, spoil.

scarce adjective *Water was scarce during the drought.* [*informal*] few and far between, [*informal*] hard to find, inadequate, infrequent, in short supply, insufficient, lacking, meagre, rare, scant, scanty, sparse, [*informal*] thin on the ground, uncommon, unusual.
OPPOSITES: SEE **plentiful**.

scarcely adverb barely, hardly, only just.

scarcity noun *a scarcity of water.* dearth, famine, inadequacy, insufficiency, lack, paucity, poverty, rarity, shortage, want.
OPPOSITES: SEE **plenty**.

scare noun *The bang gave us a nasty scare.* alarm, SEE **fright**, jolt, shock.

scare verb **1** *The bang scared us.* alarm, dismay, shake, shock, startle, unnerve.
2 *The ruffians tried to scare us.* bully, cow, daunt, dismay, SEE **frighten**, intimidate, make afraid, menace, panic, terrorize, threaten.
OPPOSITES: SEE **reassure**.

scaremonger noun alarmist.

scarf noun headscarf, muffler, shawl, stole.

scarify verb SEE **scratch** verb.

scarlet adjective SEE **red**.

scarp noun SEE **slope** noun.

scarper verb SEE **escape** verb.

scary adjective SEE **frightening**.

scathing adjective SEE **critical**.

scatter verb **1** *to scatter a crowd.* break up, disband, disintegrate, dispel, disperse, divide, send in all directions.
2 *to scatter seeds.* broadcast, disseminate, intersperse [= *scatter between other things*], shed, shower, sow, spread, sprinkle, strew, throw about.
OPPOSITES: SEE **gather**.

scatter-brained adjective absent-minded, careless, crazy, disorganized, forgetful, frivolous, inattentive, muddled, [*informal*] not with it, [*informal*] scatty, SEE **silly**, thoughtless, unreliable, unsystematic, vague.

scatty adjective SEE **scatter-brained**.

scavenge verb *to scavenge in a rubbish heap.* forage, rummage, scrounge, search.

scenario noun *the scenario of a film.* outline, plan, SEE **story**, summary.

scene noun **1** *the scene of a crime.* locale, locality, location, place, position, setting, site, situation, spot.
2 *a beautiful scene.* landscape, outlook, panorama, picture, prospect, scenery, sight, spectacle, view, vista.
3 *the scene for a play.* backdrop, scenery, set, stage.
4 *a scene from a play.* act, [*informal*] clip, episode, part, section, sequence.
5 *He made a scene because he didn't win.* argument, [*informal*] carry-on, commotion, disturbance, fuss, quarrel, row, [*informal*] to-do.

scenery noun SEE **scene**.

scenic adjective *a scenic journey.* attractive, beautiful, lovely, panoramic, picturesque, pretty, spectacular.

scent noun **1** *the scent of flowers.* fragrance, odour, perfume, redolence, SEE **smell** noun.
2 *a bottle of scent.* after-shave, eau de Cologne, lavender water, perfume.
OTHER COSMETICS: SEE **cosmetics**.
3 *The dog followed the scent.* trail.

scent verb SEE **smell** verb.

scented adjective SEE **smelling**.

sceptic noun agnostic, cynic, doubter, sceptical person [SEE **sceptical**].
OPPOSITES: SEE **believer**.

sceptical adjective *I was sceptical about the truth of his story.* cynical, disbelieving, distrustful, doubting, dubious, incredulous, mistrustful, questioning, suspicious, uncertain, unconvinced, unsure.
OPPOSITES: SEE **confident**.

scepticism noun agnosticism, cynicism, disbelief, distrust, doubt, incredulity, lack of confidence, suspicion.
OPPOSITES: SEE **faith**.

schedule noun *a schedule of events.* agenda, calendar, diary, itinerary, list, plan, programme, scheme, timetable.

schedule verb *When are we scheduled to arrive?* appoint, arrange, book, fix a time, organize, plan, programme, timetable.

scheme noun **1** *a proper scheme for running the business.* idea, method, plan, procedure, project, proposal, system.
2 *a dishonest scheme to make money.* conspiracy, [*informal*] dodge, intrigue, machinations, manœuvre, plot, [*informal*] ploy, [*informal*] racket, ruse, scheming, stratagem.
3 *a colour scheme.* arrangement, design.

scheme verb *Two boys schemed together.* collude, conspire, intrigue, plan, plot.

schism noun SEE **division**.

scholar noun **1** *a scholar of a school.* SEE **pupil**.
2 *The professor is a real scholar.* SEE **academic** noun.

scholarly adjective SEE **academic** adjective.

scholarship noun **1** *a scholarship to study at college.* award, bursary, exhibition, grant.
2 *a woman of great scholarship.* academic achievement, education, erudition, intellectual attainment, knowledge, learning, wisdom.

scholastic adjective SEE **academic** adjective.

school noun **1** See panel below.
2 *a school of whales.* SEE **group** noun, shoal.

KINDS OF SCHOOL: academy, boarding-school, coeducational school, college, comprehensive school, grammar school, high school, infant school, junior school, kindergarten, nursery school, play group, preparatory school, primary school, public school, secondary school.

PARTS OF A SCHOOL: assembly hall, cafeteria, common room, dormitory, classroom, cloakroom, foyer, gymnasium, hall, laboratory, library, office, playground, playing-field, reception, refectory, staff room, stock room.

PEOPLE WHO HELP RUN A SCHOOL: assistant, caretaker, groundsman, headmaster, headmistress, head teacher, librarian, monitor, peripatetic teacher, prefect, principal, secretary, [*plural*] staff, SEE **teacher**, technician, tutor.

---

schoolchild noun SEE **pupil**.

schooling noun SEE **education**.

schoolteacher noun SEE **teacher**.

science noun organized knowledge, systematic study.

SOME BRANCHES OF SCIENCE AND TECHNOLOGY: acoustics, aeronautics, agricultural science, anatomy, anthropology, artificial intelligence, astronomy, astrophysics, behavioural science, biochemistry, biology, biophysics, botany, chemistry, climatology, computer science, cybernetics, dietetics, domestic science, dynamics, earth science, ecology, economics, electronics, engineering, entomology, environmental science, food science, genetics, geographical science, geology, geophysics, hydraulics.

information technology, life science, linguistics, materials science, mathematics, mechanics, medical science [SEE **medicine**], metallurgy, meteorology, microbiology, mineralogy, ornithology, pathology, pharmacology, physics, physiology, political science, psychology, robotics, sociology, space technology, sports science, telecommunications, thermodynamics, toxicology, veterinary science, zoology.

---

scientific adjective *a scientific investigation.* analytical, methodical, organized, precise, systematic.

scientist noun [*informal*] boffin, researcher, scientific expert, technologist.
VARIOUS SCIENCES: SEE **science**.

scintillate verb SEE **light** noun (**give light**).

scion noun SEE **descendant**.

scissors noun SEE **cutter**.

scoff verb **1** *to scoff at someone.* SEE **jeer**.
2 [*informal*] *to scoff food.* SEE **eat**.

scold verb *to scold someone for wrongdoing.* admonish, berate, blame, castigate, censure, chide, criticize, find fault with, [*informal*] lecture, [*informal*] nag, rebuke, reprimand, reproach, reprove, [*informal*] tell off, [*informal*] tick off, upbraid.

scoop noun *an ice-cream scoop.* ladle, shovel, spoon.

scoop verb *to scoop out a hole.* dig, excavate, gouge, hollow, scrape, shovel.

scoot verb SEE **run** verb.

scope noun **1** *That kind of work is beyond my scope.* ambit, capacity, compass, competence, extent, limit, range, reach, sphere, terms of reference.
2 *scope for expansion.* chance, [*informal*] elbow-room, freedom, latitude, leeway, liberty, opportunity, outlet, room, space.

scorch verb SEE **burn** verb, **heat** verb.

scorching adjective SEE **hot**.

score noun **1** *the score in a game.* mark, number of points, reckoning, result, tally, total.
2 *a score to settle.* SEE **debt**.

score verb **1** *to score points in a game.* SEE **achieve**, add up, [*informal*] chalk up, earn, gain, [*informal*] knock up, make, win.
2 *to score a line on a surface.* cut, engrave, gouge, incise, mark, scrape, scratch, slash.
3 *to score a piece of music.* orchestrate, write out.

scorn noun *They viewed my cooking with scorn.* contempt, derision, detestation, disdain, disgust, dislike, disparagement, disrespect, mockery, ridicule.
OPPOSITES: SEE **admiration**.

scorn verb *They scorned my efforts.* be scornful about [SEE **scornful**], deride, despise, disapprove of, disdain, dislike, dismiss, hate, insult, jeer at, laugh at, look down on, make fun of, mock, reject, ridicule, [*informal*] scoff at, sneer at, spurn, taunt.
OPPOSITES: SEE **admire**.

scornful adjective *scornful laughter.* condescending, contemptuous, derisive, disdainful, dismissive, disrespectful, insulting, jeering, mocking, patronizing, sarcastic, satirical, scathing, sneering, [*informal*] snide, [*informal*] snooty, supercilious, taunting, withering (*a withering look*).
OPPOSITES: SEE **flattering**.

scotch verb SEE **end** verb.

scot-free adjective *He got off scot-free.* safe, unharmed, unhurt, unpunished, unscathed.

scoundrel noun [*Scoundrel* and synonyms are mostly used *informally.*] blackguard, blighter, good-for-nothing, heel, knave, miscreant, ne'er-do-well, rascal, rogue, ruffian, scallywag, scamp, villain.

scour verb **1** *to scour a saucepan.* buff up, burnish, clean, polish, rub, scrape, scrub, wash.
2 *I scoured the house looking for my purse.* comb, forage (through), hunt through, ransack, rummage through, search, [*informal*] turn upside down.

scourge noun, verb SEE **whip** noun, verb.

scout noun *They sent out scouts to get information.* lookout, spy.

scout verb *Wait here while I scout round.* explore, get information, investigate, look about, reconnoitre, search, [*informal*] snoop, spy.

scowl verb frown, glower.
FACIAL EXPRESSIONS: SEE **expression**.

scrabble verb *to scrabble about in the sand.* claw, dig, grope, scrape, scratch.

scraggy adjective *a weak, scraggy animal.* bony, emaciated, gaunt, lanky, lean, scrawny, skinny, starved, thin, underfed.
OPPOSITES: SEE **plump**.

scram verb SEE **depart**.

scramble noun SEE **race** noun.

scramble verb **1** *to scramble over rocks.* clamber, climb, crawl, move awkwardly.
2 *to scramble for food.* compete, contend, fight, jostle, push, scuffle, strive, struggle, tussle, vie.
3 *to scramble into your places.* dash, hasten, hurry, run, rush.
4 *to scramble eggs.* SEE **cook** verb.

scrap noun **1** *a scrap of food. a scrap of cloth.* bit, crumb, fraction, fragment, iota, mite, morsel, particle, piece, rag, shred, snippet, speck.
2 *a pile of scrap.* junk, litter, odds and ends, refuse, rubbish, salvage, waste.
3 *Two dogs had a scrap.* SEE **fight** noun.

scrap verb **1** *We scrapped our plan when we worked out the cost.* abandon, cancel, discard, [*informal*] ditch, drop, give up, jettison, throw away, write off.
2 *Those two are always scrapping.* SEE **fight** verb.

scrape noun *Don't get into any scrapes.* escapade, mischief, prank, trouble.

scrape verb **1** *to scrape your skin.* abrade, bark, graze, lacerate, scratch, scuff.
2 *to scrape something clean.* clean, file, rasp, rub, scour, scrub.
to scrape together *I scraped together enough for the bus fare.* SEE **collect**.

scrappy adjective *a scrappy programme which didn't hold my attention. scrappy work.* bitty, disjointed, fragmentary, hurriedly put together, imperfect, incomplete, inconclusive, sketchy, slipshod, unfinished, unpolished, unsatisfactory.
OPPOSITES: SEE **perfect** adjective.

scratch noun **1** *scratches on the furniture.* gash, groove, line, mark, scoring, scrape.
2 *a scratch on your skin.* graze, laceration, SEE **wound** noun.
up to scratch SEE **satisfactory**.

scratch verb *to scratch a car. to scratch your skin.* claw at, cut, damage the surface of, gouge, graze, incise, lacerate, mark, rub, scarify, score, scrape.

scrawl verb SEE **write**.

scrawny adjective SEE **scraggy**.

scream noun, verb bawl, cry, howl, roar, screech, shout, shriek, squeal, wail, yell.

scree noun stones.

screech noun, verb SEE **scream**.

screed noun SEE **writing**.

screen noun *a dividing screen.* blind, curtain, partition.

screen verb **1** *We planted a hedge to screen the manure heap.* camouflage, cloak, conceal, cover, disguise, guard, hide, mask, protect, safeguard, shade, shelter, shield, shroud, veil.
2 *All employees were screened before being appointed.* examine, investigate, vet.

screw noun **1** *a screw used in woodwork.*
OTHER FASTENERS: SEE **fastener**.
2 *the screws of a ship.* propeller.

screw verb **1** *to screw something down.* SEE **fasten**.
2 *to screw something into a spiral shape or with a spiral movement.* SEE **twist** verb.

screwy adjective SEE **mad**.

scribble verb SEE **write**.

scribe noun amanuensis, secretary, writer.

scrimmage noun SEE **fight** noun.

script noun **1** *cursive script.* handwriting.
2 *the script of a play.* screenplay, text, words.
VARIOUS KINDS OF WRITING: SEE **writing**.

scripture noun Bible, Koran, sacred writings, Word of God.

scroll noun SEE **book** noun.

scrounge verb *The stray cat scrounged scraps.* beg, cadge.

scrub verb **1** *to scrub the floor.* brush, clean, rub, scour, wash.
2 [*informal*] *to scrub your plans.* SEE **cancel**.

scruffy adjective *a scruffy appearance. scruffy clothes.* bedraggled, dirty, dishevelled, disordered, dowdy, messy, ragged, scrappy, shabby, slatternly, slovenly, tatty, ungroomed, unkempt, untidy, worn out.
OPPOSITES: SEE **smart** adjective.

scrumping noun SEE **stealing**.

scrumptious adjective SEE **delicious**.

scrunch verb SEE **crunch** verb.

scruples noun *Don't trust him—he has no scruples about cheating.* compunction, conscience, doubts, hesitation, misgivings, qualms.

scrupulous adjective **1** *a scrupulous worker. scrupulous attention to detail.* SEE **careful**, conscientious, diligent, fastidious, meticulous, minute, painstaking, precise, punctilious, rigorous, strict, systematic, thorough.
2 *a scrupulous businessman. scrupulous honesty.* ethical, fair-minded, honest, honourable, just, moral, proper, upright.
OPPOSITES: SEE **unscrupulous**.

scrutinize verb SEE **examine**.

scrutiny noun *She subjected my work to close scrutiny.* examination, inspection, investigation, search, study.

scuff verb SEE **scrape** verb.

scuffle noun, verb SEE **fight** noun, verb.

scull noun [Do not confuse with *skull*.] *the sculls of a rowing-boat.* oar, paddle.

scull verb *to scull a rowing-boat.* paddle, row.

sculpt verb SEE **sculpture** verb.

sculptor noun VARIOUS ARTISTS: SEE **artist**.

sculpture noun three-dimensional art.

KINDS OF SCULPTURE: bas-relief, bronze, bust, carving, caryatid, cast, effigy, figure, figurine, maquette, moulding, plaster cast, statue.
OTHER WORKS OF ART: SEE **art**.

---

sculpture verb *to sculpture a statue.* carve, cast, chisel, form, hew, model, mould, [*informal*] sculpt, shape.

scum noun *scum on dirty water.* film, foam, froth, impurities.

scupper verb SEE **sink** verb.

scurf noun *scurf in your hair.* dandruff, dry skin, flakes, scales.

scurrilous adjective **1** *a scurrilous attack on someone.* SEE **insulting**.
2 *scurrilous jokes.* SEE **obscene**.

scurry verb SEE **run** verb.

scuttle verb **1** *to scuttle a ship.* SEE **sink** verb.
2 *to scuttle away.* SEE **run** verb.

scythe noun billhook, sickle.

sea adjective *sea creatures. a sea voyage. a sea port.* aquatic, marine, maritime, nautical, naval, oceangoing, oceanic, saltwater, seafaring, seagoing.

sea noun [*joking*] the briny, [*poetic*] the deep, lake, ocean.

seal noun **1** sea-lion, walrus.
2 *the royal seal.* crest, emblem, impression, sign, stamp, symbol.

seal verb **1** *to seal a lid. to seal an envelope.* close, fasten, lock, secure, shut, stick down.
2 *to seal a leak.* make airtight, make waterproof, plug, stop up.
3 *to seal an agreement.* authenticate, [*informal*] clinch, conclude, confirm, decide, finalize, ratify, settle, sign, validate.

sealant noun SEE **glue** noun.

sea-lion noun seal, walrus.

seam noun **1** *the seam of a garment.* join, stitching.
2 *a seam of coal.* layer, stratum, thickness, vein.

seaman noun SEE **sailor**.

seamy adjective SEE **sordid**.

seaplane noun VARIOUS AIRCRAFT: SEE **aircraft**.

seaport noun SEE **port** noun.

sear verb SEE **burn** verb.

search noun *a search for the things we'd lost. a search for intruders.* check, examination, hunt, inspection, investigation, look, quest, scrutiny.

search verb **1** *I searched for the things we'd lost.* explore, ferret about, hunt, look, nose about, poke about, prospect, pry, seek.
2 *Security staff search all passengers.* check, examine, [*informal*] frisk, inspect, investigate, scrutinize.
3 *I searched the house for my purse.* comb, ransack, rifle, rummage through, scour.

searching adjective *searching questions.* deep, intimate, minute, penetrating, probing, sharp, thorough.
OPPOSITES: SEE **superficial**.

sea-shore noun SEE **seaside**.

seaside noun *a day at the seaside.* beach, coast, coastal resort, sands, sea-coast, sea-shore, shore.

season noun *the festive season. the holiday season.* period, phase, time.
SEASONS OF THE YEAR: autumn, spring, summer, winter.

season verb **1** *to season food.* add seasoning to, flavour, salt, spice.
2 *to season wood.* harden, mature.

seasonable adjective **1** *seasonable weather.* appropriate, normal, predictable, suitable.
2 *I'll wait for a seasonable moment to speak to her.* opportune, timely, well-timed.

seasoning noun *I don't add much seasoning to my food.* additives, condiments, flavouring.
KINDS OF SEASONING: dressing, herbs, mustard, pepper, relish, salt, SEE **sauce**, spice, vinegar.

seat noun KINDS OF SEAT: armchair, bench, chair, chaise longue, couch, deck-chair, pew, pillion, place, pouffe, reclining chair, rocking-chair, saddle, settee, settle, sofa, squab, stall, stool, throne, window seat.
ITEMS OF FURNITURE: SEE **furniture**.

seat verb **to seat yourself** SEE **sit**.

seat-belt noun safety-belt, safety-harness.

seaworthy adjective *a seaworthy ship.* safe, sound, watertight.

secateurs noun clippers, SEE **cutter**, pruning shears.

secede verb SEE **withdraw**.

secluded adjective *a secluded existence. a secluded beach.* cloistered, concealed, cut off, inaccessible, isolated, lonely, private, remote, screened, sequestered, sheltered, shut away, solitary, unfrequented, unvisited.
OPPOSITES: SEE **busy**.

seclusion noun *the seclusion of your own home. the seclusion of a hermit.* concealment, isolation, loneliness, privacy, retirement, shelter, solitariness.

second adjective *You won't get a second chance.* additional, alternative, another, duplicate, extra, further, repeated, SEE **secondary**, subsequent.

second noun **1** *The pain only lasted a second.* flash, instant, [*informal*] jiffy, moment, [*informal*] tick, [*informal*] twinkling.
2 *a second to a boxer in a fight.* assistant, helper, supporter.

second verb **1** *to second a proposal. to second someone in a fight.* assist, back, encourage, give approval to, help, promote, side with, support.
2 [pronounced se-*cond*] *to second someone to another job.* move, relocate, transfer.

secondary adjective **1** *of secondary importance.* inferior, lesser, lower, minor, second-rate, subordinate, subsidiary.
2 *a secondary line of attack.* auxiliary, extra, reinforcing, reserve, second, supplementary, supportive.
secondary school SEE **school**.

second-class adjective SEE **second-rate**.

second-hand adjective **1** *a second-hand car.* old, used.
OPPOSITES: SEE **new**.
2 *second-hand experience.* indirect, vicarious.
OPPOSITE: personal.

second-rate adjective *a second-rate performance.* commonplace, indifferent, inferior, low-grade, mediocre, middling, ordinary, poor, second-best, second-class, undistinguished, unexciting, uninspiring.

secret adjective *secret messages. secret meetings.* arcane, clandestine, classified, concealed, confidential, covert, cryptic, disguised, hidden, [*informal*] hushed up, [*informal*] hush-hush, inaccessible, intimate, invisible, occult, personal, private, secluded, SEE **secretive**, stealthy, undercover, underground, undisclosed, unknown, unpublished.
OPPOSITES: SEE **open** adjective.

secretary noun amanuensis, clerk, filing-clerk, personal assistant, scribe, shorthand-typist, stenographer, typist, word-processor operator.

secrete verb **1** *He secreted his winnings in a drawer.* SEE **hide** verb.
2 *The pores of your body secrete sweat.* SEE **discharge** verb.

secretion noun SEE **discharge** noun.

secretive adjective *secretive about his private life.* close-lipped, enigmatic, furtive, mysterious, quiet, reserved, reticent, shifty, tight-lipped, uncommunicative, unforthcoming, withdrawn.
OPPOSITES: SEE **communicative**.

sect noun *a religious sect.* cult, denomination, faction, SEE **group** noun, party.

sectarian adjective *sectarian beliefs.* bigoted, cliquish, dogmatic, exclusive, factional, fanatical, inflexible, narrow, narrow-minded, partisan, prejudiced, rigid, schismatic.

section noun *a section of a more complex whole.* bit, branch, chapter (*of a book*), compartment, component, department, division, fraction, fragment, instalment, part, passage (*from a book or piece of music*), portion, SEE **sector**, segment, slice, stage (*of a journey*), subdivision, subsection.

sector noun *a sector of a town.* area, district, division, part, quarter, region, SEE **section**, zone.

secular adjective *the secular authorities. secular music.* civil, earthly, lay, mundane, non-religious, [*formal*] temporal, worldly.
OPPOSITES: SEE **religious**.

secure adjective **1** *Is the house secure against burglars?* defended, foolproof, guarded, impregnable, invulnerable, protected, safe.
2 *During the storm we remained secure indoors.* snug, unharmed, unhurt, unscathed.
3 *Is that hook secure?* fast, firm, fixed, immovable, solid, steady, tight, unyielding.

secure verb SEE **fasten**.

security noun SEE **safety**.

sedate adjective *The procession moved at a sedate pace.* calm, collected, composed, cool, decorous, deliberate, dignified, grave, level-headed, quiet, sensible, serene, serious, slow, sober, solemn, staid, tranquil.
OPPOSITES: SEE **lively**.

sedate verb *The nurse sedated the patient.* calm, put to sleep, tranquillize, treat with sedatives.

sedative noun anodyne, barbiturate, narcotic, opiate, sleeping-pill, tranquillizer.

sedentary adjective *People in sedentary jobs need to take exercise.* immobile, inactive, seated, sitting down.
OPPOSITES: SEE **active**.

sediment noun *sediment at the bottom of a bottle.* deposit, dregs, lees, [*formal*] precipitate, remains, [*informal*] sludge.

sedition noun SEE **rebellion**.

seduce verb *to seduce someone into wicked ways.* allure, beguile, corrupt, debauch, decoy, deprave, entice, inveigle, lead astray, lure, mislead, tempt.

seduction noun **1** *the seductions of the big city.* SEE **temptation**.
2 *sexual seduction.* SEE **sex (sexual intercourse)**.

seductive adjective *a seductive dress. seductive music.* alluring, appealing, SEE **attractive**, bewitching, captivating, enticing, irresistible, provocative, [*informal*] sexy, tempting.
OPPOSITES: SEE **repulsive**.

sedulous adjective SEE **diligent**.

see verb **1** *What did you see?* [*old-fashioned*] behold, discern, discover, distinguish, [*old-fashioned*] espy, glimpse, identify, look at, make out, mark, note, notice, observe, perceive, recognize, sight, spot, spy, view, witness.
2 *I can see what you mean.* appreciate, comprehend, fathom, follow, grasp, know, realize, take in, understand.
3 *I see problems ahead.* anticipate, conceive, envisage, foresee, foretell, imagine, picture, visualize.
4 *I'll have to see what I can do.* consider, decide, investigate, reflect on, think about, weigh up.
5 *Did you see the game on Saturday?* attend, be a spectator at, watch.
6 *She's going to see him again tonight.* go out with, have a date with, meet, visit.
7 *Shall I see you home?* accompany, conduct, escort.
8 *The homeless see much misery.* endure, experience, go through, suffer, undergo.
9 *Guess who I saw in town!* encounter, face, meet, run into, visit.
to see red SEE **angry (become angry)**.
to see to SEE **attend (attend to)**.

seed noun **1** *a seed from which something will grow.* egg, germ, ovule, ovum, semen, [*plural*] spawn, sperm, spore.
2 *a seed in a fruit.* pip, stone.

seed verb *to seed a lawn.* SEE **sow** verb.

seedy adjective **1** [*informal*] *a seedy appearance.* SEE **shabby**.
2 [*informal*] *feeling seedy.* SEE **ill**.

seek verb *to seek something you've lost. to seek revenge.* ask for, aspire to, beg for, desire, hunt for, inquire after, look for, pursue, search for, solicit, strive after, want, wish for.

seem verb *She isn't as well as she seems.* appear, feel, give an impression of being, look, pretend, sound.

seemly adjective SEE **proper**.

seep verb *Oil seeped through the crack.* dribble, drip, exude, flow, leak, ooze, percolate, run, soak, trickle.

seer noun SEE **prophet**.

see-saw verb SEE **alternate** verb.

seethe verb **1** *The water in the pan began to seethe.* be agitated, boil, bubble, foam, froth up, rise, simmer, surge.
2 *She seethed with anger.* SEE **angry (be angry)**.

segment noun SEE **section**.

segregate verb *They segregated visitors from the home supporters.* cut off, isolate, keep apart, put apart, separate, set apart.

segregation noun **1** *racial segregation.* apartheid, discrimination, separation.
2 *the segregation of sick animals.* isolation, quarantine.

seismic adjective SEE **earthquake**.

seize verb **1** *to seize something in your hands.* catch, clutch, grab, grasp, grip, hold, pluck, snatch, take.
2 *to seize a person by force.* abduct, apprehend, arrest, capture, [*informal*] collar, detain, [*informal*] nab, take prisoner.
3 *to seize a country.* annex, invade.
4 *to seize property.* appropriate, commandeer, confiscate, hijack, impound, steal, take away.
OPPOSITES: SEE **release** verb.

seizure noun *to suffer a seizure.* apoplexy, attack, convulsion, epileptic fit, fit, paroxysm, spasm, stroke.

seldom adverb infrequently, rarely.
OPPOSITES: SEE **often**.

select adjective *Only a select few were invited.* choice, chosen, élite, exclusive, first-class, [*informal*] hand-picked, preferred, privileged, rare, selected, special, top-quality.
OPPOSITES: SEE **ordinary**.

select verb *to select a representative. to select your purchases.* appoint, choose, decide on, elect, nominate, opt for, pick, prefer, settle on, single out, vote for.

selection noun **1** *There's a wide selection to choose from.* assortment, SEE **range** noun, variety.
2 *Make your selection.* choice, option, pick.

selective adjective *She's very selective in what she watches on TV.* careful, [*informal*] choosy, discerning, discriminating, particular, specialized.
OPPOSITES: SEE **undiscriminating**.

self-assured adjective SEE **self-evident**.

self-catering noun SEE **accommodation**.

self-centred adjective SEE **selfish**.

self-command noun SEE **self-control**.

self-confident adjective *Try to look self-confident at the interview.* assertive, assured, bold, collected, cool, fearless, poised, positive, self-assured, self-possessed, sure of yourself.
OPPOSITES: SEE **self-conscious**.

self-conscious adjective *self-conscious in front of an audience.* awkward, bashful, blushing, coy, diffident, embarrassed, ill at ease, insecure, nervous, reserved, self-effacing, sheepish, shy, uncomfortable, unnatural.
OPPOSITES: SEE **self-confident**.

self-contained adjective **1** *a self-contained flat.* complete, separate.
2 *a self-contained person.* aloof, cold, independent, reserved, self-reliant, undemonstrative, unemotional.
OPPOSITES: SEE **sociable**.

self-control noun *He showed great self-control when they were teasing him.* calmness, composure, coolness, patience, restraint, self-command, self-discipline, will-power.

self-denial noun *Lent is a time of self-denial.* abstemiousness, fasting, moderation, self-sacrifice, temperance.
OPPOSITES: SEE **self-indulgence**.

self-employed adjective *a self-employed journalist.* free-lance, independent.

self-esteem noun SEE **pride**.

self-evident, **self-explanatory** adjectives SEE **obvious**.

self-governing adjective *a self-governing country.* autonomous, independent, sovereign.

self-important adjective SEE **pompous**.

self-indulgent adjective *a self-indulgent pursuit of pleasure.* dissipated, epicurean, extravagant, greedy, hedonistic, intemperate, pleasure-loving, profligate, SEE **selfish**, sybaritic.
OPPOSITES: SEE **abstemious**.

self-indulgence noun extravagance, greed, hedonism, pleasure, self-gratification, SEE **selfishness**.
OPPOSITES: SEE **self-denial**.

self-interest noun SEE **selfishness**.

selfish adjective *It's selfish to keep it all to yourself.* demanding, egocentric, egotistic, grasping, greedy, mean, mercenary, miserly, self-centred, self-indulgent, self-seeking, [*informal*] stingy, thoughtless, worldly.
OPPOSITES: SEE **unselfish**.

selfishness noun egotism, greed, meanness, miserliness, self-indulgence, self-

interest, self-love, self-regard, [*informal*] stinginess, thoughtlessness.
OPPOSITES: SEE **unselfishness**.

selfless adjective SEE **unselfish**.

self-possessed adjective SEE **self-confident**.

self-reliant adjective SEE **self-supporting**.

self-respect noun SEE **pride**.

self-righteous adjective *Don't feel self-righteous just because you gave an odd coin to charity.* complacent, [*informal*] holier-than-thou, pious, pompous, priggish, proud, sanctimonious, self-important, self-satisfied, sleek, smug, vain.
a self-righteous person [*informal*] goody-goody, prig.

self-sacrifice noun SEE **unselfishness**.

self-satisfied adjective SEE **self-righteous**.

self-seeking adjective SEE **selfish**.

self-sufficient adjective SEE **self-supporting**.

self-supporting adjective *a self-supporting community.* independent, self-contained, self-reliant, self-sufficient.

self-willed adjective SEE **obstinate**.

sell verb **1** *What does this shop sell?* deal in, [*informal*] keep, offer for sale, retail, stock, trade in (*He trades in electrical goods*), traffic in, vend.

VARIOUS WAYS TO SELL THINGS: auction, barter, give in part-exchange, hawk, [*informal*] knock down, peddle, [*informal*] put under the hammer, sell off, tout, trade-in (*He traded-in his old car*).

---

2 *If business is slack, we must sell our product more attractively.* advertise, market, merchandise, package, promote, [*informal*] push.

seller noun vendor.

PEOPLE WHO SELL THINGS: agent, barrow-boy, costermonger, dealer, [*old-fashioned*] hawker, market-trader, merchant, pedlar, [*informal*] rep, representative, retailer, salesman, saleswoman, shopkeeper, stockist, storekeeper, street-trader, supplier, trader, tradesman, traveller, wholesaler.
PARTICULAR SHOPS: SEE **shop**.

---

selvage noun SEE **edge** noun.

semantic adjective SEE **meaning**.

semblance noun SEE **appearance**.

semester noun SEE **time** noun.

semi-detached noun VARIOUS HOUSES: SEE **house** noun.

seminal adjective *seminal ideas.* constructive, creative, fertile, imaginative, important, innovative, new, original, productive.

senate, senator nouns SEE **government**.

send verb **1** *to send a parcel. to send a cheque.* convey, dispatch, post, remit, transmit.
2 *to send a rocket to the moon.* direct, fire, launch, propel, shoot.
to send away banish, dismiss, exile, expel.
to send out belch, broadcast, discharge, emit, give off.
to send round circulate, distribute, issue, publish.
to send up SEE **parody** verb.

send-off noun SEE **farewell**.

send-up noun SEE **parody** noun.

senile adjective SEE **old**.

senior adjective *a senior position. a senior member of the team.* chief, higher, major, older, principal, revered, superior, well-established.
OPPOSITES: SEE **junior**.

sensation noun **1** *a tingling sensation in my fingers.* awareness, feeling, sense.
2 *The robbery caused a sensation.* SEE **commotion**, excitement, furore, outrage, scandal, surprise, thrill.

sensational adjective **1** *a sensational account of a murder. the sensational experience of hang-gliding.* blood-curdling, breathtaking, exciting, hair-raising, lurid, shocking, startling, stimulating, thrilling, violent.
2 [*informal*] *a sensational football result.* amazing, SEE **extraordinary**, fabulous, fantastic, great, marvellous, remarkable, spectacular, superb, surprising, unexpected, wonderful.

sense noun **1** *She has no sense of shame.* awareness, consciousness, faculty, feeling, intuition, perception, sensation.
YOUR FIVE SENSES ARE: hearing, sight, smell, taste, touch.
2 *If you had any sense you'd stay at home.* brains, cleverness, gumption, intellect, intelligence, judgement, logic, [*informal*] nous, reason, reasoning, understanding, wisdom, wit.
3 *Did you grasp the sense of her message?* denotation, [*informal*] drift, gist, import,

interpretation, meaning, point, significance.
to make sense of SEE **understand.**

sense verb *I sensed that he was bored. The machine senses any change of temperature.* be aware (of), detect, discern, feel, guess, notice, perceive, realize, respond to, suspect, understand.
WAYS IN WHICH WE SENSE THINGS: SEE **feel, hear, see, smell, taste** verbs.

senseless adjective **1** *a senseless thing to do.* SEE **stupid.**
2 *knocked senseless.* SEE **unconscious.**

sensibility noun *artistic sensibility.* SEE **feeling.**

sensible adjective **1** *a sensible person. a sensible decision.* calm, common-sense, cool, discriminating, intelligent, judicious, level-headed, logical, prudent, rational, realistic, reasonable, sane, serious-minded, sound, straightforward, thoughtful, wise.
OPPOSITES: SEE **stupid.**
2 *sensible clothes.* comfortable, functional, [*informal*] no-nonsense, practical, useful.
OPPOSITES: SEE **fashionable, impractical.**

sensitive adjective **1** *sensitive to light.* affected (by), responsive, susceptible.
2 *sensitive to someone's problems.* considerate, perceptive, sympathetic, tactful, thoughtful, understanding.
3 *Take care what you say—he's very sensitive.* emotional, hypersensitive, thin-skinned, touchy.
4 *a sensitive skin.* delicate, fine, fragile, painful, soft, tender.
5 *a sensitive subject.* confidential, controversial, secret.
OPPOSITES: SEE **insensitive.**

sensual adjective **1** *sensual pleasures.* animal, bodily, carnal, fleshly, physical, self-indulgent, SEE **sexual**, voluptuous, worldly.
2 *a sensual expression. sensual lips.* pleasure-loving, SEE **sexy.**
OPPOSITES: SEE **ascetic.**

Sensual often implies disapproval (especially when it has sexual connotations), whereas *sensuous* does not.

---

sensuous adjective *a sensuous description. sensuous music.* affecting, appealing, beautiful, emotional, lush, rich, richly embellished.
OPPOSITES: SEE **simple.**

sentence noun **1** LINGUISTIC TERMS: SEE **language.**
2 LEGAL TERMS: SEE **law.**

sentence verb *The judge sentenced the convicted man.* condemn, pass judgement on, pronounce sentence on.

sententious adjective SEE **pompous.**

sentient adjective SEE **conscious.**

sentiment noun **1** *What are your sentiments about experiments on animals?* attitude, belief, idea, judgement, opinion, thought, view.
2 *The reader communicated the sentiment of the poem most powerfully.* emotion, feeling, SEE **sentimentality.**

The noun *sentimentality* always implies disapproval (*I hate the sentimentality of animal stories*), whereas *sentiment* does not necessarily imply disapproval.

---

sentimental adjective **1** *Old family photographs make me sentimental.* emotional, nostalgic, romantic, soft-hearted, tearful, tender, [*informal*] weepy.
2 [*uncomplimentary*] *I hate sentimental words on birthday cards.* gushing, indulgent, insincere, maudlin, mawkish, [*informal*] mushy, overdone, over-emotional, [*informal*] sloppy, [*informal*] soppy, [*informal*] sugary, tear-jerking, [*informal*] treacly, unrealistic.
OPPOSITES: SEE **cynical, realistic.**

sentimentality noun emotionalism, insincerity, [*informal*] kitsch, mawkishness, nostalgia, [*informal*] slush.

sentinel, sentry nouns guard, look-out, picket, watchman.

separable adjective *separable components.* detachable, removable.

separate adjective **1** *They kept visiting supporters separate from ours.* apart, cut off, divided, divorced, fenced off, isolated, segregated.
2 *We all have separate jobs to do. We work in separate buildings.* detached, different, discrete, distinct, free-standing, unattached, unconnected, unrelated.
3 *The islanders have their own separate government.* autonomous, free, independent, particular.

separate verb **1** *to separate people or things or places from each other.* break up, cut off, detach, disconnect, disentangle, disjoin, dissociate, divide, fence off, hive off, isolate, keep apart, part, segregate, set apart, sever, split, sunder, take apart.
OPPOSITES: SEE **unite.**
2 *Our paths separated.* diverge, fork.
OPPOSITES: SEE **merge.**
3 *to separate grain from chaff.* abstract, filter out, remove, sift out, winnow.
OPPOSITES: SEE **mix.**

4 *to separate from your spouse.* become estranged, divorce, part company, [*informal*] split up.

separation noun **1** *the separation of one thing from another.* amputation, cutting off, detachment, disconnection, dissociation, division, parting, removal, segregation, severance, splitting.
OPPOSITES: SEE **connection**.
2 *the separation of a married couple.* [*informal*] break-up, divorce, estrangement, rift, split.

septic adjective *a septic wound.* festering, infected, inflamed, poisoned, purulent, putrefying, suppurating.

septuagenarian noun SEE **old (old person)**.

sepulchral adjective SEE **funereal**.

sepulchre noun SEE **tomb**.

sequel noun *the sequel of an event or story.* consequence, continuation, [*informal*] follow-up, outcome, result, upshot.

sequence noun **1** *an unbroken sequence of events.* chain, concatenation, cycle, procession, progression, SEE **series**, succession, train.
2 *a sequence from a film.* episode, scene, section.

sequester verb SEE **confiscate**.

sequin noun decoration, spangle.

seraphic adjective SEE **angelic**.

serenade verb SEE **perform**.

serene adjective *a serene mood. serene music.* calm, contented, imperturbable, peaceful, placid, pleasing, quiet, tranquil, unclouded, unruffled, untroubled.
OPPOSITES: SEE **agitated**.

serial noun SEE **series**.

series noun **1** *a series of events.* arrangement, chain, concatenation, course, cycle, line, order, procession, programme, progression, range, row, run, sequence, set, string, succession, train.
2 *a television series.* mini-series, serial, [*informal*] soap, soap-opera.

serious adjective **1** *a serious expression.* dignified, grave, grim, humourless, long-faced, pensive, sedate, sober, solemn, staid, stern, thoughtful, unsmiling.
OPPOSITES: SEE **cheerful**.
2 *a serious discussion. serious literature.* deep, earnest, heavy, important, intellectual, profound, sincere, weighty.
OPPOSITES: SEE **frivolous**.
3 *a serious accident. a serious illness.* acute, appalling, awful, calamitous, critical, dangerous, dreadful, frightful, ghastly, grievous, hideous, horrible, nasty, severe, shocking, terrible, unfortunate, unpleasant, violent.
OPPOSITES: SEE **trivial**.
4 *a serious worker.* careful, committed, conscientious, diligent, hard-working.
OPPOSITES: SEE **casual**.

sermon noun SEE **talk** noun.

sermonize verb SEE **preach**.

serpent noun snake.

serpentine adjective SEE **twisty**.

serrated adjective *a serrated edge.* jagged, notched, saw-like, toothed.
OPPOSITES: SEE **straight**.

servant noun assistant, attendant, [*informal*] dogsbody, drudge, [*joking*] factotum, [*joking*] flunkey, helper, hireling, menial, [*informal*] skivvy, slave, vassal.

VARIOUS SERVANTS: au pair, barmaid, barman, batman, butler, chamber-maid, [*informal*] char, charwoman, chauffeur, commissionaire, cook, [*informal*] daily, errand boy, footman, home help, housekeeper, housemaid, kitchenmaid, lackey, lady-in-waiting, maid, manservant, page, parlourmaid, retainer, [*plural*] retinue, scout, slave, steward, stewardess, valet, waiter, waitress.

---

serve verb **1** *to serve the community.* aid, assist, attend, further, help, look after, minister to, work for.
2 *to serve in the armed forces.* be employed, do your duty.
3 *to serve food. to serve at table.* [*informal*] dish up, distribute, give out, officiate, wait.
4 *to serve in a shop.* assist, be an assistant, sell goods.

service noun **1** *Would you do me a small service?* assistance, benefit, favour, help, kindness, office.
2 *He spent his life in the service of the same firm.* attendance (on), employment, ministering (to), work (for).
3 *a bus service.* business, organization, provision, system, timetable.
4 *a service for a car.* check-over, maintenance, overhaul, repair, servicing.
5 *a religious service.* ceremony, liturgy, meeting, rite, worship.

VARIOUS CHURCH SERVICES: baptism, christening, communion, compline, Eucharist, evensong, funeral, Lord's Supper, marriage, Mass, matins, Requiem Mass, vespers.

---

service verb *to service a car.* check, maintain, mend, overhaul, repair, tune.

serviceable adjective *a pair of strong serviceable shoes.* dependable, durable, functional, hard-wearing, lasting, practical, strong, tough, usable.
OPPOSITES: SEE **impractical**.

serviceman, servicewoman nouns SEE **armed services**.

serviette noun napkin, table-napkin.

servile adjective *servile self-abasement.* abject, [*informal*] boot-licking, craven, cringing, fawning, flattering, grovelling, humble, ingratiating, menial, obsequious, slavish, submissive, subservient, sycophantic, unctuous.
OPPOSITES: SEE **bossy**.
to be servile be at someone's beck and call, fawn, grovel, ingratiate yourself, [*informal*] kowtow, [*informal*] lick (someone's) boots, toady.

serving noun *a serving of food.* helping, plateful, portion, ration.

servitude noun SEE **slavery**.

session noun **1** *The court is in session.* assembly, conference, discussion, hearing, meeting, sitting.
2 *a session at the swimming-baths.* period, time.

set noun **1** *a set of people. a set of tools.* batch, bunch, category, class, clique, collection, SEE **group** noun, kind, series, sort.
2 *a TV set.* apparatus, receiver.
3 *a set for a play.* scene, scenery, setting, stage.

set verb **1** *to set something in place.* arrange, assign, deploy, deposit, dispose, lay, leave, locate, lodge, park, place, plant, [*informal*] plonk, position, put, rest, set down, set out, settle, situate, stand, station.
2 *to set a gate-post in concrete.* embed, fasten, fix.
3 *to set a watch.* adjust, correct, put right, rectify, regulate.
4 *to set a question in an exam.* ask, express, formulate, frame, phrase, put forward, suggest, write.
5 *Has the jelly set?* become firm, congeal, [*informal*] gel, harden, [*informal*] jell, stiffen, take shape.
6 *to set a target. to set a date.* allocate, allot, appoint, decide, designate, determine, establish, identify, name, ordain, prescribe, settle.
to set about 1 *I set about my work.* SEE **begin**.
2 *They set about us with their fists.* SEE **attack** verb.
to set free SEE **liberate**.
to set off 1 *We set off on a journey.* SEE **depart**.
2 *They set off a bomb.* SEE **explode**.
to set on *The dogs set on him.* SEE **attack** verb.
to set on fire SEE **ignite**.
to set to SEE **begin**.
to set up SEE **establish**.

set-back noun *We were delayed by a set-back.* [*informal*] blow, complication, difficulty, disappointment, [*informal*] hitch, misfortune, obstacle, problem, reverse, snag, upset.

settee noun chaise longue, couch, sofa.

setting noun **1** *a beautiful setting for a picnic.* background, context, environment, location, place, position, site, surroundings.
2 *a setting for a drama.* backcloth, backdrop, scene, scenery, set.

settle noun SEE **seat** noun.

settle verb **1** *to settle something in place.* SEE **set** verb.
2 *They plan to settle here.* become established, colonize, immigrate, make your home, move to, occupy, people, set up home, stay.
3 *We settled on the sofa. A bird settled on the fence.* alight, come to rest, land, light, [*informal*] make yourself comfortable, [*informal*] park yourself, pause, rest, sit down.
4 *Wait until the dust settles.* calm down, clear, compact, go down, sink, subside.
5 *We settled what to do.* agree, choose, decide, establish, fix.
6 *They settled their differences.* conclude, deal with, end, reconcile, resolve, square.
7 *I settled the bill.* pay.

settlement noun **1** *a business settlement.* SEE **arrangement**.
2 *a human settlement.* colony, community, encampment, kibbutz, SEE **town**, village.

settler noun colonist, immigrant, newcomer, pioneer, squatter.

sever verb *to sever a limb. to sever a relationship.* amputate, break, break off, SEE **cut** verb, cut off, disconnect, end, part, remove, separate, split, terminate.

several adjective assorted, different, a few, many, miscellaneous, a number of, sundry, various.

severe adjective **1** *a severe ruler. a severe look.* cold-hearted, cruel, disapproving, forbidding, grim, hard, harsh, oppressive, pitiless, relentless, stern, strict, unkind, unsmiling, unsympathetic.
OPPOSITES: SEE **kind** adjective.

2 *a severe frost. severe flu.* acute, bad, drastic, extreme, great, intense, keen, serious, sharp, troublesome, violent.
OPPOSITES: SEE **mild**.
3 *severe conditions. a severe test of stamina.* arduous, dangerous, demanding, difficult, nasty, spartan, stringent, taxing, tough.
OPPOSITES: SEE **easy**.
4 *a severe style of dress.* austere, chaste, plain, simple, unadorned.
OPPOSITES: SEE **ornate**.

sew verb *to sew up a hole in your jeans.* darn, mend, repair, stitch, tack.

sewage noun effluent, waste.

sewers noun drainage, drains, sanitation, septic tank, soak-away.

sewing noun dressmaking, embroidery, mending, needlepoint, needlework, tapestry.

sex noun *a person's sex.* gender, sexuality.
to have sexual intercourse be intimate, consummate marriage, copulate, couple, fornicate, [*informal*] have sex, make love, mate, rape, unite.

KINDS OF SEXUALITY: bisexual, hermaphrodite, heterosexual, homosexual.

WORDS TO DESCRIBE SEXUAL ACTIVITY: [*old-fashioned*] carnal knowledge, coitus, consummation of marriage, copulation, coupling, fornication, incest, intercourse, intimacy, love-making, masturbation, mating, orgasm, perversion, rape, seduction, sexual intercourse, union.

---

sexism noun [*informal*] chauvinism (*male chauvinism*), SEE **prejudice** noun.

sexist adjective [*informal*] chauvinist, SEE **prejudiced**.

sexual adjective *sexual feelings.* carnal, erotic, physical, sensual, SEE **sexy**, venereal (*venereal diseases*).

sexuality noun SEE **sex**.

sexy adjective **1** *a sexy person.* attractive, desirable, [*informal*] dishy, flirtatious, seductive, sensual, [*informal*] sultry, voluptuous.
2 *sexy feelings.* amorous, erotic, lascivious, lecherous, libidinous, lustful, passionate, [*informal*] randy.
3 *sexy talk. sexy books.* aphrodisiac, erotic, SEE **obscene**, pornographic, provocative, [*informal*] raunchy, suggestive, titillating, [*informal*] torrid.

shabby adjective **1** *shabby clothes.* dingy, dirty, dowdy, drab, faded, frayed, grubby, [*informal*] moth-eaten, ragged, [*informal*] scruffy, seedy, tattered, [*informal*] tatty, threadbare, unattractive, worn, worn-out.
OPPOSITES: SEE **smart** adjective.
2 *shabby behaviour. a shabby trick.* despicable, dishonest, dishonourable, disreputable, [*informal*] low-down, mean, nasty, shameful, unfair, unfriendly, unkind, unworthy.
OPPOSITES: SEE **honourable**.

shack noun cabin, SEE **house** noun, hovel, hut, lean-to, shanty, shed.

shackle verb SEE **chain** verb.

shackles noun SEE **chain** noun.

shade noun **1** *the shade of a tree.* SEE **shadow** noun.
2 *a shade to keep the sun off.* blind, canopy, covering, parasol, screen, shelter, shield, umbrella.
3 *a pale shade of blue.* colour, hue, tinge, tint, tone.

shade verb **1** *I shaded my eyes from the sun.* conceal, hide, mask, protect, screen, shield, shroud, veil.
2 *I shaded the background with a pencil.* block in, cross-hatch, darken, fill in, make dark.

shadow noun **1** *I sat in the shadow of a tree.* darkness, dimness, gloom, [*formal*] penumbra, semi-darkness, shade, [*formal*] umbra.
2 *The sun casts shadows.* outline, shape.

shadow verb *The detective shadowed the suspect.* follow, hunt, [*informal*] keep tabs on, keep watch on, pursue, stalk, [*informal*] tag onto, tail, track, trail, watch.

shadowy adjective **1** *a shadowy figure.* dim, faint, ghostly, hazy, indistinct, nebulous, obscure, unrecognizable, vague.
2 *a shadowy path through the woods.* SEE **shady**.

shady adjective **1** *a shady spot under a tree.* cool, dark, dim, gloomy, shaded, shadowy, sheltered, sunless.
OPPOSITES: SEE **sunny**.
2 *a shady character.* dishonest, disreputable, dubious, [*informal*] fishy, shifty, suspicious, untrustworthy.
OPPOSITES: SEE **honest**.

shaft noun **1** *a wooden shaft.* arrow, column, handle, pillar, pole, post, rod, stem, stick.
2 *a shaft of light.* beam, ray.
3 *a mine-shaft.* mine, pit, working.

shaggy adjective *a shaggy beard. a shaggy texture.* bushy, fibrous, fleecy, hairy,

hirsute, rough, tousled, unkempt, untidy, woolly.
OPPOSITES: SEE **clean-shaven, smooth** adjective.

shake verb 1 *An explosion made the house shake.* convulse, heave, jump, quake, quiver, rattle, rock, shiver, shudder, sway, throb, totter, tremble, vibrate, waver, wobble.
2 *I shook my watch to get it going again.* agitate, brandish, flourish, jar, jerk, [*informal*] jiggle, [*informal*] joggle, jolt, twirl, twitch, wag, [*informal*] waggle, wave, [*informal*] wiggle.
3 *The terrible news shook us.* alarm, distress, disturb, frighten, perturb, shock, startle, unnerve, unsettle, upset.

shaky adjective 1 *shaky hands.* quivering, shaking, trembling.
2 *a shaky table.* flimsy, frail, ramshackle, rickety, rocky, unsteady, weak, wobbly.
3 *a shaky voice.* faltering, nervous, quavering, tremulous.
OPPOSITES: SEE **steady** adjective.
4 *a shaky start.* insecure, precarious, uncertain, under-confident, unimpressive, unpromising, unreliable, unsound.

shallow adjective 1 *shallow water.* [Surprisingly, there are no convenient synonyms for this common sense of *shallow.*]
2 *a shallow person, shallow arguments.* facile, foolish, frivolous, glib, insincere, puerile, silly, simple, slight, superficial, trivial, unconvincing, unscholarly, unthinkable.
OPPOSITES: SEE **deep**.

sham adjective *I saw through his sham surprise.* SEE **imitation** adjective.

sham noun *It was all a sham.* SEE **pretence**.

sham verb *He was shamming.* SEE **pretend**.

shamble verb SEE **walk** verb.

shambles noun 1 slaughter-house.
2 [*informal*] *My room is a shambles.* chaos, confusion, disorder, mess, muddle.

shame noun 1 *the shame of being found out.* degradation, discredit, disgrace, dishonour, embarrassment, guilt, humiliation, ignominy, mortification, opprobrium, remorse, stain, stigma.
2 [*informal*] *It's a shame to treat a dog so badly!* outrage, pity, scandal.

shame verb *They shamed him into admitting everything.* discomfit, disconcert, disgrace, embarrass, humble, humiliate, make ashamed [SEE **ashamed**], [*informal*] show up.

shamefaced adjective *a shamefaced expression.* abashed, SEE **ashamed**, embarrassed, [*informal*] hang-dog, mortified, penitent, repentant, self-conscious, sheepish, sorry.
OPPOSITES: SEE **shameless**.

shameful adjective *a shameful defeat. a shameful crime.* base, contemptible, degrading, discreditable, disgraceful, dishonourable, humiliating, ignominious, inglorious, outrageous, reprehensible, scandalous, unworthy, SEE **wicked**.
OPPOSITES: SEE **honourable**.

shameless adjective *He's shameless about his cheating and lying.* barefaced, bold, brazen, cheeky, cool, defiant, flagrant, hardened, impenitent, impudent, incorrigible, insolent, rude, unabashed, unashamed, unrepentant.
OPPOSITES: SEE **shamefaced**.

shampoo verb SEE **wash** verb.

shanghai verb SEE **compel**.

shanty noun *a shanty town.* SEE **shack**.

shape noun configuration, figure, form, format, model, mould, outline, pattern, silhouette.

FLAT SHAPES: circle, diamond, ellipse, heptagon, hexagon, lozenge, oblong, octagon, oval, parallelogram, pentagon, polygon, quadrant, quadrilateral, rectangle, rhomboid, rhombus, ring, semicircle, square, trapezium, trapezoid, triangle.

THREE-DIMENSIONAL SHAPES: cone, cube, cylinder, decahedron, hemisphere, hexahedron, octahedron, polyhedron, prism, pyramid, sphere.

---

shape verb *The sculptor shaped the stone.* carve, cast, cut, fashion, form, frame, give shape to, model, mould, [*informal*] sculpt, sculpture, whittle.

shapeless adjective 1 *a shapeless mass.* amorphous, formless, indeterminate, irregular, nebulous, undefined, unformed, vague.
OPPOSITE: defined.
2 *a shapeless figure.* [*informal*] dumpy, unattractive, unshapely.
OPPOSITES: SEE **shapely**.

shapely adjective *a shapely figure.* attractive, [*informal, sexist*] curvaceous, elegant, graceful, trim, [*informal, sexist*] voluptuous, well-proportioned.
OPPOSITES: SEE **shapeless**.

share noun *Everyone got a share of the cake.* allocation, allowance, bit, cut, division, fraction, helping, part, piece, portion, proportion, quota, ration, [*informal*] whack.

share verb **1** *We shared the food equally.* allocate, allot, apportion, deal out, distribute, divide, [*informal*] go halves or shares (with), halve, partake of, portion out, ration out, share out, split.
2 *If we share the work we'll finish quickly.* be involved, co-operate, join, participate, take part.

shared adjective *a shared responsibility.* collective, combined, common, co-operative, corporate, joint, united.
OPPOSITES: SEE **individual** adjective.

sharp adjective **1** *a sharp knife. a sharp point.* cutting, fine, jagged, keen, pointed, razor-sharp, sharpened, spiky.
OPPOSITES: SEE **blunt** adjective.
2 *a sharp corner. a sharp drop.* abrupt, acute, angular, hairpin (*a hairpin bend*), precipitous (*a precipitous drop*), steep, sudden, surprising, unexpected.
OPPOSITES: SEE **gradual**.
3 *a sharp picture.* clear, defined, distinct, focused, well-defined.
OPPOSITES: SEE **blurred**.
4 *a sharp frost.* extreme, heavy, intense, serious, severe, violent.
OPPOSITES: SEE **slight** adjective.
5 *a sharp pain.* acute, excruciating, painful, stabbing, stinging.
6 *a sharp tongue.* acerbic, acid, acidulous, barbed, biting, caustic, critical, hurtful, incisive, mocking, mordant, sarcastic, sardonic, scathing, trenchant, unkind, vitriolic.
OPPOSITES: SEE **kind** adjective.
7 *a sharp taste or smell.* acid, acrid, bitter, caustic, pungent, sour, tangy, tart.
OPPOSITES: SEE **bland**.
8 *a sharp mind.* acute, alert, astute, bright, clever, cute, discerning, incisive, intelligent, observant, perceptive, quick, quick-witted, shrewd, [*informal*] smart.
OPPOSITES: SEE **stupid**.
9 *a sharp sound.* clear, high, penetrating, piercing, shrill.
OPPOSITES: SEE **muffled**.

sharpen verb *to sharpen a knife.* file, grind, hone, make sharp, strop, whet.
OPPOSITE: blunt.

sharpener noun KINDS OF SHARPENER: file, grindstone, hone, pencil-sharpener, strop, whetstone.

sharp-eyed adjective SEE **observant**.

sharpshooter noun SEE **marksman**.

shatter verb *to shatter a window.* blast, break, break up, burst, crack, destroy, disintegrate, explode, pulverize, shiver, smash, splinter, split, wreck.

shattered adjective **1** *shattered by the bad news.* SEE **upset** adjective.
2 [*informal*] *shattered after all that effort.* SEE **exhausted**.

shave verb SEE **cut** verb.

shaven adjective SEE **clean-shaven**.

shawl noun scarf, stole.

sheaf noun *a sheaf of papers.* bunch, bundle.

shear verb *to shear sheep.* clip, SEE **cut** verb, strip, trim.

shears noun SEE **cutter**.

sheath noun *a sheath for a sword.* casing, covering, scabbard, sleeve.

sheathe verb *Sheathe your swords!* cocoon, cover, encase, SEE **enclose**, put away, put in a sheath.

sheath-knife noun SEE **knife** noun.

shed noun *a garden shed.* hut, lean-to, outhouse, potting-shed, shack, shelter, storehouse.
OTHER BUILDINGS: SEE **building**.

shed verb *A lorry shed its load. I shed a few tears.* cast off, discard, drop, let fall, scatter, shower, spill, throw off.

sheen noun *a nice sheen on the furniture.* brightness, burnish, gleam, gloss, lustre, patina, polish, shine.

sheep noun ewe, lamb, mutton [= *meat from sheep*], ram, wether.

sheep-fold noun SEE **enclosure**.

sheepish adjective *a sheepish look.* abashed, ashamed, bashful, coy, embarrassed, guilty, mortified, self-conscious, shamefaced, shy, timid.
OPPOSITES: SEE **shameless**.

sheer adjective **1** *sheer nonsense.* absolute, complete, out-and-out, pure, total, unmitigated, unqualified, utter.
2 *a sheer cliff.* abrupt, perpendicular, precipitous, vertical.
3 *sheer silk.* diaphanous, fine, flimsy, [*informal*] see-through, thin, transparent.

sheet noun **1** *sheets for a bed.* OTHER BEDCLOTHES: SEE **bedclothes**.
2 *a sheet of paper.* folio, leaf, page.
3 *a sheet of glass.* pane, panel, plate.
4 *a sheet of ice on a pond.* coating, covering, film, layer, skin.
5 *a sheet of water.* area, expanse, surface.

shelf noun ledge, shelving.

shell noun **1** *a hard outer shell.* carapace [= *shell of a tortoise*], case, casing, covering, crust, exterior, husk, outside, pod.
2 *a shell from a gun.* SEE **ammunition**.

shell verb *to shell the enemy.* attack, barrage, bomb, bombard, fire at, shoot at, strafe.

shellac noun, verb varnish.

shellfish noun bivalve, crustacean, mollusc.

VARIOUS SHELLFISH: barnacle, clam, cockle, conch, crab, crayfish, cuttlefish, limpet, lobster, mussel, oyster, prawn, scallop, shrimp, whelk, winkle.

---

shelter noun 1 *Where can we find shelter from the wind?* asylum, cover, haven, lee, protection, refuge, safety, sanctuary.
2 *a shelter against the wind.* barrier, cover, fence, hut, roof, screen, shield.
3 *an air-raid shelter.* bunker.

shelter verb 1 *The fence sheltered us from the wind.* defend, guard, protect, safeguard, screen, shade, shield.
2 *Is it wrong to shelter a criminal?* accommodate, give shelter to [SEE **shelter** noun], harbour, hide.

sheltered adjective 1 *a sheltered spot.* enclosed, on the leeward side, protected, quiet, screened, shielded, snug, windless.
OPPOSITE: exposed.
2 *a sheltered life.* cloistered, isolated, limited, lonely, unadventurous, unexciting, withdrawn.
OPPOSITES: SEE **adventurous**.

shelve verb 1 *They shelved their plan.* SEE **postpone**.
2 *The beach shelves gently.* SEE **slope** verb.

shemozzle noun SEE **commotion**.

shepherd noun FARM WORKERS: SEE **farm** noun.

sheriff noun SEE **official** noun.

shield noun 1 *a shield against the wind.* barrier, defence, guard, protection, safeguard, screen, shelter.
2 *a warrior's shield.* buckler, [*in heraldry*] escutcheon.

shield verb *to shield someone from danger.* cover, defend, guard, keep safe, protect, safeguard, screen, shade, shelter.

shift noun 1 *a shift in your position.* SEE **change** noun, **move** noun.
2 *working on a night shift.* group, period.
3 *a woman's shift.* SEE **dress** noun.

shift verb *to shift your position.* SEE **change** verb, **move** verb.

shiftless adjective SEE **ineffective**.

shifty adjective *I didn't trust his shifty expression.* crafty, deceitful, devious, dishonest, evasive, furtive, scheming, secretive, [*informal*] shady, [*informal*] slippery, sly, tricky, untrustworthy, wily.
OPPOSITES: SEE **straightforward**.

shilly-shally verb SEE **prevaricate**.

shimmer verb SEE **light** noun (**give light**).

shine noun *a shine on the furniture.* SEE **polish** noun.

shine verb 1 SEE **light** noun (**give light**).
2 *What do you shine at?* be clever, do well, excel.
3 [*informal*] *to shine your shoes.* SEE **polish** verb.

shining adjective 1 *a shining light.* brilliant, glittering, glowing, luminous, radiant, SEE **shiny**, sparkling.
2 *a shining example.* conspicuous, eminent, glorious, outstanding, praiseworthy, resplendent, splendid.

shingle noun 1 *shingle on the beach.* gravel, pebbles, stones.
2 *shingles on the roof.* tile.

shiny adjective *a shiny surface.* bright, burnished, dazzling, gleaming, glistening, glossy, lustrous, polished, reflective, rubbed, shining, sleek.
OPPOSITES: SEE **dull** adjective, matt.

ship noun VARIOUS SHIPS: SEE **vessel**.

ship verb *to ship goods to a foreign country.* SEE **transport** verb.

shipment noun SEE **load** noun.

shipshape adjective SEE **tidy** adjective.

shipwreck noun SEE **disaster**.

shipwright noun shipbuilder.

shire noun county.

shirk verb *to shirk your duty.* avoid, dodge, duck, evade, get out of, neglect.
to shirk work be lazy, malinger, [*informal*] skive, slack.

shirty adjective SEE **annoyed**.

shiver verb *to shiver with cold.* quake, quaver, quiver, shake, shudder, tremble, twitch, vibrate.

shoal noun 1 *a shoal of fish.* SEE **group** noun.
2 *stranded on a shoal.* sand-bank, shallows.

shock noun 1 *the shock of an explosion.* blow, collision, concussion, impact, jolt.
2 *His sudden death was a great shock.* blow, bombshell, SEE **surprise** noun.
3 *in a state of shock.* dismay, distress, fright, [*formal*] trauma, upset.

shock verb 1 *The unexpected news shocked us.* alarm, amaze, astonish, astound, confound, daze, dismay, distress, frighten, [*informal*] give someone a turn, jolt, numb, paralyse, scare, shake, stagger,

startle, stun, stupefy, surprise, [*formal*] traumatize, unnerve.
2 *The bad language shocked us.* appal, disgust, horrify, offend, outrage, repel, revolt, scandalize.

shocking adjective **1** *a shocking experience.* alarming, distressing, frightening, SEE **painful**, staggering, traumatic, unnerving, upsetting.
2 *shocking bad language.* SEE **outrageous**.

shoddy adjective **1** *shoddy goods.* cheap, flimsy, gimcrack, inferior, jerry-built, nasty, poor quality, rubbishy, tawdry, trashy.
OPPOSITES: SEE **superior**.
2 *shoddy work.* careless, messy, negligent, slipshod, sloppy, slovenly, untidy.
OPPOSITES: SEE **careful**.

shoe noun [*plural*] footwear.

KINDS OF SHOE: boot, bootee, brogue, clog, espadrille, [*plural*] galoshes, gumboot, [*informal*] lace-up, moccasin, plimsoll, pump, sabot, sandal, [*informal*] slip-on, slipper, trainer, wader, wellington.

---

shoemaker noun bootmaker, cobbler.

shoot noun *shoots of a plant.* branch, bud, new growth, offshoot, sprout, twig.

shoot verb **1** *to shoot a gun.* aim, discharge, fire.
2 *to shoot animals. to shoot someone in the street.* aim at, bombard, fire at, gun down, hit, SEE **hunt** verb, SEE **kill** verb, open fire on, [*informal*] pick off, shell, snipe at, strafe, [*informal*] take pot-shots at.
3 *He shot out of his chair.* dart, dash, hurtle, leap, move quickly, rush, streak.
4 *Plants shoot in the spring.* bud, grow, put out shoots, spring up, sprout.

shooting-range noun butts, rifle-range.

shooting star meteor.
ASTRONOMICAL TERMS: SEE **astronomy**.

shop noun boutique, cash-and-carry, department store, [*old-fashioned*] emporium, establishment, market, retailer, seller, store, wholesaler.

VARIOUS SHOPS AND BUSINESSES: antique shop, baker, bank, barber, betting shop, bookmaker, bookshop, building society, butcher, café, chandler, chemist, clothes shop, confectioner, creamery, dairy, delicatessen, DIY, draper, electrician, estate agent, fish and chip shop, fishmonger, florist, furniture store, garden-centre, greengrocer, grocer, haberdasher, hairdresser, hardware store, health-food shop, herbalist, hypermarket, insurance brokers, ironmonger, jeweller.
launderette, market, newsagent, off-licence, outfitters, pawnbroker, pharmacy, post office, poulterer, radio and TV shop, shoemaker, stationer, supermarket, tailor, take-away, tobacconist, toyshop, video-shop, vintner, watchmaker.

---

shopkeeper noun dealer, merchant, retailer, salesgirl, salesman, saleswoman, stockist, storekeeper, supplier, trader, tradesman.

shop-lifter noun SEE **thief**.

shopper noun buyer, customer.

shopping noun **1** *Christmas shopping.* buying, [*informal*] spending-spree.
2 *Put the shopping in a carrier-bag.* goods, purchases.

shopping-bag noun SEE **bag** noun.

shopping-centre noun *an indoor shopping-centre.* arcade, complex, mall, precinct.

shore noun *the shore of a lake or the sea.* bank, beach, coast, edge, foreshore, sands, seashore, seaside, shingle, [*old-fashioned*] strand.

shore verb **to shore up** SEE **support** verb.

short adjective **1** *a short piece of string.* [There is no obvious synonym for *short* in this sense.] OPPOSITES: SEE **long** adjective.
2 *a short person.* diminutive, dumpy, dwarfish, little, [*of a woman*] petite, small, squat, stubby, stumpy, tiny, [*informal*] wee, undergrown.
OPPOSITES: SEE **tall**.
3 *a short visit.* brief, cursory, curtailed, ephemeral, fleeting, momentary, passing, quick, temporary, transient, transitory.
OPPOSITES: SEE **long** adjective.
4 *a short book.* abbreviated, abridged, compact, concise, shortened, succinct, terse.
OPPOSITES: SEE **long** adjective.
5 *During the drought water was in short supply.* deficient, inadequate, insufficient, lacking, limited, meagre, scanty, scarce, sparse, wanting.
OPPOSITES: SEE **plentiful**.
6 *He was short with me when I asked for a loan.* abrupt, bad-tempered, blunt, brusque, cross, curt, gruff, grumpy, impolite, irritable, laconic, sharp, snappy,

testy, unfriendly, unkind, unsympathetic.
OPPOSITES: SEE **friendly**.

shortage noun *a shortage of water during drought.* absence, dearth, deficiency, insufficiency, lack, paucity, poverty, scarcity, shortfall, want.
OPPOSITES: SEE **plenty**.

short-change verb SEE **cheat** verb.

shortcoming noun *Bad language is one of his shortcomings.* defect, failing, fault, foible, imperfection, vice, weakness.

shorten verb *I shortened my story because it was too long.* abbreviate, abridge, compress, condense, curtail, cut down, cut short, précis, prune, reduce, summarize, telescope, trim, truncate.
OPPOSITES: SEE **lengthen**.

shorthand noun stenography.

short-lived adjective SEE **temporary**.

shortly adverb *The post will arrive shortly.* directly, presently, soon.

shorts noun SEE **trousers**.

short-tempered adjective SEE **cross** adjective.

short-term adjective *a short-term solution.* SEE **temporary**.

shot noun **1** *a shot from a gun.* ball, bang, blast, bullet, crack, discharge, pellet, round, [*informal*] slug.
2 *He's a good shot.* SEE **marksman**.
3 *a shot at goal.* attempt, effort, endeavour, [*informal*] go (*Have a go!*), hit, kick, stroke, try.
4 *The photographer took some unusual shots.* angle, photograph, picture, scene, sequence, snap.
a shot in the arm SEE **encouragement**.
a shot in the dark SEE **guess** noun.

shotgun noun SEE **gun**.

shoulder verb SEE **carry**.

shout verb bawl, bellow, [*informal*] belt (*Belt it out!*), call, cheer, clamour, cry out, exclaim, rant, roar, scream, screech, shriek, talk loudly, vociferate, yell, yelp.
OPPOSITES: SEE **whisper** verb.
OTHER WAYS TO USE YOUR VOICE: SEE **talk** verb.

shouting noun SEE **clamour** noun.

shove verb *They shoved me out of the way.* barge, crowd, drive, elbow, hustle, jostle, SEE **push**, shoulder.

shovel verb *I shovelled the snow off the path.* clear, dig, scoop, shift.

show noun **1** *a show at the theatre.* SEE **entertainment**, performance, production.
2 *an art show. a dog show.* competition, display, exhibition, presentation.
3 *a show of strength.* appearance, demonstration, façade, illusion, impression, pose, pretence, threat.
4 *He does it all for show.* exhibitionism, flamboyance, ostentation, showing off.

show verb **1** *We showed our work in public.* display, exhibit, open up, present, produce, reveal.
2 *My knee showed through a hole in my jeans.* appear, be seen, be visible, emerge, materialize, stand out.
3 *She showed me the way.* conduct, direct, guide, indicate, point out.
4 *He showed me great kindness.* bestow (upon), confer (upon), treat with.
5 *The photo shows us at work.* depict, give a picture of, illustrate, picture, portray, represent.
6 *She showed me how to do it.* describe, explain, instruct, make clear, teach, tell.
7 *The tests showed that I was right.* attest, demonstrate, evince, exemplify, manifest, prove, witness (to).
to show off SEE **boast**.
to show up SEE **appear, reveal**.

show-down noun *a show-down between two rivals.* confrontation, crisis, [*informal*] decider, decisive encounter.

shower noun **1** SEE **rain** noun.
2 douche.

shower verb *A passing bus showered mud over us.* deluge, rain, spatter, splash, spray, sprinkle.

showery adjective WORDS TO DESCRIBE WEATHER: SEE **weather** noun.

show-off noun [*informal*] big-head, boaster, braggart, conceited person [SEE **conceited**], egotist, exhibitionist, [*informal*] poser, poseur, [*informal*] showman.

showy adjective *showy clothes.* bright, conspicuous, flamboyant, flashy, garish, gaudy, [*informal*] loud, lurid, ostentatious, pretentious, striking, trumpery.
OPPOSITES: SEE **restrained**.

shred noun *not a shred of evidence.* bit, iota, jot, piece, scrap, snippet, trace.
shreds *torn to shreds.* rags, ribbons, strips, tatters.

shred verb cut to shreds, grate, tear.

shrewd adjective *a shrewd politician.* artful, astute, [*informal*] canny, clever, crafty, cunning, discerning, discriminating, ingenious, intelligent, knowing, observant, perceptive, quick-witted, sharp, sly, smart, wily, wise.
OPPOSITES: SEE **stupid**.

shrewish adjective SEE **bad-tempered**.

shriek noun, verb SEE **scream**.

shrill adjective *a shrill voice.* ear-splitting, high, high-pitched, penetrating, piercing, piping, screaming, sharp, strident, treble.
OPPOSITES: SEE **gentle, sonorous**.

shrine noun holy place.
PLACES OF WORSHIP: SEE **worship** noun.

shrink verb **1** *The pond shrank during the drought. The laundry has shrunk my jumper.* become smaller, contract, decrease, diminish, dwindle, lessen, make smaller, narrow, reduce, shorten, SEE **shrivel**.
OPPOSITES: SEE **expand**.
2 *The dog shrank when the cat spat at him.* back off, cower, cringe, flinch, hang back, quail, recoil, retire, wince, withdraw.

shrivel verb *The plants shrivelled in the heat.* become parched, dehydrate, droop, dry out, dry up, SEE **shrink**, wilt, wither, wrinkle.

shrivelled adjective SEE **wrinkled**.

shroud noun *a shroud of mist.* blanket, cover, mantle, pall, veil.

shroud verb *Mist shrouded the top of the mountain.* cloak, conceal, cover, enshroud, envelop, hide, mask, screen, swathe, veil, wrap up.

shrub noun bush, tree.

COMMON SHRUBS: azalea, berberis, blackthorn, broom, bryony, buddleia, camellia, daphne, forsythia, gorse, heather, hydrangea, japonica, jasmine, lavender, lilac, myrtle, privet, rhododendron, rosemary, rue, viburnum.

---

shrubbery noun SEE **garden**.

shrug noun, verb SEE **gesture** noun, verb.

shudder verb *I shuddered when I heard the gory details.* be horrified, convulse, quake, quiver, shake, shiver, squirm, tremble.

shuffle verb **1** *I shuffled upstairs in my slippers.* SEE **walk** verb.
2 *to shuffle cards.* jumble, mix, mix up, rearrange, reorganize.

shun verb SEE **avoid**.

shunt verb SEE **divert**.

shut verb *Shut the door.* bolt, close, fasten, latch, lock, push to, replace, seal, secure, slam.
to shut in, to shut up confine, detain, enclose, imprison, incarcerate, keep in.
to shut off cut off, isolate, segregate, separate, stop.
to shut out ban, bar, exclude, keep out, prohibit.
Shut up! Be quiet! Be silent! [*informal*] Hold your tongue! Hush! Keep quiet! [*informal*] Pipe down! Silence! Stop talking!

shutter noun *Close the shutter.* blind, louvre, screen.

shuttle verb SEE **travel** verb.

shy adjective *I was too shy to call out.* backward, bashful, cautious, chary, coy, diffident, hesitant, inhibited, modest, [*informal*] mousy, nervous, reserved, reticent, retiring, self-conscious, self-effacing, timid, timorous, wary.
OPPOSITES: SEE **assertive**.

shy verb SEE **throw**.

sibilant adjective hissing.

sibling noun brother, sister, twin.
FAMILY RELATIONSHIPS: SEE **family**.

sibyl noun SEE **prophet**.

sibylline adjective SEE **prophetic**.

sick adjective **1** *unable to work because she was sick.* ailing, bedridden, diseased, SEE **ill**, indisposed, infirm, [*informal*] laid up, [*informal*] poorly, [*informal*] queer, sickly, unwell.
2 *He feels sick.* bilious, likely to vomit, nauseous, queasy.
3 *We're sick of their rude behaviour.* annoyed (by), disgusted (by), distressed (by), nauseated (by), sickened (by), upset (by).
4 *I'm sick of that tune.* bored (with), [*informal*] fed up (with), glutted (with), sated (with), tired, weary.
to be sick SEE **vomit**.

sicken verb *The sight of people fighting sickens me.* disgust, nauseate, repel, revolt, [*informal*] turn off.

sickening adjective *sickening cruelty.* bestial, disgusting, distressing, foul, hateful, inhuman, loathsome, nasty, nauseating, nauseous, offensive, repulsive, revolting, SEE **unpleasant**, vile.

sickle verb billhook, scythe.

sickly adjective **1** *a sickly child.* ailing, delicate, feeble, frail, SEE **ill**, pallid, [*informal*] peaky, unhealthy, weak.
OPPOSITES: SEE **healthy**.
2 *sickly sweetness. sickly sentiment.* cloying, nasty, nauseating, obnoxious, syrupy, treacly, unpleasant.
OPPOSITES: SEE **refreshing**.

sickness noun **1** *a bout of sickness.* biliousness, nausea, queasiness, vomiting.
2 VARIOUS ILLNESSES: SEE **illness**.

side noun **1** *the sides of a cube.* face, facet, elevation, flank, surface.
2 *the side of a road, pool, etc.* border, boundary, brim, brink, edge, fringe, limit, margin, perimeter, rim, verge.
3 *I saw both sides of the problem.* angle, aspect, perspective, slant, standpoint, view, viewpoint.
4 *The two sides attacked each other.* army, camp, faction, team.
RELATED ADJECTIVE: lateral.

side verb *Who do you side with?* SEE **ally** verb.

side-effect noun SEE **by-product**.

sideline noun *He does decorating as a sideline.* additional activity, extra.

sidelong adjective SEE **sideways**.

side-show noun SEE **fun-fair**.

side-step verb SEE **avoid**.

side-street noun SEE **road**.

sideways adjective **1** *sideways movement.* indirect, lateral, oblique.
2 *a sideways glance.* covert, sidelong, sly, [*informal*] sneaky, unobtrusive.

sidle verb SEE **edge** verb.

siege noun blockade.

siesta noun SEE **sleep** noun.

sieve noun colander, riddle, screen, strainer.

sieve verb *Sieve out the lumps.* filter, riddle, separate, sift, strain.

sift verb **1** *to sift flour.* SEE **sieve** verb.
2 *to sift the evidence.* analyse, examine, investigate, review, scrutinize, sort out, winnow.

sigh noun, verb VARIOUS SOUNDS: SEE **sound** noun.

sight noun **1** *the power of sight.* eyesight, seeing, vision, visual perception.
2 *We live within sight of the power-station.* field of vision, range, view, visibility.
3 *The sight of home brought tears to his eyes.* appearance, glimpse, look.
4 *The procession was an impressive sight.* display, exhibition, scene, show, show-piece, spectacle.

sight verb *The look-out sighted a ship.* behold, discern, distinguish, glimpse, make out, notice, observe, perceive, recognize, see, spot.

sightless adjective SEE **blind** adjective.

sightseer noun *The castle was full of sightseers.* holiday-maker, tourist, tripper, visitor.

sign noun **1** *signs of a change in the weather.* augury, forewarning, hint, indication, intimation, omen, pointer, portent, presage, warning.
2 *a sign to begin.* cue, SEE **gesture** noun, signal, [*informal*] tip-off.
3 *a sign that someone was here.* clue, [*informal*] giveaway, proof, reminder, spoor (*of an animal*), trace, vestige.
4 *The flowers are a sign of our love.* manifestation, marker, symptom, token.
5 *We painted a sign for our sweet-stall.* advertisement, notice, placard, poster, publicity, signboard.
6 *Do you recognize the British Rail sign?* badge, cipher, device, emblem, insignia, logo, mark, symbol, trademark.

sign verb **1** *Sign your name.* autograph, endorse, inscribe, write.
2 *I signed that I was turning left.* SEE **signal** verb.
to sign off *The DJ signed off with his catch-phrase.* conclude, end, finish, say goodbye, take your leave.
to sign on *He signed on in the army.* enlist, join up, volunteer.
to sign up *They signed up several new workers.* engage, enrol, recruit, register, take on.

signal noun **1** *I gave a clear signal.* communication, cue, SEE **gesture** noun, [*informal*] go-ahead, indication, sign, [*informal*] tip-off, token, warning.

VARIOUS SIGNALS: alarm-bell, beacon, bell, burglar-alarm, buzzer, flag, flare, gong, green light, indicator, light, lights, password, red light, reveille, rocket, semaphore signal, siren, smoke-signal, [*old-fashioned*] tocsin, trafficator, traffic-lights, warning-light, whistle, winker.

---

2 *They sent a signal to say all was well.* cable, telegram, transmission.

signal verb *I signalled that I was ready.* beckon, communicate, flag, gesticulate, SEE **gesture** verb, give or send a signal [SEE **signal** noun], indicate, motion, sign, wave.

signature noun *a signature on a cheque.* autograph, endorsement, mark, name.

signboard noun SEE **sign** noun.

signet noun seal, stamp.

significance noun *the significance of wearing a red poppy.* force, implication, importance, meaning, message, point, purport, relevance, sense, signification, usefulness.

significant adjective **1** *a significant remark.* eloquent, expressive, indicative, knowing, meaningful, pregnant, revealing, symbolic, [*informal*] tell-tale.

2 *a significant moment in history.* big, considerable, SEE **important**, influential, newsworthy, noteworthy, salient, serious, sizeable, valuable, vital, worthwhile.
OPPOSITES: SEE **insignificant**.

signify verb **1** *A green light signifies "all clear".* be a sign of [SEE **sign** noun], betoken, bode, connote, denote, imply, mean, portend, presage, represent, say, spell, stand for, symbolize.
2 *Signify your agreement by raising your hand.* announce, communicate, convey, express, indicate, intimate, make known, signal, tell, transmit.

signpost noun pointer, sign.

silage noun fodder.

silence noun **1** *the silence of the night.* calm, hush, peace, quiet, quietness, stillness.
OPPOSITES: SEE **noise**.
2 *We couldn't understand her silence.* dumbness, muteness, reticence, taciturnity, uncommunicativeness.
OPPOSITES: SEE **verbosity**.

silence verb **1** *The gang silenced witnesses by intimidation.* gag, keep quiet, make silent, muzzle, shut up, suppress.
2 *The silencer is supposed to silence the engine noise.* deaden, muffle, mute, quieten.

silent adjective **1** *a silent engine.* inaudible, muffled, muted, noiseless, soundless.
2 *a silent audience.* attentive, hushed, quiet, rapt, restrained, still.
OPPOSITES: SEE **noisy**.
3 *a silent person.* dumb, laconic, [*informal*] mum (*Keep mum!*), mute, reserved, reticent, speechless, taciturn, tongue-tied, uncommunicative, unforthcoming, voiceless.
OPPOSITES: SEE **talkative**.
to be silent [*informal*] pipe down, [*informal*] shut up.

silhouette noun SEE **outline** noun.

silky adjective *A cat has silky fur.* fine, satiny, sleek, smooth, soft, velvety.

silly adjective *silly behaviour. a silly plan.* absurd, asinine, brainless, childish, crazy, daft, [*informal*] dopey, [*informal*] dotty, fatuous, feather-brained, feeble-minded, flighty, foolish, [*old-fashioned*] fond (*fond hopes*), frivolous, grotesque, [*informal*] half-baked, hare-brained, idiotic, illogical, immature, inane, infantile, irrational, [*informal*] jokey, laughable, ludicrous, mad, meaningless, mindless, misguided, naïve, nonsensical, playful, pointless, preposterous, ridiculous, scatter-brained, [*informal*] scatty, senseless, shallow, simple (*He's a bit simple*), simple-minded, simplistic, [*informal*] soppy, stupid, thoughtless, unintelligent, unreasonable, unsound, unwise, wild, witless.
OPPOSITES: SEE **serious, wise**.
a silly person halfwit, SEE **idiot**, joker, madcap, scatter-brain, simpleton, [*informal*] twerp.

silt noun *silt at the bottom of an estuary.* [*formal*] alluvium, deposit, mud, sediment, slime, sludge.

silvan adjective *a silvan landscape.* arboreal, leafy, tree-covered, wooded.

silvery adjective *a silvery sound.* SEE **clear** adjective.

simian adjective monkey-like.

similar adjective *similar in appearance.* akin, alike, analogous, comparable, compatible, congruous, corresponding, equal, equivalent, homogeneous, identical, indistinguishable, like, matching, parallel, related, resembling, the same, uniform, well-matched.
OPPOSITES: SEE **dissimilar**.

similarity noun *the similarity of twins.* affinity, closeness, congruity, correspondence, likeness, resemblance, sameness, similitude, uniformity.
OPPOSITES: SEE **difference**.

simile noun SEE **figure** noun (**figure of speech**).

simmer verb boil, SEE **cook** verb, seethe, stew.

simper verb SEE **smile** verb.

simple adjective **1** *a simple person. a simple life-style.* artless, guileless, homely, honest, humble, innocent, lowly, modest, [*uncomplimentary*] naïve, natural, sincere, straightforward, unaffected, uncomplicated, unpretentious, unsophisticated.
OPPOSITES: SEE **sophisticated**.
2 *a simple explanation.* basic, clear, direct, easy, elementary, foolproof, intelligible, lucid, understandable.
OPPOSITES: SEE **complicated**.
3 *a simple dress.* austere, classical, plain, stark, unadorned.
OPPOSITES: SEE **ornate**.
4 [*uncomplimentary*] *He's a bit simple.* SEE **silly**.

simple-minded adjective SEE **silly, unsophisticated**.

simpleton noun SEE **silly** (**silly person**).

simplify verb *They simplified the way we pay taxes.* clarify, make simple, prune, streamline.
OPPOSITES: SEE **complicate**.

simplistic adjective *a simplistic view of things.* facile, inadequate, naïve, oversimple, shallow, silly, superficial.
OPPOSITES: SEE **sophisticated**.

simulate verb **1** *to simulate a crash-landing.* SEE **reproduce**.
2 *to simulate drunkenness.* SEE **pretend**.

simulated adjective SEE **artificial**.

simultaneous adjective *I can't attend two simultaneous events.* coinciding, concurrent, contemporaneous, parallel, synchronized, synchronous.

sin noun *sin against God.* blasphemy, depravity, error, evil, guilt, immorality, impiety, iniquity, offence, sacrilege, sinfulness, transgression, [*formal*] trespass, ungodliness, unrighteousness, vice, wickedness, wrong, wrongdoing.

sin verb *to sin against God.* be guilty of sin [SEE **sin** noun], blaspheme, do wrong, err, go astray, misbehave, offend, transgress.

sincere adjective *sincere beliefs.* candid, earnest, frank, genuine, guileless, heartfelt, honest, open, real, serious, simple, straightforward, true, truthful, unaffected, wholehearted.
OPPOSITES: SEE **insincere**.

sincerity noun *I trust her sincerity.* candour, directness, frankness, genuineness, honesty, honour, integrity, openness, straightforwardness, trustworthiness, truthfulness.

sinecure noun SEE **job**.

sinewy adjective SEE **muscular**.

sinful adjective *sinful behaviour.* bad, blasphemous, corrupt, damnable, depraved, erring, evil, fallen, guilty, immoral, impious, iniquitous, irreligious, sacrilegious, ungodly, unholy, unrighteous, wicked, wrong.
OPPOSITES: SEE **righteous**.

sing verb chant, croon, descant, hum, intone, serenade, trill, warble, yodel.
MUSIC FOR SINGING: SEE **song**.

singe verb blacken, SEE **burn** verb, char, scorch.

singer noun songster, vocalist.

VARIOUS SINGERS: alto, baritone, bass, [*plural*] choir, choirboy, choirgirl, chorister, [*plural*] chorus, coloratura, contralto, crooner, folk singer, minstrel, precentor, opera singer, pop star, prima donna, soloist, soprano, tenor, treble, troubadour.

---

single adjective **1** *I got all my things into a single suitcase.* exclusive, individual, isolated, one, only, personal, separate, sole, solitary, unique.
OPPOSITE: plural.
2 *a single person.* celibate, [*informal*] free, unattached, unmarried.
OPPOSITES: SEE **married**.
a single person bachelor, spinster.

single verb **to single out** SEE **choose**.

single-handed adjective *I can't shift the piano single-handed.* alone, independently, unaided, without help.

single-minded adjective SEE **determined**.

singlet noun T-shirt, vest.

singular adjective **1** [*as grammatical term*] SEE **language**.
OPPOSITE: plural.
2 *a singular happening.* abnormal, curious, extraordinary, odd, peculiar, remarkable, uncommon, unusual.

sinister 1 *a sinister leer. a sinister groan.* disquieting, disturbing, evil, forbidding, frightening, menacing, ominous, threatening, villainous, upsetting.
2 *sinister motives.* bad, corrupt, criminal, dishonest, illegal, questionable, [*informal*] shady, suspect.

sink noun *the kitchen sink.* basin.

sink verb **1** *The sun sinks in the west.* decline, descend, disappear, drop, fall, go down, go lower, set, slip down, subside.
2 *Our spirits sank.* diminish, droop, dwindle, ebb, fail, fall, weaken.
3 *The ship sank.* become submerged, founder, go down.
4 *The attackers sank the ship.* scupper, scuttle.

sinless adjective SEE **innocent**.

sinner noun offender, reprobate, transgressor, wrongdoer.

sinuous adjective SEE **curved**.

sip noun, verb SEE **drink** noun, verb.

siphon verb SEE **pump** verb.

sir, sire nouns SEE **title** noun.

siren noun *a fire siren.* SEE **warning**.

sissy noun SEE **effeminate (effeminate man)**.

sister noun sibling.
FAMILY RELATIONSHIPS: SEE **family**.

sit verb **1** *to sit on a chair.* be seated, perch, rest, seat yourself, settle, squat.
2 *to sit for your portrait.* pose.
3 *to sit an exam.* be a candidate in, [*informal*] go in for, take, write.
4 *Parliament does not sit over Christmas.* assemble, be in session [SEE **session**], convene, meet.

site noun *a site for a new building.* campus, ground, location, place, plot, position, setting, situation, spot.

site verb SEE **situate.**

sitting noun *a sitting of Parliament.* SEE **session.**

sitting-room noun drawing-room, living-room, lounge.
OTHER ROOMS: SEE **room.**

situate verb *The house is situated in the park.* build, establish, found, locate, place, position, put, set up, site, station.

situation noun **1** *The house is in a pleasant situation.* locality, location, place, position, setting, site, spot.
2 *I was in an awkward situation when I lost my money.* circumstances, condition, plight, position, predicament.
3 *She applied for a situation in the new firm.* employment, job, position, post.

size noun amount, area, breadth, bulk, capacity, depth, dimensions, extent, gauge, height, immensity, largeness, length, magnitude, measurement, proportions, scale, volume, width.
UNITS OF SIZE: SEE **measure** noun.

sizeable adjective *sizeable helpings.* SEE **big**, considerable, decent, generous, largish, significant, worthwhile.

sizzle verb VARIOUS SOUNDS: SEE **sound** noun.

skate verb roller-skate, SEE **slide** verb.

skeleton noun bones, frame, framework, structure.

PRINCIPAL BONES IN YOUR BODY: backbone, carpus, coccyx, cranium, digit, femur, fibula, humerus, jaw, metacarpus, patella, pelvis, radius, rib, sacrum, scapula, skull, tarsal, tibia, ulna, vertebra.
SEE ALSO: **joint** noun.
OTHER PARTS OF YOUR BODY: SEE **body.**

---

sketch noun **1** *a quick sketch of someone.* description, design, diagram, draft, drawing, outline, SEE **picture** noun, plan, skeleton, vignette.
2 *a comic sketch on TV.* SEE **performance**, playlet, scene, skit, turn.

sketch verb *to sketch with crayons.* depict, draw, portray, represent.
to sketch out *I sketched out my plan.* draft, give the gist of, outline, rough out.

sketchy adjective *a sketchy essay.* bitty, imperfect, incomplete, perfunctory, rough, scrappy, undeveloped, unfinished.
OPPOSITES: SEE **perfect** adjective.

skewer verb SEE **pierce.**

skid verb *to skid on a slippery road.* aquaplane, glide, go out of control, slide, slip.

skiff noun rowing-boat.

skilful adjective *a skilful carpenter. skilful work.* able, accomplished, adept, adroit, apt, artful, brilliant, [*informal*] canny, capable, clever, competent, consummate, crafty, cunning, deft, dextrous, experienced, expert, gifted, handy, ingenious, masterly, practised, professional, proficient, shrewd, smart, talented, versatile.
OPPOSITES: SEE **unskilful.**

skill noun *the skill of a carpenter.* ability, accomplishment, adroitness, aptitude, art, capability, cleverness, competence, craft, cunning, deftness, dexterity, experience, expertise, gift, handicraft, ingenuity, knack, mastery, professionalism, proficiency, prowess, shrewdness, talent, technique, training, versatility, workmanship.

skilled adjective experienced, qualified, SEE **skilful**, trained, versed.

skim verb **1** *to skim across ice or water.* aquaplane, coast, glide, move lightly, plane, skate, ski, skid, slide, slip.
2 *to skim through a book.* look through, read quickly, scan, skip.

skimp verb SEE **economize.**

skimpy adjective SEE **scanty.**

skin noun **1** *the skin of an animal, fruit, etc.* casing, coat, coating, covering, [*formal*] epidermis, exterior, film, fur, hide, husk, membrane, outside, peel, pelt, rind, shell, surface.
2 *a person's skin.* SEE **complexion.**

skin verb *to skin an orange. to skin an animal.* flay, pare, peel, strip.

skin-deep adjective SEE **superficial.**

skinflint noun SEE **miser.**

skinny adjective *a skinny figure.* emaciated, lanky, scraggy, SEE **thin** adjective.

skip noun SEE **container.**

skip verb **1** *to skip and play.* bound, caper, cavort, dance, frisk, gambol, hop, jump, leap, prance, spring.
2 *to skip the boring bits.* forget, ignore, leave out, miss out, neglect, overlook, pass over, skim through.
3 *to skip lessons.* be absent from, cut, miss, play truant from.

skipper noun captain.

skirl noun VARIOUS SOUNDS: SEE **sound** noun.

skirmish noun, verb SEE **fight** noun, verb.

skirt noun OTHER CLOTHES: SEE **clothes.**

skirt verb *The path skirts the playing-field.* avoid, border, bypass, circle, encircle, go round, pass round, [*informal*] steer clear of, surround.

skit noun burlesque, parody, satire, sketch, spoof, [*informal*] take-off.

skittish adjective SEE **playful**.

skive verb SEE **lazy (be lazy)**.

skiver noun SEE **lazy (lazy person)**.

skivvy noun SEE **servant**.

skulduggery noun SEE **trickery**.

skulk verb SEE **loiter**.

skull noun head.
PARTS OF YOUR SKELETON: SEE **skeleton**.

sky noun *The rocket rose into the sky.* air, atmosphere, [*poetic*] blue, [*poetic*] firmament, [*poetic*] heavens, space, stratosphere, [*poetic*] welkin.

skylight noun SEE **window**.

skyline noun horizon.

skyscraper noun OTHER BUILDINGS: SEE **building**.

slab noun *a slab of rock, cake, etc.* block, chunk, hunk, lump, piece, slice, wedge.

slack adjective **1** *slack ropes.* limp, loose.
OPPOSITES: SEE **tight**.
2 *a slack attitude.* disorganized, easy-going, flaccid, idle, lax, lazy, listless, negligent, permissive, relaxed, unbusinesslike, uncaring, undisciplined.
OPPOSITES: SEE **businesslike**.
3 *slack trade.* inactive, quiet, slow, slow-moving, sluggish.
OPPOSITES: SEE **busy**.

slack verb SEE **lazy (be lazy)**.

slacken verb **1** *to slacken the tension in ropes.* ease off, loosen, relax, release.
2 *The pace slackened in the second half.* abate, decrease, ease, lessen, lower, moderate, reduce, slow down.

slacker noun SEE **lazy (lazy person)**.

slacks noun SEE **trousers**.

slake verb *to slake your thirst.* allay, cool, quench, satisfy.

slam verb **1** *to slam a door.* bang, shut.
2 [*informal*] *to slam someone's work.* SEE **criticize**.

slander noun *The slander in the papers ruined his reputation.* backbiting, calumny, defamation, denigration, insult, libel, lie, misrepresentation, obloquy, scandal, slur, smear.

slander verb *to slander someone.* blacken the name of, defame, denigrate, disparage, libel, malign, misrepresent, smear, spread tales about, tell lies about, traduce, vilify.

slanderous adjective *slanderous rumours.* abusive, cruel, damaging, defamatory, disparaging, false, hurtful, insulting, libellous, malicious, scurrilous, untrue, vicious.

slang noun argot, cant, jargon.
LINGUISTIC TERMS: SEE **language**.

slang verb SEE **insult** verb.
slanging match SEE **quarrel** noun.

slant noun **1** *Rest the ladder at a slant.* angle, diagonal, gradient, incline, list, rake, ramp, slope, tilt.
2 *I didn't like the slant they gave to the news.* bias, distortion, emphasis, imbalance, perspective, prejudice, viewpoint.

slant verb **1** *Her handwriting slants backwards.* be at an angle, be skewed, incline, lean, shelve, slope, tilt.
2 *He slanted the evidence in her favour.* bias, distort, prejudice, twist, weight.

slanting adjective *a slanting line.* angled, askew, diagonal, inclined, listing, oblique, raked, skewed, slantwise, sloping, tilted.
OPPOSITES: SEE **level** adjective, **perpendicular**.

slap verb SEE **hit** verb.

slapdash adjective SEE **careless**.

slap-happy adjective SEE **casual**.

slapstick noun SEE **comedy**.

slash verb SEE **cut** verb.

slat noun SEE **strip** noun.

slate verb [*informal*] *to slate someone's work.* SEE **criticize**.

slatternly adjective SEE **slovenly**.

slaughter noun bloodshed, butchery, carnage, SEE **killing**, massacre, murder.

slaughter verb *to slaughter men on a battlefield.* annihilate, butcher, SEE **kill**, massacre, murder, slay.

slaughter-house noun abattoir, [*old-fashioned*] shambles.

slave noun drudge, serf, SEE **servant**, thrall, vassal.

slave verb *We slaved away all day.* drudge, exert yourself, labour, [*informal*] sweat, toil, SEE **work** verb.

slave-driver noun despot, hard taskmaster, tyrant.

slaver verb dribble, drool, foam at the mouth, salivate, slobber.

slavery noun bondage, captivity, enslavement, serfdom, servitude.
OPPOSITES: SEE **freedom**.

slavish adjective **1** *slavish submission.* abject, cringing, fawning, grovelling, humiliating, menial, obsequious, servile, submissive.
OPPOSITES: SEE **proud**.

2 *a slavish imitation.* close, flattering, strict, sycophantic, unimaginative, unoriginal.
OPPOSITES: SEE **independent**.

slay verb assassinate, bump off, butcher, destroy, dispatch, execute, exterminate, [*informal*] finish off, SEE **kill**, martyr, massacre, murder, put down, put to death, slaughter.

sleazy adjective *a sleazy night-club.* dirty, disreputable, mucky, seedy, slovenly, sordid, squalid, unprepossessing.

sledge noun bob-sleigh, sled, sleigh, toboggan.

sleek adjective 1 *The cat had a sleek coat.* brushed, glossy, shiny, silky, smooth, soft, velvety, well-groomed.
OPPOSITES: SEE **unkempt**.
2 *The cat had a sleek look.* complacent, contented, self-satisfied, smug, thriving, well-fed.

sleep noun cat-nap, coma, dormancy, doze, [*informal*] forty winks, hibernation, [*informal*] kip, [*informal*] nap, rest, [*informal*] shut-eye, siesta, slumber, snooze.

sleep verb cat-nap, [*informal*] doss down, doze, [*informal*] drop off, drowse, hibernate, [*informal*] nod off, rest, slumber, snooze, [*informal*] take a nap.

sleepiness noun drowsiness, lethargy, somnolence, torpor.

sleeping adjective asleep, comatose, dormant, hibernating, [*informal*] in the land of Nod, [*informal*] off, [*informal*] out like a light, resting, slumbering, unconscious.

sleeping-car noun sleeper.

sleepless adjective *sleepless through the night.* awake, disturbed, insomniac, restless, wakeful, watchful, wide awake.

sleeplessness noun insomnia.

sleep-walker noun somnambulist.

sleepy adjective 1 *sleepy after a big meal.* comatose, [*informal*] dopey, drowsy, heavy, lethargic, ready to sleep, sluggish, somnolent, soporific, tired, torpid, weary.
2 *a sleepy little village.* inactive, quiet, restful, unexciting.
OPPOSITES: SEE **lively**.

sleigh noun SEE **sledge**.

slender adjective 1 *a slender figure.* graceful, slight, SEE **slim** adjective, svelte, thin.
OPPOSITES: SEE **fat** adjective.
2 *a slender thread.* feeble, fine, fragile, tenuous.
OPPOSITES: SEE **strong**.
3 *slender means.* inadequate, meagre, scanty.
OPPOSITES: SEE **adequate**.

sleuth noun SEE **detective**.

slice noun *a slice of bread.* SEE **piece**.

slice verb carve, SEE **cut** verb.

slick adjective *a slick bit of deception.* adroit, artful, clever, cunning, deft, dextrous, glib, plausible, quick, smart, smooth, [*informal*] tricky, wily.
OPPOSITES: SEE **clumsy**.

slide noun 1 *The children play on the slide.* chute.
2 *I take slides with my camera.* transparency.

slide verb *to slide over a slippery surface.* aquaplane, coast, glide, glissade, skate, skid, ski, skim, slip, slither, toboggan.

slight adjective 1 *a slight improvement.* imperceptible, insignificant, minor, negligible, slim (*a slim chance*), superficial, tiny, trifling, trivial, unimportant.
2 *a slight figure.* delicate, feeble, flimsy, fragile, frail, sickly, slender, SEE **slim** adjective, thin, weak.
OPPOSITES: SEE **big**.

slight noun, verb SEE **insult** noun, verb.

slightly adverb *slightly warm.* hardly, moderately, only just, scarcely.
OPPOSITES: SEE **very**.

slim adjective 1 *a slim figure.* fine, graceful, lean, narrow, slender, slight, svelte, sylphlike, SEE **thin** adjective, trim.
2 *a slim chance of winning.* SEE **slight** adjective.

slim verb become slimmer, diet, lose weight, reduce.

slime noun muck, mucus, mud, ooze, sludge.

sling verb *I slung the rubbish on the tip.* cast, chuck, fling, heave, hurl, lob, pelt, pitch, shy, throw, toss.

slink verb *He slunk away in disgrace.* creep, edge, move guiltily, slither, sneak, steal.

slinky adjective [*informal*] *a slinky dress.* clinging, close-fitting, sexy, sleek.

slip noun *I made a silly slip.* accident, [*informal*] bloomer, blunder, error, fault, inaccuracy, indiscretion, lapse, miscalculation, mistake, oversight, [*informal*] slip of the pen/tongue, [*informal*] slip-up.
to give someone the slip SEE **escape** verb.

slip verb 1 *I slipped on the wet floor.* aquaplane, coast, glide, glissade, move

out of control, skate, skid, ski, skim, slide, slip, slither.
2 *She slipped into the room without being noticed.* creep, edge, move quietly, slink, sneak, steal.
to slip away SEE **escape** verb.
to slip up SEE **blunder** verb.

slipper noun VARIOUS SHOES: SEE **shoe**.

slippery adjective 1 *Take care: the floor is slippery.* glassy, greasy, icy, lubricated, oily, [*informal*] slippy, slithery, smooth.
2 [*informal*] *a slippery customer.* SEE **devious**.

slippy adjective SEE **slippery**.

slipshod adjective SEE **careless**.

slit noun *a slit in a fence. a slit made with a knife.* breach, break, chink, crack, cut, fissure, gap, gash, hole, incision, opening, rift, slot, split, tear, vent.

slit verb *to slit with a knife.* SEE **cut** verb.

slither verb *The snake slithered away.* creep, glide, slide, slink, SEE **slip** verb, snake, worm.

sliver noun SEE **strip** noun.

slobber verb dribble, drool, salivate, slaver.

slog verb SEE **hit** verb.

slogan noun *an advertising slogan.* catchphrase, catchword, jingle, motto, SEE **saying**.

slop verb *I slopped tea in the saucer.* SEE **splash** verb.

slope noun *an upwards slope. a downwards slope.* ascent, bank, camber, cant, declivity, descent, dip, fall, gradient, hill, incline, rake, ramp, rise, scarp, slant, tilt.

slope verb 1 *The beach slopes gently.* bank, fall, rise, shelve.
2 *The leaning tower slopes to one side.* incline, lean, slant, tilt, tip.

sloppy adjective 1 *a sloppy mixture.* liquid, messy, runny, slushy, splashing about, watery, wet.
2 *sloppy work.* SEE **slovenly**.
3 *a sloppy love-story.* SEE **sentimental**.

slosh verb 1 *to slosh someone.* SEE **hit** verb.
2 *to slosh water about.* SEE **splash** verb.

slot noun 1 *Put a coin in the slot.* break, chink, crack, cut, fissure, gap, gash, groove, hole, incision, opening, rift, slit, split.
2 *TV has a weekly slot for viewers' comments.* place, space, time.

sloth noun SEE **laziness**.

slothful adjective SEE **lazy**.

slouch verb *Don't slouch in that slovenly way!* droop, loaf, lounge, shamble, slump, stoop.

slough noun SEE **bog**.

slovenly adjective *slovenly work. a slovenly appearance.* careless, disorganized, hasty, messy, shoddy, slapdash, slatternly, sloppy, thoughtless, untidy.
OPPOSITES: SEE **careful**.

slow adjective 1 *slow progress.* careful, cautious, dawdling, delayed, deliberate, dilatory, gradual, leisurely, lingering, loitering, measured, moderate, painstaking, plodding, protracted, sluggish, steady, tardy, unhurried.
OPPOSITES: SEE **fast** adjective.
2 *a slow learner.* backward, dense, dim, dull, obtuse, stupid, [*informal*] thick.
3 *a slow worker.* idle, lazy, sluggish.
to be slow dally, dawdle, delay, [*informal*] hang about, idle, lag behind, linger, loiter, move slowly, straggle, [*informal*] take your time, trail behind.

slow verb **to slow down** brake, decelerate, go slower, reduce speed.

sludge noun mud, ooze, silt, slime, slurry, slush.

slug verb SEE **hit** verb.

sluggard noun SEE **lazy (lazy person)**.

sluggish adjective *a sluggish response.* dull, idle, lazy, lethargic, lifeless, listless, phlegmatic, slothful, SEE **slow** adjective, torpid, unresponsive.
OPPOSITES: SEE **lively**.

sluice verb *I sluiced the dirt down the drain.* flush, rinse, swill, wash.

slumber noun, verb SEE **sleep** noun, verb.

slump noun *a slump in trade.* collapse, crash, decline, depression, downturn, drop, fall, recession, trough.
OPPOSITES: SEE **boom** noun.

slump verb 1 *Trade slumped after Christmas.* collapse, decline, drop, fall off, plummet, plunge, sink, worsen.
OPPOSITES: SEE **prosper**.
2 *He slumped across his desk.* be limp, collapse, droop, flop, loll, sag, slouch.

slur noun *a slur on his reputation.* SEE **slander** noun.

slur verb *to slur your words.* WAYS OF TALKING: SEE **talk** verb.

slurp verb VARIOUS SOUNDS: SEE **sound** noun.

slurry noun SEE **mud**, ooze, slime.

sly adjective *a sly trick.* artful, [*informal*] catty, conniving, crafty, cunning, deceitful, devious, [*informal*] foxy, furtive, guileful, knowing, scheming, secretive,

[*informal*] shifty, [*informal*] sneaky, [*informal*] snide, stealthy, surreptitious, tricky, underhand, wily.
OPPOSITES: SEE **straightforward**.

smack verb *to smack someone on the wrist.* SEE **hit** verb, pat, slap, spank.

small adjective **1** *a small person. small things.* [*informal*] baby, compact, concise, diminutive, [*informal*] dinky, dwarf, exiguous, fractional, infinitesimal, lilliputian, little, microscopic, midget, [*informal*] mini, miniature, minuscule, minute, petite (*a petite woman*), [*informal*] pint-sized, [*informal*] poky (*a poky room*), portable, pygmy, short, [*informal*] teeny, tiny, toy, undersized, [*informal*] wee, [*informal*] weeny.
2 *small helpings.* inadequate, insufficient, meagre, mean, measly, scanty, stingy.
3 *a small problem.* SEE **trivial**.
OPPOSITES: SEE **big**.
a small amount, a small thing bagatelle, [*informal*] chicken-feed, fragment, modicum, morsel, particle, scrap, [*informal*] smattering, snippet, soupçon, spot, trifle.
a small animal, a small person dwarf, midget, pygmy, runt, [*informal*] titch.
small arms SEE **weapons**.

smallholding noun SEE **farm** noun.

small-minded adjective *small-minded objections.* bigoted, grudging, hidebound, illiberal, intolerant, mean, narrow-minded, old-fashioned, parochial, petty, prejudiced, selfish, trivial.
OPPOSITES: SEE **broad-minded**.

smarmy adjective [*uncomplimentary*] *I hate his smarmy compliments.* SEE **obsequious**.

smart adjective **1** *a smart pace.* brisk, [*informal*] cracking, fast, forceful, quick, rapid, [*informal*] rattling, speedy, swift.
OPPOSITES: SEE **slow** adjective.
2 *a smart idea.* acute, artful, astute, bright, clever, crafty, [*informal*] cute, ingenious, intelligent, shrewd.
OPPOSITES: SEE **stupid**.
3 *a smart appearance.* chic, clean, dapper, [*informal*] dashing, elegant, fashionable, modish, [*informal*] natty, neat, [*informal*] posh, [*informal*] snazzy, spruce, stylish, tidy, trim, well-dressed.
OPPOSITES: SEE **dowdy**.

smart verb *The sting smarts.* SEE **hurt** verb.

smarten verb SEE **tidy** verb.

smash verb **1** *to smash an egg.* SEE **break** verb, crumple, crush, demolish, destroy, shatter, squash, wreck.
2 *to smash into a wall.* bang, bash, batter, bump, collide, crash, hammer, SEE **hit** verb, knock, pound, ram, slam, strike, thump, wallop.

smashing adjective SEE **excellent**.

smattering noun *a smattering of French.* SEE **small (small amount)**.

smear noun **1** *a smear of grease.* mark, smudge, streak.
2 *a smear on his good name.* SEE **slander** noun.

smear verb **1** *He smeared paint over the canvas.* dab, daub, plaster, rub, smudge, spread, wipe.
2 *The papers smeared his reputation.* attack, malign, SEE **slander** verb, vilify.

smeary adjective SEE **dirty** adjective.

smell noun aroma, bouquet, fragrance, incense, nose, odour, perfume, [*informal*] pong, redolence, reek, scent, stench, stink, whiff.
RELATED ADJECTIVE: olfactory.

smell verb **1** *Smell these roses.* scent, sniff.
2 *Those onions smell.* [*informal*] pong, reek, stink, whiff.

smelling adjective [*Smelling* is usually used not on its own but in combination with other words: *strong-smelling, sweet-smelling*, etc.] **1** *pleasant-smelling.* aromatic, fragrant, musky, odorous, perfumed, redolent, scented.
2 *strong- or unpleasant-smelling.* fetid, foul, [*informal*] high, malodorous, musty, noisome, [*informal*] off, pongy, pungent, putrid, rank, reeking, rotten, smelly, stinking, [*informal*] whiffy.
OPPOSITES: SEE **odourless**.

smelly adjective SEE **smelling**.

smile noun, verb beam, grin, SEE **laugh**, leer, simper, smirk, sneer.
FACIAL EXPRESSIONS: SEE **expression**.

smirk noun, verb SEE **smile**.

smite verb SEE **hit** verb.

smith noun blacksmith.
ARTISTS AND CRAFTSMEN: SEE **artist**.

smithereens noun SEE **fragment** noun.

smog noun SEE **fog**.

smoke noun **1** *clouds of smoke.* air pollution, exhaust, fog, fumes, gas, smog, steam, vapour.
2 *She offered me a smoke.* cheroot, cigar, cigarette, [*informal*] fag, pipe, tobacco.

smoke verb **1** *The fire was smoking.* emit smoke, fume, reek, smoulder.
2 *He smokes cigars.* inhale, puff at.

smokeless adjective clean, smoke-free.

smoke-screen noun SEE **disguise** noun.

smoky adjective *a smoky atmosphere.* clouded, dirty, foggy, grimy, hazy, sooty.
OPPOSITES: SEE **clear** adjective.

smooth adjective **1** *a smooth lawn.* even, flat, horizontal, level.
2 *a smooth sea.* calm, glassy, peaceful, placid, quiet, restful, unruffled.
3 *a cat's smooth coat. a smooth finish on the car.* glossy, polished, shiny, silken, silky, sleek, soft, velvety.
4 *a smooth ride. smooth progress.* comfortable, easy, steady, uneventful, uninterrupted.
5 *a smooth taste.* agreeable, bland, mellow, mild, pleasant.
6 *a smooth mixture.* creamy, flowing, runny.
OPPOSITE: lumpy.
7 *a smooth manner. a smooth talker.* convincing, facile, glib, insincere, plausible, polite, self-assured, self-satisfied, smug, sophisticated, suave, untrustworthy, urbane.
OPPOSITES: SEE **rough**.

smooth verb *to smooth a rough surface.* even out, file, flatten, iron, level, level off, plane, polish, press, roll out, sand down, sandpaper.

smother verb *to smother a fire. to smother someone with a pillow.* choke, cover, SEE **kill**, snuff out, stifle, strangle, suffocate, throttle.

smoulder verb SEE **burn** verb, smoke.

smudge noun *a smudge on the paper.* SEE **mark** noun.

smudge verb **1** *I smudged the ink.* blur, smear, streak.
2 *I smudged the paper.* blot, dirty, mark, stain.

smug adjective *a smug expression.* complacent, conceited, pleased, priggish, self-righteous, self-satisfied, sleek, superior.
OPPOSITES: SEE **humble** adjective.

smuggling noun VARIOUS CRIMES: SEE **crime**.

smut noun *a smut on your nose.* SEE **mark** noun.

smutty adjective *smutty jokes.* SEE **obscene**.

snack noun bite, [*informal*] elevenses, [*informal*] nibble, refreshments.
VARIOUS MEALS: SEE **meal**.

snack-bar noun buffet, café, cafeteria, fast-food restaurant.

snag noun *An unexpected snag delayed our plan.* complication, difficulty, hindrance, hitch, obstacle, problem, setback, [*informal*] stumbling-block.

snag verb SEE **tear** verb.

snake noun serpent.

VARIOUS SNAKES: adder, anaconda, boa constrictor, cobra, copperhead, flying-snake, grass snake, mamba, python, rattlesnake, sand snake, sea snake, sidewinder, tree snake, viper.

---

snap adjective *a snap decision.* SEE **sudden**.

snap verb **1** *A twig snapped.* SEE **break** verb, crack.
2 *The dog snapped at me.* bite, nip, snatch.
3 *She snapped at us.* SEE **angry (be angry)**.

snappy adjective [*informal*] *a snappy answer.* SEE **brisk**.

snapshot noun KINDS OF PHOTOGRAPH: SEE **photograph** noun.

snare noun ambush, booby-trap, [*old-fashioned*] gin, noose, trap.

snare verb *to snare animals.* catch, decoy, ensnare, net, trap.

snarl verb **1** *The dog snarled.* bare the teeth, growl.
WAYS PEOPLE SPEAK: SEE **talk** verb.
2 *The rope got snarled up in the wheels.* SEE **tangle** verb.

snatch verb *The muggers snatched her handbag.* catch, clutch, grab, grasp, pluck, seize, take, wrench away, wrest away.

snazzy adjective SEE **stylish**.

sneak verb **1** *I sneaked in without anyone seeing.* creep, move stealthily, prowl, slink, stalk, steal.
2 [*informal*] *She sneaked on me.* [*informal*] grass, inform (against), report, [*informal*] tell tales (about).

sneaking adjective **1** *a sneaking suspicion.* half-formed, intuitive, nagging, niggling, persistent, private, uncomfortable, unproved, worrying.
2 SEE **sneaky**.

sneaky adjective [*informal*] *a sneaky way of getting an advantage.* cheating, contemptible, crafty, deceitful, despicable, devious, dishonest, furtive, [*informal*] low-down, mean, nasty, shady, [*informal*] shifty, sly, sneaking, treacherous, underhand, unorthodox, untrustworthy.
OPPOSITES: SEE **straightforward**.

sneer verb boo, hiss, hoot, jeer, SEE **laugh**, scoff.
to sneer at be contemptuous of, be scornful of [SEE **scornful**], denigrate, mock, ridicule, [*informal*] sniff at, taunt.
FACIAL EXPRESSIONS: SEE **expression**.

sneering adjective SEE **scornful.**

snick noun, verb SEE **cut** noun, verb.

snicker verb SEE **snigger.**

snide adjective SEE **scornful.**

sniff verb **1** *to sniff the roses.* SEE **smell** verb.
2 *to sniff because you have a cold.* [*informal*] sniffle, snivel, snuffle.
to sniff at SEE **sneer (sneer at).**

snigger verb *to snigger at a rude joke.* chuckle, giggle, SEE **laugh**, snicker, titter.

snip noun, verb SEE **cut** noun, verb.

snipe verb *A gunman sniped at them from the roof.* fire, SEE **shoot** verb, [*informal*] take pot-shots.

snippet noun *snippets of information.* fragment, morsel, particle, piece, scrap, shred, snatch (*a snatch of a song*).

snitch verb SEE **steal.**

snivel verb *He began to snivel when he heard his punishment.* blubber, cry, grizzle, grovel, sniff, sob, weep, whimper, whine, [*informal*] whinge.

snob noun élitist, snobbish person [SEE **snobbish**].

snobbish adjective *too snobbish to eat convenience foods. a snobbish attitude to art.* condescending, disdainful, élitist, haughty, patronizing, pompous, [*informal*] posh, presumptuous, pretentious, [*informal*] snooty, [*informal*] stuck-up, superior, [*informal*] toffee-nosed.
OPPOSITES: SEE **unpretentious.**

snoop verb *Don't snoop into my affairs!* be inquisitive [SEE **inquisitive**], interfere, intrude, meddle, [*informal*] nose about, pry, sneak, spy, [*informal*] stick your nose (into).

snooper noun SEE **busybody.**

snooty adjective SEE **snobbish.**

snooze noun, verb SEE **sleep** noun, verb.

snore noun, verb VARIOUS SOUNDS: SEE **sound** noun.

snorkelling noun SEE **diving.**

snort noun, verb VARIOUS SOUNDS: SEE **sound** noun.

snout noun *an animal's snout.* face, muzzle, nose, proboscis, trunk.

snowy adjective WORDS TO DESCRIBE WEATHER: SEE **weather** noun.

snub verb *She snubbed him by ignoring his question.* be rude to, brush off, cold-shoulder, disdain, humiliate, insult, offend, [*informal*] put (someone) down, rebuff, reject, scorn, [*informal*] squash.

snuff noun SEE **tobacco.**

snuff verb *to snuff a candle.* extinguish, put out.
to snuff it SEE **die.**

snuffle verb SEE **sniff.**

snug adjective **1** *snug in bed.* comfortable, [*informal*] comfy, cosy, relaxed, safe, secure, soft, warm.
2 *The jacket was a snug fit.* close-fitting, exact, well-tailored.

snuggle verb SEE **cuddle.**

soak verb **1** *to soak something in liquid.* bathe, drench, [*informal*] dunk, immerse, [*in cooking*] marinate, pickle, souse, steep, submerge, wet thoroughly.
2 *Rain soaked the pitch.* make soaked [SEE **soaked**], penetrate, permeate, saturate.
3 *A sponge soaks up water.* absorb, take up.

soaked, soaking adjectives drenched, dripping, sodden, soggy, sopping, waterlogged, SEE **wet** adjective, wet through.
OPPOSITES: SEE **dry** adjective.

soap noun detergent.

soar verb *An eagle soared overhead.* ascend, climb, float, fly, glide, hover, rise, tower.

sob verb SEE **weep.**

sober adjective **1** *He got drunk, but you stayed sober. I spent time in sober reflection.* calm, clear-headed, composed, in control, lucid, rational, sensible, steady.
OPPOSITES: SEE **drunk, irrational.**
2 *a sober life-style.* abstemious, moderate, plain, restrained, self-controlled, staid, temperate, unexciting.
OPPOSITES: SEE **self-indulgent.**
3 *a sober occasion. sober colours.* dignified, dull, grave, peaceful, quiet, sedate, serene, serious, solemn, sombre, subdued.
OPPOSITES: SEE **frivolous.**

sobriquet noun SEE **nickname.**

soccer noun Association football.

sociable adjective *a sociable crowd of people.* affable, approachable, [*old-fashioned*] clubbable, companionable, convivial, extroverted, friendly, gregarious, hospitable, neighbourly, outgoing, SEE **social** adjective, warm, welcoming.
OPPOSITES: SEE **unfriendly.**

social adjective **1** *Humans are supposed to be social creatures.* civilized, collaborative, friendly, gregarious, organized, SEE **sociable.**
OPPOSITES: SEE **solitary.**
2 *We organized some social events.* communal, community, group, public.
OPPOSITES: SEE **individual** adjective.

social noun *a Christmas social.* dance, disco, [*informal*] do, gathering, [*informal*] get-together, SEE **party**, reception, reunion, soirée.

socialism noun POLITICAL TERMS: SEE **politics**.

socialize verb *She's got lots of friends: she likes to socialize.* associate, be sociable [SEE **sociable**], entertain, fraternize, get together, join in, mix, relate.

society noun **1** *We are part of human society.* civilization, community, nation, the public.
2 *We enjoy the society of our friends.* camaraderie, companionship, company, fellowship, friendship.
3 *a secret society.* association, brotherhood, club, fraternity, group, league, organization, sisterhood, union.

sock verb SEE **hit** verb.

sodden adjective SEE **soaked**.

sofa noun chaise longue, couch, SEE **seat** noun, settee.
OTHER FURNITURE: SEE **furniture**.

soft adjective **1** *soft rubber. soft sponge-cake. soft clay.* crumbly, cushiony, elastic, flabby, flexible, floppy, limp, malleable, mushy, plastic, pliable, pulpy, spongy, springy, squashy, supple, tender, yielding.
2 *a soft bed.* comfortable, cosy.
OPPOSITES: SEE **hard**.
3 *a soft texture.* downy, feathery, fleecy, furry, silky, sleek, smooth, velvety.
OPPOSITES: SEE **rough**.
4 *a soft voice. soft music. soft lighting.* faint, dim, low, mellifluous, muted, peaceful, soothing, subdued.
OPPOSITES: SEE **bright, loud**.
5 [*informal*] *a soft teacher.* compassionate, easygoing, indulgent, kind, lenient, permissive, sympathetic, tender-hearted, understanding.
OPPOSITES: SEE **severe**.
6 *a soft breeze. a soft touch.* delicate, gentle, light, mild.
OPPOSITES: SEE **violent**.
7 [*informal*] *a soft job. a soft option.* easy, undemanding.
OPPOSITES: SEE **difficult**.

soften verb **1** *to soften your tone.* deaden, decrease, lower, make quieter, moderate, muffle, quieten, subdue, tone down.
2 *to soften a blow.* alleviate, buffer, cushion, deflect, reduce the impact of, temper.
OPPOSITES: SEE **intensify**.
3 *to soften ingredients before mixing a cake.* dissolve, fluff up, lighten, liquefy, make softer, melt.
OPPOSITES: SEE **harden**.

soft-hearted adjective SEE **kind** adjective.

soft-pedal verb SEE **understate**.

soggy adjective **1** *a soggy towel.* drenched, saturated, soaked, sodden, sopping, wet through.
OPPOSITES: SEE **dry** adjective.
2 *soggy cake.* heavy, moist, stodgy.
OPPOSITE: light.

soil noun *the soil in the garden.* earth, ground, humus, land, loam, marl, topsoil.

soil verb *Don't soil your hands with that filthy stuff.* contaminate, defile, dirty, make dirty, pollute, stain, tarnish.

soiled adjective SEE **dirty** adjective.

soirée noun SEE **social** noun.

sojourn noun, verb SEE **stay** noun, verb.

solace noun, verb SEE **comfort** noun, verb.

solder verb SEE **fasten**, weld.

soldier noun cavalryman, centurion, commando, conscript, SEE **fighter**, guardsman, gunner, infantryman, lancer, marine, mercenary, NCO, officer, paratrooper, private, regular, rifleman, sapper, sentry, serviceman, trooper, [*plural*] troops, warrior.
RANKS IN THE ARMY: SEE **rank** noun.

sole adjective *the sole survivor.* exclusive, individual, lone, one, only, single, solitary, unique.

solecism noun SEE **mistake** noun.

solemn adjective **1** *a solemn expression.* earnest, glum, grave, grim, sedate, serious, sober, sombre, staid, thoughtful, unsmiling.
OPPOSITES: SEE **cheerful**.
2 *a solemn occasion.* awe-inspiring, ceremonious, dignified, formal, grand, holy, important, imposing, impressive, pompous, religious, stately.
OPPOSITES: SEE **frivolous**.

solemnize verb SEE **celebrate**.

solicit verb *to solicit help.* SEE **seek**.

solicitor noun lawyer.
LEGAL TERMS: SEE **law**.

solicitous adjective SEE **concerned**.

solicitude noun SEE **concern** noun.

solid adjective **1** *solid rock. frozen solid.* compact, dense, firm, fixed, hard, rigid, stable, unbending, unyielding.
OPPOSITES: SEE **fluid, powdery, soft**.
2 *solid gold.* pure, unalloyed, unmixed.
OPPOSITE: alloyed.
3 *three solid hours.* SEE **continual**, continuous, unbroken, uninterrupted.
OPPOSITES: SEE **intermittent**.

4 *a solid piece of furniture.* robust, sound, steady, SEE **strong**, sturdy, well-made.
OPPOSITES: SEE **flimsy**.
5 *a solid shape.* cubic, rounded, spherical, thick, three-dimensional.
OPPOSITE: two-dimensional.
6 *solid evidence.* concrete, genuine, physical, proven, real, tangible, weighty.
OPPOSITES: SEE **hypothetical**.
7 *solid support from friends.* complete, dependable, like-minded, reliable, trustworthy, unanimous, undivided, united.
OPPOSITES: SEE **unreliable**.

solidarity noun *We can depend on the solidarity of our team.* cohesion, harmony, like-mindedness, unanimity, unity.
OPPOSITES: SEE **disunity**.

solidify verb *The liquid solidifies as it cools down.* cake, clot, coagulate, congeal, SEE **harden**, set.
OPPOSITES: SEE **liquefy**.

Some words beginning *sol-*, including *soliloquy, solitary,* and *solo,* are related to Latin *solus = alone.* Others, including *solar, solarium,* and *solstice,* are related to Latin *sol = sun.*

---

soliloquize verb SEE **speak**.

soliloquy noun monologue, SEE **speech**.

solitary adjective **1** *a solitary existence.* alone, anti-social, cloistered, companionless, friendless, isolated, lonely, unsociable.
OPPOSITES: SEE **social** adjective.
2 *a solitary survivor.* one, only, single, sole.
3 *a solitary place.* desolate, hidden, isolated, out-of-the-way, remote, secluded, sequestered, unfrequented.
a solitary person hermit, [*informal*] loner, recluse.

solitude noun *the solitude of the wilderness.* isolation, loneliness, privacy, remoteness, retirement, seclusion.

solo adverb *to perform solo.* alone, unaccompanied.

soloist noun MUSICAL PERFORMERS: SEE **music**.

solstice noun OPPOSITE: equinox.

soluble adjective **1** *soluble in water.* dispersing, dissolving.
2 *a soluble problem.* explicable, manageable, solvable, tractable, understandable.
OPPOSITES: SEE **insoluble**.

solution noun **1** *a solution of salt in water.* blend, compound, mixture.
2 *the solution to a problem.* answer, elucidation, explanation, key, resolution, solving.

solvable adjective *a solvable problem.* SEE **soluble**.

solve verb *to solve a riddle.* answer, [*informal*] crack, decipher, elucidate, explain, find the solution to, interpret, work out.

solvent adjective *Accountants confirmed that the firm was solvent.* in credit, self-supporting, sound, viable.
OPPOSITES: SEE **bankrupt**.

sombre adjective *sombre colours. a sombre expression.* cheerless, dark, dim, dismal, doleful, drab, dull, gloomy, grave, lugubrious, melancholy, mournful, SEE **sad**, serious, sober.
OPPOSITES: SEE **cheerful**.

somersault noun forward roll.

somewhat adverb *somewhat annoyed.* fairly, moderately, [*informal*] pretty, quite, rather, [*informal*] sort of.

somnambulist noun sleep-walker.

son noun FAMILY RELATIONSHIPS: SEE **family**.

song noun lyric.

MUSIC FOR SINGING: air, anthem, aria, ballad, blues, calypso, cantata, canticle, carol, chant, chorus, descant, ditty, folk-song, hymn, jingle, lied, lullaby, madrigal, musical, number, nursery rhyme, opera, oratorio, pop song, psalm, reggae, rock, serenade, shanty, soul, spiritual, wassail.
OTHER MUSICAL TERMS: SEE **music**.

---

songster noun SEE **singer**.

sonorous adjective *a sonorous voice.* deep, full, loud, powerful, resonant, resounding, rich, ringing.
OPPOSITES: SEE **quiet, shrill**.

soon adverb [*old-fashioned*] anon, presently, quickly, shortly.

sooner adverb **1** *I wish you'd come sooner.* before, earlier.
2 *I'd sooner have an apple than sweets.* preferably, rather.

soot noun dirt, grime.

soothe verb *Quiet music soothes my nerves.* allay, appease, assuage, calm, comfort, compose, ease, mollify, pacify, quiet, relieve, salve, settle, still, tranquillize.

soothing adjective **1** *soothing ointment.* balmy, comforting, emollient, healing, mild, palliative.
2 *soothing music.* calming, gentle, peaceful, pleasant, relaxing, restful.

sooty adjective SEE **dirty** adjective.

sophisticated adjective **1** *sophisticated behaviour. sophisticated clothes.* adult, cosmopolitan, cultivated, cultured, fashionable, [*informal*] grown-up, mature, [*informal*] posh, [*uncomplimentary*] pretentious, refined, stylish, urbane, worldly.
OPPOSITES: SEE **naïve, simple.**
2 *sophisticated ideas, sophisticated machinery.* advanced, clever, complex, complicated, elaborate, hard to understand, ingenious, intricate, involved, subtle.
OPPOSITES: SEE **primitive, simple.**

sophistry noun *I wasn't taken in by his sophistry.* SEE **casuistry.**

soporific adjective *I dozed off during the soporific music.* boring, hypnotic, sedative, sleep-inducing, sleepy, somnolent.
OPPOSITES: SEE **lively, stimulating.**

sopping adjective SEE **soaked.**

soppy adjective SEE **sentimental, silly.**

soprano noun SEE **singer.**

sorbet noun fruit-ice, ice, water-ice.

sorcerer noun conjuror, enchanter, magician, necromancer, sorceress, [*old-fashioned*] warlock, witch, witch-doctor, wizard.

sorcery noun black magic, charms, conjuring, incantations, magic, necromancy, the occult, spells, voodoo, witchcraft, wizardry.

sordid adjective **1** *sordid surroundings. sordid details.* dirty, disreputable, filthy, foul, mucky, nasty, seamy, [*informal*] sleazy, [*informal*] slummy, squalid, ugly, undignified, SEE **unpleasant,** wretched.
OPPOSITES: SEE **elegant.**
2 *sordid dealings on the stock-exchange.* avaricious, corrupt, covetous, degenerate, dishonourable, immoral, mercenary, rapacious, selfish, [*informal*] shabby, shameful, unethical.
OPPOSITES: SEE **honourable.**

sore adjective **1** *a sore wound. a sore place on your skin.* aching, chafing, hurting, inflamed, painful, raw, red, sensitive, smarting, tender.
2 *She was sore about the way she'd been treated.* SEE **annoyed.**
to make sore *The continual rubbing made my skin sore.* chafe, chap, gall, hurt, inflame, redden.

sore noun *I put ointment on the sores.* abscess, boil, carbuncle, gall, gathering, graze, inflammation, laceration, pimple, rawness, spot, ulcer, SEE **wound** noun.

sorrow noun **1** *the sorrow of parting.* affliction, anguish, dejection, depression, desolation, despair, desperation, despondency, disappointment, discontent, disgruntlement, dissatisfaction, distress, [*poetic*] dolour, gloom, glumness, grief, heartache, heartbreak, heaviness, homesickness, hopelessness, loneliness, melancholy, misery, misfortune, mourning, sad feelings [SEE **sad**], sadness, suffering, tearfulness, tribulation, trouble, unhappiness, wistfulness, woe, wretchedness.
OPPOSITES: SEE **happiness.**
2 *She expressed her sorrow for what she had done.* apologies, feeling of guilt, penitence, regret, remorse, repentance.
OPPOSITE: impenitence.

sorrow verb *to sorrow at someone's misfortune.* be sorrowful [SEE **sorrowful**], be sympathetic [SEE **sympathetic**], grieve, lament, mourn, weep.
OPPOSITES: SEE **rejoice.**

sorrowful adjective *sorrowful feelings. a sorrowful expression.* broken-hearted, concerned, dejected, disconsolate, distressed, doleful, grief-stricken, heartbroken, long-faced, lugubrious, melancholy, miserable, mournful, regretful, rueful, SEE **sad,** saddened, sombre, SEE **sorry,** sympathetic, tearful, unhappy, upset, woebegone, woeful, wretched.
OPPOSITES: SEE **happy.**

sorry adjective **1** *I'm sorry for what I did.* apologetic, ashamed, conscience-stricken, contrite, guilt-ridden, penitent, regretful, remorseful, repentant, shamefaced.
2 *We were sorry for the girl who came last.* compassionate, merciful, pitying, sympathetic, understanding.
3 [*informal*] *Things were in a sorry state.* SEE **bad.**

sort noun **1** *Pop is my sort of music. The club welcomes all sorts of people.* brand, category, class, description, form, genre, group, kind, make, set, quality, type, variety.
2 *a sort of dog. a sort of wild flower.* breed, class, family, genus, race, species.
sort of [*informal*] *I feel sort of anxious.* SEE **somewhat.**

sort verb *to sort things into sets.* arrange, assort, catalogue, categorize, classify, divide, file, grade, group, organize, put in order, tidy.
OPPOSITES: SEE **mix.**

to sort out 1 *Sort out the things you need.* choose, [*informal*] put on one side, segregate, select, separate, set aside.
2 *I sorted out their problem.* attend to, clear up, cope with, deal with, find an answer to, grapple with, handle, manage, resolve, solve, tackle.

sortie noun SEE **attack** noun.

sot noun SEE **drunkard**.

sought-after adjective SEE **attractive**.

soul noun **1** *your immortal soul.* psyche, spirit.
2 [*informal*] *The poor souls had to wait ages for a bus.* SEE **person**.

soulful adjective *a soulful expression. a soulful performance.* deeply felt, eloquent, emotional, expressive, heartfelt, inspiring, moving, passionate, profound, sincere, spiritual, stirring, uplifting.
OPPOSITES: SEE **soulless**.

soulless adjective *a soulless performance.* cold, insincere, mechanical, perfunctory, routine, spiritless, superficial, trite, unemotional, unfeeling, uninspiring, unsympathetic.
OPPOSITES: SEE **soulful**.

sound adjective **1** *in a sound condition.* fit, healthy, hearty, robust, secure, solid, strong, sturdy, undamaged, well, whole.
OPPOSITES: SEE **damaged, ill**.
2 *sound advice.* coherent, convincing, correct, logical, prudent, rational, reasonable, reasoned, sensible, wise.
OPPOSITES: SEE **silly**.
3 *a sound business.* dependable, established, recognized, reliable, reputable, safe, trustworthy, viable.
OPPOSITES: SEE **disreputable**.

sound noun noise, timbre.
the science of sound acoustics.
RELATED ADJECTIVES [= *to do with sound*]: acoustic, sonic.

VARIOUS SOUNDS [Most of these words can be used either as nouns or as verbs]: bang, bark, bawl, bay, bellow, blare, bleat, bleep, boo, boom, bray, buzz, cackle, caw, chime, chink, chirp, chirrup, chug, clack, clamour, clang, clank, clap, clash, clatter, click, clink, cluck, coo, crack, crackle, crash, creak, croak, croon, crow, crunch, cry.

drone, echo, fizz, grate, grizzle, groan, growl, grunt, gurgle, hiccup, hiss, honk, hoot, howl, hum, jabber, jangle, jeer, jingle, lisp, low, miaow, moan, moo, murmur, neigh, patter, peal, ping, pip, plop, pop, purr, quack, rattle, reverberation, ring, roar, rumble, rustle.

scream, screech, shout, shriek, sigh, sizzle, skirl, slam, slurp, snap, snarl, sniff, snore, snort, sob, splutter, squawk, squeak, squeal, squelch, swish, throb, thud, thunder, tick, ting, tinkle, toot, trumpet, twang, tweet, twitter, wail, warble, whimper, whine, whinny, whir, whistle, whiz, whoop, woof, yap, yell, yelp, yodel, yowl.
SEE ALSO: **music, noise, talk** verb.

---

sound verb **1** *The signal sounded.* become audible, be heard, make a noise, resound, reverberate.
2 *They sounded the signal.* cause, create, make, make audible, produce, pronounce, utter.
3 *to sound the depth of a river. to sound out public opinion.* examine, investigate, measure, plumb, probe, test, try.

soundless adjective SEE **silent**.

soup noun KINDS OF SOUP: broth, consommé, minestrone, mulligatawny, Scotch broth, stock. [There are many other kinds of soup. Often they are named after the principal ingredient: *chicken soup, tomato soup,* etc.]

soupçon noun SEE **small (small amount)**.

sour adjective **1** *sour fruit.* acid, bitter, pungent, sharp, tangy, tart, unripe, vinegary.
OPPOSITES: SEE **sweet** adjective.
OTHER WORDS DESCRIBING TASTE: SEE **taste** verb.
2 *a sour temper. sour comments.* acerbic, bad-tempered, bitter, cynical, disagreeable, grudging, grumpy, ill-natured, irritable, jaundiced, peevish, snappy, testy, unpleasant.
OPPOSITES: SEE **kind** adjective.

source noun **1** *the source of a rumour.* author, cause, derivation, initiator, originator, starting-point.
2 *the source of a river.* beginning, head, origin, spring, start.

sourpuss noun SEE **angry (angry person)**.

souse verb SEE **soak**.

south noun GEOGRAPHICAL TERMS: SEE **geography**.

souvenir noun *a souvenir of a holiday.* keepsake, memento, reminder.

sovereign adjective **1** *sovereign power.* absolute, dominant, supreme.
2 *a sovereign state.* autonomous, independent, self-governing.

sovereign noun emperor, empress, king, monarch, queen, SEE **ruler**.

sow noun SEE **pig**.

sow verb *to sow seeds.* broadcast, plant, scatter, seed, spread.

spa noun SEE **spring** noun.

space adjective *space exploration.* extraterrestrial, interplanetary, interstellar, orbiting.
space travel astronautics.

WORDS TO DO WITH TRAVEL IN SPACE: astronaut, blast-off, booster rocket, capsule, cosmonaut, count-down, heat-shield, module, orbit, probe, re-entry, retro-rocket, rocket, satellite, spacecraft, spaceship, space-shuttle, space-station, spacesuit, splash-down, sputnik.

---

space noun **1** *interstellar space.* emptiness, endlessness, ionosphere, infinity, stratosphere, the universe.
ASTRONOMICAL TERMS: SEE **astronomy**.
2 *space to move about.* [*informal*] elbow-room, freedom, leeway, room, scope.
3 *an empty space.* area, blank, break, chasm, concourse, distance, gap, hiatus, hole, interval, lacuna, opening, place, vacuum.

space verb *to space things out.* SEE **arrange**.

spacious adjective *a spacious house.* ample, SEE **big**, capacious, commodious, extensive, large, open, roomy, sizeable.
OPPOSITES: SEE **poky, small**.

spadework noun SEE **work** noun.

spaghetti noun SEE **pasta**.

span noun *a span of time. We could look along the whole span of the lake.* breadth, compass, distance, duration, extent, length, reach, scope, stretch, width.

span verb *to span a river.* arch over, bridge, cross, extend across, pass over, reach over, straddle, stretch over, traverse.

spank verb SEE **hit** verb, slap, smack.

spanking adjective *a spanking pace.* SEE **brisk**.

spanking noun SEE **punishment**.

spar noun SEE **pole**.

spar verb box, SEE **fight** verb.

spare adjective **1** *spare players. spare food.* additional, extra, inessential, leftover, odd, remaining, superfluous, surplus, unnecessary, unneeded, unused, unwanted.
OPPOSITES: SEE **necessary**.
2 *a spare figure.* SEE **thin** adjective.

spare verb **1** *The judge did not spare the guilty man.* be merciful to, forgive, free, [*informal*] let off, pardon, release, reprieve, save.
2 *Can you spare something for charity?* afford, allow, give, give up, manage (*£10 is all I can manage*), part with, provide, sacrifice.

sparing adjective *sparing with his money.* careful, [*informal*] close, economical, frugal, mean, miserly, prudent, stingy, thrifty.
OPPOSITES: SEE **generous, wasteful**.

spark noun *a spark of light.* flash, flicker, gleam, glint, sparkle.

spark verb SEE **light** noun (**give light**).
to spark off *He sparked off an argument.* SEE **provoke**.

sparkle verb SEE **light** noun (**give light**).

sparkling adjective **1** *sparkling jewels.* brilliant, flashing, glinting, glittering, scintillating, shining, shiny, twinkling.
OPPOSITES: SEE **dull** adjective.
2 *sparkling drinks.* aerated, bubbling, bubbly, carbonated, effervescent, fizzy, foaming.
OPPOSITES: flat, still.

sparse adjective *sparse vegetation.* inadequate, light (*light traffic*), meagre, scanty, scarce, scattered, thin, [*informal*] thin on the ground.
OPPOSITES: SEE **dense**.

spartan adjective *spartan conditions.* abstemious, ascetic, austere, bare, bleak, frugal, hard, harsh, plain, rigorous, severe, simple, stern, strict.
OPPOSITES: SEE **luxurious**, pampered.

spasm noun *a spasm of coughing. a muscular spasm.* attack, contraction, convulsion, fit, jerk, paroxysm, seizure, [*plural*] throes, twitch.

spasmodic adjective *a spasmodic fault on our TV.* erratic, fitful, intermittent, irregular, occasional, [*informal*] on and off, sporadic.
OPPOSITES: SEE **continual, regular**.

spat noun gaiter.

spate noun *a spate of water.* cataract, flood, gush, rush, torrent.
OPPOSITES: SEE **trickle** noun.

spatter verb *The bus spattered water over us.* pepper, scatter, shower, slop, splash, spray, sprinkle.

speak verb articulate, communicate, converse, deliver a speech, discourse, enunciate, express yourself, hold a conversation, [*informal*] pipe up, pronounce words, say something,

soliloquize, talk, tell, use your voice, utter, verbalize, vocalize.
FOR A LONGER LIST OF SYNONYMS: SEE **talk** verb.
to speak about allude to, comment on, discuss, mention, refer to, relate.
to speak to address, harangue, lecture.
to speak your mind be honest [SEE **honest**], say what you think, speak honestly, speak out, state your opinion, voice your thoughts.

speaker noun *a speaker at a meeting.* lecturer, mouthpiece (*She can be our mouthpiece*), orator, spokesperson.

spear noun assegai, harpoon, javelin, lance, pike.

spearhead verb SEE **lead** verb.

special adjective **1** *a special occasion. a special visitor.* distinguished, exceptional, extraordinary, important, infrequent, momentous, notable, [*informal*] out-of-the-ordinary, rare, red-letter (*a red-letter day*), significant, uncommon, unusual.
OPPOSITES: SEE **ordinary**.
2 *Petrol has a special smell.* characteristic, distinctive, memorable, unique, unmistakable.
OPPOSITES: SEE **common** adjective.
3 *my special chair.* especial, individual, particular, personal.
4 *a special tool for cutting glass.* proper, specific, specialized, tailor-made.

specialist noun **1** *a science specialist. a specialist in antiques.* authority, connoisseur, expert, fancier (*a pigeon fancier*), professional, researcher.
2 *a medical specialist.* consultant.
MEDICAL SPECIALISTS: SEE **medicine**.

speciality noun *What's your speciality?* expertise, forte, [*informal*] line (*What's your line?*), special knowledge or skill, strength, strong point.

specialize verb **to specialize in** be a specialist in [SEE **specialist**], be best at, concentrate on, have a reputation for.

specialized adjective *specialized knowledge.* esoteric, expert, specialist, unfamiliar.
OPPOSITES: SEE **general**.

species noun *a species of animal.* breed, class, genus, kind, race, sort, type, variety.

specific adjective *I need specific information, not rumours.* clear-cut, definite, detailed, exact, explicit, particular, precise, special.
OPPOSITES: SEE **general**.

specify verb *Specify your requirements.* be specific about [SEE **specific**], define, detail, enumerate, identify, itemize, list, name, particularize, [*informal*] spell out, stipulate.

specimen noun *a specimen of your handwriting.* example, illustration, instance, model, pattern, representative, sample.

specious adjective *specious arguments.* SEE **misleading**.

speck noun *a speck of dirt.* bit, dot, fleck, grain, mark, mite, particle, speckle, spot, trace.

speckled adjective *speckled with patches of colour.* blotchy, brindled, dappled, dotted, flecked, freckled, mottled, patchy, spotted, spotty, stippled.

spectacle noun *a colourful spectacle. the spectacle of a coronation.* ceremonial, ceremony, colourfulness, display, exhibition, extravaganza, grandeur, magnificence, ostentation, pageantry, parade, pomp, show, spectacular effects [SEE **spectacular**], splendour.
spectacles SEE **glass (glasses)**.

spectacular adjective *a spectacular display.* SEE **beautiful**, breathtaking, colourful, dramatic, elaborate, eye-catching, impressive, magnificent, [*uncomplimentary*] ostentatious, sensational, showy, splendid, stunning.

spectator noun [*plural*] audience, bystander, [*plural*] crowd, eye-witness, looker-on, observer, onlooker, passer-by, viewer, watcher, witness.

spectral adjective SEE **ghostly**.

spectre noun SEE **ghost**.

spectrum noun SEE **range** noun.

speculate verb **1** *We speculated as to whether they would marry.* conjecture, hypothesize, make guesses, reflect, surmise, theorize, wonder.
2 *He speculates on the stock exchange.* gamble, hope to make profit, invest speculatively.

speculative adjective **1** *speculative rumours.* based on guesswork, conjectural, [*informal*] gossipy, hypothetical, suppositional, theoretical, unfounded, uninformed.
OPPOSITES: SEE **knowledgeable**.
2 *speculative investments.* chancy, [*informal*] dicey, [*informal*] dodgy, hazardous, [*informal*] iffy, risky, uncertain, unpredictable, unsafe.
OPPOSITES: SEE **safe**.

speech noun **1** *clear speech.* articulation, communication, declamation, delivery, elocution, enunciation, pronunciation, speaking, talking, using words, utterance.
2 *a speech to an audience.* address, discourse, disquisition, harangue, homily,

lecture, oration, paper (*to give a paper*), presentation, sermon, [*informal*] spiel, talk.
3 *a speech in a play.* dialogue, lines, monologue, soliloquy.
OTHER RELEVANT ENTRIES: **language, say, speak, talk** noun, verb.

speechless adjective *speechless with rage.* dumb, dumbfounded, dumbstruck, inarticulate, [*informal*] mum, mute, nonplussed, silent, thunderstruck, tongue-tied.
OPPOSITES: SEE **talkative**.

speed noun **1** *What speed were you going?* pace, rate, tempo (*the tempo of a piece of music*), velocity.
2 *I was amazed by her speed.* alacrity, celerity, fleetness, haste, hurry, quickness, rapidity, swiftness.

speed verb **1** *We sped along.* [*informal*] belt, [*informal*] bolt, canter, career, dart, dash, flash, flit, fly, gallop, hasten, hurry, hurtle, move quickly, [*informal*] nip, [*informal*] put your foot down, race, run, rush, shoot, sprint, stampede, streak, tear, [*informal*] zoom.
2 *She was speeding when the police stopped her.* break the speed limit, go too fast.
to speed up accelerate, go faster, increase speed, quicken, spurt.

speedway noun VARIOUS RACES: SEE **race** noun.

speedy adjective SEE **fast** adjective.

spell noun **1** *a magic spell.* bewitchment, charm, conjuration, conjuring, enchantment, incantation, magic formula, sorcery, witchcraft.
2 *the spell of the theatre.* allure, charm, fascination, glamour, magic.
3 *a spell of fine weather.* interval, period, phase, season, session, stint, stretch, term, time, turn.

spell verb *The rain spelt disaster for the garden-party.* foretell, indicate, mean, signal, signify, suggest.
to spell out SEE **explain**.

spellbound adjective *spellbound by the music.* bewitched, captivated, charmed, enchanted, enthralled, entranced, fascinated, hypnotized, mesmerized, transported.

spend verb **1** *I spent all my money.* [*informal*] blue, consume, [*informal*] cough up, exhaust, [*informal*] fork out, fritter, [*informal*] get through, invest, [*informal*] lash out, pay out, [*informal*] shell out, [*informal*] splurge, squander.
2 *We spent all our time talking.* fill, occupy, pass, use up, waste.

spending noun *I must cut back on my spending.* SEE **expense**.

spendthrift noun big spender, prodigal, profligate, wasteful person [SEE **wasteful**], wastrel.
OPPOSITES: SEE **miser**.

spew verb SEE **vomit**.

sphere noun **1** ball, globe, orb, spheroid.
OTHER SHAPES: SEE **shape** noun.
2 *He's an expert in his own limited sphere.* area, department, domain, field, milieu, province, range, scope, subject, territory.

spherical adjective *a spherical object.* ball-shaped, globular, rotund, round, spheroidal.

spice noun **1** *spices used in cooking.* flavouring, piquancy, seasoning.

SOME COMMON SPICES: allspice, bayleaf, capsicum, cardamom, cassia, cayenne, chilli, cinnamon, cloves, coriander, curry powder, ginger, grains of paradise, juniper, mace, nutmeg, paprika, pepper, pimento, poppy seed, saffron, sesame, turmeric.

---

2 *Seeing exotic places adds spice to a holiday.* colour, excitement, interest, zest.

spicy adjective *a spicy smell. spicy food.* highly flavoured, hot, piquant, pungent, seasoned.

spiel noun SEE **speech**.

spike noun *He tore his jeans on a spike.* barb, nail, point, projection, prong, tine (*the tines of a fork*).

spike verb *to spike something with a pin.* SEE **pierce**.

spiky adjective SEE **prickly**.

spill verb **1** *to spill milk.* overturn, slop, splash about, tip over, upset.
2 *Milk spilled out of the bottle.* brim, flow, overflow, run, pour.
3 *The lorry spilled its load.* discharge, drop, scatter, shed, tip.

spin verb **1** *A wheel spins on an axle.* gyrate, pirouette, revolve, rotate, swirl, turn, twirl, twist, wheel, whirl.
2 *Alcohol makes my head spin.* reel, swim.

spindle noun axle, rod, shaft.

spindly adjective SEE **thin** adjective.

spine noun **1** backbone, spinal column, vertebrae.
OTHER BONES OF YOUR BODY: SEE **skeleton**.
2 *A hedgehog has sharp spines.* bristle, needle, point, quill, spike.

spine-chilling adjective SEE **frightening**.

spineless adjective *a spineless coward.* cowardly, faint-hearted, feeble, helpless, irresolute, [*informal*] soft, timid, unheroic, weak, weedy.
OPPOSITES: SEE **brave**.

spinnaker noun SEE **sail** noun.

spinney noun SEE **wood**.

spin-off noun SEE **by-product**.

spinster noun SEE **unmarried**.

spiny adjective SEE **prickly**.

spiral adjective coiled, turning.
OTHER CURVING SHAPES: SEE **curved**.

spiral noun coil, screw, whorl.

spiral verb SEE **twist** verb.

spire noun *a church spire.* pinnacle, steeple.
OTHER PARTS OF A CHURCH: SEE **church**.

spirit noun **1** *a person's spirit.* mind, psyche, soul.
OPPOSITES: SEE **body**.
2 *supernatural spirits.* apparition, [*informal*] bogy, demon, devil, genie, ghost, ghoul, gremlin, hobgoblin, imp, incubus, nymph, phantasm, phantom, poltergeist, [*poetic*] shade, shadow, spectre, [*informal*] spook, sprite, sylph, vision, visitant, wraith, zombie.
3 *It took some time to get into the spirit of the party.* atmosphere, essence, feeling, mood.
4 *The athletes had great spirit.* animation, bravery, cheerfulness, confidence, courage, daring, determination, energy, enthusiasm, fortitude, [*informal*] go, [*informal*] guts, heroism, morale, motivation, optimism, pluck, valour, verve, will-power.
5 *strong spirits.* SEE **alcohol**.

spirited adjective *a spirited performance. spirited opposition.* active, animated, assertive, brave, courageous, daring, energetic, frisky, gallant, intrepid, lively, plucky, positive, sparkling, sprightly, vigorous.
OPPOSITES: SEE **spiritless**.

spiritless adjective *a spiritless performance.* apathetic, cowardly, defeatist, despondent, dispirited, dull, lacklustre, languid, lifeless, listless, melancholy, negative, unenthusiastic.
OPPOSITES: SEE **spirited**.

spiritual adjective *Are spiritual or worldly values more important?* devotional, eternal, heavenly, holy, incorporeal, other-worldly, religious, sacred, unworldly.
OPPOSITES: SEE **physical**.

spirituous adjective SEE **alcoholic**.

spit noun **1** *spit dribbling down his face.* dribble, saliva, spittle, [*formal*] sputum.
2 *a spit of land.* SEE **promontory**.

spit verb *to spit something out.* eject, spew.

spite noun *They showed their spite by not co-operating.* animosity, animus, [*informal*] bitchiness, bitterness, [*informal*] cattiness, grudge, hate, hostility, ill-feeling, malevolence, malice, malignity, rancour, resentment, spleen, vindictiveness.

spiteful adjective *spiteful remarks.* acid, [*informal*] bitchy, bitter, [*informal*] catty, cruel, cutting, hateful, hostile, hurtful, ill-natured, malevolent, malicious, nasty, poisonous, rancorous, resentful, revengeful, sharp, [*informal*] snide, sour, venomous, vicious, vindictive.

spitfire noun SEE **angry (angry person)**.

spittle noun SEE **spit** noun.

splash verb **1** *The bus splashed water over us.* shower, slop, [*informal*] slosh, spatter, spill, splatter, spray, sprinkle, squirt, wash.
2 *We splashed about in the water.* bathe, dabble, paddle, wade.
3 *The news was splashed across the front page.* display, exhibit, flaunt, [*informal*] plaster, publicize, show.
to splash out SEE **spend**.

splash-down noun SEE **landing**.

splatter verb SEE **splash**.

splay verb *to splay your feet.* make a V-shape, slant, spread.

spleen noun *He gave vent to his spleen.* SEE **spite**.

splendid adjective **1** *a splendid banquet. splendid clothes. splendid surroundings.* beautiful, brilliant, costly, dazzling, elegant, glittering, glorious, gorgeous, grand, great, handsome, imposing, impressive, lavish, luxurious, magnificent, majestic, marvellous, noble, ornate, palatial, [*informal*] posh, regal, resplendent, rich, royal, stately, sublime, sumptuous, [*informal*] super, superb, supreme, wonderful.
2 *splendid work.* admirable, excellent, first-class, SEE **good**.

splendour noun *Tourists love the splendour of a royal occasion.* brilliance, ceremony, display, glory, grandeur, magnificence, majesty, ostentation, pomp, richness, show, spectacle, stateliness, sumptuousness.

splice verb SEE **join** verb.

splinter noun *a splinter of wood.* chip, flake, fragment, shaving, [*plural*] shivers, sliver.

splinter verb *He splintered the door when he kicked it.* SEE **break** verb, chip, crack, fracture, shatter, shiver, smash, split.

split noun **1** *a split in a tree. a split in my jeans.* break, cleavage, cleft, crack, fissure. SEE **opening** noun, rent, rift, rupture, slash, slit, tear.
2 *a split in a political party. a split in a marriage.* breach, difference, dissension, divergence of opinion, division, divorce, estrangement, SEE **quarrel** noun, schism, separation.

split verb **1** *We split into two teams.* break up, divide, separate.
2 *The axe split the log. I split my jeans.* burst, chop, cleave, crack, SEE **cut** verb, rend, rip open, slice, splinter, tear.
3 *We split the profits.* allocate, allot, apportion, distribute, divide, halve, share.
4 *The roads split here.* branch, diverge, fork.
5 [*informal*] *to split on your friends.* SEE **inform (inform against)**.

splitting adjective *a splitting headache.* SEE **painful**.

splotch noun SEE **mark** noun.

splurge verb SEE **spend**.

splutter verb VARIOUS SOUNDS: SEE **sound** noun.

spoil verb **1** *Don't spoil that neat work. She spoilt her reputation.* blight, blot, blotch, bungle, damage, deface, destroy, disfigure, [*informal*] dish, harm, injure, [*informal*] make a mess of, mar, [*informal*] mess up, ruin, stain, undermine, undo, upset, vitiate, worsen, wreck.
OPPOSITES: SEE **improve**.
2 *Soft fruit spoils quickly.* become useless, decompose, go bad, go off, perish, putrefy, rot.
3 *Grandad spoils the little ones.* coddle, cosset, indulge, make a fuss of, mollycoddle, over-indulge, pamper.

spoils noun *the spoils of war.* SEE **booty**.

spoken adjective *Her spoken French is excellent.* oral, unwritten, verbal.
OPPOSITES: SEE **written**.

spokesperson noun mouthpiece, representative, spokesman, spokeswoman.

sponge verb **1** *to sponge down the car.* clean, mop, rinse, swill, wash, wipe.
2 [*informal*] *to sponge on your friends.* cadge (from), scrounge (from).

spongy adjective *spongy rubber.* absorbent, porous, soft, springy.
OPPOSITES: SEE **solid**.

sponsor noun *Our team's sponsor donated the new equipment.* backer, benefactor, donor, patron, promoter.

sponsor verb *to sponsor someone in a race. to sponsor an arts festival.* back, be a sponsor of, finance, fund, help, promote, subsidize, support.

sponsorship noun *We were able to go ahead under the sponsorship of a local firm.* aegis, [*plural*] auspices, backing, benefaction, guarantee, patronage, promotion, support.

spontaneous adjective **1** *a spontaneous display of affection.* extempore, impromptu, impulsive, unconstrained, unforced, unplanned, unpremeditated, unprepared, unrehearsed, voluntary.
2 *a spontaneous reaction.* automatic, instinctive, involuntary, natural, reflex.
OPPOSITES: SEE **premeditated**.

spoof noun SEE **satire**.

spook noun SEE **ghost**.

spooky adjective [*informal*] *a spooky big house.* creepy, eerie, frightening, ghostly, haunted, mysterious, scary, uncanny, unearthly, weird.

spool noun *a spool of cotton.* bobbin, reel.

spoon noun dessert-spoon, ladle, tablespoon, teaspoon.
OTHER ITEMS OF CUTLERY: SEE **cutlery**.

spoon-feed verb cosset, help, indulge, mollycoddle, pamper, spoil.

spoor noun *an animal's spoor.* footprints, scent, traces, track.

sport noun **1** *Sport can help you keep healthy.* exercise, games, pastime, play, recreation.
2 *They were having a bit of sport at my expense.* amusement, diversion, entertainment, fun, joking, merriment, raillery, teasing.
blood sports beagling, fishing, hunting, shooting.

VARIOUS SPORTS: aerobics, American football, angling, archery, Association football, SEE **athletics**, badminton, baseball, basketball, billiards, bobsleigh, bowls, boxing, bullfighting, canoeing, climbing, cricket, croquet, cross-country, curling.

darts, decathlon, discus, fishing, football, gliding, golf, gymnastics, hockey, hurdling, ice-hockey, javelin, jogging, keep-fit, lacrosse, marathon, SEE **martial (martial arts)**, mountaineering, netball, orienteering, pentathlon, [*informal*] ping-pong, polo, pool, pot-holing, quoits.

racing [SEE **race** noun], rock-climbing, roller-skating, rounders, rowing, Rugby, running, sailing, shot, show-jumping, skating, skiing, skin-diving, sky-diving, snooker, soccer, sprinting, squash, street-hockey, surfing or surf-riding, SEE **swimming**, table-tennis, tennis, tobogganing, trampolining, volleyball, water-polo, water-skiing, windsurfing, SEE **winter sports**, wrestling, yachting.

PLACES WHERE SPORTS TAKE PLACE: arena, boxing-ring, circuit, course, court, field, golf-course, ground, gymnasium, ice-rink, links, pitch, playing-field, race-course, race-track, stadium.

---

sporting adjective *a sporting gesture.* considerate, fair, generous, honourable, sportsmanlike.

sportive adjective SEE **playful**.

sportsperson noun contestant, participant, player, sportsman, sportswoman.

sporty adjective SEE **athletic**.

spot noun **1** *a dirty spot on your clothing.* blemish, blot, blotch, discoloration, dot, fleck, mark, smudge, speck, speckle, stain.
2 *a spot on the skin.* birthmark, boil, freckle, impetigo [= *skin disease causing spots*], mole, naevus, pimple, rash [= *spots*], sty, whitlow.
3 *a spot of rain.* bead, blob, drop.
4 *a nice spot for a picnic.* locality, location, place, point, position, site, situation.
5 [*informal*] *I'd love a spot of tea.* SEE **small (small quantity)**.
6 [*informal*] *I was in a bit of a spot.* SEE **difficulty**.

spot verb **1** *My overalls were spotted with paint.* blot, discolour, fleck, mark, mottle, smudge, spatter, speckle, stain.
2 *I spotted a rare bird.* SEE **see**.

spotless adjective **1** *spotless laundry.* SEE **clean** adjective, unmarked.
2 *a spotless reputation.* blameless, immaculate, innocent, irreproachable, pure, unblemished, unsullied, untarnished, [*informal*] whiter than white.

spotlight noun SEE **light** noun.

spotty adjective *a spotty face.* blotchy, freckled, mottled, pimply, speckled, spotted.
to be spotty erupt in spots, have a rash.

spouse noun [*joking*] better half, [*old-fashioned*] helpmate, husband, partner, wife.

spout noun *Water poured from the spout.* fountain, gargoyle, geyser, jet, lip (*of a jug*), nozzle, outlet, rose (*of a watering-can*), spray.

spout verb **1** *Water spouted through the hole.* discharge, erupt, flow, gush, jet, pour, shoot, spurt, squirt, stream.
2 [*informal*] *The lecturer spouted for hours.* SEE **talk** verb.

sprain verb *to sprain your ankle.* SEE **wound** verb.

sprawl verb **1** *We sprawled on the lawn.* flop, lean back, lie, loll, lounge, recline, relax, slouch, slump, spread out, stretch out.
2 *The village sprawled across the valley.* be scattered, spread, straggle.

spray noun **1** *a spray of water.* droplets, fountain, mist, shower, splash, sprinkling.
2 *a spray of flowers.* arrangement, bouquet, branch, bunch, corsage, posy, sprig.
3 *a paint spray.* aerosol, atomizer, spray-gun, sprinkler.

spray verb *The bus sprayed mud over us.* scatter, shower, spatter, splash, spread in droplets, sprinkle.

spray-gun noun SEE **spray** noun.

spread noun [*informal*] *an appetizing spread.* SEE **meal**.

spread verb **1** *to spread things on a table. to spread out a map.* arrange, display, lay out, open out, unfold, unroll.
2 *The epidemic spread. The stain spread.* broaden, enlarge, expand, extend, get bigger or longer or wider, lengthen, [*informal*] mushroom, proliferate, widen.
3 *to spread butter.* apply, cover a surface with.
4 *to spread news.* advertise, broadcast, circulate, diffuse, disperse, disseminate, distribute, divulge, give out, make known, pass on, pass round, proclaim, promulgate, publicize, publish, scatter, transmit.
to spread out *to spread out in a line.* fan out, scatter, SEE **straggle**.

spree noun *to go out on a spree.* [*informal*] binge, [*informal*] fling, [*informal*] orgy, outing, SEE **revelry**.

sprightly adjective *a sprightly 90-year-old.* active, agile, animated, brisk, energetic, lively, nimble, [*informal*] perky, playful, quickmoving, spirited, spry, vivacious.
OPPOSITES: SEE **lethargic**.

spring noun **1** *a clock's spring.* coil, mainspring.
2 *a spring in your step.* bounce, buoyancy, elasticity, give, liveliness.
3 *a spring of water.* fount, fountain, geyser, source (*of a river*), spa, well.

spring verb **1** *He sprang over the gate.* bounce, bound, hop, jump, leap, pounce, vault.
2 *Weeds sprang up.* appear, develop, emerge, germinate, grow, shoot up, sprout.

springy adjective bendy, elastic, flexible, pliable, resilient, spongy, stretchy, supple.
OPPOSITES: SEE **rigid**.

sprinkle verb *to sprinkle salt on food. to sprinkle water about.* drip, dust, pepper, scatter, shower, spatter, splash, spray, strew.

sprint verb SEE **run** verb.

sprite noun SEE **spirit**.

sprout noun *a sprout growing from a seed.* bud, shoot.

sprout verb *The seeds began to sprout.* bud, develop, emerge, germinate, grow, shoot up, spring up.

spruce adjective *He looked spruce in his best clothes.* clean, dapper, elegant, groomed, [*informal*] natty, neat, [*informal*] posh, smart, tidy, trim, well-dressed.
OPPOSITES: SEE **scruffy**.

spruce verb *to spruce yourself up.* SEE **tidy** verb.

spry adjective SEE **sprightly**.

spume noun SEE **froth** noun.

spunk noun SEE **courage**.

spur noun *Applause is a spur to greater effort.* encouragement, impetus, incentive, inducement, motive, prompting, stimulus.

spur verb *The applause spurred us to greater efforts.* egg on, encourage, incite, prick, prod, prompt, provide a spur [SEE **spur** noun], stimulate, urge.

spurious adjective SEE **false**.

spurn verb SEE **reject**.

spurt verb **1** *Water spurted from the hole.* SEE **squirt**.
2 *She spurted ahead.* SEE **speed** verb (**speed up**).

sputum noun dribble, saliva, spit, spittle.

spy noun *a spy working for the enemy.* contact, double agent, infiltrator, informer, mole, private detective, secret agent, snooper, undercover agent.

spy verb **1** *to spy for the enemy.* be a spy [SEE **spy** noun], be engaged in spying [SEE **spying**], eavesdrop, gather intelligence, inform, snoop.
2 *I spy with my little eye.* SEE **see**.

spying noun counter-espionage, detective work, eavesdropping, espionage, intelligence, snooping.

squab noun SEE **seat** noun.

squabble verb SEE **quarrel** verb.

squad, squadron nouns SEE **group** noun.

squalid adjective **1** *squalid surroundings.* dingy, dirty, disgusting, filthy, foul, mucky, nasty, poverty-stricken, repulsive, run-down, [*informal*] sleazy, slummy, sordid, ugly, uncared for, unpleasant, unsalubrious.
OPPOSITES: SEE **clean** adjective.
2 *squalid behaviour.* corrupt, degrading, dishonest, dishonourable, disreputable, immoral, scandalous, [*informal*] shabby, shameful, unethical.
OPPOSITES: SEE **honourable**.

squall noun SEE **storm** noun.

squally adjective SEE **stormy**.

squander verb *to squander your money.* [*informal*] blow, [*informal*] blue, dissipate, [*informal*] fritter, misuse, spend unwisely, [*informal*] splurge, use up, waste.
OPPOSITES: SEE **save**.

square adjective **1** *square corners.* right-angled.
2 *a square deal.* SEE **honest**.

square noun **1** SEE **shape** noun.
2 *a market square.* piazza, plaza.
3 [*informal*] *Don't be a square!* conformist, conservative, conventional person, die-hard, [*informal*] old fogy, [*informal*] stick-in-the-mud, traditionalist.
marked in squares chequered, criss-crossed.

square verb *to square an account.* SEE **settle** verb.

squash verb **1** *Don't squash the strawberries.* compress, crumple, crush, flatten, mangle, mash, pound, press, pulp, smash, stamp on, tread on.
2 *We all squashed into the room.* crowd, pack, squeeze.
3 *They squashed the uprising.* control, put down, quell, repress, suppress.
4 *She squashed him with a withering look.* humiliate, [*informal*] put down, silence, snub.

squashy adjective *squashy fruit.* mashed up, mushy, pulpy, shapeless, soft, spongy, squelchy, yielding.
OPPOSITES: SEE **firm** adjective.

squat adjective *a squat figure.* burly, dumpy, plump, podgy, short, stocky, thick, thickset.
OPPOSITES: SEE **slender**.

squat verb *to squat on the ground.* crouch, sit.

squawk, squeak, squeal nouns, verbs
VARIOUS SOUNDS: SEE **sound** noun.

squeamish adjective *squeamish about dirty things.* [*informal*] choosy, fastidious, finicky, particular, prim, [*informal*] prissy, scrupulous.

squeeze verb 1 *He squeezed my hand.* clasp, compress, crush, embrace, enfold, exert pressure on, grip, hug, pinch, press, squash, wring.
2 *They squeezed us into a little room.* cram, crowd, push, ram, shove, stuff, thrust, wedge.
to squeeze out *Squeeze out the last of the toothpaste.* expel, extrude, force out.

squelch verb VARIOUS SOUNDS: SEE **sound** noun.

squint verb 1 be cross-eyed, have a squint.
2 *I squinted through the keyhole.* SEE **look** verb.

squirm verb *The worm squirmed.* twist, wriggle, writhe.

squirt verb *Water squirted out. They squirted water at us.* ejaculate, gush, jet, send out, shoot, spit, spout, spray, spurt.

stab noun 1 *a stab with a dagger.* blow, jab, prick, thrust, wound, wounding.
2 *a stab of pain.* SEE **pain** noun, pang, sting, throb, twinge.
3 [*informal*] *Have a stab at it.* SEE **try** noun.

stab verb *to stab with a dagger.* bayonet, cut, injure, jab, SEE **pierce**, stick, thrust, wound.

stability noun balance, equilibrium, firmness, permanence, solidity, soundness, steadiness, strength.
OPPOSITES: SEE **instability**.

stabilize verb *to stabilize a ship. to stabilize a political regime.* balance, give stability to [SEE **stability**], keep upright, make stable [SEE **stable**], settle.
OPPOSITES: SEE **upset**.

stable adjective 1 *Make sure the tripod is stable.* balanced, firm, fixed, solid, sound, steady, strong.
2 *a stable relationship.* constant, continuing, durable, established, lasting, permanent, predictable, steadfast, unchanging, unwavering.
OPPOSITES: SEE **changeable**, unstable.

stack noun 1 *a stack of books.* heap, mound, mountain, pile, quantity.
2 *a stack of hay.* [*old-fashioned*] cock, haycock, rick, stook.
3 *a tall stack.* chimney, pillar.

stack verb *Stack the books on the table.* accumulate, assemble, build up, collect, gather, heap, load, mass, pile.

stadium noun arena, sports-ground.

staff noun 1 *She carried a staff as a sign of her authority.* cane, crosier, pole, rod, sceptre, stave, stick.
2 *the staff of a business.* assistants, crew, employees, personnel, officers, team, workers, workforce.

staff verb *The business is staffed by volunteers.* [*sexist*] man, provide with staff, run.

stag noun SEE **deer**.

stage noun 1 *the stage in a theatre.* apron, dais, performing area, platform, proscenium.
2 *a stage of a journey. a stage in your life.* juncture, leg, period, phase, point, time.

stage verb *to stage a play. to stage a demonstration.* arrange, [*informal*] get up, mount, organize, perform, present, produce, put on, set up, stage-manage.

stage-manage verb SEE **stage** verb.

stagger verb 1 *He staggered under the heavy load.* falter, lurch, reel, stumble, sway, totter, walk unsteadily, waver, wobble.
2 *The price staggered us.* alarm, amaze, astonish, astound, confuse, dismay, dumbfound, flabbergast, shake, shock, startle, stun, stupefy, surprise, worry.

stagnant adjective *stagnant water.* motionless, stale, standing, static, still.
OPPOSITE: flowing.

stagnate verb *to stagnate in the same job for years.* achieve nothing, become stale, deteriorate, idle, languish, stand still, stay still, vegetate.
OPPOSITES: SEE **progress** verb.

stagy adjective SEE **theatrical**.

staid adjective SEE **sedate** adjective.

stain noun 1 *What's that stain on your shirt?* blemish, blot, blotch, discoloration, mark, smear, spot.
2 *a wood stain.* colouring, paint, pigment, tint, varnish.

stain verb 1 *to stain something with dirty marks.* blacken, blemish, blot, contaminate, defile, dirty, discolour, make dirty, mark, smudge, soil, sully, taint, tarnish.
2 *to stain wood.* colour, dye, paint, tinge, tint, varnish.

stainless adjective 1 *a stainless reputation.* SEE **pure**.
2 *stainless steel.* rust-free.

stair noun *one stair at a time.* riser, step, tread.
stairs escalator, flight of stairs, staircase, stairway, steps.

stake noun 1 *a wooden stake.* paling, pile, pole, post, spike, stave, stick.
2 *the stake you risk when you gamble.* bet, pledge, wager.

stale adjective **1** *stale bread.* dry, hard, mouldy, old, tasteless.
2 *stale ideas.* hackneyed, out-of-date, overused, uninteresting, unoriginal, worn out.
OPPOSITES: SEE **fresh**.

stalemate noun *stalemate in negotiations.* deadlock, impasse, SEE **standstill**.

stalk noun *the stalk of a plant.* branch, shoot, stem, trunk, twig.

stalk verb **1** *The lion stalked its prey.* follow, hound, hunt, pursue, shadow, tail, track, trail.
2 *I stalked up and down.* prowl, rove, stride, strut, SEE **walk** verb.

stall noun **1** *a market stall.* booth, kiosk, stand.
2 *We sat in the stalls.* SEE **theatre**.

stall verb *Stop stalling!* delay, hang back, hesitate, pause, [*informal*] play for time, postpone, prevaricate, put off, stop, temporize.

stallion noun SEE **horse**.

stalwart adjective *stalwart supporters.* dependable, faithful, reliable, robust, staunch, strong, sturdy, tough, trustworthy, valiant.
OPPOSITES: SEE **feeble**.

stamina noun *I don't have the stamina to run long distances.* energy, resilience, staying-power.

stammer verb falter, splutter, stumble, stutter, SEE **talk** verb.

stamp noun **1** *an official stamp.* brand, hallmark, impression, imprint, mark, print, seal.
2 *a stamp on a letter.* franking, postage stamp.

stamp verb **1** *to stamp your foot.* bring down, strike, thump.
2 *to stamp a mark on something.* brand, engrave, impress, imprint, mark, print.
to stamp on *to stamp on a cigarette stub.* crush, trample, tread on.
to stamp out *to stamp out crime.* eliminate, end, eradicate, extinguish, put an end to, [*informal*] scotch, suppress.

stamp-collecting noun philately.

stampede noun *a stampede towards the exit.* charge, dash, rout, rush, sprint.

stampede verb *The cattle stampeded.* bolt, career, charge, dash, gallop, panic, run, rush, sprint, tear.

stance noun SEE **posture**.

stanch verb SEE **stop** verb.

stanchion noun SEE **pillar**.

stand noun **1** *a stand to put something on.* base, pedestal, rack, support, tripod, trivet.
2 *a newspaper stand.* booth, kiosk, stall.
3 *a stand for spectators.* grandstand, terraces.

stand verb **1** *Stand when the visitor comes.* get to your feet, get up, rise.
2 *A tree stands by our gate.* be, be situated, exist.
3 *They stood the monument on a hill.* erect, locate, position, put up, set up, situate, station.
4 *I stood my books on a shelf.* arrange, deposit, place, set upright.
5 *My offer still stands.* be unchanged, continue, remain valid, stay.
6 *I can't stand smoking in the house.* abide, bear, endure, put up with, suffer, tolerate, [*informal*] wear.
to stand by *She stood by her friends.* adhere to, be faithful to, stay with, stick to, support.
to stand for *What do your initials stand for?* be a sign for, denote, indicate, mean, represent, signify, symbolize.
to stand in for *She stood in for the regular teacher.* be a substitute for [SEE **substitute** noun], cover for, deputize for, replace, substitute for, take over from, understudy.
to stand out *He stands out in a crowd.* be obvious, be prominent, catch the eye, show, stick out.
to stand up for *Stand up for yourself.* champion, defend, fight for, help, look after, protect, shield, side with, speak up for, support.
to stand up to *They bravely stood up to the attack.* clash with, confront, defy, face up to, oppose, resist, withstand.

standard adjective *a standard procedure. a standard size.* accepted, accustomed, approved, average, basic, common, conventional, customary, established, everyday, familiar, habitual, normal, official, ordinary, orthodox, popular, recognized, regular, routine, set, staple (*a staple diet*), typical, usual.
OPPOSITES: SEE **abnormal**.

standard noun **1** *a high standard.* achievement, benchmark, criterion, example, gauge, grade, guideline, ideal, level, measure, measurement, model, norm, pattern, rule, sample, specification, touchstone, yardstick.
2 *the standard of a regiment.* banner, colours, ensign, flag, pennant.
standards *Have you no standards?* SEE **morality**.

standardize verb *Standardize your results. Standardize the presentation of your work.* average out, conform to a standard, equalize, normalize, regiment, stereotype.

stand-in noun SEE **substitute** noun.

standing noun SEE **status**.

standoffish adjective SEE **unfriendly**.

standpoint noun *Can you understand my standpoint?* angle, attitude, belief, opinion, perspective, point of view, position, stance, vantage-point, view, viewpoint.

standstill noun *We came to a standstill.* [*informal*] dead end, deadlock, halt, [*informal*] hold-up, impasse, stalemate, stop, stoppage.

stanza noun SEE **verse**.

staple adjective *our staple diet.* chief, main, principal, SEE **standard** adjective.

staple noun, verb SEE **fasten, fastener**.

star noun **1** asteroid, lodestar, nova, shooting star, sun, supernova.
RELATED ADJECTIVES: astral, stellar.
OTHER ASTRONOMICAL TERMS: SEE **astronomy**.
2 *the shape of a star.* asterisk, pentagram.
3 *a TV star.* attraction, big name, celebrity, [*informal*] draw, idol, SEE **performer**, starlet, superstar.

starboard adjective *starboard side of a ship.* right-hand (when facing forward).
OPPOSITE: port.

starch noun *starch in food.* carbohydrate.

starchy adjective [*informal*], *Don't be so starchy.* aloof, conventional, formal, prim, stiff, SEE **unfriendly**.

stare verb *Why are you staring?* gape, gaze, glare, goggle, look fixedly, peer.
to stare at contemplate, examine, eye, scrutinize, study, watch.

stark adjective **1** *a stark prospect.* SEE **grim**.
2 *a stark contrast.* SEE **absolute**.

starlight noun SEE **light** noun.

starry adjective *a starry sky.* clear, glittering, star-filled, twinkling.
OPPOSITE: starless.

starry-eyed adjective SEE **romantic**.

start noun **1** *the start of something new.* beginning, birth, commencement, creation, dawn, establishment, inauguration, inception, initiation, institution, introduction, launch, onset, opening.
OPPOSITES: SEE **finish** noun.
2 *the start of a journey.* point of departure, setting out.
3 *Having a rich mother gave her a start in life.* advantage, opportunity.
4 *The explosion gave me a nasty start.* jump, shock, surprise.
to give someone a start SEE **startle**.

start verb **1** *to start something new.* activate, begin, commence, create, embark on, engender, establish, found, [*informal*] get cracking on, give birth to, inaugurate, initiate, instigate, institute, introduce, launch, open, originate, pioneer, set up.
OPPOSITES: SEE **finish** verb.
2 *The train is ready to start.* depart, [*informal*] get going, leave, move off, set off, set out.
OPPOSITES: SEE **stop** verb.
3 *I started when the gun went off.* blench, flinch, jerk, jump, recoil, spring up, twitch, wince.
to make someone start SEE **startle**.

startle verb *The explosion startled us.* agitate, alarm, catch unawares, frighten, give you a start, jolt, make you start, scare, shake, shock, surprise, take by surprise, upset.
OPPOSITES: SEE **calm** verb.

startling adjective SEE **surprising**.

starvation noun *dying of starvation.* deprivation, famine, hunger, malnutrition, undernourishment, want.
OPPOSITES: SEE **overeating, plenty**.

starve verb *Many starved in the drought.* die of starvation [SEE **starvation**], go hungry, go without, perish.
to starve yourself diet, fast, go on hunger strike, refuse food.
OPPOSITES: SEE **overeat**.

starving adjective *starving refugees.* emaciated, famished, hungry, ravenous, starved, underfed, undernourished.

state noun **1** *in an excellent state.* [*plural*] circumstances, condition, fitness, health, mood, situation.
2 [*informal*] *He was in such a state!* agitation, excitement, [*informal*] flap, panic, plight, predicament, [*informal*] tizzy.
3 *a sovereign state.* SEE **country**, nation.

state verb *to state the obvious.* affirm, announce, assert, communicate, declare, express, formulate, proclaim, put into words, report, say, SEE **speak**, submit, voice.

stately adjective *a stately ceremony.* dignified, elegant, formal, grand, imposing, impressive, majestic, noble, pompous, regal, royal, solemn, splendid.
OPPOSITES: SEE **informal**.
a stately home SEE **palace**.

statement noun *an official statement.* account, announcement, assertion, bulletin, comment, communication, communiqué, declaration, explanation, message, notice, proclamation, proposition, report, testament, testimony, utterance.

stateroom noun VARIOUS ROOMS: SEE **room**.

statesman noun diplomat, politician.

static adjective **1** *a static caravan.* fixed, immobile, motionless, SEE **stationary**, still, unmoving.
OPPOSITES: SEE **mobile**.
2 *static sales figures.* constant, invariable, stable, stagnant, steady, unchanging.
OPPOSITES: SEE **variable**.

station noun **1** *your station in life.* calling, class, employment, occupation, place, position, post, rank, situation, standing, status.
2 *a fire station. a police station.* base, depot, headquarters, office.
3 *a radio station.* channel, company, transmitter, wavelength.
4 *a railway station.* halt, platform, stopping-place, terminus.

station verb *We stationed a look-out on the roof.* assign, garrison, locate, place, position, put, situate, stand.

stationary adjective *stationary cars.* at a standstill, at rest, halted, immobile, immovable, motionless, parked, standing, static, still, stock-still, unmoving.
OPPOSITES: SEE **moving**.

Notice the difference in spelling between *stationary* and *stationery*.

---

stationery noun paper, writing materials.
WRITING MATERIALS: SEE **write**.

statistics noun data, figures, information, numbers.

statue noun SEE **sculpture** noun.

statuesque adjective *a statuesque figure.* dignified, elegant, poised, stately, upright.

stature noun **1** *a woman of average stature.* build, height, size, tallness.
2 *a politician of international stature.* esteem, greatness, importance, prominence, recognition, significance, SEE **status**.

status noun *your status in society or in your job.* class, degree, eminence, grade, importance, level, position, prestige, rank, standing, title.

statute noun SEE **law**.

staunch adjective *a staunch supporter.* constant, dependable, faithful, firm, loyal, reliable, sound, stalwart, steadfast, strong, true, trustworthy, unswerving.
OPPOSITES: SEE **unreliable**.

stave verb **to stave off** SEE **avert**.

stay noun **1** *a stay in a hotel.* holiday, [*old-fashioned*] sojourn, stop, visit.
2 [= *a support*] SEE **support** noun.

stay verb **1** *to stay in one place.* [*old-fashioned*] abide, carry on, continue, endure, [*informal*] hang about, hold out, keep on, last, linger, live on, loiter, persist, remain, survive, [*old-fashioned*] tarry, wait.
OPPOSITES: SEE **depart**.
2 *to stay in a hotel.* be accommodated, be a guest, be housed, board, dwell, live, lodge, reside, settle, [*old-fashioned*] sojourn, stop, visit.
3 *to stay judgement.* SEE **postpone**.

steadfast adjective *steadfast support.* committed, constant, dedicated, dependable, faithful, firm, loyal, patient, persevering, reliable, resolute, staunch, steady, unchanging, unfaltering, unflinching, unswerving, unwavering.
OPPOSITES: SEE **unreliable**.

steady adjective **1** *Is the ladder steady? Baby isn't steady on her feet yet.* balanced, confident, fast, firm, immovable, poised, safe, secure, settled, solid, stable.
2 *a steady supply of water.* ceaseless, consistent, constant, continuous, dependable, incessant, non-stop, regular, reliable, uninterrupted.
3 *a steady rhythm.* even, invariable, regular, repeated, rhythmic, smooth, unbroken, unchanging, uniform, unhurried, unremitting, unvarying.
4 *a steady friend.* devoted, faithful, loyal, serious, SEE **steadfast**.
OPPOSITES: SEE **unsteady**.

steady verb *to steady a rocking boat.* balance, hold, secure, stabilize.

steal verb **1** *to steal someone's property.* appropriate, burgle, embezzle, [*informal*] filch, hijack, [*informal*] knock off, [*informal*] lift, loot, [*informal*] make off with, misappropriate, [*informal*] nick, pick someone's pocket, pilfer, pillage, [*informal*] pinch, pirate, plagiarize [= *to steal someone else's ideas*], plunder, poach, purloin, [*informal*] rip someone off, rob, shop-lift, [*informal*] sneak, [*informal*] snitch, [*informal*] swipe, take, thieve, walk off with.
SEE ALSO: **stealing**.
2 *I stole quietly upstairs.* creep, move stealthily, slink, sneak, tiptoe, SEE **walk** verb.

stealing noun VARIOUS KINDS OF STEALING: burglary, embezzlement, fraud,

hijacking, housebreaking, larceny, looting, misappropriation, mugging, [*formal*] peculation, pilfering, pillage, piracy, plagiarism [=*stealing someone else's ideas*], plundering, purloining, robbery, scrumping, shop-lifting, theft, thieving.
OTHER CRIMES: SEE **crime**.

stealthy adjective *stealthy movements.* concealed, covert, disguised, furtive, inconspicuous, quiet, secret, secretive, [*informal*] shifty, sly, sneaky, surreptitious, underhand, unobtrusive.
OPPOSITES: SEE **blatant**.

steam noun condensation, haze, mist, smoke, vapour.

steamy adjective **1** *steamy windows.* cloudy, hazy, misty.
2 *a steamy atmosphere.* close, damp, humid, moist, muggy, sultry, sweaty.

steed noun SEE **horse**.

steel noun OTHER METALS: SEE **metal**.

steep adjective **1** *a steep cliff. a steep rise.* abrupt, headlong, precipitous, sharp, sheer, sudden, vertical.
OPPOSITES: SEE **gradual**.
2 *steep prices.* SEE **exorbitant**.

steep verb *to steep in liquid.* SEE **soak**.

steeple noun spire.
OTHER PARTS OF A CHURCH: SEE **church**.

steeple-chase noun OTHER RACES: SEE **race** noun.

steer noun SEE **cattle**.

steer verb *to steer a vehicle.* be at the wheel of, control, direct, drive, guide, navigate, pilot.
to steer clear of SEE **avoid**.

steersman noun SEE **helmsman**.

stem noun *the stem of a plant.* shoot, stalk, trunk, twig.

stem verb *to stem the flow of blood from a wound.* SEE **check**.

stench noun SEE **smell** noun.

stencil noun print.

stenographer noun SEE **secretary**.

stentorian adjective SEE **loud**.

step noun **1** *I took a step forward.* footstep, pace, stride.
2 *a step into the unknown.* advance, movement, progress, progression.
3 *She explained the next step in the process.* action, manœuvre, measure, phase, stage.
4 *I stood on the step.* doorstep, rung, stair, tread (*the treads of a staircase*).
steps ladder, staircase, stairs, step-ladder.

step verb *Don't step in the mud!* put your foot, stamp, trample, tread, SEE **walk** verb.
to step in *The boss stepped in to sort things out.* SEE **intervene**.
to step on it SEE **hurry** verb.
to step up *They stepped up the pressure.* SEE **increase** verb.

stepchild, step-parent FAMILY RELATIONSHIPS: SEE **family**.

step-ladder noun steps.

steppe noun SEE **plain** noun.

stepping-stone noun SEE **crossing**.

stereo adjective stereophonic.
OPPOSITES: mono, monophonic.

stereo noun SEE **audio equipment**.

stereoscopic adjective solid-looking, three-dimensional, [*informal*] 3-D.
OPPOSITE: two-dimensional.

stereotype noun *He's my stereotype of a schoolteacher.* formula, model, pattern, stereotyped idea [SEE **stereotyped**].

stereotyped adjective *a stereotyped character in a play.* clichéd, conventional, hackneyed, predictable, standard, standardized, stock, typecast, unoriginal.
OPPOSITES: SEE **individual** adjective.

sterile adjective **1** *sterile soil.* arid, barren, dry, infertile, lifeless, unproductive.
OPPOSITES: SEE **fertile**.
2 *sterile bandages.* antiseptic, aseptic, clean, disinfected, germ-free, hygienic, sterilized, uninfected.
OPPOSITES: SEE **infected**, unsterilized.
3 *a sterile attempt to reach agreement.* abortive, fruitless, hopeless, pointless, unfruitful, unprofitable, useless.
OPPOSITES: SEE **fruitful**.

sterilize verb **1** *to sterilize medical equipment. to sterilize food.* clean, decontaminate, disinfect, fumigate, make sterile [SEE **sterile**], pasteurize, purify.
OPPOSITES: SEE **infect**.
2 *to sterilize animals so that they cannot reproduce.* castrate, geld, neuter, perform a vasectomy, spay.

sterilized adjective *sterilized bandages.* SEE **sterile**.

sterling adjective **1** *sterling silver.* SEE **genuine**.
2 *sterling qualities.* SEE **excellent**.

sterling noun SEE **money**.

stern adjective *a stern rebuke. a stern disciplinarian.* austere, authoritarian, dour, forbidding, grim, hard, harsh, inflexible, rigid, rigorous, severe, strict, unbending, unrelenting.
OPPOSITES: SEE **lenient**.

stern noun *the stern of a ship.* aft, back, rear end.

stertorous adjective SEE **harsh**.

stevedore noun docker.

stew noun *stew for dinner.* casserole, goulash, hash, hot-pot, ragout.

stew verb *to stew meat.* boil, braise, casserole, simmer.
OTHER WAYS TO COOK: SEE **cook** verb.

steward, stewardess nouns **1** *a steward on a ship.* attendant, SEE **servant**, waiter.
2 *a steward at a racecourse.* marshal, officer, official.

stick noun *dry sticks used for firewood.* branch, stalk, twig.
VARIOUS KINDS OF STICK: bar, baton, cane, club, hockey-stick, pole, rod, staff, walking-stick, wand.

stick verb **1** *to stick a pin in. to stick someone in the ribs.* dig, jab, poke, prod, punch, puncture, stab, thrust.
2 *to stick something with glue. to stick together.* adhere, affix, agglutinate, bind, bond, cement, cling, coagulate, SEE **fasten**, fuse together, glue, weld.
3 *His head stuck between the railings.* become trapped, jam, wedge.
4 [*informal*] *I can't stick snobs.* SEE **tolerate**.
to stick at [*informal*] *Stick at it!* SEE **persevere**.
to stick in *The pin won't stick in.* go in, pass through, penetrate, pierce.
to stick out *A shelf stuck out above my head.* jut, overhang, project, protrude.
to stick up *The spire sticks up above the trees.* loom, rise, stand out, tower.
to stick up for SEE **defend**.

sticker noun SEE **label** noun.

sticky adjective **1** *sticky tape.* adhesive, glued, gummed, self-adhesive.
OPPOSITE: non-adhesive.
2 *sticky fingers.* gluey, [*informal*] gooey, gummy, tacky.
OPPOSITES: SEE **clean** adjective.
3 *a sticky atmosphere.* clammy, damp, dank, humid, moist, muggy, steamy, sultry, sweaty.
OPPOSITES: SEE **dry** adjective.

stiff adjective **1** *stiff cardboard. stiff clay.* firm, hard, heavy, inflexible, rigid, solid, solidified, thick, unbending, unyielding, viscous.
OPPOSITES: SEE **soft**.
2 *stiff joints.* arthritic, immovable, painful, paralysed, rheumatic, taut, tight.
OPPOSITES: SEE **supple**.
3 *a stiff task. stiff opposition.* arduous, difficult, exacting, hard, laborious, powerful, severe, strong, stubborn, tiring, tough, uphill.
OPPOSITES: SEE **easy**.
4 *a stiff manner.* awkward, clumsy, cold, formal, graceless, inelegant, starchy, stilted, tense, ungainly, unnatural, wooden.
OPPOSITES: SEE **relaxed**.
5 *a stiff penalty.* excessive, harsh, merciless, pitiless, relentless, rigorous, strict.
OPPOSITES: SEE **lenient**.
6 *a stiff breeze.* brisk, fresh, strong.
OPPOSITES: SEE **gentle**.

stiffen verb become stiff [SEE **stiff**], congeal, harden, set, solidify, thicken, tighten.

stiff-necked adjective SEE **obstinate**.

stifle verb **1** *The heat stifled us.* asphyxiate, choke, smother, strangle, suffocate, throttle.
2 *We stifled our laughter.* check, curb, dampen, deaden, muffle, repress, restrain, silence, stop, suppress.

stifling adjective SEE **stuffy**.

stigma noun *the stigma of prison.* blot, disgrace, dishonour, reproach, shame, slur, stain.

stigmata plural noun SEE **mark** noun.

stigmatize verb *He was stigmatized as an ex-convict.* brand, condemn, label, mark, pillory, vilify.

stiletto noun SEE **dagger**.

still adjective **1** *a still evening.* calm, hushed, noiseless, peaceful, placid, quiet, restful, serene, silent, tranquil, untroubled, windless.
OPPOSITES: SEE **stormy, troubled**.
2 *Keep still!* immobile, inert, lifeless, motionless, stagnant (*stagnant water*), static, stationary, unmoving.
OPPOSITES: SEE **moving**.
3 *still drinks.* flat.
OPPOSITES: SEE **fizzy**.

still verb *She stilled my fears. He stilled the audience by raising his hand.* allay, appease, calm, lull, make still [SEE **still** adjective], pacify, quieten, settle, silence, soothe, subdue, tranquillize.
OPPOSITES: SEE **agitate**.

stillborn adjective SEE **abortive**.

stilt noun SEE **pole**.

stilted adjective *stilted language.* SEE **formal**.

stimulant noun VARIOUS DRUGS: SEE **drug** noun.

stimulate verb *to stimulate interest. to stimulate people to greater effort.* activate, arouse, encourage, excite, fan, fire, foment, galvanize, goad, incite, inflame, inspire, invigorate, prompt, provoke,

quicken, rouse, spur, stir up, titillate, urge, whet.
OPPOSITES: SEE **discourage**.

stimulating adjective *a stimulating discussion. stimulating company.* challenging, exciting, exhilarating, inspiring, interesting, intoxicating, invigorating, provoking, rousing, stirring, thought-provoking.
OPPOSITES: SEE **boring**.

stimulus noun *a stimulus to greater effort.* encouragement, fillip, goad, incentive, inducement, inspiration, prompting, provocation, spur.
OPPOSITES: SEE **discouragement**.

sting noun **1** *a wasp sting.* SEE **wound** noun.
2 *the sting of acid in a wound.* SEE **pain** noun.

sting verb **1** *Some insects can sting you.* bite, nip, SEE **wound** verb.
2 *The salt water stings.* SEE **hurt** verb, smart, tingle.

stingy adjective **1** *a stingy miser.* avaricious, cheese-paring, close, close-fisted, covetous, mean, mingy, miserly, niggardly, parsimonious, penny-pinching, tight-fisted, ungenerous.
OPPOSITES: SEE **generous**.
2 *stingy helpings.* inadequate, insufficient, meagre, [*informal*] measly, scanty, SEE **small**.
OPPOSITES: SEE **big**.

stink noun, verb SEE **smell** noun, verb.

stipulate verb SEE **insist (insist on)**.

stipulation noun SEE **condition**.

stir noun *The news caused quite a stir.* SEE **commotion**.

stir verb **1** *Stir yourself!* SEE **move** verb.
2 *Stir the ingredients thoroughly.* agitate, beat, blend, mix, whisk.
3 *The music stirred us.* affect, arouse, challenge, electrify, excite, exhilarate, fire, impress, inspire, move, rouse, stimulate, touch.
to stir up *Don't stir up any trouble!* awaken, cause, incite, instigate, kindle, provoke, set off.

stirring adjective *stirring music. a stirring speech.* affecting, dramatic, emotional, exciting, heady, impassioned, moving, rousing, spirited, stimulating, thrilling.
OPPOSITES: SEE **boring**.

stitch verb *to stitch a hole in your jeans.* darn, mend, repair, sew, tack.

stoat noun ermine.

stock adjective *a stock response.* accustomed, common, conventional, customary, expected, ordinary, predictable, regular, set, standard, staple, stereotyped, traditional, unoriginal, usual.
OPPOSITES: SEE **unexpected**.

stock noun **1** *a stock of provisions.* hoard, reserve, reservoir, stockpile, store, supply.
2 *the stock in a shop.* commodities, goods, merchandise, wares.
3 *the stock on a cattle farm.* animals, beasts, cattle, flocks, herds, livestock.
4 *descended from ancient stock.* ancestry, blood, breed, descent, extraction, family, forebears, line, lineage, parentage.
5 *We boiled bones to make stock.* broth, soup.
out of stock sold out, unavailable.

stock verb *The local shop stocks most things.* deal in, handle, [*informal*] keep, keep in stock, provide, sell, supply, trade in.

stockade noun fence, paling, palisade, wall.

stockings noun nylons, panti-hose, socks, tights.

stockist noun merchant, retailer, shopkeeper, supplier.

stockpile noun, verb SEE **store** noun, verb.

stock-pot noun SEE **saucepan**.

stockroom noun SEE **storehouse**.

stock-still adjective SEE **motionless**.

stocky adjective *a stocky figure.* compact, dumpy, short, solid, squat, stubby, sturdy, thickset.
OPPOSITES: SEE **thin** adjective.

stodgy adjective **1** *stodgy food.* filling, heavy, indigestible, lumpy, soggy, solid, starchy.
OPPOSITES: SEE **appetizing**.
2 *a stodgy lecture.* boring, dull, [*informal*] stuffy, tedious, turgid, unexciting, unimaginative, uninteresting.
OPPOSITES: SEE **lively**.

stoical adjective *a stoical response to pain.* calm, impassive, imperturbable, long-suffering, patient, philosophical, phlegmatic, resigned, stolid, uncomplaining.
OPPOSITES: SEE **excitable**.

stoke verb *to stoke a fire.* fuel, keep burning, mend, put fuel on, tend.

stole noun cape, shawl, wrap.

stolid adjective *a dependable, stolid member of the team.* heavy, impassive, SEE **stoical**, unemotional, unexciting, unimaginative, wooden.
OPPOSITES: SEE **lively**.

stomach noun abdomen, belly, [*informal*] guts, [*informal*] insides, [*uncomplimentary*] paunch, [*informal*] tummy.
OTHER PARTS OF YOUR BODY: SEE **body**.

stomach verb *I can't stomach any more of this drivel.* SEE **tolerate**.

stomach-ache noun colic, [*informal*] colly-wobbles, [*childish*] tummy-ache.

stomp verb SEE **walk** verb.

stone noun **1** *stones on the beach.* boulder, cobble, [*plural*] gravel, pebble, rock, [*plural*] scree.
KINDS OF STONE: SEE **rock** noun.
2 *stones used by builders.* block, flagstone, sett, slab.
3 *a stone to commemorate the fallen.* memorial, monolith, obelisk.
4 *a precious stone.* gem, SEE **jewel**.
5 *a plum stone.* pip, seed.

stone verb *to stone someone.* SEE **execute**.

stonewall verb SEE **obstruct**.

stony adjective **1** *a stony beach.* pebbly, rocky, rough, shingly.
2 *a stony silence. a stony response.* cold, expressionless, frigid, hard, heartless, hostile, icy, indifferent, pitiless, steely, stony-hearted, uncaring, unemotional, unfeeling, unforgiving, unfriendly, unresponsive.
OPPOSITES: SEE **emotional**.

stooge noun butt, dupe, [*informal*] fall-guy, lackey, puppet.

stook noun SEE **stack** noun.

stool noun SEE **seat** noun.

stool-pigeon noun SEE **decoy** noun.

stoop verb **1** *I stooped to go under the barrier.* bend, bow, crouch, duck, hunch your shoulders, kneel, lean, squat.
2 *She wouldn't stoop to be seen with the likes of us.* condescend, deign, lower yourself, sink.

stop noun **1** *Everything came to a stop.* cessation, conclusion, end, finish, halt, shut-down, standstill, stoppage, termination.
2 *a stop on a journey.* break, destination, pause, resting-place, station, stopover, terminus.
3 *a stop at a hotel.* [*old-fashioned*] sojourn, stay, visit.

stop verb **1** *to stop what you are doing.* break off, call a halt to, cease, conclude, cut off, desist from, discontinue, end, finish, [*informal*] knock off, leave off, [*informal*] pack in, pause, quit, refrain from, rest from, suspend, terminate.
OPPOSITES: SEE **start** verb.
2 *to stop traffic. to stop something happening.* bar, block, check, curb, delay, frustrate, halt, hamper, hinder, immobilize, impede, intercept, interrupt, [*informal*] nip in the bud, obstruct, put a stop to, stanch or staunch, stem.
3 *to stop in a hotel.* be a guest, have a holiday, [*old-fashioned*] sojourn, spend time, stay, visit.
4 *to stop a gap.* [*informal*] bung up, close, fill in, plug, seal.
5 *Wait for the bus to stop.* come to rest, draw up, halt, pull up.
6 *Stop the thief!* arrest, capture, catch, detain, hold, seize.

stop-cock noun SEE **tap** noun.

stopgap noun SEE **substitute** noun.

stoppage noun SEE **stop** noun.

stopper noun *a stopper in a bottle.* bung, cork, plug.

stopping noun *a stopping in a tooth.* filling.

storage noun SEE **storehouse**.

store noun **1** *a store of supplies.* accumulation, cache, fund, hoard, quantity, reserve, reservoir, stock, stockpile, SEE **storehouse**, supply.
2 *a grocery store.* outlet, retail business, retailers, SEE **shop**, supermarket.

store verb *to store food for future use.* accumulate, deposit, hoard, keep, lay by, lay up, preserve, put away, reserve, save, set aside, [*informal*] stash away, stockpile, stock up, stow away.

storehouse noun PLACES TO STORE THINGS: armoury, arsenal, barn, cellar, cold-storage, depot, granary, larder, pantry, repository, safe, silo, stock-room, storage, store-room, strong-room, treasury, vault, warehouse.

storey noun [Don't confuse with *story*.] *a building with six storeys.* deck, floor, level, stage, tier.

storm noun **1** *The forecast predicts a storm.* disturbance, onslaught, outbreak, stormy weather [SEE **stormy**], tempest, tumult, turbulence.
OPPOSITES: SEE **calm** noun.
2 *a storm of protest.* SEE **clamour** noun.

KINDS OF STORM: blizzard, cyclone, deluge, dust-storm, gale, hurricane, rainstorm, sandstorm, squall, thunderstorm, tornado, typhoon, whirlwind.

METEOROLOGICAL TERMS: SEE **weather** noun.

---

storm verb *The army stormed the castle.* SEE **attack** verb.

stormy adjective *stormy seas. stormy weather.* angry, blustery, choppy, gusty, raging, rough, squally, tempestuous,

thundery, tumultuous, turbulent, violent, wild, windy.
OPPOSITES: SEE **calm** adjective.

story noun **1** *the story of my life. Tell me a story.* account, chronicle, fiction, history, narration, narrative, plot, scenario, tale, yarn.
2 *a story in a newspaper.* article, [*informal*] exclusive, feature, news item, report.
3 [*informal*] *Don't tell stories.* falsehood, [*informal*] fib, lie, untruth.

VARIOUS KINDS OF STORY: anecdote, children's story, crime story, detective story, fable, fairy-tale, fantasy, folk-tale, legend, mystery, myth, novel, parable, romance, saga, science fiction or SF, thriller, [*informal*] whodunit.

OTHER KINDS OF WRITING: SEE **writing**.

---

storyteller noun author, narrator, raconteur, teller.

stoup noun SEE **basin**.

stout adjective **1** *stout rope.* reliable, robust, sound, strong, sturdy, substantial, thick, tough.
OPPOSITES: SEE **weak**.
2 *a stout person.* [*informal*] beefy, [*informal*] chubby, SEE **fat** adjective, heavy, overweight, plump, portly, solid, stocky, tubby, well-built.
OPPOSITES: SEE **thin** adjective.
3 *a stout fighter.* bold, brave, courageous, fearless, gallant, heroic, intrepid, plucky, resolute, spirited, valiant.
OPPOSITES: SEE **cowardly**.

stove noun boiler, cooker, fire, furnace, heater, oven, range.

stow verb **1** *I stow unwanted things in the attic.* SEE **store** verb.
2 *Stow the luggage in the car.* SEE **load** verb.

stowaway noun SEE **traveller**.

straddle verb *The bridge straddles the river.* SEE **span** verb.

strafe verb SEE **bombard**.

straggle verb *Some of the runners straggled behind.* dawdle, fall behind, lag, loiter, ramble, scatter, spread out, stray, string out, trail, wander.

straggling adjective *a straggling village.* disorganized, rambling, scattered, spread out.
OPPOSITES: SEE **compact** adjective.

straight adjective [Do not confuse with *strait.*] **1** *a straight line. a straight road.* aligned, direct, smooth, undeviating, unswerving.
OPPOSITES: SEE **crooked**.
2 *Put the room straight.* neat, orderly, organized, right, [*informal*] shipshape, tidy.
OPPOSITES: SEE **untidy**.
3 *a straight sequence.* consecutive, continuous, non-stop, perfect, sustained, unbroken, uninterrupted, unrelieved.
4 *straight talking.* SEE **straightforward**.
straight away at once, directly, immediately, instantly, now, without delay.

straighten verb **to straighten out** disentangle, make straight, sort out, SEE **tidy** verb, unbend, untwist.

straightforward adjective *straightforward talk. a straightforward person.* blunt, candid, direct, easy, forthright, frank, genuine, honest, intelligible, lucid, open, plain, simple, sincere, straight, truthful, uncomplicated.
OPPOSITES: SEE **devious**.

strain noun *He's been under great strain.* anxiety, difficulty, hardship, pressure, stress, tension, worry.

strain verb **1** *We strained at the ropes.* haul, pull, stretch, tighten, tug.
2 *I strained to hear what he said.* attempt, endeavour, exert yourself, make an effort, strive, struggle, try.
3 *Don't strain yourself.* exhaust, tire out, weaken, wear out, weary.
4 *I strained my neck.* damage, hurt, injure, rick, sprain, twist, wrench.
5 *to strain solids out of a liquid.* filter, percolate, riddle, separate, sieve, sift.

strained adjective *a strained expression. strained good humour.* artificial, drawn, embarrassed, false, forced, self-conscious, stiff, tense, tired, uncomfortable, uneasy, unnatural.
OPPOSITES: SEE **relaxed**.

strainer noun colander, filter, riddle, sieve.

strait adjective [Do not confuse with *straight.*] [*old-fashioned*] *the strait way.* SEE **narrow**.

strait noun *the Strait of Gibraltar.* channel, sound.
GEOGRAPHICAL TERMS: SEE **geography**.

strait-jacket verb SEE **restrain**.

strait-laced adjective SEE **prim**.

strand noun **1** *one strand of a rope.* fibre, filament, string, thread, wire.
2 [*old-fashioned*] *The tide covered the strand.* SEE **shore** noun.

strand verb **1** *to strand a ship.* beach, ground, run aground.
2 *to strand someone on an island.* abandon, desert, forsake, leave stranded [SEE **stranded**], maroon.

stranded adjective 1 *a stranded ship.* aground, beached, grounded, [*informal*] high and dry, shipwrecked, stuck.
2 *stranded in London without any money.* abandoned, alone, deserted, forsaken, helpless, in difficulties, left, lost, marooned, without help.

strange adjective 1 *a strange event. strange goings-on.* abnormal, astonishing, atypical, bizarre, curious, eerie, exceptional, extraordinary, [*informal*] funny, irregular, odd, out of the ordinary, peculiar, queer, rare, remarkable, singular, surprising, uncommon, unexpected, unheard of, unique, unnatural, untypical, unusual.
2 *We have strange neighbours.* [*informal*] cranky, eccentric, sinister, unconventional, weird, [*informal*] zany.
3 *The experts agreed it was a strange problem.* baffling, bewildering, inexplicable, insoluble, mysterious, mystifying, perplexing, puzzling, unaccountable.
4 *We travelled to some strange places.* alien, exotic, foreign, little-known, off the beaten track, outlandish, remote, unexplored, unmapped.
5 *Eating the local food was a strange experience.* different, fresh, new, novel, unaccustomed, unfamiliar.
OPPOSITES: SEE **familiar, ordinary**.

strangeness noun abnormality, bizarreness, eccentricity, eeriness, extraordinariness, irregularity, mysteriousness, novelty, oddity, oddness, outlandishness, peculiarity, queerness, rarity, singularity, unconventionality, unfamiliarity.

stranger noun *I'm a stranger here.* alien, foreigner, guest, newcomer, outsider, visitor.

strangle verb asphyxiate, choke, garotte, smother, stifle, SEE **strangulate**, suffocate, throttle.

stranglehold noun SEE **grip** noun.

strangulate verb compress, constrict, squeeze, SEE **strangle**.

strangulation noun asphyxiation, garotting, suffocation.
METHODS OF KILLING: SEE **killing**.

strap noun band, belt, strop, tawse, thong, webbing.

strap verb *to strap things together.* SEE **fasten**.

strapping adjective SEE **sturdy**.

stratagem noun SEE **trick** noun.

strategic adjective 1 *the strategic deployment of troops.* advantageous, deliberate, planned, politic, tactical.
2 [*informal*] *the strategic moment.* SEE **important**.

strategy noun *a strategy to beat the opposition.* approach, manœuvre, method, plan, plot, policy, procedure, programme, scheme, tactics.

stratosphere noun SEE **space** noun.

stratum noun *a stratum of rock.* layer, seam, thickness, vein.

straw noun corn, stalks, stubble.

strawberry noun SEE **fruit**.

stray verb 1 *Don't stray in the hills.* get lost, go astray, meander, move about aimlessly, ramble, range, roam, rove, straggle, wander.
2 *Don't stray from the point.* deviate, digress, diverge, drift.

streak noun 1 *a streak of dirt on the window.* band, line, smear, stain, strip, stripe, vein.
2 *a streak of selfishness in her character.* component, element, trace.

streak verb 1 *Rain streaked the new paint.* mark with streaks, smear, smudge, stain.
2 [*informal*] *Cars streaked past.* dash, flash, fly, gallop, hurtle, move at speed, rush, speed, sprint, tear, zoom.

streaky adjective lined, smeary, smudged, streaked, striated, stripy, veined.

stream noun 1 *a rippling stream.* beck, brook, burn, SEE **channel** noun, [*poetic*] rill, river, rivulet, streamlet, watercourse.
2 *A stream of water poured through the hole.* cataract, current, flood, flow, gush, jet, outpouring, rush, spate, surge, tide, torrent.

stream verb *Water streamed through the hole.* cascade, course, flood, flow, gush, issue, pour, run, spill, spout, spurt, squirt, surge, well.

streamer noun banner, SEE **flag** noun, pennant, pennon, ribbon.

streamlined adjective *a car with a streamlined body.* aerodynamic, efficient, graceful, sleek, smooth.
OPPOSITE: air-resistant.

street noun SEE **road**.

strength noun 1 *physical strength.* brawn, capacity, condition, energy, fitness, force, health, might, muscle, power, robustness, stamina, sturdiness, toughness, vigour.
2 *strength of purpose.* commitment, courage, firmness, resolution, spirit.
OPPOSITES: SEE **weakness**.

strengthen verb 1 *to strengthen your muscles.* build up, fortify, harden,

increase, make stronger, tone up, toughen.
2 *to strengthen a fence.* bolster, brace, buttress, prop up, reinforce, support.
3 *We need more evidence to strengthen our case.* back up, consolidate, corroborate, enhance, justify, substantiate.
OPPOSITES: SEE **weaken**.

strenuous adjective **1** *strenuous efforts.* active, committed, determined, dynamic, energetic, herculean, laborious, resolute, spirited, strong, tireless, unremitting, vigorous.
OPPOSITES: SEE **apathetic, casual**.
2 *strenuous work.* arduous, demanding, difficult, exhausting, gruelling, hard, punishing, stiff, taxing, tough, uphill.
OPPOSITES: SEE **easy**.

stress noun **1** *a time of stress.* anxiety, difficulty, hardship, pressure, strain, tension, trauma, worry.
2 *Put a stress on the important words.* accent, beat, emphasis, importance, weight.

stress verb *He stressed the importance of keeping fit.* accentuate, assert, emphasize, insist on, lay stress on, put the stress on, repeat, underline.

stressful adjective *a stressful period in my life.* anxious, difficult, tense, traumatic, worrying.
OPPOSITES: SEE **easy**.

stretch noun **1** *a stretch in prison.* period, spell, stint, term, time.
2 *a stretch of road.* distance, length.
3 *a stretch of countryside.* area, expanse, sweep, tract.

stretch verb **1** *to stretch something to make it longer or bigger or wider.* crane (*to crane your neck*), distend, draw out, elongate, expand, extend, flatten out, inflate, lengthen, open out, pull out, spread out, swell, tauten, tighten.
2 *The lake stretches into the distance.* be unbroken, continue, disappear, extend, go, spread.

stretchy adjective SEE **elastic** adjective.

strew verb SEE **scatter**.

striated adjective SEE **streaky**.

striation noun SEE **line** noun.

stricken adjective SEE **troubled**.

strict adjective **1** *strict rules.* absolute, binding, [*informal*] hard and fast, inflexible, invariable, rigid, stringent, tight, unchangeable.
OPPOSITES: SEE **flexible**.
2 *strict discipline. a strict teacher.* austere, authoritarian, autocratic, firm, harsh, merciless, [*informal*] no-nonsense, rigorous, severe, stern, stringent, tyrannical, uncompromising.
OPPOSITES: SEE **lax, lenient**.
3 *the strict truth.* accurate, complete, correct, exact, perfect, precise, right, scrupulous, true.
OPPOSITES: SEE **approximate** adjective.

stricture noun SEE **criticism**.

stride noun *Take two strides forward.* pace, step.

stride verb SEE **walk** verb.

strident adjective *a strident cry. strident voices.* clamorous, grating, harsh, jarring, loud, noisy, raucous, screeching, shrill.
OPPOSITES: SEE **soft**.

strife noun SEE **conflict** noun.

strike noun *an industrial strike.* industrial action, stoppage, withdrawal of labour.

strike verb **1** *I struck my head.* SEE **hit** verb.
2 *The invaders struck without warning.* SEE **attack** verb.
3 *The clock struck one.* chime, ring.
4 *The workforce threatened to strike.* [*informal*] come out, [*informal*] down tools, stop work, take industrial action, withdraw your labour.
5 *to strike a flag or tent.* lower, take down.

striking adjective *a striking contrast. a striking hair-do.* arresting, conspicuous, distinctive, impressive, memorable, noticeable, obvious, outstanding, prominent, showy, stunning, telling, unmistakable, unusual.
OPPOSITES: SEE **inconspicuous**.

string noun **1** *a length of string.* cord, line, rope, twine.
2 *a string of cars waiting at the lights.* file, line, procession, queue, row, succession.
3 *a string of coincidences.* chain, progression, sequence, series.

MUSICAL INSTRUMENTS WITH STRINGS: banjo, cello, clavichord, double-bass, [*informal*] fiddle, guitar, harp, harpsichord, lute, lyre, piano, sitar, spinet, ukulele, viola, violin, zither.
OTHER INSTRUMENTS: SEE **music**.

---

string verb *to string things together.* connect, join, line up, link, thread.

stringent adjective SEE **strict**.

stringy adjective *stringy meat.* chewy, fibrous, gristly, sinewy, tough.
OPPOSITES: SEE **tender**.

strip noun *a strip of carpet. a strip of wood. a strip of land.* band, belt, lath, line, narrow piece, ribbon, shred, slat, sliver, stripe, swathe.

strip verb **1** *to strip clothes, vegetation, paint, etc., off something.* clear, defoliate, denude, divest, [*old-fashioned*] doff, flay [*=strip skin off*], peel, remove, skin, take.
OPPOSITES: SEE **cover** verb.
2 *to strip to the waist.* bare yourself, expose yourself, lay yourself bare, uncover yourself.
OPPOSITES: SEE **dress** verb.
to strip down *to strip a machine down.* dismantle, take apart.
OPPOSITES: SEE **assemble**.
to strip off disrobe, get undressed, peel off, undress.
OPPOSITES: SEE **dress** verb.

stripe noun *football shirts with red and white stripes.* band, bar, line, [*formal*] striation, strip.

striped adjective banded, barred, lined, streaky, striated, stripy.

stripling noun SEE **youth**.

strive verb SEE **try** verb.

strobe, stroboscope nouns SEE **light** noun.

stroke noun **1** *a stroke with a cricket bat.* SEE **hit** noun.
2 *You can't change the world at a single stroke.* action, blow, effort, move.
3 *a stroke of the pen.* flourish, line, mark, movement, sweep.
4 [*= medical condition*] apoplexy, seizure.

stroke verb *to stroke the cat.* caress, fondle, pass your hand over, pat, pet, rub, touch.

stroll noun, verb SEE **walk** noun, verb.

strong adjective **1** *a strong person.* athletic, [*informal*] beefy, [*informal*] brawny, burly, fit, [*informal*] hale and hearty, hardy, hefty, mighty, muscular, powerful, [*informal*] strapping, sturdy, tough, well-built, wiry.
2 *a strong structure. strong materials.* durable, hard, hardwearing, heavy-duty, impregnable (*an impregnable fortress*), indestructible, permanent, reinforced, resilient, robust, sound, stout, substantial, thick, unbreakable, well-made.
3 *strong government. strong efforts.* aggressive, assertive, decisive, dependable, determined, [*uncomplimentary*] SEE **dictatorial**, domineering, fearless, firm, forceful, herculean, loyal, reliable, resolute, stalwart, staunch, steadfast, [*informal*] stout, strong-minded, strong-willed, true, unflinching, unswerving, vehement, vigorous, violent.
4 *a strong army.* formidable, invincible, large, numerous, unconquerable, well-armed, well-equipped, well-trained.
5 *a strong light.* bright, brilliant, clear, dazzling, glaring.
6 *a strong taste or smell.* highly-flavoured, hot, noticeable, obvious, overpowering, prominent, pronounced, pungent, spicy, unmistakable.
7 *strong drink.* alcoholic, concentrated, intoxicating, potent, undiluted.
8 *strong evidence.* clear-cut, cogent, compelling, convincing, evident, persuasive, plain, solid, undisputed.
9 *strong convictions.* committed, deep-rooted, deep-seated, eager, earnest, enthusiastic, fervent, fierce, genuine, intense, keen, zealous.
OPPOSITES: SEE **weak**.

stronghold noun bastion, bulwark, castle, citadel, fort, fortress, garrison.

strong-minded adjective SEE **determined**.

strongroom noun SEE **storehouse**.

strop noun SEE **strap** noun.

stroppy adjective SEE **bad-tempered**.

structure noun **1** *the structure of a poem. the structure of a living cell.* arrangement, composition, constitution, design, [*informal*] make-up, organization, plan, shape.
2 *a structure of steel and stone.* SEE **building**, construction, edifice, erection, fabric, framework, pile, superstructure.

structure verb SEE **organize**.

struggle noun **1** *a struggle to get things finished.* challenge, difficulty, effort, endeavour, exertion, labour, problem.
2 *a struggle against an enemy or opponent.* SEE **fight** noun.

struggle verb **1** *to struggle to get free.* endeavour, exert yourself, labour, make an effort, move violently, strain, strive, toil, try, work hard, wrestle, wriggle about, writhe about.
2 *to struggle with an enemy.* SEE **fight** verb.
3 *to struggle through mud.* flail, flounder, stumble, wallow.

strut noun *a wooden strut.* SEE **bar** noun.

strut verb SEE **walk** verb.

stub noun *a cigarette stub. the stub of a tree.* butt, end, remains, remnant, stump.

stub verb *to stub your toe.* SEE **hit** verb.

stubble noun **1** *stubble of corn.* stalks, straw.
2 *stubble on a man's chin.* beard, bristles, [*informal*] five-o'clock shadow, hair, roughness.

stubbly adjective *a man with a stubbly chin.* bristly, prickly, rough, unshaven.

stubborn adjective *a stubborn donkey. stubborn opposition.* defiant, difficult, disobedient, dogged, headstrong, inflexible, intractable, intransigent, mulish, obdurate, obstinate, opinionated, persistent, [*informal*] pig-headed, recalcitrant, refractory, rigid, self-willed, uncontrollable, uncooperative, unmanageable, unreasonable, unyielding, wilful.
OPPOSITES: SEE **obedient**.

stubby adjective SEE **short**.

stucco noun *stucco on the walls.* cement, mortar, plaster.

stuck adjective **1** *stuck in the mud.* bogged down, fast, fastened, fixed, immovable.
2 *stuck on a problem.* baffled, beaten, held up, [*informal*] stumped.

stuck-up adjective [*informal*] *a stuck-up snob.* arrogant, [*informal*] big-headed, bumptious, [*informal*] cocky, conceited, condescending, [*informal*] high-and-mighty, patronizing, proud, self-important, snobbish, [*informal*] snooty, supercilious, [*informal*] toffee-nosed.
OPPOSITES: SEE **modest**.

stud noun SEE **nail** noun.

student noun learner, pupil, postgraduate, scholar, undergraduate.

studied adjective *studied carelessness.* SEE **deliberate** adjective.

studio noun *an artist's studio.* workroom, workshop.

studious adjective *a studious pupil.* academic, bookish, brainy, earnest, hard-working, intellectual, scholarly, serious-minded, thoughtful.

study noun OTHER ROOMS: SEE **room**.

study verb **1** *We studied the evidence.* analyse, consider, contemplate, enquire into, examine, give attention to, investigate, learn about, look closely at, peruse, pore over, read carefully, research, scrutinize, survey, think about.
2 *to study for an examination.* [*informal*] cram, learn, [*informal*] mug up, read, [*informal*] swot, work.

stuff noun **1** *What's this stuff in the jar?* matter, substance.
2 *stuff to make a skirt.* cloth, fabric, material, textile.
3 [*informal*] *That's my stuff in the drawer.* articles, belongings, [*informal*] clobber, [*formal*] effects, [*informal*] gear, junk, objects, [*informal*] paraphernalia, possessions, [*informal*] tackle, things.

stuff verb **1** *I stuffed everything into a suitcase.* compress, cram, crowd, force, jam, pack, push, ram, shove, squeeze, stow, tuck.
2 *to stuff a cushion.* fill, pad.
to stuff yourself SEE **eat**.

stuffing noun **1** *stuffing in a cushion.* filling, padding, quilting, wadding.
2 *stuffing in a roast chicken.* forcemeat, seasoning.

stuffy adjective **1** *a stuffy room.* airless, close, fetid, fuggy, fusty, heavy, humid, muggy, musty, oppressive, stale, steamy, stifling, suffocating, sultry, unventilated, warm.
OPPOSITES: SEE **airy**.
2 [*informal*] *a stuffy old bore.* boring, conventional, dreary, dull, formal, humourless, narrow-minded, old-fashioned, pompous, prim, staid, [*informal*] stodgy, strait-laced.
OPPOSITES: SEE **informal**.

stultify verb SEE **nullify**.

stumble verb **1** *to stumble as you walk.* blunder, flounder, lurch, reel, stagger, totter, trip, tumble, SEE **walk** verb.
2 *to stumble in your speech.* falter, hesitate, stammer, stutter, SEE **talk** verb.

stumbling-block noun SEE **difficulty**.

stump verb *The riddle stumped us.* baffle, bewilder, [*informal*] catch out, confound, confuse, defeat, [*informal*] flummox, mystify, outwit, perplex, puzzle.

stumpy adjective SEE **short**.

stun verb **1** *The blow stunned him.* daze, knock out, knock senseless, make unconscious.
2 *The terrible news stunned us.* amaze, astonish, astound, bewilder, confound, confuse, dumbfound, flabbergast, numb, shock, stagger, stupefy.

stunning adjective SEE **beautiful**, **stupendous**.

stunt noun exploit, feat, trick.
stunt man daredevil, SEE **entertainer**.

stunt verb *to stunt someone's growth.* SEE **check** verb.

stupefy verb SEE **stun**.

stupendous adjective *stupendous strength. a stupendous achievement.* amazing, colossal, enormous, exceptional, extraordinary, huge, incredible, marvellous, miraculous, notable, phenomenal, prodigious, remarkable, [*informal*] sensational, singular, special, staggering, stunning, tremendous, unbelievable, wonderful.
OPPOSITES: SEE **ordinary**.

stupid adjective **1** [Note that all these words can be insulting, and some will be more insulting than others. Many are used only *informally*.] *a stupid person.* brainless, clueless, cretinous, dense, dim, dopey, drippy, dull, dumb, feeble-minded, foolish, gormless, half-witted, idiotic, ignorant, imbecilic, ineducable, irrational, irresponsible, lacking, mindless, moronic, naïve, obtuse, puerile, senseless, silly, simple, slow, slow in the uptake, slow-witted, subnormal, thick, thick-headed, thick-skulled, thick-witted, unintelligent, unthinking, unwise, vacuous, witless.

2 *a stupid thing to do.* absurd, asinine, crack-brained, crass, crazy, fatuous, [*informal*] feeble, futile, [*informal*] half-baked, ill-advised, inane, irrelevant, laughable, ludicrous, [*informal*] lunatic, [*informal*] mad, nonsensical, pointless, rash, reckless, ridiculous, thoughtless, unjustifiable.
OPPOSITES: SEE **intelligent**.

3 *stupid after a knock on the head.* dazed, in a stupor [SEE **stupor**], semi-conscious, sluggish, stunned, stupefied.

a stupid person SEE **fool** noun.

stupidity noun *I could hardly believe her stupidity.* absurdity, crassness, denseness, dullness, [*informal*] dumbness, fatuousness, folly, foolishness, idiocy, imbecility, inanity, lack of intelligence, lunacy, madness, naïvety, silliness, slowness.
OPPOSITES: SEE **intelligence**.

stupor noun coma, daze, lethargy, shock, state of insensibility, torpor, trance, unconsciousness.

sturdy adjective **1** *a sturdy person.* athletic, brawny, burly, hardy, healthy, hefty, husky, muscular, powerful, robust, stalwart, stocky, [*informal*] strapping, strong, vigorous, well-built.
OPPOSITES: SEE **weak**.

2 *a sturdy pair of shoes.* durable, solid, sound, substantial, tough, well-made.
OPPOSITES: SEE **flimsy**.

stutter verb stammer, stumble, SEE **talk** verb.

sty noun **1** pigsty.

2 *a sty on your eyelid.* SEE **spot** noun.

style noun **1** *a style of writing.* custom, habit, idiosyncrasy, manner, method, phraseology, register, tone, way, wording.

2 *the latest style in clothes.* cut, design, fashion, mode, pattern, taste, type, vogue.

3 *She dresses with great style.* chic, dress-sense, elegance, flair, flamboyance, panache, refinement, smartness, sophistication, stylishness, taste.

stylish adjective *stylish clothes.* chic, [*informal*] classy, contemporary, [*informal*] dapper, elegant, fashionable, modern, modish, [*informal*] natty, [*informal*] posh, smart, [*informal*] snazzy, sophisticated, [*informal*] trendy, up-to-date.
OPPOSITES: SEE **dowdy**.

stylus noun *the stylus of a record-player.* needle.

stymie verb SEE **obstruct**.

suave adjective SEE **smooth** adjective.

The prefix *sub-* is related to the Latin preposition *sub = under.*

---

sub-aqua adjective underwater.

subconscious adjective *subconscious awareness.* intuitive, repressed, subliminal, unacknowledged, unconscious.
OPPOSITES: SEE **conscious**.

subdivide verb SEE **divide**.

subdue verb **1** *to subdue the opposition.* beat, conquer, control, crush, defeat, master, overcome, overpower, overrun, quell, subject (*to subject a country*), subjugate, vanquish.

2 *to subdue your excitement.* check, curb, hold back, keep under, quieten, repress, restrain, suppress.

subdued adjective **1** *a subdued mood.* depressed, downcast, grave, reflective, repressed, restrained, serious, silent, sober, solemn, thoughtful.
OPPOSITES: SEE **excitable**.

2 *subdued music.* hushed, muted, peaceful, placid, quiet, soft, soothing, toned down, unobtrusive.
OPPOSITES: SEE **loud**.

subhuman adjective bestial, brutal, brutish, inhuman.
OPPOSITES: SEE **superhuman**.

subject adjective *subject nations within an empire.* captive, dependent, enslaved, oppressed, ruled, subjugated.
OPPOSITES: SEE **independent**.

subject noun **1** *a British subject.* citizen, dependant, national, passport-holder.

2 *a subject for discussion.* affair, business, issue, matter, point, question, theme, topic.

SUBJECTS WHICH STUDENTS STUDY: anatomy, archaeology, architecture, art, astronomy, biology, business, chemistry, classics, computing, craft, design, divinity, domestic science, drama, economics, education, electronics, engineering, English, environmental science, ethnology, etymology.

geography, geology, heraldry, history, languages, Latin, law, linguistics, literature, mathematics, mechanics, SEE **medicine**, metallurgy, metaphysics, meteorology, music, natural history, oceanography, ornithology.

penology, pharmacology, pharmacy, philology, philosophy, photography, physics, physiology, politics, psychology, religious studies, SEE **science**, scripture, social work, sociology, sport, surveying, technology, theology, topology, zoology.

---

subject verb 1 *to subject a country to your control.* SEE **subdue.**

2 *to subject something to close examination.* expose, submit.

subjective adjective *a subjective reaction to something.* biased, emotional, [*informal*] gut (*a gut reaction*), idiosyncratic, instinctive, intuitive, personal, prejudiced.

OPPOSITES: SEE **objective** adjective.

subjugate verb SEE **subdue.**

sublimate verb *to sublimate your emotions.* divert, purify, redirect, refine.

sublime adjective *a sublime religious experience.* ecstatic, elated, elevated, exalted, lofty, noble, spiritual, transcendent.

OPPOSITES: SEE **base** adjective.

submarine noun VARIOUS VESSELS: SEE **vessel.**

submerge verb 1 *The flood submerged the village.* cover, drown, engulf, flood, immerse, inundate, overwhelm, swamp.

2 *The submarine submerged.* dive, go under, subside.

submission noun 1 *the submission of a wrestler.* capitulation, giving in, surrender.

2 *The judge accepted counsel's submission.* argument, claim, contention, idea, presentation, proposal, suggestion, theory.

3 *cowardly submission.* SEE **submissiveness.**

submissive adjective *submissive acceptance of someone else's authority.* acquiescent, compliant, deferential, docile, humble, meek, obedient, passive, resigned, [*uncomplimentary*] SEE **servile**, supine, tame, tractable, unassertive, uncomplaining, [*uncomplimentary*] weak.

OPPOSITES: SEE **assertive.**

submissiveness noun *submissiveness to someone else's authority.* acquiescence, assent, compliance, deference, docility, meekness, obedience, passivity, resignation, submission, subservience.

submit verb 1 *to submit to an opponent.* accede, capitulate, give in, [*informal*] knuckle under, surrender, yield.

2 *to submit work to a teacher.* give in, hand in, present.

3 *to submit your views.* advance, offer, put forward, propound, SEE **state** verb, suggest.

to submit to *to submit to authority.* bow to, comply with, conform to, defer to, keep to, obey.

subnormal adjective 1 *subnormal temperatures.* low.

2 *educationally subnormal.* SEE **backward.**

subordinate adjective *subordinate rank.* inferior, junior, lesser, lower, menial, minor, secondary, subservient, subsidiary.

subordinate noun *He likes ordering subordinates about.* assistant, dependant, employee, inferior, junior, menial, servant, [*informal*] underling.

suborn verb SEE **bribe** verb.

subpoena verb SEE **summon.**

subscribe verb **to subscribe to** 1 *to subscribe to a good cause.* contribute to, donate to, give to, support.

2 *to subscribe to a magazine.* be a subscriber to, buy regularly, pay a subscription to.

3 *to subscribe to a theory or a course of action.* advocate, agree with, approve of, believe in, condone, endorse, [*informal*] give your blessing to.

subscriber noun patron, regular customer, sponsor, supporter.

subscription noun *a club subscription.* fee, SEE **payment**, regular contribution.

subsequent adjective *I made a guess, but subsequent events proved me wrong.* consequent, ensuing, following, later, next, resulting, succeeding.

OPPOSITES: SEE **previous.**

subservient adjective SEE **servile.**

subside verb 1 *The flood subsided. The pain subsided.* abate, decline, decrease, diminish, dwindle, ebb, fall, go down, lessen, melt away, moderate, recede, shrink, slacken, wear off.

2 *I subsided into a comfortable chair.* collapse, settle, sink.

OPPOSITES: SEE **rise** verb.

subsidiary adjective *of subsidiary importance.* ancillary, auxiliary, contributory, lesser, minor, secondary, SEE **subordinate** adjective.

subsidize verb *Their parents subsidized their trip abroad.* aid, back, finance, fund, promote, sponsor, support, underwrite.

subsidy noun *Public transport needs a subsidy from taxes.* backing, financial help, grant, sponsorship, support.

subsist verb SEE **exist**.

subsistence noun SEE **payment, provisions**.

substance noun 1 *What is this substance?* chemical, material, matter, stuff.
2 *the substance of an argument.* essence, gist, meaning, subject-matter, theme.
3 [*old-fashioned*] *a woman of substance.* SEE **wealth**.

substandard adjective *substandard workmanship.* [*informal*] below par, disappointing, inadequate, inferior, poor, shoddy, unworthy.

substantial adjective 1 *a substantial door.* durable, hefty, solid, sound, strong, sturdy, well-made.
OPPOSITES: SEE **flimsy**.
2 *a substantial amount of money.* big, considerable, generous, large, significant, sizeable, worthwhile.
OPPOSITES: SEE **small**.

substantiate verb SEE **confirm**.

substitute adjective 1 *a substitute player.* acting, deputy, relief, reserve, standby, surrogate, temporary.
2 *a substitute ingredient.* alternative, ersatz, imitation.

substitute noun deputy, locum [= *substitute doctor*], proxy [= *substitute voter*], relief, replacement, reserve, stand-in, stopgap, supply [= *substitute teacher*], surrogate, understudy.

substitute verb 1 *to substitute one thing for another.* change, exchange, interchange, replace, [*informal*] swop, [*informal*] switch.
2 [*informal*] *to substitute for an absent colleague.* act as a substitute [SEE **substitute** noun], deputize, stand in, understudy.

substratum noun SEE **layer**.

substructure noun SEE **base** noun.

subsume verb SEE **include**.

subterfuge noun SEE **trick** noun.

subterranean adjective *subterranean passageways.* underground.

subtitle noun *a film with subtitles.* caption.

subtle adjective 1 *subtle flavours.* delicate, elusive, faint, mild, slight, unobtrusive.
2 *a subtle hint.* gentle, indirect, tactful, understated.
3 *a subtle argument.* clever, SEE **cunning**, ingenious, refined, shrewd, sophisticated.
OPPOSITES: SEE **obvious**.

subtract verb *to subtract one number from another.* debit, deduct, remove, take away.
OPPOSITES: SEE **add**.

subtropical adjective SEE **warm** adjective.

suburban adjective *the suburban areas of a town.* residential, outer, outlying.

suburbs noun *the suburbs of a city.* fringes, outer areas, outskirts, residential areas, suburbia.

subversive adjective *subversive ideas. subversive propaganda.* challenging, disruptive, questioning, revolutionary, seditious, undermining, unsettling.
OPPOSITES: SEE **orthodox**.

subvert verb *to subvert justice.* challenge, corrupt, destroy, disrupt, overthrow, pervert, undermine.

subway noun tunnel, underpass.

succeed verb 1 *If you work hard you will succeed.* accomplish your objective, be successful, do well, flourish, [*informal*] make it, prosper, thrive.
2 *The plan succeeded.* be effective, [*informal*] catch on, produce results, work.
OPPOSITES: SEE **fail**.
3 *Elizabeth II succeeded George VI.* come after, follow, replace, take over from.

succeeding adjective *We didn't guess what would happen in the succeeding days.* coming, ensuing, following, later, next, subsequent, successive.

success noun 1 *How do you measure success?* accomplishment, achievement, attainment, fame, prosperity.
2 *The success of the plan depends on your co-operation.* completion, effectiveness, successful outcome.
3 *The plan was a success.* [*informal*] hit, [*informal*] sensation, triumph, victory, [*informal*] winner.
OPPOSITES: SEE **failure**.

successful adjective 1 *a successful business.* effective, flourishing, fruitful, lucrative, productive, profitable, profit-making, prosperous, rewarding, thriving, well-off.
2 *a successful team.* unbeaten, victorious, winning.
OPPOSITES: SEE **unsuccessful**.

succession noun *a succession of disasters.* chain, line, procession, progression, run, sequence, series, string.

successive adjective *We had rain on seven successive days.* consecutive, in succession, uninterrupted.

successor noun *the successor to the throne.* heir, inheritor, replacement.

succinct adjective SEE **concise**.

succour noun, verb SEE **help** noun, verb.

succulent adjective *succulent fruit.* fleshy, juicy, luscious, moist, rich.

succumb verb SEE **surrender**.

suck verb **to suck up** *to suck up liquid.* absorb, draw up, pull up, soak up.
to suck up to SEE **flatter**.

suckle verb SEE **feed**.

sucrose noun SEE **sugar** noun.

suction noun sucking.

sudden adjective **1** *a sudden decision.* abrupt, hasty, hurried, impetuous, impulsive, quick, rash, [*informal*] snap, swift, unconsidered.
OPPOSITES: SEE **slow** adjective.
3 *a sudden happening.* acute (*an acute illness*), sharp, startling, surprising, unexpected, unforeseen, unlooked for.
OPPOSITES: SEE **expected**.

suds noun bubbles, foam, froth, lather, soapsuds.

sue verb indict, prosecute.
LEGAL TERMS: SEE **law**.

suede noun SEE **leather**.

suffer verb **1** *to suffer pain.* bear, cope with, endure, experience, feel, go through, put up with, stand, tolerate, undergo.
2 *Did you suffer when you were ill?* experience pain [SEE **pain** noun], hurt.
3 *He suffered for his crime.* be punished, make amends, pay.
4 [*old-fashioned*] *Suffer the children to come to me.* SEE **permit** verb.

suffering noun SEE **torment** noun.

suffice verb *A cup of water sufficed to keep him alive.* be sufficient [SEE **sufficient**], [*informal*] do (*Will this do?*), serve.

sufficient adjective *sufficient money to live on.* adequate, enough, satisfactory.
OPPOSITES: SEE **insufficient**.

suffix noun OPPOSITE: **prefix**.

suffocate verb asphyxiate, choke, SEE **kill**, smother, stifle, strangle, throttle.

sugar noun FORMS OF SUGAR: brown sugar, cane sugar, caster sugar, demerara, glucose, granulated sugar, icing sugar, lump sugar, molasses, sucrose, SEE **sweets**, syrup, treacle.

sugar verb SEE **sweeten**.

sugary adjective **1** *a sugary taste.* SEE **sweet** adjective.
2 *sugary sentiments.* cloying, SEE **sentimental**, sickly.

suggest verb **1** *I suggest we go home.* advise, advocate, moot, move, propose, propound, put forward, raise, recommend.
2 *Her face suggests that she's bored.* communicate, hint, imply, indicate, insinuate, intimate, mean, signal.

suggestible adjective SEE **impressionable**.

suggestion noun **1** *I made a suggestion.* offer, plan, proposal, recommendation.
2 *a suggestion of cheating.* hint, suspicion, trace.

suggestive adjective **1** *suggestive images in a poem.* evocative, expressive, thought-provoking.
2 *suggestive jokes.* SEE **indecent**.

suicidal adjective **1** *a suicidal mood.* SEE **depressed**.
2 *a suicidal mission.* hopeless, [*informal*] kamikaze, self-destructive.

suicide noun SEE **killing**.

suit noun **1** *a suit to wear.* VARIOUS ITEMS OF CLOTHING: SEE **clothes**.
2 *a suit of cards.* set.
SUITS IN A PACK OF CARDS: clubs, diamonds, hearts, spades.
3 *a suit in a court of law.* LEGAL TERMS: SEE **law**.

suit verb **1** *What you suggest suits me.* be suitable for [SEE **suitable**], gratify, please, satisfy.
OPPOSITES: SEE **displease**.
2 *Their offer suits our requirements.* accommodate, conform to, fit in with, harmonize with, match, tally with.
3 *That colour suits you.* become, fit, look good on.

suitable adjective *a suitable present for granny.* acceptable, applicable, apposite, appropriate, apt, becoming, congenial, convenient, fit, fitting, handy, pertinent, proper, relevant, satisfactory, seemly, timely, well-chosen, well-judged, well-timed.
OPPOSITES: SEE **unsuitable**.

suitcase noun SEE **luggage**.

suite noun *a suite of rooms.* SEE **group** noun.

suitor noun SEE **lover**.

sulk verb *to sulk after a defeat.* be sullen [SEE **sullen**], brood, mope.

sulky adjective *a sulky look.* SEE **sullen**.

sullen adjective **1** *a sullen expression.* bad-tempered, churlish, cross, disgruntled, grudging, moody, morose, petulant, resentful, sad, silent, sour, stubborn, sulky, surly, uncommunicative, unfriendly, unhappy, unsociable.
OPPOSITES: SEE **cheerful**.

2 *a sullen sky.* brooding, cheerless, dark, dismal, dull, gloomy, grey, sombre.
OPPOSITES: SEE **bright**.

sully verb SEE **stain** verb.

sulphureous, sulphurous adjectives SEE **noxious**.

sultry adjective **1** *sultry weather.* close, hot, humid, [*informal*] muggy, oppressive, steamy, stifling, stuffy, warm.
OPPOSITES: SEE **cool** adjective.
2 *a sultry beauty.* dark, mysterious, sensual, SEE **sexy**, voluptuous.

sum noun *Add up the sum.* aggregate, amount, number, quantity, reckoning, result, score, tally, total, whole.
MATHEMATICAL TERMS: SEE **mathematics**.

sum verb **to sum up** SEE **summarize**.

summarize verb **1** *to summarize evidence.* make a summary of [SEE **summary** noun], outline, [*informal*] recap, recapitulate, review, sum up.
2 *to summarize a story.* abridge, condense, précis, reduce, shorten.
OPPOSITES: SEE **elaborate** verb.

summary adjective **1** *a summary account.* SEE **brief** adjective.
2 *summary justice.* SEE **hasty**.

summary noun **1** *a summary of the main points.* abstract, digest, outline, recapitulation, resumé, review, summation, summing-up.
2 *a summary of a story.* abridgement, condensation, précis, reduction, synopsis.

summation noun SEE **summary**.

summer-house noun gazebo, pavilion.

summery adjective *summery weather.* bright, SEE **hot**, sunny, tropical, warm.
OPPOSITES: SEE **wintry**.

summit noun **1** *the summit of a mountain.* apex, crown, head, height, peak, pinnacle, point, top.
OPPOSITES: SEE **foot**.
2 *the summit of your success.* acme, apogee, high point, zenith.
OPPOSITES: SEE **nadir**.

summon verb **1** *to summon someone to attend.* command, demand, invite, order, send for, [*formal*] subpoena.
2 *to summon a meeting.* assemble, call, convene, convoke, gather together, muster, rally.

summons noun LEGAL TERMS: SEE **law**.

sumptuous *a sumptuous banquet.* costly, dear, expensive, extravagant, grand, lavish, luxurious, magnificent, opulent, [*informal*] posh, rich, splendid, superb.
OPPOSITES: SEE **mean** adjective.

sun noun sunlight, sunshine.
RELATED ADJECTIVE: solar.
ASTRONOMICAL TERMS: SEE **astronomy**.

sunbathe verb bask, [*informal*] get a tan, sun yourself.

sunburn noun sunstroke, suntan, tanning.

sunburnt adjective blistered, bronzed, brown, peeling, tanned, weatherbeaten.

sunder verb SEE **part** verb.

sundown noun SEE **sunset**.

sundry adjective SEE **various**.

sun-glasses noun SEE **glass (glasses)**.

sunken adjective *a sunken area.* concave, depressed, hollow, hollowed, low.

sunless adjective *a sunless day.* cheerless, cloudy, dark, dismal, dreary, dull, gloomy, grey, overcast.
OPPOSITES: SEE **sunny**.

sunlight noun daylight, sun, sunbeams, sunshine.

sunlit adjective SEE **sunny**.

sunny adjective **1** *a sunny day.* bright, clear, cloudless, fine, summery, sunlit.
OPPOSITES: SEE **sunless**.
WORDS TO DESCRIBE WEATHER: SEE **weather** noun.
2 *a sunny smile.* SEE **cheerful**.

sunrise noun dawn, daybreak.
OTHER TIMES OF DAY: SEE **day**.

sunset noun dusk, evening, [*poetic*] gloaming, nightfall, sundown, twilight.
OTHER TIMES OF DAY: SEE **day**.

sunshade noun awning, canopy, parasol.

sunshine noun SEE **sunlight**.

suntan noun sunburn, tan.

super adjective SEE **good**.

The prefix *super-* is related to the Latin preposition *super = above, over.*

---

superabundance noun SEE **excess**.

superannuated adjective **1** *a superannuated employee.* discharged, [*informal*] pensioned off, [*informal*] put out to grass, old, retired.
2 [*informal*] *superannuated possessions,* discarded, disused, obsolete, thrown out, worn out.

superannuation noun annuity, pension.

superb adjective SEE **splendid**.

supercilious adjective SEE **superior**.

superficial adjective **1** *a superficial wound.* exterior, on the surface, shallow, skin-deep, slight, surface, unimportant.
OPPOSITE: deep.
2 *a superficial examination.* careless, casual, cursory, desultory, hasty, hurried, inattentive, [*informal*] nodding (*a nodding acquaintance*), passing, perfunctory.
OPPOSITE: SEE **thorough**.
3 *superficial arguments.* facile, frivolous, lightweight, simple-minded, simplistic, sweeping (*sweeping generalizations*), trivial, unconvincing, uncritical, unscholarly, unsophisticated.
OPPOSITES: SEE **analytical**.

superfluity noun SEE **excess**.

superfluous adjective *superfluous possessions.* excess, excessive, needless, redundant, spare, surplus, unnecessary, unwanted.
OPPOSITES: SEE **necessary**.

superhuman adjective **1** *superhuman efforts.* herculean, heroic, phenomenal, prodigious.
2 *superhuman powers.* divine, higher, metaphysical, supernatural.
OPPOSITES: SEE **subhuman**.

superimpose verb *to superimpose one thing on another.* overlay, place on top of.

superintend verb SEE **supervise**.

superintendent noun SEE **supervisor**.

superior adjective **1** *superior in rank.* greater, higher, more important, senior.
2 *superior quality.* better, choice, exclusive, fine, first-class, first-rate, select, top, unrivalled.
3 *a superior attitude.* arrogant, condescending, disdainful, haughty, [*informal*] high-and-mighty, lofty, patronizing, self-important, smug, snobbish, [*informal*] snooty, stuck-up, supercilious.
OPPOSITES: SEE **inferior**.

superlative adjective SEE **excellent, supreme**.

superman noun SEE **hero**.

supermarket noun SEE **shop**.

supernatural adjective *supernatural powers, supernatural manifestations.* abnormal, ghostly, inexplicable, magical, metaphysical, miraculous, mysterious, mystic, occult, paranormal, preternatural, psychic, spiritual, uncanny, unearthly, unnatural, weird.
SUPERNATURAL BEINGS: SEE **spirit**.

supernumerary adjective SEE **extra**.

superpower noun SEE **nation**.

superscription noun SEE **inscription**.

supersede verb SEE **replace**.

supersonic adjective SEE **fast** adjective.

superstar noun big name, celebrity, idol, SEE **performer**, star.

superstition noun *My fear of Friday 13th is just superstition.* delusion, illusion, myth, [*informal*] old wives' tale, superstitious belief [SEE **superstitious**].

superstitious adjective *superstitious beliefs.* groundless, illusory, irrational, mythical, traditional, unfounded, unprovable.
OPPOSITES: SEE **scientific**.

superstructure noun SEE **structure**.

supervise verb *to supervise a task.* administer, be in charge (of), be the supervisor (of) [SEE **supervisor**], conduct, control, direct, invigilate [= *supervise an exam*]. lead, look after, manage, organize, oversee, preside over, run, superintend, watch over.

supervision noun *the supervision of a production line. the supervision of an exam.* administration, conduct, control, invigilation, management, organization, oversight, surveillance.

supervisor noun administrator, SEE **chief** noun, controller, director, foreman, [*informal*] gaffer, head, inspector, invigilator, leader, manager, organizer, overseer, superintendent, timekeeper.

supine adjective *lying supine on the floor.* face upwards, on your back.
OPPOSITES: SEE **prone**.

supper noun VARIOUS MEALS: SEE **meal**.

supplant verb *to supplant a leader.* displace, oust, replace, [*informal*] step into the shoes of, [*informal*] topple, unseat.

supple adjective *supple leather. supple limbs.* bending, [*informal*] bendy, elastic, flexible, graceful, limber, lithe, plastic, pliable, pliant, soft.
OPPOSITES: SEE **brittle, rigid**.

supplement noun **1** *a supplement to travel first class.* additional payment, excess, surcharge.
2 *a newspaper supplement.* addendum, addition, SEE **appendix, extra, insert**.

supplement verb *I do odd jobs to supplement my income.* add to, augment, boost, complement, reinforce, [*informal*] top up.

supplementary adjective *a supplementary fare. supplementary information.* accompanying, additional, auxiliary, complementary, extra.

suppliant noun petitioner.

supplicate verb SEE **request** verb.

supplication noun SEE **request** noun.

supplier noun dealer, provider, purveyor, retailer, seller, shopkeeper, vendor, wholesaler.

supply noun *a supply of sweets.* quantity, reserve, reservoir, stock, stockpile, store.
supplies *supplies for the weekend.* equipment, food, necessities, provisions, rations, shopping.

supply verb *to supply goods.* contribute, donate, equip, feed, furnish, give, hand-over, pass on, produce, provide, purvey, sell, stock.

support noun **1** *Thank you for your support.* aid, approval, assistance, backing, contribution, co-operation, donation, encouragement, friendship, help, interest, loyalty, patronage, protection, reassurance, reinforcement, sponsorship, succour.
2 *a support to lean or rest on.* bracket, buttress, crutch, foundation, pillar, post, prop, sling, stanchion, stay, strut, trestle, truss.

support verb **1** *to support a weight.* bear, bolster, buttress, carry, give strength to, hold up, prop up, provide a support for, reinforce, shore up, strengthen, underlie, underpin.
2 *to support someone in trouble.* aid, assist, back, champion, comfort, defend, encourage, give support to [SEE **support** noun], rally round, reassure, speak up for, stand by, stand up for, take (someone's) part.
3 *to support a family.* bring up, feed, finance, fund, keep, maintain, nourish, provide for, sustain.
4 *to support a charity.* be a supporter of [SEE **supporter**], be interested in, contribute to, espouse (*to espouse a cause*), follow, give to, patronize, pay money to, sponsor, subsidize, work for.
5 *to support a point of view.* advocate, agree with, argue for, confirm, corroborate, defend, endorse, explain, justify, promote, substantiate, uphold, verify.
OPPOSITES: SEE **undermine**.
to support yourself *She supported herself on her arms.* lean, rest.

supporter noun **1** *a football supporter.* enthusiast, [*informal*] fan, fanatic, follower.
2 *a supporter of an idea. a supporter of a political party.* adherent, advocate, apologist (for), champion, defender, seconder, upholder, voter.
3 *a supporter of someone in a job or in a contest.* ally, collaborate, helper, [*old-fashioned*] henchman, second.

supportive adjective *a supportive group of friends.* caring, concerned, encouraging, helpful, interested, kind, loyal, positive, reassuring, sympathetic, understanding.
OPPOSITES: SEE **subversive**.

suppose verb **1** *I suppose you want some food.* accept, assume, believe, conclude, conjecture, expect, guess, infer, judge, postulate, presume, speculate, surmise, think.
2 *Just suppose you had lots of money.* fancy, fantasize, imagine, hypothesize, maintain, pretend.

supposed adjective *No one has ever seen the supposed monster.* alleged, assumed, conjectural, hypothetical, imagined, presumed, putative, reported, reputed, rumoured.
to be supposed to *I'm supposed to start work at 8.30.* be due to, be expected to, be meant to, be required to, have a duty to, need to, ought to.

supposition noun *a supposition, not a known fact.* assumption, conjecture, guess, [*informal*] guesstimate, hypothesis, inference, notion, opinion, presumption, speculation, surmise, theory, thought.

suppress verb **1** *to suppress a rebellion.* conquer, crush, overcome, overthrow, put an end to, put down, quash, quell, stamp out, stop, subdue.
2 *to suppress the truth. to suppress your feelings.* bottle up, censor, conceal, cover up, SEE **hide** verb, [*informal*] keep quiet about, repress, restrain, silence, smother.

suppurate verb SEE **fester**.

supremacy noun *No one could challenge her supremacy in gymnastics.* dominance, domination, lead, predominance, pre-eminence, sovereignty.

supreme adjective *Her supreme moment was winning a gold medal.* best, consummate, crowning, culminating, greatest, highest, incomparable, matchless, outstanding, paramount, predominant, pre-eminent, prime, principal, superlative, surpassing, top, ultimate, unbeatable, unbeaten, unparalleled, unrivalled, unsurpassable, unsurpassed.

surcharge noun SEE **supplement** noun.

sure adjective **1** *I'm sure that I'm right.* assured, confident, convinced, decided, definite, persuaded, positive, resolute.
2 *He's sure to come.* bound, certain, compelled, obliged, required.
3 *a sure fact.* accurate, clear, convincing, guaranteed, indisputable, inescapable, inevitable, precise, proven, true,

unchallenged, undeniable, undisputed, undoubted, verifiable.
4 *a sure ally.* dependable, effective, faithful, firm, infallible, loyal, reliable, safe, secure, solid, steadfast, steady, trustworthy, trusty, unerring, unfailing, unswerving.
OPPOSITES: SEE **uncertain**.

surety noun SEE **guarantee** noun.

surf noun SEE **wave** noun.

surface noun **1** *the outer surface.* coat, covering, crust, exterior, façade, outside, shell, skin, veneer.
OPPOSITES: SEE **centre**.
2 *A cube has six surfaces.* face, facet, plane, side.
3 *a working surface.* top, worktop.

surface verb **1** *I surfaced the wood with plastic.* coat, cover, veneer.
2 *The submarine surfaced. A problem surfaced.* appear, [*informal*] come to light, come up, emerge, materialize, rise, [*informal*] pop up.

surf-boarding noun SEE **surfing**.

surfeit noun *a surfeit of rich food.* excess, glut, over-indulgence, superfluity.

surfing noun surf-boarding, surf-riding.

surge noun **1** *a surge of water.* SEE **wave noun**.
2 *a surge of enthusiasm.* gush, increase, onrush, outpouring, rush, upsurge.

surge verb **1** *Water surged around them.* billow, eddy, gush, heave, make waves, roll, swirl.
2 *The crowd surged forward.* move irresistibly, push, rush, stampede, sweep.

surgeon noun MEDICAL PRACTITIONERS: SEE **medicine**.

surgery noun **1** *She underwent surgery.* biopsy, operation.
2 *I visited the doctor's surgery.* clinic, consulting room, health centre, infirmary, medical centre, sick-bay.

surly adjective *a surly mood, a surly answer.* bad-tempered, churlish, cross, [*informal*] crusty, gruff, [*informal*] grumpy, ill-natured, irascible, miserable, morose, peevish, rude, sulky, sullen, testy, uncivil, unfriendly, ungracious.
OPPOSITES: SEE **friendly**.

surmise noun, verb SEE **guess** noun, verb.

surmount verb SEE **deal** verb (**deal with**).

surname noun SEE **name** noun.

surpass verb *The success of the sale surpassed our expectations.* beat, better, do better than, eclipse, exceed, excel, outclass, outdo, outshine, outstrip, overshadow, top, transcend.

surpassing adjective SEE **excellent**.

surplus noun *If you've had all you want, give the surplus to others.* balance, excess, extra, remainder, residue, superfluity, surfeit.

surprise noun **1** *Imagine our surprise when she walked in.* alarm, amazement, astonishment, consternation, dismay, incredulity, wonder.
2 *Her arrival was a complete surprise.* [*informal*] bolt from the blue, [*informal*] bombshell, [*informal*] eye-opener, shock.

surprise verb **1** *The news surprised us.* alarm, amaze, astonish, astound, disconcert, dismay, shock, stagger, startle, stun, [*informal*] take aback, take by surprise, [*informal*] throw (*The unexpected news threw me*).
2 *The security officer surprised him opening the safe.* capture, catch out, [*informal*] catch red-handed, come upon, detect, discover, take unawares.

surprised adjective *I admit that I was surprised.* alarmed, amazed, astonished, astounded, disconcerted, dumbfounded, flabbergasted, incredulous, nonplussed, shocked, speechless, staggered, startled, stunned, taken aback, taken by surprise, thunderstruck.

surprising adjective *a surprising turn of events.* alarming, amazing, astonishing, astounding, disconcerting, extraordinary, incredible, [*informal*] offputting, shocking, staggering, startling, stunning, sudden, unexpected, unforeseen, unlooked for, unplanned.
OPPOSITES: SEE **predictable**.

surrender verb **1** *to surrender to an enemy.* capitulate, [*informal*] cave in, collapse, concede, fall, [*informal*] give in, resign, submit, succumb, [*informal*] throw in the towel, [*informal*] throw up the sponge, yield.
2 *to surrender your ticket.* give, hand over, relinquish.
3 *to surrender your rights.* abandon, cede, give up, renounce, waive.

surreptitious adjective *a surreptitious look at the answers.* concealed, covert, crafty, disguised, furtive, hidden, secretive, shifty, sly, [*informal*] sneaky, stealthy, underhand.
OPPOSITES: SEE **blatant**.

surrogate noun SEE **substitute** noun.

surround verb *The park is surrounded by houses.* besiege, beset, encircle, encompass, engulf, girdle, hedge in, hem in, ring, skirt.

surroundings noun *You work more happily in pleasant surroundings.* ambience, area, background, context, environment, location, milieu, neighbourhood, setting, vicinity.

surveillance noun *Police maintained a 24-hour surveillance on the building.* check, observation, scrutiny, supervision, vigilance, watch.

survey noun *a traffic survey, a land survey.* appraisal, assessment, census, count, evaluation, examination, inspection, investigation, scrutiny, study, [*formal*] triangulation.

survey verb **1** *to survey the damage after an accident.* appraise, assess, estimate, evaluate, examine, inspect, investigate, look over, scrutinize, study, view, weigh up.
2 *to survey building land.* do a survey of, map out, measure, plan out, plot, reconnoitre, [*formal*] triangulate.

survival noun *Commercial exploitation of resources threatens our survival.* continuance, continued existence.

survive verb **1** *You can't survive without water.* carry on, continue, endure, keep going, last, live, persist, remain.
OPPOSITES: SEE **die**.
2 *He survived the disasters which plagued him.* come through, live through, outlast, outlive, weather, withstand.
OPPOSITE: succumb to.

sus verb **to sus out** SEE **investigate**.

susceptible adjective *susceptible to colds.* disposed, given, inclined, liable, predisposed, prone, sensitive, vulnerable.
OPPOSITES: SEE **resistant**.

suspect adjective **1** *His evidence was suspect.* doubtful, inadequate, questionable, unconvincing, unreliable, unsatisfactory.
OPPOSITES: SEE **satisfactory**.
2 *a suspect character.* dubious, suspected, SEE **suspicious**.

suspect verb **1** *I suspect his motives.* call into question, distrust, doubt, mistrust.
2 *I suspect that he's lying.* believe, conjecture, consider, guess, imagine, infer, presume, speculate, suppose, surmise, think.

suspend verb **1** *to suspend something from a hook, etc.* dangle, hang, swing.
2 *to suspend a meeting.* adjourn, break off, defer, delay, discontinue, interrupt, postpone, put off.
3 *to suspend someone from school or from a job.* debar, dismiss, expel, send down.

suspended adjective *a suspended sentence. a suspended meeting.* adjourned, deferred, frozen, in abeyance, pending, postponed, [*informal*] put on ice, shelved.

suspense noun *The suspense was unbearable.* anticipation, anxiety, drama, excitement, expectancy, expectation, tension, uncertainty, waiting.

suspicion noun **1** *a suspicion that she was lying.* apprehension, distrust, doubt, feeling, guess, [*informal*] hunch, impression, misgiving, presentiment, qualm, uncertainty, wariness.
2 *a suspicion of a smile on his face.* hint, shadow, suggestion, tinge, touch, trace.

suspicious adjective **1** *suspicious of the evidence.* [*informal*] chary, disbelieving, distrustful, doubtful, incredulous, mistrustful, sceptical, unconvinced, uneasy, wary.
OPPOSITES: SEE **credulous**.
2 *a suspicious character.* disreputable, dubious, [*informal*] fishy, peculiar, questionable, shady, suspect, suspected, unreliable, untrustworthy.
OPPOSITES: SEE **straightforward**.

sustain verb SEE **support** verb.

sustenance noun SEE **food**.

suzerain noun SEE **ruler**.

svelte adjective SEE **slender**.

swab verb SEE **clean** verb.

swaddle verb **wrap** verb.

swag noun [*informal*] *robbers' swag.* booty, loot, plunder, takings.

swagger verb SEE **walk** verb.

swallow verb consume, SEE **drink** verb, **eat**.
to swallow up *Fog swallowed them up.* absorb, enclose, enfold, envelop, SEE **swamp** verb.

swamp noun bog, fen, marsh, marshland, mire, morass, mud, mudflats, quagmire, quicksand, saltmarsh, [*old-fashioned*] slough, wetlands.

swamp verb *A hugh wave swamped the ship.* deluge, drench, engulf, flood, inundate, overwhelm, sink, submerge, swallow up.

swampy adjective *swampy ground.* boggy, marshy, miry, muddy, soft, soggy, unstable, waterlogged, wet.
OPPOSITES: SEE **dry** adjective.

swan noun cob [=*male swan*], cygnet [=*young swan*].

swank verb see **boast**.

swanky adjective SEE **ostentatious**.

swap verb SEE **exchange** verb.

swarm noun *a swarm of bees.* SEE **group** noun.

swarm verb *People swarm to watch an accident.* cluster, congregate, crowd, flock, mass, move in a swarm, throng.
to swarm up *to swarm up a tree.* SEE **climb** verb.
to swarm with *The kitchen swarmed with ants.* abound, be alive with, be infested with, be invaded by, be overrun with, crawl, teem.

swarthy adjective *a swarthy complexion.* brown, dark, dusky, tanned.

swashbuckling adjective *a swashbuckling hero.* adventurous, aggressive, bold, daredevil, dashing, [*informal*] macho, SEE **manly, swaggering**.

swat verb *to swat a fly.* SEE **hit** verb.

swathe verb SEE **wrap** verb.

sway verb **1** *to sway in the breeze.* bend, lean from side to side, rock, roll, swing, wave.
2 *Nothing I can say will sway them.* affect, change the mind of, govern, influence, persuade.
3 *She swayed from her chosen path.* divert, go off course, swerve, veer, waver.

swear verb **1** *He swore that he would tell the truth.* affirm, attest, declare, give your word, pledge, promise, state on oath, take an oath, testify, vow.
2 *She swore when she hit her finger.* blaspheme, curse, use swearwords [SEE **swearword**].

swearword noun blasphemy, curse, expletive, [*informal*] four-letter word, oath, obscenity, profanity.
swearwords bad language, foul language, swearing.

sweat verb perspire, swelter.

sweaty adjective *sweaty hands.* clammy, damp, moist, perspiring, sticky, sweating.

sweep verb **1** *Sweep the floor.* brush, clean, clear, dust.
2 *The bus swept past.* SEE **move** verb.

sweeping adjective **1** *sweeping changes.* comprehensive, extensive, far-reaching, indiscriminate, radical, wholesale.
OPPOSITES: SEE **specific**.
2 *a sweeping statement* broad, general, oversimplified, simplistic, superficial, uncritical, undiscriminating, unqualified, unscholarly.
OPPOSITES: SEE **analytical**.

sweepstake noun SEE **gambling**.

sweet adjective **1** *a sweet taste. a sweet smell.* cloying, fragrant, luscious, mellow, perfumed, sickly, sugary, sweetened, syrupy.
OPPOSITES: SEE **acid, acrid, bitter, savoury**.
2 *sweet sounds.* [*often joking*] dulcet (*dulcet tones*), euphonious, harmonious, heavenly, melodious, musical, pleasant, silvery, soothing, tuneful.
OPPOSITES: SEE **discordant**.
3 *a sweet nature.* affectionate, attractive, charming, dear, endearing, engaging, gentle, gracious, lovable, lovely, nice, pretty, unselfish, winning.
OPPOSITES: SEE **selfish, ugly**.
sweetcorn corn on the cob, maize.

sweet noun [= *the sweet course of a meal*] [*informal*] afters, dessert, pudding.
sweets [*old-fashioned*] bon-bons, [*American*] candy, confectionery, [*childish*] sweeties, [*old-fashioned*] sweetmeats.

VARIOUS SWEETS: acid drop, barley sugar, boiled sweet, bull's-eye, butterscotch, candy, candyfloss, caramel, chewing-gum, chocolate, fondant, fruit pastille, fudge, humbug, liquorice, lollipop, marshmallow, marzipan, mint, nougat, peppermint, rock, toffee, Turkish delight.

---

sweeten verb **1** *to sweeten your coffee.* make sweeter, sugar.
2 *to sweeten someone's temper.* appease, calm, mellow, mollify, pacify, soothe.

sweetener noun VARIOUS SWEETENERS: artificial sweetener, honey, saccharine, SEE **sugar** noun, sweetening.

sweetheart noun SEE **lover**.

swell noun *an ocean swell.* SEE **wave** noun.

swell verb **1** *The balloon swelled as it filled with air.* balloon, become bigger, billow, blow up, bulge, dilate, distend, enlarge, expand, fatten, grow, inflate, puff up, rise.
2 *We invited friends to swell the numbers in the audience.* augment, boost, build up, extend, increase, make bigger.
OPPOSITES: SEE **shrink**.

swelling noun *a painful swelling.* blister, bulge, bump, hump, inflammation, knob, lump, protuberance, tumescence, tumour.

sweltering adjective SEE **hot**.

swerve verb *The car swerved to avoid a hedgehog.* change direction, deviate, dodge about, swing, take avoiding action, turn aside, veer, wheel.

swift adjective *a swift journey. a swift reaction.* agile, brisk, fast, [*old-fashioned*] fleet, fleet-footed, hasty, hurried, nimble, [*informal*] nippy, prompt, SEE **quick**, rapid, speedy, sudden.
OPPOSITES: SEE **slow** adjective.

swig verb SEE **drink** verb.

swill verb **1** *Swill the car with clear water.* bathe, clean, rinse, sponge down, wash.
2 [*informal*] *They sat there swilling champagne.* SEE **drink** verb.

swim verb *to swim in the sea.* bathe, dive in, float, go swimming, [*informal*] take a dip.
VARIOUS SWIMMING STROKES: backstroke, breaststroke, butterfly, crawl.

swimming-bath noun baths, leisure-pool, lido, swimming-pool.

swim-suit noun bathing-costume, bathing-dress, bathing-suit, bikini, swimwear, trunks.

swindle noun *I don't want to get involved in a swindle.* cheat, chicanery, [*informal*] con, deception, double-dealing, fraud, [*informal*] racket, [*informal*] rip-off, [*informal*] sharp practice, [*informal*] swizz, trickery.

swindle verb *He swindled us out of a lot of money.* [*informal*] bamboozle, cheat, [*informal*] con, deceive, defraud, [*informal*] do, double-cross, dupe, [*informal*] fiddle, [*informal*] fleece, fool, hoax, hoodwink, [*informal*] rook, trick, [*informal*] welsh (*to welsh on a bet*).

swindler noun charlatan, cheat, cheater, [*informal*] con-man, counterfeiter, double-cross, extortioner, forger, fraud, hoaxer, impostor, mountebank, quack, racketeer, [*informal*] shark, trickster, [*informal*] twister.

swine noun SEE **pig**.

swineherd noun SEE **farmer**.

swing noun *a swing in public opinion.* change, fluctuation, movement, oscillation, shift, variation.

swing verb **1** *He swung from the end of a rope.* be suspended, dangle, flap, hang loose, rock, sway, swivel, turn, twirl, wave about.
2 *The car swung from one side of the road to the other.* SEE **swerve**.
3 *During the election, support swung to the opposition.* change, fluctuate, move across, oscillate, shift, transfer, vary.

swingeing adjective **1** *a swingeing blow.* SEE **violent**.
2 *a swingeing increase in price.* SEE **exorbitant**.

swinish adjective SEE **beastly**.

swipe verb **1** *to swipe with a bat.* SEE **hit** verb.
2 [*informal*] *She swiped my pen.* SEE **steal**.

swirl verb *The water swirled round.* boil, churn, eddy, move in circles, spin, surge, twirl, twist, whirl.

swish adjective SEE **posh**.

swish noun, verb VARIOUS SOUNDS: SEE **sound** noun.

switch noun **1** *an electric switch.* circuit-breaker, light-switch, power-point.
2 [= *whip*] SEE **whip** noun.

switch verb *to switch places.* change, exchange, replace, shift, substitute, [*informal*] swap.

swivel verb *to swivel round.* gyrate, pirouette, pivot, revolve, rotate, spin, swing, turn, twirl, wheel.

swizz noun SEE **swindle** noun.

swollen adjective big, bulging, distended, enlarged, fat, full, inflated, puffy, tumescent.

swoon verb SEE **faint** verb.

swoop verb *The owl swooped down.* descend, dive, drop, fall, fly down, lunge, plunge, pounce.
to swoop on [*informal*] *The police swooped on the club.* SEE **raid** verb.

swop verb SEE **exchange** verb.

sword noun blade, broadsword, cutlass, foil, rapier, sabre, scimitar.
OTHER WEAPONS: SEE **weapons**.

swordsman noun SEE **fighter**.

sworn adjective SEE **determined**.

swot verb SEE **study** verb.

sybarite noun SEE **hedonist**.

sybaritic adjective SEE **hedonistic**.

sycophant noun flatterer, today.

sycophantic adjective SEE **flattering**.

syllabus noun course, curriculum, outline, programme of study.

symbol noun **1** *A crown is a symbol of royal power.* badge, emblem, figure, ideogram, ideograph, image, insignia, logo, monogram, motif, pictogram, pictograph, sign.
2 *symbols used in writing.* character, letter.

symbolic adjective *a symbolic image. a symbolic gesture.* allegorical, emblematic, figurative, meaningful, metaphorical, representative, significant, suggestive, token (*a token gesture*).

symbolize verb *Easter eggs symbolize the renewal of life.* be a sign of, betoken, communicate, connote, denote, indicate, mean, represent, signify, stand for, suggest.

symmetrical adjective *a symmetrical design.* balanced, even, regular.
OPPOSITES: SEE **asymmetrical**.

sympathetic adjective *sympathetic about someone's problems.* benevolent,

caring, charitable, comforting, compassionate, concerned, consoling, friendly, humane, interested, kind, merciful, pitying, soft-hearted, sorry, supportive, tender, tolerant, understanding, warm.
OPPOSITES: SEE **unsympathetic**.

sympathize verb **to sympathize with** *to sympathize with someone in trouble.* be sorry for, be sympathetic towards [SEE **sympathetic**], comfort, commiserate with, console, empathize with, feel for, identify with, pity, show sympathy for [SEE **sympathy**], understand.

sympathy noun *She showed no sympathy when I described my problem.* affinity, commiseration, compassion, condolences, consideration, empathy, feeling, fellow-feeling, kindness, mercy, pity, tenderness, understanding.

symposium noun SEE **discussion**.

symptom noun *A rash is one of the symptoms of measles.* feature, indication, manifestation, mark, sign, warning.

symptomatic adjective *Do you think violence is symptomatic of our times?* characteristic, indicative, suggestive, typical.

synagogue noun SEE **worship** noun **(place of worship)**.

synchronize verb *Synchronize your watches.* match up, set to the same time.

synchronous adjective SEE **contemporary**.

synonym noun OPPOSITE: antonym.

synthesis noun SEE **combination**.

synthesize verb SEE **combine**.

synthetic adjective *Nylon is a synthetic material.* artificial, concocted, ersatz, fabricated, fake [*informal*] made-up, man-made, manufactured, mock, simulated, unnatural.
OPPOSITES: SEE **authentic, natural**.

syringe noun hypodermic, needle.

syrup noun SEE **sugar** noun.

system noun **1** *a railway system.* network, organization, [*informal*] setup.
2 *a system for getting your work done.* arrangement, logic, method, methodology, order, plan, practice, procedure, process, routine, rules, scheme, structure, technique, theory.
3 *a system of government.* constitution, philosophy, principles, regime, science.

systematic adjective *a systematic worker. systematic organization.* businesslike, logical, methodical, ordered, orderly, organized, planned, scientific, structured.
OPPOSITES: SEE **unsystematic**.

systematize verb *You need to systematize your work routine.* arrange, classify, codify, make systematic [SEE **systematic**], organize, rationalize, standardize.

T

tab noun SEE **tag** noun.

tabernacle noun SEE **worship** noun **(place of worship)**.

table noun **1** coffee-table, dining-table, gate-leg table, kitchen table.
OTHER ITEMS OF FURNITURE: SEE **furniture**.
2 *a table of information.* catalogue, chart, diagram, graph, index, list, register, schedule, tabulation, timetable.
table tennis [*informal*] ping-pong.

tableau noun picture, representation, scene.

tablespoon noun serving spoon.
OTHER CUTLERY: SEE **cutlery**.

tablet noun **1** *a tablet of soap.* bar, block, chunk, piece, slab.
2 *The doctor prescribed some tablets.* capsule, medicine, pellet, pill.

tabloid noun SEE **newspaper**.

taboo adjective *a taboo subject.* banned, disapproved of, forbidden, prohibited, proscribed, unacceptable, unmentionable, unnameable.

taboo noun *a religious taboo.* ban, curse, prohibition, taboo subject [SEE **taboo** adjective].

tabulate verb *to tabulate information.* arrange as a table, catalogue, list, set out in columns.

tacit adjective *tacit agreement.* implicit, implied, silent, understood, unspoken, unvoiced.

taciturn adjective SEE **silent**.

tack noun **1** drawing-pin, nail, pin, tintack.
OTHER FASTENERS: SEE **fastener**.
2 *a tack in a garment.* stitch.
3 *You're on the wrong tack.* approach, SEE **direction**, policy, procedure.

tack verb **1** *to tack down a carpet.* nail, pin.
OTHER WAYS TO FASTEN THINGS: SEE **fasten**.
2 *to tack up a hem.* sew, stitch.
3 *to tack in a sailing-boat.* beat against the wind.
to tack on SEE **add**.

tackle noun **1** *fishing tackle.* apparatus, equipment, gear, implements, kit, outfit, [*joking*] paraphernalia, rig, tools.
2 *a football tackle.* attack, block, challenge, interception, intervention.

tackle verb 1 *to tackle a problem.* address yourself to, attempt, attend to, combat, confront, cope with, deal with, face up to, grapple with, handle, manage, set about, sort out, undertake.
2 *to tackle an opposing player.* attack, challenge, intercept, stop, take on.

tacky adjective *tacky paint.* gluey, sticky, wet.
OPPOSITES: SEE **dry** adjective.

tact noun *He showed tact in dealing with their embarrassment.* consideration, delicacy, diplomacy, discretion, sensitivity, tactfulness, thoughtfulness, understanding.
OPPOSITES: SEE **tactlessness**.

tactful adjective *a tactful reminder.* appropriate, considerate, delicate, diplomatic, discreet, judicious, polite, sensitive, thoughtful.
OPPOSITES: SEE **tactless**.

tactical adjective *a tactical manœuvre.* calculated, deliberate, planned, politic, prudent, shrewd, skilful, strategic.

tactics noun *The manager explained the tactics for the next game.* approach, campaign, course of action, manœuvring, plan, ploy, policy, procedure, scheme, strategy.

tactile adjective SEE **touch** noun.

tactless adjective *a tactless reference to her illness.* blundering, boorish, clumsy, gauche, heavy-handed, hurtful, impolite, inappropriate, inconsiderate, indelicate, indiscreet, inept, insensitive, misjudged, SEE **rude**, thoughtless, uncouth, undiplomatic, unkind.
OPPOSITES: SEE **tactful**.

tactlessness noun *I'm surprised by his tactlessness in discussing her illness.* gaucherie, indelicacy, indiscretion, ineptitude, insensitivity, SEE **rudeness**, thoughtlessness.
OPPOSITES: SEE **tact**.

tag noun **1** *a price tag.* docket, label, marker, slip, sticker, tab, ticket.
2 *a Latin tag.* SEE **saying**.

tag verb *to tag items in a database. to tag goods with price-labels.* identify, label, mark, ticket.
to tag on *I tagged on a PS at the end of the letter.* add, append, attach, tack on.
to tag along *We tagged along at the end of the queue.* SEE **follow**, join, [*informal*] latch on, trail, unite.

tagliatelle noun SEE **pasta**.

tail noun **1** *an animal's tail. the tail of a queue.* back, end, extremity, rear, tail-end.
2 [*informal*] *a person's tail.* SEE **bottom** noun.

tail verb *to tail a car.* follow, pursue, shadow, stalk, track, trail.
to tail off *Our enthusiasm tailed off when we got tired.* decline, decrease, dwindle, lessen, peter out, reduce, slacken, subside, wane.

tailcoat noun evening dress, [*informal*] tails.

tailor-made adjective SEE **perfect** adjective.

taint verb **1** *to taint food or water.* adulterate, contaminate, dirty, infect, poison, pollute, soil.
2 *to taint someone's reputation.* blacken, dishonour, ruin, slander, smear, stain.

take verb [*Take* has many meanings and uses. We give just the commoner ones here.]
1 *Take my hand.* clutch, grab, grasp, hold, pluck, seize, snatch.
2 *They took prisoners.* abduct, arrest, capture, catch, corner, detain, ensnare, entrap, secure.
3 *Someone took my pen.* appropriate, move, pick up, pocket, remove, SEE **steal**.
4 *Take 2 from 4.* deduct, eliminate, subtract, take away.
5 *My car takes four people.* accommodate, carry, contain, have room for, hold.
6 *We took him home.* accompany, bring, [*informal*] cart, conduct, convey, escort, ferry, fetch, guide, lead, transport.
7 *We took a taxi.* catch, engage, hire, make use of, travel by, use.
8 *She took science at college.* have lessons in, learn about, read, study.
9 *I can't take rich food. I won't take any more insults.* abide, accept, bear, brook, consume, drink, eat, endure, have, receive, [*informal*] stand, [*informal*] stomach, suffer, swallow, tolerate, undergo, withstand.
10 *It took a lot of courage to own up.* necessitate, need, require, use up.
11 *She took a new name.* adopt, assume, choose, select.
to take aback *The news took me aback.* SEE **surprise** verb.
to take after *She takes after her mother.* SEE **resemble**.
to take against *He took against me from the start.* SEE **dislike** verb.

to take back *He took back all he'd said.* SEE **withdraw.**
to take in 1 *The trick took me in.* SEE **deceive.**
2 *He takes in lodgers.* SEE **accommodate.**
3 *I hope you took in all I said.* SEE **understand.**
to take life SEE **kill.**
to take off 1 *Take off your clothes.* SEE **remove.**
2 *The mimic took off the prime minister.* SEE **imitate.**
to take on *I took on a new job.* SEE **undertake.**
to take over *I was angry when she took over my job.* SEE **usurp.**
to take part *We took part in the organization.* SEE **participate.**
to take place *The incident took place last week.* SEE **happen.**
to take to task *She took me to task for my lateness.* SEE **reprimand** verb.
to take up 1 *She's taken up a new hobby.* SEE **begin.**
2 *Studying takes up a lot of my time.* SEE **occupy.**

take-away noun OTHER MEALS: SEE **meal.**
SHOPS AND BUSINESSES: SEE **shop.**

take-off noun **1** *the take-off of an aircraft.* lift-off.
2 *a take-off of the prime minister.* SEE **imitation.**

take-over noun *a business take-over.* amalgamation, combination, incorporation, merger.

taking adjective SEE **attractive.**

takings noun *the takings of a shop.* earnings, gains, gate [= *takings at a football match*], income, proceeds, profits, receipts, revenue.

talcum noun OTHER COSMETICS: SEE **cosmetics.**

tale noun *She told us her tale.* account, anecdote, narration, narrative, relation, report, [*slang*] spiel, story, yarn.
VARIOUS KINDS OF STORY: SEE **story.**
to tell tales SEE **inform (inform against).**

talent noun *musical talent. sporting talent.* ability, accomplishment, aptitude, brilliance, capacity, expertise, flair, genius, gift, knack, [*informal*] know-how, prowess, skill.

talented adjective *a talented player.* able, accomplished, artistic, brilliant, SEE **clever**, distinguished, expert, gifted, inspired, skilful, skilled, versatile.
OPPOSITES: SEE **unskilful.**

talisman noun *a good-luck talisman.* amulet, charm, mascot.

talk noun **1** *talk between two or more people.* chat, confabulation, conference, conversation, dialogue, discussion, gossip, intercourse, palaver, words.
2 *a talk to an audience.* address, discourse, harangue, lecture, oration, presentation, sermon, speech.

talk verb **1** *As far as we know, animals can't talk.* address each other, articulate ideas, commune, communicate, confer, converse, deliver a speech, discourse, enunciate, exchange views, have a conversation, negotiate, [*informal*] pipe up, pronounce words, say something [SEE **say**], speak, tell, use language, use your voice, utter, verbalize, vocalize.
2 *Can you talk French?* communicate in, express yourself in, pronounce, speak.
3 *The police tried to get him to talk.* confess, give information, [*informal*] grass, inform, [*informal*] let on, [*informal*] spill the beans, [*informal*] squeal, [*informal*] tell tales.
to talk about allude to, comment on, discuss, mention, refer to, relate.
to talk to address, harangue, lecture.

VERBS EXPRESSING DIFFERENT MODES OF TALKING: SEE **answer**, argue, SEE **ask**, assert, complain, declaim, declare, ejaculate, exclaim, fulminate, harangue, object, plead, read aloud, recite, soliloquize, [*informal*] speechify.

WORDS EXPRESSING DIFFERENT WAYS OF TALKING [many of these words are used both as nouns and as verbs; many are used *informally*]: babble, baby-talk, bawl, bellow, blab, blarney, blether, blurt out, breathe (*Don't breathe a word!*), burble, call out, chat, chatter, chin-wag, chit-chat, clamour, croak, cry, drawl, drone, gabble, gas, gibber, gossip, grunt, harp, howl, intone, jabber, jaw, jeer, lisp, maunder, moan, mumble, murmur, mutter, natter, patter, prattle, pray, preach, rabbit, rant, rasp, rave, roar, scream, screech, shout, shriek, slur, snap, snarl, speak in an undertone, splutter, spout, squeal, stammer, stutter, tattle, tittle-tattle, utter, vociferate, wail, whimper, whine, whinge, whisper, witter, yell.

---

talkative adjective *a talkative person.* articulate, [*informal*] chatty, communicative, effusive, eloquent, expansive, garrulous, glib, gossipy, long-winded, loquacious, prolix, unstoppable, verbose, vocal, voluble, wordy.
a talkative person chatter-box, [*informal*] gas-bag, gossip, [*informal*] windbag.

tall adjective *a tall skyscraper.* SEE **big**, giant, high, lofty, towering.
OPPOSITE: SEE **short**.

tally noun SEE **reckoning**.

tally verb SEE **correspond**.

talon noun claw.

tame adjective **1** *tame animals.* amenable, biddable, compliant, disciplined, docile, domesticated, gentle, manageable, meek, obedient, safe, subdued, submissive, tractable.
OPPOSITES: SEE **wild**.
2 *a tame story.* bland, boring, dull, feeble, flat, lifeless, tedious, unadventurous, unexciting, uninspiring, uninteresting.
OPPOSITES: SEE **exciting**.

tame verb **1** *to tame a wild animal.* break in, discipline, domesticate, house-train, make tame [SEE **tame** adjective], master, train.
2 *to tame your passions.* conquer, curb, humble, keep under, quell, repress, subdue, subjugate, suppress, temper.

tamper verb **to tamper with** alter, [*informal*] fiddle about with, interfere with, make adjustments to, meddle with, tinker with.

tan adjective SEE **brown** adjective.

tan noun *I got a tan on holiday.* sunburn, suntan.

tan verb *to tan in the sun.* burn, bronze, brown, colour, darken, get tanned [SEE **tanned**].

tang noun *The flavour has quite a tang to it.* acidity, [*informal*] bite, piquancy, pungency, savour, sharpness.

tangent noun **to go off at a tangent** SEE **diverge**.

tangible adjective *tangible evidence.* actual, concrete, definite, material, palpable, physical, positive, provable, real, solid, substantial, touchable.
OPPOSITES: SEE **intangible**.

tangle noun *a tangle of string.* coil, confusion, jumble, jungle, knot, mass, muddle, twist, web.

tangle verb **1** *to tangle string or ropes.* confuse, entangle, entwine, [*informal*] foul up, interweave, muddle, ravel, [*informal*] snarl up, twist.
OPPOSITES: SEE **disentangle**.
2 *A fish was tangled in the net.* catch, enmesh, ensnare, entrap, trap.
3 *Don't tangle with those criminals.* become involved with, confront, cross.

tangled adjective **1** *a tangled situation.* complicated, confused, convoluted, entangled, intricate, involved, knotty, messy.
OPPOSITES: SEE **straightforward**.
2 *tangled hair.* dishevelled, knotted, matted, tousled, uncombed, unkempt, untidy.
OPPOSITES: SEE **tidy** adjective.

tangy adjective *a tangy taste.* acid, appetizing, bitter, fresh, piquant, pungent, refreshing, sharp, spicy, strong, tart.
OPPOSITES: SEE **bland**.

tank noun **1** *a water tank.* basin, cistern, reservoir.
OTHER CONTAINERS: SEE **container**.
2 *a fish tank.* aquarium.
3 *an army tank.* armoured vehicle.

tankard noun SEE **cup**.

tanned adjective brown, sunburnt, suntanned, weather-beaten.

tantalize verb *The delicious smell tantalized us.* entice, frustrate, [*informal*] keep on tenterhooks, lead on, provoke, taunt, tease, tempt, titillate, torment.

tantamount adjective SEE **equivalent**.

tantrum noun SEE **temper** noun.

tap noun **1** *a water tap.* [*American*] faucet, stop-cock, valve.
2 *a tap on the door.* SEE **hit** noun.

tap verb *I tapped on the door.* SEE **hit** verb, knock, rap, strike.

tape noun **1** *I tied the parcel with tape.* band, binding, braid, ribbon, strip.
2 *recording tape.* SEE **record** noun.
tape deck, tape recorder SEE **audio equipment**.

tape verb *to tape up a parcel.* SEE **fasten**.

taper noun candle, lighter, spill.

taper verb *to taper to a point.* attenuate, become narrower, narrow, thin.
to taper off *The conversation tapered off.* SEE **decrease** verb.

tape-record verb SEE **record** verb.

tar noun pitch.

tardy adjective SEE **late**, **slow** adjective.

target noun **1** *Our target was to raise £100.* aim, ambition, end, goal, hope, intention, objective, purpose.
2 *Who was the target of their criticism?* butt, object, quarry, victim.

tariff noun **1** *a hotel's tariff.* charges, menu, price-list, schedule.
2 *a tariff on imports.* customs, duty, excise, levy, tax, toll.

tarn noun SEE **lake**.

tarnish verb **1** *Acid rain tarnished the metal.* blacken, corrode, discolour.
2 *The slander tarnished his reputation.* blemish, blot, dishonour, mar, spoil, stain, sully.

tarpaulin noun SEE **covering**.
tarry verb SEE **delay** verb.
tart adjective *the tart taste of lemons.* acid, biting, piquant, pungent, sharp, sour, tangy.
OPPOSITES: SEE **bland, sweet** adjective.
tart noun flan, pastry, pie, quiche, tartlet.
task noun *We were given several tasks to do.* activity, assignment, burden, business, chore, duty, employment, enterprise, errand, imposition, job, mission, requirement, undertaking, work.
to take to task SEE **reprimand** verb.
task-force noun SEE **armed services**.
taskmaster noun SEE **employer**.
taste noun **1** *the taste of strawberries.* character, flavour, savour.
2 *I gave her a taste of my apple.* bit, bite, morsel, mouthful, nibble, piece, sample, titbit.
3 *We share the same tastes in music.* appreciation, choice, inclination, judgement, liking, preference.
4 *She is a person of taste.* breeding, culture, discernment, discretion, discrimination, education, elegance, fashion sense, finesse, good judgement, perception, polish, refinement, sensitivity, style.
in bad taste SEE **tasteless**.
in good taste SEE **tasteful**.
taste verb *Taste a bit of this!* nibble, relish, sample, savour, sip, test, try.

WORDS TO DESCRIBE HOW THINGS TASTE: acid, bitter, creamy, fresh, fruity, hot, luscious, meaty, mellow, peppery, piquant, pungent, rancid, refreshing, salty, savoury, sharp, sour, spicy, stale, strong, sugary, sweet, tangy, tart, SEE **tasteless**, SEE **tasty**, unpalatable.

---

tasteful adjective *tasteful clothes. a tasteful choice of colours.* artistic, attractive, cultivated, dignified, discerning, discreet, discriminating, elegant, fashionable, in good taste, judicious, proper, refined, restrained, sensitive, smart, stylish, well-judged.
OPPOSITES: SEE **tasteless**.
tasteless adjective **1** *tasteless food.* bland, characterless, flavourless, insipid, mild, uninteresting, watered down, watery, weak.
OPPOSITES: SEE **tasty**.
2 *a tasteless choice of colours. a tasteless joke.* crude, garish, gaudy, graceless, improper, inartistic, in bad taste, indelicate, inelegant, injudicious, [*informal*] kitsch, ugly, unattractive, undiscriminating, unfashionable, unimaginative, unpleasant, unseemly, unstylish, SEE **vulgar**.
OPPOSITES: SEE **tasteful**.
tasty adjective *tasty food.* appetizing, delicious, flavoursome, [*informal*] mouthwatering, [*informal*] nice, piquant, savoury, [*informal*] scrumptious.
OTHER WORDS TO DESCRIBE HOW THINGS TASTE: SEE **taste** verb.
OPPOSITES: SEE **tasteless**.
tattered adjective *tattered clothes.* frayed, ragged, ripped, tatty, threadbare, torn, worn out.
OPPOSITES: SEE **smart** adjective.
tatters noun *Her clothes were in tatters.* rags, ribbons, shreds, torn pieces.
tattle verb SEE **talk** verb.
tattoo noun **1** *a drum tattoo.* SEE **signal** noun.
2 *a military tattoo.* SEE **entertainment**.
3 *a tattoo on the skin.* SEE **mark** noun.
tatty adjective **1** *tatty clothes.* frayed, old, patched, ragged, ripped, scruffy, shabby, tattered, torn, threadbare, untidy, worn out.
OIPPOSITES: SEE **new**.
2 *tatty ornaments.* SEE **tawdry**.
taunt verb SEE **ridicule** verb.
taut adjective *Make sure the rope is taut.* firm, stretched, tense, tight.
OPPOSITES: SEE **slack** adjective.
tauten verb SEE **tighten**.
tautological adjective *a tautological use of words.* otiose, pleonastic, redundant, repetitious, repetitive, superfluous, tautologous, SEE **wordy**.
OPPOSITES: SEE **concise**.
tautology noun duplication, pleonasm, repetition.
tavern noun (*old-fashioned*) *They had a drink at the tavern.* [*old-fashioned*] alehouse, bar, (*joking*) hostelry, inn, [*informal*] local, pub, public house.
tawdry adjective *tawdry ornaments. a tawdry imitation.* cheap, common, eye-catching, fancy, [*informal*] flashy, garish, gaudy, inferior, meretricious, poor quality, raffish, showy, tasteless, tatty, vulgar, worthless.
OPPOSITES: SEE **superior**.
tawny adjective SEE **brown** adjective, **yellow**.
tawse noun SEE **strap** noun.
tax noun charge, imposition, levy, tariff.

VARIOUS TAXES: airport tax, community charge, customs, duty, excise, income tax, poll-tax, rates, [*old-fashioned*] tithe, toll, value-added tax.

---

tax verb **1** *to tax income, goods, etc.* impose a tax on, levy a tax on.
2 *The problem taxed me severely.* burden, exhaust, make heavy demands on, overwork, SEE **tire**.
to tax with *They taxed me with inefficiency.* accuse of, blame for, censure for, charge with, reproach for, reprove for.

taxi noun cab, [*old-fashioned*] hackney carriage, minicab.

taxonomy noun SEE **classification**.

taxpayer noun SEE **citizen**.

tea noun **1** *a cup of tea.* OTHER DRINKS: SEE **drink** noun.
2 *She invited me to tea.* OTHER MEALS: SEE **meal**.

tea-break noun SEE **break** noun.

teach verb VARIOUS WAYS TO TEACH THINGS TO OTHERS: advise, brainwash, coach, counsel, demonstrate to, discipline, drill, educate, enlighten, familiarize with, ground (someone) in, impart knowledge to, implant knowledge in, inculcate habits in, indoctrinate, inform, instruct, lecture, school, train, tutor.

teacher noun VARIOUS TEACHERS: adviser, coach, counsellor, demonstrator, don, educator, governess, guide, guru, headteacher, housemaster, housemistress, instructor, lecturer, maharishi, master, mentor, mistress, pedagogue, preacher, preceptor, professor, pundit, schoolmaster, schoolmistress, schoolteacher, trainer, tutor.

tea-chest noun SEE **box**.

teaching noun **1** VARIOUS KINDS OF TEACHING: advice, brainwashing, briefing, coaching, computer-aided learning, counselling, demonstration, distance learning, grounding, guidance, indoctrination, instruction, lecture, lesson, practical (*a science practical*), preaching, rote learning, schooling, seminar, training, tuition, tutorial, work experience, workshop (*a writing workshop*).
2 *the teachings of holy scripture.* doctrine, dogma, gospel, precept, principle, tenet.

tea-cloth noun SEE **towel** noun.

team noun **1** *a football team.* club, [*informal*] line-up, side.
2 *working as a team.* SEE **group** noun.

team verb **to team up** SEE **group** verb.

tea-party noun SEE **party**.

teapot noun ITEMS OF CROCKERY: SEE **crockery**.

tear noun **1** [rhymes with *fear*] *tears in his eyes.* droplet, tear-drop.
tears [*informal*] blubbering, crying, sobs, weeping.
to shed tears SEE **weep**.
2 [rhymes with *bear*] *a tear in my jeans.* cut, gap, gash, hole, opening, rent, rip, slit, split.

tear verb **1** *The barbed wire tore my jeans.* claw, gash, lacerate, mangle, pierce, rend, rip, rupture, scratch, shred, slit, snag, split.
2 [*informal*] *We tore to the station.* SEE **rush** verb.

tearaway noun SEE **hooligan**.

tearful adjective *tearful children. a tearful farewell.* [*informal*] blubbering, crying, emotional, lachrymose, SEE **sad**, sobbing, weeping, [*informal*] weepy.

tearing adjective [*informal*] *a tearing hurry.* SEE **impetuous**.

tea-room, tea-shop nouns SEE **café**.

tea-towel noun SEE **towel** noun.

tease verb *The cat scratches if you tease her.* [*informal*] aggravate, annoy, bait, chaff, goad, irritate, laugh at, make fun of, mock, [*informal*] needle, pester, plague, provoke, [*informal*] pull someone's leg, [*informal*] rib, SEE **ridicule** verb, tantalize, taunt, torment, vex, worry.

teasing noun *I was annoyed by their teasing.* badinage, banter, joking, mockery, provocation, raillery, [*informal*] ribbing, ridicule, taunts.

teaser noun SEE **problem**.

teat noun nipple.

technical adjective **1** *technical data. technical details.* esoteric, expert, professional, specialized.
2 *technical skill.* engineering, mechanical, scientific.

technician noun engineer, mechanic, skilled worker, [*plural*] technical staff.

technique noun *the technique you need to do a task.* art, craft, craftsmanship, dodge, expertise, facility, knack, [*informal*] know-how, manner, means, method, mode, procedure, proficiency, routine, skill, system, trick, way, workmanship.

technological adjective *technological equipment.* advanced, automated, computerized, electronic, scientific.

technology noun BRANCHES OF SCIENCE AND TECHNOLOGY: SEE **science**.

tedious adjective *a tedious journey. a tedious lecture.* boring, dreary, dull, [*informal*] humdrum, irksome, laborious,

long-winded, monotonous, slow, tiresome, tiring, unexciting, uninteresting, wearisome.
OPPOSITES: SEE **interesting**.

tedium noun *We played games to relieve the tedium of the journey.* boredom, dreariness, dullness, long-windedness, monotony, slowness, tediousness.

teem verb *The pond teemed with tadpoles.* abound (in), be full (of), be infested, be overrun (by), [*informal*] crawl, seethe, swarm.

teenager noun adolescent, boy, girl, juvenile, minor, youngster, youth.

teeny adjective SEE **small**.

teeter verb *to teeter on the brink.* SEE **waver**.

teetotal adjective *He won't drink because he's teetotal.* abstemious, abstinent, restrained, self-denying, self-disciplined, temperate.
OPPOSITES: SEE **drunken**.

teetotaller noun abstainer, non-drinker.
OPPOSITES: SEE **drunkard**.

The prefix *tele-* is from Greek *tele=far off*.

---

telecommunications noun SEE **communication**.

telegram noun cable, fax, telex, wire.

telegraph, telegraphy nouns SEE **communication**.

telepathic adjective *If you know what I'm thinking, you must be telepathic.* clairvoyant, psychic.

telephone noun [*informal*] blower, carphone, handset, phone.

telephone verb *Telephone us if you can't come.* [*informal*] buzz, call, dial, [*informal*] give (someone) a call, phone, ring.
OTHER WAYS OF COMMUNICATING: SEE **communication**.

telephonist noun switchboard operator.

telerecording noun SEE **recording**.

telescope noun SEE **optical (optical instruments)**.

telescope verb *to telescope things together.* SEE **shorten**.

telescopic adjective *a tripod with telescopic legs.* adjustable, collapsible, expanding, extending, retractable.

televise verb *They televise a lot of snooker these days.* broadcast, relay, send out, transmit.

television noun monitor, receiver, [*informal*] telly, [*informal*] the box, [*informal*] the small screen, video.
OTHER WAYS OF COMMUNICATING: SEE **communication**.

TELEVISION PROGRAMMES: cartoon, chat show, comedy, commercial, documentary, drama, SEE **entertainment**, film, interview, mini series, movie, news, panel game, play, quiz, serial, series, [*informal*] sitcom, situation comedy, [*informal*] soap, soap opera, sport.

---

telex noun SEE **telegram**.

tell verb **1** *Tell the whole story.* announce, communicate, describe, disclose, divulge, explain, impart, make known, narrate, portray, recite, recount, rehearse, relate, reveal, speak, utter.
2 *Tell me the time.* acquaint (someone) with, advise, inform, notify.
3 *Can you tell the difference?* calculate, comprehend, decide, discover, discriminate, distinguish, identify, notice, recognize, see.
4 *He told me I could trust him.* assure, promise.
5 *Tell them to stop.* command, direct, instruct, order.
to tell someone off SEE **reprimand** verb.

teller noun **1** *a teller of tales.* SEE **storyteller**.
2 *a teller in a bank.* bank clerk, cashier.

telling adjective SEE **effective, striking**.

telling-off noun SEE **reprimand** noun.

tell-tale adjective *tell-tale signs.* SEE **significant**.

temerity noun SEE **audacity**.

temper noun **1** *in a good temper. in a bad temper.* attitude, disposition, humour, mood, state of mind, temperament.
2 *He sometimes flies into a temper.* fit (of anger), fury, [*informal*] paddy, passion, rage, tantrum.
3 *Try to keep your temper.* calmness, composure, coolness, sang-froid, self-control.
4 *Beware of his temper.* anger, irascibility, irritability, peevishness, petulance, surliness, unpredictability, volatility, wrath.

temper verb *to temper your opposition to something.* SEE **moderate** verb.

temperament noun *a melancholy temperament.* character, [*old-fashioned*] complexion, disposition, [*old-fashioned*] humour, nature, personality, spirit, temper.

temperamental adjective **1** *a temperamental aversion to work.* characteristic, congenital, constitutional, inherent, innate, natural.
2 *temperamental moods.* capricious, changeable, emotional, erratic, excitable, fickle, highly strung, impatient, inconsistent, inconstant, irritable, mercurial, moody, neurotic, passionate, touchy, unpredictable, unreliable, [*informal*] up and down, variable, volatile.

temperance noun SEE **moderation.**

temperate adjective SEE **moderate** adjective.

temperature noun SCALES FOR MEASURING TEMPERATURE: Celsius, centigrade, Fahrenheit.
to have a temperature be feverish, have a fever.

tempest noun SEE **storm** noun.

tempestuous adjective SEE **stormy.**

temple noun *a temple of the gods.* SEE **worship** noun (**place of worship**).

tempo noun *the tempo of a piece of music.* pace, rhythm, speed.

temporal adjective *temporal affairs.* earthly, impermanent, materialistic, mortal, mundane, passing, secular, sublunary, terrestrial, transient, transitory, worldly.
OPPOSITES: SEE **spiritual.**

temporary adjective **1** *a temporary building. a temporary arrangement.* brief, ephemeral, evanescent, fleeting, impermanent, interim, makeshift, momentary, passing, provisional, short, short-lived, short-term, stop-gap, transient, transitory.
OPPOSITES: SEE **permanent.**
2 *temporary captain.* acting.

temporize verb SEE **delay** verb.

tempt verb *I tempted the mouse with a bit of cheese.* allure, attract, bait, bribe, coax, decoy, entice, fascinate, inveigle, lure, persuade, seduce, tantalize, woo.

temptation noun *He succumbed to the temptations of the big city.* allurement, appeal, attraction, draw, enticement, fascination, lure, pull, seduction.

tempting adjective SEE **attractive.**

tenable adjective *a tenable theory.* arguable, credible, defensible, feasible, justifiable, legitimate, logical, plausible, rational, reasonable, sensible, sound, understandable, viable.
OPPOSITES: SEE **untenable.**

tenacious adjective *a tenacious hold on something.* determined, dogged, firm, intransigent, obdurate, obstinate, pertinacious, resolute, single-minded, strong, stubborn, tight, unshakeable, unswerving, unwavering, unyielding.
OPPOSITES: SEE **weak.**

tenant noun *the tenant of a rented flat.* inhabitant, leaseholder, lessee, lodger, occupant, resident.

tend verb **1** *A shepherd tends sheep.* attend to, care for, cherish, cultivate, guard, keep, look after, manage, mind, protect, watch.
2 *Doctors tend the sick.* nurse, treat.
3 *I tend to fall asleep in the evening.* be disposed to, be inclined to, be liable to, have a tendency to [SEE **tendency**], incline.

tendency noun *a tendency to be lazy.* bias, disposition, inclination, instinct, leaning, liability, partiality, penchant, predilection, predisposition, proclivity, propensity, readiness, susceptibility, trend.

tendentious adjective SEE **prejudiced.**

tender adjective **1** *tender meat.* eatable, edible.
OPPOSITES: SEE **tough.**
2 *tender plants.* dainty, delicate, fleshy, fragile, frail, soft, succulent, vulnerable, weak.
OPPOSITES: SEE **hardy.**
3 *a tender wound.* aching, painful, sensitive, smarting, sore.
4 *a tender love-song.* emotional, moving, poignant, romantic, sentimental, touching.
OPPOSITES: SEE **cynical.**
5 *tender care.* affectionate, caring, compassionate, concerned, considerate, fond, gentle, humane, kind, loving, merciful, pitying, soft-hearted, sympathetic, tender-hearted, warm-hearted.
OPPOSITES: SEE **callous.**

tenet noun SEE **principle.**

tense adjective **1** *tense muscles.* strained, stretched, taut, tight.
2 *a tense atmosphere.* anxious, apprehensive, edgy, excited, exciting, fidgety, highly strung, jittery, jumpy, [*informal*] nail-biting, nerve-racking, nervous, restless, stressed, [*informal*] strung up, touchy, uneasy, [*informal*] uptight, worried, worrying.
OPPOSITES: SEE **relaxed.**

tense noun TENSES OF A VERB: future, imperfect, past, perfect, pluperfect, present.
LINGUISTIC TERMS: SEE **language.**

tension noun **1** *the tension of guy ropes.* strain, stretching, tautness, tightness.
OPPOSITE: slackness.
2 *the tension of waiting for an answer.* anxiety, apprehension, excitement,

nervousness, stress, suspense, unease, worry.
OPPOSITES: SEE **relaxation**.

tent noun KINDS OF TENT: bell tent, big-top, frame tent, marquee, ridge tent, tepee, trailer tent, wigwam.

tentacle noun *the tentacles of an octopus.* feeler, limb.

tentative adjective 1 *a tentative attempt.* cautious, diffident, doubtful, half-hearted, hesitant, indecisive, indefinite, nervous, timid, uncertain, [*informal*] wishy-washy.
2 *a tentative enquiry.* experimental, preliminary, provisional, speculative, uncommitted.
OPPOSITES: SEE **decisive**.

tenuous adjective *a tenuous connection. a tenuous line of argument.* fine, flimsy, insubstantial, slight, SEE **thin** adjective, weak.
OPPOSITES: SEE **strong**.

tepid adjective 1 *tepid bath-water.* lukewarm, warm.
2 *a tepid response.* SEE **apathetic**.

term noun 1 *a term in prison.* duration, period, season, span, spell, stretch, time.
2 *a school term.* [*American*] semester, session.
3 *a technical term. a foreign term.* epithet, expression, phrase, saying, title, word.
terms 1 *the terms of an agreement.* conditions, particulars, provisions, specifications, stipulations.
2 *a hotel's terms.* charges, fees, prices, rates, tariff.

termagant noun SEE **woman**.

terminal adjective *a terminal illness.* deadly, fatal, final, incurable, killing, lethal, mortal.

terminal noun 1 *a computer terminal.* VDU, work-station.
2 *a passenger terminal.* SEE **airport**, destination, terminus.
3 *an electrical terminal.* connection, connector.

terminate verb SEE **end** verb.

termination noun SEE **end** noun.

terminology noun *I didn't understand her terminology.* choice of words, jargon, language, phraseology, special terms, technical language, vocabulary.

terminus noun destination, terminal, termination.

termite noun SEE **insect**.

terrace noun *a terrace in the garden.* patio, paved area.

A number of English words, including *extraterrestrial, Mediterranean, terrain,* and *territory,* are related to Latin *terra* = *earth.*

---

terra firma noun SEE **land** noun.

terrain noun *They made slow progress across difficult terrain.* country, ground, land, landscape, SEE **territory**, topography.

terrestrial adjective *terrestrial beings.* earthly, mundane, ordinary.
OPPOSITE: extraterrestrial.

terrible adjective 1 *a terrible accident. terrible living-conditions.* appalling, distressing, dreadful, fearful, frightful, ghastly, hideous, horrible, horrific, horrifying, insupportable, intolerable, loathsome, nasty, outrageous, revolting, shocking, unbearable, unpleasant, vile.
2 [*informal*] *This coffee is terrible!* SEE **bad**.

terrific adjective [Like *terrible, terrific* is related to Latin *terrere* meaning *to frighten* and to our English word *terror*. However, the meaning of *terrific* is now vague. It is used informally to describe anything which is extreme in its own way, e.g. *We faced a terrific problem.* SEE **extreme**; *My fish was a terrific size.* SEE **big**; *We had a terrific time.* SEE **excellent**; *There was a terrific storm.* SEE **violent**.]

terrified adjective afraid, appalled, dismayed, SEE **frightened**, horrified, horror-struck, panicky, petrified, terror-stricken, unnerved.
OPPOSITES: SEE **calm** adjective.

terrify verb appal, dismay, SEE **frighten**, horrify, petrify, scare, shock, terrorize, unnerve.

terrifying adjective blood-curdling, dreadful, SEE **frightening**, hair-raising, horrifying, petrifying, [*informal*] scary, spine-chilling, traumatic, unnerving.

territory noun *enemy territory.* area, colony, SEE **country**, [*old-fashioned*] demesne, district, dominion, enclave, jurisdiction, land, preserve, province, region, sector, sphere [*sphere of influence*), state, terrain, tract, zone.

terror noun alarm, consternation, dread, SEE **fear** noun, [*informal*] funk, fright, horror, panic, shock, trepidation.

terrorist noun assassin, SEE **criminal** noun, gunman, hijacker.

terrorize verb *A criminal gang terrorized the neighbourhood.* browbeat, bully, coerce, cow, SEE **frighten**, intimidate, menace, persecute, terrify, threaten, torment, tyrannize.

terror-stricken adjective SEE **terrified**.

terse adjective *a terse comment.* SEE **brief** adjective, brusque, concise, crisp, curt, epigrammatic, incisive, laconic, pithy, short, [*informal*] snappy, succinct, to the point.
OPPOSITES: SEE **verbose**.

tessellation noun SEE **pattern**.

test noun *You have to pass a test before you get the job.* appraisal, assessment, audition, [*informal*] check-over, evaluation, examination, interrogation, investigation, probation, quiz, trial.

test verb *to test a theory. to test the quality of a product or a substance. to test a candidate.* analyse, appraise, assay, assess, audition, check, evaluate, examine, experiment with, inspect, interrogate, investigate, [*informal*] put someone through their paces, put to the test, screen, question, try out.

testament noun SEE **statement**.

testify verb *to testify in a court of law.* affirm, attest, bear witness, declare, give evidence, state on oath, swear, vouch, witness.

testimonial noun *a testimonial for an applicant for a job.* character reference, commendation, recommendation, reference.

testimony noun *testimony given in court.* affidavit, declaration, deposition, evidence, statement, submission, witness.
LEGAL TERMS: SEE **law**.

test-tube noun SEE **container**.

testy, tetchy adjectives SEE **irritable**.

tête-à-tête noun SEE **conversation**.

tether noun *an animal's tether.* chain, cord, halter, lead, leash, rope.

tether verb *to tether an animal.* chain up, SEE **fasten**, keep on a tether, restrain, rope, secure, tie up.

text noun **1** *the text of a document.* argument, contents, matter, wording.
2 *a literary text.* book, textbook, work, SEE **writing**.
3 *the text of a sermon. a text from the Bible.* motif, passage of scripture, sentence, theme, topic, verse.

textbook noun VARIOUS KINDS OF BOOK: SEE **book** noun.

textiles noun SEE **cloth**, fabric, material, stuff.

texture noun *the soft texture of velvet.* composition, consistency, feel, quality, touch.

thane noun SEE **lord**.

thank verb *to thank someone for a kindness.* acknowledge, express thanks [SEE **thanks**].

thankful adjective *thankful to be home.* appreciative, contented, grateful, happy, pleased, relieved.
OPPOSITES: SEE **ungrateful**.

thankless adjective *a thankless task.* unappreciated, unrecognized, unrewarded, unrewarding.
OPPOSITES: SEE **rewarding**.

thanks noun acknowledgement, appreciation, gratefulness, gratitude, recognition, thanksgiving.

thanksgiving noun SEE **thanks**.

thatch noun SEE **roof**.

thaw verb *The snow thawed.* become liquid, defrost, melt, soften, uncongeal, unfreeze, unthaw, warm up.
OPPOSITES: SEE **freeze**.

theatre noun auditorium, drama studio, hall, opera-house, playhouse.

THEATRICAL ENTERTAINMENTS: ballet, comedy, drama, farce, masque, melodrama, mime, music-hall, nativity play, opera, operetta, pantomime, play, tragedy.

OTHER ENTERTAINMENTS: SEE **entertainment**.

KINDS OF PERFORMANCE: command performance, dress rehearsal, first night, last night, matinée, première, preview, production, rehearsal, show.

THEATRE PEOPLE: actor, actress, backstage staff, ballerina, dancer, director, dresser, make-up artist, performer, player, producer, prompter, stage-manager, understudy, usher or usherette.

PARTS OF A THEATRE: back-stage, balcony, box-office, circle, dressing-room, foyer, front of house, gallery, [*informal*] the gods, [*old-fashioned*] pit, stage, stalls.

---

theatrical adjective **1** *I made my first theatrical appearance in a Shakespeare play.* dramatic, histrionic.
2 *He made the announcement in a theatrical manner.* demonstrative, exaggerated, melodramatic, ostentatious, pompous, self-important, showy, stagy, stilted, unnatural.
OPPOSITES: SEE **natural**.

theft noun SEE **stealing**.

theme noun **1** *the theme of a talk.* argument, idea, issue, keynote, matter, subject, text, thesis, topic.

2 *a musical theme.* air, melody, motif, [*formal*] subject, tune.

theology noun divinity, religion.

theoretical adjective *theoretical knowledge.* abstract, academic, conjectural, doctrinaire, hypothetical, ideal, notional, pure (*pure science*), speculative, unproven, untested.
OPPOSITES: SEE **applied, empirical.**

theorize verb *to theorize about a problem.* conjecture, form a theory, hypothesize, speculate.

theory noun **1** *My theory would explain what happened.* argument, assumption, belief, conjecture, explanation, guess, hypothesis, idea, notion, speculation, supposition, surmise, thesis, view.
2 *the theory of musical composition.* laws, principles, rules, science.
OPPOSITES: SEE **practice.**

Several English words like *therapeutic* and *therapy* are related to Greek *therapeia = healing.*

---

therapeutic adjective *When I was sad, music had a therapeutic effect.* beneficial, corrective, curative, healing, helpful, restorative.
OPPOSITES: SEE **harmful.**

therapist noun healer, physiotherapist, psychotherapist.

therapy noun cure, healing, remedy, tonic, treatment.

SOME KINDS OF THERAPY: chemotherapy, group therapy, hydrotherapy, hypnotherapy, occupational therapy, physiotherapy, psychotherapy, radiotherapy.
OTHER MEDICAL TREATMENT: SEE **medicine.**

---

therefore adverb accordingly, consequently, hence, so, thus.

Several English words like *thermal, thermometer,* and *Thermos* are related to Greek *therm = heat.*

---

thermal adjective SEE **hot.**

Thermos noun vacuum flask.

thesaurus noun OTHER KINDS OF BOOK: SEE **book** noun.

thesis noun **1** *She argued a convincing thesis.* argument, hypothesis, idea, premise or premiss, proposition, theory, view.
2 *He wrote a thesis about his research.* disquisition, dissertation, essay, monograph, paper, tract, treatise.

thick adjective **1** *a thick book. thick rope. a thick line.* broad, [*informal*] bulky, chunky, fat, stout, sturdy, substantial, wide.
2 *thick snow. thick cloth.* deep, heavy.
3 *a thick crowd.* dense, impenetrable, numerous, packed, solid.
4 *The place was thick with photographers.* covered, filled, swarming, teeming.
5 *thick mud. thick cream.* clotted, coagulated, concentrated, condensed, heavy, stiff, viscous.
OPPOSITES: SEE **thin** adjective.
6 [*informal*] *a thick pupil.* SEE **stupid.**

thicken verb *to thicken a sauce.* concentrate, condense, reduce, stiffen.

thicket noun SEE **wood.**

thick-headed adjective SEE **stupid.**

thickness noun **1** *a thickness of paint.* coating, layer.
2 *a thickness of rock.* seam, stratum.

thickset adjective SEE **stocky.**

thick-skinned adjective SEE **insensitive.**

thick-witted adjective SEE **stupid.**

thief noun bandit, burglar, SEE **criminal** noun, embezzler, highwayman, housebreaker, looter, mugger, pickpocket, pirate, plagiarist [*= person who steals other people's ideas*], poacher, robber, shop-lifter, stealer, swindler.

thieve verb SEE **steal.**

thieving adjective *The thieving rogue!* SEE **dishonest**, light-fingered, rapacious.

thieving noun SEE **stealing.**

thigh noun SEE **leg.**

thin adjective **1** *a thin figure.* anorexic, attenuated, bony, emaciated, flat-chested, gaunt, lanky, lean, narrow, rangy, scraggy, scrawny, skeletal, skinny, slender, slight, slim, small, spare, spindly, underweight, wiry.
OPPOSITES: SEE **fat** adjective.
2 *thin cloth.* delicate, diaphanous, filmy, fine, flimsy, insubstantial, light, sheer (*sheer silk*), wispy.
3 *thin gravy.* dilute, flowing, fluid, runny, watery.
4 *a thin crowd.* meagre, scanty, scarce, scattered, sparse.
OPPOSITES: SEE **thick.**
5 *a thin atmosphere.* rarefied.
OPPOSITES: SEE **dense.**
6 *a thin excuse.* feeble, implausible, tenuous, unconvincing.
OPPOSITES: SEE **convincing.**

thin verb *to thin paint.* dilute, water down, weaken.
to thin out 1 *The crowd thinned out.* become less dense, diminish, disperse.
2 *to thin out seedlings. to thin out a hedge.* make less dense, prune, trim, weed out.

thing noun **1** *a thing you can touch or hold.* artefact, article, body, device, entity, implement, item, object.
2 *a thing that happens.* affair, circumstance, deed, event, eventuality, happening, incident, occurrence, phenomenon.
3 *a thing on your mind. things you want to say.* concept, detail, fact, factor, idea, point, statement, thought.
4 *a thing you have to do.* act, action, job, task.
5 [*informal*] *He's got a thing about snakes.* [*informal*] hang-up, obsession, phobia, preoccupation.
things 1 *Put your things in the back of the car.* baggage, belongings, clothing, equipment, [*informal*] gear, luggage, possessions, [*informal*] stuff.
2 *Things improved when I found a place to live.* circumstances, conditions, life.

think verb **1** *I thought about my mistakes.* attend, brood, cogitate, concentrate, consider, contemplate, deliberate, give thought (to), meditate, [*informal*] mull over, muse, ponder, [*informal*] rack your brains, reason, reflect, ruminate, use your intelligence, work things out, worry.
2 *He thinks that science can explain everything.* accept, admit, be convinced, believe, conclude, deem, have faith, judge.
3 *I think she's angry.* assume, believe, be under the impression, estimate, feel, guess, imagine, presume, reckon, suppose, surmise.
to think better of *When I saw the rain, I thought better of going out.* change your mind about, reconsider, revise your opinion of.
to think out *She thought out how to do it.* analyse, answer, calculate, puzzle out, work out.
to think twice about *I'd think twice about taking a cut in wages.* be cautious, think carefully.
to think up *We thought up a plan.* conceive, concoct, create, design, devise, [*informal*] dream up, imagine, improvise, invent, make up.

thinker noun *Plato was one of the world's great thinkers.* [*informal*] brain, innovator, intellect, philosopher.

thinking adjective *She said that all thinking people would agree with her.* educated, intelligent, rational, reasonable, sensible, thoughtful.
OPPOSITES: SEE **stupid**.

thin-skinned adjective SEE **sensitive**.

thirst noun **1** *a thirst for water.* drought, dryness, thirstiness.
2 *a thirst for knowledge.* appetite, craving, desire, eagerness, hunger, itch, longing, love (of), lust, passion, urge, wish, yearning.
to have a thirst SEE **thirst** verb.

thirst verb *to thirst after* be thirsty for [SEE **thirsty**], crave, have a thirst for, hunger after, long for, need, strive after, want, wish for, yearn for.

thirsty adjective **1** *thirsty after a long walk.* dehydrated, dry, [*informal*] gasping (for a drink), panting, parched.
2 *thirsty for adventure.* avid, eager, greedy, itching, longing, yearning.

thong noun SEE **lace** noun.

thorax noun chest.

thorn noun *thorns on a rose-bush.* barb, needle, prickle, spike, spine.

thorny adjective **1** *a thorny bush.* barbed, bristly, prickly, scratchy, sharp, spiky, spiny.
OPPOSITE: thornless.
2 [*informal*] *a thorny problem.* SEE **difficult**.

thorough adjective **1** *a thorough piece of work.* assiduous, attentive, careful, comprehensive, conscientious, diligent, efficient, exhaustive, full, [*informal*] in-depth, methodical, meticulous, observant, orderly, organized, painstaking, scrupulous, systematic, thoughtful, watchful.
OPPOSITES: SEE **superficial**.
2 [*informal*] *He's a thorough rascal!* absolute, arrant, complete, downright, out-and-out, perfect, thoroughgoing, total, unmitigated, unqualified, utter.
OPPOSITES: SEE **incomplete**.

thoroughfare noun SEE **road**.

thoroughgoing adjective SEE **thorough**.

thought noun **1** *deep in thought.* [*informal*] brainwork, brooding, [*informal*] brown study (*in a brown study*), cogitation, concentration, consideration, contemplation, day-dreaming, deliberation, introspection, meditation, musing, pensiveness, reasoning, reflection, reverie, rumination, study, thinking, worrying.
2 *a clever thought.* belief, concept, conception, conclusion, conjecture, conviction, idea, notion, opinion.

3 *We had no thought of staying so long.* aim, design, expectation, intention, objective, plan, purpose.
4 *It was a nice thought to give them flowers.* attention, concern, kindness, solicitude, thoughtfulness.

thoughtful adjective 1 *a thoughtful expression.* absorbed, abstracted, anxious, attentive, brooding, contemplative, dreamy, grave, introspective, meditative, pensive, philosophical, rapt, reflective, serious, solemn, studious, wary, watchful, worried.
2 *a thoughtful piece of work.* careful, conscientious, diligent, exhaustive, methodical, meticulous, observant, orderly, organized, painstaking, scrupulous, systematic, thorough.
3 *a thoughtful kindness.* attentive, caring, concerned, considerate, friendly, good-natured, helpful, SEE **kind** adjective, obliging, public-spirited, solicitous, unselfish.
OPPOSITES: SEE **thoughtless**.

thoughtless adjective 1 *thoughtless stupidity.* absent-minded, careless, forgetful, hasty, heedless, ill-considered, impetuous, inadvertent, inattentive, injudicious, irresponsible, mindless, negligent, rash, reckless, [*informal*] scatter-brained, SEE **stupid**, unobservant, unthinking.
2 *a thoughtless insult.* cruel, heartless, impolite, inconsiderate, insensitive, rude, selfish, tactless, uncaring, undiplomatic, unfeeling, SEE **unkind**.
OPPOSITES: SEE **thoughtful**.

thrall noun SEE **slave** noun.

thrash verb 1 *to thrash with a stick.* SEE **whip** verb.
2 [*informal*] *to thrash your opponents.* SEE **defeat** verb.

thread noun 1 *threads in a piece of cloth.* fibre, filament, hair, strand.
KINDS OF THREAD: cotton, silk, thong, twine, wool, yarn.
2 *the thread of a story.* argument, continuity, course, direction, line of thought, story-line, theme.

thread verb *to thread beads.* put on a thread, string together.
to thread your way SEE **pass** verb.

threadbare adjective *threadbare clothes.* frayed, old, ragged, shabby, tattered, tatty, worn, worn-out.

threat noun 1 *threats against his life.* menace, warning.
2 *a threat of snow.* danger, forewarning, omen, portent, presage, risk, warning.

threaten verb 1 *A gang of hooligans threatened us.* browbeat, bully, SEE **frighten**, intimidate, make threats against, menace, pressurize, terrorize.
2 *The forecast threatened rain.* forebode, foreshadow, forwarn of, give warning of, portend, presage, warn of.
3 *An avalanche threatened the town.* endanger, imperil, jeopardize.
OPPOSITES: SEE **reassure**.

threatening adjective *threatening storm-clouds.* forbidding, grim, menacing, minatory, ominous, sinister, stern, unfriendly, worrying.
OPPOSITES: SEE **reassuring**.

three noun [=*a group of three*]. triad, trio, triplet, triumvirate.
RELATED ADJECTIVES: SEE **triple**.

three-cornered adjective triangular.

three-dimensional adjective rounded, solid, stereoscopic.

thresh verb **to thresh about** SEE **writhe**.

threshold noun 1 *the threshold of a house.* doorstep, doorway, entrance, sill.
2 *the threshold of a new era.* SEE **beginning**.

thrifty adjective *thrifty with your money.* careful, economical, frugal, parsimonious, provident, prudent, sparing.
OPPOSITES: SEE **extravagant**.

thrill noun *the thrill of a fun-fair.* adventure, [*informal*] buzz, excitement, [*informal*] kick, pleasure, sensation, suspense, tingle, tremor.

thrill verb *The music thrilled us.* delight, electrify, excite, rouse, stimulate, stir, titillate.
OPPOSITES: SEE **bore** verb.

thriller noun crime story, detective story, mystery, [*informal*] whodunit.
VARIOUS KINDS OF WRITING: SEE **writing**.

thrilling adjective *thrilling feats.* electrifying, exciting, extraordinary, gripping, [*informal*] hair-raising, rousing, sensational, spectacular, stimulating, stirring.
OPPOSITES: SEE **boring**.

thrive verb *Tomato plants thrive in my greenhouse.* be vigorous, burgeon, develop strongly, do well, flourish, grow, prosper, succeed.
OPPOSITES: SEE **die**.

thriving adjective *a thriving business.* affluent, alive, booming, burgeoning, developing, expanding, flourishing, growing, healthy, profitable, prosperous, successful, vigorous.
OPPOSITES: SEE **dying**.

throat noun gullet, neck, oesophagus, uvula, wind pipe.
RELATED ADJECTIVE: guttural.
OTHER PARTS OF YOUR BODY: SEE **body**.

throaty adjective *a throaty voice.* deep, gravelly, gruff, guttural, hoarse, husky, rasping, rough, thick.

throb noun **1** *a throb of toothache.* SEE **pain** noun.
2 *the throb of music.* SEE **rhythm**.

throb verb *Blood throbs through our veins.* beat, palpitate, pound, pulsate, pulse.

throes plural noun *the throes of childbirth.* convulsions, effort, labour, labour-pains, pangs, spasms.

thrombosis noun blood-clot, embolism.

throne noun OTHER SEATS: SEE **seat** noun.

throng noun, verb SEE **crowd** noun, verb.

throttle noun SEE **valve**.

throttle verb asphyxiate, choke, SEE **kill**, smother, stifle, strangle, suffocate.

throw verb **1** *to throw a ball. to throw stones at something.* bowl, [*informal*] bung, cast, [*informal*] chuck, fling, heave, hurl, launch, lob, pelt, pitch, project, propel, put (*to put the shot*), [*informal*] shy, [*informal*] sling, toss.
2 *The horse threw the rider.* dislodge, shake off, throw off, unseat.
3 [*informal*] *The unexpected question threw me.* SEE **disconcert**.
to throw away *I threw away some old clothes.* SEE **discard**.
to throw out *He threw out a gatecrasher.* SEE **expel**.
to throw up 1 *The enquiry threw up new evidence.* SEE **produce**.
2 [*informal*] SEE **vomit**.
to throw in the towel, to throw up the sponge SEE **surrender**.

throwaway adjective **1** *throwaway plastic cups.* cheap, disposable.
2 *a throwaway remark.* casual, offhand, passing, unimportant.

thrust verb **1** *to thrust someone or something forward.* drive, force, press, propel, push, send, shove, urge.
2 *to thrust with a dagger.* jab, lunge, plunge, poke, prod, stab, stick.

thud noun, verb VARIOUS SOUNDS: SEE **sound** noun.

thug noun [*informal*] bully-boy, SEE **criminal** noun, delinquent, gangster, hooligan, killer, mugger, ruffian, [*informal*] tough, trouble-maker, vandal, [*informal*] yob.

thumb verb *to thumb through a book.* SEE **browse**.
to thumb your nose at SEE **insult** verb.

thump noun, verb SEE **hit** noun, verb.

thumping adjective SEE **large**.

thunder noun, verb WORDS FOR THE SOUND OF THUNDER: clap, crack, peal, roll, rumble.

thunderous adjective SEE **loud**.

thunderstorm noun SEE **storm** noun.

thunderstruck adjective SEE **amazed**.

thus adverb accordingly, consequently, hence, so, therefore.

thwack noun, verb SEE **hit** noun, verb.

thwart verb *to thwart someone's wishes.* foil, frustrate, hinder, impede, obstruct, prevent, stand in the way of, stop.

tiara noun diadem, crown.

tic noun *a nervous tic.* SEE **twitch** noun.

tick noun, verb *the tick of a clock.* VARIOUS SOUNDS: SEE **sound** noun.
to tick someone off SEE **reprimand** verb.

ticket noun **1** *an entry ticket.* coupon, pass, permit, token, voucher.
2 *a price ticket.* docket, label, marker, tab, tag.

ticking noun SEE **cloth**.

tickle verb **1** *to tickle someone with your fingertips.* SEE **touch** verb.
2 *My foot tickles.* SEE **itch** verb.
3 [*informal*] *His antics tickled us.* SEE **amuse**.

ticklish adjective **1** *Are you ticklish?* [*informal*] giggly, responsive to tickling, sensitive.
2 *a ticklish problem.* awkward, delicate, difficult, risky, [*informal*] thorny, touchy, tricky.

tidal adjective *tidal waters.* ebbing and flowing.
OPPOSITE: tideless.
tidal wave SEE **wave** noun.

tide noun *the tides of the sea.* current, drift, ebb and flow, movement, rise and fall.

tidiness noun *I admire her tidiness.* meticulousness, neatness, order, orderliness, organization, system.
OPPOSITES: SEE **disorder**.

tidings noun [*old-fashioned*] *good tidings.* SEE **news**.

tidy adjective **1** *tidy in appearance.* neat, orderly, presentable, shipshape, smart, spick and span, spruce, straight, trim, uncluttered, well-groomed.
2 *tidy in your habits.* businesslike, careful, house-proud, methodical, meticulous, organized, systematic.
OPPOSITES: SEE **untidy**.

tidy verb *Please tidy your room.* arrange, clean up, groom (*your hair*), make tidy [SEE **tidy** adjective], neaten, put in order, set straight, smarten, spruce up, straighten, titivate.
OPPOSITES: SEE **muddle** verb.

tie verb **1** *to tie something with string.* bind, SEE **fasten**, hitch, interlace, join, knot, lash, truss up.
OPPOSITES: SEE **untie.**
2 *to tie with an opponent in a game.* be equal, be level, draw.
to tie up *to tie up a boat or an animal.* anchor, moor, secure, tether.

tier noun *seats arranged in tiers.* level, line, rank, row, stage, storey, terrace.

tiff noun SEE **quarrel** noun.

tiffin noun SEE **meal.**

tight adjective **1** *a tight fit.* close, close-fitting, fast, firm, fixed, immovable, secure, snug.
2 *a jar with a tight lid.* airtight, hermetic, impervious, sealed, watertight.
3 *tight controls.* inflexible, precise, rigorous, severe, strict, stringent.
4 *tight ropes.* rigid, stiff, stretched, taut, tense.
5 *a tight space.* compact, constricted, crammed, cramped, crowded, dense, packed.
OPPOSITES: SEE **loose.**
6 [*informal*] *tight after drinking a few beers.* SEE **drunk.**
7 [*informal*] *tight with her money.* SEE **miserly.**

tighten verb **1** *to tighten your grip.* clamp down, constrict, hold tighter, squeeze, tense.
2 *to tighten a rope.* pull tighter, stretch, tauten.
3 *to tighten a screw.* give another turn to, make tighter, screw up.
OPPOSITES: SEE **loosen.**

tight-fisted adjective SEE **miserly.**

tights noun panti-hose.

tile noun OTHER ROOFING MATERIALS: SEE **roof.**

tile verb *to tile a floor.* SEE **cover** verb.

till noun *money in the till.* cash-register.

till verb *to till the land.* SEE **cultivate.**

tiller noun *the tiller of a boat.* helm.

tilt verb **1** *to tilt to one side.* careen, incline, keel over, lean, list, slant, slope, tip.
2 *to tilt with lances.* SEE **fight** verb, joust, thrust.
at full tilt SEE **fast** adjective.

timber noun *a house built of timber.* beams, boarding, boards, deal, lath, logs, lumber, planking, planks, posts, softwood, trees, tree trunks, SEE **wood.**

timbre noun SEE **sound** noun.

time noun **1** [=*a moment in time*] date, hour, instant, juncture, moment, occasion, opportunity.
2 [=*a length of time*] duration, period, phase, season, semester, session, spell, stretch, term, while.
3 *the time of Elizabeth I.* age, days, epoch, era, period.
4 *Keep time with the music.* beat, rhythm, tempo.
RELATED ADJECTIVE: chronological.
in no time SEE **fast** adjective.
on time SEE **punctual.**

UNITS OF TIME: aeon, century, day, decade, eternity, fortnight, hour, instant, leap year, lifetime, minute, month, second, week, weekend, year.

DEVICES FOR MEASURING TIME: calendar, chronometer, clock, digital clock, digital watch, hour-glass, stop-watch, sundial, timepiece, timer, watch, wristwatch.

SPECIAL TIMES OF THE YEAR: Advent, autumn, Christmas, Easter, equinox, Hallowe'en, hogmanay, Lent, midsummer, midwinter, New Year, Passover, Ramadan, solstice, spring, summer, Whitsun, winter, Yom Kippur, yuletide.

TIMES OF THE DAY: SEE **day.**

---

time verb **1** *I timed my arrival to coincide with hers.* choose a time for, estimate, fix a time for, judge, schedule, timetable.
2 *You use a stop-watch to time a race.* clock, measure the time (of).

time-consuming adjective SEE **long** adjective.

time-honoured adjective SEE **traditional.**

timekeeper noun SEE **supervisor.**

time-lag noun SEE **interval.**

timeless adjective SEE **immortal.**

timely adjective appropriate, apt, fitting, suitable.

timepiece, timer nouns DEVICES FOR MEASURING TIME: SEE **time** noun.

time-share adjective SEE **accommodation.**

timetable noun *a timetable of events.* agenda, calendar, diary, list, programme, roster, rota, schedule.

timid adjective *Don't be timid—dive in at the deep end!* afraid, apprehensive, bashful, cowardly, coy, diffident, faint-hearted, fearful, [*informal*] mousy, nervous, pusillanimous, reserved, retiring, sheepish, shrinking, shy, spineless, tentative, timorous, unadventurous, unheroic.
OPPOSITES: SEE **bold.**

timorous adjective SEE **timid**.

timpani plural noun kettledrums.
OTHER DRUMS: SEE **drum**.

timpanist noun drummer, kettledrummer.

tin noun **1** OTHER METALS: SEE **metal**.
2 *a tin of beans.* can.
OTHER CONTAINERS: SEE **container**.

tin verb *to tin food.* can.
OTHER WAYS TO PRESERVE FOOD: SEE **preserve** verb.

tine noun SEE **prong**.

ting noun, verb VARIOUS SOUNDS: SEE **sound** noun.

tinge noun, verb SEE **colour** noun, verb.

tingle noun **1** *a tingle under the skin.* itch, itching, pins and needles, prickling, stinging, tickle, tickling.
2 *a tingle of excitement.* quiver, sensation, shiver, thrill.

tingle verb *I tingle where I sat in the nettles.* itch, prickle, sting, tickle.

tinker verb *Don't tinker with the TV.* fiddle, interfere, meddle, [*informal*] mess about, [*informal*] play about, tamper, try to mend, work amateurishly.

tinkle noun, verb VARIOUS SOUNDS: SEE **sound** noun.

tinny adjective [*informal*] *a tinny old car.* cheap, inferior, poor-quality.
OPPOSITES: SEE **solid**.

tinsel noun *decorated with tinsel.* glitter, sparkle, tin foil.

tint noun, verb SEE **colour** noun, verb.

tiny adjective *a tiny insect, a tiny amount.* diminutive, imperceptible, infinitesimal, insignificant, microscopic, midget, [*informal*] mini, miniature, minuscule, minute, negligible, pygmy, SEE **small**, [*informal*] teeny, unimportant, [*informal*] wee, [*informal*] weeny.
OPPOSITES: SEE **big**.

tip noun **1** *the tip of a pen or pencil.* end, extremity, nib, point, sharp end.
2 *the tip of a mountain or iceberg.* apex, cap, crown, head, peak, pinnacle, summit, top.
3 *a tip for the waiter.* gift, gratuity, money, [*informal*] perk, present, reward, service-charge.
4 *useful tips on how to do it.* advice, clue, hint, information, suggestion, warning.
5 *a rubbish tip.* dump, rubbish-heap.

tip verb **1** *to tip to one side.* careen, incline, keel over, lean, list, slant, slope, tilt.
2 *to tip something from a container.* dump, empty, pour out, spill, unload.
3 *to tip a waiter.* give a tip to, remunerate, reward.
to tip over *A wave tipped the boat over.* capsize, knock over, overturn, topple, turn over, upset.

tip-off noun SEE **information**.

tipple noun, verb SEE **drink** noun, verb.

tipsy adjective SEE **drunk**.

tiptoe verb SEE **walk** verb.

tiptop adjective SEE **excellent**.

tirade noun SEE **attack** noun.

tire verb *The long game tired us.* drain, enervate, exhaust, fatigue, [*informal*] finish, make tired [SEE **tired**], overtire, tax, wear out, weary.
OPPOSITES: SEE **refresh**.

tired adjective [*informal*] dead beat, [*informal*] dog-tired, [*informal*] done in, drawn [= *looking tired*], drained, drowsy, exhausted, [*informal*] fagged, fatigued, flagging, footsore, jaded, [*informal*] jet-lagged, [*slang*] knackered, listless, [*informal*] shattered, sleepy, spent, travel-weary, wearied, weary, [*informal*] whacked, worn out.
tired of *I'm tired of all this noise.* bored with, [*informal*] fed up with, impatient with, sick of, [*informal*] sick and tired.

tiredness noun drowsiness, exhaustion, fatigue, inertia, jet-lag, lassitude, lethargy, listlessness, sleepiness, weariness.

tireless adjective *a tireless worker.* determined, diligent, energetic, indefatigable, persistent, sedulous, unceasing, unflagging, untiring.
OPPOSITES: SEE **lazy**.

tiresome adjective *tiresome interruptions.* annoying, bothersome, distracting, exasperating, irksome, irritating, petty, troublesome, unwelcome, vexing, wearisome.
OPPOSITES: SEE **welcome** adjective.

tiring adjective *tiring work.* demanding, difficult, exhausting, fatiguing, hard, laborious, taxing, wearying.
OPPOSITES: SEE **refreshing**.

tiro noun SEE **inexperienced (inexperienced person)**.

tissue noun **1** *bodily tissue.* material, structure, stuff, substance.
2 *paper tissue.* tissue-paper, tracing-paper.
3 *a box of tissues.* handkerchief, napkin, serviette.

titanic adjective SEE **huge**.

titbit noun SEE **piece**.

titillate verb SEE **excite**.

titivate verb SEE **tidy** verb.

title noun **1** *the title of a picture or story.* caption, heading, name.
2 *a person's title.* appellation, designation, form of address, office, position, rank, status.
3 *the title to an inheritance.* claim, entitlement, ownership, prerogative, right.

TITLES YOU USE BEFORE SOMEONE'S NAME: Baron, Baroness, Count, Countess, Dame, Dr or Doctor, Duchess, Duke, Earl, Lady, Lord, Marchioness, Marquis, Master, Miss, Mr, Mrs, Ms, Professor, Rev or Reverend, Sir, Viscount, Viscountess.

OTHER TITLES: SEE **rank** noun, **royalty**.

TITLES YOU USE WHEN ADDRESSING PEOPLE: madam or madame, my lady, my lord, sir, sire, your grace, your honour, your majesty.

---

title verb *to title a story.* entitle, give a title to, name.

titled adjective *a titled family.* aristocratic, noble.
a titled person SEE **peer** noun.

titter verb chuckle, giggle, SEE **laugh**, snigger.

tittle-tattle verb SEE **gossip** verb.

titular adjective *the titular head of state.* formal, nominal, official, theoretical, token.
OPPOSITES: SEE **actual**.

tizzy noun [*informal*] **in a tizzy** SEE **confused**.

T-junction noun SEE **junction**.

toady noun SEE **flatterer**.

toady verb SEE **flatter**.

toast verb **1** *to toast bread.* brown, grill.
OTHER WAYS TO COOK THINGS: SEE **cook** verb.
2 *to toast a guest at a banquet.* drink a toast to, drink the health of, raise your glass to.

tobacco noun FORMS IN WHICH PEOPLE USE TOBACCO: cigar, cigarette, pipe-tobacco, plug, snuff.

toboggan noun SEE **sledge**.

tocsin noun SEE **signal** noun.

toddle verb SEE **walk** verb.

to-do noun SEE **commotion**.

toe noun digit.

toe verb **to toe the line** SEE **conform**.

tog verb **to tog yourself up** SEE **dress** verb.

together adverb all at once, at the same time, collectively, concurrently, consecutively, continuously, co-operatively, hand in hand, in chorus, in unison, jointly, shoulder to shoulder, side by side, simultaneously.
OPPOSITES: independently, separately.

toil noun [*informal*] donkey work, drudgery, effort, exertion, industry, labour, SEE **work** noun.

toil verb drudge, exert yourself, [*informal*] keep at it, labour, [*informal*] plug away, [*informal*] slave away, struggle, [*informal*] sweat, SEE **work** verb.

toilet noun **1** SEE **lavatory**.
2 SEE **washing**.

toiletries plural noun THINGS USED IN PERFORMING YOUR TOILET: SEE **cosmetics**, hair conditioner, lotion, moisturizer, rinse, shampoo, soap, talcum powder.

token noun **1** *a token of our affection.* evidence, expression, indication, mark, proof, reminder, sign, symbol, testimony.
2 *a bus-token.* counter, coupon, voucher.

tolerable adjective **1** *tolerable noise. tolerable pain.* acceptable, bearable, endurable, sufferable, supportable.
OPPOSITES: SEE **intolerable**.
2 *tolerable food. a tolerable performance.* adequate, all right, fair, mediocre, middling, [*informal*] OK, ordinary, passable, satisfactory.

tolerance noun **1** *tolerance towards those who do wrong.* broad-mindedness, charity, fairness, forbearance, forgiveness, lenience, openness, permissiveness.
2 *tolerance of others' opinions.* acceptance, sufferance, sympathy (towards), toleration, understanding.
OPPOSITES: intolerance, SEE **prejudice** noun.

tolerant adjective *tolerant of people's mistakes.* charitable, easygoing, fair, forbearing, forgiving, generous, indulgent, [*uncomplimentary*] lax, lenient, liberal, magnanimous, open-minded, patient, permissive, [*uncomplimentary*] soft, sympathetic, understanding, unprejudiced, willing to forgive.
OPPOSITES: SEE **intolerant**.

tolerate verb **1** *I can't tolerate this toothache!* abide, bear, endure, [*informal*] lump (*You'll have to lump it!*), [*informal*] put up with, [*informal*] stand, [*informal*] stick, [*informal*] stomach, suffer, [*informal*] take (*I can't take any more*), undergo.
2 *They don't tolerate smoking in the house.* accept, admit, brook, condone, countenance, make allowances for, permit,

sanction, [*informal*] wear (*You can ask, but I'm sure they won't wear it*).

toll noun *a toll to cross the bridge.* charge, duty, fee, levy, payment, tax.

toll verb *to toll a bell.* SEE **ring** verb.

tomahawk noun SEE **axe** noun.

tomb noun burial-place, catacomb, crypt, grave, gravestone, mausoleum, SEE **memorial**, sepulchre, tombstone, vault.

tomboy noun SEE **girl**.

tombstone noun SEE **tomb**.

tom-cat noun SEE **cat**.

tome noun SEE **book** noun.

tommy-gun noun OTHER GUNS: SEE **gun**.

tommy-rot noun SEE **nonsense**.

tom-tom noun OTHER DRUMS: SEE **drum**.

tonality noun *the tonality of a piece of music.* key, tonal centre.

tone noun **1** *an angry tone in her voice.* accent, expression, feel, inflection, intonation, manner, modulation, note, quality, sound, timbre.
2 *eerie music to create the right tone for a mystery.* atmosphere, character, effect, feeling, mood, spirit, style, vein.
3 *paint with a pink tone.* SEE **colour** noun.

tone verb **to tone down** *to tone down the noise.* SEE **soften**.
to tone in *to tone in with something else.* SEE **harmonize**.
to tone up *to tone up your muscles.* SEE **strengthen**.

toneless adjective *a toneless voice.* SEE **monotonous**.

tongue noun **1** PARTS OF YOUR HEAD: SEE **head** noun.
2 *a foreign tongue.* SEE **language**.

tongue-tied adjective *He can't explain because he gets tongue-tied.* dumb, inarticulate, mute, silent, speechless.

tonic noun *You need a tonic after being ill.* boost, cordial, [*formal*] dietary supplement, fillip, [*informal*] pick-me-up, restorative.

tonsure noun VARIOUS HAIR-STYLES: SEE **hair-style**.

tool noun *a tool for every job.* apparatus, appliance, contraption, contrivance, device, gadget, hardware, implement, instrument, invention, machine, utensil, weapon.

CARPENTER'S TOOLS: auger, awl, brace and bit, bradawl, chisel, clamp, cramp, drill, file, fretsaw, gimlet, glass-paper, hack-saw, hammer, jigsaw, mallet, pincers, plane, pliers, power-drill, rasp, sander, sandpaper, saw, spokeshave, T-square, vice, wrench.

GARDENING TOOLS: billhook, dibber, fork, grass-rake, hoe, lawn mower, mattock, rake, roller, scythe, secateurs, shears, sickle, spade, strimmer, trowel.

COOKING UTENSILS: SEE **cook** verb.

VARIOUS OTHER TOOLS: axe, bellows, chain-saw, chopper, clippers, crowbar, cutter, hatchet, jack, ladder, lever, penknife, pick, pickaxe, pitchfork, pocket-knife, scissors, screw-driver, shovel, sledge-hammer, spanner, tape-measure, tongs, tweezers.

---

toot noun, verb VARIOUS SOUNDS: SEE **sound** noun.

tooth noun VARIOUS TEETH: canine, eye-tooth, fang, incisor, molar, tusk, wisdom tooth.
false teeth bridge, denture, dentures, plate.
RELATED ADJECTIVE: dental.
DENTAL PROBLEMS: caries, cavity, decay, plaque, toothache.

toothache noun SEE **pain** noun.

toothed adjective *a toothed edge.* cogged, indented, jagged.

top adjective *top marks. top speed. the top performance.* best, first, foremost, greatest, highest, leading, maximum, most, topmost, winning.
OPPOSITES: SEE **bottom** adjective.
top hat [*informal*] topper.

top noun **1** *the top of a mountain.* apex, crest, crown, head, peak, pinnacle, summit, tip, vertex.
2 *the top of the table.* surface.
3 *the top of her fame.* acme, apogee, culmination, height, zenith.
4 *the top of a jar.* cap, cover, covering, lid.
OPPOSITES: SEE **bottom** noun.

top verb **1** *I topped the cake with chopped nuts.* cover, decorate, finish off, garnish.
2 *Our charity collection topped last year's record.* beat, be higher than, better, cap, exceed, excel, outdo, surpass.

topcoat noun **1** *a topcoat to wear in winter.* SEE **overcoat**.
2 *a topcoat of paint.* final coat, finish, gloss, outer coat.

toper noun SEE **drunkard**.

topic noun *a topic for discussion.* issue, matter, question, subject, talking-point, theme, [*formal*] thesis.

topical adjective *topical news.* contemporary, current, recent, up-to-date.

topmost adjective SEE **top** adjective.

topography noun *the topography of an area.* features, geography, [*informal*] lie of the land.

topper noun top hat.

topple verb 1 *The gale toppled our TV aerial.* knock down, overturn, throw down, tip over, upset.
2 *He toppled off the wall.* fall, overbalance, tumble.
3 *The opposition eventually toppled the prime minister.* oust, overthrow, unseat.

topsoil noun SEE **soil** noun.

topsy-turvy adjective SEE **untidy**.

tor noun SEE **hill**.

torch noun bicycle lamp, [*old-fashioned*] brand, electric lamp, flashlight, [*old-fashioned*] link.

torchlight noun SEE **light** noun.

toreador noun bullfighter, matador.

torment noun *the torment of toothache.* affliction, agony, anguish, distress, misery, SEE **pain** noun, persecution, plague, purgatory, scourge, suffering, torture.

torment verb *My bad tooth was tormenting me. We were tormented by flies.* afflict, annoy, bait, be a torment to, bedevil, bother, bully, distress, harass, hurt, inflict pain on, intimidate, [*informal*] nag, pain, persecute, pester, plague, tease, torture, vex, victimize, worry.

tornado noun SEE **storm** noun.

torpid adjective SEE **lethargic**.

torpor noun SEE **lethargy**.

torrent noun *a torrent of water.* cascade, cataract, deluge, downpour, flood, flow, gush, rush, spate, stream, tide.

torrential adjective *a torrential downpour.* heavy, soaking, violent.
torrential rain cloudburst, deluge, rainstorm.

torrid adjective 1 *a torrid climate.* SEE **hot**.
2 [*informal*] *a torrid love-scene.* SEE **sexy**.

torso noun *a human torso.* body, trunk.

tortuous adjective *a tortuous route. a tortuous explanation.* circuitous, complicated, convoluted, crooked, devious, indirect, involved, meandering, roundabout, twisted, twisting, winding, zigzag.
OPPOSITES: SEE **straightforward**.

torture noun 1 *Many political prisoners experience torture in prison.* cruelty, degradation, humiliation, inquisition, persecution, torment.
2 *the torture of toothache.* affliction, agony, anguish, distress, misery, plague, scourge, suffering.

torture verb 1 *to torture a prisoner.* be cruel to, brainwash, bully, cause pain to, degrade, dehumanize, humiliate, hurt, inflict pain on, intimidate, persecute, rack, torment, victimize.
2 *I was tortured by doubts.* afflict, agonize, annoy, bedevil, bother, distress, harass, [*informal*] nag, pester, plague, tease, vex, worry.

Tory noun POLITICAL TERMS: SEE **politics**.

toss verb 1 *to toss something into the air.* bowl, cast, [*informal*] chuck, fling, flip (*to flip a coin*), heave, hurl, lob, pitch, shy, sling, throw.
2 *to toss about in a storm. to toss about in bed.* bob, lurch, move restlessly, pitch, reel, rock, roll, shake, twist and turn, wallow, welter, writhe.

tot noun 1 *tiny tots.* SEE **child**.
2 *a tot of rum.* SEE **drink** noun.

tot verb **to tot up** SEE **total** verb.

total adjective 1 *The bill shows the total amount.* complete, comprehensive, entire, full, gross (*gross income*), overall, whole.
2 *Our play was a total disaster.* absolute, downright, perfect, sheer, thorough, unmitigated, unqualified, utter.

total noun *Add up the figures and tell me the total.* aggregate, amount, answer, lot, sum, totality, whole.

total verb 1 *Our shopping totalled £37.* add up to, amount to, come to, make.
2 *to total a list of figures.* add up, calculate, count, find the total of, reckon up, totalize, [*informal*] tot up, work out.

totalitarian adjective *a totalitarian regime.* authoritarian, dictatorial, one-party, oppressive, tyrannous, undemocratic, unrepresentative.
OPPOSITES: SEE **democratic**.

totality noun SEE **total** noun.

totalize verb SEE **total** verb.

totter verb *We tottered unsteadily off the ship.* dodder, falter, reel, stagger, SEE **walk** verb.

touch noun 1 *the sense of touch.* feeling, touching.
2 *I felt a touch on the arm.* caress, contact, dab, pat, stroke, tap.
3 *Working with animals requires a special touch.* ability, feel, flair, knack, manner, sensitivity, skill, style, technique, understanding, way.
4 *There's a touch of frost in the air.* hint, suggestion, suspicion, tinge, trace.
RELATED ADJECTIVE: tactile.

touch verb **1** *to touch physically.* brush, caress, contact, cuddle, dab, embrace, feel, finger, fondle, graze, handle, SEE **hit** verb, kiss, manipulate, massage, nuzzle, pat, paw, pet, push, rub, stroke, tap, tickle.
2 *to touch someone emotionally.* affect, concern, disturb, influence, inspire, move, stir, upset.
3 *Our speed touched 100 m.p.h.* attain, reach, rise to.
4 *No one could touch her performance.* [*informal*] come up to, compare with, equal, match, parallel, rival.
to touch off SEE **begin.**
to touch up SEE **improve.**

touched adjective **1** *I was touched by her kindness.* affected, moved, responsive (to), stirred, sympathetic (towards).
2 [*informal*] *He's a bit touched.* SEE **mad.**

touching adjective *a touching scene.* affecting, SEE **emotional**, moving, tender.

touchstone noun SEE **criterion.**

touchy adjective *Be careful what you say because he's touchy.* edgy, irascible, irritable, jittery, jumpy, nervous, quick-tempered, sensitive, snappy, temperamental, thin-skinned.

tough adjective **1** *tough shoes.* durable, hard-wearing, indestructible, lasting, stout, unbreakable, well-made.
OPPOSITES: SEE **delicate.**
2 *a tough physique.* [*informal*] beefy, brawny, burly, hardy, muscular, robust, stalwart, strong, sturdy.
3 *tough opposition.* invulnerable, merciless, obstinate, resilient, resistant, resolute, ruthless, stiff, stubborn, tenacious, unyielding.
OPPOSITES: SEE **weak.**
4 *tough meat.* chewy, hard, gristly, leathery, rubbery, uneatable.
OPPOSITES: SEE **tender.**
5 *a tough climb.* arduous, difficult, exacting, exhausting, gruelling, hard, laborious, stiff, strenuous.
6 *a tough problem.* baffling, intractable, [*informal*] knotty, puzzling, [*informal*] thorny.
OPPOSITES: SEE **easy.**

tough noun SEE **ruffian.**

toughen verb harden, make tougher, reinforce, strengthen.

toupee noun hair-piece, wig.

tour noun *a sight-seeing tour.* circular tour, drive, excursion, expedition, jaunt, journey, outing, ride, trip.

tour verb *to tour the beauty spots.* do the rounds of, explore, go round, make a tour of, SEE **travel** verb, visit.

tourist noun *The cathedral was full of tourists.* holiday-maker, sightseer, traveller, tripper, visitor.

tournament noun *a tennis tournament.* championship, competition, contest, match, meeting, series.

tousle verb *to tousle someone's hair.* SEE **ruffle.**

tout verb SEE **sell.**

tow verb *to tow a trailer.* drag, draw, haul, pull, trail, tug.

towel noun bath-towel, hand-towel, tea-cloth, tea-towel.

towel verb SEE **dry** verb.

tower noun KINDS OF TOWER: belfry, castle, fort, fortress, keep, minaret, skyscraper, steeple, turret.

tower verb *The castle towers above the village.* dominate, loom, rear, rise, stand out, stick up.

towering adjective **1** *a towering figure.* colossal, gigantic, high, imposing, lofty, mighty, soaring, SEE **tall.**
2 *a towering rage.* extreme, fiery, SEE **intense**, overpowering, passionate, violent.

town noun borough, city, conurbation, municipality, SEE **settlement.**

PLACES IN A TOWN: bank, SEE **building**, café, car-park, cinema, college, concert-hall, council-house, factory, filling-station, flats, garage, ghetto, hotel, SEE **house** noun, housing estate, industrial estate, leisure-centre, library, museum, office block, park, police station, post office, [*informal*] pub, recreation ground, residential area, restaurant, SEE **road**, school, SEE **shop**, shopping-centre, snack-bar, sports-centre, square, station, suburb, supermarket, theatre, warehouse.

---

townsfolk, townspeople nouns SEE **inhabitant.**

toxic adjective *toxic fumes.* dangerous, deadly, harmful, lethal, noxious, poisonous.
OPPOSITES: SEE **harmless.**

toy adjective *a toy car.* imitation, model, [*informal*] pretend, scaled down, SEE **small**, small-scale.

toy noun game, model, plaything, puzzle.

trace noun **1** *traces left by an animal.* evidence, footprint, [*informal*] give-away, hint, indication, mark, remains, sign, spoor, track, trail, vestige.

2 *a trace of jam left in the jar.* SEE **amount** noun (**small amount**).
to kick over the traces SEE **rebel** verb.

trace verb 1 *I traced my lost relatives.* detect, discover, find, get back, recover, retrieve, seek out.
2 *The hounds traced the fox across the field.* SEE **track** verb.
3 *to trace a picture.* copy, draw, go over, make a copy of, mark out, sketch.

tracery noun SEE **decoration**.

trachea noun windpipe.

tracing noun SEE **copy** noun.

track noun 1 *an animal's tracks.* footmark, footprint, mark, scent, spoor, trace, trail.
2 *a cross-country track.* bridle-path, bridle-way, cart-track, footpath, path, SEE **road**, way.
3 *a racing track.* circuit, course, dirt-track, race-track.
4 *a railway track.* SEE **railway**.
to make tracks SEE **depart**.

track verb *The hunters tracked the deer.* chase, dog, follow, hound, hunt, pursue, shadow, stalk, tail, trace, trail.
to track down discover, find, get back, recover, retrieve, trace.

tract noun 1 *a tract of land.* SEE **area**.
2 *a religious tract.* SEE 4TREATISE.

tractable adjective SEE **obedient**.

tractor noun VEHICLES: SEE **vehicle**.

trade noun 1 *international trade.* barter, business, buying and selling, commerce, dealing, exchange, industry, market, trading, traffic, transactions.
2 *trained in a trade.* calling, craft, employment, SEE **job**, [*informal*] line (*What's your line?*), occupation, profession, pursuit, work.

trade verb be involved in trade (SEE **trade** noun], do business, market goods, retail, sell, traffic (in).
to trade in *to trade in your old car.* exchange, offer in part exchange, swop.
to trade on *to trade on someone's good nature.* SEE **exploit** verb.

trader, tradesman nouns *market traders. local tradesmen.* dealer, merchant, retailer, roundsman, salesman, seller, shopkeeper, stockist, supplier, trafficker [= *trader in something illegal or suspect*], vendor.
SHOPS AND BUSINESSES: SEE **shop**.

trading noun SEE **trade** noun.

tradition noun 1 *It's a tradition to give gifts at Christmas.* convention, custom, habit, institution, practice, routine.
2 *Popular tradition portrays Richard III as a hunchback.* belief, folklore.

traditional adjective 1 *a traditional Christmas dinner.* accustomed, conventional, customary, established, familiar, habitual, historic, normal, orthodox, regular, time-honoured, typical, usual.
OPPOSITES: SEE **unconventional**.
2 *traditional stories.* folk, handed down, oral, popular, unwritten.
OPPOSITES: SEE **literary**.

traditionalist noun SEE **conservative** noun.

traduce verb SEE **denigrate**.

traffic noun 1 *road traffic.* movement, transport, transportation.
VARIOUS VEHICLES: SEE **vehicle**.
2 *traffic in drugs.* SEE **trade** noun.

traffic verb SEE **trade** verb.

trafficker noun SEE **trader**.

traffic-lights noun SEE **signal** noun.

tragedy noun 1 *"Romeo and Juliet" is a tragedy by Shakespeare.* KINDS OF WRITING: SEE **writing**.
2 *It was a tragedy when their dog was killed.* affliction, blow, calamity, catastrophe, disaster, misfortune.
OPPOSITES: SEE **comedy**.

tragic adjective 1 *a tragic accident.* appalling, awful, calamitous, catastrophic, depressing, dire, disastrous, dreadful, fatal, fearful, ill-fated, lamentable, terrible, unfortunate, unlucky.
2 *a tragic expression on her face.* bereft, distressed, grief-stricken, hurt, pathetic, piteous, pitiful, SEE **sad**, sorrowful, woeful, wretched.
OPPOSITES: SEE **comic**. adjective.

trail noun 1 *The hounds followed the fox's trail.* evidence, footprints, mark, scent, signs, spoor, traces.
2 *a nature trail.* path, pathway, SEE **road**, route, track.

trail verb 1 *to trail something behind you.* dangle, drag, draw, haul, pull, tow.
2 *to trail someone.* chase, follow, hunt, pursue, shadow, stalk, tail, trace, track down.
3 *to trail behind.* SEE **dawdle**.

train noun 1 *a railway train.* SEE **railway**.
2 *a train of events.* SEE **sequence**.

train verb 1 *to train a football team.* coach, educate, instruct, prepare, teach, tutor.
2 *to train hard.* do exercises, exercise, [*informal*] get fit, practise, prepare yourself, rehearse, [*informal*] work out.
3 *to train your sights on a target.* SEE **aim** verb.

trainee noun apprentice, beginner, cadet, learner, [*informal*] L-driver, novice, pupil, starter, student, tiro, unqualified person.

trainer noun **1** coach, instructor, teacher, tutor.
2 [= *light shoe*] SEE **shoe**.

traipse verb SEE **tramp** verb.

trait noun SEE **characteristic** noun.

traitor noun *a traitor to a cause.* apostate, betrayer, blackleg, collaborator, defector, deserter, double-crosser, informer, [*informal*] Judas, quisling, renegade, treacherous person [SEE **treacherous**], turncoat.

traitorous adjective SEE **treacherous**.

trajectory noun SEE **flight**.

tram noun tram-car.

trammel verb SEE **hamper**.

tramp noun **1** *a long tramp across country.* SEE **walk** noun.
2 *a homeless tramp.* beggar, [*informal*] destitute person, [*informal*] dosser, [*informal*] down and out, homeless person, traveller, vagabond, vagrant, wanderer.

tramp verb *We tramped across the hills.* [*informal*] foot-slog, hike, march, plod, stride, toil, traipse, trek, trudge, SEE **walk** verb, [*slang*] yomp.

trample verb *Don't trample on the flowers.* crush, flatten, squash, stamp on, tread on, walk over.

tramway noun SEE **railway**.

trance noun *lost in a trance.* day-dream, daze, dream, ecstasy, hypnotic state, reverie, spell, stupor, unconsciousness.

tranquil adjective **1** *a tranquil lake.* calm, peaceful, placid, quiet, restful, serene, still, undisturbed, unruffled.
OPPOSITES: SEE **stormy**.
2 *a tranquil mood.* collected, composed, dispassionate, [*informal*] laid-back, sedate, sober, unemotional, unexcited, untroubled.
OPPOSITES: SEE **excited**.

tranquillize verb SEE **calm** verb.

tranquillizer noun barbiturate, narcotic, opiate, sedative.

The prefix *trans-* is related to Latin *trans = across.*

---

transact verb SEE **perform**.

transaction noun *a business transaction.* SEE **deal** noun.

transcend verb SEE **surpass**.

transcendental adjective SEE **visionary** adjective.

transcribe verb *to transcribe a tape-recording.* copy out [SEE **copy** verb], take down, transliterate, write out.

transcript noun SEE **writing**.

transfer verb *to transfer from one place to another.* carry, change, convey, displace, ferry, hand over, move, relocate, remove, second (*seconded to another job*), take, transplant, transport, transpose.

transfigure verb SEE **transform**.

transfix verb SEE **pierce**.

transform verb *We transformed the attic into a games room.* adapt, alter, SEE **change** verb, convert, metamorphose, modify, rebuild, reconstruct, remodel, revolutionize, transfigure, translate, [*joking*] transmogrify, transmute, turn.

transformation noun *a transformation in her appearance.* alteration, SEE **change** noun, conversion, improvement, metamorphosis, revolution, transfiguration, transition, [*informal*] turn-about.

transfusion noun *a blood transfusion.* OTHER MEDICAL TERMS: SEE **medicine**.

transgress verb SEE **sin** verb.

transgression noun SEE **sin** noun.

transgressor noun SEE **sinner**.

transient adjective *transient visitors. a transient glimpse.* brief, evanescent, fleeting, impermanent, momentary, passing, [*informal*] quick, short, temporary, transitory.
OPPOSITES: SEE **permanent**.

transistor noun SEE **radio**.

transit noun *goods damaged in transit.* journey, movement, passage, shipment, transportation, travel.

transition noun *the transition from childhood to adulthood.* alteration, SEE **change** noun, change-over, evolution, movement, progress, progression, shift, transformation, transit.

transitory adjective SEE **transient**.

translate verb *to translate words into English.* SEE **change** verb, convert, decode, express, interpret, make a translation, paraphrase, render, transcribe.

translation noun gloss, interpretation, paraphrase, rendering, transcription, version.

translator noun interpreter, linguist.

transliterate verb SEE **transcribe**.

translucent adjective SEE **transparent**.

transmigration noun *the transmigration of souls.* reincarnation.

transmission noun **1** *the transmission of a TV programme.* broadcast, diffusion, dissemination, relaying, sending out.
2 *the transmission of goods.* carriage, conveyance, dispatch, shipment, transportation.

transmit verb *to transmit a message. to transmit radio signals.* broadcast, communicate, convey, dispatch, disseminate, emit, pass on, relay, send.
OPPOSITES: SEE **receive**.

transmogrify, transmute verbs SEE **transform**.

transparency noun slide.
OTHER PHOTOGRAPHS: SEE **photograph** noun.

transparent adjective *transparent material.* clear, crystalline, diaphanous, filmy, gauzy, limpid, pellucid, [*informal*] see-through, sheer, translucent.

transpire verb SEE **happen**.

transplant noun *a heart transplant.* operation, surgery.

transplant verb *to transplant seedlings.* move, relocate, reposition, shift, transfer, uproot.

transport noun *public transport.* conveyance, haulage, shipping, transportation.

KINDS OF TRANSPORT: SEE **aircraft**, barge, boat [SEE **vessel**], bus, cable-car, cable railway, canal, car, chair-lift, coach, cycle, ferry, horse, lorry, Metro, minibus, [*old-fashioned*] omnibus, SEE **railway**, road transport [SEE **vehicle**], sea, ship [SEE **vessel**], space-shuttle, taxi, train, tram, van, waterways.

WAYS TO TRAVEL: SEE **travel** noun.

---

transport verb *to transport goods.* bring, carry, convey, fetch, haul, move, shift, ship, take, transfer.

transportable adjective SEE **movable**.

transpose verb *to transpose letters in a word.* change, exchange, move round, rearrange, reverse, substitute, swap, switch, transfer.

transverse adjective crosswise, diagonal, oblique.

trap noun *a trap to catch someone or something.* ambush, booby-trap, gin, mantrap, net, noose, snare.

trap verb *to trap an animal. to trap a criminal.* ambush, arrest, capture, catch, corner, ensnare, entrap, snare.

trapper noun hunter.

trappings noun *The judge wore a wig and all the trappings of his position.* accessories, accompaniments, accoutrements, adornments, decorations, equipment, finery, fittings, [*informal*] gear, ornaments, [*joking*] paraphernalia, [*informal*] things, trimmings.

trash noun garbage, junk, litter, refuse, rubbish, waste.

trashy adjective SEE **worthless**.

trauma noun SEE **shock** noun.

traumatic adjective *a traumatic experience.* SEE **shocking**.

travail noun SEE **effort**.

travel noun *They say that travel broadens the mind.* globe-trotting, moving around, [*joking*] peregrination, travelling.

KINDS OF TRAVEL: cruise, drive, excursion, expedition, exploration, flight, hike, holiday, journey, march, migration, mission, outing, pilgrimage, ramble, ride, safari, sail, sea-passage, tour, trek, trip, visit, voyage, walk.

WAYS TO TRAVEL: aviate, circumnavigate the world, commute, cruise, cycle, drive, emigrate, fly, free-wheel, [*informal*] gad about, [*informal*] gallivant, hike, hitch-hike, march, migrate, motor, navigate, paddle (*paddle a canoe*), pedal, pilot, punt, ramble, ride, roam, [*poetic*] rove, row, sail, shuttle, steam, tour, trek, voyage, walk, wander.

---

travel verb *to travel to work. to travel to foreign lands.* go, journey, move, proceed, progress, [*old-fashioned*] wend.

traveller noun **1** astronaut, aviator, cosmonaut, cyclist, driver, flyer, migrant, motor-cyclist, motorist, passenger, pedestrian, sailor, voyager, walker.
2 [=*person travelling on business or to work*] commuter, [*informal*] rep, representative, salesman, saleswoman.
3 [=*person travelling for adventure or pleasure*] explorer, globe-trotter, hiker, hitch-hiker, holiday-maker, pilgrim, rambler, stowaway, tourist, tripper, wanderer, wayfarer.
4 [=*person for whom travelling is a way of life*] gypsy, itinerant, nomad, tinker, tramp, vagabond.

travelling adjective *travelling tribes.* itinerant, migrant, migratory, mobile, nomadic, peripatetic, roaming, roving, touring, vagrant, wandering.

travel-stained adjective SEE **dirty** adjective.

travel-weary adjective SEE **tired**.

traverse verb SEE **cross** verb.

travesty noun SEE **imitation**.

travesty verb SEE **imitate**.

trawl verb SEE **fish** verb.

trawler noun fishing-boat.

tray noun salver.

treacherous adjective **1** *a treacherous ally.* deceitful, disloyal, double-crossing, double-dealing, duplicitous, faithless, false, perfidious, sneaky, unfaithful, untrustworthy.
OPPOSITES: SEE **loyal**.
treacherous person SEE **traitor**.
2 *treacherous weather conditions.* dangerous, deceptive, hazardous, misleading, perilous, risky, shifting, unpredictable, unreliable, unsafe, unstable.
OPPOSITES: SEE **reliable**.

treachery noun *treachery against an ally.* betrayal, dishonesty, disloyalty, double-dealing, duplicity, faithlessness, infidelity, perfidy, SEE **treason**, untrustworthiness.
OPPOSITES: SEE **loyalty**.

treacle noun SEE **sugar** noun.

tread noun **1** *the tread of approaching feet.* footstep.
2 *the treads of a staircase.* step.

tread verb *to tread carefully.* OTHER WAYS TO WALK: SEE **walk** verb.
to tread on *She trod on my foot.* crush, squash underfoot, stamp on, step on, trample, walk on.

treason noun *treason against your country.* betrayal, mutiny, rebellion, sedition, SEE **treachery**.
OPPOSITES: SEE **loyalty**.

treasure noun *hidden treasure.* fortune, gold, hoard, jewels, riches, treasure trove, valuables, wealth.

treasure verb *She treasures the brooch granny gave her.* adore, appreciate, cherish, esteem, guard, keep safe, love, prize, value, venerate, worship.

treasury noun hoard, repository, storeroom, treasure-house, vault.

treat noun *a birthday treat.* entertainment, gift, outing, pleasure, surprise.

treat verb **1** *to treat someone kindly.* attend to, behave towards, care for, look after, use.
2 *to treat a subject thoroughly.* consider, deal with, discuss, tackle.
3 *to treat a patient. to treat a wound.* cure, dress, give treatment to [SEE **treatment**], heal, medicate, nurse, prescribe medicine for, tend.
4 *to treat food to kill germs.* process.
5 *I didn't have any money, but they were kind enough to treat me.* entertain, give (someone) a treat, pay for, provide for.

treatise noun disquisition, dissertation, essay, monograph, pamphlet, paper, thesis, tract.
OTHER KINDS OF WRITING: SEE **writing**.

treatment noun **1** *the treatment of prisoners. the treatment of a problem.* care, conduct, dealing (with), handling, management, organization, use.
2 *the treatment of illness.* cure, first aid, healing, nursing, remedy, therapy.
VARIOUS KINDS OF MEDICAL TREATMENT: SEE **medicine**, **therapy**.

treaty noun *a peace treaty.* agreement, alliance, armistice, compact, concordat, contract, convention, covenant, [*informal*] deal, entente, pact, peace, [*formal*] protocol, settlement, truce, understanding.

tree noun SOME TYPES OF TREE: bonsai, conifer, cordon, deciduous, espalier, evergreen, pollard, standard.
small tree bush, half-standard, shrub.
young tree sapling.
RELATED ADJECTIVE: arboreal.

VARIOUS TREES: ash, banian, bay, baobab, beech, birch, cacao, cedar, chestnut, cypress, elder, elm, eucalyptus, fir, fruit-tree [SEE **fruit**], gum-tree, hawthorn, hazel, holly, horse-chestnut, larch, lime, maple, oak, olive, palm, pine, plane, poplar, redwood, rowan, sequoia, spruce, sycamore, tamarisk, tulip tree, willow, yew.

---

treeless adjective *a treeless landscape.* SEE **bare** adjective.

trefoil noun clover, shamrock.

trek noun, verb SEE **travel** noun, verb.

trellis noun SEE **framework**.

tremble verb *to tremble with cold.* quake, quaver, quiver, shake, shiver, shudder, vibrate, waver.

Tremendous (like *tremble, tremor, tremulous,* etc.) is related to Latin *tremere* = *to tremble.* Sometimes *tremendous* still means *fearful,* but more often we use it informally and rather vaguely to describe things which are impressive in some way.

---

tremendous adjective **1** *a tremendous explosion.* alarming, appalling, awful,

fearful, fearsome, frightening, frightful, horrifying, shocking, terrible, terrific.
2 [*informal*] *a tremendous helping of potatoes.* SEE **big**.
3 [*informal*] *a tremendous piece of music.* SEE **excellent**.
4 [*informal*] *a tremendous achievement.* SEE **remarkable**.

tremor noun *a tremor in someone's voice.* agitation, hesitation, quavering, quiver, shaking, trembling, vibration.
an earth tremor SEE **earthquake**.

tremulous adjective **1** *We waited in tremulous anticipation.* agitated, anxious, excited, frightened, jittery, jumpy, nervous, timid, uncertain.
OPPOSITES: SEE **calm** adjective.
2 *I opened the important letter with tremulous fingers.* quivering, shaking, shivering, trembling, [*informal*] trembly, vibrating.
OPPOSITES: SEE **steady** adjective.

trench noun SEE **ditch** noun.

trench verb SEE **dig**.
trench coat SEE **overcoat**.

trenchant adjective *trenchant criticisms.* SEE **sharp**, **intelligent**.

trend noun **1** *an upward trend in prices.* bias, direction, inclination, leaning, movement, shift, tendency.
2 *the latest trend in clothes.* [*informal*] fad, fashion, mode, style, [*informal*] thing (*It's the latest thing*), way.

trendy adjective [*informal*] *trendy clothes.* contemporary, fashionable, [*informal*] in (*the in fashion*), latest, modern, stylish, up-to-date.
OPPOSITES: SEE **old-fashioned**.

trepidation noun SEE **fear** noun.

trespass noun [*old-fashioned*] *Forgive us our trespasses.* SEE **sin** noun.

trespass verb *to trespass on someone's property.* encroach, enter illegally, intrude, invade.

tress noun SEE **hair**.

trestle noun SEE **support** noun.

trestle-table noun SEE **table**.

trews noun SEE **trousers**.

trial noun **1** *a legal trial.* case, court martial, examination, hearing, tribunal.
LEGAL TERMS: SEE **law**.
2 *a trial of a new product.* attempt, experiment, test, testing, [*informal*] try-out.
3 *Appearing in public can be a trial for shy people.* affliction, burden, difficulty, hardship, ordeal, problem, tribulation, trouble, worry.

The prefix *tri-* in words like *triangle, tricycle, tripod,* etc. is related to Latin *tres = three.*

---

triangle noun VARIOUS SHAPES: SEE **shape** noun.

triangular adjective three-cornered, three-sided.

tribe noun *a close-knit tribe.* clan, dynasty, family, group, horde, nation, people, race, stock.

tribulation noun SEE **trouble** noun.

tribunal noun SEE **trial**.

tributary noun SEE **river**.

tribute noun *Her friends read moving tributes to her courage.* accolade, appreciation, commendation, compliment, eulogy, panegyric, testimony.
to pay tribute to *They paid tribute to her courage.* applaud, celebrate, commend, SEE **honour** verb, pay homage to, praise, respect.

trick noun **1** *a conjuring trick.* illusion, legerdemain, magic, sleight of hand.
2 *a deceitful trick.* cheat, [*informal*] con, deceit, deception, fraud, hoax, imposture, manœuvre, ploy, pretence, ruse, scheme, stratagem, stunt, subterfuge, swindle, trap, SEE **trickery**, wile.
3 *I never learned the trick of standing on my head.* art, craft, device, dodge, expertise, gimmick, knack, [*informal*] know-how, secret, skill, technique.
4 *He has a trick of repeating himself.* characteristic, habit, idiosyncrasy, mannerism, peculiarity, way.
5 *She played a trick on me.* joke, [*informal*] leg-pull, practical joke, prank.

trick verb *He tricked me into buying rubbish.* [*informal*] bamboozle, bluff, catch out, cheat, [*informal*] con, deceive, defraud, [*informal*] diddle, dupe, fool, hoax, hoodwink, [*informal*] kid, mislead, outwit, [*informal*] pull (someone's) leg, swindle.

trickery noun bluffing, cheating, chicanery, deceit, deception, dishonesty, fraud, [*informal*] hocus-pocus, [*informal*] jiggery-pokery, [*informal*] skulduggery, swindling, SEE **trick** noun.

trickle verb *Water trickled from a crack.* dribble, drip, flow slowly, leak, ooze, percolate, run, seep.
OPPOSITES: SEE **gush** verb.

trickster noun SEE **cheat** noun.

tricky adjective **1** *a tricky customer.* SEE **deceitful**.
2 *a tricky manœuvre.* SEE **complicated**.

tricycle noun SEE **cycle** noun.

trifle noun *It cost only a trifle.* SEE **small (small amount)**.

trifle verb *Don't trifle with me!* behave frivolously, dabble, fool about, play about.

trifling adjective *a trifling amount.* SEE **trivial**.

trigger verb **to trigger off** SEE **activate**.

trilby noun SEE **hat**.

trill verb *birds trilling in the garden.* SEE **sing**, twitter, warble, whistle.

trim adjective *a trim garden. a trim figure.* compact, neat, orderly, [*informal*] shipshape, smart, spruce, tidy, well-groomed, well-kept.
OPPOSITES: SEE **untidy**.

trim verb *to trim a hedge.* clip, crop, SEE **cut** verb, shape, shear, tidy.

trip noun *a trip to the seaside.* excursion, expedition, jaunt, journey, outing, tour, visit, voyage.
to make a trip SEE **travel** verb.

trip verb **1** *to trip along lightly.* run, skip, SEE **walk** verb.
2 *to trip over something.* catch your foot, fall, stagger, stumble, totter, tumble.

tripartite adjective SEE **triple**.

tripe noun **1** *tripe and onions.* SEE **meat**.
2 [*informal*] *She's talking tripe!* SEE **nonsense**.

triple adjective threefold, tripartite, triplicate (*Complete the form in triplicate*).

tripod noun *a camera tripod.* SEE **stand** noun, support.

tripper noun SEE **traveller**.

trite adjective *a trite remark.* SEE **commonplace**.

triumph noun **1** *a triumph over our opponents.* conquest, knock-out, victory, [*informal*] walk-over, win.
2 *The pudding I made was a triumph.* accomplishment, achievement, [*informal*] hit, master-stroke, [*informal*] smash hit, success.

triumph verb *We triumphed in the end.* be victorious, prevail, succeed, win.
to triumph over SEE **defeat** verb.

triumphant adjective **1** *We cheered the triumphant team.* conquering, dominant, successful, victorious, winning.
OPPOSITES: SEE **unsuccessful**.
2 *The losers didn't like our triumphant laughter.* boastful, [*informal*] cocky, elated, exultant, gleeful, gloating, immodest, joyful, jubilant, proud.
OPPOSITES: SEE **modest**.

trivet noun SEE **stand** noun.

trivial adjective *trivial details.* [*informal*] fiddling, [*informal*] footling, frivolous, inconsequential, inconsiderable, insignificant, little, minor, negligible, paltry, pettifogging, petty, [*informal*] piffling, silly, slight, small, superficial, trifling, trite, unimportant, worthless.
OPPOSITES: SEE **important**.

troglodyte noun cave-dweller, caveman.

trombone noun OTHER BRASS INSTRUMENTS: SEE **brass**.

troop noun SEE **group** noun.
troops *armed troops.* SEE **armed services**.

troop verb *We trooped along the road.* march, parade, SEE **walk** verb.

trooper noun SEE **soldier**.

trophy noun **1** [*plural*] *trophies of war.* booty, loot, mementoes, rewards, souvenirs, spoils.
2 *a sporting trophy.* award, cup, medal, prize.

tropical adjective *a tropical climate.* equatorial, SEE **hot**.
OPPOSITES: arctic, SEE **cold** adjective.

trot noun, verb SEE **run** noun, verb.

trotter noun SEE **foot**.

trouble noun **1** *personal troubles.* adversity, affliction, anxiety, burden, difficulty, distress, grief, hardship, SEE **illness**, inconvenience, misery, misfortune, pain, problem, sadness, sorrow, suffering, trial, tribulation, unhappiness, vexation, worry.
2 *trouble in the crowd.* bother, commotion, conflict, discontent, discord, disorder, dissatisfaction, disturbance, fighting, fuss, misbehaviour, misconduct, naughtiness, row, strife, turmoil, unpleasantness, unrest, violence.
3 *engine trouble.* break-down, defect, failure, fault, malfunction.
4 *I took a lot of trouble to get it right.* care, concern, effort, exertion, labour, pains, struggle, thought.

trouble verb *You look sad—is something troubling you?* afflict, annoy, bother, cause trouble to, concern, distress, disturb, grieve, hurt, inconvenience, interfere with, molest, pain, perturb, pester, plague, threaten, torment, upset, vex, worry.
OPPOSITES: SEE **reassure**.

troubled adjective *a troubled conscience. troubled times.* anxious, disturbed, fearful, [*informal*] fraught, guilt-ridden, insecure, perturbed, restless, stricken, uncertain, uneasy, unhappy, vexed, worried.
OPPOSITES: SEE **peaceful**.

trouble-maker noun agitator, SEE **criminal** noun, culprit, delinquent, hooligan, mischief-maker, offender, rabble-rouser, rascal, ring-leader, ruffian, vandal, wrongdoer.

troublesome adjective *troublesome insects. troublesome neighbours.* annoying, badly behaved, bothersome, disobedient, disorderly, distressing, inconvenient, irksome, irritating, naughty, [*informal*] pestiferous, pestilential, rowdy, tiresome, trying, uncooperative, unruly, upsetting, vexing, wearisome, worrisome, worrying.
OPPOSITES: SEE **helpful**.

trounce verb SEE **defeat** verb.

troupe noun SEE **group** noun.

trouper noun SEE **entertainer**.

trousers noun

KINDS OF TROUSERS: [*informal*] bags, breeches, corduroys, culottes, denims, dungarees, jeans, jodhpurs, [*old-fashioned*] knickerbockers, [*informal*] Levis, overalls, [*American*] pants, plus fours, shorts, ski-pants, slacks, [*Scottish*] trews, trunks.

OTHER GARMENTS: SEE **clothes**.

---

truancy noun absenteeism, malingering, shirking, [*informal*] skiving.

truant noun *a truant from school or work.* absentee, deserter (*from the army*), dodger, malingerer, runaway, shirker, [*informal*] skiver.
to play truant be absent, desert, malinger, [*informal*] skive, stay away.

truce noun *a truce between two warring sides.* armistice, cease-fire, moratorium, pact, peace, suspension of hostilities, treaty.

truck noun SEE **railway, vehicle**.

truculent adjective SEE **quarrelsome**.

trudge noun, verb SEE **walk** noun, verb.

true adjective **1** *a true happening. true facts. a true copy.* accurate, actual, authentic, confirmed, correct, exact, factual, faithful, genuine, proper, real, right, veracious, veritable.
2 *a true friend. true love.* constant, dependable, devoted, faithful, firm, honest, honourable, loyal, reliable, responsible, sincere, steady, trustworthy, trusty.
OPPOSITES: SEE **false**.
3 *Are you the true owner of this car?* authorized, legal, legitimate, rightful, valid.
4 *the true aim of a marksman. a true alignment.* accurate, exact, perfect, precise, [*informal*] spot-on, unerring, unswerving.
OPPOSITES: SEE **inaccurate**.

trug noun SEE **basket**.

truism noun SEE **saying**.

trump verb **to trump up** *They trumped up charges against him.* SEE **invent**.

trumpery adjective SEE **showy, worthless**.

trumpet noun OTHER BRASS INSTRUMENTS: SEE **brass**.

trumpet verb VARIOUS SOUNDS: SEE **sound** noun.

truncate verb SEE **shorten**.

truncheon noun *a policeman's truncheon.* baton, club, cudgel, staff, stick.

trundle verb *A wagon trundled up the road.* lumber, lurch, SEE **move** verb.

trunk noun **1** *a tree trunk.* bole, shaft, stalk, stem.
2 *a person's trunk.* body, frame, torso.
3 *an elephant's trunk.* nose, proboscis.
4 *a clothes' trunk.* box, case, chest, coffer, crate, suitcase.
trunks *swimming trunks.* briefs, shorts, SEE **trousers**.

truss noun **1** *a truss of hay.* SEE **bundle** noun.
2 *a truss supporting a bridge.* SEE **support** noun.

truss verb SEE **tie**.

trust noun **1** *The dog has trust in his owner.* belief, certainty, confidence, credence, faith, reliance.
2 *a position of trust.* responsibility, trusteeship.

trust verb **1** *We trust you to do your duty.* bank on, believe in, be sure of, count on, depend on, have confidence in, have faith in, rely on.
2 *I trust you are well.* assume, expect, hope, imagine, presume, suppose, surmise.
OPPOSITES: SEE **doubt** verb.

trustee noun SEE **agent**.

trustful adjective *Small children are often very trustful.* credulous, gullible, innocent, trusting, unquestioning, unsuspecting, unwary.
OPPOSITES: SEE **suspicious**.

trustworthy adjective *a trustworthy friend.* constant, dependable, faithful, honest, honourable, [*informal*] on the level, loyal, reliable, responsible, [*informal*] safe, sensible, steadfast, steady, straightforward, true, [*old-fashioned*] trusty, truthful, upright.
OPPOSITES: SEE **deceitful**.

truth noun **1** *Tell the truth.* facts, reality.

2 *I doubt the truth of her story.* accuracy, authenticity, correctness, exactness, factuality, integrity, reliability, truthfulness, validity, veracity, verity.
3 *an accepted truth.* axiom, fact, maxim, truism.
OPPOSITES: SEE **lie** noun.

truthful adjective **1** *a truthful person.* candid, credible, forthright, frank, honest, reliable, sincere, [*informal*] straight, straightforward, trustworthy, veracious.
2 *a truthful answer.* accurate, correct, proper, right, true, valid.
OPPOSITES: SEE **dishonest**.

try noun *Have a try!* attempt, [*informal*] bash, [*informal*] crack, effort, endeavour, experiment, [*informal*] go, [*informal*] shot, [*informal*] stab, test, trial.

try verb **1** *Try to do your best.* aim, attempt, endeavour, essay, exert yourself, make an effort, strain, strive, struggle, venture.
2 *We tried a new method.* [*informal*] check out, evaluate, examine, experiment with, investigate, test, try out, undertake.
3 *She tries us with her chattering.* SEE **annoy**.

trying adjective SEE **annoying**.

tub noun barrel, bath, butt, cask, drum, keg, pot, vat.
OTHER CONTAINERS: SEE **container**.

tubby adjective [*informal*] *a tubby figure.* SEE **fat** adjective.

tube noun *tubes to carry liquids.* capillary, conduit, cylinder, duct, hose, main, pipe, spout, tubing.

tuber noun SEE **root**.

tuberculosis noun consumption.

tubing noun SEE **tube**.

tuck verb *Tuck your shirt into your jeans.* cram, gather, insert, push, put away, shove, stuff.
to tuck in SEE **eat**.

tufa, tuff nouns SEE **rock** noun.

tuft noun *a tuft of grass.* bunch, clump, cluster, tuffet, tussock.

tug verb **1** *We tugged the cart behind us.* drag, draw, haul, heave, lug, pull, tow.
2 *I tugged at the rope.* jerk, pluck, twitch, wrench, yank.

tuition noun SEE **teaching**.

tumble verb **1** *I tumbled into the water.* collapse, drop, fall, flop, pitch, stumble, topple, trip up.
2 *I tumbled everything into a heap.* disarrange, jumble, mix up, roll, rumple, shove, spill, throw carelessly, toss.

tumbledown adjective *a tumbledown cottage.* badly maintained, broken down, crumbling, decrepit, derelict, dilapidated, ramshackle, rickety, ruined, shaky.

tummy noun SEE **stomach** noun.

tummy-button noun navel, umbilicus.

tumour noun SEE **growth**.

tumult noun SEE **uproar**.

tumultuous adjective *tumultuous applause.* agitated, boisterous, confused, excited, hectic, passionate, tempestuous, turbulent, unrestrained, unruly, uproarious, violent, wild.
OPPOSITES: SEE **calm** adjective.

tun noun SEE **barrel**.

tuna noun tunny.

tune noun air, melody, song, strain, theme.
MUSICAL TERMS: SEE **music**.
in tune SEE **harmonious**.

tune verb *to tune a violin. to tune an engine.* adjust, regulate, set, temper.

tuneful adjective *tuneful music.* [*informal*] catchy, mellifluous, melodious, musical, pleasant, singable.
OPPOSITES: SEE **tuneless**.

tuneless adjective *tuneless music.* atonal, boring, cacophonous, discordant, dissonant, harsh, monotonous, unmusical.
OPPOSITES: SEE **tuneful**.

tunic noun SEE **coat** noun.

tunnel noun burrow, gallery, hole, mine, passage, passageway, shaft, subway, underpass.

tunnel verb *A rabbit tunnelled under the fence.* burrow, dig, excavate, mine.

turbid adjective **1** *turbid waters.* clouded, cloudy, hazy, muddy, murky, opaque, unclear, unsettled.
OPPOSITES: SEE **clear** adjective.
2 *a turbid state of mind.* SEE **turbulent**.

turbine noun SEE **engine**.

turbulence noun SEE **turmoil**.

turbulent adjective **1** *turbulent emotions.* agitated, boisterous, confused, disordered, excited, hectic, passionate, restless, seething, turbid, unrestrained, violent, volatile, wild.
2 *a turbulent crowd.* badly behaved, disorderly, lawless, obstreperous, riotous, rowdy, undisciplined, unruly.
3 *turbulent weather.* blustery, bumpy (*a bumpy flight*), choppy (*choppy seas*), rough, stormy, tempestuous, violent, wild, windy.
OPPOSITES: SEE **calm** adjective.

tureen noun *a soup tureen.* SEE **dish** noun.

turf noun grass, lawn, [*poetic*] sward.
turf accountant [*informal*] bookie, bookmaker.

turgid adjective *a turgid style of writing.* affected, bombastic, flowery, fulsome, grandiose, high-flown, over-blown, pompous, pretentious, stilted, wordy.
OPPOSITES: SEE **lucid**.

turmoil noun *The place was in turmoil until we organized ourselves.* [*informal*] bedlam, chaos, commotion, confusion, disorder, disturbance, ferment, [*informal*] hubbub, [*informal*] hullabaloo, pandemonium, riot, row, rumpus, tumult, turbulence, unrest, upheaval, uproar, welter.
OPPOSITES: SEE **calm** noun.

turn noun **1** *a turn of a wheel.* circle, cycle, revolution, rotation, spin, twirl, whirl.
2 *a turn in the road.* angle, bend, corner, curve, deviation, hairpin bend, junction, loop, twist.
3 *a turn in someone's fortunes.* change of direction, reversal, shift, turning-point, [*informal*] U-turn.
4 *a player's turn in a game.* chance, [*informal*] go, innings, opportunity, shot.
5 *a comic turn in a concert.* SEE **performance**.
6 [*informal*] *He had a bad turn and had to go to hospital.* SEE **illness**.
to give someone a turn SEE **shock** verb.

turn verb **1** *to turn round a central point as a wheel does.* circle, gyrate, hinge, move in a circle, orbit, pivot, revolve, roll, rotate, spin, spiral, swivel, twirl, twist, whirl, yaw.
2 *to turn left or right.* change direction, corner, deviate, divert, go round a corner, negotiate a corner, steer, swerve, veer, wheel.
3 *to turn a wire round a stick.* bend, coil, curl, loop, twist, wind.
4 *We turned the attic into a games room.* adapt, alter, change, convert, make, modify, remake, remodel, transfigure, transform.
5 *The snake turned this way and that.* squirm, twist, wriggle, writhe.
to turn away *They turned uninvited guests away.* decline, dismiss, exclude, send away, [*informal*] send packing.
to turn down 1 *I turned the invitation down.* decline, refuse, reject, spurn.
2 *Turn down the heat.* decrease, lessen, reduce.
to turn into *Tadpoles turn into frogs.* become, be transformed into, change into, metamorphose into.
to turn off 1 *We turned off the main road.* branch off, deviate from, leave.
2 *Turn off the water. Turn off the light.* cut off, disconnect, put off, shut off, stop, switch off, turn out.
3 [*informal*] *She turned me off with her bossy manner.* alienate, irritate, put off, repel.
4 [*informal*] *He was so boring that I turned off.* lose interest, stop listening.
to turn on 1 *Turn on the water. Turn on the light.* connect, start, put on, switch on.
2 [*informal*] *He quite turned her on with his flattering grin.* attract, excite, [*informal*] get going, stimulate.
to turn out 1 *How did your party turn out?* befall, emerge, happen, result.
2 *We had to turn out an intruder.* eject, evict, expel, [*informal*] kick out, remove, throw out.
3 *The factory turns out hundreds of items each day.* make, manufacture, produce.
4 *Turn out the light.* SEE **turn off**.
to turn over 1 *The boat turned over.* capsize, flip, invert, keel over, overturn, turn turtle, turn upside down.
2 *I turned the problem over.* consider, contemplate, deliberate, mull over, ponder, reflect on, think about, weigh up.
to turn tail abscond, [*informal*] beat it, [*informal*] bolt, [*informal*] do a bunk, escape, flee, run away, [*informal*] take to your heels.
to turn up 1 *I turned up some interesting facts.* [*informal*] dig up, disclose, discover, expose, find, reveal, show up, unearth.
2 *Some friends turned up unexpectedly.* appear, arrive, come, [*informal*] drop in, materialize, [*informal*] pop up, visit.
3 *Turn up the volume.* amplify, increase, raise.

turncoat noun SEE **renegade**.

turning noun *a turning in the road.* SEE **corner** noun.

turning-point noun *a turning-point in your life.* crisis, crossroads, new direction, revolution, watershed.

turnover noun **1** *the turnover of a business.* cash-flow, efficiency, output, production, productivity, profits, throughput, yield.
2 *an apple turnover.* SEE **pie**.

turnstile noun entrance, exit, SEE **gate**.

turpitude noun SEE **wickedness**.

turret noun SEE **tower** noun.

tusk noun SEE **tooth**.

tussle noun, verb SEE **struggle** noun, verb.

tussock noun *a tussock of grass.* bunch, clump, cluster, tuffet, tuft.

tutelage noun SEE **protection**.

tutor noun SEE **teacher**.
tutorial noun SEE **teaching**.
tutu noun ballet-skirt.
twaddle noun SEE **nonsense**.
twang noun, verb VARIOUS SOUNDS: SEE **sound** noun.
tweak verb SEE **pinch** verb.
twee adjective SEE **quaint**.
tweet noun, verb VARIOUS SOUNDS: SEE **sound** noun.
twerp noun SEE **idiot**.
twiddle verb *to twiddle your thumbs.* fiddle with, fidget with, twirl, twist.
twig noun branch, offshoot, shoot, spray, stalk, stem, stick.
twig verb [*informal*] *I soon twigged what was happening.* SEE **realize**.
twilight noun dusk, evening, [*poetic*] eventide, [*poetic*] gloaming, gloom, half-light, nightfall, sundown, sunset.
OTHER TIMES OF DAY: SEE **day**.
twin adjective *twin statuettes on the mantelpiece.* balancing, corresponding, duplicate, identical, indistinguishable, matching, paired, similar, symmetrical.
OPPOSITES: SEE **contrasting**.
twin noun *This statue is a twin of the one in the antique shop.* clone, double, duplicate, [*informal*] lookalike, match, pair.
FAMILY RELATIONSHIPS: SEE **family**.
twine noun SEE **string** noun.
twinge noun *a twinge in your tooth.* SEE **pain** noun.
twinkle verb SEE **light** noun (**give light**).
twirl verb **1** *The dancers twirled faster and faster.* gyrate, pirouette, revolve, rotate, spin, turn, twist, wheel, whirl.
2 *I twirled my umbrella.* brandish, twiddle, wave.
twist noun **1** *a twist in a rope. a twist in the road.* bend, coil, curl, kink, knot, loop, tangle, turn, zigzag.
2 *an unexpected twist to a story.* revelation, surprise ending.
twist verb **1** *to twist and turn.* bend, coil, corkscrew, curl, curve, loop, revolve, rotate, screw, spin, spiral, turn, weave, wind, wreathe, wriggle, writhe, zigzag.
2 *The ropes became twisted.* entangle, entwine, intertwine, interweave, tangle.
3 *to twist the lid off a jar.* jerk, wrench, wrest.
4 *to twist something out of shape.* buckle, contort, crinkle, crumple, distort, warp, wrinkle.
5 *to twist the meaning of something.* alter, change, falsify, misquote, misrepresent.
twisted adjective **1** *a twisted rope. a twisted shape.* bent, coiled, contorted, corkscrew, crumpled, deformed, distorted, knotted, looped, misshapen, screwed up, tangled, warped.
2 *a twisted message.* garbled, misreported, misrepresented, misunderstood.
3 *a twisted mind.* SEE **perverted**.
twister noun SEE **swindler**.
twisty adjective [*informal*] *a twisty road.* bendy, crooked, curving, indirect, serpentine, tortuous, twisting, winding, zigzag.
OPPOSITES: SEE **straight**.
twit noun SEE **idiot**.
twitch noun *a nervous twitch.* blink, convulsion, flutter, jerk, jump, spasm, tic, tremor.
twitch verb **1** *Our dog's legs twitch while he's asleep.* fidget, flutter, jerk, jump, start, tremble.
2 *to twitch at a rope.* SEE **tug** verb.
twitter noun, verb VARIOUS SOUNDS: SEE **sound** noun.
two noun couple, duet, duo, pair, twosome.
RELATED ADJECTIVES: binary, bipartite, double, dual, duple, paired, SEE **twin** adjective, twofold.
two-dimensional adjective flat.
OPPOSITES: SEE **three-dimensional**.
two-faced adjective SEE **insincere**.
twosome noun SEE **two** noun.
tycoon noun SEE **businessman**.
type noun **1** *Things of the same type are classed together.* category, class, classification, description, designation, form, genre, group, kind, mark, set, sort, species, variety.
2 *Job is often quoted as a type of patient suffering.* embodiment, epitome, example, model, pattern, personification, standard.
3 *a book printed in large type.* characters, [*formal*] font or fount, letters, lettering, print, printing, type-face.
type verb *to type business letters.* SEE **write**.
typecast verb *to typecast an actor.* stereotype.
typescript noun SEE **document**.
typewriter noun WRITING IMPLEMENTS: SEE **write**.
typhoon noun SEE **storm** noun.
typical adjective **1** *a typical Chinese dinner.* characteristic, distinctive, particular, representative, special.
OPPOSITES: SEE **atypical**.

2 *a typical day*. average, conventional, normal, ordinary, orthodox, predictable, standard, stock, unsurprising, usual.
OPPOSITES: SEE **unusual**.

typify verb SEE **characterize**.

tyrannical adjective *a tyrannical ruler*. absolute, authoritarian, autocratic, [*informal*] bossy, cruel, despotic, dictatorial, domineering, harsh, high-handed, imperious, oppressive, overbearing, ruthless, severe, tyrannous, unjust.
OPPOSITES: SEE **liberal**.

tyrannize verb SEE **oppress**.

tyrannous adjective SEE **tyrannical**.

tyrant noun autocrat, despot, dictator, [*informal*] hard taskmaster, oppressor, SEE **ruler**, slave-driver.

tyre noun pneumatic tyre.

U

ubiquitous adjective [*Ubiquitous* is related to Latin *ubique = everywhere*.] common, commonplace, pervasive, SEE **universal**.

ugliness noun deformity, hideousness, repulsiveness, unsightliness.
OPPOSITES: SEE **beauty**.

ugly adjective **1** *ugly monsters*. deformed, disfigured, disgusting, frightful, ghastly, grisly, grotesque, gruesome, hideous, [*informal*] horrid, ill-favoured, misshapen, monstrous, nasty, objectionable, SEE **repulsive**, revolting.
2 *an ugly room. an ugly piece of furniture*. displeasing, inartistic, inelegant, plain, tasteless, unattractive, unpleasant, unsightly.
OPPOSITES: SEE **beautiful**.
3 *ugly storm clouds. in an ugly mood*. SEE **angry**, dangerous, forbidding, hostile, menacing, ominous, sinister, threatening, unfriendly.

A number of English words like *ulterior*, *ultimate*, and words with the prefix *ultra-* are related to Latin *ultra = beyond*.

---

ulterior adjective *ulterior motives*. concealed, covert, hidden, personal, private, secondary, secret, undeclared, undisclosed.
OPPOSITES: SEE **overt**.

ultimate adjective **1** *We scored in the ultimate minutes of the game*. closing, concluding, eventual, extreme, final, last, terminal.
2 *The ultimate cause of the fire was an electrical fault*. basic, fundamental, primary, root.

ultimatum noun *The enemy issued an ultimatum*. final demand.

umbra noun SEE **shadow** noun.

umbrage noun **to take umbrage** be annoyed [SEE **annoyed**], be offended.

umpire noun adjudicator, arbiter, arbitrator, judge, linesman, moderator, [*informal*] ref, referee.

umpteen adjective SEE **many**.

---

un- The prefix *un-* can be attached to a vast number of words. Sometimes it simply signifies *not* (*happy/unhappy*; *safe/unsafe*); sometimes it has the effect of reversing the action indicated by a verb (*do/undo*; *lock/unlock*). The number of words beginning with *un-* is almost unlimited: we don't have space to include all of them.

---

unabridged adjective SEE **whole**.

unacceptable adjective *unacceptable work. an unacceptable level of pollution*. inadequate, inadmissible, inappropriate, insupportable, intolerable, unsatisfactory, unsuitable.
OPPOSITE: SEE **acceptable**.

unaccompanied adjective *an unaccompanied traveller*. alone, lone, sole, solo (*a solo performer*), unescorted.

unaccountable adjective SEE **inexplicable**.

unaccustomed adjective SEE **strange**.

unadulterated adjective SEE **pure**.

unadventurous adjective **1** *an unadventurous spirit*. cautious, cowardly, spiritless, SEE **timid**, unimaginative.
2 *an unadventurous life*. cloistered, limited, protected, sheltered, unexciting.
OPPOSITES: SEE **adventurous, enterprising**.

unaided adjective single-handed, solo.

unalloyed adjective SEE **pure**.

unalterable adjective SEE **immutable**.

unambiguous adjective SEE **definite**.

unanimous adjective SEE **united**.

unanswerable adjective **1** *an unanswerable riddle*. SEE **insoluble**.
2 *an unanswerable argument*. SEE **indisputable**.

unapproachable adjective SEE **aloof**.

unarguable adjective SEE **indisputable**.

unarmed adjective SEE **undefended**.

unashamed adjective SEE **unrepentant**.

unasked adjective, adverb *It's not often someone does you a favour unasked.* spontaneous(ly), unbidden, uninvited, unprompted, unsolicited, voluntary (voluntarily).

unassuming adjective SEE **modest**.

unattached adjective [*informal*] available, free, independent, single, uncommitted, unmarried, [*informal*] unspoken for.
OPPOSITES: SEE **engaged, married**.

unattractive adjective repulsive, SEE **ugly**, uninviting, unprepossessing.
OPPOSITES: SEE **attractive**.

unauthorized adjective *The train made an unauthorized stop.* abnormal, illegal, irregular, unlawful, unusual.

unavoidable adjective **1** *an unavoidable accident.* certain, destined, fated, inescapable, inevitable, sure.
2 *an unavoidable payment.* compulsory, mandatory, necessary, obligatory, required.
OPPOSITES: SEE **unnecessary**.

unaware adjective SEE **ignorant**.

unbalanced adjective **1** *an unbalanced shape.* asymmetrical, irregular, lopsided, off-centre, uneven.
2 *an unbalanced argument.* biased, bigoted, one-sided, partial, partisan, prejudiced, unfair, unjust.
3 *an unbalanced mind.* SEE **mad**.
OPPOSITES: SEE **balanced**.

unbearable adjective *unbearable pain. an unbearable snob.* insufferable, insupportable, intolerable, unacceptable, unendurable.
OPPOSITES: SEE **tolerable**.

unbeatable adjective SEE **invincible**.

unbecoming adjective *unbecoming behaviour.* dishonourable, ill-mannered, improper, inappropriate, indecorous, indelicate, offensive, tasteless, unattractive, unbefitting, unseemly, unsuitable.
OPPOSITES: SEE **decorous**.

unbelievable adjective SEE **incredible**.

unbend verb **1** *to unbend something that has been bent.* straighten, uncurl, untwist.
OPPOSITES: SEE **bend** verb.
2 [*informal*] *to unbend in front of the TV in the evening.* loosen up, relax, rest, unwind.

unbending adjective SEE **inflexible**.

unbiased adjective *an unbiased opinion.* disinterested, enlightened, even-handed, fair, impartial, independent, just, neutral, non-partisan, objective, open-minded, reasonable, [*informal*] straight, unbigoted, undogmatic, unprejudiced.
OPPOSITES: SEE **biased**.

unbidden adjective SEE **uninvited**.

unbind verb SEE **unfasten**.

unblemished adjective SEE **spotless**.

unblock, unbolt verbs SEE **open** verb.

unblushing adjective SEE **unrepentant**.

unbosom verb **to unbosom yourself** SEE **confess**.

unbounded adjective SEE **boundless**.

unbreakable adjective SEE **indestructible**.

unbridled adjective SEE **unrestrained**.

unbroken adjective SEE **continuous, whole**.

unburden verb **to unburden yourself** SEE **confess**.

uncalled for adjective SEE **unnecessary**.

uncanny adjective SEE **eerie**.

uncared for adjective SEE **neglected**.

uncaring adjective SEE **callous**.

unceasing adjective SEE **continual**.

unceremonious adjective SEE **informal**.

uncertain adjective **1** *The outcome of the trial is uncertain.* ambiguous, arguable, conjectural, imprecise, incalculable, inconclusive, indefinite, indeterminate, speculative, unclear, unconvincing, undecided, undetermined, unforeseeable, unknown, unresolved.
2 *I'm uncertain what to believe.* agnostic, ambivalent, doubtful, dubious, [*informal*] hazy, insecure, [*informal*] in two minds, self-questioning, unconvinced, undecided, unsure, vague, wavering.
3 *My chance of success is uncertain.* [*informal*] chancy, hazardous, [*informal*] iffy, problematical, questionable, risky, [*informal*] touch and go.
4 *Our climate is uncertain.* changeable, erratic, fitful, inconstant, irregular, precarious, unpredictable, unreliable, variable.
OPPOSITES: SEE **certain**.

unchangeable adjective SEE **invariable**.

unchanging adjective SEE **constant**.

uncharitable, unchristian adjectives SEE **unkind**.

uncivil adjective SEE **rude**.

uncivilized adjective *uncivilized behaviour.* anarchic, antisocial, badly

behaved, barbarian, barbaric, barbarous, disorganized, illiterate, Philistine, primitive, savage, uncultured, uneducated, unenlightened, unsophisticated, wild.
OPPOSITES: SEE **civilized**.

uncle noun FAMILY RELATIONSHIPS: SEE **family**.
RELATED ADJECTIVE: avuncular.

unclean adjective SEE **dirty** adjective.

unclear adjective *unclear evidence. unclear meaning.* ambiguous, cryptic, doubtful, dubious, hazy, imprecise, obscure, puzzling, SEE **uncertain**, vague.
OPPOSITES: SEE **clear** adjective.

unclose verb SEE **open** verb.

unclothed adjective SEE **naked**.

uncomfortable adjective **1** *uncomfortable surroundings. an uncomfortable bed.* SEE **bleak**, comfortless, cramped, hard, inconvenient, lumpy, painful.
OPPOSITES: SEE **comfortable**.
2 *uncomfortable clothes.* formal, restrictive, stiff, tight, tight-fitting.
3 *an uncomfortable silence.* awkward, distressing, SEE **embarrassing**, nervous, restless, troubled, uneasy, worried.

uncommon adjective SEE **unusual**.

uncommunicative adjective SEE **silent**.

uncomplimentary adjective *uncomplimentary remarks.* censorious, critical, deprecatory, depreciatory, derogatory, disapproving, disparaging, pejorative, SEE **rude**, scathing, slighting, unfavourable, unflattering.
OPPOSITES: SEE **complimentary**.

uncompromising adjective SEE **inflexible**.

unconcealed adjective SEE **obvious**.

unconcerned adjective SEE **callous**.

unconditional adjective *unconditional surrender.* absolute, categorical, complete, full, outright, total, unequivocal, unlimited, unqualified, unreserved, unrestricted, whole-hearted, [*informal*] with no strings attached.
OPPOSITES: SEE **conditional**.

uncongenial adjective *I can't work in uncongenial surroundings.* alien, antipathetic, disagreeable, incompatible, unattractive, unfriendly, unpleasant, unsympathetic.
OPPOSITES: SEE **congenial**.

unconnected adjective SEE **irrelevant**, **separate** adjective.

unconquerable adjective SEE **invincible**.

unconscionable adjective **1** *an unconscionable rogue.* SEE **unscrupulous**.
2 *He kept me waiting an unconscionable time.* SEE **unjustifiable**.

unconscious adjective **1** *unconscious after a knock on the head.* anaesthetized, comatose, concussed, [*informal*] dead to the world, insensible, [*informal*] knocked out, oblivious, [*informal*] out for the count, senseless, sleeping.
2 *unconscious of her effect on others.* blind (to), oblivious, unaware, unwitting.
3 *unconscious humour.* accidental, inadvertent, unintended, unintentional.
4 *an unconscious reaction.* automatic, impulsive, instinctive, involuntary, reflex, spontaneous, unthinking.
5 *your unconscious desires.* repressed, subconscious, subliminal, suppressed.
OPPOSITES: SEE **conscious**.

unconsciousness noun coma, faint, oblivion, sleep.

uncontrollable adjective SEE **rebellious**.

unconventional adjective *unconventional ideas. an unconventional appearance.* abnormal, atypical, [*informal*] cranky, eccentric, exotic, futuristic, idiosyncratic, inventive, non-conforming, non-standard, odd, off-beat, original, peculiar, progressive, revolutionary, strange, surprising, unaccustomed, unorthodox, [*informal*] way-out, wayward, weird, zany.
OPPOSITES: SEE **conventional**.

unconvincing adjective SEE **incredible**.

uncooked adjective SEE **raw**.

uncooperative adjective *an uncooperative partner.* lazy, obstructive, recalcitrant, selfish, unhelpful, unwilling.
OPPOSITES: SEE **co-operative**.

uncoordinated adjective SEE **clumsy**.

uncouple verb SEE **disconnect**.

uncouth adjective SEE **rude**.

uncover verb **1** *to uncover something which has been concealed.* bare, disclose, disrobe, expose, reveal, show, strip, take the wraps off, undress, unmask, unveil, unwrap.
2 *to uncover something which was lost.* come across, detect, dig up, discover, exhume, locate, unearth.
OPPOSITES: SEE **cover** verb.

uncritical adjective SEE **undiscriminating**.

unctuous adjective SEE **obsequious**.

uncultivated adjective SEE **wild**.

undamaged adjective *The goods survived the journey undamaged.* faultless, [*informal*] in one piece, intact, mint (*in mint condition*), perfect, safe, sound,

unharmed, unhurt, unimpaired, uninjured, unscathed, whole, [*informal*] without a scratch.
OPPOSITES: SEE **damaged**.

undaunted adjective SEE **brave**.

undeceive verb SEE **disillusion**.

undecided adjective **1** *The outcome is still undecided.* SEE **uncertain**.
2 *an undecided manner*. SEE **hesitant**.

undefended adjective *The army withdrew and left the post undefended.* defenceless, exposed, helpless, insecure, unarmed, unfortified, unguarded, unprotected, vulnerable, weaponless.
OPPOSITES: SEE **secure** adjective.

undefiled adjective SEE **chaste**.

undefined adjective SEE **imprecise**.

undemanding adjective *undemanding work*. SEE **easy**.

undemocratic adjective *an undemocratic political system*. SEE **totalitarian**.

undemonstrative adjective SEE **aloof**.

undeniable adjective SEE **indisputable**.

Often, the prefix *under-* simply adds the notion *below, beneath, lower* to the word it is attached to (e.g. *underground, underclothes, undertone*). It can also mean *less than might be expected* (e.g. *underprivileged, understaffed*).

---

underclothes noun lingerie, underclothing, undergarments, underwear, [*informal*] undies.

VARIOUS UNDERGARMENTS: bra, braces, brassière, briefs, camiknickers, corset, drawers, garter, girdle, knickers, panties, panti-hose, pants, petticoat, slip, suspenders, tights, trunks, underpants, underskirt, vest.

OTHER GARMENTS: SEE **clothes**.

---

undercover adjective SEE **secret** adjective.

undercurrent noun *an undercurrent of hostility*. atmosphere, feeling, hint, sense, suggestion, trace, undertone.

undercut verb SEE **compete (compete against)**.

underdeveloped adjective SEE **backward**.

underdog noun SEE **subordinate** noun.

underdone adjective SEE **raw**.

underestimate verb *to underestimate difficulties*. belittle, dismiss, disparage, minimize, misjudge, underrate, undervalue.
OPPOSITES: SEE **exaggerate**.

underfed adjective SEE **hungry**.

undergarment noun SEE **underclothes**.

undergo verb *to undergo an operation*. bear, be subjected to, endure, experience, go through, put up with, submit yourself to, suffer, withstand.

undergraduate noun SEE **student**.

underground adjective **1** *an underground store*. subterranean.
2 *an underground society*. SEE **secret** adjective.
underground railway metro, tube.

undergrowth noun *undergrowth in the woods*. brush, bushes, ground cover, plants, vegetation.

underhand adjective SEE **sly**.

underlie verb SEE **support** verb.

underline verb SEE **emphasize**.

underling noun SEE **subordinate** noun.

undermine verb **1** *to undermine a wall*. burrow under, dig under, erode, excavate, mine under, sabotage, tunnel under, undercut.
OPPOSITES: underpin, SEE **support** verb.
2 *to undermine someone's confidence*. destroy, ruin, sap, weaken, wear away.
OPPOSITES: SEE **boost** verb.

underpants noun SEE **underclothes**.

underpaid adjective SEE **poor**.

underpass noun subway.

underpin verb SEE **support** verb.

underprivileged adjective deprived, destitute, disadvantaged, impoverished, needy, SEE **poor**.

underrate verb SEE **underestimate**.

undersea adjective subaquatic, submarine, underwater.

undersized adjective SEE **small**.

understand verb **1** *to understand what something means*. appreciate, apprehend, comprehend, [*informal*] cotton on to, decipher, decode, fathom, follow, gather, [*informal*] get, [*informal*] get to the bottom of, grasp, interpret, know, learn, make out, make sense of, master, perceive, realize, recognize, see, take in, [*informal*] twig.
2 *She understands animals*. empathize with, sympathize with.

understanding noun **1** *a person of quick understanding*. ability, acumen, brains, cleverness, discernment, insight, intellect, intelligence, judgement, penetration, perceptiveness, sense, wisdom.

2 *an understanding of a problem.* appreciation, apprehension, awareness, cognition, comprehension, grasp, knowledge.
3 *friendly understanding between two people.* accord, agreement, compassion, consensus, consent, consideration, empathy, fellow feeling, harmony, kindness, mutuality, sympathy, tolerance.
4 *a formal understanding between two parties.* arrangement, bargain, compact, contract, deal, entente, pact, settlement, treaty.

understate verb *to understate a problem.* belittle, [*informal*] make light of, minimize, [*informal*] play down, [*informal*] soft-pedal.
OPPOSITES: SEE **exaggerate**.

understudy noun SEE **deputy**.

understudy verb SEE **deputize**.

undertake verb **1** *to undertake to do something.* agree, consent, guarantee, pledge, promise.
2 *to undertake a task.* accept responsibility for, address, approach, attempt, attend to, begin, commence, commit yourself to, cope with, deal with, embark on, grapple with, handle, manage, tackle, take on, take up, try.

undertaker noun funeral director, [*American*] mortician.

undertaking noun SEE **enterprise**.

undertone noun SEE **undercurrent**.

undertow noun SEE **current** noun.

undervalue verb SEE **underestimate**.

underwater adjective *underwater exploration.* subaquatic, submarine, undersea.

underwear noun SEE **underclothes**.

underweight adjective SEE **light** adjective.

underworld noun SEE **hell**.

underwrite verb *to underwrite a business enterprise.* SEE **finance** verb.

undeserved adjective *undeserved punishment.* unearned, unfair, unjustified, unmerited, unwarranted.

undesirable adjective SEE **objectionable**.

undeveloped adjective SEE **backward**.

undignified adjective *an undignified rush to be first.* indecorous, inelegant, ridiculous, scrambled, unbecoming, unseemly.
OPPOSITES: SEE **dignified**.

undisciplined adjective *an undisciplined rabble.* anarchic, chaotic, disobedient, disorderly, disorganized, intractable, rebellious, uncontrolled, unruly, unsystematic, untrained, wild, wilful.
OPPOSITES: SEE **disciplined**.

undiscriminating adjective *an undiscriminating audience.* easily pleased, imperceptive, superficial, thoughtless, uncritical, undiscerning, unselective.
OPPOSITES: SEE **discriminating**.

undisguised adjective SEE **blatant**.

undisputed adjective SEE **indisputable**.

undistinguished adjective SEE **ordinary**.

undo verb **1** *to undo a fastening. to undo a parcel.* detach, disconnect, disengage, loose, loosen, open, part, separate, unbind, unbuckle, unbutton, unchain, unclasp, unclip, uncouple, unfasten, unfetter, unhook, unleash, unlock, unpick, unpin, unscrew, unseal, unshackle, unstick, untether, untie, unwrap, unzip.
2 *to undo someone's good work.* annul, cancel out, destroy, mar, nullify, quash (*to quash a decision*), reverse, ruin, spoil, undermine, vitiate, wipe out, wreck.

undoing noun SEE **ruin** noun.

undoubted adjective SEE **indisputable**.

undoubtedly adverb certainly, definitely, doubtless, indubitably, of course, surely, undeniably, unquestionably.

undreamed of adjective SEE **inconceivable**.

undress verb disrobe, divest yourself, [*informal*] peel off, shed your clothes, strip, take off your clothes, uncover yourself.
OPPOSITES: SEE **dress** verb.

undressed adjective SEE **naked**.

undue adjective SEE **excessive**.

undulating adjective SEE **wavy**.

undying adjective SEE **eternal**.

unearth verb SEE **uncover**.

unearthly adjective SEE **eerie**.

uneasy adjective **1** *an uneasy night.* disturbed, restive, restless, uncomfortable, unsettled.
OPPOSITES: SEE **comfortable**.
2 *an uneasy feeling.* anxious, apprehensive, awkward, concerned, distressing, edgy, fearful, insecure, jittery, nervous, tense, troubled, upsetting, worried.
OPPOSITES: SEE **secure** adjective.

uneconomic adjective SEE **unprofitable**.

uneducated adjective SEE **ignorant**.

unemotional adjective **1** *a doctor's unemotional approach to illness.* clinical,

cool, dispassionate, impassive, objective.
2 *an unemotional reaction to a tragedy.* apathetic, cold, frigid, hard-hearted, heartless, indifferent, unfeeling, unmoved, unresponsive.
OPPOSITES: SEE **emotional**.

unemployed adjective jobless, on the dole, out of work, redundant.
OPPOSITES: SEE **working**.

unending adjective SEE **endless**.

unendurable adjective SEE **unbearable**.

unenthusiastic adjective SEE **apathetic**.

unequal adjective 1 *unequal contributions from two participants.* different, differing, disparate, dissimilar, uneven, varying.
OPPOSITES: SEE **equal**.
2 *unequal treatment of contestants by the referee.* biased, prejudiced, unjust.
3 *an unequal contest.* ill-matched, one-sided, unbalanced, uneven, unfair.
OPPOSITES: SEE **fair** adjective.

unequalled adjective *an unequalled reputation.* incomparable, inimitable, matchless, peerless, supreme, surpassing, unmatched, unparalleled, unrivalled, unsurpassed.

unequivocal adjective SEE **definite**.

unerring adjective SEE **accurate**.

unethical adjective SEE **immoral**.

uneven adjective 1 *an uneven surface.* bent, broken, bumpy, crooked, irregular, jagged, jerky, pitted, rough, rutted, undulating, wavy.
OPPOSITES: SEE **smooth** adjective.
2 *an uneven rhythm.* erratic, fitful, fluctuating, inconsistent, spasmodic, unpredictable, variable, varying.
OPPOSITES: SEE **consistent**.
3 *an uneven load.* asymmetrical, lop-sided, unsteady.
4 *an uneven contest.* ill-matched, one-sided, unbalanced, unequal, unfair.
OPPOSITES: SEE **balanced**.

unexceptionable adjective SEE **perfect** adjective.

unexceptional, unexciting adjectives SEE **ordinary**.

unexpected adjective *an unexpected meeting.* accidental, chance, fortuitous, sudden, surprising, unforeseen, unhoped for, unlooked for, unplanned, unpredictable, unusual.
OPPOSITES: SEE **expected**.

unfailing adjective SEE **dependable**.

unfair adjective SEE **unjust**.

unfaithful adjective deceitful, disloyal, double-dealing, duplicitous, faithless, false, fickle, inconstant, perfidious, traitorous, treacherous, treasonable, unreliable, untrue, untrustworthy.
OPPOSITES: SEE **faithful**.

unfaithfulness noun 1 *unfaithfulness to your country or your party.* duplicity, perfidy, treachery, treason.
2 *unfaithfulness to a husband or wife.* adultery, infidelity.

unfamiliar adjective SEE **strange**.

unfashionable adjective dated, obsolete, old-fashioned, [*informal*] out (*Bright colours are out this year*), outmoded, passé, superseded, unstylish.
OPPOSITES: SEE **fashionable**.

unfasten verb SEE **undo**.

unfavourable adjective 1 *unfavourable criticism. unfavourable winds.* adverse, attacking, contrary, critical, disapproving, discouraging, hostile, ill-disposed, inauspicious, negative, opposing, uncomplimentary, unfriendly, unhelpful, unkind, unpromising, unpropitious, unsympathetic.
2 *an unfavourable reputation.* bad, undesirable, unenviable, unsatisfactory.
OPPOSITES: SEE **favourable**.

unfeeling adjective SEE **callous**.

unfinished adjective imperfect, incomplete, rough, sketchy, uncompleted, unpolished.
OPPOSITES: SEE **perfect** adjective.

unfit adjective 1 *A drunkard is unfit to drive. A slum is unfit to live in.* ill-equipped, inadequate, incapable, incompetent, unsatisfactory, useless.
2 *The film was unfit for children's viewing.* improper, inappropriate, unbecoming, unsuitable, unsuited.
3 *You won't play well if you're unfit.* feeble, flabby, SEE **ill**, out of condition, unhealthy.
OPPOSITES: SEE **fit** adjective.

unflagging adjective SEE **tireless**.

unflappable adjective SEE **calm** adjective.

unflattering adjective SEE **candid**.

unflinching adjective SEE **resolute**.

unfold verb SEE **open** verb.

unforeseen adjective SEE **unexpected**.

unforgettable adjective SEE **memorable**.

unforgivable adjective *an unforgivable mistake.* inexcusable, mortal (*a mortal sin*), reprehensible, shameful, unjustifiable, unpardonable, unwarrantable.
OPPOSITES: SEE **forgivable**.

unfortunate adjective SEE **unlucky**.

unfounded adjective SEE **groundless**.

unfreeze verb SEE **thaw**.

unfrequented adjective SEE **inaccessible**.

unfriendly adjective *an unfriendly welcome. unfriendly people*. aggressive, aloof, antagonistic, antisocial, cold, cool, detached, disagreeable, distant, forbidding, hostile, ill-disposed, impersonal, indifferent, inhospitable, menacing, nasty, obnoxious, offensive, reserved, rude, sour, stand-offish, [*informal*] starchy, stern, threatening, uncivil, uncongenial, unenthusiastic, unkind, unneighbourly, unsociable, unsympathetic, unwelcoming.
OPPOSITES: SEE **friendly**.

unfruitful adjective SEE **unproductive**.

unfurl verb SEE **open** verb.

ungainly adjective SEE **awkward**.

ungentlemanly adjective SEE **vulgar**.

unget-at-able adjective SEE **inaccessible**.

ungodly adjective SEE **irreligious**.

ungovernable adjective SEE **rebellious**.

ungrateful adjective *I won't give her any more if she's ungrateful*. displeased, ill-mannered, selfish, unappreciative, unthankful.
OPPOSITES: SEE **grateful**.

unguarded adjective SEE **careless**.

unguent noun SEE **ointment**.

unhappy adjective **1** *unhappy because things are not going well*. SEE **sad**.
2 *an unhappy accident*. SEE **unlucky**.
3 *an unhappy arrangement*. SEE **unsatisfactory**.

unhealthy adjective **1** *unhealthy animals*. ailing, delicate, diseased, SEE **ill**, infected, [*informal*] poorly, sick, sickly, suffering, unwell, weak.
2 *unhealthy conditions*. deleterious, dirty, harmful, insalubrious, insanitary, polluted, unhygienic, unwholesome.
OPPOSITES: SEE **healthy**.

unheard of adjective SEE **exceptional**.

unhelpful adjective *an unhelpful shop-assistant*. disobliging, inconsiderate, negative, slow, uncivil, uncooperative, unwilling.
OPPOSITES: SEE **obliging**.

unhinged adjective SEE **mad**.

unhoped for adjective SEE **unexpected**.

unhurried adjective SEE **leisurely**.

unhygienic adjective SEE **unhealthy**.

unidentifiable adjective camouflaged, disguised, hidden, SEE **unidentified**, unrecognizable.
OPPOSITES: SEE **identifiable**.

unidentified adjective *an unidentified benefactor*. anonymous, incognito, nameless, unfamiliar, unknown, unnamed, unrecognized, unspecified.
OPPOSITES: SEE **named**.

The prefix *uni-* in words like *unicorn*, *uniform*, *unisex*, etc., is related to Latin *unus=one*. (Do not confuse with words like *unidentified* and *unimaginable*, which are formed by attaching prefix *un-* to words beginning with *i*-!)

---

uniform adjective *a uniform appearance*. consistent, homogeneous, identical, indistinguishable, regular, the same, similar, single, unvarying.
OPPOSITES: SEE **different**.

uniform noun livery.

unify verb *unified by a common purpose*. amalgamate, bring together, combine, consolidate, fuse, harmonize, integrate, join, merge, unite, weld together.
OPPOSITES: SEE **separate** verb.

unilateral adjective *a unilateral decision*. one-sided.
OPPOSITE: multilateral.

unimaginable adjective SEE **inconceivable**.

unimaginative adjective *an unimaginative story*. banal, boring, derivative, dull, hackneyed, inartistic, obvious, ordinary, pedestrian, prosaic, stale, trite, uninspired, uninteresting, unoriginal.
OPPOSITES: SEE **imaginative**.

unimpeachable adjective SEE **indisputable**.

unimportant adjective *unimportant news. an unimportant mistake*. ephemeral, immaterial, inconsequential, inessential, insignificant, irrelevant, lightweight, minor, negligible, peripheral, petty, secondary, slight, SEE **small**, trifling, trivial, uninteresting, unremarkable, worthless.
OPPOSITES: SEE **important**.

unimpressive adjective SEE **ordinary**.

uninhabited adjective *an uninhabited island*. abandoned, deserted, empty, uncolonized, unoccupied, unpeopled, vacant.
OPPOSITES: SEE **inhabited**.

uninhibited adjective *uninhibited language.* abandoned, casual, frank, informal, natural, open, relaxed, spontaneous, unrepressed, unreserved, unrestrained, unselfconscious.
OPPOSITES: SEE **inhibited**.

uninspired adjective SEE **unimaginative**.

unintelligent adjective SEE **stupid**.

unintelligible adjective SEE **incomprehensible**.

unintentional adjective *an unintentional insult.* accidental, fortuitous, inadvertent, involuntary, unconscious, unintended, unplanned, unwitting.
OPPOSITES: SEE **intentional**.

uninterested adjective *uninterested pupils.* apathetic, bored, incurious, indifferent, lethargic, passive, phlegmatic, unconcerned, unenthusiastic, uninvolved, unresponsive.
OPPOSITES: SEE **interested**.

uninteresting adjective *an uninteresting book. an uninteresting voice.* boring, dreary, dry, dull, flat, monotonous, obvious, SEE **ordinary**, predictable, tedious, unexciting, uninspiring, vapid, wearisome.
OPPOSITE: SEE **interesting**.

uninterrupted adjective SEE **continuous**.

uninvited adjective *uninvited guests.* unasked, unbidden, unwelcome.

uninviting adjective SEE **unattractive**.

uninvolved adjective SEE **detached**.

union noun **1** *a union of two organizations or parties.* SEE **alliance**, amalgamation, association, coalition, conjunction, integration, joining together, merger, unification, unity.
2 *a union of two substances.* amalgam, blend, combination, compound, fusion, mixture, synthesis.
3 *a union of two people.* marriage, matrimony, partnership, wedlock.
4 *sexual union.* SEE **sex**.

unique adjective [Many people consider that *unique* correctly means *being the only one of its kind*, and that sense 2 is incorrect.] **1** [=*being the only one of its kind*] *She's proud of her ring because of its unique design.* distinctive, lone, [*informal*] one-off, peculiar, single, singular, unparalleled.
2 [*informal=rare, unusual*] SEE **unusual**.

unit noun **1** UNITS OF MEASUREMENT: SEE **measure** noun.
2 *a complete unit.* entity, item, whole.
3 *You can buy extra units to add on when you can afford them.* component, constituent, element, module, part, piece, portion, section, segment.

unite verb **1** *The manager decided to unite two departments.* amalgamate, blend, bring together, coalesce, combine, confederate, consolidate, couple, federate, fuse, harmonize, incorporate, integrate, join, link, marry, merge, unify, weld together.
OPPOSITES: SEE **separate** verb.
2 *Everyone united to support the appeal for charity.* ally, associate, collaborate, conspire, co-operate, go into partnership, join forces.
OPPOSITES: SEE **compete**.
3 *to unite in marriage* SEE **marry**.

united adjective *a united decision. a united effort.* agreed, common, collective, concerted, corporate, harmonious, joint, unanimous, undivided.
OPPOSITES: SEE **disunited**.
to be united SEE **agree**.

unity noun SEE **agreement**.

universal adjective *universal peace.* all-round, common, general, global, international, total, ubiquitous, widespread, worldwide.

universe noun cosmos, the heavens.
ASTRONOMICAL TERMS: SEE **astronomy**.

university noun SEE **college**.

unjust adjective *an unjust decision.* biased, bigoted, indefensible, inequitable, one-sided, partial, partisan, prejudiced, undeserved, unfair, unjustified, unlawful, unmerited, unreasonable, unwarranted, wrong, wrongful.
OPPOSITES: SEE **just**.

unjustifiable adjective *unjustifiable severity.* excessive, immoderate, indefensible, inexcusable, unacceptable, unconscionable, unforgivable, SEE **unjust**, unreasonable, unwarrantable.
OPPOSITES: SEE **justifiable**.

unkempt adjective SEE **untidy**.

unkind adjective [There are many other words you can use in addition to those listed here: SEE **angry**, **critical**, **cruel**, etc.] *unkind criticism. unkind treatment of animals.* [*informal*] beastly, callous, cold-blooded, cruel, discourteous, disobliging, hard, hard-hearted, harsh, heartless, hurtful, ill-natured, impolite, inconsiderate, inhumane, insensitive, malevolent, malicious, mean, merciless, nasty, pitiless, relentless, ruthless, sadistic, savage, selfish, severe, spiteful, stern, tactless, thoughtless, uncaring, uncharitable, unchristian,

unfeeling, unfriendly, unpleasant, unsympathetic, vicious.
OPPOSITES: SEE **kind** adjective.

unknown adjective 1 *unknown intruders.* anonymous, disguised, incognito, mysterious, nameless, strange, unidentified, unnamed, unrecognized, unspecified.
OPPOSITES: SEE **named**.
2 *unknown territory.* alien, foreign, uncharted, undiscovered, unexplored, unfamiliar, unmapped.
OPPOSITES: SEE **familiar**.
3 *an unknown actor.* humble, insignificant, little-known, lowly, obscure, undistinguished, unheard of, unimportant.
OPPOSITES: SEE **famous**.

unladen adjective SEE **empty**.

unladylike adjective SEE **vulgar**.

unlawful adjective SEE **illegal**.

unlearn verb SEE **forget**.

unleash verb SEE **release** verb.

unlettered adjective SEE **ignorant**.

unlike adjective SEE **dissimilar**.

unlikely adjective 1 *an unlikely story.* dubious, far-fetched, implausible, improbable, incredible, suspect, suspicious, [*informal*] tall (*a tall story*), unbelievable, unconvincing.
2 *an unlikely possibility.* distant, doubtful, faint, [*informal*] outside, remote, slight.
OPPOSITES: SEE **likely**.

unlimited adjective SEE **boundless**.

unload verb *We unloaded the cases at the station.* discharge, drop off, [*informal*] dump, empty, offload, take off, unpack.
OPPOSITES: SEE **load** verb.

unlock verb SEE **open** verb.

unlooked for adjective SEE **unexpected**.

unloved adjective abandoned, forsaken, SEE **hated**, lovelorn, neglected, rejected, spurned, uncared for, unvalued, unwanted.
OPPOSITE: loved [SEE **love** verb].

unlucky adjective 1 *an unlucky mistake.* accidental, calamitous, chance, disastrous, dreadful, tragic, unfortunate, untimely, unwelcome.
2 *an unlucky person.* [*informal*] accident-prone, hapless, luckless, unhappy, unsuccessful, wretched.
3 *13 is supposed to be an unlucky number.* cursed, ill-fated, ill-omened, ill-starred, inauspicious, jinxed, ominous, unfavourable.
OPPOSITES: SEE **lucky**.

unmanageable adjective SEE **rebellious**.

unmanly adjective SEE **effeminate**.

unmannerly adjective SEE **rude**.

unmarried adjective [*informal*] available, celibate, single, unwed.
an unmarried person [*male*] bachelor, [*female*] spinster.

unmask verb SEE **reveal**.

unmentionable adjective SEE **taboo** adjective.

unmindful adjective SEE **oblivious**.

unmistakable adjective SEE **obvious**.

unmitigated, unmixed adjectives SEE **absolute**.

unmoved adjective SEE **unemotional**.

unnamed adjective SEE **unidentified**.

unnatural adjective 1 *unnatural happenings.* abnormal, bizarre, eerie, extraordinary, fantastic, freak, inexplicable, magic, magical, odd, queer, strange, supernatural, unaccountable, uncanny, unusual, weird.
2 *unnatural feelings.* callous, cold-blooded, cruel, hard-hearted, heartless, inhuman, inhumane, monstrous, perverse, perverted, sadistic, savage, stony-hearted, unfeeling, unkind.
3 *unnatural behaviour. an unnatural accent.* actorish, affected, bogus, fake, feigned, insincere, mannered, [*informal*] phoney, pretended, [*informal*] pseudo, [*informal*] put on, self-conscious, stagey, stiff, stilted, theatrical, unspontaneous.
4 *unnatural materials.* artificial, fabricated, imitation, man-made, manufactured, simulated, synthetic.
OPPOSITES: SEE **natural**.

unnecessary adjective *Let's get rid of all the unnecessary things lying around.* dispensable, excessive, expendable, extra, inessential, needless, non-essential, redundant, superfluous, surplus, uncalled for, unjustified, unneeded, unwanted, useless.
OPPOSITES: SEE **necessary**.

unnerve verb SEE **discourage**.

unobtrusive adjective SEE **inconspicuous**.

unoccupied adjective SEE **uninhabited**.

unofficial adjective *an unofficial warning.* friendly, informal, [*informal*] off the record, private, unauthorized, unconfirmed, unlicensed.
OPPOSITES: SEE **official** adjective.

unoriginal adjective *an unoriginal joke.* banal, borrowed, conventional, copied, [*informal*] corny, derivative, hackneyed, old, orthodox, second-hand,

stale, traditional, unimaginative, uninspired, uninventive.
OPPOSITES: SEE **original**.

unorthodox adjective SEE **unconventional**.

unpaid adjective **1** *unpaid bills*. due, outstanding, owing.
2 *unpaid work*. unremunerative, voluntary.

unpalatable adjective *unpalatable food*. disgusting, inedible, nauseating, sickening, tasteless, unappetizing, SEE **unpleasant**.
OPPOSITES: SEE **palatable**.
WORDS DESCRIBING TASTE: SEE **taste** verb.

unparalleled adjective SEE **unequalled**.

unpardonable adjective SEE **unforgivable**.

unperturbed adjective SEE **untroubled**.

unpick verb SEE **undo**.

unplanned adjective SEE **spontaneous**.

unpleasant adjective [*Unpleasant* can refer to anything which displeases you: there are far more synonyms than we can give here.] abhorrent, abominable, antisocial, appalling, awful, SEE **bad**, bad-tempered, bitter, coarse, crude, detestable, diabolical, dirty, disagreeable, disgusting, displeasing, distasteful, dreadful, evil, fearful, fearsome, filthy, foul, frightful, ghastly, grim, grisly, gruesome, harsh, hateful, [*informal*] hellish, hideous, horrible, horrid, horrifying, improper, indecent, irksome, loathsome, [*informal*] lousy, malevolent, malicious, mucky, nasty, nauseating, objectionable, obnoxious, odious, offensive, repellent, repugnant, repulsive, revolting, rude, shocking, sickening, sickly, sordid, sour, spiteful, squalid, terrible, ugly, unattractive, uncouth, undesirable, unfriendly, unkind, unpalatable, unsavoury, unwelcome, upsetting, vexing, vicious, vile, vulgar.
OPPOSITES: SEE **pleasant**.

unpolished adjective SEE **rough**.

unpopular adjective *an unpopular choice. an unpopular government*. despised, disliked, hated, minority (*minority interests*), rejected, shunned, unfashionable, unloved, unwanted.
OPPOSITES: SEE **popular**.

unprecedented adjective SEE **exceptional**.

unpredictable adjective *unpredictable weather*. changeable, uncertain, unexpected, unforeseeable, SEE **variable**.
OPPOSITES: SEE **predictable**.

unprejudiced adjective SEE **unbiased**.

unpremeditated adjective SEE **spontaneous**.

unprepared adjective **1** *unprepared for bad weather*. [*informal*] caught napping, ill-equipped, unready.
2 *an unprepared speech*. SEE **spontaneous**.

unprepossessing adjective SEE **unattractive**.

unpretentious adjective *Although she was wealthy, she lived in an unpretentious house*. humble, modest, plain, simple, straightforward, unaffected, unassuming, unostentatious, unsophisticated.
OPPOSITES: SEE **pretentious**.

unprincipled adjective SEE **unscrupulous**.

unprintable adjective SEE **rude**.

unproductive adjective **1** *unproductive work*. ineffective, fruitless, futile, pointless, unprofitable, unrewarding, useless, valueless, worthless.
2 *an unproductive garden*. arid, barren, infertile, sterile, unfruitful.
OPPOSITES: SEE **productive**.

unprofessional adjective *an unprofessional attitude towards your work*. amateurish, SEE **casual**, incompetent, inefficient, irresponsible, lax, negligent, unethical, unseemly, unskilled, unworthy.
OPPOSITES: SEE **professional**.

unprofitable adjective *an unprofitable business*. loss-making, uncommercial, uneconomic, unproductive, unremunerative, unrewarding.
OPPOSITES: SEE **profitable**.

unpromising adjective SEE **unfavourable**.

unprotected adjective SEE **helpless**.

unprovable adjective SEE **questionable**, undemonstrable, unsubstantiated, unverifiable.
OPPOSITES: SEE **provable**.

unpunctual adjective behind-hand, delayed, late, overdue, tardy, unreliable.
OPPOSITES: SEE **punctual**.

unqualified adjective **1** *an unqualified worker*. SEE **amateur** adjective.
2 *an unqualified refusal*. SEE **absolute**.

unquestionable adjective SEE **indisputable**.

unravel verb SEE **disentangle**.

unreal adjective SEE **imaginary**.

unrealistic adjective **1** *an unrealistic portrait*. non-representational, unconvincing, unlifelike, unnatural, unrecognizable.

2 *an unrealistic suggestion.* fanciful, idealistic, impossible, impracticable, impractical, over-ambitious, quixotic, romantic, silly, unworkable.
3 *unrealistic prices.* SEE **exorbitant**.
OPPOSITES: SEE **realistic**.

unreasonable adjective 1 *an unreasonable person.* SEE **irrational**.
2 *an unreasonable argument.* SEE **absurd**.
3 *unreasonable prices.* SEE **excessive**.

unrecognizable adjective SEE **unidentifiable**.

unrefined adjective SEE **crude**.

unreformable, unregenerate adjectives SEE **unrepentant**.

unrelated adjective SEE **irrelevant, separate** adjective.

unrelenting adjective SEE **persistent, pitiless**.

unreliable adjective 1 *unreliable evidence.* deceptive, false, implausible, inaccurate, misleading, suspect, unconvincing.
2 *an unreliable friend.* changeable, fallible, fickle, inconsistent, irresponsible, undependable, unpredictable, unsound, unstable, untrustworthy.
OPPOSITES: SEE **reliable**.

unrelieved, unremitting adjectives SEE **persistent, pitiless**.

unrepentant adjective *an unrepentant criminal.* brazen, confirmed, hardened, impenitent, incorrigible, incurable, inveterate, SEE **irredeemable**, shameless, unashamed, unblushing, unreformable, unregenerate.
OPPOSITES: SEE **repentant**.

unreserved adjective *unreserved apologies.* SEE **absolute**.

unresisting adjective SEE **passive**.

unresolved adjective SEE **uncertain**.

unrest noun SEE **riot** noun.

unrestrained adjective SEE **wild**.

unrestricted adjective SEE **absolute**.

unripe adjective *unripe fruit.* immature, sour, unready.
OPPOSITES: SEE **ripe**.

unrivalled adjective SEE **unequalled**.

unroll verb SEE **open** verb.

unruffled adjective SEE **calm** adjective.

unruly adjective SEE **disobedient**.

unsafe adjective SEE **dangerous**.

unsaid adjective *It was what she left unsaid that worried me.* SEE **implicit**.

unsatisfactory adjective *an unsatisfactory result.* disappointing, displeasing, dissatisfying, frustrating, inadequate, incompetent, inefficient, insufficient, [*informal*] not good enough, poor, unacceptable, unhappy, unsatisfying, [*informal*] wretched.
OPPOSITES: SEE **satisfactory**.

unsavoury adjective SEE **unpleasant**.

unscathed adjective SEE **safe**.

unscrupulous adjective *unscrupulous cheating.* dishonest, dishonourable, SEE **immoral**, improper, self-interested, shameless, unconscionable.
OPPOSITES: SEE **moral** adjective.

unscrew verb SEE **unfasten**.

unscripted adjective SEE **impromptu**.

unseal verb SEE **open** verb.

unseat verb SEE **oust**.

unseemly adjective SEE **unbecoming**.

unseen adjective SEE **invisible**.

unselfish adjective altruistic, caring, charitable, considerate, disinterested, generous, humanitarian, kind, magnanimous, philanthropic, public-spirited, self-effacing, selfless, self-sacrificing, thoughtful, ungrudging, unstinting.
OPPOSITES: SEE **selfish**.

unselfishness noun altruism, consideration, generosity, kindness, magnanimity, philanthropy, self-denial, selflessness, thoughtfulness.
OPPOSITES: SEE **selfishness**.

unsettle verb SEE **disturb**.

unshakeable adjective SEE **firm** adjective.

unsightly adjective SEE **ugly**.

unskilful adjective *unskilful work.* amateurish, bungled, clumsy, crude, incompetent, inept, inexpert, maladroit, [*informal*] rough and ready, shoddy, unprofessional.
OPPOSITES: SEE **skilful**.

unskilled adjective *an unskilled worker.* inexperienced, SEE **unskilful**, unqualified, untrained.
OPPOSITES: SEE **skilled**.

unsociable adjective SEE **unfriendly**.

unsolicited adjective SEE **unasked**.

unsophisticated adjective *unsophisticated tastes.* [*uncomplimentary*] childish, childlike, ingenuous, innocent, lowbrow, naïve, plain, provincial, simple, simple-minded, straightforward, unaffected, uncomplicated, unostentatious, unpretentious, unrefined, unworldly.
OPPOSITES: SEE **sophisticated**.

unsound adjective SEE **weak**.

unsparing adjective SEE **generous**.

unspeakable adjective *unspeakable horrors.* SEE **dreadful**, indescribable, inexpressible, nameless, unutterable.

unspecified adjective SEE **unidentified**.

unstable adjective SEE **changeable**, **unsteady**.

unsteady adjective 1 *unsteady on your legs. an unsteady structure.* flimsy, frail, insecure, precarious, rickety, [*informal*] rocky, shaky, tottering, unbalanced, unsafe, unstable, wobbly.
2 *an unsteady trickle of water.* changeable, erratic, inconstant, intermittent, irregular, variable.
3 *the unsteady light of a candle.* flickering, fluctuating, quavering, quivering, trembling, tremulous, wavering.
OPPOSITES: SEE **steady** adjective.

unstinting adjective SEE **generous**.

unsubstantial adjective SEE **flimsy**.

unsubstantiated adjective SEE **unproved**.

unsuccessful adjective 1 *an unsuccessful attempt.* abortive, failed, fruitless, futile, ill-fated, ineffective, ineffectual, loss-making, sterile, unavailing, unlucky, unproductive, unprofitable, unsatisfactory, useless, vain.
2 *unsuccessful contestants in a race.* beaten, defeated, losing.
OPPOSITES: SEE **successful**.

unsuitable adjective *an unsuitable choice.* ill-chosen, ill-judged, ill-timed, inapposite, inappropriate, incongruous, inept, irrelevant, mistaken, unbefitting, unfitting, unhappy, unsatisfactory, unseasonable, unseemly, untimely.
OPPOSITES: SEE **suitable**.

unsullied adjective SEE **spotless**.

unsung adjective SEE **anonymous**.

unsure adjective SEE **uncertain**.

unsurpassed adjective SEE **unequalled**.

unsuspecting adjective SEE **credulous**.

unswerving adjective SEE **resolute**.

unsympathetic adjective *an unsympathetic response.* apathetic, cold, cool, dispassionate, hard-hearted, heartless, impassive, indifferent, insensitive, neutral, reserved, uncaring, uncharitable, unconcerned, unfeeling, uninterested, unkind, unmoved, unpitying, unresponsive.
OPPOSITES: SEE **sympathetic**.

unsystematic adjective *an unsystematic worker. unsystematic work.* anarchic, chaotic, confused, disorderly, disorganized, haphazard, illogical, jumbled, muddled, [*informal*] shambolic, [*informal*] sloppy, unmethodical, unplanned, unstructured, untidy.
OPPOSITES: SEE **systematic**.

untamed adjective SEE **wild**.

untangle verb SEE **disentangle**.

untarnished adjective SEE **spotless**.

untenable adjective SEE **indefensible**.

unthinkable adjective SEE **incredible**.

unthinking adjective SEE **thoughtless**.

untidy adjective 1 *untidy work. an untidy room.* careless, chaotic, cluttered, confused, disorderly, disorganized, haphazard, [*informal*] higgledy-piggledy, in disarray, jumbled, littered, [*informal*] messy, muddled, [*informal*] shambolic, slapdash, [*informal*] sloppy, slovenly, [*informal*] topsy-turvy, unsystematic, upside-down.
2 *untidy hair. an untidy appearance.* bedraggled, blowzy, dishevelled, disordered, rumpled, scruffy, shabby, tangled, tousled, uncared for, uncombed, ungroomed, unkempt.
OPPOSITES: SEE **tidy** adjective.

untie verb *to untie a rope.* cast off [= *to untie a boat*], disentangle, free, loosen, release, unbind, undo, unfasten, unknot, untether.

untimely adjective SEE **unsuitable**.

untiring adjective SEE **persistent**.

untold adjective SEE **boundless**, **numerous**.

untoward adjective SEE **inconvenient**.

untraceable adjective SEE **lost**.

untrained adjective SEE **unskilled**.

untrammelled adjective SEE **free** adjective.

untried adjective *an untried formula.* experimental, innovatory, new, novel, unproved, untested.
OPPOSITES: SEE **established**.

untroubled adjective *untroubled progress.* carefree, SEE **peaceful**, straightforward, undisturbed, uninterrupted, unruffled.

untrue adjective SEE **false**.

untrustworthy adjective SEE **dishonest**.

untruth noun SEE **lie** noun.

untruthful adjective SEE **lying**.

untwist verb SEE **disentangle**.

unused adjective *The shop may take back any unused items.* blank, clean, fresh, intact, mint (*in mint condition*), new, pristine, unopened, untouched, unworn.
OPPOSITES: SEE **used**.

unusual adjective *unusual events. unusual things.* abnormal, atypical, curious, [*informal*] different, exceptional,

extraordinary, [*informal*] funny, irregular, odd, out of the ordinary, peculiar, queer, rare, remarkable, singular, SEE **strange**, surprising, uncommon, unconventional, unexpected, unfamiliar, [*informal*] unheard of, [*informal*] unique, unnatural, untypical, unwonted.
OPPOSITES: SEE **usual**.

unutterable adjective SEE **indescribable**.

unveil verb SEE **uncover**.

unwanted adjective SEE **unnecessary**.

unwarrantable adjective SEE **unforgivable**.

unwarranted adjective SEE **unjustified**.

unwary adjective SEE **careless**.

unwavering adjective SEE **resolute**.

unwelcome adjective *unwelcome guests.* disagreeable, unacceptable, undesirable, unwanted.
OPPOSITES: SEE **welcome** adjective.

unwell adjective SEE **ill**.

unwholesome adjective SEE **unhealthy**.

unwieldy adjective SEE **awkward**.

unwilling adjective *unwilling helpers.* averse, backward, disinclined, grudging, half-hearted, hesitant, ill-disposed, indisposed, lazy, loath, opposed, reluctant, resistant, slow, uncooperative, unenthusiastic, unhelpful.
OPPOSITES: SEE **willing**.

unwind verb SEE **unbend**.

unwise adjective *unwise advice. an unwise thing to do.* [*informal*] daft, foolhardy, foolish, ill-advised, ill-judged, illogical, imperceptive, impolitic, imprudent, inadvisable, indiscreet, inexperienced, injudicious, irrational, irresponsible, mistaken, obtuse, perverse, rash, reckless, senseless, short-sighted, silly, SEE **stupid**, thoughtless, unintelligent, unreasonable.
OPPOSITES: SEE **wise**.

unwitting adjective SEE **unintentional**.

unwonted adjective SEE **unusual**.

unworkable adjective SEE **impractical**.

unworldly adjective SEE **spiritual**.

unworn adjective SEE **unused**.

unworthy adjective *A person who cheats is an unworthy winner.* despicable, discreditable, dishonourable, disreputable, ignoble, inappropriate, shameful, undeserving, unsuitable.
OPPOSITES: SEE **worthy**.

unwrap verb SEE **open** verb.

unwritten adjective *an unwritten message.* oral, spoken, verbal, [*informal*] word-of-mouth.
OPPOSITES: SEE **written**.

unyielding adjective SEE **firm** adjective.

unzip verb SEE **undo**.

upbraid verb SEE **reproach** verb.

upbringing noun *the upbringing of children.* breeding, bringing up, care, education, instruction, nurture, raising, rearing, teaching, training.

update verb *to update information. to update a design.* amend, bring up to date, correct, modernize, review, revise.

upgrade verb *to upgrade a computer system.* enhance, expand, improve, make better.

upheaval noun SEE **commotion**.

uphill adjective *an uphill struggle.* arduous, difficult, exhausting, gruelling, hard, laborious, stiff, strenuous, taxing, tough.

uphold verb SEE **support** verb.

upholster verb *to upholster a chair.* SEE **pad** verb.

upholstery noun SEE **padding**.

upkeep noun *The upkeep of a car is expensive.* care, keep, maintenance, running, preservation.

uplift verb SEE **raise**.

uplifting adjective *an uplifting experience.* civilizing, edifying, educational, enlightening, ennobling, enriching, good, humanizing, improving, spiritual.
OPPOSITES: SEE **degrading**.

upper adjective *an upper floor.* elevated, higher, raised, superior, upstairs.

uppermost adjective *the uppermost level.* SEE **dominant**, highest, supreme, top, topmost.

upright adjective **1** *an upright position.* erect, perpendicular, vertical.
OPPOSITES: SEE **flat** adjective.
2 *an upright judge.* conscientious, fair, good, high-minded, honest, honourable, incorruptible, just, moral, principled, righteous, [*informal*] straight, true, trustworthy, upstanding, virtuous.
OPPOSITES: SEE **corrupt** adjective.

uproar noun *There was uproar when the referee gave his controversial decision.* [*informal*] bedlam, brawling, chaos, clamour, commotion, confusion, din, disorder, disturbance, furore, [*informal*] hubbub, [*informal*] hullabaloo, [*informal*] a madhouse, noise, outburst, outcry, pandemonium, [*informal*] racket, riot, row, [*informal*] ructions, [*informal*] rumpus, tumult, turbulence, turmoil.

uproarious adjective *an uproarious comedy.* SEE **funny**.

uproot verb *to uproot plants.* destroy, eliminate, eradicate, extirpate, get rid of, [*informal*] grub up, pull up, remove, root out, weed out.

upset verb 1 *to upset a cup. to upset a boat.* capsize, destabilize, overturn, spill, tip over, topple.
OPPOSITES: SEE **stabilize**.
2 *to upset someone's plans.* affect, alter, change, confuse, defeat, disorganize, disrupt, hinder, interfere with, interrupt, jeopardize, overthrow, spoil.
OPPOSITES: SEE **assist**.
3 *to upset someone's feelings.* agitate, alarm, SEE **annoy**, disconcert, dismay, distress, disturb, excite, fluster, frighten, grieve, irritate, offend, perturb, [*informal*] rub up the wrong way, ruffle, scare, unnerve, worry.
OPPOSITES: SEE **calm** verb.

upshot noun SEE **result** noun.

upside-down adjective 1 *I can't read it if it's upside-down.* inverted, [*informal*] topsy-turvy, upturned, wrong way up.
2 *They left the room upside-down.* SEE **chaotic**.

upstanding adjective 1 *a fine upstanding youth.* SEE **well-built**.
2 *an upstanding judge.* SEE **upright**.

upstart noun nouveau riche, social climber, [*informal*] yuppie.

upsurge noun SEE **rise** noun.

uptight adjective SEE **tense** adjective.

up-to-date adjective 1 *up-to-date technology.* advanced, current, latest, modern, new, present-day, recent.
2 *up-to-date clothes.* contemporary, fashionable, [*informal*] in, modish, stylish, [*informal*] trendy.
OPPOSITES: SEE **old-fashioned**.

upturn noun SEE **rise** noun.

upward adjective *an upward path.* ascending, rising, SEE **uphill**.

urban adjective *an urban area.* built-up, densely populated, metropolitan.

urbane adjective SEE **polite, sophisticated**.

urchin noun SEE **child**.

urge noun *an urge to giggle.* compulsion, desire, eagerness, impulse, inclination, instinct, [*informal*] itch, longing, wish, yearning, [*informal*] yen.

urge verb 1 *to urge a horse over a fence.* compel, drive, force, impel, press, propel, push, spur.
2 *I urge you to make a decision.* advise, advocate, appeal to, beg, beseech, [*informal*] chivvy, counsel, [*informal*] egg on, encourage, entreat, exhort, implore, incite, induce, invite, nag, persuade, plead with, prompt, recommend, solicit, stimulate.
OPPOSITES: SEE **deter**.

urgent adjective 1 *business needing urgent attention. an urgent problem.* acute, dire (*in dire need*), essential, exigent, immediate, important, inescapable, instant, necessary, pressing, top-priority, unavoidable.
2 *urgent cries for help.* eager, earnest, importunate, insistent, persistent, persuasive.

urinal noun SEE **lavatory**.

urn noun VARIOUS CONTAINERS: SEE **container**.

usable adjective 1 *Is the lift usable today?* fit for use, functional, functioning, operating, operational, serviceable, working.
OPPOSITE: unusable.
2 *My ticket is usable only on certain trains.* acceptable, current, valid.
OPPOSITES: SEE **invalid** adjective.

use noun *What's the use of this?* advantage, application, necessity, need, [*informal*] point, profit, purpose, usefulness, utility, value, worth.

use verb 1 *to use something for a particular purpose.* administer, apply, employ, exercise, exploit, make use of, utilize, wield.
2 *to use a tool or machine.* deal with, handle, manage, operate, work.
3 *How much money did you use?* consume, exhaust, expend, spend, use up, waste.
to use up SEE **consume**.

used adjective *used cars.* second-hand.

useful adjective 1 *useful advice.* advantageous, beneficial, constructive, good, helpful, invaluable, positive, profitable, salutary, valuable, worthwhile.
2 *a useful tool.* convenient, effective, efficient, handy, powerful, practical, productive, utilitarian.
3 *a useful player.* capable, competent, effectual, proficient, skilful, successful, talented.
OPPOSITES: SEE **useless**.

useless adjective 1 *a useless search. useless advice.* fruitless, futile, hopeless, pointless, unavailing, unprofitable, unsuccessful, vain, worthless.
2 *a useless machine.* [*informal*] broken down, [*informal*] clapped out, dead, dud, ineffective, inefficient, impractical, unusable.

3 *a useless player.* incapable, incompetent, ineffectual, lazy, unhelpful, unskilful, unsuccessful, untalented.
OPPOSITES: SEE **useful**.

usher, usherette nouns attendant, sidesman.

usual adjective *our usual route home. the usual price.* accepted, accustomed, average, common, conventional, customary, everyday, expected, familiar, general, habitual, natural, normal, official, ordinary, orthodox, predictable, prevalent, recognized, regular, routine, standard, stock, traditional, typical, unexceptional, unsurprising, well-known, widespread, wonted.
OPPOSITES: SEE **unusual**.

usurer noun money-lender.

usurp verb *to usurp someone's position or rights.* appropriate, assume, commandeer, seize, steal, take, take over.

utensil noun *kitchen utensils.* appliance, device, gadget, implement, instrument, machine, tool.
VARIOUS TOOLS: SEE **tool**.

uterus noun womb.

utilitarian adjective SEE **functional**.

utilize verb SEE **use** verb.

utmost adjective SEE **extreme** adjective.

Utopian adjective SEE **ideal** adjective.

utter adjective *utter exhaustion.* SEE **absolute**.

utter verb *I didn't utter a word!* SEE **speak**.

U-turn noun SEE **about-turn**.

V

vacancy noun *a job vacancy.* opening, place, position, post, situation.

vacant adjective **1** *a vacant space.* available, bare, blank, clear, empty, free, open, unfilled, unused, usable, void.
2 *a vacant house.* deserted, uninhabited, unoccupied, untenanted.
OPPOSITES: SEE **occupied**.
3 *a vacant look.* absent-minded, abstracted, blank, dreamy, expressionless, far away, inattentive, SEE **vacuous**.
OPPOSITES: SEE **alert** adjective.

vacate verb *to vacate a room.* abandon, depart from, evacuate, give up, leave, quit, withdraw from.

vacation noun holiday, leave, time off.

vaccinate verb SEE **immunize**.

vacillate verb SEE **waver**.

vacuous adjective *a vacuous expression on his face.* apathetic, blank, empty-headed, expressionless, inane, mindless, SEE **stupid**, uncomprehending, unintelligent, vacant.
OPPOSITES: SEE **alert** adjective.

vacuum noun emptiness, space, void.
vacuum cleaner noun Hoover, [*informal*] vacuum.
vacuum flask noun Thermos.

vagabond noun SEE **vagrant**.

vagary noun *the vagaries of fortune.* caprice, fancy, fluctuation, quirk, uncertainty, unpredictability, [*informal, plural*] ups and downs, whim.
OPPOSITES: SEE **certainty**.

vagrant noun beggar, destitute person, [*informal*] down-and-out, homeless person, itinerant, tramp, traveller, vagabond, wanderer, wayfarer.

vague adjective **1** *vague remarks. a vague plan.* ambiguous, ambivalent, broad (*broad generalizations*), confused, equivocal, evasive, general, generalized, imprecise, indefinite, inexact, loose, nebulous, uncertain, unclear, undefined, unspecific, unsure, [*informal*] woolly.
2 *a vague shape in the mist.* amorphous, blurred, dim, hazy, ill-defined, indistinct, misty, shadowy, unrecognizable.
3 *a vague person.* absent-minded, careless, disorganized, forgetful, inattentive, scatter-brained, thoughtless.
OPPOSITES: SEE **definite**.

vain adjective **1** *vain about your appearance.* arrogant, boastful, [*informal*] cocky, conceited, egotistical, haughty, narcissistic, proud, self-important, self-satisfied, [*informal*] stuck-up, vainglorious.
OPPOSITES: SEE **modest**.
2 *a vain attempt.* abortive, fruitless, futile, ineffective, pointless, senseless, unavailing, unproductive, unrewarding, unsuccessful, useless, worthless.
OPPOSITES: SEE **successful**.

vainglorious noun SEE **vain**.

valediction noun SEE **farewell** noun.

valedictory adjective SEE **farewell** adjective.

valentine noun SEE **lover**.

valet noun SEE **servant**.

valetudinarian noun hypochondriac, invalid, worrier.

valiant adjective SEE **brave**.

valid adjective *a valid excuse. a valid ticket.* acceptable, allowed, approved, authentic, authorized, bona fide, convincing, current, genuine, lawful, legal, legitimate, official, permissible, permitted, proper, ratified, reasonable, rightful, sound, suitable, usable.
OPPOSITES: SEE **invalid** adjective.

validate verb *You need an official signature to validate the order.* authenticate, authorize, certify, endorse, legalize, legitimize, make valid, ratify.

valley noun canyon, chasm, coomb, dale, defile, dell, dingle, glen, gorge, gulch, gully, hollow, pass, ravine, vale.

valorous adjective SEE **brave**.

valour noun SEE **bravery**.

valuable adjective **1** *valuable jewellery.* costly, dear, expensive, generous (*a generous gift*), precious, priceless.
2 *valuable advice.* advantageous, beneficial, constructive, esteemed, good, helpful, invaluable [NB *invaluable* is not used as an opposite of *valuable*], positive, prized, profitable, treasured, useful, valued, worthwhile.
OPPOSITES: SEE **worthless**.

value noun **1** *the value of an antique.* cost, price, worth.
2 *the value of keeping fit.* advantage, benefit, importance, merit, significance, use, usefulness.
values *moral values.* SEE **principles**.

value verb **1** *The jeweller valued my watch.* assess, estimate the value of, evaluate, price, [*informal*] put a figure on.
2 *I value your advice.* appreciate, care for, cherish, esteem, [*informal*] have a high regard for, [*informal*] hold dear, love, prize, respect, treasure.

valueless adjective SEE **worthless**.

valve noun SEE **tap** noun.

vamp verb SEE **improvise**.

vandal noun barbarian, delinquent, hooligan, looter, marauder, Philistine, raider, ruffian, savage, thug, troublemaker.

vane noun weather-cock, weather-vane.

vanguard noun SEE **armed services**.
OPPOSITE: rearguard.

vanish verb *The crowd vanished.* clear, clear off, disappear, disperse, dissolve, dwindle, evaporate, fade, go away, melt away, pass.
OPPOSITES: SEE **appear**.

vanity noun SEE **pride**.

vanquish verb SEE **conquer**.

vapid adjective SEE **uninteresting**.

vaporize verb *Petrol vaporizes quickly.* dry up, evaporate, turn to vapour [SEE **vapour**].
OPPOSITES: SEE **condense**.

vapour noun fog, fumes, gas, haze, miasma, mist, smoke, steam.

variable adjective *variable moods.* capricious, changeable, erratic, fickle, fitful, fluctuating, fluid, inconsistent, inconstant, mercurial, mutable, shifting, temperamental, uncertain, unpredictable, unreliable, unstable, unsteady, [*informal*] up-and-down, vacillating, varying, volatile, wavering.
OPPOSITES: SEE **constant**.

variance noun **to be at variance** SEE **disagree**.

variant noun SEE **variation**.

variation noun *a variation from the usual.* alteration, change, deviation, difference, discrepancy, diversification, elaboration, modification, permutation, variant.

varied adjective SEE **various**.

variegated adjective SEE **dappled**.

variety noun **1** *Variety is the spice of life.* alteration, change, difference, diversity, unpredictability, variation.
2 *a variety of things.* array, assortment, blend, collection, combination, jumble, medley, miscellany, mixture, multiplicity.
3 *a variety of baked beans. a variety of dog.* brand, breed, category, class, form, kind, make, sort, species, strain, type.
a variety show SEE **entertainment**.

various adjective *balloons of various colours.* assorted, contrasting, different, differing, dissimilar, diverse, heterogeneous, miscellaneous, mixed, [*informal*] motley (*a motley crowd*), multifarious, several, sundry, varied, varying.
OPPOSITES: SEE **similar, unchanging**.

varnish noun SEE **paint** noun.

vary verb **1** *The temperature varies during the day.* change, differ, fluctuate, go up and down.
2 *You can vary the temperature by turning the knob.* adapt, adjust, alter, convert, modify, reset, transform, upset.
OPPOSITES: SEE **stabilize**.

vast adjective *a vast desert. vast amounts of money.* SEE **big**, boundless, broad, enormous, extensive, great, huge, immeasurable, immense, large, limitless, massive, measureless, never-ending, unbounded, unlimited, wide.
OPPOSITES: SEE **small**.

vat noun VARIOUS CONTAINERS: SEE **container**.

vault noun *a wine vault. the vaults of a bank.* basement, cavern, cellar, crypt, repository, strongroom, undercroft.

vault verb *to vault a fence.* bound over, clear, hurdle, jump, leap, leap-frog, spring over.

VDU noun [= *visual display unit*] display, monitor, screen.
OTHER PARTS OF COMPUTER SYSTEM: SEE **computer**.

veer verb *The car veered across the road.* change direction, dodge, swerve, tack, turn, wheel.

vegetable adjective *vegetable matter.* growing, organic.

vegetable noun

VARIOUS VEGETABLES: asparagus, bean, beet, beetroot, broad bean, broccoli, Brussels sprout, butter bean, cabbage, carrot, cauliflower, celeriac, celery, courgette, kale, kohlrabi, leek, marrow, onion, parsnip, pea, potato, pumpkin, runner bean, shallot, spinach, sugar beet, swede, tomato, turnip, zucchini.
SALAD VEGETABLES: SEE **salad**.

---

vegetarian adjective graminivorous, herbivorous, vegan.
COMPARE: carnivorous, omnivorous.

vegetate verb be inactive, do nothing, [*informal*] go to seed, idle, lose interest, stagnate.

vegetation noun foliage, greenery, growing things, growth, plants, undergrowth, weeds.

vehement adjective *a vehement denial.* animated, ardent, eager, enthusiastic, excited, fervent, fierce, forceful, heated, impassioned, intense, passionate, powerful, strong, urgent, vigorous, violent.
OPPOSITES: SEE **apathetic**.

vehicle noun conveyance.

VARIOUS VEHICLES: ambulance, armoured car, articulated lorry, breakdown vehicle, [*informal*] buggy, bulldozer, bus, cab, camper, SEE **car**, caravan, carriage, cart, [*old-fashioned*] charabanc, chariot, coach, container lorry, SEE **cycle**, double-decker bus, dump truck, dustcart, estate car, fire-engine, float, gig, go-kart, [*old-fashioned*] hackney carriage, hearse, horse-box, jeep, juggernaut, lorry, milk float, minibus, minicab, moped, motor car, [*old-fashioned*] omnibus, panda car, pantechnicon, patrol-car, [*old-fashioned*] phaeton, pick-up, removal van, rickshaw, scooter, sedan-chair, side-car, single-decker bus, sledge, snowplough, stagecoach, steam-roller, tank, tanker (*oil tanker*), taxi, traction-engine, tractor, trailer, tram, transporter, trap, trolleybus, truck, [*old-fashioned*] tumbrel, van, wagon.

PARTS OF A MOTOR VEHICLE: accelerator, accumulator, air-filter, axle, battery, big-end, bodywork, bonnet, boot, brake, bumper, carburettor, chassis, choke, clutch, cockpit, cylinder, dashboard, diesel engine, dipstick, distributor, engine, exhaust, fascia, fog-light, fuel tank, gear, gearbox, headlight, ignition, indicator, mileometer, mudguard, oil filter, piston, plug, radiator, rev counter, safety belt or seat-belt, shock-absorber, sidelight, silencer, spare wheel, sparking-plug or spark plug, speedometer, starter, steering-wheel, stop-light, tachograph, tachometer, tail-light, throttle, transmission, tyre, wheel, windscreen, windscreen-wiper, wing.

---

veil noun, verb SEE **cover** noun, verb.

vein noun **1** artery, blood vessel, capillary.
2 *in a sentimental vein.* SEE **mood**.

vellum noun SEE **paper** noun.

velocity noun SEE **speed** noun.

venal adjective SEE **corrupt** adjective.

vend verb SEE **sell**.

vendetta noun SEE **feud** noun.

vendor noun SEE **seller**.

veneer noun coating, covering, layer, surface.

veneer verb SEE **cover** verb.

venerable adjective *The cathedral is a venerable building.* aged, ancient, august, dignified, esteemed, honoured, old, respected, revered, reverenced, venerated, worthy of respect.

venerate verb SEE **respect** verb.

veneration noun SEE **respect** noun.

venereal adjective SEE **sexual**.

vengeance noun *vengeance for an injury or insult.* reprisal, retaliation, retribution, revenge, [*informal*] tit for tat.

vengeful adjective avenging, bitter, rancorous, revengeful, spiteful, unforgiving, vindictive.
OPPOSITES: SEE **forgiving**.

venial adjective *a venial sin.* SEE **forgivable**.

venom noun poison, toxin.

venomous adjective SEE **poisonous**.

vent noun *a vent in a garment. a fresh-air vent.* aperture, cut, duct, gap, hole, opening, outlet, passage, slit, split.
to give vent to SEE **vent** verb.

vent verb *to vent your anger.* SEE **express** verb, give vent to, let go, release.

ventilate verb **1** *to ventilate a room.* aerate, air, freshen.
2 *to ventilate your feelings.* SEE **express** verb.

venture noun SEE **enterprise**.

venture verb **1** *to venture a small wager. to venture an opinion.* chance, dare, gamble, put forward, risk, speculate, stake, wager.
2 *to venture out.* dare to go, risk going.

venturesome adjective SEE **adventurous**.

venue noun *a venue for a sporting event.* meeting-place, location, rendezvous.

veracious adjective SEE **true, truthful**.

verbal adjective **1** *verbal communication.* lexical, linguistic.
OPPOSITE: non-verbal.
2 *a verbal message.* oral, spoken, unwritten, word-of-mouth.
OPPOSITES: SEE **written**.

verbalize verb SEE **speak**.

verbatim adjective *a verbatim account of what was said.* exact, literal, precise, word for word.
OPPOSITE: paraphrased [SEE **paraphrase**].

verbiage noun SEE **verbosity**.

verbose adjective *a verbose speaker.* diffuse, garrulous, long-winded, loquacious, pleonastic, prolix, rambling, repetitious, talkative, tautological, unstoppable, wordy.
OPPOSITES: SEE **concise**.

verbosity noun *We became bored with his verbosity.* [*informal*] beating about the bush, circumlocution, diffuseness, garrulity, long-windedness, loquacity, periphrasis, pleonasm, prolixity, repetition, tautology, verbiage, wordiness.

verdant adjective SEE **green**.

verdict noun *the verdict of the jury.* adjudication, assessment, conclusion, decision, finding, judgement, opinion, sentence.
LEGAL TERMS: SEE **law**.

verge noun **1** *the verge of the road.* bank, edge, hard shoulder, kerb, margin, roadside, shoulder, side, wayside.
2 *on the verge of a discovery.* brink.

verifiable adjective demonstrable, provable.
OPPOSITE: unverifiable.

verify verb *to verify someone's story.* ascertain, authenticate, check out, confirm, corroborate, demonstrate the truth of, establish, prove, show the truth of, substantiate, support, uphold, validate.
OPPOSITES: SEE **discredit**.

verisimilitude noun authenticity, realism, truth to life.

veritable adjective SEE **true**.

vermilion adjective SEE **red**.

vermin noun parasites, pests.

verminous adjective SEE **infested**.

vernal adjective spring-like.

versatile adjective *a versatile player.* adaptable, all-round, gifted, resourceful, skilful, talented.

verse noun *a story in verse.* lines, metre, rhyme, stanza.

VARIOUS VERSE FORMS: blank verse, Chaucerian stanza, clerihew, couplet, free verse, haiku, hexameter, limerick, ottava rima, pentameter, quatrain, rhyme royal, sestina, sonnet, Spenserian stanza, terza rima, triolet, triplet, vers libre, villanelle.

VARIOUS METRICAL FEET: anapaest, dactyl, iamb, spondee, trochee.

VARIOUS KINDS OF POEM: SEE **poem**.

---

versed adjective **versed in** SEE **skilled**.

version noun **1** *an unbiased version of what happened.* account, description, portrayal, report, story.
2 *a modern version of the Bible.* adaptation, interpretation, paraphrase, rendering, translation.
3 *The car is an up-dated version of our old one.* design, form, kind, [*formal*] mark, model, type, variant.

vertebra noun [*plural*] **vertebrae** backbone, spine.

vertex noun SEE **top** noun.

vertical adjective **1** *a vertical position.* erect, perpendicular, upright.
2 *a vertical drop.* precipitous, sheer.
OPPOSITES: SEE **horizontal**.

vertigo noun dizziness, giddiness.

verve noun SEE **liveliness**.

very adverb acutely, enormously, especially, exceedingly, extremely,

greatly, highly, [*informal*] jolly, most, noticeably, outstandingly, particularly, really, remarkably, [*informal*] terribly, truly, uncommonly, unusually.
OPPOSITES: SEE **slightly**.

vessel noun **1** [=*container*] SEE **container**.
2 *vessels in the harbour*. boat, craft, ship.

VARIOUS VESSELS: aircraft-carrier, barge, bathysphere, battleship, brigantine, cabin cruiser, canoe, catamaran, clipper, coaster, collier, coracle, corvette, cruise-liner, cruiser, cutter, destroyer, dhow, dinghy, dredger, dugout, ferry, freighter, frigate, galleon, galley, gondola, gunboat.

houseboat, hovercraft, hydrofoil, hydroplane, ice-breaker, junk, kayak, ketch, landing-craft, launch, lifeboat, lighter, light-ship, liner, longboat, lugger, man-of-war, merchant ship, minesweeper, motor boat, narrow-boat, oil-tanker, [*old-fashioned*] packet-ship, paddle-steamer, pedalo, pontoon, power-boat, pram, privateer, punt.

quinquereme, raft, rowing-boat, sailing-boat, sampan, schooner, skiff, sloop, smack, speed-boat, steamer, steamship, sub or submarine, super-tanker, tanker, tender, torpedo boat, tramp steamer, trawler, trireme, troop ship, tug, warship, whaler, wind-jammer, yacht, yawl.

PARTS OF A VESSEL: aft, amidships, anchor, binnacle, boom, bow, bridge, bulwark, conning-tower, crow's nest, deck, fo'c'sle or forecastle, funnel, galley, gunwale, helm, hull, keel, mast, oar, paddle, poop, port, porthole, propeller, prow, quarterdeck, rigging, rudder, sail, scull, starboard, stern, tiller.

---

vestibule noun SEE **entrance** noun.

vet noun veterinary surgeon.

vet verb *to vet a person's credentials*. SEE **examine**.

veteran adjective *a veteran car*. SEE **old**.

veteran noun *a veteran of a war*. experienced soldier, old soldier, survivor.
OPPOSITES: SEE **recruit** noun.

veto noun *We couldn't act because of the boss's veto on new schemes*. ban, embargo, prohibition, refusal, rejection, [*informal*] thumbs down.
OPPOSITES: SEE **approval**.

veto verb *The boss vetoed our proposal*. ban, bar, blackball, disallow, dismiss, forbid, prohibit, refuse, reject, rule out, say no to, turn down, vote against.
OPPOSITES: SEE **approve**.

vex verb SEE **annoy**.

vexation noun SEE **annoyance**.

vexatious adjective SEE **annoying**.

vexed adjective SEE **annoyed**.

viable adjective *a viable plan*. achievable, feasible, operable, possible, practicable, practical, realistic, usable, workable.
OPPOSITES: SEE **impractical**.

viaduct noun SEE **bridge** noun.

vial noun SEE **bottle** noun.

viands plural noun SEE **food**.

vibrant adjective *vibrant with energy*. alert, alive, dynamic, electric, energetic, living, pulsating, quivering, resonant, thrilling, throbbing, trembling, vibrating, vivacious.
OPPOSITES: SEE **lifeless**.

vibrate verb *The machine vibrated as the engine turned faster*. judder, oscillate, pulsate, quake, quiver, rattle, reverberate, shake, shiver, shudder, throb, tremble, wobble.

vibration noun juddering, oscillation, pulsation, quivering, rattling, reverberation, shaking, shivering, shuddering, throbbing, trembling, tremor, wobbling.

vicar noun SEE **clergyman**.

vicarious adjective *vicarious experiences*. indirect, second-hand.

vice noun **1** *The police wage war on crime and vice*. corruption, depravity, evil, evil-doing, immorality, iniquity, sin, venality, wickedness, wrongdoing.
2 *His worst vice is his continual chattering*. bad habit, blemish, defect, failing, fault, imperfection, shortcoming, weakness.

The prefix *vice-* is related to a Latin word meaning *change*. In words like *vice-captain*, *vice-president*, and *vice-principal* it means either *person acting on behalf of* or *person next in importance to*. SEE **deputy**.

---

viceroy noun SEE **ruler**.

vicinity noun *A taxi-driver ought to know the vicinity*. area, district, environs, locality, neighbourhood, outskirts, precincts, proximity, purlieus, region, sector, territory, zone.

vicious adjective **1** *a vicious attack*. atrocious, barbaric, barbarous, beastly,

blood-thirsty, brutal, callous, cruel, diabolical, fiendish, heinous, hurtful, inhuman, merciless, monstrous, murderous, pitiless, ruthless, sadistic, savage, unfeeling, vile, violent.
2 *a vicious character.* SEE **bad**, [*informal*] bitchy, [*informal*] catty, depraved, evil, heartless, immoral, malicious, mean, perverted, rancorous, sinful, spiteful, venomous, villainous, vindictive, vitriolic, wicked.
3 *a vicious animal.* aggressive, bad-tempered, dangerous, ferocious, fierce, snappy, untamed, wild.
4 *a vicious wind.* cutting, nasty, severe, sharp, unpleasant.
OPPOSITES: SEE **gentle**.

vicissitude noun *the vicissitudes of life.* alteration, SEE **change** noun, instability, mutability, shift, uncertainty.

victim noun **1** *a victim of an accident.* casualty, fatality, injured person, patient, sufferer, wounded person.
2 *a sacrificial victim.* martyr, offering, prey, sacrifice.

victimize verb *Don't victimize the weak.* bully, cheat, discriminate against, exploit, intimidate, oppress, persecute, [*informal*] pick on, terrorize, torment, treat unfairly, [*informal*] use (*She was just using him*).

victor noun SEE **winner**.

victorious adjective *the victorious team.* champion, conquering, first, leading, prevailing, successful, top, top-scoring, triumphant, unbeaten, undefeated, winning.
OPPOSITES: SEE **defeated**.

victory noun *We celebrated our team's victory.* achievement, conquest, knockout, mastery, success, superiority, triumph, [*informal*] walk-over, win.
OPPOSITES: SEE **defeat** noun.

victuals noun SEE **food**.

video noun, verb SEE **recording** noun, **record** verb.

vie verb SEE **compete**.

view noun **1** *the view from the top of the hill.* aspect, landscape, outlook, panorama, perspective, picture, prospect, scene, scenery, spectacle, vista.
2 *I had a good view of what happened.* look, sight, vision.
3 *My view is that we should ban smoking.* attitude, belief, conviction, idea, notion, opinion, perception, thought.

view verb **1** *to view a scene.* behold, consider, contemplate, examine, eye, gaze at, inspect, observe, perceive, regard, scan, stare at, survey, witness.
2 *to view TV.* look at, see, watch.

viewer noun [*plural*] audience, observer, onlooker, spectator, watcher, witness.

viewpoint noun *Our visitor saw the problem from a foreign viewpoint.* angle, perspective, point of view, position, slant, standpoint.

vigil noun *an all-night vigil.* watch.

vigilant adjective *Be vigilant!* alert, attentive, awake, careful, observant, on the watch, on your guard, [*informal*] on your toes, wakeful, watchful, wide-awake.
OPPOSITES: SEE **negligent**.

vignette noun SEE **picture** noun.

vigorous adjective *a vigorous game. a vigorous player.* active, animated, brisk, dynamic, energetic, flourishing, forceful, full-blooded, healthy, lively, lusty, potent, red-blooded, robust, spirited, strenuous, strong, virile, vital, zestful.
OPPOSITES: SEE **feeble**.

vigour noun animation, dynamism, energy, force, forcefulness, gusto, health, life, liveliness, might, potency, power, robustness, spirit, stamina, strength, verve, [*informal*] vim, virility, vitality, zeal, zest.

vile adjective *a vile crime.* contemptible, degenerate, depraved, despicable, disgusting, evil, filthy, foul, horrible, loathsome, low, nasty, nauseating, obnoxious, offensive, odious, perverted, repellent, repugnant, repulsive, revolting, sickening, ugly, vicious, wicked.

vilify verb SEE **slander** verb.

villa noun SEE **house** noun.

village noun hamlet.
OTHER SETTLEMENTS: SEE **settlement**.

villain noun SEE **wicked (wicked person)**.

villainous adjective SEE **wicked**.

vim noun SEE **vigour**.

vindicate verb SEE **excuse** verb, **justify**.

vindictive adjective *vindictive retaliation.* malicious, nasty, punitive, rancorous, revengeful, spiteful, unforgiving, vengeful, vicious.
OPPOSITES: SEE **forgiving**.

vinegary adjective SEE **sour**.

vineyard noun SEE **plantation**.

vintage adjective *a vintage wine. a vintage Presley record.* choice, classic, fine, good, high-quality, mature, old, venerable.

vintner noun wine-merchant.

violate verb **1** *to violate a rule.* break, contravene, defy, disobey, disregard, flout, ignore, infringe, transgress.

2 *to violate someone's privacy.* abuse, disturb, invade.
3 [*of a man*] *to violate a woman.* assault, dishonour, force yourself on, rape, ravish.

violation noun *the violation of a rule.* breach, contravention, defiance, flouting, infringement, offence (against), transgression.

violent adjective 1 *a violent explosion. a violent reaction.* acute, damaging, dangerous, destructive, devastating, explosive, ferocious, fierce, forceful, furious, hard, harmful, intense, powerful, rough, savage, severe, strong, swingeing, tempestuous, turbulent, uncontrollable, vehement, wild.
2 *violent criminals. violent behaviour.* barbaric, berserk, blood-thirsty, brutal, cruel, desperate, headstrong, homicidal, murderous, riotous, rowdy, ruthless, unruly, vehement, vicious, wild.
OPPOSITES: SEE **gentle**.

violin noun fiddle.
OTHER STRINGED INSTRUMENTS: SEE **string** noun.

VIP celebrity, dignitary, important person.

virago noun SEE **woman**.

virgin noun SEE **girl, woman**.

virginal adjective SEE **chaste**.

virile adjective *a virile man* [*uncomplimentary*] macho, manly, masculine, potent, vigorous.

virtue noun 1 *We respect virtue and hate vice.* decency, goodness, high-mindedness, honesty, honour, integrity, morality, nobility, principle, rectitude, righteousness, sincerity, uprightness, worthiness.
2 *sexual virtue.* abstinence, chastity, innocence, purity, virginity.
3 *This car's main virtue is that it's cheap to run.* advantage, asset, good point, merit, [*informal*] redeeming feature, strength.
OPPOSITES: SEE **vice**.

virtuoso noun expert, prodigy.
VARIOUS MUSICIANS: SEE **music**.

virtuous adjective *virtuous behaviour.* blameless, chaste, ethical, exemplary, God-fearing, good, [*uncomplimentary*] goody-goody, high-principled, honest, honourable, innocent, irreproachable, just, law-abiding, moral, praiseworthy, pure, right, righteous, [*uncomplimentary*] smug, spotless, trustworthy, unimpeachable, upright, worthy.
OPPOSITES: SEE **wicked**.

virulent adjective 1 *a virulent infection.* deadly, lethal, noxious, poisonous, toxic, venomous.
2 *virulent abuse.* acrimonious, bitter, hostile, malicious, nasty, spiteful, vicious, vitriolic.

virus noun SEE **micro-organism**.

visa noun SEE **document**.

visage noun SEE **face** noun.

viscera noun SEE **entrails**.

viscid adjective SEE **viscous**.

viscous adjective *a viscous liquid.* gluey, sticky, syrupy, thick, viscid.
OPPOSITES: SEE **runny**.

visible adjective *visible signs of weakness.* apparent, clear, conspicuous, detectable, discernible, distinct, evident, manifest, noticeable, obvious, perceptible, plain, recognizable, unconcealed, undisguised, unmistakable.
OPPOSITES: SEE **invisible**.

vision noun 1 *The optician said I had good vision.* eyesight, sight.
2 *He claims to have seen a vision.* apparition, day-dream, delusion, fantasy, ghost, hallucination, illusion, mirage, phantasm, phantom, spectre, spirit.
3 *Statesmen need to be people of vision.* farsightedness, foresight, imagination, insight, spirituality, understanding.

visionary adjective *a visionary scheme for the future.* fanciful, farsighted, futuristic, idealistic, imaginative, impractical, prophetic, quixotic, romantic, speculative, transcendental, unrealistic, Utopian.

visionary noun *The ideas of a visionary may seem impractical to us.* dreamer, idealist, mystic, poet, prophet, romantic, seer.

visit noun 1 *a visit to friends.* call, stay.
2 *an official visit.* visitation.
3 *a visit to London.* day out (in), excursion, outing, trip.

visit verb *to visit friends.* call on, come to see, [*informal*] descend on, [*informal*] drop in on, go to see, [*informal*] look up, make a visit to, pay a call on, stay with.
to visit repeatedly frequent, haunt.

visitant noun SEE **visitor**.

visitation noun 1 *an official visitation.* SEE **visit** noun.
2 *a visitation from God.* SEE **punishment**.

visitor noun 1 *We had visitors to dinner.* caller, [*plural*] company, guest.
2 *The town is full of visitors.* holiday-maker, sightseer, tourist, tripper.
3 *a visitor from another land.* alien, foreigner, migrant, traveller, visitant.

visor noun protector, shield, sun-shield.

vista noun landscape, outlook, panorama, prospect, scene, scenery, view.

visual adjective *visual effects.* eye-catching, optical.

visualize verb *I can't visualize what heaven is like.* conceive, dream up, envisage, imagine, picture.

vital adjective **1** *the vital spark of life.* alive, animate, dynamic, life-giving, live, living.
OPPOSITES: SEE **dead**.
2 *vital information.* current, crucial, essential, fundamental, imperative, important, indispensable, necessary, relevant.
OPPOSITES: SEE **inessential**.
3 *a vital sort of person.* animated, energetic, exuberant, lively, sparkling, spirited, sprightly, vigorous, vivacious, zestful.
OPPOSITES: SEE **lifeless**.

vitality noun *full of vitality.* animation, dynamism, energy, exuberance, [*informal*] go, life, liveliness, [*informal*] sparkle, spirit, sprightliness, vigour, [*informal*] vim, vivacity, zest.

vitalize verb SEE **animate** verb.

vitiate verb SEE **spoil**.

vitreous adjective SEE **glassy**.

vitriol noun sulphuric acid.

vitriolic adjective *vitriolic criticism.* abusive, acid, biting, bitter, caustic, cruel, destructive, hostile, hurtful, malicious, savage, scathing, vicious, vindictive, virulent.

vituperate verb SEE **abuse** verb.

viva noun SEE **examination**, oral, viva voce.

vivacious adjective SEE **lively**.

vivid adjective **1** *vivid colours.* bright, brilliant, colourful, [*uncomplimentary*] gaudy, gay, gleaming, glowing, intense, shiny, showy, striking, strong, vibrant.
2 *a vivid description.* clear, graphic, imaginative, lifelike, lively, memorable, powerful, realistic.
OPPOSITES: SEE **lifeless**.

vocabulary noun **1** *I speak French, but my vocabulary is limited.* diction, lexis, words.
2 *The vocabulary in your French book gives the meanings of words.* dictionary, glossary, lexicon, word-list.

vocal adjective **1** *vocal sounds.* oral, said, spoken, sung, voiced.
2 *Usually she's quiet, but today she was quite vocal.* outspoken, SEE **talkative**, vociferous.

vocalist noun SEE **singer**.

vocalize verb SEE **speak**.

vocation noun SEE **calling**.

vociferate verb SEE **shout** verb.

vogue noun *the latest vogue in clothes.* craze, fashion, rage, style, taste, trend.
in vogue SEE **fashionable**.

voice noun *I recognized her voice.* accent, inflexion, singing, sound, speaking, speech, tone.

voice verb *to voice your thoughts.* SEE **speak**.

void adjective SEE **empty** adjective.

volatile adjective **1** *Petrol is a volatile liquid.* explosive, unstable.
2 *Beware of his volatile moods!* changeable, fickle, inconstant, lively, SEE **temperamental**, unpredictable, [*informal*] up and down, variable.
OPPOSITES: SEE **stable**.

volcano noun eruption, SEE **mountain**.

volition noun SEE **will** noun.

volley noun *a volley of missiles.* SEE **bombardment**.

volte-face noun SEE **about-turn**.

voluble adjective SEE **talkative**.

volume 1 *an encyclopaedia in ten volumes.* book, [*old-fashioned*] tome.
KINDS OF BOOK: SEE **book** noun.
2 *the volume of a container.* amount, bulk, capacity, dimensions, mass, quantity, size.

voluminous adjective SEE **large**.

voluntary adjective **1** *voluntary work.* optional, unpaid, willing.
OPPOSITES: SEE **compulsory**.
2 *a voluntary act.* conscious, deliberate, intended, intentional.
OPPOSITES: SEE **involuntary**.

volunteer verb **1** *to volunteer to clear up.* be willing, offer, propose, put yourself forward.
2 *to volunteer for military service.* SEE **enlist**.

voluptuous adjective **1** *voluptuous living.* SEE **hedonistic**.
2 [*informal*] *a voluptuous figure.* [*informal*] curvaceous, erotic, sensual, [*informal*] sexy, shapely.

voodoo noun SEE **magic** noun.

vomit verb be sick, [*informal*] bring up, disgorge, [*informal*] heave up, [*informal*] puke, regurgitate, retch, [*informal*] sick up, [*informal*] spew up, [*informal*] throw up.

voracious adjective **1** *a voracious appetite.* SEE **greedy**.
2 *a voracious reader.* SEE **eager**.

vortex noun eddy, spiral, whirlpool, whirlwind.

vote noun *a democratic vote.* ballot, election, plebiscite, poll, referendum, show of hands.

vote verb *to vote in an election.* ballot, cast your vote.
to vote for choose, elect, nominate, opt for, pick, return, select, settle on.

vouch verb **to vouch for** SEE **guarantee** verb.

voucher noun *a voucher to be exchanged for goods.* coupon, ticket, token.

vouchsafe verb SEE **grant** verb.

vow noun *a solemn vow.* assurance, guarantee, oath, pledge, promise, undertaking, word of honour.

vow verb *She vowed to be good.* give an assurance, give your word, guarantee, pledge, promise, swear, take an oath.

voyage noun, verb SEE **travel** noun, verb.

vulgar adjective **1** *vulgar language.* churlish, coarse, foul, gross, ill-bred, impolite, improper, indecent, indecorous, low, SEE **obscene**, offensive, rude, uncouth, ungentlemanly, unladylike.
OPPOSITES: SEE **polite**.
2 *a vulgar colour scheme.* common, crude, gaudy, inartistic, in bad taste, inelegant, insensitive, lowbrow, plebeian, tasteless, tawdry, unrefined, unsophisticated.
OPPOSITES: SEE **tasteful**.

vulgarize verb SEE **debase**.

vulnerable adjective **1** *The defenders were in a vulnerable position.* at risk, defenceless, exposed, unguarded, unprotected, weak, wide open.
OPPOSITES: SEE **invulnerable**.
2 *He has a vulnerable nature.* easily hurt, sensitive, thin-skinned.
OPPOSITES: SEE **resilient**.

W

wad noun *a wad of bank-notes.* bundle, lump, mass, pad, roll.

wadding noun *protective wadding.* filling, lining, packing, padding, stuffing.

waddle verb SEE **walk** verb.

wade verb *to wade through water.* paddle, SEE **walk** verb.

wafer noun SEE **biscuit**.

waffle noun [*informal*] *Cut the waffle and get to the point.* evasiveness, padding, prevarication, SEE **verbosity**, wordiness.

waffle verb *Stop waffling and get to the point.* [*informal*] beat about the bush, hedge, prevaricate.

waft verb **1** *The scent wafted on the breeze.* drift, float, travel.
2 *A breeze wafted the scent towards us.* carry, convey, transmit, transport.

wag noun [*informal*] *a bit of a wag.* SEE **comedian**.

wag verb *A dog wags its tail.* move to and fro, shake, [*informal*] waggle, wave, [*informal*] wiggle.

wage noun *weekly wages.* earnings, income, SEE **pay** noun, pay packet.

wage verb *to wage war.* carry on, conduct, engage in, fight, undertake.

wager noun, verb SEE **bet** noun, verb.

waggle verb SEE **wag** verb.

wagon noun VARIOUS VEHICLES: SEE **vehicle**.

waif noun foundling, orphan, stray.

wail verb caterwaul, complain, cry, howl, lament, moan, shriek, waul, weep, [*informal*] yowl.

waist noun *a belt round the waist.* middle, waistline.

waistband noun belt, cummerbund, girdle.

waistcoat noun VARIOUS COATS: SEE **coat** noun.

wait noun *a long wait for the bus. a wait before taking action.* SEE **delay** noun, halt, hesitation, hiatus, [*informal*] hold-up, interval, pause, postponement, rest, stay.

wait verb **1** *We waited for a signal.* [*old-fashioned*] bide, SEE **delay** verb, halt, [*informal*] hang about, hesitate, hold back, keep still, linger, mark time, pause, remain, rest, stay, stop, [*old-fashioned*] tarry.
2 *to wait at table.* serve.

waiter, waitress nouns SERVANTS: SEE **servant**.

waive verb *to waive your right to something.* abandon, disclaim, dispense with, forgo, give up, relinquish, renounce, surrender.
OPPOSITES: SEE **enforce**.

wake noun **1** [=*funeral*] SEE **funeral**.
2 *the wake of a ship.* path, track, trail, turbulence, wash.

wake verb **1** *A loud noise woke me.* arouse, awaken, call, disturb, rouse, waken.
2 *I usually wake at about 7.* become conscious, [*informal*] come to life, get up, rise, [*informal*] stir, wake up.

to wake up to *I woke up to what she was really saying.* SEE **realize.**

wakeful adjective SEE **sleepless.**

waken verb SEE **wake** verb.

waking adjective *your waking hours.* active, alert, aware, conscious, daytime. OPPOSITE: sleeping.

walk noun **1** *He had a characteristic walk.* gait.
2 *a walk in the country.* [*joking*] constitutional, hike, [*old-fashioned*] promenade, ramble, saunter, stroll, traipse, tramp, trek, trudge, [*informal*] turn (*I'll take a turn in the garden*).
3 *I made a paved walk in the garden.* aisle, alley, path, pathway, pavement.

walk verb **1** *I walk to work.* be a pedestrian, travel on foot.
SEE PANEL BELOW.
2 *Don't walk on the flowers.* stamp, step, trample, tread.
to walk away with SEE **win.**
to walk off with SEE **steal.**
to walk out SEE **quit.**
to walk out on SEE **desert** verb.

VARIOUS WAYS TO WALK: amble, crawl, creep, dodder, [*informal*] foot-slog, hike, hobble, limp, lope, lurch, march, mince, [*slang*] mooch, pace, pad, paddle, parade, [*old-fashioned*] perambulate, plod, promenade, prowl, ramble, saunter, scuttle, shamble, shuffle, slink, stagger, stalk, steal, step, [*informal*] stomp, stride, stroll, strut, stumble, swagger, tiptoe, [*informal*] toddle, totter, traipse, tramp, trample, trek, troop, trot, trudge, waddle, wade.

---

walker noun hiker, pedestrian, rambler.

walk-over noun SEE **victory.**

wall noun KINDS OF WALL: barricade, barrier, bulkhead, bulwark, dam, dike, divider, embankment, fence, fortification, hedge, obstacle, paling, palisade, parapet, partition, rampart, screen, seawall, stockade.

wall verb SEE **enclose.**

wallet noun notecase, pocket-book, pouch, purse.

wallop verb SEE **hit** verb.

wallow verb **1** *to wallow in mud.* flounder, lie, roll about, stagger about, wade, welter.
2 *to wallow in luxury.* glory, indulge yourself, luxuriate, revel, take delight.

wallpaper noun SEE **paper** noun.

wan adjective SEE **pale** adjective.

wand noun SEE **stick** noun.

wander verb **1** *to wander about the hills.* go aimlessly, meander, ramble, range, roam, rove, stray, travel about, walk, wind.
2 *to wander off course.* curve, deviate, digress, drift, err, stray, swerve, turn, twist, veer, zigzag.

wanderer noun SEE **traveller.**

wandering adjective **1** *wandering tribes.* homeless, itinerant, nomadic, peripatetic, rootless, roving, strolling, travelling, vagrant, wayfaring.
2 *wandering thoughts.* drifting, inattentive, rambling, straying.

wane verb *The evening light waned. My enthusiasm waned after a while.* decline, decrease, dim, diminish, dwindle, ebb, fade, fail, [*informal*] fall off, lessen, shrink, subside, taper off, weaken.
OPPOSITES: SEE **strengthen.**

want noun **1** *The hotel staff try to satisfy all your wants.* demand, desire, need, requirement, wish.
2 *We had to abandon our project for want of a few pounds.* absence, lack, need.
3 *Why do we tolerate want when so many are rich?* dearth, famine, hunger, insufficiency, penury, poverty, privation, scarcity, shortage.

want verb **1** *We can't always have what we want.* covet, crave, demand, desire, fancy, hanker (after), [*informal*] have a yen (for), hunger (for), [*informal*] itch (for), like [often *would like* (*I would like a drink*)], long (for), pine (for), please (*You can take what you please*), prefer, [*informal*] set your heart on, wish (for), yearn (for).
2 *That rude man wants good manners!* be short of, lack, need, require.

war noun **1** *wars between nations.* conflict, fighting, hostilities, military action, strife, warfare.
2 *a war against crime.* campaign, crusade.
to wage war SEE **fight** verb.

VARIOUS KINDS OF ACTION IN WAR: ambush, assault, attack, battle, blitz, blockade, bombardment, campaign, counterattack, espionage, guerrilla warfare, hostilities, invasion, manœuvre, negotiation, operation, resistance, retreat, siege, skirmish, surrender, withdrawal.

---

warble verb SEE **sing.**

ward noun **1** *a hospital ward.* SEE **room.**

2 *the ward of a guardian.* charge, dependant, minor.

ward verb **to ward off** *to ward off an attack.* avert, beat off, block, check, deflect, fend off, forestall, parry, push away, repel, repulse, stave off, thwart, turn aside.

warden noun SEE **official** noun.

warder noun *a prison warder.* gaoler, guard, jailer, keeper, prison officer.

wardrobe noun SEE **cupboard**.

warehouse noun depository, depot, store, storehouse.

wares plural noun *wares for sale.* commodities, goods, merchandise, produce, stock.

warhead noun VARIOUS WEAPONS: SEE **weapon**.

warlike adjective SEE **belligerent**.

warm adjective 1 *warm weather.* close, SEE **hot**, subtropical, sultry, summery, temperate, warmish.
OPPOSITES: SEE **cold** adjective.
2 *warm water.* lukewarm, tepid.
3 *warm clothes.* cosy, thermal, thick, winter, woolly.
4 *a warm welcome.* affable, affectionate, cordial, enthusiastic, fervent, friendly, genial, kind, loving, sympathetic, warm-hearted.
OPPOSITES: SEE **unfriendly**.

warm verb SEE **heat** verb, make warmer, melt, raise the temperaure (of), thaw, thaw out.
OPPOSITES: SEE **chill** verb.

warm-hearted adjective SEE **friendly**.

warmongering adjective SEE **belligerent**.

warn verb *to warn someone of danger.* advise, alert, caution, forewarn, give a warning [SEE **warning**], inform, notify, raise the alarm, remind, [*informal*] tip off.

warning noun 1 *warning of impending trouble. She just turned up without warning.* advance notice, augury, forewarning, hint, indication, notice, omen, premonition, presage, sign, signal, threat, [*informal*] tip-off.
2 *They let him off with a warning.* admonition, advice, caveat, caution, reprimand.

VARIOUS WARNING SIGNALS: alarm, alarm-bell, beacon, bell, fire-alarm, flashing lights, fog-horn, gong, hooter, red light, siren, traffic-lights, whistle.

---

warp verb *warped floor-boards.* become deformed, bend, buckle, contort, curl, curve, distort, kink, twist.

warrant noun *a search-warrant.* authority, authorization, SEE **document**, licence, permit, voucher.

warrant verb *His crime didn't warrant such a stiff punishment.* SEE **justify**.

warranty noun SEE **guarantee** noun.

warren noun *a rabbit warren.* burrow.

warring adjective SEE **belligerent**.

warrior noun SEE **fighter**.

warship noun VARIOUS VESSELS: SEE **vessel**.

wart noun SEE **spot** noun.

wary adjective *wary of possible dangers. a wary approach.* alert, apprehensive, attentive, careful, cautious, chary, circumspect, distrustful, heedful, observant, on the look-out (for), suspicious, vigilant, watchful.
OPPOSITES: SEE **reckless**.

wash noun *I have a wash as soon as I get up.* [*joking*] ablutions, bath, rinse, shampoo, shower.

wash verb 1 *to wash the car. to wash clothes.* SEE **clean** verb, cleanse, launder, mop, rinse, scrub, shampoo, sluice, soap down, sponge down, swab down, swill, wipe.
2 *to wash yourself.* bath, bathe, [*old-fashioned*] make your toilet, [*joking*] perform your ablutions, shower.
3 *The sea washes against the cliff.* flow, splash.
to wash your hands of SEE **abandon**.

washing noun dirty clothes, laundry, [*informal*] the wash.

wash-out noun SEE **failure**.

waspish adjective SEE **irritable**.

wassailing noun SEE **merrymaking**.

wastage noun SEE **waste** noun.

waste adjective 1 *waste materials.* discarded, extra, superfluous, unused, unwanted.
2 *waste land.* bare, barren, derelict, empty, overgrown, run-down, uncared for, uncultivated, undeveloped, wild.

waste noun 1 *The disposal of waste is a problem in big cities.* debris, effluent, garbage, junk, litter, refuse, rubbish, scraps, trash.
2 *waste left after you've finished something.* dregs, excess, leavings, [*informal*] left-overs, offcuts, remnants, scrap, unusable material, unwanted material, wastage.

waste verb *to waste resources.* be prodigal with, dissipate, fritter, misspend, misuse, squander, use wastefully [SEE **wasteful**], use up.
OPPOSITES: SEE **conserve** verb.
to waste away *He wasted away when he was ill.* become emaciated, become thin, become weaker, mope, pine, weaken.

wasteful adjective *a wasteful use of resources.* excessive, expensive, extravagant, improvident, imprudent, lavish, needless, prodigal, profligate, reckless, thriftless, uneconomical.
OPPOSITES: SEE **economical**.
a wasteful person SEE **spendthrift**.

wasteland noun = waste land [SEE **waste** adjective].

watch noun chronometer, clock, digital watch, stop-watch, timepiece, timer, wrist-watch.
on the watch SEE **alert** adjective.
to keep watch SEE **guard** verb.

watch verb **1** *to watch what someone does. to watch TV.* attend to, concentrate on, contemplate, eye, gaze at, heed, keep your eyes on, look at, mark, note, observe, pay attention to, regard, see, stare at, take notice of, view.
2 *Watch the baby while I pop out for a minute.* care for, defend, guard, keep an eye on, keep watch on, look after, mind, protect, safeguard, shield, supervise, tend.
to watch out, to watch your step = to be careful [SEE **careful**].

watcher noun [*plural*] audience, [*informal*] looker-on, observer, onlooker, spectator, viewer, witness.

watchful adjective SEE **observant**.

watchman noun caretaker, custodian, guard, look-out, night-watchman, security guard, sentinel, sentry.

watchword noun SEE **saying**.

water noun VARIOUS KINDS OF WATER: bath-water, brine, distilled water, drinking water, rainwater, sea-water, spa water, spring water, tap water.
VARIOUS STRETCHES OF WATER: brook, lake, lido, ocean, pond, pool, river, sea, SEE **stream** noun.
RELATED ADJECTIVES: aquatic, hydraulic.

Many English words connected with the idea of *water* are related to Latin and Greek words for water. Related to Latin *aqua* are words like *aquarium*, *aquatic*, and *aqueduct*; related to Greek *hudor* are words like *hydraulic*, *hydrofoil*, and *hydrometer*.

---

water verb *to water the garden.* dampen, douse, drench, flood, hose, irrigate, moisten, soak, souse, sprinkle, wet.
to water something down dilute, thin, weaken.

water-closet noun SEE **lavatory**.

water-colour noun SEE **paint** noun.

watercourse noun SEE **channel** noun.

waterfall noun cascade, cataract, chute, rapids, torrent, white water.

waterless adjective SEE **dry** adjective.

waterlogged adjecive *a waterlogged pitch.* full of water, saturated, soaked.

waterproof adjective *waterproof material.* damp-proof, impermeable, impervious, water-repellent, water-resistant, watertight, weatherproof.

waterproof noun *Take a waterproof— it's going to be wet.* cape, groundsheet, mackintosh, [*informal*] mac, raincoat, sou'wester.

watershed noun SEE **turning-point**.

water-splash noun ford.

watertight adjective *a watertight container.* hermetic, sealed, sound, SEE **waterproof** adjective.
OPPOSITES: SEE **leaky**.

waterway noun SEE **channel** noun.

watery adjective **1** *a watery liquid. watery gravy.* aqueous, characterless, dilute, fluid, liquid, [*informal*] runny, [*informal*] sloppy, tasteless, thin, watered down, weak.
2 *watery eyes.* damp, moist, tear-filled, tearful, [*informal*] weepy, wet.

waul verb SEE **wail**.

wave noun **1** *waves on the sea.* billow, breaker, crest, ridge, ripple, roller, surf, swell, tidal wave, undulation, wavelet, [*informal*] white horse.
2 *a wave of enthusiasm.* flood, outbreak, surge, upsurge.
3 *a new wave in the world of fashion.* advance, tendency, trend.
4 *a wave of the hand.* flourish, gesticulation, gesture, shake, signal.
5 *radio waves.* pulse, vibration.

wave verb *to wave your arms about.* brandish, flail about, flap, flourish, flutter, move to and fro, shake, sway, swing, twirl, undulate, waft, wag, waggle, wiggle.
VARIOUS WAYS TO GESTURE: SEE **gesture** verb.
to wave something aside SEE **dismiss**.

wavelength noun *Tune your radio to the right wavelength.* channel, station, waveband.

waver verb 1 *to waver when confronted by danger. to waver on the brink.* become unsteady, change, falter, SEE **hesitate**, quake, quaver, quiver, shake, shiver, shudder, sway, teeter, totter, tremble, vacillate, wobble.
2 *The light from a candle wavers.* SEE **flicker**.

wavering adjective SEE **hesitant**.

wavy adjective *a wavy line.* curling, curly, curving, rippling, sinuous, undulating, winding, zigzag.
OPPOSITES: SEE **straight**.

wax verb SEE **increase** verb.

way noun 1 *the way home.* direction, journey, SEE **road**, route.
2 *a long way.* distance, length, measurement.
3 *the way to do something.* approach, avenue, course, knack, manner, means, method, mode, path, procedure, process, system, technique.
4 *I was not used to American ways.* custom, fashion, habit, practice, routine, style, tradition.
5 *Her funny ways take some getting used to.* characteristic, eccentricity, idiosyncrasy, oddity, peculiarity.
6 *It's all right in some ways.* aspect, circumstances, detail, feature, particular, respect.

wayfarer noun SEE **traveller**.

waylay verb *He waylaid me on my way to the meeting.* accost, ambush, attack, buttonhole, detain, intercept, lie in wait for, surprise.

way-out adjective SEE **unconventional**.

wayside noun *flowers growing on the wayside.* SEE **verge**.

wayward adjective *a wayward child.* disobedient, headstrong, SEE **naughty**, obstinate, self-willed, stubborn, uncontrollable, uncooperative, wilful.
OPPOSITES: SEE **co-operative**.

WC SEE **lavatory**.

weak adjective 1 *weak materials. a weak structure.* brittle, decrepit, delicate, feeble, flawed, flimsy, fragile, frail, inadequate, insubstantial, rickety, shaky, slight, substandard, tender, thin, unsafe, unsound, unsteady.
2 *a weak constitution.* anaemic, debilitated, delicate, enervated, exhausted, feeble, flabby, frail, helpless, ill, infirm, listless, low (*feeling low today*), [*informal*] poorly, puny, sickly, slight, thin, wasted, weakly, [*uncomplimentary*] weedy.
3 *a weak leader.* cowardly, fearful, impotent, indecisive, ineffective, ineffectual, irresolute, poor, powerless, pusillanimous, spineless, timid, timorous, weak-minded.
4 *a weak position.* defenceless, exposed, unguarded, unprotected, vulnerable.
5 *a weak excuse.* feeble, lame, unconvincing, unsatisfactory.
6 *weak tea.* dilute, diluted, tasteless, thin, watery.
OPPOSITES: SEE **strong**.

weaken verb 1 *to weaken the strength of someone or something.* debilitate, destroy, diminish, emasculate, enervate, enfeeble, erode, impair, lessen, lower, make weaker, reduce, ruin, sap, soften, undermine, [*informal*] water down.
2 *Our resolve weakened.* abate, become weaker, decline, decrease, dwindle, ebb, fade, flag, give way, wane.
OPPOSITES: SEE **strengthen**.

weakling noun coward, [*informal*] milksop, [*informal*] runt, [*informal*] softie, weak person [SEE **weak**], [*informal*] weed.

weakness noun 1 *a weakness in the design of something.* blemish, defect, error, failing, fault, flaw, imperfection, mistake, shortcoming.
2 *a weakness in the foundations.* flimsiness, fragility, frailty, inadequacy, softness.
3 *a feeling of weakness.* debility, feebleness, SEE **illness**, impotence, infirmity, lassitude, vulnerability.
OPPOSITES: SEE **strength**.
4 *a weakness for chocolates.* fondness, inclination, liking, penchant, predilection, [*informal*] soft spot.

weal noun SEE **wound** noun.

wealth noun 1 *Most of his wealth is in stocks and shares.* affluence, assets, capital, fortune, [*old-fashioned*] lucre, SEE **money**, opulence, possessions, property, prosperity, riches, [*old-fashioned*] substance (*a man of substance*).
OPPOSITES: SEE **poverty**.
2 *a wealth of information.* abundance, SEE **plenty**, profusion, store.

wealthy adjective affluent, [*informal*] flush, [*informal*] loaded, moneyed, opulent, [*joking*] plutocratic, prosperous, rich, [*informal*] well-heeled, well-off, well-to-do.
OPPOSITES: SEE **poor**.
a wealthy person billionaire, capitalist, millionaire, plutocrat, tycoon.

weapons plural noun armaments, munitions, ordnance, weaponry.

TYPES OF WEAPON: artillery, automatic weapons, biological weapons, chemical weapons, firearms, missiles, nuclear weapons, small arms, strategic weapons, tactical weapons.

VARIOUS WEAPONS: airgun, arrow, atom bomb, ballistic missile, battering-ram, battleaxe, bayonet, bazooka, blowpipe, blunderbuss, bomb, boomerang, bow and arrow, bren-gun, cannon, carbine, catapult, claymore, cosh, crossbow, CS gas, cudgel, cutlass.

dagger, depth-charge, dirk, flame-thrower, foils, grenade, [*old-fashioned*] halberd, harpoon, H-bomb, howitzer, incendiary bomb, javelin, knuckleduster, lance, land-mine, laser beam, long-bow, machete, machine-gun, mine, missile, mortar, musket, mustard gas, napalm bomb, pike, pistol, pole-axe.

rapier, revolver, rifle, rocket, sabre, scimitar, shotgun, [*informal*] six-shooter, sling, spear, sten-gun, stiletto, sub-machine-gun, sword, tank, tear-gas, time-bomb, tomahawk, tommy-gun, torpedo, truncheon, warhead, water-cannon.

PLACES WHERE WEAPONS ARE STORED: armoury, arsenal, depot, magazine.

wear verb **1** *to wear clothes.* be dressed in, clothe yourself in, dress in, have on, present yourself in, put on, wrap up in.
2 *Constant tramping in and out wears the carpet.* damage, fray, injure, mark, scuff, wear away, weaken.
3 *This carpet has worn well.* endure, last, [*informal*] stand the test of time, survive.
to wear away abrade, corrode, eat away, erode, grind down, rub away.
to wear off *The effects soon wore off.* SEE **subside**.
to wear out *The effort wore me out.* SEE **weary** verb.

weariness noun SEE **tiredness**.

wearisome adjective *wearisome business.* boring, dreary, exhausting, monotonous, repetitive, tedious, tiring, SEE **troublesome**.
OPPOSITES: SEE **stimulating**.

weary adjective SEE **tired**.

weary verb SEE **tire**.

wearying adjective SEE **tiring**.

weather noun climate, the elements, meteorological conditions.
RELATED ADJECTIVE: meteorological.

FEATURES OF WEATHER: blizzard, breeze, cloud, cyclone, deluge, dew, downpour, drizzle, drought, fog, frost, gale, hail, haze, heatwave, hoar-frost, hurricane, ice, lightning, mist, rain, rainbow, shower, sleet, slush, snow, snowstorm, squall, storm, sunshine, tempest, thaw, thunder, tornado, typhoon, whirlwind, wind.

WORDS USED TO DESCRIBE WEATHER: autumnal, blustery, breezy, bright, brilliant, chilly, clear, close, cloudless, cloudy, SEE **cold**, drizzly, dry, dull, fair, fine, foggy, foul, freezing, frosty, grey, hazy, SEE **hot**, humid, icy, inclement, misty, overcast, pouring, rainy, rough, showery, slushy, snowy, spring-like, squally, stormy, sultry, summery, sunless, sunny, sweltering, teeming, thundery, torrential, turbulent, wet, wild, windy, wintry.

SOME METEOROLOGICAL TERMS: anticyclone, depression, front, isobar, isotherm, temperature.

weather verb *to weather a storm.* SEE **survive**.

weather-beaten adjective SEE **sunburnt**.

weathercock noun weather-vane.

weatherman noun forecaster, meteorologist.

weatherproof adjective SEE **waterproof**.

weave verb **1** *to weave threads.* braid, criss-cross, entwine, interlace, intertwine, interweave, knit, plait, sew.
2 *to weave a story.* compose, create, make, plot, put together.
3 *to weave your way through a crowd.* tack, [*informal*] twist and turn, wind, zigzag.

weaver noun VARIOUS CRAFTSMEN: SEE **artist**.

weaving noun VARIOUS CRAFTS: SEE **art**.

web noun *a web of intersecting lines.* criss-cross, lattice, mesh, net, network.

webbing noun band, belt, strap.

wed verb SEE **marry**.

wedding noun marriage, matrimony, [*joking*] nuptials.

PEOPLE AT A WEDDING: best man, bride, bridegroom, bridesmaid, groom, page, registrar, usher, wedding guests.

OTHER WORDS TO DO WITH WEDDINGS: confetti, honeymoon, reception, registry office, service, trousseau, wedding-ring.

wedge verb *Wedge the door open.* SEE **fasten**, jam, stick.

wedlock noun SEE **marriage**.

wee adjective SEE **small**.

weed noun wild flower, wild plant, unwanted plant.

weedy adjective **1** *a weedy garden.* overgrown, rank, unkempt, untidy, unweeded, wild.
2 [*uncomplimentary*] *a weedy child.* SEE **weak**.

weeny adjective SEE **small**.

weep verb blubber, cry, [*informal*] grizzle, moan, shed tears, snivel, sob, wail, whimper.

weepy adjective SEE **tearful**.

weigh verb **1** *to weigh something on scales.* measure the weight of.
2 *We weighed the evidence.* consider, evaluate, SEE **weigh up**.
3 *His evidence weighed with the jury.* be important, count, have weight.
to weigh down *weighed down with troubles. weighed down with shopping.* afflict, burden, depress, load, make heavy, overload, weight.
to weigh up *We weighed up the pros and cons.* assess, consider, evaluate, examine, give thought to, meditate on, mull over, ponder, study, think about.

weighing-machine noun balance, scales, spring-balance, weighbridge.

weight noun **1** *a great weight to bear.* burden, heaviness, load, mass, pressure, strain.
UNITS OF WEIGHT: SEE **measure** noun.
2 *The boss's support lent weight to our campaign.* authority, emphasis, gravity, importance, seriousness, significance, substance.

weight verb *The end of the line is weighted with a lump of lead.* ballast, hold down, keep down, load, make heavy, weigh down.

weightless adjective SEE **light** adjective.

weighty adjective **1** *a weighty load.* SEE **heavy**.
2 *a weighty problem.* SEE **serious**.

weir noun dam.

weird adjective **1** *a weird atmosphere in the dungeon.* creepy, eerie, ghostly, mysterious, scary, [*informal*] spooky, supernatural, unaccountable, uncanny, unearthly, unnatural.
OPPOSITES: SEE **natural**.
2 *a weird style of dress.* abnormal, bizarre, [*informal*] cranky, curious, eccentric, [*informal*] funny, grotesque, odd, outlandish, peculiar, queer, quirky, strange, unconventional, unusual, [*informal*] way-out, [*informal*] zany.
OPPOSITES: SEE **conventional**.

weirdie, weirdo nouns SEE **eccentric** noun.

welcome adjective *a welcome rest.* acceptable, agreeable, gratifying, much-needed, [*informal*] nice, pleasant, pleasing, pleasurable.
OPPOSITES: SEE **unwelcome**.

welcome noun *a friendly welcome.* greeting, hospitality, reception.

welcome verb **1** *She welcomed us at the door.* greet, receive.
WORDS USED TO WELCOME PEOPLE: SEE **greeting**.
2 *We welcome constructive criticism.* accept, appreciate, approve of, delight in, like, want.

welcoming adjective SEE **friendly**.

weld verb bond, cement, SEE **fasten**, fuse, join, solder, unite.

welfare noun *Nurses look after the welfare of patients.* good, happiness, health, interests, prosperity, well-being.

welkin noun SEE **sky**.

well adjective *You look well.* fit, healthy, hearty, lively, robust, sound, strong, thriving, vigorous.

well noun **1** *water from a well.* artesian well, borehole, oasis, shaft, spring, waterhole, wishing-well.
2 *oil from a well.* gusher, oil well.

well verb SEE **flow** verb.

well-behaved adjective *a well-behaved class.* co-operative, disciplined, docile, dutiful, good, hard-working, law-abiding, manageable, [*informal*] nice, SEE **obedient**, polite, quiet, well-trained.
OPPOSITES: SEE **naughty**.

well-being noun SEE **happiness, health**.

well-bred adjective SEE **polite**.

well-built adjective *a well-built young person.* athletic, big, brawny, burly, hefty, muscular, powerful, stocky, [*informal*] strapping, strong, sturdy, upstanding.
OPPOSITES: undersized, SEE **small**.

well-disposed adjective SEE **friendly**, **kind** adjective.

well-dressed adjective SEE **smart** adjective.

well-groomed adjective SEE **tidy** adjective.

well-heeled adjective SEE **wealthy**.

wellington noun SEE **shoe**.

well-known adjective **1** *a well-known person.* SEE **famous.**
2 *a well-known fact. a well-known beauty spot.* SEE **public** adjective.

well-mannered adjective SEE **polite.**

well-meaning adjective [usually implies *kind but misguided*] *His well-meaning remarks misfired.* good-natured, SEE **kind** adjective, obliging, sincere, well-intentioned, well-meant.
OPPOSITES: SEE **malicious.**

well-off adjective SEE **wealthy.**

well-read adjective SEE **educated.**

well-spoken adjective SEE **polite.**

well-to-do adjective SEE **wealthy.**

welsh verb SEE **swindle** verb.

welt noun SEE **wound** noun.

welter verb SEE **wallow.**

wench noun SEE **girl.**

wend verb SEE **go.**

west noun GEOGRAPHICAL TERMS: SEE **geography.**

western noun *I watched a western on TV.* SEE **film.**

wet adjective **1** *wet clothes. wet grass.* awash, bedraggled, clammy, damp, dank, dewy, drenched, dripping, moist, muddy, saturated, sloppy, soaked, soaking, sodden, soggy, sopping, soused, spongy, submerged, waterlogged, watery, wringing.
2 *wet weather.* drizzly, humid, misty, pouring, rainy, showery.
WORDS TO DESCRIBE WEATHER: SEE **weather** noun.
3 *wet paint.* runny, sticky, tacky.
OPPOSITES: SEE **dry** adjective.

wet noun *Come in out of the wet.* dampness, drizzle, rain.

wet verb *Wet the soil before you plant the seeds.* dampen, douse, drench, irrigate, moisten, saturate, soak, spray, sprinkle, steep, water.
OPPOSITES: SEE **dry** verb.

wether noun SEE **sheep.**

whack noun, verb SEE **hit** noun, verb.

whacked adjective SEE **tired.**

whacking adjective SEE **large.**

wharf noun SEE **landing-stage.**

wheat noun corn.
OTHER CEREALS: SEE **cereal.**

wheedle verb SEE **coax.**

wheel noun KINDS OF WHEEL: bogie, castor, cog-wheel, spinning-wheel, steering-wheel.
PARTS OF A WHEEL: axle, hub, rim, spoke, tyre.

wheel verb *Gulls wheeled overhead.* SEE **circle** verb, gyrate, move in circles.
to wheel round *He wheeled round when he heard her voice.* change direction, swerve, swing round, turn, veer.

wheeze verb breathe noisily, cough, gasp, pant, puff.

whelp noun SEE **dog** noun.

whereabouts noun SEE **location.**

wherewithal noun SEE **money.**

whet verb **1** *to whet a knife.* SEE **sharpen.**
2 *to whet someone's appetite.* SEE **stimulate.**

whetstone noun SEE **sharpener.**

whiff noun *a whiff of cigar smoke.* breath, hint, puff, SEE **smell** noun.

while noun *I saw her a short while ago.* SEE **time** noun.

whim noun *an unaccountable whim.* caprice, desire, fancy, impulse, quirk, urge.

whimper, whine verbs complain, cry, [*informal*] grizzle, groan, moan, snivel, wail, weep, whimper, [*informal*] whinge.
OTHER SOUNDS: SEE **sound** noun.

whinge verb SEE **whine.**

whinny verb neigh.
OTHER SOUNDS: SEE **sound** noun.

whip noun VARIOUS INSTRUMENTS USED FOR WHIPPING: birch, cane, cat, cat-o'-nine-tails, crop, horsewhip, lash, riding-crop, scourge, switch.

whip verb **1** *to whip someone as a punishment.* beat, birch, cane, flagellate, flog, SEE **hit** verb, lash, scourge, [*informal*] tan, thrash.
2 *to whip cream.* beat, stir vigorously, whisk.

whippet noun SEE **dog** noun.

whipping-boy noun scapegoat.

whippy adjective SEE **flexible.**

whirl noun *My mind was in a whirl.* SEE **confusion.**

whirl verb *The dancers whirled round.* SEE **circle** verb, gyrate, pirouette, reel, revolve, rotate, spin, swivel, turn, twirl, twist, wheel.

whirlpool noun eddy, vortex.

whirlwind noun cyclone, tornado, vortex.

whirr noun, verb VARIOUS SOUNDS: SEE **sound** noun.

whisk noun *an egg-whisk.* beater, mixer.

whisk verb *to whisk eggs for an omelette.* beat, mix, stir, whip.

whiskers noun *whiskers on a man's face.* bristles, hairs, moustache.

whisper noun **1** *She spoke in a whisper.* murmur, undertone.
2 *I heard a whisper that they were engaged.* gossip, hearsay, rumour.

whisper verb *Keep quiet—don't even whisper.* breathe, murmur, SEE **talk** verb.

whistle noun *the sound of a whistle.* hooter, pipe, pipes, siren.

whistle verb *to whistle a tune.* blow, pipe.
OTHER SOUNDS: SEE **sound** noun.

white adjective **1** *white sheets.* clean, spotless.
2 *shades of white.* cream, ivory, SEE **pale** adjective, snow-white, snowy, whitish.
white horses SEE **wave** noun.

whiten verb blanch, bleach, etiolate, fade, lighten, pale.

whitewash noun, verb SEE **paint** noun, verb.

whitlow noun SEE **spot** noun.

whittle verb *to whittle a piece of wood.* SEE **shape** verb.
to whittle down SEE **reduce**.

whodunit noun SEE **thriller**.

whole adjective **1** *She told us the whole story.* complete, entire, full, total, unabbreviated, unabridged, uncut, unedited, unexpurgated.
OPPOSITES: SEE **incomplete**.
2 *When we unpacked it, the clock was still whole.* in one piece, intact, integral, perfect, sound, unbroken, undamaged, undivided, unharmed, unhurt.
OPPOSITES: SEE **fragmentary**.

wholesale adjective **1** *wholesale trade.*
OPPOSITE: retail.
2 *wholesale destruction.* comprehensive, extensive, general, global, indiscriminate, mass, total, universal, widespread.

wholesome adjective *wholesome food. a wholesome atmosphere.* good, health-giving, healthy, hygienic, nourishing, nutritious, salubrious, sanitary.
OPPOSITES: SEE **unhealthy**.

whoop noun, verb VARIOUS SOUNDS: SEE **sound** noun.

whopper noun SEE **giant** noun.

whopping adjective SEE **large**.

whore noun SEE **prostitute** noun.

whorl noun coil, spiral, turn, twist.

wicked adjective *a wicked deed. a wicked person.* [*informal*] awful, bad, base, dissolute, SEE **evil** adjective, guilty, incorrigible, indefensible, insupportable, intolerable, irresponsible, lost (*a lost soul*), machiavellian, mischievous, naughty, nefarious, offensive, rascally, scandalous, shameful, sinful, sinister, spiteful, [*informal*] terrible, ungodly, unprincipled, unrighteous, vicious, vile, villainous, wrong.
OPPOSITES: SEE **moral** adjective.
a wicked person criminal, mischief-maker, sinner, villain, wretch.

wickedness noun enormity, SEE **evil** noun, guilt, heinousness, immorality, infamy, irresponsibility, [*old-fashioned*] knavery, misconduct, naughtiness, sinfulness, spite, turpitude, unrighteousness, vileness, villainy, wrong, wrongdoing.

wickerwork noun basket-work.

wicket, wicket-gate nouns SEE **gate**.

wide adjective **1** *a wide river. a wide area.* broad, expansive, extensive, large, panoramic (*a panoramic view*), spacious, vast, yawning.
2 *wide sympathies.* all-embracing, broad-minded, catholic, comprehensive, eclectic, encyclopaedic, inclusive, wide-ranging.
3 *wide trousers.* baggy, flared.
OPPOSITES: SEE **narrow**.
4 *I welcomed her with arms open wide.* extended, open, outspread, outstretched.
5 *The shot was wide.* off-course, off-target.

widen verb **1** *to widen an opening.* broaden, dilate, distend, make wider, open out, spread, stretch.
2 *to widen the scope of a business.* enlarge, expand, extend, increase.

widespread adjective *Disease was widespread.* common, endemic, extensive, far-reaching, general, global, pervasive, prevalent, rife, universal, wholesale.
OPPOSITES: SEE **uncommon**.

widow, widower nouns FAMILY RELATIONSHIPS: SEE **family**.

width noun beam (*of a ship*), breadth, diameter (*of a circle*), distance across, girth (*of a horse*), span (*of a bridge*), thickness.

wield verb **1** *to wield a tool or weapon.* brandish, flourish, handle, hold, manage, ply, use.
2 *to wield influence.* employ, exercise, have, possess.

wife noun spouse.
FAMILY RELATIONSHIPS: SEE **family**.

wig noun toupee.

wigging noun SEE **reprimand** noun.

wiggle verb SEE **wriggle**.

wigwam noun SEE **tent**.

wild adjective **1** *wild animals. wild flowers.* free, natural, uncultivated, undomesticated, untamed.
OPPOSITES: cultivated, SEE **domestic**.

2 *wild tribes.* barbaric, barbarous, savage, uncivilized.
OPPOSITES: SEE **civilized**.
3 *wild country.* deserted, desolate, [*informal*] godforsaken, overgrown, remote, rough, rugged, uncultivated, unenclosed, unfarmed, uninhabited, waste.
OPPOSITES: SEE **cultivated**.
4 *wild behaviour.* aggressive, berserk, boisterous, disorderly, ferocious, fierce, frantic, hysterical, lawless, mad, noisy, obstreperous, out of control, rabid, rampant, rash, reckless, riotous, rowdy, savage, uncontrollable, uncontrolled, undisciplined, ungovernable, unmanageable, unrestrained, unruly, uproarious, violent.
OPPOSITES: SEE **restrained**.
5 *wild weather.* blustery, stormy, tempestuous, turbulent, violent, windy.
OPPOSITES: SEE **calm** adjective.
6 *wild enthusiasm.* eager, excited, extravagant, uninhibited, unrestrained.
7 *wild notions.* crazy, fantastic, impetuous, irrational, SEE **silly**, unreasonable.
8 *a wild guess.* inaccurate, random, unthinking.

wildebeest noun gnu.

wilderness noun *an uncultivated wilderness.* desert, jungle, waste, wasteland, wilds (*out in the wilds*).

wildlife noun ANIMALS: SEE **animal** noun.

wile noun SEE **trick** noun.

wilful adjective **1** *wilful disobedience.* [*informal*] bloody-minded, calculated, conscious, deliberate, intended, intentional, premeditated, voluntary.
OPPOSITES: SEE **accidental**.
2 *a wilful character.* determined, dogged, headstrong, intransigent, obdurate, obstinate, perverse, self-willed, stubborn, uncompromising.
OPPOSITES: SEE **amenable**.

will noun **1** *the will to succeed.* aim, desire, determination, inclination, intention, purpose, resolution, resolve, volition, will-power, wish.
2 *a last will and testament.* SEE **document**.

will verb **1** *We willed her to keep going.* encourage, influence, inspire, wish.
2 *He willed his fortune to his housekeeper.* bequeath, leave, pass on.

willing adjective **1** *willing to help.* content, disposed, eager, [*informal*] game (*I'm game for anything*), inclined, pleased, prepared, ready.
2 *willing workers.* amenable, compliant, consenting, co-operative, enthusiastic, helpful, obliging.
OPPOSITES: SEE **unwilling**.

willowy adjective *a willowy figure.* SEE **graceful**.

wilt verb *The plants wilted in the heat.* become limp, droop, fade, fail, flag, flop, languish, sag, shrivel, weaken, wither.
OPPOSITES: SEE **flourish** verb.

wily adjective *Foxes are supposed to be wily creatures.* artful, astute, clever, crafty, cunning, deceptive, designing, devious, furtive, guileful, ingenious, knowing, scheming, shifty, shrewd, skilful, sly, tricky, underhand.
OPPOSITES: SEE **straightforward**.

win verb **1** *to win in a game or battle.* be victorious, be the winner [SEE **winner**], come first, SEE **conquer**, overcome, prevail, succeed, triumph.
OPPOSITES: SEE **lose**.
2 *to win a prize. to win someone's admiration.* achieve, acquire, [*informal*] carry off, [*informal*] come away with, deserve, earn, gain, get, obtain, [*informal*] pick up, receive, secure, [*informal*] walk away with.

wince noun, verb FACIAL EXPRESSIONS: SEE **expression**.

winch noun, verb SEE **hoist** noun, verb.

wind noun **1** *a blustery wind. a gentle wind.* air-current, blast, breath, breeze, cyclone, draught, gale, gust, hurricane, monsoon, puff, squall, tornado, whirlwind, [*poetic*] zephyr.
2 *wind in the stomach.* flatulence, gas.
wind instruments SEE **brass**, **woodwind**.

wind verb **1** *to wind thread on to a reel.* coil, curl, curve, furl, loop, roll, turn, twine.
2 *The road winds up the hill.* bend, curve, meander, ramble, snake, twist, [*informal*] twist and turn, zigzag.
to wind up SEE **finish** verb.

windbag noun SEE **talkative (talkative person)**.

wind-cheater noun anorak.
OTHER COATS: SEE **coat** noun.

winding adjective *a winding road.* bending, [*informal*] bendy, circuitous, curving, [*informal*] in and out, indirect, meandering, rambling, roundabout, serpentine, sinuous, snaking, tortuous, [*informal*] twisting and turning, zigzag.
OPPOSITES: SEE **straight**.

windlass noun SEE **hoist** noun.

windless adjective SEE **calm** adjective.

window noun KINDS OF WINDOW: casement, dormer, double-glazed window, embrasure, fanlight, French window, light, oriel, pane, sash window, skylight, shop window, stained-glass window, windscreen.

window-seat noun SEE **seat** noun.

windscreen noun SEE **window**.

windswept adjective *a windswept moor.* bare, bleak, desolate, exposed, unprotected, windy.
OPPOSITES: SEE **sheltered**.

windy adjective 1 *windy weather.* blowy, blustery, boisterous, breezy, draughty, gusty, squally, stormy.
OPPOSITES: SEE **calm** adjective.
2 *a windy corner.* SEE **windswept**.

wine noun SOME KINDS OF WINE: beaujolais, Burgundy, champagne, chianti, claret, dry wine, hock, Madeira, malmsey, [*informal*] plonk, port, red wine, rosé, sherry, sweet wine, vintage, white wine.
OTHER DRINKS: SEE **drink** noun.

wing noun 1 PARTS OF AIRCRAFT: SEE **aircraft**.
2 *the wing of a car.* mudguard.
PARTS OF A VEHICLE: SEE **vehicle**.
3 *a new wing of a hospital.* annexe, end, extension.
to take wing SEE **fly** verb.

wink verb 1 *to wink an eye.* bat (*didn't bat an eyelid*), blink, flutter.
OTHER GESTURES: SEE **gesture** verb.
2 *The lights winked on and off.* flash, flicker, sparkle, twinkle.

winker noun [*informal*] *the winkers on a car.* indicator, signal, [*old-fashioned*] trafficator.

winner noun [*informal*] champ, champion, conqueror, first, medallist, victor.
OPPOSITES: SEE **loser**.

winning adjective 1 *the winning team.* champion, conquering, first, leading, prevailing, successful, top, top-scoring, triumphant, unbeaten, undefeated, victorious.
OPPOSITES: SEE **losing**.
2 *a winning smile.* SEE **charming**.

winnings noun SEE **money**.

winnow verb SEE **sift**.

winsome adjective SEE **charming**.

winter noun WINTER SPORTS: bob-sleigh, ice-hockey, skating, skiing, sledging, tobogganing.

wintry adjective *wintry weather.* SEE **cold** adjective.
OPPOSITE: summery.

wipe verb *to wipe things clean.* brush, clean, dry, dust, mop, polish, rub, scour, sponge, swab, wash.
to wipe out *to wipe out an ants' nest.* SEE **destroy**.

wire noun 1 *a length of wire.* cable, coaxial cable, flex, lead, [*plural*] wiring.
2 *She sent a wire to say she couldn't come.* cable, telegram.

wireless noun SEE **radio**.

wiry adjective *a wiry figure.* lean, sinewy, strong, thin, tough.

wisdom noun astuteness, common sense, discernment, discrimination, good sense, insight, SEE **intelligence**, judgement, penetration, prudence, reason, sagacity, sense, understanding.
wisdom tooth SEE **tooth**.

wise adjective 1 *a wise judge.* astute, discerning, enlightened, erudite, informed, SEE **intelligent**, judicious, knowledgeable, penetrating, perceptive, perspicacious, philosophical, prudent, rational, reasonable, sagacious, sage, sensible, shrewd, thoughtful, understanding, well-informed.
2 *a wise decision.* advisable, appropriate, fair, just, proper, right, sound.
OPPOSITES: SEE **unwise**.
a wise person philosopher, pundit, sage.
the three wise men magi.

wiseacre noun SEE **expert** noun, know-all.

wisecrack noun, verb SEE **joke** noun, verb.

wish noun *What's your dearest wish?* aim, ambition, aspiration, craving, desire, fancy, hankering, hope, longing, objective, request, want, yearning, [*informal*] yen.

wish verb *I wish that they'd be quiet.* ask, hope.
to wish for *What do you most wish for?* aspire to, covet, crave, desire, fancy, hanker after, long for, want, yearn for.

wishy-washy adjective SEE **feeble**.

wisp noun *a wisp of hair. a wisp of cloud.* shred, strand, streak.

wispy adjective *wispy material. wispy clouds.* flimsy, fragile, gossamer, insubstantial, light, streaky, thin.

wistful adjective SEE **sad**.

wit noun 1 *a comedian's wit.* banter, cleverness, comedy, facetiousness, humour, ingenuity, jokes, puns, quickness, quips, repartee, witticisms, wordplay.
2 *She is quite a wit.* comedian, comic, humorist, jester, joker, [*informal*] wag.
3 *I didn't have the wit to understand.* SEE **intelligence**.

witch noun SEE **magician**.

witchcraft noun SEE **magic** noun.

witch-doctor noun SEE **magician**.

witchery noun SEE **magic** noun.

withdraw verb **1** *to withdraw an objection. to withdraw your troops.* call back, cancel, recall, remove, rescind, take away, take back.
2 *The attackers withdrew.* back away, draw back, fall back, leave, move back, retire, retreat, run away.
OPPOSITES: SEE **advance** verb.
3 *Some competitors withdrew at the last minute.* back out, [*informal*] chicken out, [*informal*] cry off, drop out, pull out, secede.
OPPOSITES: SEE **enter**.

withdrawn adjective SEE **reserved**.

wither verb *Plants withered in the drought.* become dry, become limp, dehydrate, desiccate, droop, dry out, dry up, fail, flag, flop, sag, shrink, shrivel, waste away, wilt.
OPPOSITES: SEE **thrive**.

withhold verb *to withhold information.* conceal, hide, hold back, keep back, keep secret, repress, retain, suppress.

withstand verb *to withstand an attack.* bear, brave, cope with, defy, endure, hold out against, last out against, oppose, [*informal*] put up with, resist, stand up to, survive, tolerate, weather (*to weather a storm*).
OPPOSITES: SEE **surrender**.

witless adjective SEE **silly**.

witness noun **1** *a witness of an accident.* bystander, eye-witness, looker-on, observer, onlooker, spectator, watcher.
2 *a witness in a legal case.* LEGAL TERMS: SEE **law**.
to bear witness SEE **testify**.

witness verb *to witness an accident.* attend, behold, be present at, look on, observe, see, view, watch.
2 *to witness in a lawcourt.* SEE **testify**.

witticism noun SEE **joke** noun.

witty adjective *a witty storyteller.* amusing, clever, comic, facetious, funny, humorous, ingenious, intelligent, quick-witted, sharp-witted, waggish.
OPPOSITES: SEE **dull** adjective.

wizard noun **1** SEE **magician**, sorcerer, [*old-fashioned*] warlock.
2 *a wizard with engines.* SEE **expert** noun.

wizardry noun SEE **magic** noun.

wizened adjective SEE **wrinkled**.

woad noun SEE **colouring**.

wobble verb be unsteady, heave, move unsteadily, oscillate, quake, quiver, rock, shake, sway, teeter, totter, tremble, vacillate, vibrate, waver.

wobbly adjective *a wobbly stone.* insecure, loose, rickety, rocky, shaky, teetering, tottering, unbalanced, unsafe, unstable, unsteady.
OPPOSITES: SEE **steady** adjective.

wodge noun SEE **lump** noun.

woe noun SEE **sorrow** noun.

woebegone, woeful SEE **sad**.

wok noun COOKING UTENSILS: SEE **cook** verb.

wold noun SEE **hill**.

wolf verb *to wolf your food.* SEE **eat**.

woman noun bride, [*old-fashioned*] dame, [*old-fashioned*] damsel, daughter, dowager, female, girl, girlfriend, [*uncomplimentary*] hag, [*uncomplimentary*] harridan, housewife, hoyden, [*uncomplimentary, old-fashioned*] hussy, lady, lass, [*formal*] madam or Madame, maid, [*old-fashioned*] maiden, matriarch, matron, mistress, mother, [*uncomplimentary*] termagant, [*uncomplimentary*] virago, virgin, widow, wife.
FAMILY RELATIONSHIPS: SEE **family**.

Some words connected with the concept *woman* are related to Greek *gune*= *woman*, e.g. *gynaecology*, *misogynist*.

---

womanly adjective SEE **feminine**.

womb noun uterus.

wonder noun **1** *We gasped with wonder.* admiration, amazement, astonishment, awe, bewilderment, curiosity, fascination, respect, reverence, surprise, wonderment.
2 *It was a wonder that she recovered.* marvel, miracle.

wonder verb *I wonder if dinner is ready?* ask yourself, be curious about, conjecture, ponder, question yourself, speculate, think.
to wonder at *We wondered at their skill.* admire, be amazed by, feel wonder at [SEE **wonder** noun], gape at, marvel at.

wonderful adjective **1** *She made a wonderful recovery.* amazing, astonishing, astounding, extraordinary, incredible, marvellous, miraculous, phenomenal, remarkable, surprising, unexpected, [*old-fashioned*] wondrous.
OPPOSITES: SEE **normal**.
2 [*informal*] *The food was wonderful.* SEE **excellent**.

wonderment noun SEE **wonder** noun.

wondrous adjective SEE **wonderful**.

wonted adjective SEE **usual**.

woo verb **1** [*old-fashioned*] *to woo a girlfriend or boyfriend.* court, make love to.

2 *The shop is wooing new customers.* attract, bring in, coax, cultivate, persuade, pursue, seek, try to get.

Some words connected with the concept *wood* are related to Latin words *arbor = tree*, *lignum = wood*, and *silva = a wood*, and to Greek *xulon = wood.* e.g. *arboreal, arboretum; ligneous, lignite; silvan, silviculture; xylophone.*

---

wood noun **1** *We went for a walk in the wood.* afforestation, coppice, copse, forest, grove, jungle, orchard, plantation, spinney, thicket, trees, woodland, woods.
2 *A carpenter works with wood.* blockboard, chipboard, deal, planks, plywood, timber.

KINDS OF WOOD OFTEN USED TO MAKE THINGS: balsa, beech, cedar, chestnut, ebony, elm, mahogany, oak, pine, rosewood, sandalwood, sapele, teak, walnut.

---

woodbine noun honeysuckle.

wooded adjective *a wooded hillside.* afforested, silvan, timbered, tree-covered, woody.

wooden adjective **1** *wooden furniture.* timber, wood.
2 *a wooden performance.* emotionless, expressionless, hard, inflexible, lifeless, rigid, stiff, unbending, unemotional, unnatural.
OPPOSITES: SEE **lively**.

woodland noun SEE **wood**.

woodman noun forester.

woodwind noun WOODWIND INSTRUMENTS: bassoon, clarinet, cor anglais, flute, oboe, piccolo, recorder.
OTHER INSTRUMENTS: SEE **music**.

woodwork noun carpentry, joinery.

woody adjective **1** *a woody substance. a woody plant.* fibrous, hard, ligneous, tough, wooden.
2 *a woody hillside.* afforested, silvan, timbered, tree-covered, wooded.

woof noun, verb VARIOUS SOUNDS: SEE **sound** noun.

woolly adjective **1** *a woolly jumper.* wool, woollen.
2 *a woolly teddybear.* cuddly, downy, fleecy, furry, fuzzy, hairy, shaggy, soft.
3 *woolly ideas.* ambiguous, blurry, confused, hazy, ill-defined, indefinite, indistinct, uncertain, unclear, unfocused, vague.

word noun **1** *A thesaurus is a book of words.* expression, term.
LINGUISTIC TERMS: SEE **language**.
2 *Have you had any word from granny?* SEE **news**.
3 *You gave me your word.* SEE **promise** noun.
word for word SEE **verbatim**.

Some English words connected with the concept *word* are related to Latin *verba = word* [e.g. *verbal, verbatim*]; or to Greek *lexis = word* [e.g. *lexical, lexicography*]; or to Greek *logos = word* [e.g. *dialogue, philology*].

---

word verb *I spent ages thinking how to word my letter.* SEE **express** verb.

wording noun *the wording of a letter.* choice of words, diction, expression, language, phraseology, phrasing, style, terminology.

word-processor noun OTHER TOOLS TO WRITE WITH: SEE **write**.

wordy adjective *a wordy lecture. a wordy speaker.* diffuse, garrulous, long-winded, loquacious, pleonastic, prolix, rambling, repetitious, talkative, tautological, unstoppable, verbose.
OPPOSITES: SEE **brief** adjective.

work noun **1** *He hates hard work.* [*informal*] donkey-work, drudgery, effort, exertion, [*informal*] fag, [*informal*] graft, [*informal*] grind, industry, labour, [*informal*] plod (*It was sheer plod*), slavery, [*informal*] slog, [*informal*] spadework, [*informal*] sweat, toil.
2 *He set me work to do.* assignment, chore, commission, homework, housework, job, project, task, undertaking.
3 *What work do you do?* business, employment, job, livelihood, living, occupation, profession, trade.
VARIOUS KINDS OF WORK: SEE **job**.

work verb **1** [*informal*] beaver away, be busy, drudge, exert yourself, [*informal*] fag, [*informal*] grind away, [*informal*] to keep your nose to the grindstone, labour, make efforts, [*informal*] peg away, [*informal*] plug away, [*informal*] potter about, slave, sweat, toil.
2 *She works her staff hard.* drive, exploit.
3 *Does your watch work? I hope my plan works.* act, be effective, function, go, operate, perform, run, succeed, thrive.
to work out *to work out answers.* SEE **calculate**.
to work up *to work up an appetite.* SEE **develop**.
worked up SEE **excited**.

workable adjective SEE **practicable**.

workaday adjecive SEE **ordinary**.

worker noun [In British society, *worker* is usually seen as being opposite to *manager* or *owner*.] artisan, coolie, craftsman, employee, [*old-fashioned*] hand, labourer, member of staff, member of the working class, navvy, operative, operator, peasant, practitioner, servant, slave, tradesman, working man, working woman, workman.
WORKERS IN SPECIFIC JOBS: SEE **job**.

work-force noun employees, staff, workers [SEE **worker**].

working adjective **1** *a working woman.* employed, in work, practising.
OPPOSITES: SEE **unemployed**.
2 *Is the machine working?* functioning, going, in use, in working order, operational, running, usable.
OPPOSITES: SEE **defective**.

workman noun SEE **worker**.

workmanlike adjective *a workmanlike job.* SEE **competent**.

workmanship noun *We admired the blacksmith's workmanship.* art, artistry, competence, craft, craftsmanship, expertise, handicraft, handiwork, skill, technique.

workshop noun factory, mill, smithy, studio, workroom.

work-shy adjective SEE **lazy**.

world noun earth, globe, planet.
GEOGRAPHICAL TERMS: SEE **geography**.

world-famous adjective SEE **famous**.

worldly adjective *worldly things. a worldly outlook.* avaricious, earthly, greedy, material, materialistic, mundane, physical, selfish, temporal.
OPPOSITES: SEE **spiritual**.

worm verb *I wormed my way through the undergrowth.* crawl, creep, slither, squirm, wriggle, writhe.

worn adjective *worn at the elbows.* frayed, moth-eaten, SEE **old**, ragged, [*informal*] scruffy, shabby, tattered, [*informal*] tatty, thin, threadbare, worn-out.

worried adjective *worried about your work. worried about a sick relative.* afraid, agitated, anxious, apprehensive, bothered, concerned, distressed, disturbed, edgy, fearful, nervous, nervy, neurotic, obsessed (by), overwrought, perplexed, perturbed, solicitous, tense, troubled, uneasy, unhappy, upset, vexed.

worrisome adjective SEE **troublesome**.

worry noun **1** *She's in a constant state of worry.* agitation, anxiety, apprehension, distress, fear, neurosis, tension, uneasiness, vexation.
2 *She has a lot of worries.* burden, care, concern, misgiving, problem, [*informal, plural*] trials and tribulations, trouble.

worry verb **1** *Don't worry me while I'm busy.* agitate, annoy, [*informal*] badger, bother, distress, disturb, [*informal*] hassle, irritate, molest, nag, perplex, perturb, pester, plague, tease, torment, trouble, upset, vex.
2 *He worries about money.* agonize, be worried [SEE **worried**], brood, exercise yourself, feel uneasy, fret.

worrying adjective *worrying symptoms.* disquieting, distressing, disturbing, perturbing, SEE **troublesome**.
OPPOSITES: SEE **reassuring**.

worsen verb **1** *to worsen a situation.* aggravate, exacerbate, make worse.
2 *My temper worsened as the day went on.* become worse, decline, degenerate, deteriorate, get worse.
OPPOSITES: SEE **improve**.

worship noun *the worship of an idol.* adoration, adulation, deification, devotion, glorification, idolatry, love, praise, reverence (for), veneration.

PLACES OF WORSHIP: abbey, basilica, cathedral, chapel, church, meeting house, minster, mosque, oratory, pagoda, sanctuary, synagogue, tabernacle, temple.

---

worship verb **1** *She worships her grandad.* adore, be devoted to, deify, dote on, hero-worship, idolize, lionize, look up to, love, revere, reverence, venerate.
2 *to worship God.* glorify, laud, [*old-fashioned*] magnify, praise, pray to.

worth noun *What's the worth of this?* cost, importance, merit, price, quality, significance, use, usefulness, utility, value.
to be worth be priced at, cost, have a value of.

worthless adjective *worthless junk. worthless advice.* frivolous, futile, [*informal*] good-for-nothing, hollow, insignificant, meaningless, meretricious, paltry, pointless, poor, [*informal*] rubbishy, [*informal*] trashy, trifling, trivial, trumpery, unimportant, unusable, useless, valueless.
OPPOSITES: SEE **valuable**, **worthwhile**.

worthwhile adjective *a worthwhile sum of money. a worthwhile effort.* advantageous, beneficial, biggish, considerable, good, helpful, important, invaluable, meaningful, noticeable, productive, profitable, rewarding, significant, sizeable, substantial, useful, valuable, SEE **worthy**.
OPPOSITES: SEE **worthless**.

worthy adjective *a worthy cause. a worthy winner.* admirable, commendable, creditable, decent, deserving, good, honest, honourable, laudable, meritorious, praiseworthy, reputable, respectable, worthwhile.
OPPOSITES: SEE **unworthy**.

would-be adjective SEE **aspiring**.

wound noun disfigurement, hurt, injury, scar.

wound verb *Several were wounded in the accident.* cause pain to, damage, disfigure, harm, hurt, injure.

KINDS OF WOUND: amputation, bite, bruise, burn, cut, fracture, gash, graze, laceration, lesion, mutilation, scab, scald, scar, scratch, sore, sprain, stab, sting, strain, weal, welt.

WAYS TO WOUND: bite, blow up, bruise, burn, claw, cut, fracture, gash, gore, graze, SEE **hit** verb, impale, knife, lacerate, maim, make sore, mangle, maul, mutilate, scald, scratch, shoot, sprain, stab, sting, strain, torture.

---

wraith noun SEE **ghost**.

wrangle noun, verb SEE **quarrel** noun, verb.

wrap noun *a warm wrap round her shoulders.* cape, cloak, mantle, shawl, stole.

wrap verb *We wrapped it in brown paper.* bind, bundle up, cloak, cocoon, conceal, cover, encase, enclose, enfold, envelop, hide, insulate, lag, muffle, pack, package, shroud, surround, swaddle, swathe, wind.
OPPOSITES: SEE **open** verb.

wrapper noun SEE **cover** noun.

wrath noun SEE **anger** noun.

wrathful adjective SEE **angry**.

wreak verb *to wreak vengeance.* SEE **inflict**.

wreathe verb *wreathed in flowers.* adorn, decorate, encircle, festoon, intertwine, interweave, twist, weave.

wreck noun **1** *a broken wreck.* shipwreck, SEE **wreckage**.
2 *the wreck of all our hopes.* demolition, destruction, devastation, overthrow, ruin, termination, undoing.

wreck verb **1** *The ship was wrecked on the rocks. He wrecked his car.* break up, crumple, crush, demolish, destroy, shatter, shipwreck, smash, [*informal*] write off.
2 *The storm wrecked our picnic.* ruin, spoil.

wreckage noun bits, debris, [*informal*] flotsam and jetsam, fragments, pieces, remains, rubble, ruins.

wrench noun *The handle turns if you give it a wrench.* jerk, pull, tug, twist, [*informal*] yank.

wrench verb *to wrench a lid off. to wrench something out of shape.* force, jerk, lever, prize, pull, strain, tug, twist, wrest, wring, [*informal*] yank.

wrest verb SEE **wring**.

wrestle verb SEE **fight** verb, grapple, struggle, tussle.

wrestler noun SEE **fighter**.

wretch noun **1** *homeless wretches.* beggar, down and out, miserable person, pauper.
2 [*uncomplimentary*] *a villainous wretch.* SEE **wicked (wicked person)**.

wretched adjective **1** *a wretched look on his face.* SEE **miserable**.
2 [*informal*] *The wretched car won't start!* SEE **unsatisfactory**.

wriggle verb *The snake wriggled away.* snake, squirm, twist, waggle, wiggle, worm, writhe, zigzag.

wring verb **1** *to wring someone's hand.* clasp, grip, shake.
2 *to wring water out of wet clothes.* compress, crush, press, squeeze, twist.
3 *to wring a promise out of someone.* coerce, exact, extort, extract, force, wrench, wrest.

wringer noun SEE **drier**.

wringing adjective SEE **wet** adjective.

wrinkle noun *wrinkles in cloth. wrinkles in your face.* corrugation, crease, crinkle, [*informal*] crow's feet [= *wrinkles at the side of your eyes*], dimple, fold, furrow, gather, line, pleat, pucker, ridge.

wrinkle verb *Don't wrinkle the carpet.* crease, crinkle, crumple, fold, furrow, make wrinkles (in), pucker up, ridge, ruck up, rumple.
OPPOSITES: SEE **smooth** verb.

wrinkled adjective *a wrinkled face. a wrinkled surface.* corrugated, creased, crinkly, crumpled, furrowed, lined, pleated, ridged, rumpled, shrivelled, wavy, wizened, wrinkly.

wrist noun SEE **arm** noun.

wristlet noun bracelet.

writ noun SEE **command** noun.

write verb *to write a shopping list. to write your thoughts. to write a book.* compile, compose, copy, correspond [=*to write letters*], doodle, draft, draw up, engrave, inscribe, jot down, note, pen, print, record, scrawl, scribble, set down, take down, transcribe, type.

TOOLS YOU WRITE WITH: ballpoint, Biro, chalk, crayon, felt-tip, fountain-pen, ink, pen, pencil, typewriter, word-processor.

THINGS YOU WRITE ON: blackboard, card, exercise book, form, jotter, notepaper, pad, paper, papyrus, parchment, postcard, stationery, writing-paper.

writer noun **1** [=*person who writes things down*] amanuensis, clerk, copyist, [*uncomplimentary*] pen-pusher, scribe, secretary, typist.

2 [=*person who creates literature or music*] author, [*joking*] bard, composer, [*uncomplimentary*] hack, poet.

VARIOUS WRITERS: biographer, columnist, copy-writer, correspondent, diarist, dramatist, essayist, ghost-writer, journalist, leader-writer, librettist, novelist, playwright, poet, reporter, scriptwriter.

writhe verb *to writhe in agony.* coil, contort, jerk, squirm, struggle, thrash about, thresh about, twist, wriggle.

writing noun **1** *Can you read this writing?* calligraphy, characters, copperplate, cuneiform, handwriting, hieroglyphics, inscription, italics, letters, longhand, notation, penmanship, printing, runes, scrawl, screed, scribble, script, shorthand.

2 *The children were busy at their writing.* authorship, composition.

writings *the writings of Shakespeare.* literary texts, literature, texts, works.

KINDS OF WRITING: article, autobiography, biography, children's literature, comedy, copy-writing, correspondence, crime story, criticism, detective story, diary, documentary, drama, editorial, epic, epistle, essay, fable, fairy story or fairy-tale, fantasy, fiction, folk-tale.

history, journalism, legal document, legend, letter, libretto, lyric, monograph, mystery, myth, newspaper column, non-fiction, novel, parable, parody, philosophy, play, SEE **poem**, propaganda, prose, reportage, romance.

saga, satire, science fiction, scientific writing, scriptwriting, SF, sketch, story, tale, thriller, tragi-comedy, tragedy, travel writing, treatise, trilogy, TV script, verse, [*informal*] whodunit, yarn.

written adjective *written evidence.* documentary, [*informal*] in black and white, inscribed, in writing, set down, transcribed, typewritten.

OPPOSITES: SEE **unwritten**.

wrong adjective **1** *He was wrong to steal. Cruelty to animals is wrong.* SEE **bad**, base, blameworthy, corrupt, criminal, crooked, deceitful, dishonest, dishonourable, evil, felonious, illegal, illicit, immoral, iniquitous, irresponsible, naughty, reprehensible, sinful, unethical, unlawful, unprincipled, unscrupulous, vicious, villainous, wicked.

2 *a wrong answer. a wrong decision.* erroneous, fallacious, false, imprecise, improper, inaccurate, incorrect, inexact, misinformed, mistaken, unacceptable, unfair, unjust, untrue, wrongful.

3 *I put on the wrong coat. He came the wrong way.* abnormal, inappropriate, incongruous, inconvenient, unconventional, unsuitable, worst.

4 *What's wrong with the car? There's something wrong here.* amiss, broken down, defective, faulty, out of order, unusable.

OPPOSITES: SEE **right** adjective.

wrong noun SEE **wrongdoing**.

to do wrong default, err, go astray, SEE **misbehave, sin** verb.

wrong verb *I wronged him when I accused him without evidence.* abuse, be unfair to, cheat, do an injustice to, harm, hurt, maltreat, misrepresent, mistreat, traduce, treat unfairly.

wrongdoer noun convict, criminal, crook, culprit, delinquent, evildoer, law-breaker, malefactor, mischief-maker, miscreant, offender, sinner, transgressor.

wrongdoing noun crime, delinquency, disobedience, evil, immorality, indiscipline, iniquity, malpractice, misbehaviour, mischief, naughtiness, offence, sin, sinfulness, wickedness.

wrongful adjective *wrongful dismissal.* SEE **unjust**.

wrongheaded adjective SEE **obstinate**.

wry adjective **1** *a wry smile.* askew, awry, bent, crooked, distorted, twisted, uneven.

2 *a wry sense of humour.* droll, dry, ironic, mocking, sardonic.

X

xenophobia noun SEE **patriotism**.

Xerox noun, verb SEE **copy** noun, verb.

xylophone noun PERCUSSION INSTRUMENTS: SEE **percussion**.

Y

yacht noun VARIOUS BOATS: SEE **vessel**.

yachtsman noun SEE **sailor**.

yam noun sweet potato.

yank verb SEE **tug** verb.

yap noun, verb VARIOUS SOUNDS: SEE **sound** noun.

yard noun 1 OTHER UNITS OF MEASUREMENT: SEE **measure** noun.
2 *a back yard.* court, courtyard, enclosure, garden, [*informal*] quad, quadrangle.

yardstick noun SEE **standard** noun.

yarn noun 1 *yarn woven into cloth.* SEE **thread** noun.
2 [*informal*] *a sailor's yarn.* anecdote, narrative, story, tale.

yashmak noun veil.

yaw verb SEE **turn** verb.

yawn noun OTHER FACIAL EXPRESSIONS: SEE **expression**.

yawning adjective *a yawning hole.* gaping, open, wide.

year noun OTHER UNITS OF TIME: SEE **time** noun.

yearly adjective *a yearly payment.* annual.

yearn verb SEE **long** verb.

yearning noun SEE **longing**.

yell noun, verb SEE **shout** noun, verb.

yellow adjective SHADES OF YELLOW: amber, chrome yellow, cream, gold, golden, orange, tawny.
OTHER COLOURS: SEE **colour** noun.

yelp noun, verb VARIOUS SOUNDS: SEE **sound** noun.

yen noun [*informal*] *a yen for sweets.* SEE **longing**.

yeoman noun SEE **farmer**.

yeti noun abominable snowman.

yield noun 1 *a good yield from our fruit-trees.* crop, harvest, produce, product.
2 *a good yield from my investment.* earnings, income, interest, profit, return.

yield verb 1 *to yield to your opponent.* acquiesce, bow, capitulate, [*informal*] cave in, cede, concede, defer, give in, give way, submit, succumb, surrender, [*informal*] throw in the towel, [*informal*] throw up the sponge.
2 *Our fruit-trees yield a big crop.* bear, grow, produce, supply.
3 *This investment yields a high interest.* earn, generate, pay out, provide, return.

yielding adjective SEE **soft**.

yob noun SEE **hooligan**.

yodel verb VARIOUS SOUNDS: SEE **sound** noun.

yoga noun SEE **meditation**.

yoke noun SEE **burden** noun, **link** noun.

yoke verb *to yoke things together.* SEE **link** verb.

young adjective 1 *young plants. young animals, young birds.* baby, early, growing, immature, newborn, undeveloped, unfledged, youngish, youthful.
2 *They're young for their age.* babyish, boyish, childish, girlish, immature, infantile, juvenile, puerile.

YOUNG PEOPLE: adolescent, baby, boy, [*uncomplimentary*] brat, child, girl, infant, juvenile, [*informal*] kid, lad, lass, [*informal*] nipper, teenager, toddler, [*uncomplimentary*] urchin, youngster, youth.

YOUNG ANIMALS: bullock, calf, colt, cub, fawn, foal, heifer, kid, kitten, lamb, leveret, piglet, puppy, whelp, yearling.

YOUNG BIRDS: chick, cygnet, duckling, fledgeling, gosling, nestling, pullet.

YOUNG FISH: elver [=*young eel*], [*plural*] fry, grilse [=*young salmon*].

YOUNG PLANTS: cutting, sapling, seedling.

---

young noun *Parents have an instinct to protect their young.* brood, family, issue, litter, offspring, progeny.

youngster noun SEE **youth**.

youth noun 1 *Grown-ups look back on their youth.* adolescence, babyhood, boyhood, childhood, girlhood, growing up, immaturity, infancy, [*informal*] teens.
2 [*often uncomplimentary*] *a noisy crowd of youths.* adolescent, boy, juvenile, [*informal*] kid, [*informal*] lad, stripling, teenager, youngster.
youth hostel SEE **accommodation**.

youthful adjective **1** *a youthful audience* SEE **young** adjective.
2 [*complimentary*] *youthful in appearance*. fresh, lively, sprightly, vigorous, well-preserved, young-looking.
3 [*uncomplimentary*] *youthful behaviour*. babyish, boyish, childish, girlish, immature, inexperienced, infantile, juvenile, puerile.

yowl noun, verb SEE **cry** noun, verb.
OTHER SOUNDS: SEE **sound** noun.

yule, yuletide nouns Christmas.

Z

zany adjective SEE **absurd, eccentric**.

zeal noun SEE **enthusiasm**.

zealot noun SEE **fanatic**.

zealous adjective *a zealous official*. conscientious, diligent, eager, earnest, enthusiastic, fanatical, fervent, keen, passionate.
OPPOSITES: SEE **apathetic**.

zebra noun VARIOUS ANIMALS: SEE **animal** noun.
zebra crossing pedestrian crossing.

zenith noun **1** *The sun was at its zenith*. highest point, meridian.
2 *He's at the zenith of his career*. acme, apex, climax, height, peak, pinnacle, top.
OPPOSITES: SEE **nadir**.

zephyr noun SEE **wind** noun.

zero noun SEE **nothing**.

zero verb **to zero in on** SEE **aim** verb.

zest noun *We tucked into the food with zest*. eagerness, energy, enjoyment, enthusiasm, liveliness, pleasure, zeal.

zigzag adjective *a zigzag route*. bendy, crooked, [*informal*] in and out, indirect, meandering, serpentine, twisting, winding.

zigzag verb *The road zigzags up the hill*. bend, curve, meander, snake, tack (*to tack against the wind*), twist, wind.

zip noun zip-fastener, [*informal*] zipper.
OTHER FASTENERS: SEE **fastener**.

zip verb **1** *Zip up your bag*. SEE **fasten**.
2 [*informal*] *She zipped along the road*. SEE **zoom**.

zippy adjective SEE **lively**.

zodiac noun astrological signs.

SIGNS OF THE ZODIAC: Aquarius [*Water-Carrier*], Aries [*Ram*], Cancer [*Crab*], Capricorn [*Goat*], Gemini [*Twins*], Leo [*Lion*], Libra [*Scales*], Pisces [*Fish*], Sagittarius [*Archer*], Scorpio [*Scorpion*], Taurus [*Bull*], Virgo [*Virgin*].

zombie noun SEE **spirit**.

zone noun *No one may enter the forbidden zone*. area, district, locality, neighbourhood, region, sector, sphere, territory, tract, vicinity.

zoo noun menagerie, safari-park, zoological gardens.
VARIOUS ANIMALS: SEE **animal** noun.

zoom verb [*informal*] *She zoomed home with her good news*. dash, hurry, hurtle, SEE **move** verb, race, rush, speed, [*informal*] whiz, [*informal*] zip.
zoom lens PHOTOGRAPHIC EQUIPMENT: SEE **photography**.

Notes

Notes

Notes

Notes

Notes

Notes

Notes

Notes

Notes

Notes

Notes

Notes

Notes